W9-AYE-374
http://www
"The new MyPHLIP (Prentice Hall's Learning on the Internet Partnership) enhanced Companion Web site includes a customizable home page, real-time news headlines, In the News (IS-related news articles summarized by a selected team of professors and supported by exercises and activities), Internet Exercises, Electronic Commerce Projects, Application Exercises, Internet Connections, Student Study Guide, International Resources, and PowerPoint presentations.
www.prenhall.com/laudon
An interactive multimedia CD-ROM will be packaged with the text. This interactive student CD-ROM includes bullet text to assist students in their understanding of the material in the text, audio and video tours, and links to the student's Web site exercises and study guide so users can continually check their progress in mastering the material."

# Management Information Systems

# MANAGEMENT INFORMATION SYSTEMS

## MANAGING THE DIGITAL FIRM

**Seventh Edition**

KENNETH C. LAUDON

*New York University*

JANE P. LAUDON

*Azimuth Information Systems*

*Upper Saddle River, New Jersey 07458*

**Library of Congress Cataloging-in-Publication Data**
Laudon, Kenneth C.
Management information systems : managing the digital firm / Kenneth C. Laudon, Jane P. Laudon. — 7th ed.
p. cm.
Includes bibliographical references and index.
ISBN 0-13-033066-3
1. Management information systems. I. Laudon, Jane Price. II. Title.

T58.6.L376 2002
658.4'038—dc21 2001021520

**Executive Editor:** Bob Horan
**Editor-in-Chief:** Natalie Anderson
**Associate Editor:** Kyle Hannon
**Editorial Assistant:** Erika Rusnak
**Director of Development:** Steve Deitmer
**Developmental Editor:** Rebecca Johnson
**Media Project Manager:** Joan Waxman
**Marketing Manager:** Sharon K. Turkovich
**Marketing Assistant:** Jason Smith
**Senior Production Editor:** Anne Graydon
**Managing Editor (Production):** Gail Steier
**Permissions Coordinator:** Suzanne Grappi
**Photo Permissions Coordinator:** Charles Morris
**Production Manager:** Arnold Vila
**Associate Director, Manufacturing:** Vincent Scelta
**Design Direction:** Cheryl Asherman; Blair Brown
**Interior Design:** Jill Little
**Cover Design:** Amanda Wilson
**Cover Illustration:** ©Guy Crittenden/SIS
**Manager, Print Production:** Christy Mahon
**Composition:** Carlisle Communications
**Full-Service Project Management:** Carlisle Publishers Services
**Printer/Binder:** RR Donnelley/Willard

Credits and acknowledgments borrowed from other sources and reproduced, with permission, in this textbook appear on appropriate page within text and on the last two pages of the book.

10 9 8 7 6 5 4 3 2 1
ISBN 0-13-033066-3

FOR

ERICA AND ELISABETH

# About The Authors

**Kenneth C. Laudon** is a Professor of Information Systems at New York University's Stern School of Business. He holds a B.A. in Economics from Stanford and a Ph.D. from Columbia University. He has authored eleven books dealing with information systems, organizations, and society. Professor Laudon has also written over forty articles concerned with the social, organizational, and management impacts of information systems, privacy, ethics, and multimedia technology.

Professor Laudon's current research is on the planning and management of large-scale information systems and multimedia information technology. He has received grants from the National Science Foundation to study the evolution of national information systems at the Social Security Administration, the IRS, and the FBI. A part of this research is concerned with computer-related organizational and occupational changes in large organizations, changes in management ideology, changes in public policy, and understanding productivity change in the knowledge sector.

Ken Laudon has testified as an expert before the United States Congress. He has been a researcher and consultant to the Office of Technology Assessment (United States Congress) and to the Office of the President, several executive branch agencies, and Congressional Committees. Professor Laudon also acts as an in-house educator for several consulting firms and as a consultant on systems planning and strategy to several Fortune 500 firms. Ken works with the Concours Group to provide advice to firms developing enterprise systems.

Ken Laudon's hobby is sailing.

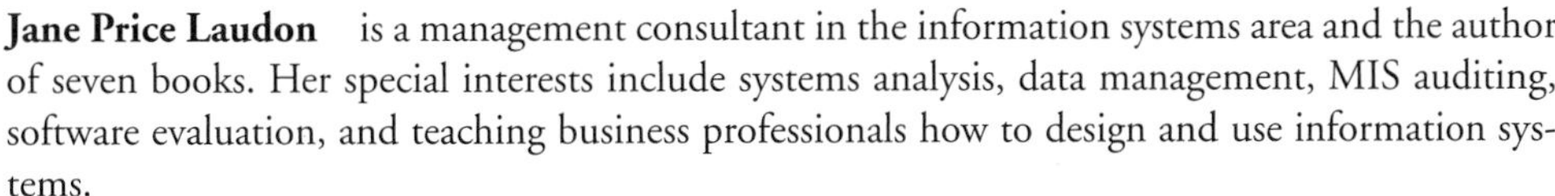

**Jane Price Laudon** is a management consultant in the information systems area and the author of seven books. Her special interests include systems analysis, data management, MIS auditing, software evaluation, and teaching business professionals how to design and use information systems.

Jane received her Ph.D. from Columbia University, her M.A. from Harvard University, and her B.A. from Barnard College. She has taught at Columbia University and the New York University Graduate School of Business. She maintains a lifelong interest in Oriental languages and civilizations.

The Laudons have two daughters, Erica and Elisabeth.

*Management Information Systems: Managing the Digital Firm* reflects a deep understanding of MIS research and teaching as well as practical experience designing and building real-world systems.

# Brief Contents

# Contents

# PART THREE BUILDING INFORMATION SYSTEMS IN THE DIGITAL FIRM 301

# PREFACE

## WELCOME TO THE DIGITAL FIRM

*Management Information Systems: Managing the Digital Firm (Seventh Edition)* is based on the premise that information systems knowledge is essential for creating competitive firms, managing global corporations, and providing useful products and services to customers. This book provides an introduction to management information systems that undergraduate and MBA students will find vital to their professional success.

## THE INFORMATION REVOLUTION IN BUSINESS AND MANAGEMENT: THE EMERGING DIGITAL FIRM

The growth of the Internet, globalization of trade, and the rise of information economies, have recast the role of information systems in business and management. The Internet is becoming the foundation for new business models, new business processes, and new ways of distributing knowledge. Companies can use the Internet and networking technology to conduct more of their work electronically, seamlessly linking factories, offices, and sales forces around the globe. Leading-edge firms such as Cisco Systems, Dell Computer, and Procter & Gamble are extending these networks to suppliers, customers, and other groups outside the organization so they can react instantly to customer demands and market shifts. Cisco Systems corporate managers can use information systems to "virtually close" their books at any time, generating consolidated financial statements based on up-to-the-minute figures on orders, discounts, revenue, product margins, and staffing expenses. Executives can constantly analyze performance at all levels of the organization. This digital integration both within the firm and without, from the warehouse to the executive suite, from suppliers to customers, is changing how we organize and manage a business firm. Ultimately these changes are leading to fully digital firms where all internal business processes and relationships with customers and suppliers are digitally enabled. In digital firms, information to support business decisions is available any time and anywhere in the organization. Accordingly, we have changed the subtitle of this text to *Managing the Digital Firm.*

## NEW TO THE SEVENTH EDITION

This edition more fully explores the digital integration of the firm and the use of the Internet to enable business processes digitally for electronic commerce and electronic business. The text provides a complete set of tools for integrating the Internet and multimedia technology into the MIS course and for promoting active problem solving. The following features and content reflect this new direction:

### NEW COVERAGE OF THE DIGITAL FIRM

Chapter 1 introduces and defines the emerging digital firm, using examples of leading-edge companies such as Cisco Systems and General Electric. Chapter 3 explains how information systems and business strategy have changed as a result of digital firm technology, and Chapter 13 describes digital firm applications of decision-support systems and executive support systems. The entire text details the management, organization, and technology issues surrounding the digital integration of the firm and the formation of industry-wide networks and global supply chains.

## DETAILED COVERAGE OF CUSTOMER RELATIONSHIP MANAGEMENT, SUPPLY CHAIN MANAGEMENT, AND ENTERPRISE SYSTEMS

Chapter 2 provides detailed treatment of customer relationship management, supply chain management, enterprise systems, and the digital integration of business processes. Subsequent chapters include additional descriptions, discussions, and case studies of these topics, emphasizing the importance of integrating information across business processes and electronically linking the firm to suppliers, customers, and other business partners. "Before and after" snapshots throughout the text illustrate how firms have changed their business processes using digital technology. (The "Before–After" diagram in Chapter 4 showing changes in procurement using Fibermarket.com is one example.)

## INCREASED COVERAGE OF ELECTRONIC COMMERCE, ELECTRONIC BUSINESS, AND THE INTERNET

The Internet, electronic commerce, and electronic business are introduced in Chapter 1 and integrated throughout the text and the entire learning package. The text now features two full chapters on these topics. Chapter 4, The Digital Firm: Electronic Commerce and Electronic Business, discusses electronic commerce, Internet business models, e-business, and the management and organizational transformations driving the move toward digital firms. Chapter 9, The Internet and the New Information Technology Infrastructure, describes the underlying technology, capabilities, and benefits of the Internet, with new coverage of the wireless Web, m-commerce, and digital firm infrastructure. Every chapter contains a Window On box or a case study devoted to electronic commerce, electronic business, or digital firm issues, as well as in-text descriptions of how Internet technology is changing a particular aspect of information systems.

## MORE ACTIVE HANDS-ON LEARNING PROJECTS AND PROBLEM SOLVING

This edition is more problem-solving- and project-oriented than earlier editions, with new active hands-on learning projects to help students make text concepts more meaningful.

### New Comprehensive Projects

We have added five new, longer comprehensive projects, each concluding a Part section of the text. These projects require students to apply text concepts to demanding problems that they might encounter as firms become more digitally integrated and Internet enabled. These projects include:

- Analyzing business processes for an enterprise system (Part I Project)
- Creating a new Internet business (Part II Project)
- Redesigning business processes (Part III Project)
- Designing an enterprise information portal (Part IV Project)
- Analyzing the total cost of ownership (TCO) of a Web site (Part V Project)

### New Hands-on Application Exercises

Each chapter now features a hands-on Application Software Exercise in which students can develop a solution using spreadsheet, database, expert system, CASE, or electronic presentation software. Some of these exercises require students to use these application software tools in conjunction with Web activities. The Application Exercises give students the opportunity to apply their software skills and text concepts to management problem solving. The complete application exercises are included in each chapter and also on the Laudon Web site along with required data files. The Application Exercises include business problems such as:

- Developing a Web page for a business (Chapter 6 and Chapter 15)
- Developing a hotel reservation database and management reporting system (Chapter 2)

- Developing a spreadsheet application for information technology risk assessment (Chapter 14)

### New Management Decision Problems

We have added a Management Decision Problem to each chapter to encourage students to apply what they have learned to a real-world management decision-making scenario. These problems can be used for practical group or individual learning both in and outside of the classroom. The problems require students to make decisions based on real-world MIS issues such as:

- Analyzing enterprise process integration (Chapter 2)
- Measuring the effectiveness of Web advertising (Chapter 4)
- Monitoring how much time employees spend on the Web (Chapter 15)

### NEW LEADING-EDGE TOPICS

In addition to the new digital firm coverage we have already described, this edition includes up-to-date treatment of topics such as:

- M-commerce and the wireless Web (Chapter 9)
- Optical networks and broadband access (Chapter 8)
- Application service providers and on-line storage service providers (Chapters 5 and 6)
- Peer-to-peer computing (Chapter 5)
- B2B exchanges (Chapter 4)
- Scalability and high-availability computing (Chapters 5, 9, and 14)
- Middleware and enterprise application integration software (Chapter 6)
- Application development for e-commerce (Chapter 10)
- XML (Chapter 6)
- Web-enabled databases and elements of SQL (Chapter 7)

## BOOK OVERVIEW

Part One is concerned with the organizational foundations of systems, their strategic role, and the organizational and management changes driving electronic commerce, electronic business, and the emerging digital firm. It provides an extensive introduction to real-world systems, focusing on their relationship to organizations, management, and business processes.

Part Two provides the technical foundation for understanding information systems, describing the hardware, software, data storage, and telecommunications technologies that comprise the organization's information technology infrastructure. Part Two concludes by describing how all of these information technologies work together with the Internet to create a new infrastructure for the digital integration of the enterprise.

Part Three focuses on the process of redesigning organizations using information systems, including reengineering of critical business processes and development of Web applications. We see systems analysis and design as an exercise in organizational design, one that requires great sensitivity to the right tools and techniques, quality assurance, and change management.

Part Four describes the role of information systems in capturing and distributing organizational knowledge and in enhancing management decision making across the enterprise. It shows how knowledge management, work group collaboration, and individual and group decision making can be supported by the use of knowledge work, group collaboration, artificial intelligence, decision-support, and executive support systems.

Part Five concludes the text by examining the special management challenges and opportunities created by the pervasiveness and power of contemporary information systems and the global connectivity of the Internet: ensuring security and control, understanding the ethical and social consequences of systems, and developing global systems. Throughout the text, emphasis is placed on using information technology to redesign the organization's products, services, procedures, jobs, and management structures; numerous examples are drawn from multinational systems and global business environments.

## CHAPTER OUTLINE

Each chapter contains the following:

- A detailed outline at the beginning to provide an overview
- An opening vignette describing a real-world organization to establish the theme and importance of the chapter
- A diagram analyzing the opening vignette in terms of the management, organization, and technology model used throughout the text
- A list of learning objectives
- Management Challenges related to the chapter theme
- Marginal glosses of key terms in the text
- An Internet Connection icon directing students to related material on the Internet
- A Management Decision Problem presenting a real-world management decision scenario
- An Application Software Exercise requiring students to use application software tools to develop solutions to real-world business problems based on chapter concepts
- A Management Wrap-Up tying together the key management, organization, and technology issues for the chapter, with questions for discussion
- A chapter summary keyed to the learning objectives
- A list of key terms that the student can use to review concepts
- Review questions for students to test their comprehension of chapter material
- A group project to develop teamwork and presentation skills
- A Tools for Interactive Learning section showing specifically how the chapter can be integrated with the Laudon Web site and optional CD-ROM edition of the text
- A chapter-ending case study that illustrates important themes

## IMPROVED COMPANION WEB SITE

This text will be accompanied by a Companion Web site that is supported by MyPHLIP. MyPHLIP stands for Prentice Hall's Learning on the Internet Partnership. This enhancement will bring your students a richer Web experience.

Features of this new site include the ability for you to customize your home page, real-time news headlines, In the News (IS-related news articles summarized by a selected team of professors and supported by exercises and activities), and Internet Exercises that are continually added to the site. These exercises encourage students' critical thinking skills as they explore business resources on the Internet and take learning MIS on the Internet to the next level.

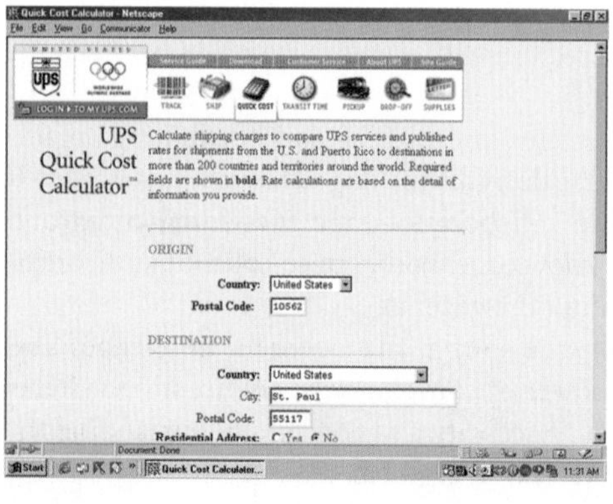

Students are presented with a problem to develop a budget for annual shipping costs. To obtain the information required for the solution, they can input data on-line and use the interactive software at this Web site to perform the required calculations or analysis.

Further enhancements have been made to the Laudon & Laudon Web site to provide a wide array of capabilities for interactive learning and management problem solving that have been carefully prepared for use with the text. They include:

### Electronic Commerce Projects for Every Chapter

On the Web site are Web-based Electronic Commerce exercises for each chapter. Students can use interactive software at various company Web sites and other Web tools to solve specific business problems related to chapter concepts.

### Interactive Study Guide and Internet Connections for Each Chapter

For each chapter of the text, the Web site features an Interactive Study Guide and Internet Connection exercise.

- The on-line Interactive Study Guide helps students review and test their mastery of chapter concepts with a series of multiple-choice, true-false, and essay questions.
- Internet Connections noted by icons in the chapter margins direct students to exercises and projects on the Laudon Web site related to organizations and concepts in that chapter.

Student responses to questions are automatically graded and can be e-mailed to the instructor.

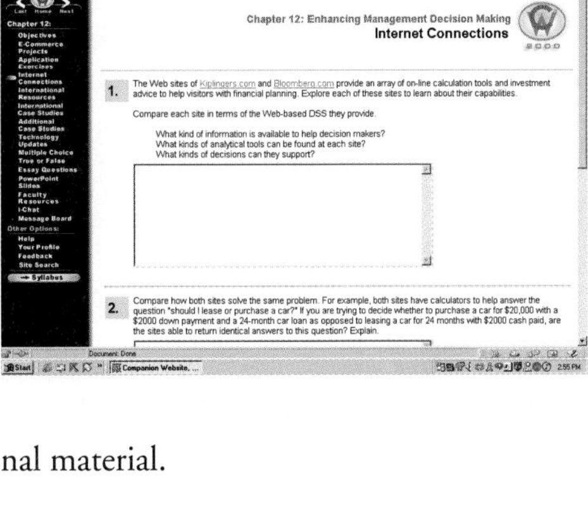

Internet Connections direct students to Web-based exercises on the Laudon Web site. Students can e-mail their work to their professors.

### Additional Case Studies

The Web site contains additional case studies with hyperlinks to the Web sites of the organizations they discuss.

### International Resources

Links to Web sites of non-U.S. countries are provided for users interested in more international material.

## UNIQUE FEATURES OF THIS TEXT FOR THE STUDENT

*Management Information Systems: Managing the Digital Firm (Seventh Edition)* has many unique features designed to create an active, dynamic learning environment.

### INTEGRATED FRAMEWORK FOR DESCRIBING AND ANALYZING INFORMATION SYSTEMS

An integrated framework portrays information systems as being composed of management, organization, and technology elements. This framework is used throughout the text to describe and analyze information systems and information system problems.

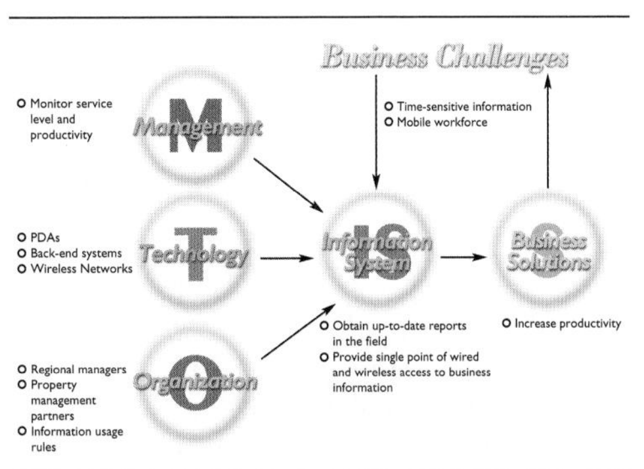


A special diagram accompanying each chapter-opening vignette illustrates how management, organization, and technology elements work together to create an information system solution to the business challenges discussed in the vignette.

### REAL-WORLD EXAMPLES

Real-world examples drawn from business and public organizations are used throughout to illustrate text concepts. More than 100 companies in the United States and nearly 100 organizations in Canada, Europe, Australia, Asia, and Africa are discussed.

Each chapter opens with a vignette illustrating the themes of the chapter by showing how a real-world organization meets a business challenge using information systems. Each chapter also contains two or three Window On boxes (Window on Management, Window on Organizations, Window on Technology) that present real-world examples illustrating the management, organization, and technology issues in the chapter. Each Window On box concludes with a section called To Think About containing questions for students to apply chapter concepts to management problem solving. The themes for each box are:

### Window on Management

Management problems raised by systems and their solution; management strategies and plans; careers and experiences of managers using systems.

### Window on Technology

Hardware, software, telecommunications, data storage, standards, and systems-building methodologies.

### Window on Organizations

Activities of private and public organizations using information systems; experiences of people working with systems.

## MANAGEMENT WRAP-UP OVERVIEWS OF KEY ISSUES

Management Wrap-Up sections at the end of each chapter summarize key issues using the authors' management, organization, and technology framework for analyzing information systems.

Management Wrap-Up provides a quick overview of the key issues in each chapter, reinforcing the authors' management, organization, and technology framework.

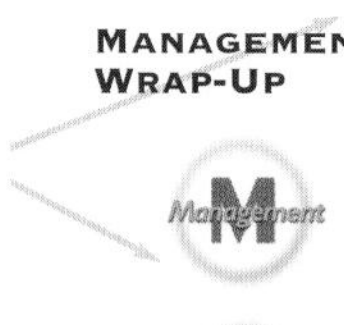

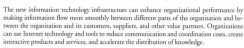

Planning the firm's IT infrastructure is a key management responsibility. Managers need to consider how the IT infrastructure supports the firm's business goals and whether the infrastructure should incorporate public infrastructures and links to other organizations. Planning should also consider the need to maintain some measure of management control as computing power becomes more widely distributed throughout the organization.

The new information technology infrastructure can enhance organizational performance by making information flow more smoothly between different parts of the organization and between the organization and its customers, suppliers, and other value partners. Organizations can use Internet technology and tools to reduce communication and coordination costs, create interactive products and services, and accelerate the distribution of knowledge.

Internet technology is providing the connectivity for the new information technology infrastructure and the emerging digital firm, using the TCP/IP reference model and other standards for retrieving, formatting, and displaying information. Key technology decisions should consider the capabilities of Internet, electronic commerce, and new wireless technologies along with connectivity, scalability, reliability, and requirements for application integration.

*For Discussion*

1. It has been said that developing an IT infrastructure for electronic commerce and electronic business is above all a business decision, as opposed to a technical decision. Discuss.
2. A fully-integrated IT infrastructure is essential for business success. Do you agree? Why or why not?

## A TRULY INTERNATIONAL PERSPECTIVE

In addition to a full chapter on managing international information systems (Chapter 16), all chapters of the text are illustrated with real-world examples from nearly one-hundred corporations in Canada, Europe, Asia, Latin America, Africa, Australia, and the Middle East. Each chapter contains at least one Window On box, case study or opening vignette drawn from a non-U.S. firm, and often more. The text concludes with four major international case studies contributed by leading MIS experts in Canada, Europe, and Singapore—Len Fertuck, University of Toronto (Canada); Gerhard Schwabe, University of Koblenz (Germany); Boon Siong Neo and Christina Soh, Nanyang Technological University (Singapore); and Scott Schneberger and Jane Movold, University of Western Ontario (Canada).

## ATTENTION TO SMALL BUSINESSES AND ENTREPRENEURS

A diamond-shaped symbol identifies in-text discussions and specially designated chapter-opening vignettes, Window On boxes, and chapter-ending case studies that highlight the experiences and challenges of small businesses and entrepreneurs using information systems.

## PEDAGOGY TO PROMOTE ACTIVE LEARNING AND MANAGEMENT PROBLEM SOLVING

*Management Information Systems: Managing the Digital Firm (Seventh Edition)* In addition to the new Comprehensive Projects, Management Decision Problems, and hands-on Application Exercises, the text contains many other features that encourage students to learn actively and to engage in management problem solving.

### Group Projects

At the end of each chapter is a group project that encourages students to develop teamwork and oral and written presentation skills. The group projects have been enhanced in this edition to make even better use of the Internet. For instance, students might be asked to work in small groups to evaluate the Web sites of two competing businesses or to develop a corporate ethics code on privacy that considers e-mail privacy and the monitoring of employees using networks.

### Management Challenges Section

Each chapter begins with several challenges relating to the chapter topic that managers are likely to encounter. These challenges are multifaceted and sometimes pose dilemmas. They make excellent springboards for class discussion. Some of these Management Challenges are: finding the right Internet business model; overcoming the organizational obstacles to building a database environment; and agreeing on quality standards for information systems.

### Case Studies

Each chapter concludes with a case study based on a real-world organization. These cases help students synthesize chapter concepts and apply this new knowledge to concrete problems and scenarios. Major international case studies and electronic case studies at the Laudon & Laudon Web site provide additional opportunities for management problem solving.

## TOOLS FOR INTERACTIVE LEARNING: TECHNOLOGY INTEGRATED WITH CONTENT

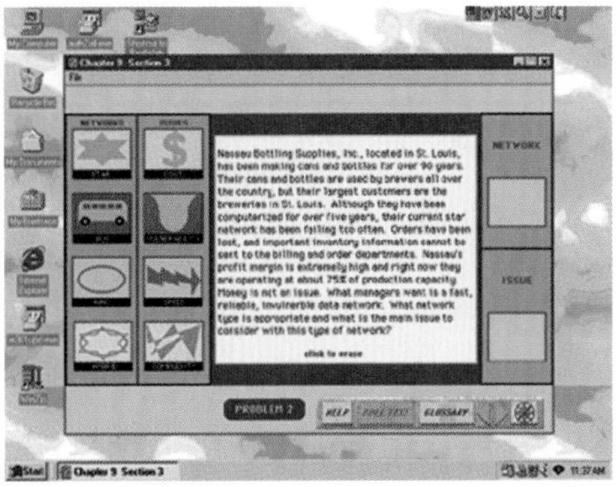

Students can reinforce and extend their knowledge of chapter concepts with interactive exercises on the CD-ROM.

An interactive CD-ROM multimedia version of the text is available to be packaged with the text. In addition to the full text and bullet-text summaries by chapter, the CD-ROM features interactive exercises, simulations, audio/video overviews explaining key concepts, on-line quizzes, hyperlinks to the exercises on the Laudon Web site, technology updates, and more. Students can use the CD-ROM as an interactive supplement or as an alternative to the traditional text.

A Tools for Interactive Learning section concluding each chapter shows students how they can extend their knowledge of each chapter with projects and exercises on the Laudon Web site and the CD-ROM multimedia edition.

Students and instructors can see at a glance exactly how Internet Connections and Electronic Commerce projects can be used to enhance student learning for each chapter. Students can also see immediately how the chapter can be used in conjunction with the optional CD-ROM.

#### TOOLS FOR INTERACTIVE LEARNING

**INTERNET CONNECTION**

The Internet Connection for this chapter will take you to the WingspanBank.com Web site where you can see how one company used the Internet to create an entirely new type of business. You can complete an exercise for analyzing this Web site's capabilities and its strategic benefits. You can also use the Interactive Study Guide to test your knowledge of this chapter and get instant feedback where you need more practice.

**ELECTRONIC COMMERCE PROJECT**

At the Laudon Web site for Chapter 3, you will find an Electronic Commerce project on competitive auto pricing and sales on the Web.

**CD-ROM**

If you use the Multimedia Edition CD-ROM with this chapter, you will find an interactive exercise asking you to apply the correct model of organizational decision making to solve a series of problems. You can also find a video clip illustrating the role of information systems in Schneider National's organization, an audio overview of the major themes of this chapter, and bullet text summarizing the key points of the chapter.

# Instructional Support Materials

## Instructor's Resource CD-ROM (0-13-061299-5)

Most of the support materials described below are now conveniently provided for adopters on the Instructor's Resource CD-ROM. The CD includes the Instructor's Resource Manual, Test Item File, Windows PH Test Manager, PowerPoint slides, and the helpful lecture tool "Image Library."

## Image Library (on Instructor's Resource CD-ROM)

The Image Library is a wonderful resource to help instructors create vibrant lecture presentations. Just about every figure and photo found in the text is provided and organized by chapter for your convenience. These images and lecture notes can be easily imported into Microsoft PowerPoint to create new presentations or to add to existing sets.

## Instructor's Manual (0-13-061298-7)

The Instructor's Manual, written by Dr. Anne Nelson of High Point University, features not only answers to review, discussion, case study, and group project questions, but also an in-depth lecture outline, teaching objectives, key terms, teaching suggestions, and Internet resources. This supplement can be downloaded from the secure faculty section of the Laudon/Laudon Web site, and is also available on the Instructor's Resource CD-ROM.

## Test Item File (0-13-061157-3)

The Test Item File is a comprehensive collection of true-false, multiple-choice, fill-in-the-blank, and essay questions, written by Dr. Lisa Miller of the University of Central Oklahoma. The questions are rated by difficulty level and answers are referenced by section. An electronic version of the Test Item File is available as the **Windows PH Test Manager** on the Instructor's Resource CD-ROM.

## PowerPoint Slides (on Web and Instructor's Resource CD-ROM)

Electronic color slides, created by Dr. Edward Fisher of Central Michigan University, are available in Microsoft PowerPoint, Version 97. The slides illuminate and build upon key concepts in the text. Both students and faculty can download the PowerPoints from the Web site, and the PowerPoints are also provided on the Instructor's Resource CD-ROM within Image Library.

## Videos

### Prentice Hall MIS Video, Volume I (0-13-027199-3)

The first video in the Prentice Hall MIS Video Library includes custom clips created exclusively for Prentice Hall featuring real companies such as Andersen Consulting, Lands' End, Lotus Development Corporation, Oracle Corporation, and Pillsbury Company.

### Prentice Hall MIS Video, Volume 2 (0-13-027929-3)

These video clips highlight real-world corporations and organizations and illustrate key concepts found in the text.

## Web Site

The Laudon/Laudon text is once again supported by an excellent Web site at **www.prenhall.com/laudon** that truly reinforces and enhances text material with Electronic Commerce Projects, hands-on Application Exercises, Internet Exercises, an Interactive Study Guide, International Resources, and PowerPoint slides. The Web site also features a secure password-protected faculty area from which instructors can download the Instructor's Manual and find suggested answers to the Internet Connections and E-Commerce Projects. The site also has an improved online syllabus tool to help professors add their own personal syllabus to the site in minutes.

Please see its complete description found earlier in this preface.

## Online Courses

### WebCT www.prenhall.com/webct

Gold Level Customer Support available exclusively to adopters of Prentice Hall courses, is provided free-of-charge upon adoption and provides you with priority assistance, training discounts, and dedicated technical support.

### BlackBoard www.prenhall.com/blackboard

Prentice Hall's abundant on-line content, combined with Blackboard's popular tools and interface, result in robust Web-based courses that are easy to implement, manage, and use—taking your courses to new heights in student interaction and learning.

### CourseCompass www.prenhall.com/coursecompass

CourseCompass is a dynamic, interactive on-line course management tool powered exclusively for Pearson Education by Blackboard. This exciting product allows you to teach market-leading Pearson Education content in an easy-to-use customizable format.

## Tutorial Software

For instructors looking for Application Software support to use with this text, Prentice Hall is pleased to offer PH Train IT and PH Assess IT for Office 2000. These exciting tutorial and assessment products are fully certified up to the expert level of the Microsoft Office User Specialist (MOUS) Certification Program. These items are not available as stand-alone items but can be packaged with the Laudon/Laudon text at an additional charge. Please go to www.prenhall.com/phit for an online demonstration of these products or contact your local Prentice Hall representative for more details.

## Software Cases

A series of optional management software cases called *Solve it! Management Problem Solving with PC Software* has been developed to support the text. *Solve it!* consists of 10 spreadsheet cases, 10 database cases, and 6 Internet projects drawn from real-world businesses, plus a data disk with the files required by the cases. The cases are graduated in difficulty. The case book contains complete tutorial documentation showing how to use spreadsheet, database, and Web browser software to solve the problems. A new version of *Solve it!* with all new cases is published every year. *Solve it!* must be adopted for an entire class. It can be purchased directly from the supplier, Azimuth Corporation, 124 Penfield Ave., Croton-on-Hudson, New York 10520 (Telephone: 914-271-6321).

# Acknowledgments

The production of any book involves many valued contributions from a number of persons. We would like to thank all of our editors for encouragement, insight, and strong support for many years, especially editors Robert Horan and David Alexander who guided the development of this edition. We remain grateful to Natalie Anderson and Mickey Cox for their support of this project. We thank Sharon K. Turkovich, senior marketing manager, for her excellent marketing work. Special thanks to Patti Arneson for her focus group and market research work for this edition.

We commend Kyle Hannon for directing the preparation of ancillary materials and Anne Graydon and Arnold Vila for production/manufacturing of this text under an extraordinarily ambitious schedule. We thank Shirley Webster for her energetic photo research work and Rebecca Johnson for her contributions as developmental editor.

Our special thanks go to Dr. Lisa Miller of Central Oklahoma University for developing the hands-on Application Exercises for this edition and the testing systems that accompany our text. We also want to thank Professor Beverly Amer of Northern Arizona University for her assistance in reviewing the Management Decision Problems and other text features, as well as Dr. Anne Nelson of High Point University and Dr. Edward Fisher of Central Michigan University for their work on supporting materials.

We remain deeply indebted to Marshall R. Kaplan for his invaluable assistance in the preparation of the text. Jiri Rodovsky and Todd Traver provided additional suggestions for improvement.

The Stern School of Business at New York University and the Information Systems Department provided a very special learning environment, one in which we and others could rethink the MIS field. Special thanks to Professors Edward Stohr, Vasant Dhar, and Alex Tuzhilin for providing critical feedback and support where deserved. Professor William H. Starbuck of the Management Department at NYU provided valuable comments and insights in our joint graduate seminar on organization theory.

The Concours Group has provided stimulation, insight, and new research on enterprise systems and industrial networks. We remain especially grateful to Dr. Edward Roche for his contributions and to Jim Ware, Walt Dulaney, Vaughn Merlyn, and Peter Boggis of the Concours Group for ideas and feedback.

Professor Gordon Everest of the University of Minnesota, Professors Al Croker and Michael Palley of Baruch College and NYU, Professor Lisa Friedrichsen of the Keller Graduate School of Management, and Professor Kenneth Marr provided additional suggestions for improvement. We continue to remember the late Professor James Clifford of the Stern School as a wonderful friend and colleague who also made valuable recommendations for improving our discussion of files and databases.

One of our goals was to write a book that was authoritative, synthesized diverse views in the MIS literature, and helped define a common academic field. A large number of leading scholars in the field were contacted and assisted us in this effort. Reviewers and consultants for *Management Information Systems: Managing the Digital Firm* are listed on the back endpapers of the book. We thank them for their contributions. Consultants for this new edition include: Professor Tom Abraham of Kean University, Professor Bob Fulkerth of Golden Gate University, Professor Minnie Ghent of Florida Atlantic University, Professor Rassule Hadidi of University of Illinois-Springfield, Professor Susan K. Lippert of George Washington University, Professor Ronald E. McGaughey of Arkansas Tech University, Professor Roger McHaney of Kansas State University, Professor Steve Newberry of Tarleton College, Professor Mary E. Rasley of Lehigh Carbon Community College, and Professor Frederick Wheeler of University of Maryland-University College.

It is our hope that this group endeavor contributes to a shared vision and understanding of the MIS field.

*—K.C.L.*
*—J.P.L.*

# PART I

# ORGANIZATIONS, MANAGEMENT, AND THE NETWORKED ENTERPRISE

chapter 1

# MANAGING THE DIGITAL FIRM

objectives

**After completing this chapter, you will be able to:**

1. *Evaluate the role of information systems in today's competitive business environment.*
2. *Define an information system from both a technical and business perspective and distinguish between computer literacy and information systems literacy.*
3. *Explain how information systems are transforming organizations and management.*
4. *Assess the relationship between the digital firm, electronic commerce, electronic business, and Internet technology.*
5. *Identify the major management challenges to building and using information systems in organizations.*

## GUESS Goes Digital

During the 1980s and early 1990s, GUESS dominated the designer jeans and casual clothing market. But by 1997 the company was gasping for air. It had started out as a family business but had mushroomed into a corporate empire that had become difficult to manage. Competitors such as Levi's and the Gap sharpened their designs to grab GUESS's market.

At that point, Paul Marciano, the company's cochair and cochief executive officer called for overhauling GUESS from head to toe. Marciano cut the workforce by 6 percent, shifting three-fourths of production from domestic to overseas plants. He set an ambitious sales target to triple sales to $2 billion by 2003. He also turned to the Internet to help him keep costs low while increasing sales.

GUESS launched a major initiative to shift its internal and external business processes to the Internet. Working with Cisco Systems, GUESS replaced a tangle of outdated networking equipment with up-to-date standardized technology. With the help of software vendors PeopleSoft and CommerceOne, GUESS created an Apparel Buying Network for GUESS's suppliers and 1000 independent retailers in the United States and many other countries. Store buyers could order merchandise directly from GUESS by entering their purchases on a private Web site called ApparelBuy.com, which is integrated with GUESS's core order processing systems. Users can track their orders through fulfillment or delivery any time of the day or night. The ApparelBuy.com system features software to maintain an on-line catalog and to integrate information from sales, inventory, and other business functions. ApparelBuy.com can detect order errors by checking catalog product numbers, correct the orders, and avoid shipping the wrong products, cutting down the number of returns. GUESS used to take one to two weeks to place and receive orders using manual, paper-based processes. With its new system, GUESS reduced its ordering process to one or two days and cut warehouse operations staff from 350 to 110 people. ApparelBuy.com is open to other companies in the fashion industry, including GUESS's competitors.

GUESS maintains a public Web site for retail customers called GUESS.com, which offers product catalogs and the ability to order merchandise on-line. This e-commerce site generates as many sales as one of the GUESS flagship stores, and GUESS expects sales to grow even more as it offers more merchandise on this site. GUESS established www.babyguess.com and www.guesskids.com as e-commerce sites for retailing infants and children's clothing and accessories.

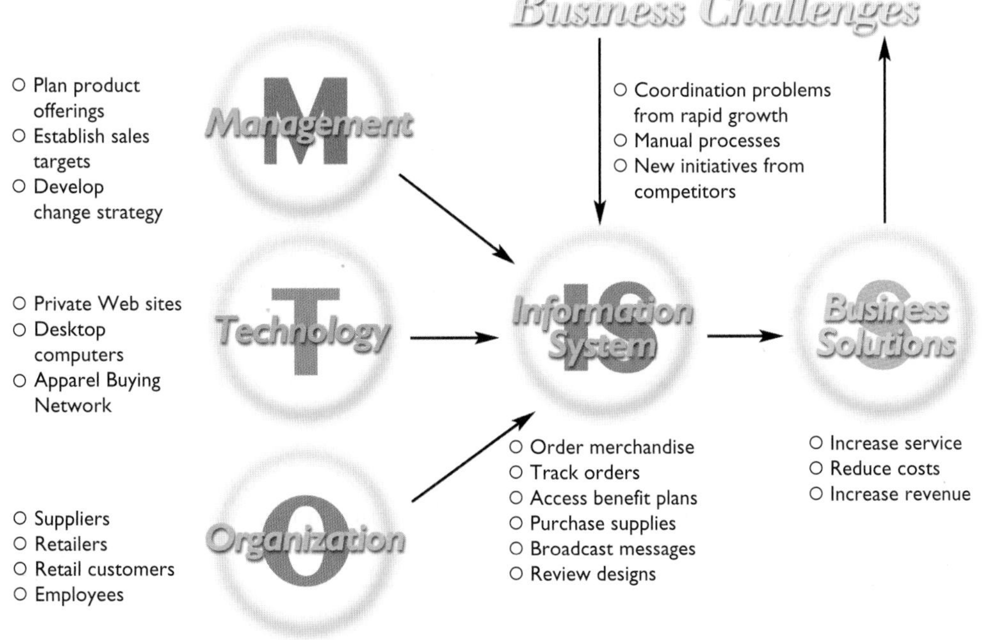


GUESS is also using Internet technology to streamline its internal business operations. GUESSExpress is an internal private network based on Internet technology that is used for purchasing supplies, reviewing architectural plans for new stores, making travel arrangements, and broadcasting messages to managers about operating instructions and company and industry trends. Employees can use GUESSExpress to access their benefits records on-line and make changes to their benefits plans.

All of these systems will eventually replace most of GUESS's telephone and fax-based processes. Management believes these systems will increase revenue and decrease costs by providing more efficient supply chain management and customer service while reducing internal administrative expenses. GUESS management is counting on the Internet to change the whole backbone of how the company does business in the twenty-first century.

**Sources:** Thomas York, "Perfect Fit," *Cisco IQ Magazine*, January/February 2001, GUESS Annual Report, March 30, 2000; and www.ApparelBuy.com.

**GUESS Goes Digital**

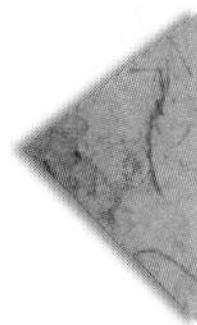

The changes taking place at GUESS exemplify the transformation of business firms throughout the world as they rebuild themselves as fully digital firms. Such digital firms use the Internet and networking technology to make data flow seamlessly among different parts of the organization, streamline the flow of work, and create electronic links with customers, suppliers, and other organizations.

All types of businesses, both large and small, are using information systems, networks, and Internet technology to conduct more of their business electronically, achieving new levels of efficiency and competitiveness. This chapter starts our investigation of information systems and organizations by describing information systems from both technical and behavioral perspectives and by surveying the changes they are bringing to organizations and management.

## 1.1 WHY INFORMATION SYSTEMS?

Today it is widely recognized that information systems knowledge is essential for managers, because most organizations need information systems to survive and prosper. Information systems can help companies extend their reach to faraway locations, offer new products and services, reshape jobs and work flows, and perhaps profoundly change the way they conduct business.

### THE COMPETITIVE BUSINESS ENVIRONMENT AND THE EMERGING DIGITAL FIRM

Four powerful worldwide changes have altered the business environment. The first change is the emergence and strengthening of the global economy. The second change is the transformation of industrial economies and societies into knowledge- and information-based service economies. The third is the transformation of the business enterprise. The fourth is the emergence of the digital firm. These changes in the business environment and climate, summarized in Table 1-1, pose a number of new challenges to business firms and their management.

### Emergence of the Global Economy

A growing percentage of the American economy—and other advanced industrial economies in Europe and Asia—depends on imports and exports. Foreign trade, both exports and imports, accounts for a little more than 25 percent of the goods and services produced in the United States, and even more in countries such as Japan and Germany. The success of firms today and in the future depends on their ability to operate globally.

**TABLE 1-1 THE CHANGING CONTEMPORARY BUSINESS ENVIRONMENT**

**Globalization**

Management and control in a global marketplace
Competition in world markets
Global work groups
Global delivery systems

**Transformation of Industrial Economies**

Knowledge- and information-based economies
New products and services
Knowledge: a central productive and strategic asset
Time-based competition
Shorter product life
Turbulent environment
Limited employee knowledge base

**Transformation of the Enterprise**

Flattening
Decentralization
Flexibility
Location independence
Low transaction and coordination costs
Empowerment
Collaborative work and teamwork

**Emergence of the Digital Firm**

Digitally enabled relationships with customers, suppliers, and employees
Core business processes accomplished via digital networks
Digital management of key corporate assets
Rapid sensing and responding to environmental changes

Today, information systems provide the communication and analytical power that firms need for conducting trade and managing businesses on a global scale. Controlling the far-flung global corporation—communicating with distributors and suppliers, operating 24 hours a day in different national environments, servicing local and international reporting needs—is a major business challenge that requires powerful information system responses.

Globalization and information technology also bring new threats to domestic business firms: Because of global communication and management systems, customers now can shop in a worldwide marketplace, obtaining price and quality information reliably 24 hours a day. To become competitive participants in international markets, firms need powerful information and communication systems.

## Transformation of Industrial Economies

The United States, Japan, Germany, and other major industrial powers are being transformed from industrial economies to knowledge- and information-based service economies, whereas manufacturing has been moving to low-wage countries. In a knowledge- and information-based economy, knowledge and information are key ingredients in creating wealth.

The knowledge and information revolution began at the turn of the twentieth century and has gradually accelerated. By 1976 the number of white-collar workers employed in offices surpassed the number of farm workers, service workers, and blue-collar workers employed in manufacturing (see Figure 1-1). Today, most people no longer work on farms or in factories but instead are found in sales, education, healthcare, banks, insurance firms, and law firms; they also provide business services, such as copying, computer programming, or making deliveries. These jobs primarily involve working with, distributing, or creating new knowledge and information. In fact, knowledge and information work now account for a significant 60 percent of the American gross national product and nearly 55 percent of the labor force.

Knowledge and information are becoming the foundation for many new services and products. **Knowledge- and information-intense products,** such as computer games, require a great deal of knowledge to produce. Entire new information-based services have sprung up, such as Lexis, Dow Jones News Service, and America Online. These fields are

**knowledge- and information-intense products**
Products that require a great deal of learning and knowledge to produce.

***Figure 1-1*** The growth of the information economy. Since the beginning of the twentieth century, the United States has experienced a steady decline in the number of farm workers and blue-collar workers who are employed in factories. At the same time, the country is experiencing a rise in the number of white-collar workers who produce economic value using knowledge and information.
*Sources:* U.S. Department of Commerce, Bureau of the Census, *Statistical Abstract of the United States, 1998,* Table 672: 1900–1970 and *Historical Statistics of the United States, Colonial Times to 1970,* Vol. 1, Series D 182–232.

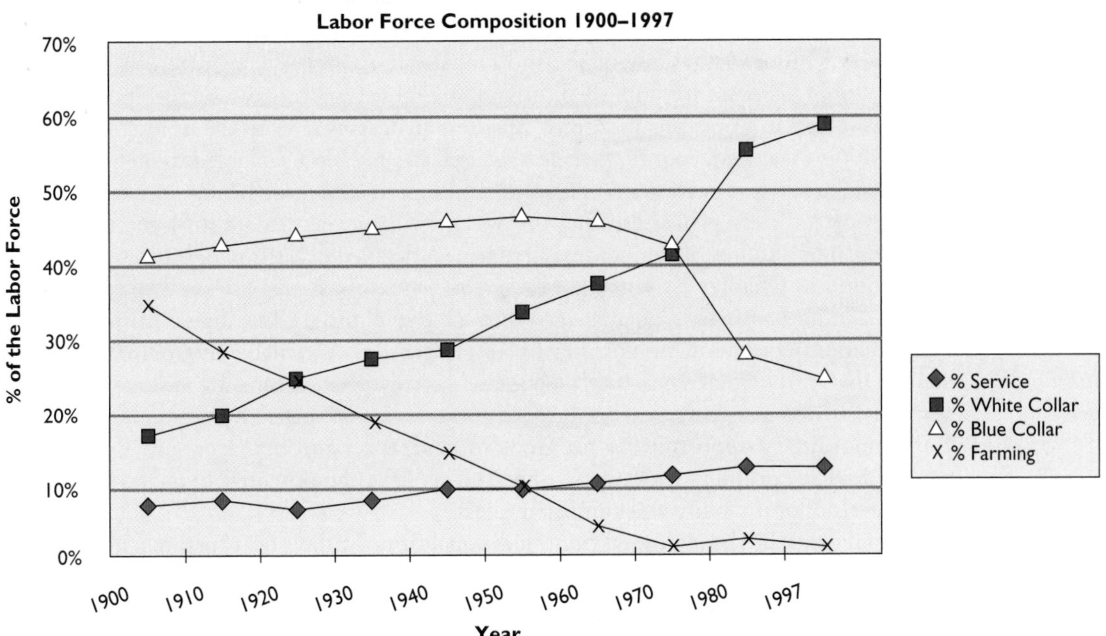

employing millions of people. Knowledge is used more intensively in the production of traditional products as well. In the automobile industry, for instance, both design and production now rely heavily on knowledge and information technology.

In a knowledge- and information-based economy, information technology and systems take on great importance. Knowledge-based products and services of great economic value, such as credit cards, overnight package delivery, and worldwide reservation systems, are based on new information technologies. Information technology constitutes more than 70 percent of the invested capital in service industries like finance, insurance, and real estate.

Across all industries, information and the technology that delivers it have become critical, strategic assets for business firms and their managers (Leonard-Barton, 1995). Information systems are needed to optimize the flow of information and knowledge within the organization and to help management maximize the firm's knowledge resources. Because employees' productivity will depend on the quality of the systems serving them, management decisions about information technology are critically important to the firm's prosperity and survival.

## Transformation of the Business Enterprise

There has been a transformation in the possibilities for organizing and managing the business enterprise. Some firms have begun to take advantage of these new possibilities.

The traditional business firm was—and still is—a hierarchical, centralized, structured arrangement of specialists that typically relied on a fixed set of standard operating procedures to deliver a mass-produced product (or service). The new style of business firm is a flattened (less hierarchical), decentralized, flexible arrangement of generalists who rely on nearly instant information to deliver mass-customized products and services uniquely suited to specific markets or customers.

The traditional management group relied—and still relies—on formal plans, a rigid division of labor, and formal rules. The new manager relies on informal commitments and networks to establish goals (rather than formal planning), a flexible arrangement of teams and individuals working in task forces, and a customer orientation to achieve coordination among employees. The new manager appeals to the knowledge, learning, and decision making of individual employees to ensure proper operation of the firm. Once again, information technology makes this style of management possible.

## The Emerging Digital Firm

The intensive use of information technology in business firms since the mid-1990s, coupled with equally significant organizational redesign, created the conditions for a new phenomenon in industrial society—the fully digital firm. The **digital firm** can be defined along several dimensions. A digital firm is one where nearly all of the organization's *significant business relationships* with customers, suppliers, and employees are digitally enabled and mediated. *Core business processes* are accomplished through digital networks spanning the entire organization or linking multiple organizations. **Business processes** refer to the unique manner in which work is organized, coordinated, and focused to produce a valuable product or service. Developing a new product, generating and fulfilling an order, or hiring an employee are examples of business processes, and the way organizations accomplish their business processes can be a source of competitive strength. (A detailed discussion of business processes can be found in Chapter 2.) *Key corporate assets*—intellectual property, core competencies, financial and human assets—are managed through digital means. In a digital firm, any piece of information required to support key business decisions is available at anytime and anywhere in the firm. Digital firms *sense and respond* to their environments far more rapidly than traditional firms, giving them more flexibility to survive in turbulent times. Digital firms offer extraordinary opportunities for global organization and management. By digitally enabling and streamlining their work, digital firms have the potential to achieve unprecedented levels of profitability and competitiveness.

**digital firm**
Organization where nearly all significant business processes and relationships with customers, suppliers, and employees are digitally enabled, and key corporate assets are managed through digital means.

**business processes**
The unique ways in which organizations coordinate and organize work activities, information, and knowledge to produce a product or service.

Digital firms are distinguished from traditional firms by their near total reliance on a set of information technologies to organize and manage. For managers of digital firms, information technology is not simply an enabler, but rather it is the core of the business and the primary management tool.

## CISCO SYSTEMS: A DIGITAL FIRM IN THE MAKING

Cisco Systems loves to advertise that it is the company on which the Internet runs. Headquartered in San Jose, California, it dominates the sale of network routers and switching equipment used for Internet infrastructure. Under the leadership of CEO John Chambers, it has become one of the most valuable companies on earth. One key to its success is that Cisco is an organization that uses the Internet in every way it can. To turn its advertising slogan around, it would be equally accurate to say that Cisco runs on the Internet.

Cisco is very close to becoming a digital firm, using Internet technology to drive every aspect of its business. Customers, suppliers, distributors, and other business partners have access to portions of Cisco's private internal Web site as well as its public Web site. More than 90 percent of Cisco's sales come via the Internet. Three-quarters of Cisco's products are manufactured by contract suppliers, and Cisco does not order based on sales projections. Instead, production is based on actual customer orders. Customers use the Cisco Web site to configure and price their systems and then to place an order. The order is routed directly to one of Cisco's manufacturers, such as Flextronics International in Singapore, which produces the product and ships it directly to the customer. The same Web site is linked directly to Federal Express and UPS so customers can track their shipments. Using this method to build products on order, Cisco has cut delivery time by 70 percent while reducing its own inventory. As Karen Brunett of Cisco's Inter-net business solutions group put it, "We don't touch the product at all." For those customers who want handholding when ordering, Cisco sales personnel gladly provide it.

Customer service also occurs on the Net. Cisco receives about 800,000 customer queries monthly, and 85 percent of those are handled satisfactorily on the Net, eliminating thousands of customer service representative positions and saving the company $600 million in the year 2000 alone. Cisco does make available personal service when the customer wants it, however. Charles Schwab Corp., for example, cannot afford network downtime under any circumstances. This giant on-line brokerage firm pays Cisco to keep engineers available by telephone 24 hours per day. Meanwhile, customer satisfaction has risen by 25 percent since 1995.

Management is on top of all financial numbers, because their computers update sales and related figures three times daily, and those numbers are instantly available over the Web on a need-to-know basis. Executives can even see net income, margins, orders, and expenses. Because they use the Internet to obtain and store all these numbers, the company can even close their books within 24 hours after the end of a quarter. Such speed is almost unheard of for a function that is usually so slow that the Securities and Exchange Commission gives companies 90 days after a quarter to report.

Similarly, human resource functions are managed through Internet technology. For example, Cisco receives about 25,000 employment applications monthly, and almost all come in through Cisco's public Web site. If the applications were submitted by paper, Cisco probably could not handle them all. Cisco employees can fill out all human resource forms, such as expense reports or changes to healthcare benefits, on the Web and update them whenever necessary. The company has also moved almost 80 percent of its training to the Web and is very pleased with the results. Cisco is even using the Internet to operate what may be the largest daycare center in northern California, where 450 youngsters can be cared for while their parents work. Parents can monitor their children on the Web while at work via cameras installed in the daycare center.

**To Think About:** How is the Internet driving organizational and management changes at Cisco? To what extent is it a digital firm?

*Sources:* Dawn Gareiss, "E-Learning Around the World," *Information Week,* February 26, 2001; Larry Carter, "Cisco's Virtual Close," Harvard Business Review, April, 2001; Scott Thurm, "Eating Their Own Dog Food," *The Wall Street Journal,* April 19, 2000; John Markoff, "Ignore the Label, It's Flextronics Inside," *The New York Times,* February 15, 2001; and Andy Serwer, "There's Something About Cisco," *Fortune,* May 15, 2000.

There are very few fully digital firms today. Yet it is the direction in which many firms are being driven by a number of business forces and opportunities. The Window on Organizations illustrates one digital firm in the making.

Moving from a traditional firm foundation toward a digital firm requires insight, skill, and patience (see the chapter ending case study). Managers need to identify the challenges facing their firms, discover the technologies that will help them meet these challenges, organize their firm and business processes to take advantage of the technology, and create management procedures and policies to implement the required changes. This book is dedicated to helping managers prepare for these tasks.

**information system**
Interrelated components working together to collect, process, store, and disseminate information to support decision making, coordination, control, analysis, and visualization in an organization.

## WHAT IS AN INFORMATION SYSTEM?

An **information system** can be defined technically as a set of interrelated components that collect (or retrieve), process, store, and distribute information to support decision making, coordination, and control in an organization. In addition to supporting decision making,

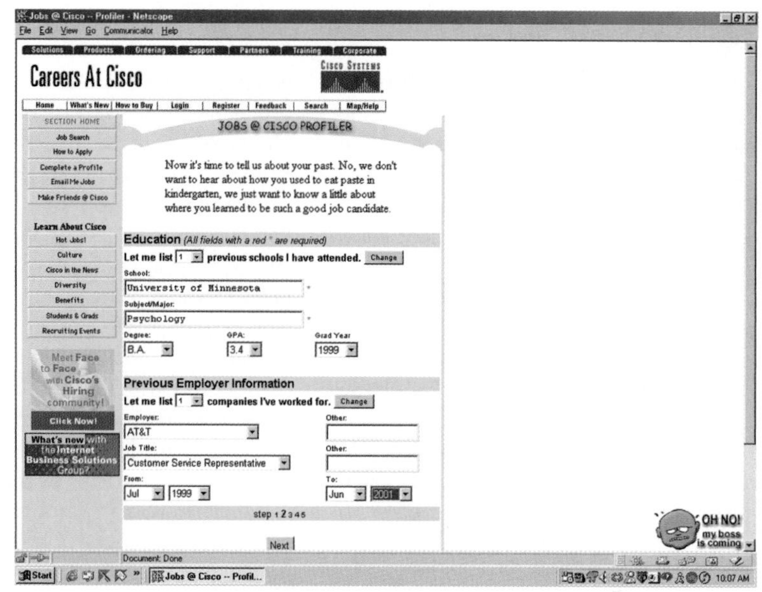


*Cisco Systems uses the Web to recruit almost all of its employees. With many of its business processes enabled by the Internet, Cisco is becoming a digital firm.*

**information**
Data that have been shaped into a form that is meaningful and useful to human beings.

**data**
Streams of raw facts representing events occurring in organizations or the physical environment before they have been organized and arranged into a form that people can understand and use.

**input**
The capture or collection of raw data from within the organization or from its external environment for processing in an information system.

**processing**
The conversion, manipulation, and analysis of raw input into a form that is more meaningful to humans.

**output**
The distribution of processed information to the people who will use it or to the activities for which it will be used.

**feedback**
Output that is returned to the appropriate members of the organization to help them evaluate or correct input.

**computer-based information systems (CBIS)**
Information systems that rely on computer hardware and software for processing and disseminating information.

**formal system**
System resting on accepted and fixed definitions of data and procedures, operating with predefined rules.

coordination, and control, information systems may also help managers and workers analyze problems, visualize complex subjects, and create new products.

Information systems contain information about significant people, places, and things within the organization or in the environment surrounding it. By **information** we mean data that have been shaped into a form that is meaningful and useful to human beings. **Data,** in contrast, are streams of raw facts representing events occurring in organizations or the physical environment before they have been organized and arranged into a form that people can understand and use.

A brief example contrasting information with data may prove useful. Supermarket checkout counters ring up millions of pieces of data, such as a product identification number or the cost of each item sold. Such pieces of data can be totaled and analyzed to provide meaningful information, such as the total number of bottles of dish detergent sold at a particular store, which brands of dish detergent are selling the most rapidly at that store or sales territory, or the total amount spent on that brand of dish detergent at that store or sales region (see Figure 1-2).

Three activities in an information system produce the information that organizations need to make decisions, control operations, analyze problems, and create new products or services. These activities are input, processing, and output (see Figure 1-3). **Input** captures or collects raw data from within the organization or from its external environment. **Processing** converts this raw input into a meaningful form. **Output** transfers the processed information to the people who will use it or to the activities for which it will be used. Information systems also require **feedback,** which is output that is returned to appropriate members of the organization to help them evaluate or correct the input stage.

In GUESS's information system for apparel buying, the raw input for an order from retailers consists of item number, item description, and amount of each item ordered along with the retailer's name and identification number. The computer processes these data by comparing each item number on the order to item numbers in GUESS's master catalog and supplying the correct item number when discrepancies are found. The system schedules the shipment of orders to the retailers, notifying the retailer if an item is out of stock. Shipping documents, invoices, and on-line reports to the retailer showing delivery date and location of the order in transit become outputs. The system thus provides meaningful information, such as lists of what items a retailer ordered, the total number of each item ordered daily by all retailers, and the total number of each item ordered by each retailer.

Our interest in this book is in formal, organizational **computer-based information systems (CBIS),** such as those designed and used by GUESS and its customers, suppliers, and employees. **Formal systems** rest on accepted and fixed definitions of data and procedures for collecting, storing, processing, disseminating, and using these data. The formal systems we

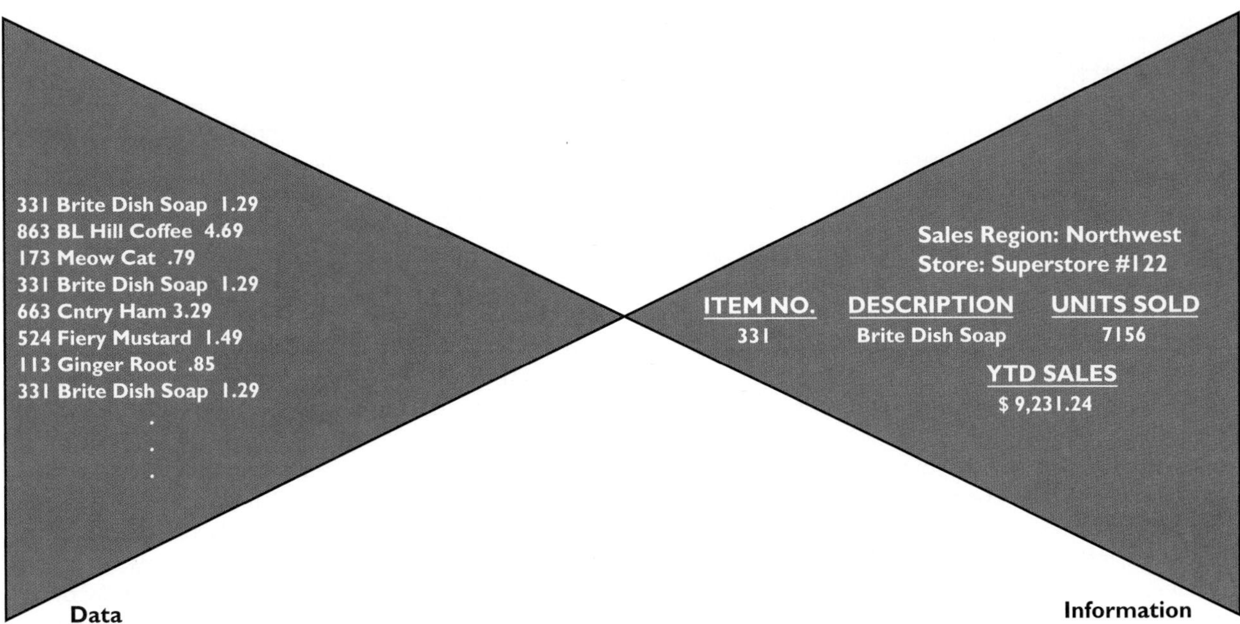


***Figure 1-2*** Data and information. Raw data from a supermarket checkout counter can be processed and organized in order to produce meaningful information, such as the total unit sales of dish detergent or the total sales revenue from dish detergent for a specific store or sales territory.

describe in this text are structured; that is, they operate in conformity with predefined rules that are relatively fixed and not easily changed. For instance, GUESS's system requires that all orders include the retailer's name, an identification number, and a unique number identifying each item ordered.

Informal information systems (such as office gossip networks) rely, by contrast, on unstated rules of behavior. There is no agreement on what is information, or on how it will be stored and processed. Such systems are essential for the life of an organization, but an analysis of their qualities is beyond the scope of this text.

Formal information systems can be either computer-based or manual. Manual systems use paper-and-pencil technology. These manual systems serve important needs, but they too are not the subject of this text. Computer-based information systems, in contrast, rely on

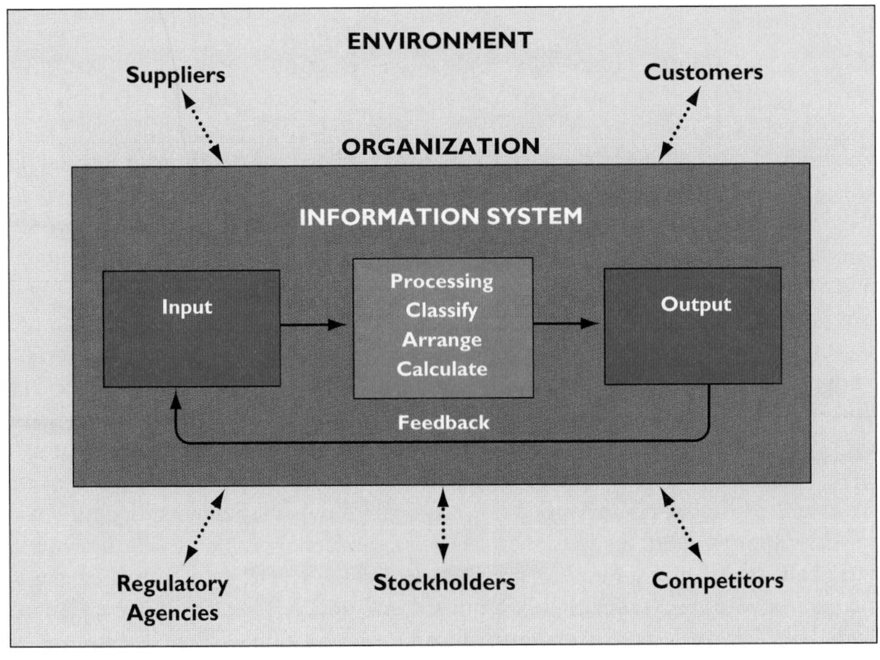


***Figure 1-3*** Functions of an information system. An information system contains information about an organization and its surrounding environment. Three basic activities—input, processing, and output—produce the information organizations need. Feedback is output returned to appropriate people or activities in the organization to evaluate and refine the input. Environmental actors such as customers, suppliers, competitors, stockholders, and regulatory agencies interact with the organization and its information systems.

## UPS COMPETES GLOBALLY WITH INFORMATION TECHNOLOGY

United Parcel Service (UPS), the world's largest air and ground package-distribution company, started out in 1907 in a closet-size basement office. Jim Casey and Claude Ryan—two teenagers from Seattle with two bicycles and one phone—promised the "best service and lowest rates." UPS has used this formula successfully for more than 90 years.

Today UPS delivers more than 13 million parcels and documents daily throughout the United States and more than 200 other countries and territories. The firm has been able to maintain its leadership in small-package delivery services in the face of stiff competition from Federal Express and Airborne Express by investing heavily in advanced information technology. Over the past decade, UPS has spent more than $1 billion a year to boost customer service while keeping costs low and streamlining its overall operations.

Using a handheld computer called a Delivery Information Acquisition Device (DIAD), UPS drivers automatically capture customers' signatures along with pickup, delivery, and time-card information. The drivers then place the DIAD into their truck's vehicle adapter, an information-transmitting device that is connected to the cellular telephone network. (Drivers may also transmit and receive information using an internal radio in the DIAD.) Package tracking information is then transmitted to UPS's computer network for storage and processing in UPS's main computers in Mahwah, New Jersey, and Alpharetta, Georgia. From there, the information can be accessed worldwide to provide proof of delivery to the customer or to respond to customer queries.

Through its automated package tracking system, UPS can monitor packages throughout the delivery process. At various points along the route from sender to receiver, a bar code device scans shipping information on the package label; the information is then fed into the central computer. Customer service representatives can check the status of any package from desktop computers linked to the central computers and are able to respond immediately to inquiries from customers. UPS customers can also access this information from the company's Web site using their own computers or wireless devices, such as pagers and cell phones.

Anyone with a package to ship can access the UPS Web site to track packages, check delivery routes, calculate shipping rates, determine time in transit, and schedule a pickup. Businesses anywhere can use the Web site to arrange UPS shipments and bill the shipments to the company's UPS account or to a credit card. The data collected at the UPS Web site are transmitted to the UPS central computer and then back to the customer after processing. UPS also provides tools that enable customers such as Cisco Systems described in the Window on Organizations, to embed UPS functions, such as tracking and cost calculation, into their own Web sites so that they can track shipments without visiting the UPS site. UPS started a new service called UPS Document Exchange to deliver business documents electronically using the Internet. The service provides a high level of security for these important documents as well as document tracking.

**To Think About:** What are the inputs, processing, and outputs of UPS's package tracking system? What technologies are used? How are these technologies related to UPS's business strategy? What would happen if these technologies were not available?

*Sources:* Rick Brooks, "Outside the Box," *The Wall Street Journal E-Commerce Section,* February 12, 2001; Bob Brewin, "FedEx, UPS Vie to Offer Wireless Tracking Services," *Computerworld,* July 3, 2000; Kelly Barron, "Logistics in Brown," *Forbes,* January 10, 2000; Art Jahnke, "Deliverance," *CIO Web Business Magazine,* July 1, 1999; and David Baum, "UPS: Keeping Track," *Oracle Magazine,* May/June 1999.

computer hardware and software technology to process and disseminate information. From this point on, when we use the term *information systems,* we will be referring to computer-based information systems—formal organizational systems that rely on computer technology. The Window on Technology describes some of the typical technologies used in computer-based information systems today.

Although computer-based information systems use computer technology to process raw data into meaningful information, there is a sharp distinction between a computer and a computer program on the one hand and an information system on the other. Electronic computers and related software programs are the technical foundation, the tools and materials, of modern information systems. Computers provide the equipment for storing and processing information. Computer programs, or software, are sets of operating instructions that direct and control computer processing. Knowing how computers and computer programs work is important in designing solutions to organizational problems, but computers are only part of an information system. A house is an appropriate analogy. Houses are built with hammers, nails, and wood, but these do not make a house. The architecture, design, setting, landscaping, and all of the decisions that lead to the creation of these features are part of the

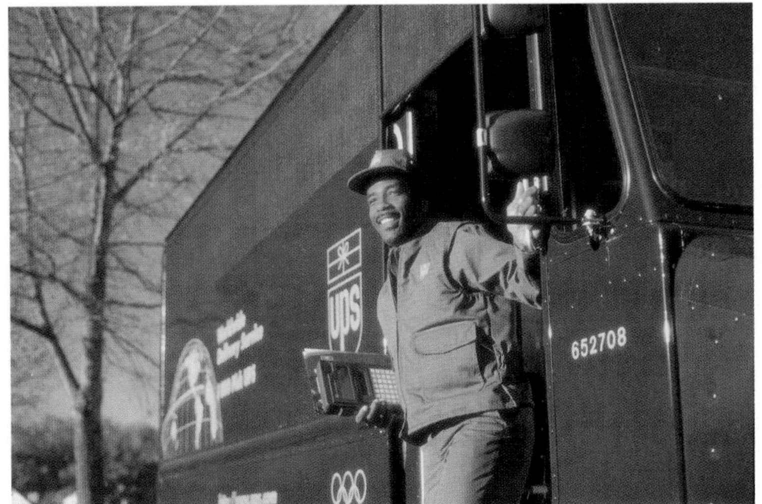


*Using a handheld computer called a Delivery Information Acquisition Device (DIAD), UPS drivers automatically capture customers' signatures along with pickup, delivery, and time-card information.*

house and are crucial for solving the problem of putting a roof over one's head. Computers and programs are the hammer, nails, and lumber of CBIS, but alone they cannot produce the information a particular organization needs. To understand information systems, one must understand the problems they are designed to solve, their architectural and design elements, and the organizational processes that lead to these solutions.

## A Business Perspective on Information Systems

From a business perspective, an information system is an organizational and management solution, based on information technology, to a challenge posed by the environment. Examine this definition closely, because it emphasizes the organizational and managerial nature of information systems: To fully understand information systems, a manager must understand the broader organization, management, and information technology dimensions of systems (see Figure 1-4) and their power to provide solutions to challenges and problems in the business environment. We refer to this broader understanding of information systems, which encompasses an understanding of the management and organizational dimensions of systems as well as the technical dimensions of systems, as **information systems literacy.**

**information systems literacy** Broad-based understanding of information systems that includes behavioral knowledge about organizations and individuals using information systems as well as technical knowledge about computers.

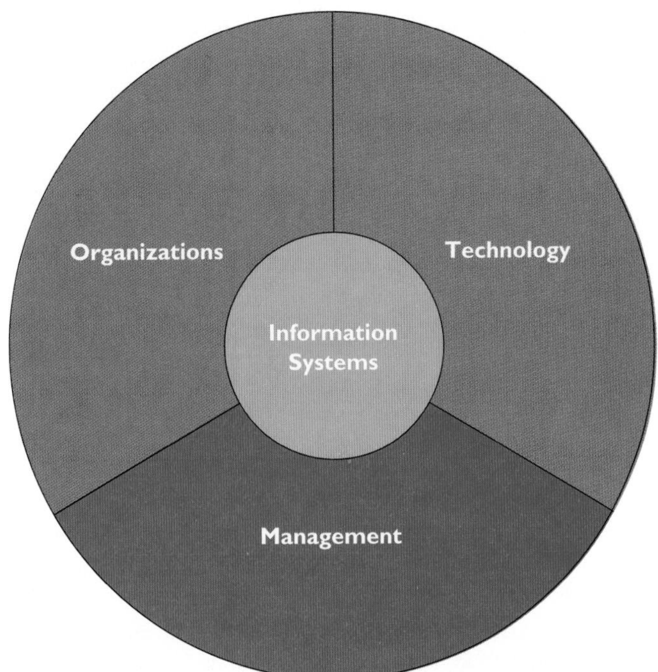


***Figure 1-4*** Information systems are more than computers. Using information systems effectively requires an understanding of the organization, management, and information technology shaping the systems. All information systems can be described as organizational and management solutions to challenges posed by the environment.

**computer literacy**
Knowledge about information technology, focusing on understanding of how computer-based technologies work.

Information systems literacy includes a behavioral as well as a technical approach to studying information systems. **Computer literacy,** in contrast, focuses primarily on knowledge of information technology.

Review the diagram at the beginning of the chapter, which reflects this expanded definition of an information system. The diagram shows how GUESS's apparel buying information system addresses the business challenges of rapid growth, intensifying competition, and inefficiencies from manual paper-based processes. The diagram also illustrates how management, technology, and organization elements work together to create the system. Each chapter of this text begins with a diagram like this one to help you analyze the opening case. You can use this diagram as a starting point for analyzing any information system or information system problem you encounter.

## Organizations

**business functions**
Specialized tasks performed in a business organization, including manufacturing and production, sales and marketing, finance, accounting, and human resources.

**standard operating procedures (SOPs)**
Formal rules for accomplishing tasks that have been developed to cope with expected situations.

**knowledge workers**
People, such as engineers or architects, who design products or services and create knowledge for the organization.

**data workers**
People, such as secretaries or bookkeepers, who process the organization's paperwork.

**production or service workers**
People who actually produce the products or services of the organization.

Information systems are an integral part of organizations. Indeed, for some companies, such as credit reporting firms, without the information system there would be no business. The key elements of an organization are its people, structure, operating procedures, politics, and culture. We introduce these components of organizations here and describe them in greater detail in Chapter 3. Organizations are composed of different levels and specialties. Their structures reveal a clear-cut division of labor. Experts are employed and trained for different functions, The major **business functions,** or specialized tasks performed by business organizations, consist of sales and marketing, manufacturing and production, finance, accounting, and human resources (see Table 1-2). Chapter 2 provides more detail on these business functions and the ways in which they are supported by information systems.

An organization coordinates work through a structured hierarchy and formal, standard operating procedures. The hierarchy arranges people in a pyramid structure of rising authority and responsibility. The upper levels of the hierarchy consist of managerial, professional, and technical employees, whereas the lower levels consist of operational personnel.

**Standard operating procedures (SOPs)** are formal rules that have been developed over a long time for accomplishing tasks. These rules guide employees in a variety of procedures, from writing an invoice to responding to customer complaints. Most procedures are formalized and written down, but others are informal work practices, such as a requirement to return telephone calls from co-workers or customers that are not formally documented. The firm's business processes, which we defined earlier, are based on its standard operating procedures. Many business processes and SOPs are incorporated into information systems, such as how to pay a supplier or how to correct an erroneous bill.

Organizations require many different kinds of skills and people. In addition to managers, **knowledge workers** (such as engineers, architects, or scientists) design products or services and create new knowledge, and **data workers** (such as secretaries, bookkeepers, or clerks) process the organization's paperwork. **Production or service workers** (such as machinists, assemblers, or packers) actually produce the organization's products or services.

Each organization has a unique culture, or fundamental set of assumptions, values, and ways of doing things, that has been accepted by most of its members. Parts of an organization's culture can always be found embedded in its information systems. For instance, the

**TABLE 1-2 MAJOR BUSINESS FUNCTIONS**

| Function | Purpose |
|---|---|
| Sales and marketing | Selling the organization's products and services |
| Manufacturing and production | Producing products and services |
| Finance | Managing the organization's financial assets (cash, stocks, bonds, etc.) |
| Accounting | Maintaining the organization's financial records (receipts, disbursements, paychecks, etc.); accounting for the flow of funds |
| Human resources | Attracting, developing, and maintaining the organization's labor force; maintaining employee records |

United Parcel Service's concern with placing service to the customer first is an aspect of its organizational culture that can be found in the company's package tracking systems.

Different levels and specialties in an organization create different interests and points of view. These views often conflict. Conflict is the basis for organizational politics. Information systems develop out of this cauldron of differing perspectives, conflicts, compromises, and agreements that are a natural part of all organizations. In Chapter 3 we examine these features of organizations in greater detail.

## Management

Managers perceive business challenges in the environment. They set the organizational strategy for responding and allocate the human and financial resources to achieve the strategy and coordinate the work. Throughout, they must exercise responsible leadership. Management's job is to "make sense" out of the many situations faced by organizations and formulate action plans to solve organizational problems.

But managers must do more than manage what already exists. They must also create new products and services and even re-create the organization from time to time. A substantial part of management responsibility is creative work driven by new knowledge and information. Information technology can play a powerful role in redirecting and redesigning the organization. Chapter 3 describes managers' activities and management decision making in detail.

It is important to note that managerial roles and decisions vary at different levels of the organization. **Senior managers** make long-range strategic decisions about products and services to produce. **Middle managers** carry out the programs and plans of senior management. **Operational managers** are responsible for monitoring the firm's daily activities. All levels of management are expected to be creative and to develop novel solutions to a broad range of problems. Each level of management has different information needs and information system requirements.

## Technology

Information technology is one of many tools managers use to cope with change. **Computer hardware** is the physical equipment used for input, processing, and output activities in an information system. It consists of the following: the computer processing unit; various input, output, and storage devices; and physical media to link these devices together. Chapter 5 describes computer hardware in greater detail.

**Computer software** consists of the detailed preprogrammed instructions that control and coordinate the computer hardware components in an information system. Chapter 6 explains the importance of computer software in information systems.

**Storage technology** includes both the physical media for storing data, such as magnetic or optical disk or tape, and the software governing the organization of data on these physical media. More detail on physical storage media can be found in Chapter 5, whereas Chapter 7 covers data organization and access methods.

**Communications technology,** consisting of both physical devices and software, links the various pieces of hardware and transfers data from one physical location to another. Computers and communications equipment can be connected in networks for sharing voice, data, images, sound, or even video. A **network** links two or more computers to share data or resources such as a printer. Chapters 8 and 9 provide more details on communications and networking technology and issues.

All of these technologies represent resources that can be shared throughout the organization and constitute the firm's **information technology (IT) infrastructure.** The information technology infrastructure provides the foundation, or platform, on which the firm can build its specific information systems. Each organization must carefully design and manage its information technology infrastructure so that it has the set of technology services it needs for the work it wants to accomplish with information systems. Chapters 5 through 9 of this text examine each major technology component of information technology infrastructure and show how they all work together to create the technology platform for the organization.

Let us return to UPS's package tracking system in the Window on Technology and identify the organization, management, and technology elements. The organization element

**senior managers**
People occupying the topmost hierarchy in an organization who are responsible for making long-range decisions.

**middle managers**
People in the middle of the organizational hierarchy who are responsible for carrying out the plans and goals of senior management.

**operational managers**
People who monitor the day-to-day activities of the organization.

**computer hardware**
Physical equipment used for input, processing, and output activities in an information system.

**computer software**
Detailed, preprogrammed instructions that control and coordinate the work of computer hardware components in an information system.

**storage technology**
Physical media and software governing the storage and organization of data for use in an information system.

**communications technology**
Physical devices and software that link various computer hardware components and transfer data from one physical location to another.

**network**
The linking of two or more computers to share data or resources, such as a printer.

**information technology (IT) infrastructure**
Computer hardware, software, data and storage technology, and networks providing a portfolio of shared information technology resources for the organization.

anchors the package tracking system in UPS's sales and production functions (the main product of UPS is a service—package delivery). It specifies the required procedures for identifying packages with both sender and recipient information, taking inventory, tracking the packages en route, and providing package status reports for UPS customers and customer service representatives. The system must also provide information to satisfy the needs of managers and workers. UPS drivers need to be trained in both package pickup and delivery procedures and in how to use the package tracking system so that they can work efficiently and effectively. UPS customers may need some training to use UPS in-house package tracking software or the UPS World Wide Web site. UPS's management is responsible for monitoring service levels and costs and for promoting the company's strategy of combining low cost and superior service. Management decided to use automation to increase the ease of sending a package via UPS and of checking its delivery status, thereby reducing delivery costs and increasing sales revenues. The technology supporting this system includes handheld computers, bar code scanners, wired and wireless communications networks, desktop computers, UPS's central computer, storage technology for the package delivery data, UPS in-house package tracking software, and software to access the World Wide Web. The result is an information system solution to the business challenge of providing a high level of service with low prices in the face of mounting competition.

## 1.2 CONTEMPORARY APPROACHES TO INFORMATION SYSTEMS

Multiple perspectives on information systems show that the study of information systems is a multidisciplinary field. No single theory or perspective dominates. Figure 1-5 illustrates the major disciplines that contribute problems, issues, and solutions in the study of information systems. In general, the field can be divided into technical and behavioral approaches. Information systems are sociotechnical systems. Though they are composed of machines, devices, and "hard" physical technology, they require substantial social, organizational, and intellectual investments to make them work properly.

### TECHNICAL APPROACH

The technical approach to information systems emphasizes mathematically based models to study information systems, as well as the physical technology and formal capabilities of these systems. The disciplines that contribute to the technical approach are computer science, management science, and operations research. Computer science is concerned with establishing theories of computability, methods of computation, and methods of efficient data storage and access. Management science emphasizes the development of models for decision-making and management practices. Operations research focuses on mathematical techniques for optimizing selected parameters of organizations such as transportation, inventory control, and transaction costs.

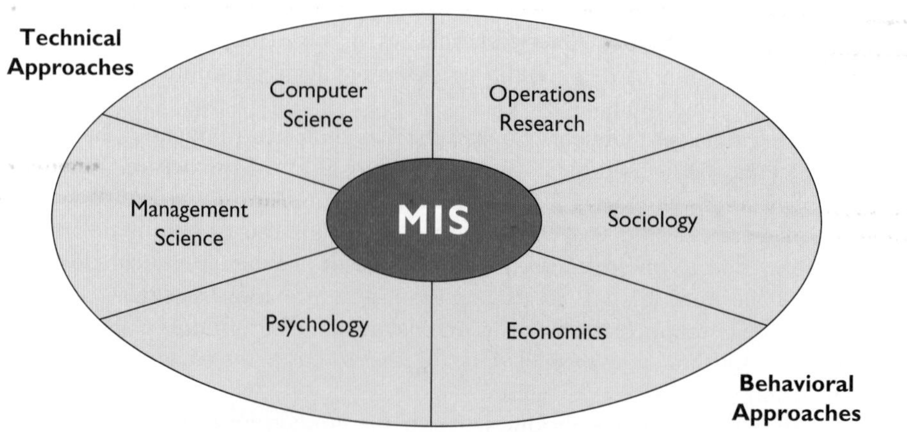


*Figure 1-5* Contemporary approaches to information systems. The study of information systems deals with issues and insights contributed from technical and behavioral disciplines.

## BEHAVIORAL APPROACH

An important part of the information systems field is concerned with behavioral issues that arise in the development and long-term maintenance of information systems. Issues such as strategic business integration, design, implementation, utilization, and management cannot be explored usefully with the models used in the technical approach. Other behavioral disciplines contribute important concepts and methods. For instance, sociologists study information systems with an eye toward how groups and organizations shape the development of systems and also how systems affect individuals, groups, and organizations. Psychologists study information systems with an interest in how human decision makers perceive and use formal information. Economists study information systems with an interest in what impact systems have on control and cost structures within the firm and within markets.

The behavioral approach does not ignore technology. Indeed, information systems technology is often the stimulus for a behavioral problem or issue. But the focus of this approach is generally not on technical solutions. Instead it concentrates on changes in attitudes, management and organizational policy, and behavior (Kling and Dutton, 1982).

## APPROACH OF THIS TEXT: SOCIOTECHNICAL SYSTEMS

The study of **management information systems (MIS)** arose in the 1970s to focus on computer-based information systems aimed at managers (Davis and Olson, 1985). MIS combines the theoretical work of computer science, management science, and operations research with a practical orientation toward building systems and applications. It also pays attention to behavioral issues raised by sociology, economics, and psychology.

**Management information systems (MIS)**
The study of information systems focusing on their use in business and management.

Our experience as academics and practitioners leads us to believe that no single perspective effectively captures the reality of information systems. Problems with systems—and their solutions—are rarely all technical or all behavioral. Our best advice to students is to understand the perspectives of all disciplines. Indeed, the challenge and excitement of the information systems field is that it requires an appreciation and tolerance of many different approaches.

Adopting a sociotechnical systems perspective helps avoid a purely technological approach to information systems. For instance, the fact that information technology is rapidly declining in cost and growing in power does not necessarily or easily translate into productivity enhancement or bottom-line profits.

In this book, we stress the need to optimize a system's performance as a whole. Both the technical and behavioral components need attention. This means that technology must be changed and designed in such a way as to fit organizational and individual needs. At times, the technology may have to be "de-optimized" to accomplish this fit. Organizations and individuals must also be changed through training, learning, and planned organizational change in order to facilitate the operation and prosperity of the technology (see, for example, Liker et al., 1987). People and organizations change to take advantage of new information technology. Figure 1-6 illustrates this process of mutual adjustment in a sociotechnical system.

TECHNOLOGY
Alternative 1
Alternative 2
Alternative 3
Final Design of Technology

ORGANIZATION
Alternative 1
Alternative 2
Alternative 3
Final Design of Organization

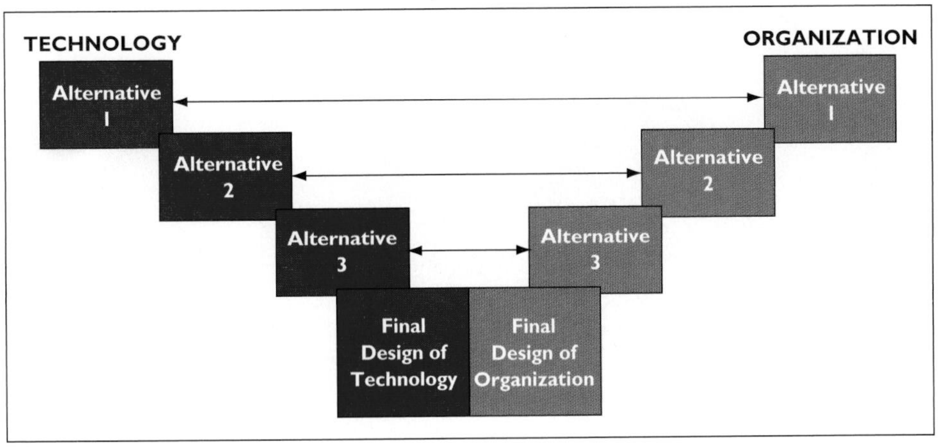

*Figure 1-6* A sociotechnical perspective on information systems. In a sociotechnical perspective, the performance of a system is optimized when both the technology and the organization mutually adjust to one another until a satisfactory fit is obtained.

## 1.3 TOWARD THE DIGITAL FIRM: THE NEW ROLE OF INFORMATION SYSTEMS IN ORGANIZATIONS

Managers cannot ignore information systems because they play such a critical role in contemporary organizations. Today's systems directly affect how managers decide, plan, and manage their employees, and increasingly shape what products are produced, where, when, and how. Therefore, responsibility for systems cannot be delegated to technical decision makers.

### THE WIDENING SCOPE OF INFORMATION SYSTEMS

Figure 1-7 illustrates the new relationship between organizations and information systems. There is a growing interdependence between business strategy, rules, and procedures on the one hand, and information systems software, hardware, databases, and telecommunications on the other. A change in any of these components often requires changes in other components. This relationship becomes critical when management plans for the future. What a business would like to do in five years often depends on what its systems will be able to do. Increasing market share, becoming the high-quality or low-cost producer, developing new products, and increasing employee productivity depend more and more on the kinds and quality of information systems in the organization.

A second change in the relationship between information systems and organizations results from the growing reach and scope of system projects and applications. Building and managing systems today involves a much larger part of the organization than it did in the past. As firms become more like "digital firms," the system enterprise extends to customers, vendors, and even industry competitors (see Figure 1-8). Where early systems produced largely technical changes that affected only a few people in the firm, contemporary systems have been bringing about managerial changes (who has what information about whom, when, and how often) and institutional "core" changes (what products and services are produced, under what conditions, and by whom). As companies move toward digital firm organizations, nearly all the firm's managers and employees—as well as customers and vendors—participate in a variety of firm systems, tied together by a digital information web. For instance, what a customer does on a firm's Web site can trigger an employee to make an on-the-spot pricing decision or alert a firm's suppliers of potential "stock out" situations.

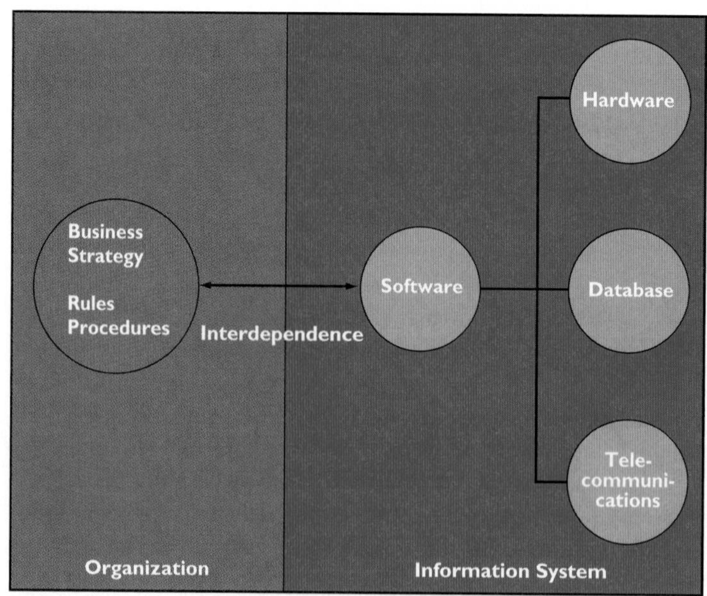


*Figure 1-7* The interdependence between organizations and information systems. In contemporary systems there is a growing interdependence between organizational business strategy, rules, and procedures and the organization's information systems. Changes in strategy, rules, and procedures increasingly require changes in hardware, software, databases, and telecommunications. Existing systems can act as a constraint on organizations. Often, what the organization would like to do depends on what its systems will permit it to do.

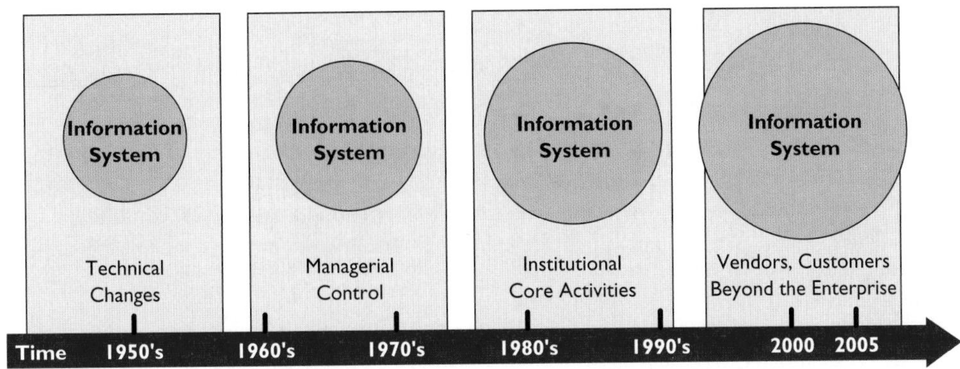


***Figure 1-8*** The widening scope of information systems. Over time, information systems have come to play a larger role in the life of organizations. Early systems brought about largely technical changes that were relatively easy to accomplish. Later systems affected managerial control and behavior, and influenced "core" institutional activities. In the digital firm era, information systems extend far beyond the boundaries of the firm to encompass vendors, customers, and even competitors.

## THE NETWORK REVOLUTION AND THE INTERNET

One reason information systems play such a large role in organizations and affect so many people is the soaring power and declining cost of computer technology. Computing power, which has been doubling every 18 months, has improved the performance of microprocessors over 25,000 times since their invention 30 years ago. With powerful, easy-to-use software, the computer can crunch numbers, analyze vast pools of data, or simulate complex physical and logical processes with animated drawings, sounds, and even tactile feedback.

The soaring power of computer technology has spawned powerful communication networks that organizations can use to access vast storehouses of information from around the world and to coordinate activities across space and time. These networks are transforming the shape and form of business enterprises, creating the foundation for the digital firm.

The world's largest and most widely used network is the **Internet.** The Internet is an international network of networks that are both commercial and publicly owned. The Internet connects hundreds of thousands of different networks from more than 200 countries around the world. More than 400 million people working in science, education, government, and business use the Internet to exchange information or perform business transactions with other organizations around the globe.

**Internet**
International network of networks that is a collection of hundreds of thousands of private and public networks.

The Internet is extremely elastic. If networks are added or removed or failures occur in parts of the system, the rest of the Internet continues to operate. Through special communication and technology standards, any computer can communicate with virtually any other computer linked to the Internet using ordinary telephone lines. Companies and private individuals can use the Internet to exchange business transactions, text messages, graphic images, and even video and sound, whether they are located next door or on the other side of the globe. Table 1-3 describes some of the Internet's capabilities.

*The Internet. This global network of networks provides a highly flexible platform for information sharing. Digital information can be distributed at almost no cost to millions of people throughout the world.*

TABLE 1-3

## WHAT YOU CAN DO ON THE INTERNET

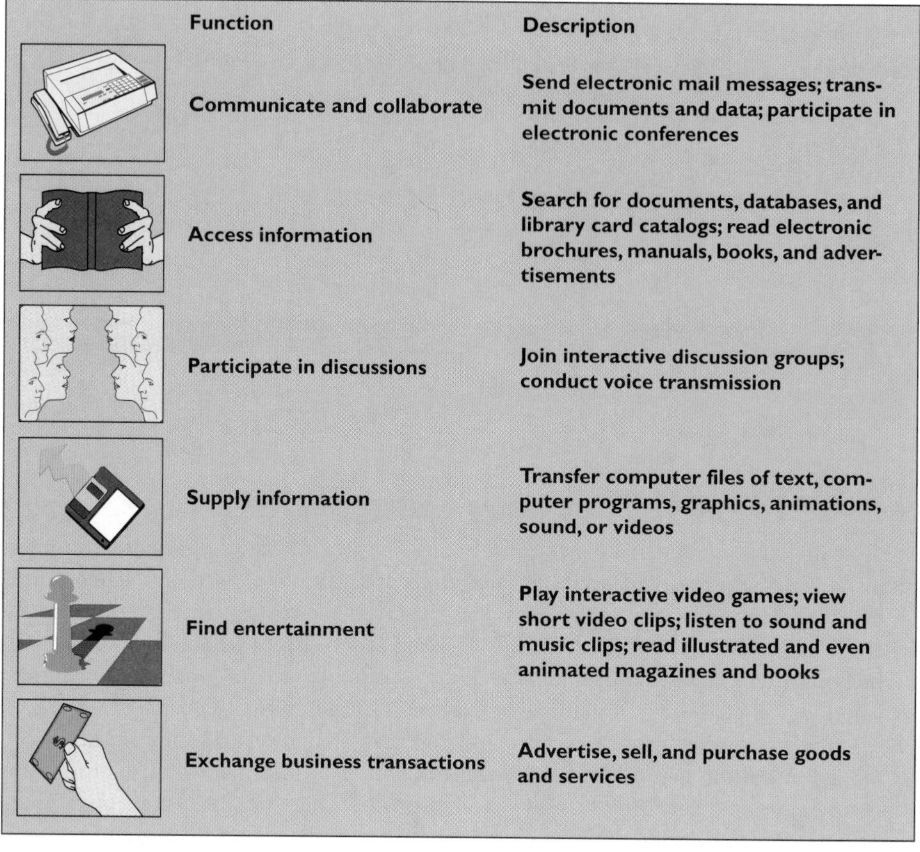

| Function | Description |
|---|---|
| Communicate and collaborate | Send electronic mail messages; transmit documents and data; participate in electronic conferences |
| Access information | Search for documents, databases, and library card catalogs; read electronic brochures, manuals, books, and advertisements |
| Participate in discussions | Join interactive discussion groups; conduct voice transmission |
| Supply information | Transfer computer files of text, computer programs, graphics, animations, sound, or videos |
| Find entertainment | Play interactive video games; view short video clips; listen to sound and music clips; read illustrated and even animated magazines and books |
| Exchange business transactions | Advertise, sell, and purchase goods and services |

The Internet is creating a new "universal" technology platform on which to build all sorts of new products, services, strategies, and organizations. It is reshaping the way information systems are being used in business and daily life. By eliminating many technical, geographic, and cost barriers obstructing the global flow of information, the Internet is inspiring new uses of information systems and new business models (see the Window on Management). The Internet provides the primary technology platform for the digital firm.

**World Wide Web**
A system with universally accepted standards for storing, retrieving, formatting, and displaying information in a networked environment.

Because it offers so many new possibilities for doing business, the Internet capability known as the **World Wide Web** is of special interest to organizations and managers. The

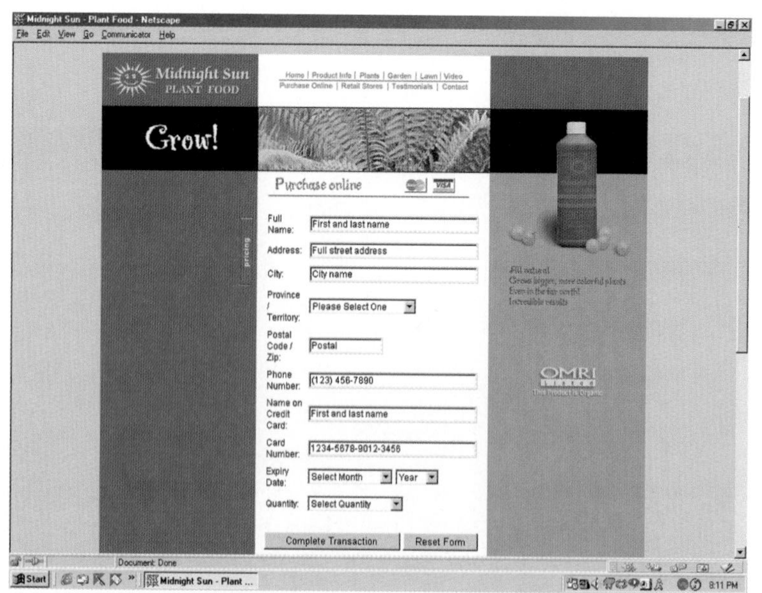


*Midnight Sun Plant Foods sells its products all over the world through its Web site. The Internet has become a source of new business models and opportunities for entrepreneurs.*

## YUKON NETREPRENEURS

How do you make a business grow when you live within the Arctic Circle? That was the problem faced by Herbie Croteau, the founder and CEO of Midnight Sun Plant Food. He lives in Faro with a population of 500. Faro is in Canada's Yukon Territories, which is two-thirds the size of Texas but only has a population of 31,000, two-thirds of which live in the capital of Whitehorse. And, of course, being north of the Arctic Circle, it has very long winters, with an average winter temperature 15 degrees below zero (Fahrenheit) and an average snowfall about five feet. A truck driver for the local zinc mine, Croteau found himself out of a job when the mine closed in 1992. To pass the time he began developing a fertilizer from local ingredients for his wife to use to feed both her indoor and her outdoor plants. When neighbors saw the size of her plants and vegetables, they began demanding he sell them some of his fertilizer, and he found himself in business.

Because Croteau lived in such a small town, his natural market was almost nonexistent. In 1993 he began bringing his fertilizer to Whitehorse, a town of 22,000 five hours away from Faro. In business terms Whitehorse also presented only a tiny market, and so by 1998 Croteau's annual sales had only grown to $10,000. However, the Internet had reached the Yukon, and when it arrived in Faro, Croteau saw it as a way to expand his business.

Yukon residents are relatively educated, with nearly 20 percent of adults holding college degrees, making it a fertile territory for the Internet. Recognizing this, a small group of computer enthusiasts founded Yknet in 1994, bringing the Internet to the region. With the help of the government and a Canadian telephone giant (Northwestel), the company eventually brought Internet service to 38 percent of Yukon households. In 1998 Croteau brought his company to the Web (www.midnightsunplantfood.com) in an attempt to broaden his market.

At first Croteau's site got only two visitors per day, and so Croteau spent much of his time searching out sites that would offer him free links to other Web sites. Quickly, his visitors rose to hundreds each week. Then his site began accepting credit cards, enabling on-line sales, and his site even included a currency converter and video testimonials from happy customers. He has already redesigned his site several times to make it easier to reach. Croteau claimed that 90 percent of the people visiting his site purchase his plant food and he expected his revenue to reach perhaps as high as $100,000 (Canadian) in 2000.

In Haines Junction another Yukon Territories business turned to the Internet for aid. Roland and Susan Shaver had founded Bear North Adventures, which offered guided snowmobile tours of the breathtaking mountains and pristine snow-covered lakes. Their problem was finding ways to publicize their magnificent territory and their tours. Investing $2,000 to establish a Web site (bearnorth.yukon.net), they can now provide visitors with many pictures of the touring area along with information on the costs. Web users find the Bear North site through links on other travel and snowmobile sites.

**To Think About:** What are the business problems that an entrepreneur can address through the use of the Internet? How essential is the Internet in the strategy and operation of these businesses? Explain.

*Source:* David H. Freedman, "Cold Comfort," *Forbes.com,* May 29, 2000; and Yukon Territories Web site, http://www.gov.yk.ca/facts.html.

World Wide Web is a system with universally accepted standards for storing, retrieving, formatting, and displaying information in a networked environment. Information is stored and displayed as electronic "pages" that can contain text, graphics, animations, sound, and video. These Web pages can be linked electronically to other Web pages, regardless of where they are located, and viewed by any type of computer. By clicking on highlighted words or buttons on a Web page, you can link to related pages to find additional information, software programs, or still more links to other points on the Web. The Web can serve as the foundation for new kinds of information systems, such as Midnight Sun Plant Food's system for placing orders over its Web site.

All of the Web pages maintained by an organization or individual are called a **Web site.** (The preceding page illustrates a page from Midnight Sun Plant Food's Web site.) Businesses are creating Web sites with stylish typography, colorful graphics, push-button interactivity, and often sound and video to disseminate product information widely, to "broadcast" advertising and messages to customers, to collect electronic orders and customer data, and increasingly to coordinate far-flung sales forces and organizations on a global scale.

**Web site**
All of the World Wide Web pages maintained by an organization or an individual.

In Chapters 4 and 9 we describe the Web and other Internet capabilities in greater detail. We also discuss relevant features of the Internet throughout the text, because the Internet affects so many aspects of information systems in organizations.

## NEW OPTIONS FOR ORGANIZATIONAL DESIGN: THE DIGITAL FIRM AND THE NETWORKED ENTERPRISE

The explosive growth in computing power and networks, including the Internet, is turning organizations into networked enterprises, allowing information to be instantly distributed within and beyond the organization. This capability can be used to redesign and reshape organizations, transforming their structure, scope of operations, reporting and control mechanisms, work practices, workflows, products, and services. The ultimate end product of these new ways of conducting business electronically is the digital firm.

### Flattening Organizations

Large, bureaucratic organizations, which primarily developed before the computer age, are often inefficient, slow to change, and less competitive than newly created organizations. Some of these large organizations have downsized, reducing the number of employees and the number of levels in their organizational hierarchies. For example, when Eastman Chemical Co. split off from Kodak in 1994, it had $3.3 billion in revenue and 24,000 full-time employees. By 2000 it generated $5 billion in revenue with only 17,000 employees (*Information Week,* 2000).

In digital firms, hierarchy and organizational levels do not disappear. But digital firms develop "optimal hierarchies" that balance the decision-making load across an organization, resulting in flatter organizations. Flatter organizations have fewer levels of management, with lower-level employees being given greater decision-making authority (see Figure 1-9). Those employees are empowered to make more decisions than in the past, they no longer work standard 9-to-5 hours, and they no longer necessarily work in an office. Moreover, such employees may be scattered geographically, sometimes working half a world away from the manager.

Contemporary information technology can make more information available to line workers so they can make decisions that had previously had been made by managers. With the emergence of global networks, such as the Internet, team members can collaborate closely even from distant locations. These changes mean that the management span of control has also been broadened, allowing high-level managers to manage and control more workers spread over greater distances. Many companies have eliminated thousands of middle managers as a result of these changes. AT&T, IBM, and General Motors are only a few of the organizations that have eliminated more than 30,000 middle managers in one fell swoop.

***Figure 1-9*** Flattening organizations. Information systems can reduce the number of levels in an organization by providing managers with information to supervise larger numbers of workers and by giving lower-level employees more decision-making authority.

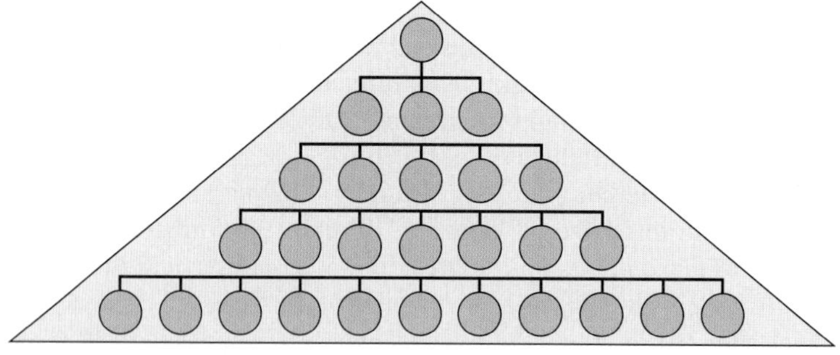

**A traditional hierarchical organization with many levels of management**

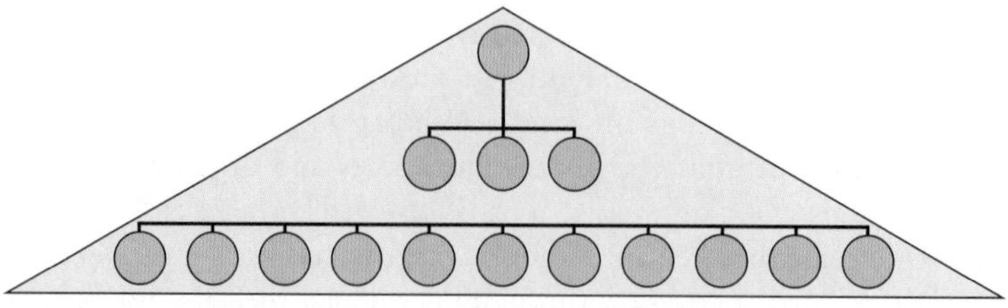

**An organization that has been "flattened" by removing layers of management**

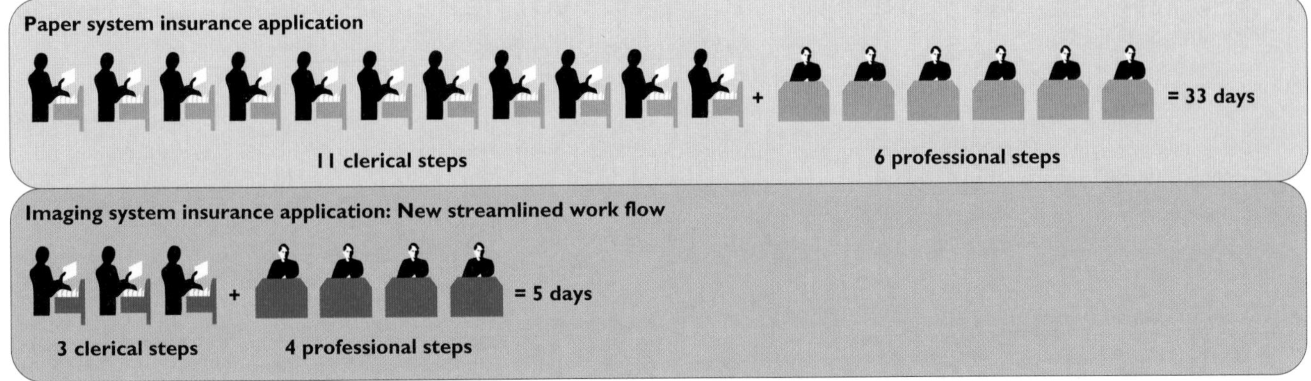


*Figure 1-10* Redesigned workflow for insurance underwriting. An application requiring 33 days in a paper system would only take 5 days using computers, networks, and a streamlined workflow.

## Separating Work from Location

Communications technology has eliminated distance as a factor for many types of work in many situations. Salespersons can spend more time in the field with customers and have up-to-date information with them while carrying less paper. Many employees can work remotely from their homes or cars, and companies can reserve space at smaller central offices for meeting clients or other employees. Entire parts of organizations can disappear. For example, inventory, and the warehouses to store it, can be eliminated as suppliers tie into the firm's computer systems and deliver only what is needed and just in time.

Collaborative teamwork across thousands of miles has become a reality as designers work on a new product together even if they are located on different continents. Ford Motor Co. has adopted a cross-continent collaborative model to design its automobiles. Supported by high-capacity communications networks and computer-aided design (CAD) software, Ford designers launched the Mustang design in Dunton, England. The design was worked on simultaneously by designers at Dearborn, Michigan, and Dunton, with some input from designers in Japan and Australia. Once the design was completed, Ford engineers in Turin, Italy, used it to produce a full-size physical model. Ford now designs other models this way and is starting to use Web technology for global collaboration (see Chapter 12).

## Reorganizing Workflows

Information systems have been progressively replacing manual work procedures with automated work procedures, workflows, and work processes. Electronic workflows have reduced the cost of operations in many companies by displacing paper and the manual routines that accompany it. Improved workflow management has enabled many corporations not only to cut costs significantly but also to improve customer service at the same time. For instance, insurance companies can reduce processing of applications for new insurance from weeks to days (see Figure 1-10).

Redesigned workflows can have a profound impact on organizational efficiency and can even lead to new organizational structures, products, and services. We discuss the impact of restructured workflows on organizational design in greater detail in Chapters 3 and 10.

## Increasing Flexibility of Organizations

Companies can use communications technology to organize in more flexible ways, increasing their ability to sense and respond to changes in the marketplace and to take advantage of new opportunities. Information systems can give both large and small organizations additional flexibility to overcome some of the limitations posed by their size. Table 1-4 describes some of the ways in which information technology can help small companies act "big" and help big companies act "small." Small organizations can use information systems to acquire some of the muscle and reach of larger organizations. They can perform coordinating activities, such as

**TABLE 1-4** **HOW INFORMATION TECHNOLOGY INCREASES ORGANIZATIONAL FLEXIBILITY**

**Small Companies**

Desktop machines, inexpensive computer-aided design (CAD) software, and computer-controlled machine tools provide the precision, speed, and quality of giant manufacturers.

Information immediately accessed by telephone and communications links eliminates the need for research staff and business libraries.

Managers can easily obtain the information they need to manage large numbers of employees in widely scattered locations.

**Large Companies**

Custom manufacturing systems allow large factories to offer customized products in small quantities.

Massive databases of customer purchasing records can be analyzed so that large companies know their customers' needs and preferences as easily as local merchants.

Information can be easily distributed down the ranks of the organization to empower lower-level employees and work groups to solve problems.

processing bids or keeping track of inventory, and many manufacturing tasks with very few managers, clerks, or production workers. For example, Beamscope Canada, a Toronto distributor of electronic and computer parts, competes effectively against global giants such as Ingram Micro Inc. and Merisel Inc. Its Beamscope Online system offers customers on-line service and 24-hour ordering capabilities (Engler, 1999).

Large organizations can use information technology to achieve some of the agility and responsiveness of small organizations. One aspect of this phenomenon is **mass customization,** where software and computer networks are used to link the plant floor tightly with orders, design, and purchasing and to finely control production machines. The result is a dynamically responsive environment in which products can be turned out in greater variety and easily customized with no added cost for small production runs. For example, Levi Strauss has equipped some of its stores with an option called Personal Pair, which allows customers to design jeans to their own specifications, rather than picking them off the rack. Customers enter their measurements into a personal computer, which then transmits the customer's specifications over a network to Levi's plants. The company is able to produce the custom jeans on the same lines that manufacture its standard items. There are almost no extra production costs, because the process does not require additional warehousing, production overruns, and inventories.

**mass customization**
Use of software and computer networks to finely control production so that products can be easily customized with no added cost for small production runs.

A related trend is micromarketing, in which information systems can help companies pinpoint tiny target markets for these finely customized products and services—as small as individualized "markets of one." We discuss micromarketing in more detail in Chapters 2 and 13.

## The Changing Management Process

Information technology is recasting the management process, providing powerful new capabilities to help managers plan, organize, lead, and control. For instance, it is now possible for managers to obtain information on organizational performance down to the level of specific transactions from almost anywhere in the organization at any time. Product managers at Frito-Lay Corporation, the world's largest manufacturer of salty snack foods, can know within hours precisely how many bags of Fritos have sold on any street in America at its customers' stores, how much they sold for, and what the competition's sales volumes and prices are. This greater availability and detail of information makes possible far more precise planning, forecasting, and monitoring than ever before.

Information technology has also opened new possibilities for leading. By distributing information through electronic networks, the new manager can effectively communicate frequently with thousands of employees and even manage far-flung task forces and teams—tasks that would be impossible in face-to-face organizations.

## Redefining Organizational Boundaries

A key feature of the emerging digital firm is the ability to conduct business across firm boundaries almost as efficiently and effectively as it can conduct business within the firm. Networked information systems allow companies to coordinate with other organizations across great distances. Transactions, such as payments and purchase orders, can be exchanged electronically among different companies, thereby reducing the cost of obtaining products and services from outside the firm. Organizations can also share business data, catalogs, or mail messages through networks. These networked information systems can create new efficiencies and new relationships between an organization, its customers, and suppliers which redefine their organizational boundaries. For example, the Chrysler Corporation is networked to suppliers, such as the Budd Company of Rochester, Michigan. Through this electronic link, the Budd Company monitors Chrysler production and ships sheet metal parts exactly when needed, preceded by an electronic shipping notice. Chrysler and its suppliers have thus become linked business partners with mutually shared responsibilities.

The information system linking Chrysler and its suppliers is called an interorganizational information system. Systems linking a company to its customers, distributors, or suppliers are termed **interorganizational systems,** because they automate the flow of information across organizational boundaries (Barrett, 1986–1987; Johnston and Vitale, 1988). Digital firms use interorganizational systems to link with suppliers, customers, and sometimes even competitors, to create and distribute new products and services without being limited by traditional organizational boundaries or physical location. For example, Cisco Systems does not manufacture the products it sells, using other companies, such as Flextronics for this purpose. Cisco uses the Internet to transmit orders to Flextronics and to monitor the status of orders as they are being shipped.

**interorganizational systems** Information systems that automate the flow of information across organizational boundaries and link a company to its customers, distributors, or suppliers.

## THE DIGITAL FIRM: ELECTRONIC COMMERCE AND ELECTRONIC BUSINESS

The changes we have described represent new ways of conducting business electronically both inside and outside the firm that can ultimately lead to digital firms. Increasingly, the Internet is providing the underlying technology for these changes. The Internet can link thousands of organizations into a single network, creating the foundation for a vast electronic marketplace. An **electronic market** is an information system that links together many buyers and sellers to exchange information, products, services, and payments. Through computers and networks, these systems function like electronic intermediaries, with lowered costs for typical marketplace transactions, such as matching buyers and sellers, establishing prices, ordering goods, and paying bills (Bakos, 1998). Buyers and sellers can complete purchase and sale transactions digitally, regardless of their location.

**electronic market** A marketplace that is created by computer and communication technologies that link many buyers and sellers.

A vast array of goods and services are being advertised, bought, and exchanged worldwide using the Internet as a global marketplace. Companies are furiously creating eye-catching electronic brochures, advertisements, product manuals, and order forms on the World Wide Web. All kinds of products and services are available on the Web, including fresh flowers, books, real estate, musical recordings, electronics, and steaks.

Many retailers maintain their own sites on the Web, such as Wine.com, an on-line source of wine and food items. Others offer their products through electronic shopping malls, such as ShopNow.com. Customers can locate products on this mall either by retailer, if they know what they want, or by product type, and then order the products directly. Even electronic financial trading has arrived on the Web for stocks, bonds, mutual funds, and other financial instruments.

Increasingly the Web is being used for business-to-business transactions as well. For example, airlines can use the Boeing Corporation's Web site to order parts electronically and check the status of their orders.

The global availability of the Internet for the exchange of transactions between buyers and sellers is fueling the growth of electronic commerce. **Electronic commerce** is the process of buying and selling goods and services electronically with computerized business

**electronic commerce** The process of buying and selling goods and services electronically, involving transactions using the Internet, networks, and other digital technologies.

transactions using the Internet, networks, and other digital technologies. It also encompasses activities supporting those market transactions, such as advertising, marketing, customer support, delivery, and payment. By replacing manual and paper-based procedures with electronic alternatives, and by using information flows in new and dynamic ways, electronic commerce can accelerate ordering, delivery, and payment for goods and services while reducing companies' operating and inventory costs.

The Internet is emerging as the primary technology platform for electronic commerce. Equally important, Internet technology is starting to facilitate the management of the rest of the business—publishing employee personnel policies, reviewing account balances and production plans, scheduling plant repairs and maintenance, revising design documents, and coordinating far-flung task forces and teams. Companies are also taking advantage of the connectivity and ease of use of Internet technology to create internal corporate networks called **intranets** that are based on Internet technology. Earlier in this chapter, the Window on Organizations described how Cisco Systems is using a private intranet to provide reports to management and human resources services to employees. The number of these private intranets for organizational communication, collaboration, and coordination is soaring. In this text, we use the term **electronic business** to distinguish these uses of Internet and digital technology for the management and coordination of other business processes from electronic commerce.

**intranet**
An internal network based on Internet and World Wide Web technology and standards.

**electronic business**
The use of Internet and other digital technology for organizational communication and coordination and the management of the firm.

**extranet**
Private intranet that is accessible to authorized outsiders.

The Window on Organizations also showed how Cisco Systems allows its suppliers and distributors access to portions of its private intranet. Private intranets extended to authorized users outside the organization are called **extranets** and firms use such networks to coordinate their activities with other firms for electronic commerce and electronic business. Table 1-5 lists some examples of electronic commerce and electronic business.

Figure 1-11 illustrates a digital firm making intensive use of Internet and digital technology for electronic commerce and electronic business. Information can flow seamlessly among different parts of the company and between the company and external entities—its customers, suppliers, and business partners. Organizations will move toward this digital firm vision as they use the Internet, intranets, and extranets to manage their internal processes and their relationships with customers, suppliers, and other external entities.

## TABLE 1-5 Examples of Electronic Commerce and Electronic Business

**Electronic Commerce**

**Drugstore.com** operates a virtual pharmacy on the Internet selling prescription medicine and over-the-counter health, beauty, and wellness products. Customers can input their orders via Drugstore.com's Web site and have their purchases shipped to them.

**Travelocity** provides a Web site that can be used by consumers for travel and vacation planning. Visitors can find out information on airlines, hotels, vacation packages, and other travel and leisure topics, and they can make airline and hotel reservations on-line through the Web site.

**Gilbarco Inc.** created an order management extranet that allows its distributors to submit purchase orders on-line for gas pumps, pump controllers, and other gas station supplies. Distributors can order parts, check on an order's status, and look up equipment training data and technical documentation.

**Electronic Business**

**Roche Bioscience** scientists worldwide use an intranet to share research results and discuss findings. The intranet also provides a company telephone directory and newsletter.

**EDS Corporation** uses an intranet to provide 70,000 employees with access to personalized health benefits information based on location, age, salary, and family status. Employees can compare the benefits of different medical plans before enrolling.

**Dream Works SKG** uses an intranet to check the daily status of projects, including animation objects, and to coordinate movie scenes.

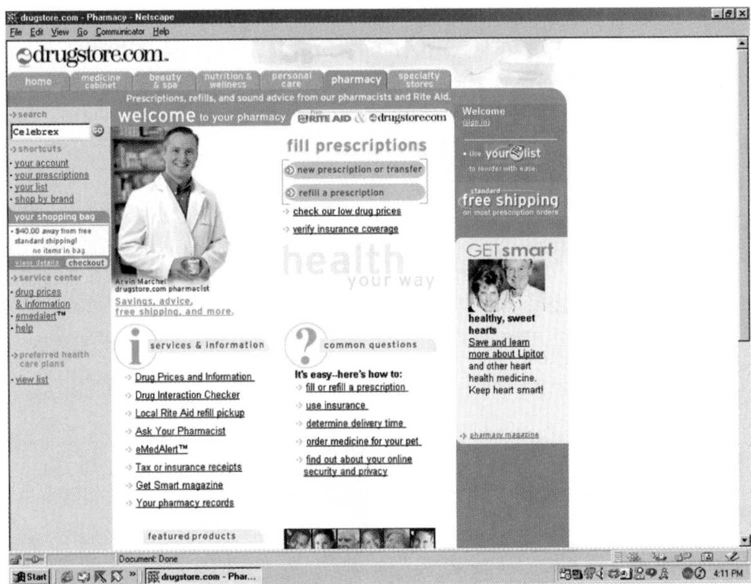


*At the Drugstore.com Web site, customers can make online purchases of prescription medicine and over-the-counter health, beauty and wellness products. The Internet is fueling the growth of electronic commerce.*

Both electronic commerce and electronic business can fundamentally change the way business is conducted. To use the Internet and other digital technologies successfully for electronic commerce, electronic business, and the creation of digital firms, organizations may have to redefine their business models, reinvent business processes, change corporate cultures, and create much closer relationships with customers and suppliers. We discuss these issues in greater detail in following chapters.

## 1.4 LEARNING TO USE INFORMATION SYSTEMS: NEW OPPORTUNITIES WITH TECHNOLOGY

Although information systems are creating many exciting opportunities for both businesses and individuals, they are also a source of new problems, issues, and challenges for managers. In this course, you will learn about both the challenges and opportunities information systems pose, and you will be able to use information technology to enrich your learning experience.

### THE CHALLENGE OF INFORMATION SYSTEMS: KEY MANAGEMENT ISSUES

Although information technology is advancing at a blinding pace, there is nothing easy or mechanical about building and using information systems. There are five key challenges confronting managers:

1. **The Strategic Business Challenge: Realizing the Digital Firm. How can businesses use information technology to become competitive, effective, and digitally enabled?** Creating a digital firm and obtaining benefits is a long and difficult journey for most organizations. Despite heavy information technology investments, many organizations are not obtaining significant business benefits, nor are they becoming digitally enabled. The power of computer hardware and software has grown much more rapidly than the ability of organizations to apply and use this technology. To fully benefit from information technology, realize genuine productivity, and take advantage of digital firm capabilities, many organizations actually need to be redesigned. They will have to make fundamental changes in organizational behavior, develop new business models, and eliminate the inefficiencies of outmoded organizational structures. If organizations merely automate what they are doing today, they are largely missing the potential of information systems.

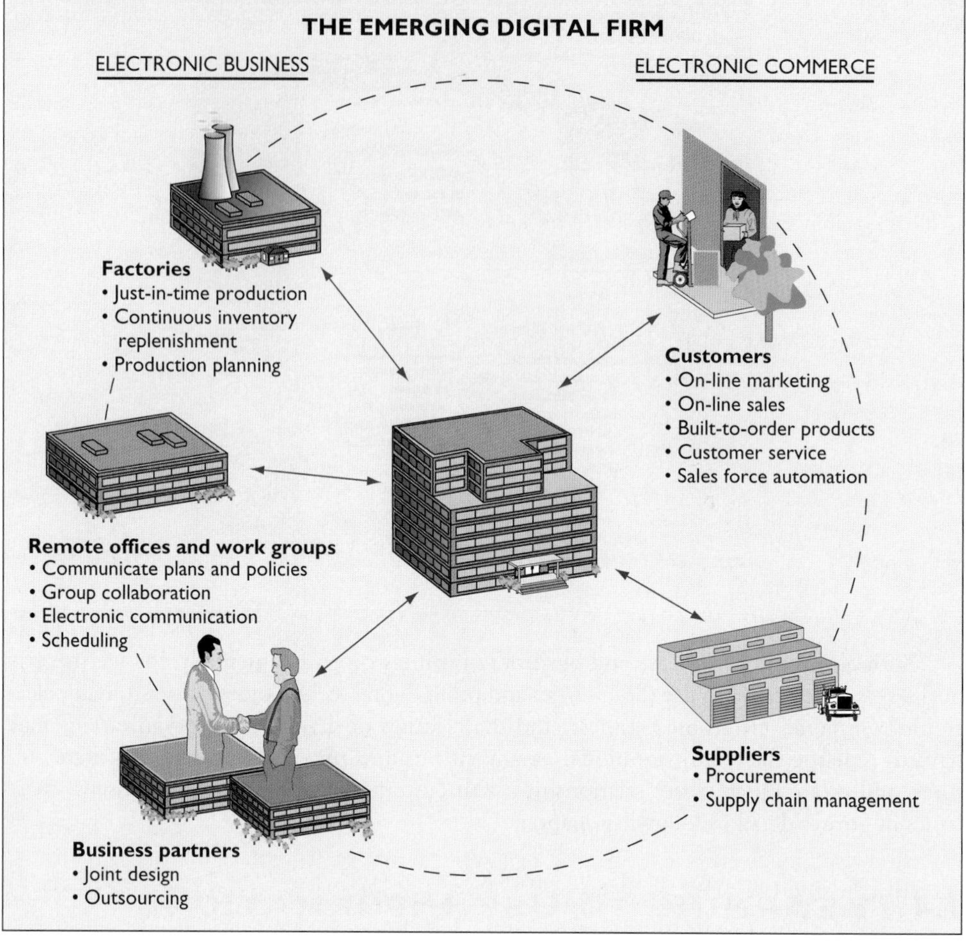


*Figure 1-11* Electronic commerce and electronic business in the emerging digital firm. Electronic commerce uses Internet and digital technology to conduct transactions with customers and suppliers, whereas electronic business uses these technologies for the management of the rest of the business.

2. **The Globalization Challenge: How can firms understand the business and system requirements of a global economic environment?** The rapid growth in international trade and the emergence of a global economy call for information systems that can support both producing and selling goods in many different countries. In the past, each regional office of a multinational corporation focused on solving its own unique information problems. Given language, cultural, and political differences among countries, this focus frequently resulted in chaos and the failure of central management controls. To develop integrated, multinational information systems, businesses must develop global hardware, software, and communications standards and create cross-cultural accounting and reporting structures (Roche, 1992).
3. **The Information Architecture and Infrastructure Challenge: How can organizations develop an information architecture and information technology infrastructure that can support their goals when business conditions and technologies are changing so rapidly?** Meeting the business and technology challenges of today's digital economy requires redesigning the organization and building a new information architecture and information technology (IT) infrastructure.

**information architecture** The particular design that information technology takes in a specific organization to achieve selected goals or functions.

**Information architecture** is the particular form that information technology takes in an organization to achieve selected goals or functions. It is a design for the business application systems that serve each functional specialty and level of the organization and the specific way that they are used by each organization. As firms move toward digital firm organizations and technologies, information architectures are increasingly being designed around business processes and clusters of system applications spanning multiple functions and organizational levels (Kalakota and Robinson, 2001). Because managers and employees directly interact with these systems, it is critical for organizational success that the information architecture meet business requirements now and in the future.

## Management Decision Problem

### PLANNING A NEW INTERNET BUSINESS

You would like to create a new business on the Web that provides cat and dog owners with advice on animal health, behavior, and nutrition and sells products such as pet beds, carriers, dishes, toys, flea treatments, and grooming aids. Your Web site would also have capabilities for pet owners to exchange electronic messages about their pets and pet care with other pet owners. In researching the U.S. market for your business, you have found the following statistics from the U.S. Commerce Department's *Statistical Abstract of the United States.*

**Household Pet Ownership by Income Level**

| Annual Income | Dog Owners | Cat Owners |
|---|---|---|
| Less than $12,500 | 14% | 15% |
| $12,500–$24,999 | 20 | 20 |
| $25,000–$39,999 | 24 | 23 |
| $40,000–$59,999 | 22 | 22 |
| Over $60,000 | 20 | 20 |
| **Total** | 100 | 100 |

**Internet Usage by Income Level**

| Annual Income | Percent Using the Internet |
|---|---|
| Less than $20,000 | 5% |
| $20,000–$49,999 | 26 |
| $50,000–$74,999 | 28 |
| $75,000 and over | 41 |
| **Total** | 100 |

1. What are the implications of this information for starting this business on the Internet?
2. What additional information might be useful to help you decide whether such a business could be profitable and what type and price range of products to sell?

Figure 1-12 illustrates the major elements of information architecture that managers will need to develop now and in the future. The architecture shows the firm's business application systems for each of the major functional areas of the organization, including sales and marketing, manufacturing, finance, accounting, and human resources. It also shows application systems supporting business processes spanning multiple organizational levels and functions within the enterprise and extending outside the enterprise to systems of suppliers, distributors, business partners, and customers. The firm's IT infrastructure provides the technology platform for this architecture. Computer hardware, software, data and storage technology, networks, and human resources required to operate the equipment constitute the shared IT resources of the firm and are available to all of its applications. Contemporary IT infrastructures are linked to public infrastructures such as the Internet. Although this technology platform is typically operated by technical personnel, general management must decide how to allocate the resources it has assigned to hardware, software, data storage, and telecommunications networks to make sound information technology investments (Weill and Broadbent, 1997, 1998).

Following are some typical questions regarding information architecture and IT infrastructure facing today's managers: Should the corporate sales data and function be distributed to each corporate remote site, or should they be centralized at headquarters? Should the organization build systems to connect the entire enterprise or separate islands of applications? Should the organization extend its infrastructure outside its boundaries to link to customers or suppliers? There is no one right answer to these questions (see Allen and Boynton, 1991). Moreover, business needs are constantly changing, which requires the IT architecture to be reassessed continually (Feeny and Willcocks, 1998).

Creating the information architecture and information technology infrastructure for a digital firm is an especially formidable task. Most companies are crippled by fragmented and incompatible computer hardware, software, telecommunications networks, and information systems that prevent information from flowing freely among different parts of the organization. Although Internet standards are solving some of these connectivity problems, creating enterprise-wide data and computing platforms is rarely as seamless as promised. Many organizations are still struggling to integrate their islands of information and technology into a coherent architecture. Chapters 5 through 9 provide more detail on information architecture and IT infrastructure issues.

4. **The Information Systems Investment Challenge: How can organizations determine the business value of information systems?** A major problem raised by the

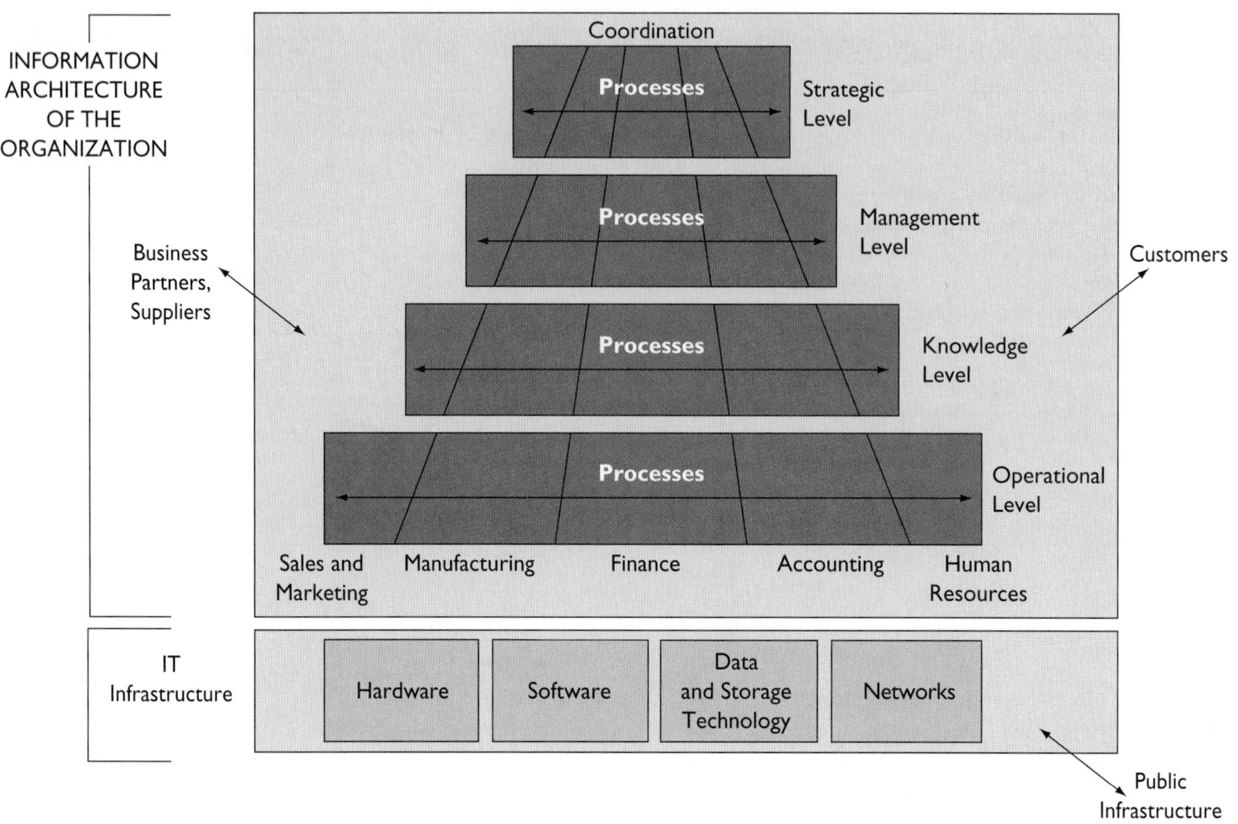


*Figure 1-12* Information architecture and information technology infrastructure. Today's managers must know how to arrange and coordinate the various computer technologies and business system applications to meet the information needs of each level of the organization, and the needs of the organization as a whole.

development of powerful, inexpensive computers involves not technology but management and organizations. It's one thing to use information technology to design, produce, deliver, and maintain new products. It's another thing to make money doing it. How can organizations obtain a sizable payoff from their investment in information systems?

Engineering massive organizational and system changes in the hope of positioning a firm strategically is complicated and expensive. Senior management can be expected to ask these questions: Are we receiving the kind of return on investment from our systems that we should be receiving? Do our competitors get more? Understanding the costs and benefits of building a single system is difficult enough; it is daunting to consider whether the entire systems effort is "worth it." Imagine, then, how a senior executive must think when presented with a major transformation in information architecture—a bold venture in organizational change costing tens of millions of dollars and taking many years.

5. **The Responsibility and Control Challenge: How can organizations ensure that their information systems are used in an ethically and socially responsible manner?** How can we design information systems that people can control and understand? Although information systems have provided enormous benefits and efficiencies, they have also introduced new problems and challenges of which managers should be aware. Table 1-6 describes some of these problems and challenges.

Many chapters of this text describe scenarios that raise these ethical issues, and Chapter 15 is devoted to this topic. A major management challenge is making informed decisions that are sensitive to the negative consequences of information systems as well to the positive ones.

## TABLE 1-6 Positive and Negative Impacts of Information Systems

| Benefits of Information Systems | Negative Impacts |
|---|---|
| Information systems can perform calculations or process paperwork much faster than people. | By automating activities that were previously performed by people, information systems may eliminate jobs. |
| Information systems can help companies learn more about the purchase patterns and preferences of their customers. | Information systems may allow organizations to collect personal details about people that violate their privacy. |
| Information systems provide new efficiencies through services such as automated teller machines (ATMs), telephone systems, or computer-controlled airplanes and air terminals. | Information systems are used in so many aspects of everyday life that system outages can cause shutdowns of businesses or transportation services, paralyzing communities. |
| Information systems have made possible new medical advances in surgery, radiology, and patient monitoring. | Heavy users of information systems may suffer repetitive stress injury, technostress, and other health problems. |
| The Internet distributes information instantly to millions of people across the world. | The Internet can be used to distribute illegal copies of software, books, articles, and other intellectual property. |

Managers will also be faced with ongoing problems of security and control. Information systems are so essential to business, government, and daily life that organizations must take special steps to ensure that they are accurate, reliable, and secure. A firm invites disaster if it uses systems that don't work as intended or that don't deliver information in a form that people can interpret correctly and use. Information systems must be designed so that they function as intended and so that humans can control the process.

Managers will need to ask: Can we apply high quality assurance standards to our information systems, as well as to our products and services? Can we build information systems that respect people's rights of privacy while still pursuing our organization's goals? Should information systems monitor employees? What do we do when an information system designed to increase efficiency and productivity eliminates people's jobs?

This text is designed to provide future managers with the knowledge and understanding required to deal with these challenges. To further this objective, each succeeding chapter begins with a Management Challenges box that outlines key issues of which managers should be aware.

## Integrating Text with Technology: New Opportunities for Learning

In addition to the changes in business and management that we have just described, we believe that information technology creates new opportunities for learning that can make the MIS course more meaningful and exciting. We have provided a Web site and an interactive multimedia CD-ROM for integrating the text with leading-edge technology.

As you read each chapter of the text, you can visit the Prentice Hall Laudon Web site (www.prenhall.com/laudon) and use the Internet for interactive learning and management problem solving. The Internet Connection icon in the chapter directs you to Web sites for which we have provided additional exercises and projects related to the concepts and organizations described in that chapter. For each chapter, you will also find an Electronic Commerce project where you can use Web research and interactive software at various company Web sites to solve specific problems. A graded on-line interactive Study Guide contains questions to help you review what you have learned and test your mastery of chapter concepts. You can also use the Laudon Web site to find links to additional on-line case studies, international resources, and technology updates.

An interactive CD-ROM multimedia version of the text features interactive exercises, simulations, audio/video overviews explaining key concepts, on-line quizzes, hyperlinks to the exercises on the Laudon Web site, technology updates, and more. You can use the CD-ROM as an interactive study guide or as an alternative to the traditional text.

Application exercises toward the end of each chapter require students to use spreadsheet, database, and other application software in hands-on projects related to chapter concepts. Students can apply the application software skills they have learned in other courses to real-world business problems. You can find these exercises before the Management Wrap-Up of each chapter and both the exercises and their data files on the Laudon Web site.

New to this edition are longer comprehensive projects concluding each major section of the text. These projects require students to apply what they have learned to more demanding problems, such as analyzing enterprise system requirements, developing an Internet business model, calculating the Total Cost of Ownership (TCO) of a Web site, redesigning business processes, and designing a corporate knowledge intranet. Some of these projects require use of the Web.

You will find a Tools for Interactive Learning section with this icon toward the end of every chapter to show how you can use the Web and interactive multimedia to enrich your learning experience.

## APPLICATION SOFTWARE EXERCISE

### WEB BROWSER AND SPREADSHEET EXERCISE: INVESTING IN ELECTRONIC RETAILING

You recently watched a news broadcast extolling the virtues of electronic commerce and the fortunes that have been made in this new form of commerce. The report mentioned such retailing companies as Amazon.com and eBay. You are interested in learning more about these companies, and would also like to learn more about other popular retailing stores.

Besides these companies, identify and investigate six additional e-tailers. For each of the eight e-tailers, locate the company's stock symbol and current selling price. This information is easily located on the Web.

Assume you want to purchase 10 shares of each company's stock. Create a spreadsheet that lists the following information: stock name, stock symbol, number of shares for each stock purchased, purchase price per share, total investment for each stock, and overall total investment. You should also create a pie chart that compares the total investment for each stock. After one week, check each stock's current value. Have any stocks gained value? Have any stocks lost value? Modify your spreadsheet to include these findings. Prepare a report for your instructor. In this report, discuss your findings regarding each company and your stock investment. Your report should include copies of your modified spreadsheet and pie chart.

## MANAGEMENT WRAP-UP

Managers are problem solvers who are responsible for analyzing the many challenges confronting organizations and for developing strategies and action plans. Information systems are one of their tools, delivering information required for solutions. Information systems both reflect management decisions and serve as instruments for changing the management process.

Information systems are rooted in organizations, an outcome of organizational structure, culture, politics, workflows, and standard operating procedures. They are instruments for organizational change, making it possible to recast these organizational elements into new business models and redraw organizational boundaries. Advances in information systems are accelerating the trend toward globalized, knowledge-driven economies, flattened, flexible, decentralized organizations, and digital firms.

A network revolution is under way. Information systems technology is no longer limited to computers but consists of an array of technologies that enable computers to be networked together to exchange information across great distances and organizational boundaries. The Internet provides global connectivity and a flexible platform for the seamless flow of information across the enterprise and between the firm and its customers and suppliers.

*For Discussion*

1. Information systems are too important to be left to computer specialists. Do you agree? Why or why not?
2. As computers become faster and cheaper and the Internet becomes more widely used, most of the problems we have with information systems will disappear. Do you agree? Why or why not?

## SUMMARY

1. *Evaluate the role of information systems in today's competitive business environment.* Information systems have become essential for helping organizations deal with changes in global economies and the business enterprise. Information systems provide firms with communication and analytic tools for conducting trade and managing businesses on a global scale. Information systems are the foundation of new knowledge-based products and services in knowledge economies and help firms manage their knowledge assets. Information systems make it possible for businesses to adopt flatter, more decentralized structures and more flexible arrangements of employees and management. Organizations are trying to become more competitive and efficient by transforming themselves into digital firms where nearly all core business processes and relationships with customers, suppliers, and employees are digitally enabled.
2. *Define an information system from both a technical and business perspective and distinguish between computer literacy and information systems literacy.* The purpose of a CBIS is to collect, store, and disseminate information from an organization's environment and internal operations to support organizational functions and decision making, communication, coordination, control, analysis, and visualization. Information systems transform raw data into useful information through three basic activities: input, processing, and output. From a business perspective, an information system represents an organizational and management solution, based on information technology, to a challenge posed by the environment.

   Computer literacy focuses on how computer-based technologies work. Information systems literacy requires an understanding of the organizational and management dimensions of information systems as well as the technical dimensions addressed by computer literacy. Information systems literacy draws on both technical and behavioral approaches to studying information systems. Both perspectives can be combined into a sociotechnical approach to systems.
3. *Explain how information systems are transforming organizations and management.* The kinds of systems built today are very important for the organization's overall performance. Information systems are driving both daily operations and organizational strategy. Powerful computers, software, and networks, including the Internet, have helped organizations become more flexible, eliminate layers of management, separate work from location, and restructure workflows, giving new powers to both line workers and management.

Information technology provides managers with tools for more precise planning, forecasting, and monitoring of the business. To maximize the advantages of information technology, there is a much greater need to plan the organization's information architecture and information technology (IT) infrastructure.

4. *Assess the relationship between the digital firm, electronic commerce, electronic business, and Internet technology.* The Internet provides the primary technology infrastructure for electronic commerce, electronic business, and the emerging digital firm. The Internet and other networks have made it possible for businesses to replace manual and paper-based processes with the electronic flow of information. In electronic commerce, businesses can exchange electronic purchase and sale transactions with each other and with individual customers. Electronic business uses the Internet and digital technology to expedite the exchange of information, which can facilitate communication and coordination both inside the organization and between the organization and its business partners. Digital firms use Internet technology intensively for electronic commerce and electronic business to manage their internal processes and relationships with customers, suppliers, and other external entities.

5. *Identify the major management challenges to building and using information systems in organizations.* There are five key management challenges in building and using information systems: (1) designing systems that are competitive, efficient, and more digitally-enabled; (2) understanding the system requirements of a global business environment; (3) creating an information architecture and IT infrastructure that support the organization's goals; (4) determining the business value of information systems; and (5) designing systems that people can control, understand, and use in a socially and ethically responsible manner.

## KEY TERMS

**Business functions, 12**
**Business processes, 6**
**Communications technology, 13**
**Computer-based information systems (CBIS), 8**
**Computer hardware, 13**
**Computer literacy, 12**
**Computer software, 13**
**Data, 8**
**Data workers, 12**
**Digital firm, 6**
**Electronic business, 24**
**Electronic commerce, 23**
**Electronic market, 23**
**Extranet, 24**
**Feedback, 8**
**Formal system, 8**
**Information, 8**
**Information architecture, 26**
**Information system, 7**
**Information systems literacy, 11**
**Information technology (IT) infrastructure, 13**
**Input, 8**
**Internet, 17**
**Interorganizational systems, 23**
**Intranet, 24**
**Knowledge- and information-intense products, 5**
**Knowledge workers, 12**
**Management information systems (MIS), 15**
**Mass customization, 22**
**Middle managers, 13**
**Network, 13**
**Operational managers, 13**
**Output, 8**
**Processing, 8**
**Production or service workers, 12**
**Senior managers, 13**
**Standard operating procedures (SOPs), 12**
**Storage technology, 13**
**Web site, 19**
**World Wide Web, 18**

## REVIEW QUESTIONS

1. Why are information systems essential in business today? Describe four trends in the global business environment that have made information systems so important.
2. Describe the capabilities of a digital firm. Why are digital firms so powerful?
3. What is an information system? Distinguish between a computer, a computer program, and an information system. What is the difference between data and information?
4. What activities convert raw data to usable information in information systems? What is their relationship to feedback?
5. What is information systems literacy? How does it differ from computer literacy?
6. What are the organization, management, and technology dimensions of information systems?
7. Distinguish between a behavioral and a technical approach to information systems in terms of the questions asked and the answers provided.
8. What major disciplines contribute to an understanding of information systems?
9. What is the relationship between an organization and its information systems? How is this relationship changing over time?
10. What are the Internet and the World Wide Web? How have they changed the role played by information systems in organizations?
11. Describe some of the major changes that information systems are bringing to organizations.
12. How are information systems changing the management process?
13. What is the relationship between the network revolution, the digital firm, electronic commerce, and electronic business?
14. What do we mean by information architecture and information technology infrastructure? Why are they important concerns for managers?
15. What are the key management challenges involved in building, operating, and maintaining information systems today?

## GROUP PROJECT

In a group with three or four classmates, find a description in a computer or business magazine of an information system used by an organization. Look for information about the company on the Web to gain further insight into the company and prepare a brief description of the business. Describe the system you have selected in terms of its inputs, processes, and outputs, and in terms of its organization, management, and technology features and the importance of the system to the company. If possible, use electronic presentation software to present your analysis to the class.

## TOOLS FOR INTERACTIVE LEARNING

### INTERNET CONNECTION

The Internet Connection for this chapter will take you to the United Parcel Service Web site, where you can complete an exercise to evaluate how UPS uses the Web and other information technology in its daily operations. You can also use the Interactive Study Guide to test your knowledge of the topics in this chapter and get instant feedback where you need more practice.

### ELECTRONIC COMMERCE PROJECT

At the Laudon Web site for Chapter 1, you will find an Electronic Commerce project that uses the interactive software at the UPS Web site to help a company calculate and budget for its shipping costs.

### CD-ROM

If you use the Multimedia Edition CD-ROM with this chapter, you will find a simulation showing you how the Internet works, a video clip illustrating UPS's package tracking system, an audio overview of the major themes of this chapter, and bullet text summarizing the key points of the chapter.

## CASE STUDY: *Can GE Remake Itself as a Digital Firm?*

General Electric (GE) is the world's largest diversified manufacturer. *Fortune* named GE "America's Most Admired Company" in 1998, 1999, and 2000. Jack Welch, GE's CEO and chairman since 1981, is often cited as the most admired CEO in the United States. Headquartered in Fairfield, Connecticut, the company consists of 20 units, including Appliances, Broadcasting (NBC), Capital, Medical Systems, and Transportation Systems. With the acquisition of Honeywell, announced in October 2000, GE became a company of $155 billion in revenue and 460,000 employees in 100 countries. Despite GE's size and old-economy businesses, *Internet Week* named GE its e-business company of 2000. Did GE transform itself into a digital firm?

At a January 1999 meeting of 500 top GE executives in Boca Raton, Florida, Welch announced a new initiative to turn GE into an Internet company. Earlier initiatives transformed GE and are partially responsible for its phenomenal rise in profit over the past two decades. Those initiatives were globalization of GE in the late 1980s, "products plus service" in 1995, which placed emphasis on customer service, and Six Sigma in 1996, a quality program that mandated GE units to use feedback from customers as the center of the program.

Welch announced that the Internet "will forever change the way business is done. It will change every relationship, between our businesses, between our customers, between our suppliers." By Internet-enabling its business processes, GE could reduce overhead costs by half, saving as much as $10 billion in the first two years. Gary Reiner, GE's corporate CIO, later explained "We are Web-enabling nearly all of the [purchasing] negotiations process, and we are targeting 100 percent of our transactions on the buy side being done electronically." On the sell side Reiner also wanted to automate as much as possible, including providing customer service and order taking.

GE had quietly been involved with the Internet years before the Boca Raton meeting, conducting more purchasing and selling on the Internet than any other noncomputer manufacturer. For example, within six months after beginning to use the Internet for purchasing in mid-1996, GE Lighting had reduced its purchasing cycle from 14 to 7 days. It also reduced its supply prices by 10 to 15 percent because of open bidding on the Internet. In 1997, seven other GE units began purchasing via the Net. The company even sold the concept to others, including Boeing and 3M.

Polymerland, GE Plastic's distribution arm, began distributing technical documentation over the Web in 1994. It put its product catalog on the Net in 1995 and in 1997 established a site for sales transactions. Its on-line system enables customers to search for product by name, number, or product characteristics, download product information, verify that the product meets their specifications, apply for credit, order, track the shipment, and even return merchandise. Polymerland's weekly on-line sales climbed from $10,000 in 1997 to $6 million in 2000.

Welch ordered all GE units to determine how dot.com companies could destroy their businesses, dubbing this project DYB (destroy your business). Welch explained that if these GE units didn't identify their weaknesses, others would. Once armed with these answers, managers were to change their units to prevent it from happening. Each of GE's 20 units created small cross-functional teams to execute the initiative. Welch also wanted them to move current operations to the Web and to uncover new Net-related business opportunities. The final product was to be an Internet-based business plan that a competitor could have used to take away their unit's customers, and a plan for changes to their unit to combat this threat. Reiner ordered GE units to "come back with alternative approaches that enhance value to the customer and reduce total costs."

The Internet initiative started by trying to change GE's culture at the very top. GE's internal newsletters and many of Welch's memos became available only on-line. To give blue-collar workers access to the Net, GE installed computer kiosks on factory floors. One thousand top managers and executives, including Welch (who also had to take typing lessons), were assigned young, skilled mentors to work with them three to four hours per week in order to make them comfortable with the Web. They had to be able to evaluate their competitors' Web sites and to use the Web in other beneficial ways. Every GE employee was given training. Welch announced in 2000, that GE would reduce administrative expenses by 30 to 50 percent (around $10 billion) within 18 months through use of the Internet.

Many projects came out of the initiative. For example GE Medical Systems, which manufactures diagnostic imaging systems, such as CAT scanners and mammography equipment, identified its DYB threat as aggregators, such as WebMD, which offered unbiased information on competing products as well as selling those products. GE products on these sites looked like just another commodity. The GE unit's major response was iCenter, a Web connection to customers' GE equipment to monitor the equipment operation at the customer site. iCenter collects data and feeds it back to each customer who can then ask questions about the operation of the equipment through the same site. GE compares a customer's operating data with the same equipment operating elsewhere to aid that customer in improving performance. In addition customers are now able to download and test upgraded software for 30 days prior to having to purchase it. The unit also began offering its equipment training classes on-line, allowing clients to take them at any time. The aggregators were also auctioning off used equipment that was in demand in poorer countries. Medical Systems established its own site to auction its own used equipment, thus opening new markets (outside the United States). GE Aircraft adapted iCenter and now monitors its customers' engines while they are in flight.

GE Power Systems then developed its Turbine Optimizer, which uses the Web to monitor any GE turbine, comparing its performance (such as fuel burn rate) with other turbines of same model anywhere in the world. Their site advises operators how to improve their turbines' performance and how much money the improvements would be worth. The operator can even schedule a service call in order to make further performance improvements.

Late in 1999 GE Transportation went live with an Internet auction system for purchasing supplies. Soon other units, including Power and Medical, adopted the system. GE later estimated the system would handle $5 billion in GE purchasing in 2000, and the company would do at least 50 percent of its purchasing on-line in 2001. The system lowers prices for GE because approved suppliers bid against each other to obtain GE contracts. It also results in fewer specification errors and speeds up the purchasing process. GE estimates it saves between 10 and 15 percent of purchasing costs altogether.

GE Appliances realized that appliances are traditionally sold through large and small retailers and that the Internet might destroy that model, turning appliances into commodities sold on big retail and auction sites. GE wanted to maintain the current system, keeping consumer loyalty to their GE brand (versus Maytag, Whirlpool, and Frigidaire). Appliances developed a point-of-sale system, which they placed in retail stores such as Home Depot, where customers enter their own orders. The retailer is paid a percentage of the sale. The product is shipped from GE directly to the customer. GE Appliances claims it can now take products from its factories and get them shipped anywhere in the United States virtually overnight on a cost-effective basis. In 2000 Appliances reported 45 percent of its sales, totaling $2.5 billion, took place on the Internet. It estimates 67 percent of its sales will be on the Internet in 2001.

The corporation and its units have issued a blizzard of press releases touting the successes of each of GE's Internet initiatives and the consequent positive effect on financial results. "In 1999, 30 percent of our orders came in via the Web," announced Marian Powell, the senior vice president for e-business at GE Capital Fleet Services. And in 2000 "we'll have over 60 percent. That's over a billion dollars in orders." CIO Reiner said, "We are not talking about incremental change. We're talking total transformation."

A January 2001 article by Mark Roberti of *The Industry Standard* was skeptical. Roberti commended GE for embracing the Internet so quickly. He also noted that "these endeavors are unlikely to make GE vastly more profitable . . . because the company isn't using the Internet to reach new markets or create major new sources of revenue." Roberti questioned the great savings through Internet-based cost cutting that GE claimed. To cut costs by moving business processes on-line, a firm "must eliminate—or redeploy—a significant number of employees" and "GE hasn't." For example, Roberti says, 60 percent of orders to GE Capital Fleet Services are now placed on-line, but it has not reduced its call center staff. GE reports that its selling, general, and administrative expenses as a percentage of sales fell for the first nine months of 2000 from 24.3 in 1999 to 23.6, a minor drop at best. Moreover, he notes caution coming from GE executives themselves. For example, although Reiner had projected a $10 billion saving over the next 18 months in 1999, in December 2000 he revised the 2001 savings to about $1.6 billion—not an insignificant sum, but far from the gigantic savings predicted. Reducing costs by having customers and employees serve themselves via the Web has proved elusive at other companies as well, such as IBM and UPS. Roberti claims that the Internet has not brought GE a significant number of new customers.

Overall, Roberti points out, "Through the third quarter of 2000, GE still hadn't demonstrated any significant improvement in its financial results that can be directly attributed to e-business." Although GE has achieved genuine progress and even leadership, the company could not be generating the savings management had been predicting. He speculates that the purpose of the continuous declarations of great savings may be to boost the price of GE's stock. Perhaps, most importantly, Roberti claims that although GE's Internet activities will give the company a boost, it will take its competitors only a few months to catch up, leaving GE without any competitive advantage.

**Sources:** Mark Roberti, "General Electric's Spin Machine," *The Industry Standard,* January 15, 2001; Meridith Levinson, "Destructive Behavior," *CIO Magazine,* July 15, 2000; Diane Brady, "GE's Welch: 'This is the Greatest Opportunity Yet,' " *Business Week,* June 28, 1999; Jon Burke, "Is GE the Last Internet Company?" *Red Herring,* December 19, 2000; Geoffrey Colvin, "How Leading Edge Are They?" *Fortune,* February 21, 2000; Cheryl Dahle, "Adventures in Polymerland," *Fast Company,* May 2000; David Bicknell, "Let There Be Light," *ComputerWeekly.com,* September 7, 2000; David Drucker, "Virtual Teams Light Up GE," *Internet Week,* April 6, 2000;David Joachim, "GE's E-Biz Turnaround Proves That Big Is Back," *Internet Week,* April 3, 2000; Mark Baard, "GE's WebCity," *Publish,* September 2000; Faith Keenan, "Giants Can Be Nimble," *Business Week,* September 18, 2000; Marianne Kolbasuk McGee, "E-Business Makes General Electric a Different Company," *InformationWeek,* January 31, 2000; and "Wake-Up Call," *Information Week,* September 18, 2000; Pamela L. Moore, "GE's Cyber Payoff," *Business Week,* April 13, 2000; Srikumar S. Rao, "General Electric, Software Vendor," *Forbes Magazine,* January 24, 2000; and Jim Rohwer, Jack Welch, Scott McNealy, John Huey, and Brent Schlender, "The Odd Couple," *Fortune,* May 1, 2000.

### *CASE STUDY QUESTIONS*

1. Summarize the business and technology conditions causing GE to launch its Internet initiative.
2. How is GE using Internet technology in its internal and external business processes?
3. What management, organization, and technology issues did GE have to address in its Internet initiative?
4. Evaluate GE's Internet initiative. Is it successful? Is the company transforming itself into a digital firm? Why or why not?

chapter 2

# Information Systems in the Enterprise

objectives

**After completing this chapter, you will be able to:**

1. *Analyze the role played by the six major types of information systems in organizations and their relationship to each other.*
2. *Describe the types of information systems supporting the major functional areas of the business.*
3. *Assess the relationship between organizations, information systems and business processes, including the processes for customer relationship management and supply chain management.*
4. *Explain how enterprise systems and industrial networks create new efficiencies for businesses.*
5. *Evaluate the benefits and limitations of enterprise systems and industrial networks.*

## Alpina Mooves Faster with Enterprise Systems

Alpina Productos Alimenticios is a privately owned dairy products company headquartered in Bogota, Colombia. It produces more than 400,000 liters of milk daily and sells more than 200 products in Colombia, Central America, and North America, including a wide array of cheeses, yogurts, milk-based beverages, fruit juices, and chilled desserts. Alpina has 21 sales agencies, plants in Venezuela and Ecuador, and 3,400 employees, which process 72 million orders and 400,000 invoices per year. The diversity of its products, the delivery volume, and the size of Alpina's market creates enormous supply chain management tasks. Dairy products require constant refrigeration and have an average shelf life of only 21 days. The company must deliver products directly to stores or distributors within 24 hours after an order has been placed.

The company wants to expand into new regional and export markets by maintaining an exceptionally high level of product quality, service, and production efficiency. It must cope with a regional economic downturn, consumer demand for lower prices, and new global and local competitors. Although Alpina was doubling sales every two years, its information systems could not support its pace of growth. Alpina had built its own series of systems that were not integrated and the systems operated in isolation from each other. The firm had no way of communicating or consolidating company-wide information.

To increase productivity and competitiveness, Alpina decided to install enterprise resource planning software, embarking in 1995 on an ambitious project to create integrated systems for industrial processes, logistics management, administrative and financial functions, and commercial functions. Alpina started its enterprise project with pieces of software from a number of different vendors but eventually used Oracle Consumer Packaged Goods (CPG) software to integrate these functions. By December 1998 Alpina had installed the Oracle CPG software in its production plants and sales agencies.

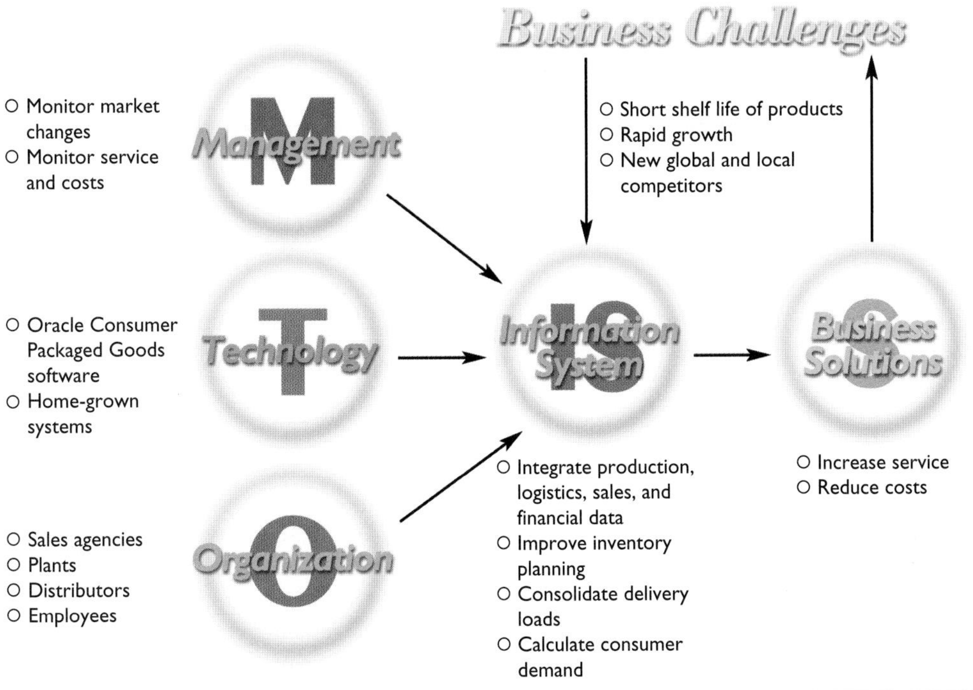


The new system has enabled Alpina to reduce its inventory through better planning and stocking of raw materials and finished products. Alpina has reduced turnaround in raw materials from 35 days to 25 days and has reduced turnaround in finished products from 8 days to 5 days. Through better supply chain management, Alpina is saving $2.7 million each year. Alpina has also reduced costs by using the information from its system to consolidate delivery loads and create more efficient delivery routes. The system's transportation planning capabilities have helped the company reduce the number of trucks at each of its major distribution centers by 15 percent, saving $200,000 annually in transport costs.

With information about past order history, Alpina's system helps customers plan and stock their shelf space, providing them with information about which products, flavors, and sizes are most in demand in their stores. Alpina is using this information to help calculate customer demand as it introduces new products in the sub-Andes region, Central America, and the United States.

**Sources:** Michael Miley, "Fast Mooving," *Profit Magazine*, February 2000 and www.alpina.com.co.

**Alpina Mooves Faster with Enterprise Systems**

**MANAGEMENT CHALLENGES**

Businesses need different types of information systems to support decision making and work activities for various organizational levels and functions. To respond to new competitive pressures, many are implementing enterprise-wide systems that integrate information and business processes from different functional areas. Alpina, for instance, needed information systems that would allow it to move its products more efficiently through its supply chain. It found a solution in building systems that could link important business processes for sales, production, and logistics. The opening vignette presents the potential rewards to firms with well-conceived systems linking the entire enterprise. Such systems typically require a significant amount of organizational and management change and raise the following management challenges:

## MANAGEMENT CHALLENGES

1. **Integration.** Although it is necessary to design different systems serving different levels, functions, and business processes in the firm, more and more firms are finding advantages in integrating systems. However, integrating systems for different organizational levels, functions, and business processes to freely exchange information can be technologically and organizationally difficult and costly. Managers need to determine what level of system integration is required and how much it is worth in dollars.
2. **Enlarging the scope of management thinking.** Most managers are trained to manage a product line, a division, or an office. They are rarely trained to optimize the performance of the organization as a whole, and often are not given the means to do so. But enterprise systems and industrial networks require managers to take a much larger view of their own behavior to include other products, divisions, departments, and even outside business firms. Investments in enterprise systems are huge, they must be developed over long periods of time, and they must be guided by a shared vision of the objectives.

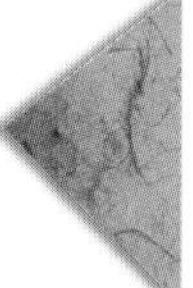

In this chapter we examine the role of the various types of information systems in organizations. First we look at ways of classifying information systems based on the organizational level they support. Next we look at systems in terms of the organizational function they serve. We then show how systems can support business processes, including processes for customer relationship management and supply chain management. Finally, we examine enterprise systems and industrial networks, which enable organizations to integrate information and business processes across entire firms and even entire industries.

## 2.1 KEY SYSTEM APPLICATIONS IN THE ORGANIZATION

Because there are different interests, specialties, and levels in an organization, there are different kinds of systems. No single system can provide all the information an organization needs. Figure 2-1 illustrates one way to depict the kinds of systems found in an organization. In the illustration, the organization is divided into strategic, management, knowledge, and operational levels and then is further divided into functional areas such as sales and marketing, manufacturing, finance, accounting, and human resources. Systems are built to serve these different organizational interests (Anthony, 1965).

### DIFFERENT KINDS OF SYSTEMS

**operational-level systems** Information systems that monitor the elementary activities and transactions of the organization.

Four main types of information systems serve different organizational levels: operational-level systems, knowledge-level systems, management-level systems, and strategic-level systems. **Operational-level systems** support operational managers by keeping track of the elementary activities and transactions of the organization, such as sales, receipts, cash deposits, payroll, credit decisions, and the flow of materials in a factory. The principal purpose of systems at this level is to answer routine questions and to track the flow of transactions through the organization. How many parts are in inventory? What happened to Mr. Williams's payment? To answer these kinds of questions, information generally must be easily available,

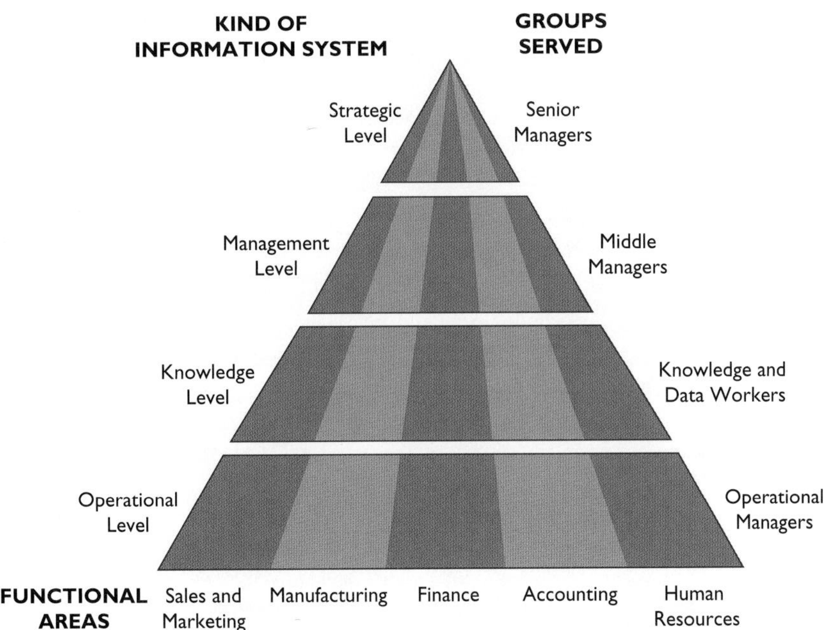


*Figure 2-1* Types of information systems. Organizations can be divided into strategic, management, knowledge, and operational levels and into five major functional areas: sales and marketing, manufacturing, finance, accounting, and human resources. Information systems serve each of these levels and functions.

current, and accurate. Examples of operational-level systems include a system to record bank deposits from automatic teller machines or one that tracks the number of hours worked each day by employees on a factory floor.

**Knowledge-level systems** support the organization's knowledge and data workers. The purpose of knowledge-level systems is to help the business firm integrate new knowledge into the business and to help the organization control the flow of paperwork. Knowledge-level systems, especially in the form of workstations and office systems, are among the most widely used applications in business today.

**knowledge-level systems** Information systems that support knowledge and data workers in an organization.

**Management-level systems** serve the monitoring, controlling, decision-making, and administrative activities of middle managers. The principal question addressed by such systems is: Are things working well? Management-level systems typically provide periodic reports rather than instant information on operations. An example is a relocation control system that reports on the total moving, house-hunting, and home financing costs for employees in all company divisions, noting wherever actual costs exceed budgets.

**management-level systems** Information systems that support the monitoring, controlling, decision-making, and administrative activities of middle managers.

Some management-level systems support nonroutine decision making. They tend to focus on less-structured decisions for which information requirements are not always clear. These systems often answer "what if" questions: What would be the impact on production schedules if we were to double sales in the month of December? What would happen to our return on investment if a factory schedule were delayed for six months? Answers to these and other questions frequently require new data from outside the organization, as well as data from inside that cannot be easily drawn from existing operational-level systems.

**Strategic-level systems** help senior management tackle and address strategic issues and long-term trends, both in the firm and in the external environment. Their principal concern is matching changes in the external environment with existing organizational capability. What will employment levels be in five years? What are the long-term industry cost trends, and where does our firm fit in? What products should we be making in five years?

**strategic-level systems** Information systems that support the long-range planning activities of senior management.

Information systems also serve the major business functions, such as sales and marketing, manufacturing, finance, accounting, and human resources. A typical organization has operational-, management-, knowledge-, and strategic-level systems for each functional area. For example, the sales function generally has a sales system on the operational level to record daily sales figures and to process orders. A knowledge-level system designs promotional displays for the firm's products. A management-level system tracks monthly sales figures by sales territory and reports on territories where sales exceed or fall below anticipated levels. A system to forecast sales trends over a five-year period serves the strategic level.

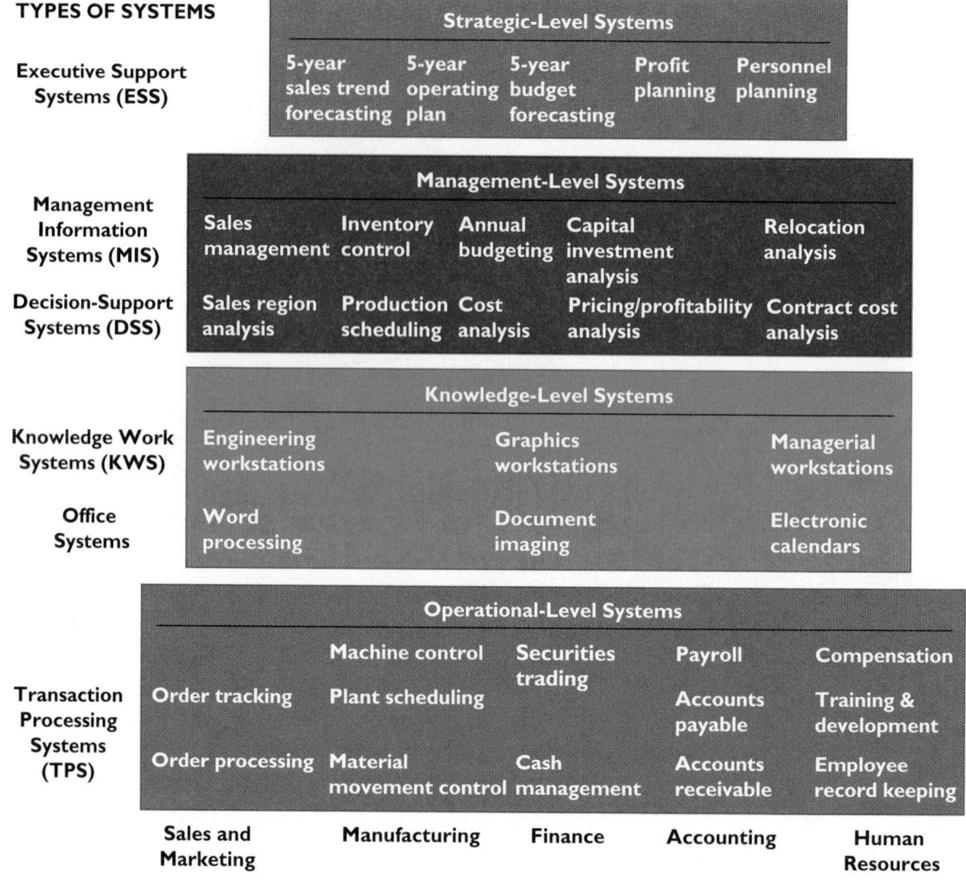


*Figure 2-2* The six major types of information systems: TPS, office systems, KWS, DSS, MIS, and ESS, showing the level of the organization and business function that each supports.

We first describe the specific categories of systems serving each organizational level and their value to the organization. Then we show how organizations use these systems for each major business function.

## SIX MAJOR TYPES OF SYSTEMS

Figure 2-2 shows the specific types of information systems that correspond to each organizational level. The organization has executive support systems (ESS) at the strategic level; management information systems (MIS) and decision-support systems (DSS) at the management level; knowledge work systems (KWS) and office systems at the knowledge level; and transaction processing systems (TPS) at the operational level. Systems at each level in turn are specialized to serve each of the major functional areas. Thus, the typical systems found in organizations are designed to assist workers or managers at each level and in the functions of sales and marketing, manufacturing, finance, accounting, and human resources.

Table 2-1 summarizes the features of the six types of information systems. It should be noted that each of the different kinds of systems may have components that are used by organizational levels and groups other than their main constituencies. A secretary may find information on an MIS, or a middle manager may need to extract data from a TPS.

### Transaction Processing Systems

**transaction processing systems (TPS)**
Computerized systems that perform and record the daily routine transactions necessary to conduct the business; they serve the organization's operational level.

**Transaction processing systems (TPS)** are the basic business systems that serve the operational level of the organization. A transaction processing system is a computerized system that performs and records the daily routine transactions necessary to conduct the business. Examples are sales order entry, hotel reservation systems, payroll, employee record keeping, and shipping.

At the operational level, tasks, resources, and goals are predefined and highly structured. The decision to grant credit to a customer, for instance, is made by a lower-level supervisor

## TABLE 2-1 CHARACTERISTICS OF INFORMATION PROCESSING SYSTEMS

| Type of System | Information Inputs | Processing | Information Outputs | Users |
|---|---|---|---|---|
| ESS | Aggregate data; external, internal | Graphics; simulations; interactive | Projections; responses to queries | Senior managers |
| DSS | Low-volume data or massive databases optimized for data analysis; analytic models and data analysis tools | Interactive; simulations; analysis | Special reports; decision analyses; responses to queries | Professionals; staff managers |
| MIS | Summary transaction data; high-volume data; simple models | Routine reports; simple models; low-level analysis | Summary and exception reports | Middle managers |
| KWS | Design specifications; knowledge base | Modeling; simulations | Models; graphics | Professionals; technical staff |
| Office systems | Documents; schedules | Document management; scheduling; communication | Documents; schedules; mail | Clerical workers |
| TPS | Transactions; events | Sorting; listing; merging; updating | Detailed reports; lists; summaries | Operations personnel; supervisors |

according to predefined criteria. All that must be determined is whether the customer meets the criteria.

Figure 2-3 depicts a payroll TPS, which is a typical accounting transaction processing system found in most firms. A payroll system keeps track of the money paid to employees. The master file is composed of discrete pieces of information (such as a name, address, or employee number) called data elements. Data are keyed into the system, updating the data elements. The elements on the master file are combined in different ways to create reports of interest to management and government agencies and to send paychecks to employees. These TPS can generate other report combinations of existing data elements.

Other typical TPS applications are identified in Figure 2-4. The figure shows that there are five functional categories of TPS: sales/marketing, manufacturing/production, finance/

*Figure 2-3* A symbolic representation for a payroll TPS.

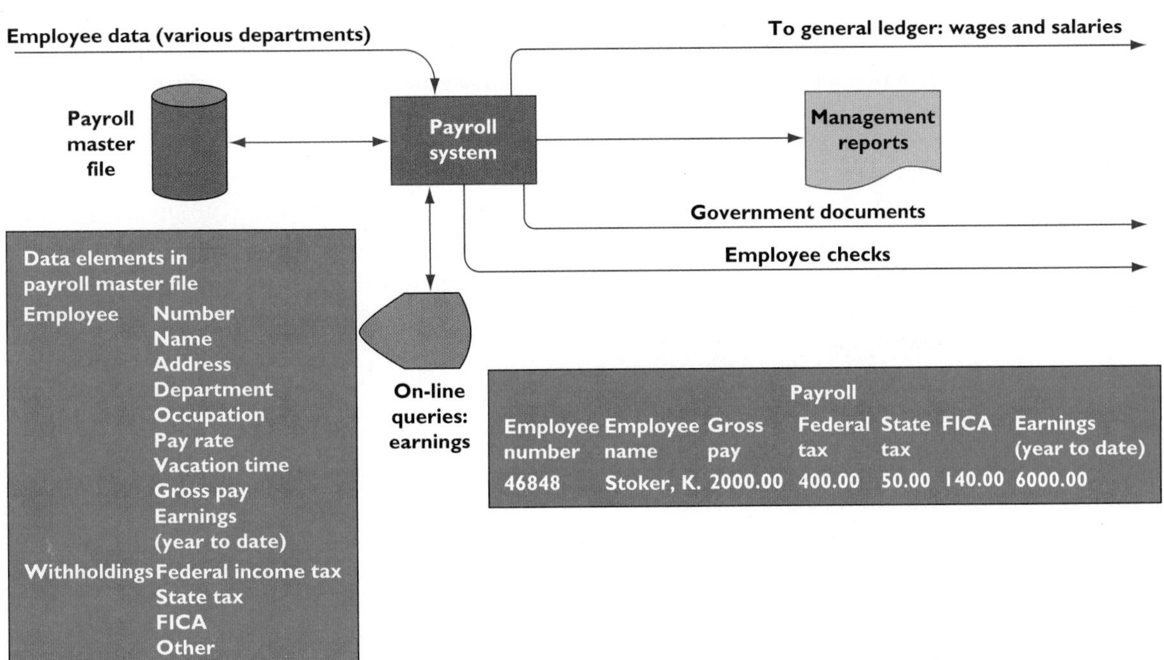

| | TYPE OF TPS SYSTEM | | | | |
|---|---|---|---|---|---|
| | Sales/ marketing systems | Manufacturing/ production systems | Finance/ accounting systems | Human resources systems | Other types (e.g., university) |
| **Major functions of system** | Sales management | Scheduling | Budgeting | Personnel records | Admissions |
| | Market research | Purchasing | General ledger | Benefits | Grade records |
| | Promotion | Shipping/receiving | Billing | Compensation | Course records |
| | Pricing | Engineering | Cost accounting | Labor relations | Alumni |
| | New products | Operations | | Training | |
| **Major application systems** | Sales order information system | Machine control systems | General ledger | Payroll | Registration system |
| | Market research system | Purchase order systems | Accounts receivable/payable | Employee records | Student transcript system |
| | Sales commission system | Quality control systems | Funds management systems | Benefit systems | Curriculum class control systems |
| | | | | Career path systems | Alumni benefactor system |

*Figure 2-4* Typical applications of TPS. There are five functional categories of TPS: sales/marketing, manufacturing/production, finance/accounting, human resources, and other types of systems specific to a particular industry. Within each of these major functions are subfunctions. For each of these subfunctions (e.g., sales management) there is a major application system.

accounting, human resources, and other types of TPS that are unique to a particular industry. The UPS package tracking system described in Chapter 1 is an example of a manufacturing TPS. UPS sells package delivery services; the system keeps track of all of its package shipment transactions.

Transaction processing systems are often so central to a business that TPS failure for a few hours can spell a firm's demise and perhaps other firms linked to it. Imagine what would happen to UPS if its package tracking system were not working! What would the airlines do without their computerized reservation systems?

Managers need TPS to monitor the status of internal operations and the firm's relations with the external environment. TPS are also major producers of information for the other types of systems. (For example, the payroll system illustrated in Figure 2-3, along with other accounting TPS, supplies data to the company's general ledger system, which is responsible for maintaining records of the firm's income and expenses and for producing reports such as income statements and balance sheets.)

## Knowledge Work and Office Systems

**knowledge work systems (KWS)**
Information systems that aid knowledge workers in the creation and integration of new knowledge in the organization.

**office systems**
Computer systems, such as word processing, electronic mail systems, and scheduling systems, that are designed to increase the productivity of data workers in the office.

**Knowledge work systems (KWS)** and **office systems** serve the information needs at the knowledge level of the organization. Knowledge work systems aid knowledge workers, whereas office systems primarily aid data workers (although they are also used extensively by knowledge workers).

In general, *knowledge workers* are people who hold formal university degrees and who are often members of a recognized profession, such as engineers, doctors, lawyers, and scientists. Their jobs consist primarily of creating new information and knowledge. Knowledge work systems (KWS), such as scientific or engineering design workstations, promote the creation of new knowledge and ensure that new knowledge and technical expertise are properly integrated into the business. *Data workers* typically have less formal, advanced educational degrees and tend to process rather than create information. They consist primarily of secretaries, bookkeepers, filing clerks, or managers whose jobs are principally to use, manipulate, or disseminate information. Office systems are information technology applications designed to increase data workers' productivity by supporting the coordinating and communicating activities of the typical office. Office systems coordinate diverse information workers, geographic units, and functional areas: The systems communicate with customers, suppliers, and other organizations outside the firm and serve as a clearinghouse for information and knowledge flows.

*Graphics designers use desktop publishing software to design a page for "La Opinion." Desktop publishing software enables users to control all aspects of the design and layout process for professional-looking publications.*

Typical office systems handle and manage documents (through word processing, desktop publishing, document imaging, and digital filing), scheduling (through electronic calendars), and communication (through electronic mail, voice mail, or videoconferencing). **Word processing** refers to the software and hardware that creates, edits, formats, stores, and prints documents (see Chapter 6). Word processing systems represent the single most common application of information technology to office work, in part because producing documents is what offices are all about. **Desktop publishing** produces professional, publishing-quality documents by combining output from word processing software with design elements, graphics, and special layout features. Companies are now starting to publish documents in the form of Web pages for easy access and distribution. We describe Web publishing in more detail in Chapter 12.

**Document imaging systems** are another widely used knowledge application. Document imaging systems convert documents and images into digital form so that they can be stored and accessed by the computer.

**word processing**
Office system technology that facilitates the creation of documents through computerized text editing, formatting, storing, and printing.

**desktop publishing**
Technology that produces professional-quality documents combining output from word processors with design, graphics, and special layout features.

**document imaging systems**
Systems that convert documents and images into digital form so that they can be stored and accessed by the computer.

## Management Information Systems

In Chapter 1, we defined management information systems as the study of information systems in business and management. The term *management information systems (MIS)* also designates a specific category of information systems serving management-level functions. **Management information systems (MIS)** serve the management level of the organization, providing managers with reports or with on-line access to the organization's current performance and historical records. Typically, they are oriented almost exclusively to internal, not environmental or external, events. MIS primarily serve the functions of planning, controlling, and decision making at the management level. Generally, they depend on underlying transaction processing systems for their data.

MIS summarize and report on the company's basic operations. The basic transaction data from TPS are compressed and are usually presented in long reports that are produced on a regular schedule. Figure 2-5 shows how a typical MIS transforms transaction-level data from sales, production, and accounting into MIS files that are used to provide managers with reports. Figure 2-6 shows a sample report from this system.

MIS usually serve managers interested in weekly, monthly, and yearly results–not day-to-day activities. MIS generally provide answers to routine questions that have been specified in advance and have a predefined procedure for answering them. For instance, MIS reports might list the total pounds of lettuce used this quarter by a fast-food chain or, as illustrated in Figure 2-6, compare total annual sales figures for specific products to planned targets. These systems are generally not flexible and have little analytical capability. Most MIS use simple routines such as summaries and comparisons, as opposed to sophisticated mathematical models or statistical techniques.

**management information systems (MIS)**
Information systems at the management level of an organization that serve the functions of planning, controlling, and decision making by providing routine summary and exception reports.

## Decision-Support Systems

**Decision-support systems (DSS)** also serve the management level of the organization. DSS help managers make decisions that are unique, rapidly changing, and not easily specified in advance. They address problems where the procedure for arriving at a solution may not be fully predefined in advance. Although DSS use internal information from TPS and MIS, they often bring in information from external sources, such as current stock prices or product prices of competitors.

**decision-support systems (DSS)**
Information systems at the organization's management level that combine data and sophisticated analytical models or data analysis tools to support nonroutine decision making.

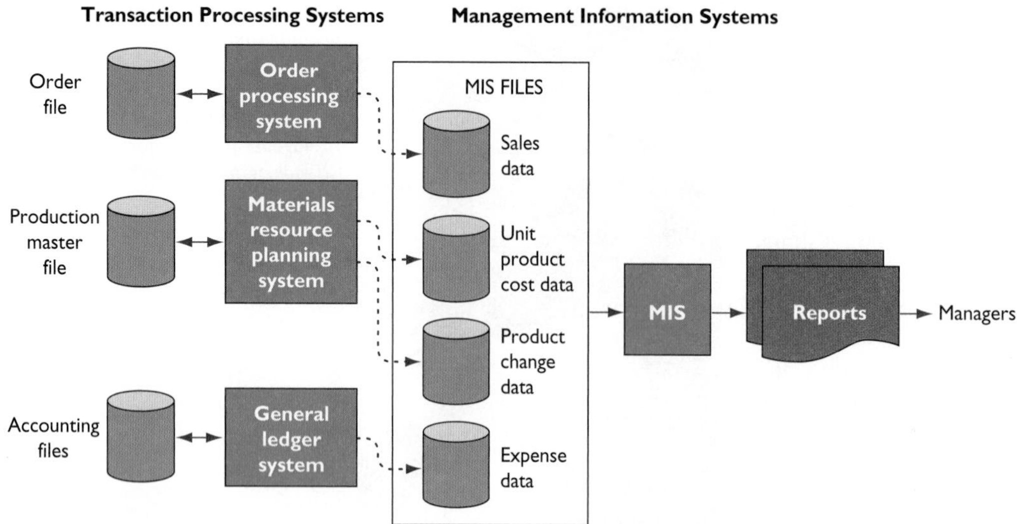


*Figure 2-5* How management information systems obtain their data from the organization's TPS. In the system illustrated by this diagram, three TPS supply summarized transaction data at the end of the time period to the MIS reporting system. Managers gain access to the organizational data through the MIS, which provides them with the appropriate reports.

Clearly, by design, DSS have more analytical power than other systems. They are built explicitly with a variety of models to analyze data, or they condense large amounts of data into a form where they can be analyzed by decision makers. DSS are designed so that users can work with them directly; these systems explicitly include user-friendly software. DSS are interactive; the user can change assumptions, ask new questions, and include new data.

An interesting, small, but powerful DSS is the voyage-estimating system of a subsidiary of a large American metals company that exists primarily to carry bulk cargoes of coal, oil, ores, and finished products for its parent company. The firm owns some vessels, charters others, and bids for shipping contracts in the open market to carry general cargo. A voyage-estimating system calculates financial and technical voyage details. Financial calculations include ship/time costs (fuel, labor, capital), freight rates for various types of cargo, and port expenses. Technical details include a myriad of factors such as ship cargo capacity, speed, port distances, fuel and water consumption, and loading patterns (location of cargo for different ports). The system can answer questions such as the following: Given a customer delivery schedule and an offered freight rate, which vessel should be assigned at what rate to maximize

*Figure 2-6* A sample report that might be produced by the MIS in Figure 2-5.

Consolidated Consumer Products Corporation
Sales by Product and Sales Region: 2001

| PRODUCT CODE | PRODUCT DESCRIPTION | SALES REGION | ACTUAL SALES | PLANNED | ACTUAL VS. PLANNED |
|---|---|---|---|---|---|
| 4469 | Carpet Cleaner | Northeast | 4,066,700 | 4,800,000 | 0.85 |
| | | South | 3,778,112 | 3,750,000 | 1.01 |
| | | Midwest | 4,867,001 | 4,600,000 | 1.06 |
| | | West | 4,003,440 | 4,400,000 | 0.91 |
| | TOTAL | | 16,715,253 | 17,550,000 | 0.95 |
| 5674 | Room Freshener | Northeast | 3,676,700 | 3,900,000 | 0.94 |
| | | South | 5,608,112 | 4,700,000 | 1.19 |
| | | Midwest | 4,711,001 | 4,200,000 | 1.12 |
| | | West | 4,563,440 | 4,900,000 | 0.93 |
| | TOTAL | | 18,559,253 | 17,700,000 | 1.05 |

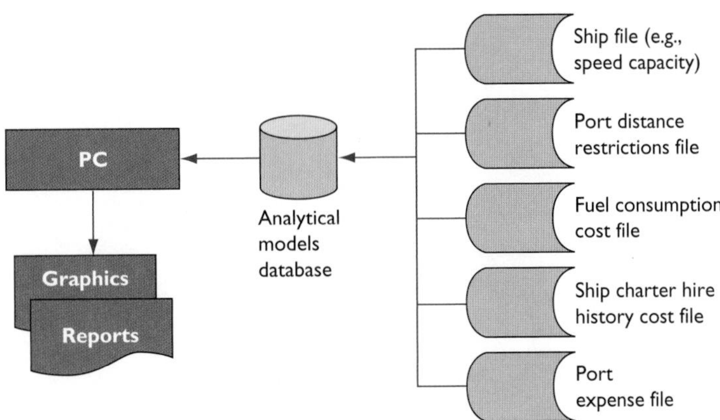


***Figure 2-7*** Voyage estimating decision-support system. This DSS operates on a powerful PC. It is used daily by managers who must develop bids on shipping contracts.

profits? What is the optimum speed at which a particular vessel can optimize its profit and still meet its delivery schedule? What is the optimal loading pattern for a ship bound for the U.S. West Coast from Malaysia? Figure 2-7 illustrates the DSS built for this company. The system operates on a powerful desktop personal computer, providing a system of menus that makes it easy for users to enter data or obtain information. We describe other types of DSS in Chapter 13.

## Executive Support Systems

Senior managers use **executive support systems (ESS)** to make decisions. ESS serve the strategic level of the organization. They address nonroutine decisions requiring judgment, evaluation, and insight because there is no agreed-on procedure for arriving at a solution. ESS create a generalized computing and communications environment rather than providing any fixed application or specific capability. ESS are designed to incorporate data about external events such as new tax laws or competitors, but they also draw summarized information from internal MIS and DSS. They filter, compress, and track critical data, emphasizing the reduction of time and effort required to obtain information useful to executives. ESS employ the most advanced graphics software and can deliver graphs and data from many sources immediately to a senior executive's office or to a boardroom.

**executive support systems (ESS)**
Information systems at the organization's strategic level designed to address nonroutine decision making through advanced graphics and communications.

Unlike the other types of information systems, ESS are not designed primarily to solve specific problems. Instead, ESS provide a generalized computing and communications capacity that can be applied to a changing array of problems. Whereas many DSS are designed to be highly analytical, ESS tend to make less use of analytical models.

Questions ESS assist in answering include the following: In what business should we be? What are the competitors doing? What new acquisitions would protect us from cyclical business swings? Which units should we sell to raise cash for acquisitions? Figure 2-8 illustrates a model of an ESS. It consists of workstations with menus, interactive graphics, and communications capabilities that can access historical and competitive data from internal corporate systems and external databases such as Dow Jones News/Retrieval or the Gallup Poll. Because ESS are designed to be used by senior managers who may have little direct contact or experience with computer-based information systems, they incorporate easy-to-use graphic interfaces. More details on leading-edge applications of DSS and ESS can be found in Chapter 13.

## RELATIONSHIP OF SYSTEMS TO ONE ANOTHER

Figure 2-9 illustrates how the systems serving different levels in the organization are related to one another. TPS are typically a major source of data for other systems, whereas ESS are primarily a recipient of data from lower-level systems. The other types of systems may exchange data with each other as well. Data may also be exchanged among systems serving different functional areas. For example, an order captured by a sales system may be transmitted to a manufacturing system as a transaction for producing or delivering the product specified in the order.

It is definitely advantageous to have some measure of integration among these systems so that information can flow easily between different parts of the organization. But integration

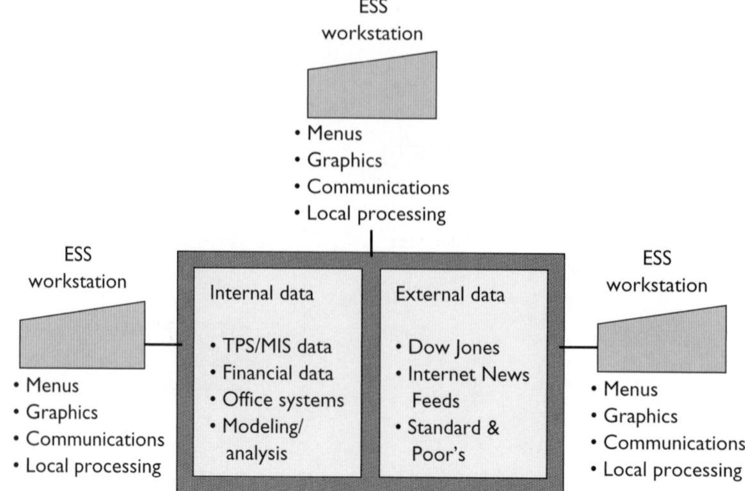


*Figure 2-8* Model of a typical executive support system. This system pools data from diverse internal and external sources and makes them available to executives in an easy-to-use form.

costs money, and integrating many different systems is extremely time consuming and complex. Each organization must weigh its needs for integrating systems against the difficulties of mounting a large-scale systems integration effort. The discussion of enterprise systems in Section 2.3 treats this issue in greater detail.

## 2.2 SYSTEMS FROM A FUNCTIONAL PERSPECTIVE

Information systems can be classified by the specific organizational function they serve as well as by organizational level. We now describe typical information systems that support each of the major business functions and provide examples of functional applications for each organizational level.

### SALES AND MARKETING SYSTEMS

The sales and marketing function is responsible for selling the organization's products or services. Marketing is concerned with identifying the customers for the firm's products or services, determining what they need or want, planning and developing products and services to

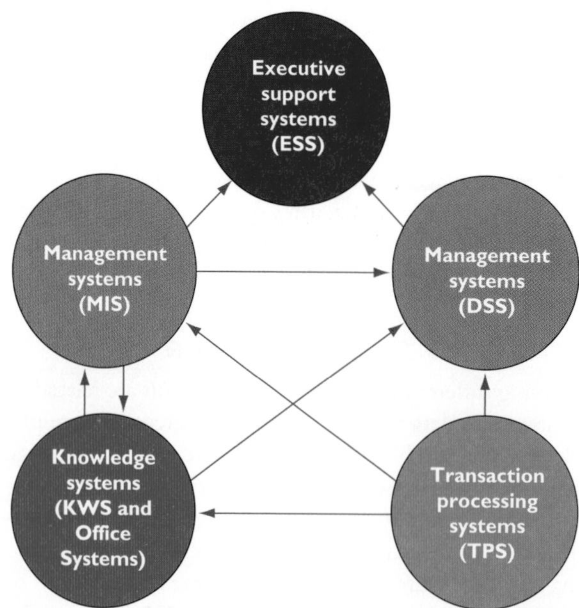


*Figure 2-9* Interrelationships among systems. The various types of systems in the organization have interdependencies. TPS are a major producer of information that is required by the other systems which, in turn, produce information for other systems. These different types of systems are only loosely coupled in most organizations.

**TABLE 2-2** EXAMPLES OF SALES AND MARKETING INFORMATION SYSTEMS

| System | Description | Organizational Level |
|---|---|---|
| Order processing | Enter, process, and track orders | Operational |
| Market analysis | Identify customers and markets using data on demographics, markets, consumer behavior, and trends | Knowledge |
| Pricing analysis | Determine prices for products and services | Management |
| Sales trend forecasting | Prepare 5-year sales forecasts | Strategic |

meet their needs, and advertising and promoting these products and services. Sales is concerned with contacting customers, selling the products and services, taking orders, and following up on sales. **Sales and marketing information systems** support these activities.

**sales and marketing information systems**
Systems that help the firm identify customers for the firm's products or services, develop products and services to meet customer needs, promote products and services, sell the products and services, and provide ongoing customer support.

Table 2-2 shows that information systems are used in sales and marketing in a number of ways. At the strategic level, sales and marketing systems monitor trends affecting new products and sales opportunities, support planning for new products and services, and monitor the performance of competitors. At the management level, sales and marketing systems support advertising and promotional campaigns and pricing decisions. They analyze sales performance and the performance of the sales staff. Knowledge-level sales and marketing systems support market research and marketing analysis workstations. At the operational level, sales and marketing systems assist in locating and contacting prospective customers, tracking sales, processing orders, and providing customer service support.

Review Figure 2-6. It shows the output of a typical sales information system at the management level. The system consolidates data about each item sold (such as the product code, product description, and amount of sales) for further management analysis. Company managers examine these sales data to monitor sales activity and buying trends. The Window on Management describes some typical sales and marketing systems that might be found in a small business.

## MANUFACTURING AND PRODUCTION SYSTEMS

The manufacturing and production function is responsible for actually producing the firm's goods and services. Manufacturing and production activities deal with the planning, development, and maintenance of production facilities; the establishment of production goals; the acquisition, storage, and availability of production materials; and the scheduling of equipment, facilities, materials, and labor required to fashion finished products. **Manufacturing and production information systems** support these activities.

**manufacturing and production information systems**
Systems that deal with the planning, development, and production of products and services and with controlling the flow of production.

Table 2-3 shows some typical manufacturing and production information systems arranged by organizational level. Strategic-level manufacturing systems deal with the firm's

**TABLE 2-3** EXAMPLES OF MANUFACTURING AND PRODUCTION INFORMATION SYSTEMS

| System | Description | Organizational Level |
|---|---|---|
| Machine control | Control the actions of machines and equipment | Operational |
| Computer-aided design (CAD) | Design new products using the computer | Knowledge |
| Production planning | Decide when and how many products should be produced | Management |
| Facilities location | Decide where to locate new production facilities | Strategic |

## How Southstream Seafoods Lands the Big Customers

According to Mark Soderstrom, president of Southstream Seafoods, anyone can sell fish. He believes that his company does it better than anyone else, thanks to powerful customer contact and sales information systems. Southstream Seafoods is based in Warwick, Rhode Island, and is an importer and wholesaler of frozen seafood that sells primarily to food-service distributors and restaurant chains. The company has been in business for more than 10 years and has 20 employees.

To stay ahead of competitors in a tough business, Southstream installed a customer relationship management (CRM) system with software from Sage Inc. The system keeps track of Southstream's customers, phone calls, and sales transactions and helps management measure the efficiency and productivity of the sales force.

Selling fish is challenging for both wholesalers and retailers because fish prices constantly go up and down, with factors such as weather or availability affecting the business within a few days. Soderstrom turned this problem into an opportunity to serve his customers better than competitors by broadcasting information about changing market prices to customers so they can make better business decisions. Southstream configured the contact management portion of the system so that with a click of a button, sales staff could send out information only to specified customers. The customer records in the system include check boxes indicating which types of fish they purchase. The check boxes enable Southstream to locate only those customers, for instance, who purchase Alaskan cod. Southstream can then send a fax about changes in Alaskan cod prices only to those customers who actually use the product. Southstream uses the system to fax market information to about half of its 1,000 customers each week.

The average Southstream sales representative handles between 75 and 125 active accounts. When making each call, the salesperson enters sales information, including quantity, price, and shipping information into the system. The salesperson can also use the system to set callback dates and reminder alarms. The system records the duration of each call and makes all of the information available to a manager or Southstream's shipping department. If the shipping department gets a call indicating that a customer's fish hasn't arrived on time, the shipping department can enter the customer's name and immediately see what that customer has just purchased and when delivery is expected.

Soderstrom can generate reports from the system to analyze the efficiency of his sales staff and find ways of better servicing customer accounts. The system can show him exactly what each salesperson has done, listing all of his or her phone calls, sales, and the results of phone calls. Using this information, Soderstrom might find that one sales representative is spending too much time on a customer with a historically low volume of purchases and recommend that the salesperson allocate more time to a customer with more purchasing potential. Using only 10 sales representatives and 2 people in the shipping department, Southstream sells and ships about one million pounds of fish each week. Without the system, the company would need a staff twice as big to do the job.

**To Think About:** What kinds of systems for sales and marketing are described here? How do these systems support the sales and marketing function? What organizational levels are supported by these systems?

*Sources:* Angela R. Garber, "Hook, Line, and Sinker," *Small Business Computing*, February 2000; and www.southstream.com.

*Southstream Seafoods uses information systems to alert customers to changing market prices for fish. Sales and marketing information systems can help companies provide better customer service.*

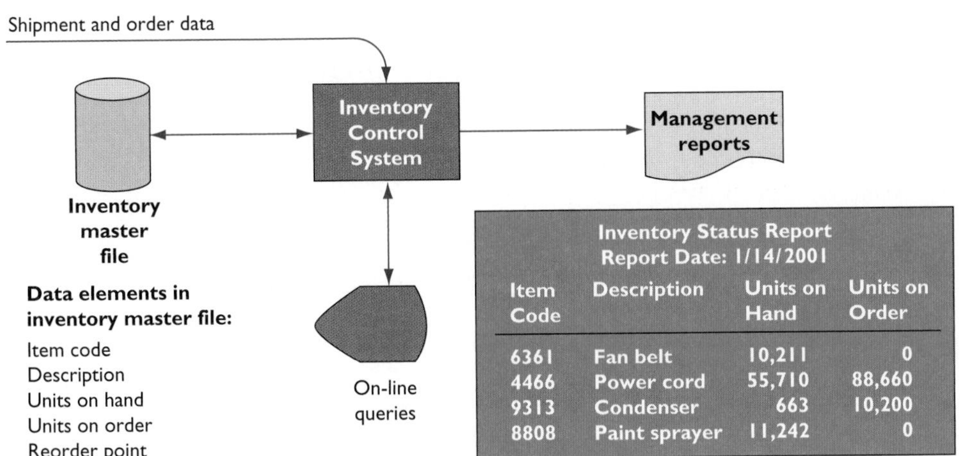


| Item Code | Description | Units on Hand | Units on Order |
|---|---|---|---|
| 6361 | Fan belt | 10,211 | 0 |
| 4466 | Power cord | 55,710 | 88,660 |
| 9313 | Condenser | 663 | 10,200 |
| 8808 | Paint sprayer | 11,242 | 0 |

***Figure 2-10*** Overview of an inventory system. This system provides information about the number of items available in inventory to support manufacturing and production activities.

long-term manufacturing goals, such as where to locate new plants or whether to invest in new manufacturing technology. At the management level, manufacturing and production systems analyze and monitor manufacturing and production costs and resources. Knowledge manufacturing and production systems create and distribute design knowledge or expertise to drive the production process, and operational manufacturing and production systems deal with the status of production tasks.

Most manufacturing and production systems use some sort of inventory system, illustrated in Figure 2-10. Data about each item in inventory, such as the number of units depleted because of a shipment or purchase or the number of units replenished by reordering or returns, are either scanned or keyed into the system. The inventory master file contains basic data about each item, including the unique identification code for each item, the description of the item, the number of units on hand, the number of units on order, and the reorder point (the number of units in inventory that triggers a decision to reorder to prevent a stockout). Companies can estimate the number of items to reorder or they can use a formula for calculating the least expensive quantity to reorder called the *economic order quantity.* The system produces reports such as the number of each item available in inventory, the number of units of each item to reorder, or items in inventory that must be replenished.

## FINANCE AND ACCOUNTING SYSTEMS

The finance function is responsible for managing the firm's financial assets, such as cash, stocks, bonds, and other investments, in order to maximize the return on these financial assets. The finance function is also in charge of managing the capitalization of the firm (finding new financial assets in stocks, bonds, or other forms of debt). In order to determine whether the firm is getting the best return on its investments, the finance function must obtain a considerable amount of information from sources external to the firm.

The accounting function is responsible for maintaining and managing the firm's financial records–receipts, disbursements, depreciation, payroll–to account for the flow of funds in a firm. Finance and accounting share related problems–how to keep track of a firm's financial assets and fund flows. They provide answers to questions such as these: What is the current inventory of financial assets? What records exist for disbursements, receipts, payroll, and other fund flows?

Table 2-4 shows some of the typical **finance and accounting information systems** found in large organizations. Strategic-level systems for the finance and accounting function establish long-term investment goals for the firm and provide long-range forecasts of the firm's financial performance. At the management level, information systems help managers oversee and control the firm's financial resources. Knowledge systems support finance and accounting by providing analytical tools and workstations for designing the right mix of investments to maximize returns for the firm. Operational systems in finance and accounting track the flow of funds in the firm through transactions such as paychecks, payments to vendors, securities reports, and receipts. Review Figure 2-3, which illustrates a payroll system, a typical accounting TPS found in all businesses with employees.

**finance and accounting information systems** Systems that keep track of the firm's financial assets and fund flows.

**TABLE 2-4** EXAMPLES OF FINANCE AND ACCOUNTING INFORMATION SYSTEMS

| System | Description | Organizational Level |
|---|---|---|
| Accounts receivable | Track money owed the firm | Operational |
| Portfolio analysis | Design the firm's portfolio of investments | Knowledge |
| Budgeting | Prepare short-term budgets | Management |
| Profit planning | Plan long-term profits | Strategic |

### HUMAN RESOURCES SYSTEMS

**human resources information systems** Systems that maintain employee records; track employee skills, job performance, and training; and support planning for employee compensation and career development.

The human resources function is responsible for attracting, developing, and maintaining the firm's workforce. **Human resources information systems** support activities such as identifying potential employees, maintaining complete records on existing employees, and creating programs to develop employees' talents and skills.

Strategic-level human resources systems identify the employee requirements (skills, educational level, types of positions, number of positions, and cost) for meeting the firm's long-term business plans. At the management level, human resources systems help managers monitor and analyze the recruitment, allocation, and compensation of employees. Knowledge systems for human resources support analysis activities related to job design, training, and the modeling of employee career paths and reporting relationships. Human resources operational systems track the recruitment and placement of the firm's employees (see Table 2-5).

Figure 2-11 illustrates a typical human resources TPS for employee record keeping. It maintains basic employee data, such as the employee's name, age, sex, marital status, address, educational background, salary, job title, date of hire, and date of termination. The system can produce a variety of reports, such as lists of newly hired employees, employees who are terminated or on leaves of absence, employees classified by job type or educational level, or employee job performance evaluations. Such systems are typically designed to provide data that can satisfy federal and state record keeping requirements for Equal Employment Opportunity (EEO) and other purposes.

## 2.3 INTEGRATING FUNCTIONS AND BUSINESS PROCESSES: ENTERPRISE SYSTEMS AND INDUSTRIAL NETWORKS

Organizations are finding benefits from using information systems to coordinate activities and decisions spanning multiple functional areas across entire firms and even entire industries.

### BUSINESS PROCESSES AND INFORMATION SYSTEMS

The systems we have described support flows of work and activities called *business processes,* which we introduced in Chapter 1. Business processes refer to the manner in which work is organized, coordinated, and focused to produce a valuable product or service. On the one

**TABLE 2-5** EXAMPLES OF HUMAN RESOURCES INFORMATION SYSTEMS

| System | Description | Organizational Level |
|---|---|---|
| Training and development | Track employee training, skills, and performance appraisals | Operational |
| Career pathing | Design career paths for employees | Knowledge |
| Compensation analysis | Monitor the range and distribution of employee wages, salaries, and benefits | Management |
| Human resources planning | Plan the long-term labor force needs of the organization | Strategic |

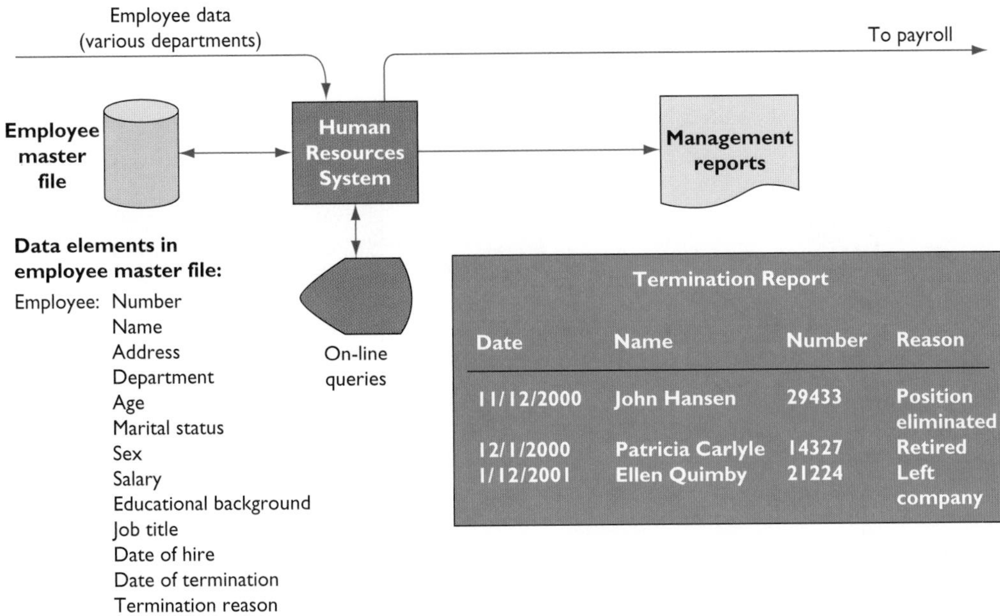


*Figure 2-11* An employee record keeping system. This system maintains data on the firm's employees to support the human resources function.

hand, business processes are concrete workflows of material, information, and knowledge–sets of activities. On the other hand, business processes represent unique ways in which organizations coordinate work, information, and knowledge, and the ways in which management chooses to coordinate work. Table 2-6 describes typical business processes for each of the functional areas.

Although each of the major business functions has its own set of business processes, many other business processes are cross-functional, transcending the boundaries between sales, marketing, manufacturing, and accounting. These cross-functional processes cut across the traditional organizational structure, grouping employees from different functional specialties to complete a piece of work. For example, the order fulfillment process at many companies requires cooperation among the sales function (receiving the order, entering the order), the accounting function (credit checking and billing for the order), and the manufacturing and production function (assembling and shipping the order). Figure 2-12 illustrates

## TABLE 2-6 EXAMPLES OF BUSINESS PROCESSES

| Functional Area | Business Process |
|---|---|
| Manufacturing and production | Assembling the product |
| | Checking for quality |
| | Producing bills of materials |
| Sales and marketing | Identifying customers |
| | Making customers aware of the product |
| | Selling the product |
| Finance and accounting | Paying creditors |
| | Creating financial statements |
| | Managing cash accounts |
| Human resources | Hiring employees |
| | Evaluating employees' job performance |
| | Enrolling employees in benefits plans |

*Figure 2-12* The order fulfillment process. Generating and fulfilling an order is a multistep process involving activities performed by the sales, manufacturing and production, and accounting functions.

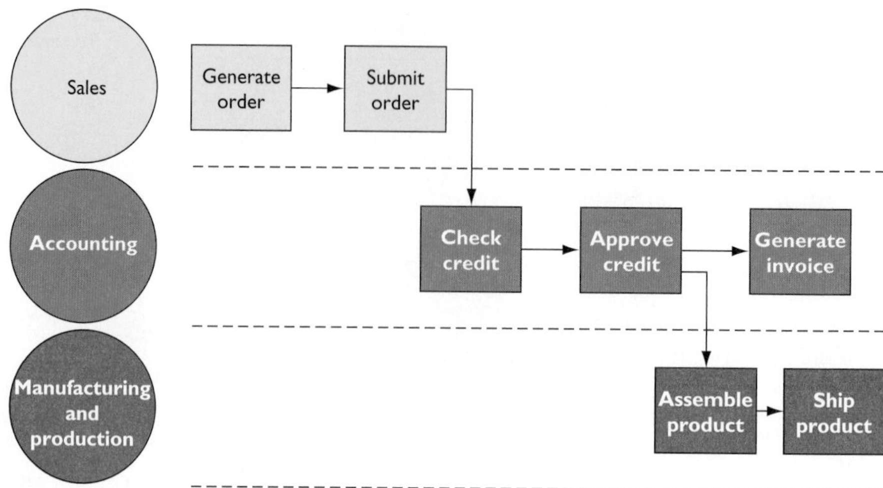


how this cross-functional process might work. Information systems support these cross-functional processes as well as processes for the separate business functions.

Information systems can help organizations achieve great efficiencies by automating parts of these processes or by helping organizations rethink and streamline these processes. However, redesigning business processes requires careful analysis and planning. When systems are used to strengthen the wrong business model or business processes, the business can become more efficient at doing what it should not do. As a result, the firm becomes vulnerable to competitors who may have discovered the right business model. Therefore, one of the most important strategic decisions that a firm can make is not deciding how to use computers to improve business processes, but instead to first understand what business processes need improvement (Keen, 1997). Chapter 10 treats this subject in greater detail, because it is fundamental to systems analysis and design.

## Customer Relationship Management and Supply Chain Management

Electronic commerce, global competition, and the rise of digital firms have made companies think strategically about their business processes for managing their relationships with customers and suppliers. Consumers can now use the Web to comparison shop and switch companies on a moment's notice. To survive, businesses need to find ways of providing more value and service to customers at lower cost. Many believe the solution lies in improving business processes for interacting with customers and for producing and delivering products or services.

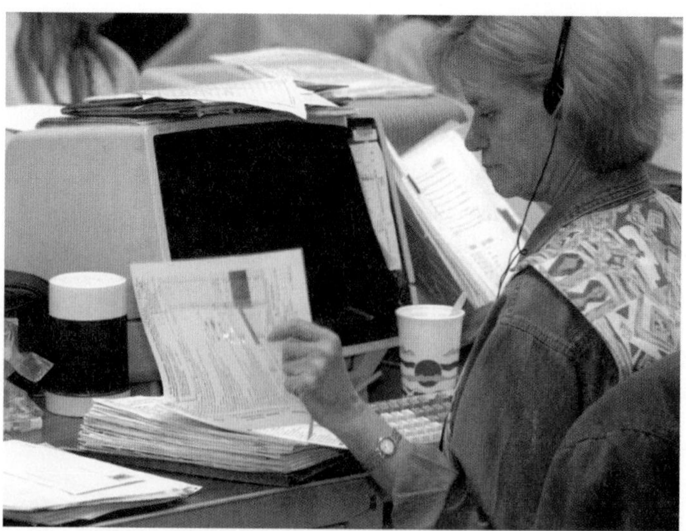

*Keying data from tax returns into the Internal Revenue Service computer system is an important activity in the tax collection process. Business processes coordinate work, information, and knowledge.*

## Customer Relationship Management (CRM)

Instead of treating customers as exploitable sources of income, businesses are now viewing them as long-term assets to be nurtured through customer relationship management (CRM). **Customer relationship management (CRM)** focuses on managing all of the ways that a firm deals with its existing and potential new customers. CRM is both a business and technology discipline that uses information systems to coordinate all of the business processes surrounding the firm's interactions with its customers in sales, marketing, and service. The ideal CRM system provides end-to-end customer care from receipt of an order acquisition through product delivery.

**customer relationship management**
Business and technology discipline to coordinate all of the business processes for dealing with customers.

In the past, a firm's processes for sales, service, and marketing were highly compartmentalized and did not share much essential customer information. Some information on a specific customer might be stored and organized in terms of that person's account with the company. Other pieces of information about the same customer might be organized by products that were purchased. There was no way to consolidate all of this information to provide a unified view of a customer across the company. CRM tools try to solve this problem by integrating the firm's customer-related processes and consolidating customer information from multiple communication channels–the telephone, e-mail, wireless devices, or the Web—so that the firm can put one coherent face to the customer (see Figure 2-13).

Good CRM systems consolidate customer data from multiple sources and provide analytical tools for answering questions such as: What is the value of a particular customer to the firm over his or her lifetime? Who are our most loyal customers? (It costs six times more to sell to a new customer than to an existing customer.) (Kalakota and Robinson, 2001). Who are our most profitable customers? (Typically 80–90% of a firm's profits are generated by 10–20% of its customers.) What do these profitable customers want to buy? Firms can then use the answers to acquire new customers, provide better service and support, customize their offerings more precisely to customer preferences, and provide ongoing value to retain profitable customers. Chapters 3, 4, 9, and 13 provide additional detail on customer relationship management applications and technologies.

**supply chain management**
Coordination of all the activities and information flows involved in buying, making, and moving a product.

## Supply Chain Management

To deliver the product more rapidly to the customer at lower cost, firms are also trying to streamline their business processes for supply chain management. **Supply chain management** is the close linkage of activities involved in buying, making, and moving a product. It integrates supplier, distributor, and customer logistics requirements into one cohesive process to reduce time, redundant effort, and inventory costs (see Figure 2-14). The **supply chain** is a network of facilities for procuring materials, transforming raw materials into intermediate

**supply chain**
Network of facilities for procuring materials, transforming raw materials into products, and distributing finished products to customers.

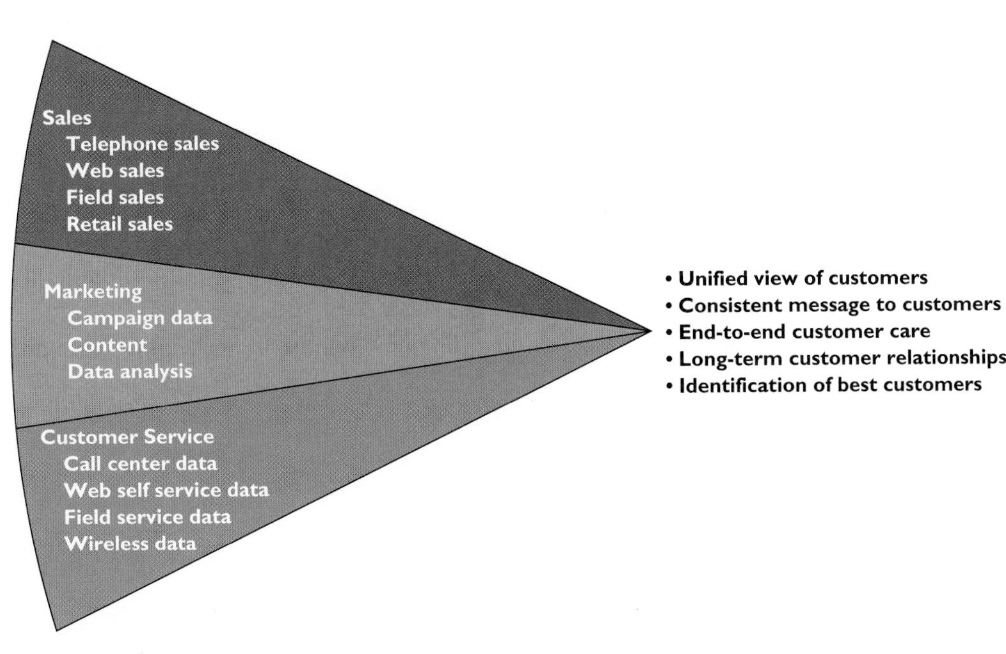


*Figure 2-13* Customer relationship management applies technology to look at customers from a multifaceted perspective. CRM uses a set of integrated applications to address all aspects of the customer relationship, including customer service, sales, and marketing.

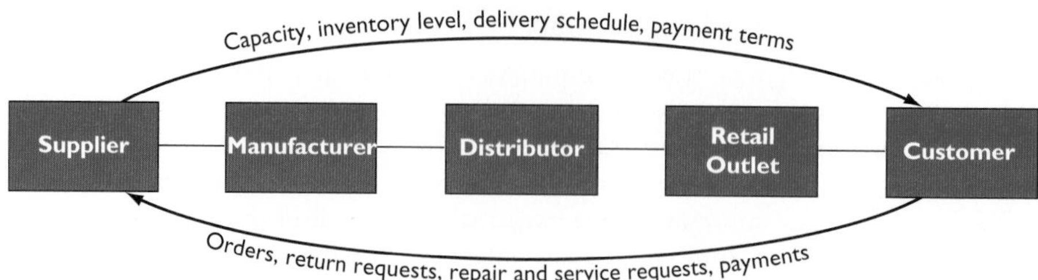


***Figure 2-14*** Supply chain management. The major entities in the supply chain use the flow of information to coordinate the activities involved in buying, making, and moving a product.

and finished products, and distributing the finished products to customers. It links manufacturing plants, distribution centers, conveyances, retail outlets, people, and information through processes such as procurement or logistics to supply goods and services from source through consumption. Goods or services start out as raw materials and move through the company's logistics and production systems until they reach customers. To manage the supply chain, a company tries to eliminate redundant steps, delays, and the amount of resources tied up along the way.

Companies that skillfully manage their supply chains get the right amount of their products from their source to their point of consumption with the least amount of time and the lowest cost. Information systems make supply chain management more efficient by helping companies coordinate, schedule, and control procurement, production, inventory management, and delivery of products and services to customers. Information systems can integrate demand planning, production forecasting, materials requisition, order processing, inventory allocation, order fulfillment, transportation services, receiving, invoicing, and payment. Table 2-7 describes how companies can benefit from using information systems for supply chain management.

Supply chain management systems can be built using intranets, extranets, or special supply chain management software. The Window on Organizations shows how Hewlett-Packard benefited from a sophisticated supply chain management system that used Internet technology.

## ENTERPRISE SYSTEMS

A large organization typically has many different kinds of information systems that support different functions, organizational levels, and business processes. Most of these systems, built around different functions, business units, and business processes, do not "talk" to each other, and managers might have a hard time assembling the data they would need for a comprehensive, overall picture of the organization's operations. For instance, sales personnel might not be able to tell at the time they placed an order whether the items that were ordered were in inventory; customers could not track their orders; and manufacturing could not communicate eas-

### HOW INFORMATION SYSTEMS CAN FACILITATE SUPPLY CHAIN MANAGEMENT

| Information systems can help participants in the supply chain |
|---|
| Decide when and what to produce, store, and move |
| Rapidly communicate orders |
| Track the status of orders |
| Check inventory availability and monitor inventory levels |
| Track shipments |
| Plan production based on actual customer demand |
| Rapidly communicate changes in product design |
| Provide product specifications |
| Share information about defect rates and returns |

## Supply Chain Management Keeps Inventory Fresh at HP

Why is the PC business like the fresh fruit business? Jean-Luc Meyer, a PC group marketing manager at Hewlett-Packard (HP), claims "Every day fresh fruit becomes less valuable because it gets a little rotten. In the PC business, every day prices go down." New computer technology develops so quickly that computers sitting on the shelf become technically outdated. To help the company sell its computers at full price, HP created a sophisticated supply chain management system that produces PCs to order and gets them to customers within 48 hours.

The new system automates much of the process. Orders are placed via computers that in turn forward the data to HP's production and delivery computer systems. Some of these systems are linked to the systems of HP's suppliers. Synnex, located in Fremont, California, is a contract manufacturer of PCs for a number of companies, including HP. When orders arrive at Synnex, computers immediately check the credit of the customer placing the order. Simultaneously they validate the order configuration to make sure it works (so no one wastes time building a computer with incompatible, duplicate, or missing components). Assuming everything checks out, the order is automatically forwarded to a computer that controls production. That computer prints out an instruction ticket for the assembly technician while simultaneously forwarding a parts order to Synnex's warehouse. The software to be included with the purchased computer is loaded onto that computer's storage unit and then the whole parts order with the ticket are shipped to the technician's workstation. One worker assembles the computer and then connects it to a computer that tests it. The new computer is then boxed, tagged, and shipped. Using the bar code on the ticket, even the delivery is monitored by computer. Much of the information in this process is communicated through the Internet.

HP's supply chain management system enables customers to receive their new computers very rapidly while HP reduces production errors. The system also reduces inventory–parts, goods in process, and completed products. Knowing exactly what computers to build helps HP reduce its pipeline of products awaiting the arrival of orders. To keep inventory low, HP makes the supply chain data available to parts suppliers and to production contractors (since many HP PCs are produced by outside manufacturers, such as Synnex).

For computers manufactured by contract producers, HP thus maintains virtually no inventory. Prior to supply chain management software, Synnex maintained four weeks of parts inventory. With the new automated system, their parts inventory has been cut to two weeks. The supply chain management software even monitors the parts inventory and automatically orders more parts when inventory gets low.

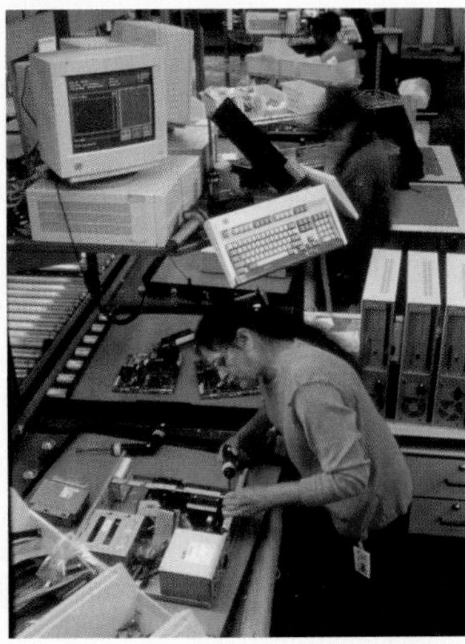

*HP is using supply chain management software in other parts of its business, and can now efficiently manage its supply chain for plastic parts.*

**To Think About:** How has HP's supply chain management system changed the way the company runs its business? It has been said that building a world-class supply chain management system is neither cheap nor easy. Why?

*Sources:* Rory J. O'Connor, "Keeping Inventory Fresh," *Upside*, June 2000; and eCompany Staff, "Supply-Chain Software: Hewlett Packard," *eCompany*, November 2000.

ily with finance to plan for new production. This fragmentation of data in hundreds of separate systems could thus have a negative impact on organizational efficiency and business performance. Figure 2-15 illustrates the traditional arrangement of information systems.

Systems for customer relationship management and supply chain management are a step forward in solving this problem. Many organizations are also building **enterprise systems,** also known as enterprise resource planning (ERP) systems, to provide firmwide integration. Enterprise software models and automates many business processes, such as filling an order or scheduling a shipment, with the goal of integrating information across the company and eliminating complex, expensive links between computer systems in different areas of the business. Information that was previously fragmented in different systems can seamlessly flow throughout the firm so that it can be shared by business processes in manufacturing,

**enterprise systems** Firmwide information systems that integrate key business processes so that information can flow freely between different parts of the firm.

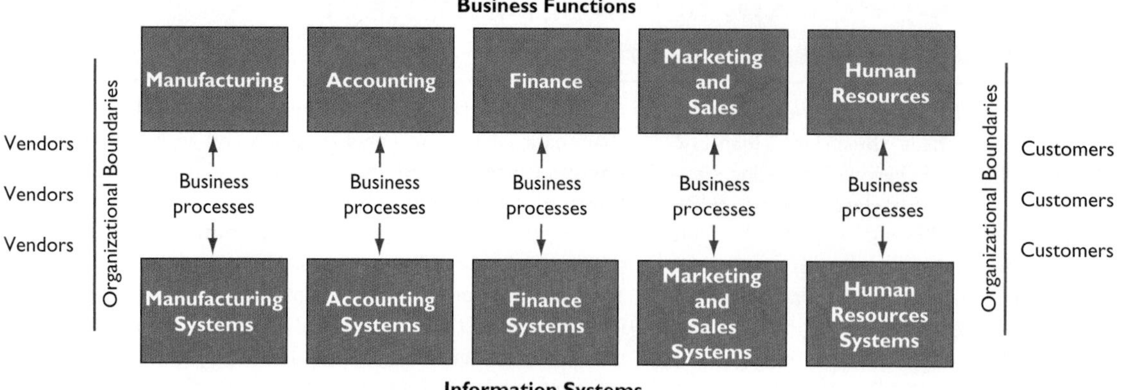


*Figure 2-15* Traditional view of systems. In most organizations today, separate systems built over a long period of time support discrete business processes and discrete business functions. The organization's systems rarely include vendors and customers.

accounting, human resources, and other areas of the firm. Discrete business processes from sales, production, finance, and logistics can be integrated into company-wide business processes that flow across organizational levels and functions. An enterprise-wide technical platform serves all processes and levels. Figure 2-16 illustrates how enterprise systems work

The enterprise system collects data from various key business processes (see Table 2-8) and stores the data in a single comprehensive data repository where they can be used by other parts of the business. Managers emerge with more precise and timely information for coordinating the daily operations of the business and a firmwide view of business processes and information flows.

For instance, when a sales representative in Brussels enters a customer order, the data flows automatically to others in the company who need to see it. The factory in Hong Kong receives the order and begins production. The warehouse checks its progress on-line and schedules the shipment date. The warehouse can check its stock of parts and replenish whatever the factory has depleted. The enterprise system stores production information, where it can be accessed by customer service representatives to track the progress of the order through every step of the manufacturing process. Updated sales and production data automatically flow to the accounting department. The system transmits information for calculating the salesperson's commission to the payroll department. The system also automatically recalculates the company's balance sheets, accounts receivable and payable ledgers, cost center accounts, and available cash. Corporate headquarters in London can view up-to-the-minute data on sales, inventory, and production at every step of the process as well as updated sales and production forecasts and calculations of product cost and availability.

*Figure 2-16* Enterprise systems. Enterprise systems can integrate the key business processes of an entire firm into a single software system that allows information to flow seamlessly throughout the organization. These systems may include transactions with customers and vendors.

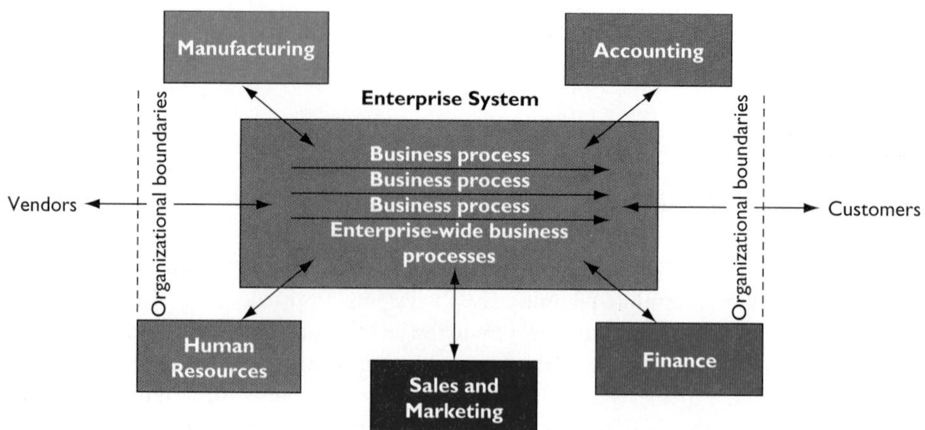

### TABLE 2-8 BUSINESS PROCESSES SUPPORTED BY ENTERPRISE SYSTEMS

**Manufacturing processes,** including inventory management, purchasing, shipping, production planning, material requirements planning, and plant and equipment maintenance

**Financial and accounting processes,** including accounts payable, accounts receivable, cash management and forecasting, product-cost accounting, cost-center accounting, asset accounting, general ledger, and financial reporting

**Sales and marketing processes,** including order processing, pricing, shipping, billing, sales management, and sales planning

**Human resource processes,** including personnel administration, time accounting, payroll, personnel planning and development, benefits accounting, applicant tracking, and travel expense reporting

## BENEFITS AND CHALLENGES OF ENTERPRISE SYSTEMS

Enterprise systems promise to integrate the diverse business processes of a firm into a single integrated information architecture but they present major challenges.

### Benefits of Enterprise Systems

Enterprise systems promise to greatly change four dimensions of business: firm structure, management process, technology platform, and business capability.

***Firm Structure and Organization: One Organization*** Companies can use enterprise systems to support organizational structures that were not previously possible or to create a more disciplined organizational culture. For example, they might use enterprise systems to integrate the corporation across geographic or business unit boundaries or to create a more uniform organizational culture in which everyone uses similar processes and information. An enterprise-enabled organization does business the same way worldwide, with functional boundaries deemphasized in favor of cross-functional coordination and information flowing freely across business functions.

***Management: Firmwide Knowledge-based Management Processes*** In addition to automating many essential business transactions, such as taking orders, paying suppliers, or changing employee benefits status, enterprise systems can also improve management report-

## MANAGEMENT DECISION PROBLEM

**ANALYZING ENTERPRISE PROCESS INTEGRATION**

Management at your agricultural chemicals corporation has been dissatisfied with production planning. Production plans are created using best guesses of demand for each product which are based on how much of each product has been ordered in the past. If a customer places an unexpected order or requests a change to an existing order after it has been placed, there is no way to adjust the production plans. The company may have to tell customers it can't fill their orders or may run up extra costs maintaining additional inventory to prevent stock-outs.

At the end of each month, orders are totaled and manually keyed into the company's production planning system. Data from the past month's production and inventory systems are manually entered into the firm's order management system. Analysts from the sales department and from the production department analyze the data from their respective systems to determine what the sales targets and what the production targets should be for the next month. These estimates are usually different. The analysts then get together at a high-level planning meeting to revise the production and sales targets to take into account senior management's goals for market share, revenues, and profits. The outcome of the meeting is a finalized production master schedule.

The entire production planning process takes 17 business days to complete. Nine of these days are required to enter and validate the data. The remaining days are spent developing and reconciling the production and sales targets and finalizing the production master schedule.

1. Draw a diagram of the production planning process.
2. Analyze the problems this process creates for the company.
3. How could an enterprise system solve these problems? In what ways could it lower costs? Diagram what this process might look like if the company implemented enterprise software.

ing and decision making. Information supplied by an enterprise system is structured around cross-functional business processes and it can be obtained rapidly. For example, an enterprise system might help management more easily determine which products are most or least profitable. No longer would general managers be stuck without any hard data on firm performance, or data that applies only to their own immediate department. An enterprise system could supply management with better data about business processes and overall organizational performance.

***Technology: Unified Platform*** Enterprise systems promise to provide firms with a single, unified, and all-encompassing information system technology platform and environment. Enterprise systems promise to create a single, integrated repository that gathers data on all the key business processes. The data have common, standardized definitions and formats that are accepted by the entire organization. You will learn more about the importance of standardizing organizational data in Chapter 7.

***Business: More Efficient Operations and Customer-driven Business Processes*** Enterprise systems can help create the foundation for a customer-driven or demand organization. By integrating discrete business processes such as sales, production, finance, and logistics, the entire organization can efficiently respond to customer requests for products or information, forecast new products, and build and deliver them as demand requires. Manufacturing has better information to produce only what customers have ordered, to procure exactly the right amount of components or raw materials to fill actual orders, to stage production, and to minimize the time that components or finished products are in inventory. Using enterprise systems to capture unit cost and quality data, firms can improve the quality of their products and services.

## The Challenge of Enterprise Systems

Although enterprise systems can improve organizational coordination, efficiency, and decision making, they have proven very difficult to build. They require not only large technology investments but also fundamental changes in the way the business operates. Companies need to rework their business processes to make information flow smoothly between them. Employees must take on new job functions and responsibilities. Enterprise systems require complex pieces of software and large investments of time, money, and expertise. Enterprise systems raise serious challenges for firms: a daunting implementation process, surviving a cost/benefit analysis, inflexibility, and realizing strategic value.

***Daunting Implementation*** Enterprise systems bring dramatic changes to business. They require not only deep-seated technological changes but also fundamental changes in the way the business operates. Business processes change dramatically, as do organizational structure and culture. Firms implementing enterprise systems have to come up with organization-wide definitions of data, retrain thousands of workers, and redesign their fundamental business processes, all at once, while carrying on business as usual. It might take a large company three to five years to fully implement all of the organizational and technology changes required by an enterprise system. Organizations that do not understand that such changes will be required or that are unable to make them will have problems implementing enterprise systems, or they may not be able to achieve a higher level of functional and business process integration.

***High Up-front Costs and Future Benefits*** The costs of enterprise systems are large, up-front, highly visible, and often politically charged. Although the costs to build the system are obvious, the benefits often cannot be precisely quantified at the beginning of an enterprise project. One reason is that the benefits often accrue from employees using the system after it is completed and gaining the knowledge of business operations heretofore impossible to learn.

***Inflexibility*** Enterprise system software tends to be complex and difficult to master, with a worldwide shortage in people with the expertise to install and maintain it. The software is deeply intertwined with corporate business processes. If companies need to make major changes to the software, the entire system will have to be changed. Because enterprise systems are integrated, it is difficult to make a change in only one part of the business without affecting other parts as well. There is the prospect that the new enterprise systems could eventually

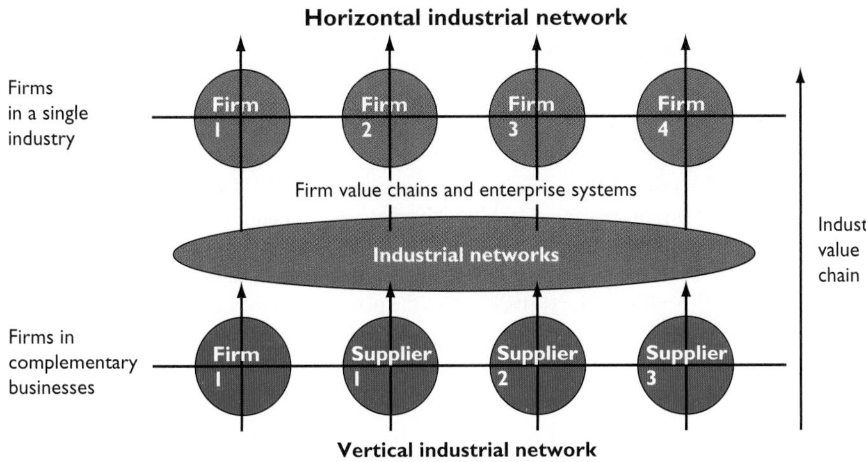


***Figure 2-17*** Industrial networks. Industrial networks link the enterprise systems of firms in an entire industry into an industry-wide system. Horizontal industrial networks link firms in the same industry, including competitors, whereas vertical industrial networks link a firm with suppliers in the same industry.

prove as brittle and hard to change as the old systems they replaced–a new kind of "digital concrete" that could, over time, bind firms to outdated business processes and systems.

***Realizing Strategic Value*** Companies may also fail to achieve strategic benefits from enterprise systems if integrating business processes using the generic models provided by standard ERP software prevents the firm from using unique business processes that had been sources of advantage over competitors. If an enterprise system is not compatible with the way the company does business, the company may lose a better way of performing a key business process that may be related to its competitive advantage. Enterprise systems promote centralized organizational coordination and decision making, which may not be the best way for some firms to operate. There are companies that clearly do not need the level of integration provided by enterprise systems (Davenport, 2000, 1998). Chapter 11 provides more detail on the organizational and technical challenges to enterprise system implementation.

## Extended Enterprises and Industrial Networks

In some industries, companies are extending their enterprise systems beyond the boundaries of the firm to share information and coordinate business processes with other firms in their industry. **Industrial networks,** which are sometimes called *extended enterprises,* link together the enterprise systems of firms in an entire industry (see Figure 2-17). For instance, Procter & Gamble (P&G), the world's largest consumer goods company, developed an integrated industry-wide system that coordinated grocery store point-of-sale systems with grocery store warehouses, shippers, its own manufacturing facilities, and its suppliers of raw materials. This single industry spanning system effectively allows P&G to monitor the movement of all its products from raw materials to customer purchase. P&G uses data collected from point-of-sale terminals to trigger shipments to retailers of items that customers have purchased and that need restocking. Electronic links to suppliers enable P&G to order materials from its own suppliers when its inventories are low. The system helps P&G reduce its inventory by allowing the company to produce products as they are demanded by retailers. P&G is implementing an Ultimate Supply System that uses Internet technology to link retailers and suppliers to its private corporate intranet (see the Chapter 3 opening vignette). By having retailers and suppliers integrate their systems with P&G's systems, P&G hopes to reduce product cycle time by half, and to slash inventory and systems costs.

**industrial networks**
Networks linking systems of multiple firms in an industry. Also called extended enterprises.

There are two kinds of industrial networks. **Vertical industrial networks** integrate the operations of the firm with its suppliers and can be used for supply chain management. **Horizontal industrial networks** link firms across an entire industry including competitors. An example would be the OASIS network of utility industry firms, which uses the Web to help members sell surplus electrical power. A few industrial networks coordinate the activities of competitors. For example, Yamaha Europe, Honda, Aprilia, and Piaggio, competing manufacturers of motor scooters, are now working together to share suppliers. They hope to ultimately reduce the number of suppliers, which will boost the production efficiency in the remaining group, and they all expect to realize savings from their cooperation (Abramson,

**vertical industrial networks**
Networks for integrating the operations of a firm with its suppliers.

**horizontal industrial networks**
Networks for linking firms across an entire industry.

## TABLE 2-9 Examples of Industrial Networks

| Organization(s) | Type of Industrial Network | Description |
|---|---|---|
| Coca-Cola | Vertical | Installed an enterprise system using SAP software and extended the system to its bottling partners. Coke and its partners can pool resources, share sales information, and leverage their combined size to obtain lower raw material costs. The extended enterprise system enables them to react rapidly to market changes and deploy products efficiently to the places where they are most likely to sell. |
| OASIS | Horizontal | Web sites link U.S. electrical utility companies in regional power pool groups to sell their surplus power to wholesalers and locate the transmission facilities for moving the power between its source and the customer. |
| General Mills, Kellogg, Land O'Lakes, Monsanto | Horizontal | Shared Internet system enables large package foods manufacturers to share excess shipping capacity, reducing logistics costs. |
| Safeway UK | Vertical | Has electronic links to suppliers where it can share information about forecasts, shelf space, and inventory, so they can track demand for their products, adjust production, and adjust the timing and size of deliveries. The suppliers can download Safeway's information into their enterprise systems or production planning systems. Suppliers send Safeway information about product availability, production capacity, and inventory levels. |

1999). Table 2-9 provides examples of both types of industrial networks. Most industrial networks today are vertical and do not link together competitors in the same industry.

Many of these industrial networks are currently dedicated to supply chain management. Enterprise systems have primarily focused on helping companies manage their internal manufacturing, financial, and human resource processes and were not originally designed to support supply chain management processes involving entities outside the firm. However, enterprise software vendors are starting to enhance their products so that firms can link their enterprise systems with external vendors, suppliers, manufacturers, distributors, and retailers.

Enterprise systems can produce the integration among internal supply chain processes, such as sales, inventory, and production, that makes it easier for the firm to coordinate its activities with manufacturing partners and customers. Manufacturing can be informed of exactly what to produce, based on sales orders, and reduce the need to keep excess stock in inventory. If participants in the supply chain use the same enterprise software systems, their systems can exchange data without manual intervention. Companies can also use Internet technology to create industrial networks, because it provides a platform where systems from different companies can seamlessly exchange information.

## Application Software Exercise

### Database Exercise: Tracking Reservations at Monroe's Midnight Inn

Monroe's Midnight Inn is a family-owned and operated bed and breakfast. After inheriting the Monroe mansion eight years ago, James and Peggy Monroe decided to renovate the mansion and establish a bed and breakfast. The bed and breakfast has 14 rooms: 5 overlook a private lake, 5 overlook the woods, and the remaining 4 rooms overlook the gardens. Room rates are based on room choice, length of stay, and number of guests per room. Guests staying for 7 days or more are given a 15 percent discount on their daily room rates. A maximum of four guests are permitted in each room, with each additional guest charged $20 per day.

Business has grown steadily during the past eight years. In the early years, the establishment was frequented primarily by couples; however, the bed and breakfast now caters to a variety of clientele, including families, executives, and locals. The bed and breakfast's growing popularity is because, in part, of its location, the activities available to its visitors, and its affordability.

Currently, all records are manually kept. This manual record keeping system has caused many problems for James and Peggy. For instance, only last week Peggy had two families booked in the Washington room. Luckily, she was able to reassign one of the families to the Lincoln room and avoid upsetting a valuable customer. Similarly, James does not have immediate access to management information about the bed and breakfast's operations. He would like to have information about current room occupancy, average length of stay, and weekly income by room.

Using the information provided in the scenario and in the accompanying tables on the Laudon Web site, prepare a simple database to track reservations and generate management reports. In addition to the 10 transactions provided in the table, add at least 10 more transactions to the database. You may make any assumptions you believe are necessary; however, please document these assumptions in writing and provide them to your professor.

In addition to the data already provided, what additional data should be captured and stored in the database? As mentioned previously, James requires managerial information about the bed and breakfast's operations. What reports would provide the necessary information? Identify at least two other reports that would be beneficial for James. Prepare these reports.

## MANAGEMENT WRAP-UP

Enterprise systems and industrial networks require management to take a firmwide view of business processes and information flows. Managers need to determine which business processes should be integrated, the short- and long-term benefits of this integration, and the appropriate level of financial and organizational resources to support this integration.

There are many types of information systems in an organization that support different organizational levels, functions, and business processes. Some of these systems, such as those for customer relationship management and supply chain management, span more than one function or business process. Enterprise systems integrating information from different organizational functions and business processes often require extensive organizational change.

Information systems that create firm- or industry-wide information flows and business processes require major technology investments and planning. Firms must have an information technology (IT) infrastructure that can support organization-wide or industry-wide computing.

*For Discussion*

1. Review the payroll TPS illustrated in Figure 2-3. How could it provide information for other types of systems in the firm?
2. Adopting an enterprise system is a key business decision as well as a technology decision. Do you agree? Why or why not? Who should make this decision?

## SUMMARY

1. *Analyze the role played by the six major types of information systems in organizations and their relationship to each other.* There are six major types of information systems in contemporary organizations that are designed for different purposes and different audiences. Operational-level systems are transaction processing systems (TPS), such as payroll or order processing, that track the flow of the daily routine transactions that are necessary to conduct business. Knowledge-level systems support clerical, managerial, and professional workers. They consist of office systems for increasing data workers' productivity and knowledge work systems for enhancing knowledge workers' productivity. Management-level systems (MIS and DSS) provide the management control level with reports and access to the organization's current performance and historical records. Most MIS reports condense information from TPS and are not highly analytical. Decision-support systems (DSS) support management decisions when these decisions are

unique, rapidly changing, and not specified easily in advance. They have more advanced analytical models and data analysis capabilities than MIS and often draw on information from external as well as internal sources.

Executive support systems (ESS) support the strategic level by providing a generalized computing and communications environment to assist senior management's decision making. They have limited analytical capabilities but can draw on sophisticated graphics software and many sources of internal and external information.

The various types of systems in the organization exchange data with one another. TPS are a major source of data for other systems, especially MIS and DSS. ESS primarily receive data from lower-level systems. The different systems in an organization have traditionally been loosely integrated.

2. *Describe the types of information systems supporting the major functional areas of the business.* At each level of the organization there are information systems supporting the major functional areas of the business. Sales and marketing systems help the firm identify customers for the firm's products or services, develop products and services to meet customer needs, promote products and services, sell the products and services, and provide ongoing customer support. Manufacturing and production systems deal with the planning, development, and production of products and services, and control the flow of production. Finance and accounting systems keep track of the firm's financial assets and fund flows. Human resources systems maintain employee records, track employee skills, job performance, and training; and support planning for employee compensation and career development.

3. *Assess the relationship between organizations, information systems and business processes, including the processes for customer relationship management and supply chain management.* Business processes refer to the manner in which work is organized, coordinated, and focused to produce a valuable product or service. Business processes are concrete workflows of material, information, and knowledge, and they also represent unique ways in which organizations coordinate work, information, and knowledge, and the ways in which management chooses to coordinate work. Although each of the major business functions has its own set of business processes, many other business processes are cross-functional, such as fulfilling an order. Information systems can help organizations achieve great efficiencies by automating parts of these processes or by helping organizations rethink and streamline these processes, especially those for customer relationship management and supply chain management. Customer relationship management uses information systems to coordinate all of the business processes surrounding a firm's interactions with its customers. Supply chain management is the close linkage of activities involved in buying, making, and moving a product. Information systems make supply chain management more efficient by helping companies coordinate, schedule, and control procurement, production, inventory management, and delivery of products and services to customers.

4. *Explain how enterprise systems and industrial networks create new efficiencies for businesses.* Enterprise systems integrate the key business processes of a firm into a single software system so that information can flow seamlessly throughout the organization, improving coordination, efficiency, and decision making. Industrial networks link other organizations in the same industry in a single industry-wide system. Vertical industrial networks consist of an organization and its suppliers, whereas horizontal industrial networks consist of competitors in the same industry.

5. *Evaluate the benefits and limitations of enterprise systems and industrial networks.* Enterprise systems and industrial networks promise efficiencies from better coordination of both internal and external business processes. Enterprise systems can help create a uniform organization in which everyone uses similar processes and information, and measures their work in terms of organization-wide performance standards. An enterprise system could supply management with better data about business processes and overall organizational performance. Enterprise systems feature a single information technology platform where data definitions are standardized across the organization. The coordination of sales, production, finance, and logistics processes provided by enterprise systems helps organizations respond rapidly to customer demands.

The reality is that firm- and industry-wide systems are very difficult to implement successfully. They require extensive organizational change, use complicated technologies, and require large up-front costs for long-term benefits that are difficult to quantify in advance. Once implemented, enterprise systems are very difficult to change. Management vision and foresight are required to take a firm- and industry-wide view of problems and to find solutions that realize strategic value from the investment.

## KEY TERMS

**Customer relationship management (CRM), 53**
**Decision-support systems (DSS), 43**
**Desktop publishing, 43**
**Document imaging systems, 43**
**Enterprise systems, 55**
**Executive support systems (ESS), 45**
**Finance and accounting information systems, 49**
**Horizontal industrial networks, 59**
**Human resources information systems, 50**
**Industrial networks, 59**
**Knowledge-level systems, 39**
**Knowledge work systems (KWS), 42**
**Management information systems (MIS), 43**
**Management-level systems, 39**

**Manufacturing and production information systems, 47**
**Office systems, 42**
**Operational-level systems, 38**
**Sales and marketing information systems, 47**
**Strategic-level systems, 39**
**Supply chain, 53**
**Supply chain management, 53**
**Transaction processing systems (TPS), 40**
**Vertical industrial networks, 59**
**Word processing, 43**

## REVIEW QUESTIONS

1. Identify and describe the four levels of the organizational hierarchy. What types of information systems serve each level?
2. List and briefly describe the major types of systems in organizations.
3. What are the five types of TPS in business organizations? What functions do they perform? Give examples of each.
4. Describe the functions performed by knowledge work and office systems and some typical applications of each.
5. What are the characteristics of MIS? How do MIS differ from TPS? From DSS?
6. What are the characteristics of DSS? How do they differ from those of ESS?
7. Describe the relationship between TPS, office systems, KWS, MIS, DSS, and ESS.
8. List and describe the information systems serving each of the major functional areas of a business.
9. What is a business process? Give two examples of business processes for functional areas of the business and one example of a cross-functional process.
10. What is customer relationship management? Why is it so important to businesses? How do information systems facilitate customer relationship management?
11. What is supply chain management? What activities does it comprise? Why is it so important to businesses?
12. How do information systems facilitate supply chain management?
13. What are enterprise systems? How do they change the way an organization works?
14. What are the benefits and challenges of implementing enterprise systems?
15. What are industrial networks? Define and describe the two types of industrial networks.
16. How can organizations benefit from participating in industrial networks?

## GROUP PROJECT

With a group of three or four other students, select a business using an industrial network for supply chain management. Use the Web, newspapers, journals, and computer or business magazines to find out more about that organization and its use of information technology to provide links to other organizations. If possible, use presentation software to present your findings to the class.

## TOOLS FOR INTERACTIVE LEARNING

### INTERNET CONNECTION

The Internet Connection for this chapter will take you to a series of Web sites used in business-to-business electronic commerce where you can complete an exercise to evaluate the use of the Web in supply chain management. You can also use the Interactive Study Guide to test your knowledge of the topics in this chapter and get instant feedback when you need more practice.

### ELECTRONIC COMMERCE PROJECT

At the Laudon Web site for Chapter 2 you will find an electronic commerce project where you can use a series of Web sites to help a company plan and budget for a sales conference.

### CD-ROM

If you use the Multimedia Edition CD-ROM with this chapter, you can complete an interactive exercise to analyze an enterprise system implementation. You can also find an audio overview of the major themes of this chapter and bullet text summarizing the key points of the chapter.

## CASE STUDY *Owens-Corning's Enterprise System Struggle*

In the early 1990s Owens-Corning was a U.S. leader in the production and sale of such building materials as insulation, siding, and roofing, but management wanted the company to grow. The company had only two possible paths to growth: offering a fuller range of building materials, or becoming a global force. To increase its range of products Owens-Corning decided to acquire other companies. To become a global force, management realized the company would need to become a global enterprise that could coordinate the activities of all of its units in many different countries.

Headquartered in Toledo, Ohio, Owens-Corning had been divided along product lines, such as fiberglass insulation, exterior siding, and roofing materials. Each unit operated as a distinct entity with its own set of information systems. (The company had more than 200 archaic, inflexible, and isolated systems.) Each plant had its own product lines, pricing schedules, and trucking carriers. Owens-Corning customers had to place separate telephone calls for each product ordered–one each for siding, roofing, and insulation. The company operated like a collection of autonomous fiefdoms.

Owens-Corning management believed that these problems could be solved by implementing an enterprise system. The company selected enterprise software from SAP AG to serve as the foundation for a broad company overhaul. "The primary intent with SAP was to totally integrate our business systems on a global basis so everyone was operating on the same platform with the same information," said Dennis Sheets, sourcing manager for the insulation and roofing business. Sheets wanted to centralize purchasing. "Prior to SAP," he said, "we were buying widgets all over the world without any consolidated knowledge of how much we were buying and from whom. Now [using SAP's R/3 software] we can find out how many widgets we're using, where they're being purchased, and how much we paid for them, [allowing] us to consolidate the overall acquisition process." Now, he added, "we can . . . make better business decisions and better buys." Sheets expected the company's material and supply inventories to drop by 25 percent as a result.

However, the project to install SAP's enterprise system would ultimately cost Owens-Corning about $100 million and take several years, too expensive and time consuming to be justified only by the reasons given by Sheets. The company hoped that the new system would also enable it to digest acquisitions more easily. Owens-Corning wanted to acquire other companies to expand its product line so it could increase sales from $2.9 billion in 1992 to $5 billion within a few years. That meant that Owens-Corning would have to digest the archaic, inflexible systems from the companies it purchased. If Owens-Corning were to become a global enterprise, it would need a flexible system that would enable the company to access all of its data in an open and consolidated way.

ERP experts point out that simply converting to ERP systems does not solve companies' problems. "Unless a company does a lot of thinking about what its supply chain strategy is and articulating what its business processes are, these tools are going to be of little use," explained Mark Orton, of the New England Supplier Institute in Boston.

Owens-Corning's project began with its insulation group, and those on the project team understood this. They undertook a redesign process before implementing SAP's R/3. They set up cross-functional teams to identify the handoffs and touch points between the various functions. For example, the process that runs from the time the firm needs to buy something through the payment issuance to the supplier touches logistics and accounting. The teams also kept in close contact with suppliers who needed to know what Owens-Corning would require of them. As a result of the redesign, purchasing decisions were moved from the plants up to a regional level, enabling commodity specialists to use their expertise and the leverage of buying for a larger base to improve Owens-Corning's purchasing position.

How did the first ERP project go? During a weekend in March 1997 a team of about 60 people transferred legacy data into the SAP system, and on Monday morning the company went live. When Owens-Corning first went live with SAP, overall productivity and customer service dropped sharply during the first six months. "When you put in something like SAP, it's not a mere systems change," said David Johns, Owens-Corning's director of global development. "You're changing the way people have done their jobs for the past 20 years."

The first problems that surfaced were technical. According to Johns, application response time had increased from seconds before ERP to minutes under the new system. Other technical problems also emerged. For example, Johns said the system wasn't working the way it was supposed to. Johns believes the source of these problems was inadequate testing. The team further tuned the software, and during the next weeks response time reduced to an acceptable level. Slowly the software began operating smoothly.

However, after Owens-Corning fixed some of the technical problems, it saw that this was much bigger than a technology problem. There were problems in the business, problems with the way people's new roles had been defined, communication and change management issues, and business process issues. For example, the SAP system demanded that the entire corporation adopt a single product list and a single price list. Staff members initially resisted. Owens-Corning employees had not been properly trained and they were overwhelmed, resulting in a lot of errors. Johns explained that at Owens-Corning "we underestimated the impact that swapping out all our old systems would have on our people." Users had indeed been properly trained on their own functions, but ERP systems are integrated, and the users did not understand the impact their work was having on other departments.

ERP systems are complex and errors ripple throughout the system. When using the old systems, employees had time to correct data entry mistakes, and if they were not caught, they only affected the local function. However, now that they were using R/3, data that are used by the entire company are immediately updated. Thus, for example, the data flow instantly from sales to purchasing, production, and logistics systems. Johns offered another example. "If you're at a warehouse, and you don't tell the system when a truck is leaving the dock, the truck can still leave, but the customer will never get an invoice for the goods. Accounting won't find out later because the transaction will never get to them." Such errors can be costly. To motivate users to work with more care, they needed to know how their errors would affect other workers and even company profitability.

To address this problem the company quickly instituted a new training approach. Training now would include information on the larger system and its complexities, so users would understand the impact of their work. Under the new training regimen, all employees were denied access to the system until they had passed a test and became certified. Those who failed the test had to return to training until they could pass it. About 20 percent of Owens-Corning employees never passed the test and had to change jobs. This job shifting was massive and time consuming, causing organizational disruption. Whereas the original project budgeted training for 7 percent of overall costs, training eventually consumed 13 percent of the budget.

Customers also suffered. Owens-Corning had been known for its excellent customer service, but the quality of that service declined sharply after the SAP system went live. Many customers were shocked, and some began turning to other suppliers. Owens-Corning began losing important customers. The company was forced to devote a great deal of personnel time rebuilding relations with its customers while simultaneously repairing both its organization and the software installation.

ERP implementation problems of this type are common. According to Barry Wilderman of the Meta Group, ERP projects often result in a negative return on investment (ROI) for five or more years. Why? Because ERP systems are so complex. The company may not understand all that needs to be done in preparation. Moreover, these systems are expensive, and testing and training often get cut for budgetary reasons. Not only do employees need to become accustomed to new ways of doing business, but customers and suppliers may need to change their business processes as well.

How successful was the whole project? Management believes it has been a success. Johns said, "We made each mistake only once. Each deployment [in the rollout] got better." For instance, "We do a lot more testing now before we go live," he said, "to make sure that all the different pieces of the system work together." Customers now have a single point of contact for all orders. With Owens-Corning's old system, it didn't know what inventory was in stock. Employees would have to check around and get back to the customer. Now the firm can see what inventory is available, when it will be produced, and who is the lowest cost carrier. It can commit to the customer before hanging up the phone. The changes have been massive, with about 10,000 people involved with the reengineering effort.

The ERP system's rollout was completed in 2000. During those years, Owens-Corning acquired and integrated 17 companies, successfully expanding their product offerings. Company sales have reached $5 billion annually. Because of the new system, Owens-Corning has been able to reduce its inventory significantly, while centralizing coordination of various functions and divisions. Lot size and machine allocations have become more efficient. The company can perform production planning and control globally because it has one uniform system with which to work. The integrated system lets the company leverage common carriers and take advantage of overlapping transportation routes. Managers can use the system to identify its biggest suppliers across the entire company and use that information to negotiate bulk discounts. A customer needs to call only one location to place an order. Factory production managers no longer have to concern themselves with taking customer orders, tracking logistics or after-sales service. Because centralization applied not only to U.S. operations but also to foreign activities, the corporation has been transformed into a truly globalized enterprise.

In the autumn of 2000, Owens-Corning filed for Chapter 11 bankruptcy protection which was caused by a massive liability from the settlement of asbestos-related lawsuits. The company is also facing softening demand for some of its products. Nevertheless, the firm is investing in a series of e-business initiatives designed to optimize its supply chain operations. It is installing Web-based versions of its SAP R/3 enterprise software and a new logistics system that will enable its workers to use the Web to check the status of shipments, interact with the carriers, and input data. These new system projects should improve Owens-Corning's customer relationship management and business collaboration capabilities while further improving data accuracy and reducing operational costs.

**Sources:** Marc L. Songini, "Owens Corning Pushes E-business Projects Despite Financial Struggles," *Computerworld,* January 25, 2001; Rajagopal Palaniswamy and Tyler Frank, "Enhancing Manufacturing Performance with ERP Systems," *Information Systems Management,* Summer 2000; SAP, "Owens Corning Builds Its Internet Future with mySAP.com," September 14, 2000, www.sap.com; Christopher Koch, "From Team Techie to Enterprise Leader," *CIO Magazine,* October 15, 1999; Tom Stein, "Making ERP Add Up," *Information Week,* May 24, 1999, and "Key Work: Integration," *Information Week,* September 22, 1997; Tim Minahan, "Enterprise Resource Planning: Strategies Not Included," *Purchasing,* July 16, 1998; Janice Fioravante, "ERP Orchestrates Change," *Beyond Computing,* October 1998; Bruce Caldwell and Tom Stein, "Beyond ERP," *Information Week,* October 12, 1998; John E. Ettlie, "The ERP Challenge," *Automotive Manufacturing & Production,* June 1998; and Joseph B. White, Don Clark, and Silvio Ascarelli, "Program of Pain," *Wall Street Journal,* March 14, 1997.

### *CASE STUDY QUESTIONS*

1. Describe the problems Owens-Corning had with its information systems prior to installing its enterprise system. What management, organization, and technology factors were responsible for those problems?
2. What management, organization, and technology problems did Owens-Corning face in putting their enterprise system into effect?
3. How did implementing an enterprise system change the way Owens-Corning ran its business?
4. Was installing an enterprise system the right solution for Owens-Corning? Explain.

chapter

# 3 Information Systems, Organizations, Management, and Strategy

objectives

**After completing this chapter, you will be able to:**

1. *Identify the salient characteristics of organizations.*
2. *Analyze the relationship between information systems and organizations.*
3. *Contrast the classical and contemporary models of managerial activities and roles.*
4. *Describe how managers make decisions in organizations.*
5. *Evaluate the role of information systems in supporting various levels of business strategy.*

## Procter & Gamble's Internet Gamble Starts to Pay Off

Procter & Gamble Co. (P&G), the 163-year-old consumer goods giant, has traditionally aimed at doubling its sales every decade and has usually succeeded—until recently. During the past five years, annual sales growth has slowed from 5 to 2.6 percent. A. G. Lafley, P&G's new CEO, is trying to revitalize the company to make faster and better decisions, cut red tape, wring costs out of systems and procedures, and fuel innovation. A key component in P&G's ambitious change program is the use of Internet technology to drive inefficiencies out of its supply chain, forge new relationships with consumers, and pull in new revenue from one-to-one marketing and electronic commerce.

P&G has launched dozens of Web sites to promote old brands and build new ones, hoping to deepen its relationship with consumers in the process. PG.com, its main corporate Web site, links to numerous other subsites devoted to P&G products, such as Tide, Pampers, or Mr. Clean. If consumers enter details at Tide.com about a coffee stain, the site offers on-line advice on how to remove it. P&G's MoreThanACard.com allows visitors to create custom gift packages using P&G products for $25. Reflect.com targets upscale women by letting them design their own custom-blended cosmetics. An icon of a stylized test tube and beaker on PG.com invites visitors to send new product suggestions to the company. By using the Internet to interact with customers, P&G has cut its marketing research costs by 50 to 75 percent.

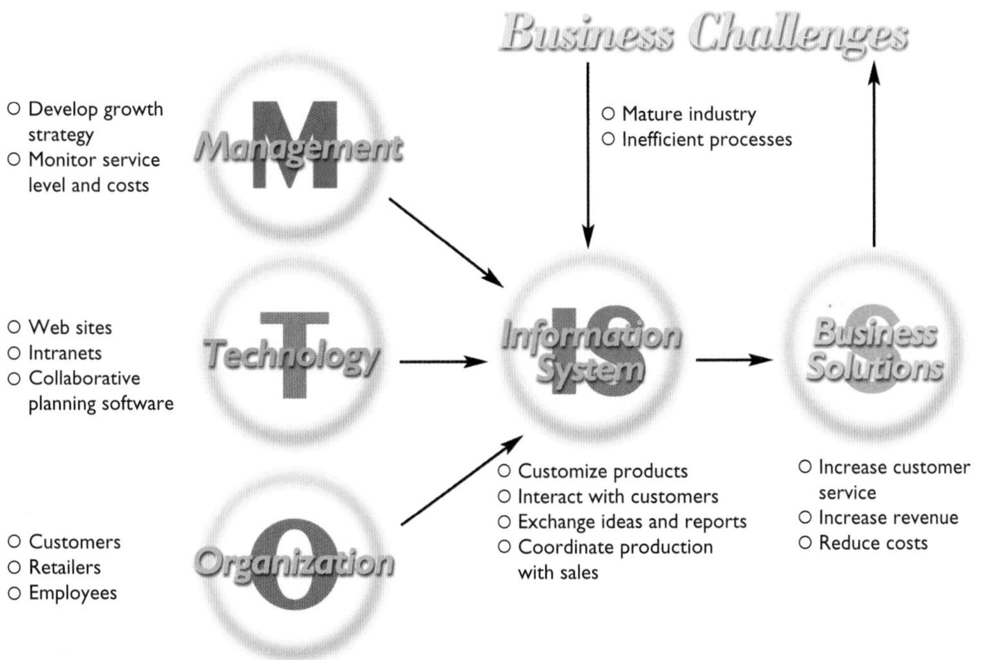


P&G had a reputation for a very insular, bureaucratic culture. Rivals called P&G employees "Proctoids." P&G's management hopes its Internet and intranet initiatives will loosen things up, encouraging employees to be more creative and to take more initiative. An internal InnovationNet intranet allows users to post reports, charts, and videos to a common shared repository and to contact other people working on similar problems and issues. Another intranet called MyIdea provides a forum for employees to publicize their ideas for improving the company.

To slash inventory and cycle time, P&G instituted a collaborative planning, forecasting, and replenishment (CPFR) system in which it shares sales forecasts with its retailers such as Kmart, Target, and Wal-Mart in the United States and Dansk, Sainsbury, and Tesco in Europe. If actual sales are in line with forecasts, the system automatically orders items to replenish what has been sold in stores. If the results are sharply different from forecasts, the system automatically notifies companies about such "exceptions," allowing company planners to adjust orders to accommodate spikes or dips in demand. Early tests showed that the CPFR system helped P&G reduce inventory by 10 percent and cycle time (the time required to get a product from the assembly line to the retailer's shelf) by 10 percent. Sales increased by 2 percent as well, because P&G was able to use the information in the system to take immediate actions to prevent out-of-stock items.

**Sources:** Kayte VanScoy, "Can the Internet Hot-Wire P&G?" *Smart Business Magazine,* January 2001; Noah Schachtman, "Trading Partners Collaborate to Increase Sales," *Information Week,* October 9, 2000; and Clinton Wilder, "Redefining Business," *Information Week,* October 16, 2000.

**Procter & Gamble's Internet Gamble Starts to Pay Off**

**MANAGEMENT CHALLENGES**

Procter & Gamble's experience illustrates the interdependence of business environments, organizational culture, management strategy, and information systems. P&G developed a series of Internet-based information systems in response to changes in competitive pressures from its surrounding environment, but its systems effort could not succeed without a significant amount of organizational and management change. The new information system is changing the way P&G runs its business and makes management decisions. Procter & Gamble's experience raises the following management challenges:

## MANAGEMENT CHALLENGES

1. **Sustainability of competitive advantage.** The competitive advantages strategic systems confer do not necessarily last long enough to ensure long-term profitability. Because competitors can retaliate and copy strategic systems, competitive advantage isn't always sustainable. Markets, customer expectations, and technology change. The Internet can make competitive advantage disappear very quickly as virtually all companies can use this technology. (Porter, 2001; Yoffie and Cusumano, 1999). Classic strategic systems such as American Airlines, SABRE computerized reservation system, Citibank's ATM system, and Federal Express's package tracking system benefited by being the first in their industries. Then rival systems emerged. Information systems alone cannot provide an enduring business advantage. Systems which were originally intended to be strategic frequently become tools for survival, something required by every firm to stay in business, or they may even inhibit organizations from making the strategic changes essential for future success (Eardley, Avison, and Powell, 1997).
2. **Fitting technology to the organization (or vice-versa).** On the one hand, it is important to align information technology to the business plan, to the firm's business processes, and to senior management's strategic business plans. Information technology is, after all, supposed to be the servant of the organization. On the other hand, these business plans, processes, and management strategy all may be very outdated or incompatible with the envisioned technology. In such instances, managers will need to change the organization to fit the technology or to adjust both the organization and the technology to achieve an optimal "fit."

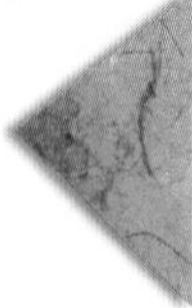

This chapter explores the relationships between organizations, management, information systems, and business strategy. We introduce the features of organizations that you will need to understand when you design, build, and operate information systems. We also scrutinize the role of a manager and the management decision-making process, identifying areas where information systems can enhance managerial effectiveness. We conclude by examining the problems firms face from competition and the ways in which information systems can provide competitive advantage.

## 3.1 ORGANIZATIONS AND INFORMATION SYSTEMS

Information systems and organizations influence one another. On the one hand, information systems must be aligned with the organization to provide information that important groups within the organization need. On the other hand, the organization must be aware of and open itself to the influences of information systems in order to benefit from new technologies.

The interaction between information technology and organizations is very complex and is influenced by a great many mediating factors, including the organization's structure, standard operating procedures, politics, culture, surrounding environment, and management decisions (see Figure 3-1). Managers must be aware that information systems can markedly alter life in the organization. They cannot successfully design new systems or understand existing systems without understanding organizations. Managers decide what systems will be built, what they will do, how they will be implemented, and so forth. Sometimes, however, the outcomes are the result of pure chance and of both good and bad luck.

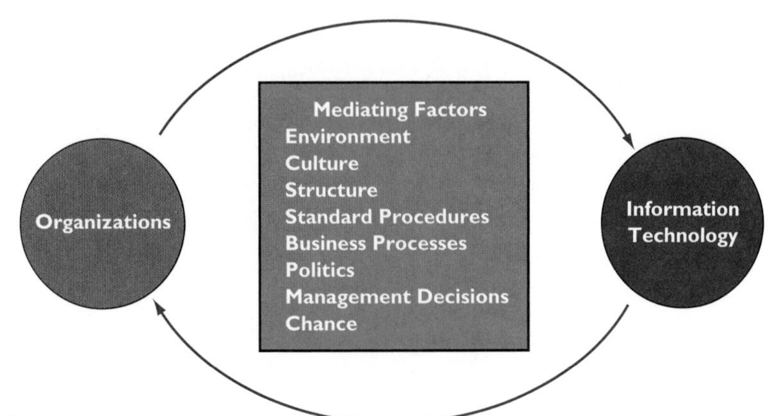


***Figure 3-1*** The two-way relationship between organizations and information technology. This complex two-way relationship is mediated by many factors, not the least of which are the decisions made—or not made—by managers. Other factors mediating the relationship are the organizational culture, bureaucracy, politics, business processes, and pure chance.

## WHAT IS AN ORGANIZATION?

An **organization** is a stable, formal, social structure that takes resources from the environment and processes them to produce outputs. This technical definition focuses on three elements of an organization. Capital and labor are primary production factors provided by the environment. The organization (the firm) transforms these inputs into products and services in a production function. The products and services are consumed by environments in return for supply inputs (see Figure 3-2). An organization is more stable than an informal group (such as a group of friends that meets every Friday for lunch) in terms of longevity and routineness. Organizations are formal legal entities, with internal rules and procedures, that must abide by laws. Organizations are also social structures, because they are a collection of social elements, much as a machine has a structure—a particular arrangement of valves, cams, shafts, and other parts.

**organization (technical definition)**
A stable, formal, social structure that takes resources from the environment and processes them to produce outputs.

This definition of organizations is powerful and simple, but it is not very descriptive or even predictive of real-world organizations. A more realistic behavioral definition of an **organization** is that it is a collection of rights, privileges, obligations, and responsibilities that are delicately balanced over a period of time through conflict and conflict resolution (see Figure 3-3). In this behavioral view of the firm, people who work in organizations develop customary ways of working; they gain attachments to existing relationships; and they make arrangements with subordinates and superiors about how work will be done, how much work will be done, and under what conditions. Most of these arrangements and feelings are not discussed in any formal rule book.

**organization (behavioral definition)**
A collection of rights, privileges, obligations, and responsibilities that are delicately balanced over a period of time through conflict and conflict resolution.

How do these definitions of organizations relate to information system technology? A technical view of organizations encourages us to focus on the way inputs are combined into outputs when technology changes are introduced into the company. The firm is seen as infinitely malleable, with capital and labor substituting for each other quite easily. But the more realistic behavioral definition of an organization suggests that building new information

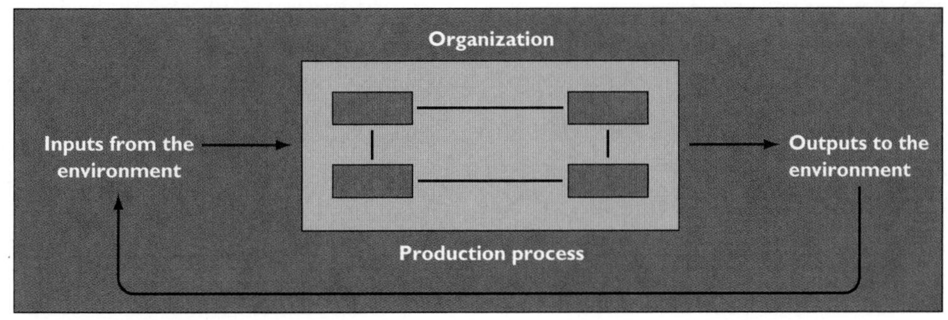


***Figure 3-2*** The technical microeconmic definition of the organization. In the microeconomic definition of organizations, capital and labor (the primary production factors provided by the environment) are transformed by the firm through the production process into products and services (outputs to the environment). The products and services are consumed by the environment, which supplies additional capital and labor as inputs in the feedback loop.

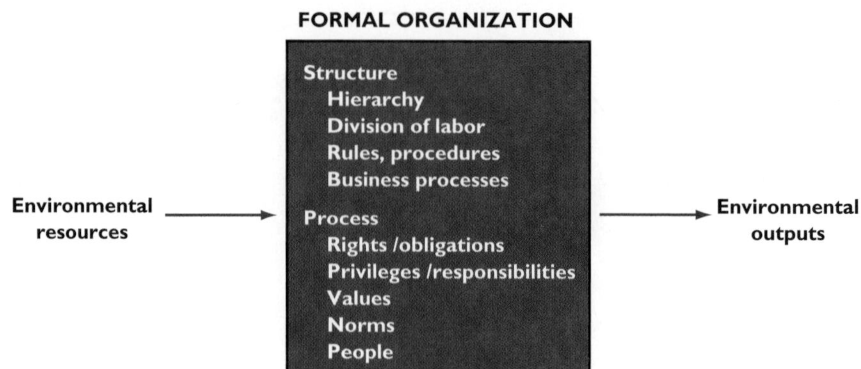


***Figure 3-3*** The behavioral view of organizations. The behavioral view of organizations emphasizes group relationships, values, and structures.

systems or rebuilding old ones involves much more than a technical rearrangement of machines or workers—that some information systems change the organizational balance of rights, privileges, obligations, responsibilities, and feelings that has been established over a long period of time.

Technological change requires changes in who owns and controls information, who has the right to access and update that information, and who makes decisions about whom, when, and how. For instance, Procter & Gamble's collaborative planning and forecasting system provides both retailers and P&G managers with more information to make production decisions. This more complex view forces us to look at the way work is designed and the procedures that are used to achieve outputs.

The technical and behavioral definitions of organizations are not contradictory. Indeed, they complement each other: The technical definition tells us how thousands of firms in competitive markets combine capital, labor, and information technology, whereas the behavioral model takes us inside the individual firm to see how that technology affects the organization's inner workings. Section 3.2 describes how each of these definitions of organizations can help explain the relationship between information systems and organizations.

Some features of organizations are common to all organizations; others distinguish one organization from another. Let us look first at the features common to all organizations.

## COMMON FEATURES OF ORGANIZATIONS

You might not think that Apple Computer, United Airlines, and the Aspen (Colorado) Police Department have much in common, but they do. In some respects, all modern organizations are alike because they share the characteristics that are listed in Table 3-1. A German sociologist, Max Weber, was the first to describe these "ideal-typical" characteristics of organizations in 1911. He called organizations **bureaucracies** that have certain "structural" features.

**bureaucracy**
Formal organization with a clear-cut division of labor, abstract rules and procedures, and impartial decision making that uses technical qualifications and professionalism as a basis for promoting employees.

According to Weber, all modern bureaucracies have a clear-cut division of labor and specialization. Organizations arrange specialists in a hierarchy of authority in which everyone is accountable to someone and authority is limited to specific actions. Authority and action are further limited by abstract rules or procedures (standard operating procedures, or SOPs) that are interpreted and applied to specific cases. These rules create a system of impartial and universalistic decision making; everyone is treated equally. Organizations try to hire and pro-

### TABLE 3-1 STRUCTURAL CHARACTERISTICS OF ALL ORGANIZATIONS

Clear division of labor
Hierarchy
Explicit rules and procedures
Impartial judgments
Technical qualifications for positions
Maximum organizational efficiency

mote employees on the basis of technical qualifications and professionalism (not personal connections). The organization is devoted to the principle of efficiency: maximizing output using limited inputs.

According to Weber, bureaucracies are prevalent because they are the most efficient form of organization. Other scholars have supplemented Weber, identifying additional features of organizations. All organizations develop standard operating procedures, politics, and cultures.

## Standard Operating Procedures

Organizations that survive over time become very efficient, producing a limited number of products and services by following standard routines. These standard routines become codified into reasonably precise rules, procedures, and practices called **standard operating procedures (SOPs)** that are developed to cope with virtually all expected situations. Some of these rules and procedures are written, formal procedures. Most are "rules of thumb" to be followed in selected situations.

**standard operating procedures (SOPs)**
Precise rules, procedures, and practices developed by organizations to cope with virtually all expected situations.

These standard operating procedures have a great deal to do with the efficiency that modern organizations attain. For instance, in the assembly of a car, managers and workers develop complex standard procedures to handle the thousands of motions in a precise fashion, permitting the finished product to roll off the assembly line. Any change in SOPs requires an enormous organizational effort. Indeed, the organization may need to halt the entire production process before the old SOPs can be retired.

Difficulty in changing standard operating procedures is one reason Detroit automakers had been slow to adopt Japanese mass-production methods. For many years, U.S. automakers followed Henry Ford's mass-production principles. Ford believed that the cheapest way to build a car was to churn out the largest number of autos by having workers repeatedly perform a simple task. By contrast, Japanese automakers have emphasized "lean production" methods whereby a smaller number of workers, each performing several tasks, can produce cars with less inventory, less investment, and fewer mistakes. Workers have multiple job responsibilities and are encouraged to stop production in order to correct a problem.

## Organizational Politics

People in organizations occupy different positions with different specialties, concerns, and perspectives. As a result, they naturally have divergent viewpoints about how resources, rewards, and punishments should be distributed. These differences matter to both managers and employees, and they result in political struggle, competition, and conflict within every organization. Political resistance is one of the great difficulties of bringing about organizational change—especially the development of new information systems. Virtually all information systems that bring about significant changes in goals, procedures, productivity, and personnel are politically charged and will elicit serious political opposition.

## Organizational Culture

All organizations have bedrock, unassailable, unquestioned (by the members) assumptions that define their goals and products. **Organizational culture** is this set of fundamental assumptions about what products the organization should produce, how it should produce them, where, and for whom. Generally, these cultural assumptions are taken totally for granted and are rarely publicly announced or spoken about (Schein, 1985).

**organizational culture**
The set of fundamental assumptions about what products the organization should produce, how and where it should produce them, and for whom they should be produced.

You can see organizational culture at work by looking around your university or college. Some bedrock assumptions of university life are that professors know more than students, the reason students attend college is to learn, and classes follow a regular schedule. Organizational culture is a powerful unifying force that restrains political conflict and promotes common understanding, agreement on procedures, and common practices. If we all share the same basic cultural assumptions, then agreement on other matters is more likely.

At the same time, organizational culture is a powerful restraint on change, especially technological change. Most organizations will do almost anything to avoid making changes in basic assumptions. Any technological change that threatens commonly held cultural assumptions usually meets a great deal of resistance. However, there are times when the only sensible thing to do is to employ a new technology that directly opposes an existing organizational culture. When this occurs, the technology is often stalled while the culture slowly adjusts.

## UNIQUE FEATURES OF ORGANIZATIONS

Although all organizations have common characteristics, no two organizations are identical. Organizations have different structures, goals, constituencies, leadership styles, tasks, and surrounding environments.

### Different Organizational Types

One important way in which organizations differ is in their structure or shape. The differences among organizational structures are characterized in many ways. Mintzberg's classification, described in Table 3-2, identifies five basic kinds of organizations (Mintzberg, 1979).

### Organizations and Environments

Organizations reside in environments from which they draw resources and to which they supply goods and services. Organizations and environments have a reciprocal relationship. On the one hand, organizations are open to, and dependent on, the social and physical environment that surrounds them. Without financial and human resources—people willing to work reliably and consistently for a set wage or revenue from customers—organizations could not exist. Organizations must respond to legislative and other requirements imposed by government, as well as the actions of customers and competitors. On the other hand, organizations can influence their environments. Organizations form alliances with others to influence the political process; they advertise to influence customer acceptance of their products.

Figure 3-4 shows that information systems play an important role in helping organizations perceive changes in their environments, and also in helping organizations act on their environments. Information systems are key instruments for *environmental scanning,* helping managers identify external changes that might require an organizational response.

Environments generally change much faster than organizations. The main reasons for organizational failure are an inability to adapt to a rapidly changing environment and a lack of resources—particularly among young firms—to sustain even short periods of troubled times (Freeman et al., 1983). New technologies, new products, and changing public tastes and values (many of which result in new government regulations) put strains on any organization's culture, politics, and people. Most organizations do not cope well with large environmental shifts. The inertia built into an organization's standard operating procedures, the political conflict raised by changes to the existing order, and the threat to closely held cultural values typically inhibit organizations from making significant changes. It is not surprising that only 10 percent of the Fortune 500 companies in 1919 still exist today.

**TABLE 3-2 ORGANIZATIONAL STRUCTURES**

| Organizational Type | Description | Example |
|---|---|---|
| Entrepreneurial structure | Young, small firm in a fast-changing environment. It has a simple structure and is managed by an entrepreneur serving as its single chief executive officer. | Small start-up business |
| Machine bureaucracy | Large bureaucracy existing in a slowly changing environment, producing standard products. It is dominated by a centralized management team and centralized decision making. | Midsize manufacturing firm |
| Divisionalized bureaucracy | Combination of multiple machine bureaucracies, each producing a different product or service, all topped by one central headquarters. | Fortune 500 firms such as General Motors |
| Professional bureaucracy | Knowledge-based organization where goods and services depend on the expertise and knowledge of professionals. Dominated by department heads with weak centralized authority. | Law firms, school systems, hospitals |
| Adhocracy | "Task force" organization that must respond to rapidly changing environments. Consists of large groups of specialists organized into short-lived multidisciplinary teams and has weak central management. | Consulting firms such as the Rand Corporation |

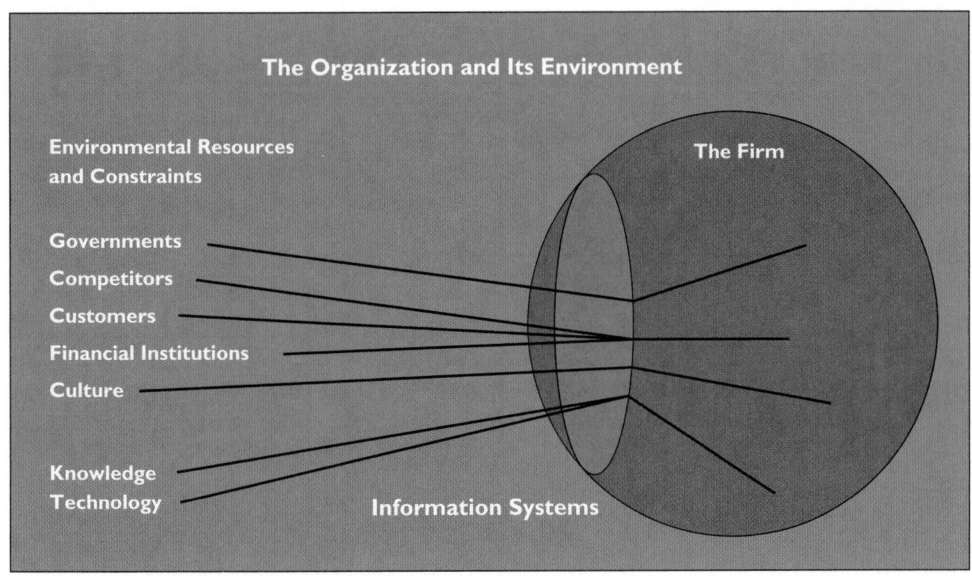


***Figure 3-4*** Environments and organizations have a reciprocal relationship. Environments shape what organizations can do, but organizations can influence their environments and decide to change environments altogether. Information technology plays a critical role in helping organizations perceive environmental change and in helping organizations act on their environment. Information systems act as a filter between organizations and their environments. They do not necessarily reflect reality, but instead refract environmental change through a number of built-in biases.

## Other Differences Among Organizations

Organizations have different shapes or structures for many other reasons also. They differ in their ultimate goals and the types of power used to achieve them. Some organizations have coercive goals (e.g., prisons); others have utilitarian goals (e.g., businesses). Still others have normative goals (universities, religious groups). Organizations also serve different groups or have different constituencies, some primarily benefiting their members, others benefiting clients, stockholders, or the public. The nature of leadership differs greatly from one organization to another—some organizations may be more democratic or authoritarian than others. Another way organizations differ is by the tasks they perform and the technology they use. Some organizations perform primarily routine tasks that could be reduced to formal rules that require little judgment (such as manufacturing auto parts), whereas others (such as consulting firms) work primarily with nonroutine tasks.

As you can see in Table 3-3, the list of unique features of organizations is longer than the common features list. It stands to reason that information systems will have different impacts on different types of organizations. Different organizations in different circumstances will experience different effects from the same technology. The Window on Organizations shows, for example, how Japan's unique environment, culture, and organizational characteristics have affected Internet use and electronic commerce. Only by close analysis of a specific organization can a manager effectively design and manage information systems.

**TABLE 3-3** SUMMARY OF SALIENT FEATURES OF ORGANIZATIONS

| Common Features | Unique Features |
|---|---|
| Formal structure | Organizational type |
| Standard operating procedures (SOPs) | Environments |
| Politics | Goals |
| Culture | Power |
| | Constituencies |
| | Function |
| | Leadership |
| | Tasks |
| | Technology |
| | Business processes |

## E-commerce, Japanese Style

In Japan, many people don't have credit cards or are reluctant to give out their credit card numbers over the Internet. Internet access charges are very high compared to the United States and other countries. Although many Japanese people own PCs, most still don't surf the Web from their homes. So how can e-commerce flourish? The answer, at least for now, lies in the old neighborhood convenience store.

Convenience stores—called "conbini"—have a special place in Japan. Most people have very tiny homes or apartments with minimal space for storage or refrigerators. Frequent shopping is a necessity. Japanese convenience stores are very small, averaging about 100 square meters and outside the radar of Japanese regulators. Thus, they can be more responsive to changing customer tastes than larger competitors. What's more, most conbini are open around the clock. There are more than 33,000 convenience stores throughout Japan and the average Seven-Eleven store attracts 900 visitors each day.

The ubiquity and popularity of these stores make them attractive partners for e-commerce companies that need marketing and promotion. The convenience stores don't have promotional expenses, because so many customers come to them on their own. People can pay by cash for e-commerce goods when they pick them up at the convenience stores and the product orders can be handled by the conbinis' existing distribution systems. A newcomer would have trouble finding temporary warehousing to store goods for delivery to customers, but convenience stores already have warehouses and can act as the final pick-up point. The conbini also provide computer terminals with Internet access. According to Kenyu Adachi, director of the Ministry of Trade and Industry distribution division, "Without the convenience store, e-commerce in Japan would have more trouble taking off."

And the convenience stores are counting on the Internet, too. With no more room to expand physically and relentless competition from new stores, the neighborhood convenience store is betting on e-commerce to keep afloat. By offering access to e-commerce sites, the convenience stores can expand their range of product offerings without expanding their space. All of the major Japanese convenience store chains have adopted Internet strategies.

Seven-Eleven Japan, the country's largest convenience store chain, lets a customer select titles from the eShopping Books Web site. Several days later the customer can pick up the selection and pay for it at the local Seven-Eleven. eShopping Books uses Seven-Eleven's warehouses and pays for the books only after they have been sold, so it does not bear the cost of warehousing merchandise. Its cost structure may be even lower than Amazon.com's.

**To Think About:** What factors explain why convenience stores are centers of Internet use and electronic commerce in Japan?

*Sources:* Stephanie Strom, "E-commerce the Japanese Way," *The New York Times*, March 18, 2000; and "The Web@Work/Lawson Co.," *The Wall Street Journal*, March 13, 2000.

## 3.2 The Changing Role of Information Systems in Organizations

Information systems have become integral, on-line, interactive tools deeply involved in the minute-to-minute operations and decision making of large organizations. We now describe the changing role of systems in organizations and how it has been shaped by the interaction of organizations and information technology.

### Information Technology Infrastructure and Information Technology Services

One way that organizations can influence how information technology will be used is through decisions about the technical and organizational configuration of systems. Previous chapters described the ever-widening role of information systems in organizations. Supporting this widening role have been changes in information technology (IT) infrastructure, which we defined in Chapter 1. During the 1950s, organizations were dependent on computers for a few critical functions. The 1960s witnessed the development of large, centralized machines. By the late 1970s and into the 1980s IT infrastructure became complex, and information systems included telecommunications links to distribute information. Today's new IT infrastructure is designed to make information flow across the enterprise and includes links to customers, vendors, and public infrastructures, including the Internet. Each organization determines how its infrastructure will be configured.

Another way that organizations have affected information technology is through decisions about who will design, build, and maintain the organization's IT infrastructure. These decisions determine how information technology services will be delivered.

The formal organizational unit or function responsible for technology services is called the **information systems department.** The information systems department is responsible for maintaining the hardware, software, data storage, and networks that comprise the firm's IT infrastructure.

The information systems department consists of specialists such as programmers, systems analysts, project leaders, and information systems managers (see Figure 3-5). **Programmers** are highly trained technical specialists who write the software instructions for the computer. **Systems analysts** constitute the principal liaison between the information systems group and the rest of the organization. It is the systems analyst's job to translate business problems and requirements into information requirements and systems. **Information systems managers** are leaders of teams of programmers and analysts, project managers, physical facility managers, telecommunications managers, and heads of office system groups. They are also managers of computer operations and data entry staff. Also external specialists, such as hardware vendors and manufacturers, software firms, and consultants frequently participate in the day-to-day operations and long-term planning of information systems.

In many companies, the information systems department is headed by a **chief information officer (CIO).** The CIO is a senior management position to oversee the use of information technology in the firm.

**End users** are representatives of departments outside of the information systems group for whom information system applications are developed. These users are playing an increasingly larger role in the design and development of information systems.

In the early years, the information systems group was composed mostly of programmers and performed very highly specialized but limited technical functions. Today, a growing proportion of staff members are systems analysts and network specialists, with the information systems department acting as a powerful change agent in the organization. The information systems department suggests new business strategies and new information-based products and services and coordinates both the development of the technology and the planned changes in the organization.

In the past, firms generally built their own software and managed their own computing facilities. Today, many firms are turning to external vendors to provide these services (see Chapters 5, 6, 9, and 10) and using their information systems departments to manage these service providers.

**information systems department**
The formal organizational unit that is responsible for the information systems function in the organization.

**programmers**
Highly trained technical specialists who write computer software instructions.

**systems analysts**
Specialists who translate business problems and requirements into information requirements and systems, acting as liaison between the information systems department and the rest of the organization.

**information systems managers**
Leaders of the various specialists in the information systems department.

**chief information officer (CIO)**
Senior manager in charge of the information systems function in the firm.

**end users**
Representatives of departments outside the information systems group for whom applications are developed.

## HOW INFORMATION SYSTEMS AFFECT ORGANIZATIONS

How have changes in information technology affected organizations? To find answers, we draw on research and theory based on both economic and behavioral approaches.

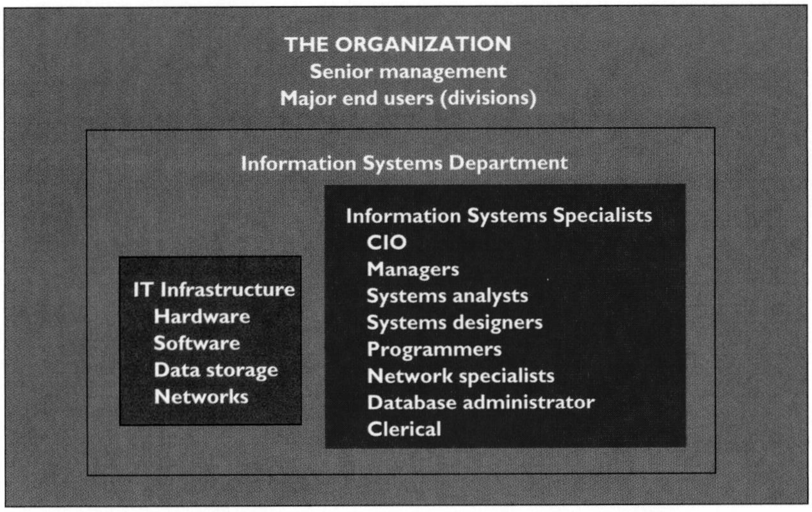

THE ORGANIZATION
Senior management
Major end users (divisions)

Information Systems Department

IT Infrastructure
Hardware
Software
Data storage
Networks

Information Systems Specialists
CIO
Managers
Systems analysts
Systems designers
Programmers
Network specialists
Database administrator
Clerical

*Figure 3-5* Information technology services. Many types of specialists and groups are responsible for the design and management of the organization's information technology (IT) infrastructure.

## Economic Theories

From an economic standpoint, information system technology can be viewed as a factor of production that can be freely substituted for capital and labor. As the cost of information system technology falls, it is substituted for labor, which historically has been a rising cost. Hence, in the **microeconomic model of the firm,** information technology should result in a decline in the number of middle managers and clerical workers as information technology substitutes for their labor.

**microeconomic model of the firm**
Model of the firm that views information technology as a factor of production that can be freely substantiated for capital and labor.

Information technology also helps firms contract in size, because it can reduce transaction costs—the costs incurred when a firm buys on the marketplace what it cannot make itself. According to **transaction cost theory,** firms and individuals seek to economize on transaction costs, much as they do on production costs. Using markets is expensive (Williamson, 1985; Coase, 1937) because of costs such as locating and communicating with distant suppliers, monitoring contract compliance, buying insurance, obtaining information on products, and so forth. Traditionally, firms have tried to reduce transaction costs by getting bigger, hiring more employees, or buying their own suppliers and distributors, as General Motors used to do.

**transaction cost theory**
Economic theory stating that firms grow larger because they can conduct marketplace transactions internally more cheaply than they can with external firms in the marketplace.

Information technology, especially the use of networks, can help firms lower the cost of market participation (transaction costs), making it worthwhile for firms to contract with external suppliers instead of using internal sources. For example, by using computer links to external suppliers, the Chrysler Corporation can achieve economies by obtaining more than 70 percent of its parts from the outside. Figure 3-6 shows that as transaction costs decrease, firm size (the number of employees) should shrink because it becomes easier and cheaper for the firm to contract the purchase of goods and services in the marketplace rather than to make the product or service itself. Firm size can stay constant or contract even if the company increases its revenues.

Information technology also can reduce internal management costs. According to **agency theory,** the firm is viewed as a "nexus of contracts" among self-interested individuals rather than as a unified, profit-maximizing entity (Jensen and Meckling, 1976). A principal (owner) employs "agents" (employees) to perform work on his or her behalf. However, agents need constant supervision and management, because they otherwise will tend to pursue their own interests rather than those of the owners. As firms grow in size and scope, agency costs or coordination costs rise, because owners must expend more and more effort supervising and managing employees.

**agency theory**
Economic theory that views the firm as a nexus of contracts among self-interested individuals who must be supervised and managed.

Information technology, by reducing the costs of acquiring and analyzing information, permits organizations to reduce agency costs, because it becomes easier for managers to oversee a greater number of employees. Figure 3-7 shows that by reducing overall management costs, information technology allows firms to increase revenues while shrinking the numbers of middle management and clerical workers. We have seen examples in earlier chapters where information technology expanded the power and scope of small organizations by allowing them to perform coordinating activities, such as processing orders or keeping track of inventory, with very few clerks and managers.

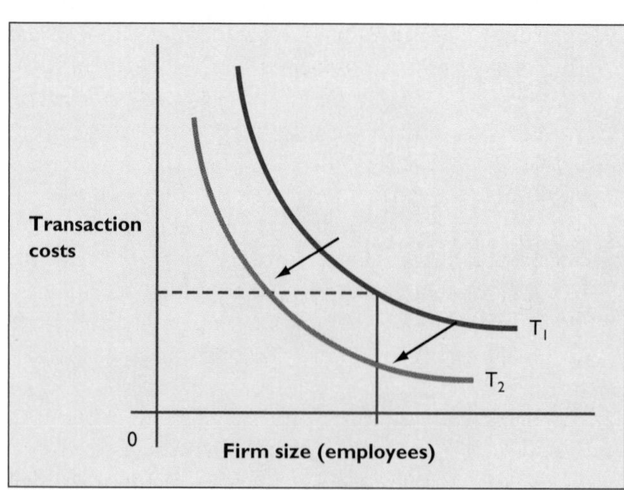


*Figure 3-6* The transaction cost theory of the impact of information technology on the organization. Firms traditionally grew in size in order to reduce transaction costs. IT potentially reduces the costs for a given size, shifting the transaction cost curve inward, opening up the possibility of revenue growth without increasing size, or even revenue growth accompanied by shrinking size.

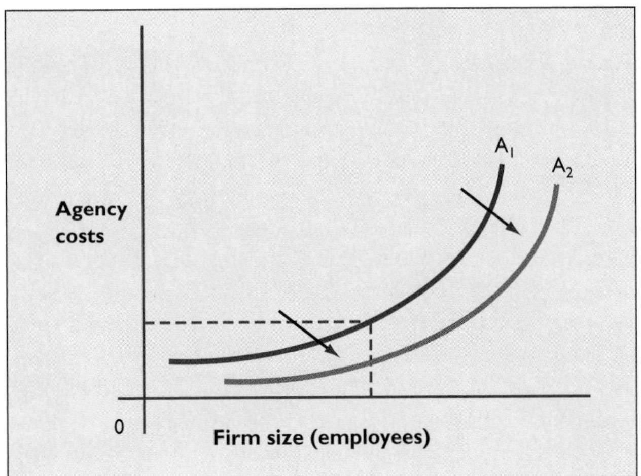


***Figure 3-7*** The agency cost theory of the impact of information technology on the organization. As firms grow in size and complexity, traditionally they experience rising agency costs. IT shifts the agency cost curve down and to the right, allowing firms to increase size while lowering agency costs.

## Behavioral Theories

Although economic theories try to explain how large numbers of firms act in the marketplace, behavioral theories from sociology, psychology, and political science are more useful for describing the behavior of individual firms. Behavioral research has found little evidence that information systems automatically transform organizations, although the systems may be instrumental in accomplishing this goal once senior management decides to pursue this end.

Behavioral researchers have theorized that information technology could change the hierarchy of decision making in organizations by lowering the costs of information acquisition and broadening the distribution of information (Malone, 1997). Information technology could bring information directly from operating units to senior managers, thereby eliminating middle managers and their clerical support workers. Alternatively, information technology could distribute information directly to lower-level workers, who could then make their own decisions based on their own knowledge and information without any management intervention. Some research even suggests that computerization increases the information given to middle managers, empowering them to make more important decisions than in the past, thus reducing the need for large numbers of lower-level workers (Shore, 1983).

In postindustrial societies, authority increasingly relies on knowledge and competence, and not on mere formal position. Hence, the shape of organizations should "flatten," because professional workers tend to be self-managing; and decision making should become more decentralized as knowledge and information become more widespread throughout (Drucker, 1988). Information technology may encourage adhocracies and "task force" networked organizations in which groups of professionals come together—face-to-face or electronically—for short periods of time to accomplish a specific task (e.g., designing a new automobile); once the task is accomplished, the individuals join other task forces. More firms may operate as **virtual organizations,** where work no longer is tied to geographic location. Virtual organizations use networks to link people, assets, and ideas. They can ally with suppliers, customers, and sometimes even competitors to create and distribute new products and services without being limited by traditional organizational boundaries or physical location. For example, Calyx and Corolla is a networked virtual organization selling fresh flowers directly to customers, bypassing traditional florists. The firm takes orders via telephone or from its Web site and transmits them to grower farms which ship them in Federal Express vans directly to the customers.

**virtual organization**
Organization using networks to link people, assets and ideas to create and distribute products and services without being limited to traditional organizational boundaries or physical location.

Who makes sure that self-managed teams do not head off in the wrong direction? Who decides which person works on what team and for how long? How can managers judge the performance of someone who is constantly rotating from team to team? How do people know where their careers are headed? New approaches for evaluating, organizing, and informing workers are required; and not all companies can make virtual work effective (Davenport and Pearlson, 1998).

No one knows the answers to these questions, and it is not clear that all modern organizations will undergo this transformation. General Motors, for example, may have many self-managed knowledge workers in certain divisions, but it still will have a manufacturing division

*In virtual offices, employees do not work from a permanent location. Here, work spaces are temporary with employees moving from desk to desk as vacancies open.*

structured as a large, traditional bureaucracy. In general, the shape of organizations historically changes with the business cycle and with the latest management fashions. When times are good and profits are high, firms hire large numbers of supervisory personnel; when times are tough, they let go many of these same people.

Another behavioral approach views information systems as the outcome of political competition between organizational subgroups for influence over the organization's policies, procedures, and resources (Laudon, 1974; Kling, 1980; Keen, 1981; Laudon, 1986). Information systems inevitably become bound up in organizational politics, because they influence access to a key resource—namely, information. Information systems can affect who does what to whom, when, where, and how in an organization. For instance, a major study of FBI efforts to develop a national computerized criminal history system (a single national listing of the criminal histories, arrests, and convictions of more than 36 million individuals in the United States) found that the state governments strongly resisted the FBI's efforts. This information would enable the federal government, and the FBI in particular, to monitor how states use criminal histories. The states resisted the development of this national system quite successfully (Laudon, 1986).

Because information systems potentially change an organization's structure, culture, politics, and work, there is often considerable resistance to them when they are introduced. There are several ways to visualize organizational resistance. Leavitt (1965) used a diamond shape to illustrate the interrelated and mutually adjusting character of technology and organization (see Figure 3-8). Here, changes in technology are absorbed, deflected, and defeated by organizational task arrangements, structures, and people. In this model, the only way to bring about change is to change the technology, tasks, structure, and people simultaneously. Other authors have spoken about the need to "unfreeze" organizations before introducing an innovation, quickly implementing it, and "refreezing," or institutionalizing, the change (Kolb, 1970; Alter and Ginzberg, 1978).

***Figure 3-8*** Organizational resistance and the mutually adjusting relationship between technology and the organization. Implementing information systems has consequences for task arrangements, structures, and people. According to this model, in order to implement change, all four components must be changed simultaneously.
(*Source:* Leavitt, 1965.)

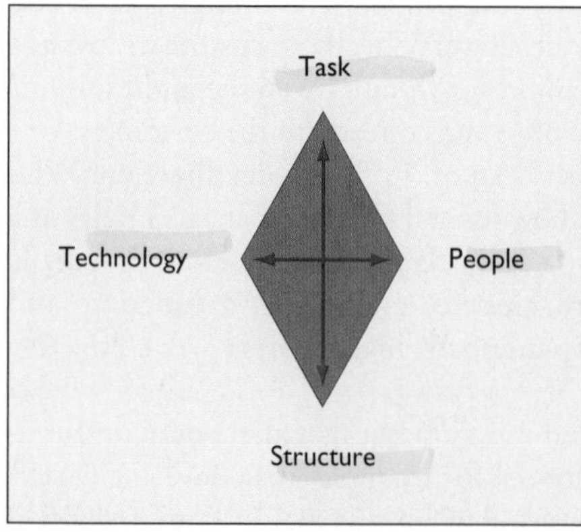


## The Internet and Organizations

The Internet, especially the World Wide Web, is beginning to have an important impact on the relationships between firms and external entities, and even on the organization of business processes inside a firm. The Internet increases the accessibility, storage, and distribution of information and knowledge for organizations. In essence, the Internet is capable of dramatically lowering the transaction and agency costs facing most organizations. For instance, brokerage firms and banks in New York can now "deliver" their internal operations procedures manuals to their employees at distant locations by posting them on their corporate Web site, saving millions of dollars in distribution costs. A global sales force can receive nearly instant price and product information updates via the Web or instructions from management via e-mail. Vendors of some large retailers can access retailers' internal Web sites directly for up-to-the-minute sales information and initiate replenishment orders instantly.

Businesses are rapidly rebuilding some of their key business processes based on Internet technology and making this technology a key component of their IT infrastructures. If prior networking is any guide, one result will be simpler business processes, fewer employees, and much flatter organizations than in the past.

### IMPLICATIONS FOR THE DESIGN AND UNDERSTANDING OF INFORMATION SYSTEMS

In order to reap the benefits of technology, changes in organizational culture, values, norms, and interest-group alignments must be managed with as much planning and effort as technology changes. In our experience, the central organizational factors to consider when planning a new system are these:

- The environment in which the organization must function.
- The structure of the organization: hierarchy, specialization, standard operating procedures.
- The organization's culture and politics.
- The type of organization.
- The nature and style of leadership.
- The extent of top management's support and understanding.
- The principal interest groups affected by the system.
- The kinds of tasks, decisions, and business processes that the information system is designed to assist.
- The sentiments and attitudes of workers in the organization who will be using the information system.
- The history of the organization: past investments in information technology, existing skills, important programs, and human resources.

## 3.3 MANAGERS, DECISION MAKING, AND INFORMATION SYSTEMS

To determine how information systems can benefit managers, we must first examine what managers do and what information they need for their decision making and other functions. We must also understand how decisions are made and what kinds of decisions can be supported by formal information systems.

### THE ROLE OF MANAGERS IN ORGANIZATIONS

Managers play a key role in organizations. Their responsibilities range from making decisions, to writing reports, to attending meetings, to arranging birthday parties. We can better understand managerial functions and roles by examining classical and contemporary models of managerial behavior.

#### Classical Descriptions of Management

The **classical model of management,** which describes what managers do, was largely unquestioned for the more than 70 years since the 1920s. Henri Fayol and other early writers first described the five classical functions of managers as planning, organizing, coordinating, deciding, and controlling. This description of management activities dominated management thought for a long time, and it is still popular today.

**classical model of management**
Traditional description of management that focused on its formal functions of planning, organizing, coordinating, deciding, and controlling.

Although these terms actually describe managerial functions, they are unsatisfactory as a description of what managers actually do. The terms do not address what managers do when

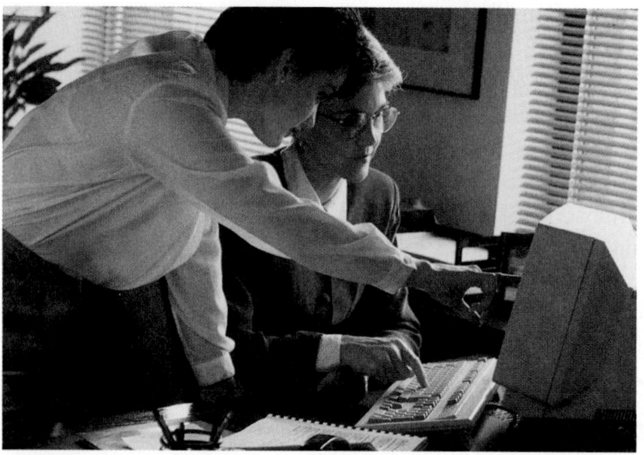

*A corporate chief executive learns how to use a computer. Many senior managers lack computer knowledge or experience and require systems that are extremely easy to use.*

they plan, decide things, and control the work of others. We need a more fine-grained understanding of how managers actually behave.

## Behavioral Models

Contemporary behavioral scientists have observed that managers do not behave as the classical model of management led us to believe. Kotter (1982), for example, describes the morning activities of the president of an investment management firm.

7:35 A.M. Richardson arrives at work, unpacks her briefcase, gets some coffee, and begins making a list of activities for the day.

7:45 A.M. Bradshaw (a subordinate) and Richardson converse about a number of topics and exchange pictures recently taken on summer vacations.

8:00 A.M. They talk about a schedule of priorities for the day.

8:20 A.M. Wilson (a subordinate) and Richardson talk about some personnel problems, cracking jokes in the process.

8:45 A.M. Richardson's secretary arrives, and they discuss her new apartment and arrangements for a meeting later in the morning.

8:55 A.M. Richardson goes to a morning meeting run by one of her subordinates. Thirty people are there, and Richardson reads during the meeting.

11:05 A.M. Richardson and her subordinates return to the office and discuss a difficult problem. They try to define the problem and outline possible alternatives. She lets the discussion roam away from and back to the topic again and again. Finally, they agree on a next step.

**behavioral models**
Descriptions of management based on behavioral scientists' observations of what managers actually do in their jobs.

In this example, it is difficult to determine which activities constitute Richardson's planning, coordinating, and decision making. **Behavioral models** state that the actual behavior of managers appears to be less systematic, more informal, less reflective, more reactive, less well organized, and much more frivolous than students of information systems and decision making generally expect it to be.

Observers find that managerial behavior actually has five attributes that differ greatly from the classical description: First, managers perform a great deal of work at an unrelenting pace—studies have found that managers engage in more than 600 different activities each day, with no break in their pace. Second, managerial activities are fragmented; most activities last for less than nine minutes; only 10 percent of the activities exceed one hour in duration. Third, managers prefer speculation, hearsay, gossip—they want current, specific, and ad hoc information (printed information often will be too old). Fourth, they prefer oral forms of communication to written forms because oral media provide greater flexibility, require less effort, and bring a faster response. Fifth, managers give high priority to maintaining a diverse and complex web of contacts that acts as an informal information system.

From his real-world observations, Kotter argues that effective managers are actually involved in only three critical activities:

- First, general managers spend significant time establishing personal agendas and both short- and long-term goals.
- Second—and perhaps most important—effective managers spend a great deal of time building an interpersonal network composed of people at virtually all organizational levels, from warehouse staff to clerical support personnel to other managers and senior management.
- Third, Kotter found that managers use their networks to execute personal agendas to accomplish their own goals.

Analyzing managers' day-to-day behavior, Mintzberg found that it could be classified into 10 managerial roles. **Managerial roles** are expectations of the activities that managers should perform in an organization. Mintzberg found that these managerial roles fell into three categories: interpersonal, informational, and decisional.

**managerial roles**
Expectations of the activities that managers should perform in an organization.

***Interpersonal Roles*** Managers act as figureheads for the organization when they represent their companies to the outside world and perform symbolic duties such as giving out employee awards. Managers act as leaders, attempting to motivate, counsel, and support subordinates. Managers also act as a liaison between various organizational levels; within each of these levels, they serve as a liaison among the members of the management team. Managers provide time and favors, which they expect to be returned.

**interpersonal roles**
Mintzberg's classification for managerial roles where managers act as figureheads and leaders for the organization.

***Informational Roles*** Managers act as the nerve centers of their organization, receiving the most concrete, up-to-date information and redistributing it to those who need to be aware of it. Managers are, therefore, information disseminators and spokespersons for their organization.

**informational roles**
Mintzberg's classification for managerial roles where managers act as the nerve centers of their organizations, receiving and disseminating critical information.

***Decisional Roles*** Managers make decisions. They act as entrepreneurs by initiating new kinds of activities; they handle disturbances arising in the organization; they allocate resources to staff members who need them; and they negotiate conflicts and mediate between conflicting groups in the organization.

**decisional roles**
Mintzberg's classification for managerial roles where managers initiate activities, handle disturbances, allocate resources, and negotiate conflicts.

Table 3-4, based on Mintzberg's role classifications, is one look at where systems can and cannot help managers. The table shows that information systems do not yet contribute a great deal to important areas of management life. These areas will provide great opportunities for future systems efforts.

## MANAGERS AND DECISION MAKING

Decision making is often a manager's most challenging role. Information systems have helped managers communicate and distribute information; however, they have provided

### TABLE 3-4 MANAGERIAL ROLES AND SUPPORTING INFORMATION SYSTEMS

| Role | Behavior | Support Systems |
|---|---|---|
| Interpersonal Roles | | |
| Figurehead | → | None exist |
| Leader | Interpersonal → | None exist |
| Liaison | → | Electronic communication systems |
| Informational Roles | | |
| Nerve center | → | Management information systems, ESS |
| Disseminator | Information → | Mail, office systems |
| Spokesperson | processing → | Office and professional systems, workstations |
| Decisional Roles | | |
| Entrepreneur | → | None exist |
| Disturbance handler | Decision → | None exist |
| Resource allocator | making → | DSS systems |
| Negotiator | → | None exist |

*Source:* Kenneth C. Laudon and Jane P. Laudon; and Mintzberg, 1971.

**strategic decision making** Determining the long-term objectives, resources, and policies of an organization.

**management control** Monitoring how efficiently or effectively resources are utilized and how well operational units are performing.

**operational control** Deciding how to carry out specific tasks specified by upper and middle management and establishing criteria for completion and resource allocation.

**knowledge-level decision making** Evaluating new ideas for products, services, ways to communicate new knowledge, and ways to distribute information throughout the organization.

**unstructured decisions** Nonroutine decisions in which the decision maker must provide judgment, evaluation, and insights into the problem definition; there is no agreed-upon procedure for making such decisions.

**structured decisions** Decisions that are repetitive, routine, and have a definite procedure for handling them.

only limited assistance for management decision making. Because decision making is an area that system designers have sought most of all to affect (with mixed success), we now turn our attention to this issue.

## The Process of Decision Making

Decision making can be classified by organizational level, corresponding to the strategic, management, knowledge, and operational levels of the organization introduced in Chapter 2. **Strategic decision making** determines the objectives, resources, and policies of the organization. Decision making for **management control** is principally concerned with how efficiently and effectively resources are used and how well operational units are performing. **Operational control** decision making determines how to carry out the specific tasks set forth by strategic and middle-management decision makers. **Knowledge-level decision making** deals with evaluating new ideas for products and services, ways to communicate new knowledge, and ways to distribute information throughout the organization.

Within each of these levels of decision making, researchers classify decisions as structured and unstructured. **Unstructured decisions** are those in which the decision maker must provide judgment, evaluation, and insights into the problem definition. Each of these decisions are novel, important, and nonroutine, and there is no well-understood or agreed-on procedure for making them (Gorry and Scott-Morton, 1971). **Structured decisions,** by contrast, are repetitive and routine and involve a definite procedure for handling them so that they do not have to be treated each time as if they were new. Some decisions are semistructured; in such cases, only part of the problem has a clear-cut answer provided by an accepted procedure.

Combining these two views of decision making produces the grid shown in Figure 3-9. In general, operational control personnel face fairly well-structured problems. In contrast, strategic planners tackle highly unstructured problems. Many of the problems knowledge workers encounter are fairly unstructured as well. Nevertheless, each level of the organization contains both structured and unstructured problems.

## Stages of Decision Making

Making decisions consists of several different activities. Simon (1960) described four different stages in decision making: intelligence, design, choice, and implementation.

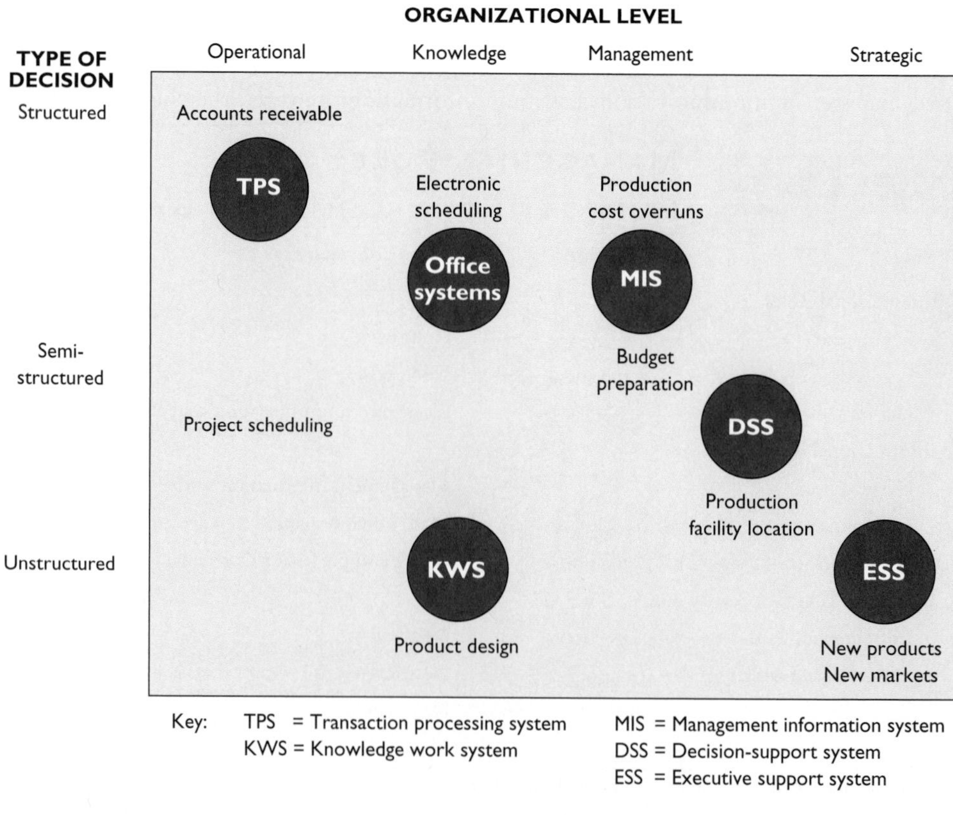

*Figure 3-9* Different kinds of information systems at the various organization levels support different types of decisions.

**Intelligence** consists of identifying and understanding the problems occurring in the organization—why the problem, where, and with what effects. Traditional MIS systems that deliver a wide variety of detailed information can help identify problems, especially if the systems report exceptions.

During solution **design,** the individual designs possible solutions to the problems. Smaller DSS systems are ideal in this stage of decision making, because they operate on simple models, can be developed quickly, and can be operated with limited data.

**Choice** consists of choosing among solution alternatives. Here, the decision maker might need a larger DSS system to develop more extensive data on a variety of alternatives and complex models or data analysis tools to account for all of the costs, consequences, and opportunities.

During solution **implementation,** when the decision is put into effect, managers can use a reporting system that delivers routine reports on the progress of a specific solution. Support systems can range from full-blown MIS systems to much smaller systems, as well as project-planning software operating on personal computers.

In general, the stages of decision making do not necessarily follow a linear path. Think again about the decision you made to attend a specific college. At any point in the decision-making process, you may have to loop back to a previous stage (see Figure 3-10). For instance, one can often come up with several designs but may not be certain about whether a specific design meets the requirements for the particular problem. This situation requires additional intelligence work. Alternatively, one can be in the process of implementing a decision, only to discover that it is not working. In such a case, one is forced to repeat the design or choice stage.

**intelligence**
The first of Simon's four stages of decision making, when the individual collects information to identify problems occurring in the organization.

**design**
Simon's second stage of decision making, when the individual conceives of possible alternative solutions to a problem.

**choice**
Simon's third stage of decision making, when the individual selects among the various solution alternatives.

**implementation**
Simon's final stage of decision making, when the individual puts the decision into effect and reports on the progress of the solution.

## Individual Models of Decision Making

A number of models attempt to describe how people make decisions. Some of these models focus on individual decision making, whereas others focus on decision making in groups.

The basic assumption behind individual models of decision making is that human beings are in some sense rational. The **rational model** of human behavior is built on the idea that people engage in basically consistent, rational, value-maximizing calculations. Under this model, an individual identifies goals, ranks all possible alternative actions by their contributions to those goals, and chooses the alternative that contributes most to those goals.

**rational model**
Model of human behavior based on the belief that people, organizations, and nations engage in basically consistent, value-maximizing calculations or adaptations within certain constraints.

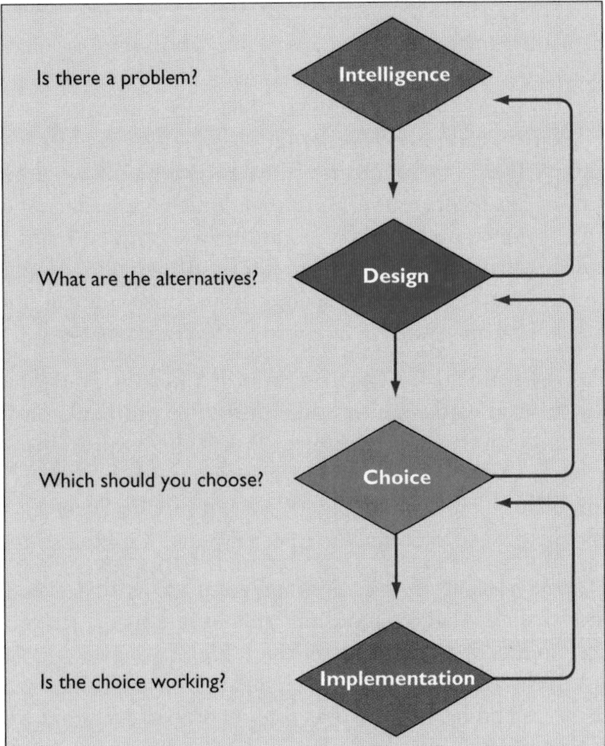


*Figure 3-10* The decision-making process. Decisions are often arrived at after a series of iterations and evaluations at each stage in the process. The decision maker often must loop back through one or more of the stages before completing the process.

Criticisms of this model show that in fact people cannot specify all of the alternatives, and that most individuals do not have singular goals and so are unable to rank all alternatives and consequences. Many decisions are so complex that calculating the choice (even if done by computer) is virtually impossible. One modification to the rational model states that instead of searching through all alternatives, people actually choose the first available alternative that moves them toward their ultimate goal. Another modification alters the rational model by suggesting that in making policy decisions, people choose policies most like the previous policy (Lindblom, 1959). Finally, some scholars point out that decision making is a continuous process in which final decisions are always being modified.

Modern psychology has further qualified the rational model by research that finds that humans differ in how they maximize their values and in the frames of reference they use to interpret information and make choices. **Cognitive style** describes underlying personality dispositions toward the treatment of information, the selection of alternatives, and the evaluation of consequences. McKenney and Keen (1974) described two decision-making cognitive styles: systematic versus intuitive types. **Systematic decision makers** approach a problem by structuring it in terms of some formal method. They evaluate and gather information in terms of their structured method. **Intuitive decision makers** approach a problem with multiple methods, using trial and error to find a solution. They tend not to structure information gathering or evaluation. Neither style is considered superior to the other. There are different ways of being rational. More recent psychological research shows that humans have built-in biases that can distort decision making. People can be manipulated into choosing alternatives that they might otherwise reject simply by changing the frame of reference (Tversky and Kahneman, 1981).

**cognitive style**
Underlying personality dispositions toward the treatment of information, selection of alternatives, and evaluation of consequences.

**systematic decision makers**
Cognitive style that describes people who approach a problem by structuring it in terms of some formal method.

**intuitive decision makers**
Cognitive style that describes people who approach a problem with multiple methods in an unstructured manner, using trial and error to find a solution.

## Organizational Models of Decision Making

Decision making often is not performed by a single individual but by entire groups or organizations. **Organizational models of decision making** take into account the structural and political characteristics of an organization. Bureaucratic, political, and even "garbage can" models have been proposed to describe how decision making takes place in organizations. We shall now consider each of these models.

**organizational models of decision making**
Models of decision making that take into account the structural and political characteristics of an organization.

***Bureaucratic Models*** According to **bureaucratic models of decision making,** an organization's most important goal is the preservation of the organization itself. The reduction of uncertainty is another major goal. Policy tends to be incremental, only marginally different from the past, because radical policy departures involve too much uncertainty. These models depict organizations generally as not "choosing" or "deciding" in a rational sense. Rather, according to bureaucratic models, whatever organizations do is the result of standard operating procedures (SOPs) honed over years of active use.

Organizations rarely change these SOPs, because they may have to change personnel and incur risks (who knows if the new techniques work better than the old ones?). Although senior management and leaders are hired to coordinate and lead the organization, they are effectively trapped by the organization's standard solutions. Some organizations do, of course, change; they learn new ways of behaving; and they can be led. But all of these changes require a long time. Look around and you will find many organizations doing pretty much what they did 10, 20, or even 30 years ago.

**bureaucratic models of decision making**
Models of decision making where decisions are shaped by the organization's standard operating procedures (SOPs).

***Political Models of Organizational Choice*** Power in organizations is shared; even the lowest-level workers have some power. In **political models of decision making,** what an organization does is a result of political bargains struck among key leaders and interest groups. Organizations do not come up with "solutions" that are "chosen" to solve some "problem." They come up with compromises that reflect the conflicts, the major stakeholders, the diverse interests, the unequal power, and the confusion that constitute politics.

**political models of decision making**
Models of decision making where decisions result from competition and bargaining among the organization's interest groups and key leaders.

***"Garbage Can" Model*** A more recent theory of decision making, called the **"garbage can" model,** states that organizations are not rational. Decision making is largely accidental and is the product of a stream of solutions, problems, and situations that are randomly associated.

**"garbage can" model**
Model of decision making that states that organizations are not rational and that decisions are solutions that become attached to problems for accidental reasons.

If this model is correct, it should not be surprising that the wrong solutions are applied to the wrong problems in an organization or that, over time, a large number of organizations make critical mistakes that lead to their demise. Exxon Corporation's delayed response to the 1989

Alaska oil spill is an example. Within an hour after the Exxon tanker *Valdez* ran aground in Alaska's Prince William Sound on March 29, 1989, workers were preparing emergency equipment; however, the aid was not dispatched. Instead of sending out emergency crews, the Alyeska Pipeline Service Company (which was responsible for initially responding to oil spill emergencies) sent the crews home. The first full emergency crew did not arrive at the spill site until at least 14 hours after the shipwreck, by which time the oil had spread beyond effective control. Yet enough equipment and personnel had been available to respond effectively. Much of the 10 million gallons of oil fouling the Alaska shoreline in the worst tanker spill in American history could have been confined had Alyeska acted more decisively (Malcolm, 1989).

### Implications for System Design

The research on decision making shows that it is not a simple process even in the rational individual model. Information systems do not make the decision for humans but rather support the decision-making process. How this is done will depend on the types of decisions, decision makers, and frames of reference.

Research on organizational decision making should alert students of information systems to the fact that decision making in a business is a group and organizational process. Systems must be built to support group and organizational decision making. As a general rule, information systems designers should design systems that have the following characteristics:

- They are flexible and provide many options for handling data and evaluating information.
- They are capable of supporting a variety of styles, skills, and knowledge.
- They are powerful in the sense of having multiple analytical and intuitive models for the evaluation of data and the ability to keep track of many alternatives and consequences.
- They reflect understanding of group and organizational processes of decision making.
- They are sensitive to the bureaucratic and political requirements of systems.

## 3.4 Information Systems and Business Strategy

Certain types of information systems have become especially critical to firms' long-term prosperity and survival. Such systems, which are powerful tools for staying ahead of the competition, are called *strategic information systems.*

### What Is a Strategic Information System?

**Strategic information systems** change the goals, operations, products, services, or environmental relationships of organizations to help them gain an edge over competitors. Systems that have these effects may even change the business of organizations. For instance, State Street Bank and Trust Co. of Boston transformed its core business from traditional banking services, such as customer checking and savings accounts and loans, to electronic record keeping and financial information services, providing data processing services for securities and mutual funds, and services for pension funds to monitor their money managers.

**strategic information systems**
Computer systems at any level of the organization that change goals, operations, products, services, or environmental relationships to help the organization gain a competitive advantage.

Strategic information systems should be distinguished from strategic-level systems for senior managers that focus on long-term, decision-making problems. Strategic information systems can be used at all organizational levels and are more far-reaching and deep-rooted than the other kinds of systems we have described. Strategic information systems profoundly alter the way a firm conducts its business or the very business of the firm itself. As we will see, organizations may need to change their internal operations and relationships with customers and suppliers in order to take advantage of new information systems technology.

Traditional models of strategy are being modified to accommodate the impact of digital firms and new information flows. Before the emergence of the digital firm, business strategy emphasized competing head-to-head against other firms in the same marketplace. Today, the emphasis is increasingly on exploring, identifying, and occupying new market niches before competitors act; understanding the customer value chain better; and learning faster and more deeply than competitors.

There is generally no single all-encompassing strategic system, but instead there are a number of systems operating at different levels of strategy—the business, the firm, and the industry level. For each level of business strategy, there are strategic uses of systems. And for each level of business strategy, there is an appropriate model used for analysis.

## BUSINESS-LEVEL STRATEGY AND THE VALUE CHAIN MODEL

At the business level of strategy, the key question is, "How can we compete effectively in this particular market?" The market might be light bulbs, utility vehicles, or cable television. The most common generic strategies at this level are (1) to become the low-cost producer, (2) to differentiate your product or service, and (3) to change the scope of competition by either enlarging the market to include global markets or narrowing the market by focusing on small niches not well served by competitors. Digital firms provide new capabilities for supporting business-level strategy by managing the supply chain, building efficient customer "sense and respond" systems, and participating in "value webs" to deliver new products and services to market.

### Leveraging Technology in the Value Chain

**value chain model**
Model that highlights the primary or support activities that add a margin of value to a firm's products or services where information systems can best be applied to achieve a competitive advantage.

**primary activities**
Activities most directly related to the production and distribution of a firm's products or services.

**support activities**
Activities that make the delivery of a firm's primary activities possible. Consist of the organization's infrastructure, human resources, technology, and procurement.

**value web**
Digitally enabled network of a firm and its suppliers and business partners.

At the business level the most common analytic tool is value chain analysis. The **value chain model** highlights specific activities in the business where competitive strategies can be best applied (Porter, 1985) and where information systems are most likely to have a strategic impact. The value chain model identifies specific, critical leverage points where a firm can use information technology most effectively to enhance its competitive position. Exactly where can it obtain the greatest benefit from strategic information systems—what specific activities can be used to create new products and services, enhance market penetration, lock in customers and suppliers, and lower operational costs? This model views the firm as a series or "chain" of basic activities that add a margin of value to a firm's products or services. These activities can be categorized as either primary activities or support activities.

**Primary activities** are most directly related to the production and distribution of the firm's products and services that create value for the customer. Primary activities include inbound logistics, operations, outbound logistics, sales and marketing, and service. Inbound logistics include receiving and storing materials for distribution to production. Operations transforms inputs into finished products. Outbound logistics entail storing and distributing finished products. Marketing and sales includes promoting and selling the firm's products. The service activity includes maintenance and repair of the firm's goods and services. **Support activities** make the delivery of the primary activities possible and consist of organization infrastructure (administration and management), human resources (employee recruiting, hiring, and training), technology (improving products and the production process), and procurement (purchasing input).

Organizations have competitive advantage when they provide more value to their customers or when they provide the same value to customers at a lower price. An information system could have a strategic impact if it helped the firm provide products or services at a lower cost than competitors or if it provided products and services at the same cost as competitors but with greater value. The value activities that add the most value to products and services depend on the features of each particular firm.

Internet technology has extended the concept of a firm's value chain to include all the firm's suppliers and business partners into a single value web. A **value web** is a collection of independent firms who use information technology to coordinate their behavior so as to collectively produce a product or service for a market. Well before the digital era, companies such as automobile manufacturers had relationships with key suppliers from whom they purchased coal, steel, glass, and parts. But today's value webs are much more powerful, using digitally enabled networks not only to purchase supplies but also to closely coordinate production of many independent firms.

For instance, in the Italian sweater industry, Bennetton is the design, marketing, and distribution side of a much larger number of independent firms who collectively produce sweaters and other apparel for the U.S. market. Dyers, weavers, assemblers—all operating as independent businesses—obtain production information from Bennetton systems and efficiently produce the ingredients needed for the Bennetton marketing business.

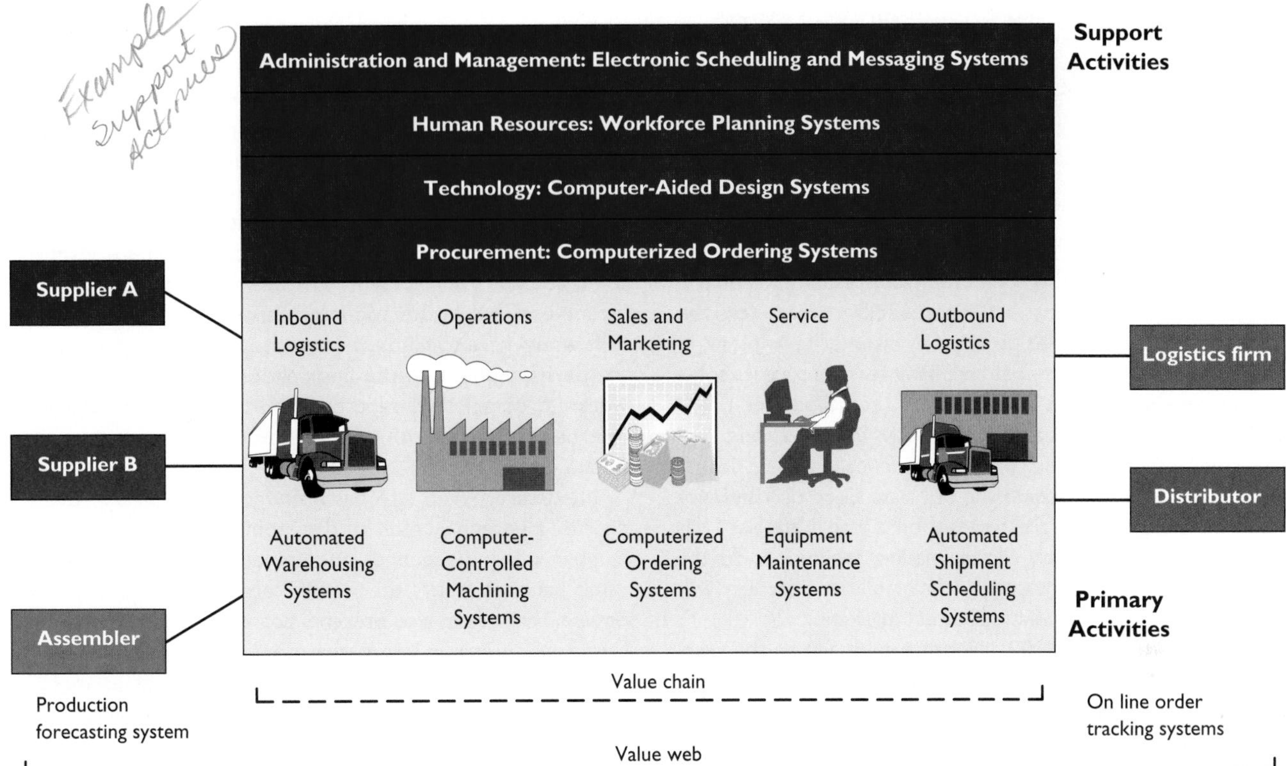


*Figure 3-11* The value chain and the value web. Various examples of strategic information systems for the primary and support activities of a firm and of its value web that would add a margin of value to a firm's products or services.

Figure 3-11 illustrates the activities of the value chain and the value web, showing examples of strategic information systems that could be developed to make each of the value activities more cost effective.

The industrial networks we introduced in Chapter 2 form the infrastructure for value webs. A firm can achieve a strategic advantage by providing value, not only through its internal value chain processes but also through powerful, efficient ties to value web partners as well.

Businesses should try to develop strategic information systems for both the internal value chain activities and the external value web activities that add the most value. A strategic analysis might, for example, identify sales and marketing activities where information systems could provide the greatest boost. The analysis might recommend a system to reduce marketing costs by targeting marketing campaigns more efficiently or by providing information for developing products more finely attuned to a firm's target market. A series of systems, including some linked to systems of other value web partners, might be required to create a strategic advantage. The Window on Technology describes how NextCard developed systems for such purposes.

We will now show how information technology at the business level helps the firm reduce costs, differentiate product, and serve new markets.

## Information System Products and Services

Firms can use information systems to create unique new products and services that can be easily distinguished from those of competitors. Strategic information systems for **product differentiation** can prevent the competition from responding in kind so that firms with these differentiated products and services no longer have to compete on the basis of cost.

**product differentiation** Competitive strategy for creating brand loyalty by developing new and unique products and services that are not easily duplicated by competitors.

Many of these information technology–based products and services have been created by financial institutions. Citibank developed automatic teller machines (ATMs) and bank debit cards in 1977. Citibank became at one time the largest bank in the United States.

Window on Technology

## NextCard Direct Markets with the Internet

Most people in the United States already have too many credit cards. If they already have three or four credit cards, why would they want another one? This has been the challenge of NextCard, an Internet-only credit card issuer, and so far it has succeeded, thanks to new direct marketing efficiencies provided by Internet technology.

The credit card industry has had many years of success soliciting customers via direct mail. (About three billion credit card solicitations are mailed yearly in the United States.) Credit card firms constantly tinker with the mailings, tweaking their design, wording, and even the positioning of MasterCard or Visa logos to see what triggers the greatest response rate. NextCard has transferred some of these direct-mailing techniques to the Internet while taking advantage of capabilities that are way beyond the reach of conventional direct marketing.

NextCard runs about 100 different banner ads on the Web, based on its stock of 2,000 different designs. In any given month, NextCard ads appear about three billion different times on 200 different Web sites of other companies, amounting to 200,000 tests in a year. Within a two-week period NextCard has 200,000 different opportunities to gauge what combination of design and Web site positioning is most likely to elicit a credit card application, and the exact cost to the company of such advertisements. NextCard even has tools to monitor what Web banner ads generate the most profitable customers, the amount of balances from a customer's other credit card accounts transferred to NextCard, and whether customers stay after their low introductory rates expire.

Signing up for a credit card is often an impulse move. By placing its ads on other Web sites of interest to potential credit card users, NextCard creates opportunities for individuals to transact at the precise moment when they are most likely to be interested in a credit card. Once a visitor to an affiliated Web site clicks on a NextCard banner ad, that person is transported to NextCard's Web site where he or she can immediately apply for a NextCard. In the non-Internet world, a credit card applicant would have to fill out a physical application form, mail it in (or perhaps phone in the information), and wait for days or weeks to obtain credit approval and the card itself. Thanks to Internet technology, all of these events can now take place instantaneously.

NextCard's Web site has software that can approve (or decline) a potential credit card customer and issue a NextCard number within 30 seconds, and immediately transfer the applicant's balances from other credit card accounts to NextCard on-line. The system also presents approved cardholders with at least two options on terms, such as interest rates, airline tickets, or other rewards. Although other dot.com businesses are falling by the wayside, NextCard is starting to become profitable.

To Think About: What is the relationship of Internet technology to NextCard's business model and business strategy? How is NextCard using value chain strategy?

*Sources:* Paul Beckett, "NextCard Is a Dot-Com Rarity: Its Online Ads Prove Effective," *The Wall Street Journal,* January 29, 2001; Jason Black, "Sales by Association," *Internet World,* February 1, 2001.

Citibank ATMs were so successful that Citibank's competitors were forced to counterstrike with their own ATM systems. Citibank, Wells Fargo Bank, and others have continued to innovate by providing on-line electronic banking services so that customers can do most of their banking transactions with home computers linked to proprietary networks or the Internet. Some companies such as WingspanBank.com have used the Web to set up "virtual banks" offering a full array of banking services without any physical branches. (Customers mail in their deposits.) NextCard, described in the Window on Technology, is another example of a new Internet-based financial product.

Manufacturers and retailers are starting to use information systems to create products and services that are custom-tailored to fit the precise specifications of individual customers. Dell Computer Corporation sells directly to customers using build-to-order manufacturing. Individuals, businesses, and government agencies can buy computers directly from Dell customized with exactly the features and components they need. They can place their orders directly using a toll-free telephone number or Dell's Web site. Once the Dell factory receives an order, it assembles the computer based on the configuration specified by the customer. Chapter 1 describes other instances in which information technology is creating customized products and services while retaining the cost efficiencies of mass-production techniques.

**focused differentiation** Competitive strategy for developing new market niches for specialized products or services where a business can compete in the target area better than its competitors.

### Systems to Focus on Market Niche

Businesses can create new market niches by identifying a specific target for a product or service that it can serve in a superior manner. Through **focused differentiation,** the firm can provide a specialized product or service for this narrow target market better than competitors.

**TABLE 3-5 HOW BUSINESSES ARE USING CUSTOMER DATA ANALYSIS**

| Organization | Application |
|---|---|
| Canadian Imperial Bank of Commerce (CIBC) | Customer profitability system helps the bank identify its most profitable customers so that it can offer them special sales and services. |
| Stein Roe Investors | Analyzes data generated by visitors to its Web site to create profiles of existing and prospective customers. The company can use these profiles to target potential customers with content, advertising, and incentives geared to their interests, such as retirement planning. |
| American Express | Analyzes data from hundreds of billions of credit card purchases to create "one-to-one" marketing campaigns. Customers receive personalized messages promoting goods and services in which they have shown interest along with their credit card bills. |
| U.S. West Communications | Analyzes data from billing operations and external sources to derive customer trends and needs based on household characteristics such as family size, median ages of family members, types of spending patterns, and location. Its findings helped the company increase customer service and reduce the number of lost customers by 45 percent. |

An information system can give companies a competitive advantage by producing data for finely tuned sales and marketing techniques. Such systems treat existing information as a resource that the organization can "mine" to increase profitability and market penetration. Information systems enable companies to finely analyze customer buying patterns, tastes, and preferences so that they efficiently pitch advertising and marketing campaigns to smaller and smaller target markets.

Sophisticated software tools find patterns in large pools of data and infer rules from them that can be used to guide decision making. For example, mining data about purchases at supermarkets might reveal that when potato chips are purchased, soda is also purchased 65 percent of the time. When there is a promotion, soda is purchased 85 percent of the time people purchase potato chips. This information could help firms design better sales promotions or product displays. Table 3-5 describes how businesses are benefiting from customer data analysis. More detail on this topic can be found in Chapters 7 and 13.

The data come from a range of sources—credit card transactions, demographic data, purchase data from checkout counter scanners at supermarkets and retail stores, and data collected when people access and interact with Web sites. Analysis of such data can help one-to-one marketers create personal messages based on individualized preferences. The level of fine-grained customization provided by these data analysis systems parallels that for mass customization described in Chapter 1.

The cost of acquiring a new customer has been estimated to be five times that of retaining an existing customer. By carefully examining transactions of customer purchases and activities, firms can identify profitable customers and win more of their business. Likewise, companies can use these data to identify nonprofitable customers (Clemons and Weber, 1994). Companies that skillfully use customer data will focus on identifying the most valued customers and use data from a variety of sources to understand their needs (Davenport, Harris, and Kohli, 2001).

## Supply Chain Management and Efficient Customer Response Systems

Digital firms have the capabilities to go far beyond traditional strategic systems for taking advantage of digital links with other organizations. A powerful business-level strategy available to digital firms involves linking the value chains of vendors and suppliers to the firm's value chain. Integration of value chains can be carried further by digital firms through linking the customer's value chain to the firm's value chain in an "efficient customer response system." Firms using systems to link with customers and suppliers can reduce their inventory costs while responding rapidly to customer demands.

By keeping prices low and shelves well stocked using a legendary inventory replenishment system, Wal-Mart has become the leading retail business in the United States. Wal-Mart's "continuous replenishment system" sends orders for new merchandise directly to

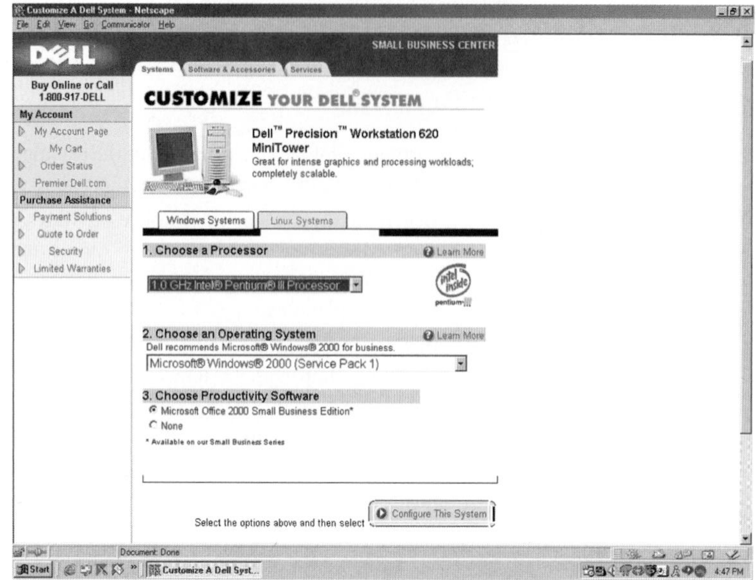


*At Dell Computer Corporation's Web site, customers can select the options they want and order their computer custom-built to these specifications. Dell's build-to-order system is a major source of competitive advantage.*

suppliers as soon as consumers pay for their purchases at the cash register. Point-of-sale terminals record the bar code of each item passing the checkout counter and send a purchase transaction directly to a central computer at Wal-Mart headquarters. The computer collects the orders from all Wal-Mart stores and transmits them to suppliers. Suppliers can also access Wal-Mart's sales and inventory data using Web technology. Because the system can replenish inventory with lightning speed, Wal-Mart does not need to spend much money on maintaining large inventories of goods in its own warehouses. The system also allows Wal-Mart to adjust purchases of store items to meet local customer demands. Competitors such as Kmart spend 21 percent of sales on overhead. But by using systems to keep operating costs low, Wal-Mart pays only 15 percent of sales revenue for overhead.

Wal-Mart's continuous replenishment system is an example of efficient supply chain management, which we introduced in Chapter 2. To manage the supply chain, a company tries to eliminate delays and cut the amount of resources tied up along the way. This can be accomplished by streamlining the company's internal operations or by asking suppliers to put off delivery of goods—and their payments—until the moment they are needed.

**efficient customer response system**
System that directly links consumer behavior back to distribution, production, and supply chains.

Supply chain management systems can not only lower inventory costs but can also deliver the product or service more rapidly to the customer. Supply chain management can thus be used to create **efficient customer response systems** that respond to customer demands more efficiently. An efficient customer response system directly links consumer

## MANAGEMENT DECISION PROBLEM

### ANALYZING CUSTOMER ACQUISITION COSTS

Companies that sell products directly to consumers over the Web need to measure the effectiveness of their Web site as a sales channel. Web sites are often expensive to build and maintain and firms want to know if they are getting a good return on their investment. One way of measuring Web site effectiveness is by analyzing new customer acquisition costs. In other words, how much must the company spend in advertising, marketing, or promotional discounts to turn an on-line browser into an on-line buyer? Are the firm's customer acquisition costs higher or lower than for other companies selling on-line? (The average new customer acquisition cost for companies that only sell online is $42 per customer although such costs may be higher or lower for certain types of businesses.) If new customer acquisition costs continue to rise, this could be an indicator that the company is facing higher marketing costs because of increased competition. Here is the information on quarterly new customer acquisition costs for four different Web companies:

**New Customer Acquisition Costs: July 1, 2000 to July 1, 2001**

| Company | Q3'00 | Q4'00 | Q1'01 | Q2'01 |
|---|---|---|---|---|
| Internet Software City | 81.82 | 84.70 | 92.98 | 142.65 |
| Online Garage Sale | 8.79 | 9.22 | 10.60 | 7.73 |
| Books and More Books | 24.77 | 26.88 | 31.20 | 36.17 |
| Online Travel and Vacation | 5.11 | 5.14 | 5.98 | 5.61 |

1. Are any of these companies experiencing customer acquisition problems? Explain your answer.
2. What can companies facing competitive pressure do to lower their customer acquisition costs and compete more effectively in a virtual environment?

behavior back to distribution, production, and supply chains. Wal-Mart's continuous replenishment system provides such efficient customer response. Dell Computer Corporation's build-to-order system, described earlier, is an example of efficient customer response triggered by activities on the Web.

*Wal-Mart's continuous inventory replenishment system uses sales data captured at the checkout counter to transmit orders to restock merchandise directly to its suppliers. The system enables Wal-Mart to keep costs low while fine-tuning its merchandise to meet customer demands.*

The convenience and ease of using these information systems raise **switching costs** (the cost of switching from one product to a competing product), which discourages customers from going to competitors. For example, Baxter Healthcare International's "stockless inventory" and ordering system uses supply chain management to create an efficient customer response system. Participating hospitals become unwilling to switch to another supplier because of the system's convenience and low cost. Baxter supplies nearly two-thirds of all products used by U.S. hospitals. Terminals tied to Baxter's own computers are installed in hospitals. When hospitals want to place an order, they do not need to call a salesperson or send a purchase order—they simply use a Baxter computer terminal on-site to order from the full Baxter supply catalog. The system generates shipping, billing, invoicing, and inventory information, and the hospital terminals provide customers with an estimated delivery date. With more than 80 distribution centers in the United States, Baxter can make daily deliveries of its products, often within hours of receiving an order.

**switching costs**
The expense a customer or company incurs in lost time and expenditure of resources when changing from one supplier or system to a competing supplier or system.

Baxter delivery personnel no longer drop off their cartons at a loading dock to be placed in a hospital storeroom. Instead, they deliver orders directly to the hospital corridors, dropping them at nursing stations, operating rooms, and supply closets. This has created in effect a "stockless inventory," with Baxter serving as the hospitals' warehouse.

Figure 3-12 compares stockless inventory with the just-in-time supply method and traditional inventory practices. Whereas just-in-time inventory allows customers to reduce their inventories by ordering only enough material for a few days' inventory, stockless inventory allows them to eliminate their warehoused inventories entirely. All inventory responsibilities shift to the

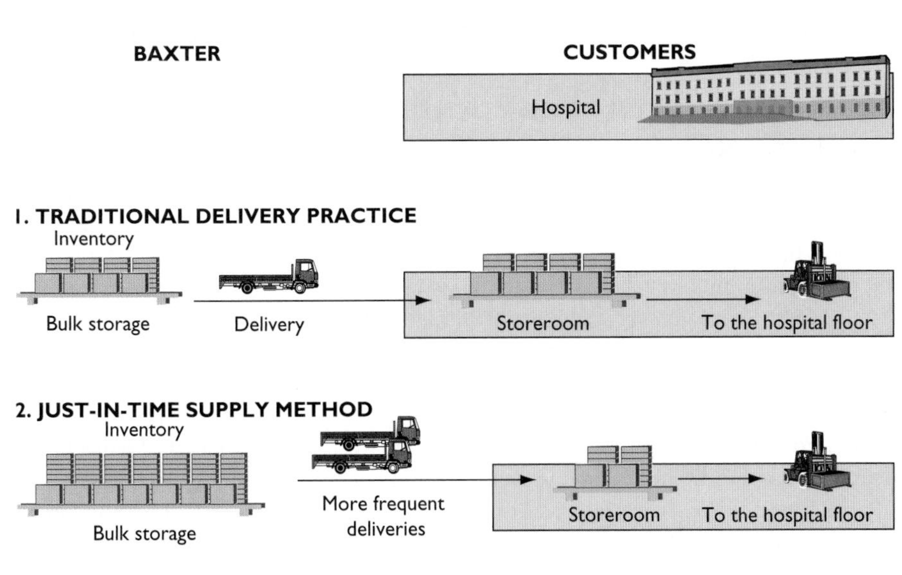


*Figure 3-12* Stockless inventory compared to traditional and just-in-time supply methods. The just-in-time supply method reduces inventory requirements of the customer, whereas stockless inventory allows the customer to eliminate inventories entirely. Deliveries are made daily, sometimes directly to the departments that need supplies.

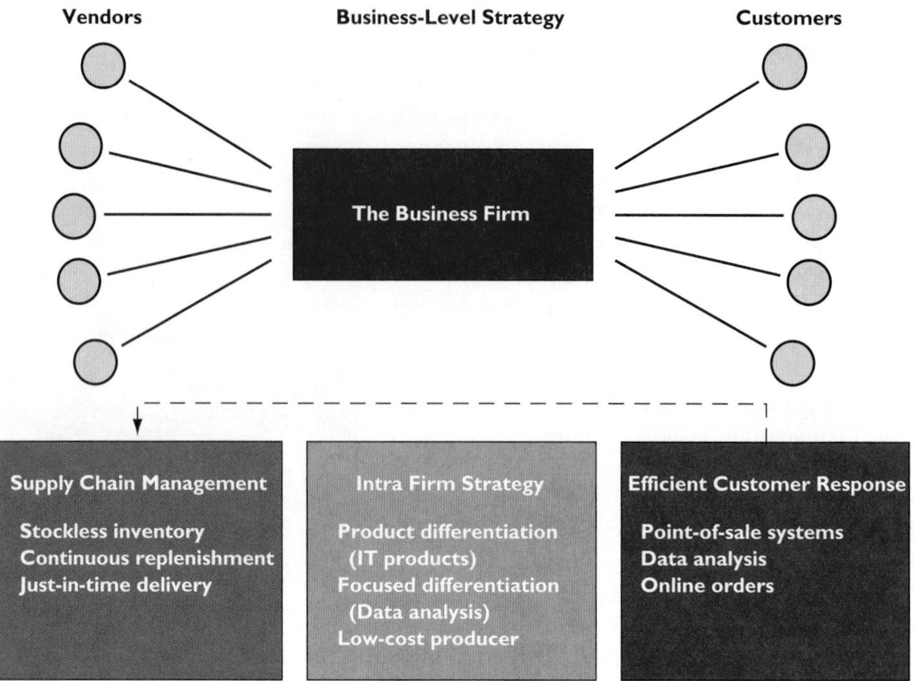


***Figure 3-13*** Business-level strategy. Efficient customer response and supply chain management systems are often interrelated, helping firms "lock in" customers and suppliers while lowering operating costs. Other types of systems can be used to support product differentiation, focused differentiation, and low-cost producer strategies.

distributor, who manages the supply flow. The stockless inventory is a powerful instrument for "locking in" customers, thus giving the supplier a decided competitive advantage.

Supply chain management and efficient customer response systems are two examples of how emerging digital firms can engage in business strategies not available to traditional firms. Both types of systems require network-based information technology infrastructure investment and software competence to make customer and supply chain data flow seamlessly among different organizations. Both types of systems have greatly enhanced the efficiency of individual digital firms and the U.S. economy as a whole by moving toward a *demand-pull production system,* and away from the traditional *supply-push economic system* in which factories were managed on the basis of 12-month official plans rather than on near-instantaneous customer purchase information. Figure 3-13 illustrates the relationships between supply chain management, efficient customer response, and the various business-level strategies.

## FIRM-LEVEL STRATEGY AND INFORMATION TECHNOLOGY

A business firm is typically a collection of businesses. Often, the firm is organized financially as a collection of strategic business units, and the returns to the firm are directly tied to strategic business unit performance. The questions are, "How can the overall performance of these business units be achieved?" and "How can information technology contribute?"

There are two answers in the literature to these questions: synergy and core competency. The idea driving synergies is that when some units can be used as inputs to other units, or two organizations can pool markets and expertise, these relationships can lower costs and generate profits. Recent bank and financial firm mergers, such as the merger of Chemical Bank and Chase Manhattan Corp., Wells Fargo and Norwest Corp., Deutsche Bank and Bankers Trust, and Citicorp and Travelers Insurance occurred precisely for this purpose.

How can IT be used strategically here? One use of information technology in these synergy situations is to tie together the operations of disparate business units so that they can act as a whole. For example, Citigroup can cross market the financial products of both Citicorp and Travelers to customers. Such systems would lower retailing costs, increase customer access to new financial products, and speed up the process of marketing new instruments.

### Enhancing Core Competencies

A second concept for firm-level strategy involves the notion of "core competency." The argument is that the performance of all business units can increase insofar as these business units develop, or create, a central core of competencies. A **core competency** is an activity at which a firm is a world-class leader. Core competencies may involve being the world's best fiber-optic manufacturer, the best miniature parts designer, the best package delivery service, or the best thin film manufacturer. In general, a core competency relies on knowledge that is gained over many years of experience (embedded knowledge) and a first-class research organization or simply key people who follow the literature and stay abreast of new external knowledge.

**core competency**
Activity at which a firm excels as a world-class leader.

How can IT be used to advance or create core competencies? Any system that encourages the sharing of knowledge across business units enhances competency. Such systems might encourage or enhance existing competencies and help employees become aware of new external knowledge; such systems might also help a business leverage existing competencies to related markets.

## INDUSTRY-LEVEL STRATEGY AND INFORMATION SYSTEMS: COMPETITIVE FORCES AND NETWORK ECONOMICS

Firms together comprise an industry, such as the automotive industry, telephone, television broadcasting, and forest products industries, to name a few. The key strategic question at this level of analysis is, "How and when should we compete as opposed to cooperate with others in the industry?" Whereas most strategic analyses emphasize competition, a great deal of money can be made by cooperating with other firms in the same industry or firms in related industries. For instance, firms can cooperate to develop industry standards in a number of areas; they can cooperate by working together to build customer awareness, and to work collectively with suppliers to lower costs (Shapiro and Varian, 1999). The three principal concepts for analyzing strategy at the industry level are information partnerships, the competitive forces model, and network economics.

### Information Partnerships

Firms can form information partnerships, and even link their information systems to achieve unique synergies. In an **information partnership,** both companies can join forces, without actually merging, by sharing information (Konsynski and McFarlan, 1990). American Airlines has an arrangement with Citibank to award one mile in its frequent flier program for every dollar spent using Citibank credit cards. American benefits from increased customer loyalty, and Citibank gains new credit card subscribers and a highly creditworthy customer base for cross-marketing. Northwest Airlines has a similar arrangement with U.S. Bank. American and Northwest have also allied with MCI, awarding frequent flier miles for each dollar of long-distance billing.

**information partnership**
Cooperative alliance formed between two or more corporations for the purpose of sharing information to gain strategic advantage.

Such partnerships help firms gain access to new customers, creating new opportunities for cross-selling and targeting products. Companies that have been traditional competitors may find such alliances to be mutually advantageous. Baxter Healthcare International offers its customers medical supplies from competitors and office supplies through its electronic ordering channel.

### The Competitive Forces Model

In the **competitive forces model,** which is illustrated in Figure 3-14, a firm faces a number of external threats and opportunities: the threat of new entrants into its market, the pressure from substitute products or services, the bargaining power of customers, the bargaining power of suppliers, and the positioning of traditional industry competitors.

**competitive forces model**
Model used to describe the interaction of external influences, specifically threats and opportunities, that affect an organization's strategy and ability to compete.

Competitive advantage can be achieved by enhancing the firm's ability to deal with customers, suppliers, substitute products and services, and new entrants to its market, which in turn may change the balance of power between a firm and other competitors in the industry in the firm's favor.

How can information systems be used to achieve strategic advantage at the industry level? By working with other firms, industry participants can use information technology to develop industry-wide standards for exchanging information or business transactions electronically (see Chapters 6 and 9), which force all market participants to subscribe to similar standards. Earlier we described how firms can benefit from value webs with complementary firms in the industry. Such efforts increase efficiency at the industry level as well as at the

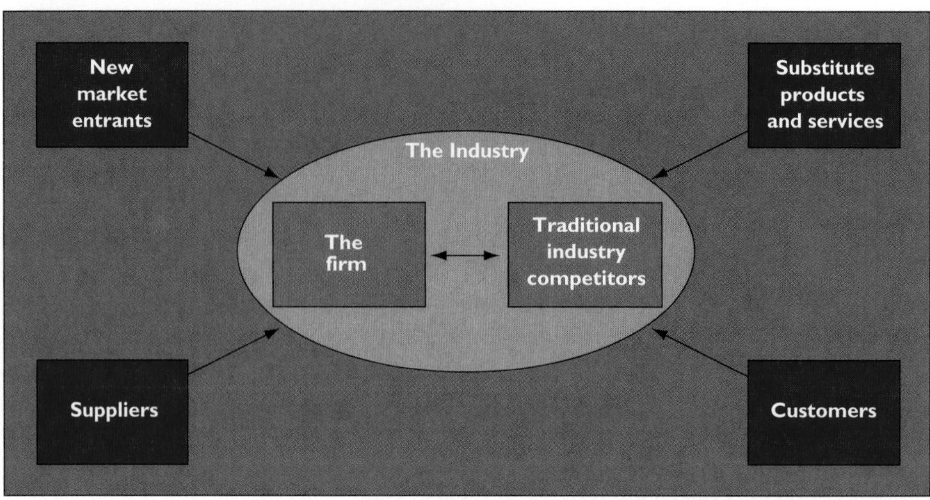


**Figure 3-14** The competitive forces model. There are various forces that affect an organization's ability to compete and, therefore, greatly influence a firm's business strategy. There are threats from new market entrants and from substitute products and services. Customers and suppliers wield bargaining power. Traditional competitors constantly adapt their strategies to maintain their market position.

business level—making substitute products less possible and perhaps raising entry costs—thus discouraging new entrants. Also, industry members can build industry-wide, IT-supported consorti, symposia, and communications networks to coordinate activities vis-à-vis government agencies, foreign competition, and competing industries.

An example of such industry-level cooperation can be found in the Chapter 4 Window on Organizations describing Covisint, an electronic exchange shared by the major automobile manufacturers for procurement of auto parts. Although the Big 3 U.S. auto manufacturers aggressively compete on such factors as design, service, quality, and price, they can raise the industry's productivity by working together to create an integrated supply chain. Covisint enables all manufacturers and suppliers to trade on a single Internet site, sparing manufacturers the cost of setting up their own Web-based marketplaces.

In the digital firm era, the competitive forces model needs some modification. The traditional Porter model assumes a relatively static industry environment, relatively clear-cut industry boundaries, and a relatively stable set of suppliers, substitutes, and customers. Instead of participating in a single industry, today's firms are much more aware that they participate in "industry sets"—multiple related industries that consumers can choose from to obtain a product or service (see Figure 3-15). For instance, automobile companies compete against other automobile companies in the "auto industry," but they also compete against many other industries in the transportation industry "set," which includes train, plane, and bus transportation companies. Success or failure for a single auto company may depend on the success or failure of various other industries. Colleges may think they are in competition with other traditional colleges, but, in fact, they are also in competition with electronic distance learning universities, publishing companies who have created on-line college courses, and private training firms who offer technical certificates—all of whom are members of a

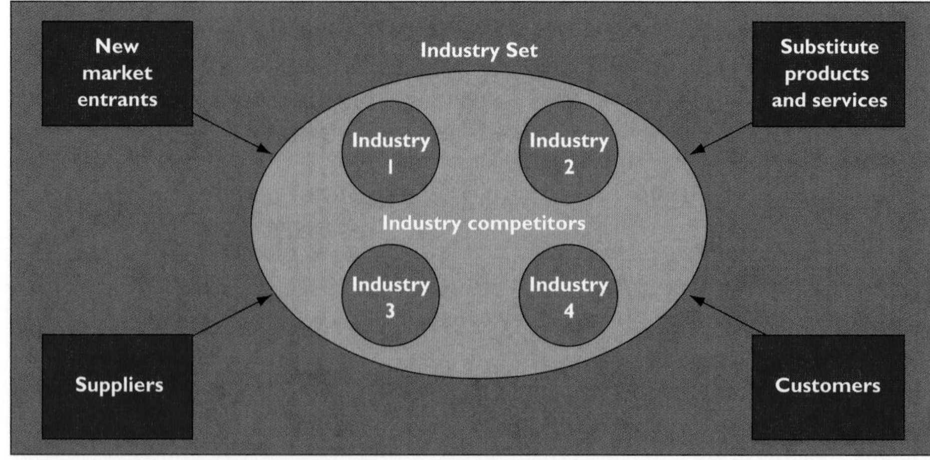


**Figure 3-15** The new competitive forces model. The digital firm era requires a more dynamic view of the boundaries between firms, customers, and suppliers, with competition occurring among industry sets.

much larger "education industry set." In the digital era we can expect greater emphasis on building strategies to compete—and cooperate—with members of the firm's industry set.

Nevertheless, the competitive forces model remains a valid model for analyzing strategy, even considering the impact of the Internet. Internet technology has affected industry structure by providing technologies that make it easier for rivals to compete on price alone and for new competitors to enter the market. Profits have also been dampened because the Internet dramatically increases the information available to customers for comparison shopping, thus raising their bargaining power. Although the Internet can provide benefits such as new channels to customers and new operating efficiencies, firms cannot achieve competitive advantage with this technology unless they have skillfully integrated Internet initiatives into their overall strategy and operations. In the age of the Internet, the traditional competitive forces are still at work, but competitive rivalry has become much more intense. (Porter, 2001).

### Network Economics

A third strategic concept useful at the industry level is **network economics.** In traditional economics—the economics of factories and agriculture—production experiences diminishing returns. The more any given resource is applied to production, the lower the marginal gain in output, until a point is reached where the additional inputs produce no additional outputs. This is the law of diminishing returns, and it is the foundation for most of modern economics.

**network economics**
Model of strategic systems at the industry level based on the concept of a network where adding another participant entails zero marginal costs but can create much larger marginal gain.

In some situations the law of diminishing returns does not work. For instance, in a network, the marginal costs of adding another participant are about zero, whereas the marginal gain is much larger. The larger the number of subscribers in a telephone system, or the Internet, the greater the value to all participants. It's no more expensive to operate a television station with 1,000 subscribers than with 10 million subscribers. And the value of a community of people grows with size, whereas the cost of adding new members is inconsequential.

From this network economics perspective, information technology can be strategically useful. Internet sites can be used by firms to build "communities of users"—like-minded customers who want to share their experiences. This can build customer loyalty and enjoyment, and build unique ties to customers. Microsoft Corporation—the world's dominant PC software manufacturer—uses information technology to build communities of software developers around the world. Using the Microsoft Developer's Network, these small software development firms work closely with Microsoft to debug its operating system software, provide new applications ideas and extensions, supply customers with tips and new software applications, and in general participate in a powerful and useful network.

## USING SYSTEMS FOR COMPETITIVE ADVANTAGE: MANAGEMENT ISSUES

Strategic information systems often change the organization as well as its products, services, and operating procedures, driving the organization into new behavior patterns. Using technology effectively for strategic benefit requires careful planning and management.

### Managing Strategic Transitions

Adopting the kinds of strategic systems described in this chapter generally requires changes in business goals, relationships with customers and suppliers, internal operations, and information architecture. These sociotechnical changes, affecting both social and technical elements of the organization, can be considered **strategic transitions**—a movement between levels of sociotechnical systems.

**strategic transitions**
A movement from one level of sociotechnical system to another. Often required when adopting strategic systems that demand changes in the social and technical elements of an organization.

Such changes often entail blurring of organizational boundaries, both external and internal. Suppliers and customers may become intimately linked and may share each other's responsibilities. For instance, in Baxter International's stockless inventory system, Baxter has assumed responsibility for managing its customers' inventories (Johnston and Vitale, 1988). Managers will need to devise new business processes for coordinating their firms' activities with those of customers, suppliers, and other organizations. The organizational change requirements surrounding new information systems are so important that they merit attention throughout this text. Chapters 10 and 11 examine organizational change issues in great detail.

## What Managers Can Do

Information systems are too important to be left entirely to a small technical group in the corporation. Managers must take the initiative to identify the types of systems that would provide a strategic advantage to the firm. Some of the important questions managers should ask themselves are as follows:

- What are some of the forces at work in the industry? What strategies are being used by industry leaders?
- How is the industry currently using information and communication technology? Which organizations are the industry leaders in the application of information systems technology? What kinds of systems are applicable to the industry?
- What are the direction and nature of change within the industry? From where are the momentum and change coming?

Once the nature of information systems technology in the industry is understood, managers should turn to their organization and ask other important questions:

- Is the organization behind or ahead of the industry in its application of information systems?
- What is the current business strategic plan, and how does that plan mesh with the current strategy for information services?
- Does the firm have sufficient technology and capital to develop a strategic information systems initiative? (Kettinger et al. 1994)
- Where would new information systems provide the greatest value to the firm?
- Are there strategic benefits from using Internet technology in operations, marketing, or customer service for this specific firm? (Feeny, 2001).

Once these issues have been considered, managers can gain a keen insight into whether their firms are ready for strategic information systems.

## Application Software Exercise

### Spreadsheet Exercise: Determining Monthly Loan Payments for Roberto's Place

Roberto's Place is a chain of pizza delivery stores, owned and operated by Roberto Lunsford. Customers often remark on the quality, variety, and low price of Roberto's pizzas. For each store, Roberto has three delivery vehicles. During the past year, Roberto has noticed an increase in the repair and maintenance costs associated with several of his delivery vehicles. Under normal circumstances, Roberto purchases two cars each year. However, because of the increased repair and maintenance problems, he must now purchase at least six new vehicles.

After visiting several dealerships, he determines that each vehicle will cost approximately $20,000. He knows that he can borrow up to $125,000 from a local bank; the interest rate is about 9 percent; he will need to arrange financing for at least four years, and he has $25,000 available for a down payment. Organize this information in a spreadsheet. What is Roberto's approximate monthly payment?

If Roberto finances his new pizza delivery vehicles for five years instead of four years, what is the new monthly payment? If Roberto wishes to keep his payment below $2,000 a month, should he finance the loan for five years instead of four years? What is the difference in monthly payments? Also, what is the difference in total interest between the two years?

After speaking with a loan officer at the local bank, Roberto is told that the available interest rates vary between 7.5 and 9 percent. Using your spreadsheet product's help feature, investigate how to build input tables. Next, build one input table, outlining the interest rates and associated monthly payments. Your interest rates should increase in quarter percent increments. Prepare a written analysis of your findings. What recommendations would you give Roberto?

## MANAGEMENT WRAP-UP

Information technology provides tools for managers to carry out both their traditional and newer roles, allowing them to monitor, plan, and forecast with more precision and speed than ever before and to respond rapidly to the changing business environment. Finding ways to use information technology to achieve competitive advantage at the business, firm, and industry level is a key management responsibility. In addition to identifying the business processes, core competencies, and the relationships with others in the industry that can be enhanced with information technology, managers need to oversee the sociotechnical changes required to implement strategic systems.

Each organization has a unique constellation of information systems that result from its interaction with information technology. Contemporary information technology can lead to major organizational changes—and efficiencies—by reducing transaction and agency costs and can also be a source of competitive advantage. Developing meaningful strategic systems generally requires extensive changes in organizational structure, culture, and business processes that often encounter resistance.

Information technology offers new ways of organizing work and using information that can promote organizational survival and prosperity. Technology can be used to differentiate existing products, create new products and services, nurture core competencies, and reduce operational costs. Selecting an appropriate technology for the firm's competitive strategy is a key decision.

*For Discussion*

1. A number of information system experts have claimed that there is no such thing as a sustainable strategic advantage. Do you agree? Why or why not?
2. How has the Internet changed the management process?

## SUMMARY

1. *Identify the salient characteristics of organizations.* All modern organizations are hierarchical, specialized, and impartial. They use explicit standard operating procedures to maximize efficiency. All organizations have their own culture and politics arising from differences in interest groups. Organizations differ in goals, groups served, social roles, leadership styles, incentives, surrounding environments, and types of tasks performed. These differences create varying types of organizational structures.
2. *Analyze the relationship between information systems and organizations.* The impact of information systems on organizations is not unidirectional. Information systems and the organizations in which they are used interact with and influence each other. The introduction of a new information system will affect organizational structure, goals, work design, values, competition between interest groups, decision making, and day-to-day behavior. At the same time, information systems must be designed to serve the needs of important organizational groups and will be shaped by the organization's structure, tasks, goals, culture, politics, and management. The power of information systems to transform organizations radically by flattening organizational hierarchies has not yet been demonstrated for all types of organizations, but information technology can reduce transaction and agency costs. The Internet has a potentially large impact on organizational structure and business processes, because it can further reduce transaction and agency costs.
3. *Contrast the classical and contemporary models of managerial activities and roles.* Early classical models of management stressed the functions of planning, organizing, coordinating, deciding, and controlling. Contemporary research has examined the actual behavior of managers to show how managers get things done.
   Mintzberg found that managers' real activities are highly fragmented, variegated, and brief in duration, with managers moving rapidly and intensely from one issue to another. Other behavioral research has found that managers spend considerable time pursuing personal agendas and goals and that contemporary managers shy away from making grand, sweeping policy decisions.
4. *Describe how managers make decisions in organizations.* Decisions can be structured, semistructured, or unstructured, with structured decisions clustering at the operational level of the organization and unstructured decisions at the

strategic planning level. The nature and level of decision making are important factors in building information systems for managers.

Decision making itself is a complex activity at both the individual and the organizational levels. Individual models of decision making assume that human beings can accurately choose alternatives and consequences based on the priority of their objectives and goals. The rigorous rational model of individual decision making has been modified by behavioral research that suggests that rationality is limited. People select alternatives biased by their cognitive style and frame of reference. Organizational models of decision making illustrate that real decision making in organizations takes place in arenas where many psychological, political, and bureaucratic forces are at work. Thus, organizational decision making may not necessarily be rational.

5. *Evaluate the role of information systems in supporting various levels of business strategy.* A strategic information system changes the goals, operations, products, services, or environmental relationships of organizations to help them gain an edge over competitors. Information systems can be used to support strategy at the business, firm, and industry level. At the business level of strategy, information systems can be used to help firms become the low-cost producer, differentiate products, or serve new markets. Information systems can also be used to "lock in" customers and suppliers using efficient customer response and supply chain management applications. Value chain analysis is useful at the business level to highlight specific activities in the business where information systems are most likely to have a strategic impact.

At the firm level, information systems can be used to achieve new efficiencies or to enhance services by tying together the operations of disparate business units so that they can function as a whole or by promoting the sharing of knowledge across business units. At the industry level, systems can promote competitive advantage by facilitating cooperation with other firms in the industry, creating consortiums or communities for sharing information, exchanging transactions, or coordinating activities. The competitive forces model, information partnerships, and network economics are useful concepts for identifying strategic opportunities for systems at the industry level.

Not all strategic systems make a profit; they can be expensive and risky to build. Many strategic information systems are easily copied by other firms, so that strategic advantage is not always sustainable. Implementing strategic systems often requires extensive organizational change and a transition from one sociotechnical level to another. Such changes are called *strategic transitions* and are often difficult and painful to achieve.

## KEY TERMS

**Agency theory, 76**
**Behavioral models, 80**
**Bureaucracy, 70**
**Bureaucratic models of decision making, 84**
**Chief information officer (CIO), 75**
**Choice, 83**
**Classical model of management, 79**
**Cognitive style, 84**
**Competitive forces model, 93**
**Core competency, 93**
**Decisional roles, 93**
**Design, 83**
**Efficient customer response system, 90**
**End users, 75**
**Focused differentiation, 88**
**"Garbage can" model, 84**
**Implementation, 83**
**Information partnership, 93**
**Information systems department, 75**
**Information systems managers, 75**
**Informational roles, 81**
**Intelligence, 83**
**Interpersonal roles, 81**
**Intuitive decision makers, 84**
**Knowledge-level decision making, 82**
**Management control, 82**
**Managerial roles, 81**
**Microeconomic model of the firm, 76**
**Network economics, 95**
**Operational control, 82**
**Organization, 69**
**Organizational culture, 71**
**Organizational models of decision making, 84**
**Political models of decision making, 84**
**Primary activities, 86**
**Product differentiation, 87**
**Programmers, 75**
**Rational model, 83**
**Standard operating procedures (SOPs), 71**
**Strategic decision making, 82**
**Strategic information systems, 85**
**Strategic transitions, 95**
**Structured decisions, 82**
**Support activities, 86**
**Switching costs, 91**
**Systematic decision makers, 84**
**Systems analysts, 75**
**Transaction cost theory, 76**
**Unstructured decisions, 82**
**Value chain model, 86**
**Value web, 86**
**Virtual organization, 77**

## REVIEW QUESTIONS

1. What is an organization? Compare the technical definition of organizations with the behavioral definition.
2. What features do all organizations have in common? In what ways can organizations differ?
3. How has information technology infrastructure in organizations evolved over time?
4. How are information technology services delivered in organizations? Describe the role played by programmers, systems analysts, information systems managers, and the chief information officer (CIO).
5. Describe the major economic theories that help explain how information systems affect organizations.

6. Describe the major behavioral theories that help explain how information systems affect organizations.
7. Why is there considerable organizational resistance to the introduction of information systems?
8. Compare the descriptions of managerial behavior in the classical and behavioral models.
9. What specific managerial roles can information systems support? Where are information systems particularly strong in supporting managers, and where are they weak?
10. What are the four stages of decision making described by Simon?
11. Describe each of the organizational models of decision making. How would the design of systems be affected by the choice of model employed?
12. What is the impact of the Internet on organizations and the process of management?
13. What is a strategic information system? What is the difference between a strategic information system and a strategic-level system?
14. Describe appropriate models for analyzing strategy at the business level, and the types of strategies and information systems that can be used to compete at this level.
15. How can information system support strategies at the firm level?
16. How can the competitive forces, information partnerships, and network economics be used to identify strategies at the industry level?
17. Why are strategic information systems difficult to build?
18. How can managers find strategic applications in their firms?

## GROUP PROJECT

With a group of three or four students, select a company described in *The Wall Street Journal, Fortune, Forbes,* or another business publication. Visit the company's Web site to find out additional information about that company and to see how the firm is using the Web. On the basis of this information, analyze the business. Include a description of the organization's features, such as important business processes, culture, structure, and environment, as well as its business strategy. Suggest strategic information systems appropriate for that particular business, including those based on Internet technology, if appropriate. If possible, use electronic presentation software to present your findings to the class.

## TOOLS FOR INTERACTIVE LEARNING

### INTERNET CONNECTION

The Internet Connection for this chapter will take you to the WingspanBank.com Web site where you can see how one company used the Internet to create an entirely new type of business. You can complete an exercise for analyzing this Web site's capabilities and its strategic benefits. You can also use the Interactive Study Guide to test your knowledge of this chapter and get instant feedback where you need more practice.

### ELECTRONIC COMMERCE PROJECT

At the Laudon Web site for Chapter 3, you will find an Electronic Commerce project on competitive auto pricing and sales on the Web.

### CD-ROM

If you use the Multimedia Edition CD-ROM with this chapter, you will find an interactive exercise asking you to apply the correct model of organizational decision making to solve a series of problems. You can also find a video clip illustrating the role of information systems in Schneider National's organization, an audio overview of the major themes of this chapter, and bullet text summarizing the key points of the chapter.

## CASE STUDY *Rand McNally Maps Out a Trip to a Digital Future*

In 1856 William Rand and Andrew McNally founded a small printing shop in Chicago, which they called Rand McNally. The company did not begin printing maps until 1916, but it has been the leader in maps ever since, credited with creating the mapping conventions for our current numbered highway system. In 1924 Rand McNally published its first *Rand McNally Road Atlas.* The various versions of this atlas have sold 150 million copies in the years since, making it the all-time best selling map product from any publisher. Today Rand McNally has 1,200 employees, mostly at its Skokie, Illinois, headquarters.

Through the following decades the company continued to develop and maintain its position as the most well known and respected publisher of geographic and travel information. As recently as 1999 it sold 46 million maps, which accounted for more than half of all printed maps sold in the United States. Of course Rand McNally also produces many other products such as globes, a wide range of geographic educational materials, travel-planning software, and products for trucking fleet route planning and optimization. Its products are currently sold in more than 46,000 outlets, including 29 of its own retail stores.

As the digital economy developed at the beginning of the 1990s, Rand McNally's management did not understand the full impact of the new Internet and other computer-related developments. The company did respond to changing business conditions by producing travel and address location software it then sold on CD-ROMs. It also established a modest Web site in 1994 in order to support its customers' use of its CDs. However, the Internet soon offered many other opportunities, and Rand McNally failed to maintain its leadership and pioneering spirit.

AEA Investors purchased Rand McNally in 1997 expecting the company to modernize itself using new technologies such as the Internet. Despite new ownership and leadership, little changed as the company remained staid and unwilling to take risks, apparently because of fear of losing money. "We proposed putting maps on-line, but senior management was not interested," observed Jim Ferguson who later became director of product management for Rand McNally.com.

When they realized that nothing was changing, the investors intervened and, in July 1999, appointed Richard J. Davis as president and CEO. Davis already had 25 years of experience managing emerging high-tech companies, including seven years with Donnelley Cartographic Services and GeoSystems. (GeoSystems was the company that established MapQuest, Rand McNally's chief competitor in the new on-line environment.) Davis said his goal was to develop technology solutions and corporate growth rising above the historical 5 to 6 percent range.

Davis immediately brought in Chris Heivly to head up the recently created RandMcNally.com group. Heivly promptly put Rand McNally maps and address-to-address driving directions on the Web. Prior to the arrival of Davis and Heivly, management had feared that putting the company's maps on-line would undercut the sales of the company's traditional paper maps, something MapQuest, then still known as GeoSystems, had risked doing in 1996.

The most important goal of the new management was to transform Rand McNally from a map company into a travel planning and advisory service so that it would not become obsolete. Management plans included:

- Making Rand McNally's Web site indispensable to travelers.
- Updating map products for the fast-growing Net environment.
- Linking the company Web site and products to other services on the Net.
- Generating more bricks-and-mortar store business from Web site visitors.
- Remaining overwhelmingly a business-to-consumer company and not try to become a business-to-business company.

To accomplish these objectives, the company had to address two needs that all types of travelers experience: the need for quick information about travel conditions and recommendations on meeting those needs along the way. To accomplish this, the Web site must not only help travelers to plan the trip but travelers must also be able to bring the Internet with them as they travel. Travelers need on-line road maps, detailed driving instructions, and road condition updates while they are on the road, which means they will have to be delivered through wireless technology as soon as it matures. The Rand McNally Web site also needed to work with third parties to provide other travel information, such as timely weather and hotel reservations. The site also had to have a very user-friendly interface, one that could be used comfortably by people who are not highly skilled Internet users. Profitability remained a critical goal for both management and the investors. Profitability requires services that are good enough that customers will be willing to pay for them.

Rand McNally's main on-line competition was MapQuest whose Web site has been highly successful. In March 2000, the site had 5.5 million visitors who viewed and printed its electronic maps. During the same period Rand McNally had only 255,000 visitors. In addition MapQuest had partnered with many corporate and Internet business forces whose visitors need to use maps on their sites, for example to locate their stores. These giants include AOL, Excite, Yahoo, Ford, Wal-Mart and many, many others. "We put out more maps in 36 hours than are sold in the United States in a year," proclaimed MapQuest CEO Mike Mulligan. At the end of 1999, the company was sold to AOL for $1.1 billion.

Davis understood that he needed to shake up the very staid and conservative corporate culture dominating Rand McNally. He wanted to make the company agile again so it would be able to resume its leadership in the digital age. He tried to give all employees the feeling that they had a stake in the success of the entire company, both the print and digital arms. In the process he personally met with more than 900 employees to sell his vision of the company's future. He responded personally to e-mails he received from employees, and as he walked through the halls, he greeted employees by name. He also made opportunities for longtime employees to join the new Internet group, although few took advantage of the opportunity.

As Rand McNally tried to become a major force on the Internet, its advantages were clear. It was an old, very well known and highly respected name in the field of travel and maps. The company was profitable and, therefore, had income from existing sales, enabling it to take the necessary time and spend the needed funds to design and develop its new businesses. Some of the technology that Rand McNally wanted to use, such as wireless travel services, was still not well developed, so no company had yet achieved a genuine lead. Also the need for on-line maps to aid and orient people was growing extremely rapidly.

Heivly and Davis both believed that MapQuest had weaknesses, and these too were Rand McNally advantages. They believed that Rand McNally maps were more accurate than those of MapQuest. Moreover, they concluded, MapQuest driving instructions were overly detailed, contained much information that was out of date, and usually did not select the most appropriate route to travel. Nor, in their minds, did MapQuest have the reputation and respect of and the personal relationship with the American people that Rand McNally had. "We've been on the backseat of everyone's car in America," said Heivly.

Davis reorganized the company into three divisions: RandMcNally.com, a unit that services businesses, and a unit that services consumers. However, the key to the future in the eyes both of management and of the investors was Rand McNally.com. In order to break into the Internet competition and become a force rapidly, Davis decided to create an auto club similar to the American Automobile Association (AAA) with its more than 40 million members to entice Internet visitors to pay something for their use of the Rand McNally Web site. Management's expectation is that once customers pay for one service, they will be willing to pay for other products and services as well. The auto club was planned to provide standard services, including emergency roadside service and a network of repair shops. Rather than taking on AAA head on, management chose to create affinity groups such as recreational vehicle drivers and Corvette owner clubs. Management also wanted to create links for users while they were on the road using Net-capable mobile phones, car navigation systems, and other wireless devices when they become mature enough.

The Web site is linked to the RandMcNally.com store where visitors can purchase the more than 3,500 products that are sold in the bricks-and-mortar stores. Visitors can print customized free maps and address-to-address driving instructions. The "Plan a Trip" section has an improved ability to search out what travelers want on their trips. For example the site can answer such questions as "name art museums within 25 miles of the trip." Visitors can also store their personalized trip plans and information on-line. At the time of launching, the site carried information on more than 1,100 U.S. cities, 379 national parks, and 4,000 other points of interest and local events. The site also supplies continuously updated weather information and twice monthly updates on road construction projects that might interfere with travel. Finally, it contains trip-planning checklists as well as a section that offers materials and ideas on traveling with children.

The print products have been affected as well. The *Rand McNally Road Atlas* has changed its rear cover so that it no longer advertises other companies' products. It gave up the revenue in order to advertise its own Web site. A travel atlas for children is one of a number of new print products growing out of the development of its Web site. Rand McNally has also jumped into the GPS (global positioning system) market in a big way, selling GPS products to visitors who want to keep track of their current position for various reasons. For example, they sell a device that attaches to the Palm computer and another that attaches to a laptop PC. Both will pinpoint one's current location.

The early experience at Rand McNally is that the Web site is drawing more visitors. Consumers attracted to RandMcNally.com have also shown up at the firm's retail stores. But Rand McNally still has a long way to go to catch up to its more Net-savvy competitors. Has it found the right success formula for the Internet age?

**Sources:** Miguel Helft, "A Rough Road Trip to the Net," *The Industry Standard,* June 5, 2000; Bruce and Marge Brown, "Rand McNally TripMaker Deluxe 2000," *PC Magazine,* November 17, 2000; and Rand McNally press releases, http://www.randmcnally.com/rcm/company/, July 29, 1999; September 6, 2000; September 20, 2000; November 14, 2000.

### *CASE STUDY QUESTIONS*

1. Evaluate Rand McNally's use of the value chain and competitive forces models.
2. What was Rand McNally's business strategy? What were the causes, both internal and external, that caused Rand McNally to change this strategy?
3. What organization, management, and technology issues did the company face in attempting to change its business strategy?
4. Evaluate Rand McNally's new business strategy and the role of information systems in this strategy. Do you think it will prove to be successful?

chapter

# 4 The Digital Firm: Electronic Commerce and Electronic Business

objectives

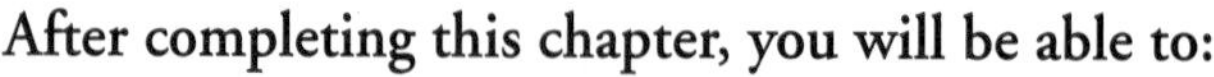

**After completing this chapter, you will be able to:**

1. *Explain how Internet technology has transformed organizations and business models.*
2. *Compare the categories of electronic commerce and describe how electronic commerce is changing consumer retailing and business-to-business transactions.*
3. *Evaluate the principal electronic payment systems.*
4. *Demonstrate how Internet technology can support electronic business and supply chain management.*
5. *Assess the managerial and organizational challenges posed by electronic commerce and electronic business.*

## SwissAir Takes Flight as a Digital Firm

Everyone realizes the airline business is fiercely competitive. Airlines compete on price, scheduling, and product. SwissAir has tried to pull ahead of the pack by focusing on customer care while reducing operating costs. Internet technology is making it possible to realize this strategy.

SwissAir's first Web site in 1995 was very static, providing basic flight and aircraft information on-line. Since then SwissAir has made many enhancements to the Web site and has enthusiastically embraced Internet business. Customers can now use the Web site to book and pay for airline tickets on-line, and check departures and arrivals. Top customers can bypass lines at the airport gate by checking in on the Web site up to 24 hours before their flight. Since implementing these features, SwissAir's sales have climbed steadily, especially among frequent business travelers who appreciate the convenience of booking and paying for their tickets on-line. SwissAir has found that its average price per on-line ticket is actually higher than the average ticket sold in person or over the telephone. Web site traffic has soared from 250,000 visitors per month to two million.

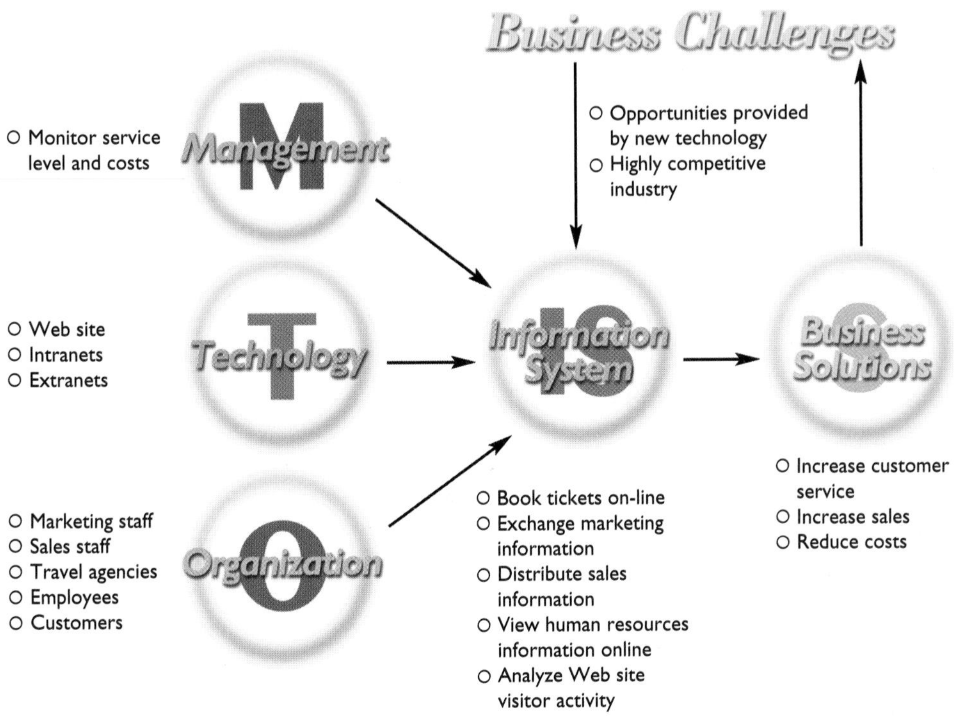


The company was so pleased by its e-commerce success that it is Internet-enabling its internal business processes. SwissAir set up corporate intranets for sales, marketing, and human resources and extended elements of these private intranets to its outside suppliers and partners. The marketing intranet provides new reports, tools, and design guidelines to help SwissAir's marketing staff in 150 cities improve their marketing campaigns. Marketing staff can exchange meeting minutes and presentations with its Qualiflyer Group, an alliance of 40 independent air carriers. SwissAir and its partners share information about upcoming marketing campaigns and try to develop similar themes and promotions.

SwissAir's sales intranet provides its salespeople with sales leads, statistics, libraries of best practices, access to incentive programs, discussion groups, and collaborative workspaces. The sales staff can use a Sales Ticket capability on the intranet to display bulletins about unfilled airplane seats around the world to their colleagues and travel agents who could help them fill those seats. SwissAir is providing travel agencies with fare data from its intranet. (Travel agents are an important source of SwissAir's business.) Data about fares that used to be distributed by paper can be electronically loaded from the intranet into the agents' own in-house information systems.

SwissAir's human resources intranet provides employees with updates of corporate policy, expense forms, job listings, and organization charts to help them work more efficiently and generate new ideas. About 90 percent of SwissAir's human resources forms are now available on its intranet.

**SwissAir Takes Flight as a Digital Firm**

**MANAGEMENT CHALLENGES**

SwissAir continues to make improvements to its Web site. The current upgrade enables visitors to redeem frequent flyer miles and features one-to-one marketing capabilities to recognize the customer every time that person visits the Web site. SwissAir can analyze Web site visitor activity to learn what customers are looking for on the Web. Andy Guenthard, SwissAir's general manager for electronic commerce, calls the Web site a "24 hours-per-day, seven-days-per-week focus group."

**Sources:** Gene Koprowski, "Taking Flight," *IQ Magazine*, September/October 2000; and Cheryl Rosen, "SwissAir Takes Customer Data Airborne," *Information Week*, November 20, 2000.

## MANAGEMENT CHALLENGES

Like SwissAir, many companies are starting to use the Internet to communicate with both their customers and suppliers, creating new digital electronic commerce networks that bypass traditional distribution channels. They are using Internet technology to streamline their internal business processes as well. Digitally enabling business processes and relationships with other organizations can help companies achieve new levels of competitiveness and efficiency, but they raise the following management challenges:

1. **Electronic commerce and electronic business require a complete change of mind-set.** Digital firms require new organizational designs and management processes. To implement electronic commerce and electronic business successfully, companies must examine, and perhaps redesign, an entire business process rather than throw new technology at existing business practices. Companies must consider a different organizational structure, changes in organizational culture, a different support structure for information systems, different procedures for managing employees and networked processing functions, and perhaps a different business strategy.

2. **Finding a successful Internet business model.** Companies have raced to put up Web sites in the hope of increasing earnings through electronic commerce. However, many, if not most, electronic commerce sites have yet to turn a profit or to make a tangible difference in firms' sales and marketing efforts. Cost savings or access to new markets promised by the Web may not materialize. Companies need to think carefully about whether they can create a genuinely workable business model on the Internet and how the Internet relates to their overall business strategy. Electronic commerce requires different strategies for ordering, advertising, and customer support than traditional ones (Chaudhury, Mallick, and Rao, 2001).

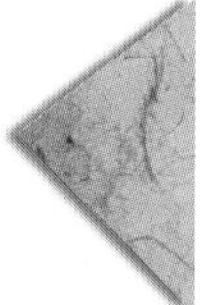

Internet technology is creating a universal technology platform for buying and selling goods and for driving important business processes inside the firm. It has inspired new ways of organizing and managing that are transforming businesses and the use of information systems in everyday life. Along with bringing many new benefits and opportunities, electronic commerce and electronic business have created a new set of management challenges. We describe these challenges so that organizations can understand the management, organization, and technology issues that must be addressed to benefit from electronic commerce, electronic business, and the emerging digital firm.

## 4.1 ELECTRONIC COMMERCE, ELECTRONIC BUSINESS, AND THE EMERGING DIGITAL FIRM

Throughout this edition, we emphasize the benefits of integrating information across the enterprise, creating an information technology infrastructure where information can flow seamlessly from one part of the organization to another and from the organization to its customers, suppliers, and business partners. The emerging digital firm requires this level of information integration, and companies increasingly depend on such an infrastructure today to remain efficient and competitive. Internet technology has emerged as the key enabling technology for digital integration.

## INTERNET TECHNOLOGY AND THE DIGITAL FIRM

For a number of years, companies used proprietary systems to integrate information from their internal systems and to link to their customers and trading partners. Such systems were expensive and based on technology standards that only a few could follow. The Internet is rapidly becoming the infrastructure of choice for electronic commerce, because it offers businesses an even easier way to link with other businesses and individuals at a very low cost. It provides a universal and easy-to-use set of technologies and technology standards that can be adopted by all organizations, no matter what computer system or information technology platform they are using.

Trading partners can directly communicate with each other, bypassing intermediaries and inefficient multilayered procedures. Web sites are available to consumers 24 hours a day. Some information-based products, such as software, music, and videos, can actually be physically distributed via the Internet. Vendors of other types of products and services can use the Internet to distribute the information surrounding their wares, such as product pricing, options, availability, and delivery time. The Internet can replace existing distribution channels or extend them, creating outlets for attracting and serving customers who otherwise would not patronize the company. For example, Web-based discount brokerages have attracted new customers who could not afford paying the high commissions and fees charged by conventional brokerage and financial services firms.

Companies can use Internet technology to radically reduce their transaction costs. Chapter 3 introduced the concept of transaction costs, which include the costs of searching for buyers and sellers, collecting information on products, negotiating terms, writing and enforcing contracts, and arranging transportation. Information on buyers, sellers, and prices for many products is immediately available on the Web. For example, manually processing a purchase order can cost $100 to $125, whereas purchasing goods via an Internet marketplace can reduce those costs by nearly 80 percent. Figure 4-1 provides other examples of transaction cost reductions from the Internet. Handling transactions electronically can reduce transaction costs and delivery time for some goods, especially those that are purely digital (such as software, text products, images, or videos) because these products can be distributed over the Internet as electronic versions.

Equally important, Internet technology is providing the infrastructure for electronic business because its technology and technology standards can also be used to make information flow seamlessly from one part of the organization to another. Internet technology provides a much lower cost and easier to use alternative for coordination activities than proprietary networks. Managers can use e-mail and other Internet communication capabilities to oversee large numbers of employees, to manage many tasks and subtasks in projects, and to coordinate the work of multiple teams working in different parts of the world. Internet standards can be used

**DISTRIBUTION SAVINGS ON E-GOODS IS DRAMATIC**

E-commerce Savings by Category

| | Traditional System | Internet | Percent Savings |
|---|---|---|---|
| Airline Tickets | $8 | $1 | 87% |
| Banking | $1.08 | $0.13 | 89% |
| Bill Payment | $2.22 to $3.32 | $0.65 to $1.10 | 71% to 67% |
| Term Life-Insurance Policy | $400 to $700 | $200 to $350 | 50% |
| Software | $15 | $0.20 to $0.50 | 97% to 99% |

SOURCE: OECD FROM VARIOUS INDUSTRY SOURCES

*Figure 4-1* Internet technology can radically reduce transaction costs in many industries.

*Source:* "Distribution Savings on E-Goods is Dramatic," from "Spotlight: The Economic Impact of E-Commerce," *The Industry Standard,* May 15, 1999. Reprinted by permission.

to link disparate systems, such as ordering and logistics tracking, that previously could not communicate with each other. The Internet also reduces other agency costs, such as the cost to coordinate activities of the firm with suppliers and other external business partners. The low-cost connectivity and universal standards provided by Internet technology are the driving force behind the explosion of electronic business and the emergence of the digital firm.

## NEW BUSINESS MODELS AND VALUE PROPOSITIONS

The Internet has introduced major changes in the way companies conduct business. It has brought about a dramatic drop in the cost of creating, sending, and storing information while making that information more widely available. Millions of people can exchange massive amounts of information directly, instantly, and almost for free.

In the past, information about products and services was usually tightly bundled with the physical value chain for those products and services. If a consumer wanted to find out about the features, price, and availability of a refrigerator or an automobile, for instance, that person had to visit a retail store that sold those products. The cost of comparison shopping was very high, because people had to physically travel from store to store.

The Internet has changed that relationship. Once everyone is connected electronically, information about products and services can flow on its own directly and instantly to consumers. The traditional link between the flow of the product and the flow of product-related information can be broken. Information is not limited to traditional physical methods of delivery. Customers can find out about products on their own on the Web and buy directly from product suppliers instead of using intermediaries, such as retail stores.

**business model**
An abstraction of what and how the enterprise delivers a product or service, showing how the enterprise creates wealth.

This unbundling of information from traditional value chain channels is having a disruptive effect on old business models and creating new business models as well. A **business model** describes how the enterprise delivers a product or service, showing how the enterprise creates wealth. Some of the traditional channels for exchanging product information have become unnecessary or uneconomical, and business models based on the coupling of information with products and services may no longer be necessary.

For example in pre-Internet retailing days, people who wanted to purchase books had to go to a physical bookstore in order to learn about what titles were available, the books' contents, and prices. The bookstore had a monopoly on this information. When Amazon.com opened as an on-line bookstore, it provided visitors to its Web site with a vast electronic catalog containing close to three million titles, along with tables of contents, reviews, and other information about those titles. People could order books directly from their desktop computers. Amazon.com was able to sell books at lower cost, because it did not have to pay rent, employee salaries, warehousing, and other overhead to maintain physical retail bookstores. (Amazon had almost no inventory costs, because it relied on book distributors to stock most of its books.) Traditional booksellers who maintained physical storefronts were threatened. Selling books and other goods directly to consumers on-line without using physical storefronts represents a new business model. Publishers are now challenging this business model by selling digital, electronic books directly to consumers without any intermediaries at all.

Financial service business models underwent a similar revolution. In the past, people wishing to purchase stocks or bonds had to pay high commissions to full-service brokers such as Merrill Lynch. Individual investors relied on these firms both to execute their trading transactions and to provide them with investment information. It was difficult for individual investors to obtain stock quotes, charts, investment news, historical data, investment advice, and other financial information on their own. Such information can now be found in abundance on the Web, and investors can use financial Web sites to place their own trades directly for very small transaction fees. The unbundling of financial information from trading has sharply reduced the need for full-service retail brokers.

**information asymmetry**
Situation in which the relative bargaining power of two parties in a transaction is determined by one party possessing more information essential to the transaction than the other party.

### The Changing Economics of Information

The Internet shrinks information asymmetry. An **information asymmetry** exists when one party in a transaction has more information that is important for the transaction than the other party. That information can determine relative bargaining power. For example, until auto retailing sites appeared on the Web, there was a pronounced information asymmetry

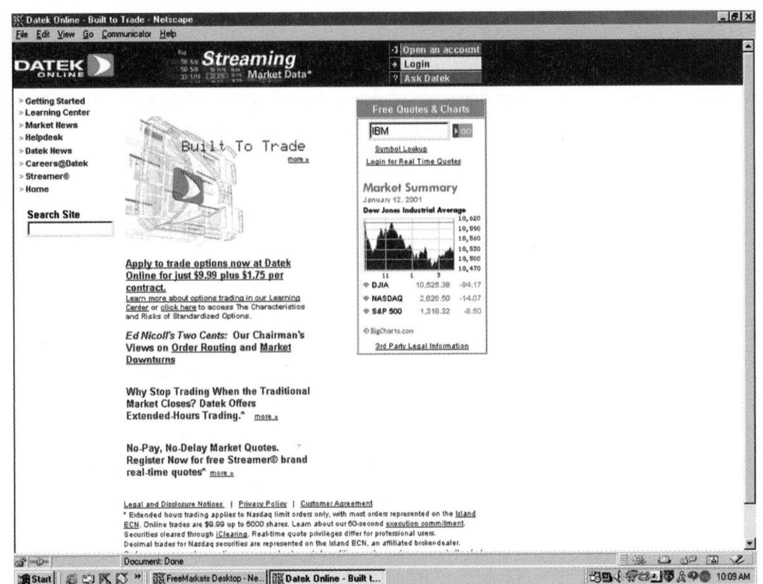


*Internet brokerage firms such as Datek Online deliver real-time market quotes and other investment information directly to users' desktops. Customers can place their own trades online for a fraction of the cost of using a traditional full-service broker.*

between auto dealers and customers. Only the auto dealers knew the manufacturers' prices, and it was difficult for consumers to shop around for the best price. Auto dealers' profit margins depended on this asymmetry of information. Now consumers have access to a legion of Web sites providing competitive pricing information, and the majority of auto buyers use the Internet to shop around for the best deal. Thus, the Web has reduced the information asymmetry surrounding an auto purchase. The Internet has also helped businesses seeking to purchase from other businesses to reduce information asymmetries and to locate better prices and terms.

Before the Internet, businesses had to make trade-offs between the richness and reach of their information. **Richness** refers to the depth and detail of information—the amount of information the business can supply to the customer as well as information the business collects about the customer. **Reach** refers to how many people a business can connect with and how many products it can offer those people. Rich communication occurs, for example, when a sales representative meets with a customer, sharing information that is very specific to that interaction. Such an interaction is very expensive for a business, because it can only take place with a small audience. Newspaper and television ads can reach millions of people quite inexpensively, but the information they provide is much more limited. It used to be prohibitively expensive for traditional businesses to have both richness and reach. Few, if any, companies could afford to provide highly detailed, customized information to a large mass audience. The Internet has transformed the richness and reach relationship (see Figure 4-2). Using the Internet and Web multimedia capabilities, companies can quickly and inexpensively provide detailed product information and detailed information specific to each customer to very large numbers of people simultaneously (Evans and Wurster, 2000).

Internet-enabled relationships between richness and reach are changing internal operations as well. Organizations can now exchange rich, detailed information among large numbers of people, making it easier for management to coordinate more jobs and tasks. In the past, management's span of control had to be much narrower because rich communication could only be channeled among a few people at a time using cumbersome manual paper-based processes. Digitally-enabled business processes have become new sources organizational efficiency, reducing operating costs while improving the accuracy and timeliness of customer service.

**richness**
Measurement of the depth and detail of information that a business can supply to the customer as well as information the business collects about the customer.

**reach**
Measurement of how many people a business can connect with and how many products it can offer those people.

Richness
New levels of richness and reach attainable
ENABLERS
• Explosion of connectivity
• Dissemination of standards
Reach

***Figure 4-2*** The changing economics of information. In the past, companies have had to trade off between the richness and reach of their information. Internet connectivity and universal standards for information sharing radically lower the cost of providing rich, detailed information to large numbers of people, reducing the trade-off.

Reprinted by permission of Harvard Business School Press. From: *Blown to Bits: How The New Economics of Information Transforms Strategy* by Philip B. Evans and Thomas Wurster. Boston, MA 2000, pp. 31. Copyright © 2000 by Harvard Business School Press.

## Internet Business Models

The Internet can help companies create and capture profit in new ways by adding extra value to existing products and services or by providing the foundation for new products and services. Table 4-1 describes some of the most important Internet business models that have emerged. All in one way or another add value: They provide the customer with a new product or service; they provide additional information or service along with a traditional product or service; or they provide a product or service at a much lower cost than traditional means.

Some of these new business models take advantage of the Internet's rich communication capabilities. eBay is an on-line auction forum, using e-mail and other interactive features of the Web. People can make on-line bids for items, such as computer equipment, antiques and collectibles, wine, jewelry, rock concert tickets, and electronics, that are posted by sellers

**TABLE 4-1 INTERNET BUSINESS MODELS**

| Category | Description | Examples |
|---|---|---|
| Virtual storefront | Sells physical goods or services on-line instead of through a physical storefront or retail outlet. Delivery of nondigital goods and services takes place through traditional means. | Amazon.com<br>Wine.com<br>WingspanBank.com |
| Marketplace concentrator | Concentrates information about products and services from multiple providers at one central point. Purchasers can search, comparison-shop, and sometimes complete the sales transaction. | ShopNow.com<br>DealerNet<br>Industrial Mall<br>InsureMarket |
| On-line exchange | Bid–ask system where multiple buyers can purchase from multiple sellers. | Asia Capacity Exchange<br>Covisint<br>E-Steel<br>Fibermarket |
| Information broker | Provides product, pricing, and availability information. Some facilitate transactions, but their main value is the information they provide. | PartNet<br>Travelocity |
| Transaction broker | Buyers can view rates and terms, but the primary business activity is to complete the transaction. | E*TRADE<br>Ameritrade |
| Auction | Provides electronic clearinghouse for products where price and availability are constantly changing, sometimes in response to customer actions. | eBay<br>Ubid<br>BigEquip.com |
| Reverse auction | Consumers submit a bid to multiple sellers to buy goods or services at a buyer-specified price. | Priceline.com<br>ImportQuote.com |
| Aggregator | Groups of people who want to purchase a particular product sign up and then seek a volume discount from vendors. | MobShop.com |
| Digital product delivery | Sells and delivers software, multimedia, and other digital products over the Internet. | Regards.com<br>PhotoDisc |
| Content provider | Creates revenue by providing content. The customer may pay to access the content, or revenue may be generated by selling advertising space or by having advertisers pay for placement in an organized listing in a searchable database. | Wall Street Journal Interactive<br>Salon.com<br>TheStreet.com |
| On-line service provider | Provides service and support for hardware and software users. | PCSupport.com<br>@Backup<br>Xdrive.com |
| Virtual community | Provides on-line meeting place where people with similar interests can communicate and find useful information. | Geocities<br>FortuneCity<br>Tripod |
| Portal | Provides initial point of entry to the Web along with specialized content and other services. | Yahoo<br>Barrabas |
| Syndicator | Aggregates content or applications from multiple sources and resells them to other companies. | Thinq<br>Screaming Media |

from around the world. The system accepts bids for items entered on the Internet, evaluates the bids, and notifies the highest bidder. eBay collects a small commission on each listing and sale.

Business-to-business auctions are proliferating as well. BigEquip.com has Web-based auction services for business-to-business sales of used construction equipment. Many business-to-business sites have sprung up to help companies dispose of surplus inventory. On-line bidding, also known as **dynamic pricing,** is expected to grow rapidly, representing as much as 40 percent of total on-line transactions by 2004, because buyers and sellers can interact so easily through the Internet to determine what an item is worth at any particular moment (Dalton, 1999).

**dynamic pricing**
Pricing of items based on real-time interactions between buyers and sellers that determine what an item is worth at any particular moment.

The Internet has created on-line communities, where people with similar interests can exchange ideas from many different locations. Some of these virtual communities are providing the foundation for new businesses. Tripod, Geocities, and FortuneCity (which started out in the United Kingdom) provide communities for people wishing to communicate with others about arts, careers, health and fitness, sports, business, travel, and many other interests. Members can post their own personal Web pages, participate in on-line discussion groups, and join on-line "clubs" with other like-minded people. A major source of revenue for these communities is providing ways for corporate clients to target customers, including the placement of banner ads on their Web sites. A **banner ad** is a graphic display on a Web page used for advertising. The banner is linked to the advertiser's Web site so that a person clicking on the banner will be transported to a Web page with more information about the advertiser.

**banner ad**
Graphic display on a Web page used for advertising. The banner is linked to the advertiser's Web site so that a person clicking on it will be transported to the advertiser's Web site.

Even traditional retailing businesses are enhancing their Web sites with chat, message boards, and community-building features as a means of encouraging customers to spend more time, return more frequently, and hopefully make more purchases on-line. For example, iGo.com, a Web site selling mobile computing technology, found that its average sales shot up more than 50 percent after it added the ability to communicate interactively on-line with customer service representatives (Bannan, 2000).

The Web's information resources are so vast and rich that special business models called **portals** have emerged to help individuals and organizations locate information more efficiently. A portal is a Web site or other service that provides an initial point of entry to the Web or to internal company data. Yahoo is an example. It provides a directory of information on the Internet along with news, sports, weather, telephone directories, maps, games, shopping, e-mail, and other services. There are also specialized portals to help users with specific interests. For example, Barrabas is a bilingual portal for mountaineering and snow sports featuring weather reports, ski trail reports, a magazine, expert reviews, advice, instruction, and on-line

**portal**
Web site or other service that provides an initial point of entry to the Web or to internal company data.

*Fortune City is an Internet business based on on-line communities for people sharing similar interests, such as sports, health, or music. The company generates revenue from advertising banners on its Web pages.*

shopping for 14,000 items of skiing and mountaineering gear. (Companies are also building their own internal portals to provide employees with streamlined access to corporate information resources—see Chapter 12.)

Yahoo and other portals and Web content sites often combine content and applications from many different sources and service providers. Other Internet business models use syndication as well to provide additional value. For example, E*TRADE, the discount Web trading site, purchases most of its content from outside sources such as Reuters (news), Bridge Information Systems (quotes), and BigCharts.com (charts). Companies can also purchase electronic commerce services such as shopping cart ordering and payment systems from syndicators to use on their Web sites. On-line **syndicators** who aggregate content or applications from multiple sources, package them for distribution, and resell them to third-party Web sites have emerged as another new Internet business model (Werbach, 2000). The Web makes it much easier for companies to aggregate, repackage, and distribute information and information-based services.

**syndicator**
Business aggregating content or applications from multiple sources, packaging them for distribution, and reselling them to third-party Web sites.

Chapter 6 describes application service providers who provide software that runs over the Web. *Virtual desktop* services that provide on-line calendars, calculators, address books, word processing, and other office-productivity software, as well as facilities to store users' data on remote computers, are proliferating.

Most of the business models described in Table 4-1 are called **pure-play** business models, because they are based purely on the Internet. These firms did not have an existing bricks-and-mortar business when they designed their Internet business. However, many existing retail firms such as L.L. Bean, Office Depot, R.E.I., or The Wall Street Journal have developed Web sites as extensions of their traditional bricks-and-mortar businesses. Such businesses represent a hybrid **clicks-and-mortar** business model.

**pure-play**
Business model based solely on the Internet.

**clicks-and-mortar**
Business model where the Web site is an extension of a traditional bricks-and-mortar businesses.

## 4.2 ELECTRONIC COMMERCE

Although most commercial transactions still take place through conventional channels, rising numbers of consumers and businesses are using the Internet for electronic commerce. Projections show that by 2004, more than 640 million people, representing 14 percent of the world's population, will be active Internet users, and total e-commerce spending could reach $3 trillion to $4 trillion (Enos, 2000).

### CATEGORIES OF ELECTRONIC COMMERCE

There are alternative ways in which electronic commerce transactions can be classified. One is by looking at the nature of the participants in the electronic commerce transaction. The three major electronic commerce categories are business-to-consumer e-commerce (B2C), business-to-business e-commerce (B2B), and consumer-to-consumer electronic commerce (C2C).

- **Business-to-consumer (B2C) electronic commerce** involves retailing products and services to individual shoppers. Barnes&Noble.com, which sells books, software, and music to individual consumers, is an example of B2C e-commerce.
- **Business-to-business (B2B) electronic commerce** involves the sales of goods and services among businesses. Milpro.com, Milacron Inc.'s Web site for selling cutting tools, grinding wheels, and metal working fluids to more than 100,000 small machining businesses, is an example of B2B e-commerce.
- **Consumer-to-consumer (C2C) electronic commerce** involves consumers selling directly to other consumers. For example, eBay, the giant Web auction site, allows people to sell their goods to other consumers by auctioning them off to the highest bidder.

**business-to-consumer (B2C) electronic commerce**
Electronic retailing of products and services directly to individual consumers.

**business-to-business (B2B) electronic commerce**
Electronic sales of goods and services among businesses.

**consumer-to-consumer (C2C) electronic commerce**
Consumers selling goods and services electronically to other consumers.

Another way of classifying electronic commerce transactions is in terms of the participants' physical connection to the Web. Until recently, almost all e-commerce transactions took place over wired networks. Now cell phones and other wireless handheld digital appliances are Internet enabled so that they can be used to send e-mail or access Web sites. Companies are rushing to offer new sets of Web-based products and services that can be accessed by these wireless devices. For example, in Britain, customers of Virgin Mobile can use their cell phones to browse Virgin's Web site and purchase compact disks, wine, TV sets, and washing machines. Swedish mobile phone users can track stocks and receive travel information by linking to special Web sites providing wireless services. The use of handheld wireless devices for purchasing goods and services has been termed **mobile commerce** or **m-commerce.** Both business-to-business and business-to-consumer e-commerce transactions can take place using m-commerce technology. Chapter 9 discusses m-commerce and wireless Web technology in detail.

**mobile commerce (m-commerce)**
The use of wireless devices, such as cell phones or handheld digital information appliances, to conduct e-commerce transactions over the Internet.

## CUSTOMER-CENTERED RETAILING

The Internet provides companies with new channels of communication and interaction that can create closer yet more cost-effective relationships with customers in sales, marketing, and customer support. Companies can use the Web to provide ongoing information, service, and support, creating positive interactions with customers that can serve as the foundation for long-term relationships and encourage repeat purchases.

### Direct Sales over the Web

Manufacturers can sell their products and services directly to retail customers, bypassing intermediaries such as distributors or retail outlets. Eliminating intermediaries in the distribution channel can significantly reduce purchase transaction costs. Operators of virtual storefronts, such as Amazon.com or Wine.com, do not have large expenditures for rent, sales staff, and the other operations associated with a traditional retail store. Airlines can sell tickets directly to passengers through their own Web sites or through travel sites such as Travelocity without paying commissions to travel agents.

To pay for all the steps in a traditional distribution channel, a product may have to be priced as high as 135 percent of its original cost to manufacture (Mougayar, 1998). Figure 4-3 illustrates how much savings can result from eliminating each of these layers in the distribution process. By selling directly to consumers or reducing the number of intermediaries, companies can achieve higher profits while charging lower prices. The elimination of organizations or business process layers responsible for intermediary steps in a value chain is called **disintermediation.**

**disintermediation**
The elimination of organizations or business process layers responsible for certain intermediary steps in a value chain.

The Internet is accelerating disintermediation in some industries and creating opportunities for new types of intermediaries in others. In certain industries, distributors with warehouses of goods, or intermediaries such as real estate agents, may be replaced by new intermediaries or "infomediaries" specializing in helping Internet users efficiently obtain product and price information, locate on-line sources of goods and services, or manage or maximize the value of the information captured about them in electronic commerce transactions

*Figure 4-3* The benefits of disintermediation to the consumer. The typical distribution channel has several intermediary layers, each of which adds to the final cost of a product, such as a sweater. Removing layers lowers the final cost to the consumer.

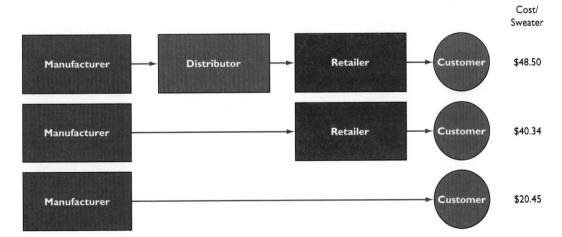

(Hagel III and Singer, 1999). The information brokers listed in Table 4-1 are examples. The process of shifting the intermediary function in a value chain to a new source is called **reintermediation.**

**reintermediation**
The shifting of the intermediary role in a value chain to a new source.

## Interactive Marketing and Personalization

Marketers can use the interactive features of Web pages to hold consumers' attention or to capture detailed information about their tastes and interests for one-to-one marketing (see Chapter 3). Web sites have become a bountiful source of detailed information about customer behavior, preferences, needs, and buying patterns that companies can use to tailor promotions, products, services, and pricing. Some customer information may be obtained by asking visitors to "register" on-line and provide information about themselves, but many companies are also collecting customer information by using software tools that track the activities of Web site visitors. Companies can use special Web site auditing software capable of tracking the number of times visitors request Web pages, the Web pages of greatest interest to visitors after they have entered the sites, and the paths visitors followed as they clicked from Web page to Web page. Companies then can analyze this information about customer interests and behavior to develop more precise profiles of existing and potential customers.

For instance, TravelWeb, a Web site offering electronic information on more than 16,000 hotels in 138 countries and an on-line reservation capability, tracks the origin of each user and the screens and Web page links he or she uses to learn about customer preferences. The Hyatt hotel chain found that Japanese users are most interested in the resort's golf facilities, valuable information in shaping market strategies and for developing hospitality-related products.

Communications and product offerings can be tailored precisely to individual customers. Generic Web sites that force users to wade through options and content that are irrelevant to

## MANAGEMENT DECISION PROBLEM

### MEASURING THE EFFECTIVENESS OF WEB ADVERTISING

You head an Internet company called Baby Boomers On-line, which features articles of interest to people age 40 to 60 on subjects such as travel, discount shopping, health, and financial planning and links to Web sites selling related products and services. Your revenue comes from banner ads, which other companies place on your Web site for a fee. You would like to generate more revenue by raising your advertising rates. You can do this by increasing the quantity and quality of visitors to your site in order to justify charging more for ads placed there. One way to measure the success of ads placed on a Web site is by measuring the *click-through rate,* which is the percentage of ads that Web visitors viewed on a Web page and then clicked on to explore. Software on the computer running your Web site provided the following weekly report.

**Web Usage Report for the Week Ending February 16, 2001**

| Ad Title | Ad Views | Ad Clicks | Click-through Rate (%) |
|---|---|---|---|
| Soy Foods and Vitamins | 321 | 19 | |
| Budget Trips Inc. | 674 | 228 | |
| Budget Books On-line | 79 | 5 | |
| No-Frills Getaways | 945 | 311 | |
| Computers for Less | 118 | 5 | |
| Boomer Financial Planners Inc. | 63 | 16 | |

1. Calculate the click-through rate (expressed as a percentage) for each ad by dividing the number of ad clicks by the number of ad views. *Ad clicks* are the number of times a visitor clicks on a banner ad to access the advertiser's Web site. *Ad views* are the number of times visitors call up a page with a banner during a specific time period, such as a day or a week. Rank-order the ads with the highest click-through rates.
2. What categories of ads are the most successful at your Web site? Least successful? Using this information, what kinds of companies should you be soliciting as advertisers on your site?
3. According to industry news sources, more than 27 percent of the visitors to the Travelocity Web site were age 50 or older, as were more than 31 percent of the visitors to Priceline.com, which offers discount airline tickets. How can you use this information to increase click-throughs and revenues at your own Web site?

them are considered frustrating. Firms can create unique personalized Web sites that display content or ads for products or services of special interest to each user, improving the customer's experience and creating additional value (see Figure 4-4). By using **Web personalization** technology to modify the Web pages presented to each customer, marketers can achieve the benefits of using individual salespeople at dramatically lower costs. Personalization can also help firms form lasting relationships with customers by providing individualized content, information, and services. Here are some examples:

*Figure 4-4* Firms can create unique personalized Web sites that display content or ads for products or services of special interest to individual users, improving the customer experience and creating additional value.

**Web personalization**
The tailoring of Web content directly to a specific user.

- Amazon.com retains information on each customer's purchases. When a customer returns to the Amazon.com Web site, that person will be greeted with a Web page recommending books based on that person's purchase history or past purchases of other buyers with similar histories.
- American Airlines is using personalization to reduce its cost structure by encouraging customers to manage their frequent flyer accounts and purchase tickets through its Web site instead of from a travel agent. American Airlines can create individual "travel agencies" for its customers on the Web, informing them, for example, that if they take one more domestic flight this year, they can achieve platinum frequent flyer status next year. American expects to sell $500 million worth of tickets from its Web site.
- Dell Computer allows users to create their own personal "Dell sites," where Dell can offer them special prices and deals based on the information they provide about their interests and computing requirements. Users can buy exactly what they want without having to call a representative, hunt down the products available, and try to work out deals.

Many other Web sites are using personalization technologies to deliver Web pages with content and banner ads geared to the specific interests of the visitor. Chapters 9, 13, and 15

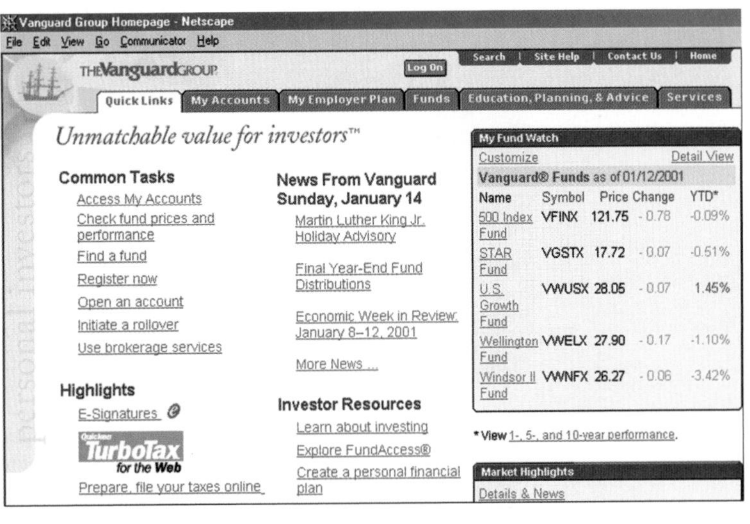


*Web sites can tailor their content to the specific interests of individual visitors. The Vanguard Group home page can be personalized to display mutual fund information of special interest to the user.*

describe additional technologies that gather the information on Web site visitors to make such personalized advertising and customer interaction possible. They also describe how companies are trying to combine Web visitor data with customer data from other sources such as off-line purchases, customer service records, or product registrations to create detailed profiles of individuals. Critics worry that companies gathering so much personal information on Web site visitors pose a threat to individual privacy, especially when much of this information is gathered without the customer's knowledge. Chapter 15 provides a detailed discussion of Web site privacy issues raised by these practices.

The cost of customer surveys and focus groups is very high. Learning how customers feel or what they think about one's products or services through electronic visits to Web sites is much cheaper. Web sites providing product information also lower costs by shortening the sales cycle and reducing the amount of time sales staff must spend in customer education. The Web shifts more marketing and selling activities to the customer, because customers fill out their own on-line order forms. By using the Web to provide vendors with more precise information about their preferences and suggestions for improving products and services, customers are being transformed from passive buyers to active participants in creating value (Prahalad and Ramaswamy, 2000).

## M-Commerce and Next Generation Marketing

Within the next few years, the Web will be accessible from almost anywhere, as consumers turn to wireless telephones, handheld digital appliances, interactive television, or other information appliances to link to the Internet. Chapter 9 discusses m-commerce and new wireless Internet devices in greater detail. Travelers will be able to access the Internet in automobiles, airports, hotels, and train stations. Mobile commerce will provide businesses with additional channels for reaching customers and with new opportunities for personalization. Location tracking software in some of these devices will enable businesses to track users' movements and supply information, advertisements, and other services while they are on the go, such as local weather reports or directions to the nearest restaurant. Instead of focusing on how to bring a customer to a Web site, marketing strategies will shift to finding ways of bringing the message directly to the customer at the point of need (Kenny and Marshall, 2000). Figure 4-5 illustrates how personalization can be extended via the ubiquitous Internet and m-commerce.

*Figure 4-5* Customer personalization with the ubiquitous Internet. Companies can use mobile, wireless devices to deliver new, value-added services directly to customers at any time and place, extending personalization and deepening the relationship.

| Target | Platform | When | Content and Service |
|---|---|---|---|
| Traveler | Computer-equipped car  | Whenever car is moving | Provide maps, driving directions, weather reports, ads for nearby restaurants and hotels. |
| Parent | Cell phone  | During school days | Notify about school-related closings:<br>Hello, Caroline. Your children's school is closing early.<br>Press 1 for closure reason<br>Press 2 for weather reports<br>Press 3 for traffic reports |
| Stock Broker | Pager  | During trading days. Notify if unusually high trading volume. | Summary portfolio analysis showing changes in positions for each holding. |

## Customer Self-Service

The Web and other network technologies are inspiring new approaches to customer service and support. Many companies are using their Web sites and e-mail to answer customer questions or to provide customers with helpful information. The Web provides a medium through which customers can interact with the company, at their convenience, and find information on their own that previously required a human customer support expert. Automated self-service or other Web-based responses to customer questions cost one-tenth the price of a live customer service representative on the telephone.

Companies are realizing substantial cost savings from Web-based customer self-service applications. American, Northwest, and other major airlines have created Web sites where customers can review flight departure and arrival times, seating charts, and airport logistics, check frequent-flyer miles, and purchase tickets on-line. Yamaha Corporation of America has reduced customer calls concerning questions or problems by allowing customers to access technical solutions information from the service and support area of its Web site. If customers can't find answers on their own, they can send e-mail to a live technician. Chapter 1 described how customers of UPS can use its Web site to track shipments, calculate shipping costs, determine time in transit, and arrange for a package pickup. FedEx and other package delivery firms provide similar Web-based services.

New products are even integrating the Web with customer call centers, where customer service problems have been traditionally handled over the telephone. A **call center** is an organizational department responsible for handling customer service issues by telephone and other channels. For example, visitors can click on a "push to talk" link on the Lands' End Web site that lets a user request a phone call. The user enters his or her telephone number and a call-center system directs a customer service representative to place a voice telephone call to the user's phone. Some systems also let the customer interact with a service representative by entering questions on the Web while talking on the phone at the same time.

**call center**
An organizational department responsible for handling customer service issues by telephone and other channels.

## BUSINESS-TO-BUSINESS ELECTRONIC COMMERCE: NEW EFFICIENCIES AND RELATIONSHIPS

The fastest growing area of electronic commerce is not retailing to individuals but the automation of purchase and sale transactions from business to business. Some analysts estimate that B2B transactions represent 80 percent of all e-commerce transactions and could represent as much as 87 percent by 2004. That year worldwide B2B e-commerce revenues could reach nearly $2.8 trillion (Enos, 2000). For a number of years, companies have used proprietary electronic data interchange (EDI) systems for this purpose; now they are turning to the Web and Internet technology. By eliminating inefficient, paper-based processes for locating suppliers, ordering supplies, or delivering goods, and by providing more opportunities for finding the lowest priced products and services, business-to-business Web sites can save participants anywhere from 5 to 45 percent. B2B commerce can also reduce errors in commerce-related documents from 20 percent down to less than 1 percent (Keen, 2000).

Corporate purchasing traditionally has been based on long-term relationships with one or two suppliers. The Internet makes information about alternative suppliers more accessible so that companies can find the best deal from a wide range of sources, including those overseas. A purchasing manager might consult the Web when he or she needs to buy from an unfamiliar supplier or locate a new type of part. Identifying and researching potential trading partners is one of the most popular procurement activities on the Internet. Suppliers themselves can use the Web to research competitors' prices on-line. Organizations also can use the Web to solicit bids from suppliers on-line. Table 4-2 describes some examples of business-to-business electronic commerce.

For business-to-business electronic commerce, companies can use their own Web sites, like Alliant Exchange, or they can conduct sales through Web sites set up as on-line marketplaces. On-line marketplaces, also termed **electronic hubs** or *e-hubs* represent some of the new Internet business models we introduced earlier in this chapter. Using on-line marketplaces, companies can link up to many buyers without having to create point-to-point connections to each and can potentially find new customers. Many marketplaces have capabilities

**electronic hub (e-hub)**
On-line business-to-business marketplace.

## TABLE 4-2 EXAMPLES OF BUSINESS-TO-BUSINESS ELECTRONIC COMMERCE

| Business | Electronic Commerce Applications |
|---|---|
| HealthSouth Corporation | Uses the MedCenterDirect.com Web system to purchase supplies from many different vendors, track inventories, and monitor spending electronically. HealthSouth can use MedCenterDirect.com's SmartOrder system to track supplies on-line and link their inventory data with scheduling. The system also helps HealthSouth make sure each of its 2,000 locations purchases from preferred suppliers by flagging noncontract items. |
| U.S. General Services Administration | The procurement arm of the U.S. federal government created an ordering system called GSA Advantage, which allows federal agencies to buy everything through its Web site. The Web site lists more than 220,000 products. By using the Web, agencies can see all of their purchasing options and make choices based on price and delivery. |
| Alliant Exchange | Alliant built a Web-based system called AlliantLink.com that allows its 100,000 customers, who are primarily restaurant personnel, to order from its catalog of 180,000 products. Chefs can use Alliant.Link.com to reserve meat, potatoes, cookware, and other food and restaurant supplies and have them delivered by the following day. |
| General Electric Information Services | Operates a Trading Process Network (TPN) where GE and other subscribing companies can solicit and accept bids from selected suppliers over the Internet. TPN is a secure Web site developed for internal GE use that now is available to other companies for customized bidding and automated purchasing. GE earns revenue by charging subscribers for the service and by collecting a fee from the seller if a transaction is completed. |

for integrating product information stored in disparate vendor systems. Companies purchasing products don't have to manage four or five different systems for buying from various suppliers and can save money by comparing prices and purchasing from a wide range of companies (Dalton, 1999).

**exchange**
Type of on-line marketplace where multiple buyers can purchase from multiple sellers using a bid–ask system.

One type of on-line marketplace called an exchange has attracted special interest, because so many businesses are turning to Internet exchanges to automate their purchases and sales. **Exchanges** are on-line marketplaces where multiple buyers can purchase from multiple sellers using a bid–ask system (see Figure 4-6). E-Steel is an example. Buyers log in and create inquiries, specifying details, terms, and suppliers for the steel they wish to purchase. Suppliers respond with specifications for their wares. Buyers can also search for certain types of steel, solicit bids, and negotiate on-line with suppliers. There are several categories of exchanges. *Vertical exchanges,* also known as industry exchanges, are set up to service specific industries, such as the automobile, forest products, or energy industries. Vertical exchanges are also available for the chemical and plastic, machine tool, telecommunications, paper, and loan and mortgage industries. E-Steel is a vertical exchange for the metals industry. *Horizontal exchanges* focus on specific functions that can be found in many different industries, such as purchasing office equipment or maintenance, repair, and operating (MRO) supplies. MRO.com is an example. Companies can also create their own private exchanges, called *branded exchanges,* in order to add value for customers by providing marketplace services. For example, Cable & Wireless Hong Kong Telecom (CWHKT), a full-service communications provider, created an exchange for the Greater China region. The exchange provides services for increasing purchasing and supply chain efficiencies for a broad range of industries.

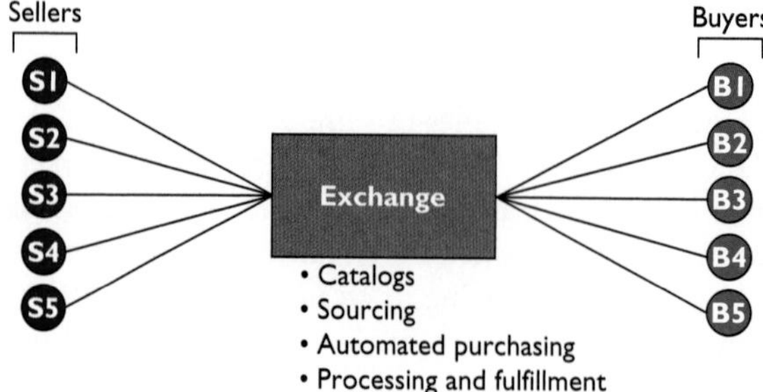


*Figure 4-6* Exchanges are on-line marketplaces where multiple buyers can purchase from multiple sellers using a bid–ask system.

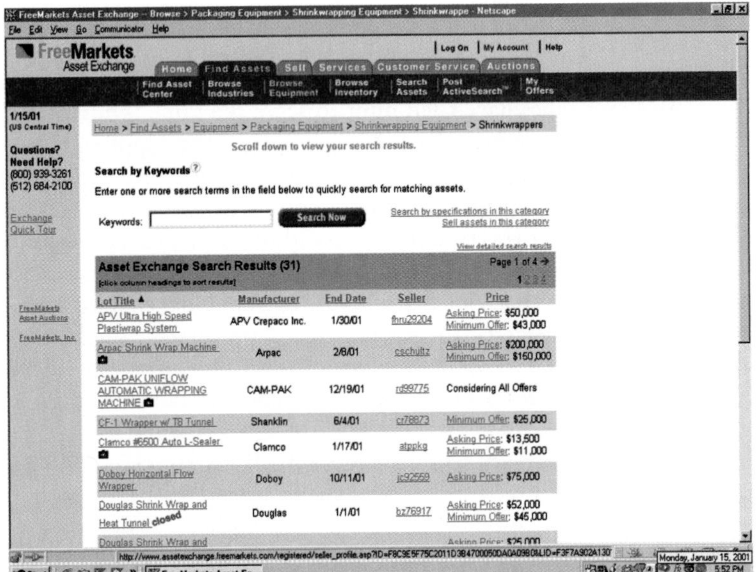


*Free Markets Inc. runs an on-line Asset Exchange where buyers and sellers can negotiate asset sales on-line.*

By enabling buyers and sellers to share information about supply, demand, and production, exchanges can sharply reduce inefficiencies among all the participants in the supply chain—suppliers, manufacturers, distributors, logistics companies, and even billing companies. Figure 4-7 shows how the business processes for procuring recovered paper in the forest products industry became more streamlined by using Fibermarket, an exchange for the forest products industry. To sell recovered paper (wastepaper), for example, suppliers would first use the telephone or fax on a daily, weekly, or monthly basis to source mill capacity and determine into what paper mills to sell. They would then arrange a carrier, negotiate price, schedule shipments, fill out bills of lading, and bill the customer. The customer would reconcile the receipt of goods against a mill receiving report. Using Fibermarket, all of these

***Figure 4-7*** Before–after diagram of change in procurement of recovered paper. Fibermarket is an e-marketplace for forest products, such as paper, pulp, recovered fiber, solid wood, and related building products. All supply chain participants, including suppliers, manufacturers, distributors, logistics companies, and billing companies can perform more efficiently by automatically accessing the information they need when they need it. Instead of linear one-way communication, all participants have a 360-degree, many-to-many view. This exchange reduces the time and costs involved in purchasing and selling pulp and recovered fiber.

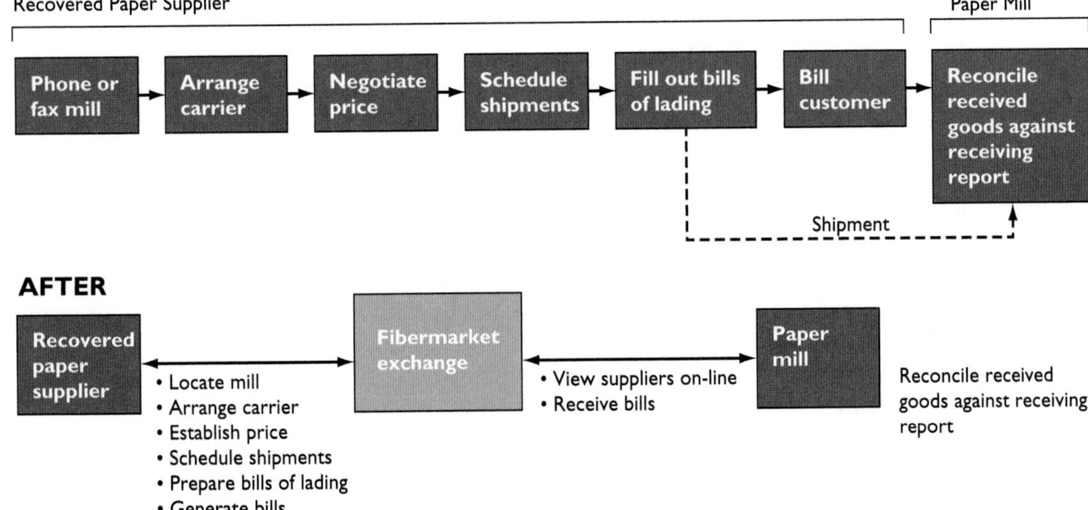

steps can take place automatically. Orders are brokered and prices set on-line, and participants have a real-time view of supply and demand.

Exchanges are proliferating, but analysts believe that many cannot be sustained. Numerous exchanges have been built to serve the same industry and not all can survive. Exchanges facilitate competitive bidding among many suppliers to provide purchasers with the lowest price. Suppliers may be reluctant to participate in exchanges if their profit margins erode. Moreover, companies, especially those with lean production systems, must consider the timing of deliveries, customization, and other factors besides price when making purchases. Most B2B exchanges support relatively simple transactions that cannot address these complexities (Wise and Morrison, 2000). Realizing benefits from more sophisticated B2B services requires changes to organizational processes, culture and behavior (Andrew, Blackburn and Sirkin, 2000). The Window on Organizations explores some of the challenges facing exchanges as they struggle to become sustainable business models.

## The Digital Firm in Action: Marshall Industries' Virtual Distribution System

Electronic commerce is changing the role of distributors, which traditionally served as intermediaries between manufacturers and customers. To survive, distributors may need to find other ways of providing value. Marshall Industries, the world's fourth-largest distributor of industrial electronic components and production supplies, reinvented itself by converting almost all of the processes it performs physically to a digital service on the Internet (El Sawy, Malhotra, Gosain, and Young, 1999). This is how its new "virtual" distribution environment works.

Marshall's customers and suppliers can access its intranet to obtain customized information. For example, high-tech companies can see information about their own accounts, such as sales reports, inventory levels, and design data. They also can accept or reject price quotes or order training materials. A personal knowledge-assistant process called Plugged-in allows customers to specify the product categories in which they are interested. They only receive information specific to their interests.

Visitors can view more than 100,000 pages of data sheets, up-to-date pricing, and inventory information from 150 major suppliers, and information on 170,000 parts numbers. They can quickly locate products in Marshall's on-line catalog using a sophisticated search engine. The site links to the United Parcel Service (UPS) Web site, where customers can track the status of their shipments. Sales representatives have secure intranet access so they can check sales and activity status only in their territory.

When a customer places an order, the system verifies price and quantity and initiates a real-time credit authorization and approval. As soon as the order is approved, the system sends an automated request to the warehouse for scheduling. The system then sends the customer an order acknowledgment accompanied by relevant shipping and logistics information from UPS. Messages about order status are automatically broadcast to the customer. The system thus integrates the entire process of placing and receiving an order.

Other features of Marshall's Web site provide additional service and value. Visitors can access a free "Electronic Design Center" to test and run their designs over the Internet. For example, an engineer might use Marshall's Web site to test Texas Instruments' (TI) digital signal processors (DSPs) for the design of a new piece of multimedia hardware. (DSP chips improve the performance of high-tech products such as computer hard disks, headphones, and power steering in cars.) At the site, the engineer can find technical specifications and even simulate designs using TI chips. The engineer would download sample code, modify the code to suit the product being built, test it on a "virtual chip" attached to the Web, and analyze its performance. If the engineer liked the results, Marshall could download his or her code, burn it into physical chips, and send back samples for designing prototypes. The entire process would take minutes.

Marshall's Web site provides after-sale training so that engineers do not have to attend special training classes or meetings in faraway locations. Marshall links to NetSeminar, a Web site where Marshall's customers can register for and receive educational programs developed for them by their suppliers using video, audio, and real-time chat capabilities.

## CAN COVISINT SUCCEED AS AN AUTO INDUSTRY EXCHANGE?

On February 25, 2000, General Motors, Ford, and DaimlerChrysler announced the formation of a new automotive industry business-to-business trading exchange called Covisint. The three rivals agreed to work cooperatively on this exchange to squeeze excess costs out of the process of purchasing auto parts. (General Motors and Ford together spend about $250 billion a year on purchasing raw materials and components.) Lower prices would be achieved by requiring suppliers to bid for orders together over the Covisint Web site and by reducing the cost of each purchase order transaction. (Covisint is expected to reduce the transaction cost of each purchase order from $100 to $10 or $20.) Covisint includes an analysis tool to help the manufacturers weigh competing bids from suppliers using attributes such as quality, price, and delivery date. The automobile producers believe they will save billions every year, trimming costs by $1,200 to $3,000 per car. The rival automakers believe they could realize additional savings by sharing one common industry exchange rather than bearing the costs of setting up their own exchanges. Covisint could also provide savings to suppliers by providing a low-cost point of entry for trading with manufacturers. Covisint is controlled by the Big Three automobile manufacturers (later joined by Renault and Nissan Motors) and two companies supplying the software to power the Web site—Oracle, which is Ford's software teammate, and Commerce One, which has partnered with General Motors.

Covisint has been controversial from the beginning and many observers and analysts have expressed doubt that it can ever succeed. The U.S. Federal Trade Commission (FTC) started investigating whether the giant automobile manufacturers were using Covisint to control parts prices. The two giant software vendors have been squabbling over specifications. Probably the main reason for skepticism has been the lack of participation by most of the approximately 40,000 auto industry suppliers. Covisint's board is made up only of representatives of the automobile producers and so excludes parts suppliers. Eventually, Covisint did agree to the formation of a Customer Advisory Council of suppliers who will have some input into decisions. Another issue is that many of the 8,000 or so first-tier suppliers (those who sell directly to the automobile companies) had already built their own private exchanges to be used with their lower-tier suppliers. Covisint has now assured these suppliers that Covisint is being designed to enable the suppliers to use their own exchanges in conjunction with Covisint. Another concern of the suppliers is that Covisint would impose high transaction fees. (As of this writing that issue has not been resolved.) Yet another issue is that the suppliers fear their products will become commodities, that they will lose the benefit of loyalty to their brands. The reaction of Covisint is that suppliers will be given the opportunity to build their own company-branded portals on the site. Still another problem is the lack of communication; thousands of suppliers have little or no information on Covisint. One advantage seen by the smaller suppliers is that Covisint will enable them to participate in e-commerce; previously more than 60 percent of them could not afford their own electronic networks.

On September 12, the FTC announced the end of its Covisint investigation, enabling the exchange to proceed. The approval was tentative, however, because, the FTC said, Covisint was not yet in operation and did not even have bylaws or operating rules. The FTC announced they would be monitoring its operation, because "the founders represent such a large share of the automobile market, the Commission cannot say that implementation of the Covisint venture will not cause competitive concerns." Soon thereafter, the Bundeskartellamt, the German equivalent of the FTC, also granted its approval.

**To Think About:** Do you think Covisint can succeed? If so, how and why? If not, why not? What management, organization and technology problems confronted the Covisint project?

*Sources:* Bill Robinson, "Driving the Automotive Industry," *Cisco IQ Magazine,* January/February 2001; Ruhan Memishi, "Covisint's Starts and Stops," *Internet World,* January 1, 2001; Clare Ansberry, "Let's Build an Online Supply Network," *Wall Street Journal,* April 17, 2000; Dow Jones Newswires, "Honda Considers Joining Covisint Parts Exchange," *Wall Street Journal,* November 21, 2000; "Covisint: Reinventing Procurement and Supply," *New York Times,* November 6, 2000; Paul Elias, "Feds Can't Call Covisint Antitrust-worthy—Yet," *Red Herring Magazine,* September 12, 2000; Gail Kachadourian, "Covisint Is Up and Running," *Automotive News,* October 9, 2000; Steve Konicki, "Covisint's Rough Road," *Information Week,* August 7, 2000; and Sarah L. Roberts-Witt, "Proposed Auto Exchange Hits Bumps," *Knowledge Management,* July 2000.

## ELECTRONIC COMMERCE PAYMENT SYSTEMS

Special **electronic payment systems** have been developed to handle ways of paying for goods electronically on the Internet. Electronic payment systems for the Internet include systems for credit card payments, digital cash, electronic wallets, person-to-person payment systems, smart cards, electronic checks, and electronic billing systems.

**electronic payment system** The use of digital technologies, such as credit cards, smart cards, debit cards, and Internet-based payment systems, to pay for products and services electronically.

The more sophisticated electronic commerce software (see Chapter 9) has capabilities for processing credit card purchases on the Web. Businesses can also contract with services such as PC Authorize, Web Authorize, and IC Verify to process their credit card transactions. These services accept merchant transactions containing customer credit card information,

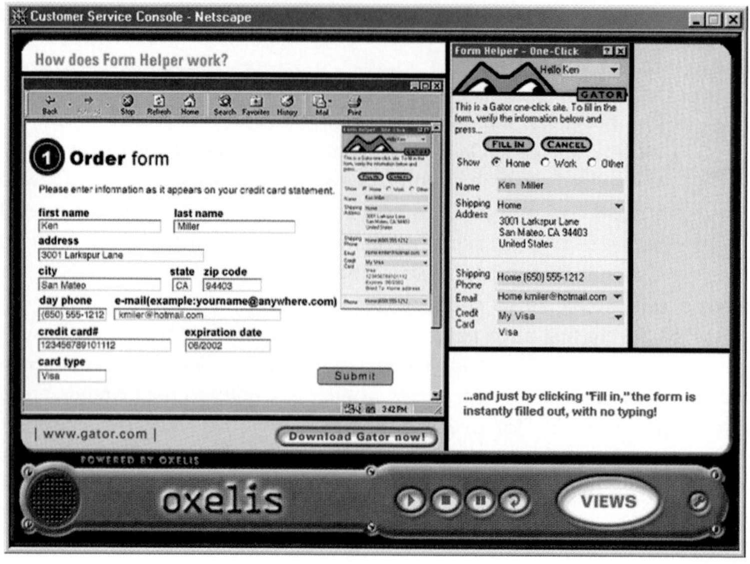


*Gator (www.gator.com) is a digital wallet system which stores personal information securely on the user's computer. When the user encounters a registration or order form on the Web, Gator Form Helper pops up and fills in the form with one or just a few clicks.*

authenticate the credit card to make sure that it is valid and that funds are available, and arrange for the bank that issued the credit card to deposit money for the amount of the purchase in the merchant's bank account. Chapter 14 describes the technologies for secure credit card processing in more detail.

**digital wallet**
Software that stores credit card, electronic cash, owner identification, and address information and provides these data automatically during electronic commerce purchase transactions.

Digital wallets make paying for purchases over the Web more efficient by eliminating the need for shoppers to repeatedly enter their address and credit card information each time they buy something. A **digital wallet** stores credit card, electronic cash, and owner identification information and provides that information at an electronic commerce site's "checkout counter." The digital wallet enters the shopper's name, credit card number, and shipping information automatically when invoked to complete the purchase. Amazon.com's 1-Click shopping, which enables a consumer to automatically fill in shipping and credit card information by clicking one button, uses digital wallet technology. Other digital wallet systems include Microsoft Passport, Gator, and America Online's Quick Checkout.

**micropayment**
Payment for a very small sum of money, often $1.00 or less.

**electronic cash (e-cash)**
Currency represented in electronic form that can be exchanged with another e-cash user or retailer over the Internet.

**Micropayment** systems have been developed for purchases of less than $10 that would be too small for conventional credit card payments. If one needed to pay an Internet service $1.50 to search for a specific piece of information or several dollars to reprint an article, electronic cash or smart cards would be useful for this purpose. **Electronic cash** or **e-cash** (also known as digital cash) is currency represented in electronic form that is moving outside the normal network of money (paper currency, coins, checks, credit cards.) Users are supplied with client software and can exchange money with another e-cash user over the Internet or with a retailer accepting e-cash. CyberCash, e-Coin, Flooz.com, and InternetCash.com offer digital cash services. In addition to facilitating micropayments, digital cash can be useful for people who don't have credit cards and wish to make Web purchases or for people who want to give gift certificates for on-line shopping.

**smart card**
A credit card-size plastic card that stores digital information and that can be used for electronic payments in place of cash.

Smart cards offer an alternative system for processing micropayments, because the smart card's microchip can contain electronic cash as well as other information. A **smart card** is a plastic card the size of a credit card that stores digital information. The smart card can store health records, identification data, or telephone numbers or it can serve as an "electronic purse" in place of cash. The Mondex smart card contains electronic cash and can be used to transfer funds to merchants in physical storefronts and to merchants on the Internet. Mondex cards can accept electronic cash transferred from users' bank accounts over the Web. The card requires use of a special card reading and writing device whenever the card needs to be "recharged" with cash or whenever the card needs to transfer cash to either an on-line or

## TABLE 4-3 EXAMPLES OF ELECTRONIC PAYMENT SYSTEMS FOR E-COMMERCE

| Payment System | Description | Commercial Example |
|---|---|---|
| Credit cards | Secure services for credit card payments on the Internet that protect information transmitted among users, merchant sites, and processing banks | PC Authorize<br>Web Authorize<br>IC Verify |
| Electronic cash (e-cash) | Digital currency that can be used for micropayments | Flooz.com<br>e-Coin |
| Person-to-person payment systems | Send money via the Web to individuals who are not set up to accept credit card payments | PayPal<br>BillPoint<br>Yahoo PayDirect |
| Digital wallet | Software that stores credit card and other information to facilitate payment for goods on the Web | Passport, Gator, AOL Quick Checkout |
| Electronic check | Check with secure digital signature | NetChex |
| Smart card | Microchip that stores electronic cash to use for on-line and off-line micropayments | Mondex |
| Electronic bill payment | Supports electronic payment for on-line and physical store purchases of goods or services after the purchase has taken place | CheckFree<br>Billserve.com |

off-line merchant. Internet users must attach a Mondex reader to their PC to use the card. To pay for Web purchase, the user would swipe the smart card through the card reader.

Micropayment systems have been developed to let consumers bill small purchases to their credit cards or telephone bills. Qpass collects all of a consumer's tiny purchases for monthly billing on a credit card. The New York Times uses Qpass to bill consumers wishing to access articles from its NYTimes.com Web site. ECharge and Trivnet let consumers charge small purchases to their monthly telephone bills.

New Web-based **person-to-person payment systems** have sprung up to serve people who want to send money to vendors or individuals who are not set up to accept credit card payments. The party sending money uses his or her credit card to create an account with the designated payment at a Web site dedicated to person-to-person payments. The recipient "picks up" the payment by visiting the Web site and supplying information about where to send the payment (a bank account or a physical address). PayPal, Billpoint, and Yahoo's PayDirect are popular person-to-person payment systems.

**person-to-person payment system**
Electronic payment system for people who want to send money to vendors or individuals who are not set up to accept credit card payments.

On-line merchants and financial service companies offer bill presentment and payment services over the Web as well as over proprietary networks. These services support payment for on-line and physical store purchases of goods or services after the purchase has taken place. They notify purchasers about bills that are due, present the bills, and process the payments. Some of these services, such as CheckFree, consolidate subscriber bills from various sources so that they can all be paid at one time.

Payment systems, such as NetChex, that use electronic checks are also available. These checks are secured with a digital signature that can be verified and can be used for payments in electronic commerce. Electronic check systems are especially useful in business-to-business electronic commerce. Table 4-3 summarizes the features of these payment systems.

The process of paying for products and services purchased on the Internet is complex and merits additional discussion. We discuss electronic commerce security in detail in Chapter 14. Figure 4-8 provides an overview of the key information flows in electronic commerce.

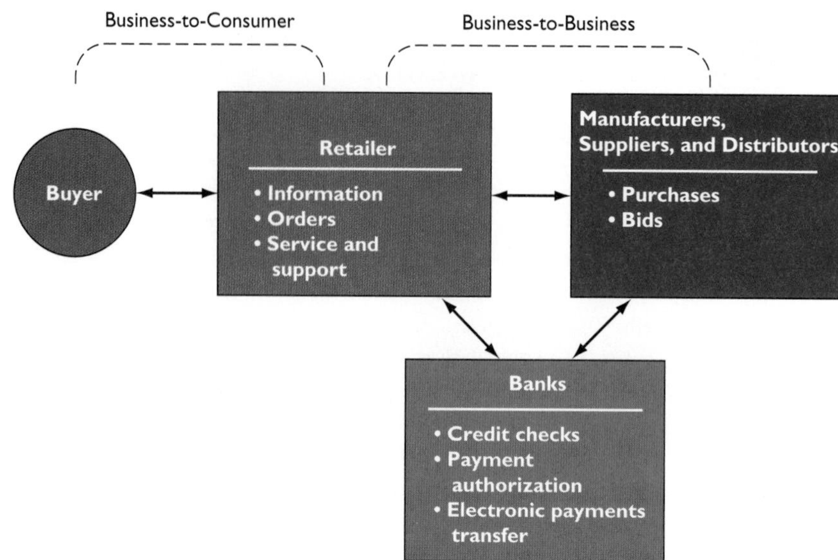


*Figure 4-8* Electronic commerce information flows. Individuals can purchase goods and services electronically from on-line retailers, who in turn can use electronic commerce technologies to link directly to their suppliers or distributors. Electronic payment systems are used in both business-to-consumer and business-to-business electronic commerce.

## 4.3 ELECTRONIC BUSINESS AND THE DIGITAL FIRM

Businesses are finding some of the greatest benefits of Internet technology come from applications that lower agency and coordination costs. Although companies have used internal networks for many years to manage and coordinate internal business processes, intranets quickly are becoming the technology of choice for electronic business.

### HOW INTRANETS SUPPORT ELECTRONIC BUSINESS

Intranets are inexpensive, scalable to expand or contract as needs change, and accessible from most computing platforms. Whereas most companies, particularly the larger ones, must support a multiplicity of computer platforms that cannot communicate with each other, intranets provide instant connectivity, uniting all computers into a single, virtually seamless, network system. Web software presents a uniform interface, which can be used to integrate many different processes and systems throughout the company. Companies can connect their intranet to internal company transaction systems, enabling employees to take actions central to a company's operations. For instance, customer service representatives for U.S. West can access the firm's main customer system through the corporate intranet to turn on services such as call waiting or to check installation dates for new phone lines, all while the customer is on the telephone.

Intranets can help organizations create a richer, more responsive information environment. Internal corporate applications based on the Web page model can be made interactive using a variety of media, text, audio, and video. A principal use of intranets has been to create on-line repositories of information that can be updated as often as required. Product catalogs, employee handbooks, telephone directories, or benefits information can be revised immediately as changes occur. This "event-driven" publishing allows organizations to respond more rapidly to changing conditions than traditional paper-based publishing, which requires a rigid production schedule. Made available via intranets, documents always can be up to date, eliminating paper, printing, and distribution costs. For instance, Sun Healthcare, a chain of nursing and long-term care facilities headquartered in Albuquerque, New Mexico, saved $400,000 in printing and mailing costs when it put its corporate newsletter on an intranet. The newsletter is distributed to 69,000 employees in 49 states (Mullich, 1999).

Intranets have provided cost savings in other application areas as well. U.S. West saves $300,000 per year with an intranet application that automatically notifies service representatives of expiring service contracts. The intranet only cost $17,000 to build (Jahnke, 1998).

**TABLE 4-4 ORGANIZATIONAL BENEFITS OF INTRANETS**

| |
|---|
| Connectivity: accessible from most computing platforms |
| Can be tied to internal corporate systems |
| Can create interactive applications with text, audio, and video |
| Scalable to larger or smaller computing platforms as requirements change |
| Easy to use, universal Web interface |
| Low start-up costs |
| Richer, more responsive information environment |
| Reduced information distribution costs |

Conservative studies of returns on investment (ROIs) from intranets show ROIs of 23 percent to 85 percent, and some companies have reported ROIs of more than 1,000 percent.

The intranet provides a universal e-mail system, remote access, group collaboration tools, an electronic library, an application-sharing system, and a company communications network. Some companies are using their intranets for virtual conferencing. Table 4-4 summarizes the organizational benefits of using intranets.

## INTRANETS AND GROUP COLLABORATION

Intranets provide a rich set of tools for creating collaborative environments in which members of an organization can exchange ideas, share information, and work together on common projects and assignments regardless of their physical location. For example, Noranda Inc., a large Canadian mining company, uses an intranet to keep track of its mineral exploration research in a dozen offices in North and South America, Australia, and Europe.

Some companies are using intranets to create enterprise collaboration environments linking diverse groups, projects, and activities throughout the organization. The Global Village intranet of U.S. West (which merged with Qwest Communications International) is a prominent example. Here are just a few of its capabilities:

- A sales consultant in Chicago can check events throughout the company. He pulls up News of the Day, an internal newsletter.
- A project manager can click on the lab page to inspect software being developed for a new service. He can test the software from his own computer.
- Repair technicians can share a map showing damage to phone lines caused by ice storms and collectively explore a strategy for repairing them.
- An executive can log onto the intranet from her home after dinner to catch up with e-mail and check out the next day's schedule for her project team.
- An engineer researching the design of a new network component can link to the public Internet via a gateway built into the Global Village home page. She surfs the Web to locate possible suppliers, then returns to the company intranet to inform her colleagues via e-mail about what she has found.

These intranet applications have enabled U.S. West to improve communications and streamline business processes, saving the company millions of dollars each year. Chapter 12 provides a detailed discussion of intranets in collaborative work.

## INTRANET APPLICATIONS FOR ELECTRONIC BUSINESS

Intranets are springing up in all the major functional areas of the business, allowing the organization to manage more of its business processes electronically. Figure 4-9 illustrates some of the intranet applications that have been developed for finance and accounting, human resources, sales and marketing, and manufacturing and production.

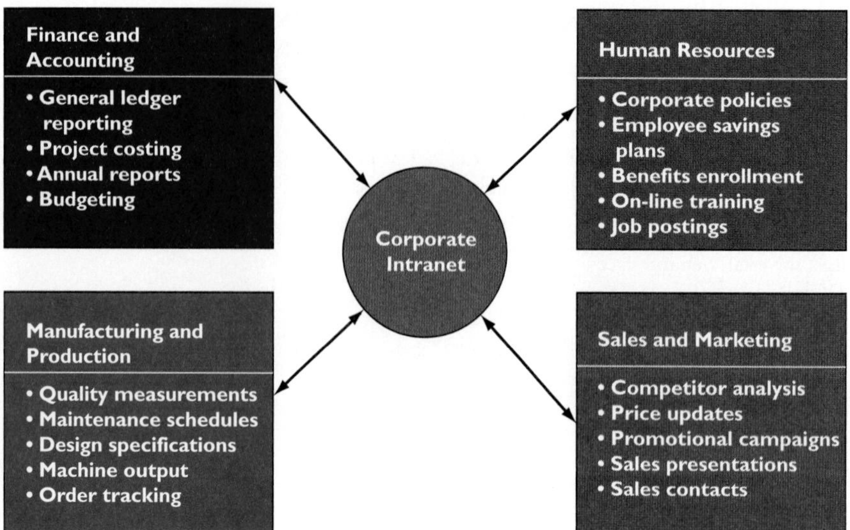


*Figure 4-9* Functional applications of intranets. Intranet applications have been developed for each of the major functional areas of the business.

## Finance and Accounting

Many organizations have extensive TPS that collect operational data on financial activities, but their traditional management reporting systems, such as general ledger systems and spreadsheets, often cannot bring this detailed information together for decision making and performance measurement. Intranets can be very valuable for finance and accounting, because they can provide an integrated view of financial and accounting information on-line in an easy-to-use format. Table 4-5 provides some examples.

## Human Resources

One of the principal responsibilities of human resources departments is to keep employees informed of company issues as well as to provide information about their personnel records and employee benefits. Human resources can use intranets for on-line publishing of corporate policy manuals, job postings and internal job transfers, company telephone directories, and training classes. Employees can use an intranet to enroll in healthcare, employee savings, and other benefit plans if it is linked to the firm's human resources or benefits system or to take on-line competency tests. (See the Window on Technology.) Human resource departments can rapidly deliver information about upcoming events or company developments to

**TABLE 4-5 INTRANETS IN FINANCE AND ACCOUNTING**

| Organization | Intranet Application |
|---|---|
| Charles Schwab | SMART reporting and analysis application provides managers with a comprehensive view of Schwab financial activities, including a risk-evaluation template that helps managers assess nine categories of risk. Schwab's intranet also delivers the FinWeb General Ledger reporting system on-line in an easy-to-digest format. |
| U.S. Department of Agriculture Rural Development | Intranet makes information about its loan and grant programs for rural and small communities available to its 7,200 employees. Employees can use the intranet to find out which projects have been funded in a specific local area. |
| Pacific Northwest National Laboratory | Intranet Web Reporting System provides financial statistics for laboratory activities, including current costs charged to each project, number of hours spent on each project by individual employees, and how actual costs compare to projected costs. Lab employees can use the intranet to perform ad hoc queries on financial data. |

## TABLE 4-6 INTRANETS IN HUMAN RESOURCES

| Organization | Intranet Application |
|---|---|
| Cigna Corp. | Employees can use the corporate intranet to check the balance and allocate funds in their 401k savings plans, look up a healthcare provider, and enroll on-line in company benefit plans. The benefits enrollment tool includes a "Decision Aide" that prompts employees to answer basic questions about their healthcare benefits preferences and then guides them to appropriate plans. |
| Sandia National Laboratories | Tech Web intranet posts a weekly newsletter and an employee directory on-line. Employees can use the intranet for time and expense calculations and for project management. |
| Sun Healthcare | Sunweb intranet provides virtual on-line tours of its facilities for new hires. Nurses and other employees can receive on-line training, including video clips. A three-dimensional cartoon figure called "Sunny" guides employees through intranet pages and explains the types of courses that are available. |

employees using electronic bulletin boards or e-mail broadcasts. Table 4-6 lists examples of how intranets are used in the area of human resources.

## Sales and Marketing

Earlier we described how the Internet and the Web can be used for selling to individual customers and to other businesses. Internet technology also can be applied to the internal management of the sales and marketing function. One of the most popular applications for corporate intranets is to oversee and coordinate the activities of the sales force. Sales staff can dial in for updates on pricing, promotions, rebates, or customers or to obtain information about competitors. They can access presentations and sales documents and customize them for customers. The chapter-opening vignette describes the capabilities of SwissAir's sales intranet.

Haworth Inc. of Holland, Michigan, which makes office furniture, customized ERoom, a Web-based collaboration tool for sales force support. ERoom provides project-based collaboration sites where documents and threaded discussions can be stored. Haworth created "virtual workspaces" dedicated to sales reporting, sales strategy development, sales forecasting, field sales processes, and education and training. The system helps salespeople in many different countries work together on multinational accounts (Deckmyn, 1999).

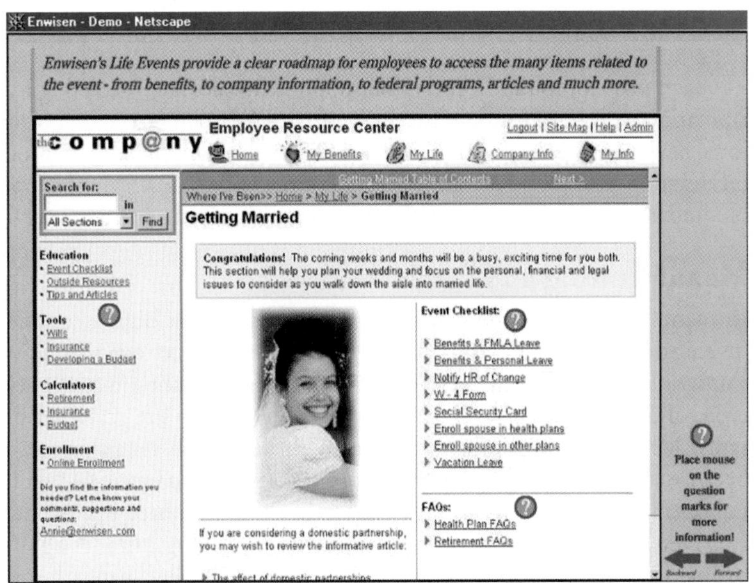


*Enwisen's Employee Information System enables employees to maintain their own human resources data over a corporate intranet. Self-service human resources intranets can give employees more control over their own information while reducing human resources administration costs.*

## SELF-SERVICE INTRANETS FOR HUMAN RESOURCES

Many companies are installing self-service human resources (HR) systems on their intranets, and the results are benefiting both the companies and their employees. A recent survey by Watson Wyatt Worldwide found that more than 79 percent of corporations are now using their intranets to deliver HR-related services to their employees. One reason for the popularity is because in our globalized economy, employees of many corporations are spread throughout the country or the world.

LSI Logic Corp. of Milpitas, California, is a producer of semiconductors. Its staff of about 6,500 is located in 16 countries around the world. In 1998 the company decided to install an ERP system, R/3 from SAP. One of R/3's attractions was the self-service HR tools it included. Employees now use LSI's intranet to maintain their own human resources data, such as changes in marriage status, new babies, or changes of address. They also use this system to enroll in insurance programs, apply for newly posted internal jobs, and handle many other HR tasks, all without using paper. In this way many transcription errors are eliminated, and the HR staff spends much less time on strictly clerical tasks. Because the LSI Logic system is Web-based, employees can also use the system to access Internet content from medical providers and benefits-plan partners. Thus, by using intranets, HR departments have given employees more control over their own records and benefits while freeing up HR employees to focus more on strategic issues.

Self-service HR technology has even been applied to the job application process. E*TRADE Group Inc., the on-line stock trading company headquartered in Menlo Park, California, has 3,000 employees distributed all over the United States. About half of E*TRADE's employees are difficult-to-find skilled information technologists such as Web designers. Because employees are scattered, most HR functions, including new-employee requests and the processing and tracking of candidates, are, of necessity, decentralized. Arnnon Geshuri who is in charge of workforce management software at E*TRADE, claims the "shelf life" of an attractive IT candidate in a tight market is about 48 hours. If the company cannot hire the candidate by then, it is likely that the candidate will have already accepted an offer elsewhere. Therefore, the whole applicant tracking process must be automated to eliminate the slow paper process.

The software E*TRADE uses to automate the process is Icarian's Workforce, a distributed, Web-based product that is running on the company's intranet. The software automatically takes in applicant information from job sources including headhunters and on-line job sites. Managers are able to access this information to aid them in locating potential candidates. The software tracks all applicants from requisition through interviewing and offers to the final signature for a new hire. All this data is integrated with the company's Oracle HR system.

To Think About: What are the benefits of using intranets for human resources applications? What management, technology, and organization issues must be addressed when installing an intranet-based, self-service human resources system in a national or international organization?

*Sources:* Bob MacAvoy, "Employee Investments," *Cisco IQ Magazine*, January/February 2001 and "Electrifying Human Resources," *Cisco IQ Magazine*, July/August 2000; and Norbert Turek, "Automation Transforms Human Resources," *Information Week*, July 10, 2000.

Compaq Computer Corporation supports its sales and marketing teams with intranet collaboration tools from Conjoin Inc. of Bedford, Massachusetts. Using Conjoin's Field First salesforce software, Compaq's sales representatives can call up specific product and competitive information posted by the marketing department. They can use the intranet to retrieve, assemble, and customize materials for clients very rapidly ("Compaq Intranet Case Study," 2001.)

### Manufacturing and Production

In manufacturing, information-management issues are highly complex, involving massive inventories, capturing and integrating real-time production data flows, changing relationships with suppliers, and volatile costs. The manufacturing function typically uses multiple types of data, including graphics as well as text, which are scattered in many disparate systems. Manufacturing information is often very time sensitive and difficult to retrieve, because files must be continuously updated. Developing intranets that integrate manufacturing data under a uniform user interface is more complicated than in other functional areas.

Despite these difficulties, companies are launching intranet applications for manufacturing. Intranets coordinating the flow of information between lathes, controllers, inventory systems, and other components of a production system can make manufacturing information more accessible to different parts of the organization, increasing precision and lowering costs. Table 4-7 describes some of these uses.

## TABLE 4-7 INTRANETS IN MANUFACTURING AND PRODUCTION

| Organization | Intranet Application |
|---|---|
| Noranda Inc. | Intranet for its Magnola magnesium production facility in Quebec monitors plant operations remotely using a virtual control panel and video cameras. |
| Sony Corporation | Intranet delivers financial information to manufacturing personnel so that workers can monitor the production line's profit-and-loss performance and adapt performance accordingly. The intranet also provides data on quality measurements, such as defects and rejects, as well as maintenance and training schedules. |
| Duke Power | Intranet provides on-line access to a computer-aided engineering tool for retrieving equipment designs and operating specifications that allows employees to view every important system in the plant at various levels of detail. Different subsets of systems can be formatted together to create a view of all the equipment in a particular room. Maintenance technicians, plant engineers, and operations personnel can use this tool with minimal training. |
| Rockwell International | Intranet improves process and quality of manufactured circuit boards and controllers by establishing home pages for its Milwaukee plant's computer-controlled machine tools that are updated every 60 seconds. Quality control managers can check the status of a machine by calling up its home page to learn how many pieces the machine output that day, what percentage of an order that output represents, and to what tolerances the machine is adhering. |

### COORDINATION AND SUPPLY CHAIN MANAGEMENT

Intranets can also be used to simplify and integrate business processes spanning more than one functional area. These cross-functional processes can be coordinated electronically, increasing organizational efficiency and responsiveness. One area of great interest to companies is the use of Internet technology to facilitate supply chain management.

Chapter 2 introduced the concept of supply chain management, which integrates procurement, production, and logistics processes to supply goods and services from their source to final delivery to the customer. The supply chain links material suppliers, distributors, retailers, and customers, as well as manufacturing facilities.

In the pre-Internet environment, supply chain coordination was hampered by the difficulties of making information flow smoothly between many different kinds of systems servicing different parts of the supply chain, such as purchasing, materials management, manufacturing, and distribution. Enterprise systems could supply some of this integration for internal business processes, but such systems are difficult and costly to build. Some of this integration can be supplied using Internet technology. Firms can use intranets to improve coordination among their internal supply chain processes, and they can use extranets to coordinate supply chain processes shared with their business partners (see Figure 4-10). An

*Figure 4-10* Intranet linking supply chain functions. Intranets can be used to integrate information from isolated business processes so that they can be coordinated for supply chain management. Access to private corporate intranets can be extended to distributors, suppliers, logistics services, and customers to improve coordination of external supply chain processes.

## TABLE 4-8 EXAMPLES OF WEB-BASED SUPPLY CHAIN MANAGEMENT APPLICATIONS

| Organization | Supply Chain Management Application |
|---|---|
| Acma Computers | Uses Datasweep Advantage Web-based supply chain management tool to track work orders for specific customers on-line, flag and manage product shortages, manage change orders, and monitor production and quality information throughout the product lifecycle. Increased on-time delivery of units from 78 to 96 percent. |
| Eastman Chemical Corporation | Uses Logility Inc.'s Web-based Demand Chain Voyager software on its intranet to enable more than 240 sales reps to access and share forecasts. Is providing key customers with its software so they can work collaboratively with sales reps on forecasting. |
| SMTC Manufacturing | Uses Web-based OrderIT software to enable customers for its circuit boards and computer components to check the status of orders. Customers can also check SMTC's master production schedule to help them respond to changing customer demand. |
| Chrysler Corporation | Supplier Partner Information Network (SPIN) allows 3,500 of Chrysler's 12,000 suppliers to access portions of its intranet, where they can access the most current data on design changes, parts shortages, packaging information, and invoice tracking. Chrysler can use the information from SPIN to reassign workers so that shortages do not hold up assembly lines. Chrysler believes SPIN has reduced the time to complete various business processes by 25 to 50 percent. |

extranet is a private intranet that is extended to authorized users outside the company. Many of the industrial networks we introduced in Chapter 2, which link a company's systems with those of other companies in its industry, are based on extranets for streamlining supply chain management.

Through a Web interface, a manager can tap into suppliers' systems to see if inventory and production capabilities match demand for the manufacturer's products. Business partners can use Web-based supply chain management tools to collaborate on-line on forecasts. Sales representatives can tap into suppliers' production schedules and logistics information to monitor customers' order status. As extended supply chains start sharing production, scheduling, inventory, forecasting, and logistics information on-line instead of by phone or fax, companies can respond more accurately to changing customer demand. The low cost of providing this information with Web-based tools instead of costly proprietary systems encourages companies to share critical business information with a greater number of suppliers. Table 4-8 provides examples of Web-based supply chain management applications.

The Web-based B2B marketplaces and exchanges we described earlier also provide supply chain management functions. When completed, Covisint, the giant automotive industry exchange described in the Window on Organizations, will help the participating auto manufacturers view their supply chains as components move through the system. Purchase orders,

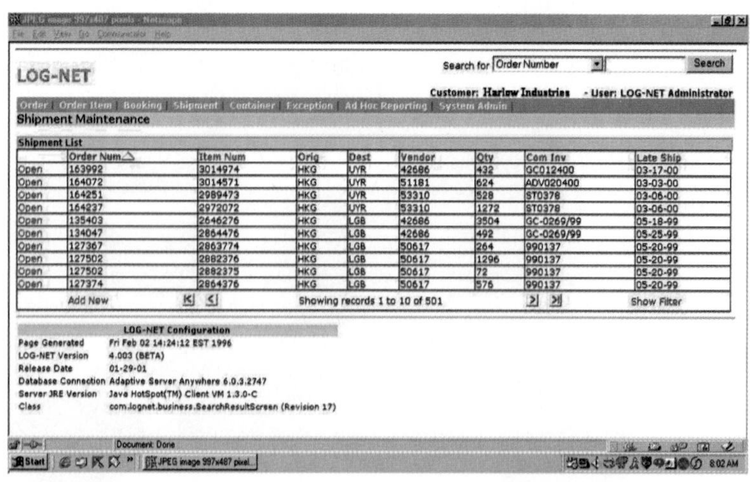


*LOG-NET Inc. provides software for tracking purchase orders and shipments from any location over the Internet. Companies can use such Web-based tools to improve their supply chain management.*

supplier ship dates, and production schedules are all available on the Covisint Web site. The auto manufacturers and their suppliers can use this real-time information to reduce their inventories and respond more quickly to customers.

Internet-based supply chain management applications are clearly changing the way businesses work internally and with each other. In addition to reducing costs, these supply chain management systems provide more responsive customer service, allowing the workings of the business to be driven more by customer demand. Earlier supply chain management systems were driven by production master schedules based on forecasts or best guesses of demand for products. With new flows of information made possible by Web-based tools, supply chain management can follow a demand-driven model.

## 4.4 Management Challenges and Opportunities

Although electronic commerce and electronic business offer organizations a wealth of new opportunities, they also present managers with a series of challenges. Many new Internet business models have yet to prove enduring sources of profit. Web-enabling business processes for electronic commerce and electronic business requires far-reaching organizational change. The legal environment for electronic commerce has not yet been solidified, and companies pursuing electronic commerce must be vigilant about security and consumer privacy.

### Unproven Business Models

Not all companies make money on the Web. Hundreds of retail dot-com firms, including Garden.com, Chinese Books Cyberstore, Productopia.com, and Pets.com, have closed their doors. Fleetscape.com, M-Xchange.com, IndustrialVortex.com, and other exchanges have shut down. Dot-com stock prices collapsed after many of these companies failed to generate enough revenue to sustain their costly marketing campaigns, infrastructure, and staff salaries, losing money on every sale they made. Business models built around the Internet are new and largely unproven. The chapter ending case study on the failure of Boo.com is devoted to this topic.

Doing business over the Internet is not necessarily more efficient or cost effective than traditional business methods. Virtual retailers may not need to pay for costly storefronts and retail workers, but they often require heavy outlays for warehousing, customer service call centers, and customer acquisition.

Challenges also confront businesses that are trying to use the Web to supplement or enhance a traditional business model. Many businesses are finding that it is not enough to "get on the Web." Businesses that are unclear about their on-line strategy can waste thousands and even millions of dollars building and maintaining a Web site that fails to deliver the desired results. Even successful Web sites can incur very high costs. For example, Recreational Equipment Inc. (REI), the famous vendor of outdoor gear headquartered in Kent, Washington, has bricks-and-mortar retail stores, hefty catalog sales, and a profitable Web site that dominates its market. It has high payroll expenditures to pay for the skilled technical staff supporting the Web site and additional shipping expenses to make sure Web orders are delivered to customers in a timely fashion. REI has spent more than $15 million on upgrading and remodeling its Web site in four years.

### Business Process Change Requirements

Electronic commerce and electronic business require careful orchestration of the firm's divisions, production sites, and sales offices, as well as close relationships with customers, suppliers, and other business partners in its network of value creation. Essential business processes must be redesigned and more closely integrated, especially those for supply chain management. Traditional boundaries between departments and divisions, as well as companies and suppliers can be an impediment to collaboration and relationship-building. The digitally enabled enterprise must transform the way it conducts business on many levels to act rapidly and with precision.

## Controlling Channel Conflict

When Canada's largest book retailer, Chapters Inc., decided it had to establish a Web site, it created another way for its customers to purchase its products. Unfortunately, it also created the threat of channel conflict. Chapters Inc. had several strong reasons for selling on the Web. First, management feared it was losing sales to Web sites such as Amazon.com. Second, research showed that, in general, Web customers are new to a given company, having never purchased at the stores of the site owners. And third, management believed the Web would enable it to expand into new areas, such as used and out-of-print books. However, a Web site could steal customers from its own bricks-and-mortar stores, and Chapters management wanted a strategy to avoid channel conflict.

Chapters decided to integrate its Web site with its stores to give its customers good experiences regardless of which channel they chose. To prevent cross-channel rivalry, the company created a special new "retail ambassador" position to troubleshoot the relationship between the two channels and to ensure that both organizations took a holistic view of the customer retail experience.

The new Chapters Web site gives its visitors information on books and enables them to shop on-line, much as other Internet booksellers do. In addition, however, the company uses the Web to improve the experiences of in-store customers by placing computer kiosks in each store linked to the specific store's inventory. Each kiosk is so easy to use that even customers with no Web experience can discover whether a book is in stock and, if so, determine its shelf location. Customers can also order books that are not in stock using the kiosks and have the books delivered to their homes. Because the kiosks' back ends are integrated with Chapters' e-commerce systems, all customer service functions are integrated, enabling customers to return on-line purchases at any store. Soon the company will start selling other products through the kiosks and the Web, including e-books, videos, CDs, and DVDs.

Has Chapters' integrated approach been effective? According to David Hainline, chief operating officer of Chapters Online, consumers rated its bookstores the number one retail brand in Canada in 1999. Chapters Online has been able to stop the leakage of its business to other on-line booksellers. Management is obviously pleased.

Other companies have had more difficulty managing channel conflict. When Levi Straus & Co. began selling its Levi and Dockers brands on-line, it was potentially stealing business from the very retail stores where most people purchase Levi products. After a year Levi Straus abandoned on-line sales, converting its Web site to information only, thus eliminating the channel conflict. When Avon Products, the $5 billion cosmetics company, experienced powerful on-line competition from Estee Lauder Inc., it decided it must begin selling on-line. In the United States Avon mainly sells its products through about 500,000 independent saleswomen who go door to door announcing "Avon calling." These reps felt threatened when their customers suddenly had another venue to purchase Avon cosmetics. In this case, Avon management concluded it could not abandon Web sales and so decided to give the reps a commission from its on-line sales to their customers. The reps did not find the solution to be totally satisfactory—they are receiving a much lower percentage than if their customers had purchased directly from them. Only time will tell if Avon's solution has been successful in addressing Avon's channel conflict.

**To Think About:** What management, organization, and technology issues should be addressed when considering whether to use the Web for direct sales to consumers?

*Sources:* Stephanie Wilkinson, "Melding Clicks and Bricks," *Datamation,* August 29, 2000; Alorie Gilbert and Beth Bacheldor, "The Big Squeeze," *Information Week,* March 27, 2000; and Minda Zetlin, "Channel Conflicts," *Computerworld,* September 25, 2000.

management

**channel conflict**
Competition between two or more different distribution chains used to sell the products or services of the same company.

## Channel Conflicts

Using the Web for on-line sales and marketing may create **channel conflict** with the firm's traditional channels, especially for less information-intensive products that require physical intermediaries to reach buyers. The firm's sales force and distributors may fear that their revenues will drop as customers make purchases directly from the Web or that they will be displaced by this new channel. The Window on Management describes how several companies are dealing with this problem.

Channel conflict is an especially troublesome issue in business-to-business electronic commerce, where customers buy directly from manufacturers via the Web instead of through distributors or sales representatives. Milacron Inc. operates one of heavy industry's most extensive Web sites for selling machine tools to contract manufacturers. To minimize negative repercussions from channel conflict, Milacron is paying full commissions to its reps for on-line sales made in their territory, even if they had not done any work on the sale or met

## TABLE 4-9 DIGITALLY ENABLING THE ENTERPRISE: TOP QUESTIONS FOR MANAGERS

1. How much digital integration does our business need to remain competitive? How can the digital integration provided by Internet technology change our business model? Should we change our business model?
2. How can we measure the success of digitally enabling the enterprise? Will the benefits outweigh the costs?
3. How will business processes have to be changed to use Internet technology seriously for electronic commerce or electronic business? How much process integration is required?
4. How will we have to recast our relationships with customers, suppliers, and other business partners to take advantage of digitally enabled business processes?
5. Do we have the appropriate information technology infrastructure for digitally enabling our business? How can we integrate Internet applications with existing applications and data?
6. What technical skills and employee training will be required to use Internet technology?
7. Are we doing enough to protect the security and privacy of customers we reach electronically?

the buyer. Other companies are devising solutions such as offering only a portion of their full product line on the Web. Using alternative channels created by the Internet requires very careful planning and management.

### LEGAL ISSUES

Laws governing electronic commerce are still being written. Legislatures, courts, and international agreements are just starting to settle such issues as the legality and force of e-mail contracts, the role of electronic signatures, and the application of copyright laws to electronically copied documents. Moreover, the Internet is global, and is used by individuals and organizations in hundreds of different countries. If a product were offered for sale in Thailand via a Web site stored on a computer in Singapore and the purchaser lived in Hungary, whose law would apply? The legal and regulatory environment for electronic commerce has not been fully established.

### SECURITY AND PRIVACY

Internet-based systems are even more vulnerable to penetration by outsiders than private networks, because the Internet was designed to be open to everyone. Any information, including e-mail, passes through many computer systems on the Internet before it reaches its destination. It can be monitored, captured, and stored at any of these points along the route. Valuable data that might be intercepted include credit card numbers and names, private employee data, marketing plans, sales contracts, product development and pricing data, negotiations between companies, and other data that might be of value to the competition. Hackers, vandals, and computer criminals have exploited Internet weaknesses to break into computer systems, causing harm by stealing passwords, obtaining sensitive information, electronic eavesdropping, or "jamming" corporate Web sites to make them inaccessible. We explore Internet security, computer crime, and technology for secure electronic payments in greater detail in Chapters 14 and 15.

The Web provides an unprecedented ability to learn about and target customers. But the same capability can also undermine individual privacy. Through the use of Web site monitoring software and other technology for tracking Web visitors, companies can gather detailed information about individuals without their knowledge. In other instances, Web site visitors knowingly supply personal information, such as their names, addresses, e-mail addresses, and special interests, in exchange for access to sites without realizing how the organization that owns the site may use the information. Companies collecting detailed customer information over the Web will need to balance their desire to profit from such information with the need to safeguard individual privacy.

Digitally enabling the enterprise with Internet technology requires careful management planning. Table 4-9 lists what we believe are the top questions managers should ask when exploring the use of the Internet for electronic commerce and electronic business.

## APPLICATION SOFTWARE EXERCISE

### SPREADSHEET AND ELECTRONIC PRESENTATION SOFTWARE EXERCISE: ANALYZING WEB MARKETING CAMPAIGNS

Your firm has been attempting to increase the number of on-line customers by placing advertising banners for your Web site at other Web sites. When users click on these banner ads, they are automatically transported to your Web site. Data from this advertising campaign are summarized in the weekly Marketing Trends Report produced by your Web site analysis software, which can be found on the Laudon Web site for Chapter 4.

- Total visitors are the number of people who visited your Web site by clicking on a banner ad for your site that was placed on an affiliated Web site.
- Total shoppers are the number of visitors referred by banner ads who reached a page in your Web site designated as a shopping page.
- Total attempted buyers are the number of potential buyers referred by banner ads who reached a Web page designated as a page for summarizing and paying for purchases.
- Total buyers are the number of buyers referred by banner ads who actually placed an order from your Web site.

Management would like to use these data to identify which Web sites directed the most visitors to your Web site and which sites were the most effective in referring visitors who actually became buyers.

Use spreadsheet software to do the following:

1. For each referring Web site, calculate the conversion rate, which is the percentage of visitors who actually became buyers.
2. Calculate the total number of visitors, shoppers, attempted buyers, and buyers who came to your site that week.
3. Prepare a bar graph for management showing which Web sites provided the most visitors and which provided the highest conversion rates.
4. Create an electronic slide of your graph using electronic presentation software.

## MANAGEMENT WRAP-UP

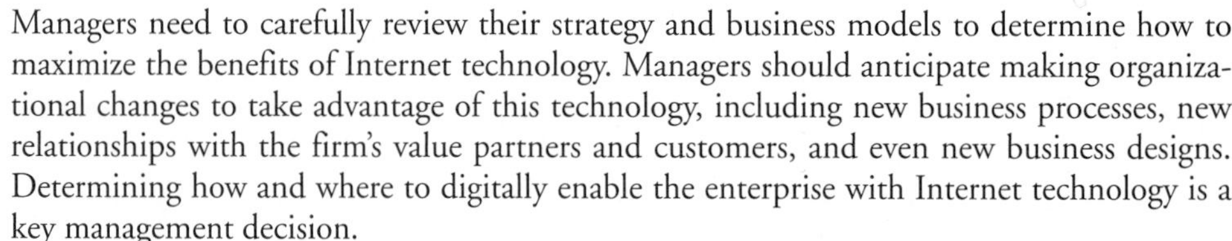

Managers need to carefully review their strategy and business models to determine how to maximize the benefits of Internet technology. Managers should anticipate making organizational changes to take advantage of this technology, including new business processes, new relationships with the firm's value partners and customers, and even new business designs. Determining how and where to digitally enable the enterprise with Internet technology is a key management decision.

The Internet can dramatically reduce transaction and agency costs and is fueling new business models. By using the Internet and other networks for electronic commerce, organizations can exchange purchase and sale transactions directly with customers and suppliers, eliminating inefficient intermediaries. Organizational processes can be streamlined by using the Internet and intranets to make communication and coordination more efficient. To take advantage of these opportunities, organizational processes must be redesigned.

Internet technology has created a universal computing platform that has become the primary infrastructure for electronic commerce, electronic business, and the emerging digital firm. Web-based applications integrating voice, data, video, and audio are providing new products, services, and tools for communicating with employees and customers. Intranets enable companies to make information flow between disparate systems, business processes, and parts of the organization.

*For Discussion*

1. How does the Internet change consumer and supplier relationships?
2. The Internet may not make corporations obsolete, but they will have to change their business models. Do you agree? Why or why not?

## SUMMARY


1. *Explain how Internet technology has transformed organizations and business models.* The Internet is rapidly becoming the infrastructure of choice for electronic commerce and electronic business, because it provides a universal and easy-to-use set of technologies and technology standards that can be adopted by all organizations, no matter what computer system or information technology platform they are using. Internet technology provides a much lower cost and easier to use alternative for coordination activities than proprietary networks. Companies can use Internet technology to radically reduce their transaction costs.

   The Internet radically reduces the cost of creating, sending, and storing information while making that information more widely available. Information is not limited to traditional physical methods of delivery. Customers can find out about products on their own on the Web and buy directly from product suppliers instead of using intermediaries such as retail stores. This unbundling of information from traditional value chain channels is having a disruptive effect on old business models and creating new business models as well. Some of the traditional channels for exchanging product information have become unnecessary or uneconomical, and business models based on the coupling of information with products and services may no longer be necessary.

   The Internet shrinks information asymmetry and has transformed the richness and reach relationship. Using the Internet and Web multimedia capabilities, companies can quickly and inexpensively provide detailed product information and detailed information specific to each customer to very large numbers of people simultaneously. The Internet can help companies create and capture profit in new ways by adding extra value to existing products and services or by providing the foundation for new products and services. Many different business models for electronic commerce on the Internet have emerged, including virtual storefronts, marketplace concentrators, information brokers, portals, content providers, digital content delivery, on-line exchanges, auctions, syndicators, and on-line service providers.

2. *Compare the categories of electronic commerce and describe how electronic commerce is changing consumer retailing and business-to-business transactions.* The three major type of electronic commerce are business-to-consumer (B2C), business-to-business (B2B), and consumer-to-consumer (C2C). Another way of classifying electronic commerce transactions is in terms of the participants' physical connection to the Web. Conventional e-commerce transactions, which take place over wired networks can be distinguished from mobile commerce or m-commerce, the purchase of goods and services using handheld wireless devices.

   The Internet provides a universally available set of technologies for electronic commerce that can be used to create new channels for marketing, sales, and customer support and to eliminate intermediaries in buy and sell transactions. Interactive capabilities on the Web can be used to build closer relationships with customers in marketing and customer support. Firms can use various Web personalization technologies to deliver Web pages with content geared to the specific interests of each user, including technologies to deliver personalized information and ads through m-commerce channels. Companies can also reduce costs and improve customer service by using Web sites to provide helpful information as well as e-mail and even telephone access to customer service representatives.

   B2B e-commerce generates efficiencies by enabling companies to electronically locate suppliers, solicit bids, place orders, and track shipments in transit. Businesses can use their own Web sites to conduct B2B e-commerce or use on-line marketplaces. Exchanges are on-line marketplaces where multiple buyers can purchase from multiple sellers using a bid–ask system. The two major types of exchanges are vertical exchanges for specific industries and horizontal exchanges providing functions for many different industries such as providing maintenance, repair, and operating supplies.

3. *Evaluate the principal electronic payment systems.* The principal electronic payment systems for Internet commerce are credit cards, electronic cash (e-cash), digital wallets, electronic checks, person-to-person payment systems, smart cards, and electronic billing systems. Smart cards and e-cash are useful for small micropayments. Electronic checking and billing systems are useful in business-to-business electronic commerce.

4. *Demonstrate how Internet technology can support electronic business and supply chain management.* Private, internal corporate networks called intranets can be created using Internet connectivity standards. Extranets are private intranets that are extended to selected organizations or individuals outside the firm. Intranets and extranets are forming the underpinnings

of electronic business by providing a low-cost technology for integrating different systems and different business processes in the enterprise. Organizations can use intranets to create collaboration environments for coordinating work and information sharing, and they can use intranets to make information flow between different functional areas of the firm. Intranets also provide a low-cost alternative for improving coordination among organizations' internal supply chain processes. Extranets can be used to coordinate supply chain processes shared with external organizations.

5. *Assess the managerial and organizational challenges posed by electronic commerce and electronic business.* Many new business models based on the Internet have not yet found proven ways to generate profits or reduce costs. Digitally enabling a firm for electronic commerce and electronic business requires far-reaching organizational change, including the redesign of business processes; recasting relationships with customers, suppliers, and other business partners; and new roles for employees. Channel conflicts may erupt as the firm turns to the Internet as an alternative outlet for sales. Security, privacy, and legal issues pose additional electronic commerce challenges.

## KEY TERMS

**Banner ad, 109**
**Business model, 106**
**Business-to-business (B2B) electronic commerce, 110**
**Business-to-consumer (B2C) electronic commerce, 110**
**Call center, 115**
**Channel conflict, 130**
**Clicks-and-mortar, 110**
**Consumer-to-consumer (C2C) electronic commerce, 110**
**Digital wallet, 120**
**Disintermediation, 111**
**Dynamic pricing, 109**
**Electronic cash (e-cash), 120**
**Electronic hub (e-hub), 115**
**Electronic payment system, 119**
**Exchange, 116**
**Information asymmetry, 106**
**Micropayment, 120**
**Mobile commerce (m-commerce), 111**
**Person-to-person payment system, 121**
**Portal, 109**
**Pure-play, 110**
**Reach, 107**
**Reintermediation, 112**
**Richness, 107**
**Smart card, 120**
**Syndicator, 110**
**Web personalization, 113**

## REVIEW QUESTIONS

1. What are the advantages of using the Internet as the infrastructure for electronic commerce and electronic business?
2. How is the Internet changing the economics of information and business models?
3. Name and describe six Internet business models for electronic commerce. Distinguish between a pure-play Internet business model and a clicks-and-mortar business model.
4. Name and describe the various categories of electronic commerce.
5. How can the Internet facilitate sales and marketing to individual customers? Describe the role played by Web personalization.
6. How can the Internet help provide customer service?
7. How can Internet technology support business-to-business electronic commerce?
8. What are exchanges? Why do they represent an important business model for B2B e-commerce?
9. Name and describe the principal electronic payment systems used on the Internet.
10. Why are intranets so useful for electronic business?
11. How can intranets support organizational collaboration?
12. Describe the uses of intranets for electronic business in sales and marketing, human resources, finance and accounting, and manufacturing and production.
13. How can companies use Internet technology for supply chain management?
14. Describe the management challenges posed by electronic commerce and electronic business on the Internet.
15. What is channel conflict? Why is it becoming a growing problem in electronic commerce?

## GROUP PROJECT

Form a group with three or four of your classmates. Select two businesses that are competitors in the same industry and using their Web sites for electronic commerce. Visit their Web sites. You might compare, for example, the Web sites for virtual banking created by Citibank and Wells Fargo Bank, or the Internet trading Web sites of E*TRADE and Ameritrade. Prepare an evaluation of each business's Web site in terms of its functions, its user friendliness, and how well it supports the company's business strategy. Which Web site does a better job? Why? Can you make some recommendations to improve these Web sites? If possible, use electronic presentation software to present your findings to the class.

## Tools for Interactive Learning

### Internet Connection

The Internet Connection for this chapter will take you to Wine.com and other Web sites where you can complete an exercise to evaluate virtual storefronts. You can also use the Interactive Study Guide to test your knowledge of the topics in this chapter and get instant feedback where you need more practice.

### Electronic Commerce Project

At the Laudon Web site for Chapter 4, you will find an Electronic Commerce project where you can build an electronic commerce storefront.

### CD-ROM

If you purchase and use the Multimedia Edition CD-ROM with this chapter you can complete an interactive exercise for analyzing Internet business models. You can also find an audio overview of the major themes of this chapter and bullet text summarizing the key points of the chapter.

## Case Study *Boo.com: Poster Child for Dot.com Failure?*

Boo.com arrived on the Internet scene promising its investors and on-line shoppers the treat of a profitable Web site offering high-quality, stylish, designer sportswear that could be purchased easily from the office or home. Thanks to advanced widespread publicity, Boo.com became, perhaps, the most eagerly awaited Internet IPO (initial public offering of stock) of its time. However, the company declared bankruptcy only six months after its Web site had been launched and before the company could ever undertake an IPO. Investors lost an estimated $185 million, while shoppers faced a system too difficult for most to use. Many people are still wondering how it could have all gone so wrong so swiftly.

The idea for Boo.com came from two 28-year-old Swedish friends, Ernst Malmsten and Kajsa Leander, who had already established and later sold Bokus.com, which is the world's third-largest on-line bookstore after Amazon.com and Barnes&Noble.com. The two were joined by Patrik Hedelin, an investment banker at HSBC Holdings.

Boo.com planned to sell trendy fashion products over the Web, offering such brands as North Face, Adidas, Fila, Vans, Cosmic Girl, and Donna Karan. The Boo.com business model differed from other Internet start-ups in that its products would be sold at full retail price rather than at a discount. Malmsten labeled his target group as "cash-rich, time-poor."

The Boo Web site enabled shoppers to view every product in full-color, three-dimensional images. Visitors could zoom in on individual products, rotating them 360 degrees to view them from any angle. The site's advanced search engine allowed customers to search for items by color, brand, price, style, and even sport. The site featured a universal sizing system based on size variations among brands and countries. Visitors were able to question Miss Boo, an animated figure offering fashion advice based on locale or on a specific activity (such as trekking in Nepal). Boo.com also made available a telephone customer service advice line. In addition Boo was to feature an independently run fashion magazine to report on global fashion trends. Those who purchased products from Boo.com earned "loyalty points," which they could use to obtain discounts on future purchases.

The company offered free delivery within one week and also free returns for dissatisfied customers. The Web site was fluent in seven languages (two of which were American and British English). Local currencies were accepted from 18 countries, and in those countries national taxes were also calculated and collected. "Boo.com will revolutionize the way we shop. . . . It's a completely new lifestyle proposition, " Ms. Leander proclaimed.

The founders planned to advertise its site broadly both prior to and after launching. "We are building a very strong brand name for Boo.com," stated Malmsten. "We want to be the style editors for people with the best selection of products. We decided from day one that we would want to create a global brand name."

Although many important financial firms rejected investment in Boo.com, J. P. Morgan & Co., an old-line investment bank, decided to back the project even though it had done no start-ups for many decades. According to the *New York Times,* Morgan liked the concept "because Boo wouldn't undercut traditional retailers with cut-rate pricing as many e-retailers do." The Morgan bankers were also impressed by the two founders who had previously successfully launched an Internet company (Bokus.com). They also were impressed by promised rewards of "55 percent gross margins and profitability within two years," according to the *Times.* Morgan found other early-stage investors, including Alessandro Benetton (son of the CEO of Benetton), Bain Capital (a Boston high-tech venture capital company), Bernard Arnault (who has made a fortune in luxury goods), Goldman Sachs, and the very wealthy Hariri family of Lebanon.

With start-up funds in hand, Malmsten and Leander set a target date of May 1999 for launching the Web site. Boo planned to develop both its complex Internet platform and customer-fulfillment systems from scratch. Management originally planned to launch in the United States and five European countries simultaneously but soon expanded the number of countries to 18. It also wanted a system that would handle 100 million Web visitors at once. When the launch date began to loom close, management committed $25 million to an advertising budget, a huge sum for a start-up. The company chose to advertise in expensive but trendy fashion magazines such as *Vanity Fair* as well as on cable television and the Internet. Malmsten and Leander even managed to appear on the cover of *Fortune* magazine before the Web site was launched.

With so much technical development to be accomplished, the company moved the target date back to June 21. As June approached management decided to open satellite offices in Munich, Paris, New York, and Amsterdam. Several hundred people were hired to take orders from these offices once the site went live. However, the launch date had to be postponed again because of incomplete Web site development, and so many of the staff sat idle for months. "With all those trophy offices, Boo looked more like a 1950s multinational than an Internet start-up," claimed Marina Galanti, a Boo marketing director.

By September the company had spent $70 million, and Boo undertook more fund-raising. With the prelaunch advertising campaign completed months earlier, the Web site was finally launched in early November. The promised mass marketing blitz never materialized. With the original advertising campaign long over, observers commented that raising people's interest while delaying the opening resulted in many disappointed and alienated potential customers. Moreover, the site reviews were terrible. At launch time, 40 percent of the site's visitors could not even gain access. The site was full of errors, even causing visitors' computers to freeze. The site design, which had been advertised as revolutionary, was slow and very difficult to use. Only one in four attempts to make a purchase worked. Users of Macintosh computers could not even log on because Boo.com was incompatible with them. Users without high-speed Internet connections found that navigating the site was painfully slow, because the flashy graphics and interactive features took so long to load. Angry customers jammed Boo.com's customer support lines. Sales in the first three months amounted to only about $880,000, and expenses heavily topped $1 million per month. The Boo plan quickly began unraveling.

In December, J. P. Morgan's representative on Boo.com's board of directors resigned, leaving no one from Morgan to advise the company. In late December with sales lagging badly and the company running out of cash, Malmsten was unable to raise enough additional investment, causing Boo to begin selling its clothing at a 40 percent discount. This changed Boo's public image and its target audience. However, Boo's advertising did not change to reflect this strategy shift.

On January 25, 2000 Boo.com announced a layoff of 70 employees, starting its decline from a reported high of about 450 persons, a huge number for a start-up. In late February, J. P. Morgan resigned as a Boo.com advisor. According to reports, it feared being sued by angry investors. In March, when sales reached $1.1 million, Boo was still spending far more than its income. In April, Internet stocks plunged on the stock market, and plans for a Boo IPO were shelved. Finally, on May 17, Malmsten hired a firm to liquidate the company, announcing his decision the next day. He also indicated that the company had many outstanding bills it could not pay.

One problem leading to Boo.com's bankruptcy was its lack of planning and control. "When you strip away the sexy dot.com aspect and the technology out of it, these are still businesses that need the fundamentals—budgeting, planning, and execution," observed Jim Rose, CEO of QXL.com PLC, an on-line auction house. "To roll out in 18 countries simultaneously, I don't think even the biggest global companies like IBM or General Motors would take that on." Boo's offices were rented in high-priced areas such as London's Carnaby Street and in New York's West Village. Numerous reports surfaced of employees flying first class and staying in five-star hotels. Reports even surfaced that communications that could have gone by regular mail were routinely sent by Federal Express.

Many in the financial community noted the lack of oversight by the board. Management controlled most of the board seats, with only four being allocated to investors. However, those four investor representatives rarely attended board meetings. Moreover, none had any significant retail or Internet experience. The board failed to offer management the supervision it clearly needed.

Serious technical problems contributed as well. Developing their own software proved slow and expensive. The plan required rich, complex graphics so visitors could view products from any angle. The technicians also had to develop a complex virtual inventory system, because Boo maintained very little inventory of its own. Boo's order basket was particularly intricate, because items were actually ordered from the manufacturer, not from Boo, so that one customer might have a basket containing items coming from four or five different sources. The site also had to enable its customers to communicate in any one of seven languages and to convert 18 different currencies and calculate taxes from 18 different countries.

Industry analysts observed that 99 percent of European and 98 percent of U.S. homes lack the high-capacity Internet connections required to easily access the graphics and animation on the Boo.com site. No Apple Macintosh computer could access the site. Navigating the site presented visitors special problems. Web pages existed that did nothing, such as one visitors reported that displayed only a strange message that read "Nothing happens on this page—except that you may want to bookmark it." Product descriptions were displayed in tiny one-square inch windows, making descriptions not only difficult to read but also difficult to scroll through. Boo developed its own, very unorthodox, scrolling method that people found unfamiliar and difficult to use. Moreover, interface navigation was too complex. The Boo hierarchical menus required precise accuracy, because visitors making a wrong choice had no alternative but to return to the top to start over again. Moreover, the icons were miniscule.

One annoying aspect of the site was the constant presence of Miss Boo. Although she was developed to give style advice to browsers and buyers, she was constantly injected regardless of whether the visitor desired her. Many visitors reacted as they might have if they were shopping in a bricks-and-mortar store and had a live clerk hovering over them, commenting without stop.

On June 18, Fashionmall.com purchased most of the remnants of Boo.com, including its brand name, Web address, advertising materials, and on-line content. (Bright Station PLC purchased the company's software for taking orders in multiple languages to market to other on-line businesses that want to sell to consumers in other countries.) "What we really bought is a brand that has phenomenal awareness world-wide," explained Kate Buggeln, the president of Fashionmall.com's Boo division. The company plans to use the Boo brand name to add a high-end site similar to its long-existing clothing site. The new

Boo.com was launched on October 30, 2000 with a shoestring $1 million budget. The site is much less ambitious than its earlier incarnation, acting primarily as a portal, and it does not own any inventory. Its design is much less graphics-intensive and flashy, enabling visitors to browse smoothly and easily through its pages. It features about 400 items for sale ferreted out by a network of fashion scouts as appealing to upscale buyers under age 31. Rather than getting bogged down in taking orders and shipping goods, Boo will direct customers to the Web sites that sell the merchandise they wish to purchase. Buggeln is optimistic about Boo.com's chances of success this time.

**Sources:** Michelle Slatalla, "Boo.com Tries Again, Humbled and Retooled," *New York Times,* January 11, 2001; Andrew Ross Sorkin, "Boo.com, Online Fashion Retailer, Goes Out of Business" *New York Times,* May 19, 2000; Stephanie Gruner, "Trendy Online Retailer Is Reduced to a Cautionary Tale for Investors," *Wall Street Journal,* May 19, 2000; Sarah Ellison, "Boo.com: Buried by Badly Managed Buzz," *Wall Street Journal,* May 23, 2000; David Walker, "Talk About a Real Boo-boo," *Sydney Morning Herald,* May 30, 2000; Andrew Ross Sorkin, "Fashionmall.com Swoops in for the Boo.com Fire Sale," *New York Times,* June 2, 2000; Bernhard Warner, "Boo.com Trims its Bottom Line," *The Industry Standard,* January 25, 2000; Polly Sprenger, "Boo Founder: Don't Cry for Me," *The Industry Standard,* February 11, 2000; Rikke Sternberg, "All About the Brand," *BizReport,* April 3, 2000; Polly Sprenger, "More Creaks and Groans at Boo.com," *The Industry Standard,* May 4, 2000; Christopher Cooper and Erik Portanger, " 'Miss Boo' and Her Makeovers," *Wall Street Journal,* June 27, 2000; Stephanie Gruner, "Resurrection of Boo May Prove Existence of Dot-com Afterlife," *Wall Street Journal Europe,* September 6, 2000; Suzanne Kapner, "Boo.com, Online Fashion Flop, Is Ready to Rise from Ashes," *New York Times,* October 17, 2000; Suzie Amer, "If You Build It, Will They Come?" *Forbes ASAP,* May 25, 1999; Lauren Goldstein, "Boo.com," *Fortune.com,* July 7, 1999; and Polly Sprenger, "Where Is Boo.com," *The Industry Standard,* September 17, 1999.

### *CASE STUDY QUESTIONS*

1. Analyze Boo.com's business model. How did it differ from more conventional retail Web site strategies? Why do you think the founders and investors of Boo were drawn to this unusual strategy?
2. What problems did Boo.com encounter trying to implement its business model? What management, organization, and technology factors contributed to these problems?
3. What could Boo.com have done differently that might have made the project successful?

# Part I Project

# Analyzing Business Processes for an Enterprise System

Your firm manufactures specialty chemicals and dyestuffs used in plastics, fibers, and coatings. It operates five different production facilities in the southeastern United States, with corporate headquarters in Memphis, Tennessee.

Rapid time-to-market of new products, strong customer service, and low costs are essential for remaining competitive in the chemical industry. Management is looking for ways to make the company operate more efficiently and would like to start by examining order processing.

This is how the firm's order processing works. A customer can call, fax, or mail in an order. A customer service representative writes down order information on an order pad. This information includes the customer name, shipping address, billing address, product number, product description, quantity, and shipping instructions (such as to call the receiving manager to make an appointment for delivery). After gathering all the relevant information, the representative confirms the entire order with the customer.

While taking down the order information, the customer service representative accesses the company's order entry system and checks the inventory for each product ordered. The customer service representative first checks the warehouse closest to the customer's shipping address. If the product is not available there, the representative checks another warehouse. If the order is placed on the telephone, the customer service representative suggests a delivery date, which is four to five business days away. If the customer needs the order sooner, the customer service representative queries the existing order entry information system to see which warehouse might have the inventory to fulfill the order. Generally, the order will be filled by the warehouse closest to the customer's shipping address.

All current orders are collected manually and entered into the firm's order entry system. The order will not be accepted by the system unless it includes the customer's identification number, shipping address, and billing address. (If the order is from a new customer, the system can assign a new customer number.) If the order has a delivery date of 8 to 10 business days in the future, the order form will be held manually for several days and then input into the system. If an order is for more than 10 days in the future, it will be treated as a back order when it is input into the system. The system generates a back order report daily to remind customer service representatives of orders that they have on back order.

When each order has been entered, the system performs a credit check on the customer. Some customers are assigned "credit hold" status and are not shipped their orders until payment has been received for the purchase. Other customer orders are processed immediately, and the customer pays for the purchase after receiving the shipment and an invoice. A report on credit holds is forwarded to the credit department, and the customer service representatives receive a daily report on orders placed on credit hold.

Different business units at your company use different identification systems for the same products. In other words, corporate headquarters might use a different product number for a product such as purple dye 211, than the product identification number used at the plant at which it was manufactured.

1. Diagram the order process. What are the outputs of this process?
2. What other major business processes outside of the order process are likely to be impacted by the order process? Explain.
3. How could this process be made more efficient? Draw a diagram of your proposed process and information changes.
4. Prepare descriptions of two reports from this system: one that would be important to the order entry staff and one that would be important to corporate management.
5. Your company is thinking about installing enterprise software. You would like to learn more about enterprise software and how it could handle your order entry process. Explore the Solutions Map for the chemical industry on the SAP Web site (www.sap.com), paying special attention to the processes for Customer Relationship Management. Which SAP processes are likely to address the activities in order processing that we have described? What questions would you ask to determine whether SAP's software could handle your order process?

You have heard that enterprise software might not be able to handle the following situations:

- When the system checks for available inventory, it treats batches of chemicals that are still undergoing quality control inspection as available inventory as well as material in inventory that has already passed quality control inspection.
- There is no way to automatically check customer records to determine which qualify for sales tax exemptions.
- The system assigns a date for back orders of items that are currently out of stock rather than the original requested date on the customer order.

What impact might this lack of functionality have on order processing in other parts of the company? How could you determine how serious a problem this creates? What questions would you ask?

# PART II

# INFORMATION TECHNOLOGY INFRASTRUCTURE

chapter

# 5 Managing Hardware Assets

objectives

**After completing this chapter, you will be able to:**

1. *Identify the hardware components in a typical computer system and their role in processing information.*
2. *Describe the principal storage, input, and output technologies for computer systems and interactive multimedia.*
3. *Compare the capabilities of mainframes, midrange computers, PCs, workstations, servers, and supercomputers.*
4. *Evaluate different arrangements of computer processing, including client/server computing, network computers, and peer-to-peer computing.*
5. *Analyze important issues in managing hardware technology assets.*

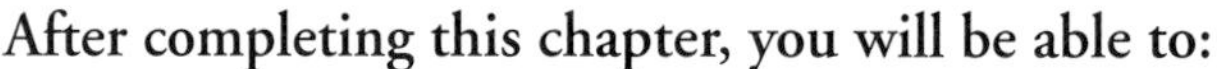

## Battling the Megadealers with the Right Computers

Employees and managers at West Coast Office Interiors, a small office furniture company in the San Francisco Bay area, used to face a grim work environment. The company relied on a hodgepodge of "clunky" computers, none of which ran the same software. The servers were outdated. One piece of software for drawing furniture layouts required too much computer memory to run and constantly overloaded the system. Accounting software that could run on one of the computers was inefficient as well, requiring employees to manually key in new inventory entries, which could amount to thousands in one day. Sometimes the office manager had to work 18-20-hour days just to keep up with the paperwork.

To make matters worse, West Coast was competing with a sales force of four against "megadealers" who each had more than 20 people in their sales staff. West Coast's tiny sales staff had no computer support in the field. On a typical sales call, a sales representative would have to draw an office layout for a customer by hand, then go back to the office to see if the requested furniture was in stock. Then the sales rep would enter the data into the memory-hogging layout software, print out the result, and take it back to the customer. The process of preparing a proposal could take up to a week. In the office furniture business, closing a deal with a customer requires vendors to develop proposals quickly, and West Coast did not have the tools to be competitive.

Cy Sidun, who was West Coast's vice president and general manager at that time, wanted to supply everyone with laptop computers that could link to a new computer system in the main office. The major stumbling block was price—$300,000, which was way too expensive for a firm such as West Coast with only $8 million in annual sales. Fortunately, he was able to lease the equipment from

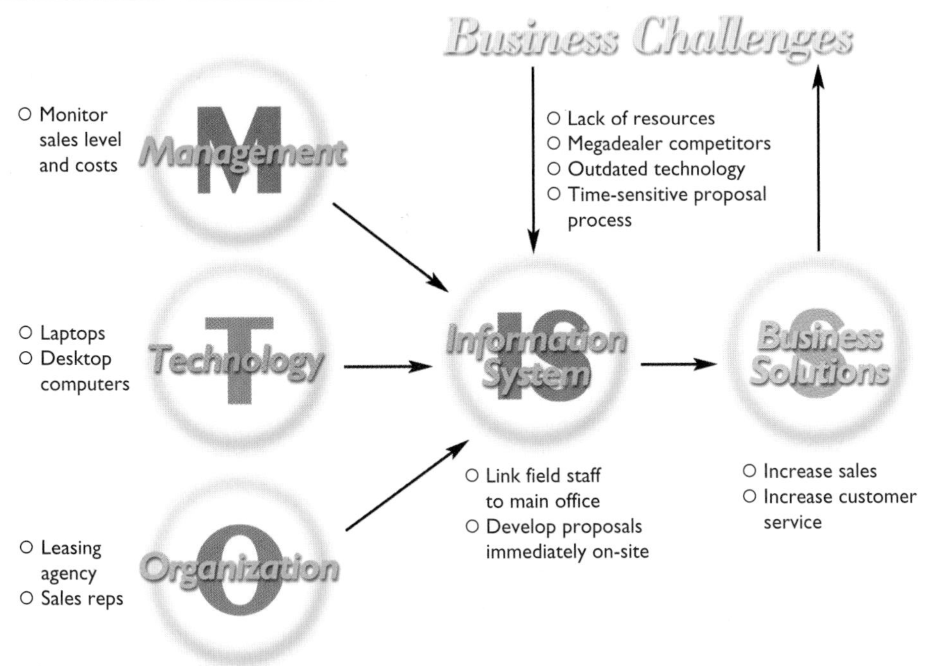


CenterBeam, which specializes in hardware, software, and information systems consulting to small and emerging businesses. West Coast leased all new desktop computers and about six laptop computers for the sales staff to use on sales calls. The salespeople can now develop proposals immediately on-site. CenterBeam charges $200 per month to help support and maintain the system. Sidun likens his new information technology solution to a miracle.

**Sources:** Michael Grebb, "If It Ain't Broke, Fix It Anyway," *Small Business Computing,* November 2000; and "West Coast Office Interiors Gains Technological Advantage with CenterBeam," CenterBeam Inc., 2000-2001, www.CenterBeam.com.

## Battling the Megadealers with the Right Computers

### MANAGEMENT CHALLENGES

By shifting to more up-to-date computer hardware, West Coast Office Interiors was able to provide more computing power for its operations. To select the right computers, West Coast Office Interiors' management needed to understand how much computer processing capacity its business processes required, how to evaluate the price and performance of various types of computers, and the financial and business rationale for hardware technology investments. Management also had to plan for future processing requirements and understand how the computer worked with related storage, input/output, and communications technology. Selecting appropriate computer hardware raises the following management challenges:

## MANAGEMENT CHALLENGES

1. **The centralization versus decentralization debate.** A long-standing issue among information system managers and CEOs has been the question of how much to centralize or distribute computing resources. Should processing power and data be distributed to departments and divisions, or should they be concentrated at a single location using a large central computer? Client/server computing facilitates decentralization, but network computers and mainframes support a centralized model. Which is the best for the organization? Each organization will have a different answer based on its own needs. Managers need to make sure that the computing model they select is compatible with organizational goals.
2. **Making wise technology purchasing decisions.** Computer hardware technology advances much more rapidly than other assets of the firm. Soon after having made an investment in hardware technology, managers find the completed system is obsolete and too expensive, given the power and lower cost of new technology. In this environment it is very difficult to keep one's own systems up to date. A considerable amount of time must be spent anticipating and planning for technological change.

Successful use of information systems to support an organization's business goals requires an understanding of computer processing power and the capabilities of hardware devices. By understanding the role of hardware technology in the organization's information technology infrastructure, managers can make sure that their firms have the processing capability they need to accomplish the work of the firm and to meet future business challenges.

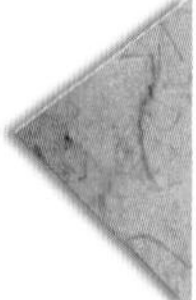

In this chapter we describe the typical hardware configuration of a computer system, explaining how a computer works and how computer processing power and storage capacity are measured. We then compare the capabilities of various types of computers and related input, output, and storage devices. We conclude by discussing the major issues in the management of hardware assets for the firm.

## 5.1 COMPUTER HARDWARE AND INFORMATION TECHNOLOGY INFRASTRUCTURE

Computer hardware technology constitutes the underlying physical foundation for the firm's information technology (IT) infrastructure. The other components of IT infrastructure—software, data, and networks—require computer hardware for their storage or operation. Although managers and business professionals do not need to be computer technology experts, they should have a basic understanding of how computer hardware works and its role in the organization's IT infrastructure so that they can make technology decisions that benefit organizational performance and productivity.

### THE COMPUTER SYSTEM

A contemporary computer system consists of a central processing unit, primary storage, secondary storage, input devices, output devices, and communications devices (see Figure 5-1).

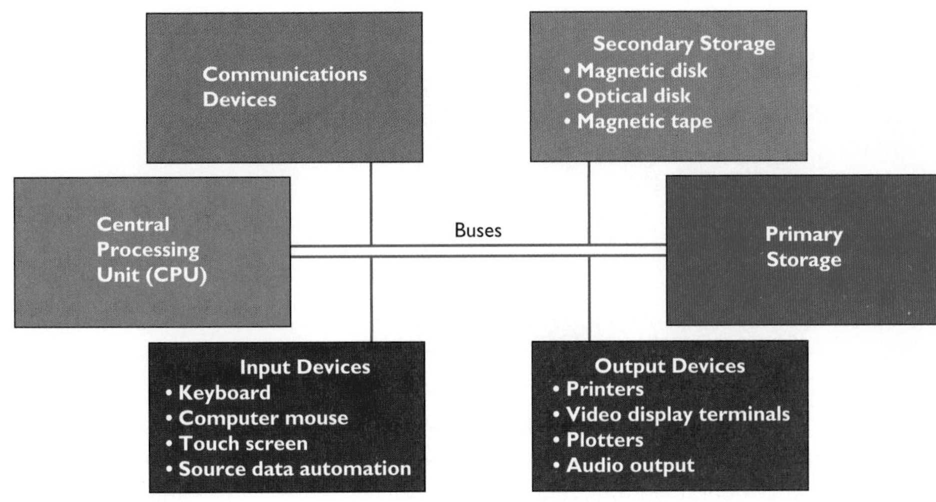


*Figure 5-1* Hardware components of a computer system. A contemporary computer system can be categorized into six major components. The central processing unit (CPU) manipulates data and controls the other parts of the computer system; primary storage temporarily stores data and program instructions during processing; secondary storage stores data and instructions when they are not used in processing; input devices convert data and instructions for processing in the computer; output devices present data in a form that people can understand; and communications devices control the passing of information to and from communications networks.

The central processing unit manipulates raw data into a more useful form and controls the other parts of the computer system. Primary storage temporarily stores data and program instructions during processing, whereas secondary storage devices (magnetic and optical disks, magnetic tape) store data and programs when they are not being used in processing. Input devices, such as a keyboard or mouse, convert data and instructions into electronic form for input into the computer. Output devices, such as printers and video display terminals, convert electronic data produced by the computer system and display them in a form that people can understand. Communications devices provide connections between the computer and communications networks. Buses are circuitry paths for transmitting data and signals among the parts of the computer system.

**bit**
A binary digit representing the smallest unit of data in a computer system. It can only have one of two states, representing 0 or 1.

## HOW COMPUTERS REPRESENT DATA

**byte**
A string of bits, usually eight, used to store one number or character in a computer system.

In order for information to flow through a computer system and be in a form suitable for processing, all symbols, pictures, or words must be reduced to a string of binary digits. A binary digit is called a **bit** and represents either a 0 or a 1. In the computer, the presence of an electronic or magnetic signal means one, and its absence signifies zero. Digital computers operate directly with binary digits, either singly or strung together to form bytes. A string of eight bits that the computer stores as a unit is called a **byte.** Each byte can be used to store a decimal number, a symbol, a character, or part of a picture (see Figure 5-2).

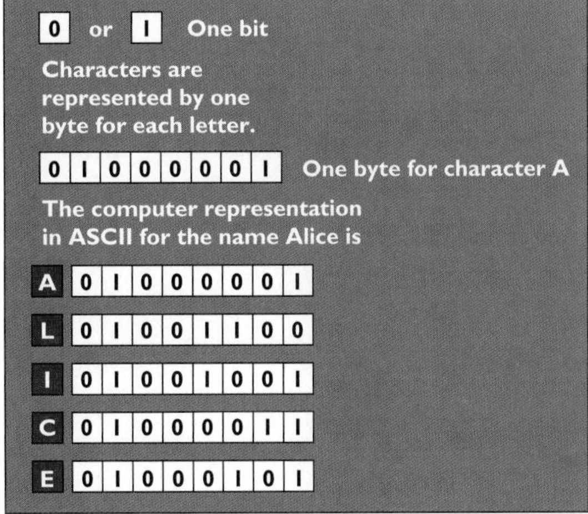


*Figure 5-2* Bits and bytes. Bits are represented by either a 0 or 1. A string of eight bits constitutes a byte, which represents a character. The computer's representation for the word "ALICE" is a series of five bytes, where each byte represents one character (or letter) in the name.

Figure 5-3 shows how decimal numbers are represented using binary digits. Each position in a decimal number has a certain value. Any number in the decimal system (base 10) can be reduced to a binary number. The binary number system (base 2) can express any number as a power of the number 2. The table at the bottom of the figure shows how the translation from binary to decimal works. By

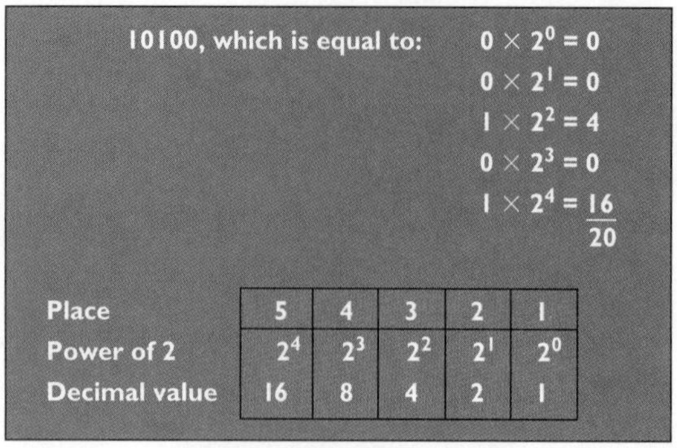

| 10100, which is equal to: | | | | | $0 \times 2^0 = 0$ |
|---|---|---|---|---|---|
| | | | | | $0 \times 2^1 = 0$ |
| | | | | | $1 \times 2^2 = 4$ |
| | | | | | $0 \times 2^3 = 0$ |
| | | | | | $1 \times 2^4 = 16$ |
| | | | | | 20 |

| Place | 5 | 4 | 3 | 2 | 1 |
|---|---|---|---|---|---|
| Power of 2 | $2^4$ | $2^3$ | $2^2$ | $2^1$ | $2^0$ |
| Decimal value | 16 | 8 | 4 | 2 | 1 |

***Figure 5-3*** The binary number system. Each decimal number has a certain value that can be expressed as a binary number. The binary number system can express any number as a power of the number 2.

**EBCDIC (Extended Binary Coded Decimal Interchange Code)**
Binary code representing every number, alphabetic character, or special character with eight bits, used primarily in IBM and other mainframe computers.

**ASCII (American Standard Code for Information Interchange)**
A seven- or eight-bit binary code used in data transmission, PCs, and some large computers.

**pixel**
The smallest unit of data for defining an image in the computer. The computer reduces a picture to a grid of pixels. The term *pixel* comes from picture element.

**central processing unit (CPU)**
Area of the computer system that manipulates symbols, numbers, and letters, and controls the other parts of the computer system.

**primary storage**
Part of the computer that temporarily stores program instructions and data being used by the instructions.

using a binary number system, a computer can express all numbers as groups of zeroes and ones. In addition to representing numbers, a computer must represent alphabetic characters and many other symbols used in natural language, such as $ and &. Manufacturers of computer hardware have developed standard binary codes for this purpose.

Two common codes are EBCDIC and ASCII. The **Extended Binary Coded Decimal Interchange Code (EBCDIC**—pronounced ib-si-dick) was developed by IBM in the 1950s, and it represents every number, alphabetic character, or special character with eight bits. **ASCII,** which stands for the **American Standard Code for Information Interchange,** was developed by the American National Standards Institute (ANSI) to provide a standard code that could be used by many different manufacturers in order to make machinery compatible. ASCII was originally designed as a seven-bit code, but most computers use eight-bit versions. EBCDIC is used in IBM and other large mainframe computers, whereas ASCII is used in data transmission, PCs, and some larger computers. Table 5-1 shows how some letters and numbers would be represented using EBCDIC and ASCII. Other coding systems are being developed to represent a wider array of foreign languages.

How can a computer represent a picture? The computer stores a picture by creating a grid overlay of the picture. Each single point in this grid, or matrix, is called a **pixel** (picture element) and consists of a number of bits. The computer then stores this information on each pixel. A high-resolution computer display monitor has a 1024 × 768 SVGA (super-video graphics array) standard grid, creating more than 700,000 pixels. Whether processing pictures or text, modern computers operate by reducing such data into bits and bytes.

## THE CPU AND PRIMARY STORAGE

The **central processing unit (CPU)** is the part of the computer system where the manipulation of symbols, numbers, and letters occurs, and it controls the other parts of the computer system (see Figure 5-4). Located near the CPU is **primary storage** (sometimes called primary memory or main memory), where data and program instructions are stored temporarily during processing. Three kinds of buses link the CPU, primary storage, and the other devices in the computer system. The data bus moves data to and from primary storage. The address bus transmits signals for locating a given address in primary storage, indicating where data should be placed. The control bus transmits signals specifying whether to read or write

**TABLE 5-1 EXAMPLES OF ASCII AND EBCDIC CODES**

| Character or Number | ASCII-8 Binary | EBCDIC Binary |
|---|---|---|
| A | 01000001 | 11000001 |
| E | 01000101 | 11000101 |
| Z | 01011010 | 11101001 |
| 0 | 00110000 | 11110000 |
| 1 | 00110001 | 11110001 |
| 5 | 00110101 | 11110101 |

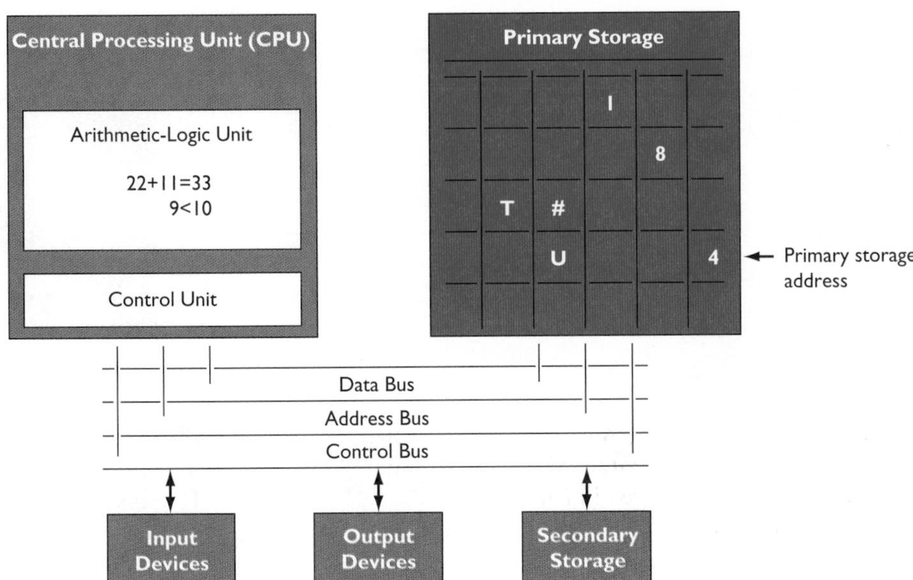


*Figure 5-4* The CPU and primary storage. The CPU contains an arithmetic-logic unit and a control unit. Data and instructions are stored in unique addresses in primary storage that the CPU can access during processing. The data bus, address bus, and control bus transmit signals between the central processing unit, primary storage, and other devices in the computer system.

data to or from a given primary storage address, input device, or output device. The characteristics of the CPU and primary storage are very important in determining a computer's speed and capabilities.

## The Arithmetic-Logic Unit and Control Unit

Figure 5-4 also shows that the CPU consists of an arithmetic-logic unit and a control unit. The **arithmetic-logic unit (ALU)** performs the computer's principal logical and arithmetic operations. It adds, subtracts, multiplies, and divides, determining whether a number is positive, negative, or zero. In addition to performing arithmetic functions, an ALU must be able to determine when one quantity is greater than or less than another and when two quantities are equal. The ALU can perform logic operations on the binary codes for letters as well as numbers.

The **control unit** coordinates and controls the other parts of the computer system. It reads a stored program, one instruction at a time, and directs other components of the computer system to perform the program's required tasks. The series of operations required to process a single machine instruction is called the **machine cycle.** Older computers and PCs have machine cycle times measured in **microseconds** (one-millionth of a second). More powerful machines have machine cycle times measured in **nanoseconds** (billionths of a second) or picoseconds (trillionths of a second). Another measure of machine cycle time is by MIPS, or millions of instructions per second.

**arithmetic-logic unit (ALU)** Component of the CPU that performs the computer's principal logic and arithmetic operations.

**control unit** Component of the CPU that controls and coordinates the other parts of the computer system.

**machine cycle** Series of operations required to process a single machine instruction.

**microsecond** One-millionth of a second.

**nanosecond** One-billionth of a second.

## Primary Storage

Primary storage has three functions. It stores all or part of the program that is being executed. Primary storage also stores the operating system programs that manage the operation of the computer. (These programs are discussed in Chapter 6.) Finally, the primary storage area holds data that the program is using. Data and programs are placed in primary storage before processing, between processing steps, and after processing has ended, prior to being returned to secondary storage or released as output.

Figure 5-5 (on p. 146) illustrates primary storage in an electronic digital computer. Internal primary storage is often called **RAM,** or **random access memory.** It is called RAM because it can directly access any randomly chosen location in the same amount of time.

Figure 5-5 shows that primary memory is divided into storage locations called bytes. Each location contains a set of eight binary switches or devices, each of which can store one bit of information. The set of eight bits found in each storage location is sufficient to store one letter, one digit, or one special symbol (such as $) using either EBCDIC or ASCII. Each byte has a unique address, similar to a mailbox, indicating where it is located in RAM. The

**RAM (random access memory)** Primary storage of data or program instructions that can directly access any randomly chosen location in the same amount of time.

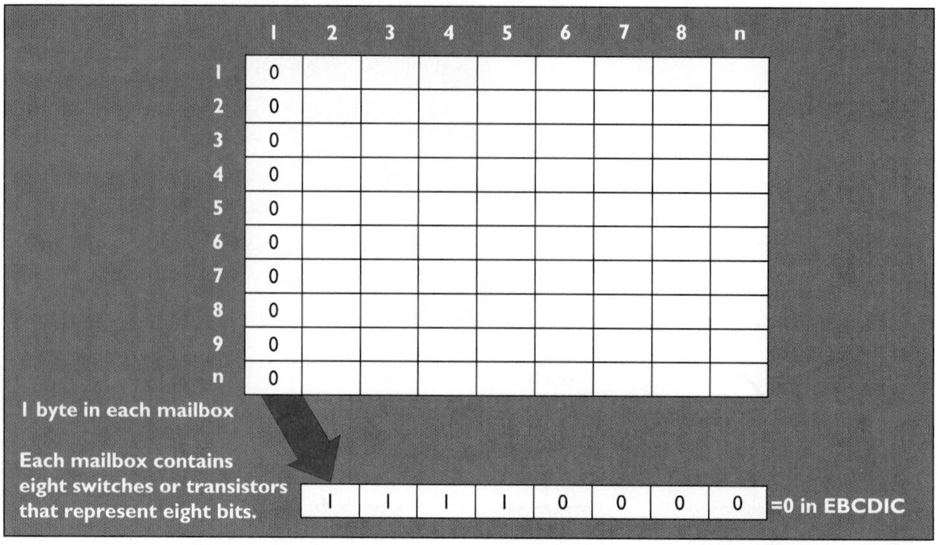

*Figure 5-5* Primary storage in the computer. Primary storage can be visualized as a matrix. Each byte represents a mailbox with a unique address. In this example, mailbox [n,1] contains eight bits representing the number 0 (as coded in EBCDIC).

| | 1 | 2 | 3 | 4 | 5 | 6 | 7 | 8 | n |
|---|---|---|---|---|---|---|---|---|---|
| 1 | 0 | | | | | | | | |
| 2 | 0 | | | | | | | | |
| 3 | 0 | | | | | | | | |
| 4 | 0 | | | | | | | | |
| 5 | 0 | | | | | | | | |
| 6 | 0 | | | | | | | | |
| 7 | 0 | | | | | | | | |
| 8 | 0 | | | | | | | | |
| 9 | 0 | | | | | | | | |
| n | 0 | | | | | | | | |

1 byte in each mailbox

Each mailbox contains eight switches or transistors that represent eight bits.

| 1 | 1 | 1 | 1 | 0 | 0 | 0 | 0 | =0 in EBCDIC |
|---|---|---|---|---|---|---|---|---|

computer can remember where the data in all of the bytes are located simply by keeping track of these addresses.

Computer storage capacity is measured in bytes. Table 5-2 lists computer storage capacity measurements. One thousand bytes (actually 1024 storage positions) is called a **kilobyte.** One million bytes is called a **megabyte,** one billion bytes is called a **gigabyte,** and one trillion bytes is called a **terabyte.**

Primary storage is composed of semiconductors. A **semiconductor** is an integrated circuit made by printing thousands and even millions of tiny transistors on a small silicon chip. There are several different kinds of semiconductor memory used in primary storage. RAM is used for short-term storage of data or program instructions. RAM is volatile: Its contents will be lost when the computer's electric supply is disrupted by a power outage or when the computer is turned off. **ROM,** or **read-only memory,** can only be read from; it cannot be written to. ROM chips come from the manufacturer with programs already burned in, or stored. ROM is used in general-purpose computers to store important or frequently used programs, such as computing routines for calculating the square roots of numbers.

## MICROPROCESSORS AND PROCESSING POWER

Contemporary CPUs also use semiconductor chips called **microprocessors,** which integrate all of the memory, logic, and control circuits for an entire CPU onto a single chip. The speed and performance of a computer's microprocessors help determine a computer's processing power. Some popular microprocessors are listed in Table 5-3. You may see chips labeled as 8-bit, 16-bit, or 32-bit devices. These labels refer to the **word length,** or the number of bits that the computer can process at one time. A 32-bit chip can process 32 bits or 4 bytes of data in a single machine cycle. A 64-bit chip can process 64 bits or 8 bytes in a single cycle. The larger the word length, the greater the computer's speed.

A second factor affecting chip speed is cycle speed. Every event in a computer must be sequenced so that one step logically follows another. The control unit sets a beat to the chip.

### TABLE 5-2 COMPUTER STORAGE CAPACITY

| | |
|---|---|
| Byte | String of eight bits |
| Kilobyte | 1,000 bytes[a] |
| Megabyte | 1,000,000 bytes |
| Gigabyte | 1,000,000,000 bytes |
| Terabyte | 1,000,000,000,000 bytes |

[a]Actually 1024 storage positions.

**kilobyte**
One thousand bytes (actually 1,024 storage positions). Unit of computer storage capacity.

**megabyte**
Approximately one million bytes. Unit of computer storage capacity.

**gigabyte**
Approximately one billion bytes. Unit of computer storage capacity.

**terabyte**
Approximately one trillion bytes. Unit of computer storage capacity.

**semiconductor**
An integrated circuit made by printing thousands and often millions of tiny transistors on a small silicon chip.

**ROM (read-only memory)**
Semiconductor memory chips that contain program instructions. These chips can only be read from; they cannot be written to.

**microprocessor**
Very large-scale integrated circuit technology that integrates the computer's memory, logic, and control on a single chip.

**word length**
The number of bits that the computer can process at one time. The larger the word length, the greater the computer's speed.

**TABLE 5-3 EXAMPLES OF MICROPROCESSORS**

| Name | Microprocessor Manufacturer | Word Length | Data Bus Width | Clock Speed (MHz) | Used In |
|---|---|---|---|---|---|
| Pentium | Intel | 32 | 64 | 75–200 | IBM and other PCs |
| Pentium II | Intel | 32 | 64 | 233–450 | PCs |
| Pentium III | Intel | 32 | 64 | 900+ | High-end PCs, servers, and workstations |
| PowerPC | Motorola, IBM, Apple | 32 or 64 | 64 | 100–700+ | PCs and workstations |
| Alpha 21364 | Compaq | 64 | 64 | 1,000+ | Compaq workstations and servers |
| AMD Athlon | Advanced Micro Devices | 32 | 64 | 1,000+ | High-end PCs and workstations |
| Pentium 4 | Intel | 32 | 64 | 1,500 | High-end PCs, servers, and workstations |

This beat is established by an internal clock and is measured in **megahertz** (abbreviated MHz, which stands for millions of cycles per second). The Intel 8088 chip, for instance, originally had a clock speed of 4.47 megahertz, whereas the Intel Pentium III chip has a clock speed that ranges from 450 to over 900 megahertz and the Pentium 4 chip clock speed is more than 1 gigahertz.

**megahertz**
A measure of cycle speed, or the pacing of events in a computer; one megahertz equals one million cycles per second.

A third factor affecting speed is the **data bus width.** The data bus acts as a highway between the CPU, primary storage, and other devices, determining how much data can be moved at one time. The 8088 chip used in the original IBM personal computer, for example, had a 16-bit word length but only an 8-bit data bus width. This meant that data were processed within the CPU chip itself in 16-bit chunks but could only be moved 8 bits at a time between the CPU, primary storage, and external devices. However, the Alpha chip has both a 64-bit word length and a 64-bit data bus width. To have a computer execute more instructions per second and work through programs or handle users expeditiously, it is necessary to increase the processor's word length, the data bus width, or the cycle speed—or all three.

**data bus width**
The number of bits that can be moved at one time between the CPU, primary storage, and the other devices of a computer.

Microprocessors can be made faster by using **reduced instruction set computing (RISC)** in their design. Conventional chips, based on complex instruction set computing, have several hundred or more instructions hard-wired into their circuitry, and they may take several clock cycles to execute a single instruction. If the little-used instructions are eliminated, the remaining instructions can execute much faster. RISC computers have only the most frequently used instructions embedded in them. A RISC CPU can execute most instructions in a single machine cycle and sometimes multiple instructions at the same time.

**reduced instruction set computing (RISC)**
Technology used to enhance the speed of microprocessors by embedding only the most frequently used instructions on a chip.

*The Pentium 4 chip has a clock speed of more than 1 gigahertz.*

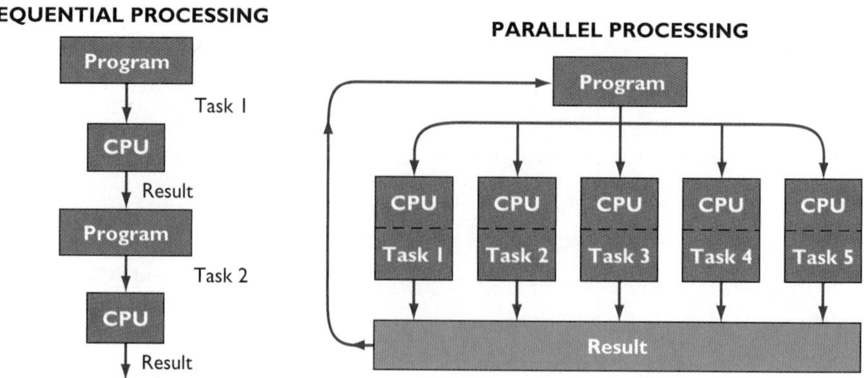


**Figure 5-6** Sequential and parallel processing. During sequential processing, each task is assigned to one CPU that processes one instruction at a time. In parallel processing, multiple tasks are assigned to multiple processing units to expedite the result.

RISC is most appropriate for scientific and workstation computing, where there are repetitive arithmetic and logical operations on data or applications calling for three-dimensional image rendering.

Microprocessors optimized for multimedia and graphics have been developed to improve processing of visually intensive applications. Recent Intel, AMD and other microprocessors include a set of additional instructions called **MMX (MultiMedia eXtension)** to increase performance in many applications featuring graphics and sound. Multimedia applications such as games and video run more smoothly, with more colors, and perform more tasks simultaneously than other microprocessors if software can take advantage of MMX instructions. For example, multiple channels of audio, high-quality video or animation, and Internet communication could all be running in the same application.

**MMX (MultiMedia eXtension)**
Set of instructions built into a microprocessor to improve processing of multimedia applications.

### MULTIPLE PROCESSORS AND PARALLEL PROCESSING

Many computers use multiple processors to perform their processing work. For example, PCs often use a **coprocessor** to speed processing by performing specific tasks such as mathematical calculations or graphics processing so that the CPU is free to do other processing.

**coprocessor**
Additional processor that enhances performance by performing specific tasks to free the CPU for other processing activities.

Processing can also be speeded by linking several processors to work simultaneously on the same task. Figure 5-6 compares parallel processing to serial processing used in conventional computers. In **parallel processing,** multiple processing units (CPUs) break down a problem into smaller parts and work on it simultaneously. Getting a group of processors to attack the same problem at once requires both rethinking the problems and special software that can divide problems among different processors in the most efficient way possible, providing the needed data, and reassembling the many subtasks to reach an appropriate solution.

**parallel processing**
Type of processing in which more than one instruction can be processed at a time by breaking down a problem into smaller parts and processing them simultaneously with multiple processors.

**Massively parallel computers** have huge networks of hundreds or even thousands of processor chips interwoven in complex and flexible ways to attack large computing problems. As opposed to parallel processing, where small numbers of powerful but expensive specialized chips are linked together, massively parallel machines chain hundreds or thousands of inexpensive, commonly used chips to break problems into many small pieces and solve them. For instance, Wal-Mart stores use a massively parallel machine to sift through an inventory and sales trend database with 24 trillion bytes of data.

**massively parallel computers**
Computers that use hundreds or thousands of processing chips to attack large computing problems simultaneously.

## 5.2 STORAGE, INPUT, AND OUTPUT TECHNOLOGY

The capabilities of computer systems depend not only on the speed and capacity of the CPU but also on the speed, capacity, and design of storage, input, and output technology. Storage, input, and output devices are called *peripheral devices* because they are outside the main computer system unit.

## SECONDARY STORAGE TECHNOLOGY

Most of the information used by a computer application is stored on secondary storage devices located outside of the primary storage area. **Secondary storage** is used for relatively long-term storage of data outside the CPU. Secondary storage is nonvolatile and retains data even when the computer is turned off. The most important secondary storage technologies are magnetic disk, optical disk, and magnetic tape.

**secondary storage**
Relatively long-term, nonvolatile storage of data outside the CPU and primary storage.

### Magnetic Disk

The most widely used secondary-storage medium today is **magnetic disk.** There are two kinds of magnetic disks: floppy disks (used in PCs) and **hard disks** (used on large commercial disk drives and PCs). Large mainframe or midrange systems have multiple hard disk drives because they require immense disk storage capacity in the gigabyte and terabyte range. PCs also use **floppy disks,** which are removable and portable, with a storage capacity up to 2.8 megabytes, and they have a much slower access rate than hard disks. Removable disk drives such as those manufactured by Iomega and Syquest are becoming popular backup storage alternatives for PC systems.

Magnetic disks on both large and small computers permit direct access to individual records so that data stored on the disk can be directly accessed regardless of the order in which the data were originally recorded. Disk storage is often referred to as a **direct access storage device (DASD).** Disk technology is useful for systems requiring rapid and direct access to data.

Disk drive performance can be further enhanced by using a disk technology called **RAID (Redundant Array of Inexpensive Disks).** RAID devices package more than a hundred disk drives, a controller chip, and specialized software into a single large unit. Such an array appears to the computer as a single logical unit consisting of multiple disk drives. Traditional disk drives deliver data from the disk drive along a single path, but RAID delivers data over multiple paths simultaneously, improving disk access time and reliability. For most RAID systems, data on a failed disk can be restored automatically without the computer system having to be shut down.

**magnetic disk**
A secondary storage medium in which data are stored by means of magnetized spots on a hard or floppy disk.

**hard disk**
Magnetic disk resembling a thin, metallic platter used in large computer systems and in most PCs.

**floppy disk**
Removable magnetic disk storage primarily used with PCs.

**direct access storage device (DASD)**
Magnetic disk technology that permits the CPU to locate a record directly.

**RAID (Redundant Array of Inexpensive Disks)**
Disk storage technology to boost disk performance by packaging more than 100 smaller disk drives with a controller chip and specialized software in a single, large unit to deliver data over multiple paths simultaneously.

### Optical Disks

Optical disks, also called compact disks or laser optical disks, user laser technology to store data at densities many times greater than those of magnetic disks. They are available for both PCs and large computers. Optical disks can store massive quantities of data, including not only text but also pictures, sound, and full-motion video, in a highly compact form.

The most common optical disk system used with PCs is called **CD-ROM (compact disk read-only memory).** A 4.75-inch compact disk for PCs can store up to 660 megabytes, nearly 300 times more than a high-density floppy disk. Optical disks are most appropriate for applications where enormous quantities of unchanging data must be stored compactly for easy retrieval, or for storing graphic images and sound.

CD-ROM is read-only storage. No new data can be written to it; it can only be read. CD-ROM has been most widely used for reference materials with massive amounts of data, such as encyclopedias and directories, and for storing multimedia applications that combine text, sound, and images. For example, U.S. census demographic data and financial databases from Dow Jones or Dun & Bradstreet are available on CD-ROM.

**WORM (write once/read many)** and **CD-R (compact disk-recordable)** optical disk systems allow users to record data only once on an optical disk. Once written, the data cannot be erased but can be read indefinitely. CD-R technology allows individuals and organizations to create their own CD-ROMs at a low cost using a special CD-R recording device. New CD-RW (CD-ReWritable) technology has been developed to allow users to create rewritable optical disks. Rewritable optical disk drives are not yet competitive with magnetic disk storage for most applications but are useful for applications requiring large volumes of storage where the information is only occasionally updated.

**Digital video disks (DVDs),** also called digital versatile disks, are optical disks the same size as CD-ROMs but of even higher capacity. They can hold a minimum of 4.7 gigabytes of

**CD-ROM (compact disk read-only memory)**
Read-only optical disk storage used for imaging, reference, and other applications with massive amounts of unchanging data and for multimedia.

**WORM (write once/read many)**
Optical disk system that allows users to record data only once; data cannot be erased but can be read indefinitely.

**CD-R (compact disk-recordable)**
Optical disk system that allows individuals and organizations to record their own CD-ROMs.

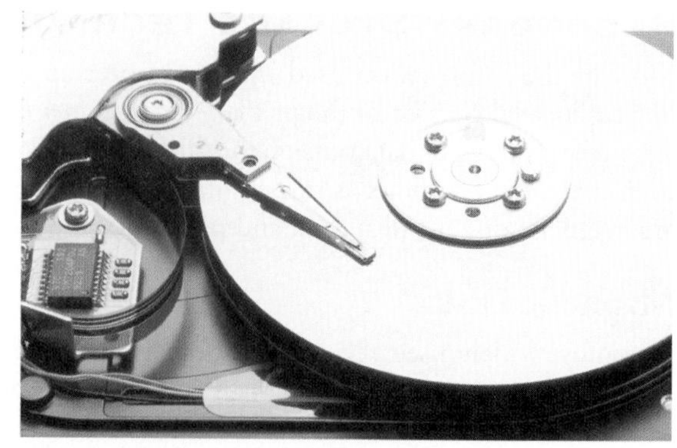

*Secondary storage devices such as floppy disks, optical disks, and hard disks are used to store large quantities of data outside the CPU and primary storage. They provide direct access to data for easy retrieval.*

**digital video disk (DVD)** High-capacity, optical storage medium that can store full-length videos and large amounts of data.

data, enough to store a full-length, high-quality motion picture. DVDs are used to store movies and multimedia applications with large amounts of video and graphics, but they may replace CD-ROMs, because they can store large amounts of digitized text, graphics, audio, and video data.

## Magnetic Tape

**magnetic tape** Inexpensive, older secondary-storage medium in which large volumes of information are stored sequentially by means of magnetized and nonmagnetized spots on tape.

**Magnetic tape** is an older storage technology that still is used for secondary storage of large volumes of information. More and more organizations are moving away from using the old reel-to-reel magnetic tapes and instead are using mass-storage tape cartridges that hold far more data (up to 35 gigabytes) than the old magnetic tapes. These cartridges are part of automated systems that store hundreds of such cartridges and select and mount them automatically using sophisticated robotics technology. Contemporary magnetic tape systems are used for archiving data and for storing data that are needed rapidly but not instantly.

The principal advantages of magnetic tape include its inexpensiveness, its relative stability, and its ability to store very large quantities of information. The principal disadvantages of magnetic tape are its sequentially stored data and its relative slowness compared to the speed of other secondary storage media. In order to find an individual record stored on magnetic tape, such as an employment record, the tape must be read from the beginning up to the location of the desired record.

## New Storage Alternatives: Storage Area Networks (SANs) and On-line Storage Service Providers (SSPs)

To meet the escalating demand for data-intensive multimedia, Web, and other services, the amount of data that companies need to store is increasing from 75 to 150 percent every year. Companies are turning to new kinds of storage infrastructures to deal with their mushrooming storage requirements and their difficulties managing large volumes of data.

**storage area network (SAN)** A high-speed network dedicated to storage, which connects different kinds of storage devices, such as tape libraries and disk arrays.

***Storage Area Networks*** Storage area networks (SANs) can provide a solution for companies with the need to share information across applications and computing platforms. A **storage area network (SAN)** is a high-speed network dedicated to storage, which connects different kinds of storage devices, such as tape libraries and disk arrays. The network moves data among pools of servers and storage devices, creating an enterprise-wide infrastructure for data storage. Many companies are storing vital information on servers at many different locations, and SANs can make data available to all servers attached to them. The SAN creates a large central pool of storage that can be shared by multiple servers so that users can rapidly share data across the SAN. Every user in a company can access data from any server in the organization. Figure 5-7 illustrates how a SAN works. The SAN storage devices are located on their own network and are connected using a high-transmission technology, such as Fibre Channel. The SAN supports communication between any server and the storage unit as well as between different storage devices in the network.

SANs can be expensive and difficult to manage. More machines have to function correctly to get work done and coordinate their work over a network (Gibson and Van Meter, 2000). SANs are very useful for companies that need rapid data access for widely distributed users and have the money to make long-term investments in their storage infrastructures.

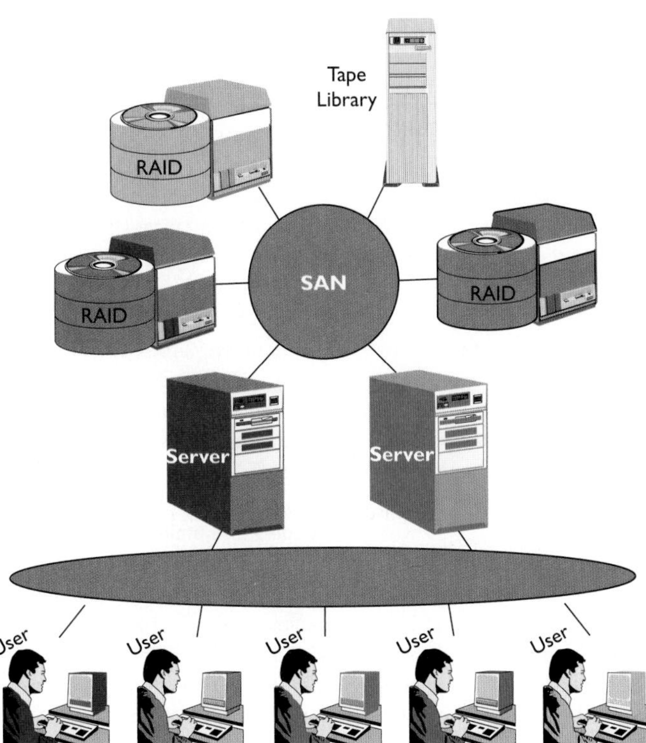


*Figure 5-7* A storage area network (SAN). The SAN stores data on many different types of storage devices, providing data to the enterprise. Users can share data across the SAN.

***On-line Storage Service Providers*** Storage needs are growing so rapidly that many organizations no longer view computer storage as traditional hardware. Instead they view storage through the model of a utility such as electricity or water. With utilities, we use what we need and pay for what we use. Following the utility model, some companies are no longer providing their own data storage. Instead they store their data elsewhere, renting this capability from a storage service provider. A **storage service provider (SSP)** is a third-party provider that rents out storage space to subscribers over the Web. Storage service providers sell storage as a pay-per-use utility, allowing customers to store and access their data without having to purchase and maintain their own storage technology. (Similar outsourced service providers exist for software, as described in Chapter 6.) The Window on Management describes some of the benefits of using a storage service provider.

**storage service provider (SSP)**
Third-party provider that rents out storage space to subscribers over the Web, allowing customers to store and access their data without having to purchase and maintain their own storage technology.

## INPUT AND OUTPUT DEVICES

Human beings interact with computer systems largely through input and output devices. Input devices gather data and convert them into electronic form for use by the computer, whereas output devices display data after they have been processed.

### Input Devices

Keyboards remain the principal method of data entry for entering text and numerical data into a computer. However, pointing devices, such as the computer mouse and touch screens, are becoming popular for issuing commands and making selections in today's highly graphic computing environment.

**computer mouse**
Handheld input device whose movement on the desktop controls the position of the cursor on the computer display screen.

***Pointing Devices*** A **computer mouse** is a handheld device with point-and-click capabilities that is usually connected to the computer by a cable. The computer user can move the mouse around on a desktop to control the cursor's position on a computer display screen, pushing a button to select a command. The mouse also can be used to "draw" images on the screen. Trackballs and touch pads often are used in place of the mouse as pointing devices on laptop PCs.

**touch screen**
Input device technology that permits the entering or selecting of commands and data by touching the surface of a sensitized video display monitor with a finger or a pointer.

**Touch screens** allow users to enter limited amounts of data by touching the surface of a sensitized video display monitor with a finger or a pointer. Touch screens often are found in information kiosks in retail stores, restaurants, and shopping malls.

## STORAGE SERVICE PROVIDERS: DATA STORAGE BECOMES A UTILITY

The ever-increasing use of e-mail, graphics, video, sound, and electronic commerce documents has created a giant problem for many companies: How can they store so much data? According to Dataquest Gartner of Lowell, Massachusetts, storage requirements will double every year for a number of years, with many companies unable to estimate their future data storage needs. Moreover, data storage and the management of stored data are growing more complex almost daily, leading to a rapidly growing shortage of technical experts in data storage. To meet these growing data storage problems, companies can turn to storage service providers (SSPs).

Most SSPs store a company's data on their equipment at their sites. They operate like electric utilities: A company uses what storage it needs and is billed monthly for that usage. SSPs obtain and manage the hardware, software, and staff for data storage. Companies can use an SSP service to replace or supplement their in-house storage infrastructure. To be successful, SSPs must offer very high availability and reliability and also must keep up with the latest technology. SSPs are responsible for monitoring the stored data and for managing their own capacity, response time, and reliability. SSPs also offer archive and retrieval services and disaster recovery. The standard cost at present is about $50,000 per managed terabyte per month, although some vendors offer it for as low as $30,000. These costs are starting to drop as more companies enter this new field.

SSP customers benefit in several ways. They no longer have to purchase hardware and software to store their data and will not need to maintain an expert storage support staff. They also eliminate the cost of building and maintaining their own storage infrastructure. The thought of escalating storage costs makes fee-for-storage very appealing, because the costs of using SSPs are fairly predictable.

Internet start-ups have been the first users of SSPs. Many of them store massive amounts of data and yet are limited by their venture capital. By following the SSP route they can use their limited funds for more fundamental initiatives, such as designing Web sites and products, and building quality management. For example, New York-based Flooz, a purveyor of on-line gift currency, contracted with StorageNetworks Inc. of Fremont, California, to manage its data storage. In return for a monthly fee, StorageNetworks houses Flooz's data in a storage area network (SAN). By using a SSP, Flooz obtains top-quality, reliable data storage without expending exorbitant internal resources building and maintaining a new storage infrastructure.

Large, established companies are more hesitant to try SSPs, often using them for less-important data as a test. These companies have existing data centers, including their required infrastructures, so their cost savings are less. In addition, they fear a loss of control over their critical data. Finally, they fear for the security of data that are stored off-site. They also have the same fundamental fear as with any outsourcing—that the SSP staff serves many masters who do not take ownership of the data as seriously as their internal staffs do.

**To Think About:** What management, technology, and organization issues would an established company face in transferring its data storage to an SSP?

*Sources:* Stephanie Wilkinson, "Phone Bill, Electricity Bill, Storage Bill?" *Datamation,* October 24, 2000; Philip Gordon, "Convenient Online Storage," *Information Week,* July 3, 2000; Nick Wredon, "Outsourcing Options; A Hard Sell," *Information Week,* October 2, 2000; Lisa Kalis, "The Storage Space," *Red Herring Magazine,* March 1, 2000; and Tom Stein, "The New Rage for Storage," *Red Herring Magazine,* March 1, 2000.

management

**source data automation**
Input technology that captures data in computer-readable form at the time and place the data are created.

**optical character recognition (OCR)**
Form of source data automation in which optical scanning devices read specially designed data off source documents and translate the data into digital form for the computer.

***Source Data Automation*** **Source data automation** captures data in computer-readable form at the time and place they are created. The principal source data automation technologies are optical character recognition, magnetic ink character recognition, pen-based input, digital scanners, voice input, and sensors.

**Optical character recognition (OCR)** devices translate specially designed marks, characters, and codes into digital form. The most widely used optical code is the **bar code,** which is used in point-of-sale systems in supermarkets and retail stores. Bar codes also are used in hospitals, libraries, military operations, and transportation facilities. The codes can include time, date, and location data in addition to identification data. The information makes them useful for analyzing the movement of items and determining what has happened to them during production or other processes. (The discussion of the United Parcel Service in Chapter 1 shows how valuable bar codes can be for this purpose.)

**Magnetic ink character recognition (MICR)** technology is used primarily in check processing for the banking industry. The bottom portion of a typical check contains characters identifying the bank, checking account, and check number that are preprinted using a special magnetic ink. A MICR reader translates these characters into digital form for the computer.

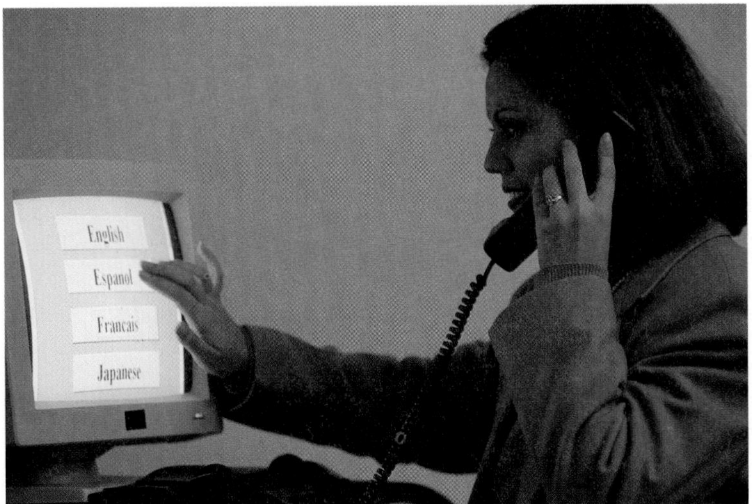


*Touch screens allow users to enter small amounts of data by touching words, numbers, or specific points on the screen.*

Handwriting-recognition devices such as pen-based tablets, notebooks, and notepads are promising new input technologies, especially for people working in the sales or service areas or for those who have traditionally shunned computer keyboards. These **pen-based input** devices convert the motion made by an electronic stylus pressing on a touch-sensitive tablet screen into digital form. For instance, the United Parcel Service replaced its drivers' clipboard with a battery-powered Delivery Information Acquisition Device (DIAD) to capture signatures (see the Chapter 1 Window on Technology) along with other information required for pickup and delivery.

**Digital scanners** translate images such as pictures or documents into digital form and are an essential component of image-processing systems. **Voice input devices** convert spoken words into digital form for processing by the computer. Voice recognition devices allow people to enter data into the computer without using their hands, making them useful for inspecting and sorting items in manufacturing and shipping and for dictation. Microphones and tape cassette players can serve as input devices for music and other sounds.

**Sensors** are devices that collect data directly from the environment for input into a computer system. For instance, farmers can use sensors to monitor the moisture of the soil in their fields to help them with irrigation (Garber, 2000).

## Batch and On-line Input and Processing

The manner in which data are input into the computer affects how the data can be processed. Information systems collect and process information in one of two ways: through batch or through on-line processing. In **batch processing,** transactions, such as orders or payroll time cards, are accumulated and stored in a group, or batch, until the time when, because of some reporting cycle, it is efficient or necessary to process them. This was the only method of processing until the early 1960s, and it is still used today in older systems or some systems with massive volumes of transactions. In **on-line processing,** which is now very common, the user enters transactions into a device (such as a data entry keyboard or bar code reader) that is directly connected to the computer system. The transactions usually are processed immediately.

The demands of the business determine the type of processing. If the user needs periodic or occasional reports or output, as in payroll or end-of-year reports, batch processing is most efficient. If the user needs immediate information and processing, as in an airline or hotel reservation system, then the system should use on-line processing.

Figure 5-8 compares batch and on-line processing. Batch systems often use tape as a storage medium, whereas on-line processing systems use disk storage, which permits immediate access to specific items. In batch systems, transactions are accumulated in a **transaction file,** which contains all the transactions for a particular time period. Periodically, this file is used to update a **master file,** which contains permanent information on entities. (An example is a payroll master file with employee earnings and deduction data. It is updated with

**bar code**
Form of OCR technology widely used in supermarkets and retail stores in which identification data are coded into a series of bars.

**magnetic ink character recognition (MICR)**
Input technology that translates characters written in magnetic ink into digital codes for processing.

**pen-based input**
Input devices such as tablets, notebooks, and notepads consisting of a flat-screen display tablet and a penlike stylus that digitizes handwriting.

**digital scanners**
Input devices that translate images, such as pictures or documents, into digital form for processing.

**voice input devices**
Technology that converts the spoken word into digital form for processing.

**sensors**
Devices that collect data directly from the environment for input into a computer system.

**batch processing**
A method of collecting and processing data in which transactions are accumulated and stored until a specified time when it is convenient or necessary to process them as a group.

**on-line processing**
A method of collecting and processing data in which transactions are entered directly into the computer system and processed immediately.

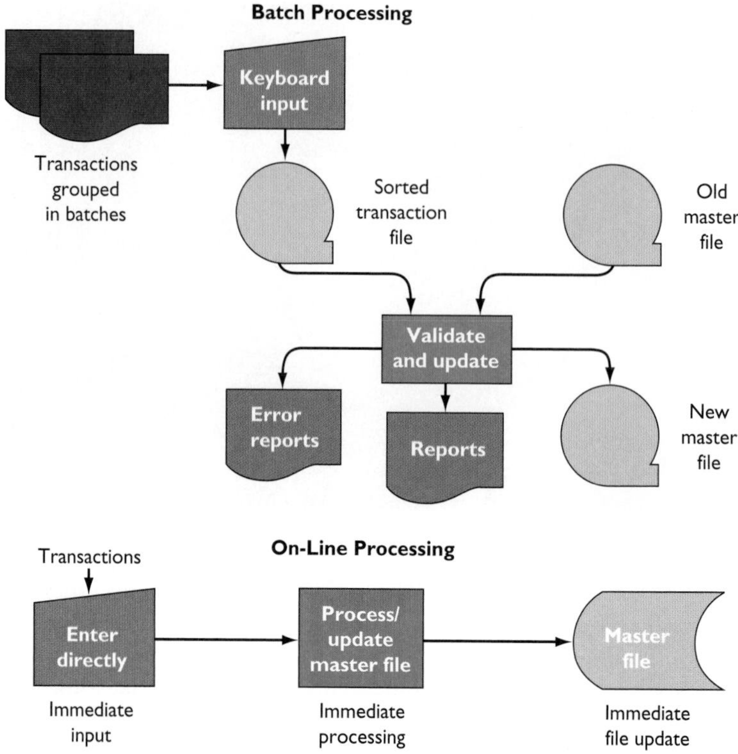


*Figure 5-8* A comparison of batch and on-line processing. In batch processing, transactions are accumulated and stored in a group. Because batches are processed on a regular interval basis, such as daily, weekly, or monthly, information in the system will not always be up to date. A typical batch-processing job is payroll preparation. In on-line processing, transactions are input immediately and usually processed immediately. Information in the system is generally up to date. A typical on-line application is an airline reservation system.

weekly time-card transactions.) Adding the transaction data to the existing master file creates a new master file. In on-line processing, transactions are entered into the system immediately using a keyboard, pointing device, or source data automation, and the system usually responds immediately. The master file is updated continually. In on-line processing, there is a direct connection to the computer for input and output.

**transaction file**
In batch systems, a file in which all transactions are accumulated to await processing.

**master file**
A file containing permanent information that is updated during processing by transaction data.

## Output Devices

The major data output devices are cathode ray tube terminals, sometimes called video display terminals, or VDTs, and printers.

**cathode ray tube (CRT)**
A screen, also referred to as a video display terminal (VDT) that provides a visual image of both user input and computer output.

The **cathode ray tube (CRT)** is probably the most popular form of information output in modern computer systems. It works much like a television picture tube, with an electronic gun shooting a beam of electrons to illuminate the pixels on the screen. The more pixels per screen, the higher the resolution, or clarity, of the image on the screen. Laptop computers use flat panel displays, which are less bulky than CRT monitors.

**printer**
A computer output device that provides paper hard-copy output in the form of text or graphics.

**Printers** produce a printed hard copy of information output. They include impact printers (such as a dot matrix printer) and nonimpact printers (laser, inkjet, and thermal transfer printers). Most printers print one character at a time, but some commercial printers print an entire line or page at a time. In general, impact printers are slower than nonimpact printers.

**plotter**
Output device using multicolored pens to draw high-quality, graphic documents.

High-quality graphics documents can be created using **plotters** with multicolored pens to draw (rather than print) computer output. Plotters are much slower than printers but are useful for outputting large-size charts, maps, or drawings.

**voice output device**
A converter of digital output data into spoken words.

A **voice output device** converts digital output data into intelligible speech. For instance, when you call for information on the telephone, you may hear a computerized voice respond with the telephone number you requested.

Audio output such as music and other sounds can be delivered by speakers connected to the computer. Microfilm and microfiche have been used to store large quantities of output as microscopic filmed documents, but they are being replaced by optical disk technology.

### INTERACTIVE MULTIMEDIA

The processing, input, output, and storage technologies we have described can be used to create interactive multimedia applications that integrate sound, full-motion video, or animation with graphics and text. **Multimedia** technologies facilitate the integration of two or more types of media, such as text, graphics, sound, voice, full-motion video, still video, or animation, into a computer-based application. Multimedia is becoming the foundation of new consumer products and services, such as electronic books and newspapers, electronic classroom-presentation technologies, full-motion video conferencing, imaging, graphics design tools, and computer games. Many Web sites use multimedia.

*Multimedia combines text, graphics, sound, and video into a computer-based experience that permits two-way communication. Many organizations use this technology for interactive training.*

PCs today come with built-in multimedia capabilities, including a high-resolution color monitor; a CD-ROM drive or DVD drive to store video, audio, and graphic data; and stereo speakers for amplifying audio output.

The most difficult element to incorporate into multimedia information systems has been full-motion video, because so much data must be brought under the digital control of the computer. The massive amounts of data in each video image must be digitally encoded, stored, and manipulated electronically, using techniques that compress the digital data.

**multimedia**
The integration of two or more types of media such as text, graphics, sound, full-motion video, or animation into a computer-based application.

The possibilities of this technology are endless, but multimedia seems especially well suited for training and presentations. For training, multimedia is appealing because it is interactive and permits two-way communication. People can use multimedia training sessions any time of the day, at their own pace. Instructors can easily integrate words, sounds, pictures, and both live and animated video to produce lessons that capture students' imaginations. For example, Duracell, the $2.6 billion battery manufacturer, used an interactive multimedia program to teach new employees at its Chinese manufacturing facility how to use battery-making machinery. Workers could use computer simulations to "stop," "start," and control equipment.

Interactive Web pages replete with graphics, sound, animations, and full-motion video have made multimedia popular on the Internet. For example, visitors to the CNN Interactive Web site can access news stories from CNN, photos, on-air transcripts, video clips, and audio clips. The video and audio clips are made available using **streaming technology,** which allows audio and video data to be processed as a steady and continuous stream

**streaming technology**
Technology for transferring data so that they can be processed as a steady and continuous stream.

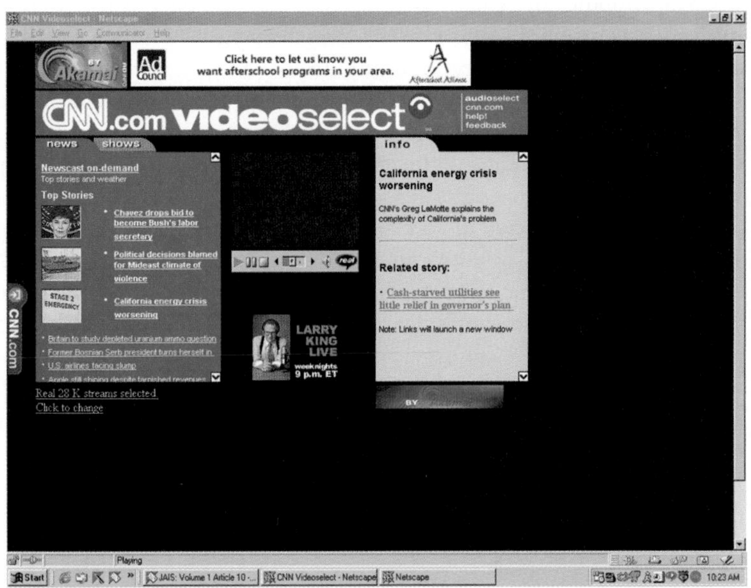


*CNN.com is a multimedia Web site providing news and live video 24 hours a day. Web sites can incorporate multimedia elements such as graphics, sound, animation, and full-motion video.*

**TABLE 5-4 EXAMPLES OF MULTIMEDIA WEB SITES**

| Web Site | Description |
|---|---|
| TerraQuest | Provides interactive tours of exotic destinations including maps, film clips, photos, and on-line discussions |
| CNN.com | Provides news, including live video, 24 hours a day |
| Lands' End | Allows shoppers to create a "personal model" allowing them to "try on" clothes from their computer screens |
| VideoSonicNet | Provides streaming music videos on demand as well as music news, reviews, and radio broadcasts |

as they are downloaded from the Web. (RealAudio and RealVideo are widely used streaming technology products on the Web.) Table 5-4 lists examples of other multimedia Web sites. If Internet transmission capacity and streaming technology continue to improve, Web sites could provide broadcast functions that compete with television along with new two-way interactivity.

Multimedia Web sites are also being used to sell digital products, such as digitized music clips. A compression standard known as **MP3** (also called **MPEG3**), which stands for Motion Picture Experts Group, audio layer 3, can compress audio files down to one-tenth or one-twelfth of their original size with virtually no loss in quality. Visitors to Web sites such as MP3.com can download MP3 music clips over the Internet and play them on their own computers.

**MP3 (MPEG3)**
Compression standard that can compress audio files for transfer over the Internet with virtually no loss in quality.

## 5.3 CATEGORIES OF COMPUTERS AND COMPUTER SYSTEMS

Computers represent and process data the same way, but there are different classifications. We can use size and processing speed to categorize contemporary computers as mainframes, midrange computers, PCs, workstations, and supercomputers. Managers need to understand the capabilities of each of these types of computers and why some types are more appropriate for certain processing work than others.

### CATEGORIES OF COMPUTERS

A **mainframe** is the largest computer, a powerhouse with massive memory and extremely rapid processing power. It is used for very large business, scientific, or military applications where a computer must handle massive amounts of data or many complicated processes. A **midrange computer** is less powerful, less expensive, and smaller than a mainframe; it is capable of supporting the computing needs of smaller organizations or of managing networks of other computers. Midrange computers can be **minicomputers,** which are used in systems for universities, factories, or research laboratories; or they can be **servers,** which are used for managing internal company networks or Web sites. Server computers are specifically optimized to support a computer network, enabling users to share files, software, peripheral devices (such as printers), or other network resources. Servers have large memories and disk-storage capacity, high-speed communications capabilities, and powerful CPUs.

Servers have become important components of firm's IT infrastructure because they provide the hardware platform for electronic commerce. By adding special software, they can be customized to deliver Web pages, process purchase and sales transactions, or exchange data with systems inside the company. Organizations with heavy electronic commerce requirements and massive Web sites are running their Web and electronic commerce applications on multiple servers in **server farms** in computing centers run by commercial vendors such as IBM. Large electronic commerce sites, such as Amazon.com or Dell.com, rely on server farms with sophisticated capabilities to balance computer loads and handle millions of purchases, inquiries, and other transactions.

**mainframe**
Largest category of computer, used for major business processing.

**midrange computer**
Middle-size computer capable of supporting the computing needs of small organizations or of managing networks of other computers.

**minicomputer**
Middle-range computer used in systems for universities, factories, or research laboratories.

**server**
Computer specifically optimized to provide software and other resources to other computers over a network.

**server farm**
Large group of servers maintained by a commercial vendor and made available to subscribers for electronic commerce and other activities requiring heavy use of servers.

A **personal computer (PC),** which is sometimes referred to as a microcomputer, is one that can be placed on a desktop or carried from room to room. Smaller laptop PCs are often used as portable desktops on the road. PCs are used as personal machines as well as in business. A **workstation** also fits on a desktop but has more powerful mathematical and graphics-processing capability than a PC and can perform more complicated tasks than a PC in the same amount of time. Workstations are used for scientific, engineering, and design work that requires powerful graphics or computational capabilities.

**personal computer (PC)**
Small desktop or portable computer.

**workstation**
Desktop computer with powerful graphics and mathematical capabilities and the ability to perform several complicated tasks at once.

A **supercomputer** is a highly sophisticated and powerful computer that is used for tasks requiring extremely rapid and complex calculations with hundreds of thousands of variable factors. Supercomputers traditionally have been used in scientific and military work, such as classified weapons research and weather forecasting, which use complex mathematical models, but they are starting to be used in business for the manipulation of vast quantities of data. Supercomputers use parallel processing and can perform billions and even trillions of calculations per second, many times faster than the largest mainframe. For example, on-line brokerage giant Charles Schwab & Co. uses an IBM RS/6000 SP supercomputer with 2,000 processors to deliver Web pages to as many as 95,000 simultaneous visitors to its Web site and to process transactions entered through the Web site. The supercomputer allows Schwab to handle a high transaction volume, to meet unpredictable demands, and to execute customer trades and changes to accounts instantly (Anthes, 2000).

**supercomputer**
Highly sophisticated and powerful computer that can perform very complex computations extremely rapidly.

The problem with this classification scheme is that the capacity of the machines changes so rapidly. Powerful PCs have sophisticated graphics and processing capabilities similar to workstations. PCs still cannot perform as many tasks at once as mainframes, midrange computers, or workstations (see the discussion of operating systems in Chapter 6), nor can they be used by as many people simultaneously as the larger machines. Even these distinctions will become less pronounced in the future. The most powerful workstations have some of the capabilities of earlier mainframes and supercomputers.

## COMPUTER NETWORKS AND CLIENT/SERVER COMPUTING

**distributed processing**
The distribution of computer processing work among multiple computers linked by a communications network.

**centralized processing**
Processing that is accomplished by one large central computer.

Today, stand-alone computers have been replaced by computers in networks for most processing tasks. The use of multiple computers linked by a communications network for processing is called **distributed processing.** In contrast with **centralized processing,** in which all processing is accomplished by one large central computer, distributed processing distributes the processing work among PCs, midrange computers, and mainframes linked together.

**client/server computing**
A model for computing that splits processing between "clients" and "servers" on a network, assigning functions to the machine most able to perform the function.

One widely used form of distributed processing is **client/server computing.** Client/server computing splits processing between "clients" and "servers." Both are on the network, but each machine is assigned functions it is best suited to perform. The **client** is the user point-of-entry for the required function and is normally a desktop computer, workstation, or laptop computer. The user generally interacts directly only with the client portion of the application, often to input data or retrieve data for further analysis. The *server* provides the client with services. The server could be a mainframe or another desktop computer, but specialized server computers are often used in this role. Servers store and process shared data and also perform back-end functions not visible to users, such as managing network activities. Figure 5-9 illustrates the client/server computing concept. Computing on the Internet uses the client/server model (see Chapter 9).

**client**
The user point-of-entry for the required function in client/server computing. Normally, a desktop computer, workstation, or laptop computer.

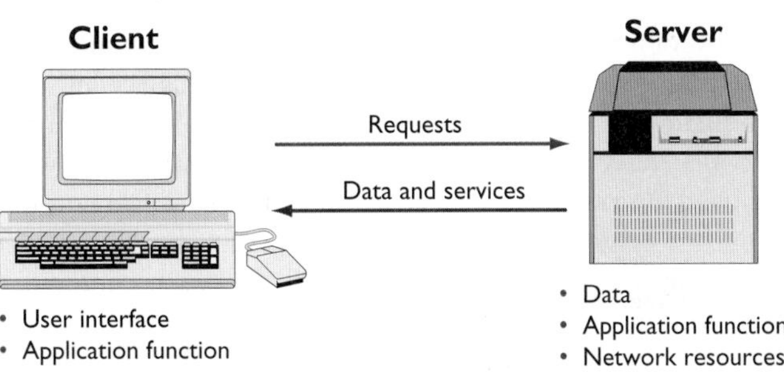


***Figure 5-9*** Client/server computing. In client/server computing, computer processing is split between client machines and server machines linked by a network. Users interface with the client machines.

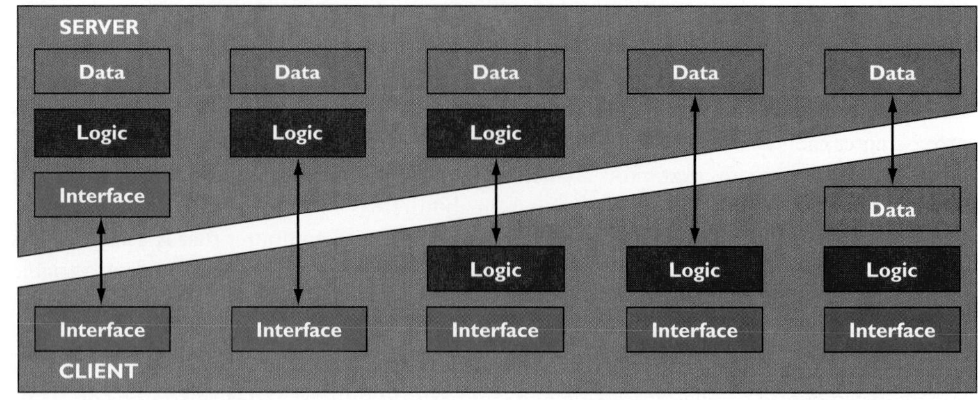


***Figure 5-10*** Types of client/server computing. There are various ways in which an application's interface, logic, and data management components can be divided among the clients and servers in a network.

Figure 5-10 illustrates five different ways that the components of an application could be partitioned between the client and the server. The interface component is essentially the application interface—how the application appears visually to the user. The application logic component consists of the processing logic, which is shaped by the organization's business rules. (An example might be that a salaried employee is only to be paid monthly.) The data management component consists of the storage and management of the data used by the application.

The exact division of tasks depends on the requirements of each application, including its processing needs, the number of users, and the available resources. For example, client tasks for a large corporate payroll might include inputting data (such as enrolling new employees and recording hours worked), submitting data queries to the server, analyzing the retrieved data, and displaying results on the screen or on a printer. The server portion will fetch the entered data and process the payroll. It also will control access so that only authorized users can view or update the data.

**downsizing**
The process of transferring applications from large computers to smaller ones.

In some firms client/server networks with PCs have actually replaced mainframes and minicomputers. The process of transferring applications from large computers to smaller ones is called **downsizing.** Downsizing has many advantages. Memory and processing power on a PC costs a fraction of their equivalent on a mainframe. The decision to downsize involves many factors in addition to the cost of computer hardware, including the need for new software, training, and perhaps new organizational procedures.

## NETWORK COMPUTERS

**network computer (NC)**
Simplified desktop computer that does not store software programs or data permanently. Users download whatever software or data they need from a central computer over the Internet or an organization's own internal network.

In one form of client/server computing, client processing and storage capabilities are so minimal that the bulk of computer processing occurs on the server. The term *thin client* is sometimes used to refer to the client in this arrangement. Thin clients with minimal memory, storage, and processor power and which are designed to work on networks are called **network computers (NCs).** Users download whatever software or data they need from a central computer over the Internet or an organization's internal network. The central computer also saves information for the user and makes it available for later retrieval, effectively eliminating the need for secondary storage devices such as hard disks, floppy disks, CD-ROMs, and their drives. A network computer may consist of little more than a stripped-down PC, a monitor, a keyboard, and a network connection.

If managed properly, both network computers and client/server computing can reduce the cost of information technology resources. Proponents of network computers believe NCs can reduce hardware costs, because they are less expensive to purchase than PCs with local processing and storage, and because they can be administered and updated from a central network server. Software programs and applications would not have to be purchased, installed, and upgraded for each user because software would be delivered and maintained from one central point. Network computers thus could increase management control over the organization's computing function. So much data and information are being delivered through the Web that computers do not necessarily need to store their own content.

*Designed to work on networks, network computers are thin clients with minimal memory, storage, and processor power. Both network computers and client/server computing can reduce the cost of information technology resources.*

Network computers are finding additional uses as application software that can be rented over the Web becomes widely available (see Chapter 6).

Not everyone agrees that network computers will bring benefits. Some researchers believe that centralizing control over computing would stifle worker initiative and creativity. PCs have become so cheap and plentiful ($500 and even less if additional services are purchased with the machine) that many question whether the savings promised by network computers will actually be realized. If a network failure occurs, hundreds or thousands of employees would not be able to use their computers, whereas people could keep on working if they had full-function PCs. Full-function PCs are more appropriate for situations where end users have varied application needs that require local processing. Companies should closely examine how network computers would fit into their information technology infrastructure.

## PEER-TO-PEER COMPUTING

Another form of distributed processing, called **peer-to-peer computing,** puts processing power back on users' desktops, linking these computers so that they can share processing tasks. Individual PCs, workstations, or other computers can share data, disk space, and even processing power for a variety of tasks when they are linked in a network, including the Internet. The peer-to-peer computing model stands in contrast to the network computing model because processing power resides only on individual desktops and these computers work together without a server or any central controlling authority. It has been estimated that most companies—and individuals—use less than 25 percent of their processing and storage capacity. Peer-to-peer computing taps the unused disk space or processing power on PC or workstation networks for large computing tasks that can now only be performed by large, expensive server computers or even supercomputers. The Window on Technology describes how some companies benefited from using this computing approach.

**peer-to-peer computing**
Form of distributed processing that links computers via the Internet or private networks so that they can share processing tasks.

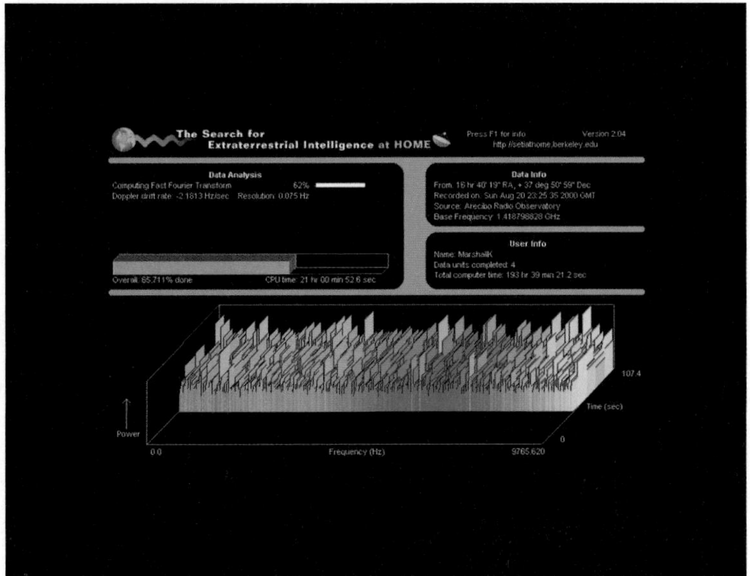


*Screen shot from a volunteer for the SETI@home project. The user's laptop computer is processing SETI data without any noticeable impact on other work.*

Window on Technology

## Creating Virtual Massively Parallel Computers Via Peer-to-Peer Computing

Did you know that about 90 percent of the processing power of most computers goes unused? Most computers are used weekdays only and sit idle during coffee breaks, lunch, meetings, nights, and weekends. When they are processing, most tasks only use a small portion of available computer power. The revolutionary concept growing out of peer-to-peer computing is that by distributing small portions of giant processing tasks among many computers, their unused processing power can be employed to good advantage. In effect peer-to-peer technology can be used to create virtual massively parallel computers.

Peer-to-peer technology is neither complex nor technologically new. All it does is establish direct links between two computers so they can "talk" to each other without going through a third party such as a server. What is new is that the connections between computers are now being established through the Internet as well as through private networks. Direct connections now can easily be established between any two computers selected from thousands and even millions that are on-line.

One well-known example of peer-to-peer distributed processing is the SETI@home project, begun in the spring of 1999 to search for extraterrestrial intelligence. Everyday the world's largest radio telescope, located in Arecibo, Puerto Rico, sweeps the sky recording digital noises traveling through space. Astronomers collect about 50 gigabytes of data per day. The data then must be searched for regular patterns that might indicate transmission by intelligent beings. However, searching through a year's worth of this data would take a large computer as much as 100,000 years, too large a task for ordinary means. The solution was using the peer-to-peer model to create a virtual massively parallel computer.

The data gathered in Arecibo are forwarded to the University of California at Berkeley where they are broken into work units of perhaps 350 kilobytes each, producing about 150,000 units daily. Each unit is then downloaded to one of the two million volunteers who allow their computers to process the data whenever their full power is not being used. Once the unit is searched (about 20 hours on a Pentium 400 MHz machine), the results are uploaded to the SETI computer for review. This analysis is only possible because of the massively parallel computing that occurs on the computers of all the volunteers.

This model is not applicable to all huge applications. It is useful only for large, data-intensive projects. Computer chip manufacturer Intel began using this approach in 1990 to reduce the cost of chip design. It linked 10,000 computers globally, thus eliminating the need to purchase several mainframes within two years. Energy companies gather immense amounts of geographic and seismic data that must be analyzed prior to digging for oil, gas, or coal. Oil giant Amerada Hess in New York is using the peer-to-peer model through its own network, connecting 200 desktop computers to analyze seismic data. The company cancelled the purchase of two IBM supercomputers as a result. According to CIO Richard Ross, Amerada Hess is "running seven times the throughput at a fraction of the cost." His company has also carried the concept one step further, joining the storage of these desktops to create a giant data repository.

**To Think About:** Suggest other industries that might use the peer-to-peer concept of computing, and explain why they might by appropriate for using this technology. What are some of the drawbacks or problems of this approach?

*Sources:* Aaron Ricadela, "Power to the PC," *Information Week*, January 15, 2001; Jennifer Di Sabatino, "What's So New About Peer-to-Peer?" *Computerworld*, November 20, 2000; Paul McDougall, "The Power of Peer-to-Peer," *Information Week*, August 28, 2000; and Kathleen Melymuka, "IT on the 'Outer Limits,' " *Computerworld*, July 3, 2000.

## 5.4 Managing Hardware Assets

As you can tell from this chapter, selection and use of computer hardware technology can have a profound impact on business performance. Computer hardware technology thus represents an important organizational asset that must be properly managed. Managers need to balance the cost of acquiring hardware resources with the need to provide a responsive and reliable platform for delivering information systems applications. We now describe the most important issues in managing hardware technology assets: understanding the new technology requirements for electronic commerce and the digital firm, determining the total cost of ownership (TCO) of technology assets, and identifying technology trends impacting the organization's information technology infrastructure.

### Hardware Technology Requirements for Electronic Commerce and the Digital Firm

Electronic commerce and electronic business are placing heavy new demands on hardware technology because organizations are replacing so many manual and paper-based processes with electronic ones. Companies are processing and storing vast quantities of data for data-intensive applications, such as video or graphics, as well as for electronic commerce. Much larger processing and storage resources are required to handle the surge in digital transactions flowing between different parts of firms and between firms and their customers and suppliers.

## The Strategic Role of Storage Technology in the Digital Firm

Although electronic commerce and electronic business may be reducing the role of paper, data of all types (such as purchase orders, invoices, requisitions, and work orders) must be stored electronically and available whenever needed. Customers and suppliers doing business electronically want to place their orders, check their accounts, and do their research at any hour of the day or night, and they demand 24-hour availability. For business to occur 24 hours a day anywhere in our electronic world, all possibly relevant data must be stored for on-line access, and all these data must be backed up.

For example, on-line banking has become very important at Chase Manhattan Bank, forcing Chase to change its check-handling method. Until recently, the bank stored its 12 million daily checks on microfilm and microfiche, which were not available on-line. Now Chase creates a digital image of each check that is stored on-line for 45 days, after which it is archived to a fast tape system. Customers can now view any recent check within one to two seconds. Each check requires about 40,000 bytes, so Chase needs more than 20 gigabytes to store checks at current levels in a business that is expanding fast. Electronic commerce and electronic business have put new strategic emphasis on technologies that can store vast quantities of transaction data and make them immediately available on-line.

## Capacity Planning and Scalability

As firms' electronic commerce and electronic business activities expand, they must carefully review their servers and other infrastructure components to make sure they can handle increasing numbers of transactions and users while maintaining a high level of performance and availability. Managers and information systems specialists need to pay more attention to hardware capacity planning and scalability than they have in the past. **Capacity planning** is the process of predicting when a computer hardware system becomes saturated. It considers factors such as the maximum number of users that the system can accommodate, the impact of existing and future software applications, and performance measures such as minimum response time for processing business transactions. Capacity planning ensures that adequate computing resources are available for work of different priorities and that the firm has enough computing power for its current and future needs. For example, the Nasdaq stock exchange performs ongoing capacity planning to identify peaks in the volume of stock trading transactions and to ensure it has enough computing capacity to handle large surges in volume when trading is very heavy (Robinson, 2000).

**capacity planning**
The process of predicting when a computer hardware system becomes saturated to ensure that adequate computing resources are available for work of different priorities, and that the firm has enough computing power for its current and future needs.

Although capacity planning is performed by information system specialists, input from business managers is essential. Capacity planners try to establish an optimum level of service for current and future applications. Outages and delayed response times translate into lost customers and lost revenue. Business managers need to determine acceptable levels of computer response time and availability for the firm's mission-critical systems to maintain the level of business performance they expect. New applications, mergers and acquisitions, and changes in business volume all impact computer work load and must be taken into account when planning hardware capacity.

Electronic commerce and electronic business both call for scalable IT infrastructures that have the capacity to grow with the business. Servers need to provide the processing power to keep electronic commerce up and running as Web site visitors and customers grow in number. Delivering large Web pages with graphics over the Internet or private intranets can create performance bottlenecks. **Scalability** refers to the ability of a computer, product, or system to expand to serve a larger number of users without breaking down. There are several approaches to achieving scalability. One is to scale up, replacing, for example, a small server with a larger multiprocessor server or even a mainframe. Another approach is to scale out, which involves adding a large number of smaller servers. The choice of approach depends on the nature of the application or set of applications requiring upgraded hardware capacity.

**scalability**
The ability of a computer, product, or system to expand to serve a larger number of users without breaking down.

## MANAGEMENT DECISION PROBLEM

### HARDWARE CAPACITY PLANNING FOR ELECTRONIC COMMERCE

Your company implemented its own electronic commerce site using its own hardware and software, and business is growing rapidly. The company Web site has not experienced any outages and customers are always able to have requests for information or purchase transactions processed very rapidly. Your information systems department has instituted a formal operations review program that continuously monitors key indicators of system usage that affect processing capacity and response time. The accompanying report illustrates two of those indicators: daily CPU usage and daily I/O usage for the system. I/O usage measures the number of times a disk has been read.

Your server supports primarily U.S. customers who access the Web site during the day and early in the evening. I/O usage should be kept below 70 percent if the CPU is very busy so that the CPU does not waste machine cycles looking for data. I/O usage is high between 1 A.M. and 6 A.M. because the firm backs up its data stored on disk when the CPU is not busy.

1. Anticipated increases in your e-commerce business during the next year are expected to increase CPU usage and I/O usage by 20 percent between 1 P.M. and 9 P.M. and by 10 percent during the rest of the day. Does your company have enough processing capacity to handle this increased load? Explain your answer.
2. What would happen if your organization did not pay attention to capacity issues?

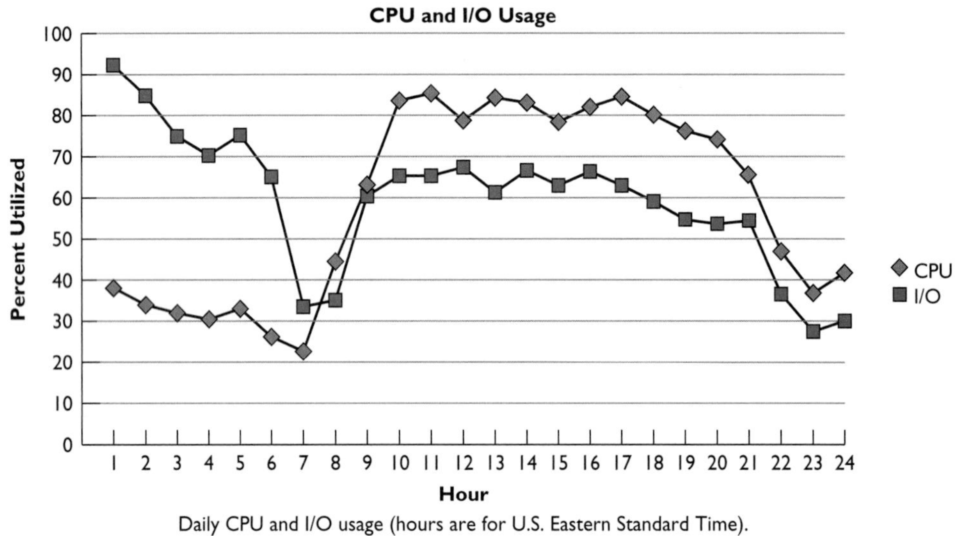


Daily CPU and I/O usage (hours are for U.S. Eastern Standard Time).

## HARDWARE ACQUISITION AND THE TOTAL COST OF OWNERSHIP (TCO) OF TECHNOLOGY ASSETS

**total cost of ownership (TCO)**
Designates the total cost of owning technology resources, including initial purchase costs, the cost of hardware and software upgrades, maintenance, technical support, and training.

The purchase and maintenance of computer hardware equipment is but one of a series of cost components that managers must consider when selecting and managing technology assets. The actual cost of owning technology resources includes both direct and indirect costs, including the original purchase costs of computers and software; hardware and software upgrades; and maintenance, technical support, and training. The **total cost of ownership (TCO)** model can be used to analyze these direct and indirect costs to help firms determine the actual cost of specific technology implementations. Table 5-5 lists and describes the most important total cost of ownership components.

When all these cost components are considered, the TCO for a PC might run up to three times the original purchase price of the equipment. "Hidden costs" for support staff and additional network management may make distributed client/server architectures more expensive than centralized mainframe architectures. CheckFree, a leading provider of electronic consumer bill payment and other financial services used TCO analysis when deciding on a new computing architecture to support plans to expand its bill payment and banking services to 50 million customers. CheckFree's original plan called for a multitiered client/server architecture with distributed servers. But by examining the total cost of ownership, management found that distributed architecture would have cost twice as much over time as a centralized mainframe environment, because it required extra technical support and was more likely to have service interruptions (Brannigan, 1999; Paul, 1998.)

**TABLE 5-5** COMPONENTS OF THE TOTAL COST OF OWNERSHIP (TCO) OF TECHNOLOGY ASSETS

**Hardware acquisition:** Purchase price of computer hardware equipment, including computers, terminals, storage, printers

**Software acquisition:** Purchase or license of software for each user

**Installation:** Cost to install computers and software

**Training:** Cost to provide training to information system specialists and end users

**Support:** Cost to provide ongoing technical support, help desks

**Maintenance:** Cost to upgrade the hardware and software

**Infrastructure:** Cost to acquire, maintain, and support related infrastructure, such as networks and specialized equipment (such as storage back-up units)

A key to reducing TCO is to create a comprehensive asset management plan. Many organizations cannot measure the total cost of ownership of their technology assets because these assets have never been inventoried. Organizations need to catalog and manage their hardware and software assets. Software tools are now available to help identify and track these technology assets. Some of these tools even show managers what assets are breaking down and why, and when these assets should be cycled out of service. The chapter ending case study provides more discussion of this topic.

## MONITORING TECHNOLOGY TRENDS

Computing technology continues to change at a blinding pace, requiring managers to constantly monitor technology trends and make decisions about upgrading the firm's information technology infrastructure. New hardware technologies can provide new ways of organizing work and sources of new products and services.

### Microminiaturization and Information Appliances

During the past 40 years, each decade has seen computing costs drop by a factor of 10 and capacity increase by a factor of at least 100, allowing computers to become progressively smaller and more powerful. Today's microprocessors can put a mainframe-like processing power on a desktop, a briefcase, and even into a shirt pocket, and technology will soon be able to produce computers the size of a thumbnail. These advances in microprocessor technology have fueled the growth of microminiaturization—the proliferation of computers that are so small, fast, and cheap that they have become ubiquitous. For instance, many of the intelligent features that have made automobiles, stereos, toys, watches, cameras, and other equipment easy to use are based on microprocessors. The future will see even more intelligence built into everyday devices as well as miniaturized computers. Billions of tiny computers embedded in other objects will be used to monitor and shape their physical surroundings (Tennenhouse, 2000).

More computing work will be performed by small handheld computers and portable information appliances. Unlike a PC, which is a general-purpose device capable of performing many different kinds of tasks, an **information appliance** is customized to perform only a few specialized tasks very well with a minimum of effort. Such information appliances include mobile phones with e-mail and Internet access, wireless handheld computing devices, and television set-top boxes that can access the Web and provide e-mail and home shopping services. Chapters 8 and 9 describe the capabilities of these information appliances in greater detail. These specialized computing devices are less expensive and difficult to use than PCs, and they provide enough capabilities for communication or accessing the Web to meet many peoples' computing needs. Some of the devices can run business applications as well as send e-mail or maintain names and addresses. PCs will play a smaller role in both personal and corporate computing as information appliances, handheld computing devices, and embedded computers become more widely used. Managers will need to manage these new computing resources and find the best way of incorporating them into the firm's information

**information appliance**
A computing device customized to perform only a few specialized tasks very well with a minimum of effort.

technology infrastructure. Data stored on mobile computing devices and appliances will need to be coordinated with data stored in the main corporate computers.

## Social Interfaces

Computer technology is becoming so powerful and integrated into daily experiences that it can appear almost invisible to the user. Social interfaces are being developed to model the interaction between people and computers using familiar human behavior. People increasingly will interact with the computer in more intuitive and effortless ways—through writing, speech, touch, eye movement, and other gestures (Selker, 1996).

Voice-recognition technology is moving closer to human, natural speech. Commercial, continuous-speech voice-recognition products have vocabularies large enough for general business use. These social interfaces will make it easier for organizations to incorporate computing devices into their work practices and business processes. People will use voice or other social interfaces to interact with corporate information systems.

# APPLICATION SOFTWARE EXERCISE

### SPREADSHEET EXERCISE: IDENTIFYING HARDWARE REQUIREMENTS

Each semester the management information systems department at your university encourages its new majors to attend an orientation seminar. During the seminar, students are provided with helpful information, such as how to establish an e-mail account, select a personal computer system, and join the local Association of Information Technology Professionals (AITP) chapter. You have attended several of these orientations and have found them valuable. Often current and former students are asked to participate in the orientations.

One afternoon Dr. Janice Martinez, your favorite MIS professor, stops by the lab to speak with you. She mentions that she is in charge of the upcoming orientation and would like you to speak at next month's seminar. In particular, she would like you to advise new students on the type of computer system they should consider purchasing. She would like you to discuss the minimum requirements that would be necessary, as well as identify possible upgrades for the system. During your presentation, you should discuss issues such as processor type and speed, RAM, hard drives, monitors, CD-ROM drives, and price.

In order to prepare your personal computer requirements presentation, identify the minimum requirements that a student computer system should have. Next, identify at least three computer systems that you would recommend to your fellow students. What features does each system have? What are the advantages and disadvantages of each system? For each system identified, what are the upgrade options? How much will the upgrades cost? Summarize your findings in a spreadsheet. Based on your findings, use presentation software to prepare a presentation that you could give to the orientation group. If time permits, share your findings with the class. How are your recommendations similar to those of your classmates? How do your recommendations differ from those of your classmates?

## MANAGEMENT WRAP-UP

Selecting computer hardware technology for the organization is a key business decision, and it should not be left to technical specialists alone. General managers should understand the capabilities of various computer processing, input, output, and storage options, as well as price/performance relationships. They should be involved in hardware-capacity planning, technology asset management, and decisions to distribute computing, downsize, or use network computers.

Computer hardware technology can either enhance or impede organizational performance. Computer hardware selection should consider how well the technology meshes with the organization's culture and structure as well as its information-processing requirements.

Information technology today is not limited to computers but must be viewed as an array of digital devices networked together. Organizations have many computer processing options to choose from, including mainframes, workstations, PCs, and network computers and many different ways of configuring hardware components to create systems.

*For Discussion*

1. What management, organization, and technology issues should be considered when selecting computer hardware?
2. What factors would you consider in deciding whether to switch from centralized processing on a mainframe to client/server processing?

## SUMMARY

1. *Identify the hardware components in a typical computer system and their role in processing information.* The modern computer system has six major components: a central processing unit (CPU), primary storage, input devices, output devices, secondary storage, and communications devices. Computers store and process information in the form of binary digits called bits. A string of eight bits is called a byte. There are several coding schemes for arranging binary digits into characters. The most common are EBCDIC and ASCII. The CPU is the part of the computer where the manipulation of symbols, numbers, and letters occurs. The CPU has two components: an arithmetic-logic unit and a control unit. The arithmetic-logic unit performs arithmetic and logical operations on data, whereas the control unit controls and coordinates the computer's other components.

   The CPU is closely tied to primary memory, or primary storage, which stores data and program instructions temporarily before and after processing. Several different kinds of semiconductor memory chips are used with primary storage: RAM (random access memory) is used for short-term storage of data and program instructions, whereas ROM (read-only memory) permanently stores important program instructions.

   Computer processing power depends, in part, on the speed of microprocessors, which integrate the computer's logic and control on a single chip. Microprocessors' capabilities can be gauged by their word length, data bus width, and cycle speed. Most conventional computers process one instruction at time, but computers with parallel processing can process multiple instructions simultaneously.
2. *Describe the principal storage, input, and output technologies for computer systems and interactive multimedia.* The principal forms of secondary storage are magnetic disk, optical disk, and magnetic tape. Magnetic disk permits direct access to specific records. Disk technology is used in on-line processing. Optical disks can store vast amounts of data compactly. CD-ROM disk systems can only be read from, but rewritable optical disk systems are becoming available. Tape stores records in sequence and only can be used in batch processing.

   The principal input devices are keyboards, computer mice, touch screens, magnetic ink, optical character recognition, pen-based instruments, digital scanners, sensors, and voice input. The principal output devices are video display terminals, printers, plotters, voice output devices, microfilm, and microfiche. In batch processing, transactions are accumulated and stored in a group until the time when it is efficient or necessary to process them. In on-line processing, the user enters transactions into a device that is directly connected to the computer system. The transactions are usually processed immediately. Multimedia integrates two or more types of media, such as text, graphics, sound, full-motion video, or animation into a computer-based application.
3. *Compare the capabilities of mainframes, midrange computers, PCs, workstations, servers, and supercomputers.* Depending on their size and processing power, computers are categorized as mainframes, midrange computers, PCs, workstations, or supercomputers. Mainframes are the largest computers; midrange computers can be minicomputers used in factory, university, or research lab systems or servers providing software and other resources to computers on a network. PCs are desktop or laptop machines; workstations are desktop machines with powerful mathematical and graphic capabilities; and supercomputers are sophisticated, powerful computers that can perform massive and complex computations rapidly. Because of continuing advances in microprocessor technology, the distinctions between these types of computers are constantly changing.
4. *Evaluate different arrangements of computer processing, including client/server computing, network computers, and peer-to-peer computing.* Computers can be networked together to distribute processing among different machines. In the client/server model of computing, computer processing is split between "clients" and "servers" connected via a network.

Each function of an application is assigned to the machine best suited to perform that function. The exact division of tasks between client and server depends on the application. Network computers are pared-down desktop machines with minimal or no local storage and processing capacity. They obtain most or all of their software and data from a central network server. Whereas network computers help organizations maintain central control over computing, peer-to-peer computing puts processing power back on users' desktops, linking individual PCs, workstations, or other computers through the Internet or private networks to share data, disk space and even processing power for a variety of tasks.

5. *Analyze important issues in managing hardware technology assets.* Electronic commerce and electronic business have put new strategic emphasis on technologies that can store vast quantities of transaction data and make them immediately available on-line. Managers and information systems specialists need to pay special attention to hardware capacity planning and scalability to ensure that the firm has enough computing power for its current and future needs while determining the total cost of ownership (TCO) of information technology resources. Managers also need to track technology trends that might require changes in the firm's information technology infrastructure, including the assignment of more corporate computing tasks to small handheld computers and information appliances, and the use of social interfaces.

## KEY TERMS

**Arithmetic-logic unit (ALU), 145**
**ASCII (American Standard Code for Information Interchange), 144**
**Bar code, 152**
**Batch processing, 153**
**Bit, 143**
**Byte, 143**
**Capacity planning, 161**
**Cathode ray tube (CRT), 154**
**CD-R (compact disk-recordable), 149**
**CD-ROM (compact disk read-only memory), 149**
**Central processing unit (CPU), 144**
**Centralized processing, 157**
**Client, 157**
**Client/server computing, 157**
**Computer mouse, 151**
**Control unit, 145**
**Coprocessor, 148**
**Data bus width, 147**
**Digital scanner, 153**
**Digital video disk (DVD), 149**
**Direct access storage device (DASD), 149**
**Distributed processing, 157**
**Downsizing, 158**
**EBCDIC (Extended Binary Coded Decimal Interchange Code), 144**
**Floppy disk, 149**
**Gigabyte, 146**
**Hard disk, 149**
**Information appliance, 163**
**Kilobyte, 146**
**Machine cycle, 145**
**Magnetic disk, 149**
**Magnetic ink character recognition (MICR), 152**
**Magnetic tape, 150**
**Mainframe, 156**
**Massively parallel computers, 148**
**Master file, 153**
**Megabyte, 146**
**Megahertz, 147**
**Microprocessor, 146**
**Microsecond, 145**
**Midrange computer, 156**
**Minicomputer, 156**
**MMX (MultiMedia eXtension), 148**
**MP3 (MPEG3), 156**
**Multimedia, 155**
**Nanosecond, 145**
**Network computer (NC), 158**
**On-line processing, 153**
**Optical character recognition (OCR), 152**
**Parallel processing, 148**
**Peer-to-peer computing, 159**
**Pen-based input, 153**
**Personal computer (PC), 157**
**Pixel, 144**
**Primary storage, 144**
**Plotter, 154**
**Printer, 154**
**RAM (random access memory), 145**
**RAID (Redundant Array of Inexpensive Disks), 149**
**Reduced instruction set computing (RISC), 147**
**ROM (read-only memory), 146**
**Scalability, 161**
**Secondary storage, 141**
**Semiconductor, 146**
**Sensors, 153**
**Server, 156**
**Server farm, 156**
**Source data automation, 152**
**Storage area network (SAN), 150**
**Storage service provider (SSP), 151**
**Streaming technology, 155**
**Supercomputer, 157**
**Terabyte, 146**
**Total cost of ownership (TCO), 162**
**Touch screen, 151**
**Transaction file, 153**
**Voice input device, 153**
**Voice output device, 154**
**Word length, 146**
**Workstation, 157**
**WORM (write once/read many), 149**

## REVIEW QUESTIONS

1. What are the components of a contemporary computer system?
2. Distinguish between a bit and a byte, and describe how information is stored in primary memory.
3. What are ASCII and EBCDIC, and why are they used?
4. Name the major components of the CPU and describe the function of each.
5. What are the different types of semiconductor memory, and when are they used?
6. Name and describe the factors affecting a microprocessor's speed and performance.
7. Distinguish between serial, parallel, and massively parallel processing.
8. List the most important secondary storage media. What are the strengths and limitations of each?

9. List and describe the major input devices.
10. List and describe the major output devices.
11. What is the difference between batch and on-line processing? Diagram the difference.
12. What is multimedia? What technologies are involved?
13. What is the difference between a mainframe, a minicomputer, a server, and a PC? Between a PC and a workstation?
14. What are downsizing and client/server processing?
15. What is a network computer? How does it differ from a conventional PC? Compare the network computer and peer-to-peer models of computing.
16. Why should managers pay attention to the total cost of ownership (TCO) of technology resources? How would using the TCO model affect computer hardware purchase decisions?
17. Why should managers be interested in computer storage, scalability, and hardware capacity planning?
18. Name two hardware technology trends and explain their implications for business organizations.

## GROUP PROJECT

Experts predict that notebook computers will soon have 10 times the power of a current personal computer, with a touch-sensitive color screen that one can write on or draw on with a stylus, or type on when a program displays a keyboard. Each will have a small, compact, rewritable, removable CD-ROM that can store the equivalent of a set of encyclopedias. In addition, the computers will have voice-recognition capabilities, including the ability to record sound and give voice responses to questions. The computers will be able to carry on a dialogue by voice, graphics, typed words, and displayed video graphics. Thus, affordable computers will be about the size of a thick pad of letter paper and just as portable and convenient, but with the intelligence of a computer and the multimedia capabilities of a television set.

Form a group with three or four of your classmates and develop an analysis of the impacts such developments would have on one of these areas: university education, corporate sales and marketing, manufacturing, or management consulting. Explain why you think the impact will or will not occur. If possible, use electronic presentation software to present your findings to the class.

## TOOLS FOR INTERACTIVE LEARNING

### INTERNET CONNECTION

The Internet Connection for this chapter will direct you to a series of Web sites where you can complete an exercise to survey the products and services of major computer hardware vendors and the use of Web sites in the computer hardware industry. You can also use the Interactive Study Guide to test your knowledge of the topics in this chapter and get instant feedback where you need more practice.

### ELECTRONIC COMMERCE PROJECT

At the Laudon Web site for Chapter 5, you will find an Electronic Commerce project for buying and financing a home purchase.

### CD-ROM

If you use the Multimedia Edition CD-ROM with this chapter, you can view a simulation of a program executing on a computer. You can also find a video clip by Intel showing the evolution of computer hardware, an audio overview of the major themes of this chapter, and bullet text summarizing the key points of the chapter.

## CASE STUDY *Managing Technology Assets Pays Off for American Home Products*

In early 2000 pharmaceutical giant American Home Products (AHP) released its annual report. To no one's surprise, it showed a 1999 loss of more than $1.2 million versus a 1998 profit of almost $2.5 million. The $13.5 billion (annual sales) healthcare company is well known for such products as Premarin, the most prescribed drug in the United States. Nonetheless, the Madison, New Jersey, corporation had been under a news spotlight ever since 1997 headlines revealed that its very popular diet drugs, dexfenfluramine and fenfluramine (known as fen-phen) caused heart damage in some users. The drugs were quickly withdrawn, and, of course, the lawsuits immediately began. The 1999 loss was the result of a one-time charge that became necessary when AHP in October 1999 settled a class action lawsuit by about 200,000 former fen-phen users.

However, the fen-phen lawsuits were not the only financial problems facing AHP. The company also had been facing the same profit problems as the rest of the pharmaceutical industry. The whole industry was under increasing pressure as healthcare costs were ballooning in the United States. The explosive growth of managed care in the 1990s meant the insurance companies were using their powerful weight to force pharmaceutical houses to lower prices. They felt similar pressure as a result of the reform

reform of Medicare and increasing global competition. Starting in the mid-1990s, companies that are part of the pharmaceutical industry had been trying to avoid a profit squeeze by reducing their operating costs. To achieve such reductions, they have turned to enterprise resource planning, E-commerce, reform, and consolidation of their networks. The companies have also turned to other areas that have not received as much attention. For example, Bruce Faden, the vice president and CIO of AHP, added another dimension when he pointed out that, "Every pharmaceutical company is looking at improving its supply chain." AHP has looked to yet other areas to cut its costs during the past few years, one of which is its management of its computer-related assets.

Like so many large corporations, until recently, AHP has actually barely attempted to manage its computer assets. The problem came to be very much on the mind of Derek Bluestone when he became the pharmaceutical division's senior manager for global IT sourcing and acquisitions. Each site within his division managed its own hardware and software in its own way, using the spreadsheets or data management software of its choice. Some were even still using old-fashioned paper and pencil. Company executives had no way of knowing what assets the division actually owned, why they had been purchased, how much they had cost, and how they were being used now—if at all.

This decentralized and disorderly approach to asset management led to many problems. Lack of procurement centralization resulted in duplication, the loss of volume discounts, and the purchase of too many different and often incompatible systems, all of which needed support. The same was true of software; far too many software brands were performing the same functions, all of which needed maintenance. Analysts were unable to track vendor performance. In fact, they could not even determine if the software maintenance vendors were adhering to contractual spending limits. The dollar value of the computer-related assets in the company is immense, with as many as 30,000 personal computers alone, each of which uses multiple software packages. Obtaining and maintaining the information on so many machines can be very complex and yet is vital. For example, analysts have estimated that simply to move or reconfigure a computer can cost between $300 and $1,800 per machine. At that cost, with the right information, the responsible persons might decide to replace it rather than to move or reconfigure it, but such information was usually not available. One example Bluestone offered shows the complexities. AHP may have a mainframe with 50 or more software licenses on it, and each one of those licenses has a maintenance stream. For the mainframe hardware, there's a maintenance contract and cost stream. There are contracts for each one of those licenses with specific terms and conditions that need to be managed and adhered to. Without a great deal of organized information, costs and even contract execution could not be controlled or monitored or even understood.

Bluestone was eager to take action. He estimated that with the proper information, his division could save about $1 million over three years, and that was only in hardware costs. Moreover, that, he said, was a conservative estimate. Further, the reduction of soft costs would add even more savings. As an example of soft costs, he pointed out, with a proper asset management system, managing IT leases or reconciling invoices would be easier and less expensive. Also, the time spent within each unit doing inventories would be eliminated, which would result in a financial savings. In addition, during the past few years AHP has been making more and more use of application service providers (ASPs). An application service provider (ASP) is a business that runs software for subscribing companies from remote computer centers via the Internet or a private network. Instead of buying and installing software programs, subscribing companies can rent the same functions from these services (see Chapter 6). Using ASPs has added to Bluestone's concerns about asset management. "From an overall process perspective, asset management will become even more critical for enterprises considering ASP hosting," he said.

AHP management had recognized the overall need to cut costs, and in 1997 with the help of Bluestone, it finally decided that enterprise asset management was a core information technology responsibility. Management took steps to make that happen, having the pharmaceutical division's 12-member global IT sourcing group take charge of the project. The group quickly realized that assets needed to be tracked right from their beginning. For each piece of hardware and software they wanted to maintain such data as the purchase cost, the group budget that paid for it, the reason for the purchase, maintenance costs through its life, and all related costs such as software it used, service, upgrades, and add-ons. In early 1998 the project group selected software that would enable the company to capture and maintain the data it needed and so to track assets as needed. The main package, Argis, produced by Pittsburgh-based Janus Technologies, was used in conjunction with NetCensus from Tally Systems of Lebanon, New Hampshire. Using them together, the company was able to check on any asset and even link software and hardware asset records. "Effectively, we are able to look up a server to see what software is running, maintenance renewal dates and maintenance caps, and the specific grant of use of the license," explained Bluestone.

Once the software had been purchased, the question quickly arose as to how to install the new asset management system. AHP decided to take an incremental approach, at first installing it only in its pharmaceutical division's 20 U.S. sites. Bluestone explained his philosophy, stating that when you go to a unit and install such as system, "You are inviting yourself into each functional group's work stream, and each one entails a completely different process. You have to understand how people use their assets and leverage the resources within those groups to get the data in the form you need." The time and staff needed to do this led Bluestone to conclude that only a phased approach could possibly be successful. The team decided it would plan to extend the system to the rest of the units worldwide within the following one to two years.

Did the project results live up to expectations? As of the spring of 2000 it was too early to cite any cost savings. Establishing asset management is a long, slow process, and identifying savings will take time. Bluestone has certainly been pleased with the results.

The pharmaceutical division now has a single system for recording and managing all its hardware and software assets. However, Bluestone and his team are not satisfied and have visions of further change. They have begun phasing in enhancements to both Argis and NetCensus. And they want to make use of the Internet to make asset management information available to senior IT management and to the company's IT clients as well. They also want to link the asset management system with the company's problem management system.

**Sources:** Karen Schwartz, "Controlled Substances," *CIO Magazine,* June 1, 2000; "AHP Says Fen-Phen Settlement Is Win-Win," *Forbes,* August 29, 2000; Lenny Liebmann, "Drug Companies Use IT to Cure What Ails Them," *TechWeb,* September 27, 1999; Sam Jaffe, "The Cloud over American Home Products Dissipates," *BusinessWeek,* October 11, 1999; "American Home Products Annual Report," http://www.ahp.com/annrpt99; and "American Home Products, Corporation," *The Industry Standard,* http://www.thestandard.com/companies.

### *CASE STUDY QUESTIONS*

1. What problems did American Home Products have with its IT infrastructure? Why? How was its business affected by not having an information technology asset management program?
2. What management, organization, and technology issues do you think Bluestone faced as he planned and executed the project to install an asset management system in the pharmaceutical division?
3. What are the management and organizational benefits of a technology asset management system? Do you see any downside to using such a system, and if so, what?
4. It has been said that technology asset management requires an organization to change the way it does business. Do you agree? Why or why not?

chapter

# 6 Managing Software Assets

objectives

**After completing this chapter, you will be able to:**

1. *Describe the major types of software.*
2. *Examine the functions of system software and compare leading PC operating systems.*
3. *Analyze the strengths and limitations of the major application programming languages and software tools.*
4. *Describe contemporary approaches to software development.*
5. *Identify important issues in the management of organizational software assets.*

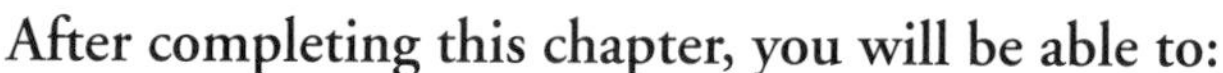

## Renting Software on the Web: A Lifeline for Medcom

Medcom, based in Jacksonville, Florida, is an administrator of health insurance plans for businesses that have elected to "self-fund." Although this 50-employee firm was in the business of providing human resources functions to other companies, it did not have an official human resources department to manage its own employees and benefit plans. Laurie Dalsgaard, Medcom's human resources coordinator, found this out when she joined the company in 1998: All of Medcom's human resource information was kept on pieces of paper stored in her file cabinet. The payroll department and other department managers had duplicate copies of these paper forms as well, keeping track of them with their own procedures.

Dalsgaard became responsible for maintaining the employee paperwork, with data on names, dependents, salaries, health insurance coverage, and life insurance plans, and for making sure that employees have appropriate health insurance, life insurance, and flexible spending options. Because everything was paper based, the information was fragmented and disorganized. Dalsgaard was spending between 20 and 25 hours per week just pushing papers and tracking down employees. When an employee was hired, she had to fill out sheets of paper and place them in a hard file folder. When an employee had any change in status, such as a marriage, change of address, termination, or change in health insurance coverage, Dalsgaard would have to fill out a new batch of forms.

To bring order and better management to Medcom's employee record keeping, Dalsgaard turned to Employease, an Internet-based application service provider of human resources software. The software allows companies to manage current and historical human resources and benefits information across divisions, locations, carriers, and benefit plans and to maintain information such as enrollment and claims forms, internal and external contact information, and links to other Web sites. Companies using Employease do not have to purchase, install, update, or maintain software. They can access entire human resources systems via the Internet and standard Web browser software. Employease makes all the updates to the system, sending companies electronic messages about the changes. Employease charges Medcom a maintenance fee of less than $5.50 per employee per month to use the software.

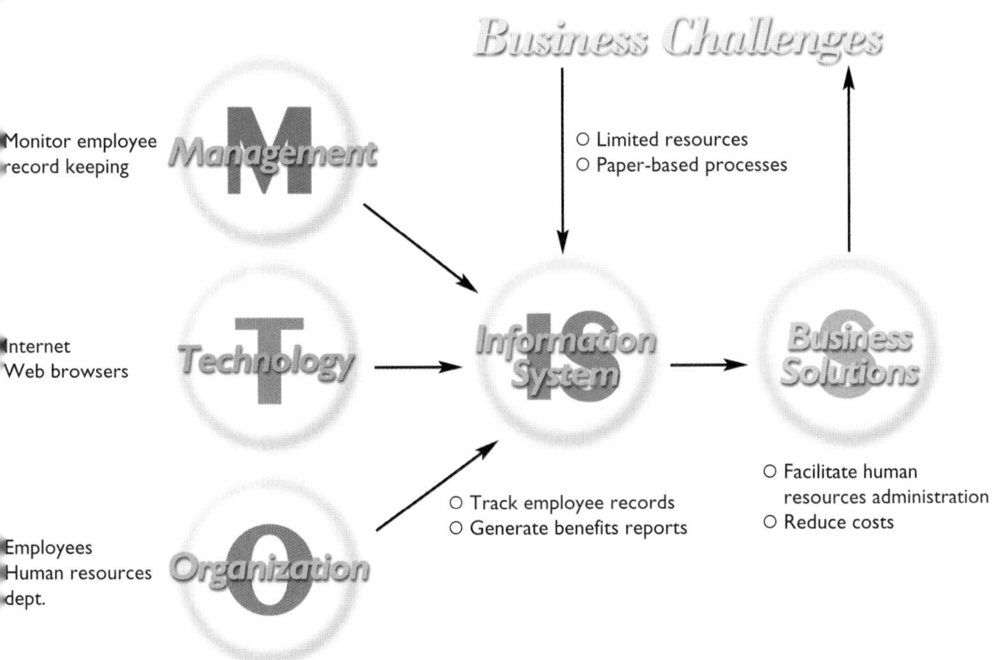


Dalsgaard was able to use Employease to automate Medcom's paperwork so that the company could administer its own accounts and benefits plans. The system keeps track of all employee records, including healthcare enrollment information. Dalsgaard can use the system to report on employee benefits eligibility, benefit election confirmation statements, and employee census data. The Employease system has also simplified processes such as issuing employee identification cards. The payoff to Medcom is clear.

**Sources:** Angela R. Garber, "Free Your Time," *Small Business Computing,* May 2000; and www. Employease.com.

**Renting Software on the Web: A Lifeline for Medcom**

**MANAGEMENT CHALLENGES**

Many businesses like Medcom have access to computer hardware. What prevented Laurie Dalsgaard from efficiently managing Medcom's human resources information was the lack of appropriate software. To find the software it needed, Medcom had to know the capabilities of various types of software, and it had to select human resources software that met its specific business requirements and that was affordable and easy to use. The Employease human resources software Medcom selected transformed a jumble of tangled paperwork into manageable information and became an important technology asset. Selecting and developing the right software can improve organizational performance, but it raises the following management challenges:

## MANAGEMENT CHALLENGES

1. **Increasing complexity and software errors.** Although some software for desktop systems and for some Internet applications can be rapidly generated, a great deal of what software will be asked to do remains far-reaching and sophisticated, requiring programs that are large and complex. Large and complex systems tend to be error prone, with software errors or "bugs" that may not be revealed for years despite exhaustive testing and actual use. Researchers do not know if the number of bugs grows exponentially or proportionately to the number of lines of code, nor can they tell for certain whether all segments of a complex piece of software will always work in total harmony. The process of designing and testing software that is reliable and "bug-free" is a serious quality control and management problem (see Chapter 14).
2. **The application backlog.** Advances in computer software have not kept pace with the breathtaking productivity gains in computer hardware. Developing software has become a major preoccupation for organizations. A great deal of software must be intricately crafted. Moreover, the software itself is only one component of a complete information system that must be carefully designed and coordinated with other people, as well as with organizational and hardware components. The "software crisis" is actually part of a larger systems analysis, design, and implementation issue, which will be treated in detail later. Despite the gains from fourth-generation languages, personal desktop software tools, object-oriented programming, and software tools for the World Wide Web, many businesses continue to face a backlog of two to three years in developing the information systems they need, or they will not be able to develop them at all.

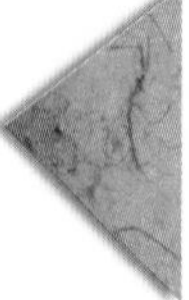

To play a useful role in the firm's information technology (IT) infrastructure, computer hardware requires instructions provided by computer software. This chapter shows how software turns computer hardware into useful information systems, describes major software types, and presents new approaches to software development and acquisition. It also introduces some key issues for managing software as an organizational asset in the firm's information technology infrastructure.

# 6.1 WHAT IS SOFTWARE?

**software**
The detailed instructions that control the operation of a computer system.

**Software** is the detailed instructions that control the operation of a computer system. Without software, computer hardware could not perform the tasks we associate with computers. The functions of software are to (1) manage the computer resources of the organization, (2) provide tools for human beings to take advantage of these resources, and (3) act as an intermediary between organizations and stored information. Selecting appropriate software for the organization is a key management decision.

## SOFTWARE PROGRAMS

**program**
A series of statements or instructions to the computer.

A software **program** is a series of statements or instructions to the computer. The process of writing or coding programs is termed *programming,* and individuals who specialize in this task are called *programmers.* A program must be stored in the computer's primary storage

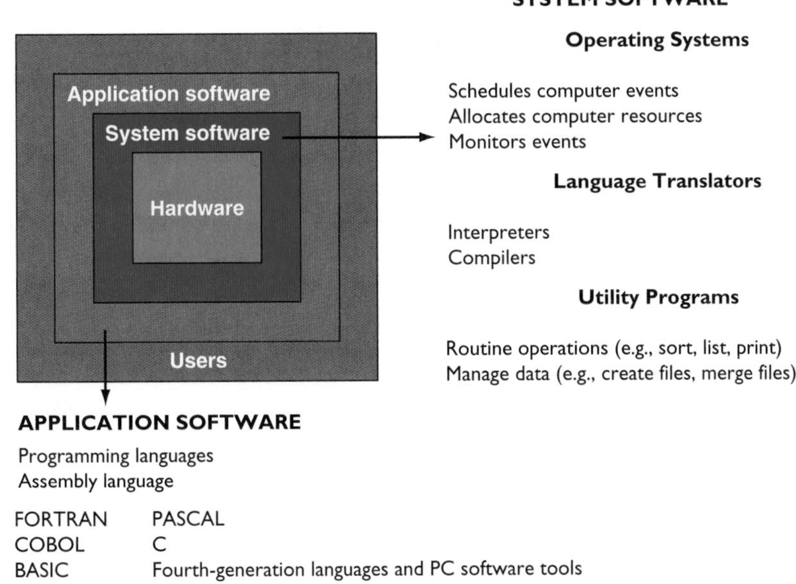


***Figure 6-1*** The major types of software. The relationship between the system software, application software, and users can be illustrated by a series of nested boxes. System software—consisting of operating systems, language translators, and utility programs—controls access to the hardware. Application software, such as the programming languages and "fourth-generation" languages, must work through the system software to operate. The user interacts primarily with the application software.

along with the required data in order to execute, or have its instructions performed by the computer. Once a program has finished executing, the computer hardware can be used for another task when a new program is loaded into memory.

### Major Types of Software

There are two major types of software: system software and application software. Each kind performs a different function. **System software** is a set of generalized programs that manage the computer's resources, such as the central processor, communications links, and peripheral devices. Programmers who write system software are called *system programmers.*

**system software**
Generalized programs that manage the computer's resources, such as the central processor, communications links, and peripheral devices.

**Application software** describes the programs that are written for or by users to apply the computer to a specific task. Software for processing an order or generating a mailing list is application software. Programmers who write application software are called *application programmers.*

**application software**
Programs written for a specific application to perform functions specified by end users.

The types of software are interrelated and can be thought of as a set of nested boxes, each of which must interact closely with the other boxes surrounding it. Figure 6-1 illustrates this relationship. The system software surrounds and controls access to the hardware. Application software must work through the system software in order to operate. End users work primarily with application software. Each type of software must be specially designed to a specific machine to ensure its compatibility.

## 6.2 System Software

System software coordinates the various parts of the computer system and mediates between application software and computer hardware. The system software that manages and controls the computer's activities is called the **operating system.** Other system software consists of computer language translation programs that convert programming languages into machine language and utility programs that perform common processing tasks.

**operating system**
The system software that manages and controls the activities of the computer.

### Functions of the Operating System

One way to look at the operating system is as the system's chief manager. Operating system software decides which computer resources will be used, which programs will be run, and the order in which activities will take place.

An operating system performs three functions. It allocates and assigns system resources; it schedules the use of computer resources and computer jobs; and it monitors computer system activities.

### Allocation and Assignment

The operating system allocates resources to the application jobs in the execution queue. It provides locations in primary memory for data and programs and controls the input and output devices such as printers, terminals, and telecommunication links.

### Scheduling

Thousands of pieces of work can be going on in a computer simultaneously. The operating system decides when to schedule the jobs that have been submitted and when to coordinate the scheduling in various areas of the computer so that different parts of different jobs can be worked on at the same time. For instance, while a program is executing, the operating system is scheduling the use of input and output devices. Not all jobs are performed in the order they are submitted; the operating system must schedule these jobs according to organizational priorities. On-line order processing may have priority over a job to generate mailing lists and labels.

### Monitoring

The operating system monitors the activities of the computer system. It keeps track of each computer job and may also keep track of who is using the system, of what programs have been run, and of any unauthorized attempts to access the system. Information system security is discussed in detail in Chapter 14.

## Multiprogramming, Virtual Storage, Time Sharing, and Multiprocessing

How is it possible for 1,000 or more users sitting at remote terminals to use a computer information system simultaneously if, as we stated in the previous chapter, most computers can execute only one instruction from one program at a time? How can computers run thousands of programs? The answer is that the computer has a series of specialized operating system capabilities.

**multiprogramming**
A method of executing two or more programs concurrently using the same computer. The CPU executes only one program but can service the input/output needs of others at the same time.

**multitasking**
The multiprogramming capability of primarily single-user operating systems, such as those for PCs.

**multithreading**
The ability of an operating system to execute different parts of the same program simultaneously.

**virtual storage**
Handing programs more efficiently by dividing the programs into small fixed- or variable-length portions with only a small portion stored in primary memory at one time.

### Multiprogramming

The most important operating system capability for sharing computer resources is **multiprogramming.** Multiprogramming permits multiple programs to share a computer system's resources at any one time through concurrent use of a CPU. By concurrent use, we mean that only one program is actually using the CPU at any given moment but that the input/output needs of other programs can be serviced at the same time. Two or more programs are active at the same time, but they do not use the same computer resources simultaneously. With multiprogramming, a group of programs takes turns using the processor.

Figure 6-2 shows how three programs in a multiprogramming environment can be stored in primary storage. The first program executes until an input/output event is read in the program. The CPU then moves to the second program until an input/output statement occurs. At this point, the CPU switches to the execution of the third program, and so forth, until eventually all three programs have been executed. In this manner, many different programs can be executing at the same time, although different resources within the CPU are actually being used.

Multiprogramming on single-user operating systems such as those in personal computers is called **multitasking. Multithreading** is the ability of an operating system to execute different parts of the same program, called *threads,* simultaneously. For example, a word processing program may be formatting one document while checking the spelling and grammar of another document.

### Virtual Storage

**Virtual storage** handles programs more efficiently because the computer divides the programs into small fixed- or variable-length portions, storing only a small portion of the program in primary memory at one time. If only two or three large programs can be read into memory, a certain part of main memory generally remains underutilized, because the pro-

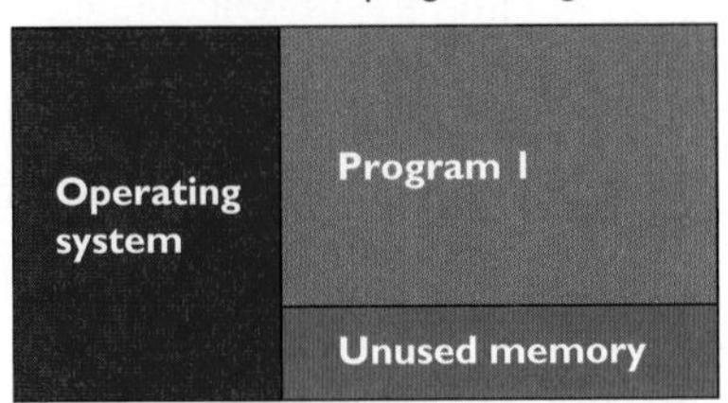


*Figure 6-2* Single-program execution versus multiprogramming. In multiprogramming, the computer can be used much more efficiently because a number of programs can be executing concurrently. Several complete programs are loaded into memory. This memory management aspect of the operating system greatly increases throughput by better management of high-speed memory and input/output devices.

grams add up to less than the total amount of primary storage space available and only a small number of programs can reside in primary storage at any given time.

Only a few statements of a program actually execute at any given moment. Virtual storage breaks a program into a number of fixed-length portions called pages or into variable-length portions called segments. Each of these portions is relatively small (a page is approximately two to four kilobytes). This permits a very large number of programs to reside in primary memory, because only one page of each program is actually located there (see Figure 6-3), using this resource more efficiently. All other program pages are stored on a peripheral disk unit until they are ready for execution.

## Time Sharing

**Time sharing** is an operating system capability that allows many users to share computer processing resources simultaneously. It differs from multiprogramming in that the CPU spends a fixed amount of time on one program before moving on to another. In a time-sharing environment, thousands of users are each allocated a tiny slice of computer time. In this time slot, each user is free to use the computer to perform any required operation; at the end of this period, another user is given a tiny time slice of the CPU. This arrangement permits many users to be connected to a CPU simultaneously, with each receiving only a tiny amount of CPU time. But because the CPU is operating at the nanosecond level, a CPU can accomplish a great deal of work in a thousandth of a second.

**time sharing**
The sharing of computer resources by many users simultaneously by having the CPU spend a fixed amount of time on each user's program before proceeding to the next.

## Multiprocessing

**Multiprocessing** is an operating system capability that links together two or more CPUs to work in parallel in a single computer system. The operating system can assign multiple CPUs to execute different instructions from the same program or from different programs

**multiprocessing**
An operating system feature for executing two or more instructions simultaneously in a single computer system by using multiple central processing units.

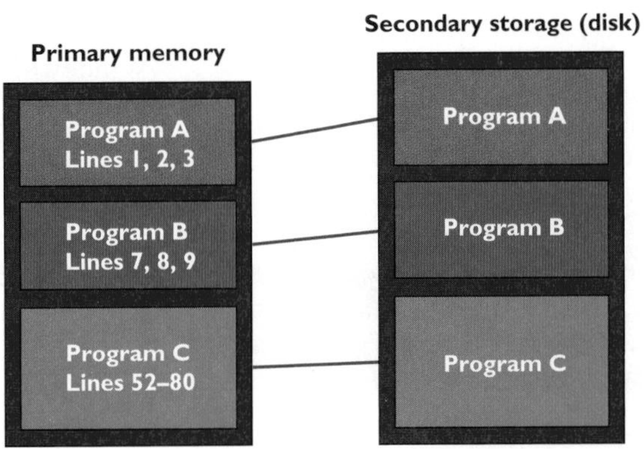


*Figure 6-3* Virtual storage. Virtual storage is based on the fact that, in general, only a few statements in a program can actually be used at any given moment. In virtual storage, programs are broken down into small sections called pages. Individual program pages are read into memory only when needed. The rest of the program is stored on disk until it is required. In this way, very large programs can be executed by small machines, or a large number of programs can be executed concurrently by a single machine.

simultaneously, dividing the work between the CPUs. Whereas multiprogramming uses concurrent processing with one CPU, multiprocessing uses simultaneous processing with multiple CPUs.

**source code**
Program instructions written in a high-level language that must be translated into machine language to be executed by the computer.

**compiler**
Special system software that translates a high-level language into machine language for execution by the computer.

**object code**
Program instructions that have been translated into machine language so that they can be executed by the computer.

**interpreter**
A special translator of source code into machine code that translates each source code statement into machine code and executes them, one at a time.

**utility program**
System software consisting of programs for routine, repetitive tasks, which can be shared by many users.

**graphical user interface (GUI)**
The part of an operating system users interact with that uses graphic icons and the computer mouse to issue commands and make selections.

## LANGUAGE TRANSLATION AND UTILITY SOFTWARE

System software includes special language translator programs that translate high-level language programs written in programming languages such as COBOL, FORTRAN, or C into machine language that the computer can execute. This type of system software is called a compiler or interpreter. The program in the high-level language before translation into machine language is called **source code.** A **compiler** translates source code into machine code called **object code.** Just before execution by the computer, the object code modules are joined with other object code modules in a process called linkage editing. The resulting load module is what is actually executed by the computer. Figure 6-4 illustrates the language translation process.

Some programming languages such as BASIC do not use a compiler but an **interpreter,** which translates each source code statement one at a time into machine code during execution and executes it. Interpreter languages are very slow to execute because they are translated one statement at a time.

An assembler is similar to a compiler, but it is used to translate only assembly language (see Section 6.3) into machine code.

System software includes **utility programs** for routine, repetitive tasks, such as copying, clearing primary storage, computing a square root, or sorting. If you have worked on a computer and have performed such functions as setting up new files, deleting old files, or formatting diskettes, you have worked with utility programs. Utility programs are prewritten programs that are stored so that they can be shared by all users of a computer system and can be used rapidly in many different information system applications when requested.

## GRAPHICAL USER INTERFACES

When users interact with a computer, even a PC, the interaction is controlled by an operating system. Users communicate with an operating system through the user interface of that operating system. The **graphical user interface,** often called a GUI, makes extensive use of icons, buttons, bars, and boxes to issue operating system commands. It has become the dominant model for the user interface of PC operating systems and for many types of application software.

Older PC operating systems such as DOS, described in the following section, were command-driven, requiring the user to type in text-based commands using a keyboard. An operating system with a graphical user interface uses graphic symbols called icons to depict programs, files, and activities. For example, a file could be deleted by moving the cursor to a trash icon. Many graphical user interfaces use a system of pull-down menus to help users select commands and pop-up boxes to help users select among command options. Windowing features allow users to create, stack, size, and move around boxes of information. A complex series of commands can be issued simply by linking icons.

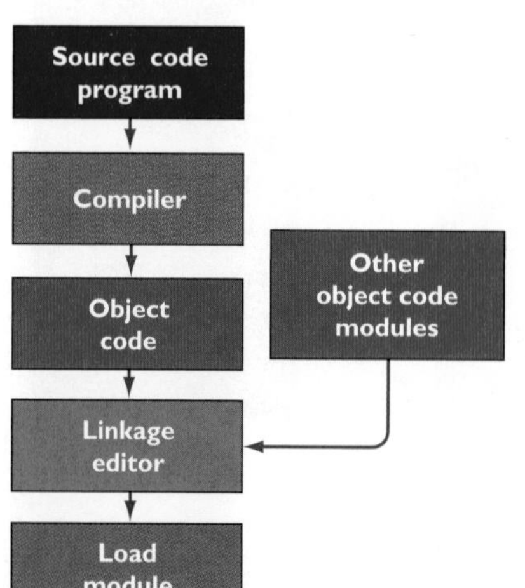


*Figure 6-4* The language translation process. The source code in a high-level language program is translated by the compiler into object code so that the instructions can be "understood" by the machine. These are grouped into modules. Prior to execution, the object code modules are joined together by the linkage editor to create the load module. It is the load module that is actually executed by the computer.

## PC OPERATING SYSTEMS

Like any other software, PC software is based on specific operating systems and computer hardware. A software package written for one PC operating system generally cannot run on another. Table 6-1 compares the leading PC operating systems: Windows XP, Windows 98, Windows Me, Windows 95, Windows 2000, Windows CE, OS/2, Unix, Linux, the Macintosh operating system, and DOS.

## TABLE 6-1 LEADING PC OPERATING SYSTEMS

| Operating System | Features |
|---|---|
| Windows XP | Reliable, robust operating system with versions for both home and corporate users. Features support of Internet and multimedia and improved networking, security, and corporate management capabilities. |
| Windows ME, Windows 98, and Windows 95 | 32-bit operating system for personal computing with a streamlined graphical user interface. Has multitasking and powerful networking capabilities and can be integrated with the information resources of the Web. |
| Windows 2000 | 32-bit operating system for PCs, workstations, and network servers. Supports multitasking, multiprocessing, intensive networking, and Internet services for corporate computing. |
| Windows CE | Pared-down version of the Windows operating system for handheld computers and wireless communication devices. |
| OS/2 | Operating system for IBM PCs that can take advantage of the 32-bit microprocessor. Supports multitasking and networking. |
| Unix | Used for powerful PCs, workstations, and midrange computers. Supports multitasking, multiuser processing, and networking. Is portable to different models of computer hardware. |
| Linux | Free, reliable alternative to Unix and Windows 2000 that runs on many different types of computer hardware and provides source code that can be modified by software developers. |
| Mac OS | Operating system for the Macintosh computer. Supports networking and multitasking and has powerful multimedia capabilities. Supports connecting to and publishing on the Internet. |
| DOS | Operating system for older IBM and IBM-compatible PCs. Limits program use of memory to 640 kilobytes. |

Microsoft's **Windows 98** is a genuine 32-bit operating system that can address data in 32-bit chunks and run programs that take up more than 640 kilobytes of memory. It provides a streamlined graphical user interface that arranges icons to provide instant access to common tasks. Windows 98 features multitasking, multithreading, and powerful networking capabilities, including the capability to integrate fax, e-mail, and scheduling programs. **Windows 95** was an earlier version of this operating system.

**Windows 98**
32-bit operating system that is closely integrated with the Internet and that supports multitasking, multithreading, and networking.

**Windows 95**
Earlier version of the Windows 32-bit operating system.

Windows 98 is faster and more integrated with the Internet than Windows 95, with support for additional hardware technologies such as MMX, digital video disk (DVD—see Chapter 5), videoconferencing cameras, scanners, TV tuner-adapter cards, and joysticks. It provides capabilities for optimizing hardware performance and file management on the hard disk and enhanced three-dimensional graphics. The most visible feature of Windows 98 is the integration of the operating system with Web browser software. Users can work with the traditional Windows interface or use the Web browser interface to display information. The user's hard disk can be viewed as an extension of the World Wide Web so that a document residing on the hard disk or on the Web can be accessed the same way. Small applet programs (see the discussion of Java in Section 6.4) on the Windows desktop can automatically retrieve information from specific Web sites whenever the user logs onto the Internet. Windows 98 also includes a group collaboration tool called NetMeeting and FrontPage Express, a tool for creating and storing Web pages.

Microsoft has provided an enhanced Windows operating system for consumer users called **Windows Millennium Edition (Windows Me).** It features tools to let users edit video recordings and put them up on the Web and tools to simplify home networking of two or more PCs. A media player bundled with Windows Me can record, store, and play CDs, digital music downloaded from the Internet, and videos. Windows Me users can also import, store, and share photos. Windows Me has improved capabilities for safeguarding critical files.

**Windows Millennium Edition (Windows Me)**
Enhanced Windows operating system for consumer users featuring tools for working with video, photos, music, and home networking.

**Windows 2000** is another 32-bit operating system developed by Microsoft with features that make it appropriate for applications in large networked organizations. Earlier versions of this operating system were known as Windows NT (for New Technology). Windows 2000 is used as an operating system for high-performance desktop and laptop computers and network servers. Windows 2000 shares the same graphical user interface as the other Windows operating systems, but it has more powerful networking, multitasking, and memory-management capabilities. Windows 2000 can support software written for Windows and it can provide mainframe-like computing power for new applications with massive memory and file requirements. It can even support multiprocessing with multiple CPUs.

**Windows 2000**
Powerful operating system developed by Microsoft for use with 32-bit PCs, workstations, and network servers. Supports networking, multitasking, multiprocessing, and Internet services.

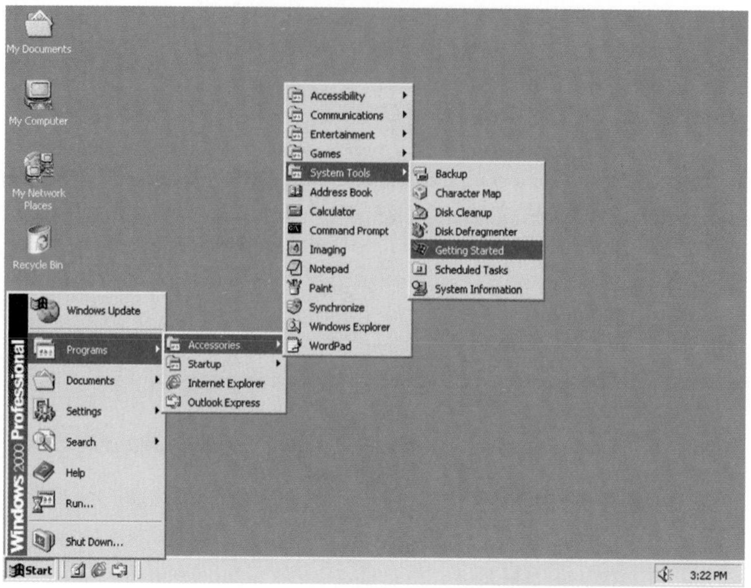


*Microsoft's Windows 2000 is a powerful operating system with a graphical user interface for high-performance desktop and laptop computers and network servers.*

There are two basic versions of Windows 2000—a Professional version for users of stand-alone or client desktop and laptop computers and several server versions designed to run on network servers and provide network management functions, including tools for creating and operating Web sites and other Internet services.

**Windows XP** (for eXPerience) combines the reliability and robustness of Windows 2000 with the ease of use of Windows 98/Me. The Windows XP Home Edition is for home users and the Windows XP Professional Edition targets mobile and business users.

**Windows CE**
Portable and compact operating system designed to run on small handheld computers, personal digital assistants, or wireless communication devices.

**Windows XP**
Powerful new Windows operating system that provides reliability, robustness, and ease of use for both corporate and home PC users.

**Windows CE** has some of the capabilities of Windows, including its graphical user interface, but it is designed to run on small handheld computers, personal digital assistants, or wireless communication devices such as pagers and cellular phones. It is a portable and compact operating system requiring very little memory. Information appliances and consumer devices can use this operating system to share information with Windows-based PCs and to connect to the Internet.

**OS/2**
Powerful operating system used with 32-bit IBM/PCs or workstations that supports multitasking, networking, and very memory-intensive applications.

**OS/2** is a robust 32-bit operating system for powerful IBM or IBM-compatible PCs with Intel microprocessors. OS/2 is used for complex, memory-intensive applications or those that require networking, multitasking, or large programs. OS/2 provides powerful desktop computers with mainframe-operating-system capabilities, such as multitasking and supporting multiple users in networks, and it supports networked multimedia and pen computing applications. OS/2 has its own graphical user interface and desktop and server versions.

**Unix**
Operating system for all types of computers, which is machine independent and supports multiuser processing, multitasking, and networking. Used in high-end workstations and servers.

**Unix** is an interactive, multiuser, multitasking operating system developed by Bell Laboratories in 1969 to help scientific researchers share data.Unix was developed to connect various machines together and is highly supportive of communications and networking. Unix is often used on workstations and servers and provides the reliability and scalability for running large systems on high-end servers. Unix can run on many different kinds of computers. Application programs that run under Unix can be ported from one computer to run on a different computer with little modification.

Unix is considered powerful but very complex, with a legion of commands. Graphical user interfaces have been developed for Unix. Unix cannot respond well to problems caused by the overuse of system resources such as jobs or disk space. Unix also poses some security problems, because multiple jobs and users can access the same file simultaneously. Vendors have developed different versions of Unix that are incompatible, thereby limiting software portability.

**Linux**
Reliable and compactly designed operating system that is an offshoot of Unix and which can run on many different hardware platforms; is available free or at very low cost. Used as alternative to Unix and Windows 2000.

**Linux** is a Unix-like operating system that runs on Intel, Motorola, Alpha, SPARC, and Mips processors. Linux can be downloaded from the Internet free of charge or purchased for a small fee from companies that provide additional tools for the software. Because it is free, reliable, compactly designed, and capable of running on many different hardware platforms, it has become popular during the past few years among sophisticated computer users and businesses as an alternative to Unix and Windows 2000. Major application software vendors are starting to provide versions that can run on Linux. The source code for Linux is available along with the operating system software so that it can be modified by software developers to fit their particular needs.

**open-source software**
Software that provides free access to its program code, allowing users to modify the program code to make improvements or fix errors.

Linux is an example of **open-source software,** which provides all computer users with free access to its source code so that they can modify the code to fix errors or to make improvements. Open-source software such as Linux is not owned by any company or individual. A global network of programmers and users manages and modifies the software, usually without being paid to do so. The Window on Organizations describes how organizations are starting to benefit from this new operating system.

**Mac OS**
Operating system for the Macintosh computer that supports multitasking, has access to the Internet, and has powerful graphics and multimedia capabilities.

**Mac OS,** the operating system for the Apple Macintosh computer, features multitasking, powerful multimedia and networking capabilities, and a mouse-driven graphical user interface. New features of this operating system allow users to connect to, explore, and publish on the Internet and World Wide Web; use Java software (see Section 6.4); and load Chinese, Japanese, Korean, Indian, Hebrew, and Arabic fonts for use in Web browser software (see Section 6.3). Mac OS X, the newest generation Apple operating system, has a new Unix-based foundation for additional reliability, superior graphics, and open-source features.

**DOS**
Operating system for older 16-bit PCs based on the IBM personal computer standard.

**DOS** is a 16-bit operating system that is used today only with older PCs based on the IBM PC standard because so much available application software was written for systems using DOS. DOS itself does not support multitasking and limits the size of a program in memory to 640 kilobytes. The newer Microsoft Windows operating systems can run pro-

## WHY LINUX?

Burlington Coat Factory, the $2 billion clothing discounter based in Burlington, New Jersey, decided to take the plunge with Linux and installed this new operating system on 1,150 computers in its 280 stores. Why would such a large company opt for a new shareware operating system that can be downloaded free from the Internet?

According to Mike Prince, Burlington's CIO, Linux was attractive both for its price and its performance. Burlington expects to save thousands of dollars in each store by not buying a commercial operating system. Prince also believes Linux is more stable than Windows 2000/NT and will be less costly to support. The company has used Unix for many years and did not need to learn new skills to use Linux. Burlington runs Linux on Dell Computer servers in its stores networked to the company's inventory system, which runs on a server running Sun Solaris, a version of Unix.

Cendant Corporation, a $5.3 billion travel services, real estate, and direct marketing company has deployed Linux servers and workstations in 60 percent of the 4,500 Days Inn, Howard Johnson, and Super 8 motels connected to its Unix reservation management system. Scott Gibson, Cendant's vice president of hotel information technology, observes that Linux's stability and ease of administration have been "remarkable." Because Cendant's franchisees have no information systems specialists on the premises, the reliability of Linux is especially important.

Small firms are discovering that Linux may be a good choice for them as well. Linux can save small companies money because it runs well on older, less powerful machines and laptops. For example, the James G. Murphy Co. in Kenmore, Washington, which auctions heavy equipment, used cars, and tools, uses a server running Linux to record all of its auction bids and payments for goods. Some of Murphy's auctions draw more than 1,000 bidders, and the results would be disastrous if the system crashed. With Linux as its operating system, it never has. Murphy runs auctions on customer sites as far away as Texas and Virginia and uses IBM laptop PCs running Linux and the auction software there too.

Even the Chinese government has embraced Linux. The government does not want to depend excessively on one vendor, Microsoft, and pay high prices for its operating system software when it can obtain Linux for free. The fact that Linux is publicly available and open to user modifications provides assurance that any security the government wants to build into its computer systems will not have undetected vulnerabilities. The government expects Linux will be running on half of China's Internet servers and one-third of its desktop computers by the end of 2001.

Yet many organizations have not jumped on the Linux bandwagon. Not all business application software can run on Linux and the operating system is used primarily on servers providing Web, e-mail, file-sharing or printing services or to run custom applications that only require a simple interface.

**To Think About:** Should a company select Linux as its operating system for its major business applications? What management, organization, and technology factors would have to be addressed when making that decision?

*Sources:* Aaron Ricadela, "Linux Is Useful, But Still Can't Crack Windows," *Information Week,* February 5, 2001 and "Linux Comes Alive," *Information Week,* January 24, 2000; Dan Orzech, "Bidding on Linux," *Inc. Technology 2000,* no. 2; Craig S. Smith, "Fearing Control by Microsoft, China Backs the Linux System," *The New York Times,* July 8, 2000.

grams written for DOS as well as newer software. DOS is command-driven, but it can present a graphical user interface by using the early Microsoft **Windows,** a highly popular graphical user interface shell that runs in conjunction with the DOS operating system.

**Windows**
A graphical user interface shell that runs in conjunction with the DOS PC operating system.

## 6.3 APPLICATION SOFTWARE

Application software is primarily concerned with accomplishing the tasks of end users. Many different languages can be used to develop application software. Each has different strengths and drawbacks. Managers should understand how to evaluate and select software tools and programming languages that are appropriate for their organization's objectives.

### PROGRAMMING LANGUAGES

**machine language**
A programming language consisting of the 1s and 0s of binary code.

The first generation of computer languages consisted of **machine language,** which requires the programmer to write all program instructions in the 0s and 1s of binary code and to specify storage locations for every instruction and item of data used. Programming in machine language was a very slow, labor-intensive process. As computer hardware improved and processing speed and memory size increased, programming languages changed from machine language to languages that have been easier for humans to understand and use. From the mid-1950s to the mid-1970s, high-level programming languages emerged, allowing programs to be written with regular words using sentencelike statements. We now briefly describe the most important high-level languages.

#### Assembly Language

**assembly language**
A programming language developed in the 1950s that resembles machine language but substitutes mnemonics for numeric codes.

**Assembly language** is the next level of programming language up from machine language, and it is considered a "second-generation" language. Like machine language, assembly language (Figure 6-5) is designed for a specific machine and specific microprocessors. Assembly language makes use of certain mnemonics (e.g., load, sum) to represent machine language instructions and storage locations. Although assembly language gives programmers great control, it is costly in terms of programmer time; it is also difficult to read, debug, and learn. Assembly language is used primarily today in system software.

#### Third-Generation Languages: FORTRAN, COBOL, BASIC, Pascal, and C

Third-generation languages specify instructions as brief statements that are more like natural language than assembly language. They are less efficient in the use of computer resources than earlier languages; they are easier to write and understand and have made it possible to create software for business and scientific problems. Important third-generation languages include FORTRAN, COBOL, C, BASIC, and Pascal.

**FORTRAN (FORmula TRANslator)**
A programming language developed in 1956 for scientific and mathematical applications.

***FORTRAN*** **FORTRAN (FORmula TRANslator)** (Figure 6-6) was developed in 1956 to provide an easier way of writing scientific and engineering applications. FORTRAN is especially useful in processing numeric data. Many kinds of business applications can be written in FORTRAN, and contemporary versions provide sophisticated structures for controlling program logic. FORTRAN is not very good at providing input/output efficiency or in printing and working with lists. The syntax is very strict and keying errors are common, making the programs difficult to debug.

**COBOL (COmmon Business Oriented Language)**
Major programming language for business applications because it can process large data files with alphanumeric characters.

***COBOL*** **COBOL (COmmon Business Oriented Language)** (Figure 6-7) came into use in the early 1960s. It was developed by a committee representing both government and industry. Rear Admiral Grace M. Hopper was a key committee member who played a major role in COBOL development. COBOL was designed with business administration in mind, for processing large data files with alphanumeric characters (mixed alphabetic and numeric data), and for performing repetitive tasks such as payroll. It is poor at complex mathematical calculations. Also, there are many versions of COBOL, and not all are compatible with each other.

**BASIC (Beginners All-purpose Symbolic Instruction Code)**
A general-purpose programming language used with PCs and for teaching programming.

***BASIC and Pascal*** BASIC and Pascal are used primarily in education to teach programming. **BASIC (Beginners All-purpose Symbolic Instruction Code)** was developed in 1964

```
AR 5, 3
```

*Figure 6-5* Assembly language. This sample assembly language command adds the contents of register 3 to register 5 and then stores the result in register 5.

```
READ (5,100) ID, QUANT, PRICE
TOTAL = QUANT * PRICE
```

*Figure 6-6* FORTRAN. This sample FORTRAN program code is part of a program to compute sales figures for a particular item.

```
MULTIPLY QUANT-SOLD BY UNIT-PRICE GIVING SALES-TOTAL.
```

*Figure 6-7* COBOL. This sample COBOL program code is part of a routine to compute total sales figures for a particular item.

by John Kemeny and Thomas Kurtz to teach students at Dartmouth College how to use computers. BASIC is easy to use, demonstrates computer capabilities well, and requires only a small interpreter. However, BASIC does few computer processing tasks well even though it does them all, and different versions of BASIC exist.

Named after Blaise Pascal, the seventeenth-century mathematician and philosopher, **Pascal** was developed by the Swiss computer science professor Niklaus Wirth of Zurich in the late 1960s. With sophisticated structures to control program logic and a simple, powerful set of commands, Pascal is used primarily in computer science courses to teach sound programming practices.

**Pascal**
A programming language used on PCs and used to teach sound programming practices in computer science courses.

***C and C++*** C is a powerful and efficient language developed at AT&T's Bell Labs in the early 1970s. It combines machine portability with tight control and efficient use of computer resources, and it can work on a variety of computers. It is used primarily by professional programmers to create operating system and application software, especially for PCs.

C++ is a newer version of C that is object-oriented (see Section 6.4). It has all the capabilities of C plus additional features for working with software objects. C++ is used for developing application software.

**C**
A powerful programming language with tight control and efficiency of execution; it is portable across different microprocessors and is used primarily with PCs.

**C++**
Object-oriented version of the C programming language.

## FOURTH-GENERATION LANGUAGES AND PC SOFTWARE TOOLS

**Fourth-generation languages** consist of a variety of software tools that enable end users to develop software applications with minimal or no technical assistance or that enhance professional programmers' productivity. Fourth-generation languages tend to be nonprocedural or less procedural than conventional programming languages. Procedural languages require specification of the sequence of steps, or procedures, that tell the computer what to do and how to do it. Nonprocedural languages need only specify what has to be accomplished rather than provide details about how to carry out the task. Thus, a nonprocedural language can accomplish the same task with fewer steps and lines of program code than a procedural language. Some of these nonprocedural languages are **natural languages** that enable users to communicate with the computer using conversational commands resembling human speech. Natural language development is one of the concerns of artificial intelligence (see Chapter 12).

There are seven categories of fourth-generation languages: query languages, report generators, graphics languages, application generators, very high-level programming languages, application software packages, and PC tools. Figure 6-8 illustrates the spectrum of these tools and some commercially available products in each category.

**fourth-generation language**
A programming language that can be employed directly by end users or less-skilled programmers to develop computer applications more rapidly than conventional programming languages.

**natural language**
Programming language that is very close to human language.

### Query Languages

**Query languages** are high-level languages for retrieving data stored in databases or files. They are usually interactive, on-line, and capable of supporting requests for information that

**query language**
A high-level computer language used to retrieve specific information from databases or files.

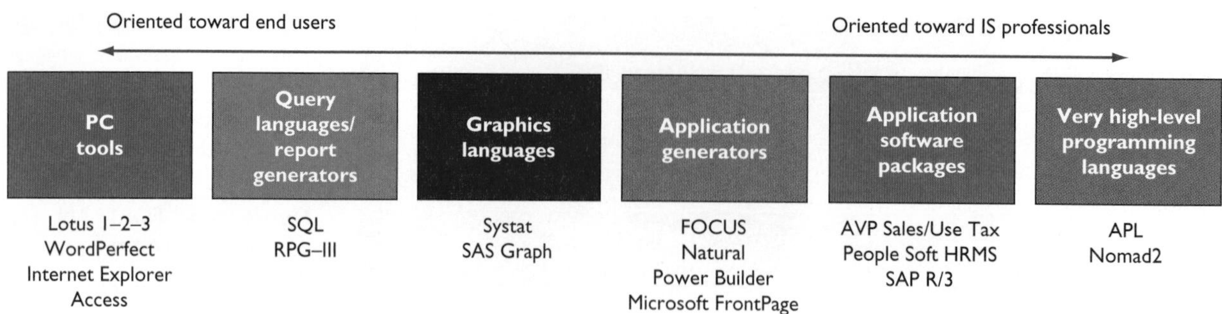


*Figure 6-8* Fourth-generation languages. The spectrum of major categories of fourth-generation languages; commercially available products in each category are illustrated. Tools range from those that are simple and designated primarily for end users to complex tools designed for information systems professionals.

are not predefined. They are often tied to database management systems (see Chapter 7) or some of the PC software tools described later in this section. For instance, the query

SELECT ALL WHERE age >40 AND name = "Wilson"

requests all records where the name is "Wilson" and the age is more than 40. Chapter 7 provides more detail on Structured Query Language (SQL), which has become a standard query language.

## Report Generators

**report generator**
Software that creates customized reports in a wide range of formats that are not routinely produced by an information system.

**Report generators** are software for creating customized reports. They extract data from files or databases and create reports in many formats. Report generators generally provide more control over the way data are formatted, organized, and displayed than query languages. The more powerful report generators can manipulate data with complex calculations and logic before they are output. Some report generators are extensions of database or query languages.

## Graphics Languages

**graphics language**
A computer language that displays data from files or databases in graphic format.

**Graphics languages** retrieve data from files or databases and display them in graphic format. Users can ask for data and specify how they are to be charted. Some graphics software can perform arithmetic or logical operations on data as well. SAS and Systat are examples of powerful analytical graphics software.

## Application Generators

**application generator**
Software that can generate entire information system applications; the user specifies what needs to be done, and the application generator creates the appropriate program code.

**Application generators** contain preprogrammed modules that can generate entire applications, greatly speeding development. A user can specify what needs to be done, and the application generator will create the appropriate code for input, validation, update, processing, and reporting. Most full-function application generators consist of a comprehensive, integrated set of development tools: a query language, screen painter, graphics generator, report generator, decision support/modeling tools, security facilities, a high-level programming language, and tools for defining and organizing data. Application generators now include tools for developing full-function Web sites.

## Very High-Level Programming Languages

**very high-level programming language**
A programming language that uses fewer instructions than conventional languages. Used primarily as a professional programmer productivity tool.

**Very high-level programming languages** are designed to generate program code with fewer instructions than conventional languages such as COBOL or FORTRAN. Programs and applications based on these languages can be developed in much shorter periods of time. End users can employ simple features of these languages. However, these languages are designed primarily as productivity tools for professional programmers. APL and Nomad2 are examples of these languages.

## Application Software Packages

A **software package** is a prewritten, precoded, commercially available set of programs that eliminates the need for individuals or organizations to write their own software programs for certain functions. There are software packages for system software, but the vast majority of package software is application software.

**software package**
A prewritten, precoded, commercially available set of programs that eliminates the need to write software programs for certain functions.

Application software packages consist of prewritten application software that is marketed commercially. These packages are available for major business applications on mainframes, midrange computers, and PCs. Table 6-2 provides examples of applications for which packages are commercially available. Although application packages for large complex systems must be installed by technical specialists, many application packages, especially those for PCs, are marketed directly to end users. Systems development based on application packages is discussed in Chapter 10.

## PC Software Tools

Some of the most popular and productivity-promoting software tools are the general-purpose application packages that have been developed for PCs. The most widely used PC tools include word processing, spreadsheet, data management, presentation graphics, and e-mail software as well as integrated software packages, Web browsers, and groupware.

***Word Processing Software*** **Word processing software** stores text data electronically as a computer file rather than on paper. The word processing software allows the user to make changes in the document electronically in memory. This eliminates the need to retype an entire page to incorporate corrections. The software has formatting options to make changes in line spacing, margins, character size, and column width. Microsoft Word and WordPerfect are popular word processing packages. Figure 6-9 illustrates a Microsoft Word screen displaying text, spelling and grammar checking, and major menu options.

**word processing software**
Software that handles electronic storage, editing, formatting, and printing of documents.

Most word processing software has advanced features that automate other writing tasks: spelling checkers, style checkers (to analyze grammar and punctuation), thesaurus programs, and mail merge programs, which link letters or other text documents with names and addresses in a mailing list. The newest versions of this software can create and access Web pages.

Although today's word processing programs can turn out very polished-looking documents, businesses that need to create highly professional-looking brochures, manuals, or books will likely use desktop publishing software for this purpose. **Desktop publishing software** allows for more control over the placement of text, graphics, and photos in the layout of a page than does word processing software. Users of this software can design the layout; determine spacing between letters, words, and lines; reduce or enlarge graphics; or rearrange blocks of text and graphics, producing finished documents that look like those created by a

**desktop publishing software**
Software that produces professional quality documents with design, graphics, and special layout features.

**TABLE 6-2 EXAMPLES OF APPLICATION SOFTWARE PACKAGES**

| | |
|---|---|
| Accounts receivable | Job costing |
| Bond and stock management | Library systems |
| Computer-aided design (CAD) | Life insurance |
| Electronic commerce storefront | Mailing labels |
| E-mail | Mathematical/statistical modeling |
| Enterprise resource planning (ERP) | Order processing |
| Groupware | Payroll |
| Healthcare | Process control |
| Hotel management | Tax accounting |
| Internet telephone | Web browser |
| | Word processing |

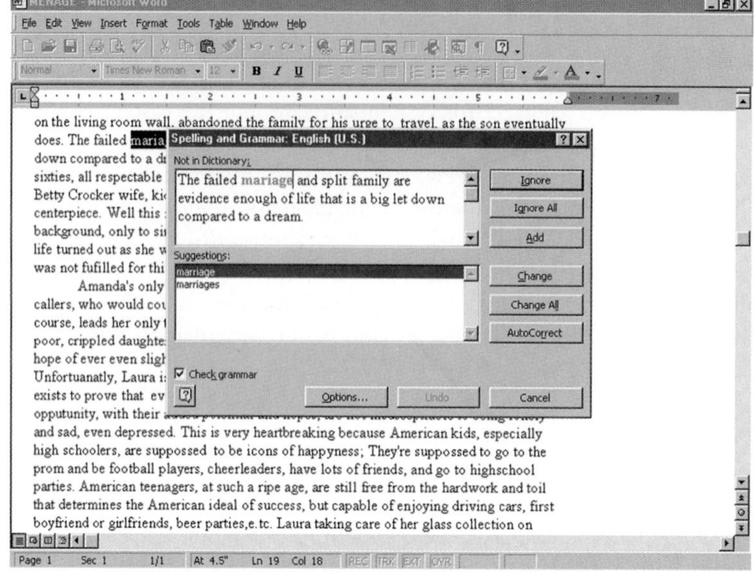

*Figure 6-9* Text and the spell-checking option in Microsoft Word. Word processing software provides many easy-to-use options to create and output a text document to meet a user's specifications.
*Source:* Courtesy of Microsoft.

professional print shops. Adobe Pagemaker and QuarkXpress are two popular desktop publishing packages.

**spreadsheet**
Software displaying data in a grid of columns and rows, with the capability of easily recalculating numerical data.

***Spreadsheets*** Electronic **spreadsheet** software provides computerized versions of traditional financial modeling tools such as the accountant's columnar pad, pencil, and calculator. An electronic spreadsheet is organized into a grid of columns and rows. The power of the electronic spreadsheet is evident when one changes a value or values because all other related values on the spreadsheet will be automatically recomputed.

Spreadsheets are valuable for applications in which numerous calculations with pieces of data must be related to each other. Spreadsheets also are useful for applications that require modeling and "what-if" analysis. After the user has constructed a set of mathematical relationships, the spreadsheet can be recalculated instantaneously using a different set of assumptions. A number of alternatives can easily be evaluated by changing one or two pieces of data without having to rekey in the rest of the worksheet. Many spreadsheet packages include graphics functions that can present data in the form of line graphs, bar graphs, or pie charts. The most popular spreadsheet packages are Microsoft Excel and Lotus 1-2-3. The newest versions of this software can read and write Web files.

Figure 6-10 illustrates the output from a spreadsheet for a breakeven analysis and its accompanying graph.

**data management software**
Software used for creating and manipulating lists, creating files and databases to store data, and combining information for reports.

***Data Management Software*** Although spreadsheet programs are powerful tools for manipulating quantitative data, **data management software** is more suitable for creating and manipulating lists and for combining information from different files. PC data management packages have programming features and easy-to-learn menus that enable nonspecialists to build small information systems.

Data management software typically has facilities for creating files and databases and for storing, modifying, and manipulating data for reports and queries. A detailed treatment of data management software and database management systems can be found in Chapter 7. Popular data management software for the personal computer includes Microsoft Access, which has been enhanced to publish data on the Web. Figure 6-11 shows a screen from Microsoft Access illustrating some of its capabilities.

**presentation graphics**
Software to create professional-quality graphics presentations that can incorporate charts, sound, animation, photos, and video clips.

***Presentation Graphics*** **Presentation graphics** software allows users to create professional-quality graphics presentations. This software can convert numeric data into charts and other types of graphics and can include multimedia displays of sound, animation, photos, and video clips. The leading presentation graphics packages include capabilities for computer-generated slide shows and for translating content for the Web. Microsoft PowerPoint, Lotus Freelance Graphics, and Aldus Persuasion are popular presentation graphics packages.

| | | | | | |
|---|---|---|---|---|---|
| Total fixed cost | 19,000.00 | | | | |
| Variable cost per unit | 3.00 | | | | |
| Average sales price | 17.00 | | | | |
| Contribution margin | 14.00 | | | | |
| Breakeven point | 1,357 | | | | |
| | Custom Neckties Pro Forma Income Statement | | | | |
| Units sold | 0.00 | 679 | 1,357 | 2,036 | 2,714 |
| Revenue | 0 | 11,536 | 23,071 | 34,607 | 46,143 |
| Fixed cost | 19,000 | 19,000 | 19,000 | 19,000 | 19,000 |
| Variable cost | 0 | 2,036 | 4,071 | 6,107 | 8,143 |
| Total cost | 19,000 | 21,036 | 23,071 | 25,107 | 27,143 |
| Profit/Loss | (19,000) | (9,500) | 0 | 9,500 | 19,000 |

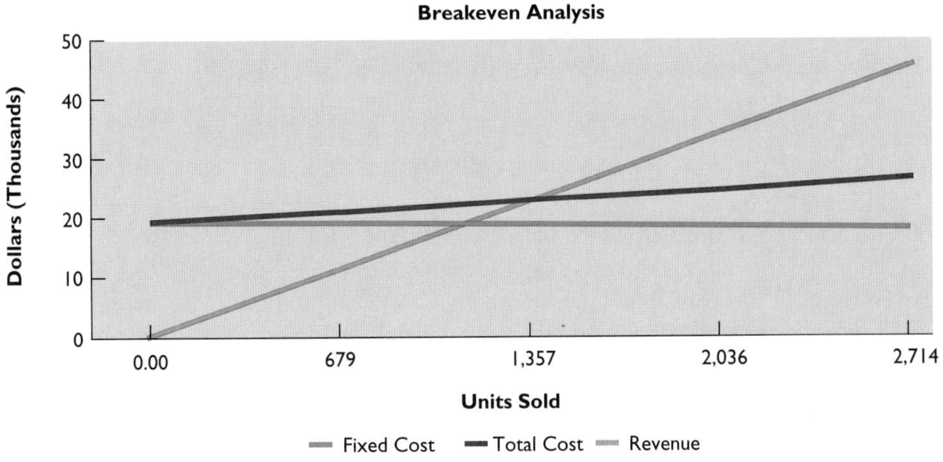


*Figure 6-10* Spreadsheet software. Spreadsheet software organizes data into columns and rows for analysis and manipulation. Contemporary spreadsheet software provides graphing abilities for clear visual representation of the data in the spreadsheets. This sample breakeven analysis is represented as numbers in a spreadsheet as well as a line graph for easy interpretation.

***Integrated Software Packages and Software Suites*** **Integrated software packages** combine the functions of the most important PC software packages, such as word processing, spreadsheets, presentation graphics, and data management. This integration provides a more general-purpose software tool and eliminates redundant data entry and data maintenance. For example, the breakeven analysis spreadsheet illustrated in Figure 6-10 could be reformatted into a polished report with word processing software without separately keying the data into both programs. Integrated packages are a compromise. Although they can do many things well, they generally do not have the same power and depth as single-purpose packages.

**integrated software package** A software package that provides two or more applications, such as word processing and spreadsheets, providing for easy transfer of data between them.

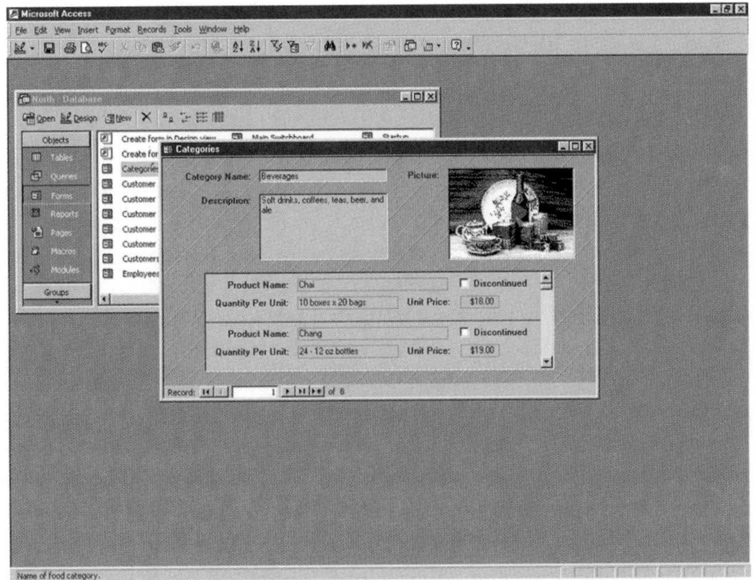


*Figure 6-11* Data management software. This screen from Microsoft Access illustrates some of its powerful capabilities for managing and organizing information.

*Users can create professional-looking electronic presentations incorporating text, diagrams, and other multimedia elements using presentation graphics software. This slide was created with Microsoft PowerPoint.*

Integrated software packages should be distinguished from software suites, which are collections of application software sold as a unit. Microsoft Office is an example. This software suite contains Word word processing software, Excel spreadsheet software, Access database software, PowerPoint presentation graphics software, and Outlook, a set of tools for e-mail, scheduling, and contact management. **Office 2000** and **Office XP** contain additional capabilities to support collaborative work on the Web. Documents created with Office tools can be viewed with a Web browser and published on a Web server. Office XP users can access information from the Web and insert it in documents and manage their e-mail accounts from a single view. Software suites have some features of integrated packages, such as the ability to share data among different applications, but they consist of full-featured versions of each type of software.

**Office 2000 and Office XP** Integrated software suites with capabilities for supporting collaborative work on the Web or incorporating information from the Web into documents.

***E-mail Software*** **Electronic mail (e-mail)** is used for the computer-to-computer exchange of messages and is an important tool for communication and collaborative work. A person can use a networked computer to send notes or lengthier documents to a recipient on the same network or a different network. Many organizations operate their own electronic-mail systems, but communications companies such as MCI and AT&T offer these services, as do commercial on-line information services such as America Online and services on the Internet.

**electronic mail (e-mail)** The computer-to-computer exchange of messages.

Web browsers and the PC software suites have e-mail capabilities, but specialized e-mail software packages such as Eudora are also available for use on the Internet. In addition to providing electronic messaging, many e-mail software packages have capabilities for routing messages to multiple recipients, message forwarding, and attaching text documents or multimedia to messages.

***Web Browsers*** **Web browsers** are easy-to-use software tools for displaying Web pages and for accessing the Web and other Internet resources. Web browser software features a point-and-click graphical user interface that can be employed throughout the Internet to access and display information stored on computers at other Internet sites. Browsers can display or present graphics, audio, and video information as well as traditional text, and they allow you to click on-screen buttons or highlighted words to link to related Web sites. Web browsers have become the primary interface for accessing the Internet or for using networked systems based on Internet technology. You can see examples of Web browser software by looking at the illustrations of Web pages in each chapter of this text.

**Web browser** An easy-to-use software tool for accessing the World Wide Web and the Internet.

The two leading commercial Web browsers are Microsoft's Internet Explorer and Netscape Navigator, which is available as part of the Netscape Communicator software suite. They include capabilities for using e-mail, file transfer, on-line discussion groups, and bulletin boards, along with other Internet services. Newer versions of these browsers contain support for Web publishing and work group computing. (See the following discussion of groupware.)

## TABLE 6-3 GROUPWARE CAPABILITIES

| |
|---|
| Group writing and commenting |
| Electronic mail distribution |
| Scheduling meetings and appointments |
| Shared files and databases |
| Shared time lines and plans |
| Electronic meetings and conferences |

***Groupware*** **Groupware** provides functions and services to support the collaborative activities of work groups. Groupware includes software for information-sharing, electronic meetings, scheduling, and e-mail, and a network to connect the members of the group as they work on their own desktop computers, often in widely scattered locations. Table 6-3 describes groupware capabilities.

**groupware**
Software that provides functions and services that support the collaborative activities of work groups.

Groupware enhances collaboration by allowing the exchange of ideas electronically. All the messages on a topic can be saved in a group, and stamped with the date, time, and author. All of these messages can be followed in a **thread** to see how a discussion evolved. (A thread is a series of messages in an on-line discussion that have been posted as replies to each other.) Any group member can review the ideas of others at any time and add to them, or individuals can post a document for others to comment on or edit. Members can post requests for help, allowing others to respond. Finally, if a group so chooses, members can store their work notes on the groupware so that all others in the group can see what progress is being made, what problems occur, and what activities are planned. The leading commercial groupware product has been Lotus Notes from the Lotus Development Corporation. The Internet is rich in capabilities to support collaborative work. Recent versions of Microsoft Internet Explorer and Netscape Communicator include groupware functions, such as e-mail, electronic scheduling and calendaring, audio and data conferencing, and electronic discussion groups and databases (see Chapters 8 and 12). Microsoft's Office 2000 and Office XP software suites include groupware features using Web technology. Powerful Web-based groupware features can also be found in products such as Opentext's Livelink.

**thread**
A series of messages in on-line discussions on a specified topic that have been posted as replies to each other. Each message in a thread can be read to see how a discussion evolved.

## SOFTWARE FOR ENTERPRISE INTEGRATION: ENTERPRISE SOFTWARE AND MIDDLEWARE

Chapters 2 and 3 discussed the growing organizational need to integrate functions and business processes to improve organizational control, coordination, and responsiveness by allowing

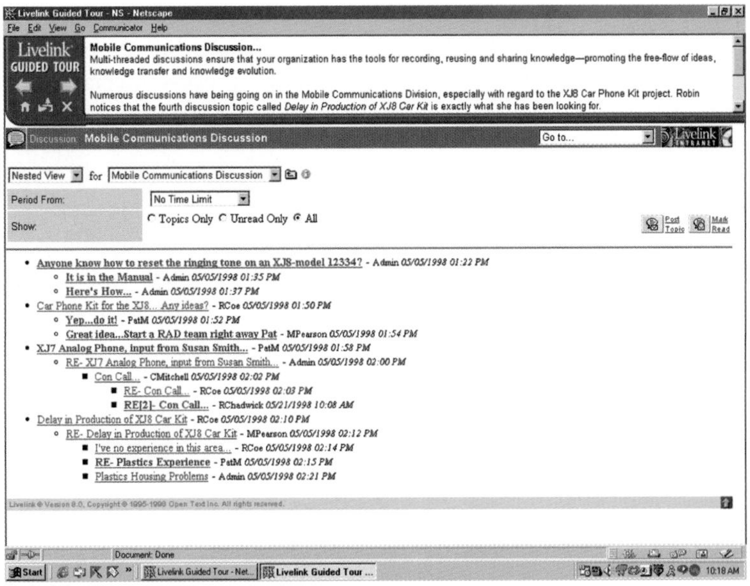

*Groupware facilitates collaboration by enabling members of a group to share documents, schedule meetings and discuss activities, events, and issues. Illustrated are capabilities for following a threaded discussion.*

data and information to flow more freely between different parts of the organization. Poorly integrated applications can create costly inefficiencies or slow customer service, which become competitive liabilities. Alternative software solutions are available to promote enterprise integration.

One alternative, which we introduced in Chapter 2, is to replace isolated systems that cannot communicate with each other with an enterprise software package. Chapter 2 introduced enterprise systems. **Enterprise software** consists of a set of interdependent modules for applications such as sales and distribution, financial accounting, investment management, materials management, production planning, plant maintenance, and human resources that allow data to be used by multiple functions and business processes for more precise organizational coordination and control. The modules can communicate with each other directly by sharing a common repository of data. Contemporary enterprise systems use a client/server computing architecture. Major enterprise software vendors include SAP, Oracle, PeopleSoft, and Baan. These vendors are now enhancing their products to provide more capabilities for supply chain management and exchange of data with other enterprises.

**enterprise software**
Set of integrated modules for applications such as sales and distribution, financial accounting, investment management, materials management, production planning, plant maintenance, and human resources, that allow data to be used by multiple functions and business processes.

Individual companies can implement all of the enterprise software modules offered by a vendor or select only the modules of interest to them. They can also configure the software they select to match the way they do business. For example, they could configure the software to track revenue by product line, geographical unit, or distribution channel. However, the enterprise software may not be able to support some companies' unique business processes and often requires firms to change the way they work. Chapter 11 describes the challenges of implementing enterprise software in greater detail.

Most firms cannot jettison all of their existing systems and create enterprise-wide integration from scratch. Many existing legacy mainframe applications are essential to daily operations and very risky to change, but they can be made more useful if their information and business logic can be integrated with other applications (Noffsinger, Niedbalski, Blanks, and Emmart, 1998). One way to integrate various legacy applications is to use special software called **middleware** to create an interface or bridge between two different systems. Middleware is software that connects two otherwise separate applications, allowing them to communicate with each other and to pass data between them (see Figure 6-12). Middleware may consist of custom software written in-house or a software package. There are many different types of middleware. One important use of middleware is to link client and server machines in client/server computing and increasingly to link a Web server to data stored on another computer. This allows users to request data from the computer in which they are stored using forms displayed on a Web browser, and it enables the Web server to return dynamic Web pages based on information users request.

**middleware**
Software that connects two disparate applications, allowing them to communicate with each other and to exchange data.

Instead of custom-writing software to connect one application to another, companies can purchase **enterprise application integration software** to connect disparate applications or application clusters. Enterprise application integration is the process of tying together multiple applications to support the flow of information across multiple business units and systems. Enterprise application integration software can consist of middleware for passing data between two different systems or business process integration tools that link applications together through business process modeling. The software allows system builders to model their business processes graphically and define the rules that applications should follow to make these processes work. The software then generates the underlying program code to link existing applications to each other to support those processes. Because the enterprise application integration software is largely independent of the individual applications it connects, the organization can change its business processes and grow without requiring changes to the applications. A few enterprise application integration tools allow multiple businesses to integrate their systems into an extended supply chain.

**enterprise application integration software**
Software that ties together multiple applications to support enterprise integration.

*Figure 6-12* Middleware. Middleware is software that can be used to pass commands and data between two disparate applications so that they can work together.

## 6.4 Contemporary Tools for Software Development

A growing backlog of software projects and the need for businesses to fashion systems that are flexible or that can run over the Internet have stimulated approaches to software development based on object-oriented programming tools and new programming languages such as Java, hypertext markup language (HTML), and Extensible Markup Language (XML).

### Object-oriented Programming

Traditional software development methods have treated data and procedures as independent components. A separate programming procedure must be written every time someone wants to take an action on a particular piece of data. The procedures act on data that the program passes to them.

#### What Makes Object-oriented Programming Different?

**Object-oriented programming** combines data and the specific procedures that operate on those data into one object. The object combines data and program code. Instead of passing data to procedures, programs send a message for an object to perform a procedure that is already embedded into it. (Procedures are termed *methods* in object-oriented languages.) The same message may be sent to many different objects, but each will implement that message differently.

**object-oriented programming**
An approach to software development that combines data and procedures into a single object.

For example, an object-oriented financial application might have Customer objects sending debit and credit messages to Account objects. The Account objects in turn might maintain Cash-on-Hand, Accounts-Payable, and Accounts-Receivable objects.

An object's data are hidden from other parts of the program and can only be manipulated from inside the object. The method for manipulating the object's data can be changed internally without affecting other parts of the program. Programmers can focus on what they want an object to do, and the object decides how to do it.

An object's data are encapsulated from other parts of the system, so each object is an independent software building block that can be used in many different systems without changing the program code. Thus, object-oriented programming is expected to reduce the time and cost of writing software by producing reusable program code or software chips that can be reused in other related systems. Future software work can draw on a library of reusable objects, and productivity gains from object-oriented technology could be magnified if objects were stored in reusable software libraries and explicitly designed for reuse (Fayad and Cline, 1996). However, such benefits are unlikely to be realized unless organizations develop appropriate standards and procedures for reuse (Kim and Stohr, 1998). Objects that can be assembled into complete systems are becoming commercially available through networks. These network-based software services should lead to further software economies for firms.

Object-oriented programming has spawned a new programming technology known as **visual programming.** With visual programming, programmers do not write code. Rather, they use a mouse to select and move around programming objects, copying an object from a library into a specific location in a program, or drawing a line to connect two or more objects. Visual Basic is a widely used visual programming tool for creating applications that run on Microsoft Windows.

**visual programming**
The construction of software programs by selecting and arranging programming objects rather than by writing program code.

#### Object-oriented Programming Concepts

Object-oriented programming is based on the concepts of class and inheritance. Program code is not written separately for every object but for classes, or general categories, of similar objects. Objects belonging to a certain class have the features of that class. Classes of objects in turn can inherit all the structure and behaviors of a more general class and then add variables and behaviors unique to each object. New classes of objects are created by choosing an existing class and specifying how the new class differs from the existing class, instead of starting from scratch each time.

**class**
The feature of object-oriented programming in which all objects belonging to a certain class have all of the features of that class.

**Classes** are organized hierarchically into superclasses and subclasses. For example, a car class might have a vehicle class for a superclass, so that it would inherit all the methods and

*With visual programming tools such as IBM's Visual Age Generator, working software programs can be created by drawing, pointing, and clicking instead of writing program code.*

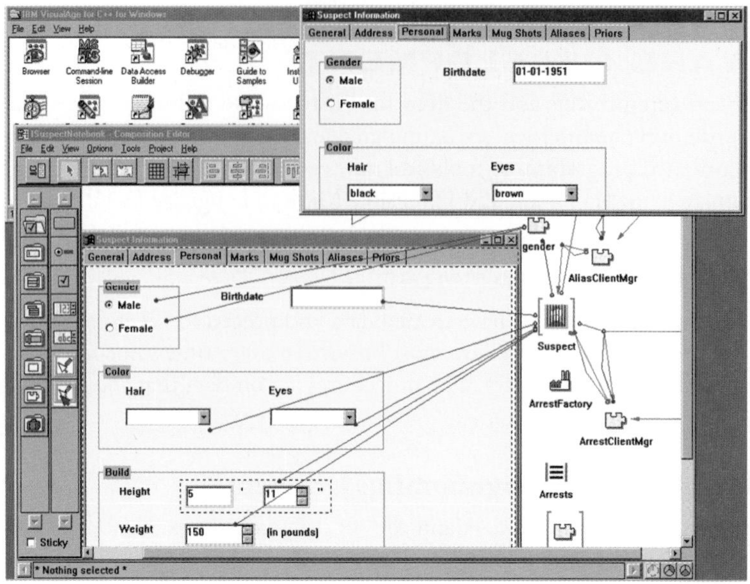


data previously defined for vehicle. The design of the car class would only need to describe how cars differ from vehicles. A banking application could define a Savings-Account object that is very much like a Bank-Account object with a few minor differences. Savings-Account inherits all the Bank-Account's state and methods and then adds a few extras.

**inheritance**
The feature of object-oriented programming in which a specific class of objects receives the features of a more general class.

We can see how class and **inheritance** work in Figure 6-13, which illustrates a tree of classes concerning employees and how they are paid. Employee is the common ancestor of the other four classes. Nonsalaried and Salaried are subclasses of Employee, whereas Temporary and Permanent are subclasses of Nonsalaried. The variables for the class are in the top half of the box, and the methods are in the bottom half. Dark-shaded items in each box are inherited from some ancestor class. (For example, by following the tree upward, we can see that Name and ID in the Nonsalaried, Salaried, Temporary, and Permanent subclasses are inherited from the Employee superclass [ancestor class].) Lighter-shaded methods, or class variables, are unique to a specific class and they override, or redefine, existing methods.

*Figure 6-13* Class, subclasses, and overriding. This figure illustrates how a message's method can come from the class itself or from an ancestor class. Class variables and methods are shaded when they are inherited from above.

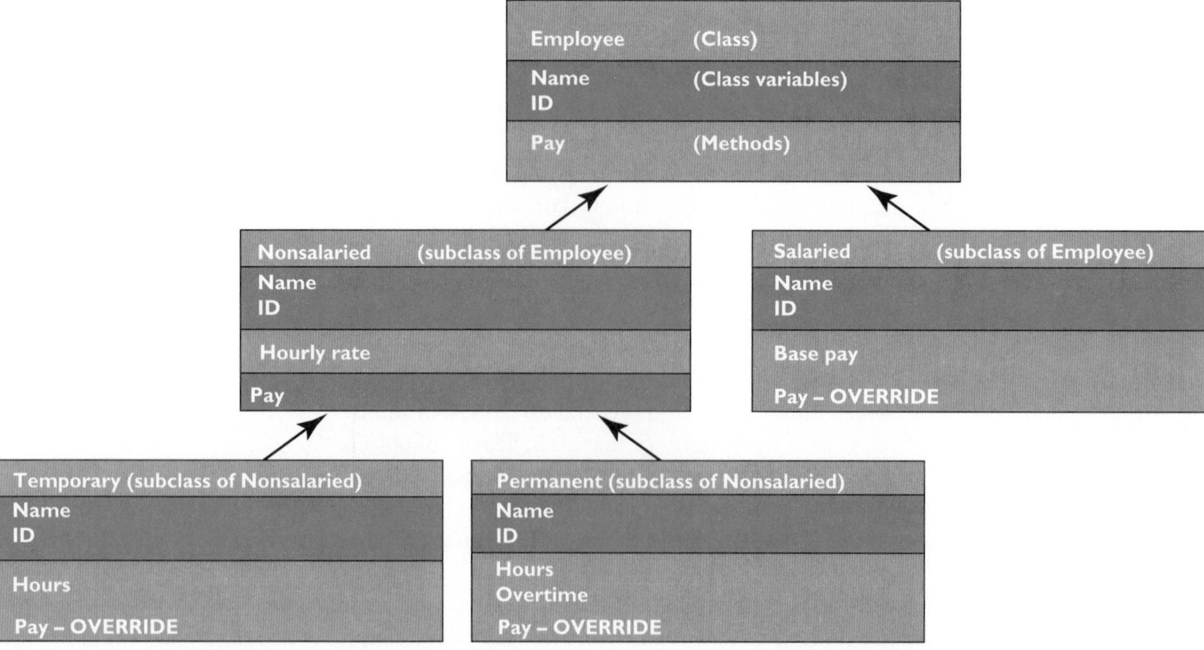

When a subclass overrides an inherited method, its object still responds to the same message, but it executes its definition of the method rather than its ancestor's. Whereas Pay is a method inherited from some superclass, the method Pay-OVERRIDE is specific to the Temporary, Permanent, and Salaried classes.

Object-oriented software can be custom programmed or it can be developed with rapid-application development tools, which can potentially cost 30 to 50 percent less than traditional program development methods. Some of these tools provide visual programming environments in which developers can create ready-to-use program code by "snapping" together prebuilt objects. Other tools generate program code that can be compiled to run on a variety of computing platforms.

## JAVA

**Java** is a platform-independent object-oriented programming language developed by Sun Microsystems. Java software is designed to run on any computer or computing device, regardless of the specific microprocessor or operating system it uses. A Macintosh PC, an IBM personal computer running Windows, a Compaq server running Unix, and even a smart cellular phone or information appliance can share the same Java application.

**Java**
Programming language that can deliver only the software functionality needed for a particular task as a small applet downloaded from a network; it can run on any computer and operating system.

Java can be used to create miniature programs called *applets* designed to reside on centralized network servers. The network delivers only the applets required for a specific function. With Java applets residing on a network, a user can download only the software functions and data that he or she needs to perform a particular task, such as analyzing the revenue from one sales territory. The user does not need to maintain large software programs or data files on his or her desktop machine. When the user is finished with processing, the data can be saved through the network. Java can be used with network computers because it enables all processing software and data to be stored on a network server, downloaded via a network as needed, and then placed back on the network server.

Java is also a very robust language that can handle text, data, graphics, sound, and video, all within one program if needed. Java applets often are used to provide interactive capabilities for Web pages. For example, Java applets can be used to create animated cartoons or real-time news tickers for a Web site, or to add a capability to a Web page to calculate a loan payment schedule on-line in response to financial data input by the user. (Microsoft's **ActiveX** sometimes is used as an alternative to Java for creating interactivity on a Web page. ActiveX is a set of controls that enables programs or other objects, such as charts, tables, or animations, to be embedded within a Web page. However, ActiveX lacks Java's machine independence and was designed for a Windows environment.)

**ActiveX**
A set of controls for the Windows software environment that enables programs or other objects such as charts, tables, or animations to be embedded within a Web page.

Companies are starting to develop more extensive Java applications running over the Internet or over their private networks because such applications can potentially run in Windows, Unix, IBM mainframe, Macintosh, and other environments without having to be rewritten for each computing platform. Sun Microsystems terms this phenomenon *write once, run anywhere.* Java allows PC users to manipulate data on networked systems using Web browsers, reducing the need to write specialized software. Table 6-4 describes how businesses can benefit from Java's capabilities.

### TABLE 6-4 HOW BUSINESSES ARE USING JAVA

| Organization | Java Application |
|---|---|
| Priceline.com | Uses Java in its demand collection system, which takes requests for airline tickets over its Web site, distributes them to the airlines, collects the best fares for customers, and books and issues the tickets. |
| Home Depot | Uses Java to write new applications such as automatically sending applications for employment to all of its 840 stores because it can roll out the software more easily on more than 50,0000 computing devices throughout the company. |
| Lincoln National Reassurance | Uses Java to extend its business systems to clients. LincStar application lets insurers use their Web browsers to access information on whether Lincoln National will assume additional risk on a particular individual. |
| General Motors | Uses Java applets on its Web site to help visitors select vehicles they might want to purchase. |

Despite these benefits, Java has not yet fulfilled its early promise to revolutionize software development and use. Programs written in current versions of Java tend to run slower than "native" programs written for a specific operating system. Vendors such as Microsoft are supporting alternative versions of Java that include subtle differences that affect Java's performance in different pieces of hardware and operating systems. Without a standard version of Java, true platform independence cannot be achieved.

## HYPERTEXT MARKUP LANGUAGE (HTML) AND XML

**hypertext markup language (HTML)**
Page description language for creating Web pages and other hypermedia documents.

**Web server**
Software that manages user requests for Web pages on the computer where they are stored and that delivers the page to the user's computer.

**Hypertext markup language (HTML)** is a page description language for creating hypertext or hypermedia documents such as Web pages. (See the discussions of hypermedia in Chapter 7 and of Web pages in Chapter 9.) HTML uses instructions called tags (see Figure 6-14) to specify how text, graphics, video, and sound are placed on a document and to create dynamic links to other documents and objects stored in the same or remote computers. With these links in place, a user need only point at a highlighted key word or graphic, click on it, and immediately be transported to another document. **Web server** software manages the requests for these HTML documents on the computer where they are stored and delivers the document to the user's computer.

HTML programs can be custom written, but they also can be created using the HTML authoring capabilities of Web browsers or of popular word processing, spreadsheet, data management, and presentation graphics software packages. HTML editors such as Claris Home Page and Adobe PageMill are powerful HTML authoring tool programs for creating Web pages.

An extension to HTML called dynamic HTML enables Web pages to react to user input without having to send additional requests to the Web server. Web pages using dynamic HTML appear less static and more like active and alive applications.

### XML

**XML (extensible markup language)**
General-purpose language that describes the structure of a document and supports links to multiple documents, allowing data to be manipulated by the computer. Used for both Web and non-Web applications.

**XML,** which stands for **eXtensible Markup Language,** is a new specification originally designed to improve usefulness of Web documents. It is actually a further development of HTML. Whereas HTML only determines how text and images should be displayed on a Web document, XML describes what the data in these documents mean. XML makes the information in documents usable in computer programs. Any piece of information on a document or Web page can be given an XML tag to describe what the data mean. In XML, a number is not just a number; the XML tag specifies whether the number represents a price, a date, or a ZIP code.

For example, an HTML tag to highlight the price of a sweater in bold on a Web page would be <b>$39</b. The number has no context. But an XML tag could designate that $39 is a price by labeling it with a tag such as <price>$39<price>. XML can also describe the meaning of nonnumerical data, such as the sweater's color or style, for instance. Figure 6-14 illustrates the differences between HTML and XML.

By tagging selected elements of the content of documents for their meanings, XML makes it possible for computers to automatically manipulate and interpret data and perform operations on the data without human intervention. The XML tags and the standardized procedures for interpreting them can accompany the information wherever it goes. Web

| Plain English | HTML | XML |
|---|---|---|
| Sport utility vehicle | <TITLE>Automobile</TITLE> | <AUTOMOBILETYPE="Sport utility vehicle"> |
| ABC Gremlin 300X SUV | <BODY> | <MANUFACTURER>ABC</MANUFACTURER> |
| | <UL> | <LINE>Gremlin</LINE> |
| | <LI>ABC Gremlin 300X SUV | <MODEL>300X SUV</MODEL> |
| 4 passenger | <LI>4 passenger | >PASSENGER UNIT="PASS">4</PASSENGER> |
| 145 maximum speed | <LI>145 maximum speed | <SPEED UNIT="MPH">145</SPEED> |
| $19,280 | <LI>$19,280 | <PRICE CURRENCY="USD">19,280</PRICE> |
| | </UL></BODY> | |

*Figure 6-14* Comparing HTML with XML. HTML is used to display a Web page and tells where words should be placed and which words should be bold or italic. XML describes what the words mean.

*Source:* "Putting it all in Context," from Computerworld, November 23, 1999. 

## BUILDING BUSINESS WEBS WITH XML

In the fast-paced world of electronic commerce and electronic business, companies can benefit by being able to respond to customers, partners, and suppliers quickly. XML provides a new tool to accomplish this, because it helps disparate applications identify and use a variety of information from otherwise incompatible sources.

The North American division of BASF Corporation, the German chemical giant, started using XML to communicate among different internal applications. Now it uses XML to realize supply chain savings by providing cross-company cooperation. BASF's business partners want direct integration between their enterprise systems and its own. BASF can't unilaterally dictate XML standards for its industry because its vendors, suppliers, and customers need the ability to work with BASF's competitors as well. So BASF is cooperating with its rivals Dow Chemical Company and E. I. duPont de Nemours to develop standards for transactions, such as purchase orders or invoices, that would benefit everyone in the chemical industry.

Even without standards in place, BASF is piloting three XML initiatives using ECOutlook.com of Houston as an application service provider. BASF is using ECOutlook's system to automatically send and receive purchase orders, allow customers to track shipments while they are in transit, and obtain current chemical inventory levels from customers for automatic ordering. As part of the order tracking application, ECOutlook reads information off the Web site of the transportation carrier used by BASF to ship its orders. When a BASF customer uses BASF's Web site to request shipping information, the BASF site requests the data from ECOutlook. The ECOutlook system then goes to the appropriate shipper's Web site, extracts the information using a BASF software script, and returns it to BASF so that BASF can display it for the customer. Using XML allows the information to be understood and formatted by whatever application receives it. The technology separates presentation from content. BASF can determine the format of the data that it receives from its trading partners and determine the format of the data that reaches them.

Yet for all of its benefits, XML may not yet work for some companies. XML standards have not been developed for some industries. Use of XML can be affected by other features of a firm's information technology infrastructure. Siemens AG, the German computer and telecommunications company, decided against using XML for a global knowledge network to link its 6,900 salespeople around the world even though it was the technology of choice. Network transmission capacity in many of the 160 countries where Siemens has offices is so slow that application processing performance and reliability were negatively impacted by the extra time required to encode and decode XML messages. (Searching a large XML document can rapidly consume processing resources.) Siemens had to build the system with another software tool.

**To Think About:** How does XML support electronic commerce and electronic business. What management, organization, and technology issues need to be addressed when adopting XML for enterprise and interenterprise communication?

*Sources:* Andy Patrizio, "XML Passes from Development to Implementation," *Information Week,* March 26, 2001; Erik Sherman, "XML Moves into the Mainstream," *Datamation,* October 17, 2000; and Stuart J. Johnston, "XML Drives Development," *The Industry Standard,* July 17, 2000.

browsers and computer programs, such as order processing or ERP software, can follow programmed rules for applying and displaying the data.

For example, documents or Web pages describing the price of the sweater could be easily accessed by buyers searching for a sweater that cost $39 or less. Data on Web pages describing new automobiles being offered for sale could include information such as brand, price, number of doors, color, and engine power, which could be tagged so that someone could use these data to submit a purchase order for a new car and have the data located automatically by a computer program to process the order. The Window on Technology describes how some businesses are benefiting from using XML.

XML is already becoming a serious technology for Web-based applications and could open the way for a whole new class of Internet software and services. The key to XML is the setting of standards (or vocabulary) that enable both sending and receiving parties to describe data the same way. The impact of XML will be felt more strongly over time as more and more industries develop their own widely accepted standards. Each standard is contained in an XML Document Type Definition (DTD), usually simply called a dictionary. For example, RosettaNet is an XML dictionary developed by 34 leading companies within the PC industry. It defines all properties of a personal computer, such as modems, monitors, and cache memory. As a result the entire PC industry is now able to speak the same language. The entire supply chain of the industry can now easily be linked. XML is supported by the latest versions of Microsoft and Netscape Internet browsers, making Web site data more usable.

The impact of XML extends far beyond the Web, facilitating companies' access to their own legacy data. Companies are now able to integrate legacy data quickly and cheaply into newer programs merely by assigning each piece of data an XML name. XML has strategic impacts as well. Companies can now give their suppliers and customers access to their own data without high application development costs, thus better integrating their operations.

**XHTML (extensible hypertext markup language)** Hybrid between HTML and XML that provides more flexibility than HTML and the ability to create Web pages that can be read by many different computing platforms and Net display devices.

**XHTML (Extensible Hypertext Markup Language)** is a hybrid between HTML and XML that has been recommended as a replacement for HTML by the World Wide Web Consortium (which works with business and government to create Web standards). XHTML reformulates HTML with XML document-type definitions, giving it additional flexibility and the ability to create Web pages that can be read by many different computing platforms and Net display devices.

## 6.5 Managing Software Assets

Software costs represent one of the largest information technology expenditures in most firms—amounting to more than double the expenditures for computer hardware—and thus software represents another major technology asset. At many points in their careers, managers will be required to make important decisions concerning the selection, purchase, and utilization of their organization's software assets. Following are some important software issues of which they should be aware.

### Rent or Build Decisions: Using Application Service Providers

Technology expenditures will increasingly focus on ways to use software to cut down on "people" costs as opposed to computer hardware costs by increasing the ease with which users can interact with the hardware and software. More organizations are using software packages, fourth-generation languages, and object-oriented tools because such software lowers "people" costs by reducing the need for custom-crafted software written by skilled computer programmers. Renting software and software services from other companies can lower some of these "people" costs even more.

#### Application Service Providers (ASPs)

Chapter 5 described hardware capabilities for providing data and software programs to desktop computers over networks. It is clear that software will be increasingly delivered and used over networks. On-line application service providers (ASPs) are springing up to provide these software services over the Web and over private networks. An **application service provider (ASP)** is a business that delivers and manages applications and computer services from remote computer centers to multiple users via the Internet or a private network. Instead of buying and installing software programs, subscribing companies can rent the same functions from these services. Users would pay for the use of this software either on a subscription or per transaction basis. For example, companies can pay $5 per month per user (plus a one-time start-up fee of $5,000) to rent travel and entertainment (T&E) expense reporting software from ExpensAble.com instead of buying and installing T&E programs on their computers. The ASP creates a single solution that can be rented, replacing all or part of a customer's IT infastructure. The ASP's solution combines package software applications and all of the related hardware, system software, network, and other infrastructure services that the customer would have to purchase, integrate, and manage on its own. The ASP customer interacts with a single entity instead of an array of technologies and service vendors.

**application service provider (ASP)** Company providing software that can be rented by other companies over the Web or a private network.

The "timesharing" services of the 1970s, which ran applications for functions such as payroll on their computers for other companies, were an earlier version of this application hosting. But today's ASPs run a wider array of applications than these earlier services and deliver many of the software services over the Web. At these Web-based services, servers perform the bulk of the processing and the only essential program needed by users is their Web browser. Table 6-5 lists examples of ASPs. Large- and medium-size businesses are using these services for enterprise systems, sales force automation, or financial management, whereas

**TABLE 6-5 EXAMPLES OF APPLICATION SERVICE PROVIDERS**

| Application Service Provider | Service | Customer Access |
|---|---|---|
| Oracle Business On-line | Provides Oracle applications for financials, manufacturing, distribution, and human resources for small and medium-size companies using hardware and technical services from Hewlett-Packard and Sun Microsystems. | Web, private networks |
| Telecomputing ASA (Norway) | Offers complete suite of desktop applications such as Microsoft Office, e-mail, and Web access. Also provides enterprise system, e-commerce, and custom applications. | Private networks |
| Corio Inc. | Hosts enterprise resource planning (ERP) applications from PeopleSoft, focusing primarily on midsize companies. | Web, private networks |
| Salesforce.com | Provides software on the Web to help sales representatives track leads, manage contacts, create reports, and measure their performance against other sales reps in the company. | Web |

small businesses are using them for functions such as invoicing, tax calculations, electronic calendars, and accounting. Employease.com, described in the chapter opening vignette, is an ASP providing human resource software.

Companies are turning to this "software utility" model as an alternative to developing their own software. Some companies will find it much easier to "rent" software from another firm and avoid the expense and difficulty of installing, operating, and maintaining complex systems, such as enterprise resource planning (ERP). The ASP contracts guarantee a level of service and support to ensure that the software is available and working at all times. For example, Telecomputing ASA charges $349 per seat per month for a three- to five-year contract that includes a guarantee of a 99.7 percent service level. Today's Internet-driven business environment is changing so rapidly that getting a system up and running in three months instead of six could make the difference between success and failure. Application service providers also enable small and medium-size companies to use applications that they otherwise could not afford.

Companies considering the software utility model need to carefully assess application service provider costs and benefits, weighing all management, organizational, and technology issues. In some cases, the cost of renting software can add up to more than purchasing and maintaining the application in-house. Yet, there may be benefits to paying more for software through an ASP if this decision allows the company to focus on core business issues instead of technology challenges. More detail on application service providers can be found in the chapter ending case study and in Chapter 10.

## SOFTWARE MAINTENANCE

After software has been created for the organization, it usually has to be modified over time to incorporate new information requirements. Because of the way software is currently designed, this maintenance process is very costly, time consuming, and challenging to manage. In most information systems departments more than 50 percent of staff time is spent maintaining the software for existing systems. Chapter 14 provides more detail on this topic.

At the end of the millennium, an unusually large maintenance problem called the Year 2000 Problem emerged. The **Year 2000 Problem,** sometimes referred to as the millennium bug or the **Y2K** problem, was the inability of software programs to handle any dates other than those of the twentieth century—years that begin with "19." Many older computer programs (and even some recent PC programs) stored dates as six digits, two digits each for the day, month, and year (MM–DD–YY) to save computer storage space. With dates represented this way, computers could interpret the year following 1999 as 1900 rather than 2000, creating errors in any software that was time sensitive. To solve the problem before 2000 arrived, organizations combed through their programs to locate all coding in which dates were used. It is estimated that organizations spent $400 billion to $600 billion worldwide to fix this problem.

**Year 2000 (Y2K) problem**
Inability of software programs to handle dates other than those of the twentieth century that begin with "19" because the software represented years with only two digits. Presented a massive maintenance problem for most organizations.

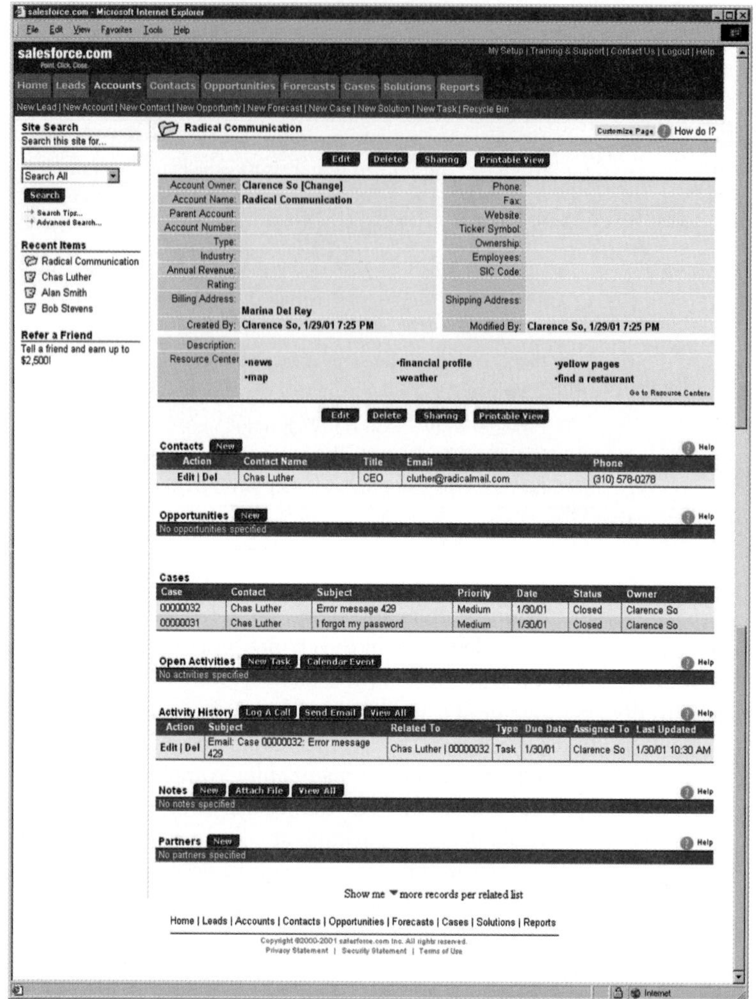


*Salesforce.com is an application service provider delivering software for sales force automation and customer relationship management as a subscription service on-line. Users can track leads, manage contacts, measure their performance, and share sales information across the company.*

## Selecting Software for the Organization

Although managers need not become programming specialists, they should be able to use clear criteria in selecting application and system software for the organization. The most important criteria are as follows.

## Management Decision Problem

**EVALUATING AN APPLICATION SERVICE PROVIDER**

Your company has grown from 40 to 200 employees in the past two years. All of your human resources record keeping, such as processing hired and terminated employees, documenting promotions, and enrolling employees in medical and dental insurance plans used to be performed manually, but your two-person human resources department is swamped with paperwork. You are looking at two options to automate these functions. One is to purchase a client/server human resources package to run on the company's midrange computer. The other is to use an application service provider that runs human resources software over the Web. The company's human resource department has PCs with Web browser software and Internet access. Your information systems staff consists of two people.

The human resources software package that best fits your needs costs $9,500 to purchase. One information systems specialist with an annual salary of $65,000 would have to spend 4 hours per 40-hour work week supporting the program and applying upgrades as they became available. Upgrades cost $1,000 each and the vendor provides one upgrade every year after the first year the package is purchased.

The application service provider you have identified charges $1,500 to set up the system initially and $5 per month for each employee in the firm. You do not need to purchase any additional hardware to run the system and the vendor is responsible for supporting the system.

1. What are the costs of each option in the first year?
2. Which option is less expensive over a three-year period?
3. Which option would you select? Why? What factors would you use in making a decision? What are the risks of each approach?

## Appropriateness

Some languages are general-purpose languages that can be used on a variety of problems, whereas others are special-purpose languages suitable for only limited tasks. COBOL has been excellent for business data processing but poor at mathematical calculations. Language selection involves identifying the organizational use for the software and the users. Application software should also be easy to maintain and change, and flexible enough so that it can grow with the organization. These organizational considerations have direct long-term cost implications.

## Efficiency

Although less important than in the past, the efficiency with which a language compiles and executes remains a consideration when purchasing software. Some programming languages are more efficient in the use of machine time than others and there are instances where such considerations outweigh personnel costs. Languages with slow compilers or interpreters, such as BASIC or Java or fourth-generation languages may prove too slow and expensive in terms of machine time for systems that must handle many thousands of transactions per second (see Chapter 10).

## Compatibility

Application software must be able to run on the firm's hardware and operating system platform. Likewise, the firm's operating system software must be compatible with the software required by the firm's mainstream business applications. Mission-critical applications typically have large volumes of transactions to process and require robust operating systems that can handle large complex software programs and massive files.

## Support

In order to be effective, a programming language must be easy for the firm's programming staff to learn, and the staff should have sufficient knowledge of that software so that they can provide ongoing support for all of the systems based on that software. It is also important to purchase package software that has widespread use in other organizations and is supported by many consulting firms and services. Another kind of support is the availability of software editing, debugging, and development aids.

# APPLICATION SOFTWARE EXERCISE

### WEB PAGE DEVELOPMENT TOOL EXERCISE: DEVELOPING A WEB PAGE

Tony Jilnek, a good friend of yours, owns and operates a local barbershop. On several occasions, Tony has mentioned that he would like to build a Web page for his barbershop, but does not know where to begin. You recall that Netscape has an on-line Web page building tool at http://home.bigstep.netscape.com/ to help people like Tony get started with Web page development. The on-line home page building tool is a great tool for beginners, since it enables them to build simple Web pages very quickly using Netscape Communicator, Netscape Navigator Gold or Microsoft Internet Explorer.

Follow the on-line instructions for selecting and customizing a template. Begin by clicking on "Try Us for Free," and then click on "Test Drive." Finally, use the information provided below to build the Jilnek's Barbershop Web page.

**a.** Pick the design you prefer.

**b.** Choose either a preset color combination or select your own color combination.

**c.** Select a font for both your headline and your body text.

**d.** Now pick the layout you would like to use.

e. Select from one of the 25 pictures offered. You will be asked to search for a barbershop picture later in the exercise.

f. Write a headline that site visitors will see. You will be able to enter the title and introduction later.

g. The introduction should read, "Jilnek's Barbershop is located in San Francisco. The barbershop is family owned, and has been in operation since the 1950s." You may want to add "Jilnek's Barbershop is open 6 days a week, Monday through Saturday from 7 A.M. to 7 P.M. Appointments are not necessary."

h. Write a way to contact you on the Internet. A hot link might be: *The Shop* and *Timbo's Barbershop Web Server.* Use your current e-mail address as the e-mail link for Jilnek's Barbershop.

i. The introduction should read, "Jilnek's Barbershop is located in San Francisco, California. The barbershop is family owned and has been in operation since the 1950s."

j. Next enter information that will enable the software to create a map for those who wish to go to your business. You may enter any address in the U.S. or Canada (it need not be in San Francisco for this example, although it would have to be correct for an actual Web site.)

k. Enter the proper business name and create a Web address and write a screen name.

l. Build your Web page. Your instructor will provide you with instructions on how to save and print your Web page.

m. After examining the initial Web page, you realize that graphics will enhance the Web page. Using a browser of your choice, locate and download a picture of a barber pole. Also, try to locate a picture of an old barber chair or barber tools. Save these images to a disk, preferably to the same location where the Jilnek Web page is currently stored.

n. Using the help feature of a Web page editor of your choice, research how to insert and delete images on a Web page.

o. Modify the Jilnek's Barbershop Web page to include the graphics that you downloaded. Insert the images where you think appropriate. Save and print this final version of the Jilnek's Barbershop Web page.

## MANAGEMENT WRAP-UP

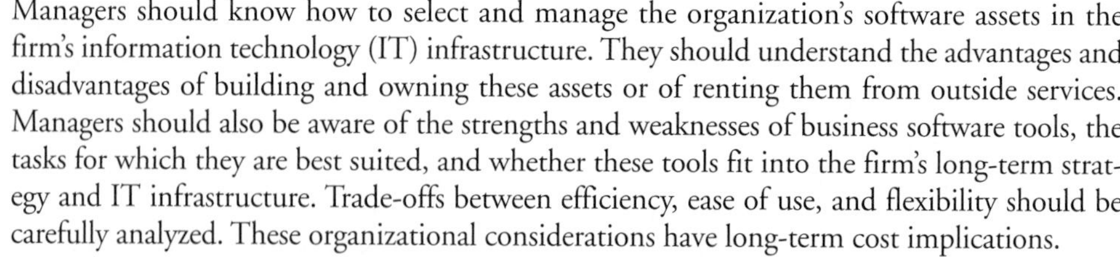
Managers should know how to select and manage the organization's software assets in the firm's information technology (IT) infrastructure. They should understand the advantages and disadvantages of building and owning these assets or of renting them from outside services. Managers should also be aware of the strengths and weaknesses of business software tools, the tasks for which they are best suited, and whether these tools fit into the firm's long-term strategy and IT infrastructure. Trade-offs between efficiency, ease of use, and flexibility should be carefully analyzed. These organizational considerations have long-term cost implications.

Software can either enhance or impede organizational performance, depending on the software tools and services selected and how they are used. Organizational needs should drive software selection. Software tools selected should be easy for the firm's information systems (IS) staff to learn and maintain and be flexible enough to grow with the organization. Software for non-IS specialists should have easy-to-use interfaces and be compatible with the firm's other software tools. Software services provided by outside vendors should fit into organizational computing plans.

A range of system and application software technologies is available to organizations. Key technology decisions include the appropriateness of the software tool for the problem to be addressed; compatibility with the firm's hardware and other components of the IT infrastructure; the efficiency of the software for performing specific tasks; vendor support of software packages and software services; and capabilities for debugging, documentation, and reuse.

*For Discussion*

1. Why is selecting both system and application software for the organization an important management decision?
2. Should organizations use application service providers (ASPs) for all of their software needs? Why or why not?

## SUMMARY

1. *Describe the major types of software.* The major types of software are system software and application software. Each serves a different purpose. System software manages the computer resources and mediates between application software and computer hardware. Application software is used by application programmers and some end users to develop specific business applications. Application software works through system software, which controls access to computer hardware.
2. *Examine the functions of system software and compare leading PC operating systems.* System software coordinates the various parts of the computer system and mediates between application software and computer hardware. The system software that manages and controls the activities of the computer is called the operating system. Other system software includes computer-language translation programs that convert programming languages into machine language and utility programs that perform common processing tasks.

   The operating system acts as the chief manager of the information system, allocating, assigning, and scheduling system resources and monitoring the use of the computer. Multiprogramming, multitasking, virtual storage, time sharing, and multiprocessing enable system resources to be used more efficiently so that the computer can attack many problems at the same time.

   Multiprogramming (multitasking in PC environments) allows multiple programs to use the computer's resources concurrently. Virtual storage splits up programs into small portions so that the main memory can be used more efficiently. Time sharing enables many users to share computer resources simultaneously by allocating each user a tiny slice of computing time. Multiprocessing is the use of two or more CPUs linked together working in tandem to perform a task.

   In order to be executed by the computer, a software program must be translated into machine language via special language-translation software—a compiler, an assembler, or an interpreter.

   PC operating systems have developed sophisticated capabilities such as multitasking and support for multiple users on networks. Leading PC operating systems include Windows XP, Windows 98 and Windows Me, Windows CE, Windows 2000, OS/2, Unix, Linux, Mac OS, and DOS. PC operating systems with graphical user interfaces have gained popularity over command-driven operating systems.
3. *Analyze the strengths and limitations of the major application programming languages and software tools.* The general trend in software is toward user-friendly, high-level languages that both increase professional programmer productivity and make it possible for amateurs to use information systems.

   Conventional programming languages include assembly language, FORTRAN, COBOL, C, BASIC, and Pascal. Conventional programming languages make more efficient use of computer resources than fourth-generation languages and each is designed to solve specific types of problems.

   Fourth-generation languages include query languages, report generators, graphics languages, application generators, very high-level programming languages, application software packages, and PC software tools. They are less procedural than conventional programming languages and enable end users to perform many software tasks that previously required technical specialists. Popular PC software tools include word processing, spreadsheet, data management, presentation graphics, and e-mail software along with Web browsers and groupware. Enterprise software, middleware, and enterprise application integration software are all software tools for promoting enterprise-wide application integration.
4. *Describe contemporary approaches to software development.* Object-oriented programming combines data and procedures into one object, which can act as an independent software building block. Each object can be used in many different systems without changing program code.

   Java is an object-oriented programming language designed to operate on the Internet. It can deliver precisely the software functionality needed for a particular task as a small applet that is downloaded from a network. Java can run on any computer and operating system. HTML is a page description language for creating Web pages. XML is a language for creating structured documents in which data are tagged for meanings. The tagged data in XML documents can be manipulated and used by other computer systems.
5. *Identify important issues in the management of organizational software assets.* Software represents a major organizational asset that should be carefully managed. Managers need to balance the costs and benefits of developing software in-house versus renting the software from an application service provider. Software maintenance can account for more than 50 percent of information system costs. Criteria such as efficiency, compatibility with the organization's technology platform, support, and whether the software language or tool is appropriate for the problems and tasks of the organization should govern software selection.

## KEY TERMS

**ActiveX, 191**
**Application generator, 182**
**Application service provider (ASP), 194**
**Application software, 173**
**Assembly language, 180**
**BASIC (Beginners All-purpose Symbolic Instruction Code), 180**
**C, 181**
**C++, 181**
**Class, 189**
**COBOL (COmmon Business Oriented Language), 180**
**Compiler, 176**
**Data management software, 184**
**Desktop publishing software, 183**
**DOS, 179**
**Electronic mail (e-mail), 186**
**Enterprise application integration software, 188**
**Enterprise software, 188**
**FORTRAN (FORmula TRANslator), 180**
**Fourth-generation language, 181**
**Graphical user interface (GUI), 176**
**Graphics language, 182**
**Groupware, 187**
**Hypertext markup language (HTML), 192**
**Inheritance, 190**
**Integrated software package, 185**
**Interpreter, 176**
**Java, 191**
**Linux, 178**
**Machine language, 180**
**Mac OS, 179**
**Middleware, 188**
**Multiprocessing, 175**
**Multiprogramming, 174**
**Multitasking, 174**
**Multithreading, 174**
**Natural language, 181**
**Object code, 176**
**Object-oriented programming, 189**
**Office 2000 and Office XP, 186**
**Open-source software, 179**
**Operating system, 173**
**OS/2, 178**
**Pascal, 181**
**Presentation graphics, 184**
**Program, 172**
**Query language, 181**
**Report generator, 182**
**Software, 172**
**Software package, 183**
**Source code, 176**
**Spreadsheet, 184**
**System software, 173**
**Thread, 187**
**Time sharing, 175**
**Unix, 178**
**Utility program, 176**
**Very high-level programming language, 182**
**Virtual storage, 174**
**Visual programming, 189**
**Web browser, 186**
**Web server, 192**
**Windows, 180**
**Windows CE, 178**
**Windows 95, 177**
**Windows 98, 177**
**Windows Millennium Edition (Windows Me), 177**
**Windows XP, 178**
**Windows 2000, 177**
**Word processing software, 183**
**XHTML (Extensible Hypertext Markup Language), 194**
**XML (eXtensible Markup Language), 192**
**Year 2000 problem (Y2K), 195**

## REVIEW QUESTIONS

1. What are the major types of software? How do they differ in terms of users and uses?
2. What is the operating system of a computer? What does it do?
3. Describe multiprogramming, virtual storage, time sharing, and multiprocessing. Why are they important for the operation of an information system?
4. What is the difference between an assembler, a compiler, and an interpreter?
5. Define and describe graphical user interfaces.
6. Compare the major PC operating systems.
7. Name three high-level programming languages. Describe their strengths and weaknesses.
8. Define fourth-generation languages and list the seven categories of fourth-generation tools.
9. What is the difference between fourth-generation languages and conventional programming languages?
10. What is the difference between an application generator and an application software package? Between a report generator and a query language?
11. Name and describe the most important PC software tools.
12. Name and describe the kinds of software that can be used for enterprise integration.
13. What is object-oriented programming? How does it differ from conventional software development?
14. What is Java? Why are firms building applications using this language?
15. What are HTML and XML? Compare their capabilities. Why are they important?
16. Name and describe three issues in managing software assets.
17. Why are organizations using application service providers? What benefits do they provide?
18. What criteria should be used when selecting software for the organization?

## GROUP PROJECT

Which is the better Internet software tool, Internet Explorer or Netscape Communicator? Your instructor will divide the class into two groups to research this question. To prepare your analysis, use articles from computer magazines and the Web and examine the software's features and capabilities. If possible, use presentation software to present your findings to the class.

## TOOLS FOR INTERACTIVE LEARNING

### INTERNET CONNECTION

The Internet Connection for this chapter will direct you to a series of Web sites of computer software vendors where you can complete an exercise to analyze the capabilities of various types of computer software. You can also use the Interactive Study Guide to test your knowledge of the topics in this chapter and get instant feedback where you need more practice.

### ELECTRONIC COMMERCE PROJECT

At the Laudon Web site for Chapter 6, you will find an Electronic Commerce project for logistics planning.

### CD-ROM

If you use the Multimedia Edition CD-ROM with this chapter, you can complete an interactive exercise asking you to select the appropriate programming language or application software for a series of business problems. You can also find a video clip illustrating the capabilities of geographic information system (GIS) software, an audio overview of the key themes of this chapter, and bullet text summarizing the key points of the chapter.

## CASE STUDY *Sunburst Hotels International Turns to an Application Service Provider*

When Sunburst Hotels International Inc. was spun off in late 1997, the company had no IT infrastructure, and CIO Charles Warczak had to create it. Sunburst earned about $114 million in 1997 by owning and operating 87 hotels in 27 states, including some Comfort Inns and EconoLodges. He knew his company could not perform all the many complex functions required without the support of application packages. Choice Hotels International Corp., Sunburst's former parent company, was using an enterprise resource planning (ERP) system from PeopleSoft, and Warczak wanted to use the same system. The major problem he faced was the costs. Warczak calculated that to acquire and install the ERP package he wanted, the company would have had to spend $1.5 million on capital expenses (mainly computer hardware and software) up front, a hefty cost for the small, newly independent company. And that was only the beginning of his projected costs. In this case study we examine his problem and the method he selected to solve it.

Installing a new ERP system can be very expensive, particularly for a start-up or a new spin-off. In Sunburst's case, Warczak met with both IS and finance personnel at Choice to determine Sunburst's needs and costs. They ultimately concluded that Sunburst needed to spend well over $1 million up front on hardware and software, including both computers and networking. In addition, they would need to purchase Oracle data management software for $500,000 to support the PeopleSoft ERP system. And these were only part of the cost.

Complex computer systems require highly skilled staffs to run and maintain them, and Warczak estimated that the cost of such a staff for his small corporation would be about $500,000. However, the immediate problem was even tougher: how to locate and hire such a staff in the first place. Skilled technicians are in short supply and so finding and hiring them was a substantial challenge. Warczak needed staff skilled in PeopleSoft software, and the competition for experienced ERP technicians was fierce everywhere but particularly so in the greater Washington D.C. area (Sunburst headquarters are in Silver Springs, Maryland, a Washington suburb). Networking experts were also difficult to locate and hire. However, hiring such a skilled staff would not solve the problem because once hired, Warczak would have to face the challenge of keeping employees who are in such high demand. "We'd have a real tough time holding on to people who are experts in, say, the accounts payable module," said Warczak. And, thinking about additional long-range costs, he added, "There's a lot of cost with high turnover."

Being bottom-line oriented, Warczak did not like all of this cost because he believed that "Everything at the corporate office including IT is an overhead [expense]." However, the company had another major concern as well. ERP software is extremely complex and a successful implementation can be a very long and arduous process. Judging by implementations at other corporations, Sunburst was facing a minimum implementation period of six to eight months. However, Sunburst had an example closer to home. Choice had faced the same problem a year earlier (prior to the Sunburst spin-off) when it installed PeopleSoft. Although they were ultimately pleased with the software, the implementation "was a disaster," according to Warczak. "There were lots of cost overruns." He added that once the implementation was completed, "functionality was terrible" because of technical problems and the long learning curve for creating an infrastructure.

With all this information and experience, the decision was not difficult. Warczak opted to outsource his ERP system. However, because he did not want to turn over to outsiders the computer system and all the vital ongoing tasks the hotel relied on, he chose a route that had only recently become available: an application service provider (ASP). ASPs are different because they own and operate the computer hardware and software and rent usage on the computer application to customers through the Web or a private network. The customer, in this case Sunburst, pays the ASP and uses the system as if it owned it, but the ASP actually operates and maintains both the software and hardware.

Companies have been renting software in this way since 1997, and software renters include PeopleSoft, J. D. Edwards & Co., Great Plains Software Inc., and Oracle Corp. Sunburst selected a lesser-known ASP, USinternetworking Inc. (USi) of nearby Annapolis, Maryland, and signed a five-year contract that began on April 1, 1999. Let us look at the benefits for Sunburst of going this route.

The fundamental change, out of which every other benefit flows, is that Sunburst did not have to purchase and own its computers (except for PCs or network computers). The company also did not have to buy the PeopleSoft and Oracle software. In addition, the costs of building and maintaining a network were eliminated because Sunburst accesses its ERP via the Web. The only Sunburst costs, in addition to the monthly rental, are for PCs, Web browsers, and telephone lines to connect to the Web. Thus, most of Sunburst's infrastructure startup costs were eliminated. The company did have the normal personnel costs connected to converting from the old system (in this case Choice's system) to the new one and learning the new system. Sunburst has not released the amount of its monthly fee, but USi says its charges range from $50,000 to $200,000, depending on the number of PeopleSoft modules the customer uses. Some ASPs charge not by the module but by the number of users, typically charging $3 to $500 per user per month. This approach enables small companies to pay less, with their costs growing only as their companies grows.

Staff costs were all but eliminated by going to an ASP because PeopleSoft software is owned and supported by USi. However, customers of ASPs usually do assign one or more persons as full-time supervisors of the system, making certain it is running properly and the staff of the renting company is using it properly. This same person (or group) usually is assigned as liaison to the ASP. By using an ASP, Sunburst also dodged the other staffing problem. The company did not have to face the fierce competition for skilled technicians—that was USi's problem and it already had its staff in place.

Even the implementation was much quicker than it would otherwise have been. The software was already working, ready for the Sunburst staff to access it. Sunburst's PeopleSoft ERP system was up and running in only three months and went live in April 1999.

Using an ASP has another benefit for many organizations. Companies are able to move slowly into using an ASP's software, trying out one function of the software package at a time. In that way they can determine whether the particular package is right for them without major up-front costs (a benefit Sunburst did not need because they learned the package when they were part of Choice, and they knew it was a good fit).

Using an ASP does present risks. Some companies are concerned because this type of service is so new. Companies that are risk averse may want to wait a year or two until ASPs have a longer track record. Security is a risk in the minds of many, particularly when a company has to access its sensitive data via the Internet. Dick Lefebvre, the vice president of information technology at auto parts producer Simpson Industries Inc. in Plymouth, Michigan, had precisely that concern. He wanted to use the J. D. Edwards ERP system through IBM Global Services, a company now also in the ASP business. To solve the problem, he decided not to use the Web, but instead connect to IBM Global through a private line. Leasing a private line is expensive, however, and his costs were, perhaps, 10 times the cost of using the Web. Lefebvre was willing to pay the price in order to be certain that competitors could not capture vital information about the parts that his company produces. However, other companies are very secure using the Internet. Typically, they are using multiple firewalls and encryption to protect their data.

One other fear common to all outsourcing is that their companies will be locked into the outside vendor, placing them at the vendor's mercy. Only time will tell for certain whether this is true, but using an ASP is different and risk may be reduced more with an ASP than with traditional outsourcing. The main difference is that the software the company is using (PeopleSoft in the case of Sunburst) does not belong exclusively to the ASP (USi in this example). Sunburst is able to leave USi and take their business to another ASP that is running PeopleSoft's ERP. And ultimately, if the company (Sunburst) cannot make it work with any ASP, it can travel the original road, purchasing the software and hardware itself, bringing the whole operation inside.

**Sources:** Jenny C. McCune, "ASPs@Your Service," *Beyond Computing,* January/February 2000; Peter Fabris, "Network Computer Revival?" and "A New Lease," *CIO Web Business Magazine,* May 1, 1999; Lee Gomes, "Somebody Else's Problem," *The Wall Street Journal,* November 15, 1999; and Paul Keegan, "Is This the Death of Packaged Software?" *Upside,* October 1999.

### *CASE STUDY QUESTIONS*

1. Why was a complex ERP system so vital to Sunburst?
2. Describe the problems that caused Sunburst to decide to go outside to an ASP. What other reasons might they have had for taking that step?
3. What management, organizational, and technical issues did Warczak have to consider when installing an ERP?
4. What management, organizational, and technical issues did Warczak have to consider when planning to outsource the ERP to an ASP?

chapter

# 7 MANAGING DATA RESOURCES

**After completing this chapter, you will be able to:**

1. *Describe basic file organization concepts and the problems of the traditional file environment.*
2. *Describe how a database management system organizes information.*
3. *Compare the principal types of databases.*
4. *Identify important database design principles and the managerial and organizational requirements of a database environment.*
5. *Evaluate new database trends.*

## Famous Footware Steps Smartly with Better Data

Since its founding, Famous Footware, a chain of shoe stores with 860 locations in 49 states, has been guided by the goal of having "the right style of shoe in the right store for sale at the right price." Until recently, this goal was difficult to attain. The firm lacked the right capabilities for monitoring the performance of each store's product mix and promotional campaigns, and for rapidly adjusting inventory. Famous Footware had an Oracle database running on IBM AS/400 servers containing gigabytes of data from more than 600,000 daily transactions and regular weekly reports. But the system was outdated, reflecting an earlier time when management structures were more centralized and hierarchical and companies did not have to respond immediately to marketplace changes. It could only produce standard reports.

As times changed, Famous Footware needed a better way to analyze its data. The company would have to assign a special programmer to help a user create a new nonstandard report, draining IT productivity. Moreover, the system could not deliver the necessary information when needed. Marketing personnel could not evaluate the effectiveness of every promotion and, thus, could not always identify approaches that were not working. Company executives could not obtain granular distribution data for improving inventory management. After a sale period, management would find that one group of stores had sold out of an item, whereas others still had inventory, which had to be marked down to move the remaining goods.

To improve the quality of information from its core business systems for more accurate decision-making, Famous Footware then developed a data warehouse using tools from ShowCase Solutions Corp. in Rochester, Minnesota. The system extracts sales and inventory data to the data warehouse where it can be better organized for analysis and can be queried using ShowCase's Strategy suite of ad hoc reporting and query tools. These tools enable users to create the reports they need. Merchandisers can now monitor sales trends while sales are still ongoing and can redistribute items so that stores don't run out. This information improves profit margins, because fewer items sell at closeout prices and inventory can be optimized. The marketing department can perform detailed comparative and historical analyses to measure the effectiveness of

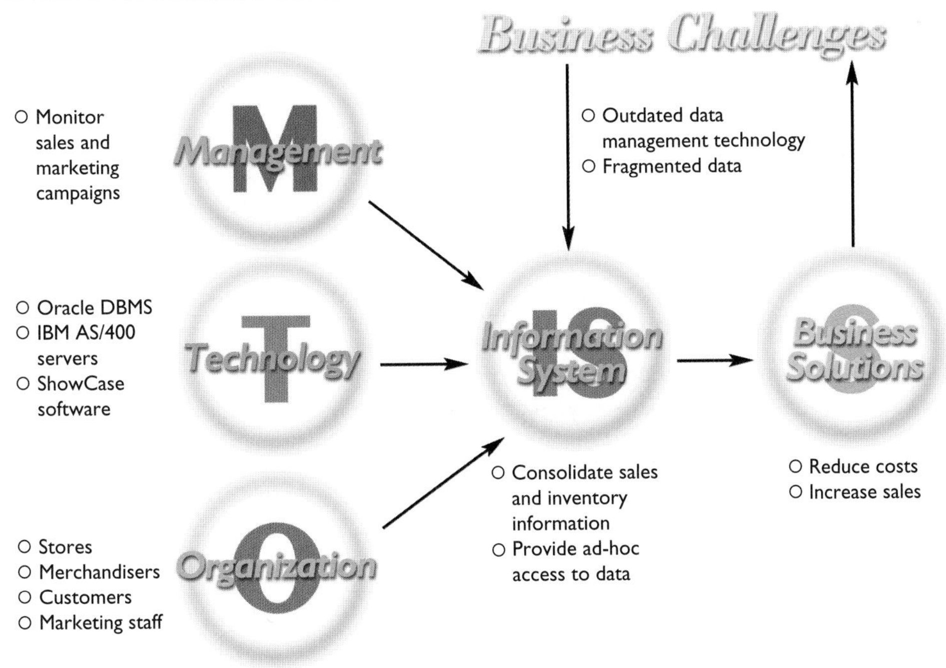


its ad campaigns. Using more targeted marketing, Famous Footware has reduced its marketing budget as well.

**Sources:** Mary Eisenhart, "Stepping Smartly," *Knowledge Management,* August 2000; Beth Stackpole, "Wash Me," *CIO Magazine,* February 15, 2001; and www.spssshowcase.com.

**Famous Footware Steps Smartly with Better Data**

**MANAGEMENT CHALLENGES**

## MANAGEMENT CHALLENGES

Famous Footware's system illustrates how much the effective use of information depends on how data are stored, organized, and accessed. Proper delivery of information not only depends on the capabilities of computer hardware and software but also on the organization's ability to manage data as an important resource. Famous Footware's inability to assemble inventory and sales data required for monitoring the performance of sales and promotional campaigns led to disorganized and inefficient marketing and distribution processes that impaired organizational performance. It has been very difficult for organizations to manage their data effectively. Two challenges stand out:

1. **Organizational obstacles to a database environment.** Implementing a database requires widespread organizational change in the role of information (and information managers), the allocation of power at senior levels, the ownership and sharing of information, and patterns of organizational agreement. A database management system (DBMS) challenges the existing power arrangements in an organization and for that reason often generates political resistance. In a traditional file environment, each department constructed files and programs to fulfill its specific needs. Now, with a database, files and programs must be built that take into account the full organization's interest in data (Wixom and Watson, 2001). Although the organization has spent the money on hardware and software for a database environment, it may not reap the benefits it should because it is unwilling to make the requisite organizational changes.

2. **Cost/benefit considerations.** The costs of moving to a database environment are tangible, up-front, and large in the short term (three years). Most firms buy a commercial DBMS package and related hardware. The software alone can cost a half million dollars for a full-function package with all options. New hardware may cost an additional $1 million to $2 million. Designing an enterprise-wide database that integrates all the organization's data can be a lengthy and costly process. It soon becomes apparent to senior management that a database system is a huge investment.

Unfortunately, the benefits of the DBMS are often intangible, back loaded, and long term (five years). Many millions of dollars have been spent over the years designing and maintaining existing systems. People in the organization understand the existing system after long periods of training and socialization. For these reasons, and despite the clear advantages of the DBMS, the short-term costs of developing a DBMS often appear to be as great as the benefits. Managers, especially those unfamiliar with (and perhaps unfriendly to) systems, tend to severely discount the obvious long-term benefits of the DBMS.

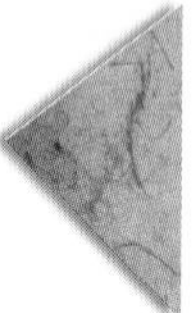

This chapter examines the managerial and organizational requirements as well as the technologies for managing data as a resource. Organizations need to manage their data assets very carefully to make sure that they can be easily accessed and used by managers and employees across the organization. First, we describe traditional file management and the problems it has created for organizations. Then we describe the technology of database management systems, which can overcome many of the drawbacks of traditional file management and provide the firmwide integration of information required for digital firm applications. We include a discussion of the managerial and organizational requirements for successfully implementing a database environment.

## 7.1 ORGANIZING DATA IN A TRADITIONAL FILE ENVIRONMENT

An effective information system provides users with timely, accurate, and relevant information. This information is stored in computer files. When the files are properly arranged and maintained, users can easily access and retrieve the information they need.

You can appreciate the importance of file management if you have ever written a term paper using 3 × 5 index cards. No matter how efficient your storage device (a metal box or a rubber band), if you organize the cards randomly, your term paper will have little or no organization. Given enough time, you could put the cards in order, but your system would be more efficient if you set up your organizational scheme early. If your scheme is flexible enough and well documented, you can extend it to account for any changes in your viewpoint as you write your paper.

The same need for file organization applies to firms. Well-managed, carefully arranged files make it easy to obtain data for business decisions, whereas poorly managed files lead to chaos in information processing, high costs, poor performance, and little, if any, flexibility. Despite the use of excellent hardware and software, many organizations have inefficient information systems because of poor file management. In this section we describe file organization concepts and the problems with traditional file management methods.

**field**
A grouping of characters into a word, a group of words, or a complete number, such as a person's name or age.

**record**
A group of related fields.

**file**
A group of records of the same type.

**database**
A group of related files.

**entity**
A person, place, thing, or event about which information must be kept.

**attribute**
A piece of information describing a particular entity.

**key field**
A field in a record that uniquely identifies instances of that record so that it can be retrieved, updated, or sorted.

## FILE ORGANIZATION TERMS AND CONCEPTS

A computer system organizes data in a hierarchy that starts with bits and bytes and progresses to fields, records, files, and databases (see Figure 7-1). A bit represents the smallest unit of data a computer can handle. A group of bits, called a byte, represents a single character, which can be a letter, a number, or another symbol. A grouping of characters into a word, a group of words, or a complete number (such as a person's name or age) is called a **field.** A group of related fields, such as the student's name, the course taken, the date, and the grade, comprises a **record;** a group of records of the same type is called a **file.** For instance, the student records in Figure 7-1 could constitute a course file. A group of related files makes up a **database.** The student course file illustrated in Figure 7-1 could be grouped with files on students' personal histories and financial backgrounds to create a student database.

A record describes an entity. An **entity** is a person, place, thing, or event on which we maintain information. An order is a typical entity in a sales order file, which maintains information on a firm's sales orders. Each characteristic or quality describing a particular entity is called an **attribute.** For example, order number, order date, order amount, item number, and item quantity would each be an attribute of the entity order. The specific values that these attributes can have can be found in the fields of the record describing the entity order (see Figure 7-2).

Every record in a file should contain at least one field that uniquely identifies that record so that the record can be retrieved, updated, or sorted. This identifier field is called a **key field.** An example of a key field is the order number for the order record illustrated in Figure 7-2 or an employee number or social security number for a personnel record (containing employee data such as the employee's name, age, address, job title, and so forth).

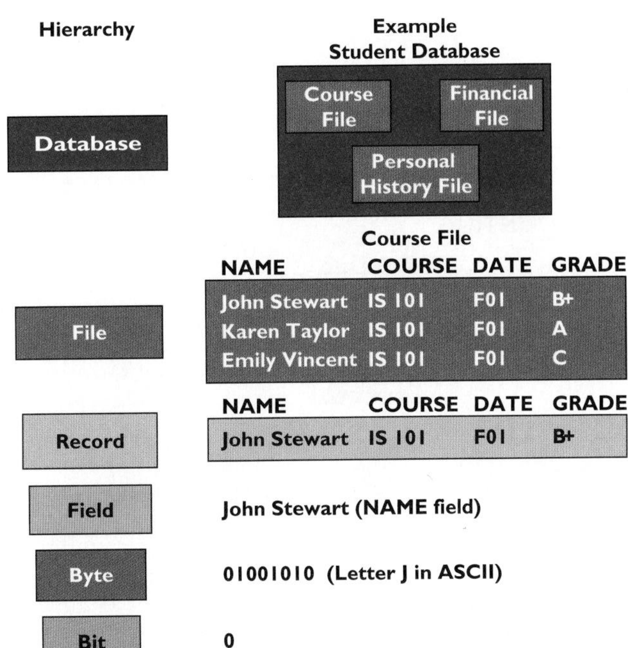


*Figure 7-1* The data hierarchy. A computer system organizes data in a hierarchy that starts with the bit, which represents either a 0 or a 1. Bits can be grouped to form a byte to represent one character, number, or symbol. Bytes can be grouped to form a field, and related fields can be grouped to form a record. Related records can be collected to form a file, and related files can be organized into a database.

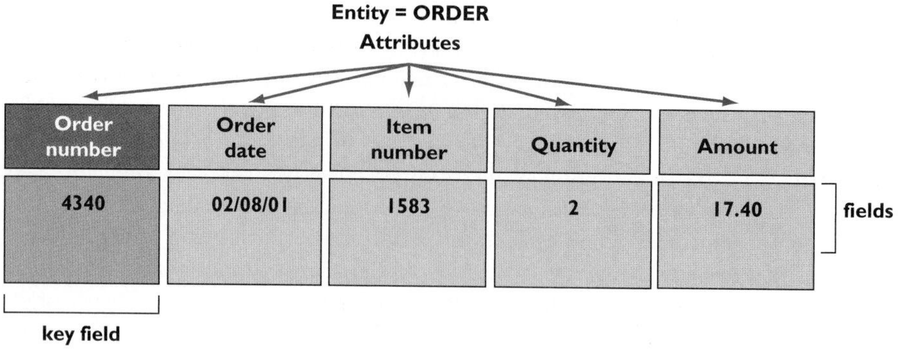

Entity = ORDER

Attributes

| Order number | Order date | Item number | Quantity | Amount |
|---|---|---|---|---|
| 4340 | 02/08/01 | 1583 | 2 | 17.40 |

key field (Order number); fields (values row)

*Figure 7-2* Entities and attributes. This record describes the entity called ORDER and its attributes. The specific values for order number, order date, item number, quantity, and amount for this particular order are the fields for this record. Order number is the key field because each order is assigned a unique identification number.

## PROBLEMS WITH THE TRADITIONAL FILE ENVIRONMENT

Most organizations began information processing on a small scale, automating one application at a time. Systems tended to grow independently and not according to some grand plan. Each functional area tended to develop systems in isolation from other functional areas. Accounting, finance, manufacturing, human resources, and marketing all developed their own systems and data files. Figure 7-3 illustrates the **traditional file environment** approach to information processing.

**traditional file environment** A way of collecting and maintaining data in an organization that leads to each functional area or division creating and maintaining its own data files and programs.

Each application, of course, required its own files and its own computer program to operate. For example, the human resources functional area might have a personnel master file, a payroll file, a medical insurance file, a pension file, a mailing list file, and so forth until tens, perhaps hundreds, of files and programs existed. In the company as a whole, this process led to multiple master files created, maintained, and operated by separate divisions or departments.

As this process goes on for five or ten years, the organization is saddled with hundreds of programs and applications, with no one who knows what they do, what data they use, and who is using the data. The organization is collecting the same information in far too many files. The resulting problems are data redundancy, program-data dependence, inflexibility, poor data security, and inability to share data among applications.

### Data Redundancy and Confusion

**data redundancy** The presence of duplicate data in multiple data files.

**Data redundancy** is the presence of duplicate data in multiple data files. Data redundancy occurs when different divisions, functional areas, and groups in an organization indepen-

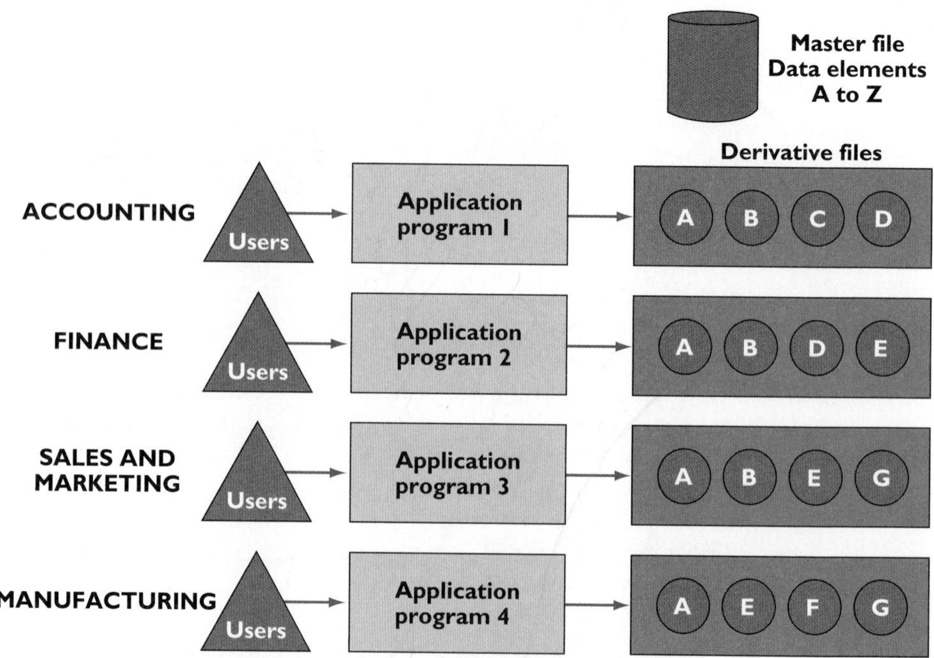


*Figure 7-3* Traditional file processing. The use of a traditional approach to file processing encourages each functional area in a corporation to develop specialized applications. Each application requires a unique data file that is likely to be a subset of the master file. These subsets of the master file lead to data redundancy, processing inflexibility, and wasted storage resources.

dently collect the same piece of information. For instance, within the commercial loans division of a bank, the marketing and credit information functions might collect the same customer information. Because it is collected and maintained in so many different places, the same data item may have different meanings in different parts of the organization. Simple data items such as the fiscal year, employee identification, and product code can take on different meanings as programmers and analysts work in isolation on different applications.

### Program-Data Dependence

**Program-data dependence** is the tight relationship between data stored in files and the specific programs required to update and maintain those files. Every computer program has to describe the location and nature of the data with which it works. In a traditional file environment, any change in data requires a change in all programs that access the data. Changes, for instance, in tax rates or ZIP-code length require changes in programs. Such programming changes may cost millions of dollars to implement in programs that require the revised data.

**program-data dependence**
The close relationship between data stored in traditional files and the software programs that update and maintain those files. Any change in data organization or format requires a change in all the programs associated with those files.

### Lack of Flexibility

A traditional file system can deliver routine scheduled reports after extensive programming efforts, but it cannot deliver ad hoc reports or respond to unanticipated information requirements in a timely fashion. As illustrated by the chapter-opening description of Famous Footwear, the information required by ad hoc requests is somewhere in the system but too expensive to retrieve. Several programmers would have to work for weeks to put together the required data items in a new file.

### Poor Security

Because there is little control or management of data, access to and dissemination of information may be out of control. Management may have no way of knowing who is accessing or even making changes to the organization's data.

### Lack of Data Sharing and Availability

The lack of control over access to data in this confused environment does not make it easy for people to obtain information. Because pieces of information in different files and different parts of the organization cannot be related to one another, it is virtually impossible for information to be shared or accessed in a timely manner. Information cannot flow freely across different functional areas or different parts of the organization.

## 7.2 THE DATABASE APPROACH TO DATA MANAGEMENT

Database technology can cut through many of the problems a traditional file organization creates. A more rigorous definition of a **database** is a collection of data organized to serve many applications efficiently by centralizing the data and minimizing redundant data. Rather than storing data in separate files for each application, data are stored physically to appear to users as being stored in only one location. A single database services multiple applications. For example, instead of a corporation storing employee data in separate information systems and separate files for personnel, payroll, and benefits, the corporation could create a single common human resources database. Figure 7-4 illustrates the database concept.

**database (rigorous definition)**
A collection of data organized to service many applications at the same time by storing and managing data so that they appear to be in one location.

### DATABASE MANAGEMENT SYSTEMS

A **database management system (DBMS)** is simply the software that permits an organization to centralize data, manage them efficiently, and provide access to the stored data by application programs. The DBMS acts as an interface between application programs and the physical data files. When the application program calls for a data item such as gross pay, the DBMS finds this item in the database and presents it to the application program. Using traditional data files, the programmer would have to specify the size and format of each data element used in the program and then tell the computer where they were located.

**database management system (DBMS)**
Special software to create and maintain a database and enable individual business applications to extract the data they need without having to create separate files or data definitions in their computer programs.

The DBMS relieves the programmer or end user from the task of understanding where and how the data are actually stored by separating the logical and physical views of the data.

*Figure 7-4* The contemporary database environment. A single human resources database serves multiple applications and also allows a corporation to easily draw together all the information for various applications. The database management system acts as the interface between the application programs and the data.

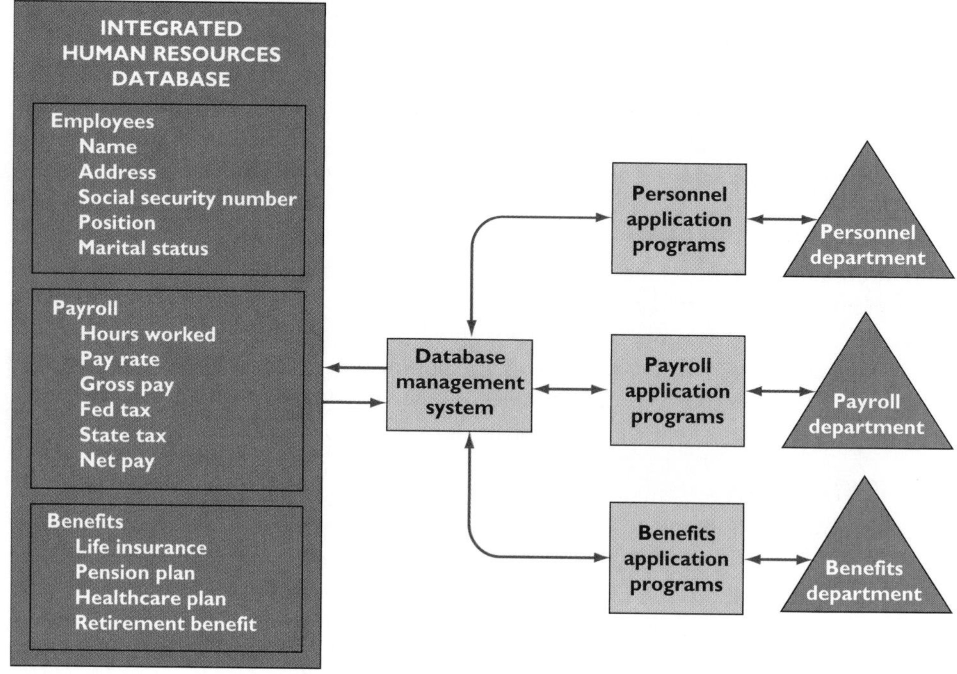


**logical view**
A representation of data as they would appear to an application programmer or end user.

**physical view**
The representation of data as they would be actually organized on physical storage media.

**data definition language**
The component of a database management system that defines each data element as it appears in the database.

**data manipulation language**
A language associated with a database management system that end users and programmers use to manipulate data in the database.

**Structured Query Language (SQL)**
The standard data manipulation language for relational database management systems.

**data dictionary**
An automated or manual tool for storing and organizing information about the data maintained in a database.

The **logical view** presents data as they would be perceived by end users or business specialists, whereas the **physical view** shows how data are actually organized and structured on physical storage media. Although there is only one physical view of the data, there can be many different logical views. The database management software makes the physical database available for different logical views presented for various application programs. For example, an employee retirement benefits program might use a logical view of the human resources database illustrated in Figure 7-4 that requires only the employee's name, address, social security number, pension plan, and retirement benefits data.

A database management system has three components:

- A data definition language
- A data manipulation language
- A data dictionary

The **data definition language** is the formal language programmers use to specify the content and structure of the database. The data definition language defines each data element as it appears in the database before that data element is translated into the forms required by application programs.

Most DBMS have a specialized language called a **data manipulation language** that is used in conjunction with some conventional third- or fourth-generation programming language to manipulate the data in the database. This language contains commands that permit end users and programming specialists to extract data from the database to satisfy information requests and develop applications. The most prominent data manipulation language today is **Structured Query Language,** or **SQL.** Complex programming tasks cannot be performed efficiently with typical data manipulation languages. However, most mainframe DBMS are compatible with COBOL, FORTRAN, and other third-generation programming languages, permitting greater processing efficiency and flexibility.

The third element of a DBMS is a **data dictionary.** This is an automated or manual file that stores definitions of data elements and data characteristics, such as usage, physical representation, ownership (who in the organization is responsible for maintaining the data), authorization, and security. Many data dictionaries can produce lists and reports of data use, groupings, program locations, and so on. Figure 7-5 illustrates a sample data dictionary report that shows the size, format, meaning, and uses of a data element in a human resources database. A

```
NAME: AMT-PAY-BASE
FOCUS NAME: BASEPAY
PC NAME:     SALARY

DESCRIPTION: EMPLOYEE'S ANNUAL SALARY

SIZE: 9 BYTES
TYPE: N      (NUMERIC)
DATE CHANGED: 01/01/95
OWNERSHIP: COMPENSATION
UPDATE SECURITY: SITE PERSONNEL
ACCESS SECURITY: MANAGER, COMPENSATION PLANNING AND RESEARCH
                 MANAGER, JOB EVALUATION SYSTEMS
                 MANAGER, HUMAN RESOURCES PLANNING
                 MANAGER, SITE EQUAL OPPORTUNITY AFFAIRS
                 MANAGER, SITE BENEFITS
                 MANAGER, CLAIMS PAYING SYSTEMS
                 MANAGER, QUALIFIED PLANS
                 MANAGER, SITE EMPLOYMENT/EEO
BUSINESS FUNCTIONS USED BY: COMPENSATION
                            HR PLANNING
                            EMPLOYMENT
                            INSURANCE
                            PENSION
                            401K

PROGRAMS USING: PI01000
                PI02000
                PI03000
                PI04000
                PI05000

REPORTS USING: REPORT 124 (SALARY INCREASE TRACKING REPORT)
               REPORT 448 (GROUP INSURANCE AUDIT REPORT)
               REPORT 452 (SALARY REVIEW LISTING)
               PENSION REFERENCE LISTING
```

***Figure 7-5*** Sample data dictionary report. The sample data dictionary report for a human resources database provides helpful information such as the size of the data element, which programs and reports use it, and which group in the organization is the owner responsible for maintaining it. The report also shows some of the other names that the organization uses for this piece of data.

**data element** represents a field. In addition to listing the standard name (AMT-PAY-BASE), the dictionary lists the names that reference this element in specific systems and identifies the positions, business functions, programs, and reports that use this data element.

**data element**
A field.

By creating an inventory of data contained in the database, the data dictionary serves as an important data management tool. For instance, business users could consult the dictionary to find out exactly what pieces of data are maintained for the sales or marketing function or even to determine all the information maintained by the entire enterprise. The dictionary could supply business users with the name, format, and specifications required to access data for reports. Technical staff could use the dictionary to determine what data elements and files must be changed if a program is changed.

Most data dictionaries are entirely passive; they simply report. More advanced types are active; changes in the dictionary can be automatically used by related programs. For instance, to change ZIP codes from five to nine digits, one could simply enter the change in the dictionary without having to modify and recompile all application programs using ZIP codes.

In an ideal database environment, the data in the database are defined only once and used for all applications whose data reside in the database, thereby eliminating data redundancy and inconsistency. Application programs, which are written using a combination of the data manipulation language of the DBMS and a conventional programming language, request data elements from the database. Data elements called for by the application programs are found and delivered by the DBMS. The programmer does not have to specify in detail how or where the data are to be found.

A DBMS can reduce program-data dependence along with program development and maintenance costs. Access and availability of information can be increased because users and programmers can perform ad hoc queries of data in the database. The DBMS allows the organization to centrally manage data, its use, and security.

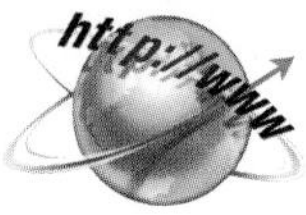


## TYPES OF DATABASES

Contemporary DBMS use different database models to keep track of entities, attributes, and relationships. Each model has certain processing advantages and certain business advantages.

### Relational DBMS

**relational DBMS**
A type of logical database model that treats data as if they were stored in two-dimensional tables. It can relate data stored in one table to data in another as long as the two tables share a common data element.

**tuple**
A row or record in a relational database.

The most popular type of DBMS today for PCs as well as for larger computers and mainframes is the **relational DBMS.** The relational data model represents all data in the database as simple two-dimensional tables called relations. The tables appear similar to flat files, but the information in more than one table can be easily extracted and combined. Sometimes the tables are referred to as files.

Figure 7-6 shows a supplier table, a part table, and an order table. In each table the rows are unique records and the columns correspond to fields. Another term for a row or record in a relation is a **tuple.** Often a user needs information from a number of relations to produce a report. Here is the strength of the relational model: It can relate data in any one file or table to data in another file or table as long as both tables share a common data element.

To demonstrate, suppose we wanted to find in the relational database in Figure 7-6 the names and addresses of suppliers who could provide us with part 137 or part 152. We would need information from two tables: the supplier table and the part table. Note that these two files have a shared data element: Supplier_Number.

In a relational database, three basic operations are used to develop useful sets of data: select, project, and join. The *select* operation creates a subset consisting of all records in the file that meet stated criteria. Select creates, in other words, a subset of rows that meet certain criteria. In our example, we want to select records (rows) from the part table with part 137 or 152. The *join* operation combines relational tables to provide the user with more information than is available in individual tables. In our example we want to join the now-shortened part table (only parts 137 or 152 will be presented) and the supplier table into a single new result table.

The *project* operation creates a subset consisting of columns in a table, permitting the user to create new tables (also called views) that contain only the information required. In our example, we want to extract from the new result table only the following columns: Part_Number, Supplier_Number, Supplier_Name, and Supplier_Address. (See Figure 7-7.)

Leading mainframe relational database management systems include IBM's DB2 and Oracle from the Oracle Corporation. DB2, Oracle, and Microsoft SQL Server are used as DBMS for midrange computers. Microsoft Access is a PC relational database management system, and Oracle Lite is a DBMS for small handheld computing devices.

Table (Relation) — Columns (Fields) — Rows (Records, Tuples)

ORDER

| Order_Number | Order_Date | Delivery_Date | Part_Number | Part_Amount | Order_Total |
|---|---|---|---|---|---|
| 1634 | 02/02/01 | 02/22/01 | 152 | 2 | 144.50 |
| 1635 | 02/12/01 | 02/28/01 | 137 | 3 | 79.70 |
| 1636 | 02/13/01 | 03/01/01 | 145 | 1 | 24.30 |

PART

| Part_Number | Part_Description | Unit_Price | Supplier_Number |
|---|---|---|---|
| 137 | Door latch | 22.50 | 4058 |
| 145 | Door handle | 26.25 | 2038 |
| 150 | Door seal | 6.00 | 4058 |
| 152 | Compressor | 70.00 | 1125 |

SUPPLIER

| Supplier_Number | Supplier_Name | Supplier_Address |
|---|---|---|
| 4058 | CBM Inc. | 44 Winslow, Gary IN 44950 |
| 2038 | Ace Inc. | Rte. 101, Essex NJ 07763 |
| 1125 | Bryant Corp. | 51 Elm, Rochester NY 11349 |

*Figure 7-6* The relational data model. Each table is a relation and each row or record is a tuple. Each column corresponds to a field. These relations can easily be combined and extracted to access data and produce reports, provided that any two share a common data element. In this example, the ORDER file shares the data element "Part_Number" with the PART file. The PART and SUPPLIER files share the data element "Supplier_Number."

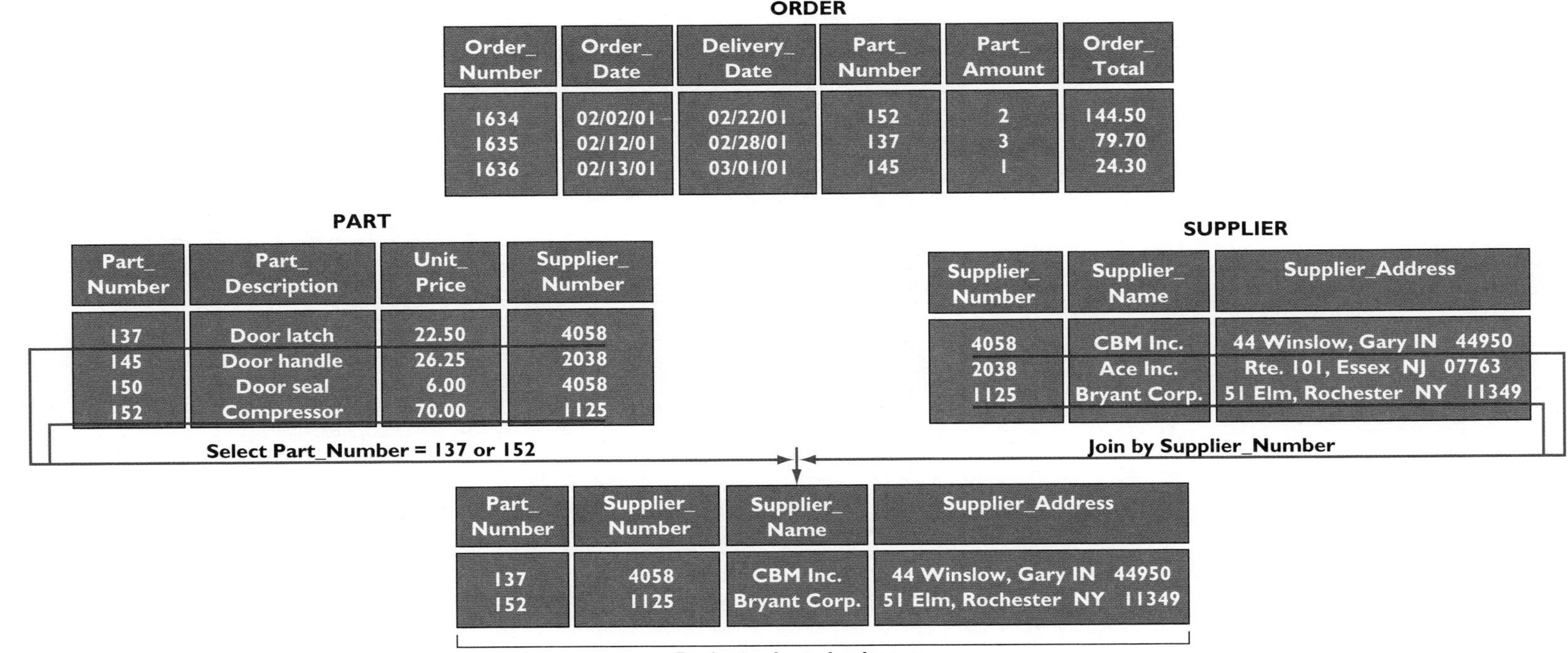


*Figure 7-7* The three basic operations of a relational DBMS. The select, project, and join operations allow data from two different tables to be combined and only selected attributes to be displayed.

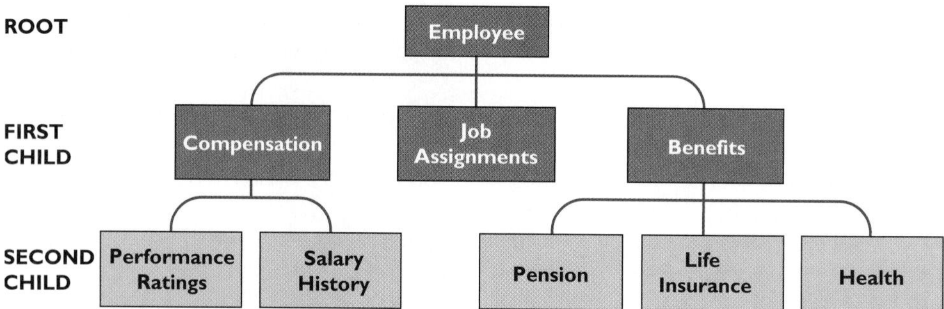


*Figure 7-8* A hierarchical DBMS for a human resources system. The hierarchical database model looks like an organizational chart or a family tree. It has a single root segment (Employee) connected to lower-level segments (Compensation, Job Assignments, and Benefits). Each subordinate segment, in turn, may connect to other subordinate segments. Here, Compensation connects to Performance Ratings and Salary History. Benefits connects to Pension, Life Insurance, and Health Care. Each subordinate segment is the child of the segment directly above it.

## Hierarchical and Network DBMS

One can still find older systems that are based on a hierarchical or network data model. The **hierarchical DBMS** presents data to users in a treelike structure. Within each record, data elements are organized into pieces of records called segments. To the user, each record looks like an organization chart with one top-level segment called the root. An upper segment is connected logically to a lower segment in a parent–child relationship. A parent segment can have more than one child, but a child can have only one parent.

**hierarchical DBMS**
Older logical database model that organizes data in a treelike structure. A record is subdivided into segments that are connected to each other in one-to-many, parent–child relationships.

Figure 7-8 shows a hierarchical structure that might be used for a human resources database. The root segment is Employee, which contains basic employee information such as name, address, and identification number. Immediately below it are three child segments: Compensation (containing salary and promotion data), Job Assignments (containing data about job positions and departments), and Benefits (containing data about beneficiaries and benefit options). The Compensation segment has two children below it: Performance Ratings (containing data about employees' job performance evaluations) and Salary History (containing historical data about employees' past salaries). Below the Benefits segment are child segments for Pension, Life Insurance, and Health, containing data about these benefit plans.

Whereas hierarchical structures depict one-to-many relationships, **network DBMS** depict data logically as many-to-many relationships. In other words, parents can have multiple children, and a child can have more than one parent. A typical many-to-many relationship for a network DBMS is the student–course relationship (see Figure 7-9). There are many courses in a university and many students. A student takes many courses and a course has many students.

**network DBMS**
An older logical database model that is useful for depicting many-to-many relationships.

Hierarchical and network DBMS are considered outdated and are no longer used for building new database applications. They are much less flexible than relational DBMS and do not support ad hoc, English language-like inquiries for information. All paths for accessing data must be specified in advance and cannot be changed without a major programming effort. For instance, if you queried the human resources database illustrated in Figure 7-8 to find out the names of the employees with the job title of administrative assistant, you would discover that there is no way that the system can find the answer in a reasonable amount of time. This path through the data was not specified in advance.

Relational DBMS, in contrast have much more flexibility in providing data for ad hoc queries, combining information from different sources, and providing capability to add new data and records without disturbing existing programs and applications. However, these systems can be slowed down if they require many accesses to the data stored on disk to carry out

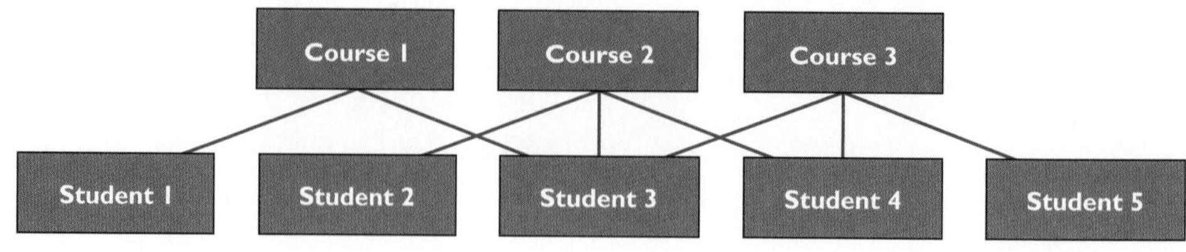


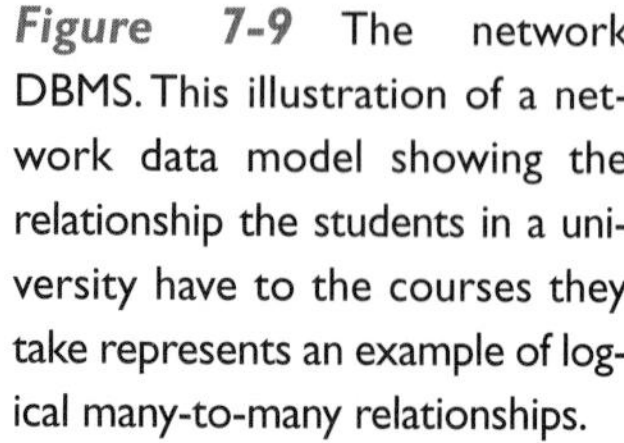
*Figure 7-9* The network DBMS. This illustration of a network data model showing the relationship the students in a university have to the courses they take represents an example of logical many-to-many relationships.

the select, join, and project commands. Selecting one part number from among millions, one record at a time, can take a long time. Of course, the database can be tuned to speed up prespecified queries.

Hierarchical DBMS can still be found in large legacy systems that require intensive high-volume transaction processing. A **legacy system** is a system that has been in existence for a long time and that continues to be used to avoid the high cost of replacing or redesigning it. Banks, insurance companies, and other high-volume users continue to use reliable hierarchical databases such as IBM's IMS (Information Management System), developed in 1969. As relational products acquire more muscle, firms will shift away completely from hierarchical DBMS, but this will happen over a long period of time.

**legacy system**
A system that has been in existence for a long time and that continues to be used to avoid the high cost of replacing or redesigning it.

## Object-Oriented Databases

Conventional database management systems were designed for homogeneous data that can be easily structured into predefined data fields and records organized in rows or tables. But many applications today and in the future will require databases that can store and retrieve not only structured numbers and characters but also drawings, images, photographs, voice, and full-motion video. Conventional DBMS are not well suited to handling graphics-based or multimedia applications. For instance, design data in a computer-aided design (CAD) database consist of complex relationships among many types of data. Manipulating these kinds of data in a relational system requires extensive programming to translate the complex data structures into tables and rows. An **object-oriented DBMS,** however, stores the data and procedures as objects that can be automatically retrieved and shared.

**object-oriented DBMS**
An approach to data management that stores both data and the procedures acting on the data as objects that can be automatically retrieved and shared; the objects can contain multimedia.

Object-oriented database management systems (OODBMS) are becoming popular, because they can be used to manage the various multimedia components or Java applets used in Web applications, which typically integrate pieces of information from a variety of sources. OODBMS also are useful for storing data types, such as recursive data. (An example would be parts within parts as found in manufacturing applications.) Finance and trading applications often use OODBMS because they require data models that must be easy to change to respond to new economic conditions.

Although object-oriented databases can store more complex types of information than relational DBMS, they are relatively slow compared with relational DBMS for processing large numbers of transactions. Hybrid **object-relational DBMS** are now available to provide capabilities of both object-oriented and relational DBMS. A hybrid approach can be accomplished in three different ways: by using tools that offer object-oriented access to relational DBMS, by using object-oriented extensions to existing relational DBMS, or by using a hybrid object-relational database management system.

**object-relational DBMS**
A database management system that combines the capabilities of a relational DBMS for storing traditional information and the capabilities of an object-oriented DBMS for storing graphics and multimedia.

## QUERYING DATABASES: ELEMENTS OF SQL

Structured query language (SQL) is the principal data manipulation language for relational DBMS and a major tool for querying, reading, and updating a relational database. There are versions of SQL that can run on almost any operating system and computer, so that computers are able to exchange data by passing SQL commands to each other. End users and information systems specialists can use SQL as an interactive query language to access data from databases, and SQL commands can also be embedded in application programs written in COBOL, C, and other programming languages.

We now describe the most important basic SQL commands. Convention calls for certain SQL reserved words with special meanings, such as SELECT and FROM, to be capitalized and for SQL statements to be written in multiple lines. Most SQL statements to retrieve data contain the following three clauses:

| | |
|---|---|
| SELECT | Lists the columns from tables that the user would like to see in a result table |
| FROM | Identifies the tables or views from which the columns will be selected |
| WHERE | Includes conditions for selecting specific rows (records) within a single table and conditions for joining multiple tables |

| Part_ Number | Part_ Description | Unit_ Price |
|---|---|---|
| 137 | Door latch | 22.50 |
| 145 | Door handle | 26.25 |
| 150 | Door seal | 6.00 |
| 152 | Compressor | 70.00 |

***Figure 7-10*** The results of using the SELECT statement to select only the columns Part_Number, Part_Description, and Unit_Price from all rows in the PART table.

## The SELECT Statement

The SELECT statement is used to query data from a relational table for specific information. The general form for a SELECT statement, retrieving specified columns for all of the rows in the table is

```
SELECT Column_Name, Column_Name, . . .
FROM Table_Name;
```

The columns to be obtained are listed after the keyword SELECT and the table to be used is listed after the keyword FROM. Note that column and table names do not have spaces and must be typed as one word or with an underscore and that the statement ends with a semi-colon. Review Figure 7-6. Suppose you wanted to see the Part_Number, Part_Description, and Unit_Price for each part in the PART table. You would specify:

```
SELECT Part_Number, Part_Description, Unit_Price
FROM PART;
```

Figure 7-10 illustrates the results of your projection.

## Conditional Selection

The WHERE clause is used to specify that only certain rows of the table are displayed, based on the criteria described in that WHERE clause. Suppose, for example, you wanted to see the same data only for parts in the part table with unit prices less than $25. You would specify:

```
SELECT Part_Number, Part_Description, Unit_Price
FROM PART
WHERE Unit_Price < 25.00;
```

Your query would return the results illustrated in Figure 7-11.

## Joining Two Tables

Suppose we wanted to obtain information on the names, identification numbers, and addresses of suppliers for each part in the database. We can do this by joining the PART table with the SUPPLIER table and then extracting the required information. The query would look like this:

```
SELECT PART.Part_Number, SUPPLIER.Supplier_Number, SUPPLIER.Supplier_Name,
    SUPPLIER.Supplier_Address
FROM PART, SUPPLIER
WHERE PART.Supplier_Number = SUPPLIER.Supplier_Number;
```

The results would look like those shown in Figure 7-12. And if we only wanted to see the name, address, and supplier numbers for the suppliers of part 137 or 152, the query would be as follows:

```
SELECT PART.Part_Number, SUPPLIER.Supplier_Number, SUPPLIER.Supplier_Name,
    SUPPLIER.Supplier_Address
FROM PART, SUPPLIER
WHERE PART.Supplier_Number = SUPPLIER.Supplier_Number AND Part_Number = 137 OR
    Part_Number = 152;
```

| Part_ Number | Part_ Description | Unit_ Price |
|---|---|---|
| 137 | Door latch | 22.50 |
| 150 | Door seal | 6.00 |

***Figure 7-11*** The results of using a conditional selection to select only parts that meet the condition of having unit prices less than $25.

| Part_ Number | Supplier_ Number | Supplier_ Name | Supplier_Address |
|---|---|---|---|
| 137 | 4058 | CBM Inc. | 44 Winslow, Gary IN 44950 |
| 145 | 2038 | Ace Inc. | Rte. 101, Essex NJ 07763 |
| 150 | 4058 | CBM Inc. | 44 Winslow, Gary IN 44950 |
| 152 | 1125 | Bryant Corp. | 51 Elm, Rochester NY 11349 |

*Figure 7-12* A projection from joining the PART and SUPPLIER tables.

The results would look like the result of the join operation depicted in Figure 7-7. Note that several conditions can be expressed in the WHERE clause.

## 7.3 CREATING A DATABASE ENVIRONMENT

In order to create a database environment, one must understand the relationships among the data, the type of data that will be maintained in the database, how the data will be used, and how the organization will need to change to manage data from a company-wide perspective. We now describe important database design principles and the management and organizational requirements of a database environment.

### DESIGNING DATABASES

To create a database, one must go through two design exercises: a conceptual design and a physical design. The conceptual or logical design of a database is an abstract model of the database from a business perspective, whereas the physical design shows how the database is actually arranged on direct access storage devices. Logical design requires a detailed description of the business information needs of the actual end users of the database. Ideally, database design will be part of an overall organizational data planning effort (see Chapter 10).

The conceptual database design describes how the data elements in the database are to be grouped. The design process identifies relationships among data elements and the most efficient way of grouping data elements together to meet information requirements. The process also identifies redundant data elements and the groupings of data elements required for specific application programs. Groups of data are organized, refined, and streamlined until an overall logical view of the relationships among all the data elements in the database emerges.

**entity-relationship diagram**
A methodology for documenting databases illustrating the relationship between various entities in the database.

**normalization**
The process of creating small stable data structures from complex groups of data when designing a relational database.

Database designers document the conceptual data model with an **entity-relationship diagram,** illustrated in Figure 7-13. The boxes represent entities and the diamonds represent relationships. The 1 or M on either side of the diamond represents the relationship among entities as either one-to-one, one-to-many, or many-to-many. Figure 7-13 shows that the entity ORDER can have more than one PART and a PART can only have one SUPPLIER. Many parts can be provided by the same supplier. The attributes for each entity are listed next to the entity and the key field is underlined.

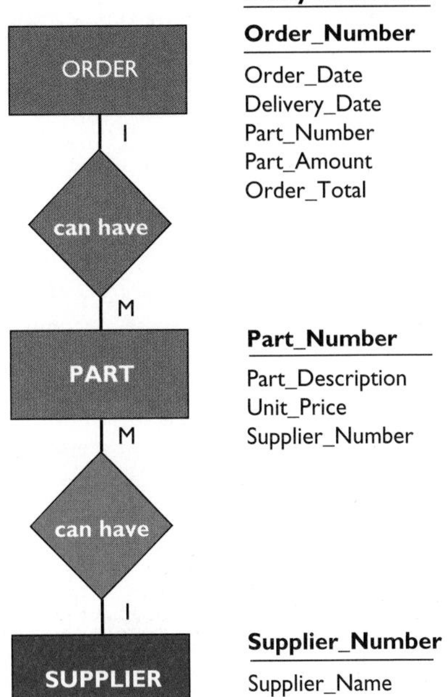


*Figure 7-13* An entity-relationship diagram. This diagram shows the relationships between the entities ORDER, PART, and SUPPLIER that were used to develop the relational database illustrated in Figure 7-6.

To use a relational database model effectively, complex groupings of data must be streamlined to eliminate redundant data elements and awkward many-to-many relationships. The process of creating small, stable data structures from complex groups of data is called **normalization.** Figures 7-14 and 7-15 illustrate this process. In the particular business modeled here, an order can have more than one part but each part is provided by only one supplier. If we built a relation called ORDER with all the fields included here, we would have to repeat the name, description, and price of each part on the order and the name and address of each part vendor. This relation contains what are called repeating groups because there can be many parts and suppliers for each order, and it actually describes multiple entities—parts and suppliers

ORDER

| Order_ Number | Part_ Amount | Part_ Number | Part_ Description | Unit_ Price | Supplier_ Number | Supplier_ Name | Supplier_ Address | Order_ Date | Delivery_ Date | Order_ Total |
|---|---|---|---|---|---|---|---|---|---|---|

*Figure 7-14* An unnormalized relation for ORDER. In an unnormalized relation there are repeating groups. For example, there can be many parts and suppliers for each order. There is only a one-to-one correspondence between Order_Number and Order_Date, Order_Total, and Delivery_Date.

as well as orders. A more efficient way to arrange the data is to break down ORDER into smaller relations, each of which describes a single entity. If we go step by step and normalize the relation ORDER, we emerge with the relations illustrated in Figure 7-15.

If a database has been carefully considered, with a clear understanding of business information needs and usage, the database model will most likely be in some normalized form. Many real-world databases are not fully normalized because this may not be the most sensible way to meet business information requirements. Note that the relational database illustrated in Figure 7-6 is not fully normalized because there could be more than one part for each order. The designers chose to not use the four relations described in Figure 7-15, because most of the orders handled by this particular business are only for one part. The designers might have believed that for this particular business it was inefficient to maintain four different tables.

## DISTRIBUTING DATABASES

Database design also considers how the data are to be distributed. Information systems can be designed with a centralized database that is used by a single central processor or by multiple processors in a client/server network. Alternatively, the database can be distributed. A **distributed database** is one that is stored in more than one physical location. Parts of the database are stored physically in one location, and other parts are stored and maintained in other locations. There are two main ways of distributing a database (see Figure 7-16). The central database (see Figure 7-16a) can be partitioned so that each remote processor has the necessary data to serve its local area. Changes in local files can be justified with the central database on a batch basis, often at night. Another strategy is to replicate the central database (Figure 7-16b) at all remote locations. For example, Lufthansa Airlines replaced its centralized mainframe database with a replicated database to make information more immediately available to flight dispatchers. Any change made to Lufthansa's Frankfort DBMS is automatically replicated in New York and Hong Kong. This strategy also requires updating of the central database on off hours.

**distributed database**
A database that is stored in more than one physical location. Parts or copies of the database are physically stored in one location, and other parts or copies are stored and maintained in other locations.

Distributed systems reduce the vulnerability of a single, massive central site. They increase service and responsiveness to local users and often can run on smaller less expensive computers. Distributed systems, however, are dependent on high-quality telecommunications lines, which themselves are vulnerable. Moreover, local databases can sometimes depart from central data standards and definitions, and they pose security problems by

*Figure 7-15* A normalized relation for ORDER. After normalization, the original relation ORDER has been broken down into four smaller relations. The relation ORDER is left with only three attributes and the relation ORDERED_PARTS has a combined, or concatenated, key consisting of Order_Number and Part_Number.

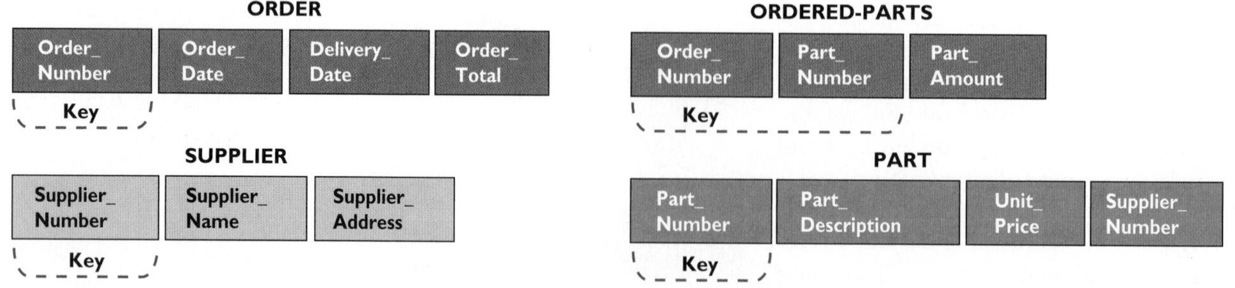

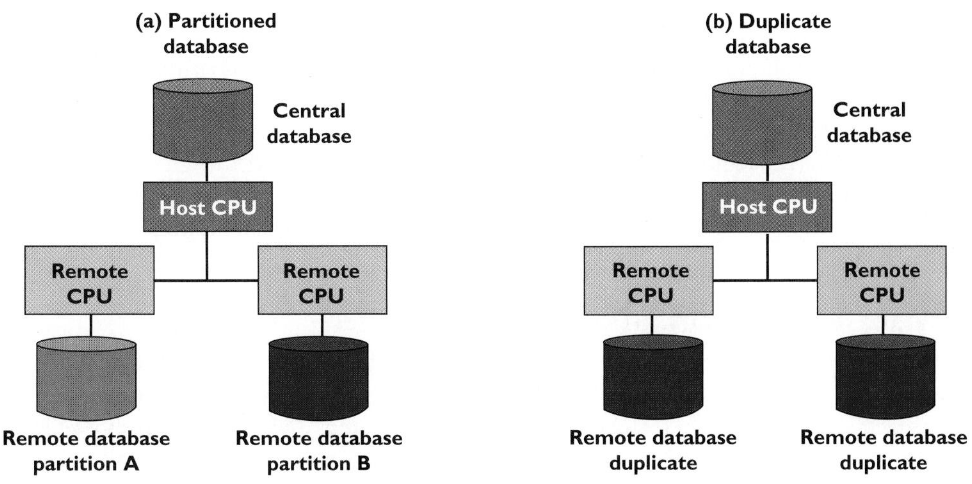


*Figure 7-16* Distributed databases. There are alternative ways of distributing a database. The central database can be partitioned (a) so that each remote processor has the necessary data to serve its own local needs. The central database also can be duplicated (b) at all remote locations.

widely distributing access to sensitive data. Database designers need to weigh these factors in their decisions.

## MANAGEMENT REQUIREMENTS FOR DATABASE SYSTEMS

Much more is required for the development of database systems than simply selecting a logical database model. The database is an organizational discipline, a method, rather than a tool or technology. It requires organizational and conceptual change. Without management support and understanding, database efforts fail. The critical elements in a database environment are (1) data administration, (2) data planning and modeling methodology, (3) database technology and management, and (4) users. This environment is depicted in Figure 7-17.

### Data Administration

Database systems require that the organization recognize the strategic role of information and begin actively to manage and plan for information as a corporate resource. This means that the organization must develop a **data administration** function with the power to define information requirements for the entire company and to have direct access to senior management. The chief information officer (CIO) or vice president of information becomes the primary advocate in the organization for database systems.

**data administration**
A special organizational function for managing the organization's data resources, concerned with information policy, data planning, maintenance of data dictionaries, and data quality standards.

Data administration is responsible for the specific policies and procedures through which data can be managed as an organizational resource. These responsibilities include developing information policy, planning for data, overseeing logical database design and data dictionary development, and monitoring how information system specialists and end-user groups use data.

**information policy**
Formal rules governing the maintenance, distribution, and use of information in an organization.

The fundamental principle of data administration is that all data are the property of the organization as a whole. Data cannot belong exclusively to any one business area or organizational unit. All data are to be made available to any group that requires them to fulfill its mission. An organization needs to formulate an **information policy** that specifies its rules for sharing, disseminating, acquiring, standardizing, classifying, and inventorying information throughout the organization. Information policy lays out specific procedures and accountabilities, specifying which organizational units share information, where information can be distributed, and who has responsibility for updating and maintaining the information. Although data administration is a very important organizational function, it has proved very challenging to implement.

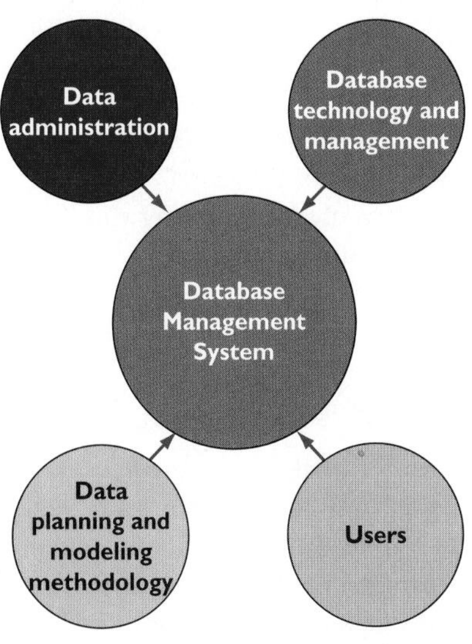


*Figure 7-17* Key organizational elements in the database environment. For a database management system to flourish in any organization, data administration functions and data planning and modeling methodologies must be coordinated with database technology and management. Resources must be devoted to training end users to use databases properly.

### Data Planning and Modeling Methodology

The organizational interests served by the DBMS are much broader than those in the traditional file environment; therefore, the organization requires enterprise-wide planning for data. Enterprise analysis, which addresses the information requirements of the entire organization (as opposed to the requirements of individual applications), is needed to develop databases. The purpose of enterprise analysis is to identify the key entities, attributes, and relationships that constitute the organization's data. These techniques are described in greater detail in Chapter 10.

### Database Technology, Management, and Users

Databases require new software and a new staff specially trained in DBMS techniques, as well as new data management structures. Most corporations develop a database design and management group within the corporate information system division that is responsible for defining and organizing the structure and content of the database and maintaining the database. In close cooperation with users, the design group establishes the physical database, the logical relations among elements, and the access rules and procedures. The functions it performs are called **database administration.**

**database administration**
Refers to the more technical and operational aspects of managing data, including physical database design and maintenance.

A database serves a wider community of users than traditional systems. Relational systems with fourth-generation query languages permit employees who are not computer specialists to access large databases. In addition, users include trained computer specialists. To optimize access for nonspecialists, more resources must be devoted to training end users.

## 7.4 DATABASE TRENDS

Organizations are installing powerful data analysis tools and data warehouses to make better use of the information stored in their databases and are taking advantage of database technology linked to the World Wide Web. We now explore these developments.

### MULTIDIMENSIONAL DATA ANALYSIS

Sometimes managers need to analyze data in ways that traditional database models cannot represent. For example, a company selling four different products—nuts, bolts, washers, and screws—in the East, West, and Central regions, might want to know actual sales by product for each region and might also want to compare them with projected sales. This analysis requires a multidimensional view of data.

To provide this type of information, organizations can use either a specialized multidimensional database or a tool that creates multidimensional views of data in relational databases. Multidimensional analysis enables users to view the same data in different ways using multiple dimensions. Each aspect of information—product, pricing, cost, region, or time period—represents a different dimension. So a product manager could use a multidimensional data analysis tool to learn how many washers were sold in the East in June, how that compares with the previous month and the previous June, and how it compares with the sales forecast. Another term for multidimensional data analysis is **on-line analytical processing (OLAP).**

**on-line analytical processing (OLAP)**
Capability for manipulating and analyzing large volumes of data from multiple perspectives.

Figure 7-18 shows a multidimensional model that could be created to represent products, regions, actual sales, and projected sales. A matrix of actual sales can be stacked on top of a matrix of projected sales to form a cube with six faces. If you rotate the cube 90 degrees one way, the face showing will be product versus actual and projected sales. If you rotate the cube 90 degrees again, you can see region versus actual and projected sales. If you rotate 180 degrees from the original view, you can see projected sales and product versus region. Cubes can be nested within cubes to build complex views of data.

### DATA WAREHOUSES AND DATAMINING

Decision makers need concise, reliable information about current operations, trends, and changes. What has been immediately available at most firms is current data only (historical data were available through special IS reports that took a long time to produce). Data often are fragmented in separate operational systems such as sales or payroll so that different managers make decisions from incomplete knowledge bases. Users and information system spe-

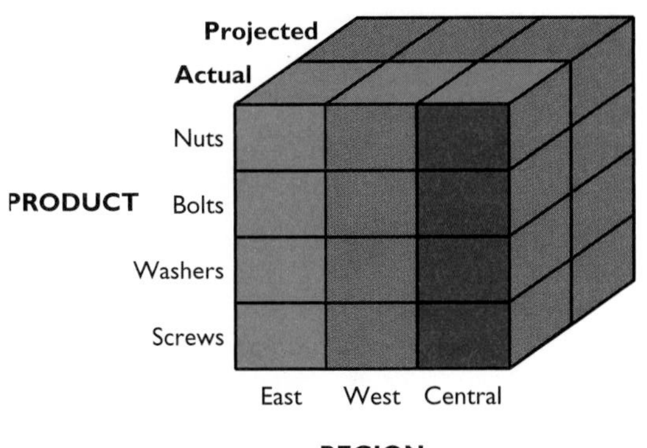


*Figure 7-18* Multidimensional data model. The view that is showing is product versus region. If you rotate the cube 90 degrees, the face that will be showing is product versus actual and projected sales. If you rotate the cube 90 degrees again, you can see region versus actual and projected sales. Other views are possible. The ability to rotate the data cube is the main technique for multidimensional reporting. It is sometimes called "slice and dice."

cialists may have to spend inordinate amounts of time locating and gathering data (Watson and Haley, 1998). Data warehousing addresses this problem by integrating key operational data from around the company in a form that is consistent, reliable, and easily available for reporting. All information can be retrieved from a single location and the data warehouse can be designed to provide an enterprise-wide view of this information.

## What Is a Data Warehouse?

A **data warehouse** is a database that stores current and historical data of potential interest to managers throughout the company. The data originate in many core operational systems and external sources, including Web site transactions, each with different data models. They may include legacy systems, relational or object-oriented DBMS applications, and new technology such as HTML Web sites or XML documents. The data from these diverse systems are copied into the data warehouse database as often as needed—hourly, daily, weekly, monthly. The data are standardized into a common data model and consolidated so that they can be used across the enterprise for management analysis and decision making. As more and more corporate data comes from changing external information sources such as the Web, data warehouse technology will need to find ways of incorporating changing data structures (Rundensteiner, Koeller and Zhang, 2000). The data are available for anyone to access as needed but cannot be altered. Figure 7-19 illustrates the data warehouse concept. The data warehouse must be carefully designed by both business and technical specialists to make sure it can provide the right information for critical business decisions. The firm may need to change its business processes to benefit from the information in the data warehouse (Cooper, Watson, Wixom, and Goodhue, 2000).

**data warehouse**
A database, with reporting and query tools, that stores current and historical data extracted from various operational systems and consolidated for management reporting and analysis.

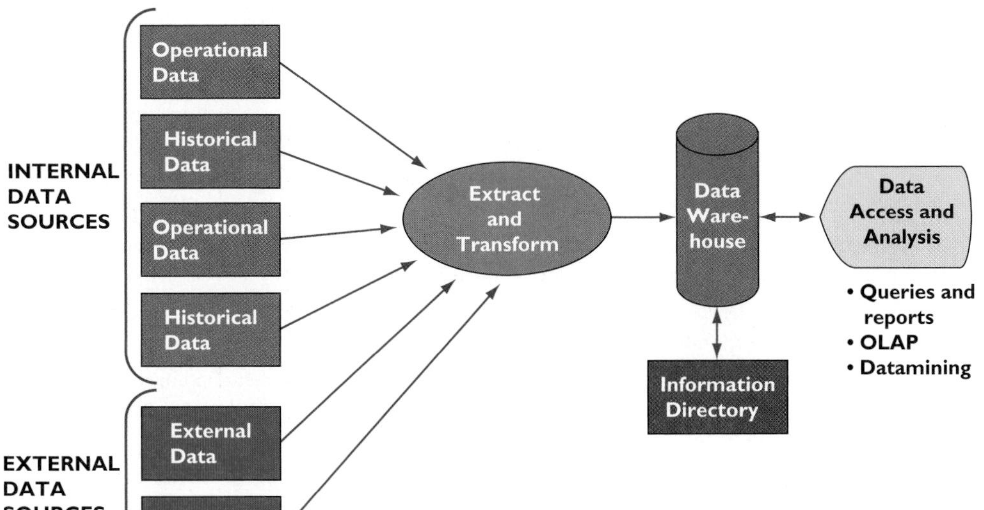


*Figure 7-19* Components of a data warehouse. A data warehouse extracts current and historical data from operational systems inside the organization. These data are combined with data from external sources and reorganized into a central database designed for management reporting and analysis. The information directory provides users with information about the data available in the warehouse.

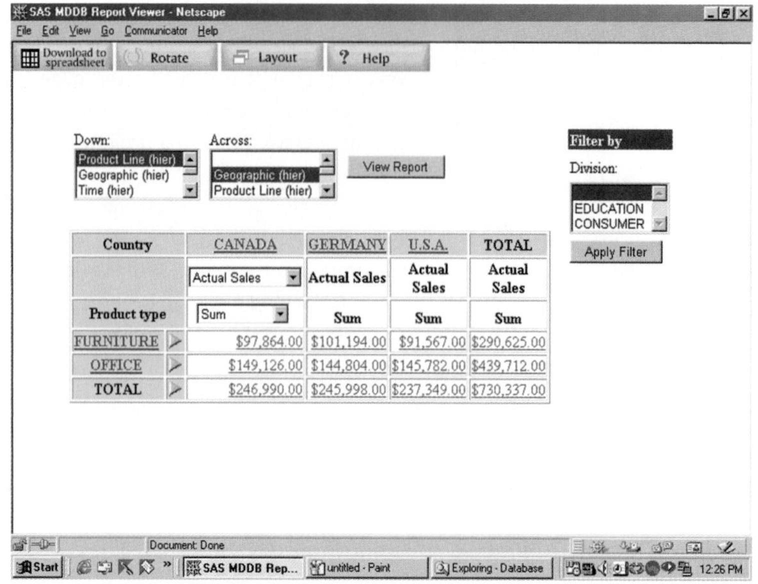


*The SAS MDDP Report Viewer offers a Web interface for viewing and manipulating multidimensional databases produced with SAS software using business dimensions such as time, geography or product. Online analytical processing (OLAP) gives users quick, unlimited views of multiple relationships in large quantities of summarized data.*

**data mart**
A smaller data warehouse containing only a portion of the organization's data for a specified function or population of users.

Companies can build enterprise-wide data warehouses where a central data warehouse serves the entire organization, or they can create smaller, decentralized warehouses called data marts. A **data mart** is a subset of a data warehouse in which a summarized or highly focused portion of the organization's data is placed in a separate database for a specific population of users. For example, a company might develop marketing and sales data marts to deal with customer relationship management. A data mart typically focuses on a single subject area or line of business, so it usually can be constructed more rapidly and at a lower cost than an enterprise-wide data warehouse. However, complexity, costs, and management problems will rise if an organization creates too many data marts.

## Datamining

**datamining**
Analysis of large pools of data to find patterns and rules that can be used to guide decision making and predict future behavior.

A data warehouse system provides a range of ad hoc and standardized query tools, analytical tools, and graphical reporting facilities, including tools for OLAP and datamining. **Datamining** software tools find hidden patterns and relationships in large pools of data and infer rules from them that can be used to predict future behavior and guide decision making. Datamining helps companies engage in one-to-one marketing where personalized or individualized messages can be created based on individual preferences. Table 7-1 describes how some organizations are benefiting from datamining. These systems can perform high-level analyses of patterns or trends, but they can also drill into more detail where needed.

### TABLE 7-1 How Businesses Are Using Datamining

| Organization | Datamining Application |
|---|---|
| ShopKo Stores | Uses datamining to discover cause-and-effect relationships between store items and customer buying habits. Increases sales by arranging merchandise to appeal to customer buying patterns. |
| Nordstrom | Uses data mining to analyze data generated by visitors to its Web site. Uses the results to customize advertising and content to individual customers and to improve on-line customer service. |
| KeyCorp. | Mines data on 3.3 million households and 7 million customers in its data warehouse to find the response rate of its direct mail marketing campaigns and to identify unprofitable products. This bank is also using datamining to profile customers for cross-selling, loyalty, and retention programs. |
| Verizon Wireless | Analyzes Verizon's customer database to identify new customers so that customer service representatives can find out if they need special help or services. Also uses datamining to identify mobile phone customers who might benefit from switching calling plans and mails them special promotions. Verizon uses such initiatives to increase customer satisfaction and thus reduce customer churn. |

## MANAGEMENT DECISION PROBLEM

### CREATING COMPANY-WIDE DATA STANDARDS

Your industrial supply company wants to create a data warehouse where management can obtain a single, corporatewide view of critical sales information to identify best-selling products in specific geographic areas, key customers, and sales trends. Your sales and product information are stored in several different systems: a divisional sales system running on a Unix server and a corporate sales system running on an IBM mainframe. You would like to create a single, standard format that consolidates these data from both systems. The following format has been proposed.

| Product_ID | Product_Description | Cost_per_Unit | Units_Sold | Sales_Region | Division | Customer_ID |
|---|---|---|---|---|---|---|

The following are sample files from the two systems that would supply the data for the data warehouse:

**Mechanical Parts Division Sales System**

| Prod_No | Product_Description | Cost_per_Unit | Units_Sold | Sales_Region | Customer_ID |
|---|---|---|---|---|---|
| 60231 | 4″ Steel bearing | 5.28 | 900,245 | N.E. | Anderson |
| 85773 | SS assembly unit | 12.45 | 992,111 | M.W. | Kelly Industries |

**Corporate Sales System**

| Product_ID | Product_Description | Unit_Cost | Units_Sold | Sales_Territory | Division |
|---|---|---|---|---|---|
| 60231 | Bearing, 4″ | 5.28 | 900,245 | Northeast | Parts |
| 85773 | SS assembly unit | 12.02 | 992,111 | Midwest | Parts |

1. What business problems are created by not having these data in a single standard format?
2. How easy would it be to create a database with a single, standard format that could store the data from both systems? Identify the problems that would have to be addressed.
3. Should the problems be solved by database specialists or general business managers? Explain.
4. Who should have the authority to finalize a single, company-wide format for this information in the data warehouse? Explain your answer.

Datamining is both a powerful and profitable tool, but it poses challenges to the protection of individual privacy. Datamining technology can combine information from many diverse sources to create a detailed "data image" about each of us—our income, our driving habits, our hobbies, our families, and our political interests. The question of whether companies should be allowed to collect such detailed information about individuals is explored in Chapter 15.

## Benefits of Data Warehouses

Data warehouses not only offer improved information, they make it easy for decision makers to obtain it. They even include the ability to model and remodel the data. It has been estimated that 70 percent of the world's business information resides on mainframe databases, many of which are for older legacy systems. Many of these legacy systems are critical production applications that support the company's core business processes. As long as these systems can efficiently process the necessary volume of transactions to keep the company running, firms are reluctant to replace them to avoid disrupting critical business functions and high system replacement costs. Many of these legacy systems use hierarchical DBMS or even older nondatabase files where information is difficult for users to access. Data warehouses enable decision makers to access data as often as they need to without affecting the performance of the underlying operational systems. Many organizations are making access to their data warehouses even easier by using Web technology.

Organizations have used the information gleaned from data warehouses using OLAP and datamining to help them refocus their businesses. For example, PostBanken Norway built a data warehouse that included both internal data and data from external sources such as the public register of households. The company used these data to relate mortgage holders to variables such as age, sex, number of financial products used, and income. The results of the analysis showed that the prime candidates for mortgages were individuals aged 41 to 45, but the bank had been targeting its marketing campaigns toward people under the age of 30. By using the information from the data warehouse, PostBanken improved the quality of sales

## MANAGING CUSTOMER DATA FOR ABN AMRO BANK

Banking is a complex business, particularly when you are as big as the fourteenth-largest bank in the world, have $414 billion in assets, and are operating in a number of countries. ABN AMRO Bank, NV, which is headquartered in Amsterdam, the Netherlands, is also the largest foreign bank in North America with 550 individual clients and assets of $155 billion. Its holdings in the United States include LaSalle bank group in Chicago, Standard Federal Bank in Troy, Michigan, European American Bank in New York, and the financial services firm of Alleghany Asset Management. In this age of very large, complex corporations, all operating in an environment of globalization, the bank found it very difficult to manage its corporate customer relations or even to understand who its customers were and what services they were using.

ABN AMRO has multiple divisions and subsidiaries, each of which operates in multiple locations and maintains its own separate banking relationships with customers. A customer might have accounts with several different ABN AMRO subsidiaries. How can the bank manage these complex customer relationships? ABN AMRO's Chicago-based North American management team took what seemed to it the obvious step. It installed a customer data warehouse.

The bank contracted with consulting firm Ernst and Young to manage its project. The project goal was to bring together the customer data from ABN AMRO's many branches and subsidiaries for enterprise-wide reporting and analysis. To make the new system easily usable, the project focused on the user interface, selecting a product from Cognos of Burlington, Massachusetts, because it was both flexible and intuitive. The project was nicknamed CRISP (Corporate Relationship Information System Platform), and it proved to be a success.

Using such a data warehouse, managers found they could bring the data together so as to better understand the firm's total relationship with each customer. Managers are now able to see what products its customers are using. They can identify which bank branches the customer is working with and the total amount of capital absorbed by each banking relationship. Management is even able to see reports on all customer contacts with individual companies regardless of the bank location or customer organizational unit.

Bank management now is able to take a more relationship-oriented approach to its customers. That means management is able to monitor general customer patterns and trends, regardless of how widespread the customer's organization is. Managers can easily compare the customer's current activities with its past activities and thereby spot any emerging trends, whether positive or negative. Also important has been the ability of managers to judge the risk exposure of the overall customer as well as the profitability of that customer's business with the bank. CRISP has also enabled management to monitor its own performance—its profitability, its revenue by product line; and the concentration of its commitments by geography, industry, and company.

ABN AMRO employees report that the project has enabled them to make faster decisions and to react more quickly when needed. It has improved employee productivity and thereby freed up staff to spend more time developing new customers and strengthening existing customer relations. It has even reduced report generation costs.

**To Think About:** Describe the business and environmental changes and forces that caused ABN AMRO in North America to turn to a data warehouse. What management, organization, and technology issues do you think the bank faced in making the project a success?

*Sources:* Sean Reid, "Warehousing Customer Data," *Strategic Vision,* Summer 2000 and "Big Boost for ABN Fund Firm," cnnfn.com, October 18, 2000.

leads and the conversion of leads to actual sales. In six months, sales increased by 360 percent (Woods and O'Rourke, 2000). The Window on Organizations shows how ABN AMRO Bank, NV benefited from a data warehouse.

## DATABASES AND THE WEB

Database technology plays an important role in making organizations' information resources available on the World Wide Web. We now explore the role of hypermedia databases in the Web and the growing use of Web sites to access information stored in conventional databases inside the firm.

**hypermedia database**
An approach to data management that organizes data as a network of nodes linked in any pattern the user specifies; the nodes can contain text, graphics, sound, full-motion video, or executable programs.

### The Web and Hypermedia Databases

Web sites store information as interconnected pages containing text, sound, video, and graphics using a hypermedia database. The **hypermedia database** approach to information

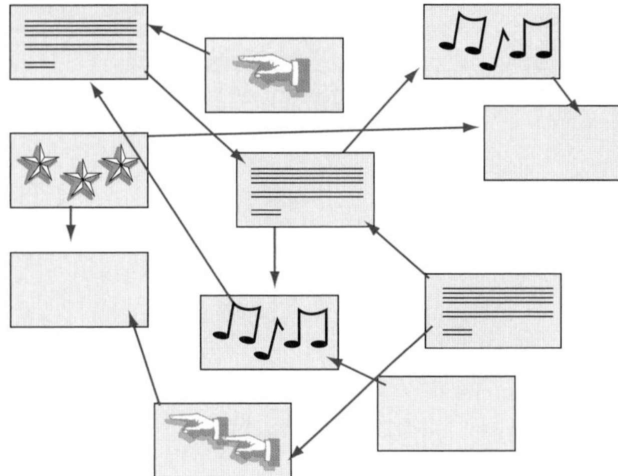

***Figure 7-20*** A hypermedia database. In a hypermedia database, the user can choose his or her own path to move from node to node. Each node can contain text, graphics, sound, full-motion video, or executable programs.

management stores chunks of information in the form of nodes connected by links the user specifies (see Figure 7-20). The nodes can contain text, graphics, sound, full-motion video, or executable computer programs. Searching for information does not have to follow a predetermined organizational scheme. Instead, one can branch instantly to related information in any kind of relationship the author establishes. The relationship between records is less structured than in a traditional DBMS.

The hypermedia database approach enables users to access topics on a Web site in whatever order they wish. For instance, from the Web page from the U.S. National Oceanic and Atmospheric Administration (NOAA) illustrated below, one could branch to other Web pages by clicking on the topics in the left column. In addition to welcoming visitors to NOAA, these Web pages provide more information on NURP (National Undersea Research Program), News from the Deep, Undersea Research Centers, Funding Opportunities, Education, Research Highlights and Products, Undersea Technologies, and Undersea Web sites. The links from the on-screen page to the other related Web pages are highlighted in blue. We provide more detail on these and other features of Web sites in Chapter 9.

## Linking Internal Databases to the Web

A series of middleware and other software products has been developed to help users gain access to organizations' legacy data through the Web. For example, a customer with a Web browser might want to search an on-line retailer's database for pricing information. Figure 7-21 illustrates how that customer might access the retailer's internal database over the Web. The user

*From the U.S. National Oceanic and Atmospheric Administration (NOAA) Web page, you can branch to other Web pages by clicking on the topics in the left column. Web sites store information as interconnected pages containing text, sound, video, and graphics using a hypermedia approach to data management.*

*The Environmental Protection Agency (EPA) Web site allows employees and the general public to access its Envirofacts data warehouse. More and more organizations are using the Web to provide an interface to internal databases.*

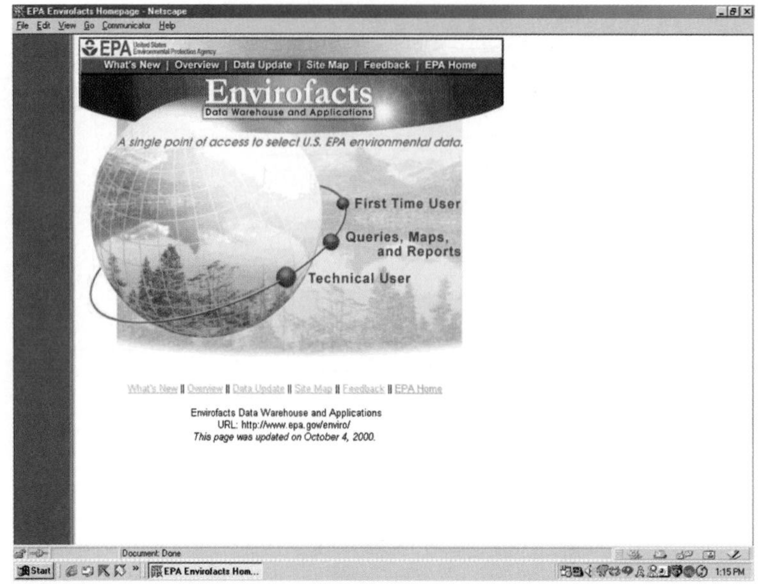


would access the retailer's Web site over the Internet using Web browser software on his or her client PC. The user's Web browser software would request data from the organization's database, using HTML commands to communicate with the Web server. Because many back-end databases cannot interpret commands written in HTML, the Web server would pass these requests for data to special software that would translate HTML commands into SQL so that they could be processed by the DBMS working with the database. The DBMS receives the SQL requests and provides the required data. The middleware would transfer information from the organization's internal database back to the Web server for delivery in the form of a Web page to the user.

**application server**
Software that handles all application operations between browser-based computers and a company's back-end business applications or databases.

Figure 7-21 shows that the software working between the Web server and the DBMS could be an application server, a custom program, or a series of software scripts. An **application server** is a software program that handles all application operations, including transaction processing and data access, between browser-based computers and a company's back-end business applications or databases. The application server takes requests from the Web server, runs the business logic to process transactions based on those requests and provides connectivity to the organization's back-end systems and databases. *Common Gateway Interface (CGI)* is a specification for transferring information between a Web server and a program designed to accept and return data. The program could be written in any programming language, including C, Perl, Java, or Visual Basic.

There are a number of advantages to using the Web to access an organization's internal databases. Web browser software is extremely easy to use, requiring much less training than even user-friendly database query tools. The Web interface requires no changes to the internal database. Companies leverage their investments in older systems because it costs much less to add a Web interface in front of a legacy system than to redesign and rebuild the system to improve user access.

Accessing corporate databases through the Web is creating new efficiencies and opportunities, in some cases even changing the way business is being done. Some companies have created new businesses based on access to large databases via the Web. Others are using Web

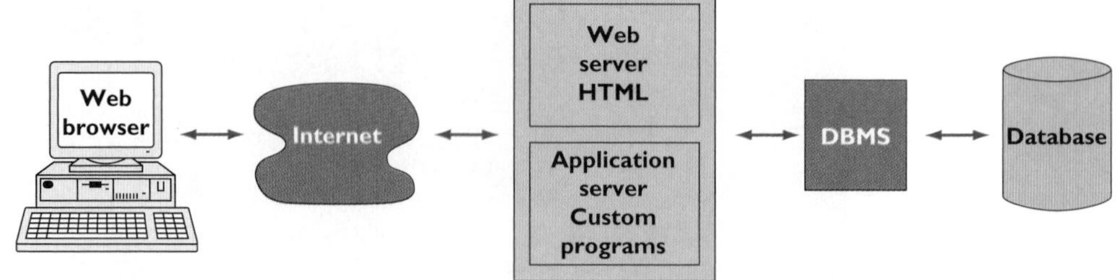


***Figure 7-21*** Linking internal databases to the Web. Users can access and organization's internal database through the Web using their desktop PCs and Web browser software.

## LINKING LEGACY DATABASES THROUGH THE INTERNET

Royal & SunAlliance Financial wanted to sell its customers both life insurance and investment services. However, the Oakville, Ontario, Canada, company faced a major obstacle. Its customer data were stored in two completely separate databases running on two independent mainframes. Given this situation, Royal and SunAlliance CEO Clive Smith observed that the firm can't tell which investment-product clients also have life insurance policies and vice versa. In addition the firm faced the data integrity problem that accompanies customer data being stored on multiple databases. If a change had to be made to the personal information in a customer's life insurance policy, it would have to be made in the other database as well.

Companies facing this problem have only two possible solutions. They could convert all existing data into a single new database, a long and expensive process, or they could connect the existing databases so they can be accessed as if they had been converted. Royal & SunAlliance turned to Unifi software, a product of DWL Inc. of Toronto, Canada. Unifi automates the process of linking existing databases and then makes the data available through a Web interface, leaving the existing databases intact. David Stahl, Royal & SunAlliance's CIO, estimated that building links to the data themselves would have taken 18 months. By using Unifi, the entire process only took six to seven months.

Insurance is not the only business that faces the need addressed by DWL. The Body Shop of Littlehampton, England, has employed DWL to create the appearance of a single system out of its many product databases. The Body Shop, which specializes in natural cosmetics and toiletries, has more than 1,700 stores in 48 countries. It is working on integrating its e-commerce Web site with existing retail and catalog operations to save costs. Many Body Shop sales take place through its retail store outlets. Prior to implementing DWL software in February 2000, it would mail monthly catalogs to its many stores worldwide. This expensive process provided outdated data. Now, the data are all on-line, with accurate and up-to-date information on product availability, internal catalogs, and new offers flowing seamlessly from headquarters to the stores. The Body Shop expects to save hundreds of thousands of dollars by having the information for more accurate orders and swifter delivery.

Both Royal & SunAlliance and The Body Shop are also benefiting from using Unifi's Internet access to their databases. Instead of accessing their databases with expensive proprietary systems, they can use PCs, a Web browser, and a secure protected Internet connection for the task. Before switching to Unifi, Royal & SunAlliance employees communicated through old, hardwired technology across leased telephone lines and terminal screens with special codes that required a lot of training. Unifi's Internet interface is easy to use and requires no training. Scalability is an additional benefit. "With the old technology, we could roll out only a limited number of lines to the offices," says Smith. "With this technology, the number of users is limitless."

**To Think About:** How did Unifi software change the way these companies conducted their businesses? Also, suggest other businesses that would benefit from the use of such software.

*Sources:* Andy Patrizio, "Legacy Data: One Solution for Two Big Problems," *Information Week,* June 6, 2000; and Ian Lynch, "The Body Shop Rethinks E-Commerce Plan," vunet.com, December 20, 2000.

technology to provide employees with integrated firmwide views of information (see the Window on Technology). The major enterprise system vendors have enhanced their software so that users can access enterprise data through a Web interface. Table 7-2 describes some of these applications of Web-enabled databases.

## TABLE 7-2 EXAMPLES OF WEB-ENABLED DATABASES

| Organization | Use of Web-enabled Database |
|---|---|
| IGo.com | Web site is linked to a giant relational database housing information about batteries for computers and other portable electronic devices. Visitors can immediately find on-line information about each electronic device and the batteries and parts it uses and place orders for these parts over the Web. |
| Mobilia.com | Web site links to a database of car memorabilia, including listings for 18,000 model cars. Visitors can search the database for specific model cars or other auto memorabilia. |
| Thomas Register Advanced Order Online | Web site links to Thomas' database of more than 157,000 companies, 400,000 products, 8,000 product catalogs, and 785,000 CAD drawings searchable by product, part number, or brand name. Visitors can search for products, view a company's catalog, request price quotes, make purchases on-line using a credit card or company purchasing card, and track orders. |

## Application Software Exercise

### Database Exercise: Building a Relational Database at Sylvester's Bike Shop

Bicycles have always fascinated Sylvester Jones. Sylvester has won several local, state, and regional bike races, once even competing in the Tour de France. His genuine interest in bicycling and racing led him to open Sylvester's Bike Shop, located in San Francisco, California. Although the store has been open only for a month, Sylvester's bicycle sales have been brisk. Sylvester sells road, mountain, hybrid, leisure, and children's bicycles. Currently, Sylvester purchases his bikes from three suppliers, but plans to add new suppliers in the near future.

Sylvester expects his business to continue to grow and realizes a database will prove useful both now and in the future. Initially, he would like the database to house information about his suppliers and products. The database will contain two tables, a supplier table and a product table. Sylvester also recognizes the benefit of establishing a relationship between the two tables. He would like to perform several queries and produce several managerial reports based on the data contained in the two tables. In the future, he would like to keep information about his customers and will eventually build tables, queries, and reports to achieve this objective.

Using the information in the tables found in the Laudon Web site for Chapter 7, build a simple database for Sylvester. You may wish to use your DBMS's help feature to review the topics of relationships, queries, reporting, and table structures. Once you have built the database, perform the following activities.

1. Prepare a report that identifies the five most expensive bicycles. The report should list the bicycles in descending order from most expensive to least expensive. What is the quantity on hand for each? What is the profit margin for each?
2. Prepare a report that lists each supplier, its products, quantity on hand, and associated reorder levels. The report should be sorted alphabetically by supplier. Within each supplier category, the products should be sorted alphabetically.
3. Prepare a report listing only the bicycles that are low in stock.

## Management Wrap-Up

Selecting an appropriate data model and data management technology for the organization is a key management decision. Managers will need to evaluate the costs and benefits of implementing a database environment and the capabilities of various DBMS or file management technologies. Management should ascertain that organizational databases are designed to meet management information objectives and the organization's business needs.

The organization's data model should reflect its key business processes and decision-making requirements. Data planning may need to be performed to make sure that the organization's data model delivers information efficiently for its business processes and enhances organizational performance. Designing a database is an organizational endeavor.

Multiple database and file management options are available for organizing and storing information. Key technology decisions should consider the efficiency of accessing information, flexibility in organizing information, type of information to be stored and arranged, compatibility with the organization's data model, and compatibility with the organization's hardware and operating systems.

*For Discussion*

1. It has been said that you do not need database management software to create a database environment. Discuss.
2. To what extent should end users be involved in the selection of a database management system and database design?

## SUMMARY

1. *Describe basic file organization concepts and the problems of the traditional file environment.* A computer system organizes data in a hierarchy that starts with bits and bytes and progresses to fields, records, files, and databases. A record describes an entity, which is a person, place, thing, or event on which we maintain information. Each characteristic or quality describing a particular entity is called an attribute. A file is a group of related records. By allowing different functional areas and groups in the organization to maintain their own files independently, the traditional file environment creates problems such as data redundancy and inconsistency, program-data dependence, inflexibility, poor security, and lack of data sharing and availability.
2. *Describe how a database management system organizes and manages information.* A database management system (DBMS) is the software that permits centralization of data and data management. A DBMS includes a data definition language, a data manipulation language, and a data dictionary capability. The most important feature of the DBMS is its ability to separate the logical and physical views of data. The user works with a logical view of data. The DBMS software translates user queries into queries that can be applied to the physical view of the data. The DBMS retrieves information so that the user does not have to be concerned with its physical location. This feature separates programs from data and from the management of data.
3. *Compare the principal types of databases.* The principal types of databases today are relational DBMS and object-oriented DBMS. Relational systems are very flexible for supporting ad hoc requests for information and for combining information from different sources. They support many-to-many relationships among entities and are efficient for storing alphanumeric data that can be organized into structured fields and records. Object-oriented DBMS can store graphics and other types of data in addition to conventional text data to support multimedia applications.
4. *Identify important database design principles and the management and organizational requirements of a database environment.* Designing a database requires both a logical design and a physical design. The process of creating small, stable data structures from complex groups of data when designing a relational database is called normalization. Database design considers whether a complete database or portions of the database can be distributed to more than one location to increase responsiveness and reduce vulnerability and costs. There are two major types of distributed databases: replicated databases and partitioned databases.

   Developing a database environment requires much more than selecting technology. It requires a change in the corporation's attitude toward information. The organization must develop a data administration function and a data planning methodology. There is political resistance in organizations to many key database concepts, especially to sharing of information that has traditionally been controlled exclusively by one organizational group.
5. *Evaluate new database trends.* New tools and technologies provide users with more powerful means to analyze the information in databases and to take advantage of the information resources on the World Wide Web. Multidimensional data analysis, also known as on-line analytical processing (OLAP), can represent relationships among data as a multidimensional structure, which can be visualized as cubes of data and cubes within cubes of data, allowing for more sophisticated data analysis. Data can be more conveniently analyzed across the enterprise by using a data warehouse, in which current and historical data are extracted from many different operational systems and consolidated for management decision making. Datamining analyzes large pools of data, including the contents of data warehouses, to find patterns and rules that can be used to predict future behavior and guide decision making. Hypermedia databases allow data to be stored in nodes linked together in any pattern the user establishes and are used for storing information at Web sites. Conventional databases can be linked to the Web to facilitate user access to the data.

## KEY TERMS

**Application server, 226**
**Attribute, 207**
**Data administration, 219**
**Data definition language, 210**
**Data dictionary, 210**
**Data element, 211**
**Data manipulation language, 210**
**Data mart, 222**
**Data redundancy, 208**
**Data warehouse, 221**
**Database, 207**
**Database (rigorous definition), 209**
**Database administration, 220**
**Database management system (DBMS), 209**
**Datamining, 222**
**Distributed database, 218**
**Entity, 207**
**Entity-relationship diagram, 217**
**Field, 207**
**File, 207**
**Hierarchical DBMS, 214**
**Hypermedia database, 224**
**Information policy, 219**
**Key field, 207**
**Legacy system, 215**
**Logical view, 210**
**Network DBMS, 214**
**Normalization, 217**
**Object-oriented DBMS, 215**
**Object-relational DBMS, 215**
**On-line analytical processing (OLAP), 220**
**Physical view, 210**
**Program-data dependence, 209**
**Record, 207**
**Relational DBMS, 212**
**Structured Query Language (SQL), 210**
**Traditional file environment, 208**
**Tuple, 212**

## REVIEW QUESTIONS

1. Why is file management important for overall system performance?
2. List and describe each of the components in the data hierarchy.
3. Define and explain the significance of entities, attributes, and key fields.
4. List and describe some of the problems of the traditional file environment.
5. Define a database and a database management system.
6. Name and briefly describe the three components of a DBMS.
7. What is the difference between a logical and a physical view of data?
8. List some benefits of a DBMS.
9. Describe the principal types of databases and the advantages and disadvantages of each.
10. Name and describe the three most important SQL commands.
11. What is normalization? How is it related to the features of a well-designed relational database?
12. What is a distributed database, and what are the two main ways of distributing data?
13. What are the four key organizational elements of a database environment? Describe each briefly.
14. Describe the capabilities of on-line analytical processing (OLAP) and datamining.
15. What is a data warehouse? How can it benefit organizations?
16. What is a hypermedia database? How does it differ from a traditional database? How is it used for the Web?
17. How can users access information from a company's internal databases via the Web?

## GROUP PROJECT

Review Figure 7-4, which provides an overview of a human resources database. Some additional information that might be maintained in such a database are an employee's date of hire, date of termination, number of children, date of birth, educational level, sex code, social security tax, Medicare tax, year-to-date gross pay, net pay, amount of life insurance coverage, healthcare plan payroll-deduction amount, life insurance plan payroll-deduction amount, and pension plan payroll-deduction amount.

Form a group with three or four of your classmates. Prepare two sample reports using the data in the database that might be of interest to either the employer or the employee. What pieces of information should be included on each report? In addition, prepare a data dictionary entry for one of the data elements in the database similar to the entry illustrated in Figure 7-5.

Your group's analysis should determine what business functions use this data element, which function has the primary responsibility for maintaining the data element, and which positions in the organization can access the data element. If possible, use electronic presentation software to present your findings to the class.

## TOOLS FOR INTERACTIVE LEARNING

### INTERNET CONNECTION

The Internet Connection for this chapter will direct you to a series of Web sites where you can complete an exercise to evaluate various commercial database management system products. You can also use the Interactive Study Guide to test your knowledge of the topics in this chapter and get instant feedback where you need more practice.

### ELECTRONIC COMMERCE PROJECT

At the Laudon Web site for Chapter 7, you will find an Electronic Commerce project for setting up a business in Australia that requires searches of on-line databases.

### CD-ROM

If you use the Multimedia Edition CD-ROM with this chapter, you can complete an interactive exercise asking you to select the appropriate database management system for a series of business problems. You can also find a video clip illustrating the THOR satellite tracking application based on a relational database management system, an audio overview of the major themes of this chapter, and bullet text summarizing the key points of the chapter.

## Case Study: *Ford and Firestone's Tire Recall: The Costliest Information Gap in History*

On August 9, 2000, Bridgestone/Firestone Inc. announced it would recall more than 6.5 million tires, most of which had been mounted as original equipment on Ford Motor Co. Explorers and other Ford light trucks. Bridgestone/Firestone had become the subject of an intense federal investigation of 46 deaths and more than 300 incidents where Firestone tires allegedly shredded on the highway. The Firestone tires affected were 15-inch Radial ATX and Radial ATX II tires produced in North America and certain Wilderness AT tires manufactured at the firm's Decatur, Illinois, plant. This tire recall was the second biggest in history, behind only Firestone's recall of 14.5 million radial tires in 1978. The 1978 tire recall financially crippled the company for years, and the August 2000 recall threatened to do the same. Consumers, the federal government, and the press wanted to know: Why didn't Ford and Firestone recognize this problem sooner? Let us look at the series of events surrounding the tire recall and the role of information management.

*1988*—Financially weakened from its 1978 tire recall, Firestone agreed to be acquired by Bridgestone Tires, a Japanese firm. To increase its sales, Firestone became a supplier of tires for Ford Motors' new sport utility vehicle (SUV), the Explorer.

*March 11, 1999*—In response to a Ford concern about tire separations on the Explorer, Bridgestone/Firestone (Firestone) sent a confidential memo to Ford claiming that less than 0.1 percent of all Wilderness tires (which are used on the Explorer) have been returned under warranty for all kinds of problems. The note did not list tire separations separately but did say this "rate of return is extremely low and substantiates [Firestone's] belief that this tire performs exceptionally well in the U.S. market."

*August 1999*—Ford Motors announced a recall in 16 foreign countries of all tires that have shown a tendency to fail mainly because of a problem of tread separation. The failures were primarily on the Ford Explorer, and the largest number of tires recalled was in Saudi Arabia. Firestone produced most of the tires. (A year earlier, Ford had noted problems with tread separation on Firestone tires mounted on Explorers in Venezuela and had sent samples of the failed tires to Bridgestone for analysis.) Ford did not report the recall to U.S. safety regulators, because such reporting was not required.

**Early Year 2000**

*February 2000*—Firestone announced its "great pride in the quality and durability of our products." This announcement was in response to an investigation by KHOU-TV in Houston, Texas, into three fatal incidents involving Firestone Radial ATX tires on Ford Explorers. Firestone further stated, "We monitor the performance of all of our tires and, having manufactured more than 12 million Radial ATX tires, we have full confidence in them." The company then offered a free inspection to all owners of Firestone tires.

*May 2, 2000*—Three days after another fatal accident involving Firestone/Ford Explorer tread separations, the National Highway Transportation Safety Administration (NHTSA) opened a full investigation into possible defects with the Firestone ATX, ATX II, and Wilderness tires. The agency listed 90 complaints nationwide including 34 crashes and 24 injuries or deaths. NHTSA also learned of the foreign recalls.

**August 2000**

*August 4*—Sears Roebuck and Co. announced it would cease selling Firestone's ATX, ATX II, and Wilderness tires. At this point the NHTSA had 193 complaints about the tires, including 21 deaths. Firestone reiterated its belief that the tires are safe. Ford stated it was still investigating and could not respond yet.

*August 9*—At a news conference, Firestone announced that it would recall about 6.5 million tires on light trucks and SUVs, because they had been implicated in more than 40 fatalities. The company said it would replace all listed tires on any vehicle regardless of their condition or age. Firestone did say it continued to stand by the tires. Gary Crigger, executive vice president of Bridgestone/Firestone Inc., explained the recall by saying, "At Bridgestone/Firestone, nothing is more important to us than the safety of our customers. We felt we must take this extraordinary step as a precaution to ensure consumer safety and consumer confidence in our brands." One Japanese analyst estimated the recall would cost the company as much as $500 million.

Firestone emphasized the importance of maintaining the proper inflation pressure. Firestone recommended a pressure of 30 pounds per square inch (psi) whereas Ford recommended a range of 26 to 30 psi. Ford claimed its tests showed the tire performed well at 26 psi and the lower pressure provides a smoother ride. Ford also said, "[Ford] has determined that the vehicle maintains good performance characteristics at [30 psi]." However, Firestone claimed underinflation could put too much pressure on the tire, contributing to a higher temperature and causing the belts to separate.

Ford pointed out that although NHTSA had not closed its investigation, the two companies did not want to wait to act. NHTSA had by then received 270 complaints, including 46 deaths and 80 injuries, about these tires peeling off their casings when Ford SUVs and some trucks traveled at high speeds.

*August 10*—Press reports asked why Ford did not act within the United States when it took action to replace tires on more than 46,000 Explorers sold overseas.

*August 13*—The *Washington Post* reported that the Decatur, Illinois, Firestone plant, source of many of the recalled tires, "was rife with quality-control problems in the mid-1990s." It said, "workers [were] using questionable tactics to speed production and managers giving short shrift to inspections." The article cited former employees who were giving testimony in lawsuits against Firestone.

*August 15*—The NHTSA announced it now linked 62 deaths to the recalled Firestone tires. It also had received more than 750 complaints on these tires.

**September 2000**

*September 4*—The U.S. Congress opened hearings on the Firestone and Ford tire separation problem. Congressional investigators released a memo from Firestone to Ford dated March 12, 1999, in which Firestone expressed "major reservations" about a

Ford plan to replace Firestone tires overseas. A Ford representative at the hearing argued it had no need to report the replacement program to the U.S. Department of Transportation because it was addressing a customer satisfaction problem and not a safety issue. The spokesperson added, "We are under no statutory obligations [to report overseas recalls] on tire actions."

Ford CEO Nasser testified before a joint congressional hearing that "this is clearly a tire issue and not a vehicle issue." He pointed out that "there are almost 3 million Goodyear tires on Ford Explorers that have not had a tread separation problem. So we know that this is a Firestone tire issue." However, he emphasized that Ford feels "a responsibility to do our best to prevent . . . this from ever happening again." He offered to work with the tire industry to develop and implement an "early warning system" to detect signs of tire defects earlier. He said, "This new system will require that tire manufacturers provide comprehensive real-world data on a timely basis."

Nasser said his company did not know of the problem until a few days prior to the announcement of the recall because "tires are the only component of a vehicle that are separately warranted." He said his company had "virtually pried the claims data from Firestone's hands and analyzed it." Ford had not obtained warranty data on tires the same way it does for brakes, transmissions, or any other part of a vehicle. It was Firestone that had collected the tire warranty data. Ford thus lacked a database that could be used to determine whether reports of incidents with one type of tire could indicate a special problem relative to tires on other Ford vehicles. Ford only obtained the tire warranty data from Firestone on July 28. A Ford team with representatives of the legal, purchasing, and communication departments; safety experts; and Ford's truck group worked intensively with experts from Firestone to try to find a pattern in the tire incident reports. They finally determined that the problem tires originated in a Decatur, Illinois, plant during a specific period of production and that the bulk of tire separation incidents had occurred in Arizona, California, Texas, and Florida, all hot states. This correlated with the circumstances surrounding tire separations overseas. Firestone's database on damage claims had been moved to Bridgestone's American headquarters in Nashville in 1988 after Firestone was acquired by Bridgestone. The firm's database in warranty adjustments, which was regularly used by Firestone safety staff, remained at Firestone's former headquarters in Akron, Ohio.

After the 1999 tire recalls in Saudi Arabia and other countries, Nasser asked Firestone to review data on U.S. customers. Firestone assured Ford "that there was no problem in this country," and, Nasser added, "our data, as well as government safety data, didn't show anything either." Nonetheless he asked Firestone for an evaluation of tires in Texas, Nevada, and Arizona, where the most failures were occurring. Again, Firestone found no problems. Nasser said Ford only became concerned when it "saw Firestone's confidential claims data." He added, "If I have one regret, it is that we did not ask Firestone the right questions sooner."

*September 8*—The *New York Times* released its own analysis of the Department of Transportation's Fatality Analysis Reporting System (FARS). FARS is one of the few tools available to the government to independently track defects that cause fatal accidents. The *Times* found "that fatal crashes involving Ford Explorers were almost three times as likely to be tire related as fatal crashes involving other sport utility vehicles." The newspaper's analysis also said, "The federal data shows no tire-related fatalities involving Explorers from 1991 to 1993 and a steadily increasing number thereafter which may reflect that tread separation becomes more common as tires age."

Their analysis brought to light difficulties in finding patterns in the data that would have alerted various organizations to a problem earlier. Ford and Firestone said they had not detected such a pattern in the data and the NHTSA said they had looked at a variety of databases without finding the tire flaw pattern. According to the *Times,* without having a clear idea of what one is looking for makes it much harder to find the problem. The *Times* did have the advantage of hindsight when it analyzed the data.

The Department of Transportation databases independently track defects that contribute to fatal accidents, with data on about 40,000 fatalities each year. However, they no longer contain anecdotal evidence from garages and body shops, because they no longer have the funding to capture this information. They only have information on type of vehicle, not the type of tire, involved in a fatality. Tire involvement in fatal accidents is common because tires, in the normal course of their life, will contribute to accidents as they age, so that accidents where tires may be a factor are usually not noteworthy. In comparison, Sue Bailey, the administrator of highway safety, pointed out that accidents with seat belt failures stand out because seat belts should never fail. Safety experts note that very little data is collected on accidents resulting only in nonfatal injuries even though there are six to eight times more such accidents than fatal accidents. Experts also note that no data are collected on the even more common accidents with only property damage. If more data were collected, the *Times* concluded, "trends could be obvious sooner." Until Firestone announced its tire recall in August 2000, NHTSA had received only five complaints per year concerning Firestone's ATX, ATX II, and Wilderness AT tires out of 50,000 complaints of all kinds about vehicles.

Although Firestone executives had testified simply that Firestone's warranty claim data did not show a problem with the tires, Firestone documents made public by congressional investigators showed that in February Firestone officials were already concerned with rising warranty costs for the now-recalled tires.

*September 12*—Yoichiro Kaizaki, president of Bridgestone (parent of Firestone) acknowledged inadequate attention to quality control. "The responsibility for the problem lies with Tokyo," he said. "We let the U.S. unit use its own culture. There was an element of mistake in that."

*September 19*—*USA Today* reported that in more than 80 tire lawsuits against Firestone since 1991, internal Firestone documents and sworn testimony have been kept secret as part of the Firestone settlements. Observers noted that had these documents been made public at the time, many of the recent deaths might have been avoided.

*September 22*—The Firestone tires that were at the center of the recalled tires passed all U.S. government-required tests, causing NHTSA head Sue Bailey to say, "Our testing is clearly outdated."

During September, both Bridgestone and Firestone announced they would install supply chain information systems to prevent anything similar happening in the future. Firestone started spending heavily to overhaul its claims database to make it more usable for safety analysis. Other tire manufacturers have beefed up programs to redesign their plant and manufacturing processes to make safer products at lower cost.

*January 2001*—Yoichiro Kaizaki, the president and chief executive of the Bridgestone Corporation resigned.

**Sources:** Timothy Aeppel, "Under Glare of Recall, Tire Makers Are Giving New Technology a Spin," *The Wall Street Journal,* March 23, 2001; Keith Bradsher, "Firestone Engineers Offer a List of Causes for Faulty Tires," *The New York Times,* December 19, 2000; Miki Tanikawa, "Chief of Bridgestone Says He Will Resign," *The New York Times,* January 12, 2001; Matthew L. Wald and Josh Barbanel, "Link Between Tires and Crashes Went Undetected in Federal Data," *The New York Times,* September 8, 2000; Robert L. Stimson, Karen Lundegaard, Norhiko Shirouzu, and Jenny Heller, "How the Tire Problem Turned into a Crisis for Firestone and Ford," *The Wall Street Journal,* August 10, 2000; Mark Hall, "Information Gap," *Computerworld,* September 18, 2000; Keith Bradsher, "Documents Portray Tire Debacle as a Story of Lost Opportunities," *The New York Times,* September 10, 2000; Ed Foldessy and Stephen Power, "How Ford, Firestone Let the Warnings Slide By as Debacle Developed," *The Wall Street Journal,* September 6, 2000; Ford Motor Company, "Bridgestone/Firestone Announces Voluntary Tire Recall," Ford Motor Company, August 9, 2000; Edwina Gibbs, "Bridgestone Sees $350 Million Special Loss, Stock Dives," Yahoo.com, August 10, 2000; John O'Dell and Edmund Sanders, "Firestone Begins Replacement of 6.4 Million Tires," *Los Angeles Times,* August 10, 2000; James V. Grimaldi, "Testimony Indicates Abuses at Firestone," *Washington Post,* August 13, 2000; Dina ElBoghdady, "Broader Tire Recall Is Urged," *Detroit News,* August 14, 2000; "Ford Report Recommended Lower Tire Pressure," *Associated Press,* August 20, 2000; Caroline E. Mayer, James V. Grimaldi, Stephen Power, and Robert L. Simison, "Memo Shows Bridgestone and Ford Considered Recall over a Year Ago," *The Wall Street Journal,* September 6, 2000; Timothy Aeppel, Clare Ansbery, Milo Geyelin, and Robert L. Simison, "Ford and Firestone's Separate Goals, Gaps in Communication Gave Rise to Tire Fiasco," *The Wall Street Journal,* September 6, 2000; Matthew L. Wald, "Rancor Grows Between Ford and Firestone," *The New York Times,* September 13, 2000; Keith Bradsher, "Questions Raised About Ford Explorer's Margin of Safety," *The New York Times,* September 16, 2000; "Sealed Court Records Kept Tire Problems Hidden," *USA Today,* September 19, 2000; Tim Dobbyn, "Firestone Recall Exposes Flaws in Government Tests," *New York Daily News,* September 22, 2000; and Bridgestone/Firestone, Inc., "Statement of February 4, 2000," Tire-defects.com.

### *CASE STUDY QUESTIONS*

*1.* Briefly summarize the problems and major issues in this case.

*2.* To what extent was this crisis an information management problem? What role did databases and data management play?

*3.* Explain why the growing trend of deaths was not noticed for a very long time. Why do you think it took so long for the issue to come to the attention of the general public?

*4.* List the different databases the parties had at their disposal as the problem grew, and list the data elements in those databases that were key to finding the tread separation problem earlier. Ignoring for the moment all other data problems, what critical data elements were these organizations not storing? For each one indicate why you think it was critical and why it was not being stored.

*5.* Make a list of useful questions that these organizations might have asked of the databases but did not. Discuss why you think they did not ask these questions.

*6.* Evaluate the types of data collected and the questions asked in analyzing the data by each of the key organizations (Firestone, Ford, the U.S. government, and the legal community).

*7.* How did the relationship between Bridgestone/Firestone, Ford, the U.S. government, and the legal community affect the development of the problem? The decisions on action that needed to be taken?

*8.* What data-related changes and improvements did the various parties and reporters suggest? Name other changes you believe should be made.

chapter

# 8 Telecommunications and Networks

objectives

**After completing this chapter, you will be able to:**

1. *Describe the basic components of a telecommunications system.*
2. *Calculate the capacity of telecommunications channels and evaluate transmission media.*
3. *Compare the various types of telecommunications networks.*
4. *Evaluate alternative network services.*
5. *Identify the principal telecommunications applications for supporting electronic commerce and electronic business.*

## Toronto's Electronic Child Health Network Connects Remote Healthcare Workers

The patients of the Hospital for Sick Children in Toronto, Canada, are especially difficult to treat. Many have severe problems such as heart disease, cancer, or conditions requiring complex surgery, but they live up to 100 miles away from Toronto and often move around a lot during the course of their treatment. In trying to provide care for these children, the Hospital for Sick Children found that the linkages among the hospitals it worked with was very poor. When these hospitals had to refer patients to the Hospital for Sick Children or when the hospital sent patients back to them, systems for moving information with the patient were very primitive or nonexistent. Patient records had to be mailed, faxed, or sent by courier.

To promote better patient care, the Hospital for Sick Children created an electronic Child Health Network (eCHN) linking it to three community hospitals, a homecare service, and a dozen physicians. The system is a secure network based on IBM's Health Data Network, a suite of software and hardware products that extracts information from the health records of each of the participating organizations. The system extracts information from the patient record systems of all of these organizations into a single chart that can be accessed by any of the participants using a Web browser. Five IBM RS/6000 servers link five eCHN sites, including a community hospital 60 miles away, with the admissions, registration, and critical information systems of the Hospital for Sick Children.

eCHN also provides a private Web site where remote healthcare workers can update their clinical skills. Some remote hospitals have only two pediatricians.

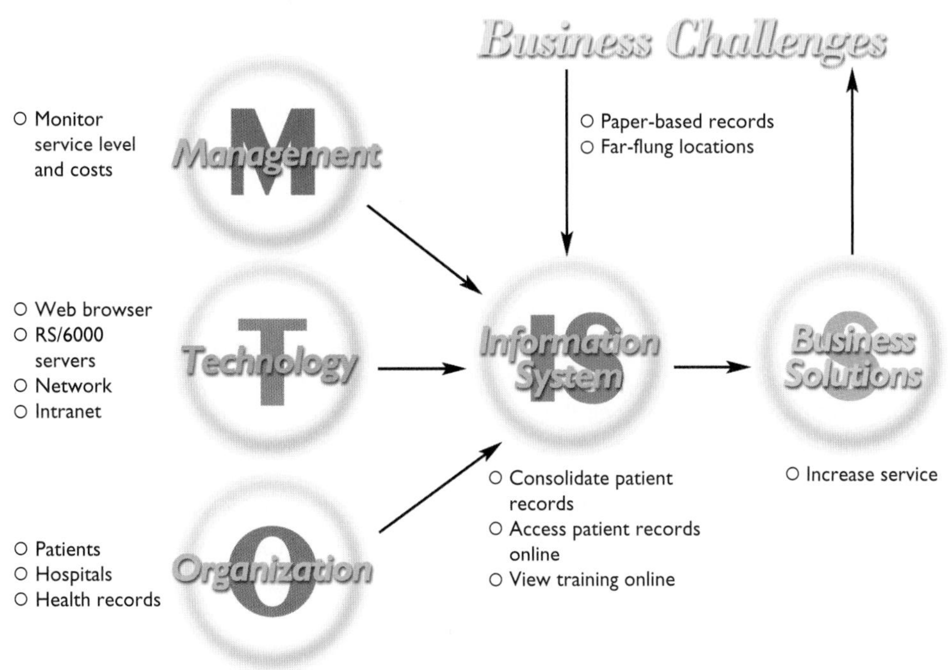


Using eCHN, they can view the seminars and teaching rounds of the Toronto Hospital for Sick Children over streaming video at their convenience.

**Sources:** Walter A. Kleinschrod, "Keeping Workers Connected," *Beyond Computing,* June 2000; and *CHN News,* Vol. 11, December 2000.

## Toronto's Electronic Child Health Network Connects Remote Healthcare Workers

**MANAGEMENT CHALLENGES**

The members of the electronic Child Health Network, like many organizations all over the world, have found ways to benefit from communications technology to coordinate their internal activities and to communicate more efficiently with other organizations. It would be virtually impossible to conduct business today without using communications technology; applications of networks and communications technology for electronic business and electronic commerce are multiplying. However, incorporating communications technology into today's applications and information technology infrastructure raises several management challenges:

## MANAGEMENT CHALLENGES

1. **Managing LANs.** Although local area networks appear to be flexible and inexpensive ways of delivering computing power to new areas of the organization, they must be carefully administered and monitored. LANs are especially vulnerable to network disruption, loss of essential data, access by unauthorized users, and infection from computer viruses (see Chapter 14). Dealing with these problems requires special technical expertise that is not normally available in end-user departments and is in very short supply.

2. **Managing bandwidth.** Networks are the foundation of electronic commerce and the digital firm. Without network infrastructures that offer fast, reliable access, companies would lose many on-line customers and jeopardize relationships with suppliers and business partners as well. Although telecommunication transmission costs are rapidly declining, total network transmission capacity (bandwidth) requirements are growing at a rate of more than 40 percent each year. If more people use networks or the firm implements data-intensive applications that require high-capacity transmission, a firm's network costs can easily spiral upward. Balancing the need to ensure network reliability and availability against mushrooming network costs is a central management concern.

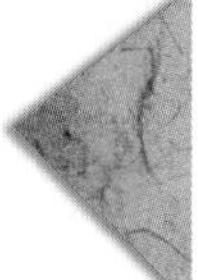

Most of the information systems we use today require networks and communications technology. Companies large and small from all over the world are using networked systems and the Internet to locate suppliers and buyers, to negotiate contracts with them, and to service their trades. Applications of networks are multiplying in research, organizational coordination, and control. Networked systems are fundamental to electronic commerce, electronic business, and the emerging digital firm.

Today's computing tasks are so closely tied to networks that some believe "the network is the computer." This chapter describes the components of telecommunications systems, showing how they can be arranged to create various types of networks and network-based applications that can increase an organization's efficiency and competitiveness.

## 8.1 THE TELECOMMUNICATIONS REVOLUTION

**telecommunications**
The communication of information by electronic means, usually over some distance.

**Telecommunications** is the communication of information by electronic means, usually over some distance. Previously, telecommunications meant voice transmission over telephone lines. Today, a great deal of telecommunications transmission is digital data transmission, using computers to transmit data from one location to another. We are currently in the middle of a telecommunications revolution that is spreading communications technology and telecommunications services throughout the globe.

### THE MARRIAGE OF COMPUTERS AND COMMUNICATIONS

Telecommunications used to be a monopoly of either the state or a regulated private firm. In the United States, American Telephone and Telegraph (AT&T) provided virtually all telecommunications services. Telecommunications in Europe and in the rest of the world traditionally has been administered primarily by a state post, telephone, and telegraph (PTT) authority. The U.S. monopoly ended in 1984 when the Justice Department forced AT&T to give up its monopoly and allow competing firms to sell telecommunications services and equipment. The 1996 Telecommunications Deregulation and Reform Act widened deregulation by freeing telephone companies, broadcasters, and cable companies to enter each other's markets. Other areas of the world are starting to open up their telecommunications services to competition as well.

Thousands of companies have sprung up to provide telecommunications products and services, including local and long-distance telephone services, cellular phones and wireless communication services, data networks, cable TV, communications satellites, and Internet services. Managers are continually faced with decisions on how to incorporate these services and technologies into their information systems and business processes.

### THE INFORMATION SUPERHIGHWAY

Deregulation and the marriage of computers and communications also have made it possible for telephone companies to expand from traditional voice communications into new information services, such as those providing transmission of news reports, stock reports, television programs, and movies. These efforts are laying the foundation for the **information superhighway,** a vast web of high-speed digital telecommunications networks delivering information, education, and entertainment services to offices and homes. The networks comprising the highway are national or worldwide in scope and are accessible by the general public rather than restricted to use by a specific organization or set of organizations such as corporations. Some analysts believe the information superhighway will have as profound an impact on economic and social life in the twenty-first century as railroads and interstate highways did in the past.

**information superhighway** High-speed digital telecommunications networks that are national or worldwide in scope and accessible by the general public rather than restricted to specific organizations.

The information superhighway concept is broad and rich, providing new ways for organizations and individuals to obtain and distribute information that virtually eliminate the barriers of time and place. Uses of this new superhighway for electronic commerce and electronic business are quickly emerging. The most well known and easily the largest implementation of the information superhighway is the Internet.

Another aspect of the information superhighway is the national computing network proposed by the U.S. federal government. The Clinton administration envisioned this network linking universities, research centers, libraries, hospitals, and other institutions that need to exchange vast amounts of information while being accessible in homes and schools.

## 8.2 COMPONENTS AND FUNCTIONS OF A TELECOMMUNICATIONS SYSTEM

A **telecommunications system** is a collection of compatible hardware and software arranged to communicate information from one location to another. Figure 8-1 illustrates the components of a typical telecommunications system. Telecommunications systems can transmit text, graphic images, voice, or video information. This section describes the major components of telecommunications systems. Subsequent sections describe how the components can be arranged into various types of networks.

**telecommunications system** A collection of compatible hardware and software arranged to communicate information from one location to another.

### TELECOMMUNICATIONS SYSTEM COMPONENTS

The following are essential components of a telecommunications system:

1. Computers to process information.
2. Terminals or any input/output devices that send or receive data.
3. Communications channels, the links by which data or voice are transmitted between sending and receiving devices in a network. Communications channels use various communications media, such as telephone lines, fiber-optic cables, coaxial cables, and wireless transmission.
4. Communications processors, such as modems, multiplexers, controllers, and front-end processors, which provide support functions for data transmission and reception.
5. Communications software, which controls input and output activities and manages other functions of the communications network.

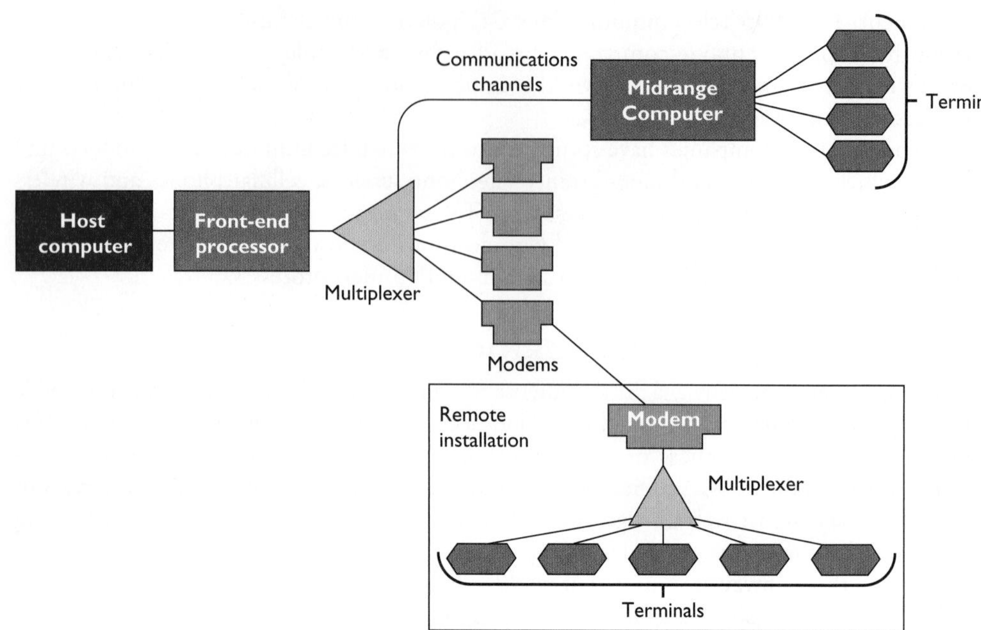


*Figure 8-1* Components of a telecommunications system. This figure illustrates some of the hardware components that would be found in a typical telecommunications system. They include computers, terminals, communications channels, and communications processors, such as modems, multiplexers, and the front-end processor. Special communications software controls input and output activities and manages other functions of the communications system.

## FUNCTIONS OF TELECOMMUNICATIONS SYSTEMS

In order to send and receive information from one place to another, a telecommunications system must perform a number of separate functions. The system transmits information, establishes the interface between the sender and the receiver, routes messages along the most efficient paths, performs elementary processing of the information to ensure that the right message gets to the right receiver, performs editorial tasks on the data (such as checking for transmission errors and rearranging the format), and converts messages from one speed (say, the speed of a computer) into the speed of a communications line or from one format to another. Finally, the telecommunications system controls the flow of information. Many of these tasks are accomplished by computer.

A telecommunications network typically contains diverse hardware and software components that work together to transmit information. Different components in a network can communicate by adhering to a common set of rules that enable them to talk to each other. This set of rules and procedures governing transmission between two points in a network is called a **protocol.** Each device in a network must be able to interpret the other device's protocol. The principal functions of protocols in a telecommunications network are to identify each device in the communication path, to secure the attention of the other device, to verify correct receipt of the transmitted message, to verify that a message requires retransmission because it cannot be correctly interpreted, and to perform recovery when errors occur.

**protocol**
A set of rules and procedures that govern transmission between the components in a network.

**analog signal**
A continuous waveform that passes through a communications medium; used primarily for voice communications.

**digital signal**
A discrete waveform that transmits data coded into two discrete states as 1-bits and 0-bits, which are represented as on–off electrical pulses; used for data communications.

**modem**
A device for translating digital signals into analog signals and vice versa.

## TYPES OF SIGNALS: ANALOG AND DIGITAL

Information travels through a telecommunications system in the form of electromagnetic signals. Signals are represented in two ways: analog and digital signals. An **analog signal** is represented by a continuous waveform that passes through a communications medium. Analog signals are used to handle voice communications and to reflect variations in pitch.

A **digital signal** is a discrete, rather than a continuous, waveform. It transmits data coded into two discrete states: 1-bits and 0-bits, which are represented as on–off electrical pulses. Most computers communicate with digital signals, as do many local telephone companies and some larger networks. However, if a traditional telephone network is set up to process analog signals, a digital signal cannot be processed without some alterations. All digital signals must be translated into analog signals before they can be transmitted in an analog system. The device that performs this translation is called a **modem.** (Modem is an abbreviation for MOdulation/DEModulation.) A modem translates a computer's digital signals into analog form for transmission over ordinary telephone lines, or it translates analog signals back into digital form for reception by a computer (see Figure 8-2).

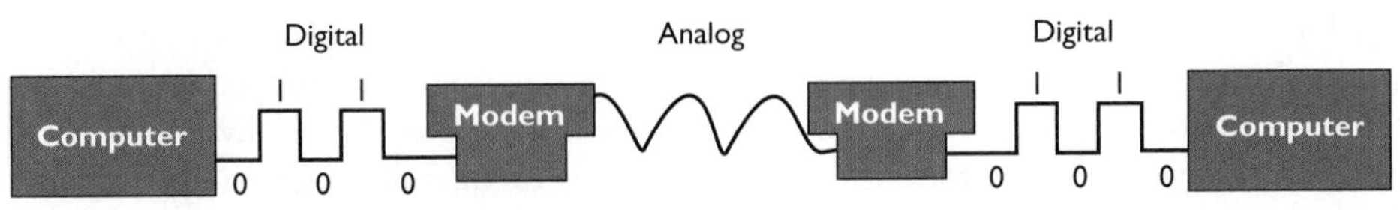


*Figure 8-2* Functions of the modem. A modem is a device that translates digital signals from a computer into analog form so that they can be transmitted over analog telephone lines. The modem also is used to translate analog signals back into digital form for the receiving computer.

## COMMUNICATIONS CHANNELS

Communications **channels** are the means by which data are transmitted from one device in a network to another. A channel can use different kinds of telecommunications transmission media: twisted wire, coaxial cable, fiber optics, terrestrial microwave, satellite, and other wireless transmission. Each has advantages and limitations. High-speed transmission media are more expensive in general, but they can handle higher volumes, which reduces the cost per bit. For instance, the cost per bit of data can be lower via satellite link than via leased telephone line if a firm uses the satellite link 100 percent of the time. There is also a wide range of speeds possible for any given medium depending on the software and hardware configuration.

**channels**
The links by which data or voice are transmitted between sending and receiving devices in a network.

### Twisted Wire

**Twisted wire** consists of strands of copper wire twisted in pairs and is the oldest transmission medium. Most of the telephone systems in a building rely on twisted wires installed for analog communication, but they can be used for digital communication as well. Although it is low in cost and already is in place, twisted wire is relatively slow for transmitting data, and high-speed transmission causes interference called crosstalk. However, new software and hardware have raised the twisted-wire transmission capacity to make it useful for local and wide area computer networks as well as telephone systems.

**twisted wire**
A transmission medium consisting of pairs of twisted copper wires; used to transmit analog phone conversations but can be used for data transmission.

### Coaxial Cable

**Coaxial cable,** such as that used for cable television, consists of thickly insulated copper wire, which can transmit a larger volume of data than twisted wire. It often is used in place of twisted wire for important links in a telecommunications network because it is a faster, more interference-free transmission medium, with speeds of up to 200 megabits per second. However, coaxial cable is thick, is hard to wire in many buildings, and cannot support analog phone conversations. It must be moved when computers and other devices are moved.

**coaxial cable**
A transmission medium consisting of thickly insulated copper wire; can transmit large volumes of data quickly.

### Fiber Optics and Optical Networks

**Fiber-optic cable** consists of thousands of strands of clear glass fiber, each the thickness of a human hair, which are bound into cables. Data are transformed into pulses of light, which are sent through the fiber-optic cable by a laser device at a rate from 500 kilobits to several trillion bits per second. Fiber-optic cable is considerably faster, lighter, and more durable than wire media and is well suited to systems requiring transfers of large volumes of data. However, fiber-optic cable is more difficult to work with, more expensive, and harder to install.

**fiber-optic cable**
A fast, light, and durable transmission medium consisting of thin strands of clear glass fiber bound into cables. Data are transmitted as light pulses.

Until recently, fiber-optic cable has been used primarily as the high-speed network **backbone,** whereas twisted wire and coaxial cable have been used to connect the backbone to individual businesses and households. A backbone is the part of a network that handles the major traffic. It acts as the primary path for traffic flowing to or from other networks. Now competitive local exchange carriers are working on bringing fiber all the way into the basement of buildings so they can provide a variety of new services to business and eventually residential customers. These **optical networks** can transmit all types of traffic—voice, data, and video—over fiber cables and provide the massive bandwidth for new types of services and software. Using optical networks, on-demand video, software downloads, and high-quality digital audio can be accessed using set-top boxes and other information appliances without any degradation in quality or delays.

**backbone**
Part of a network handling the major traffic and providing the primary path for traffic flowing to or from other networks.

**optical network**
Networking technologies for transmitting data in the form of light pulses.

For example, Bredbandsbolaget AB, a Swedish local telecommunications carrier, is running fiber to apartment blocks and wiring buildings to give each household a dedicated 10 megabits per second connection upgradable to 100 megabits per second if required. Users pay 200 Swedish kroner ($25 per month) for the connection and Internet access and an additional charge for hundreds of TV channels, programmable TV, video on demand, telephone services, games, and software rentals. Delays are so infrequent on the Bredbandsbolaget network that customers can't tell whether they are working with software programs delivered over the network or those running on their own hardware. Thus Bredbandsbolaget can offer games and software rental without the user downloading programs, and customers don't need high-powered PCs to use the services (Heywood, 2000).

Currently, fiber optic networks are slowed down by the need to convert electrical data to optics to send it over a fiber line and then reconvert it back. The long-term goal is to create pure optical networks in which light packets shuttle digital data at tremendous speed without ever converting them to electrical signals. Many new optical technologies are in development for this purpose. Next-generation optical networks will also boost capacity by using **dense wavelength division multiplexing (DWDM).** DWDM boosts transmission capacity by using many different colors of light, or different wavelengths, to carry separate streams of data over the same fiber strand at the same time. DWDM combines up to 160 wavelengths per strand and can transmit up to 6.4 terabits per second over a single fiber. This technology will enable communications service providers, such as AT&T, to add bandwidth to an existing fiber optic network without having to lay more fiber optic cable. Before wavelength division multiplexing, optical networks could only transmit a single wavelength per strand.

**dense wavelength division multiplexing (DWDM)**
Technology for boosting transmission capacity of optical fiber by using many different wavelengths to carry separate streams of data over the same fiber strand at the same time.

## Wireless Transmission

Wireless transmission that sends signals through air or space without any physical tether has become an increasingly popular alternative to tethered transmission channels such as twisted wire, coaxial cable, and fiber optics. Today, common technologies for wireless data transmission include microwave transmission, communication satellites, pagers, cellular telephones, personal communication services (PCS), smart phones, personal digital assistants (PDAs), and mobile data networks.

**microwave**
A high-volume, long-distance, point-to-point transmission in which high-frequency radio signals are transmitted through the atmosphere from one terrestrial transmission station to another.

The wireless transmission medium is the electromagnetic spectrum, illustrated in Figure 8-3. Some types of wireless transmission, such as microwave or infrared, by nature occupy specific spectrum frequency ranges, measured in megahertz (MHz). Other types of wireless transmissions are actually functional uses, such as cellular telephones and paging devices, that have been assigned a specific range of frequencies by national regulatory agencies and international agreements. Each frequency range has its own strengths and limitations, and these have helped determine the specific function or data communications niche assigned to it.

**satellite**
The transmission of data using orbiting satellites to serve as relay stations for transmitting microwave signals over very long distances.

*Fiber-optic cable can transmit data that have been transformed into pulses of light at speeds of up to 6 terabits per second. Fiber optic technology is used in high-capacity optical networks.*

**Microwave** systems, both terrestrial and celestial, transmit high-frequency radio signals through the atmosphere and are widely used for high-volume, long-distance, point-to-point communication. Microwave signals follow a straight line and do not bend with the curvature of the earth; therefore, long-distance terrestrial transmission systems require that transmission stations be positioned 25 to 30 miles apart, adding to the expense of microwave.

This problem can be solved by bouncing microwave signals off **satellites,** which serve as relay stations for microwave signals transmitted from terrestrial stations. Communication satellites are cost effective for transmitting large quantities of data over very long distances. Satellites are typically used for communications in large, geographically dispersed organizations that

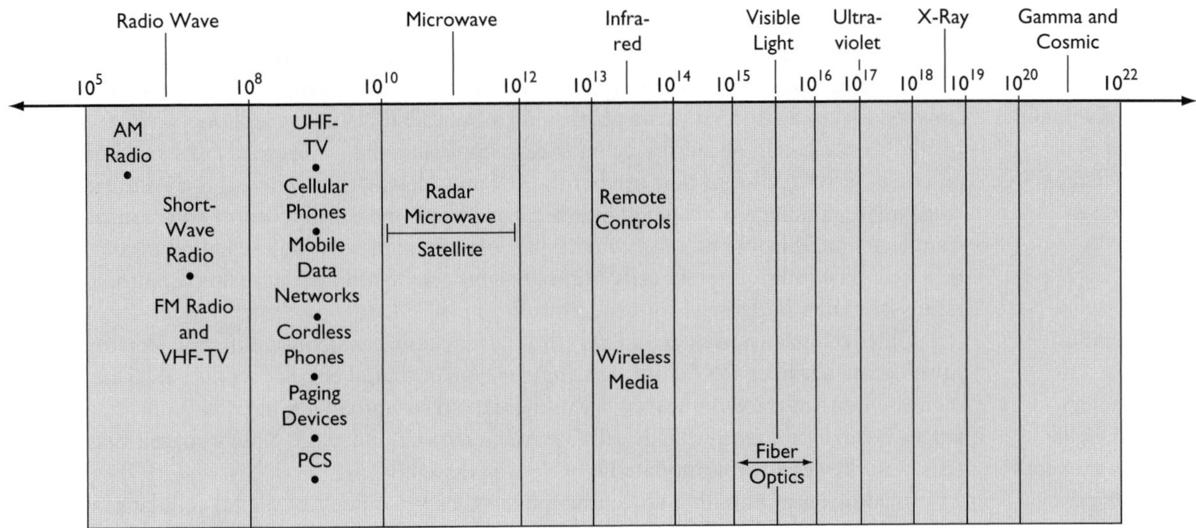


***Figure 8-3*** Frequency ranges for communications media and devices. Each telecommunications transmission medium or device occupies a different frequency range, measured in megahertz, on the electromagnetic spectrum.

would be difficult to tie together through cabling media or terrestrial microwave. For instance, Amoco uses satellites for real-time data transfer of oil field exploration data gathered from searches of the ocean floor. Exploration ships transfer these data using geosynchronous satellites to central computing centers in the United States for use by researchers in Houston, Tulsa, and suburban Chicago. Figure 8-4 illustrates how this system works.

Conventional communication satellites move in stationary orbits approximately 22,000 miles above the earth. A newer satellite medium, the low-orbit satellite, is beginning to be deployed. These satellites travel much closer to the earth and are able to pick up signals from weak transmitters. They also consume less power and cost less to launch than conventional satellites. With such wireless networks, businesspeople will be able to travel virtually anywhere in the world and have access to full communication capabilities including videoconferencing and multimedia-rich Internet access.

Other wireless transmission technologies are being used in situations requiring remote access to corporate systems and mobile computing power. **Paging systems** have been used for several decades, originally only beeping when the user received a message and requiring the user to telephone an office to learn about the message. Today, paging devices can send and receive short alphanumeric messages that the user reads on the pager's screen. Paging is useful for communicating with mobile workers such as repair crews; one-way paging also can provide an inexpensive way of communicating with workers in offices. For example,

**paging system**
A wireless transmission technology in which the pager beeps when the user receives a message; used to transmit short alphanumeric messages.

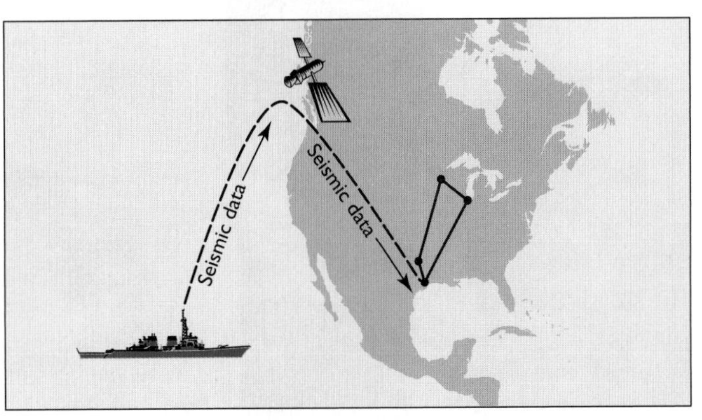


***Figure 8-4*** Amoco's satellite transmission system. Satellites help Amoco transfer seismic data between oil exploration ships and research centers in the United States.

Computer Associates distributes two-way pagers with its CA Unicenter software, which allows computer network operators to monitor and respond to problems.

**cellular telephone**
A device that transmits voice or data, using radio waves to communicate with radio antennas placed within adjacent geographic areas called cells.

**Cellular telephones** work by using radio waves to communicate with radio antennas (towers) placed within adjacent geographic areas called cells. A telephone message is transmitted to the local cell by the cellular telephone and then is handed off from antenna to antenna—cell to cell—until it reaches the cell of its destination, where it is transmitted to the receiving telephone. As a cellular signal travels from one cell into another, a computer that monitors signals from the cells switches the conversation to a radio channel assigned to the next cell. The radio antenna cells normally cover eight-mile hexagonal cells, although their radius is smaller in densely populated localities.

**personal communication services (PCS)**
A digital cellular technology that uses lower-power, higher-frequency radio waves than does analog cellular technology.

Older cellular systems are analog and newer cellular systems are digital. **Personal communication services (PCS)** are one popular type of digital cellular service. PCS are entirely digital. They can transmit both voice and data and operate in a higher frequency range than analog cellular telephones. PCS cells are much smaller and more closely spaced than analog cells, and they can accommodate higher traffic demands.

**smart phone**
Wireless phone with voice, text, and Internet capabilities.

In addition to handling voice transmission, newer models of digital cellular phones can handle voice mail, e-mail, and faxes; save addresses; access a private corporate network; and access information from the Internet. These **smart phones** are being equipped with Web browser software that lets digital cellular phones or other wireless devices access Web pages formatted to send text or other information that is suitable for tiny screens. Some smart phone models offer larger screens and keypads to make Internet access easier. Chapter 9 provides a detailed discussion of how these devices are being used for wireless Internet work.

**personal digital assistants (PDA)**
Small, pen-based, handheld computers with built-in wireless telecommunications capable of entirely digital communications transmission.

**Personal digital assistants (PDA)** are small, pen-based, handheld computers capable of entirely digital communications transmission. They have built-in wireless telecommunications capabilities as well as work-organization software. A well-known example is the Palm VII connected organizer. It can display and compose e-mail messages and provide Internet access. The handheld device includes applications such as an electronic scheduler, address book, and expense tracker and can accept data entered with a special stylus through an on-screen writing pad. The Window on Organizations illustrates Safeway U.K. using PDAs in an electronic commerce application for grocery shopping.

**mobile data networks**
Wireless networks that enable two-way transmission of data files cheaply and efficiently.

Wireless networks explicitly designed for two-way transmission of data files are called **mobile data networks.** These radio-based networks transmit data to and from handheld computers. Another type of mobile data network is based on a series of radio towers constructed specifically to transmit text and data. Ardis (owned by American Mobile Satellite

*The Palm VII PDA, Nokia 7100 series mobile phone and BlackBerry pager are examples of handheld devices for wireless communication. Some of these devices can provide wireless access to the Internet.*

## SAFEWAY U.K. AUTOMATES HOME GROCERY SHOPPING

Anita Morgan likes to keep her house well stocked with groceries, but she no longer has to cruise down supermarket aisles. Nor does she even have to figure out what items she wants. Using a Palm III personal digital assistant (PDA) connected to her telephone, she can submit her order to a computer at the headquarters of Safeway PLC in Middlesex, England, and have the goods packaged and waiting for her to pick up at her convenience. Custom-written software by IBM examines the details of Mrs. Morgan's previous orders stored in Safeway's mainframe database and creates a personalized shopping list based on her buying patterns. The software also suggests other items she might like to try. If Mrs. Morgan wants to purchase something she hasn't ordered from Safeway before and has an empty box or wrapper lying around, she can swipe its bar code into a scanner built into the PDA for Safeway and add the item to her order. And if she doesn't have the item on hand or it lacks a bar code—an apple, for instance—she can describe the item in a free-format field that is transmitted to Safeway as an e-mail: "Five apples."

After Morgan edits her order, she attaches the PDA to her telephone and dials an IBM server in Warwick that is connected to Safeway's IBM OS/390 mainframe. She attaches a note to her order indicating that she will pick up her groceries at a Safeway store in nearby Basingstroke the following afternoon between 3 P.M. and 5 P.M. The next morning, a Safeway Easi-Order specialist at the Basingstroke store logs onto the Warwick server and prints out all the orders that are scheduled for pickup that day. Then the specialist goes up and down the supermarket aisles filling the orders. The specialist logs each item in the order by scanning its bar code with a handheld scanner. After completing each order, the specialist brings it to a holding area in the front of the store, plugs the scanner into a docking station that reads the order, and holds the information until Mrs. Morgan arrives. When Mrs. Morgan picks up her order, she swipes her Safeway account card at the same station. The system matches the order data with her customer data and sends both back to the Warwick server for transmittal to the Safeway mainframe to update the database.

About 1,000 customers at two U.K. Safeways started using the Easi-Order system and six more stores joined the program in 2001. When Safeway first launched the Easi-Order program, its management was concerned that it might lose incremental business of customers making impulse purchases as they cruise through supermarket aisles. Instead, the company found that people allocate only a finite time to shop and they forget things. The Easi-Order program has actually increased customer purchases by 15 to 20 percent. The program has proven so successful that Safeway is giving its customers free Palm Pilots equipped with its customized scanners. Safeway plans to enhance the system to include automated recipes so that customers clicking on a specific recipe would have all the required ingredients automatically added to their shopping carts.

**To Think About:** How did communications technology help Safeway PLC pursue its business strategy? How did the Easi-Order system change the way Safeway conducted its business?

*Sources:* Gary H. Anthes, "Easi-Order," *Computerworld,* March 20, 2000; and Cheryl Rosen, "Here's My Order—And Don't Forget the Milk," *Information Week,* November 13, 2000.

Corp.) is a publicly available network that uses such media for national two-way data transmission. Otis Elevators uses the Ardis network to dispatch repair technicians around the country from a single office in Connecticut and to receive their reports.

Wireless networks and transmission devices are more expensive, slower, and more error prone than transmission over wired networks (Varshney and Vetter, 2000). However, the major digital cellular networks are upgrading the speed of their services (see Chapter 9). (Satellite systems such as Teledesic are also spending billions to provide high-capacity data transmission speeds for multimedia-heavy wireless Internet use.) Bandwidth and energy supply in wireless devices require careful management from both hardware and software standpoints (Imielinski and Badrinath, 1994). Security and privacy will be more difficult to maintain because wireless transmissions can be easily intercepted (see Chapter 14).

Data cannot be transmitted seamlessly between different wireless networks if they use incompatible standards. For example, digital cellular service in the United States is provided by different operators using one of several competing digital cellular technologies (CDMA, GSM 1900, and TDMA IS-136) that are incompatible with each other. Many digital cellular handsets that use one of these technologies cannot operate in countries outside North America, which operate at different frequencies with another set of standards. We provide a detailed discussion of these standards and other standards for networking in Chapter 9.

## Transmission Speed

**baud**
A change in signal from positive to negative or vice versa that is used as a measure of transmission speed.

**bandwidth**
The transmission capacity of a communications channel as measured by the difference between the highest and lowest frequencies that can be transmitted by that channel.

The total amount of information that can be transmitted through any telecommunications channel is measured in bits per second (BPS). Sometimes this is referred to as the baud rate. A **baud** is a binary event representing a signal change from positive to negative or vice versa. The baud rate is not always the same as the bit rate. At higher speeds a single signal change can transmit more than one bit at a time, so the bit rate generally will surpass the baud rate.

One signal change, or cycle, is required to transmit one or several bits per second; therefore, the transmission capacity of each type of telecommunications medium is a function of its frequency. The number of cycles per second that can be sent through that medium is measured in hertz (see Chapter 5). The range of frequencies that can be accommodated on a particular telecommunications channel is called its **bandwidth.** The bandwidth is the difference between the highest and lowest frequencies that can be accommodated on a single channel. The greater the range of frequencies, the greater the bandwidth and the greater the channel's transmission capacity. Table 8-1 compares the transmission speed and relative costs of the major types of transmissions media.

## COMMUNICATIONS PROCESSORS AND SOFTWARE

**front-end processor**
A special-purpose computer dedicated to managing communications for the host computer in a network.

**concentrator**
Telecommunications computer that collects and temporarily stores messages from terminals for batch transmission to the host computer.

**controller**
A specialized computer that supervises communications traffic between the CPU and the peripheral devices in a telecommunications system.

**multiplexer**
A device that enables a single communications channel to carry data transmissions from multiple sources simultaneously.

Communications processors, such as front-end processors, concentrators, controllers, multiplexers, and modems, support data transmission and reception in a telecommunications network. In a large computer system, the **front-end processor** is a special-purpose computer dedicated to communications management and is attached to the main, or host, computer. The front-end processor performs communications processing such as error control, formatting, editing, controlling, routing, and speed and signal conversion.

A **concentrator** is a programmable telecommunications computer that collects and temporarily stores messages from terminals until enough messages are ready to be sent economically. The concentrator bursts signals to the host computer.

A **controller** is a specialized computer that supervises communications traffic between the CPU and peripheral devices such as terminals and printers. The controller manages messages from these devices and communicates them to the CPU. It also routes output from the CPU to the appropriate peripheral device.

A **multiplexer** is a device that enables a single communications channel to carry data transmissions from multiple sources simultaneously. The multiplexer divides the communications channel so that it can be shared by multiple transmission devices. The multiplexer may divide a high-speed channel into multiple channels of slower speed or may assign each transmission source a very small slice of time for using the high-speed channel.

Special telecommunications software residing in the host computer, front-end processor, and other processors in the network is required to control and support network activities. This software is responsible for functions such as network control, access control, transmission control, error detection/correction, and security. More detail on security software can be found in Chapter 14.

### TABLE 8-1 TYPICAL SPEEDS AND COSTS OF TELECOMMUNICATIONS TRANSMISSION MEDIA

| Medium | Speed | Cost |
|---|---|---|
| Twisted wire | 300 BPS–10MBPS | Low |
| Microwave | 256 KBPS–100MBPS | |
| Satellite | 256 KBPS–100MBPS | |
| Coaxial cable | 56 KBPS–200MBPS | |
| Fiber-optic cable | 500 KBPS–up to 6+ TBPS | High |

BPS = bits per second; KBPS = kilobits per second; MBPS = megabits per second; GBPS = gigabits per second; TBPS = terabits per second

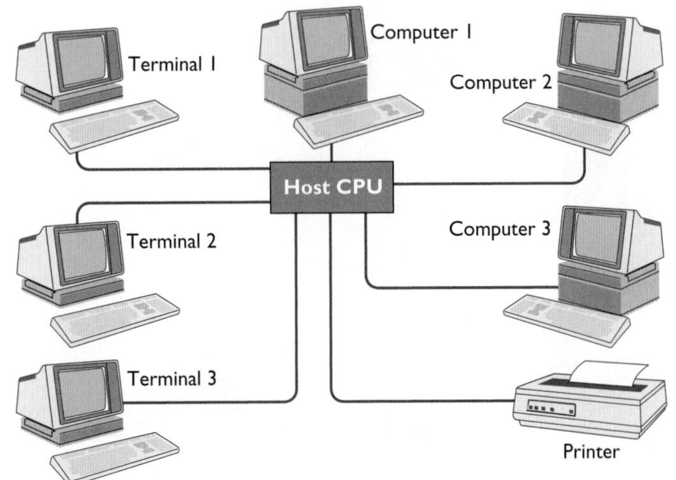


*Figure 8-5* A star network topology. In a star network configuration, a central host computer acts as a traffic controller for all other components of the network. All communication between the smaller computers, terminals, and printers must first pass through the central computer.

## 8.3 COMMUNICATIONS NETWORKS

A number of different ways exist to organize telecommunications components to form a network and hence provide multiple ways of classifying networks. Networks can be classified by their shape, or **topology.** Networks also can be classified by their geographic scope and the type of services provided. This section describes different ways of looking at networks.

**topology**
The shape or configuration of a network.

**star network**
A network topology in which all computers and other devices are connected to a central host computer. All communications between network devices must pass through the host computer.

**bus network**
Network topology linking a number of computers by a single circuit with all messages broadcast to the entire network.

**ring network**
A network topology in which all computers are linked by a closed loop in a manner that passes data in one direction from one computer to another.

### NETWORK TOPOLOGIES

One way of describing networks is by their shape, or topology. As illustrated in Figures 8-5 to 8-7, the three most common topologies are the star, bus, and ring.

### The Star Network

The **star network** (see Figure 8-5) consists of a central host computer connected to a number of smaller computers or terminals. This topology is useful for applications where some processing must be centralized and some can be performed locally. One problem with the star network is its vulnerability. All communication between points in the network must pass through the central computer. Because the central computer is the traffic controller for the other computers and terminals in the network, communication in the network will come to a standstill if the host computer stops functioning.

### The Bus Network

The **bus network** (see Figure 8-6) links a number of computers by a single circuit made of twisted wire, coaxial cable, or fiber-optic cable. All of the signals are broadcast in both directions to the entire network, with special software to identify which components receive each message (there is no central host computer to control the network). If one of the computers in the network fails, none of the other components in the network are affected. However, the channel in a bus network can handle only one message at a time, so performance can degrade if there is a high volume of network traffic. When two computers transmit messages simultaneously, a "collision" occurs, and the messages must be resent.

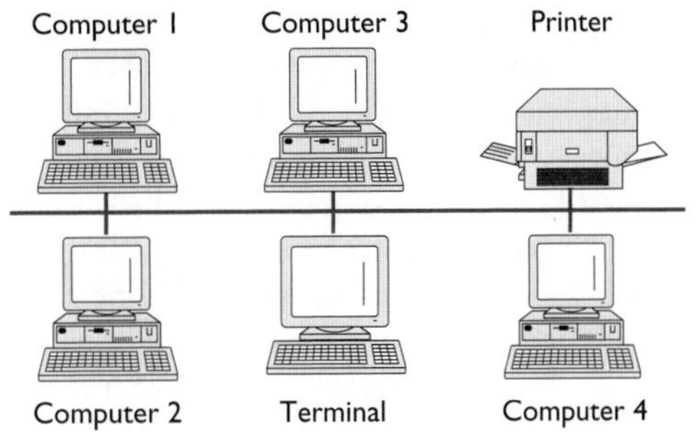


*Figure 8-6* A bus network topology. This topology allows for all messages to be broadcast to the entire network through a single circuit. There is no central host, and messages can travel in both directions along the cable.

### The Ring Network

Like the bus network, the **ring network** (see Figure 8-7) does not rely on a central

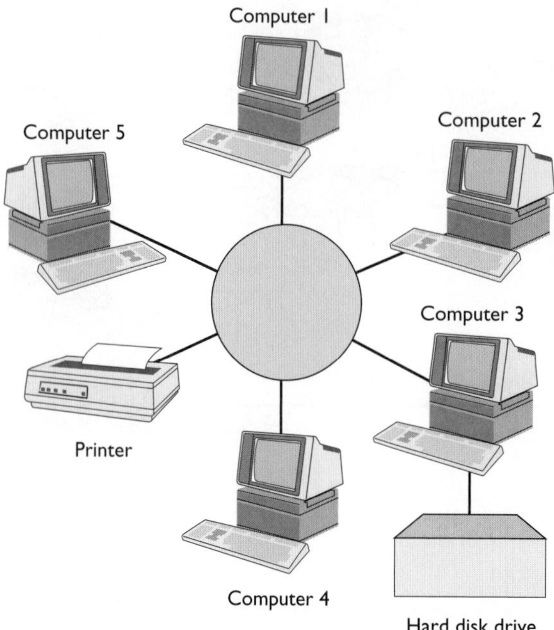


*Figure 8-7* A ring network topology. In a ring network configuration, messages are transmitted from computer to computer, flowing in a single direction through a closed loop. Each computer operates independently so that if one fails, communication through the network is not interrupted.

host computer and will not necessarily break down if one of the component computers malfunctions. Each computer in the network can communicate directly with any other computer, and each processes its own applications independently. However, in ring topology, the connecting wire, cable, or optical fiber forms a closed loop. Data are passed along the ring from one computer to another and always flow in one direction. Both ring and bus topologies are used in local area networks (LANs), which are discussed in the next section.

## PRIVATE BRANCH EXCHANGES, LOCAL AREA NETWORKS (LANS), AND WIDE AREA NETWORKS (WANS)

Networks may be classified by geographic scope into local networks and wide area networks. Wide area networks encompass a relatively wide geographic area, from several miles to thousands of miles, whereas local networks link local resources, such as computers and terminals in the same department or building of a firm. Local networks consist of private branch exchanges and local area networks.

### Private Branch Exchanges

**private branch exchange (PBX)**
A central switching system that handles a firm's voice and digital communications.

A **private branch exchange (PBX)** is a special-purpose computer designed for handling and switching office telephone calls at a company site. Today's PBXs can carry voice and data to create local networks. PBXs can store, transfer, hold, and redial telephone calls, and they also can be used to switch digital information among computers and office devices. Using a PBX, you can write a letter on a PC in your office, send it to the printer, then dial up the local copying machine and have multiple copies of your letter created.

The advantage of digital PBXs over other local networking options is that they do not require special wiring. A PC connected to a network by telephone can be plugged or unplugged anywhere in a building, using the existing telephone lines. Commercial vendors support PBXs, so the organization does not need special expertise to manage them.

The geographic scope of PBXs is limited, usually to several hundred feet, although the PBX can be connected to other PBX networks or to packet switched networks (see the discussion of packet switching later in this chapter) to encompass a larger geographic area. The primary disadvantages of PBXs are that they are limited to telephone lines and they cannot easily handle very large volumes of data.

## AVIS FUELS EFFICIENCY WITH A WIRELESS LAN

Avis Group Holdings has been a leader in using wireless technology in the car rental business. In 1984 it provided its lot attendants with handheld radio terminals to capture data about rental cars as they were returned. Now it wants to speed up customer check-ins and car returns even more by using more high-powered transmission technology.

In July 2000 Avis started rolling out high-speed wireless LANs for about 700 of its car rental locations. The LANs allow Avis personnel to capture digital signatures and billing data from customers in real time and transmit signed documents directly to the firm's enterprise system. The billing data are first transmitted to wireless LAN access points at an airport. From there they are transmitted to a local PC or server, which in turn transmits the data to the firm's enterprise system. Avis's earlier handheld terminals had a transmission capacity of only 8 kilobits per second, which was too low for transmitting digital signatures and other data-intensive applications. The new wireless LANs can transmit data at a rate of 11 megabits per second. The new handhelds also include a bar code scanner and a one-handed keyboard that gives Avis agents more flexibility than the older models.

Symbol Technologies of Holtsville, New York, is providing the technology for the new wireless LAN system, which includes Symbol model 7500 handheld terminals running the Microsoft Windows CE operating system. Avis selected the Symbol Windows CE handhelds because they are flexible, programmable, and can be easily enhanced. It did not want to be locked into something it could not easily change. For example, Avis would like to incorporate the wireless LAN technology into its airport shuttle bus fleet so that customers can check in while proceeding to the Avis rental lot. The terminal on the shuttle would transmit the data to the Avis corporate system once it comes within range of the LAN, which could be several hundred feet.

The Symbol LAN uses the Wireless Ethernet Compatibility Alliance standard, which is endorsed by more than 30 manufacturers. Avis could potentially create partnerships with public-access wireless LAN firms such as MobileStar Network Corporation in Richardson, Texas, and Waport Inc. in Austin, Texas. These firms have set up wireless LANs at major airports to provide travelers with high-speed Internet access for a fee. Avis could potentially receive revenue from partnering with these firms if customers can use the network. Avis is also developing wireless applications for its rental cars. Avis licensed General Motors' OnStar voice-activated onboard computing system, which enables drivers to receive e-mail or new reports from the Internet in their vehicles. The company is also developing applications that would let customers use cell phones or wireless PDAs to rent vehicles or report mileage.

**To Think About:** How do mobile technology and wireless LANs support Avis's business strategy?

*Sources:* Bob Brewin, "Avis Goes Wireless to Fuel Efficiency," *Computerworld*, July 24, 2000, and Tischelle George, "Avis Avoids Mishaps on Acquisition Space," *Information Week*, September 11, 2000.

## Local Area Networks

A **local area network (LAN)** encompasses a limited distance, usually one building or several buildings in close proximity. Most LANs connect devices located within a 2,000-foot radius, and they have been widely used to link PCs. LANs require their own communications channels.

**local area network (LAN)** A telecommunications network that requires its own dedicated channels and that encompasses a limited distance, usually one building or several buildings in close proximity.

LANs generally have higher transmission capacities than PBXs, using bus or ring topologies and a high bandwidth. They are recommended for applications transmitting high volumes of data and other functions requiring high transmission speeds, including video transmissions and graphics. LANs often are used to connect PCs in an office to shared printers and other resources or to link computers and computer-controlled machines in factories.

LANs are more expensive to install than PBXs and are more inflexible, requiring new wiring each time a LAN is moved. One way to solve this problem is to create a wireless LAN, such as that described in the Window on Technology. LANs are usually controlled, maintained, and operated by end users. This means that the user must know a great deal about telecommunications applications and networking.

Figure 8-8 illustrates one model of a LAN. The server acts as a librarian, storing programs and data files for network users. The server determines who gets access to what and in what sequence. Servers may be powerful PCs with large hard disk capacity, workstations, midrange computers, or mainframes, although specialized computers are available for this purpose.

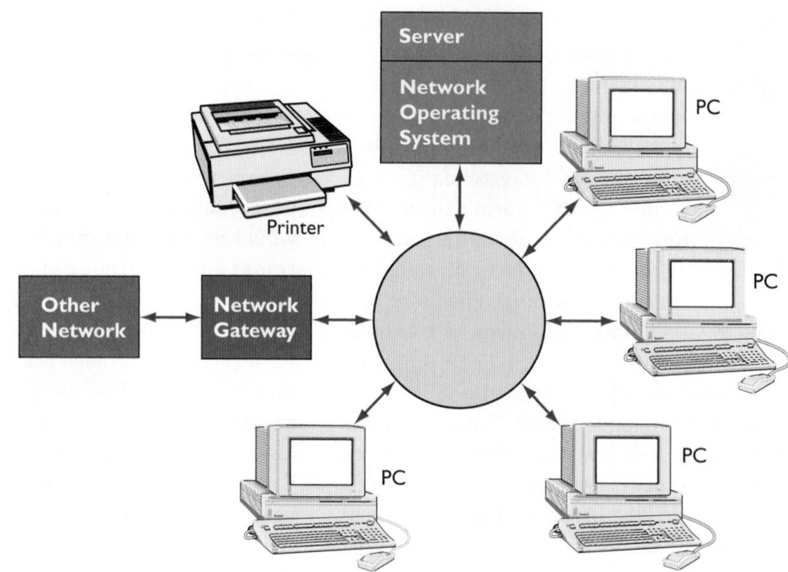


*Figure 8-8* A local area network (LAN). A typical local area network connects computers and peripheral devices that are located close to each other, often in the same building.

**gateway**
A communications processor that connects dissimilar networks by providing the translation from one set of protocols to another.

**router**
Device that routes packets of data from one network to another.

**network operating system (NOS)**
Special software that routes and manages communications on the network and coordinates network resources.

**peer-to-peer network**
Network architecture that gives equal power to all computers on the network; used primarily in small networks.

**wide area network (WAN)**
Telecommunications network that spans a large geographical distance. May consist of a variety of wired, satellite, and microwave technologies.

**switched lines**
Telephone lines that a person can access from a terminal to transmit data to another computer, the call being routed or switched through paths to the designated destination.

**dedicated lines**
Telephone lines that are continuously available for transmission by a lessee. Typically conditioned to transmit data at high speeds for high-volume applications.

The network gateway connects the LAN to public networks, such as the telephone network, or to other corporate networks so that the LAN can exchange information with networks external to it. A **gateway** is generally a communications processor that can connect dissimilar networks by translating from one set of protocols to another. A **router** is used to route packets of data and to determine the next point in a network to which the data should be sent.

LAN technology consists of cabling (twisted wire, coaxial, or fiber-optic cable) or wireless technology that links individual computer devices, network interface cards (which are special adapters serving as interfaces to the cable), and software to control LAN activities. The LAN network interface card specifies the data transmission rate, the size of message units, the addressing information attached to each message, and network topology (Ethernet uses a bus topology, for example).

LAN capabilities also are defined by the **network operating system (NOS).** The network operating system can reside on every computer in the network, or it can reside on a single designated server for all the applications on the network. The NOS routes and manages communications on the network and coordinates network resources. Novell NetWare, Microsoft Windows 2000 Server and Windows 2000 Enterprise Server, and IBM's OS/2 Warp Server are popular network operating systems.

LANs may take the form of client/server networks, in which the server provides data and application programs to "client" computers on the network (see the Chapter 5 discussion of client/server computing) or they may use a peer-to-peer architecture. A **peer-to-peer network** treats all processors equally and is used primarily in small networks. Each computer on the network has direct access to each other's workstations and shared peripheral devices.

## Wide Area Networks (WANs)

**Wide area networks (WANs)** span broad geographical distances, ranging from several miles to entire continents. WANs may consist of a combination of switched and dedicated lines, microwave, and satellite communications. **Switched lines** are telephone lines that a person can access from his or her terminal to transmit data to another computer, the call being routed or switched through paths to the designated destination. **Dedicated lines,** or nonswitched lines, are continuously available for transmission, and the lessee typically pays a flat rate for total access to the line. The lines can be leased or purchased from common carriers or private communications media vendors. Most existing WANs are switched. Amoco's network for transmitting seismic data illustrated in Figure 8-4 is a WAN. When individual business firms maintain their own wide area networks, the firm is responsible for telecommunications content and management. However, private wide area networks are expensive to maintain, and firms may not have the resources to manage their own wide area networks. In such instances, companies may choose to use commercial network services to communicate over vast distances.

## NETWORK SERVICES AND BROADBAND TECHNOLOGIES

In addition to topology and geographic scope, networks can be classified by the types of service they provide.

### Value-Added Networks (VANs)

Value-added networks are an alternative to firms designing and managing their own networks. **Value-added networks (VANs)** are private, multipath, data-only, third-party-managed networks that can provide economies in the cost of service and in network management because they are used by multiple organizations. The value-added network is set up by a firm that is in charge of managing the network. That firm sells subscriptions to other firms wishing to use the network. Subscribers pay only for the amount of data they transmit plus a subscription fee. The network may use twisted-pair lines, satellite links, and other communications channels leased by the value-added carrier.

**value-added network (VAN)** Private, multipath, data-only, third-party-managed network that multiple organizations use on a subscription basis.

The term *value added* refers to the extra value added to communications by the telecommunications and computing services these networks provide to clients. Customers do not have to invest in network equipment and software or perform their own error checking, editing, routing, and protocol conversion. Subscribers may achieve savings in line charges and transmission costs because the costs of using the network are shared among many users. The resulting costs may be lower than if the clients had leased their own lines or satellite services. (Maintaining a private network may be most cost effective for organizations with a high communications volume.) International VANs have representatives with language skills and knowledge of various countries' telecommunications administrations and can arrange access to lines and equipment abroad.

### Other Network Services

Traditional analog telephone service is based on circuit switching, where a direct connection must be maintained between two nodes in a network for the duration of the transmission session. **Packet switching** is a basic switching technique that can be used to achieve economies and higher speeds in long-distance transmission. VANs and the Internet use packet switching. Packet switching breaks up a lengthy block of text into small, fixed bundles of data called packets. (The X.25 packet switching standard uses packets of 128 bytes each.) The packets include information for directing the packet to the right address and for checking transmission errors along with the data. Data are gathered from many users, divided into small packets, and transmitted via various communications channels. Each packet travels independently through the network. Packets of data originating at one source can be routed through different paths in the network before being reassembled into the original message when they reach their destination. Figure 8-9 illustrates how packet switching works.

**packet switching** Technology that breaks blocks of text into small, fixed bundles of data and routes them in the most economical way through any available communications channel.

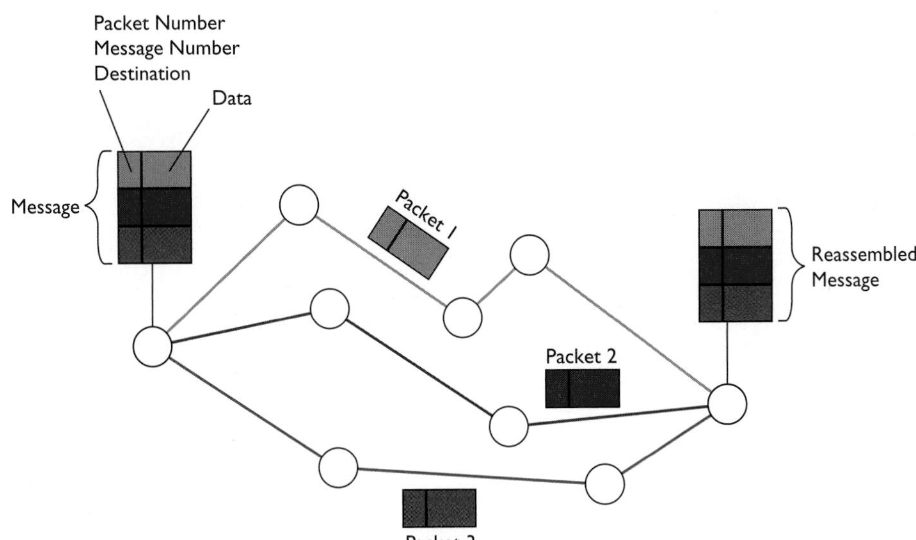


***Figure 8-9*** Packed-switched networks and packet communications. Data are grouped into small packets, which are transmitted independently via various communication channels and reassembled at their final destination.

**frame relay**
A shared network service technology that packages data into bundles for transmission but does not use error-correction routines. Cheaper and faster than packet switching.

**asynchronous transfer mode (ATM)**
A networking technology that parcels information into eight-byte cells, allowing data to be transmitted between computers from different vendors at any network speed.

**Integrated Services Digital Network (ISDN)**
International standard for transmitting voice, video, image, and data to support a wide range of service over the public telephone lines.

**digital subscriber line (DSL)**
A group of technologies providing high-capacity transmission over existing copper telephone lines.

**cable modem**
Modem designed to operate over cable TV lines to provide high-speed access to the Web or corporate intranets.

**Frame relay** is a shared network service that is faster and less expensive than packet switching and can achieve transmission speeds up to 1.544 megabits per second. Frame relay packages data into frames that are similar to packets, but it does not perform error correction. It works well on reliable lines that do not require frequent retransmissions because of errors.

Most corporations today use separate networks for voice, private-line services, and data, each of which is supported by a different technology. A service called **asynchronous transfer mode (ATM)** may overcome some of these problems, because it can seamlessly and dynamically switch voice, data, images, and video among users. ATM also promises to tie LANs and wide area networks together more easily. (LANs generally are based on lower-speed protocols, whereas WANs operate at higher speeds.) ATM technology parcels information into uniform cells, each with 53 groups of 8 bytes, eliminating the need for protocol conversion. It can pass data between computers from different vendors and permits data to be transmitted at any speed the network handles. ATM can transmit up to 2.5 gigabits per second.

**Integrated Services Digital Network (ISDN)** is an international standard for dial-up network access that integrates voice, data, image, and video services in a single link. There are two levels of ISDN service: Basic Rate ISDN and Primary Rate ISDN. Each uses a group of B (bearer) channels to carry voice or data along with a D (delta) channel for signaling and control information. Basic Rate ISDN can transmit data at a rate of 128 kilobits per second on an existing local telephone line. Organizations and individuals requiring simultaneous voice or data transmission over one physical line might choose this service. Primary Rate ISDN offers transmission capacities in the megabit range and is designed for those who use extensive telecommunications services.

Other high-capacity services include digital subscriber line (DSL) technologies, cable modems, and T1 lines. Like ISDN, **digital subscriber line (DSL)** technologies operate over existing copper telephone lines to carry voice, data, and video, but they have higher transmission capacities than ISDN. There are several categories of DSL. Asymmetric digital subscriber line (ADSL) supports a transmission rate of 1.5 to 9 megabits per second when receiving data and up to 640 kilobits per second when sending data. Symmetric digital subscriber line (SDSL) supports the same transmission rate for sending and receiving data of up to 3 megabits per second. **Cable modems** are modems designed to operate over cable TV lines. They can provide high-speed access to the Web or corporate intranets of up to 4 megabits per second. However, cable modems use a shared line so that transmission will slow down if many local users share the cable line. A cable modem at present has stronger capa-

**TABLE 8-2** NETWORK SERVICES

| Service | Description | Bandwidth |
|---|---|---|
| X.25 | Packet-switching standard that parcels data into packets of 128 bytes | Up to 1.544 MBPS |
| Frame relay | Packages data into frames for high-speed transmission over reliable lines but does not use error-correction routines | Up to 1.544 MBPS |
| ATM (asynchronous transfer mode) | Parcels data into uniform cells to allow high-capacity transmission of voice, data, images, and video between different types of computers | 25 MPBS–2.5 GBPS |
| ISDN | Digital dial-up network access standard that can integrate voice, data, and video services | Basic Rate ISDN: 128 KBPS; Primary Rate ISDN: 1.5 MBPS |
| DSL (digital subscriber line) | Series of technologies for high-capacity transmission over copper wires | ADSL—up to 9 MBPS for receiving and up to 640 KBPS for sending data; SDSL—up to 3 MBPS for both sending and receiving |
| T1 | Dedicated telephone connection with 24 channels for high-capacity transmission | 1.544 MBPS |
| Cable modem | Service for high-speed transmission of data over cable TV lines that are shared by many users | Up to 4 MBPS |

bilities for receiving data than for sending data. A **T1 line** is a dedicated telephone connection comprising 24 channels that can support a data transmission rate of 1.544 megabits per second. Each of these 64-kilobit-per-second channels can be configured to carry voice or data traffic. These services often are used for high-capacity Internet connections. Table 8-2 summarizes these network services.

High-speed transmission technologies are sometimes referred to as **broadband.** The term *broadband* is also used to designate transmission media that can carry multiple channels simultaneously over a single communications medium.

**T1 line**
A dedicated telephone connection comprising 24 channels that can support a data transmission rate of 1.544 megabits per second. Each channel can be configured to carry voice or data traffic.

**broadband**
High-speed transmission technology. Also designates a communications medium that can transmit multiple channels of data simultaneously.

### NETWORK CONVERGENCE

Most companies maintain separate networks for voice, data, and video, but products are now available to create **converged networks** which can deliver voice, data, and video in a single network infrastructure. These multiservice networks can potentially reduce networking costs by eliminating the need to provide support services and personnel for each different type of network. Multiservice networks can be attractive solutions for companies running multimedia applications such as video collaboration, voice-data call centers, distance learning (see the following section), or unified messaging, or for firms with high costs for voice services. (**Unified messaging** systems combine voice messages, e-mail, and fax so they can all be obtained from one system.)

**converged network**
Network with technology to enable voice and data to run over a single network.

**unified messaging**
System combining voice messages, e-mail, and fax so that they can all be obtained from a single system.

## 8.4 ELECTRONIC COMMERCE AND ELECTRONIC BUSINESS TECHNOLOGIES

Baxter International, described in Chapter 3, realized the strategic significance of telecommunications. The company placed its own computer terminals in hospital supply rooms. Customers could dial up a local VAN and send their orders directly to the company. Other companies also are achieving strategic benefits by developing electronic commerce and electronic business applications based on networking technologies.

Electronic mail (e-mail), groupware, voice mail, facsimile machines (fax), digital information services, teleconferencing, dataconferencing, videoconferencing, and electronic data interchange are key applications for electronic commerce and electronic business, because they provide network-based capabilities for communication, coordination, and speeding the flow of purchase and sale transactions.

## MANAGEMENT DECISION PROBLEM

### CHOOSING AN INTERNET CONNECTION SERVICE

You run a graphic design company with 15 employees that does page layout and illustrations for magazine and book publishers in many different parts of the United States. You want to take advantage of network services to send files of your illustrations and layout work for your clients to review. The average size of each graphics file you transmit is four megabytes and an average of 25 of these files are sent to clients each day. Schedules are tight and productivity can be impacted if all of your network resources are tied up transmitting files. You are also on a very tight budget. The following network services are available in your area. At its current size, your business could use one dedicated telephone line with software that enables up to 20 employees to share Internet use.

| Option | Transmission Capacity | Cost |
|---|---|---|
| Dial-up service with 56 KBPS analog modems for each employee | 56 KBPS | $40 per month for Internet service + basic $35 per month phone charge |
| ISDN line | 128 KBPS | $100 per month + $300 installation fee |
| Cable modem | 1–2 MBPS | $75 per month + $125 installation fee |
| Synchronous DSL | 512 KBPS sending and receiving | $100 for DSL modem + $175 per month fee |
| T1 line | 1.5 MBPS | $1,200 per month |

1. What is the average amount of time your business would spend daily transmitting files for each of these options?
2. Which of these options is most appropriate for your company? Why?
3. If your business expanded and you had 60 employees and 100 files to transmit daily, which option would you choose?

## ELECTRONIC MAIL AND GROUPWARE

We described the capabilities of electronic mail, or e-mail, in Chapter 6. E-mail eliminates telephone tag and costly long-distance telephone charges, expediting communication between different parts of an organization. Nestlé SA, the Swiss-based multinational food corporation, installed an e-mail system to connect its 60,000 employees in 80 countries. Nestlé's European units can use the e-mail system to share information about production schedules and inventory levels in order to ship excess products from one country to another.

Many organizations operate their own internal e-mail systems, but communications companies such as MCI and AT&T offer these services, as do commercial on-line information services such as America Online and services for accessing the Internet (see Chapter 9). The chapter ending case study looks at the privacy of e-mail messages from a different perspective, examining whether monitoring employee use of e-mail, the Internet, and other network facilities is ethical.

Although e-mail has become a valuable tool for communication, groupware provides additional capabilities for supporting enterprise-wide communication and collaborative work. Individuals, teams, and work groups at different locations in the organization can use groupware to participate in discussion forums and work on shared documents and projects. More details on the use of groupware for collaborative work can be found in Chapters 6 and 12.

## VOICE MAIL AND FAX

**voice mail**
A system for digitizing a spoken message and transmitting it over a network.

**facsimile (fax)**
A machine that digitizes and transmits documents with both text and graphics over telephone lines.

A **voice mail** system digitizes the sender's spoken message, transmits it over a network, and stores the message on disk for later retrieval. When the recipient is ready to listen, the messages are reconverted to audio form. Various store-and-forward capabilities notify recipients that messages are waiting. Recipients have the option of saving these messages for future use, deleting them, or routing them to other parties.

**Facsimile (fax)** machines can transmit documents containing both text and graphics over ordinary telephone lines. A sending fax machine scans and digitizes the document image. The digitized document is transmitted over a network and reproduced in hard copy form by a receiving fax machine. The process results in a duplicate, or facsimile, of the original.

**teleconferencing**
The ability to confer with a group of people simultaneously using the telephone or electronic-mail group communication software.

## TELECONFERENCING, DATACONFERENCING, AND VIDEOCONFERENCING

People can meet electronically, even though they are hundreds or thousands of miles apart, by using teleconferencing, dataconferencing, or videoconferencing. **Teleconferencing** allows

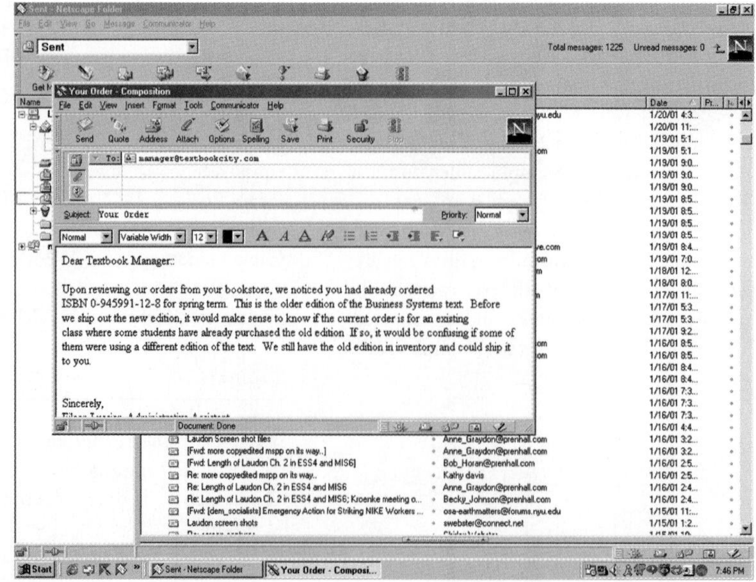


*Netscape Communicator includes e-mail functions such as attaching files, displaying messages, and providing logs of all incoming and outgoing messages. E-mail has become an important tool for organizational communication.*

a group of people to confer simultaneously via telephone or via electronic-mail group communication software. Teleconferencing that includes the ability of two or more people at distant locations to work on the same document or data simultaneously is called **dataconferencing.** With dataconferencing, users at distant locations are able to edit and modify data (text, such as word processing documents; numeric, such as spreadsheets; and graphic) files. Teleconferencing in which participants see each other over video screens is termed video teleconferencing, or **videoconferencing.**

**dataconferencing**
Teleconferencing in which two or more users are able to edit and modify data files simultaneously.

**videoconferencing**
Teleconferencing in which participants see each other over video screens.

These forms of electronic conferencing are growing in popularity because they save travel time and cost. Legal firms might use videoconferencing to take depositions and to convene meetings among lawyers in different branch offices. Videoconferencing can help companies promote remote collaboration from different locations or fill in personnel expertise gaps. Electronic conferencing is useful for supporting telecommuting, enabling home workers to meet with or collaborate with their counterparts working in the office or elsewhere.

Videoconferencing usually has required special videoconference rooms and video cameras, microphones, television monitors, and a computer equipped with a codec device that converts video images and analog sound waves into digital signals and compresses them for transfer over communications channels. Another codec on the receiving end reconverts the digital signals back into analog for display on the receiving monitor. PC-based, desktop videoconferencing systems in which users can see each other and simultaneously work on the same document are reducing videoconferencing costs so that more organizations can benefit from this technology.

Desktop videoconferencing systems typically provide a local window, in which you can see yourself, and a remote window to display the individual with whom you are communicating. Most desktop systems provide audio capabilities for two-way, real-time conversations and a whiteboard. The whiteboard is a shared drawing program that lets multiple users collaborate on projects by modifying images and text on-line. Software products such as Microsoft NetMeeting (a feature of the Windows 98 operating system), Netscape Communicator's Conference, and CU-SeeMe (available in both shareware and commercial versions) provide low-cost tools for desktop videoconferencing over the Internet.

## DIGITAL INFORMATION SERVICES AND DISTANCE LEARNING

Powerful and far-reaching digital information services enable networked PC and workstation users to obtain information from outside the firm instantly without leaving their desks. Stock prices, periodicals, competitor data, industrial supplies catalogs, legal research, news articles, reference works, and weather forecasts are some of the information that can be accessed on-line. Many of these services provide capabilities for electronic mail, electronic bulletin boards, on-line discussion groups, shopping, and travel reservations as well as

*With PC desktop videoconferencing systems, users can see each other and simultaneously work on the same document. Organizations are using video conferencing to improve coordination and save travel time and costs.*

## TABLE 8-3 COMMERCIAL DIGITAL INFORMATION SERVICES

| Provider | Type of Service |
|---|---|
| America Online | General interest/business information |
| Prodigy | General interest/business information |
| Microsoft Network | General interest/business information |
| Dow Jones News Retrieval | Business/financial information |
| Dialog | Business/scientific/technical information |
| Lexis | Legal research |
| Nexis | News/business information |

Internet access. Table 8-3 describes the leading commercial digital information services. The following chapter describes how organizations can access even more information resources using the Internet.

Organizations can also use communications technology to run distance learning programs where they can train employees in remote locations without requiring the employees to be physically present in a classroom. **Distance learning** is education or training delivered over a distance to individuals in one or more locations. Although distance learning can be accomplished with print-based materials, the distance learning experience is increasingly based on information technology, including videoconferencing, satellite or cable television, or interactive multimedia, including the Web. Some distance learning programs use *synchronous communication,* where teacher and student are present at the same time during the instruction, even if they are in different places. Other programs use *asynchronous communication,* where teacher and student don't have person-to-person interaction at the same time or place. For example, students might access a Web site to obtain their course materials and communicate with their instructors via e-mail.

**distance learning**
Education or training delivered over a distance to individuals in one or more locations.

## ELECTRONIC DATA INTERCHANGE

**Electronic data interchange (EDI)** is a key technology for electronic commerce because it allows the computer-to-computer exchange between two organizations of standard transac-

**electronic data interchange (EDI)**
The direct computer-to-computer exchange between two organizations of standard business transaction documents.

*America Online gives subscribers access to extensive information resources, including news reports, travel, weather, education, financial services, and information on the Web. Companies and individuals can use such digital information services to obtain information instantly from their desktops.*

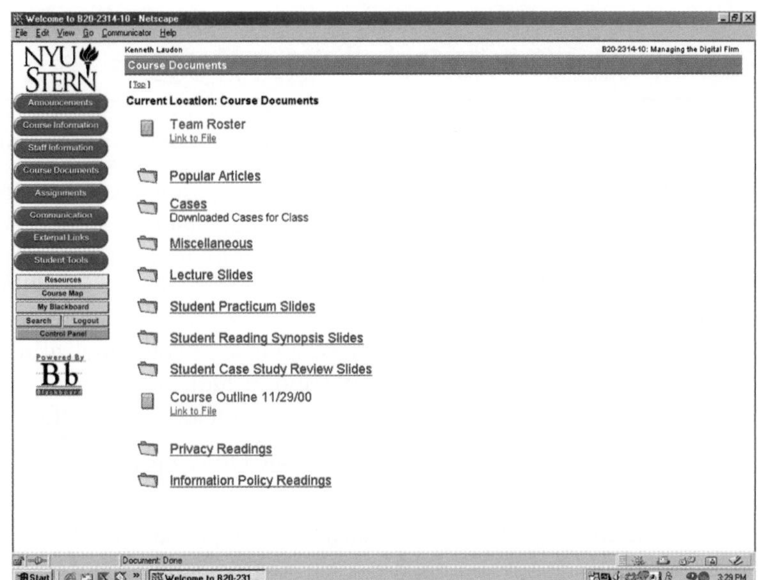


*Instructors can use Blackboard Web-based software to provide their students with course materials, virtual assessments, and a dedicated academic resource center on the Web. Such tools can be used to support distance learning.*

tion documents such as invoices, bills of lading, or purchase orders. EDI lowers transaction costs because transactions can be automatically transmitted from one information system to another through a telecommunications network, eliminating the printing and handling of paper at one end and the inputting of data at the other. EDI also may provide strategic benefits by helping a firm lock in customers, making it easier for customers or distributors to order from them rather than from competitors. EDI can curb inventory costs by minimizing the amount of time components are in inventory.

EDI differs from electronic mail in that it transmits an actual structured transaction (with distinct fields such as the transaction date, transaction amount, sender's name, and recipient's name) as opposed to an unstructured text message such as a letter. Figure 8-10 illustrates how EDI works. Organizations can most fully benefit from EDI when they integrate the data supplied by EDI with applications such as accounts payable, inventory control, shipping, and production planning (Premkumar, Ramamurthy, and Nilakanta, 1994) and when they have carefully planned for the organizational changes surrounding new business processes. Management support and training in the new technology are essential (Raymond and Bergeron, 1996). Companies also must standardize the form of the transactions they use with other firms and comply with legal requirements for verifying that the transactions are authentic. Many organizations prefer to use private networks for EDI transactions, but they are increasingly turning to the Internet for this purpose (see Chapters 4 and 9).

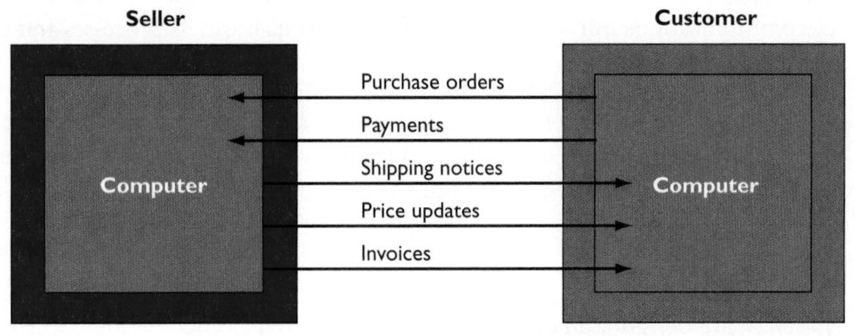


***Figure 8-10*** Electronic data interchange (EDI). Companies can use EDI to automate electronic commerce transactions. Purchase orders and payments can be transmitted directly from the customer's computer to the seller's computer. The seller can transmit shipping notices, price changes, and invoices electronically back to the customer.

## APPLICATION SOFTWARE EXERCISE

### WEB BROWSER EXERCISE: SURFING FOR INFORMATION ON THE WEB

The World Wide Web is a vast repository of information, and vast amounts of information are now retrievable from the Web. The following questions are designed to help you learn more about information technology and test your information retrieval skills.

At the time of this writing, answers to each of the following questions were available on the World Wide Web. Some of the answers you will find quickly; others may take longer to locate. Once you have found the answers, summarize your answers in a report, and submit the report to your professor. You should also include in your report the uniform resource locater (URL) addresses for the Web sites where you located the information.

1. When and where did BMW's Technology Office open? What is the Technology Office's purpose?
2. Locate an article that discusses analog and digital signals. How does the article differentiate analog signals from digital signals?
3. When was the Electronic Communications Act passed? What are its major provisions?
4. When and where is the next IEEE International Conference on Networks scheduled?
5. What is the purpose of the National Telecommunications and Information Administration?
6. What is the purpose of the European Union?
7. When was the International Standards Organization founded? What is its purpose? How does it formulate its standards?
8. Visit an on-line store and determine how much it would cost to set up a PC desktop videoconferencing system.
9. How much does it cost to subscribe to America Online, Prodigy, and Microsoft Network? Compare and contrast the features provided by each service.
10. What is the Internet Society's mission?

## MANAGEMENT WRAP-UP

Managers need to be continuously involved in telecommunications decisions, because so many important business processes are based on telecommunications and networks. Management should identify the business opportunities linked to telecommunications technology and establish the business criteria for selecting the firm's telecommunications platform.

Telecommunications technology enables organizations to reduce transaction and coordination costs, promoting electronic commerce and electronic business. The organization's telecommunications infrastructure should support its business processes and business strategy.

Communications technology is intertwined with all the other information technologies and deeply embedded in contemporary information systems. Networks are becoming more pervasive and powerful, with capabilities to transmit voice, data, and video over long distances. Many alternative network designs, transmission technologies, and network services are available to organizations.

*For Discussion*

1. Network design is a key business decision as well as a technology decision. Why?
2. If you were an international company with global operations, what criteria would you use to determine whether to use a value-added network (VAN) service or a private wide area network (WAN)?

## SUMMARY

1. *Describe the basic components of a telecommunications system.* A telecommunications system is a set of compatible devices that are used to develop a network for communication from one location to another by electronic means. The essential components of a telecommunications system are computers, terminals, other input/output devices, communications channels, communications processors (such as modems, multiplexers, controllers, and front-end processors), and telecommunications software. Different components of a telecommunications network can communicate with each other with a common set of rules termed protocols. Data are transmitted throughout a telecommunications network using either analog signals or digital signals. A modem is a device that translates analog signals to digital signals and vice versa.
2. *Calculate the capacity of telecommunications channels and evaluate transmission media.* The capacity of a telecommunications channel is determined by the range of frequencies it can accommodate. The higher the range of frequencies, called *bandwidth,* the higher the capacity (measured in bits per second). The principal transmission media are twisted copper telephone wire, coaxial copper cable, fiber-optic cable, and wireless transmission using microwave, satellite, low-frequency radio waves, or infrared waves.
3. *Compare the various types of telecommunications networks.* Networks can be classified by their shape or configuration. The three common network topologies are the star network, the bus network, and the ring network. In a star network, all communications must pass through a central computer. The bus network links a number of devices to a single channel and broadcasts all of the signals to the entire network, with special software to identify which components receive each message. In a ring network, each computer in the network can communicate directly with any other computer but the channel is a closed loop. Data are passed along the ring from one computer to another. Networks can also be classified by their geographic scope. Local area networks (LANs) and private branch exchanges (PBXs) are used to link offices and buildings in close proximity. Wide area networks (WANs) span a broad geographical distance, ranging from several miles to continents, and are private networks that are independently managed.
4. *Evaluate alternative network services.* Another way of classifying networks is in terms of the type of services they provide. Value-added networks (VANs) also encompass a wide geographic area but are managed by a third party, which sells the services of the network to other companies. VANs and the Internet use packet switching, which achieves economies and higher speeds in long-distance transmission by breaking messages into small packets that are sent independently along different paths in a network and then reassembled at their destination. Frame relay is a shared network service that is faster and less expensive than packet switching because it does not perform error correction routines.

   **Asynchronous transfer mode (ATM)** can seamlessly and dynamically switch voice, data, images, and video between users and tie LANs and wide area networks together. ATM technology parcels information into uniform cells, each with 53 groups of 8 bytes, eliminating the need for protocol conversion. ATM can transmit up to 2.5 GBPS.

   **Integrated Services Digital Network (ISDN)** is an international standard for dial-up network access that integrates voice, data, image, and video services in a single link. Basic Rate ISDN can transmit data at a rate of 128 kilobits per second on an existing local telephone line.

   Other high-capacity services include digital subscriber line (DSL) technologies, cable modems, and T1 lines. These services often are used for high-capacity Internet connections. Like ISDN, DSL technologies operate over existing copper telephone lines to carry voice, data, and video, but they have higher transmission capacities than ISDN. Asymmetric digital subscriber line (ADSL) supports a transmission rate of 1.5 to 9 megabits per second when receiving data and up to 640 kilobits per second when sending data. Symmetric digital subscriber line (SDSL) supports the same transmission rate for sending and receiving data of up to 3 megabits per second. Cable modems are modems designed to operate over cable TV lines. They can provide high-speed access to the Web or corporate intranets of up to 4 megabits per second. A T1 line is a dedicated telephone connection comprising 24 channels that can support a data transmission rate of 1.544 megabits per second. Each of these 64-kilobit-per-second channels can be configured to carry voice or data traffic.
5. *Identify the principal telecommunications applications for supporting electronic commerce and electronic business.* The principal telecommunications applications for electronic commerce and electronic business are electronic mail, voice mail, fax, digital information services, distance learning, teleconferencing, dataconferencing, videoconferencing, electronic data interchange (EDI), and groupware. Electronic data interchange is the computer-to-computer exchange between two organizations of standard transaction documents such as invoices, bills of lading, and purchase orders.

## KEY TERMS

**Analog signal, 238**
**Asynchronous transfer mode (ATM), 250**
**Backbone, 239**
**Bandwidth, 244**
**Baud, 244**
**Broadband, 251**
**Bus network, 245**
**Cable modem, 250**
**Cellular telephone, 242**
**Channels, 239**
**Coaxial cable, 239**
**Concentrator, 244**
**Controller, 244**
**Converged network, 251**
**Dataconferencing, 253**
**Dedicated lines, 248**
**Dense wavelength division multiplexing (DWDM), 240**
**Digital signal, 238**
**Digital subscriber line (DSL), 250**
**Distance learning, 254**
**Electronic data interchange (EDI), 254**
**Facsimile (fax), 252**
**Fiber-optic cable, 239**
**Frame relay, 250**
**Front-end processor, 244**
**Gateway, 248**
**Information superhighway, 237**
**Integrated Services Digital Network (ISDN), 250**
**Local area network (LAN), 247**
**Microwave, 240**
**Mobile data networks, 242**
**Modem, 238**
**Multiplexer, 244**
**Network operating system (NOS), 248**
**Optical network, 239**
**Packet switching, 249**
**Paging system, 241**
**Peer-to-peer network, 248**
**Personal communication services (PCS), 242**
**Personal digital assistants (PDA), 242**
**Private branch exchange (PBX), 246**
**Protocol, 238**
**Ring network, 245**
**Router, 248**
**Satellite, 240**
**Smart phone, 242**
**Star network, 245**
**Switched lines, 248**
**T1 line, 251**
**Telecommunications, 236**
**Telecommunications system, 237**
**Teleconferencing, 252**
**Topology, 245**
**Twisted wire, 239**
**Unified messaging, 251**
**Value-added network (VAN), 249**
**Videoconferencing, 253**
**Voice mail, 252**
**Wide area network (WAN), 248**

## REVIEW QUESTIONS

1. What is the significance of telecommunications deregulation for managers and organizations?
2. What is a telecommunications system? What are the principal functions of all telecommunications systems?
3. Name and briefly describe each of the components of a telecommunications system.
4. Distinguish between an analog and a digital signal.
5. Name the different types of telecommunications transmission media and compare them in terms of speed and cost.
6. Name and describe the technologies used for wireless transmission.
7. What are optical networks? Why are they becoming important?
8. What is the relationship between bandwidth and a channel's transmission capacity?
9. Name and briefly describe the different kinds of communications processors.
10. Name and briefly describe the three principal network topologies.
11. Distinguish between a PBX and a LAN.
12. What are the components of a typical LAN? What are the functions of each component?
13. List and describe the various network services.
14. Distinguish between a WAN and a VAN.
15. Define the following: modem, baud, protocol, converged network, and broadband.
16. Name and describe the telecommunications applications that can support electronic commerce and electronic business.

## GROUP PROJECT

With a group of two or three of your fellow students, describe in detail the ways that telecommunications technology can provide a firm with competitive advantage. Use the companies described in Chapter 3 or other chapters you have read so far to illustrate the points you make, or select examples of other companies using telecommunications from business or computer magazines. If possible, use electronic presentation software to present your findings to the class.

## TOOLS FOR INTERACTIVE LEARNING

### INTERNET CONNECTION

The Internet Connection for this chapter will take you to the Rosenbluth Travel Web site where you can complete an exercise to analyze how Rosenbluth International uses the Web and communications technology in its daily operations. You can also use the Interactive Study Guide to test your knowledge of the topics in the chapter and get instant feedback where you need more practice.

## ELECTRONIC COMMERCE PROJECT

At the Laudon Web site for Chapter 8, you can find an Electronic Commerce project to assist customers in making tire purchases.

## CD-ROM

If you use the Multimedia Edition CD-ROM with this chapter, you can perform an interactive exercise to select an appropriate network topology for a series of business scenarios and identify the main issue your selection presents to management. You also can find a video demonstrating the capabilities of personal communication services, an audio overview of the major themes of this chapter, and bullet text summarizing the key points of the chapter.

# CASE STUDY *Monitoring Employees on Networks: Unethical or Good Business?*

In the past few years the Internet has become deeply embedded in our business and personal lives. However, corporate managements have been slow to realize that their employees are using their corporate facilities to surf the Net and to use e-mail for personal reasons, and such personal use can be disruptive and costly. The problem has raised serious ethical issues. Is it ethical for employees to use the Net at work for personal purposes, as they often were accustomed to doing with the telephone? Are employers obligated to bear the costs of the private use of their facilities by their employees? Is it ethical for employers to monitor private activities of employees as long as those employees are meeting their work goals?

When employers first became aware of employees using the Internet for personal purposes, the major concern was that employees would visit pornography sites that might offend other employees, perhaps even leading to lawsuits. Then concern grew over too many visits to sport sites and retail outlets. However, it has turned out that the problem is far larger than a little bit of time on a few sites. A number of studies have concluded that at least 25 percent of employee on-line time is spent on nonwork-related surfing. Moreover, investment monitoring and trading has become the most popular nonwork-related Web activity performed by employees on the job, and these visits are apparently mushrooming. New technology, particularly Web technology, makes it easy for people not only to trade but also to research and monitor their own investments much as professionals have always done.

E-mail usage has also exploded as people the world over turn to it for speedy, convenient, and inexpensive business and personal communications. Not surprisingly, the use of e-mail for personal reasons at the workplace has also grown. Managements fear that racist, sexually explicit, or other potentially offensive material might create problems in the workplace and could even result in adverse publicity and harassment lawsuits brought by workers. Companies also fear the loss of trade secrets through e-mail. Personal use of e-mail can even clog the company's network so that the business work cannot be carried out. At Lockheed Martin Corp. an employee sent an e-mail message concerning an upcoming religious holiday to all of the company's 150,000 employees, locking up the entire network for six hours.

A study by the American Management Association concluded that 27 percent of large U.S. companies are now monitoring employee e-mail in some way compared to only 15 percent in 1997. If employees are using company Internet facilities for personal reasons, how much can it cost? The most obvious cost is the loss of time and employee productivity when employees are focusing on personal rather than company business. If you want to calculate the cost to a company, multiply the estimated average amount employees are paid for an hour's work by the number of hours lost for the average employee, and then multiply the results by the number of employees involved. The cost can be very large indeed.

An often-ignored but potentially critical cost is the effect personal Internet activities can have on the availability of the company's network bandwidth. If personal traffic is too high, it interferes with the company's ability to carry on its business. The company may then have to expand its bandwidth, an expensive and time-consuming activity. Norcross, Georgia, civil-engineering firm Wolverton & Associate Inc. installed Telemate.Net monitoring software and found that broadcast.com was the third most visited site and consumed 4 percent of the company's bandwidth. Employees were using it to download music for themselves. E*Trade, which soaked up another 3 percent of Wolverton's bandwidth, is just one of many on-line securities trading sites that employees were visiting. Douglas Dahlberg, Wolverton's IT manager, points out that bandwidth is critical to the company's operations, because Wolverton engineers regularly send very large data-laden CAD files to their clients through e-mail.

Too much time on personal business, Internet or not, can mean lost revenue or overcharges to clients. Some employees may be charging time they spend trading stocks or pursuing other personal business to clients, thus overcharging the clients.

When employees access the Web using employer facilities, anything they do on the Web, including anything illegal, carries the company's name. Therefore, the employer can be traced and held liable. However, even if the company is found not to be liable, responding to lawsuits will cost the company tens of thousands of dollars at a minimum. In addition, lawsuits often result in adverse publicity for the company regardless of outcome. Even if lawsuits do not result, companies are often embarrassed by the publicity that can surround the on-line actions by a company's employees. Problems can arise not only from illegalities but also through very legal activities, such as employee participation in chat rooms society finds unacceptable. For example, employee participation in white power or anti-Semitic chat rooms can produce a public relations nightmare.

How have the managers of some companies addressed these problems? Consultants in this field recommend that companies begin with a written corporate policy. (Studies show that relatively few companies have written Internet-usage policies that specifically address such problems as on-line investing during work.)

What should these policies contain? They must include explicit ground rules, rules written in clear, easily understood language. They should state, by position or level, who has the right to access what and under what circumstances they may access it. Naturally, the rules must be tailored to the specific organization, because different companies may need to access different Web materials as part of their businesses.

Some companies want to ban all personal activities—zero tolerance. American Fast Freight policy, for example, bans any on-line activity "not specifically and exclusively work related." Many companies reject this zero-tolerance approach because they believe they must allow employees the ability to conduct some personal business during working hours. Bell South had once instituted a zero-tolerance policy, but it softened that policy in the summer of 1998. Management had received many complaints from its employees. For example, some said they were afraid to give their business e-mail address for simple things like weekend soccer club notifications. Under Bell South's new policy, when employees log on they must read a warning about misuse of the Internet and e-mail and then click "OK" before they are allowed to continue. In this manner employees are repeatedly reminded to limit their personal activities. Employees also know by the warning screen that they might be monitored.

Clear policy rules and guidelines can be very difficult to write. An individual act, such as a visit to a stockbroker to execute an order, may be acceptable, whereas repeated visits in order to monitor that stock might not be. Many find it impossible to draw a clear line between what is acceptable and what constitutes too much. For example Boeing Corp. specifically allows employees to use the Internet, e-mail, and even fax machines for personal purposes, but the guidelines are vague, saying the use must be of "reasonable duration and frequency." Such blurry terms may be difficult for employees and employers to apply fairly.

How valuable are policies and warnings? They do warn employees, which hopefully reduces misuse. At the same time, they protect the company from any lawsuits by employees if the company does take action. In one instance Columbia/MCAHealthcare Corp. warned employees that, "It is sometimes necessary for authorized personnel to access and monitor their contents," adding that "in some situations the company may be required to publicly disclose e-mail messages, even those marked private." Some companies follow a potentially more effective strategy, combining policies and warnings with filtering or monitoring software.

One approach that some companies use is to block all employee access to specific sites. Other solutions short of total blockage also exist. Dahlberg solved his music-downloading problem by removing RealAudio music playing capability from all of Wolverton's systems.

Another approach used by many companies is to limit the Web sites employees can visit. SurfWatch software can be used by employers to allow visits to certain sites, such as investment sites, only during specific hours, such as during the lunch hour and before and after normal working hours.

Many companies are turning to software packages to monitor the Internet activities of their employees. Content Technologies produces a software package titled MailSweeper that automatically examines outgoing e-mail messages for language that the company wants to ban or at least to examine. Fearing uses of the Internet for other-than-business purposes, George Brandt, the business manager at KBHK-TV, San Francisco, decided to use Elron CommandView Internet Manager to monitor employee Internet usage. This software monitors Internet usage, records the data, and then enables managers to print detailed analyses of that usage. Managers can determine who visits what sites, how often an individual or a group visits any specific site and how long those visits are. At first Brandt found extensive recreational surfing. Soon, however, once people were fully aware that they were being monitored, such usage clearly declined, and concurrently, employee productivity increased.

A number of corporations are trying to limit on-line personal activity to an acceptable amount of time rather than trying to shut if off completely. This policy is a natural extension of one many employers followed well before the Internet was available when they allowed employees to take care of personal business during working hours within limits. In the minds of many, an absolute ban could create a situation in which employees would simply try to subvert the policy, thus creating an even worse problem. Cellular One developed a rule-of-thumb measure of how much time is reasonable. Employees spending more than half an hour on personal or recreational browsing will likely end up on a list of potential Internet abusers. The individuals who are judged as having abused the privilege may have their Internet access taken away. American Fast Freight established a new policy that prohibits employees from visiting on-line investing sites during working hours but allows it during lunch and before and after work.

Some companies are occasionally turning to the ultimate punishment, firing employees judged to be offenders. Some managers consider that firing sends a strong, quick message to the remaining employees. In July 2000 Dow Chemical fired 50 workers and disciplined 200 others after an investigation of employee e-mail found that employees at all levels had sent pornography and violent images from company computers. The New York Times Company fired more than 20 employees from its Norfolk, Virginia, payroll center in early December 1999 for "inappropriate and offensive" e-mails.

No solution is problem free. Instituting any policy can create a great deal of controversy and may even result in lawsuits, particularly if employees have not been clearly warned about a new policy. Oftentimes, employers hear charges of unethical or improper spying from their staffs. Even warnings do not always work. Wolverton's Dahlberg warned the company's small staff of only 36 employees that they would be monitored before the company installed the monitoring software. But warnings "just mustn't sink in," said Dahlberg. "I can see every little Web page you read—and still there were problems."

**Sources:** Sally McGrane, "A Little E-Mail (Or a Lot of It) Eases the Workday," *The New York Times,* March 8, 2001; "Dow Chemical Fires 50 Workers After E-mail Investigation," *SiliconValley.com,* July 27, 2000; Jesse Berst, "How to Spy on Your Employees," *MSNBC Technology,* August 21, 2000; "U.S. Web Use Mostly at Work," Reuters, April 6, 2000; Michael J. McCarthy, "Web Surfers Beware: The Company Tech May Be a Secret Agent," *The Wall Street Journal,* January 10, 2000, "How One Firm Tracks Ethics Electronically," *The Wall Street Journal,* October 21, 1999, "Now the Boss Knows Where You're Clicking," *The Wall Street Journal,* October 21, 1999, and "Virtual Morality: A New Workplace Quandary," *The Wall Street Journal,* October 21, 1999; Stacy Collett, "Net Managers Battle Online Trading Boom," *Computerworld,* July 5, 1999; Robert D. Hershey Jr., "Some Abandon the Water Cooler for Stock Trading on the Internet," *The New York Times,* May 20, 1999; and Nick Wingfield, "More Companies Monitor Employees' E-mail," *The Wall Street Journal,* December 2, 1999.

### *CASE STUDY QUESTIONS*

1. Is it ethical for employers simply to check e-mail on a fishing expedition (that is, without having any specific reason to suspect that the employee has a problem that needs to be addressed)? Explain your answer.
2. If employees complain about an undue invasion of privacy, how can management determine whether the employees' complaints are legitimate?
3. Write a rationale that would ban all employee personal use of the Internet, including e-mail and the Web.
4. Evaluate as an effective tool a zero-tolerance position (firing of employees any time an Internet access rule is broken). If you do not believe zero tolerance is an appropriate policy, under what circumstances would you support firing an employee for using the Internet or e-mail while on the job?
5. Write what you consider to be an effective e-mail and Web-use policy for a company. Briefly describe the company and explain your reasoning for its details.

chapter

# 9 The Internet and the New Information Technology Infrastructure

objectives

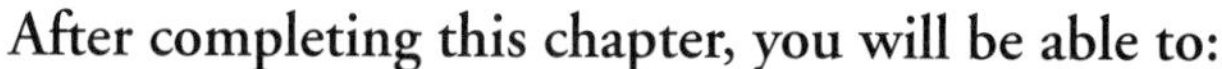

**After completing this chapter, you will be able to:**

1. *Identify the features of the new information technology (IT) infrastructure and important connectivity standards.*
2. *Describe how the Internet works and identify its major capabilities.*
3. *Evaluate the benefits the Internet offers organizations.*
4. *Describe the principal technologies for supporting electronic commerce.*
5. *Analyze the management problems raised by the new IT infrastructure and suggest solutions.*

## On the Road with AMB Property Management

Regional managers at AMB Property Management, a San Francisco real estate investment trust, spend between 40 and 60 percent of their working lives on the road. They require time-sensitive financial information in order to do their jobs, yet they can't always get to their desktops. The company found a solution by equipping them with Palm VII handheld wireless devices.

The Palm devices include wireless portal tools that allows users to access information from a wireless portal server using wireless networks and equipment. Managers can use the portal to obtain up-to-date reports on vacancies, lease expirations, payments due the company, and other critical operational data. These data are the same data that other AMB managers and property management partners can access from their desktops and they are never more than one day old.

AMB organized this information according to markets and geographic locations to make it easier for managers to find the detailed information they need in their jobs.

AMB uses Coreport from Corechange Inc. to provide the framework for managing access to business information and applications through a single point of access for both wired desktops and wireless devices. Coreport incorporates rules for determining who in the organization is authorized to access its information and what applications and pieces of information each user is allowed to see. Coreport can translate data from an organization's internal back-end systems into HTML, XML, and Voice HTML, a new standard for translating text to speech. The software can present the same personalized user experience on a wide range of wireless devices, including Pocket PC, Palm, and Rim systems as well as Web-enabled cell phones using the Wireless Application Protocol (WAP) and I-mode standards.

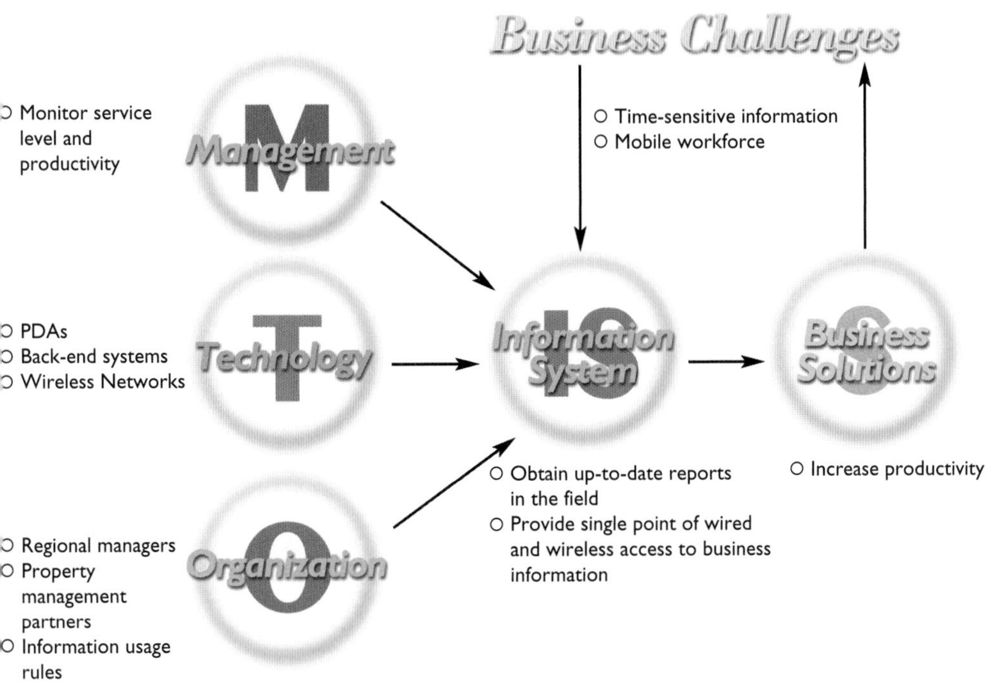


**Sources:** Peter Ruber, "Business Information at Hand," *Knowledge Management,* January 2001; and "Corechange Launches Coreport 3g," Corechange Public Relations, January 23, 2001.

## MANAGEMENT CHALLENGES

Like AMB Property Management, many companies are extending their information technology (IT) infrastructures to include mobile computing devices, access to the Internet, and electronic links to other organizations. Electronic commerce, electronic business, and the emerging digital firm require a new IT infrastructure that can integrate information from a variety of sources and applications. However, using Internet technology and this new IT infrastructure to digitally enable the firm raises the following management challenges:

1. **Taking a broader perspective to infrastructure development.** Electronic commerce, electronic business, and the digital firm require an IT infrastructure that can coordinate commerce-related transactions and operational activities across business processes and perhaps link the firm to others in its industry. The new IT infrastructure for the digitally-enabled firm connects the whole enterprise and links with other infrastructures, including those of other organizations and the public Internet. Management can no longer think in terms of isolated networks and applications, or technologies confined to organizational boundaries.

2. **Selecting technologies for the new IT infrastructure.** Internet technology, XML, and Java can only provide limited connectivity and application integration. Many firms have major applications where disparate hardware, software, and network components must be coordinated through other means. Networks based on one standard may not be able to be linked to those based on another without additional equipment, expense, and management overhead. Mobile computing devices may need to be integrated with corporate databases. Integrating business applications requires software tools that can support the firm's business processes and data structures, and these may not always provide the level of application integration desired. Networks that meet today's requirements may lack the connectivity for domestic or global expansion in the future. Managers may have trouble choosing the right set of technologies for the firm's IT infrastructure.

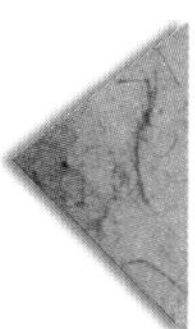

# 9.1 THE NEW INFORMATION TECHNOLOGY (IT) INFRASTRUCTURE FOR THE DIGITAL FIRM

Today's firms can use the information technologies we have described in previous chapters to create an information technology (IT) infrastructure capable of coordinating the activities of entire firms and even entire industries. By enabling companies to radically reduce their agency and transaction costs, this new IT infrastructure provides a broad platform for electronic commerce, electronic business, and the emerging digital firm. This new IT infrastructure is based on powerful networks and Internet technology.

## ENTERPRISE NETWORKING AND INTERNETWORKING

Figure 9-1 illustrates the new IT infrastructure. The new IT infrastructure uses a mixture of computer hardware supplied by different vendors. Large, complex databases that need central storage are found on mainframes or specialized servers, whereas smaller databases and parts of large databases are loaded on PCs and workstations. Client/server computing often is used to distribute more processing power to the desktop. The desktop itself has been extended to a larger workspace that includes mobile personal information devices such as programmable cell phones, personal digital assistants (PDAs), pagers, and other information appliances. This new IT infrastructure also incorporates public infrastructures, such as the telephone system, the Internet, and public network services. Internet technology plays a pivotal role in this new infrastructure as the main communication channel with customers, employees, vendors, and distributors.

In the past, firms generally built their own software and developed their own computing facilities. As today's firms move toward this new infrastructure, their information systems

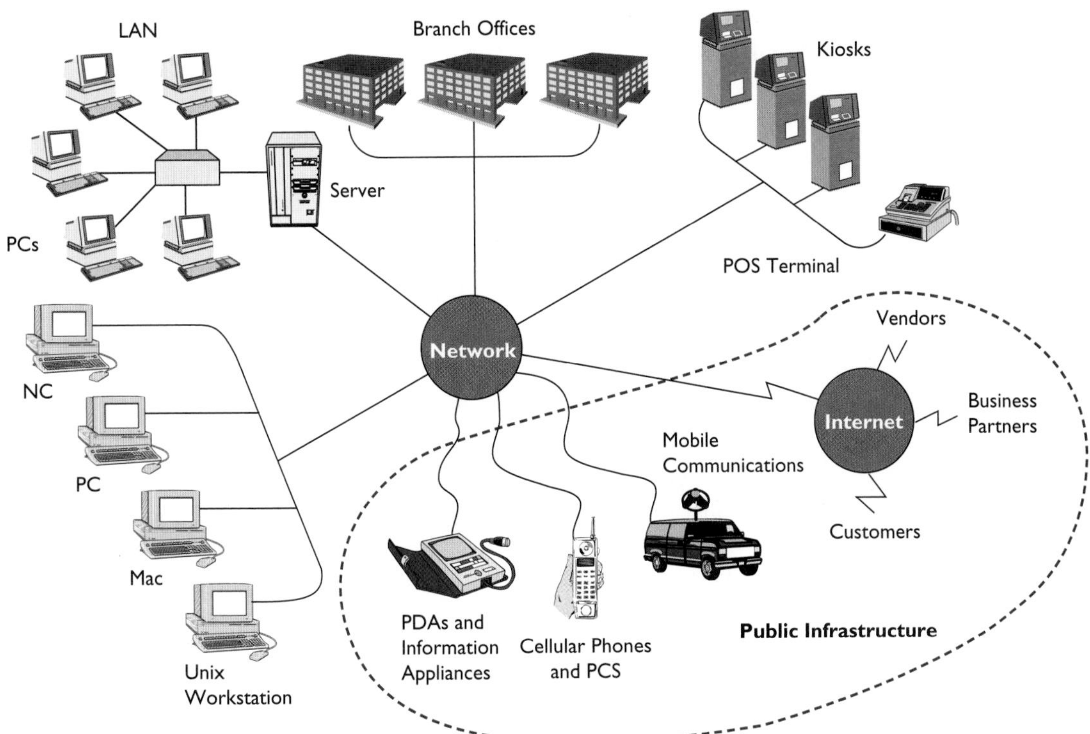


*Figure 9-1* The new information technology (IT) infrastructure: The new IT infrastructure links desktop workstations, network computers, LANs, and server computers in an enterprise network so that information can flow freely between different parts of the organization. The enterprise network may also be linked to kiosks, point-of-sale (POS) terminals, PDAs and information appliances, digital cellular telephones and PCS, and mobile computing devices as well as to the Internet using public infrastructures. Customers, suppliers, and business partners may also be linked to the organization through this new IT infrastructure.

departments are changing their roles to managers of software packages and software and networking services provided by outside vendors.

Through enterprise networking and internetworking, information flows smoothly between all of these devices within the organization and between the organization and its external environment. In **enterprise networking,** the organization's hardware, software, network, and data resources are arranged to put more computing power on the desktop and to create a company-wide network linking many smaller networks. The system is a network. In fact, for all but the smallest organizations the system is composed of multiple networks. A high-capacity backbone network connects many local area networks and devices.

**enterprise networking**
An arrangement of the organization's hardware, software, network, and data resources to put more computing power on the desktop and create a company-wide network linking many smaller networks.

The backbone may be connected to the networks of other organizations outside the firm, to the Internet, to the networks of public telecommunication service providers or to other public networks. The linking of separate networks, each of which retains its own identity, into an interconnected network, is called **internetworking.**

**internetworking**
The linking of separate networks, each of which retains its own identity, into an interconnected network.

Vienna University in Austria illustrates enterprise networking and internetworking in the new IT infrastructure. The university's network consists of 3,500 computers, including an IBM Enterprise System/9000 mainframe, Unix workstations, and thousands of PCs. A backbone network uses Cisco routers to connect various university departments to the university's Computer Center, where traffic is routed to other universities in Vienna, to the Austrian Academic Network (ACOnet), Austria's national research network, and to the public Internet.

Other organizations are using the new information IT infrastructure to provide telecommuters and other employees with mobile computing capabilities and remote access to corporate information systems.

## STANDARDS AND CONNECTIVITY FOR DIGITAL INTEGRATION

**connectivity**
A measure of how well computers and computer-based devices communicate and share information with one another without human intervention.

The new IT infrastructure is most likely to increase productivity and competitive advantage when digitized information can move seamlessly through the organization's web of electronic networks, connecting different kinds of machines, people, sensors, databases, functional divisions, departments, and work groups. This ability of computers and computer-based devices to communicate with one another and "share" information in a meaningful way without human intervention is called **connectivity.** Internet technology, XML, and Java software provide some of this connectivity, but these technologies cannot be used as a foundation for all of the organization's information systems. Most organizations still use proprietary networks. They need to develop their own connectivity solutions to make different kinds of hardware, software, and communications systems work together.

**open systems**
Software systems that can operate on different hardware platforms because they are built on public nonproprietary operating systems, user interfaces, application standards, and networking protocols.

Achieving connectivity requires standards for networking, operating systems, and user interfaces. Open systems promote connectivity because they enable disparate equipment and services to work together. **Open systems** are built on public, nonproprietary operating systems, user interfaces, application standards, and networking protocols. In open systems, software can operate on different hardware platforms and in that sense can be "portable." Java software, described in Chapter 6, can promote an open system environment. The Unix operating system supports open systems, because it can operate on many different kinds of computer hardware. However, there are different versions of Unix and no one version has been accepted as an open systems standard. Linux also supports open systems.

### Models of Connectivity for Networks

**Transmission Control Protocol/Internet Protocol (TCP/IP)**
U.S. Department of Defense reference model for linking different types of computers and networks; used in the Internet.

There are different models for achieving connectivity in telecommunications networks. The **Transmission Control Protocol/Internet Protocol (TCP/IP)** model was developed by the U.S. Department of Defense in 1972 and is used in the Internet. Its purpose was to help scientists link disparate computers. Figure 9-2 shows that TCP/IP has a five-layer reference model.

1. *Application:* Provides end-user functionality by translating the messages into the user/host software for screen presentation.
2. *Transmission Control Protocol (TCP):* Performs transport, breaking application data from the end user down into TCP packets called datagrams. Each packet consists of a header with the address of the sending host computer, information for putting the data back together, and information for making sure the packets do not become corrupted.
3. *Internet Protocol (IP):* The Internet Protocol receives datagrams from TCP and breaks the packets down further. An IP packet contains a header with address information and carries TCP information and data. IP routes the individual datagrams from the sender to the recipient. IP packets are not very reliable, but the TCP level can keep resending them until the correct IP packets get through.
4. *Network interface:* Handles addressing issues, usually in the operating system, as well as the interface between the initiating computer and the network.
5. *Physical net:* Defines basic electrical-transmission characteristic for sending the actual signal along communications networks.

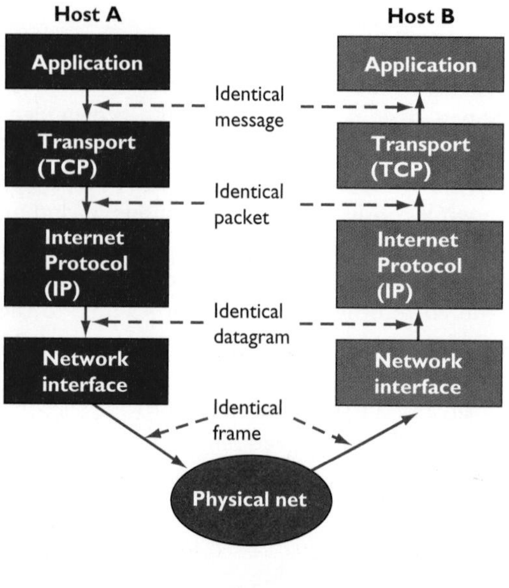

*Figure 9-2* The Transmission Control Protocol/Internet Protocol (TCP/IP) reference model. This figure illustrates the five layers of the TCP/IP reference model for communications.

Two computers using TCP/IP would be able to communicate even if they were based on different hardware and software platforms. Data sent from one computer to the other would pass downward through all five layers, starting with the sending computer's application layer and passing through the physical net. After the data reached the recipient host computer, they would travel up the layers. The TCP level would assemble the data into a format the receiving host computer could use. If the receiving computer found a damaged packet, it would ask the sending computer to retransmit it. This process would be reversed when the receiving computer responded.

The **Open Systems Interconnect (OSI)** model is an alternative model developed by the International Standards Organization for linking different types of computers and networks. It was designed to support global networks with large volumes of transaction processing. Like TCP/IP, OSI enables a computer connected to a network to communicate with any other computer on the same network or a different network, regardless of the manufacturer, by establishing communication rules that permit the exchange of information between dissimilar systems. OSI divides the telecommunications process into seven layers.

**Open Systems Interconnect (OSI)**
International reference model for linking different types of computers and networks.

Equipment makers are starting to develop standards for small, high-speed, wireless networks to serve offices, campuses, or homes that could provide high-speed data connections of up to two million bits per second. One standard under development, code-named **bluetooth,** allows high-speed, radio-based communication among wireless phones, pagers, computers, and other handheld devices within any 100-foot area so that these devices could operate each other without direct user intervention. For example, a person could highlight a telephone number on a Palm PDA and automatically activate a call on a digital telephone. A mobile device could transmit a file wirelessly to a printer to produce a hard copy document. People could also synchronize all of their mobile devices wirelessly with desktop computers in their offices and homes. Wireless digital cellular handset manufacturers are working on standards for wireless Internet access (see section 9.3).

**bluetooth**
Networking standard for high-speed, radio-based communication within a small area between wireless handheld devices and computers.

Other connectivity-promoting standards have been developed for graphical user interfaces, electronic mail, packet switching, and electronic data interchange (EDI). Any manager wishing to achieve some measure of connectivity in his or her organization should try to use these standards when designing networks, purchasing hardware and software, or developing information system applications.

## 9.2 THE INTERNET: INFORMATION TECHNOLOGY INFRASTRUCTURE FOR THE DIGITAL FIRM

The Internet is perhaps the most well-known, and the largest, implementation of internetworking, linking hundreds of thousands of individual networks all over the world. The Internet has a range of capabilities that organizations are using to exchange information internally or to communicate externally with other organizations. Internet technology is providing the primary infrastructure for electronic commerce, electronic business, and the emerging digital firm.

### WHAT IS THE INTERNET?

The Internet began as a U.S. Department of Defense network to link scientists and university professors around the world. Even today individuals cannot connect directly to the Net, although anyone with a computer, a modem, and the willingness to pay a small monthly usage fee can access it through an Internet Service Provider. An **Internet Service Provider (ISP)** is a commercial organization with a permanent connection to the Internet that sells temporary connections to subscribers. Individuals also can access the Internet through such popular on-line services as Prodigy and America Online and through networks established by such giants as Microsoft and AT&T.

**Internet Service Provider (ISP)**
A commercial organization with a permanent connection to the Internet that sells temporary connections to subscribers.

One of the most puzzling aspects of the Internet is that no one owns it and it has no formal management organization. As a creation of the Defense Department for sharing research data, this lack of centralization was purposeful, to make it less vulnerable to wartime or terrorist attacks. To join the Internet, an existing network needs only to pay a small registration fee and agree to certain standards based on the TCP/IP reference model. Costs are low because the Internet owns nothing and so has no costs to offset. Each organization, of course, pays for its own networks and its own telephone bills, but those costs usually exist independent of the

## TABLE 9-1 EXAMPLES OF INTERNET CLIENT PLATFORMS

| Device | Description | Example |
|---|---|---|
| PC | General purpose computing platform that can perform many different tasks, but can be complex to use | Dell, Compaq, IBM PCs |
| Net PC | Network computer with minimal local storage and processing capability; designed to use software and services delivered over networks and the Internet | Sun Ray |
| Pager | Provides limited e-mail and Web browsing | BlackBerry (blackberry.net) |
| Smart Phone | Has a small screen and keyboard for browsing the Web and exchanging e-mail in addition to providing voice communication | Nokia 7110 |
| Game Machine | Game machine with a modem, keyboard, and capabilities to function as a Web access terminal | Sega Dreamcast (sega.com) |
| PDA | Wireless handheld personal digital assistant with e-mail and Internet service | Palm VII |
| E-mail machine | Tablet with keyboard that provides textual e-mail capabilities; requires linking to an e-mail service | Mailstation (www.cidco.com) |
| Set top box | Provides Web surfing and e-mail capabilities using a television set and a wireless keyboard | WebTV (www.webtv.com) |

Internet. Regional Internet companies have been established to which member networks forward all transmissions. These Internet companies route and forward all traffic, and the cost is still only that of a local telephone call. The result is that the costs of e-mail and other Internet connections tend to be far lower than equivalent voice, postal, or overnight delivery, making the Net a very inexpensive communications medium. It is also a very fast method of communication, with messages arriving anywhere in the world in a matter of seconds or a minute or two at most. We now briefly describe the most important Internet capabilities.

## INTERNET TECHNOLOGY AND SERVICES

The Internet is based on client/server technology. Individuals using the Net control what they do through client applications such as Web browser software. All the data, including e-mail messages and Web pages, are stored on servers. A client uses the Internet to request information from a particular Web server on a distant computer and the server sends the requested information back to the client via the Internet.

Client platforms today include not only PCs and other computers but also a wide array of handheld devices and information appliances, some of which can even provide wireless Internet access. Table 9-1 lists examples of some of these devices, most of which were described in Chapters 5 and 8. Experts believe that the role of the PC or desktop computer as the Internet client is diminishing as people turn to these easy-to-use specialized information appliances to connect to the Internet.

Servers dedicated to the Internet or even to specific Internet services are the heart of the information on the Net. Each Internet service is implemented by one or more software programs. All of the services may run on a single server computer, as illustrated in Figure 9-3, or different services may be allocated to different machines. There may be only one disk storing the data for these services, or there may be multiple disks for each type, depending on the amount of information being stored.

Web server software receives requests for Web pages from the client and accesses the Web pages from the disk where they are stored. Web servers can also access other information from an organization's internal information system applications and their associated databases and return that information to the client in the form of Web pages if desired. Specialized middleware, including application servers, is used to manage the interactions between the Web server and the organization's internal information systems for processing orders, tracking inventory, maintaining product catalogs, and other electronic commerce functions. For example, if a customer filled out an on-line form on a Web page to order a

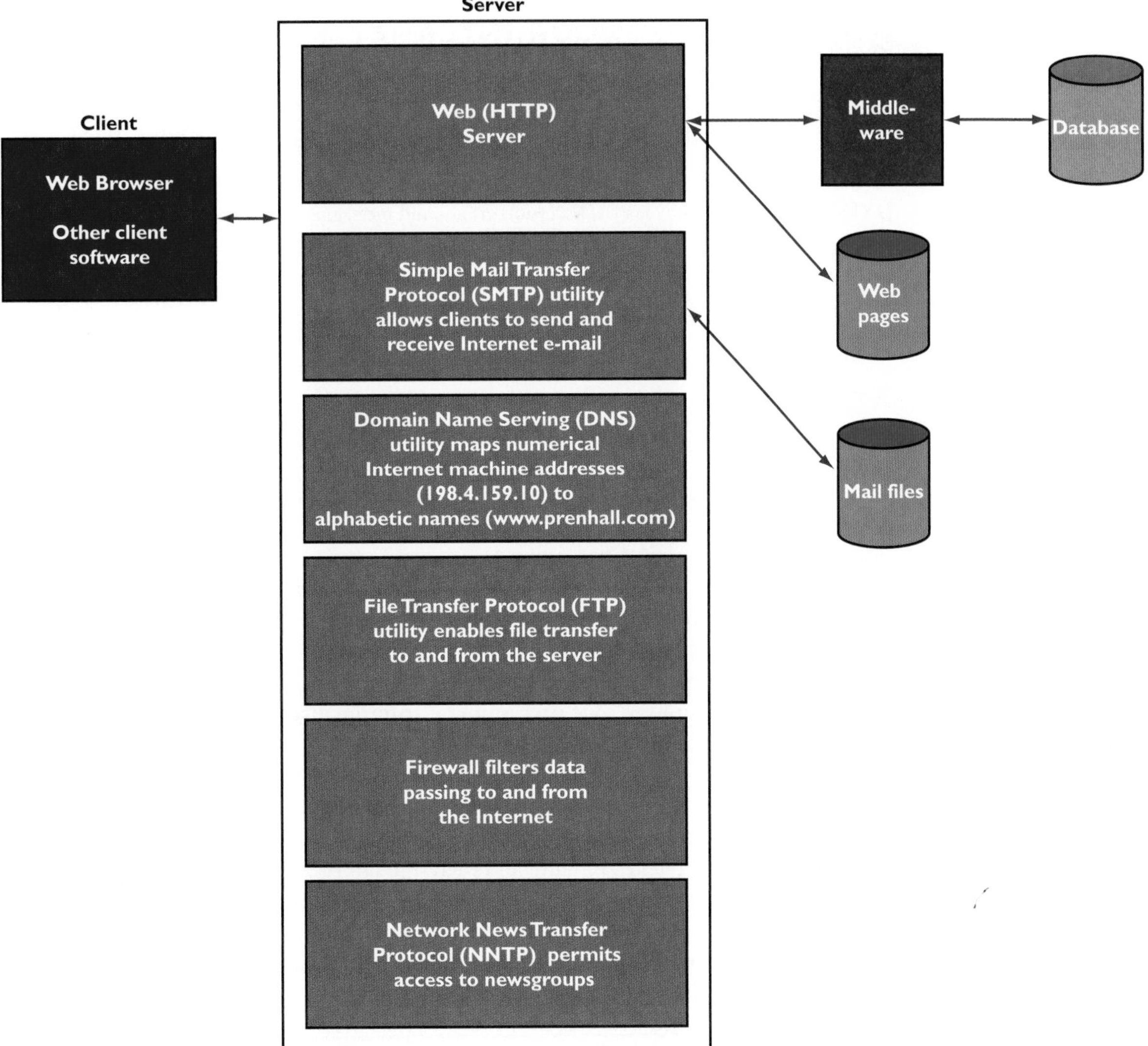


***Figure 9-3*** Client/server computing on the Internet. Client computers running Web browser and other software can access an array of services on servers via the Internet. These services may all run on a single server or on multiple specialized servers.

product such as a light fixture, the middleware would translate the request on the Web page into commands that could be used by the company's internal order processing system and customer database.

The most important Internet services for business include e-mail, Usenet newsgroups, LISTSERVs, chatting, Telnet, FTP, gophers, and the World Wide Web. They can be used to retrieve and offer information. Table 9-2 lists these capabilities and describes the functions they support.

## Internet Tools for Communication

***Electronic Mail (E-mail).*** The Net has become the most important e-mail system in the world because it connects so many people worldwide, creating a productivity gain that observers have compared to Gutenberg's development of movable type in the fifteenth century. Organizations use it to facilitate communication between employees and offices, and to communicate with customers and suppliers.

Researchers use this facility to share ideas, information, and even documents. E-mail over the Net also has made possible many collaborative research and writing projects, even though the participants are thousands of miles apart. With proper software, the user finds it

## TABLE 9-2 MAJOR INTERNET SERVICES

| Capability | Functions Supported |
|---|---|
| E-mail | Person-to-person messaging; document sharing |
| Usenet newsgroups | Discussion groups on electronic bulletin boards |
| LISTSERVs | Discussion groups and messaging using e-mail mailing list servers |
| Chatting | Interactive conversations |
| Telnet | Log on to one computer system and do work on another |
| FTP | Transfer files from computer to computer |
| Gophers | Locate information using a hierarchy of menus |
| World Wide Web | Retrieve, format, and display information (including text, audio, graphics, and video) using hypertext links |

**domain name**
The unique name of a node on the Internet.

**Internet Protocol (IP) address**
Four-part numeric address indicating a unique computer location on the Internet.

**Domain Name System (DNS)**
A hierarchical system of servers maintaining databases enabling the conversion of domain names to their IP addresses.

**Usenet**
Forums in which people share information and ideas on a defined topic through large electronic bulletin boards where anyone can post messages that others can see and to which they can respond.

**LISTSERV**
On-line groups using e-mail broadcast from mailing list servers for discussions and messaging.

easy to attach documents and multimedia files when sending a message to someone or to broadcast a message to a predefined group.

Figure 9-4 illustrates the components of an Internet e-mail address. The portion of the address to the left of the @ symbol in a Net e-mail address is the name or identifier of the specific individual or organization. To the right of the @ symbol is the domain name. The **domain name** is the name that identifies a unique node on the Internet. The domain name corresponds to a unique four-part numeric **Internet Protocol (IP) address** for each computer connected to the Internet. (For example, the domain name www.prenhall.com has the IP address 198.4.159.10.) A **Domain Name System (DNS)** maps domain names to their IP addresses.

The domain name contains subdomains separated by a period. The domain that is farthest to the right is the top level domain, and each domain to the left helps further define the domain by network, department, and even specific computer. The top level domain name may be either a country indicator or a function indicator, such as *com* for a commercial organization or *gov* for a government institution. All e-mail addresses end with a country indicator except those in the United States, which ordinarily does not use one. In Figure 9-4, *it,* the top level domain, is a country indicator, indicating that the address is in Italy. *Edu* indicates that the address is an educational institution; *univpisa* (in this case, University of Pisa) indicates the specific location of the host computer.

***Usenet Newsgroups (Forums).*** **Usenet** newsgroups are worldwide discussion groups in which people share information and ideas on a defined topic such as radiology or rock bands. Discussion takes place in large electronic bulletin boards where anyone can post messages for others to read. Many thousands of groups exist discussing almost all conceivable topics. Each Usenet site is financed and administered independently.

***LISTSERV.*** A second type of public forum, **LISTSERV,** allows discussions or messaging to be conducted through predefined groups but uses e-mail mailing list servers instead of bulletin boards for communications. If you find a LISTSERV topic you are interested in, you may

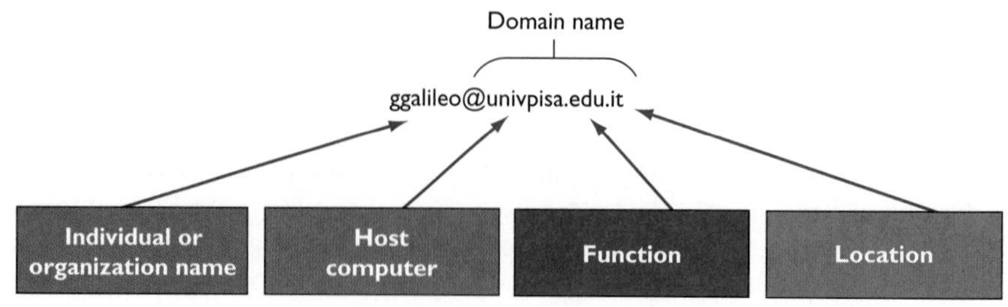


*Figure 9-4* Analysis of an Internet address. In English, the e-mail address of physicist and astronomer Galileo Galilei would be translated as "G. Galileo @ University of Pisa, educational institution, Italy." The domain name to the right of the @ symbol contains a country indicator, a function indicator, and the location of the host computer.

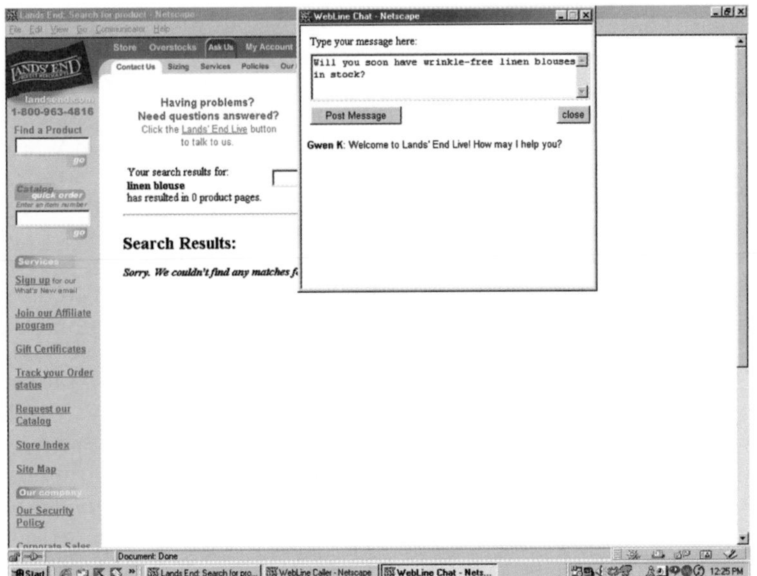


*The Lands' End Web site provides on-line chat capabilities to answer visitors' questions and to help them find items they are looking for. Chat services can help Web sites attract customers.*

subscribe. From then on, through your e-mail, you will receive all messages sent by others concerning that topic. You can, in turn, send a message to your LISTSERV and it will automatically be broadcast to the other subscribers. Many thousands of LISTSERV groups exist.

***Chatting.*** **Chatting** allows two or more people who are simultaneously connected to the Internet to hold live, interactive conversations. Chat groups are divided into channels, and each is assigned its own topic of conversation. The first generation of chat tools was for written conversations in which participants type their remarks using their keyboard and read responses on their computer screen. Systems featuring voice chat capabilities, such as those offered by Yahoo Chat are now becoming popular.

**chatting**
Live, interactive conversations over a public network.

A new enhancement to chat service called **instant messaging** even allows participants to create their own private chat channels. The instant messaging system alerts a person whenever someone on his or her private list is on-line so that the person can initiate a chat session with that particular individual. There are several competing instant messaging systems including Yahoo Messenger and America Online's Instant Messenger. Some of these systems can provide voice-based instant messages so that a user can click on a "talk" button and have an on-line conversation with another person.

**instant messaging**
Chat service that allows participants to create their own private chat channels so that a person can be alerted whenever someone on his or her private list is on-line to initiate a chat session with that particular individual.

Chatting can be an effective business tool if people who can benefit from interactive conversations set an appointed time to "meet" and "talk" on a particular topic. Many on-line retailers are enhancing their Web sites with chat services to attract visitors, to encourage repeat purchases, and to improve customer service.

***Telnet.*** **Telnet** allows someone to be on one computer system while doing work on another. Telnet is the protocol that establishes an error-free, rapid link between the two computers, allowing you, for example, to log on to your business computer from a remote computer when you are on the road or working from your home. You can also log in and use third-party computers that are accessible to the public, such as using the catalog of the U.S. Library of Congress. Telnet uses the computer address you supply to locate the computer you want to reach and connect you to it.

**Telnet**
Network tool that allows someone to log on to one computer system while doing work on another.

## Information Retrieval on the Internet

Information retrieval is a second basic Internet function. Many hundreds of library catalogs are on-line through the Internet, including those of such giants as the Library of Congress, the University of California, and Harvard University. In addition, users are able to search many thousands of databases that have been opened to the public by corporations, governments, and nonprofit organizations. Many use the Internet to locate and download some of the free, quality computer software that has been made available by developers on computers all over the world.

The Internet is a voluntary, decentralized effort with no central listing of participants or sites, much less a listing of the data located at those sites, so a major problem is finding what you need from among the storehouses of data found in databases and libraries. Here we introduce two major methods of accessing computers and locating files. We discuss additional information-retrieval methods in the section on the World Wide Web.

**file transfer protocol (FTP)**
Tool for retrieving and transferring files from a remote computer.

***FTP.*** **File transfer protocol (FTP)** is used to access a remote computer and retrieve files from it. FTP is a quick and easy method if you know the remote computer site where the file is stored. After you have logged on to the remote computer, you can move around directories that have been made accessible for FTP to search for the file(s) you want to retrieve. Once files are located, FTP makes transfer of the file to your own computer very easy.

**gopher**
A tool that enables the user to locate information stored on Internet servers through a series of easy-to-use, hierarchical menus.

***Gophers.*** Most files and digital information that are accessible through FTP also are available through gophers. A **gopher** is a computer client tool that enables the user to locate information stored on Internet gopher servers through a series of easy-to-use, hierarchical menus. The Internet has many thousands of gopher server sites throughout the world. Each gopher site contains its own system of menus listing subject-matter topics, local files, and other relevant gopher sites. One gopher site might have as many as several thousand listings within its menus. When you use gopher software to search a specific topic and select a related item from a menu, the server will automatically transfer you to the appropriate file on that server or to the selected server on which it is located. Once on that server, the process continues; you are presented with more menus of files and other gopher site servers that might interest you. You can move from site to site, narrowing your search as you go, locating information anywhere in the world. With descriptive menu listings linked to other gopher sites, you do not need to know in advance where relevant files are stored or the exact FTP address of a specific computer.

## NEXT GENERATION INTERNET: BROADBAND AND INTERNET2

Sound, graphics, and full-motion video are now important features of Web-based computing. However, these all require immense quantities of data, greatly slowing down transmission and the downloading of Web pages. During peak periods of usage, Internet traffic slows to a crawl, and ISPs cannot keep up with the demand. The public Internet in its current form is not reliable or robust enough for many business-critical applications.

**Internet2**
Research network with new protocols and transmission speeds that provides an infrastructure for supporting high-bandwidth Internet applications.

Higher bandwidth alternatives are under development. Scientists at nearly 200 universities and scores of affiliated companies are working on a new version of the Internet, known as Internet2. **Internet2** is a research network with new protocols and transmission speeds that are much higher than the current Internet. The Internet2 infrastructure is based on a series of interconnected *gigaPoPs,* which are regional high-speed points-of-presence that serve as aggregation points for traffic from participating institutions. (Several gigaPoPs in operation support at least 1 gigabit per second information transfer.) These gigaPoPs in turn are connected to the National Science Foundation's high-performance Backbone Network infrastructure, which will soon operate at two gigabits per second.

Much of the work on Internet2 is being coordinated by a consortium of universities and companies called the University Corporation for Advanced Internet Development (UCAID). Another consortium, Next Generation Internet (NGI), is also working on a high-capacity network that would connect research facilities across the United States to support next-generation applications in energy research, national security, and medical research. NGI is government sponsored and comprises research agencies such as the Defense Advanced Research Projects Agency (DARPA), the Department of Energy, the National Aeronautics and Space Administration (NASA), and the National Institute of Standards and Technology.

In addition to testing a more advanced version of the Internet Protocol, and finding new ways to route broadcast messages, Internet2 is focusing on developing protocols for permitting different quality-of-service levels. Today's Internet transmissions are "best effort"—packets of data arrive when they arrive without any regard to the priority of their contents. Under Internet2 different types of packets could be assigned different levels of priority as they travel over the network. For example, packets for applications such as videoconferenc-

**TABLE 9-3 INTERNET2 INFRASTRUCTURE**

| |
|---|
| 10–100 MBPS to the desktop |
| 500 MBPS to campus (domain) backbone |
| 155 MBPS connection to gigaPoP |
| 2+ gigabits per second (GBPS) backbones |

ing, which need to arrive simultaneously without any break in service, could be assigned high priority for immediate delivery. E-mail messages, which do not have to be delivered instantaneously, could be delivered when capacity was available. The new Internet will have the reliability and security features of private leased-line networks with much more bandwidth, enabling companies to distribute video, audio, three-dimensional animations, and data signals in broadcast fashion with minimal disruptions. Web sites will be able to offer applications such as distance learning, digital libraries, 180-degree life-size video teleconferencing, and three-dimensional simulations, that are much more interactive and data intensive than today's Internet applications without any degradation in performance. High-quality video could be part of every application, along with interactivity and high-quality sound.

As Internet2 components and high-speed network technologies come into the commercial mainstream, companies will have to rethink how they work, how they build and sell products, and how they manage their network assets. Internet2 connection speeds are in the hundreds of megabits per second (MBPS) range (see Table 9-3), with at least 100 MBPS connections to servers and at least 10 MBPS to the desktop. Broadband access technologies such as DSL and cable modem will be essential.

## 9.3 The World Wide Web

The World Wide Web (the Web) is at the heart of the explosion in the business use of the Net. The Web is a system with universally accepted standards for storing, retrieving, formatting, and displaying information using a client/server architecture. The Web combines text, hypermedia, graphics, and sound. It can handle all types of digital communication, making it easy to link resources that are half-a-world apart. The Web uses graphical user interfaces for easy viewing. It is based on a standard hypertext language called Hypertext Markup Language (HTML), which formats documents and incorporates dynamic links to other documents stored in the same or remote computers. (We described HTML in Chapter 6). Using these links, the user need only point at a highlighted keyword or graphic, click on it, and immediately be transported to another document, probably on another computer somewhere else in the world. Users are free to jump from place to place following their own logic and interest.

Web browser software is programmed according to HTML standards (see Chapter 6). The standard is universally accepted, so anyone using a browser can access any of the millions of Web sites. Browsers use hypertext's point-and-click ability to navigate or *surf*—move from site to site on the Web—to another desired site. The browser also includes an arrow or back button to enable the user to retrace his or her steps, navigating back, site by site.

Those who offer information through the Web must establish a **home page**—a text and graphical screen display that usually welcomes the user and explains the organization that has established the page. For most organizations, the home page leads users to other pages, with all the pages of a company being known as a *Web site.* For a corporation to establish a presence on the Web, therefore, it must set up a Web site of one or more pages. Most Web pages offer a way to contact the organization or individual. The person in charge of an organization's Web site is called a **Webmaster.**

To access a Web site, the user must specify a **uniform resource locator (URL),** which points to the address of a specific resource on the Web. For instance, the URL for Prentice Hall, the publisher of this text, is

http://www.prenhall.com

**home page**
A World Wide Web text and graphical screen display that welcomes the user and explains the organization that has established the page.

**Webmaster**
The person in charge of an organization's Web site.

**uniform resource locator (URL)**
The address of a specific resource on the Internet.

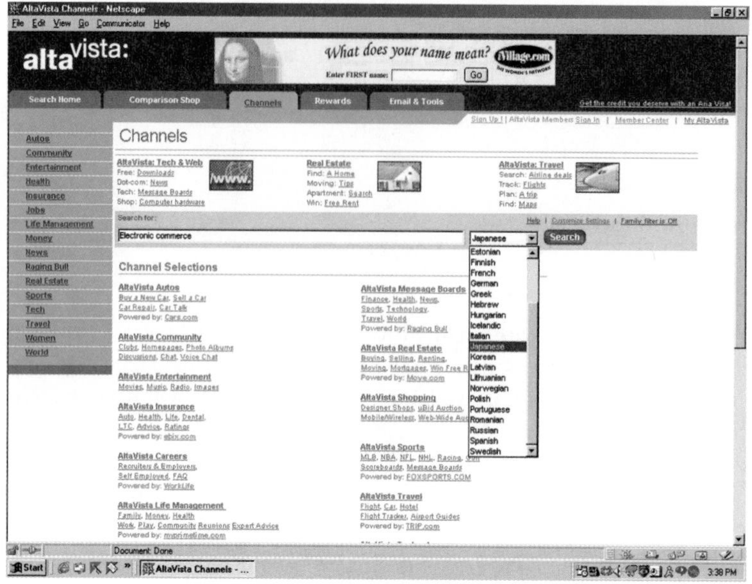


*Figure 9-5* AltaVista provides a powerful search engine for accessing Web information resources and is a major Internet portal. Users can search for sites of interest by entering keywords or by exploring the categories.

**hypertext transport protocol (http)**
The communications standard used to transfer pages on the Web. Defines how messages are formatted and transmitted.

*Http* stands for **hypertext transport protocol,** which is the communications standard used to transfer pages on the Web. Http defines how messages are formatted and transmitted and what actions Web servers and browsers should take in response to various commands. *Www.prenhall.com* is the domain name identifying the Web server storing the Web pages.

## SEARCHING FOR INFORMATION ON THE WEB

Locating information on the Web is a critical function, with the more than one billion Web pages in existence expected to double in eight months. No comprehensive catalog of Web sites exists. The principal methods of locating information on the Web are Web site directories, search engines, and broadcast or "push" technology.

Several companies have created directories of Web sites and their addresses, providing search tools for finding information. Yahoo is an example. People or organizations submit sites of interest, which then are classified. To search the directory, you enter one or more keywords and see displayed a list of categories and sites with those keywords in the title.

**search engine**
A tool for locating specific sites or information on the Internet.

Other search tools do not require Web sites to be preclassified and will search Web pages on their own automatically. Such tools, called **search engines,** can find Web sites that may be little known. They contain software that looks for Web pages containing one or more of the search terms; then they display matches ranked by a method that usually involves the location and frequency of the search terms. (Some search engine sites use human experts to help with the ranking.) These search engines do not display information about every site on the Web, but they create indexes of the Web pages they visit. The search engine software then locates Web pages of interest by searching through these indexes. AltaVista, Lycos, and GO.com are examples of these search engines. Some are more comprehensive or current than others, depending on how their components are tuned, and some also classify Web sites by subject categories (see Figure 9-5). Specialized search tools are also available to help users locate specific types of information easily. For example, Google is tuned to find the home pages of companies and organizations. Some Web sites for locating information, such as Yahoo and AltaVista, have become so popular and easy to use that they also serve as portals for the Internet (see Chapter 4).

**shopping bot**
Software with varying levels of built-in intelligence to help electronic commerce shoppers locate and evaluate products or services they might wish to purchase.

There are two ways of identifying Web pages to be tracked by search engines. One is to have Web page owners register their URLs with search engine sites. The other is to use software agents known as spiders, bots, and Web crawlers to traverse the Web and identify the Web pages for indexing. Chapter 12 details the capabilities of software agents with built-in intelligence, which can also help users search the Internet for shopping information. **Shopping bots** help people interested in making a purchase filter and retrieve information about products of interest, evaluate competing products according to criteria they have established, and negotiate with vendors for price and delivery terms (Maes, Guttman, and

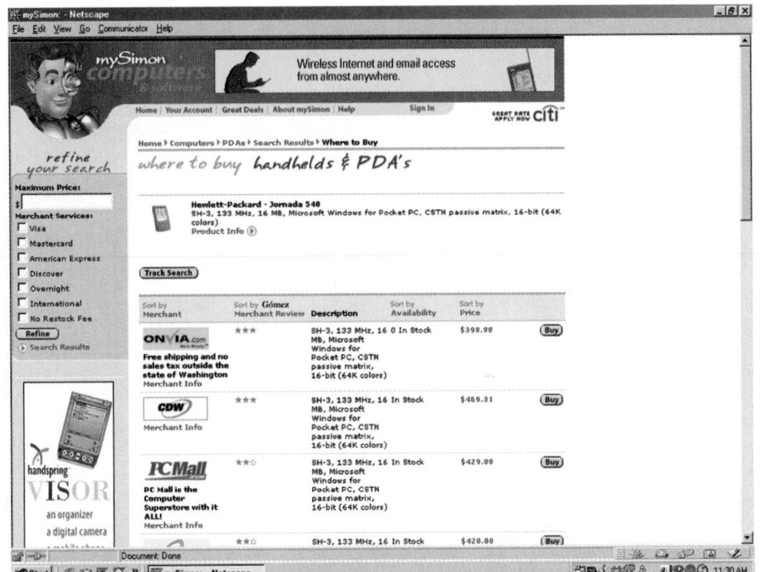


*MySimon is a shopping bot that can search virtual retailers for price and availability of products specified by the user. Displayed here are the results for a search of prices and sources for a PDA.*

Moukas, 1999). Yahoo and Excite, two of the major Web search services, now offer "shopping agents" for a few merchandise categories, such as music, books, electronics, and toys. To use these agents, the consumer enters the desired product into an on-line shopping form. Using this information, the shopping agent searches the Web for product pricing and availability. It returns a list of sites that sell the item along with pricing information and a purchase link. Table 9-4 compares various types of electronic commerce agents.

Intelligent agent technology can also facilitate business-to-business transactions. For example, agents could help suppliers collect bids on their products from customers, assist credit decisions, negotiate contract terms, and make shipping arrangements (Papazoglou, 2001).

## Broadcast and "Push" Technology

Instead of spending hours surfing the Web, users can have the information they are interested in delivered automatically to their desktops through **"push" technology.** A computer broadcasts information of interest directly to the user, rather than having the user "pull" content from Web sites.

**"push" technology**
Method of obtaining relevant information on networks by having a computer broadcast information directly to the user based on prespecified interests.

Special client software allows the user to specify the categories of information he or she wants to receive, such as news, sports, financial data, and so forth, and how often this information should be updated. After finding the kind of information requested, push server programs serve it to the push client. The streams of information distributed through push technology are

### TABLE 9-4 Examples of Electronic Commerce Agents

| Agent | Description |
| --- | --- |
| MySimon | Real-time shopping bot that searches more than 1,000 affiliated and unaffiliated merchants in 90 categories; collects a 3 to 10 percent finders fee on sales |
| BestWebBuys.com | Compares prices for best deals on books, music, and bicycles |
| Metaprices.com | Searches for prices of books, CDs, videos, and software. Includes capabilities for wireless access and personal shopping lists |
| AuctionBot | Allows sellers to set up their own auctions where buyers and sellers can place bids according to the protocols and parameters that have been established for the auction. Using AuctionBot, sellers create auctions by selecting the type of auction and parameters (such as clearing time or number of sellers) they wish to use; AuctionBot then manages the buyer bidding according to the specified parameters. |

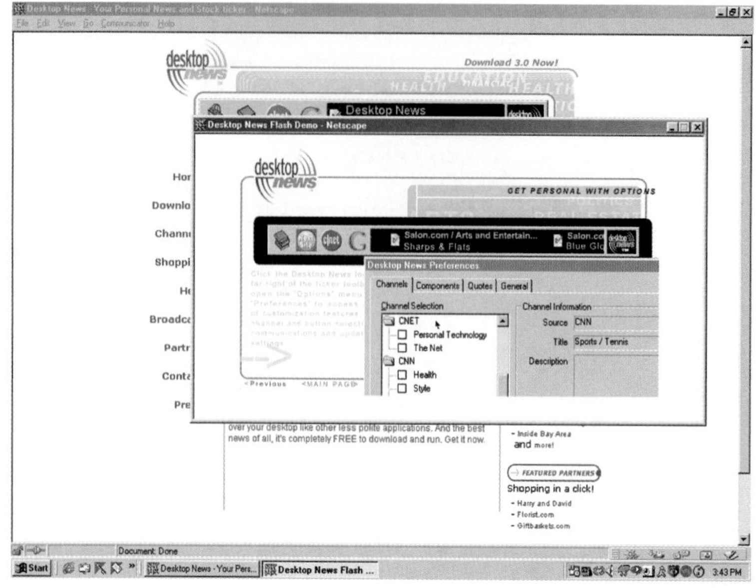

*Delivering information through "push" technology. Desktop News delivers a continuous stream of news and information from Web sites selected by users directly to their desktops as a customizable ticker toolbar.*

known as *channels.* Microsoft's Internet Explorer and Netscape Communicator include push tools that automatically download Web pages, inform the user of updated content, and create channels of user-specified sites. Using push technology to transmit information to a select group of individuals is one example of **multicasting.** (LISTSERVs sending e-mail to members of specific mailing lists is another.)

**multicasting**
Transmission of data to a selected group of recipients.

On-line marketplaces and exchanges can use push services to alert buyers to price changes and special deals. Companies are using push technology to set up their own internal push channels to broadcast important information on their own private networks. For example, Mannesmann o.tel.o GmbH, one of the largest telecommunications providers in Germany, has developed an application using BackWeb's push delivery service that broadcasts new press releases about competitors' products as soon as the information appears on the Internet.

## INTRANETS AND EXTRANETS

Organizations can use Internet networking standards and Web technology to create private networks called *intranets.* We introduced intranets in Chapter 1, explaining that an intranet is an internal organizational network that can provide access to data across the enterprise. It uses the existing company network infrastructure along with Internet connectivity standards and software developed for the World Wide Web. Intranets can create networked applications that can run on many different kinds of computers throughout the organization, including mobile handheld computers and wireless remote access devices.

### Intranet Technology

Although the Web is open to anyone, the intranet is private and is protected from public visits by **firewalls**—security systems with specialized software to prevent outsiders from invading private networks. The firewall consists of hardware and software placed between an organization's internal network and an external network, including the Internet. The firewall is programmed to intercept each message packet passing between the two networks, examine its characteristics, and reject unauthorized messages or access attempts. We provide more detail on firewalls in Chapter 14.

**firewall**
Hardware and software placed between an organization's internal network and an external network to prevent outsiders from invading private networks.

Intranets require no special hardware and can run over any existing network infrastructure. Intranet software technology is the same as that of the World Wide Web. Intranets use HTML to program Web pages and to establish dynamic, point-and-click hypertext links to other pages. The Web browser and Web server software used for intranets are the same as those on the Web. A simple intranet can be created by linking a client computer with a Web browser to a computer with Web server software via a TCP/IP network. A firewall keeps out unwanted visitors.

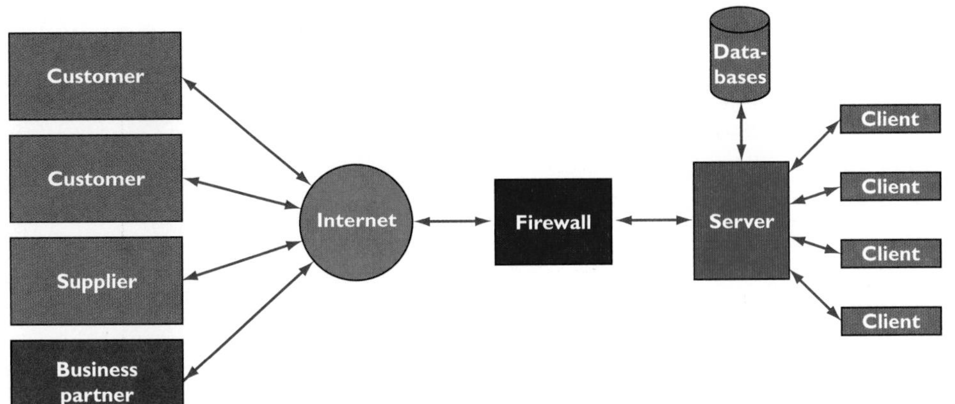


***Figure 9-6*** Model of an extranet. In this model of one type of extranet, selected customers, suppliers, and business partners can access portions of a company's private intranet from the public Internet. A firewall allows access only to authorized outsiders.

## Extranets

Some firms are allowing people and organizations outside the firm to have limited access to their internal intranets. Private intranets that are extended to authorized users outside the company are called *extranets,* which we also introduced in Chapter 1. For example, authorized buyers could link to a portion of a company's intranet from the public Internet to obtain information about the cost and features of its products. The company can use firewalls to ensure that access to its internal data is limited and remains secure; firewalls can also authenticate users, making sure that only authorized people can access the site.

Extranets are especially useful for linking organizations with customers or business partners. They often are used for providing product-availability, pricing, and shipment data; electronic data interchange (EDI); or for collaborating with other companies on joint development or training efforts. Figure 9-6 illustrates one way that an extranet might be set up.

## The Wireless Web

Chapter 4 introduced *m-commerce,* the use of the Internet for purchasing goods and services as well as sending and receiving messages using handheld wireless devices. With cell phones, PDAs, and other wireless computing devices becoming Internet-enabled, many believe m-commerce represents the next wave of Internet computing.

Web-enabled wireless devices will not replace the PC, but will enable millions of people to access the Internet while on the go. M-commerce will become a significant subset of e-commerce. Businesses will increasingly incorporate wireless Internet access into their information technology infrastructures so that employees can access information wherever they are, and make decisions instantly without being tethered to a desk or computer.

**wireless Web**
Web-based applications enabling users to access digital information from the Internet using wireless mobile computing devices.

Web content will be reformatted for wireless devices and new content and services will be developed specifically for those devices. **Wireless Web** applications enable mobile users to access digital information from the Internet and be connected anywhere, any time, any place. Specialized portals steer users of Web-enabled wireless devices to the information they are most likely to need.

The wireless Web is not a mobile version of the fixed line Internet—it's an entirely new medium. M-commerce technology and services could make the Internet ubiquitous, enmeshing individuals in Web information services wherever they go. The Web will evolve into a vast pool of data resources that can be accessed in many different ways as opposed to a collection of distinct pages.

Table 9-5 describes what are likely to be the most popular categories of m-commerce services and applications. Location-based applications are of special interest, because they take advantage of the unique capabilities of mobile technology. Whenever a user is connected to the Internet via a wireless device (cell phone, PDA, laptop), the transmission technology can be leveraged to determine that person's location and beam location-specific services or product information. For example, drivers could use this capability to obtain local weather data and local traffic information along with alternate route suggestions and descriptions of nearby restaurants.

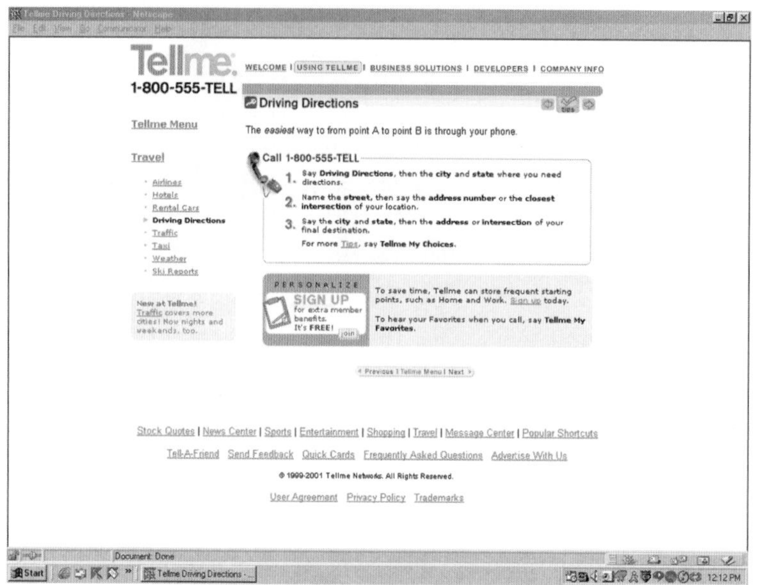


*TellMe is a portal providing direct access to the Web using voice commands with wireless devices. It can provide driving directions and other location-based services.*

**Wireless Application Protocol (WAP)**
System of protocols and technologies that lets cell phones and other wireless devices with tiny displays, low bandwidth connections, and minimal memory access Web-based information and services.

**Wireless Markup Language (WML)**
Markup language for wireless Web sites, which is based on XML and optimized for tiny displays.

**microbrowser**
Web browser software with a small file size that can work with low memory constraints and tiny screens of handheld wireless devices and low bandwidth of wireless networks.

Although m-commerce is only beginning to become popular in the United States, millions of users in Japan and Scandinavia already use cell phones to purchase goods, trade files, and get updated weather and sports reports. The Window on Organizations describes some of these m-commerce applications.

## Wireless Web Standards

There are a plethora of standards governing every area of wireless communications. The two main standards for the wireless Web are Wireless Application Protocol (WAP) and I-mode (see Figure 9-7).

**Wireless Application Protocol (WAP)** is a system of protocols and technologies that lets cell phones and other wireless devices with tiny displays, low bandwidth connections, and minimal memory access Web-based information and services. WAP uses **Wireless Markup Language (WML),** which is based on XML (see Chapter 6) and optimized for tiny displays. Like XML, WML describes data rather than only the way data are displayed. A person with a WAP-compliant phone uses the built-in microbrowser to make a request in WML. A **microbrowser** is an Internet browser with a small file size that can work with low memory constraints of handheld wireless devices and low bandwidth of wireless networks. The request is passed to a WAP gateway, which retrieves the information from an Internet server in either standard HTML format or WML. The gateway translates HTML content back into WML so that it can be received by the WAP client. The complexity of the translation process can affect the speed of information delivery.

WML requires much less bandwidth and processing power than HTML and fits within tiny display screens. WAP supports most wireless network standards and operating systems for handheld computing devices such as PalmOS and Windows CE.

### TABLE 9-5 M-COMMERCE SERVICES AND APPLICATIONS

| M-commerce Service | Application |
|---|---|
| Information-based services | Instant messaging, e-mail, searching for a movie or restaurant using a cell phone or handheld PDA |
| Transaction-based services | Purchasing stocks, concert tickets, music, or games; searching for the best price of an item using a cell phone and buying it in a physical store or on the Web |
| Personalized services | Services that anticipate what you want based on your location or data profile, such as providing updated airline flight information or beaming coupons for nearby restaurants |

## It's Becoming a Wireless World

In parts of Europe and Japan, m-commerce is flourishing. Consumers are using their cell phones as "electronic wallets" to shop, bank, and even pay their rent. Here are some examples.

Estonian Mobile Phone Co. offers a service that enables subscribers to use their mobile phones to pay for parking spaces. After pulling into a parking space, they merely tap a few keys on the phone, and the screen displays a message confirming that the parking fee has been charged to their "virtual account." Parking attendants can check for payment by entering the driver's license plate number into their mobile devices to check the virtual account.

Spain's Telefonica SA is teaming up with Banco Bilbao Vizcaya Argentaria SA to provide a wireless payment system that enables users to purchase inexpensive products such as soft drinks or newspapers by pressing a few keys on their mobile phones. The cost of the purchase is automatically deducted from the customer's bank account. Subscribers to Italy's Omnitel, a unit of Vodafone Air Touch PLC, can use their cell phones to participate in wireless auctions for holiday packages, high-tech gear, and other products.

Japan already has dozens of mobile phone services for which consumers are willing to pay. NTT DoCoMo Inc., the wireless arm of Nippon Telegraph and Telephone Co., offers a wireless Internet service that has already attracted 15 million subscribers. Subscribers receive an Internet-enabled cell phone with which they can send and receive e-mail and access numerous Web sites formatted for tiny screens. For example, 28-year-old Takayo Yamamoto uses her cell phone to send e-mail to friends, check train schedules, obtain movie listings, and read Japan's largest daily newspaper. Other Japanese users can browse through restaurant guides, purchase tickets on Japan Airlines, trade stocks via DLJ Direct Inc., or view new cartoons.

The small keypads on mobile phones make it difficult for users to type in Web addresses. Subscribers to Japanese Web services can obtain menus of services tailored to their specific interests. Customers can sign onto a service with the click of a button without having to find and key in a complete Web address.

Some of these services are free; those that aren't, such as the newspaper, are bundled together and charged to users' monthly telephone bill. The subscription fee for each Japanese wireless Internet service is about $3 per month. This microbilling system is simple for users and profitable for m-commerce service providers. According to Toby Rhodes, an analyst with Nikko Salomon Smith Barney in Tokyo, "it's a new business model." Most owners of Web sites for PCs in the United States provide the Web contents for free, and they believe consumers will balk if they start charging for their services. They are still struggling to become profitable. But Japan's mobile phone-based Internet services charge for content, adding their fees to subscribers' cellular telephone bills. People who would ordinarily resist paying for Web services apparently are willing to subscribe to wireless Web services, because payment is so convenient.

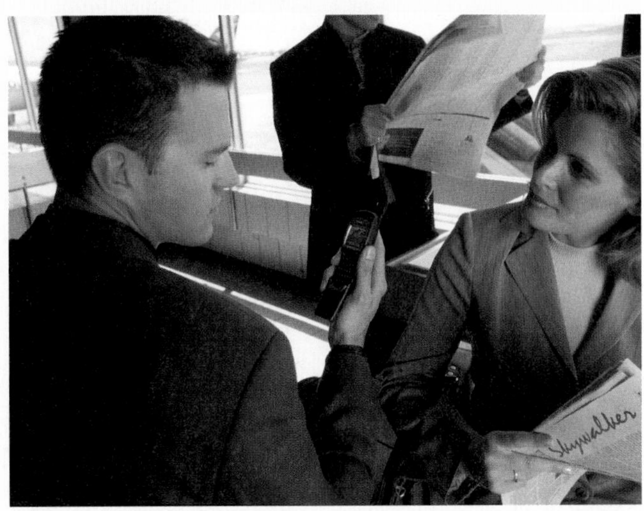

**To Think About:** What types of businesses can benefit from supplying m-commerce services?

*Sources:* Simon Romero. "Weak Reception," *The New York Times*, January 29, 2001; Samuel Greengard, "All for One," *Internet World*, March 1, 2001; Gautam Naik, "M-commerce: Mobile and Multiplying," *The Wall Street Journal*, August 18, 2000; and Miki Tanikawa, "Phone Surfing for a Few Yen," *The New York Times*, August 19, 2000.

**I-mode** is a rival standard developed by Japan's NTT DoCoMo mobile phone network. It is widely used in Japan and is being introduced to Europe. I-mode uses compact HTML to deliver content, making it easier for businesses to convert their HTML Web sites to mobile service. I-mode uses packet switching, allowing users to be constantly connected to the network and content providers to broadcast relevant information to users. (WAP users have to dial in to see if a site has changed.) I-mode can handle color graphics not available on WAP handsets, although WAP is being modified to handle color graphics.

**I-mode**
Standard developed by Japan's NTT DoCoMo mobile phone network for enabling cell phones to received Web-based content and services.

## M-commerce Challenges

Rollout of m-commerce services has not been as rapid in the United States as it has been in Japan and Europe. Keyboards and screens on cell phones are tiny and awkward to use. The

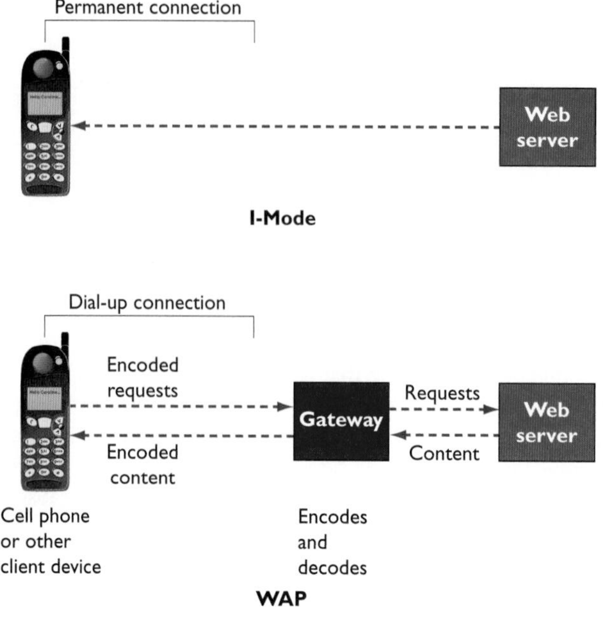


***Figure 9-7*** WAP versus I-mode. WAP and I-mode are two competing standards for accessing information from the wireless Web.

data transfer speeds on existing wireless networks are very slow, ranging from 9.6 to 14.4 KBPS, compared to 56 KBPS for a dial-up connection to the Internet via a PC. Each second waiting for data to download costs the customer money—as much as 69 cents per minute. Most Internet-enabled phones have minimal memory and limited power supplies (Vetter, 2001). Web content for wireless devices is in the form of text with very little graphics. Not enough Web sites have reconfigured their services to display only the few lines of text that can be accommodated by cell phone screens.

Unlike Europe, U.S. wireless networks are based on several incompatible technologies. (Europe uses the GSM standard, whereas wireless carriers in the United States primarily use CDMA or TDMA standards.) For the wireless Web to take off, more Web sites need to be designed specifically for wireless devices, and wireless devices need to be more Web friendly.

**voice portal**
Portal that can accept voice commands for accessing information from the Web.

Some of the limitations of m-commerce may be overcome by using voice recognition technology. **Voice portals** accept voice commands for accessing information from the Web. Voice portals offer customers a combination of content and services, with users accessing the content by speaking into a telephone. The user can orally request information such as stock quotes, weather reports, airline schedules, or news stories (see Table 9-6). Sophisticated voice recognition software processes the requests, which are translated back into speech for the customer.

M-commerce will also benefit from faster wireless networks. Cellular network providers are speeding up their services, preparing new versions of the three main digital standards that will double their speed. Third-generation (3G) mobile communication networks will offer transmission speeds of up to two MBPS. Faster wireless networks will make it possible to stream high-quality video and audio to mobile devices along with new services. The Window on Technology describes other technology advances that will facilitate m-commerce and the opportunities they provide for entrepreneurs.

## ORGANIZATIONAL BENEFITS OF INTERNET AND WEB TECHNOLOGY

The Internet, intranets, and extranets are becoming the principal platforms for electronic commerce, electronic business, and the digital firm because this technology provides so many benefits. The Internet's global connectivity, ease of use, low cost, and multimedia capa-

**TABLE 9-6 EXAMPLES OF VOICE PORTALS**

| Voice Portal | Services |
|---|---|
| HeyAnita | Users can send and receive e-mail by speaking; recognizes voice commands in English, Korean, Mandarin Chinese, and Spanish |
| TellMe Networks Inc. | Users can contact taxis, friends, and specific hotels |
| BeVocal | Provides location services such as tracking down local FedEx offices or providing driving instructions |
| Audiopoint Inc. | Provides up-to-the-minute Capitol Hill updates along with local weather, sports, and news for the Washington, D.C. area |

## M-COMMERCE INSPIRES A NEW WAVE OF NET STARTUPS

Building the Internet infrastructure has proven to be an extraordinary opportunity for entrepreneurship. New companies are popping up to develop the software and services needed to make the wireless Web a success. Entrepreneurs are identifying segments of the wireless business in which they believe they can supply value. Argo Interactive Group, a company with only 28 employees located in Chichester in the United Kingdom, decided it would address the problem of too little bandwidth that all wireless companies face. Although Argo cannot provide more bandwidth, it can help reduce the amount of bandwidth needed for any transmission by lessening the quantity of data needed to accomplish the specific task. Its software product, ActiGate, reduces or eliminates the HTML in wireless transmission that is so vital to the full Web displays on desktop and laptop computers. Because wireless devices vary widely, from the operating systems to screen size and shape, Argo also offers software that tailors messages to the specific device that will be receiving it. That way, someone using a wireless PDA with a vertical three-inch screen isn't restricted to the data that would fit the three-line display screen on a cell phone.

Iobox, a new company located in Helsinki, Finland, and employing only 40 persons, identified a way to make wireless devices more useful to business employees. Using Iobox software, individuals can enter personal data such as one's calendar or address book onto the company's Web site and then access and use them via a cell phone when away from the office. The software also enables the user to go from an entry such as an anniversary reminder to a site at which the user can order flowers or a gift to be sent.

Webraska, a company of 30 employees located in Poissy, France, has identified geographic needs and makes available a service for WAP phones that provides real-time traffic data along with alternate route suggestions. Although users originally had to enter their locations manually, the company is switching to GPS (global positioning system) technology that automatically identifies the location. Once that transition has been made, Webraska provides information about parking lots, gas stations, restaurants, hotels, and other services in the area. To achieve this, the company has joined with hotel networks, tourist guides, and auto clubs.

One Helsinki company with 35 employees, WapIT, decided to offer a wide range of information that European mobile phone users find important. The company maintains a wireless portal offering both its own Web services and those of more than 100 other content providers with whom it has partnered. In this way WapIT can truly satisfy most content demands wireless device users want. For example, their offerings include address books, emergency telephone numbers, and calendars, plus package tracking, and even sports data, horoscopes, and shoe size conversions.

In Korea, employees are forbidden to trade stocks on office PCs. Seoul-based Infobank offers a secure wireless trading platform for mobile phone users. Infobank currently charges South Korean securities firms a flat monthly fee for using its technology but will soon charge fees for every stock trade. South Korean investors are taking advantage of this technology to trade stocks while driving, shopping, and eating, making South Korea the country with the highest percentage of mobile stock trading in the world.

**To Think About:** How do the technologies described here facilitate m-commerce? How could businesses use these technologies?

*Sources:* Fred Sandsmark, "Five Hot Wireless Startups," *Red Herring,* April 2000; and Neel Chowdhury, "Infobank: Stock Trading on the Run," *Fortune,* October 9, 2000.

bilities can be used to create interactive applications, and provide services and products. By using Internet technology, organizations can reduce communication and transaction costs, enhance coordination and collaboration, and accelerate the distribution of knowledge. Table 9-7 summarizes these benefits.

## Connectivity and Global Reach

The value of the Internet lies in its ability to easily and inexpensively connect so many people from so many places all over the globe. Anyone who has an Internet address can log on to a computer and reach any other computer on the network, regardless of location, computer type, or operating system.

The Internet's global connectivity and ease of use can provide companies with access to businesses or individuals who ordinarily would be outside their reach. Companies can link directly to suppliers, business partners, or individual customers at the same low cost, even if they are halfway around the globe. The Internet provides a low-cost medium for forming global alliances. The Web provides a standard interface and inexpensive global access, which can be used to create interorganizational systems among almost any organizations (Isakowitz, Bieber, and Vitali, 1998).

| TABLE 9-7 INTERNET BENEFITS TO ORGANIZATIONS |
|---|
| Connectivity and global reach |
| Reduced communication costs |
| Lower transaction costs |
| Reduced agency costs |
| Interactivity, flexibility, and customization |
| Accelerated distribution of knowledge |

The Internet has made it easier and less expensive for companies to coordinate their staffs when opening new markets or working in isolated places, because they do not have to build their own networks. Small companies who ordinarily would find the cost of operating or selling abroad too expensive will find the Internet especially valuable.

## Reduced Communication Costs

Before the Net, organizations had to build their own wide area networks or subscribe to a value-added network (VAN) service. Employing the Internet, although far from cost free, is certainly more cost effective for many organizations than building one's own network or paying VAN subscription fees. Thus, the Internet can help organizations reduce operational costs or minimize operational expenses while extending their activities.

For example, Schlumberger Ltd., the New York and Paris oil-drilling equipment and electronics producer, operates in 85 countries. Using the Net, employees in remote locations use e-mail to stay in close contact with management at a very low cost. Schlumberger has found that since it converted to the Net from its own network, overall communications costs have dropped. E-mail has reduced voice communication and overnight delivery service charges (employees attach complete documents to their e-mail messages).

**Internet telephony** Technologies that use the Internet Protocol's packet-switched connections for voice service.

**voice over IP (VoIP)** Facilities for managing the delivery of voice information using the Internet Protocol (IP).

**virtual private network (VPN)** A secure connection between two points across the Internet to transmit corporate data. Provides a low-cost alternative to a private network.

Hardware and software have been developed for **Internet telephony,** allowing companies to use the Internet for telephone voice transmission. (Internet telephony products sometimes are called IP telephony products.) **Voice over IP** technology, abbreviated VoIP, uses the Internet Protocol (IP) to deliver voice information in digital form using packet switching, avoiding the tolls charged by the circuit-switched telephone network. For example, Science Applications International Corporation implemented voice over IP service spanning the United States and Europe at a cost of 0.4 cents per minute, one-tenth the cost of low-cost long distance rates on circuit-switched telephone networks (Sweeney, 2000). New high-bandwidth networks will eliminate many of the early sound quality problems of this technology and enable the integration of voice with other Internet services. Users will be able to communicate by talking as well as by typing when they access a Web site.

Internet technology can also reduce communication costs by allowing companies to create virtual private networks as low-cost alternatives to private WANs. A **virtual private network (VPN)** is a secure connection between two points across the Internet and is available through ISPs. The VPN provides many features of a private network at a much lower cost than using private leased telephone lines or frame-relay connections. Companies can save on long-distance communication costs, because workers can access remote locations for the cost of making a local call to an ISP. Figure 9-8 illustrates how a virtual private network works using point-to-point tunneling protocol (PPTP), which is one of several competing protocols used to protect data transmitted over the public Internet. Companies are starting to use VPNs to reduce their wide area networking expenses. For example, the Forum Corporation, a Boston-based global training and consulting firm, saves $6,000 per month by using a VPN instead of leased lines to link to its Hong Kong office (Wallace, 1999). We describe the benefits of VPNs for companies operating internationally in Chapter 16.

## Lower Transaction Costs

Businesses have found that conducting transactions electronically can be done at a fraction of the cost of paper-based processes. Using Internet technology reduces these transaction costs even further. For example, BeamScope Canada Inc. of Richmond Hill, Ontario, finds it can

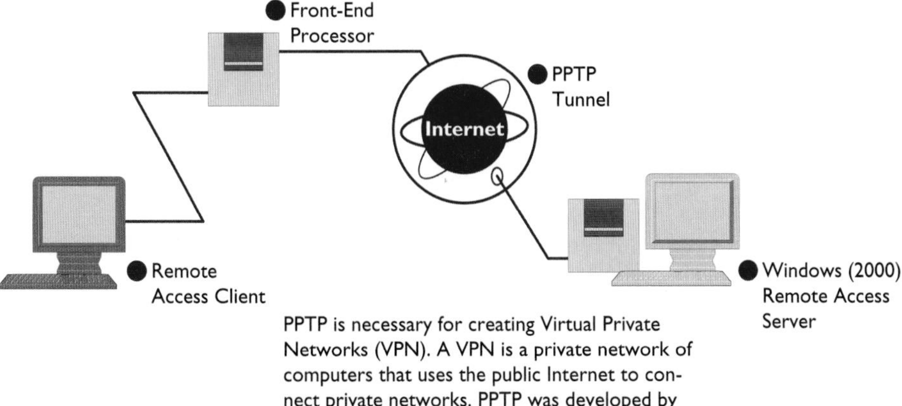


PPTP is necessary for creating Virtual Private Networks (VPN). A VPN is a private network of computers that uses the public Internet to connect private networks. PPTP was developed by Microsoft Corp. and several remote access vendor companies.

❶ The remote client makes a point-to-point connection to the front-end processor via a modem.

❷ The front-end processor connects to the remote access server, establishing a secure "tunnel" connection over the Internet. This connection then functions as the network backbone.

❸ The remote access server handles the account management and supports data encryption through IP, IPX, or NetBEUI protocols.

***Figure 9-8*** Point-to-point tunneling protocol (PPTP) in a virtual private network. Point-to-point tunneling protocol encodes information for transmission across the Internet, which uses the Internet Protocol (IP). In a process called tunneling, PPTP wraps various protocols inside the IP so that non-IP data can travel through an IP network. By adding this "wrapper" around a network message to hide its content, organizations can create a private connection that travels through the public Internet.
*Source:* "Point-to-Point Tunneling Protocol," From *Computerworld,* August 2, 1999. Copyright 1999 *Computerworld Inc.* Reprinted with the permission of *Computerworld Magazine.*

process Web orders for about 80 cents versus $5 to $15 for live orders. Each time Federal Express clients use FedEx's Web site to track the status of their packages instead of inquiring by telephone, FedEx saves $8, amounting to a $2 million savings in operating costs each year. Figure 4-1 in Chapter 4 provides more examples of Internet transaction cost savings.

## Reduced Agency Costs

As organizations expand and globalization continues, the need to coordinate activities in remote locations is becoming more critical. The Internet reduces agency costs—the cost of managing employees and coordinating their work—by providing low-cost networks and inexpensive communication and collaboration tools that can be used on a global scale. Schlumberger, Cisco Systems, Nike Inc., and Millipore are among many companies using the Net for this purpose.

## MANAGEMENT DECISION PROBLEM

### REDUCING AGENCY COSTS

Your company has 3000 employees and is looking for ways to reduce some of its operating costs. You have prepared the following list of operating expenses.

| | |
|---|---|
| Telephone costs | $750,000 per year |
| Employee policy handbooks | $8.75 per handbook for printing and distribution |
| Employee benefits counseling | $80 per hour meeting |

You are hoping you can reduce some of these costs by using Internet technology to build an intranet for the firm. The intranet would do the following:

- Provide e-mail communication among employees worldwide.
- Provide employee handbooks that could be published and revised electronically and accessed from each employee's desktop computer.
- Enable employees to select and revise their medical and life insurance plans on-line through their computers.

You believe that employees could use e-mail to accomplish 40% of the communication that is taking place over the telephone. All employees are required to review their health benefits and re-enroll in their benefits plans once per year. New employee handbooks are distributed to each employee once a year. The intranet would cost $600,000 to develop and $100,000 annually to maintain. No new hardware or networking infrastructure would be required since employees already use networked desktop PCs.

1. How would the intranet make the management process more efficient?
2. How much would the intranet reduce agency costs? Is the intranet worthwhile to build?
3. Are there any other benefits that could be produced by the intranet? Are there any disadvantages to using the intranet?

### Interactivity, Flexibility, and Customization

Internet tools can create interactive applications that can be customized for multiple purposes and audiences. Web pages have capabilities for interacting with viewers that cannot be found in traditional print media. Visitors attracted by alluring displays of text, graphics, video, and sound also can click on hot buttons to make selections, take actions, or pursue additional information. Companies can use e-mail, chat rooms, and electronic discussion groups to create ongoing dialogues with their customers, using the information they have gathered to tailor communication precisely to fit the needs of each individual. They can create **dynamic pages** that reflect each customer's interests, based on information the customer has supplied to the Web site. The content of a dynamic page changes in response to user input at a Web site.

**dynamic page**
Web page with content that changes in response to information a visitor supplies to a Web site.

### Accelerated Distribution of Knowledge

In today's information economy, rapid access to knowledge is critical to the success of many companies. The Internet helps with this problem. Organizations are using e-mail and on-line databases to gain immediate access to information resources in key areas such as business, science, law, and government. With blinding speed, the Internet can link a lone researcher sitting at a computer screen to mountains of data (including graphics) all over the world, which would be otherwise too expensive and too difficult to tap. For example, scientists can obtain photographs taken by NASA space probes within an hour of the pictures being taken. It has become easy and inexpensive for corporations to obtain the latest U.S. Department of Commerce statistics, current weather data, and laws of legal entities worldwide.

In addition to accessing public knowledge resources on the Internet and the Web, companies can create internal Web sites (intranets) as repositories of their own organizational knowledge. Multimedia Web pages can organize this knowledge, giving employees easy access to information and expertise. Web browser software provides a universal interface for accessing information resources from internal corporate databases as well as external information sources.

## 9.4 SUPPORT TECHNOLOGY FOR ELECTRONIC COMMERCE AND ELECTRONIC BUSINESS

Businesses seriously pursuing electronic commerce and electronic business need special tools for maintaining their Web sites. These tools include Web server and electronic commerce server software, customer tracking and personalization tools, Web content management tools, and Web site performance monitoring tools.

### WEB SERVERS AND ELECTRONIC COMMERCE SERVERS

Chapter 6 introduced *Web servers* as the software necessary to run Web sites, intranets, and extranets. The core capabilities of Web server software revolve around locating and managing stored Web pages. Web server software locates the Web pages requested by client computers by translating the URL Web address into the physical file address for the requested Web page. The Web server then sends the requested pages to the client. Many Web servers also include tools for authenticating users; support for FTP, search engines and indexing programs; and capabilities for capturing Web site visitor information in log files. (Each request to the server for a file is recorded as an entry in the Web server log and is called a **hit.**) Apache HTTP Server, Microsoft's Internet Information Server (IIS), and Netscape's Enterprise Server (NES) are currently the most popular Web servers. The Apache and Netscape Web servers work with most operating systems, whereas Internet Information Server is designed for Microsoft operating systems and software tools. Management should examine carefully the servers available in order to determine which server offers the functionality that best fits the needs of the organization's Web site.

**hit**
An entry into a Web server's log file generated by each request to the server for a file.

Web server computers range in size from small desktop PCs to mainframes, depending on the size of the Web sites. The Web server computer must be large enough to handle the Web server software and the projected traffic of the particular site. Servers differ in their performance of various Web functions. For example some servers will load a static Web page faster than other servers whereas others will deliver dynamic Web page content more quickly. Similarly, systems differ in their scalability, a major issue if a company is looking forward to quick growth.

Specialized **electronic commerce server software** provides functions essential for e-commerce Web sites, often running on computers dedicated to this purpose. Functions the software must perform for both business-to-consumer (B2C) and business-to-business (B2B) e-commerce include the following:

**electronic commerce server software**
Software that provides functions essential for running e-commerce Web sites, such as setting up electronic catalogs and storefronts and processing customer purchases.

- Setting up electronic storefronts and electronic catalogs to display product and pricing information.
- Designing electronic shopping carts so customers can collect the items they wish to purchase.
- Making shipping arrangements.
- Linking to electronic payment processing systems.
- Displaying product availability and tracking shipments.
- Connecting to back-office systems where necessary.
- Reporting on both the business transacted through the site and the functioning of that site.

Systems designed for small B2C e-commerce usually include wizards and templates to aid in the setting up of the storefronts and catalogs. However, high-end B2C and B2B systems requires the help of IT professionals for installation and support.

B2B e-commerce software must support tasks that are more complex than those for B2C commerce. B2B software must be able to access information on visitors' contract agreements, order histories, payment records, geographic location(s), and even industries. Although B2C prices are usually fixed, B2B prices are negotiable because they are affected by many contract factors, including volume, logistics preferences, and warranty coverages. B2B software must also support payments made by check and letters of credit as well as payments by credit cards. No single vendor can meet all of the requirements for buying and selling, linking transactions to order fulfillment, manufacturing and supply chains, inventory replenishment, and transportation. E-commerce sites usually must work with more than one system. Table 9-8 on the next page describes examples of leading e-commerce software vendors.

## Customer Tracking and Personalization Tools

Customer tracking and personalization tools have several main goals:

- Collecting and storing data on the behavior of on-line customers and combining that data with data already stored in the company's back-office systems.
- Analyzing the data in order better to understand the behavior of on-line customers.
- Identifying developing customer trends.

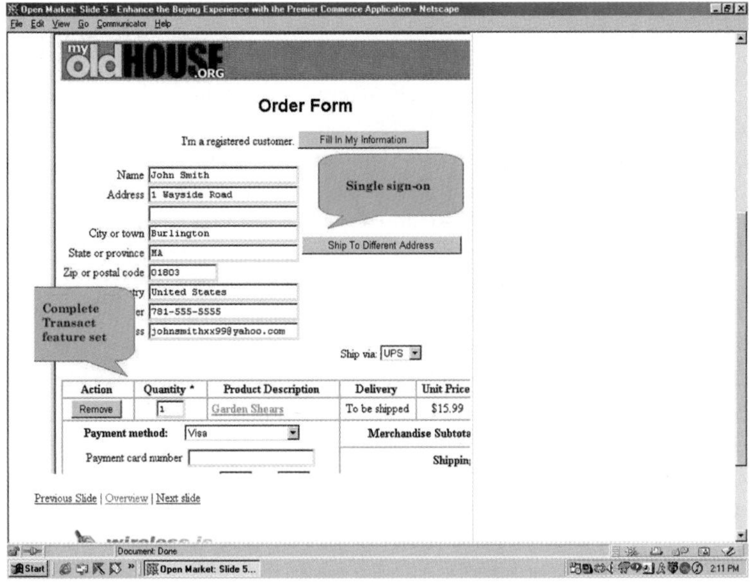


*Open Market offers an integrated suite of applications for e-commerce management and content management. Business can use these tools to quickly develop full-function e-commerce sites.*

## TABLE 9-8 EXAMPLES OF ELECTRONIC COMMERCE SERVERS

| Product | Description | Vendor |
|---|---|---|
| Commerce Server and BizTalk Server | Rapid development of e-commerce applications based on Microsoft architecture; strong enterprise application integration and B2B capabilities | Microsoft |
| Open Market Transact | E-commerce engine, order processing, content management, and catalog systems, with capabilities for integrating with back-end applications | Open Market |
| Websphere Commerce Suite | Tools for building sophisticated e-commerce applications, including pricing, e-billing, scalability, and connectivity to other applications; requires professional developer assistance | IBM |
| Customer Interaction System | Platform for building e-branding and e-marketing around commerce transactions | Blue Martini Software |
| One-to-One Retail (B2C) and One-to-One Business Commerce (B2B) | E-commerce tools with strong personalization, content management, marketing, and reporting capabilities | BroadVision |
| Spectra | E-commerce developer toolkit working with ColdFusion application server; can provide back-end integration with in-house applications | Allaire |

Chapter 4 described some of the benefits of personalizing Web sites to deliver content specific to each user. Alternative approaches for providing Web site personalization include clickstream tracking, check-box personalization, collaborative filtering software, and rules-based systems.

**clickstream tracking**
Tracking data about customer activities at Web sites and storing them in a log.

On-line personalization systems use **clickstream tracking** tools to collect data on customer activities at Web sites and store them in a log. The tools record the site that users last visited before coming to a particular Web site and where these users go when they leave a site. They also record the specific pages visited on a site, the time spent on each page of the site, the types of pages visited, and what the visitors purchased. Web sites can also populate databases with explicit data gained when visitors fill out registration forms on the site or purchase products. This approach is called *check-box personalization,* because users often check their interests on an on-line checklist at the Web site.

**collaborative filtering**
Tracking users' movements on a Web site, comparing the information gleaned about a user's behavior to data about other customers with similar interests to predict what the user would like to see next.

**Collaborative filtering** software tracks users' movements on a Web site, comparing the information it gains about a user's behavior to data about other customers with similar interests in order to predict what the user would like to see next. The software then makes recommendations to users based on their assumed interests. For example, Amazon.com uses collaborative filtering software to prepare personalized book recommendations: "Customers who bought this book also bought. . . ."

Segmentation and rules-based systems use business rules to deliver certain types of information based on a user's profile. They classify users into smaller groups, or segments, based on these rules. The software uses demographic, geographic, or other information to divide, or segment, large populations into smaller groups. Data such as income level, geographic location, or purchasing history are aggregated to identify groups of people. Web sites using such personalization systems deliver content based on applying "if this, then that" rules in processing. Broadvision's electronic commerce system for offering personalized content to Web site visitors is a rules-based product.

**Webhousing**
Storing data collected from Web site visitors in a special data warehouse for this purpose.

Data collected from Web site visitors can be stored in a special data warehouse called a Webhouse. The process is known as **Webhousing.** Some Webhouses make it possible to combine the clickstream data with both back-office data and relevant external data to gain a fuller understanding of each customer. The goal of collecting all these data is to enable the company to unearth customer preferences and trends. Chapter 13 provides additional details on Web customer data analysis.

## Web Content Management Tools

**Web content management tools** exist because many companies have Web sites with thousands or hundreds of thousands of pages, a task too great for a Webmaster to manage. Web content management software has emerged to assist the Webmaster and other responsible staff in the collection, assembly, and management of the content on a Web site, intranet, or extranet.

**Web content management tools**
Software that facilitates the collection, assembly, and management of content on a Web site, intranet, or extranet.

The materials on Web sites are often very complex and include many forms of data such as documents, graphics, and sound. Often the content must be dynamic, with parts of it capable of changing depending on circumstances, such as the identification of the visitor, the day of the month, the price of a product, or the requests of the visitor. In addition, any complex site requires the use of multiple computer languages. Material to be displayed must be able to be prepared or modified off-line and then updated instantly as often as needed. Another complication is that changes often must be published in multiple forms in order to be displayed on computers, personal digital assistants, and Web-enabled phones. Web content management tools must also be able to roll back the contents to an earlier version. And, of course, all of this must be done with neither technical nor content error so that the site will always remain up and operating. Finally Web content management software must include some form of access control (security) so that only those responsible for the specific content are able to update or change it.

## Web Performance Monitoring Tools

Most Web sites are plagued by problems such as slow performance, major outages, content errors, broken links between Web pages, transaction failures, and slow-loading pages. These problems have grown exponentially as numerous Web sites have mushroomed into many thousands or tens of thousands of pages with graphics and advertising. To address these problems, companies can use their own **Web site performance monitoring tools** or they can rely on Web site performance monitoring services.

**Web site performance monitoring tools**
Software for overseeing the speed of downloading Web pages, performing Web transactions, identifying broken links between Web pages, and for pinpointing other Web site problems and bottlenecks.

A central concern at all Web sites is speed—how long does it take for a connection to be established, for a visitor to transfer from another site to your site and to transfer from one page to another within your site. Web site performance monitoring tools measure the response times of specific transactions, such as inquiries, checking out, or authorizing credit through a credit card. They can pinpoint the location of bottlenecks that slow down the reaction of a Web site, such as performance problems at the Web or application server, a specific database, or a network router. Some tools test the site scalability through stressing the site by creating many test site visitors. Some tools also identify the causes for slow page loading speeds, such as loading too many banners, too many dense graphics files, or disk-space problems.

These tools can be used to identify missing links or missing graphics. Some tools compare one site with similar measurements at other Web sites that are top-rated for performance to help companies measure the quality of their own sites.

No single software tool exists that monitors all the functions we have described here. Companies that use these tools often purchase multiple packages or enlist external vendor specialists to do performance measurements for them. Most of these companies offer consulting services when problems do appear so that the Web site owner is able to get quick help in solving its problems.

## Web Hosting Services

Companies that lack the financial or technical resources to operate their own Web sites or electronic commerce services can use Web hosting services. A **Web hosting service** maintains a large Web server computer or a series of servers and provides fee-paying subscribers with space to maintain their Web sites. The subscribing companies may create their own Web pages or have the hosting service or a Web design firm create them.

**Web hosting service**
Company with large Web server computers to maintain the Web sites of fee-paying subscribers.

Web hosting services offer solutions to small companies that do not have the resources to operate their own Web sites or to companies that still are experimenting with electronic commerce. Companies with fewer Web site needs often outsource their sites to an ISP's computer.

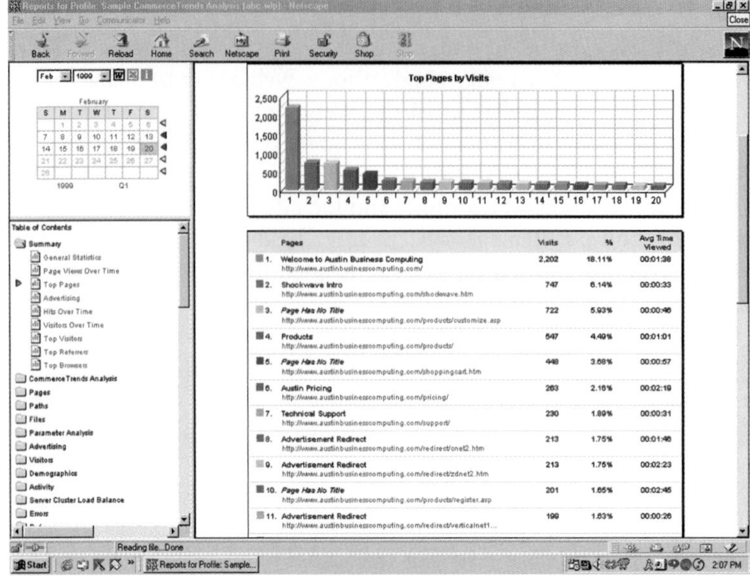


*WebTrends offers sophisticated Web site analysis and reporting tools for businesses of all sizes. Illustrated here is a report showing the most frequently viewed pages of a Web site.*

For $25 to $200 per month, they receive disk storage space for their Web pages and the software for running their Web site, including e-mail services, and in some cases, software for basic electronic commerce transactions. Such services cost much less than running one's own Web site and provide technical staff to design, develop, manage, and support the site.

Companies can also use specialized e-commerce application service providers to set up and operate their e-commerce sites. Companies such as Freemerchant.com provide free e-commerce sites to small businesses with very simple e-commerce requirements that can use a predefined template for displaying and selling their wares. Yahoo! Store and Bigstep.com offer e-commerce storefronts for a low monthly charge.

Many large companies use Web hosting services because they offer highly experienced technical staff and servers in multiple global locations, along with backup server capacity to ensure 100 percent Web site availability. Companies such as IBM Global Services, LoudCloud, and Exodus Communications provide fully managed Web hosting services. High-end managed hosting can range from $50,000 to $1 million per month.

## 9.5 MANAGEMENT ISSUES AND DECISIONS

An information technology infrastructure for digitally enabling the enterprise requires coordinating many different types of computing and networking technologies, public and private infrastructures, and organizational processes. Careful management and planning are essential.

### THE CHALLENGE OF MANAGING THE NEW INFORMATION TECHNOLOGY INFRASTRUCTURE

Implementing enterprise networking and the new information technology infrastructure has created problems as well as opportunities for organizations. Managers need to address these problems to create an IT infrastructure for digitally enabling their firms.

Electronic commerce and e-business are forcing companies to reassess their IT infrastructures in order to remain competitive. Many organizations are saddled with a maze of old legacy applications, hardware, and networks that don't connect with each other. In order to support enterprise-wide business processes that can smoothly link to customers or suppliers via the Internet, they must rebuild their information architectures and IT infrastructures. Five problems stand out: loss of management control over information systems, connectivity and application integration problems, the need for organizational change, the hidden costs

TABLE 9-9

| |
|---|
| Loss of management control over systems |
| Connectivity and application integration problems |
| Organizational change requirements |
| Hidden costs of enterprise computing |
| Scalability, reliability, security |

of enterprise computing, and the difficulty of ensuring infrastructure scalability, reliability and security (see Table 9-9).

## Loss of Management Control

Managing information systems technology and corporate data are proving much more difficult in a distributed environment because of the lack of a single, central point where needed management can occur. Distributed client/server networks, new mobile wireless networks, and Internet computing have enabled end users to become independent sources of computing power capable of collecting, storing, and disseminating data and software. Data and software no longer are confined to the mainframe and under the management of the traditional information systems department but reside on many different computing platforms throughout the organization.

An enterprise-wide IT infrastructure requires that the business know where all of its data are located and ensure that the same piece of information, such as a product number, is used consistently throughout the organization (see Chapter 7). These data may not always be in a standard format or they may reside on incompatible computing platforms. However, observers worry that excess centralization and management of information resources will stifle end users' independence and creativity and reduce their ability to define their own information needs. The dilemma posed by the enterprise networking and the new IT infrastructure is one of central-management control versus end-user creativity and productivity.

## Connectivity and Application Integration

We have already described the connectivity problems created by incompatible networks and standards, including connectivity problems for wireless networks. Digital firm organizations depend on enterprise-wide integration of their business processes and applications so that they can obtain their information from any point in the value chain. An order from a Web site should be able to trigger events automatically in the organization's accounting, inventory, and distribution applications in order to speed the product swiftly to the customer. This end-to-end process and application integration is extremely difficult to achieve and beyond the reach of many firms. For example, the National Association of Manufacturers reported that 90 percent of its members—including large firms with more than $1 billion in annual sales—could not even process orders electronically. They have to print out order information from their Web sites to input it into their transaction systems (Keen, 2000).

## Organizational Change Requirements

Enterprise-wide computing provides an opportunity to reengineer the organization into a more effective unit, but it will only create problems or chaos if the underlying organizational issues are not fully addressed (Duchessi and Chengalur-Smith, 1998). Behind antiquated legacy infrastructures are old ways of doing business, which must also be changed to work effectively in a new enterprise-wide IT infrastructure.

Infrastructure and architecture for a business that can respond to rapid marketplace and industry changes require changes in corporate culture and organizational structure that are not easy to make. It took several years of hard work and large financial investments for IBM to Web-enable its business processes and convince disparate business units to adopt a "One

IBM" mind-set where everyone uses common tools. Sun Microsystems, the networking technology giant, experienced a painful two-year conversion of its own information systems to make them run on its own networks (Kanter, 2001).

## Hidden Costs of Enterprise Computing

Many companies have found that the savings they expected from distributed client/server computing did not materialize because of unexpected costs. Hardware-acquisition savings resulting from significantly lower costs of MIPS on PCs often are offset by high annual operating costs for additional labor and time required for network and system management. Considerable time must be spent on tasks such as network maintenance; data backup; technical problem solving; and hardware, software, and software-update installations. Gains in productivity and efficiency from equipping employees with wireless mobile computing devices must be balanced against increased costs associated with integrating these devices into the firm's IT infrastructure and providing technical support.

## Scalability, Reliability, and Security

Companies seeking to digitally enable their business require robust IT infrastructures providing plentiful bandwidth and storage capacity for transmitting and maintaining all of the data generated by electronic commerce and electronic business transactions. Scalability has emerged as a critical infrastructure issue. Managers need to develop strategies for dealing with steadily increasing loads placed on company networks, from increased traffic and from bandwidth-hungry applications such as audio, streaming video, and graphics. Network infrastructures need to handle not only current e-commerce demands but they must also be able to scale rapidly to meet future demands while providing high levels of performance and availability for mission-critical applications.

Networks have dense layers of interacting technology. Enterprise networking is highly sensitive to different versions of operating systems and network management software, with some applications requiring specific versions of each. It is difficult to make all of the components of large, heterogeneous networks work together as smoothly as management envisions. **Downtime**—periods of time in which the system is not operational—remains much more frequent in distributed systems than in established mainframe systems and should be considered carefully before taking essential applications off a mainframe.

**downtime**
Period of time in which an information system is not operational.

Security is of paramount importance in firms with extensive networking and electronic transactions with individuals or other businesses outside organizational boundaries. Networks present end users, hackers, and thieves with many points of access and opportunities to steal or modify data. Systems linked to the Internet are even more vulnerable because the Internet was designed to be open to everyone. Wireless computing devices linked to corporate applications create additional areas of vulnerability. We discuss these issues in greater detail in Chapter 14.

# SOME SOLUTIONS

Organizations can meet the challenges posed by the new IT infrastructure by planning for and managing the business and organizational changes; increasing end-user training; asserting data administration disciplines; and considering connectivity, application integration, bandwidth, and cost controls in their technology planning.

## Managing the Change

To gain the full benefit of any new technology, organizations must carefully plan for and manage the change. Business processes may need to be reengineered to accompany infrastructure changes (see Chapter 10). For example, equipping the sales force with wireless handheld devices for entering orders in the field provides an opportunity for management to review the sales process to see if redundant order entry activities or a separate order entry staff can be eliminated. Management must address the organizational issues that arise from shifts in staffing, function, power, and organizational culture attending a new IT infrastructure.

## Education and Training

A well-developed training program can help end users overcome problems resulting from the lack of management support and understanding of networked computing (Westin et al., 1985; Bikson et al., 1985). Technical specialists will need training in Web site, wireless, and client/server development and in network support methods.

## Data Administration Disciplines

The role of data administration (see Chapter 7) becomes even more important when networks link many different applications, business areas, and computing devices. Organizations must systematically identify where their data are located, which group is responsible for maintaining each piece of data, and which individuals and groups are allowed to access and use the data. They need to develop specific policies and procedures to ensure that their data are accurate, available only to authorized users, and properly backed up.

## Planning for Connectivity and Application Integration

Senior management must take a long-term view of the firm's IT infrastructure and information architecture, making sure both can support the level of process and information integration for current and future needs. Infrastructure planning should consider how much connectivity would be required to digitally enable core strategic business processes. To what extent should network services be standardized throughout the organization? Will the firm be communicating with customers and suppliers using different technology platforms? How should wireless mobile computing networks be integrated with the rest of the firm?

Although some connectivity problems can be solved by using intranets or the Internet, the firm will need to establish standards for other systems and applications that are enterprise-wide. Management can establish policies to keep networks and telecommunications services as homogeneous as possible, setting standards for data, voice, e-mail, and videoconferencing services along with hardware, software, and network operating systems.

An enterprise-wide architecture for integrated business applications and processes cannot be created through piecemeal changes. It represents a long-term endeavor that should be supported by top management and coordinated with the firm's strategic plans.

# APPLICATION SOFTWARE EXERCISE

### SPREADSHEET, WEB BROWSER, AND PRESENTATION SOFTWARE EXERCISE: RESEARCHING WEB SITE DEVELOPMENT COMPANIES AT JEWEL OF THE WEB

Ralph and Janice Lorenzo have been designing and selling custom jewelry for the past 25 years. A jewelry business that was once operated out of their home has since expanded to a shop located in San Antonio, Texas. They specialize in animal-design jewelry and have built collections around Freddy the Frog, Betty the Cat, and Tommy Teddy Bear. Items in each collection include an assortment of wrist and ankle bracelets, necklaces, rings, and earrings.

Ralph and Janice have heard about electronic commerce and are interested in opening an on-line jewelry store, called Jewel of the Web. Because the Lorenzos have limited knowledge about starting an on-line business, they decided to identify and research companies specializing in Web site development and hosting services. Initially, Jewel of the Web will have seven jewelry categories consisting of 25 products each. It will accept credit cards, and will provide free shipping via all major carriers. The system should collect statistical data, such as the number of hits per day, the number of pages viewed, and peak traffic times.

Your task is to help Ralph and Janice perform their research. Locate three companies specializing in Web site development and hosting services. For each company researched, what would the company charge to build and host the Jewel of the Web on-line store? What are the monthly operating costs associated with Jewel of the Web? Which company do you recommend? Why? Organize your findings in a spreadsheet(s). Also, prepare a written report and slide presentation about your findings. When preparing your analysis, you are free to make necessary assumptions; however, these assumptions must be clearly stated in your written report.

## MANAGEMENT WRAP-UP

Planning the firm's IT infrastructure is a key management responsibility. Managers need to consider how the IT infrastructure supports the firm's business goals and whether the infrastructure should incorporate public infrastructures and links to other organizations. Planning should also consider the need to maintain some measure of management control as computing power becomes more widely distributed throughout the organization.

The new information technology infrastructure can enhance organizational performance by making information flow more smoothly between different parts of the organization and between the organization and its customers, suppliers, and other value partners. Organizations can use Internet technology and tools to reduce communication and coordination costs, create interactive products and services, and accelerate the distribution of knowledge.

Internet technology is providing the connectivity for the new information technology infrastructure and the emerging digital firm, using the TCP/IP reference model and other standards for retrieving, formatting, and displaying information. Key technology decisions should consider the capabilities of Internet, electronic commerce, and new wireless technologies along with connectivity, scalability, reliability, and requirements for application integration.

*For Discussion*

1. It has been said that developing an IT infrastructure for electronic commerce and electronic business is above all a business decision, as opposed to a technical decision. Discuss.
2. A fully-integrated IT infrastructure is essential for business success. Do you agree? Why or why not?

## SUMMARY

1. *Identify the features of the new information technology (IT) infrastructure and important connectivity standards.* The new information technology (IT) infrastructure uses a mixture of computer hardware supplied by different vendors, including mainframes, PCs, and servers, which are networked to each other. More desktop processing power is available through client/server computing and mobile personal information devices that provide remote access to the desktop from outside the organization. The new IT infrastructure also incorporates public infrastructures, such as the telephone system, the Internet, and public network services and electronic devices.

   Connectivity is a measure of how well computers and computer-based devices can communicate with one another and "share" information in a meaningful way without human intervention. It is essential in enterprise networking in the new IT infrastructure that different hardware, software, and network components work together to transfer information seamlessly from one part of the organization to another. TCP/IP and OSI are important reference models for achieving connectivity in networks. Each divides the communications process into layers. Unix is an operating system standard that can be used to create open systems as can the Linux operating system. Connectivity also can be achieved by using Internet technology, XML and Java.
2. *Describe how the Internet works and identify its major capabilities.* The Internet is a worldwide network of networks that uses the client/server model of computing and the TCP/IP network reference model. Using the Net, any computer (or computing appliance) can communicate with any other computer connected to the Net throughout the world. The Internet has no central management. The Internet is used for communications, including e-mail; public forums on thousands of topics; and live, interactive conversations. It also is used for information retrieval from hundreds of libraries and thousands of library, corporate, government, and nonprofit databases. It has developed into an effective way for individuals and organizations to offer information and products through a web of graphical user interfaces and easy-to-use

links worldwide. Major Internet capabilities include e-mail, Usenet, LISTSERV, chatting, Telnet, FTP, gophers, and the World Wide Web.

3. *Evaluate the benefits the Internet offers organizations.* Many organizations use the Net to reduce communications costs when they coordinate organizational activities and communicate with employees. Researchers and knowledge workers are finding the Internet a quick, low-cost way to gather and disperse knowledge. The global connectivity and low cost of the Internet help organizations lower transaction and agency costs, allowing them to link directly to suppliers, customers, and business partners and to coordinate activities on a global scale with limited resources. The Web provides interactive multimedia capabilities that can be used to create new products and services and closer relationships with customers. Communication can be customized to specific audiences.
4. *Describe the principal technologies for supporting electronic commerce.* Businesses need a series of software tools for maintaining an electronic commerce Web site. Web server software locates and manages Web pages stored on Web server computers. Electronic commerce server software provides capabilities for setting up electronic storefronts and arranging for payments and shipping. Customer tracking and personalization tools collect, store, and analyze data on Web site visitors to improve understanding of customer behavior. Content management tools facilitate the collection, assembly, and management of Web site content. Web site performance monitoring tools monitor the speed of Web site transactions and identify Web site performance problems. Businesses can use an external vendor's Web hosting service as an alternative to maintaining their own Web sites.
5. *Analyze the management problems raised by the new IT infrastructure and suggest solutions.* Problems posed by the new IT infrastructure include loss of management control over systems; the need to carefully manage organizational change; connectivity and application integration challenges; the difficulty of ensuring network scalability, reliability, and security; and controlling the hidden costs of enterprise computing. Solutions include planning for and managing the business and organizational changes associated with enterprise-wide computing; increasing end-user training; asserting data administration disciplines; and considering connectivity, application integration and bandwidth when planning the IT infrastructure.

## KEY TERMS

**Bluetooth, 267**
**Chatting, 271**
**Clickstream tracking, 286**
**Collaborative filtering, 286**
**Connectivity, 266**
**Domain name, 270**
**Domain Name System (DNS), 270**
**Downtime, 290**
**Dynamic page, 284**
**Electronic commerce server software, 285**
**Enterprise networking, 265**
**File transfer protocol (FTP), 272**
**Firewall, 276**
**Gopher, 272**
**Hit, 284**
**Home page, 273**
**Hypertext transport protocol (http), 274**
**I-mode, 279**
**Instant messaging, 271**
**Internet Protocol (IP) address, 270**
**Internet Service Provider (ISP), 267**
**Internet telephony, 282**
**Internet2, 272**
**Internetworking, 265**
**LISTSERV, 270**
**Microbrowser, 278**
**Multicasting, 276**
**Open systems, 266**
**Open Systems Interconnect (OSI), 267**
**"Push" technology, 275**
**Search engine, 274**
**Shopping bot, 274**
**Telnet, 271**
**Transmission Control Protocol/Internet Protocol (TCP/IP), 266**
**Uniform resource locator (URL), 273**
**Usenet, 270**
**Virtual private network (VPN), 282**
**Voice over IP (VoIP), 282**
**Voice portal, 280**
**Web content management tools, 287**
**Web hosting service, 287**
**Web site performance monitoring tools, 287**
**Webhousing, 286**
**Webmaster, 273**
**Wireless Application Protocol (WAP), 278**
**Wireless Markup Language (WML), 278**
**Wireless Web, 277**

## REVIEW QUESTIONS

1. What are the features of the new information technology (IT) infrastructure?
2. Why is connectivity so important for the digital firm? List and describe the major connectivity standards for networking and the Internet.
3. What is the Internet? List and describe alternative ways of accessing the Internet.
4. List and describe the principal Internet capabilities.
5. What is Internet2? How does it differ from the first-generation Internet? What benefits does it provide?
6. Why is the World Wide Web so useful for individuals and businesses?
7. List and describe alternative ways of locating information on the Web.
8. What are intranets and extranets? How do they differ from the Web?
9. What is the wireless Web? How does it differ from the conventional Web?
10. List and describe the types of m-commerce services and applications supported by the wireless Web.

11. Compare the WAP and I-mode wireless Web standards.
12. Describe the organizational benefits of Internet and Web technology.
13. List and describe the principal technologies for supporting electronic commerce.
14. Under what conditions should firms consider Web hosting services?
15. Describe five problems posed by the new information technology (IT) infrastructure.
16. Describe some solutions to the problems posed by the new IT infrastructure.

## GROUP PROJECT

Form a group with three or four of your classmates. Prepare an evaluation of the wireless Internet capabilities of the Palm VII and the HP Jornada PocketPC handheld computing devices. Your analysis should consider the purchase cost of each device, any additional software required to make it Internet enabled, the cost of wireless Internet services, and what Internet services are available for each device. You should also consider the other capabilities of each device, including the ability to integrate with existing corporate or PC applications. Which device would you select? What criteria would you use to guide your selection? If possible, use electronic presentation software to present your findings to the class.

## TOOLS FOR INTERACTIVE LEARNING

### INTERNET CONNECTION

The Internet Connection for this chapter will take you to a series of Web sites where you can evaluate tools for providing wireless Web access. You can also use the Interactive Study guide to test your knowledge of the topics in the chapter and get instant feedback where you need more practice.

### ELECTRONIC COMMERCE PROJECT

At the Laudon Web site for Chapter 9, you will find an Electronic Commerce project where you can evaluate various Web search engines for business research.

### CD-ROM

If you use the Multimedia Edition CD-ROM with this chapter, you can complete an interactive exercise that requires you to select the appropriate Internet service for a series of problems. You can also find a video demonstrating the Internet services provided by Apple Computer, an audio overview of the major themes of this chapter, and bullet text summarizing the key points of the chapter.

## CASE STUDY *General Motors Drives down the Information Highway*

General Motors (GM) is the world's largest automaker, with 338,000 employees in 35 countries. GM vehicle brands include Chevrolet, Pontiac, Oldsmobile, Buick, Cadillac, Saturn, Saab, and GMC Trucks. GM also has vehicle production relationships with Opel, Vauxhall, Subaru, and Alfa Romeo. Its nonvehicle ventures include Allison Transmission (manufacturer of medium and heavy-duty transmissions), GM Locomotives, and a 35 percent share of Hughes Electronics (producer of satellites and communications). GM's subsidiary, GM Acceptance Corp. (GMAC) is a major financing organization that specializes in financing GM vehicle purchases and home mortgages.

GM's auto sales have been declining, from about 60 percent of the U.S. vehicle market in the 1970s, to only 28 percent today. GM continues to face stiff competition from Ford, DaimlerChrysler, and the Japanese, all of whom have lower production costs—and cars with better styling and quality. The latest indication of GM's problems came on December 12, 2000, when GM announced it would be phasing out the Oldsmobile over the next several years.

GM's sheer size has proved to be one of its greatest burdens. For 70 years, GM operated along the lines laid down by CEO Alfred Sloan. Sloan separated the firm into five separate operating groups and divisions (Chevrolet, Pontiac, Oldsmobile, Buick, and Cadillac). Each division functioned as a semiautonomous company with its own marketing operations. GM remained a far-flung vertically integrated corporation that at one time manufactured up to 70 percent of its own parts. This model of top-down control and decentralized execution had once been a powerful source of competitive advantage, enabling GM to build cars at a lower cost than its rivals. Over time, however, it worked against the company. Domestic competitors, such as Chrysler, were able to make vehicles at lower costs, because they could purchase their parts from outside vendors and bargain on pricing. GM was not able to move quickly to update its selection and styling, and the quality of its cars lagged behind Japanese and even U.S. rivals.

GM's information systems reflected its welter of bureaucracies. At one time, GM had more than 100 mainframes and 34 computer centers but had no centralized system to link computer operations or to coordinate operations from one department to another. The design group could not interact with production engineers via computer. GM had more than 16 different electronic mail systems, 28 different word processing systems, and a jumble of factory floor systems that could not communicate with management. Most of these systems were running on completely incompatible equipment.

Since the early 1980s GM's management has tried to standardize and integrate its systems. GM first used Electronic Data Systems (EDS) of Dallas (which it had briefly owned) to consolidate its computing centers into 21 uniform information-processing centers. EDS then consolidated 100 different GM networks into the world's largest private digital telecommunications network. In 1993, EDS replaced GM's hodgepodge of desktop models, network operating systems, and application development tools with standard hardware and software for office technology. GM has also been replacing 30 different materials and scheduling systems with one integrated system to handle inventory, manufacturing, and financial data.

GM's current Chief Information Officer Ralph Szygenda has continued to work on streamlining the firm's information architecture and information technology infrastructure. Under his leadership, GM continued to trim the number of vendors of hardware, software, and services for its desktops and networks and to develop common business processes and systems. Szygenda's information systems group replaced more than 50 systems with standard, packaged software for personnel, payroll, and material management, including enterprise software to tie together human resources management and financial systems. GM replaced 26 different CAD/CAM systems with a single system from EDS. Customer data had been fragmented among thousands of disparate databases and data warehouses maintained by GM's car and truck divisions, and its leasing, home mortgage, and credit units. Szygenda initiated projects to integrate and standardize these data to provide a complete company-wide picture of the entire customer experience. Now GM knows which customers purchase vehicles frequently using GM financing and can link each order to a customer's entire car buying history. Before consolidating legacy systems and databases, this information would have been impossible to obtain.

In August 1999 GM added a new division devoted to the use of the Internet and e-commerce, known as e-GM. Mark Hogan was named the head of the division and a corporate group vice president. In February 2000, 47-year-old Rick Wagoner was appointed CEO of GM, replacing Jack Smith. At that time Wagoner stated his intention to focus on innovative products and services and the development of e-business. Wagoner's management team believes that by intensively weaving Internet technology into all of its business processes, GM can become a smarter, leaner, faster company more in tune with customers. It also hopes this technology will help GM reduce from 24 months to 12 months the time to design, engineer and manufacture a new vehicle. GM management also believes that Internet technology could cut up to 10 percent of the cost of making a vehicle by eliminating supply chain inefficiencies. GM would use the savings produced from this skillful use of technology to increase spending on its vehicle designs. Although GM has the broadest vehicle lineup in the industry (49 models), it has lacked the resources to keep its models fresh.

Internet technology could be the catalyst for GM to reconstruct its entire value chain, transforming itself into a customer-focused business that provides many different electronic services to consumers as well as cars. Indeed, more and more of GM's revenue comes from other sources, including the Internet. For instance, in April 2000 GM announced it would move into the world of on-line mortgages, cellular services, and information delivery, as well as selling its vehicle-based Internet technology. Ultimately, some think, all of this might make it the world's largest e-commerce company. Let us examine some of GM's Internet initiatives.

**Selling Vehicles On-line**

Laws in most states make it extremely difficult for anyone other than licensed auto dealerships to sell new vehicles, thanks to the lobbying power of the National Auto Dealers Association (NADA).

In March 1999, GM established GMBuyPower.com, an informational Web site for GM car shoppers. By autumn 2000, with the site receiving about one million hits per month, the company decided to use the site to try selling vehicles on line. This decision was partly in response to growing sales through such Web sites as Autobytel.com. GM is working on pilot programs to enable customers to purchase vehicles on-line through local dealerships. The dealers are concerned about GM trying to bypass them by selling vehicles on-line, a channel conflict.

Dealers are vital to GM for several other reasons, including their role in vehicle inventory. The auto manufacturers make a "guesstimate" as to the number of each model to produce each year and in what color and with what options. The dealers in turn decide which of these vehicles they think they can sell and then make their purchases. Only then do customers begin to purchase, selecting from dealer inventories. To make the system work, the industry maintains about a two-month inventory of new vehicles. The value of GM's inventory is usually about $40 billion, making inventory costs very high. The dealers hold most of this inventory and so assume much of the risk and expense of owning the vehicles.

**Building Vehicles to Order**

Auto producers are anxious to make cars that customers have actually ordered. "Build-to-order" would greatly reduce finished vehicle inventory costs as well as generate other production cost savings, potentially saving GM $20 billion per year. GM is so committed to build-to-order that it has assigned 200 people the goal of selling 80 percent of all GM new car purchases built-to-order within three years. Achieving its goal will require heavy reliance on its Internet infrastructure and extensive organizational change. The company will have to be able to take orders on-line, link its factories and suppliers on-line, change designs so the vehicles can be built more easily using modules, and greatly reduce shipping times. Although GM is experimenting with on-line sales, the company has yet to achieve individually scheduled car orders or significantly reduce order-to-delivery times (which now run around 6 weeks).

In order to reduce procurement and inventory costs, GM and other major auto manufacturers have established Covisint (see the Window on Organizations in Chapter 4), a massive on-line exchange. GM spends $87 billion per year on raw materials and components and believes the exchange could cut the cost of producing each vehicle by perhaps $1,000 (estimates vary) as well as reduce order-to-delivery time.

The Internet will play a smaller role in developing GM's ability to switch to modular construction. Such a switch is necessary because of the current need to deliver about 3,000 parts for every vehicle. The company has already established an experimental modular assembly plant in Latin America. However, union problems are likely to be a big issue, because modular building will almost certainly lower the income of autoworkers. Delivery remains a problem. Delivering a vehicle takes time, unlike a smaller item, such as a computer for example, which can be put into a box and delivered speedily by FedEx or UPS.

**Locate-to-Order**

Build-to-order is not yet a reality, and so the immediate problem is quickly finding the desired car, a strategy known as locate-to-order. To facilitate this approach, GM must create a regional inventory of the pool of available vehicles using the Internet. The pool will be displayed on the Net so potential buyers can select the car they want regardless of its location. Customers then buy it through their local dealer. Ultimately, however, GM will have to build-to-order because inventory cost savings are so compelling.

**OnStar**

Another information age venture GM has established is its wholly owned subsidiary, OnStar. It is a vehicle-based cellular communications system that includes a GPS (global positioning system), which keeps the system constantly informed as to the location of the vehicle on the road. OnStar provides such services as emergency roadside assistance, stolen-vehicle tracking, and concierge support such as making dinner reservations.

One new feature for 2001 includes OnStar Personal Calling, which enables drivers to make and receive calls hands-free with voice-activated phones. Another new service is OnStar Virtual Advisor, which allows users to retrieve personal data on the Web, including e-mail, news, stock quotes, and traffic and road condition reports within a given radius of the driver's location. Whether the hardware is standard or an option, any user of OnStar pays an annual subscription fee, ranging from $199 to $399 depending on the services.

The company expects OnStar quickly to become a significant source of revenue. By the end of 2001, the company predicts it will be serving one million subscribers. In 2000 GM licensed OnStar first to Honda Corp. and then to Toyota. OnStar's revenue is projected to climb to $6 billion by 2004. GM may also make its services available outside of vehicles through such technology as the Palm PDA.

**Internal Uses**

General Motors is using its Internet infrastructure for more standard uses as well. It created an intranet portal called Socrates that allows users to search all of GM's internal sites from one starting point. Today 100,000 GM employees around the globe can access more than 500 internal GM sites through this portal. Employees can use Socrates to access their human resources information, participate in on-line training programs, and search through a repository of best practices. Socrates has capabilities for enabling employees to tailor the information they obtain to their own needs. GM is even subsidizing the cost of home access for its employees, because it wants to make the Internet a more integral part of their daily lives.

Ralph Szygenda has said that, "The [automobile production] company that links design, procurement and sales—and puts it all together electronically—wins." Will his words be borne out? Can GM use the Internet to transform its hidebound bureaucracy? Two decades of restructuring and reorganization have brought about deep changes at GM, resulting in the paring down of waste in an overbloated organization. But GM failed to reverse its declining market share. GM risks falling behind Ford as the leader in U.S. sales. Despite shedding tens of thousands of workers, chopping billions of dollars per year off costs, and eliminating models, GM still struggles to earn net income of more than three cents on the dollar. Although GM currently is not experiencing a financial crisis, it remains under heavy pressure to boost its mediocre profit margins.

Overall, GM has invested about $1.6 billion in streamlining its IT infrastructure and architecture along with various e-commerce and e-business initiatives. These changes have already reduced GM's IT budget by $800 million each year since 1996. But will this be enough to boost profits over the long run? Information technology spending at GM is more than $4.5 billion, slightly below 3 percent of total revenue. But Ford and Chrysler only spend from 1 to 2 percent of revenue on IT.

**Sources:** Lee Copeland, "GM Adds Stock Trading to OnStar Service," *The Industry Standard,* February 15, 2001; Gregory L. White, "In Order to Grow, GM Finds That the Order of the Day Is Cutbacks," *The Wall Street Journal,* December 18, 2000; Keith Bradsher, "G.M. Phaseout of Olds Is at Center of a Range of Cutbacks," *The New York Times,* December 13, 2000; Dale Buss, "Custom Cars Stuck in Gridlock," *The Industry Standard,* October 16, 2000, and "The Race to be Wired," *The Industry Standard,* September 4, 2000; Lee Copeland, "Automakers Put Workers Online," *Computerworld,* November 3, 2000, "General Motors' CIO Touts Corporate Benefits Portal," *Computerworld,* November 27, 2000, "GM Now Sells Web Technology, Not Just Cars," *Computerworld,* June, 5, 2000, and "GM Shuts Doors on GMDriverSite.com," *Computerworld,* September 4, 2000; Sari Kalin, "Overdrive," *CIO Web Business Magazine,* July 1, 2000; Julia King and Lee Copeland, "GM Retools for E-commerce That Goes Well Beyond Cars," *Computerworld,* April 17, 2000; Todd Lassa, "General Motors Is Making a Major Internet Play, and It's Put a Real 'Car Guy' Behind the Wheel. But Can He Drive an E-business?" *Internet World Magazine,* March 1, 2000; Kathleen Melymuka, "GM Deal for Web-based Dealership Software Falls Through," *Computerworld,* November 16, 2000; Robert L. Simison, "GM Retools to Sell Custom Cars Online," *The Wall Street Journal,* February 22, 2000; Paul Strassmann, "GM's Info Gamble," *Computerworld,* June 5, 2000; Lauren Gibbons Paul, "The Biggest Gamble Yet," *CIO Magazine,* April 15, 2000; Steve Ulfelder, "Internet Drag Race," *Computerworld,* March 6, 2000; Ken Yamada, "Shop Talk: Car Dealers, Customers Both Win on Web," *Red Herring,* September 26, 2000; Eric Young, "Stalled on the Digital Highway," *The Industry Standard,* September 4, 2000; Jennifer Zaino, "OnStar Expands Services for Drivers," *Information Week,* November 14, 2000.

### *CASE STUDY QUESTIONS*

1. Describe the competitive business environment in which General Motors (GM) is operating.
2. Describe the relationship between GM's organization and its information technology infrastructure. What management, organization, and technology factors influenced this relationship?
3. Evaluate GM's current business strategy in response to its competitive environment. What is the role of Internet technology in that strategy? How successful is that strategy?
4. What management, organization, and technology issues do you think GM has had to face and will need to solve in implementing its Internet strategy?
5. How will GM have to redesign its business processes to be able to compete successfully and achieve a leading role in the new economy?
6. In GM's drive to sell cars on-line and to build-to-order, what are some of the problems that technology cannot address?

# Part II Project
# Creating a New Internet Business

We have prepared a list of new businesses that could benefit from going on the Web. Select one of the businesses from the list and develop an Internet strategy for that business. You will need to identify the Internet business model to be pursued, use the Internet to research and analyze markets and competitors, and design part of the Web site for that business.

## Virtual Tour of Electronic Commerce Sites

To prepare for this project, you can review Internet business models by taking the Virtual Tour of Electronic Commerce Sites, which can be found on the Laudon Web site. The tour takes you to nine different Web sites, each using the Web in a different way for electronic commerce. Each represents a different business model for using the Internet. The Virtual Tour itinerary includes the following:

| Business Model | Description | Organization | URL |
|---|---|---|---|
| Virtual Storefront | Sells physical goods on-line instead of through a physical storefront or retail outlet. The goods are shipped directly to the customer. | Amazon.com | www.amazon.com |
| Information Broker | Provides primarily product, pricing, and availability information. The final purchase transaction is usually conducted elsewhere. | Travelocity | www.travelocity.com |
| Marketplace Concentrator | Concentrates information about products and services from multiple providers at one central point. Purchasers can search, comparison shop, and sometimes complete the sales transaction. | InsWeb | www.insweb.com |
| Transaction Broker | Provides services that allow people to complete transactions, such as buying and selling securities. | E*TRADE | www.etrade.com |
| Electronic Clearinghouse | Provides an auctionlike setting, allowing purchase of products where price and availability constantly change. | eBay | www.ebay.com |
| Digital Product Delivery | Products that are entirely digital, such as software or multimedia, can be both sold and delivered over the Internet. | PhotoDisc | www.photodisc.com |
| Content Provider | Creates on-line content on the Web. The site generates revenue by selling the content or by selling on-line advertising space. | Wall Street Journal Interactive | www.wsj.com |
| Reverse Auction | Customers submit bids to multiple sellers to buy goods or services at a buyer-specified price. | Priceline.com | www.priceline.com |
| Online Service Provider | Web sites where hardware and software users can obtain on-line service and support. | Xdrive.com | www.xdrive.com |

## SELECTING AN INTERNET BUSINESS MODEL AND DESIGNING A WEB STRATEGY

The five businesses we describe are fictitious but are based on real-world scenarios. Review each of them. Then select one business and answer the following questions:

1. What Internet business model would be appropriate for the company to follow in creating a Web site?
2. In what ways can the company benefit from a Web site? What functions should it perform for the company (marketing, sales, customer support, internal communications, etc.)?
3. In what other ways might the company use the Internet for its own benefit?
4. Prepare functional specifications for the company's use of the Web and the Internet. Include links to and from other sites in your design.
5. Prepare a cost–benefit analysis of a proposal to implement the company's use of the Internet.

For each of the five businesses, we list a Web site of a real-world company in the same or a related business to help you understand that type of business. Visit the Web site related to the business you have selected and review it carefully.

**Business 1: InfoInc**

InfoInc is a start-up company that would like to provide a service by offering easy access to needed information in specialized fields, such as accounting, finance, or medicine. Although its business plan calls for moving into a number of fields, InfoInc would like to begin by addressing the needs of people in the accounting and tax field. Its first two target groups are accounting professionals and the general public. For the general public, the plan is to provide a Web site with advice on various issues, such as tax laws and IRA savings rules. The site would also contain links to other sites where visitors will be able to obtain advice on such issues as how to establish a new business. For accounting professionals, such as CPAs (certified public accountants) and corporate financial officers, InfoInc would like to offer more detailed information services. In addition, the company wants to provide capabilities that might help the CPA and financial officer manage their e-mail, voice mail, and fax.

Web reference: WebMD Inc. (http://webmd.com/)

**Business 2: Aerospace Metal Alloys**

Aerospace Metal is a distributor of exotic steel, aluminum, and titanium alloys to the aerospace industry and to other specialty industries. These metals, such as kovar and inconel, must meet exceptionally exacting standards, because they become parts in airplanes, rockets, industrial furnaces, and other high-performance products. Aerospace sells raw materials produced in the form of bars, sheets, rings, and forgings. In turn, Aerospace customers use these materials to fabricate their final products. Many Aerospace customers are actually parts suppliers to end-product assemblers such as Boeing Aircraft. Aerospace Metal maintains a sales staff to sell the metals, and the company stores its products in seven warehouses around the United States. They obtain their products from steel and metal manufacturers throughout North America. If a customer requests a product not carried by Aerospace, Aerospace will specially order it from an appropriate supplier.

Web reference: Specialty Steel and Storage (http://www.steelforge.com)

**Business 3: Columbiana**

Columbiana is a small, independent island in the Caribbean. It is underdeveloped and is off the tourist path for most visitors to that area, despite its many tourist attractions. The island has a unique history, with Indian ruins going back 800 years and with many historical buildings, forts, and other sites built during its centuries as a British colony. A few first-class hotels have been built along some of its beautiful white beaches, and less expensive accommodations are also available along beaches in several towns and near several fishing villages. Its rain forests, rivers, striking mountains, and volcano cone all could be of interest to tourists. In addition, it has many restaurants that specialize in native dishes and fresh fish. The government not only wants to increase tourism but it also wants to increase trade by developing new markets for its tropical agricultural products. In addition, its leaders hope to attract investment capital so that unemployed residents can find jobs. Two major airlines have regular flights to Columbiana, as do several small Caribbean airlines. The island is on the tourist itinerary of only one cruise ship company. The Web site will not transact any business, but it will offer information and links to other appropriate sites.

Web reference: Dominica (http://dominica.dm)

**Business 4: Portable Energy Inc.**

Millions of electronic products exist today that rely partially or fully on batteries. These batteries are replaced in massive numbers. Moreover, many portable equipment users are beginning to rely on rechargeable batteries to reduce long-range expenses. People needing replacement or rechargeable batteries can go to a variety of places to purchase them, but the search for such batteries can be difficult and very time consuming, and the price paid can be very high. Portable Energy's founder, seeing a market niche that was not being exploited, decided to establish a new business. The heart of the business is a database listing more than 5,000 batteries and the products in which they are used. Portable Energy began operations as a catalog company, installing a free 800 telephone number to take orders and to answer potential customers' technical questions. The company initially relied on advertisements in magazines read by business travelers to attract customers. This enabled it to reach enough users of portable devices to build the base for a small company. Portable Energy also opened a small retail store in the Silicon Valley area. However, the company is looking to expand geographically, to reach potential customers around the world, as the engine for a major increase in sales. In addition the CEO is also seeking ways to cut sales and customer support costs while maintaining or improving service quality. To achieve these goals, the company has decided to establish a Web site.

Web reference: iGo.com (http://www.igo.com)

**Business 5: Brawny Luggage Inc.**

Brawny began as a single luggage store in a small city in the Atlanta region. The goal of the store was to develop a reputation as a center of expertise on professional and vacation luggage needs. The owner also planned for the store to become known as a center for consistently low luggage prices. To accomplish these objectives, Brawny carried a wide range of products, and it emphasized having a highly trained staff. Brawny did so well that the company began opening stores in other neighborhoods and soon found itself becoming a large regional chain. Management believes that the key to the company's success is the staff's understanding of their customers' needs. The stores carry an enormous selection of products from every major luggage manufacturer as well as a wide range of related products, including business cases, tote bags, and travel accessories. The emergence of the World Wide Web is believed by management to be a great opportunity both to better service customers in its own region and to fill the luggage needs of customers elsewhere in the country and throughout the world. Brawny management also believes that the correct Web strategy will facilitate the company's opening of more stores making it a nationwide chain.

Web reference: The Luggage Factory (http://www.luggagefactoryoutlet.com/)

# PART III

# Building Information Systems in the Digital Firm

chapter

# 10 Redesigning the Organization with Information Systems

objectives

**After completing this chapter, you will be able to:**

1. *Demonstrate how building new systems can produce organizational change.*
2. *Explain how the organization can develop information systems that fit its business plan.*
3. *Identify the core activities in the systems development process.*
4. *Appraise alternatives for building systems: the traditional systems lifecycle, prototyping, application software packages, end-user development, and outsourcing.*
5. *Evaluate the use of object-oriented software development and rapid application development (RAD) in building contemporary systems.*

## TVA Nuclear Designs a New Maintenance Work System

For most companies, improper machine maintenance might mean a little downtime on the factory floors or a few missed orders. For the Tennessee Valley Authority (TVA) nuclear division, the stakes are much higher. In the heavily regulated and safety-conscious energy industry, machine maintenance can spell the difference between life and death.

Located in the seven-state Tennessee Valley region of the United States, the TVA supplies energy to nearly eight million customers from fossil, hydroelectric, and nuclear power sources. The three TVA Nuclear facilities provide about 20 percent of TVA's generating capacity. The safety and health of the public and TVA employees receive top priority in the operation and maintenance of TVA nuclear plants.

After analyzing TVA Nuclear's major business processes, senior management determined that the machine maintenance process required major improvement. It was using outdated software and maintenance work was heavily paper based. Whatever systems did exist to support this process did not "speak to" each other or share a common interface. Maintenance workers had to rely on documents, such as vendor manuals, drawings, and formal work instructions, to perform their jobs. More than 14,000 work orders are written each year at the Browns Ferry nuclear plant alone. For all of its nuclear plants, TVA Nuclear estimated it spent nearly $49 million annually generating, planning, and performing maintenance work orders.

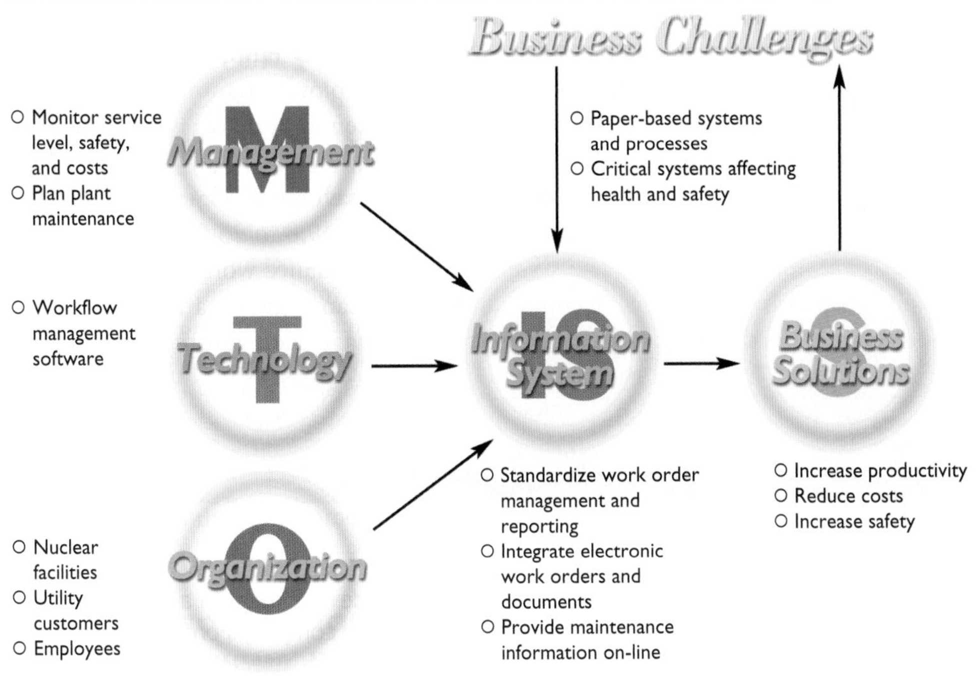


TVA executives assembled a project team from various groups at the Browns Ferry nuclear plant, with input from the two other nuclear plants in the TVA network. The team started by analyzing TVA's existing systems and business processes, looking for places to consolidate work and identifying performance metrics they most wanted to improve. They then charted the existing work order and procedures-management processes, spending more than 350 hours interviewing plant employees. To find models of good practices that they could use as guidelines, the team benchmarked the maintenance processes of 15 utilities and 6 other companies.

The team found that the planning and execution of maintenance work orders was closely linked to procedures management and document workflow. For instance, a typical work order was handwritten and came attached to various paper copies of machine diagrams, documentation, and instruction procedures. Although most of TVA Nuclear's work is planned two months to a year in advance, it constantly receives new procedural updates. The handwritten work orders could not keep up with the procedural revisions.

After six months of full-time work, the project team had designed a new work process that combined maintenance-order workflow with procedural document management. TVA Nuclear then built two integrated systems that would support the new process by linking procedural documents electronically to the work management system. TVA Nuclear outsourced the systems-building effort to a vendor called System Works, who then used the software it created for TVA to develop a commercial software package it could sell to other organizations.

*(continued)*

**TVA Nuclear Designs a New Maintenance Work System**

**MANAGEMENT CHALLENGES**

## TABLE 10-1 INFORMATION SYSTEMS PLAN

**1. Purpose of the Plan**

Overview of plan contents
Changes in firm's current situation
Firm's strategic plan
Current business organization
Key business processes
Management strategy

**2. Strategic Business Plan**

Current situation
Current business organization and future organization
Changing environments
Major goals of the business plan

**3. Current Systems**

Major systems supporting business functions and processes
Current infrastructure capabilities
- Hardware
- Software
- Database
- Telecommunications

Difficulties meeting business requirements
Anticipated future demands

**4. New Developments**

New system projects
- Project descriptions
- Business rationale

New infrastructure capabilities required
- Hardware
- Software
- Database
- Telecommunications and Internet

**5. Management Strategy**

Acquisition plans
Milestones and timing
Organizational realignment
Alliances with value partners
Internal reorganization
Management controls
Personnel strategy

**6. Implementation Plan**

Anticipated difficulties in implementation
Progress reports

**7. Budget Requirements**

Requirements
Potential savings
Financing
Acquisition cycle

## Enterprise Analysis (Business Systems Planning)

**enterprise analysis**
An analysis of organization-wide information requirements that looks at the entire organization in terms of organizational units, functions, processes, and data elements; helps identify the key entities and attributes in the organization's data.

**Enterprise analysis** (also called *business systems planning*) argues that the firm's information requirements can only be understood by looking at the entire organization in terms of organizational units, functions, processes, and data elements. Enterprise analysis can help identify the key entities and attributes of the organization's data.

The central method used in the enterprise analysis approach is to take a large sample of managers and ask them how they use information, where they get their information, what their environments are like, what their objectives are, how they make decisions, and what their data needs are.

The results of this large survey of managers are aggregated into subunits, functions, processes, and data matrices. Data elements are organized into logical application groups—groups of data elements that support related sets of organizational processes. Figure 10-1 is an output of enterprise analysis conducted by the Social Security Administration as part of a massive systems redevelopment effort. It shows what information is required to support a particular process, which processes create the data, and which use them. The shaded boxes in the figure indicate a logical application group. In this case, actuarial estimates, agency plans, and budget data are created in the planning process, suggesting that an information system should be built to support planning.

| Logical Application Groups | Processes / Data Classes | Actuarial estimates | Agency plans | Budget | Program regs./policy | Admin. regs./policy | Labor agreements | Data standards | Procedures | Automated systems documentation | Educational media | Public agreements | Intergovernmental agreements | Grants | External | Exchange control | Administrative accounts | Program expenditures | Audit reports | Organization/position | Employee identification | Recruitment/placement | Complaints/grievances | Training resources | Security | Equipment utilization | Space utilization | Supplies utilization | Workload schedules | Work measurement | Enumeration I.D. | Enumeration control | Earnings | Employer I.D. | Earnings control | Claims characteristics | Claims control | Decisions | Payment | Collection/waiver | Notice | Inquiries control | Quality appraisal |
|---|---|---|---|---|---|---|---|---|---|---|---|---|---|---|---|---|---|---|---|---|---|---|---|---|---|---|---|---|---|---|---|---|---|---|---|---|---|---|---|---|---|---|---|
| PLANNING | Develop agency plans |C|C|C|U|U||||||||U|||||||||||||||||||||||||||||||
| PLANNING | Administer agency budget |C|C|C|U|U||||||U|U|U||U|U|U||U|U|||||U|U|U||U||U|||U||U|||U||U|U|
| PLANNING | Formulate program policies |U|U||C||||U|||||||U||||U|||||||||||||||||||||||U|||||U|
| PLANNING | Formulate admin. policies ||U||U|C|C||U||||||U||||U|U|||U||||||||||||||||||||||||
| PLANNING | Formulate data policies ||U|U||U||C|U|U|||||||||||||||U|U|U|U||||||||||||||||||
| PLANNING | Design work processes ||U||U|U|||C|C||U|U||||||U||||||||||||||||||||||U|||||U|
| GENERAL MANAGEMENT | Manage public affairs ||U||U|U|||U||C|C|C|||||||||||||||||||||||||||||||||
| GENERAL MANAGEMENT | Manage intrgovt. affairs |U|U||U|U|||U||U||C|C|C||||||||||||||||||U|U||U|U||U|||U|||||
| GENERAL MANAGEMENT | Exchange data ||||U||||U|||U|U|U|U|C|U|U||||||||||||||U|||||||||||||||
| GENERAL MANAGEMENT | Maintain admin. accounts |||U||U|||U|||U|U||||C||||U|||||U|U|U||||||||U|||U|||||
| GENERAL MANAGEMENT | Maintain prog. accounts |||U|U||||U|||U|U|||||C||||||||||||||U|||U||U|U|U|U||U||
| GENERAL MANAGEMENT | Conduct audits ||||U|U|||U|U||||||U|U|C||U||||||||U|||||||||||||||
| GENERAL MANAGEMENT | Establish organizations |||U||U|||U|||||||||||C|U||||||||U|U||||||||||||||U|
| GENERAL MANAGEMENT | Manage human resources |||U||U|U||U|||||||||||C|C|C|C|C|||||||||||||||||||||
| GENERAL MANAGEMENT | Provide security ||||U|U||U|U|U|||||||||||||||C|C|C|C||U||||||||||||||
| GENERAL MANAGEMENT | Manage equipment |||U||U||U|U|U|||||||||||||||C|C|C|C||||||||||||||||
| GENERAL MANAGEMENT | Manage facilities |||U||U|||U|||||||||||||||||U|U|C|||||||||||||||||||
| GENERAL MANAGEMENT | Manage supplies |||U||U|||U|||||||||||||||||C|U|U|C||||||||||||||||
| GENERAL MANAGEMENT | Manage workloads |U||U|U|U|||U|||||||U||||||||||U|U|U|C|C||U|||U||U|||||U|U|
| PROGRAM ADMIN. | Issue Social Security nos. ||||||||U||||U||U||||||||||||||||C|C|||||||||||
| PROGRAM ADMIN. | Maintain earnings ||||||||U||||U|U|U||||||||||||||||U||C|C|C|U||||||||
| PROGRAM ADMIN. | Collect claims information ||||U|U|||U||||||U||||||||||||||||U|U||||C|C|U|U|U||||
| PROGRAM ADMIN. | Determine elig./entlmt. ||||||||U||||||||||||||||||||||U|U|U|||U||C|U|U||||
| PROGRAM ADMIN. | Compute payments ||||U||||U|||||||||U|||||||||||||U||U|||U||U|C|C||||
| PROGRAM ADMIN. | Administer debt mgmt. ||||U||||U|||||||||U|||||||||||||||||||||U|C||||
| SUPPORT | Generate notices ||||||||U||||||U|||||||||||||||U||U|||U||U|U|U|C|||
| SUPPORT | Respond to prog. inquiries ||||U||||U||U|||||||||||||||||||U||U|U||U||U|U|U|U|C||
| SUPPORT | Provide quality assessment ||||U|U|||U|U|||||||||||||||||||||U||U|||U||U|||U||C|

KEY

C = creators of data U = users of data

*Figure 10-1* Process/data class matrix. This chart depicts which data classes are required to support particular organizational processes and which processes are the creators and users of data.

The weakness of enterprise analysis is that it produces an enormous amount of data that is expensive to collect and difficult to analyze. Most of the interviews are conducted with senior or middle managers, with little effort to collect information from clerical workers and supervisory managers. Moreover, the questions frequently focus not on management's critical objectives and where information is needed, but rather on what existing information is used. The result is a tendency to automate whatever exists. But, in many instances, entirely new approaches to how business is conducted are needed, and these needs are not addressed.

## Strategic Analysis or Critical Success Factors

The strategic analysis, or critical success factors, approach argues that an organization's information requirements are determined by a small number of **critical success factors (CSFs)** of managers. If these goals can be attained, the firm's or organization's success is assured (Rockart, 1979; Rockart and Treacy, 1982). CSFs are shaped by the industry, the firm, the manager, and the broader environment. An important premise of the strategic analysis approach is that there are a small number of objectives that managers can easily identify and on which information systems can focus.

**critical success factors (CSFs)**
A small number of easily identifiable operational goals shaped by the industry, the firm, the manager, and the broader environment that are believed to assure the success of an organization. Used to determine the information requirements of an organization.

## TABLE 10-2 Critical Success Factors and Organizational Goals

| Example | Goals | CSF |
|---|---|---|
| Profit concern | Earnings/share | Automotive industry |
| | Return on investment | Styling |
| | Market share | Quality dealer system |
| | New product | Cost control |
| | | Energy standards |
| Nonprofit | Excellent healthcare | Regional integration with other hospitals |
| | Meeting government regulations | Improved monitoring of regulations |
| | Future health needs | Efficient use of resources |

*Source:* Rockart (1979).

The principal method used in CSF analysis is personal interviews—three or four—with a number of top managers to identify their goals and the resulting CSFs. These personal CSFs are aggregated to develop a picture of the firm's CSFs. Then systems are built to deliver information on these CSFs. (See Table 10-2 for an example of CSFs. For the method of developing CSFs in an organization, see Figure 10-2.)

The strength of the CSF method is that it produces a smaller data set to analyze than does enterprise analysis. Only top managers are interviewed, and the questions focus on a small number of CSFs rather than a broad inquiry into what information is used or needed. It is especially suitable for top management and for the development of DSS and ESS. Unlike enterprise analysis, the CSF method focuses organizational attention on how information should be handled.

The method's primary weakness is that the aggregation process and the analysis of the data are art forms. There is no particularly rigorous way in which individual CSFs can be aggregated into a clear company pattern. Second, there is often confusion among interviewees (and interviewers) between *individual* and *organizational* CSFs. They are not necessarily the same. What can be critical to a manager may not be important for the organization. Moreover, this method is clearly biased toward top managers because they are the ones (generally the only ones) interviewed.

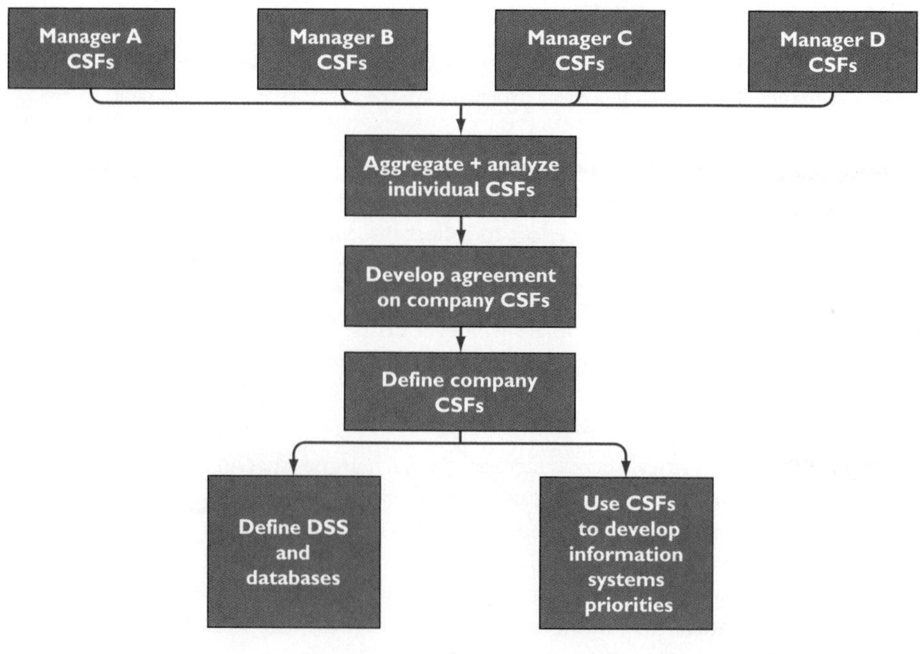


***Figure 10-2*** Using CSFs to develop systems. The CSF approach relies on interviews with key managers to identify their CSFs. Individual CSFs are aggregated to develop CSFs for the entire firm. Systems can then be built to deliver information on these CSFs.

**TABLE 10-3** HOW INFORMATION TECHNOLOGY CAN TRANSFORM ORGANIZATIONS

| Information Technology | Organizational Change |
|---|---|
| Global networks | International division of labor: The operations of a firm and its business processes are no longer determined by location; the global reach of firms is extended; the firm can link its industries to those of customers and value partners in far-flung locations; costs of global coordination decline. Transaction costs decline. |
| Enterprise networks | Collaborative work and teamwork: The organization of work can now be coordinated across divisional boundaries; the costs of management (agency costs) decline. Multiple tasks can be worked on simultaneously from different locations. |
| Distributed computing | Empowerment: Individuals and work groups now have the information and knowledge to act. Business processes can be streamlined. Management costs decline. Hierarchy and centralization decline. |
| Portable computing | Virtual organizations: Work is no longer tied to physical location. Knowledge and information can be delivered anywhere they are needed, anytime. Work becomes portable. |
| Multimedia and graphical interfaces | Accessibility: Everyone in the organization—even senior executives—can access information and knowledge. Organizational costs decline as workflows move from paper to digital image, documents, and voice. Complex knowledge objects can be stored and represented as objects containing graphics, audio, video, or text. |

## SYSTEMS DEVELOPMENT AND ORGANIZATIONAL CHANGE

New information systems can be powerful instruments for organizational change, enabling organizations to redesign their structure, scope, power relationships, workflows, products, and services. Table 10-3 describes some of the ways that information technology is being used to transform organizations and business processes.

### The Spectrum of Organizational Change

Information technology can promote various degrees of organizational change, ranging from incremental to far-reaching. Figure 10-3 shows four kinds of structural organizational change that are enabled by information technology: (1) automation, (2) rationalization, (3) reengineering, and (4) paradigm shifts. Each carries different rewards and risks.

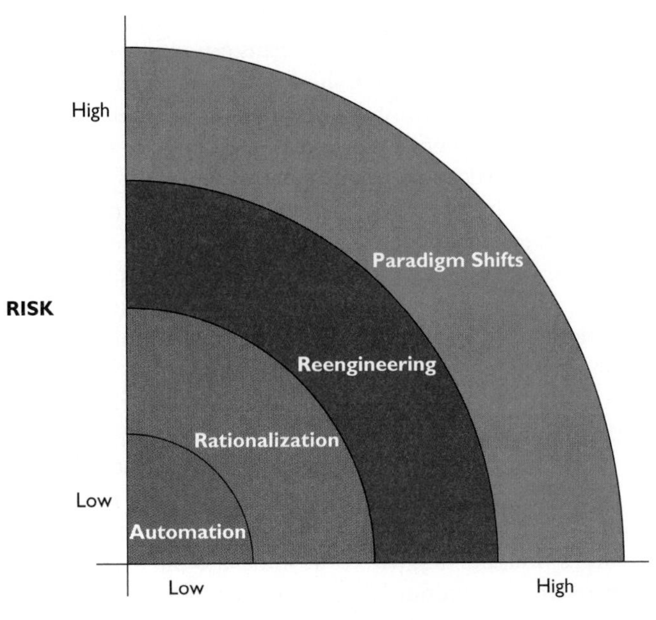


*Figure 10-3* Organizational change carries risks and rewards. The most common forms of organizational change are automation and rationalization. These relatively slow-moving and slow-changing strategies present modest returns but involve little risk. Faster and more comprehensive change—like reengineering and paradigm shifts—carry high rewards but offer a substantial chance of failure.

**automation**
Using the computer to speed up the performance of existing tasks.

The most common form of IT-enabled organizational change is **automation.** The first applications of information technology involved assisting employees in performing their tasks efficiently and effectively. Calculating paychecks and payroll registers, giving bank tellers instant access to customer deposit records, and developing a nationwide network of airline reservation terminals for airline reservation agents are all examples of early automation.

**rationalization of procedures**
The streamlining of standard operating procedures, eliminating obvious bottlenecks, so that automation makes operating procedures more efficient.

A deeper form of organizational change—one that follows quickly from early automation—is **rationalization of procedures.** Automation frequently reveals new bottlenecks in production and makes the existing arrangement of procedures and structures painfully cumbersome. Rationalization of procedures is the streamlining of standard operating procedures, eliminating obvious bottlenecks, so that automation can make operating procedures more efficient. For example, TVA Nuclear's new system is effective not only because it uses computer technology but also because its design allows the organization to operate more efficiently. The procedures of TVA Nuclear, or any organization, must be rationally structured to achieve this result. TVA Nuclear had to have standard identification numbers for each work order and standard rules for matching work orders with drawings and other documents. Without a certain amount of rationalization in TVA Nuclear's organization, its computer technology would have been useless.

**business process reengineering**
The radical redesign of business processes, combining steps to cut waste and eliminating repetitive, paper-intensive tasks in order to improve costs, quality, and service, and to maximize the benefits of information technology.

A more powerful type of organizational change is **business process reengineering,** in which business processes are analyzed, simplified, and redesigned. Using information technology, organizations can rethink and streamline their business processes to improve speed, service, and quality. Business process reengineering reorganizes workflows, combining steps to cut waste and eliminating repetitive, paper-intensive tasks (sometimes the new design eliminates jobs as well). It is much more ambitious than rationalization of procedures, requiring a new vision of how the process is to be organized.

A widely cited example of business process reengineering is Ford Motor Company's *invoiceless processing.* Ford employed more than 500 people in its North American Accounts Payable organization. The accounts payable clerks spent most of their time resolving discrepancies between purchase orders, receiving documents, and invoices. Ford reengineered its accounts payable process, instituting a system wherein the purchasing department enters a purchase order into an on-line database that can be checked by the receiving department when the ordered items arrive. If the received goods match the purchase order, the system automatically generates a check for accounts payable to send to the vendor. There is no need for vendors to send invoices. After reengineering, Ford was able to reduce headcount in accounts payable by 75 percent and produce more accurate financial information (Hammer and Champy, 1993).

Rationalizing procedures and redesigning business processes are limited to specific parts of a business. New information systems can ultimately affect the design of the entire organization, by transforming how the organization carries out its business or even the nature of the business itself. For instance, Schneider National, the largest carrier of full-truckload cargoes in North America, used new information systems to change its business model. Schneider created a new business managing the logistics for other companies. Its Schneider Brokerage Web Site allows shippers to select from thousands of approved carriers in the United States, Canada, and Mexico. Baxter International's stockless inventory system (described in Chapter 2) transformed Baxter into a working partner with hospitals and into a manager of its customers' supplies. This more radical form of business change is called a **paradigm shift.** A paradigm shift involves rethinking the nature of the business and the nature of the organization itself. The Window on Technology illustrates how Cemex used digital technology to make such organizational changes and move toward a digital firm organization.

**paradigm shift**
Radical reconceptualization of the nature of the business and the nature of the organization.

Paradigm shifts and reengineering often fail because extensive organizational change is so difficult to orchestrate (see Chapter 11). Why then do so many corporations entertain such radical change? Because the rewards are equally high (see Figure 10-3). In many instances firms seeking paradigm shifts and pursuing reengineering strategies achieve stunning, order-of-magnitude increases in their returns on investment (or productivity). Some of these success stories, and some failure stories, are included throughout this book.

Window on Technology

## CEMEX BECOMES A DIGITAL FIRM

Cemex, based in Monterrey, Mexico, is a 90-year-old company that sells cement and ready-mix concrete. It's an asset-intensive, low-efficiency business with unpredictable demand. Dispatchers took orders for 8,000 grades of mixed concrete and forwarded them to six regional mixing plants, each with its own fleet of trucks. Customers routinely changed half of their orders, often hours before delivery, and these orders might have to be rerouted because of weather change, traffic jams, or problems with building permits. Cemex's phone lines were often jammed as customers, truckers, and dispatchers tried to get orders straight. Many orders were lost.

Lorenzo Zambrano, a grandson of the founder of the company, took over the business in 1985 and decided to apply information technology to these problems. He and Cemex chief information officer Gelacio Iniguez developed a series of systems that would enable Cemex to manage unforecastable demand better than its competitors.

Zambrano and Iniguez used ideas gleaned from visits to U.S. companies such as Federal Express, Exxon, and Houston's 911 emergency dispatch system to see how other organizations anticipated demand for their services. They built a system linking Cemex delivery trucks to a global positioning satellite system to help dispatchers monitor the location, direction, and speed of every vehicle. This information helps Cemex send the right truck to deliver a specific grade of cement or redirect deliveries when prompted by last-minute changes. The company has reduced average delivery time from 3 hours to 20 minutes, realizing huge savings in fuel, maintenance, and personnel costs. Cemex now uses 35 percent fewer trucks to deliver the same amount of concrete. Customers are willing to pay premium prices to Cemex, because they do not have to keep work crews idle waiting for concrete deliveries to arrive.

Cemex's production facilities used to operate independently, without precise knowledge of customer demand. A satellite communications system called CemexNet now electronically links all the firm's production facilities and coordinates them from a central clearinghouse.

Customers, distributors, and suppliers can use the Internet to place orders, check shipment delivery times, and review payment records without having to telephone a customer service representative. Zambrano and his managers now have access to almost every detail about Cemex operations within 24 hours, whereas competitors are working with month-old data. Cemex's productivity and profitability have outpaced all of their major rivals in Mexico, and production output has grown sixfold since 1985. Cemex has become the world's third-largest concrete manufacturer.

**To Think About:** How did digital technology transform the way Cemex ran its business? It has been said that Cemex has refocused efforts from managing assets to managing information. Explain. To what extent is Cemex a digital firm?

*Sources:* Adrian J. Slywotzky and David J. Morrison, "Concrete Solution," *The Industry Standard,* August 28, 2000; and John A. Byrne, "Management by Web," *Business Week,* August 28, 2000.

# 10.2 BUSINESS PROCESS REENGINEERING AND TOTAL QUALITY MANAGEMENT (TQM)

Many companies today are focusing on building new information systems where they can improve their business processes. Some of these system projects represent radical restructuring of business processes, whereas others entail more incremental change.

## BUSINESS PROCESS REENGINEERING

If organizations rethink and radically redesign their business processes before applying computing power, they can potentially obtain very large payoffs from their investments in information technology. The home mortgage industry is a leading example in the United States of how major corporations have implemented business process reengineering. The application process for a home mortgage traditionally required about six to eight weeks and cost about $3,000. The goal of many mortgage banks has been to lower that cost to $1,000 and the time to obtain a mortgage to about one week. Leading mortgage banks such as BankBoston, Countrywide Funding Corporation, and Banc One Corporation have redesigned the mortgage application process.

The mortgage application process is divided into three stages: origination, servicing, and secondary marketing. Figure 10-4 illustrates how business process reengineering has been used in each of these stages.

In the past, a mortgage applicant filled out a paper loan application. The bank entered the application into its computer system. Specialists such as credit analysts and underwriters from perhaps eight different departments accessed and evaluated the application individually. If the loan application was approved, the closing was scheduled. After the closing, bank specialists dealing with insurance or funds in escrow serviced the loan. This "desk-to-desk" assembly-line approach might take up to 17 days.

Leading banks have replaced the sequential desk-to-desk approach with a speedier "work cell" or team approach. Now, loan originators in the field enter the mortgage application directly into laptop computers. Software checks the application transaction to make sure that all of the information is correct and complete. The loan originators transmit the loan applications using a dial-up network to regional production centers. Instead of working on the application individually, the credit analysts, loan underwriters, and other specialists convene electronically, working as a team to approve the mortgage. Some banks provide customers with a nearly instant credit lock-in of a guaranteed mortgage so they can find a house that meets their budget immediately. Such preapproval of a credit line is truly a radical reengineering of the traditional business process.

After closing, another team of specialists sets up the loan for servicing. The entire loan application process can take as little as two days. Loan information is easier to access than before, when the loan application could be in eight or nine different departments. Loan originators also can dial into the bank's network to obtain information on mortgage loan costs or to check the status of a loan for the customer.

By redesigning their approach to mortgage processing, mortgage banks have achieved remarkable efficiencies. They have not focused on redesigning a single business process, but, instead, they have reexamined the entire set of logically connected processes required to obtain a mortgage. Instead of automating the previous method of mortgage processing, the banks have completely rethought the entire mortgage application process.

## Workflow Management

To streamline the paperwork in the mortgage application process, banks have turned to workflow and document management software. By using this software to store and process documents electronically, organizations can redesign their workflow so that documents can be worked on simultaneously or moved more easily and efficiently from one location to another. The process of streamlining business procedures so that documents can be moved easily and efficiently is called **workflow management.** Workflow and document management software automates processes such as routing documents to different locations, securing approvals, scheduling, and generating reports. Two or more people can work simultaneously on the same document, allowing much quicker completion time. Work need not be delayed because a file is out or a document is in transit. And with a properly designed indexing system, users will be able to retrieve files in many different ways, based on the content of the document.

**workflow management**
The process of streamlining business procedures so that documents can be moved easily and efficiently from one location to another.

### STEPS IN EFFECTIVE REENGINEERING

To reengineer effectively, senior management needs to develop a broad strategic vision that calls for redesigned business processes. For example, Mitsubishi Heavy Industries management looked for breakthroughs to lower costs and accelerate product development that would enable the firm to regain world market leadership in shipbuilding. The company redesigned its entire production process to replace expensive, labor-intensive tasks with

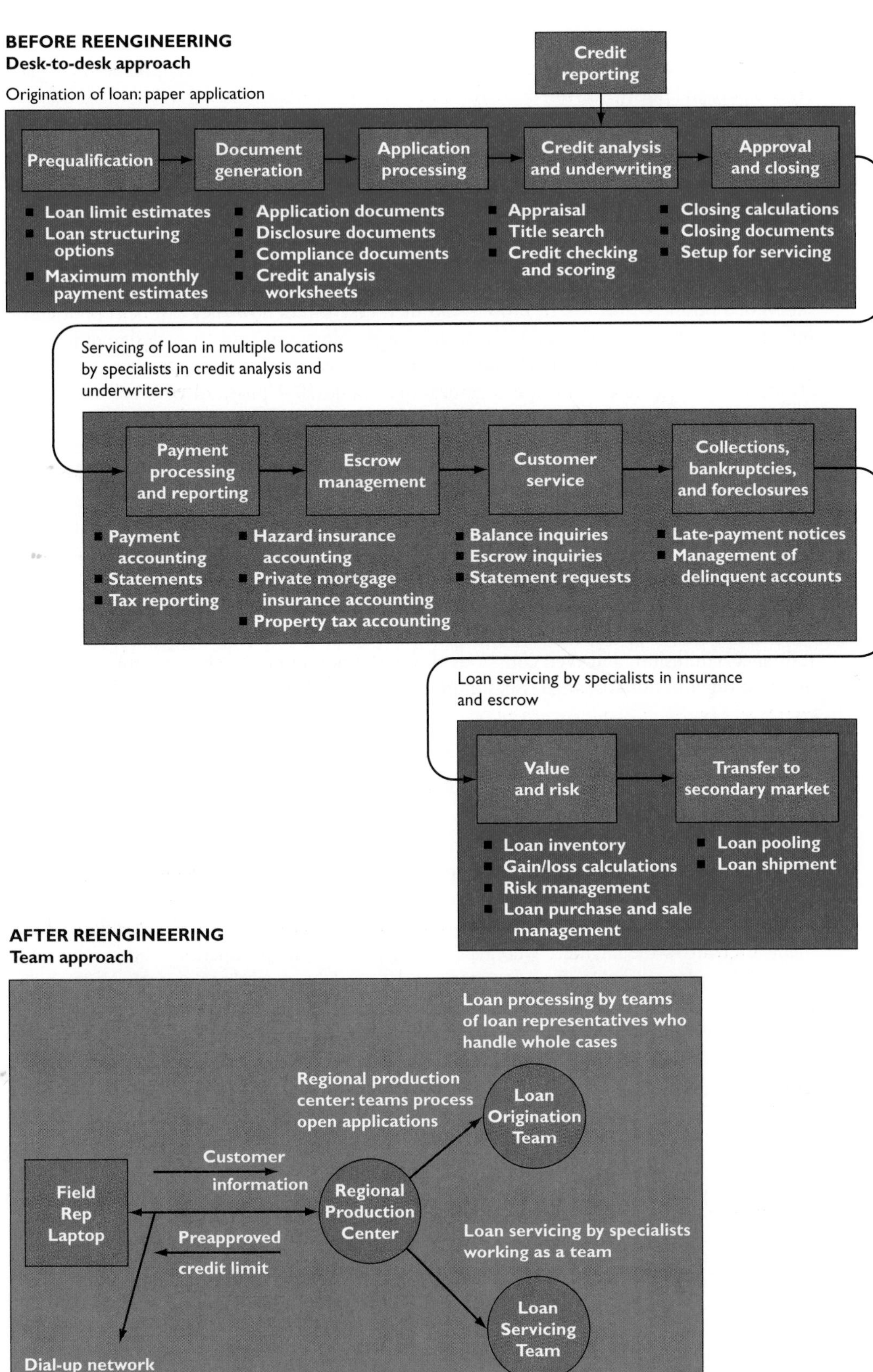


*Figure 10-4* Redesigning mortgage processing in the United States. By redesigning their mortgage processing systems and the mortgage application process, mortgage banks can reduce the costs of processing the average mortgage from $3,000 to $1,000 and reduce the time of approval from six weeks to one week or less. Some banks are even preapproving mortgages and locking interest rates on the same day as the customer applies.

robotic machines and computer-aided design tools. Companies should identify a few core business processes to be redesigned, focusing on those with the greatest potential payback (Davenport and Short, 1990).

Management must understand and measure the performance of existing processes as a baseline. If, for example, the objective of process redesign is to reduce time and cost in developing a new product or filling an order, the organization needs to measure the time and cost consumed by the unchanged process. For example, before reengineering, it cost C. R. England & Sons Inc. $5.10 to send an invoice; after processes were reengineered the cost per invoice dropped to 15 cents (Davidson, 1993).

The conventional method of designing systems establishes the information requirements of a business function or process and then determines how they can be supported by information technology. However, information technology can create new design options for various processes because it can be used to challenge long-standing assumptions about work arrangements that used to inhibit organizations. Table 10-4 provides examples of innovations that have overcome these assumptions using companies discussed in the text. Information technology should be allowed to influence process design from the start.

Following these steps does not automatically guarantee that reengineering will always be successful. The organization's information technology (IT) infrastructure should have capabilities to support business process changes that span boundaries between functions, business units, or firms (Broadbent, Weill, and St. Clair, 1999). The majority of reengineering projects do not achieve breakthrough gains in business performance. A reengineered business process or a new information system inevitably affects jobs, skill requirements, workflows, and reporting relationships (Teng, Jeong, and Grover, 1998). Fear of these changes breeds resistance, confusion, and even conscious efforts to undermine the change effort. We examine these organizational change issues more carefully in Chapter 11.

## PROCESS IMPROVEMENT AND TOTAL QUALITY MANAGEMENT

**total quality management (TQM)**
A concept that makes quality control a responsibility to be shared by all people in an organization.

In addition to increasing organizational efficiency, companies are also changing their business processes to improve the quality in their products, services, and operations. Many are using the concept of **total quality management (TQM)** to make quality the responsibility of all people and functions within an organization. TQM holds that the achievement of quality control is an end in itself. Everyone is expected to contribute to the overall improvement of quality—the engineer who avoids design errors, the production worker who spots defects, the sales representative who presents the product properly to potential customers, and even the secretary who avoids typing mistakes. TQM derives from quality management concepts developed by American quality experts such as W. Edwards Deming and Joseph Juran, but it was popularized by the Japanese. Studies have repeatedly shown that the earlier in the business cycle a problem is eliminated, the less it costs the company. Thus, quality

**TABLE 10-4 NEW PROCESS DESIGN OPTIONS WITH INFORMATION TECHNOLOGY**

| Assumption | Technology | Options | Examples |
|---|---|---|---|
| Field personnel need offices to receive, store, and transmit information | Wireless communications | People can send and receive information from wherever they are | Avis |
| Information can appear only in one place at one time | Shared databases | People can collaborate on the same project from scattered locations; information can be used simultaneously wherever it is needed | Banc One<br>U.S. West (Qwest) |
| People are needed to ascertain where things are located | Automatic identification and tracking technology | Things can tell people where they are | United Parcel Service<br>Synnex |
| Businesses need reserve inventory to prevent stockouts | Networks, extranets, and EDI | Just-in-time delivery and stockless supply | Baxter International<br>Wal-Mart |

improvements cannot only raise the level of product and service quality, but they can also lower costs.

## How Information Systems Contribute to Total Quality Management

TQM is considered to be more incremental than business process reengineering (BPR) because its efforts often focus on making a series of continuous improvements rather than dramatic bursts of change. Sometimes, however, processes may have to be fully reengineered to achieve a specified level of quality. Information systems can help firms achieve their quality goals by helping them simplify products or processes, meet benchmarking standards, make improvements based on customer demands, reduce cycle time, and increase the quality and precision of design and production.

**Simplifying the product or the production process.** The fewer steps in a process, the less time and opportunity for an error to occur. Ten years ago, 1-800-FLOWERS, a multimillion-dollar telephone and Web-based floral service with a global reach, was a much smaller company that spent too much on advertising because it could not retain its customers. It had poor service, inconsistent quality, and a cumbersome, manual, order-taking process. Telephone representatives had to write the order, obtain credit card approval, determine which participating florist was closest to the delivery location, select a floral arrangement, and forward the order to the florist. Each step in the manual process increased the chance of human error, and the whole process took at least a half hour. Owners Jim and Chris McCann installed a new computer system that downloads orders taken at telecenters into a central computer and electronically transmits them to local florists. Orders are more accurate and arrive at the florist within one to two minutes.

**Benchmarking.** Many companies have been effective in achieving quality by setting strict standards for products, services, and other activities, and then measuring performance against those standards. This procedure is called **benchmarking.** Companies may use external industry standards, standards set by other companies, internally developed high standards, or some combination of the three. L.L. Bean, Inc., the Freeport, Maine, outdoors catalog company, used benchmarking to achieve an order-shipping accuracy of 99.9 percent. Its old batch order fulfillment system could not handle the surging volume and variety of items to be shipped. After studying German and Scandinavian companies with leading-edge order fulfillment operations, L.L. Bean carefully redesigned its order fulfillment process and information systems so that orders could be processed as soon as they were received and shipped out within 24 hours.

**benchmarking**
Setting strict standards for products, services, or activities and measuring organizational performance against those standards.

**Use customer demands as a guide to improving products and services.** Improving customer service, making customer service the number one priority, will improve the quality of the product itself. Delta Airlines decided to focus more on its customers, installing a customer care system at its airport gates. For each flight, the airplane seating chart, reservations, check-in information, and boarding data are linked in a central database. Airline personnel can track which passengers are on board regardless of where they checked in and use this information to make sure that passengers reach their destinations quickly even if delays cause them to miss connecting flights.

**Reduce cycle time.** Reducing the amount of time from the beginning of a process to its end (cycle time) usually results in fewer steps. Shorter cycles mean that errors are often caught earlier in production (or logistics or design or whatever the function), often before the process is complete, eliminating many hidden costs. Iomega Corporation in Roy, Utah, a manufacturer of disk drives, was spending $20 million a year to fix defective drives at the end of its 28-day production cycle. Reengineering the production process allowed the firm to reduce cycle time to a day and a half, eliminating this problem and winning the prestigious Shingo Prize for Excellence in American Manufacturing.

**Improve the quality and precision of the design.** Computer-aided design (CAD) software has made dramatic quality improvements possible in a wide range of businesses from aircraft manufacturing to production of razor blades. Alan R. Burns, head of the Airboss Company in Perth, Australia, used CAD to invent and design a new modular tire made up of a series of replaceable modules or segments so that if one segment were damaged, only that segment, not the whole tire, would need replacing. Burns established quality performance measurements for such key tire characteristics as load, temperature, speed, wear life, and traction. He entered these data into a CAD software package, which he used to design the modules. Using the software he was able iteratively to design and test until he was satisfied with the results. He did not need to develop an actual working model until the iterative design process was almost complete. Because of the speed and accuracy of the CAD software, the product he produced was of much higher quality than would have been possible through manual design and testing.

**Increase the precision of production.** For many products, one key way to achieve quality is make the production process more precise and decrease the amount of variation from one part to another. GE Medical Systems performed a rigorous quality analysis to improve the reliability and durability of its Lightspeed diagnostic scanner. It broke the processes of designing and producing the scanner into many distinct steps and established optimum specifications for each component part. By understanding these processes precisely, engineers learned that a few simple changes would significantly improve the product's reliability and durability.

## *10.3* Overview of Systems Development

Whatever their scope and objectives, new information systems are an outgrowth of a process of organizational problem solving. A new information system is built as a solution to some type of problem or set of problems the organization perceives it is facing. The problem may be one where managers and employees realize that the organization is not performing as well as expected, or it may come from the realization that the organization should take advantage of new opportunities to perform more successfully.

**systems development** The activities that go into producing an information systems solution to an organizational problem or opportunity.

The activities that go into producing an information system solution to an organizational problem or opportunity are called **systems development.** Systems development is a structured kind of problem solving with distinct activities. These activities consist of systems analysis, systems design, programming, testing, conversion, and production and maintenance.

**systems analysis** The analysis of a problem that the organization will try to solve with an information system.

Figure 10-5 illustrates the systems development process. The systems development activities depicted here usually take place in sequential order. But some of the activities may need to be repeated or some may be taking place simultaneously, depending on the approach to system building that is being employed (see Section 10.4). Note also that each activity involves interaction with the organization. Members of the organization participate in these activities and the systems development process creates organizational changes.

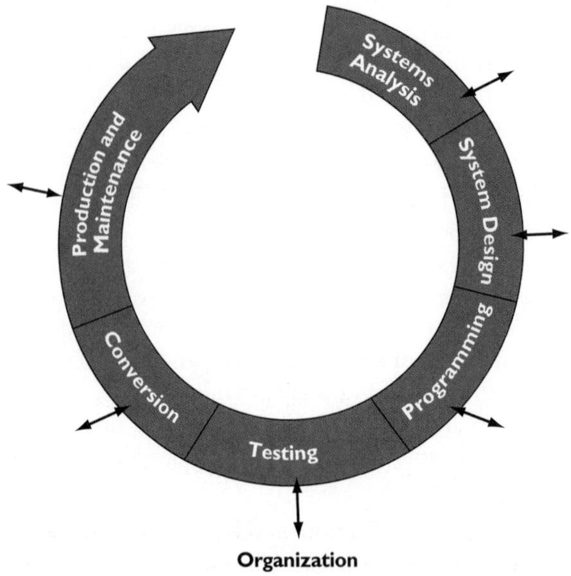

*Figure 10-5* The systems development process. Each of the core systems development activities entails interaction with the organization.

### Systems Analysis

**Systems analysis** is the analysis of the problem that the organization will try to solve with an information system. It consists of defining the problem, identifying its causes, specifying the solution, and identifying the information requirements that must be met by a system solution.

The systems analyst creates a road map of the existing organization and systems, identifying the primary owners and users of data in the organization. These stakeholders have a direct interest in the information affected by the new system. In addition to these organizational aspects, the analyst also briefly describes the existing hardware and software that serve the organization.

From this organizational analysis, the systems analyst details the problems of existing systems. By examining documents, work papers, and procedures; observing system operations; and interviewing key users of the systems, the analyst can identify the problem areas and objectives a solution would achieve. Often the solution requires building a new information system or improving an existing one.

The systems analysis includes a **feasibility study** to determine whether that solution is feasible, or achievable, from a financial, technical, and organizational standpoint. The feasibility study determines whether the proposed system is a good investment, whether the technology needed for the system is available and can be handled by the firm's information systems specialists, and whether the organization can handle the changes introduced by the system.

**feasibility study**
As part of the systems analysis process, the way to determine whether the solution is achievable, given the organization's resources and constraints.

Normally, the systems analysis process identifies several alternative solutions that the organization can pursue. The process then assesses the feasibility of each. A written systems proposal report describes the costs and benefits, advantages and disadvantages of each alternative. It is up to management to determine which mix of costs, benefits, technical features, and organizational impacts represents the most desirable alternative.

## Establishing Information Requirements

Perhaps the most challenging task of the systems analyst is to define the specific information requirements that must be met by the system solution selected. At the most basic level, the **information requirements** of a new system involve identifying who needs what information, where, when, and how. Requirements analysis carefully defines the objectives of the new or modified system and develops a detailed description of the functions that the new system must perform. Faulty requirements analysis is a leading cause of systems failure and high systems development costs (see Chapter 11). A system designed around the wrong set of requirements will either have to be discarded because of poor performance or will need to undergo major modifications. Section 10.4 describes alternative approaches to eliciting requirements that help minimize this problem.

**information requirements**
A detailed statement of the information needs that a new system must satisfy; identifies who needs what information, and when, where, and how the information is needed.

In many instances, building a new system creates an opportunity to redefine how the organization conducts its daily business. Some problems do not require an information system solution but instead need an adjustment in management, additional training, or refinement of existing organizational procedures. If the problem is information related, systems analysis still may be required to diagnose the problem and arrive at the proper solution.

# SYSTEMS DESIGN

Systems analysis describes what a system should do to meet information requirements, and **systems design** shows how the system will fulfill this objective. The design of an information system is the overall plan or model for that system. Like the blueprint of a building or house, it consists of all the specifications that give the system its form and structure.

**systems design**
Details how a system will meet the information requirements determined by the systems analysis.

The systems designer details the system specifications that will deliver the functions identified during systems analysis. These specifications should address all of the managerial, organizational, and technological components of the system solution. Table 10-5 lists the types of specifications that would be produced during systems design.

Like houses or buildings, information systems may have many possible designs. Each design represents a unique blend of technical and organizational components. What makes one design superior to others is the ease and efficiency with which it fulfills user requirements within a specific set of technical, organizational, financial, and time constraints.

## The Role of End Users

User information requirements drive the entire system-building effort. Users must have sufficient control over the design process to ensure that the system reflects their business priorities and information needs, not the biases of the technical staff. Working on design increases users' understanding and acceptance of the system, reducing problems caused by power transfers, intergroup conflict, and unfamiliarity with new system functions and procedures. As we describe in Chapter 11, insufficient user involvement in the design effort is a major

## TABLE 10-5 DESIGN SPECIFICATIONS

- Output
  - Medium
  - Content
  - Timing
- Input
  - Origins
  - Flow
  - Data entry
- User interface
  - Simplicity
  - Efficiency
  - Logic
  - Feedback
  - Errors
- Database design
  - Logical data relations
  - Volume and speed requirements
  - File organization and design
  - Record specifications
- Processing
  - Computations
  - Program modules
  - Required reports
  - Timing of outputs
- Manual procedures
  - What activities
  - Who performs them
  - When
  - How
  - Where
- Controls
  - Input controls (characters, limit, reasonableness)
  - Processing controls (consistency, record counts)
  - Output controls (totals, samples of output)
  - Procedural controls (passwords, special forms)
- Security
  - Access controls
  - Catastrophe plans
  - Audit trails
- Documentation
  - Operations documentation
  - Systems documents
  - User documentation
- Conversion
  - Transfer files
  - Inititate new procedures
  - Select testing method
  - Cut over to new system
- Training
  - Select training techniques
  - Develop training modules
  - Identify training facilities
- Organizational changes
  - Task redesign
  - Job design
  - Process design
  - Office and organization structure design
  - Reporting relationships

cause of system failure. However, some types of systems require more user participation in design than others, and Section 10.4 shows how alternative systems development methods address the user participation issue.

*Building successful information systems requires close cooperation among end users and information systems specialists throughout the systems development process.*

## Completing the Systems Development Process

The remaining steps in the systems development process translate the solution specifications established during systems analysis and design into a fully operational information system. These concluding steps consist of programming, testing, conversion, production, and maintenance.

### Programming

During the **programming stage,** system specifications that were prepared during the design stage are translated into software program code. On the basis of detailed design documents for files, transaction and report layouts, and other design details, specifications for each program in the system are prepared. Organizations write the software programs themselves or purchase application software packages for this purpose.

### Testing

Exhaustive and thorough **testing** must be conducted to ascertain whether the system produces the right results. Testing answers the question, "Will the system produce the desired results under known conditions?"

The amount of time needed to answer this question has been traditionally underrated in systems project planning (see Chapter 14). Testing is time consuming: Test data must be carefully prepared, results reviewed, and corrections made in the system. In some instances parts of the system may have to be redesigned. The risks of glossing over this step are enormous.

Testing an information system can be broken down into three types of activities: unit, system, and acceptance testing. **Unit testing,** or program testing, consists of testing each program separately in the system. It is widely believed that the purpose of such testing is to guarantee that programs are error free, but this goal is realistically impossible. Testing should be viewed instead as a means of locating errors in programs, focusing on finding all the ways to make a program fail. Once they are pinpointed, problems can be corrected.

**System testing** tests the functioning of the information system as a whole. It tries to determine if discrete modules will function together as planned and whether discrepancies exist between the way the system actually works and the way it was conceived. Among the areas examined are performance time, capacity for file storage and handling peak loads, recovery and restart capabilities, and manual procedures.

**Acceptance testing** provides the final certification that the system is ready to be used in a production setting. Systems tests are evaluated by users and reviewed by management. When all parties are satisfied that the new system meets their standards, the system is formally accepted for installation.

The systems development team works with users to devise a systematic test plan. The **test plan** includes all of the preparations for the series of tests we have just described.

Figure 10-6 shows an example of a test plan. The general condition being tested is a record change. The documentation consists of a series of test-plan screens maintained on a database (perhaps a PC database) that is ideally suited to this kind of application.

### Conversion

**Conversion** is the process of changing from the old system to the new system. Four main conversion strategies can be employed: the parallel strategy, the direct cutover strategy, the pilot study strategy, and the phased approach strategy.

In a **parallel strategy** both the old system and its potential replacement are run together for a time until everyone is assured that the new one functions correctly. This is the safest conversion approach, because, in the event of errors or processing disruptions, the old system can still be used as a backup. However, this approach is very expensive, and additional staff or resources may be required to run the extra system.

The **direct cutover** strategy replaces the old system entirely with the new system on an appointed day. At first glance, this strategy seems less costly than the parallel conversion strategy. However, it is a very risky approach that can potentially be more costly than parallel activities if serious problems with the new system are found. There is no other system on which to fall back. Dislocations, disruptions, and the cost of corrections may be enormous.

The **pilot study** strategy introduces the new system to only a limited area of the organization, such as a single department or operating unit. When this pilot version is complete

**programming stage**
The process of translating the system specifications prepared during the design stage into program code.

**testing**
The exhaustive and thorough process that determines whether the system produces the desired results under known conditions.

**unit testing**
The process of testing each program separately in the system. Sometimes called program testing.

**system testing**
Tests the functioning of the information system as a whole in order to determine if discrete modules will function together as planned.

**acceptance testing**
Provides the final user and management certification that the system is ready to be used in a production setting.

**test plan**
Prepared by the development team in conjunction with the users; it includes all of the preparations for the series of tests to be performed on the system.

**conversion**
The process of changing from the old system to the new system.

**parallel strategy**
A safe and conservative conversion approach where both the old system and its potential replacement are run together for a time until everyone is assured that the new one functions correctly.

**direct cutover**
A risky conversion approach where the new system completely replaces the old one on an appointed day.

| Procedure | Address and Maintenance "Record Change Series" | | Test Series 2 | | |
|---|---|---|---|---|---|
| | Prepared By: | Date: | Version: | | |
| Test Ref. | Condition Tested | Special Requirements | Expected Results | Output On | Next Screen |
| 2 | Change records | | | | |
| 2.1 | Change existing record | Key field | Not allowed | | |
| 2.2 | Change nonexistent record | Other fields | "Invalid key" message | | |
| 2.3 | Change deleted record | Deleted record must be available | "Deleted" message | | |
| 2.4 | Make second record | Change 2.1 above | OK if valid | Transaction file | V45 |
| 2.5 | Insert record | | OK if valid | Transaction file | V45 |
| 2.6 | Abort during change | Abort 2.5 | No change | Transaction file | V45 |

***Figure 10-6*** A sample test plan to test a record change. When developing a test plan, it is imperative to include the various conditions to be tested, the requirements for each condition tested, and the expected results. Test plans require input from both end users and information system specialists.

**pilot study**
A strategy to introduce the new system to a limited area of the organization until it is proven to be fully functional; only then can the conversion to the new system across the entire organization take place.

**phased approach**
Introduces the new system in stages either by functions or by organizational units.

**documentation**
Descriptions of how an information system works from either a technical or end-user standpoint.

**production**
The stage after the new system is installed and the conversion is complete; during this time the system is reviewed by users and technical specialists to determine how well it has met its original goals.

**maintenance**
Changes in hardware, software, documentation, or procedures to a production system to correct errors, meet new requirements, or improve processing efficiency.

and working smoothly, it is installed throughout the rest of the organization, either simultaneously or in stages.

The **phased approach** strategy introduces the new system in stages, either by functions or by organizational units. If, for example, the system is introduced by functions, a new payroll system might begin with hourly workers who are paid weekly, followed six months later by adding salaried employees (who are paid monthly) to the system. If the system is introduced by organizational units, corporate headquarters might be converted first, followed by outlying operating units four months later.

Moving from an old system to a new one requires that end users be trained to use the new system. Detailed **documentation** showing how the system works from both a technical and end-user standpoint is finalized during conversion time for use in training and everyday operations. Lack of proper training and documentation contributes to system failure, so this portion of the systems development process is very important.

## Production and Maintenance

After the new system is installed and conversion is complete, the system is said to be in **production.** During this stage the system will be reviewed by both users and technical specialists to determine how well it has met its original objectives and to decide whether any revisions or modifications are in order. Changes in hardware, software, documentation, or procedures to a production system to correct errors, meet new requirements, or improve processing efficiency are termed **maintenance.**

Studies of maintenance have examined the amount of time required for various maintenance tasks (Lientz and Swanson, 1980). Approximately 20 percent of the time is devoted to debugging or correcting emergency production problems; another 20 percent is concerned with changes in data, files, reports, hardware, or system software. But 60 percent of all maintenance work consists of making user enhancements, improving documentation, and recoding system components for greater processing efficiency. The amount of work in the third category of maintenance problems could be reduced significantly through better systems analysis and design practices. Table 10-6 summarizes the systems development activities.

# 10.4 ALTERNATIVE SYSTEM-BUILDING APPROACHES

Systems differ in terms of their size and technological complexity, and in terms of the organizational problems they are meant to solve. Because there are different kinds of systems, a number of methods have been developed to build systems. This section describes these alternative methods: the traditional systems lifecycle, prototyping, application software packages, end-user development, and outsourcing.

## TABLE 10-6 SYSTEMS DEVELOPMENT

| Core Activity | Description |
|---|---|
| Systems analysis | Identify problem(s) |
| | Specify solution |
| | Establish information requirements |
| Systems design | Create design specifications |
| Programming | Translate design specifications into program code |
| Testing | Unit test |
| | Systems test |
| | Acceptance test |
| Conversion | Plan conversion |
| | Prepare documentation |
| | Train users and technical staff |
| Production and maintenance | Operate the system |
| | Evaluate the system |
| | Modify the system |

## TRADITIONAL SYSTEMS LIFECYCLE

The **systems lifecycle** is the oldest method for building information systems and is still used today for medium or large complex systems projects. The lifecycle for an information system has six stages: (1) project definition, (2) systems study, (3) design, (4) programming, (5) installation, and (6) postimplementation. Figure 10-7 illustrates these stages. Each stage consists of basic activities that must be performed before the next stage can begin.

The lifecycle methodology has a very formal division of labor between end users and information systems specialists. Technical specialists such as systems analysts and programmers

**systems lifecycle**
A traditional methodology for developing an information system that partitions the systems development process into formal stages that must be completed sequentially with a very formal division of labor between end users and information systems specialists.

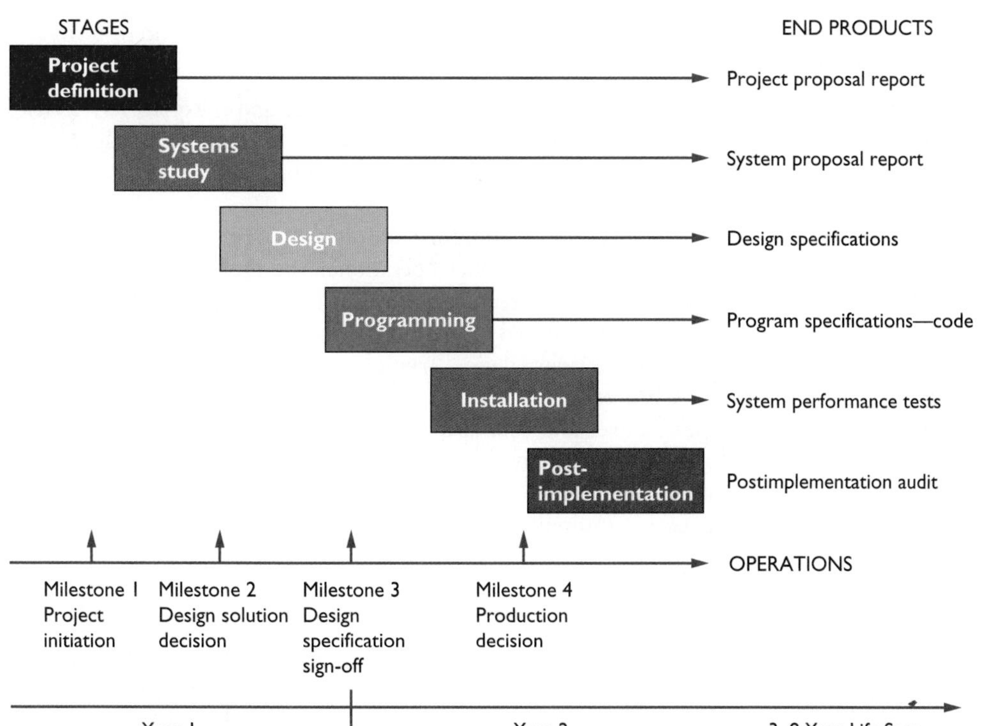


***Figure 10-7*** The lifecycle methodology for systems development. The lifecycle methodology divides systems development into formal stages with specific milestones and products at each stage.

are responsible for much of the systems analysis, design, and implementation work; end users are limited to providing information requirements and reviewing the technical staff's work.

## Stages of the Systems Lifecycle

The **project definition** stage determines whether the organization has a problem and whether that problem can be solved by building a new information system or by modifying an existing one. The **systems study** stage analyzes the problems of existing systems (manual or automated) in detail, identifies objectives to be attained by a solution to these problems, and describes alternative solutions. Much of the information gathered during the systems study phase will be used to determine information system requirements.

The **design** stage produces the design specifications for the solution. The lifecycle emphasizes formal specifications and paperwork, so many design documents are generated during this stage. The **programming** stage translates the design specifications produced during the design stage into software program code. Systems analysts work with programmers to prepare specifications for each program in the system.

The **installation** stage consists of the final steps to put the new or modified system into operation: testing, training, and conversion. The **postimplementation** stage consists of using and evaluating the system after it is installed and is in production. Users and technical specialists will go through a formal postimplementation audit that determines how well the new system has met its original objectives and whether any revisions or modifications are required. After the system has been fine-tuned it will need to be maintained while it is in production to correct errors, meet requirements, or improve processing efficiency. Over time, the system may require so much maintenance to remain efficient and meet user objectives that it will come to the end of its useful life span. Once the system's lifecycle comes to an end, a completely new system is called for and the lifecycle may begin again.

## Limitations of the Lifecycle Approach

The systems lifecycle is still useful for building large complex systems that require a rigorous and formal requirements analysis, predefined specifications, and tight controls over the systems-building process. However, the systems lifecycle approach is costly, time consuming, and inflexible. Volumes of new documents must be generated and steps repeated if requirements and specifications need to be revised. Because of the time and cost to repeat the sequence of lifecycle activities, the methodology encourages freezing of specifications early in the development process, discouraging change. The lifecycle approach is also not suitable for many small desktop systems, which tend to be less structured and more individualized.

### PROTOTYPING

**Prototyping** consists of building an experimental system rapidly and inexpensively for end users to evaluate. By interacting with the prototype, users can get a better idea of their information requirements. The prototype endorsed by the users can be used as a template to create the final system.

The **prototype** is a working version of an information system or part of the system, but it is meant to be only a preliminary model. Once operational, the prototype will be further refined until it conforms precisely to users' requirements. Once the design has been finalized, the prototype can be converted to a polished production system.

The process of building a preliminary design, trying it out, refining it, and trying again has been called an **iterative** process of systems development because the steps required to build a system can be repeated over and over again. Prototyping is more explicitly iterative than the conventional lifecycle, and it actively promotes system design changes. It has been said that prototyping replaces unplanned rework with planned iteration, with each version more accurately reflecting users' requirements.

## Steps in Prototyping

Figure 10-8 shows a four-step model of the prototyping process, which consists of the following:

**Step 1:** *Identify the user's basic requirements.* The system designer (usually an information systems specialist) works with the user only long enough to capture his or her basic information needs.

**project definition**
A stage in the systems lifecycle that determines whether the organization has a problem and whether the problem can be solved by launching a system project.

**systems study**
A stage in the systems lifecycle that analyzes the problems of existing systems, defines the objectives a solution will attain, and evaluates various solution alternatives.

**design**
A stage in the systems lifecycle that produces the design specifications for the system solution.

**programming**
A stage in the systems lifecycle that translates the design specifications produced during the design stage into software program code.

**installation**
A stage in the systems lifecycle consisting of testing, training, and conversion; the final steps required to put a system into operation.

**postimplementation**
The final stage of the systems lifecycle in which the system is used and evaluated while in production and is modified to make improvements or meet new requirements.

**prototyping**
The process of building an experimental system quickly and inexpensively for demonstration and evaluation so that users can better determine information requirements.

**prototype**
The preliminary working version of an information system for demonstration and evaluation purposes.

**Step 2:** *Develop an initial prototype.* The system designer creates a working prototype quickly, using fourth-generation software, interactive multimedia, or computer aided software engineering (CASE) tools (described in Chapter 14.)

**Step 3:** *Use the prototype.* The user is encouraged to work with the system in order to determine how well the prototype meets his or her needs and to make suggestions for improving the prototype.

**Step 4:** *Revise and enhance the prototype.* The system builder notes all changes the user requests and refines the prototype accordingly. After the prototype has been revised, the cycle returns to Step 3. Steps 3 and 4 are repeated until the user is satisfied.



***Figure 10-8*** The prototyping process. The process of developing a prototype can be broken down into four steps. Because a prototype can be developed quickly and inexpensively, system builders can go through several iterations, repeating steps 3 and 4, to refine and enhance the prototype before arriving at the final operational one.

When no more iterations are required, the approved prototype then becomes an operational prototype that furnishes the final specifications for the application. Sometimes the prototype itself is adopted as the production version of the system.

**iterative**
A process of repeating over and over again the steps to build a system.

## Advantages and Disadvantages of Prototyping

Prototyping is most useful when there is some uncertainty about requirements or design solutions. Prototyping is especially helpful in designing an information system's **end-user interface** (the part of the system that end users interact with, such as on-line display and data-entry screens, reports, or Web pages). When prototyping encourages end-user participation in building a system, it is more likely to produce systems that fulfill user requirements.

**end-user interface**
The part of an information system through which the end user interacts with the system, such as on-line screens and commands.

However, rapid prototyping can gloss over essential steps in systems development. If the completed prototype works reasonably well, management may not believe there is a need for reprogramming, redesign, or full documentation and testing to build a polished production system. Some of these hastily constructed systems may not easily accommodate large quantities of data or a large number of users in a production environment. Prototyping may also slow the development process if there are large numbers of end users to satisfy (Hardgrove, Wilson, and Eastman 1999).

# Application Software Packages

Information systems can be built using software from **application software packages,** which we introduced in Chapter 6. There are many applications that are common to all business organizations—for example, payroll, accounts receivable, general ledger, or inventory control. For such universal functions with standard procedures, a generalized system will fulfill the requirements of many organizations.

**application software package**
A set of prewritten, precoded application software programs that are commercially available for sale or lease.

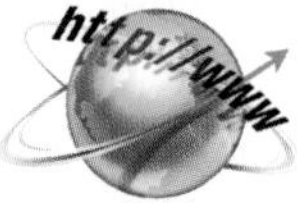


If a software package can fulfill most of an organization's requirements, the company does not have to write its own software. The company can save time and money by using the prewritten, predesigned, pretested software programs from the package. Package vendors supply much of the ongoing maintenance and support for the system, providing enhancements to keep the system in line with ongoing technical and business developments.

If an organization has unique requirements that the package does not address, many packages include capabilities for customization. **Customization** features allow a software package to be modified to meet an organization's unique requirements without destroying the integrity of the packaged software. If a great deal of customization is required, additional programming and customization work may become so expensive and time consuming that

**customization**
The modification of a software package to meet an organization's unique requirements without destroying the package software's integrity.

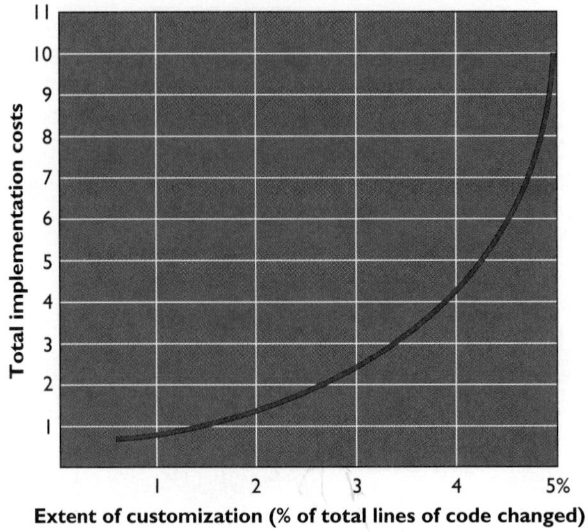

*Figure 10-9* The effects of customizing a software package on total implementation costs. As the modifications to a software package rise, so does the cost of implementing the package. Savings promised by the package can be whittled away by excessive changes.

they eliminate many of the advantages of software packages. Figure 10-9 shows how package costs in relation to total implementation costs rise with the degree of customization. The initial purchase price of the package can be deceptive because of these hidden implementation costs.

## Selecting Software Packages

When a system is developed using an application software package, systems analysis will include a package evaluation effort. The most important evaluation criteria are the functions provided by the package, flexibility, user-friendliness, hardware and software resources, database requirements, installation and maintenance effort, documentation, vendor quality, and cost. The package evaluation process often is based on a **Request for Proposal (RFP),** which is a detailed list of questions submitted to packaged software vendors.

**Request for Proposal (RFP)** A detailed list of questions submitted to vendors of software or other services to determine how well the vendor's product can meet the organization's specific requirements.

When a software package solution is selected, the organization no longer has total control over the system design process. Instead of tailoring the system design specifications directly to user requirements, the design effort will consist of trying to mold user requirements to conform to the features of the package. If the organization's requirements conflict with the way the package works and the package cannot be customized, the organization will have to adapt to the package and change its procedures.

## MANAGEMENT DECISION PROBLEM

### PRICING A SOFTWARE PACKAGE

Your rapidly growing pharmaceutical company has 24 sales representatives, annual sales of $20 million, and an extensive inventory of products that it markets to hospitals and healthcare facilities. The sales department has used glossy brochures, printed catalogs, and PowerPoint presentations to present information to customers about products but you would like to be able to create custom catalogs and PowerPoint presentations for customer sales calls that are tailored to different selling situations. You have found a sales software package called PowerSales that provides these capabilities and that can link automatically into the firm's enterprise resource planning (ERP) system to reflect changes in pricing, availability, and new products. The software also provides sales managers with forecasts and detailed reports of each sales call. The package vendor has suggested the following pricing option:

**Base software**
One-time installation charge: $115,000
Annual license charge: $75,000

**Custom content (one-time charges) for the entire sales force**
Specific product promotions and product introduction: $130,000
Product line overview presentations: $65,000
Sales skills training: $57,500

Your company plans to use the same content for two years. After determining the initial software configuration, the package vendor supplies a consultant to guide the customization process, working with the client to provide text graphics, animation, audio, and video content for the system. The cost of the consultant is $2,000 per day. You have been told that it would take about 50 days of consulting time to customize and complete the package implementation. Your firm would not need to purchase any new hardware to run the package, but you would need an information systems specialist at an annual salary of $75,000 to spend 20 hours per month supporting the package.

1. What are the total costs of using this package for the first year? For two years?
2. The package vendor claims that after implementing the package, its customers have increased sales by an average of 10 percent over two years. How much increase in sales revenue should your company anticipate if you implement this package?
3. What additional information would be useful to guide your purchase decision? Should your firm purchase this package? Explain.

## END-USER DEVELOPMENT

Some types of information systems can be developed by end users with little or no formal assistance from technical specialists. This phenomenon is called **end-user development.** Using fourth-generation languages, graphics languages, and PC software tools, end users can access data, create reports, and develop entire information systems on their own, with little or no help from professional systems analysts or programmers. Many of these end-user developed systems can be created much more rapidly than with the traditional systems lifecycle. Figure 10-10 illustrates the concept of end-user development.

**end-user development** The development of information systems by end users with little or no formal assistance from technical specialists.

### Benefits and Limitations of End-user Development

Many organizations have reported gains in application development productivity by using fourth-generation tools that in a few cases have reached 300 to 500 percent. (Glass, 1999; Green, 1984–85; Harel, 1985). Allowing users to specify their own business needs improves requirements gathering and often leads to a higher level of user involvement and satisfaction with the system. However, fourth-generation tools still cannot replace conventional tools for some business applications, because they cannot easily handle the processing of large numbers of transactions or applications with extensive procedural logic and updating requirements.

End-user computing also poses organizational risks because it occurs outside of traditional mechanisms for information system management and control. When systems are created rapidly, without a formal development methodology, testing and documentation may be inadequate. Control over data can be lost in systems outside the traditional information systems department (see Chapter 7). When users create their own applications and files, it becomes increasingly difficult to determine where data are located and to ensure that the same piece of information is used consistently throughout the organization.

### Managing End-user Development

To help organizations maximize the benefits of end-user applications development, management should control the development of end-user applications by requiring cost justifications of end-user information system projects and by establishing hardware, software, and quality standards for user-developed applications.

When end-user computing first became popular, organizations used information centers to promote standards for hardware and software so that end users would not introduce many disparate and incompatible technologies into the firm (Fuller and Swanson, 1992). **Information centers** are special facilities housing hardware, software, and technical specialists

**information center** A special facility within an organization that provides training and support for end-user computing.

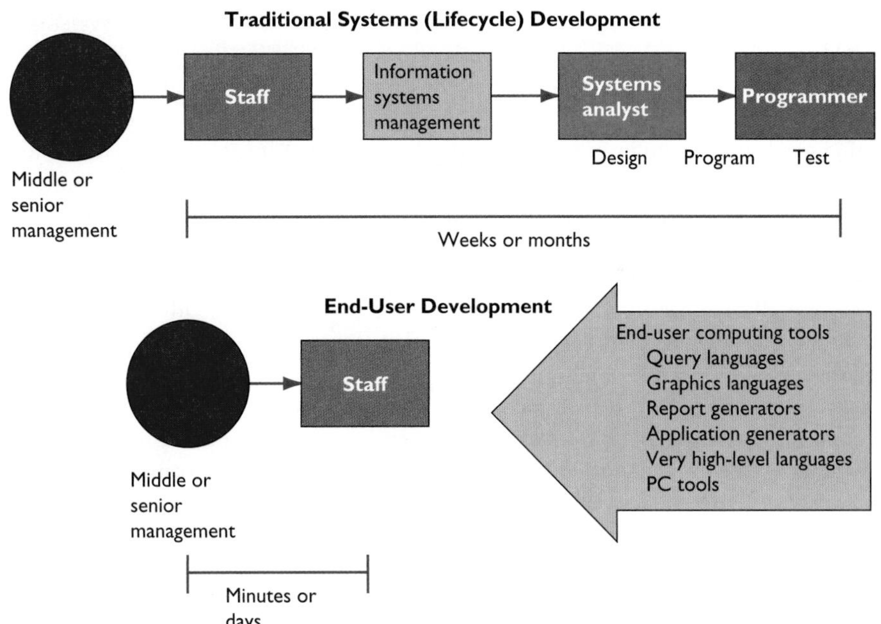


*Figure 10-10* End-user versus system lifecycle development. End users can access computerized information directly or develop information systems with little or no formal technical assistance. On the whole, end-user developed systems can be completed more rapidly than those developed through the conventional systems lifecycle.
*Source:* Application Development Without Programmers, by James Martin, 1982. Reprinted by permission of Prentice-Hall, Inc., Upper Saddle River, NJ.

*NetObjects Fusion MX allows users to plan, create, and maintain a powerful Web site without writing a single line of program code.*

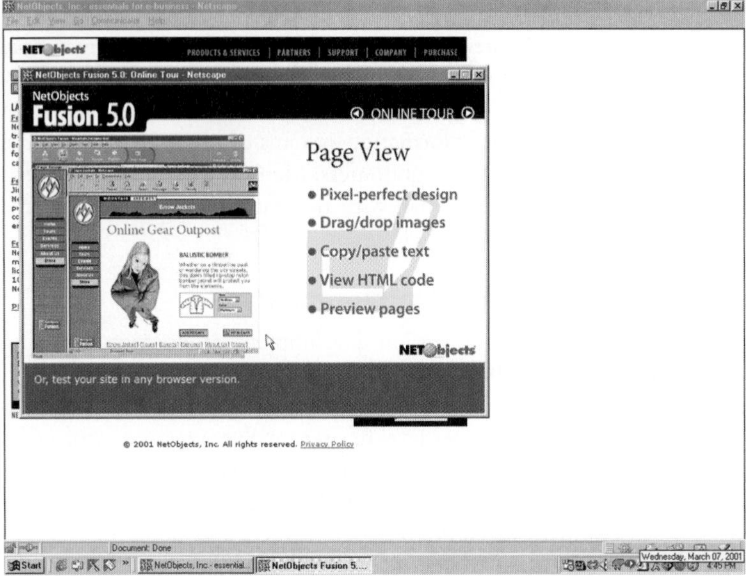


to supply end users with tools, training, and expert advice so they can create information system applications on their own or increase their productivity. The role of information centers is diminishing as end users become more computer literate, but organizations still need to closely monitor and manage end-user development.

## Outsourcing

**outsourcing**
The practice of contracting computer center operations, telecommunications networks, or applications development to external vendors.

If a firm does not want to use its internal resources to build or operate information systems, it can hire an external organization that specializes in providing these services to do the work. The process of turning over an organization's computer center operations, telecommunications networks, or applications development to external vendors is called **outsourcing.** The application service providers (ASPs) described in Chapter 6 are one form of outsourcing. Subscribing companies use the software and computer hardware provided by the ASP as the technical platform for their system. In another form of outsourcing, a company hires an external vendor to design and create the software for its system, but that company would operate the system on its own computer. The Window on Management describes how one start-up company benefited from outsourcing its Web site.

Outsourcing has become popular because some organizations perceive it as more cost-effective than maintaining their own computer center or information systems staff. The provider of outsourcing services benefits from economies of scale (the same knowledge, skills, and capacity can be shared with many different customers) and is likely to charge competitive prices for information systems services. Outsourcing allows a company with fluctuating needs for computer processing to pay for only what it uses rather than to build its own computer center, which would be underutilized when there is no peak load. Some firms outsource because their internal information systems staff cannot keep pace with technological change or innovative business practices or because they want to free up scarce and costly talent for activities with higher payback.

Not all organizations benefit from outsourcing, and the disadvantages of outsourcing can create serious problems for organizations if they are not well understood and managed (Earl, 1996). When a firm allocates the responsibility for developing and operating its information systems to another organization, it can lose control over its information systems function. If the organization lacks the expertise to negotiate a sound contract, the firm's dependency on the vendor could result in high costs or loss of control over technological direction (Lacity, Willcocks, and Feeny, 1996). Firms should be especially cautious when using an outsourcer to develop or to operate applications that give it some type of competitive advantage. Table 10-7 compares the advantages and disadvantages of each of the system-building alternatives.

## An E-commerce Site Overnight

When Peter Hunt had trouble finding instructions, lumber, and tools for building his son a tree house, he realized he had a great idea for a new business. Why not provide a hardware store for woodworkers, plumbers, contractors, and home improvement enthusiasts on the Web? Hunt partnered with Richard T. Takata, who had been in the hardware business for 24 years to set up CornerHardware.com. This virtual hardware store would not only sell supplies but also provide how-to information in a friendly "do-it-yourself" atmosphere reminiscent of the kind of old-fashioned corner hardware stores that used to be found in every small town.

By the summer of 1999 Hunt and Takata had amassed funding for their venture but realized they had to move quickly to set up their Web site. Brick-and-mortar giants such as Sears, Home Depot and Ace Hardware had already set up electronic commerce sites, and there were new Internet-based competitors such as HomeWarehouse.com racing to market. Corner Hardware.com had to be up and running by March 2000.

CornerHardware.com's Web site was a large, complex, leading-edge project. It had to have a capability for processing order transactions and for displaying descriptions and images of 37,000 products. It would also offer how-to articles, visitor message boards, animated step-by-step project instructions, a large on-line glossary of hardware terms, a powerful search engine, and live on-line customer service. Using interactive windows, customers could chat on-line with customer service representatives. This high level of service and attention to customers would distinguish Hunt and Takata's Web site from other on-line competitors.

Hunt and Takata had neither the time nor the resources to hire their own information systems staff to do this work. They outsourced the project to Xuma, a San Francisco-based company that hosts and develops Web sites. Xuma specializes in creating large flexible electronic commerce sites using a combination of standard and optional software components for e-commerce activities. By providing a Web site platform loaded with preintegrated e-commerce features, such as credit card processing and tax management, Xuma can quickly create a Web site and save companies the trouble of assembling the software themselves. Xuma promised systems and databases that were scalable to accommodate CornerHardware.com's future growth, and they agreed to deliver the system within six months.

Xuma was able to build the CornerHardware.com Web site rapidly with its preexisting software components. When CornerHardware.com's competitors launched their Web sites earlier than expected, the firm asked Xuma to launch the Web site six weeks earlier than planned. The day before the Web site was launched, Hunt asked for an additional search path for customers to view products and information. A Xuma engineer furiously worked on the new function, finishing it hours before launch time. Xuma asked for 10 more days to test the site to make absolutely sure it would perform as expected. CornerHardware.com was not able to provide digital photographs of all of its 37,000 products by launch time, and settled for posting a representative sampling from each category. Initially, the site had no capability for issuing returns to customers' credit cards. But in February 2000, CornerHardware.com's public launch went off without any major glitches. Since then, the company has seen a steady growth in visitors and in purchases of big-ticket items such as bathroom vanities and power tools. Xuma continues to run the Web site.

**To Think About:** What are the management benefits of outsourcing the development of a Web site? What are the disadvantages?

*Sources:* Anne Stuart, "Nailing IT," *Inc.Technology 2000,* no. 2, June 2000; and Alexei Oreskovic, "Reboot: A Toast to the Host," *The Industry Standard,* March 27, 2000.

management

## Object-oriented Software Development and Rapid Application Development (RAD)

Chapter 6 explained that object-oriented programming combines data and the specific procedures that operate on those data into one object. Object-oriented programming is part of a larger approach to systems development called object-oriented software development. **Object-oriented software development** differs from traditional system-building approaches by shifting the focus from separately modeling business processes and data to combining data and procedures into unified objects. The system is viewed as a collection of classes and objects and includes the relationships among them. The objects are defined, programmed, documented, and saved as building blocks for future applications. While object-oriented models of systems are not necessarily more usable than process-oriented models, organizations are increasingly turning to object-oriented software development in the hope of building systems that are more flexible and easier to maintain (Agarwal, De, Sinha, and Tanniru, 2000).

**object-oriented software development**
An approach to software development that shifts the focus from modeling processes and data to combining data and procedures to create objects.

**TABLE 10-7 COMPARISON OF SYSTEMS-DEVELOPMENT APPROACHES**

| Approach | Features | Advantages | Disadvantages |
|---|---|---|---|
| Systems lifecycle | Sequential step-by-step formal process<br>Written specification and approvals<br>Limited role of users | Necessary for large complex systems and projects | Slow and expensive<br>Discourages changes<br>Massive paperwork to manage |
| Prototyping | Requirements specified dynamically with experimental system<br>Rapid, informal, and iterative process<br>Users continually interact with the prototype | Rapid and relatively inexpensive<br>Useful when requirements uncertain or when end-user interface is very important<br>Promotes user participation | Inappropriate for large, complex systems<br>Can gloss over steps in analysis, documentation, and testing |
| Applications software package | Commercial software eliminates need for internally developed software programs | Design, programming, installation, and maintenance work reduced<br>Can save time and cost when developing common business applications<br>Reduces need for internal information systems resources | May not meet organization's unique requirements<br>May not perform many business functions well<br>Extensive customization raises development costs |
| End-user development | Systems created by end users using fourth-generation software tools<br>Rapid and informal<br>Minimal role of information systems specialists | Users control systems-building<br>Saves development time and cost<br>Reduces application backlog | Can lead to proliferation of uncontrolled information systems and data<br>Systems do not always meet quality assurance standards |
| Outsourcing | Systems build and sometimes operated by external vendor | Can reduce or control costs<br>Can produce systems when internal resources are not available or technically deficient | Loss of control over the information systems function<br>Dependence on the technical direction and prosperity of external vendors |

Objects are reusable, so object-oriented software development is expected to reduce the time and cost of writing software because organizations can reuse software objects that have already been created as building blocks for other applications. New systems can be created by using some existing objects, changing others, and adding a few new objects. Object-oriented development is very useful for creating Web applications. Of course, no organization will see savings from reusability until it builds up a library of objects to draw on and understands which objects have broad use. Object-oriented frameworks have been developed to provide reusable semicomplete applications that the organization can further customize into finished applications (Fayad and Schmidt, 1997). However, information systems specialists must learn a completely new way of modeling a system. Conversion to an object-oriented approach may require large-scale organizational investments, which management must balance against the anticipated payoffs.

## Rapid Application Development (RAD)

**rapid application development (RAD)** Process for developing systems in a very short time period by using prototyping, fourth-generation tools, and close teamwork among users and systems specialists.

Object-oriented software tools, reusable software, prototyping, and fourth-generation tools are helping system builders create working systems much more rapidly than they could using traditional system-building methods and software tools. The term **rapid application development (RAD)** is used to describe this process of creating workable systems in a very short period of time. RAD can include the use of visual programming and other tools for building graphical user interfaces, iterative prototyping of key system elements, the automation of program code generation, and close teamwork among end users and information systems

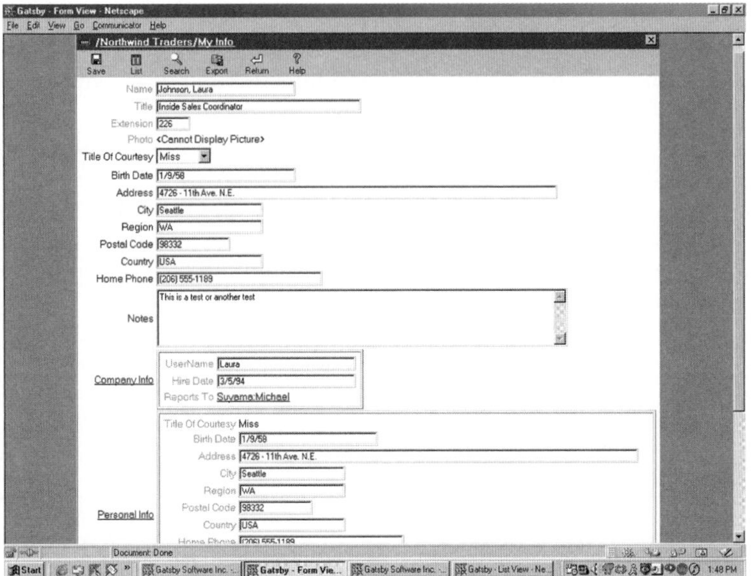


*Gatsby Database Explorer generates a user-friendly interface to Microsoft Access and SQL Server databases that allows users to edit, view and search database content over an intranet or extranet. This RAD development tool enables companies to create rapid solutions without special programming.*

specialists. Simple systems often can be assembled from prebuilt components. The process does not have to be sequential, and key parts of development can occur simultaneously. While systems or parts of systems can be built very quickly with RAD tools and methods, system-builders will still need careful requirements planning and modeling to ensure the systems deliver long-term benefits (Agarwal, Prasad, Tanniru, and Lynch, 2000).

Sometimes a technique called **joint application design (JAD)** is used to accelerate the generation of information requirements and to develop the initial systems design. JAD brings end users and information systems specialists together in an interactive session to discuss the system's design. Properly prepared and facilitated, JAD sessions can significantly speed the design phase while involving users at an intense level.

**joint application design (JAD)**
Process to accelerate the generation of information requirements by having end users and information systems specialists work together in intensive interactive design sessions.

## APPLICATION DEVELOPMENT FOR THE DIGITAL FIRM

Electronic commerce, electronic business, and the emerging digital firm pose new challenges for system-building. Technologies and business conditions are changing so rapidly that agility has become a critical success factor and primary goal of system design. Businesses need software components that can be added, modified, replaced, or reconfigured to enable them to respond rapidly to new opportunities. To remain competitive, some firms feel pressured to design, develop, test, and deploy Internet or intranet applications in a matter of weeks or months.

In the past, systems development would be based on a formal design document containing functional specifications that was handed off to a development team. Alternatively, applications might be loosely designed and iteratively developed with multiple passes going to users for review and revision. Such development processes often took months or years and were ill-suited to the pace and profile of Internet or intranet projects. Traditional methods did not address the new features of Internet-based applications, which might have multiple tiers of clients and servers with different operating systems linked to transaction processing systems, as well as business processes that had to be coordinated with those of customers or suppliers.

Companies are adopting a shorter, more informal development process for many of their e-commerce and e-business applications, one that provides fast solutions that do not disrupt their core transaction processing systems and organizational databases. They are relying more heavily on fast-cycle techniques such as JAD, prototypes, and standardized software components that can be assembled into a complete set of services for e-commerce and e-business. For example, many firms are using preassembled components for supply chain management, electronic storefronts, and customer care as well as middleware tools (see Chapters 6 and 7) to link their legacy applications to new Web interfaces.

E-commerce and e-business require systems planning and systems analysis based on a broader view of the organization, one that encompasses business processes extending beyond firm boundaries (Fingar, 2000). Firms can no longer execute their business and system plans alone because they need to forge new electronic relationships with suppliers, distributors, and customers. Their business processes often need to be integrated with customer and supplier business processes.

Building digital firm applications requires firms to respond to a hyper-change business and technology environment where information system applications can quickly become obsolete. Older development methods were based on a much more static view of systems. Organizations now need to be able to add, change, and retire their technology capabilities very rapidly. New processes for continuous improvement of applications and IT infrastructures have become essential.

## APPLICATION SOFTWARE EXERCISE:

### WEB BROWSER AND PRESENTATION SOFTWARE EXERCISE: COMPARING SECURITY FEATURES AT FRIEND-IN-NEED FOUNDATION

Several years ago, Ricardo Juarez established the privately funded Friend-in-Need Foundation. The primary purpose of this organization is to provide donations, assistance, and counseling to families or individuals who can demonstrate need based on several criteria. As the foundation continues to grow, so do its data management problems. Because the foundation is small, many of its records are kept in notebooks, file folders, and locked cabinets. This record keeping method presents many problems, especially in the area of control.

Every Friend-in-Need Foundation employee has access to all the foundation's data, thus creating security, ethical, and general concerns for the foundation's management. Ricardo realizes that a database management system may help alleviate many of his data management and control problems. He asks you to investigate, on the Web, three database management systems and prepare a written report, comparing the strengths and weaknesses of each database management system's security features. In addition to providing a general overview of each database management system's security features, he would like you to specifically address the following areas:

1. Security accounts and levels of security
2. Types of permissions
3. Controlling the look and feel of the database
4. Securing a replicated database
5. Creating and updating passwords

In addition to these areas, what additional security features do the database management systems provide? Summarize your findings in a written report and use a presentation software package to prepare a presentation based on these findings.

## MANAGEMENT WRAP-UP

Selection of a systems-building approach can have a large impact on the time, cost, and end product of systems development. Managers should be aware of the strengths and weaknesses of each systems-building approach and the types of problems for which each is best suited.

Organizational needs should drive the selection of a systems-building approach. The impact of application software packages and of outsourcing should be carefully evaluated before they are selected because these approaches give organizations less control over the systems-building process.

Various software tools are available to support the systems-building process. Key technology decisions should be based on the organization's familiarity with the technology and its compatibility with the organization's information requirements, IT infrastructure, and information architecture.

*For Discussion*

1. Why is selecting a systems development approach an important business decision? Who should participate in the selection process?
2. Some have said that the best way to reduce system development costs is to use application software packages or fourth-generation tools. Do you agree? Why or why not?

## SUMMARY

1. *Demonstrate how building new systems can produce organizational change.* Building a new information system is a form of planned organizational change that involves many different people in the organization. Because information systems are sociotechnical entities, a change in information systems involves changes in work, management, and the organization. Four kinds of technology-enabled change are (1) automation, (2) rationalization of procedures, (3) business process reengineering, and (4) paradigm shift, with far-reaching changes carrying the greatest risks and rewards. Many organizations are attempting business process reengineering to redesign workflows and business processes in the hope of achieving dramatic productivity breakthroughs.
2. *Explain how the organization can develop information systems that fit its business plan.* Organizations should develop information systems plans that describe how information technology supports the attainment of their business goals. The plans indicate the direction of systems development, the rationale, implementation strategy, and budget. Enterprise analysis and critical success factors (CSFs) can be used to elicit organization-wide information requirements that must be addressed by the plans.
3. *Identify the core activities in the systems development process.* The core activities in systems development are systems analysis, systems design, programming, testing, conversion, production, and maintenance. Systems analysis is the study and analysis of problems of existing systems and the identification of requirements for their solution. Systems design provides the specifications for an information system solution, showing how its technical and organizational components fit together.
4. *Appraise alternatives for building systems: the traditional systems lifecycle, prototyping, application software packages, end-user development, and outsourcing.* The traditional systems lifecycle—the oldest method for building systems—breaks the development of an information system into six formal stages: (1) project definition, (2) systems study, (3) design, (4) programming, (5) installation, and (6) postimplementation. The stages must proceed sequentially and have defined outputs; each requires formal approval before the next stage can commence. The system lifecycle is useful for large projects that need formal specifications and tight management control over each stage of system-building. However, this approach is very rigid and costly and is not well suited for unstructured, decision-oriented applications where requirements cannot be immediately visualized.

   Prototyping consists of building an experimental system rapidly and inexpensively for end users to interact with and evaluate. The prototype is refined and enhanced until users are satisfied that it includes all of their requirements and can be used as a template to create the final system. Prototyping encourages end-user involvement in systems development and iteration of design until specifications are captured accurately. The rapid creation of prototypes can result in systems that have not been completely tested or documented or that are technically inadequate for a production environment.

Developing an information system using an application software package eliminates the need for writing software programs when developing an information system. Using a software package cuts down on the amount of design, testing, installation, and maintenance work required to build a system. Application software packages are helpful if a firm does not have the internal information systems staff or financial resources to custom-develop a system. To meet an organization's unique requirements, packages may require extensive modifications that can substantially raise development costs.

End-user development is the development of information systems by end users, either alone or with minimal assistance from information systems specialists. End-user-developed systems can be created rapidly and informally using fourth-generation software tools. The primary benefits of end-user development are improved requirements determination, reduced application backlog, and increased end-user participation in, and control of, the systems development process. However, end-user development, in conjunction with distributed computing, has introduced new organizational risks by propagating information systems and data resources that do not necessarily meet quality assurance standards and that are not easily controlled by traditional means.

Outsourcing consists of using an external vendor to build (or operate) a firm's information systems. The work is done by the vendor rather than by the organization's internal information systems staff. Outsourcing can save application development costs or allow firms to develop applications without an internal information systems staff. However, firms risk losing control over their information systems and becoming too dependent on external vendors.

5. *Evaluate the use of object-oriented software development and rapid application development (RAD) in building contemporary systems.* Object-oriented software development is expected to reduce the time and cost of writing software and of making maintenance changes, because it models a system as a series of reusable objects that combine both data and procedures. Rapid application development (RAD) uses object-oriented software, visual programming, prototyping, and fourth-generation tools for very rapid creation of systems.

## KEY TERMS

**Acceptance testing, 319**
**Application software package, 323**
**Automation, 310**
**Benchmarking, 315**
**Business process reengineering, 310**
**Conversion, 319**
**Critical success factors (CSFs), 307**
**Customization, 323**
**Design, 322**
**Direct cutover, 319**
**Documentation, 320**
**End-user development, 325**
**End-user interface, 323**
**Enterprise analysis, 306**
**Feasibility study, 317**
**Information center, 325**
**Information requirements, 317**
**Information systems plan, 305**
**Installation, 322**
**Iterative, 323**
**Joint application design (JAD), 329**
**Maintenance, 320**
**Object-oriented software development, 327**
**Outsourcing, 326**
**Paradigm shift, 310**
**Parallel strategy, 319**
**Phased approach, 320**
**Pilot study, 320**
**Postimplementation, 322**
**Production, 320**
**Programming, 322**
**Project definition, 322**
**Prototype, 322**
**Prototyping, 322**
**Programming stage, 319**
**Rapid application development (RAD), 328**
**Rationalization of procedures, 310**
**Request for Proposal (RFP), 324**
**Systems analysis, 316**
**Systems design, 317**
**Systems development, 316**
**Systems lifecycle, 321**
**Systems study, 322**
**System testing, 319**
**Test plan, 319**
**Testing, 319**
**Total quality management (TQM), 314**
**Unit testing, 319**
**Workflow management, 312**

## REVIEW QUESTIONS

1. Why can an information system be considered planned organizational change?
2. What are the major categories of an information systems plan?
3. How can enterprise analysis and critical success factors be used to establish organization-wide information system requirements?
4. Describe each of the four kinds of organizational change that can be promoted with information technology.
5. What is business process reengineering? What steps are required to make it effective?
6. What is the difference between systems analysis and systems design? What activities do they comprise?
7. What are information requirements? Why are they difficult to determine correctly?
8. Why is the testing stage of systems development so important? Name and describe the three stages of testing for an information system.
9. What role do programming, conversion, production, and maintenance play in systems development?
10. What is the traditional systems lifecycle? Describe each of its steps and its advantages and disadvantages for system-building.
11. What do we mean by information system prototyping? What are its benefits and limitations? List and describe the steps in the prototyping process.
12. What is an application software package? What are the advantages and disadvantages of developing information systems based on software packages?
13. What do we mean by end-user development? What are its advantages and disadvantages? Name some policies and procedures for managing end-user development.
14. What is outsourcing? Under what circumstances should it be used for building information systems?
15. What is the difference between object-oriented software development and traditional software development? What are the advantages of using object-oriented software development in building systems?
16. What is rapid application development (RAD)? How can it help system builders?

## GROUP PROJECT

With three or four of your classmates, select a system described in this text that uses the Web. Examples might be Midnight Sun Plant Food in Chapter 1; Rand McNally in Chapter 3; or Chapters Inc. in Chapter 4. Review the Web site for the system you select. Use what you have learned from the Web site and the description in this book to prepare a report describing some of the design specifications for the system you select. If possible, use electronic presentation software to present your findings to the class.

## TOOLS FOR INTERACTIVE LEARNING

### INTERNET CONNECTION

The Internet Connection for this chapter will direct you to the SAP Web site where you can complete an exercise to evaluate the capabilities of this major, multinational, software package and learn more about enterprise resource planning. You can also use the Interactive Study Guide to test your knowledge of the topics in this chapter and get instant feedback where you need more practice.

### ELECTRONIC COMMERCE PROJECT

At the Laudon Web site for Chapter 10, you will find an Electronic Commerce Project requiring you to create a banner and then search for a Web hosting service.

### CD-ROM

If you use the Multimedia Edition CD-ROM with this chapter, you can complete two interactive exercises. The first asks you to select the appropriate information technology solution to improve a series of business processes. The second exercise requires you to perform a systems analysis for a multidivisional corporation experiencing revenue slowdown. You can also find a video clip on the Andersen Smart Store and Retail Place illustrating the innovative use of technology to rethink the delivery of goods and services, an audio overview of the chapter, and bullet text summarizing the key points of the chapter.

## CASE STUDY *Under Construction: A New System for Toromont Industries*

Toromont Industries Ltd. is headquartered in Toronto, Canada, and is one of the largest dealerships for Caterpillar heavy-construction equipment in North America. Toromont also makes process systems, industrial and recreational equipment, and operates a series of energy plants supplying Ontario's deregulated electricity market. Two-thirds of Toromont's revenue, which amounted to U.S $494 million in 1999, comes from its equipment group, which rents and sells heavy construction and mining equipment and parts. Toromont has more than 2,000 employees throughout North America.

Toromont's success has not been based on selling more tractors, parts, and engines but on selling the kind of service that leads customers to purchase 10-year contracts. The contracts call for Toromont to supply them with heavy equipment and maintain that equipment. Customers do not need to purchase such equipment, which can amount to $150,000 per earth-moving machine, nor do they have to maintain their own warehouses or mechanics. Toromont supplies the machines and guarantees they will be maintained in top condition for the life of the contract.

Toromont faces stiff competition. Many heavy-construction and mining equipment firms, including Komatsu, John Deere, and even Caterpillar itself, are putting more emphasis on customer service by selling parts on-line over the Internet. There are also Web sites such as Equipmentsite.com, Point2.com, and Equipmentrader.com, which are clearinghouses for heavy-construction equipment, parts, and services. The Internet appears to be turning heavy-construction equipment into a commodity. "With so many others vying for your customers' attention, how do you convince them to buy from you instead of from a discount place on the Internet?" asks Rob Kugel, an analyst with FAC/Equities in Burlingame, California.

Toromont's management believes that the company can stay ahead of these competitors by offering the best possible customer service through a new on-line system for ordering and maintaining equipment and for tracking customer accounts. The system, ideally, would provide more interactive personalized service than could be obtained from any of its competitors. For example, the system could provide oil quality and other maintenance statistics on-line that could help customers determine prefailure conditions faster, reducing the chances of costly downtime or worker injuries on construction jobs. Customers could get quick answers to questions, such as how fast they can obtain the part they need, when their equipment needs to go into the repair shop for maintenance, and how much they owe on their accounts.

Toromont's senior management wants an interactive customer service capability as soon as possible and is willing to keep things simple to get this capability up and running. It doesn't want customers to see the same generic information. Each Toromont client should be able to see precisely the information that is specific to their company. Toromont currently provides customers with oil analyses and maintenance updates on their machines but must deliver this information via fax.

The new system should not only provide this information on-line but should also be able to deliver e-mail and pager alerts to customers, technicians, and machine operators. Toromont would also like to offer personalized real-time price quotes for parts and service based on the customer's size and contract. Customers should be able to use the system to access sales and service data, update their information, check outstanding invoices, and place orders. That would require the new system to access information housed in Toromont's basic operational systems running on an IBM AS/400 midrange computer. But management does not want to rewrite the software for these back-end systems or to have the new system interfere with the data in the AS/400 database.

Toromont's legacy back-end order entry and billing system is written in COBOL and uses a DB2 database running on an IBM AS/400 model 720 computer. The system supports order entry for parts and machine sales, service work-order processing, warranty, and inventory, and is integrated with a financial subsystem from Baan, a leading enterprise software vendor. The company has an IP network connecting 700 users to both local and wide area networks and uses frame relay to connect 18 locations to corporate headquarters near Toronto. Customers order parts by telephoning Toromont's parts department. They must also use the telephone to check part prices, part availability, and the status of machines in for service.

Toromont management would like to make better use of the Internet and wonders how it could be incorporated in its system solution. It is willing to devote 25 percent of its information technology budget and wants the project completed in six months.

**Sources:** Claudia Graziano, "Under Construction," *Information Week,* February 7, 2000; and www.toromont.com.

### *CASE STUDY QUESTIONS*

1. Analyze Toromont and its business model using the competitive forces and value chain models.
2. How well did Toromont's systems support its business model? What management, organization, and technology factors were responsible for its problems?
3. Propose a system solution for Toromont. Your analysis should describe the objectives of the solution, the requirements to be met by the new system (or series of systems), and the feasibility of your proposal. Include an overview of the systems you would recommend and explain how those systems would address the problems listed in your goals. Your analysis should consider organizational and management issues to be addressed by the solution as well as technology issues.
4. If you were the systems analyst for this project, list five questions you would ask during interviews to elicit the information you need for your systems study report.
5. What method would you use to develop your system solution? Why?

# chapter 11 Understanding the Business Value of Systems and Managing Change

objectives

**After completing this chapter, you will be able to:**

1. *Evaluate models for determining the business value of information systems.*
2. *Analyze the principal causes of information system failure.*
3. *Analyze the change management requirements for building successful systems.*
4. *Select appropriate strategies to manage the system implementation process.*

## Omni Hotels New Customer System Fizzles Out

In the mid-1990s, Omni Hotels struggled with lackluster performance. The Hampton, New Hampshire, hotel chain's executive team pinned the company's financial future on a new guest recognition system that was supposed to boost customer loyalty and drive repeat sales. The system would enable the hotel to reward repeat guests with gifts or room upgrades as they checked in and note guest preferences for future visits and promotions. The marketing department enthusiastically promoted the system to customers and hotel managers.

Thomas Murphy, CIO of Royal Caribbean Cruises in Miami, was Omni's vice president of information technology at that time. He tried to get Omni's vice presidents together in one room to define the system requirements. The executives couldn't be bothered with such details and sent their underlings to take their place. When the information systems department presented a prototyped demonstration of the system, managers from marketing, sales, and operations began fighting over what capabilities the system should have. No one could agree on when and how guests should receive gifts. The system had been designed without any input from Omni's business units, and had no rules for granting the rewards.

The marketing department had not informed Omni's CEO about what it was doing, and his expectations were wildly different from what was being developed. The CEO envisioned a grandiose system that could never be built in the allotted time frame. Communication had been poor between Omni's middle managers and its executive team, because the turnover rate in Omni's executive team had been high for a number of years.

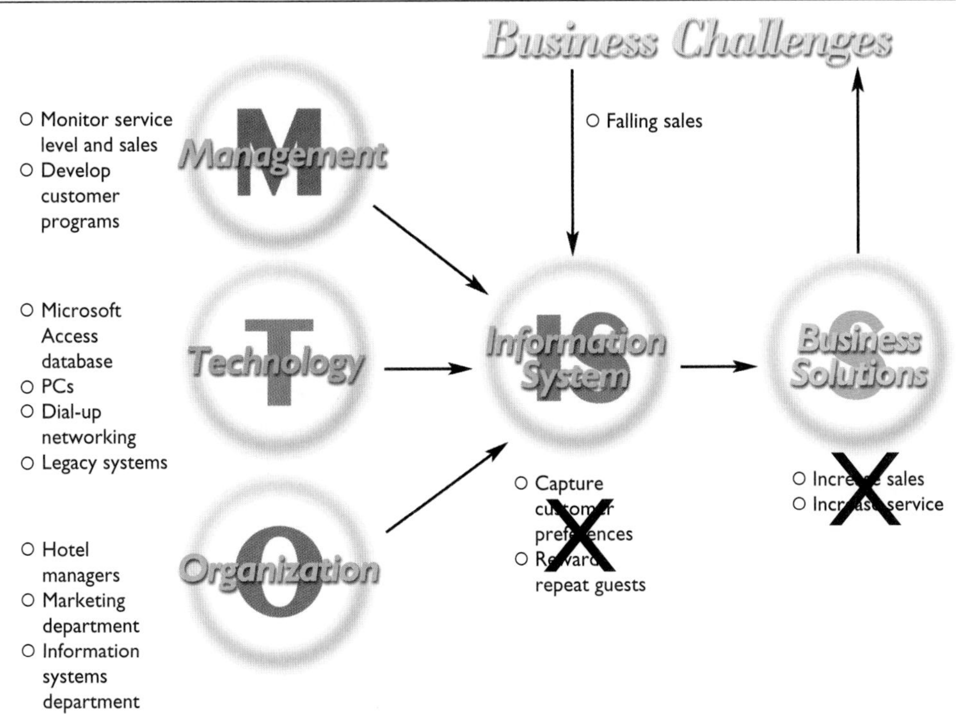


Serious technical problems emerged. The software had initially been developed on a Microsoft Access database, which could not be scaled to service Omni's 40 hotels. It took an hour each morning to update the database using a PC at the front desk. Users had to access the system through sluggish dial-up networking.

Murphy's team spent a month trying to redesign the system to satisfy all the warring interest groups as well as the CEO. The system was supposed to be rapid and easy to use, with improved reporting and interfaces to other legacy systems.

When the system went live a month behind schedule, the hotels hated it. Hotel managers had never been consulted about the project, and they resented having to use their budgets for bottles of wine and other expensive gifts to guests. The system was slow, difficult to use, and had little business value. The hotels received no training or documentation to show them how to use the system. Six months later, the system was scrapped and Omni Hotels had lost $250,000.

Omni Hotels is not alone. At least half of all information system projects are failures. Companies could be wasting as much as 50% of their information systems resources on projects that have to be abandoned.

**Sources:** Polly Schneider, "Another Trip to Hell," *CIO Magazine,* February 15, 2000; and Barbara Ponolski, "Stop Wasting Your Workers," *Computerworld,* June 26, 2000.

**Omni Hotels New Customer System Fizzles Out**

**MANAGEMENT CHALLENGES**

## MANAGEMENT CHALLENGES

One of the principal challenges posed by information systems is making sure they can deliver genuine business benefits. Organizations need to find ways of measuring the business value of their information systems and to ensure that these systems actually deliver the benefits they promise. There is a very high failure rate among information systems projects because organizations have incorrectly assessed their business value or because firms have failed to manage the organizational change process surrounding the introduction of new technology. Omni's experience is actually very common. Successful system-building requires skillful planning and change management, and you should be aware of the following management challenges:

1. **Determining benefits of a system when they are largely intangible.** As the sophistication of systems grows, they produce fewer tangible and more intangible benefits. By definition, there is no solid method for pricing intangible benefits. Organizations could lose important opportunities if they only use strict financial criteria for determining information systems benefits. However, organizations could make very poor investment decisions if they overestimate intangible benefits.
2. **Dealing with the complexity of large-scale systems projects.** Large-scale systems, including enterprise systems, that affect large numbers of organizational units and staff members and that have extensive information requirements and business process changes are difficult to oversee, coordinate, and plan for. Implementing such systems, which have multiyear development periods, is especially problem ridden because the systems are so complex. In addition, there are few reliable techniques for estimating the time and cost to develop large-scale information systems. Guidelines presented in this chapter are helpful but cannot guarantee that a large information system project can be precisely planned with accurate cost figures.

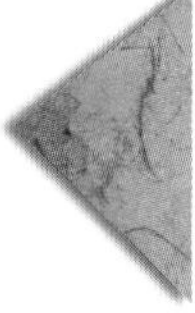

In this chapter we examine various ways of measuring the business value provided by information systems, describing both financial and nonfinancial models. We then examine the role of change management in successful system implementation. Finally, we present strategies for reducing the risks in systems projects and improving project management.

## 11.1 UNDERSTANDING THE BUSINESS VALUE OF INFORMATION SYSTEMS

Information systems can have several different values for business firms. A consistently strong information technology infrastructure can, over the long term, play an important strategic role in the life of the firm. Looked at less grandly, information systems can permit firms simply to survive.

It is important also to realize that systems can have value but that the firm may not capture all or even some of the value. Although system projects can result in firm benefits such as profitability and productivity, some or all of the benefit can go directly to the consumer in the form of lower prices or more reliable services and products (Hitt and Brynjolfsson, 1996). Society can reward firms that enhance consumer surplus by allowing them to survive or by rewarding them with increases in business revenues. Competitors who fail to enrich consumers will not survive. Benefits from information technology investments can also be reduced if firms do not consider the costs of organizational change associated with new systems and make these changes effectively. (Ryan and Harrison, 2000; Irani and Love, 2000–2001). But from a management point of view, the challenge is to retain as much of the benefit of systems investments as is feasible in current market conditions.

The value of systems from a financial view comes down to one question: Does a particular IS investment produce sufficient returns to justify its costs? There are many problems with this approach, not the least of which is how to estimate benefits and count the costs.

## TRADITIONAL CAPITAL BUDGETING MODELS

Capital budgeting models are one of several techniques used to measure the value of investing in long-term capital investment projects. The process of analyzing and selecting various proposals for capital expenditures is called **capital budgeting.** Firms invest in capital projects to expand production, to meet anticipated demand or to modernize production equipment to reduce costs. Firms also invest in capital projects for many noneconomic reasons, such as to install pollution control equipment or to convert to a human resources database to meet some government regulations. Information systems are considered long-term capital investment projects. Six capital budgeting models are used to evaluate capital projects:

**capital budgeting**
The process of analyzing and selecting various proposals for capital expenditures.

The payback method

The accounting rate of return on investment (ROI)

The cost-benefit ratio

The net present value

The profitability index

The internal rate of return (IRR)

All capital budgeting methods rely on measures of cash flows into and out of the firm. The investment cost is an immediate cash outflow caused by the purchase of the capital equipment. In subsequent years, the investment may cause additional cash outflows that will be balanced by cash inflows resulting from the investment. Cash inflows take the form of increased sales of more products (for reasons including new products, higher quality, or increasing market share) or reduction in costs of production and operation. The difference between cash outflows and cash inflows is used for calculating the financial worth of an investment. Once the cash flows have been established, several alternative methods are available for comparison among different projects and decision making about the investment.

Financial models assume that all relevant alternatives have been examined, that all costs and benefits are known, and that these costs and benefits can be expressed in a common metric, specifically, money. When one has to choose among many complex alternatives, these assumptions are rarely met in the real world, although they may be approximated. Table 11-1 lists some of the more common costs and benefits of systems. **Tangible benefits** can be quantified and assigned a monetary value. **Intangible benefits,** such as more efficient

**tangible benefits**
Benefits that can be quantified and assigned monetary value; they include lower operational costs and increased cash flows.

**intangible benefits**
Benefits that are not easily quantified; they include more efficient customer service or enhanced decision making.

### TABLE 11-1 COSTS AND BENEFITS OF INFORMATION SYSTEMS

| Costs | Intangible Benefits |
|---|---|
| Hardware | Improved asset utilization |
| Telecommunications | Improved resource control |
| Software | Improved organizational planning |
| Services | Increased organizational flexibility |
| Personnel | More timely information |
| | More information |
| **Tangible Benefits (cost savings)** | Increased organizational learning |
| Increased productivity | Legal requirements attained |
| Lower operational costs | Enhanced employee goodwill |
| Reduced workforce | Increased job satisfaction |
| Lower computer expenses | Improved decision making |
| Lower outside vendor costs | Improved operations |
| Lower clerical and professional costs | Higher client satisfaction |
| Reduced rate of growth in expenses | Better corporate image |
| Reduced facility costs | |

customer service or enhanced decision making, cannot be immediately quantified but may lead to quantifiable gains in the long run.

## Limitations of Financial Models

Many well-known problems emerge when financial analysis is applied to information systems (Dos Santos, 1991). Financial models do not express the risks and uncertainty of their own cost and benefit estimates. Costs and benefits do not occur in the same time frame—costs tend to be upfront and tangible, whereas benefits tend to be back loaded and intangible. Inflation may affect costs and benefits differently. Technology—especially information technology—can change during the course of the project, causing estimates to vary greatly. Intangible benefits are difficult to quantify. These factors wreak havoc with financial models.

The difficulties of measuring intangible benefits give financial models an application bias: Transaction and clerical systems that displace labor and save space always produce more measurable, tangible benefits than management information systems, decision-support systems, or computer-supported collaborative work systems (see Chapters 12 and 13.)

There is some reason to believe that investment in information technology requires special consideration in financial modeling. Capital budgeting historically concerned itself with manufacturing equipment and other long-term investments such as electrical generating facilities and telephone networks. These investments had expected lives of more than 1 year and up to 25 years. However, information systems differ from manufacturing systems in that their expected life is shorter. The very high rate of technological change in computer-based information systems means that most systems are seriously out of date in five to eight years (if not earlier). The high rate of technological obsolescence in budgeting for systems means simply that the payback period must be shorter and the rates of return higher than typical capital projects with much longer useful lives.

The bottom line with financial models is to use them cautiously and to put the results into a broader context of business analysis. Let us look at an example to see how these problems arise and can be handled. The following case study is based on a real-world scenario, but the names have been changed.

### CASE EXAMPLE: PRIMROSE, MENDELSON, AND HANSEN

Primrose, Mendelson, and Hansen is a 250-person law partnership on Manhattan's West Side with branch offices in London, Los Angeles, and Paris. Founded in 1923, Primrose has excelled in corporate, taxation, environmental, and health law. Its litigation department is also well known.

## The Problem

The firm occupies three floors of a new building. Many partners still have four-year-old PCs on their desktops but rarely use them except to read e-mail. Virtually all business is conducted face to face in the office or when partners meet directly with clients on the clients' premises. Most of the law business involves marking up (editing), creating, filing, storing, and sending documents. In addition, the tax, pension, and real estate groups do a considerable amount of spreadsheet work.

With overall business off 15 percent since 1999, the chairman, Edward W. Hansen III, is hoping to use information systems to cope with the flood of paperwork, enhance service to clients, and slow the growth in administrative costs.

First, the firm's income depends on billable hours, and every lawyer is supposed to keep a diary of work for specific clients in 30-minute intervals. Generally, senior lawyers at this firm charge about $500 an hour for their time. Unfortunately, lawyers often forget what they have been working on and must go back to reconstruct their time diaries. The firm hopes that there will be some automated way of tracking billable hours.

Second, much time is spent communicating with clients around the world, with other law firms both in the United States and overseas and with the Primrose branch offices. The fax machine has become the communication medium of choice, generating huge bills and developing lengthy queues. The firm looks forward to using some sort of secure e-mail, perhaps Lotus Notes or even the Internet. Law firms are wary of breaches in the security of confidential client information.

Third, Primrose has no client database! A law firm is a collection of fiefdoms—each lawyer has clients and keeps the information about them private. This, however, makes it impossible for management to determine who is a client of the firm, who is working on a deal with whom, and so forth. The firm maintains a billing system, but the information is too difficult to search. What Primrose needs is an integrated client management system that will take care of billing and hourly charges, and make client information available to others in the firm. Even overseas offices want to have information on who is taking care of a particular client in the United States.

Fourth, there is no system to track costs. The head of the firm and the department heads who compose the executive committee cannot identify what the costs are, where the money is being spent, who is spending it, and how the firm's resources are being allocated. A decent accounting system that could identify the cash flows and the costs a bit more clearly than the existing journal would be a big help.

## The Solution

Information systems could obviously have some survival value and, perhaps, could grant a strategic advantage to Primrose if a system were correctly built and implemented. We will not go through a detailed systems analysis and design here. Instead, we will sketch the solution that, in fact, was adopted, showing the detailed costs by department and estimated benefits.

The technical solution adopted was to create a local area network composed of 300 fully configured Pentium 4 multimedia desktop PCs with CD-ROM drives, three Windows 2000 servers, and an Ethernet 10 MBPS (megabit per second) local area network on a coaxial cable. The network connects all the lawyers and their secretaries to a single integrated system yet permits each lawyer to configure his or her desktop with specialized software and hardware. The older machines were given away to charity.

All desktop machines were configured with Windows 2000 and Office 2000 software, and the servers ran Windows 2000. Lotus Notes was chosen to handle client accounting, document management, group collaboration, and e-mail, because it provided an easy-to-use interface and secure links to external networks (including the Internet). The Internet was rejected as an e-mail technology because of its uncertain security. The Primrose local area network is linked to external networks so that the firm can obtain information online from Lexis (a legal database) and several financial database services.

The new system required Primrose to hire a director of systems. Two systems personnel were required to operate the system and train lawyers. An outside trainer was also hired for a short period.

Figure 11-1 shows the estimated costs and benefits of the system. The system had an actual investment cost of $1,733,100 in the first year (year 0) and total cost over six years of $3,690,600. The estimated benefits total $6,420,000 after six years. Was the investment worthwhile? If so, in what sense? There are financial and nonfinancial answers to these questions. Let us look at the financial models first. They are depicted in Figure 11-2.

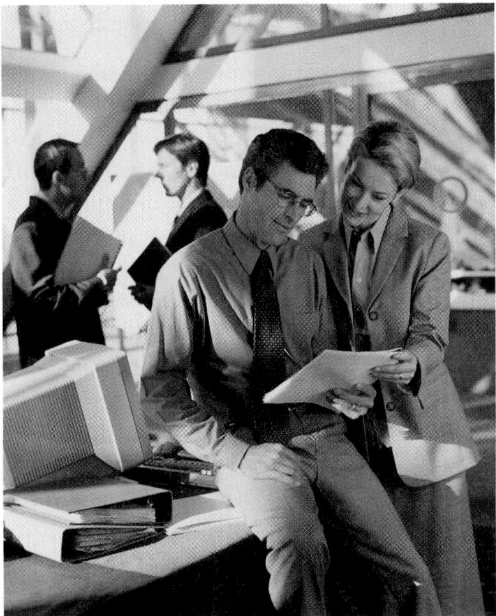

*Information systems can provide attorneys with legal data to expedite their research.*

**Estimated Costs and Benefits 2001-2006**

| | A | B | C | D | E | F | G | H | I | J | K | L |
|---|---|---|---|---|---|---|---|---|---|---|---|---|
| 1 | Year : | | | | 0 | 1 | 2 | 3 | 4 | 5 | | |
| 2 | | | | | 2001 | 2002 | 2003 | 2004 | 2005 | 2006 | | |
| 3 | **Costs Hardware** | | | | | | | | | | | |
| 4 | | Servers | | 3@ 20000 | 60,000 | 10,000 | 10,000 | 10,000 | 10,000 | 10,000 | | |
| 5 | | PCs | | 300@3000 | 900,000 | 10,000 | 10,000 | 10,000 | 10,000 | 10,000 | | |
| 6 | | Network cards | | 300@100 | 30,000 | 0 | 0 | 0 | 0 | 0 | | |
| 7 | | Scanners | | 6@100 | 600 | 500 | 500 | 500 | 500 | 500 | | |
| 8 | | | | | | | | | | | | |
| 9 | Telecommunications | | | | | | | | | | | |
| 10 | | Routers | | 10@500 | 5,000 | 1,000 | 1,000 | 1,000 | 1,000 | 1,000 | | |
| 11 | | Cabling | | 150,000 | 150,000 | 0 | 0 | 0 | 0 | 0 | | |
| 12 | | Telephone connect costs | | 50,000 | 50,000 | 50,000 | 50,000 | 50,000 | 50,000 | 50,000 | | |
| 13 | | | | | | | | | | | | |
| 14 | Software | | | | | | | | | | | |
| 15 | | Database | | 15,000 | 15,000 | 15,000 | 15,000 | 15,000 | 15,000 | 15,000 | | |
| 16 | | Network | | 10,000 | 10,000 | 2,000 | 2,000 | 2,000 | 2,000 | 2,000 | | |
| 17 | | Groupware | | 300@500 | 150,000 | 3,000 | 3,000 | 3,000 | 3,000 | 3,000 | | |
| 18 | | | | | | | | | | | | |
| 19 | Services | | | | | | | | | | | |
| 20 | | Lexis | | 50,000 | 50,000 | 50,000 | 50,000 | 50,000 | 50,000 | 50,000 | | |
| 21 | | Training | | 300hrs@75/hr | 22,500 | 10,000 | 10,000 | 10,000 | 10,000 | 10,000 | | |
| 22 | | Director of Systems | | 100,000 | 100,000 | 100,000 | 100,000 | 100,000 | 100,000 | 100,000 | | |
| 23 | | Systems Personnel | | 2@70000 | 140,000 | 140,000 | 140,000 | 140,000 | 140,000 | 140,000 | | |
| 24 | | Trainer | | 1@50000 | 50,000 | 0 | 0 | 0 | 0 | 0 | | |
| 25 | | | | | | | | | | | | |
| 26 | **Total Costs** | | | | 1,733,100 | 391,500 | 391,500 | 391,500 | 391,500 | 391,500 | 3,690,600 | |
| 27 | Benefits | | | | | | | | | | | |
| 28 | | 1. Billing enhancements | | | 300,000 | 500,000 | 600,000 | 600,000 | 600,000 | 500,000 | | |
| 29 | | 2. Reduced paralegals | | | 50,000 | 100,000 | 150,000 | 150,000 | 150,000 | 150,000 | | |
| 30 | | 3. Reduced clerical | | | 50,000 | 100,000 | 100,000 | 100,000 | 100,000 | 100,000 | | |
| 31 | | 4. Reduced messenger | | | 15,000 | 30,000 | 30,000 | 30,000 | 30,000 | 30,000 | | |
| 32 | | 5. Reduced telecommunications | | | 5,000 | 10,000 | 10,000 | 10,000 | 10,000 | 10,000 | | |
| 33 | | 6. Lawyer efficiencies | | | 120,000 | 240,000 | 360,000 | 360,000 | 360,000 | 360,000 | | |
| 34 | | | | | | | | | | | | |
| 35 | **Total Benefits** | | | | 540,000 | 980,000 | 1,250,000 | 1,250,000 | 1,250,000 | 1,150,000 | 6,420,000 | |

Sheet1 Sheet2 Sheet3

*Figure 11-1* Costs and benefits of the Legal Information System. This spreadsheet analyzes the basic costs and benefits of implementing an information system for the law firm. The costs for hardware, telecommunications, software, services, and personnel are analyzed over a six-year period.

## The Payback Method

**payback method**
A measure of the time required to pay back the initial investment on a project.

The **payback method** is quite simple: It is a measure of the time required to pay back the initial investment of a project. The payback period is computed as

$$\frac{\text{Original investment}}{\text{Annual net cash inflow}} = \text{Number of years to pay back}$$

In the case of Primrose, it will take more than two years to pay back the initial investment. (Because cash flows are uneven, annual cash inflows are summed until they equal the original investment in order to arrive at this number.) The payback method is popular because of its simplicity and power as an initial screening method. It is especially good for high-risk projects in which the useful life of a project is difficult to determine. If a project pays for itself in two years, then it matters less how long after two years the system lasts.

The weakness of this measure is its virtues: The method ignores the time value of money, the amount of cash flow after the payback period, the disposal value (usually zero with computer systems), and the profitability of the investment.

## Accounting Rate of Return on Investment (ROI)

**accounting rate of return on investment (ROI)**
Calculation of the rate of return on an investment by adjusting cash inflows produced by the investment for depreciation. Approximates the accounting income earned by the investment.

Firms make capital investments to earn a satisfactory rate of return. Determining a satisfactory rate of return depends on the cost of borrowing money, but other factors can enter into the equation. Such factors include the historic rates of return expected by the firm. In the long run, the desired rate of return must equal or exceed the cost of capital in the marketplace. Otherwise, no one will lend the firm money.

The **accounting rate of return on investment (ROI)** calculates the rate of return from an investment by adjusting the cash inflows produced by the investment for depreciation. It gives an approximation of the accounting income earned by the project.

**Estimated Costs and Benefits 2001-2006**

| | A | B | C | D | E | F | G | H | I | J | K | L |
|---|---|---|---|---|---|---|---|---|---|---|---|---|
| 1 | Year : | | | 0 | 1 | 2 | 3 | 4 | 5 | | | |
| 2 | Net Cash Flow (not including orig. investment) | | | 540,000 | 588,500 | 858,500 | 858,500 | 858,500 | 758,500 | | | |
| 3 | Net Cash Flow (including orig. investment) | | | -1,193,100 | 588,500 | 858,500 | 858,500 | 858,500 | 758,500 | | | |
| 4 | | | | | | | | | | | | |
| 5 | (1) Payback Period = 2.5 years | | | | | Cumulative Cash Flow | | | | | | |
| 6 | Initial investment = 1,733,100 | | | Year 0 | 540,000 | 540,000 | | | | | | |
| 7 | | | | Year 1 | 588,500 | 1,128,500 | | | | | | |
| 8 | | | | Year 2 | 858,500 | 1,987,000 | | | | | | |
| 9 | | | | Year 3 | 858,500 | 2,845,500 | | | | | | |
| 10 | | | | Year 4 | 858,500 | 3,704,000 | | | | | | |
| 11 | | | | Year 5 | 758,500 | 4,462,500 | | | | | | |
| 12 | | | | | | | | | | | | |
| 13 | (2) Accounting rate of return | | | | | | | | | | | |
| 14 | | | | | | | | | | | | |
| 15 | (Total benefits-Total Costs-Depreciation)/Useful life | | | | Total Benefits | 6,420,000 | | | | | | |
| 16 | ---------------------------------------------------------------- | | | | Total Costs | 3,690,600 | | | | | | |
| 17 | Total initial investment | | | | Depreciation | 1,733,100 | | | | | | |
| 18 | | | | Tot. benefits-tot. costs-depreciation | | 996,300 | | | | | | |
| 19 | | | | | Life | 6 years | | | | | | |
| 20 | | | | | | | | | | | | |
| 21 | | | | | Initial investment | | 1,733,100 | | | | | |
| 22 | ROI = | (996,300/6) | 9.58% | | | | | | | | | |
| 23 | | 1,733,100 | | | | | | | | | | |
| 24 | | | | | | | | | | | | |
| 25 | (3) Cost-Benefit Ratio | | Total Benefits | 6,420,000 | 1.74 | | | | | | | |
| 26 | | | Total Costs | 3,690,600 | | | | | | | | |
| 27 | | | | | | | | | | | | |
| 28 | (4) Net Present Value | | | | | | | | | | | |
| 29 | | = NPV (0.05,D8:I8)-1,733,100 | | | 2,001,529 | | | | | | | |
| 30 | | | | | | | | | | | | |
| 31 | (5) Profitability Index | | | | | | | | | | | |
| 32 | | PV/Investment | 3,734,629/1,733,100 | | 2.15 | | | | | | | |
| 33 | | | | | | | | | | | | |
| 34 | (6) Internal Rate of Return | | | | | | | | | | | |
| 35 | | | | | | | | | | | | |
| 36 | | = IRR(D9:I9) | | | 55% | | | | | | | |

Sheet1 Sheet2 Sheet3

*Figure 11-2* Financial models. To determine the financial basis for a project, a series of financial models helps determine the return on invested capital. These calculations include the payback period, the accounting rate of return (ROI), the cost–benefit ratio, the net present value, the profitability index, and the internal rate of return (IRR).

To find the ROI, first calculate the average net benefit. The formula for the average net benefit is as follows:

$$\frac{(\text{Total benefits} - \text{Total cost} - \text{Depreciation})}{\text{Useful life}} = \text{Net benefit}$$

This net benefit is divided by the total initial investment to arrive at ROI (rate of return on investment). The formula is

$$\frac{\text{Net benefit}}{\text{Total initial investment}} = \text{ROI}$$

In the case of Primrose, the average rate of return on the investment is 9.58 percent, which could be a good return on investment, if the cost of capital [the prime rate] is around 7 to 8 percent, and returns on invested capital in corporate bonds are at about 8 percent.

The weakness of ROI is that it can ignore the time value of money. Future savings are simply not worth as much in today's dollars as are current savings. However, ROI can be modified (and usually is) so that future benefits and costs are calculated in today's dollars. (The present value function on most spreadsheets will perform this conversion.)

## Net Present Value

Evaluating a capital project requires that the cost of an investment (a cash outflow usually in year 0) be compared with the net cash inflows that occur many years later. But these two kinds of inflows are not directly comparable because of the time value of money. Money you have been promised to receive three, four, and five years from now is not worth as much as money received today. Money received in the future has to be discounted by some appropriate percentage rate—usually the prevailing interest rate, or sometimes the cost of capital. **Present value** is the value in current dollars of a payment or stream of payments to be received in the future. It can be calculated by using the following formula:

**present value**
The value, in current dollars, of a payment or stream of payments to be received in the future.

$$\text{Payment} \times \frac{1 - (1 + 1 \text{ interest})^{-n}}{\text{Interest}} = \text{Present value}$$

Thus, to compare the investment (made in today's dollars) with future savings or earnings, you need to discount the earnings to their present value and then calculate the net present value of the investment. The **net present value** is the amount of money an investment is worth, taking into account its cost, earnings, and the time value of money. The formula for net present value is

**net present value**
The amount of money an investment is worth, taking into account its cost, earnings, and the time value of money.

Present value of expected cash flows − Initial investment cost = Net present value

In the case of Primrose, the present value of the stream of benefits is $3,734,629 and the cost (in today's dollars) is $1,733,100, giving a net present value of $2,001,529. In other words, the net present value of the investment is $2,001,529 over a six-year period. For a $1.7 million investment today, the firm will receive more than $2 million. This is a very good rate of return on an investment.

## Cost–Benefit Ratio

A simple method for calculating the returns from a capital expenditure is to calculate the **cost–benefit ratio,** which is the ratio of benefits to costs. The formula is

**cost–benefit ratio**
A method for calculating the returns from a capital expenditure by dividing total benefits by total costs.

$$\frac{\text{Total benefits}}{\text{Total costs}} = \text{Cost–benefit ratio}$$

In the case of Primrose, the cost–benefit ratio is 1.74, meaning that the benefits are 1.74 times greater than the costs. The cost–benefit ratio can be used to rank several projects for comparison. Some firms establish a minimum cost–benefit ratio that must be attained by capital projects. The cost–benefit ratio can, of course, be calculated using present values to account for the time value of money.

## Profitability Index

One limitation of net present value is that it provides no measure of profitability. Neither does it provide a way to rank order different possible investments. One simple solution is provided by the profitability index. The **profitability index** is calculated by dividing the present value of the total cash inflow from an investment by the initial cost of the investment. The result can be used to compare the profitability of alternative investments.

**profitability index**
Used to compare the profitability of alternative investments; it is calculated by dividing the present value of the total cash inflow from an investment by the initial cost of the investment.

$$\frac{\text{Present value of cash inflows}}{\text{Investment}} = \text{Profitability index}$$

In the case of Primrose, the profitability index is 2.15. Projects can be rank ordered on this index, permitting firms to focus on only the most profitable projects.

## Internal Rate of Return (IRR)

Internal rate of return (IRR) is a variation of the net present value method. It takes into account the time value of money. **Internal rate of return (IRR)** is defined as the rate of return or profit that an investment is expected to earn. IRR is the discount (interest) rate that will equate the present value of the project's future cash flows to the initial cost of the project (defined here as a negative cash flow in year 0 of $1,193,100). In other words, the value of $R$ (discount rate) is such that Present value − Initial cost = 0. In the case of Primrose, the IRR is 55%.

**internal rate of return (IRR)**
The rate of return or profit that an investment is expected to earn.

## Results of the Capital Budgeting Analysis

Using methods that take into account the time value of money, the Primrose project is cash-flow positive over the time period and returns more benefits than it costs. Against this analysis, one might ask what other investments would be better from an efficiency and effectiveness standpoint? Also, one must ask if all the benefits have been calculated. It may be that this investment is necessary for the survival of the firm or necessary to provide a level of service demanded by its clients. What are other competitors doing? In other words, there may be other intangible and strategic business factors to take into account.

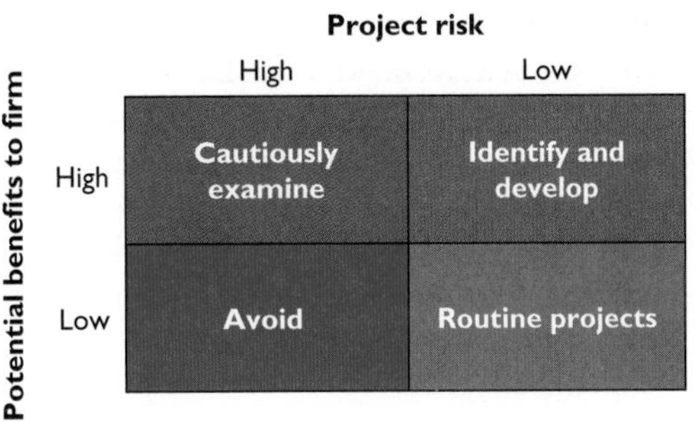


*Figure 11-3* A system portfolio. Companies should examine their portfolio of projects in terms of potential benefits and likely risks. Certain kinds of projects should be avoided altogether and others developed rapidly. There is no ideal mix. Companies in different industries have different profiles.

## STRATEGIC CONSIDERATIONS

Other methods of selecting and evaluating information system investments involve nonfinancial and strategic considerations. When the firm has several alternative investments from which to select, it can use portfolio analysis and scoring models. It can apply real options pricing models to IT investments that are highly uncertain. Several of these methods can be used in combination.

### Portfolio Analysis

Rather than using capital budgeting, a second way of selecting among alternative projects is to consider the firm as having a portfolio of potential applications. Each application carries risks and benefits. The portfolio can be described as having a certain profile of risk and benefit to the firm (see Figure 11-3). Although there is no ideal profile for all firms, information-intensive industries (e.g., finance) should have a few high-risk, high-benefit projects to ensure that they stay current with technology. Firms in noninformation-intensive industries should focus on high-benefit, low-risk projects.

Risks are not necessarily bad. They are tolerable as long as the benefits are commensurate. Section 11.2 describes the factors that increase the risks of systems projects.

Once strategic analyses have determined the overall direction of systems development, a **portfolio analysis** can be used to select alternatives. Obviously, one can begin by focusing on systems of high benefit and low risk. These promise early returns and low risks. Second, high-benefit, high-risk systems should be examined; low-benefit, high-risk systems should be totally avoided; and low-benefit, low-risk systems should be reexamined for the possibility of rebuilding and replacing them with more desirable systems having higher benefits.

**portfolio analysis**
An analysis of the portfolio of potential applications within a firm to determine the risks and benefits and select among alternatives for information systems.

### Scoring Models

A quick and sometimes compelling method for arriving at a decision on alternative systems is a **scoring model.** Scoring models give alternative systems a single score based on the extent to which they meet selected objectives (Matlin, 1989; Buss, 1983).

**scoring model**
A quick method for deciding among alternative systems based on a system of ratings for selected objectives.

In Table 11-2 the firm must decide among three alternative office systems: (1) an IBM AS/400 client/server system with proprietary software, (2) a Unix-based client/server system

**TABLE 11-2** SCORING MODEL USED TO CHOOSE AMONG ALTERNATIVE OFFICE SYSTEMS[A]

| Criterion | Weight | AS/400 | | Unix | | Windows 2000 | |
|---|---|---|---|---|---|---|---|
| Percentage of user needs met | 0.40 | 2 | 0.8 | 3 | 1.2 | 4 | 1.6 |
| Cost of the initial purchase | 0.20 | 1 | 0.2 | 3 | 0.6 | 4 | 0.8 |
| Financing | 0.10 | 1 | 0.1 | 3 | 0.3 | 4 | 0.4 |
| Ease of maintenance | 0.10 | 2 | 0.2 | 3 | 0.3 | 4 | 0.4 |
| Chances of success | 0.20 | 3 | 0.6 | 4 | 0.8 | 4 | 0.8 |
| Final score | | | 1.9 | | 3.2 | | 4.0 |
| Scale: 1 = low, 5 = high | | | | | | | |

[a]One of the major uses of scoring models is in identifying the criteria of selection and their relative weights. In this instance, an office system based on Windows 2000 appears preferable.

using an Oracle database, and (3) a Windows 2000 client/server system using Windows and Lotus Notes. Column 1 lists the criteria that decision makers may apply to the systems. These criteria are usually the result of lengthy discussions among the decision-making group. Often the most important outcome of a scoring model is not the score but simply agreement on the criteria used to judge a system (Ginzberg, 1979; Nolan, 1982). Column 2 lists the weights that decision makers attach to the decision criteria. The scoring model helps to bring about agreement among participants concerning the rank of the criteria. Columns 3, 5, and 7 use a 1-to-5 scale (lowest to highest) to express the judgments of participants on the relative merits of each system. For example, concerning the percentage of user needs that each system meets, a score of 1 for a system argues that this system when compared with others being considered will be low in meeting user needs.

As with all objective techniques, there are many qualitative judgments involved in using the scoring model. This model requires experts who understand the issues and the technology. It is appropriate to cycle through the scoring model several times, changing the criteria and weights, to see how sensitive the outcome is to reasonable changes in criteria. Scoring models are used most commonly to confirm, to rationalize, and to support decisions, rather than as the final arbiters of system selection.

If Primrose had other alternative systems projects to select from, it could have used the portfolio and scoring models as well as financial models to establish the business value of its systems solution.

Primrose did not have a portfolio of applications that could be used to compare the proposed system. Senior lawyers believed the project was low in risk using well-understood technology. They believed the rewards were even higher than the financial models stated, because the system might enable the firm to expand its business. For instance, the ability to communicate with other law firms, with clients, and with the international staff of lawyers in remote locations was not even considered in the financial analysis.

## Real Options Pricing Models

Some information system projects are highly uncertain. Their future revenue streams are unclear and their up-front costs are high. Suppose, for instance, that a firm is considering a $20 million investment to upgrade its information technology infrastructure. If this infrastructure were available, the organization would have the technology capabilities to respond to future problems and opportunities. Although the costs of this investment can be calculated, not all of the benefits of making this investment can be established in advance. But if the firm waits a few years until the revenue potential becomes more obvious, it might be too late to make the infrastructure investment. In such cases, managers might benefit from using real options pricing models to evaluate information technology investments.

**real options pricing models** Models for evaluating information technology investments with uncertain returns by using techniques for valuing financial options.

**Real options pricing models** use the concept of options valuation borrowed from the financial industry. An option is essentially the right, but not the obligation, to act at some future date. A typical call option, for instance, is a financial option in which a person buys the right (but not the obligation) to purchase an underlying asset (usually a stock) at a definite price (strike price) for a limited period of time. For instance, at the time of this writing, for $1.05 one could purchase the right (a call option) to buy 100 shares of Ford common stock at $30 per share for a period of two months until April 2001. If, after two months has elapsed, the price of Ford stock did not rise above $30, you would not exercise the option, and the value of the option would fall to zero on the strike date. If, however, the price of Ford common stock rises to, say, $60 per share, you could purchase the stock for the strike price of $30, and pocket the profit of $30 per share.

Real options involving investments in capital projects are different from financial options in that they cannot be traded on a market and they differ in value based on the firm in which they are made. Thus, an investment in an enterprise system will have very different real option values in different firms because the ability to derive value from even identical enterprise systems depends on firm factors, such as prior expertise, skilled labor force, market conditions, and other factors. Nevertheless, several scholars have argued that real options theory can be useful when considering highly uncertain IT investments and that potentially the same techniques for valuing financial options can be used (Benaroch and Kauffman, 2000;

## MANAGEMENT DECISION PROBLEM

### EVALUATING ERP SYSTEMS WITH A SCORING MODEL

Your company, Audio Direct, sells parts used in audio systems for cars and trucks and is growing very fast. Your management team has decided that the firm can speed up product delivery to customers and lower inventory and customer support costs by installing an enterprise resource planning (ERP) system. Two enterprise software vendors have responded to your request for proposal (RFP) and have submitted reports showing which of your detailed list of requirements can be supported by their systems. Audio Direct attaches the most importance to capabilities for sales order processing, inventory management, and warehousing. The information systems staff prepared the following matrix comparing the vendors' capabilities for these functions. It shows the percentage of requirements for each function that each alternative ERP system can provide. It also shows the weight, or relative importance, the company attaches to each of these functions.

1. Calculate each ERP vendor's score by multiplying the percentage of requirements for each function by the weight for that function.
2. Calculate each ERP vendor's total score for each of the three major functions (order processing, inventory management, and warehousing). Then calculate the grand total for each vendor.
3. On the basis of vendor scores, which ERP vendor would you select?
4. Are there any other factors, including intangible benefits, that might affect your decision?

| Function | Weight | ERP System A % | ERP System A Score | ERP System B % | ERP System B Score |
|---|---|---|---|---|---|
| 1.0 Order Processing | | | | | |
| 1.1 On-line order entry | 4 | 67 | | 73 | |
| 1.2 On-line pricing | 4 | 81 | | 87 | |
| 1.3 Inventory check | 4 | 72 | | 81 | |
| 1.4 Customer credit check | 3 | 66 | | 59 | |
| 1.5 Invoicing | 4 | 73 | | 82 | |
| Total Order Processing | | | | | |
| 2.0 Inventory Management | | | | | |
| 2.1 Production forecasting | 3 | 72 | | 76 | |
| 2.2 Production planning | 4 | 79 | | 81 | |
| 2.3 Inventory control | 4 | 68 | | 80 | |
| 2.4 Reports | 3 | 71 | | 69 | |
| Total Inventory Management | | | | | |
| 3.0 Warehousing | | | | | |
| 3.1 Receiving | 2 | 71 | | 75 | |
| 3.2 Picking/packing | 3 | 77 | | 82 | |
| 3.3 Shipping | 4 | 92 | | 89 | |
| Total Warehousing | | | | | |
| Grand Total | | | | | |

Taudes, Feurstein, and Mild, 2000). (Calculation of real option values for IT projects is beyond the scope of this text. )

Real options pricing models (ROPM) offer an approach to thinking about information technology projects that takes into account the value of management learning over time and the value of delaying investment. In real options theory, the value of the IT project (real option) is a function of the value of the underlying IT asset (present value of expected revenues from the IT project), the volatility of the value in the underlying asset, the cost of converting the option investment into the underlying asset (the exercise price), the risk free interest rate, and the options' time to maturity (length of time the project can be deferred).

The real options model addresses some of the limitations of the discounted cash flow models we described earlier, which essentially call for investing in an information technology project only when the value of the discounted cash value of the investment is greater than zero. The ROPM allows managers to systematically take into account the volatility in the value of IT projects over time, the optimal timing of the investment, and the changing cost of implementation as technology prices decline over time. Briefly, the ROPM places a value on management learning and the use of an unfolding investment technique (investing in chunks) based on learning over time.

The disadvantages of this model are primarily in estimating all the key variables, especially the expected cash flows from the underlying asset and changes in the cost of implementation. Several rule of thumb approaches are being developed (McGrath and MacMillan, 2000). ROPM can be useful when there is no experience with a technology and its future is highly uncertain.

## 11.2 The Importance of Change Management in Information System Success and Failure

The introduction or alteration of an information system has a powerful behavioral and organizational impact. It transforms how various individuals and groups perform and interact. Changes in the way that information is defined, accessed, and used to manage the organization's resources often lead to new distributions of authority and power. This internal organizational change breeds resistance and opposition and can lead to the demise of an otherwise good system.

A very large percentage of information systems fail to deliver benefits or to solve the problems for which they were intended because the process of organizational change surrounding system-building was not properly addressed. Successful system-building requires careful change management.

**system failure**
An information system that either does not perform as expected, is not operational at a specified time, or cannot be used in the way it was intended.

**user interface**
The part of the information system through which the end user interacts with the system; type of hardware and the series of on-screen commands and responses required for a user to work with the system.

### Information System Problem Areas

The problems causing information **system failure** fall into multiple categories, as illustrated by Figure 11-4. The major problem areas are design, data, cost, and operations.

### Design

The actual design of the system fails to capture essential business requirements or improve organizational performance. Information may not be provided quickly enough to be helpful; it may be in a format that is impossible to digest and use; or it may represent the wrong pieces of data.

The way in which nontechnical business users must interact with the system may be excessively complicated and discouraging. A system may be designed with a poor **user interface.** The user interface is the part of the system with which end users interact. For example, an input form or an on-line data entry screen may be so poorly arranged that no one wants to submit data. The procedures to request on-line information retrieval may be so unintelligible that users are too frustrated to make requests. Web sites may discourage visitors from exploring further if Web pages are cluttered and poorly arranged or users can't easily find the information they are seeking. A number of studies have found that close to 50 percent of Web shoppers give up purchasing items on-line because a site was too difficult to navigate and they could not locate products on the Web site (Lohse and Spiller, 1999). The Window on Organizations details how these user interfaces can impact electronic commerce.

An information system will be judged a failure if its design is not compatible with the structure, culture, and goals of the organization as a whole.

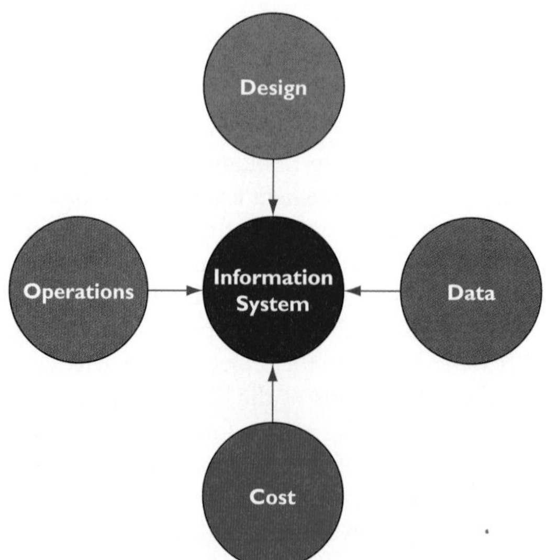


*Figure 11-4* Information system problem areas. Problems with an information system's design, data, cost, or operations can be evidence of a system failure.

*CarsDirect.com redesigned its Web site to make it easier to use. A well-designed user interface contributes to system success.*

## WEB SITES STRIVE FOR USABILITY

At the end of January 2000, CarsDirect.com, an on-line auto store, saw the number of visitors to its Web site double. This surge in visitors was not the result of heavy advertising expenditures or more powerful information systems technology. CarsDirect.com had merely redesigned its Web site.

The new CarsDirect.com site is sleeker and easier on the eye, with new tools, such as the ability to connect to a live customer service representative with a single mouse click. CarsDirect.com also added software to help it understand the behavior of potential customers. The software helps the company track what pages users are accessing and the points where they are leaving the site so that they can monitor how customers are reacting.

When it comes to Web sites, design matters. Usability and good looks count. Good design can make a Web site stand out among dozens of competitors. A well-designed Web site can boost traffic and sales and keep customers coming back. If visitors have a good experience on a Web site, they are much more likely to make a purchase. And if customers can't understand or easily find the information on a Web site, they'll get frustrated and turn to a competitor. The Web makes switching costs extraordinarily low, with competition only a mouse click away.

Studies of user behavior on the Web have found that people have a low tolerance for difficult designs and slow sites. They don't want to wait to see a Web page. They won't want to spend time deciphering a home page. E-commerce firms must make sure that users can easily download a page from their Web sites, find an item, make a purchase, and navigate through page after page without losing track of where they started. Sadly, the majority of Web sites today are difficult to use. Usability studies have found a success rate of less than 50 percent. That means that when a person is asked to perform a simple task on an average Web site, he or she will most likely fail.

Success in e-commerce can be measured by multiplying the number of people who visit a Web site times the conversion rate—the percentage of visitors who become customers. It's expensive and difficult for most companies to get people to visit their Web sites in the first place. To double the success of a site, firms must either double the number of visitors or double the conversion rate. Instead of doubling the advertising budget to increase site visitors, companies could spend much less to raise conversion rates by redesigning their Web sites using a human-centered design process.

Fidelity Investments, the largest U.S. mutual fund manager, spends more on technology than any of its rivals, focusing on product usability. Its Fidelity Center for Applied Technology features two usability labs where Fidelity tests the human interface design of its Web site and other technologies for delivering its services. Fidelity even uses eye-tracking tests to track how people are viewing the pixels on its Web pages, so it can fine-tune its Web site to eliminate every wasteful click. Fidelity.com is a complex site with many features and usability experts constantly work at making navigating its 30,000 pages as easy as possible.

**To Think About:** What organization and technology issues affect the usability of a Web site? Why is Web site usability so important in electronic commerce?

*Sources:* Danny Hakim, "A High-tech Vision Lifts Fidelity," *The New York Times,* September 17, 2000; Beth Bacheldor, "The Art of E-biz," *Information Week,* February 14, 2000; and Jakob Nielsen and Donald A. Norman, "Usability on the Web Isn't a Luxury," *Information Week,* February 14, 2000.

Historically, information system design has been preoccupied with technical issues at the expense of organizational concerns. The result has often been information systems that are technically excellent but incompatible with their organization's structure, culture, and goals. Without a close organizational fit, such systems have created tensions, instability, and conflict.

### Data

The data in the system may have a high level of inaccuracy or inconsistency. The information in certain fields may be erroneous or ambiguous, or they may not be broken out properly for business purposes. Information required for a specific business function may be inaccessible because the data are incomplete.

### Cost

Some systems operate quite smoothly, but the cost to implement and run them on a production basis is way over budget. Other system projects may be too costly to complete. In both cases, the excessive expenditures cannot be justified by the demonstrated business value of the information they provide.

### Operations

The system does not run well. Information is not provided in a timely and efficient manner because the computer operations that handle information processing break down. Jobs that abort too often lead to excessive reruns and delayed or missed schedules for delivery of information. An on-line system may be operationally inadequate because the response time is too long.

Some of these problems can be attributed to technical features of information systems, but most stem from organizational factors (Keil, Cule, Lyytinen, and Schmidt, 1998). System-builders need to understand these organizational issues and learn how to manage the change associated with a new information system.

## Change Management and the Concept of Implementation

**implementation**
All organizational activities working toward the adoption, management, and routinization of an innovation.

**change agent**
In the context of implementation, the individual acting as the catalyst during the change process to ensure successful organizational adaptation to a new system or innovation.

To effectively manage the organizational change surrounding the introduction of a new information system, one must examine the process of implementation. **Implementation** refers to all organizational activities working toward the adoption, management, and routinization of an innovation such as a new information system. In the implementation process, the systems analyst is a **change agent.** The analyst not only develops technical solutions but also redefines the configurations, interactions, job activities, and power relationships of various organizational groups. The analyst is the catalyst for the entire change process and is responsible for ensuring that the changes created by a new system are accepted by all parties involved. The change agent communicates with users, mediates between competing interest groups, and ensures that the organizational adjustment to such changes is complete.

One model of the implementation process is the Kolb/Frohman model of organizational change. This model divides the process of organizational change into a seven-stage relationship between an organizational *consultant* and his or her *client.* (The consultant corresponds to the information system designer and the client to the user.) The success of the change effort is determined by how well the consultant and client deal with the key issues at each stage (Kolb and Frohman, 1970). Other models of implementation describe the relationship as one between designers, clients, and decision makers, who are responsible for managing the implementation effort to bridge the gap between design and utilization (Swanson, 1988). Recent work on implementation stresses the need for flexibility and improvisation with organizational actors not limited to rigid prescribed roles (Markus and Benjamin, 1997; Orlikowski and Hofman, 1997).

## Causes of Implementation Success and Failure

Implementation outcome can be largely determined by the following factors:

- The role of users in the implementation process
- The degree of management support for the implementation effort

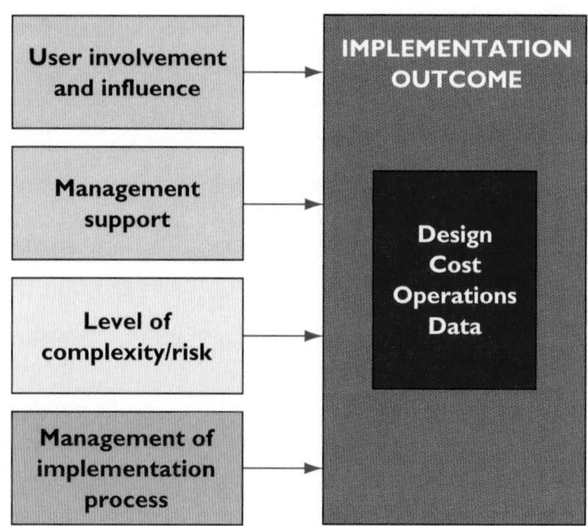


***Figure 11-5*** Factors in information system success or failure. The implementation outcome can be largely determined by the users' role, the degree of management support, the level of risk and complexity in the implementation project, and the quality of management of the implementation process. Evidence of success or failure can be found in the areas of design, cost, operations, or data of the information system.

- The level of complexity and risk of the implementation project
- The quality of management of the implementation process

These are largely behavioral and organizational issues and are illustrated in Figure 11-5.

## User Involvement and Influence

User involvement in the design and operation of information systems has several positive results. First, if users are heavily involved in systems design, they have more opportunities to mold the system according to their priorities and business requirements and more opportunities to control the outcome. Second, they are more likely to react positively to the completed system, because they have been active participants in the change process itself. It is often difficult to get users involved in a development project if they are pressed for time. Even when such involvement is limited, hands-on experience with the system helps users appreciate its benefits and encourages useful suggestions for improvement (De and Ferrat, 1998).

Incorporating the user's knowledge and expertise leads to better solutions. However, users often take a very narrow and limited view of the problem to be solved and may overlook important opportunities for improving business processes or innovative ways to apply information technology. The skills and vision of professional system designers are still required much in the same way that the services of an architect are required when building a new house (Markus and Keil, 1994).

The relationship between consultant and client has traditionally been a problem area for information system implementation efforts. Users and information systems specialists tend to have different backgrounds, interests, and priorities. This is referred to as the **user–designer communications gap.** These differences lead to divergent organizational loyalties, approaches to problem solving, and vocabularies. Information systems specialists, for example, often have a highly technical orientation to problem solving. They look for elegant and sophisticated technical solutions in which hardware and software efficiency is optimized at the expense of ease of use or organizational effectiveness. Users prefer systems that are oriented to solving business problems or facilitating organizational tasks. Often the orientations of both groups are so at odds that they appear to speak in different tongues. These differences are illustrated in Table 11-3, which depicts the typical concerns of end users and technical specialists (information system designers) regarding the development of a new information system. Communication problems between end users and designers are a major reason why user requirements are not properly incorporated into information systems and why users are driven out of the implementation process.

**user–designer communications gap** The difference in backgrounds, interests, and priorities that impede communication and problem solving among end users and information systems specialists.

Systems development projects run a very high risk of failure when there is a pronounced gap between users and technicians and when these groups continue to pursue different goals (see the chapter opening vignette). Under such conditions, users are often driven out of the implementation process. Because they cannot comprehend what the technicians are saying, users conclude that the entire project is best left in the hands of the information specialists alone. With so many implementation efforts guided by purely technical considerations, it is no wonder that many systems fail to serve organizational needs.

**TABLE 11-3 THE USER–DESIGNER COMMUNICATIONS GAP**

| User Concerns | Designer Concerns |
|---|---|
| Will the system deliver the information I need for my work? | How much disk storage space will the master file consume? |
| How quickly can I access the data? | How many lines of program code will it take to perform this function? |
| How easily can I retrieve the data? | How can we cut down on CPU time when we run the system? |
| How much clerical support will I need to enter data into the system? | What is the most efficient way of storing this piece of data? |
| How will the operation of the system fit into my daily business schedule? | What database management system should we use? |

## Management Support and Commitment

If an information systems project has the backing and commitment of management at various levels, it is more likely to be perceived positively by both users and the technical information services staff. Both groups will believe that their participation in the development process will receive higher-level attention and priority. They will be recognized and rewarded for the time and effort they devote to implementation. Management backing also ensures that a systems project will receive sufficient funding and resources to be successful. Furthermore, all the changes in work habits and procedures and any organizational realignments associated with a new system depend on management backing to be enforced effectively. If a manager considers a new system to be a priority, the system will more likely be treated that way by his or her subordinates (Doll, 1985; Ein-Dor and Segev, 1978).

However, management support can backfire sometimes. Sometimes management becomes overcommitted to a project, pouring excessive resources into a systems development effort that is failing or that should never have been undertaken in the first place (Newman and Sabherwal, 1996).

## Level of Complexity and Risk

Systems differ dramatically in their size, scope, level of complexity, and organizational and technical components. Some systems development projects are more likely to fail or suffer delays because they carry a much higher level of risk than others.

Researchers have identified three key dimensions that influence the level of project risk (McFarlan, 1981). These include project size, project structure, and the level of technical experience of the information systems staff and project team.

**Project size** The larger the project—as indicated by the dollars spent, the size of the implementation staff, the time allocated to implementation, and the number of organizational units affected—the greater the risk. Therefore, an $8 million project lasting for two years and affecting five departments in 20 operating units and 120 users will be much riskier than a $30,000 project for two users that can be completed in two months. Another risk factor is the company's experience with projects of given sizes. If a company is accustomed to implementing large, costly systems, the risk of implementing the $8 million project will be lowered. The risk may even be lower than that of another firm attempting a $200,000 project when the firm's average project cost has been about $50,000. On the whole, however, very large-scale system projects show a failure rate that is 50 to 75 percent higher than for other projects because such projects are so complex and difficult to control. The behavioral characteristics of the system—who owns the system and how much it influences business processes—contribute to the complexity of large-scale system projects just as much as technical characteristics such as the number of lines of program code, length of project, and budget (The Concours Group, 2000; Laudon, 1989; U.S. General Services Administration, 1988).

**TABLE 11-4 DIMENSIONS OF PROJECT RISK**

| Project Structure | Project Technology Level | Project Size | Degree of Risk |
|---|---|---|---|
| High | Low | Large | Low |
| High | Low | Small | Very low |
| High | High | Large | Medium |
| High | High | Small | Medium-low |
| Low | Low | Large | Low |
| Low | Low | Small | Very low |
| Low | High | Large | Very high |
| Low | High | Small | High |

**Project structure** Some projects are more highly structured than others. Their requirements are clear and straightforward so the outputs and processes can be easily defined. Users know exactly what they want and what the system should do; there is almost no possibility of them changing their minds. Such projects run a much lower risk than those where requirements are relatively undefined, fluid, and constantly changing; where outputs cannot be easily fixed because they are subject to users' changing ideas; or where users cannot agree on what they want.

**Experience with technology** The project risk will rise if the project team and the information system staff lack the required technical expertise. If the team is unfamiliar with the hardware, system software, application software, or database management system proposed for the project, it is highly likely that the project will experience technical problems or take more time to complete because of the need to master new skills.

These dimensions of project risk will be present in different combinations for each implementation effort. Table 11-4 shows that eight different combinations are possible, each with a different degree of risk. The higher the level of risk, the more likely it is that the implementation effort will fail.

## Management of the Implementation Process

The development of a new system must be carefully managed and orchestrated. Often basic elements of success are forgotten. Training to ensure that end users are comfortable with the new system and fully understand its potential uses is often sacrificed or forgotten in systems development projects. If the budget is strained at the very beginning, toward the end of a project there will likely be insufficient funds for training (Bikson et al., 1985).

The conflicts and uncertainties inherent in any implementation effort will be magnified when an implementation project is poorly managed and organized. As illustrated in Figure 11-6, a systems development project without proper management will most likely suffer these consequences:

- Cost overruns that vastly exceed budgets
- Unexpected time slippage
- Technical shortfalls resulting in performance that is significantly below the estimated level
- Failure to obtain anticipated benefits

How badly are projects managed? On average, private sector projects are underestimated by one-half in terms of budget and time required to deliver the complete system promised in the system plan. A very large number of projects are delivered with missing functionality (promised for delivery in later versions). Between 30 and 40% of all software projects are "runaway" projects that far exceed original schedule and budget projections and fail to perform as

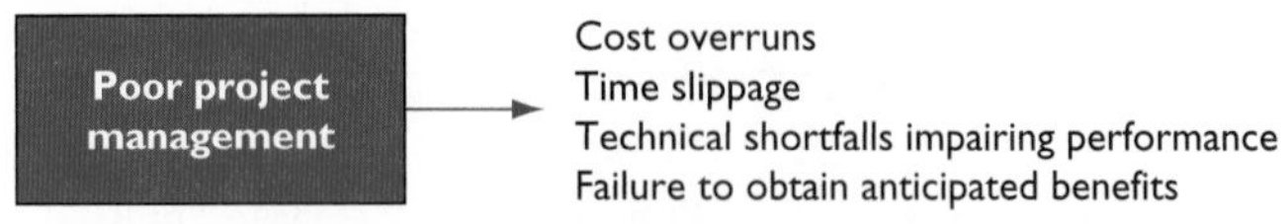


*Figure 11-6* Consequences of poor project management. Without proper management, a systems development project will take longer to complete and most often will exceed the budgeted cost. The resulting information system will most likely be technically inferior and may not be able to demonstrate any benefits to the organization.

originally specified (Keil, Mann, and Rai, 2000). Why are projects managed so poorly and what can be done about it? Here we discuss some possibilities.

**Ignorance and optimism** The techniques for estimating the length of time required to analyze and design systems are poorly developed. Most applications are "first time" (i.e., there is no prior experience in the application area). The larger the scale of systems, the greater the role of ignorance and optimism. The net result of these factors is that estimates tend to be optimistic, "best case," and wrong. It is assumed that all will go well when in fact it rarely does.

**man-month**
The traditional unit of measurement used by systems designers to estimate the length of time to complete a project. Refers to the amount of work a person can be expected to complete in a month.

**The mythical man-month** The traditional unit of measurement used by systems designers to project costs is the **man-month.** Projects are estimated in terms of how many man-months will be required. However, adding more workers to projects does not necessarily reduce the elapsed time needed to complete a systems project (Brooks, 1974). Unlike cotton picking—when tasks can be rigidly partitioned, communication between participants is not required, and training is unnecessary—systems analysis and design involve many *tasks that are sequentially linked, cannot be performed in isolation, and require extensive communication and training.* Adding labor to software projects can often slow down delivery as the communication, learning, and coordination costs escalate and detract from the output of participants. For comparison, imagine what would happen if five amateur spectators were added to one team in a championship professional basketball game? The team composed of only five professional basketball players would probably do much better in the short run than the team with five professionals and five amateurs.

**Falling behind: bad news travels slowly upward** Among projects in all fields, slippage in projects, failure, and doubts are often not reported to senior management until it is too late (Keil and Robey, 2001). The CONFIRM project, a very large-scale information systems project to integrate hotel, airline, and rental car reservations, is a classic example. It was sponsored by the Hilton Hotels, Budget Rent-a-Car, and Marriott Corporation and developed by AMR Information Services, Inc., a subsidiary of American Airlines Corporation. The project was very ambitious and technically complex, employing a staff of 500. Members of the CONFIRM project management team did not immediately come forward with accurate information when the project started encountering problems coordinating various transaction processing activities. Clients continued to invest in a project that was faltering because they were not informed of its problems with database, decision-support, and integration technologies.

## CHANGE MANAGEMENT CHALLENGES FOR ENTERPRISE SYSTEMS AND BUSINESS PROCESS REENGINEERING (BPR)

Given the challenges of innovation and implementation, it is not surprising to find a very high failure rate among enterprise system and business process reengineering (BPR) projects, which typically require extensive organizational change and which may require replacing old technologies and legacy systems that are deeply rooted in many interrelated business processes (Lloyd, Dewar, and Pooley, 1999). A number of studies have indicated that 70 percent of all business processing reengineering projects fail to deliver promised benefits. Likewise, a high percentage of enterprise resource planning projects fail to be fully implemented or to meet the goals of their users even after three years of work (Gillooly, 1998).

Many enterprise system and reengineering projects have been undermined by poor implementation and change management practices that failed to address employees' concerns about change. Dealing with fear and anxiety throughout the organization; overcoming resistance by key managers; changing job functions, career paths, and recruitment practices; and training have posed greater threats to reengineering than the difficulties companies faced visualizing and designing breakthrough changes to business processes.

Enterprise systems create myriad interconnections among various business processes and data flows to ensure that information in one part of the business can be obtained by any other unit, to help people eliminate redundant activities, and to make better management decisions. Massive organizational changes are required to make this happen. Information that was previously maintained by different systems and different departments or functional areas must be integrated and made available to the company as a whole. Business processes must be tightly integrated, jobs must be redefined, and new procedures must be created throughout the company. Employees are often unprepared for new procedures and roles (Davenport, 1998, 2000).

### System Implications of Mergers and Acquisitions

Mergers and acquisitions have been proliferating because they are a major growth engine for businesses. Potentially, firms can cut costs significantly by merging with competitors, reduce risks by expanding into different industries (e.g., conglomerating), and create a larger pool of competitive knowledge and expertise by joining forces with other players. There are also economies of time: A firm can gain market share and expertise very quickly through acquisition rather than building over the long term.

Although some firms, such as General Electric, are quite successful in carrying out mergers and acquisitions (M&As), research has found that more than 70 percent of all M&As result in a decline in shareholder value, and often lead to divestiture at a later time (Braxton Associates, 1997; *Economist,* 1997). A major reason why mergers and acquisitions fail is the difficulty of integrating the systems of different companies. Mergers and acquisitions are deeply affected by the organizational characteristics of the merging companies as well as by their IT infrastructures. Combining the information systems of two different companies usually requires considerable organizational change and complex system projects to manage. If the integration is not properly managed, firms can emerge with a tangled hodgepodge of inherited legacy systems built by aggregating the systems of one firm after another. Without a successful systems integration, the benefits anticipated from the merger cannot be realized, or, worse, the merged entity cannot execute its business processes and loses customers.

When a company targeted for acquisition has been identified, information systems managers will need to identify the realistic costs of integration; the estimated benefits of economies in operation, scope, knowledge, and time; and any problematic systems that would require major investments to integrate. In addition, IT managers can critically estimate any likely costs and organizational changes required to upgrade IT infrastructure or to make major system improvements to support the merged companies. The Window on Management describes how TransCanada dealt with these issues.

## 11.3 Managing Implementation

Not all aspects of the implementation process can be easily controlled or planned (Alter and Ginzberg, 1978). However, the chances for system success can be increased by anticipating potential implementation problems and applying appropriate corrective strategies. Various project management, requirements gathering, and planning methodologies have been developed for specific categories of problems. Strategies have also been devised for ensuring that users play an appropriate role throughout the implementation period and for managing the organizational change process.

### Controlling Risk Factors

Implementers should adopt a contingency approach to project management, handling each project with the tools, project management methodologies, and organizational linkages geared to its level of risk (McFarlan, 1981).

## Managing the TransCanada Megamerger

TransCanada PipeLines Limited is a North American Leader in natural gas transmission and marketing, moving 6.6 billion cubic feet of natural gas per day throughout Canada and the northern United States. It is also the product of the largest merger in Canadian history, formed from the union of TransCanada PipeLines Ltd. and Nova Corp. on July 1, 1998. The two had been the giants of Canadian natural gas and accompanying businesses. The emerging company (also called TransCanada PipeLines Ltd. and located in Calgary, Alberta) had revenue of $17 billion (Canadian) and 4,500 employees. The challenge for Russ Wells, TransCanada's new CIO, was to find a way to merge both companies' information technology infrastructures successfully.

The organizational differences between the two companies were immense. On the one hand, TransCanada's 250 IT employees were mostly allocated to various business units, with a separate information systems group for each business unit. All did have to follow standards and architecture set by a central group, however, and a central organization provided common services such as telecommunications. On the other hand, Nova had outsourced almost all IT work. Its only internal group consisted of 18 employees who were responsible for governance and architecture.

Although both companies had some common desktop software, such as Microsoft Office and Windows NT (the earlier version of Windows 2000), their information technology infrastructures were very different. Nova ran Oracle software, Microsoft Internet Explorer, Windows NT, and Visual Basic and was in the midst of a multiyear implementation of SAP enterprise software. TransCanada used Sun Microsystems' Forte and Java tools as well as software from Sybase, Novell, and Netscape Communications. TransCanada did not have a single enterprise system for the company, preferring best-of-breed applications for each business area.

Wells had to plan and begin to execute changes before senior management had developed a clear vision of the newly merged company. His plan called for devoting the first year to merging systems and platforms while postponing organizational restructuring until the second year. While Wells waited to make changes in the new company's IT organization, IT staff members started to worry about their jobs. Many became almost paranoid. Rumors flew about whether the new company would outsource everything or whether the SAP enterprise system or best-of-breed applications would become new company standards.

Wells responded by setting up a decision board that included business leaders from the newly merged company. The group collectively devised decision criteria for TransCanada's new information technology infrastructure, which would be based primarily on cost. A working committee then tried to objectively evaluate alternatives. Employees accepted their findings because they could see exactly how decisions were made.

Wells moved rapidly to create a reorganization plan that combined features of both merging companies' information systems groups and left most employees with jobs. Consultants that had previously been used by Nova were assigned a set of tasks but were placed under the direction of internal TransCanada staff. TransCanada would make its own strategic and architecture decisions. Hardware commodity services, such as supporting computers and telecommunications, would be outsourced to IBM, which had performed that task for Nova. The new IT structure was in place in February 1999. The main lesson Wells and TransCanada learned was to keep staff well informed at all stages of a change.

TransCanada's management believes its new information technology infrastructure is working very well. The company has been able to complete several mission-critical projects on time and on budget and the information technology budget for fiscal 2000 is 12.5 percent lower than premerger expenses in 1998.

**To Think About:** What management, organization, and technology issues were posed by the TransCanada merger? Evaluate the role of Wells and TransCanada management in dealing with these issues.

*Source:* Kathleen Melymuka, "Rules of Engagement," *Computerworld,* July 24, 2000; and "Cisco and TransCanada," Cisco Systems, January 24, 2001.

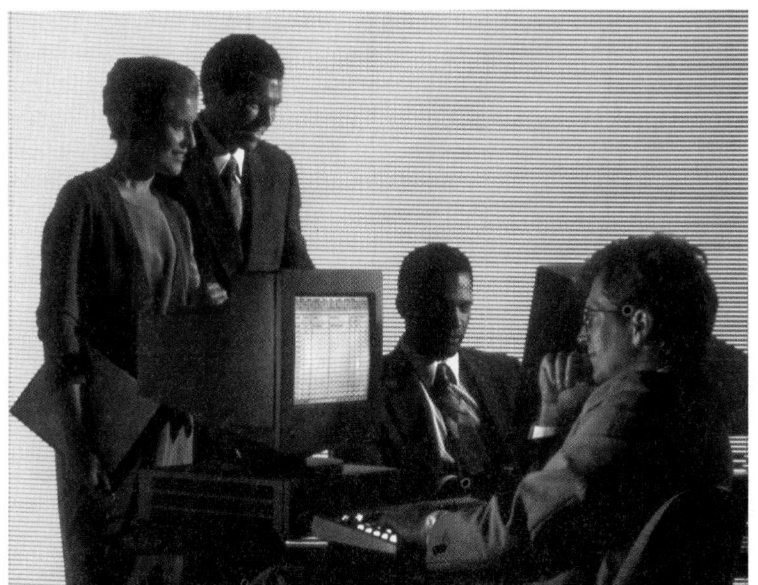

*This project team of professionals is using computing tools to enhance communication, analysis, and decision making.*

## Managing Technical Complexity

Projects with *high levels of technology* benefit from **internal integration tools.** The success of such projects depends on how well their technical complexity can be managed. Project leaders need both heavy technical and administrative experience. They must be able to anticipate problems and develop smooth working relationships among a predominantly technical team. The team should be under the leadership of a manager with a strong technical and project management background and team members should be highly experienced. Team meetings should take place frequently, with routine distribution of meeting minutes concerning key design decisions. Essential technical skills or expertise not available internally should be secured from outside the organization.

**internal integration tools**
Project management technique that ensures that the implementation team operates as a cohesive unit.

## Formal Planning and Control Tools

Large projects will benefit from appropriate use of **formal planning** and **formal control tools.** With project management techniques, such as PERT (Program Evaluation and Review Technique) or Gantt charts, a detailed plan can be developed. (PERT lists the specific activities that make up a project, their duration, and the activities that must be completed before a specific activity can start. A Gantt chart, such as that illustrated in Figure 11-7, visually represents the sequence and timing of different tasks in a development project as well as their resource requirements.) Tasks can be defined and resources budgeted.

These project management techniques can help managers identify bottlenecks and determine the impact that problems will have on project completion times. They can also help system developers partition implementation into smaller, more manageable segments with defined, measurable business results (Fichman and Moses, 1999). Standard control techniques will successfully chart the progress of the project against budgets and target dates, so deviations from the plan can be spotted.

**formal planning tools**
Project management technique that structures and sequences tasks, budgeting time, money, and technical resources required to complete the tasks.

**formal control tools**
Project management technique that helps monitor the progress toward completion of a task and fulfillment of goals.

## Increasing User Involvement and Overcoming User Resistance

Projects with relatively *little structure* must involve users fully at all stages. Users must be mobilized to support one of many possible design options and to remain committed to a single design. **External integration tools** consist of ways to link the work of the implementation team to users at all organizational levels. For instance, users can become active members of the project team, take on leadership roles, and take charge of installation and training.

Unfortunately, systems development is not an entirely rational process. Users leading design activities have used their position to further private interests and to gain power rather than to promote organizational objectives (Franz and Robey, 1984). Users may not always be involved in systems projects in a productive way.

**external integration tools**
Project management technique that links the work of the implementation team to that of users at all organizational levels.

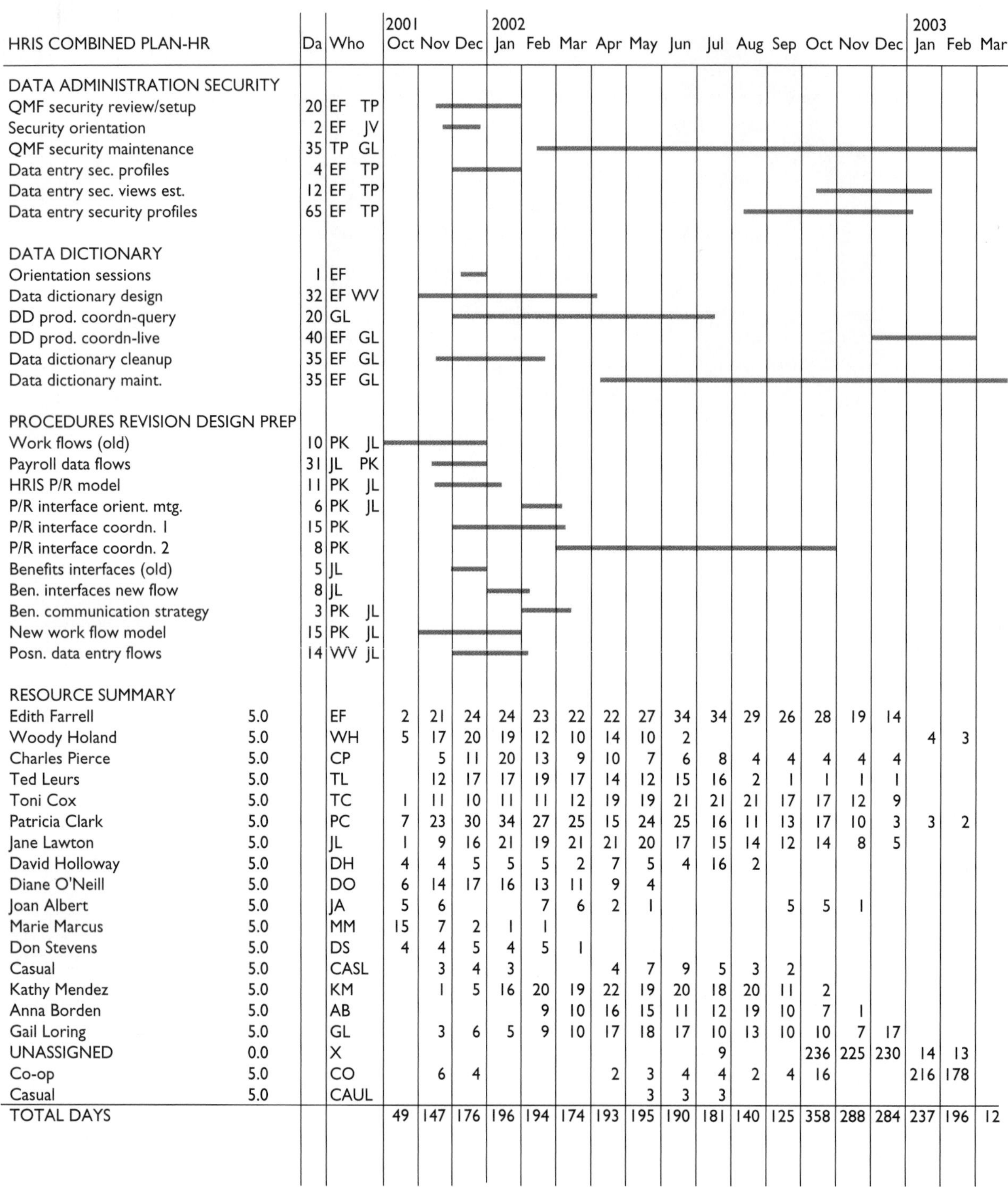

| HRIS COMBINED PLAN-HR | | Da | Who | 2001 Oct | Nov | Dec | 2002 Jan | Feb | Mar | Apr | May | Jun | Jul | Aug | Sep | Oct | Nov | Dec | 2003 Jan | Feb | Mar |
|---|---|---|---|---|---|---|---|---|---|---|---|---|---|---|---|---|---|---|---|---|---|
| DATA ADMINISTRATION SECURITY | | | | | | | | | | | | | | | | | | | | | |
| QMF security review/setup | | 20 | EF TP | | | | | | | | | | | | | | | | | | |
| Security orientation | | 2 | EF JV | | | | | | | | | | | | | | | | | | |
| QMF security maintenance | | 35 | TP GL | | | | | | | | | | | | | | | | | | |
| Data entry sec. profiles | | 4 | EF TP | | | | | | | | | | | | | | | | | | |
| Data entry sec. views est. | | 12 | EF TP | | | | | | | | | | | | | | | | | | |
| Data entry security profiles | | 65 | EF TP | | | | | | | | | | | | | | | | | | |
| DATA DICTIONARY | | | | | | | | | | | | | | | | | | | | | |
| Orientation sessions | | 1 | EF | | | | | | | | | | | | | | | | | | |
| Data dictionary design | | 32 | EF WV | | | | | | | | | | | | | | | | | | |
| DD prod. coordn-query | | 20 | GL | | | | | | | | | | | | | | | | | | |
| DD prod. coordn-live | | 40 | EF GL | | | | | | | | | | | | | | | | | | |
| Data dictionary cleanup | | 35 | EF GL | | | | | | | | | | | | | | | | | | |
| Data dictionary maint. | | 35 | EF GL | | | | | | | | | | | | | | | | | | |
| PROCEDURES REVISION DESIGN PREP | | | | | | | | | | | | | | | | | | | | | |
| Work flows (old) | | 10 | PK JL | | | | | | | | | | | | | | | | | | |
| Payroll data flows | | 31 | JL PK | | | | | | | | | | | | | | | | | | |
| HRIS P/R model | | 11 | PK JL | | | | | | | | | | | | | | | | | | |
| P/R interface orient. mtg. | | 6 | PK JL | | | | | | | | | | | | | | | | | | |
| P/R interface coordn. 1 | | 15 | PK | | | | | | | | | | | | | | | | | | |
| P/R interface coordn. 2 | | 8 | PK | | | | | | | | | | | | | | | | | | |
| Benefits interfaces (old) | | 5 | JL | | | | | | | | | | | | | | | | | | |
| Ben. interfaces new flow | | 8 | JL | | | | | | | | | | | | | | | | | | |
| Ben. communication strategy | | 3 | PK JL | | | | | | | | | | | | | | | | | | |
| New work flow model | | 15 | PK JL | | | | | | | | | | | | | | | | | | |
| Posn. data entry flows | | 14 | WV JL | | | | | | | | | | | | | | | | | | |
| RESOURCE SUMMARY | | | | | | | | | | | | | | | | | | | | | |
| Edith Farrell | 5.0 | | EF | 2 | 21 | 24 | 24 | 23 | 22 | 22 | 27 | 34 | 34 | 29 | 26 | 28 | 19 | 14 | | | |
| Woody Holand | 5.0 | | WH | 5 | 17 | 20 | 19 | 12 | 10 | 14 | 10 | 2 | | | | | | | 4 | 3 | |
| Charles Pierce | 5.0 | | CP | | 5 | 11 | 20 | 13 | 9 | 10 | 7 | 6 | 8 | 4 | 4 | 4 | 4 | 4 | | | |
| Ted Leurs | 5.0 | | TL | | 12 | 17 | 17 | 19 | 17 | 14 | 12 | 15 | 16 | 2 | 1 | 1 | 1 | 1 | | | |
| Toni Cox | 5.0 | | TC | 1 | 11 | 10 | 11 | 11 | 12 | 19 | 19 | 21 | 21 | 21 | 17 | 17 | 12 | 9 | | | |
| Patricia Clark | 5.0 | | PC | 7 | 23 | 30 | 34 | 27 | 25 | 15 | 24 | 25 | 16 | 11 | 13 | 17 | 10 | 3 | 3 | 2 | |
| Jane Lawton | 5.0 | | JL | 1 | 9 | 16 | 21 | 19 | 21 | 21 | 20 | 17 | 15 | 14 | 12 | 14 | 8 | 5 | | | |
| David Holloway | 5.0 | | DH | 4 | 4 | 5 | 5 | 5 | 2 | 7 | 5 | 4 | 16 | 2 | | | | | | | |
| Diane O'Neill | 5.0 | | DO | 6 | 14 | 17 | 16 | 13 | 11 | 9 | 4 | | | | | | | | | | |
| Joan Albert | 5.0 | | JA | 5 | 6 | | | 7 | 6 | 2 | 1 | | | | 5 | 5 | 1 | | | | |
| Marie Marcus | 5.0 | | MM | 15 | 7 | 2 | 1 | 1 | | | | | | | | | | | | | |
| Don Stevens | 5.0 | | DS | 4 | 4 | 5 | 4 | 5 | 1 | | | | | | | | | | | | |
| Casual | 5.0 | | CASL | | 3 | 4 | 3 | | | 4 | 7 | 9 | 5 | 3 | 2 | | | | | | |
| Kathy Mendez | 5.0 | | KM | | 1 | 5 | 16 | 20 | 19 | 22 | 19 | 20 | 18 | 20 | 11 | 2 | | | | | |
| Anna Borden | 5.0 | | AB | | | | | 9 | 10 | 16 | 15 | 11 | 12 | 19 | 10 | 7 | 1 | | | | |
| Gail Loring | 5.0 | | GL | | 3 | 6 | 5 | 9 | 10 | 17 | 18 | 17 | 10 | 13 | 10 | 10 | 7 | 17 | | | |
| UNASSIGNED | 0.0 | | X | | | | | | | | | | 9 | | | 236 | 225 | 230 | 14 | 13 | |
| Co-op | 5.0 | | CO | | 6 | 4 | | | | 2 | 3 | 4 | 4 | 2 | 4 | 16 | | | 216 | 178 | |
| Casual | 5.0 | | CAUL | | | | | | | | 3 | 3 | 3 | | | | | | | | |
| TOTAL DAYS | | | | 49 | 147 | 176 | 196 | 194 | 174 | 193 | 195 | 190 | 181 | 140 | 125 | 358 | 288 | 284 | 237 | 196 | 12 |

***Figure 11-7*** Formal planning and control tools help to manage information systems projects successfully. This Gantt chart was produced by a commercially available project management software package. It shows the task, person-days, and initials of each responsible person, as well as the start and finish dates for each task. The resource summary provides a good manager with the total person-days for each month and for each person working on the project to successfully manage the project. The project described here is a data administration project.

Participation in implementation activities may not be enough to overcome the problem of user resistance. The implementation process demands organizational change. Such change may be resisted, because different users may be affected by the system in different ways. Whereas some users may welcome a new system because it brings changes they perceive as beneficial to them, others may resist these changes because they believe the shifts are detrimental to their interests (Joshi, 1991).

If the use of a system is voluntary, users may choose to avoid it; if use is mandatory, resistance will take the form of increased error rates, disruptions, turnover, and even sabotage. Therefore, the implementation strategy must not only encourage user participation and involvement, it must also address the issue of counterimplementation (Keen, 1981). **Counterimplementation** is a deliberate strategy to thwart the implementation of an information system or an innovation in an organization.

**counterimplementation**
A deliberate strategy to thwart the implementation of an information system or an innovation in an organization.

Strategies to overcome user resistance include user participation (to elicit commitment as well as to improve design), user education and training, management edicts and policies, and providing better incentives for users who cooperate. The new system can be made more user-friendly by improving the end-user interface. Users will be more cooperative if organizational problems are solved prior to introducing the new system.

## DESIGNING FOR THE ORGANIZATION

Because the purpose of a new system is to improve the organization's performance, the systems development process must explicitly address the ways in which the organization will change when the new system is installed, including installation of intranets, extranets, and Internet applications. In addition to procedural changes, transformations in job functions, organizational structure, power relationships, and behavior will all have to be carefully planned. When technology-induced changes produce unforeseen consequences, the organization can benefit by improvising to take advantage of new opportunities. Information systems specialists, managers, and users should remain open-minded about their roles in the change management process and not adhere to rigid, narrow perceptions (Orlikowski and Hofman, 1997; Markus and Benjamin, 1997). Table 11-5 lists the organizational dimensions that would need to be addressed for planning and implementing many systems.

Although systems analysis and design activities are supposed to include an organizational impact analysis, this area has traditionally been neglected. An **organizational impact analysis** explains how a proposed system will affect organizational structure, attitudes, decision making, and operations. To integrate information systems successfully with the organization, thorough and fully documented organizational impact assessments must be given more attention in the development effort.

**organizational impact analysis**
Study of the way a proposed system will affect organizational structure, attitudes, decision making, and operations.

### Allowing for the Human Factor

The quality of information systems should be evaluated in terms of user criteria rather than the criteria of the information systems staff. In addition to targets such as memory size, access rates, and calculation times, systems objectives should include standards for user performance. For example, an objective might be that data entry clerks learn the procedures and codes for four new on-line data entry screens in a half-day training session.

**TABLE 11-5 ORGANIZATIONAL FACTORS IN SYSTEMS PLANNING AND IMPLEMENTATION**

| |
|---|
| Employee participation and involvement |
| Job design |
| Standards and performance monitoring |
| Ergonomics (including equipment, user interfaces, and the work environment) |
| Employee grievance resolution procedures |
| Health and safety |
| Government regulatory compliance |

**ergonomics**
The interaction of people and machines in the work environment, including the design of jobs, health issues, and the end-user interface of information systems.

Areas where users interface with the system should be carefully designed, with sensitivity to ergonomic issues. **Ergonomics** refers to the interaction of people and machines in the work environment. It considers the design of jobs, health issues, and the end-user interface of information systems. The impact of the application system on the work environment and job dimensions must be carefully assessed. One noteworthy study of 620 Social Security Administration claims representatives showed that the representatives with on-line access to claims data experienced greater stress than those with serial access to the data via teletype. Even though the on-line interface was more rapid and direct than teletype, it created much more frustration. Representatives with on-line access could interface with a larger number of clients per day. This changed the dimensions of the job for claims representatives. The restructuring of work—involving tasks, quality of working life, and performance—had a more profound impact than the nature of the technology itself (Turner, 1984).

### Sociotechnical Design

Most contemporary systems-building approaches tend to treat end users as essential to the systems-building process but playing a largely passive role relative to other forces shaping the system such as the specialist system designers and management. A different tradition rooted in the European social democratic labor movement assigns users a more active role, one that empowers them to codetermine the role of information systems in their workplace (Clement and Van den Besselaar, 1993).

This tradition of participatory design emphasizes participation by the individuals most affected by the new system. It is closely associated with the concept of sociotechnical design. A **sociotechnical design** plan establishes human objectives for the system that lead to increased job satisfaction. Designers set forth separate sets of technical and social design solutions. The social design plans explore different work group structures, allocation of tasks, and the design of individual jobs. The proposed technical solutions are compared with the proposed social solutions. Social and technical solutions that can be combined are proposed as sociotechnical solutions. The alternative that best meets both social and technical objectives is selected for the final design. The resulting sociotechnical design is expected to produce an information system that blends technical efficiency with sensitivity to organizational and human needs, leading to high job satisfaction (Mumford and Weir, 1979). Systems with compatible technical and organizational elements are expected to raise productivity without sacrificing human and social goals.

**sociotechnical design**
Design to produce information systems that blend technical efficiency with sensitivity to organizational and human needs.

## "Fourth-Generation" Project Management

Traditional techniques for managing projects deal with problems of size and complexity by breaking large projects into subprojects; assigning teams, schedules, and milestones to each; and focusing primarily on project mechanics rather than on business results. These techniques are inadequate for enterprise systems and other large-scale system projects with extremely complex problems of organizational coordination and change management, complex and sometimes unfamiliar technology, and continually changing business requirements. A new "fourth-generation" of project management techniques is emerging to address these challenges.

In this model, project planning assumes an enterprise-wide focus, driven by the firm's strategic business vision and technology architecture. Project and subproject managers focus on solving problems and meeting challenges as they arise rather than on simply meeting formal project milestones. It may be useful for organizations to establish a separate program office to manage subprojects, coordinate the entire project effort with other ongoing projects, and coordinate the project with ongoing changes in the firm's business strategy, information technology architecture and infrastructure, and business processes (The Concours Group, 2000).

## APPLICATION SOFTWARE EXERCISE

### SPREADSHEET EXERCISE: CAPITAL BUDGETING AT SPARKLING CLEAN

Sparkling Clean, a janitorial supply manufacturer, is primarily known for its commercial laundry soap line, Forever Springtime. Currently, the inventory control system at Sparkling Clean is adequate. However, in recent strategic planning meetings, the company's management team has discussed the necessity of upgrading its information systems. As part of her duties, Katrina Cordova, a lead analyst at Sparkling Clean, was assigned the task of investigating design strategies for the new information system. Part of her duties requires her to prepare a financial analysis worksheet.

Because you are Katrina's assistant, she asks you to prepare a financial worksheet that summarizes the costs, benefits, and financial analysis associated with the project. Although Katrina is still in the process of identifying the new system's costs and benefits, she feels you can begin working on the spreadsheet using the data on the Laudon Web site for Chapter 11. The remaining costs and benefits will be added later. Prepare an initial financial analysis worksheet for Katrina. Make sure your worksheet uses the capital budgeting models of cost-benefit ratio, net present value, and accounting rate of return on investment (ROI). Use a discount rate of 12 percent, and assume a useful life of four years.

## MANAGEMENT WRAP-UP

Managers must link systems development to the organization's strategy and identify precisely which systems should be changed to achieve large-scale benefits for the organization as a whole. Two principal reasons for system failure are inadequate management support and poor management of the implementation process. Managers should fully understand the level of complexity and risk in new systems projects as well as their potential business value.

Building an information system is a process of planned organizational change. Many levels of organizational change are possible. Implementing enterprise systems and redesigning business processes are high-risk endeavors because they require far-reaching organizational changes that are often resisted by members of the organization. Eliciting user support and maintaining an appropriate level of user involvement at all stages of system building are essential.

Selecting the right technology for a system solution that fits the problem's constraints and the organization's information technology infrastructure is a key business decision. Systems sometimes fail because the technology is too complex or sophisticated to be easily implemented or because system builders lack the requisite skills or experience to work with it. Managers and systems builders should be fully aware of the risks and rewards of various technologies as they make their technology selections.

*For Discussion*

1. It has been said that when we design an information system we are redesigning the organization. What are the ramifications of this statement?
2. It has been said that most systems fail because system builders ignore organizational behavior problems. Why?

## SUMMARY


1. *Evaluate models for understanding the business value of information systems.* Capital budgeting models such as the payback method, accounting rate of return on investment (ROI), cost–benefit ratio, net present value, profitability index, and internal rate of return (IRR) are the primary financial models for determining the business value of information systems. Portfolio analysis and scoring models include nonfinancial considerations and can be used to evaluate alternative information systems projects. Real options pricing models, which apply the same techniques for valuing financial options to systems investments, can be useful when considering highly uncertain IT investments.
2. *Analyze the principal causes of information system failure.* The principal causes of information system failure are (1) insufficient or improper user participation in the systems development process, (2) lack of management support, (3) high levels of complexity and risk in the systems development process, and (4) poor management of the implementation process. There is a very high failure rate among business process reengineering and enterprise resource planning projects because they require extensive organizational change. Integrating disparate IT infrastructures of merging companies is also difficult to accomplish successfully.
3. *Analyze the change management requirements for building successful systems.* Building an information system is a process of planned organizational change that must be carefully managed. The term *implementation* refers to the entire process of organizational change surrounding the introduction of a new information system. One can better understand system success and failure by examining different patterns of implementation. Especially important is the relationship between participants in the implementation process, notably the interactions between system designers and users. Conflicts between the technical orientation of system designers and the business orientation of end users must be resolved. The success of organizational change can be determined by how well information systems specialists, end users, and decision makers deal with key issues at various stages in implementation.
4. *Select appropriate strategies to manage the system implementation process.* Management support and control of the implementation process are essential, as are mechanisms for dealing with the level of risk in each new systems project. Some companies experience organizational resistance to change. Project risk factors can be brought under some control by a contingency approach to project management. The level of risk in a systems development project is determined by three key dimensions: (1) project size, (2) project structure, and (3) experience with technology. The risk level of each project will determine the appropriate mix of external integration tools, internal integration tools, formal planning tools, and formal control tools to be applied.

   Appropriate strategies can be applied to ensure the correct level of user participation in the systems development process and to minimize user resistance. Information system design and the entire implementation process should be managed as planned organizational change. Participatory design emphasizes the participation of the individuals most affected by a new system. Sociotechnical design aims for an optimal blend of social and technical design solutions. "Fourth-generation" project management techniques focus on meeting challenges as they arise rather than meeting formal milestones, and can be applied to complex large-scale system projects.


## KEY TERMS

**Accounting rate of return on investment (ROI), 342**
**Capital budgeting, 339**
**Change agent, 350**
**Cost–benefit ratio, 344**
**Counterimplementation, 359**
**Ergonomics, 360**
**External integration tools, 357**
**Formal control tools, 357**
**Formal planning tools, 357**
**Implementation, 350**
**Intangible benefits, 339**
**Internal integration tools, 357**
**Internal rate of return (IRR), 344**
**Man-month, 354**
**Net present value, 344**
**Organizational impact analysis, 359**
**Payback method, 342**
**Portfolio analysis, 345**
**Present value, 344**
**Profitability index, 344**
**Real options pricing models, 346**
**Scoring model, 345**
**Sociotechnical design, 360**
**System failure, 348**
**Tangible benefits, 339**
**User–designer communications gap, 351**
**User interface, 348**

## REVIEW QUESTIONS

1. Name and describe the principal capital budgeting methods used to evaluate information system projects.
2. What are the limitations of financial models for establishing the value of information systems?
3. Describe how portfolio analysis and scoring models can be used to establish the worth of systems.
4. How can real options pricing models be used to help evaluate information technology investments?
5. Why do builders of new information systems need to address change management?
6. What kinds of problems are evidence of information system failure?

7. Why is it necessary to understand the concept of implementation when managing the organizational change surrounding a new information system?
8. What are the major causes of implementation success or failure?
9. What is the user–designer communication gap? What kinds of implementation problems can it create?
10. Why is there such a high failure rate among enterprise resource planning (ERP) and business process reengineering (BPR) projects?
11. What role do information systems play in the success or failure of mergers and acquisitions?
12. What dimensions influence the level of risk in each systems development project?
13. What project management techniques can be used to control project risk?
14. What strategies can be used to overcome user resistance to systems development projects?
15. What organizational considerations should be addressed by information system design?

## GROUP PROJECT

Form a group with two or three other students. Write a description of the implementation problems you might expect to encounter for the information system you designed for the Part III business process redesign project which follows this chapter. Write an analysis of the steps you would take to solve or prevent these problems. Alternatively, you could describe the implementation problems that might be expected for one of the systems described in the Window on boxes or chapter ending cases in this text. If possible, use electronic presentation software to present your findings to the class.

## TOOLS FOR INTERACTIVE LEARNING

### INTERNET CONNECTION

The Internet Connection for this chapter will direct you to a series of Web sites where you can complete an exercise to evaluate user interfaces and user-system interactions. You can also use the Interactive Study Guide to test your knowledge of the topics in this chapter and get instant feedback when you need more practice.

### ELECTRONIC COMMERCE PROJECT

At the Laudon Web site for Chapter 11, you can complete an Electronic Commerce project to redesign business processes to participate in an electronic marketplace.

### CD-ROM

If you use the Multimedia Edition CD-ROM with this chapter, you can complete an interactive exercise to analyze the sources of a series of system problems and to identify the implementation stage when they occurred. You can also find an audio overview of the major themes of this chapter and bullet text summarizing the key points of the chapter.

## CASE STUDY *Hershey's Enterprise System Creates Halloween Tricks*

Hershey Foods Corp. of Hershey, Pennsylvania, was founded in 1894 and recorded $4.4 billion in sales in 1998, including its chocolate candies and other brands such as Reese's Peanut Butter Cups, Milk Duds, and Good and Plenty. Altogether the company sells approximately 3,300 candy products including variations in sizes and shapes. Candy is a very seasonal product, with Halloween and Christmas accounting for about 40 percent of annual candy sales, making the fourth quarter crucial to Hershey's profitability. Hershey's largest continuous challenge may be its ability to rack up its multibillion dollars in sales 50 cents or one dollar at a time, requiring huge numbers of its products to be sold. Such quantities means Hershey must have very reliable logistics systems.

Traditionally, the food and beverage industry has had a very low ratio of information technology (IT) spending to total revenue, ranging between 1.1 and 1.5 percent and a very low profit margin. As the year 2000 approached, many companies chose to solve their year 2000 (Y2K) problems by replacing their legacy systems rather than spending a lot of money to retain them by fixing the Y2K problems within them.

According to Hershey vice president of information systems, Rick Bentz, Hershey began to modernize its software and hardware in early 1996. The project, dubbed Enterprise 21, was scheduled to take four years (until early 2000). Enterprise 21 had several goals, including upgrading and standardizing the company's hardware and moving from a mainframe-based network to a client/server environment. The company replaced 5,000 desktop computers and also moved to TCP/IP networking based on newly installed network hardware. Bentz noted that benchmark studies by the Grocery Manufacturers of America showed that Hershey needed to be able to use and share its data much more efficiently. More and more retailers were demanding that suppliers such as Hershey fine-tune their deliveries so that they could lower their inventory costs.

Hershey's information systems management set as a goal a move to an ERP system using software from SAP AG of Walldorf, Germany. SAP was to be complemented with software from Manugistics Group Inc. of Rockville, Maryland. Manugistics would support production forecasting and scheduling, as well as transportation management. In addition the company decided to install software from Siebel Systems Inc. of San Mateo, California. Siebel's software would aid Hershey in managing customer relations and in tracking the effectiveness of its marketing activities. Management believed that the project would help Hershey better execute its business strategy of emphasizing its core mass-market candy business.

A necessary piece of Enterprise 21 was the installation of bar coding systems at all six U.S. production plants in 1999. Bar coding was necessary so the company could track all incoming and outgoing materials to improve logistics management while controlling production costs. Enterprise 21 required Hershey to switch to the new SAP system and its associated software in April of 1999, an annual period of low sales. This new target meant the company had 39 months to complete the project instead of the original 48 months. Although some SAP modules were actually put into production in January, the project ran behind the aggressive schedule, and the full system did not come on-line until mid-July. Included in the delayed conversion were SAP's critical order processing and billing systems, along with the Siebel and Manugistics systems. The timing meant that Hershey would be facing a major problem because Halloween orders were already arriving by mid-July. The information systems staff chose to convert all these new systems using the direct cutover strategy in which the whole system goes live all at once to enable Hershey to fill its Halloween orders on schedule. By the time of the conversion the whole project had cost Hershey $112 million.

Problems arose for Hershey when the cutover strategy did not work, because serious problems emerged immediately. As a result many Hershey customers found their shelves empty as Halloween approached. Bruce Steinke, the candy buyer for Great North Foods, a regional distributor in Alpena, Michigan, had placed an order for 20,000 pounds of Hershey's candy and found his warehouse short just prior to Halloween. As a result 100 of Great North's 700 customers had no Hershey candy when Halloween arrived. The shortage meant not only a drop in Hershey's sales but Great North (and other Hershey distributors) also lost credibility as its retail customers.

The shortages also meant the loss of precious, highly contested shelf space. Randall King, the candy buyer for the Winston–Salem, North Carolina-based Lowes Foods chain, had to deal with the shortage problem. He told his 81 supermarkets to fill their empty Hershey candies shelves with other candies, and he even suggested that they turn to Mars brand candies. Retailers predicted that Hershey's lost shelf space would be hard to win back. So Hershey's long-range sales were also being placed at risk by the logistics failures.

Hershey itself did not publicly acknowledge the problem until mid-September when it announced that something was wrong with its new computer systems. It did indicate that Hershey employees were having trouble entering new orders into the system. In addition, once the system was up, the company stated that order details were not being properly transmitted to the warehouses where they could be filled. Hershey did announce that it expected the problem to be solved in time for Christmas shipments. However, industry analysts, such as William Leach of Donaldson, Lufkin & Jenrette, were quick to note that should the company fail to make that deadline, the problems would likely seriously cut into not only Christmas sales but also Valentine's Day and perhaps Easter shipments, two other crucial candy sales holidays.

As soon as the admission of problems was announced, questions immediately arose as to the causes of those problems. Kevin McKay, the CEO of SAP in the United States, denied any problems with SAP's systems, saying, "If it was a system issue, I'd point directly to a system issue." He also made it clear that SAP was operating smoothly for Hershey's much smaller Canadian unit. Tom Crawford, the general manager of SAP America's consumer products business unit, verified that his consultants were at Hershey sites to help resolve the problems. But, he made it clear, "There are really no software issues per se." Crawford explained that his consultants "are just making sure they [Hershey employees] are using the business processes [built into the software] correctly." Manugistics also said it was working with Hershey on "business process improvements." Brian Doyle, an IBM spokesperson, pointed to "the business process transformation under way at Hershey" as a possible cause, which, he said, "is an enormously complex undertaking." He noted major changes in the way Hershey employees were doing their job, which implied the need for more and different training than Hershey's staff had originally received.

It was obvious that the problem was not in candy production. At the time of the cutover Hershey had an eight-day supply of products in its warehouses, a higher-than-usual supply in anticipation of possible minor problems with the new systems. However, within three weeks of turning on the new systems, shipments were more than two weeks late. Hershey began telling its customers to allow 12 days for delivery (the usual turnaround time was 6 days). Even that schedule proved to be too aggressive, because Hershey could not deliver goods so quickly. Company spokespersons told financial analysts in late October that computer system problems had already reduced sales by $100 million in the third quarter.

When word of these problems became public, Hershey's stock price went into a sharp slide. By late October, its price had fallen to $47.50, down 35 percent from $74 one year earlier. During the same period the Dow Jones Industrial Average had risen by 25 percent. Third-quarter earnings dropped from $.74 to $.62. Hershey Chairman and CEO Kenneth L. Wolfe admitted that "third-quarter sales and earnings declined primarily as a result of problems encountered since the July start-up of new business processes in the areas of customer service, warehousing and order fulfillment." He added, "These problems resulted in lost sales and significantly increased freight and warehousing costs." Hershey Senior Vice President Michael Pasquale pointed out that, "Clearly, our customer relations have been strained." Although Wolfe admitted the problems were taking longer to fix than expected, he did state his expectation that fourth-quarter sales and earnings would bounce back. In late October key individuals within Hershey held a two-day meeting to review the new system and produce a list of changes needed. Wolfe demanded that the changes involved "need to be tested before we put them in," possibly implying a lack of adequate testing prior to the original cutover.

In early February 2000 Hershey reported an 11 percent decline in sales and profits for its fourth quarter 1999. Wolfe again pointed to order processing, which, this time around, had caused many retailers to not even place orders. He said that although system changes and increased personnel experience with the new software had reduced the problems, Hershey's has "not yet fully returned to historical customer service levels."

Although Hershey has released very little information on the troubled implementation, observers continue to speculate on the key question: What went wrong? Some point to the pushing forward of the target date—trying to accomplish too much in the allotted time frame. Others believe that inadequate time and attention were allocated to testing prior to Hershey's new systems going live in July. Still other analysts point to the use of the direct cutover method. "These systems tie together in very intricate ways," stated AMR Research Inc. analyst Jim Shepherd, "and things that work fine in testing can turn out to be a disaster [when you go live]." Finally, some analysts point their finger at training. A. Blanton Godfrey, CEO of the Juran Institute, a consulting firm based in Wilton, Connecticut, says that only 10 to 15 percent of ERP implementations go smoothly. He claims that the difference for them is better training. Some observers believe that lack of education on the whys of the system and how the many pieces of the full system fit together are possibly the reason order entry difficulties created warehouse problems.

**Sources:** Jennifer DiSabatino, "Hershey Hires Outsider to Fill New CEO Job," *Computerworld,* December 15, 2000; Charles Waltner, "New Recipe for IT Implementation," *Information Week,* September 27, 2000; Craig Stedman, "IT Woes Contribute to Hershey, Profits Decline," *Computerworld,* February 2, 2000 and "Failed ERP Gamble Haunts Hershey," *Computerworld,* November 1, 1999; Polly Schneider, "Another Trip to Hell," *CIO Magazine,* February 15, 2000; Malcolm Wheatley, "ERP Training Stinks," *CIO Magazine,* June 1, 2000; Emily Nelson and Evan Ramstad, "Hershey's Biggest Dud Has Turned Out to Be Its New Technology," *The Wall Street Journal,* October 29, 1999; Hershey Foods Corporate Investor Relations, "Hershey Foods Announces Third Quarter Results," www.corporate-ir.net/, October 25, 1999; and Stacy Collett, "Hershey Earnings Drop as New Warehouse, Order Systems Falter," *Computerworld,* October 27, 1999.

### *CASE STUDY QUESTIONS*

1. Analyze Hershey's business model using the competitive forces and value chain models. Was an ERP system and related software a good solution to Hershey's problems? Explain your responses.
2. Classify and describe the problems with the Enterprise 21 project using the categories described in this chapter on the causes of system failure. What management, organization, and technology factors caused these problems? Explain.
3. What role did enterprise software play in the failure? Were Hershey's system problems the fault of the software vendors, Hershey, or both? Explain.
4. Evaluate the risks of the project as seen at its outset, and then outline its key risk factors. Describe the steps you would have taken during the planning stage of the project to control those factors.

# Part III Project

# Redesigning Business Processes for Healthlite Yogurt Company

Healthlite Yogurt Company, a U.S. market leader in yogurt and related health products, is experiencing sharp growing pains. Healthlite's sales have tripled during the past five years. However, new local competitors, offering fast delivery from local production centers and lower prices, are challenging Healthlite for retail shelf space with a bevy of new products. Healthlite needs to justify its share of shelf space to grocers and is seeking additional shelf space for its new yogurt-based products such as frozen desserts and low-fat salad dressings. Yogurt has a very short shelf life measured in days, and it must be moved very quickly.

Healthlite's corporate headquarters is in Danbury, Connecticut. Corporate has a central mainframe computer that maintains most of the major business databases. All production takes place in processing plants that are located in New Jersey, Massachusetts, Tennessee, Illinois, Colorado, Washington, and California. Each processing plant has its own minicomputer, which is connected to the corporate mainframe. Customer credit verification is maintained at corporate headquarters, where customer master files are maintained and order verification or rejection is determined. Once processed centrally, order data are then fed to the appropriate local processing plant minicomputer.

Healthlite has 20 sales regions, each with approximately 30 sales representatives and a regional sales manager. Healthlite has a 12-person marketing group at corporate headquarters. Each salesperson is able to store and retrieve data for assigned customer accounts using a terminal in the regional office linked to the corporate mainframe. Reports for individual salespeople (printouts of orders, rejection notices, customer account inquiries, etc.) and for sales offices are printed in the regional offices and mailed to them.

Sometimes, the only way to obtain up-to-date sales data is for managers to make telephone calls to subordinates and then piece the information together. Data about sales and advertising expenses, promotional campaigns, and customer shelf space devoted to Healthlite products are maintained manually at the regional offices. The central computer contains only consolidated, company-wide files for customer account data and order and billing data.

The existing order processing system requires sales representatives to write up hard-copy tickets to place orders through the mail or by fax. Each ticket lists the amount and kind of product ordered by the customer account. Approximately 20 workers at Healthlite corporate headquarters open, sort, and enter 500,000 order tickets per week into the system. Frequently, orders are delayed when the fax machines break down. Order information is transmitted every evening from the mainframe to a minicomputer at each of Healthlite's processing sites. The daily order specifies the total yogurt and yogurt product demand for each processing center. The processing center then produces the amount and type of yogurt and yogurt-related products ordered and ships out the orders. Shipping managers at the processing centers assign the shipments to various transportation carriers, who deliver the products to receiving warehouses located in the regions.

A year ago, growth in new products and sales had reached a point where the firm was choking on paper. For each order, a salesperson filled out at least two forms per account. Some sales representatives have more than 80 customers. As it became bogged down in paper, Healthlite saw increased delays in the processing of its orders. Because yogurt is a fresh food product, it could not be held long in inventory. Yet Healthlite had trouble shipping the right goods to the right places on time. It was taking between 4 and 14 days to process and ship an order, depending on mail delivery rates. Healthlite also found accounting discrepancies of $1.5 million annually between the sales force and headquarters.

Communication between sales managers and sales representatives has been primarily through the mail or by telephone. For example, regional sales managers have to send representatives letters with announcements of promotional campaigns or pricing discounts. Sales representatives have to write up their monthly reports of sales calls and then mail this information to regional headquarters.

Healthlite is considering new information system solutions. First of all, the firm would like to solve the current order entry crisis and develop immediately a new order processing system. Management would also like to make better use of information systems to support sales and marketing activities and to take advantage of new Web-based information technologies. In particular, management wants a sales-oriented Web site to help market the products but is unsure how this will fit into the sales effort. Management wants to know how these new technologies can assist the local groceries and large chains who sell the product to the actual consumer.

Senior management is looking for a modest reduction in employee head count as new, more effective systems come online to help pay for the investment in new systems. Although senior management wants the company to deploy contemporary systems, they do not want to experiment with new technologies and are only comfortable using technology that has proven itself in real-world applications.

## SALES AND MARKETING INFORMATION SYSTEMS: BACKGROUND

Sales orders must be processed and related to production and inventory. Sales of products in existing markets must be monitored, and new products must be developed for new markets. Firms need sales and marketing information in order to do product planning, make pricing decisions, devise advertising and other promotional campaigns, and forecast market potential for new and existing products. They must also monitor the efficiency of the distribution of their products and services. The sales function of a typical business captures and processes customer orders which are used to produce invoices for customers and data for inventory and production. A typical invoice is illustrated here.

***Healthlite Yogurt Inc.***

*Customer:*
Highview Supermarket
223 Highland Avenue
Ossining, New York 10562

*Order Number:* 679940
*Customer Number:* #00395
*Date:* 04/15/01

| *Quantity* | SKU# | *Description* | *Unit Price* | *Amount* |
|---|---|---|---|---|
| 100 | V3392 | 8 oz Vanilla | .44 | 44.00 |
| 50 | S4456 | 8 oz Strawberry | .44 | 22.00 |
| 65 | L4492 | 8 oz Lemon | .44 | 28.60 |
| *Shipping* | | | | 10.00 |
| *Total Invoice:* | | | | $104.60 |

Data from order entry are used by a firm's accounts receivable system and by the firm's inventory and production systems. The production planning system, for instance, builds its daily production plans based on the prior day's sales. The number and type of product sold determines how many units to produce and when.

Sales managers need information to plan and monitor the performance of the sales force. Management also needs information on the performance of specific products, product lines, or brands. Price, revenue, cost, and growth information can be used for pricing decisions, for evaluating the performance of current products, and for predicting the performance of future products.

From basic sales and invoice data, a firm can produce a variety of reports with valuable information to guide sales and marketing work. For weekly, monthly, or annual time periods, information can be gathered on which retail outlets order the most, on what the average order amount is, on which products move slowest and fastest, on which salespersons sell the most and least, on which geographic areas purchase the most (and least) of a given product, and on how current sales of a product compare to last year's sales.

## THE ASSIGNMENT

Either alone, or with a group of three or four of your classmates, develop a proposal for redesigning Healthlite's business processes for sales, marketing, and order processing that would make the company more competitive. Your report should include the following:

- An overview of the organization—its structure, products, and major business processes for sales, marketing, and order processing.
- An analysis of Healthlite's problems: What are Healthlite's problems? How are these problems related to existing business processes and systems? What management, organization, and technology factors contributed to these problems?
- An overall management plan for improving Healthlite's business and system situation. This would include a list of objectives, a time frame, major milestones, and an assessment of the costs and benefits of implementing this plan.
- Identification of the major changes in business processes required to achieve your plan.
- Identification of the major new technology components of your plan that are required to support the new business processes. If your solution requires a new system or set of systems, describe the functions of these systems; what pieces of information these systems should contain; and how this information should be captured, organized, and stored.
- A sample data entry screen or report for one of the new systems, if proposed.
- A description of the steps you would take as a manager to handle the conversion from the old system to the new.
- Quality assurance measures.

Your report should also describe the organizational impact of your solution. Consider human interface issues, the impact on jobs and interest groups, and any risks associated with implementing your solution. How will you implement your solution to take these issues into account?

It is important to establish the scope of the system project. It should be limited to order processing and related sales and marketing business processes. You do not have to redesign Healthlite's manufacturing, accounts receivable, distribution, or inventory control systems for this project.

# PART IV

# MANAGEMENT AND ORGANIZATIONAL SUPPORT SYSTEMS FOR THE DIGITAL FIRM

chapter

# 12 Managing Knowledge: Knowledge Work and Artificial Intelligence

objectives

**After completing this chapter, you will be able to:**

1. *Assess the importance of knowledge management in contemporary organizations.*
2. *Describe the applications that are most useful for distributing, creating, and sharing knowledge in the firm.*
3. *Evaluate the role of artificial intelligence in knowledge management.*
4. *Demonstrate how organizations can use expert systems and case-based reasoning to capture knowledge.*
5. *Explain how organizations can use neural networks and other intelligent techniques to improve their knowledge base.*

## Roche Labs Markets Smarter by Integrating Knowledge

Pressures on pharmaceutical firms have never been greater. In addition to wrestling with competitors and cost-cutting health maintenance organizations (HMOs), pharmaceutical firms without enough new drugs in the pipeline must figure out ways of wringing out more profits from existing products to sustain their growth rates. Roche Laboratories, the North American division of F. Hoffman-La Roche Ltd. of Switzerland, hoped that improving its marketing process would provide the answer.

Roche Laboratories maintains a 60-person professional services group within its medical affairs division that supports the launching of new drugs as they reach doctors and patients. The group prepares medical response databases and documentation to help the Roche sales force answer questions from physicians, HMOs, and patients about 70 different drugs, such as their benefits, side effects, and interactions with other medications. After a product is released, the professional services group also monitors how physicians use the drug, looking for unintended positive side effects that could lead to new products and new markets.

To do their work effectively, the professional services group needs up-to-date documentation and expertise. The answers to most of the questions typically posed by doctors, salespeople, and patients can be found in sources within the company, but the information is difficult to locate and assemble. For example, Roche's scientists maintain the information on toxicity and drug interactions, its safety group maintains clinical trial data, and its regulatory division has the Federal Drug Administration filings. There is no easy way to search across these islands of information. Like other pharmaceutical firms, Roche maintained mountains of documents but had no unified information system that operated across departments.

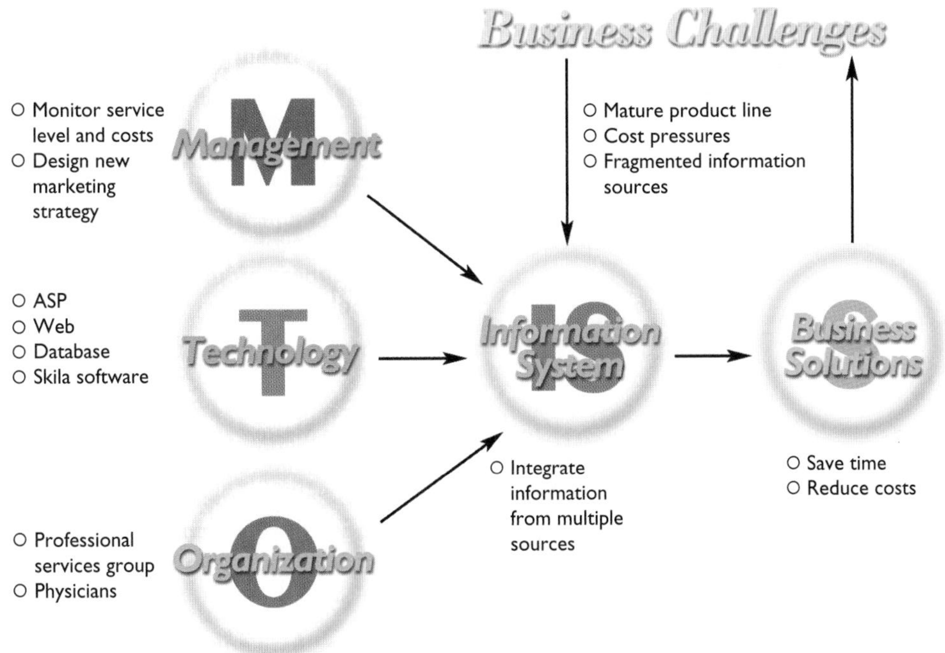


And because the pharmaceutical industry is highly regulated, there are many rules restricting sharing information.

Through an application service provider (ASP), Roche Labs started using a Web-based knowledge management system from Skila Inc. of Mahwah, New Jersey, called the Global Healthcare Intelligence Platform to integrate documents from multiple repositories. The system gathers relevant information from global news sources, specialty publishers, healthcare Web sites, government sources, and the firm's proprietary internal information systems. The software indexes, organizes, links, and updates the information as it moves through the system. Users can search multiple sources and drill down through layers of detail to see relationships among pieces of data. The system captures and retains this information in a database where it can be shared with other members of the organization. The system has helped the medical affairs division work more efficiently and spot problems and opportunities. For instance, the group found out about a fake Hong Kong version of Roche's Xenical, a medication that blocks fat absorption from food, and quickly alerted Roche about patent infringement. Roche is now starting to integrate the proprietary information from other divisions with medical affairs.

**Sources:** Dawne Shand, "Medical Marketing Gets Smarter," *Knowledge Management,* October 2000; and www.skila.com.

Roche Laboratories' Global Healthcare Intelligence Platform is one example of how systems can be used to leverage organizational knowledge by making it more easily available. In an information economy, capturing and distributing intelligence and knowledge and enhancing group collaboration have become vital to organizational innovation and survival. Special systems can be used for managing organizational knowledge, but they raise the following management challenges:

## Management Challenges

1. **Designing information systems that genuinely enhance knowledge—sharing and knowledge worker productivity.** Information systems that truly enhance the productivity of knowledge workers may be difficult to build because the manner in which information technology can enhance higher-level tasks, such as those performed by managers and professionals (i.e., scientists or engineers), is not always clearly understood. Some aspects of organizational knowledge cannot be captured easily or codified, especially tacit knowledge, or the information that organizations finally manage to capture may become outdated as environments change (Stenmark, 2000; Malhotra, 1998). Knowledge-sharing programs can spiral out of control, with managers and employees spending too much of their time sharing ideas with other groups. Firms need to carefully focus their knowledge sharing capabilities so that they produce specific business results. (Hansen and Von Octinger, 2001).

2. **Creating robust expert systems.** Expert systems must be changed every time there is a change in the organizational environment. Each time there is a change in the rules experts use, they must be reprogrammed. It is difficult to provide expert systems with the flexibility of human experts. Many thousands of businesses have undertaken experimental projects in expert systems, but only a small percentage have created expert systems that actually can be used on a production basis.

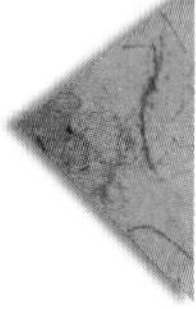

This chapter examines information system applications specifically designed to help organizations create, capture, and distribute knowledge and information. First, we examine information systems for supporting information and knowledge work. Then we look at the ways that organizations can use artificial intelligence technologies for capturing and storing knowledge and expertise.

## 12.1 Knowledge Management in the Organization

Chapter 1 described the emergence of the information economy and the digital firm, in which the major source of wealth and prosperity is the production and distribution of information and knowledge, and firms increasingly rely on digital technology to enable business processes. For example, 55 percent of the U.S. labor force consists of knowledge and information workers, and 60 percent of the gross domestic product of the United States comes from the knowledge and information sectors, such as finance and publishing.

In an information economy, knowledge-based core competencies—the two or three things that an organization does best—are key organizational assets. Producing unique products or services or producing them at a lower cost than competitors is based on superior knowledge of the production process and superior design. Knowing how to do things effectively and efficiently in ways that other organizations cannot duplicate is a primary source of profit and a factor in production that cannot be purchased in external markets. Some management theorists believe that these knowledge assets are as important for competitive advantage and survival, if not more important, than physical and financial assets.

As knowledge becomes a central productive and strategic asset, organizational success increasingly depends on the firm's ability to produce, gather, store, and disseminate knowledge. With knowledge, firms become more efficient and effective in their use of scarce resources. Without knowledge, firms become less efficient and effective in their use of resources and ultimately fail.

**organizational learning**
Creation of new standard operating procedures and business processes that reflect organizations' experience.

How do firms obtain knowledge? Like humans, organizations create and gather knowledge through a variety of **organizational learning** mechanisms. Through trial and error, careful measurement of planned activities, and feedback from customers and the environment in general, organizations create new standard operating procedures and business processes that reflect their experience. This is called "organizational learning." Arguably, organizations that can sense and respond to their environments rapidly will survive longer than organizations that have poor learning mechanisms.

Knowledge management increases the ability of the organization to learn from its environment and to incorporate knowledge into its business processes. **Knowledge management** refers to the set of processes developed in an organization to create, gather, store, maintain, and disseminate the firm's knowledge. Information technology plays an important role in knowledge management as an enabler of business processes aimed at creating, storing, maintaining, and disseminating knowledge. Developing procedures and routines—business processes—to optimize the creation, flow, learning, protection, and sharing of knowledge in the firm has become a core management responsibility.

**knowledge management**
The set of processes developed in an organization to create, gather, store, maintain, and disseminate the firm's knowledge.

Companies cannot take advantage of their knowledge resources if they have inefficient processes for capturing and distributing knowledge or if they fail to appreciate the value of the knowledge they already possess. Some corporations have created explicit knowledge management programs for protecting and distributing knowledge resources that they have identified and for discovering new sources of knowledge. These programs are often headed by a **chief knowledge officer (CKO).** The chief knowledge officer is a senior executive who is responsible for the firm's knowledge management program. The CKO helps design programs and systems to find new sources of knowledge or to make better use of existing knowledge in organizational and management processes (Earl and Scott, 1999).

**chief knowledge officer (CKO)**
Senior executive in charge of the organization's knowledge management program.

## SYSTEMS AND INFRASTRUCTURE FOR KNOWLEDGE MANAGEMENT

All the major types of information systems described in this text facilitate the flow of information and the management of a firm's knowledge. Earlier chapters have described systems that help firms understand and respond to their environments more effectively, notably enterprise systems, external and internal networks, databases, datamining, and communication-based applications. The concept of a "digital firm" refers to a firm with substantial use of information technology to enhance its ability to sense and respond to its environment.

Although all the information systems we have described help an organization sense and respond to its environment, some technologies uniquely and directly address the organizational learning and management task. Office systems, knowledge work systems (KWS), group collaboration systems, and artificial intelligence applications are especially useful for knowledge management because they focus on supporting information and knowledge work and on defining and capturing the organization's knowledge base. This knowledge base may include (1) structured, internal knowledge (explicit knowledge), such as product manuals or research reports; (2) external knowledge of competitors, products, and markets, including competitive intelligence; and (3) informal, internal knowledge, often called **tacit knowledge,** which resides in the minds of individual employees but has not been documented in structured form (Davenport, DeLong, and Beers, 1998).

**tacit knowledge**
Expertise and experience of organizational members that has not been formally documented.

Information systems can promote organizational learning by capturing, codifying, and distributing both explicit and tacit knowledge. Once information has been collected and organized in a system, it can be reused many times. Companies can use information systems to codify their best practices and make knowledge of these practices widely available to employees. **Best practices** are the most successful solutions or problem-solving methods that have been developed by a specific organization or industry. In addition to improving existing work practices, the knowledge can be preserved as organizational memory to train future employees or to help them with decision making. **Organizational memory** is the stored learning from an organization's history that can be used for decision making and other purposes. Information systems can also provide networks for linking people so that individuals with special areas of expertise can be easily identified and tacit knowledge can be shared.

**best practices**
The most successful solutions or problem-solving methods that have been developed by a specific organization or industry.

**organizational memory**
The stored learning from an organization's history that can be used for decision making and other purposes.

Figure 12-1 illustrates the information systems and information technology (IT) infrastructure for supporting knowledge management. Office systems help disseminate and coordinate the flow of information in the organization. Knowledge work systems support the activities of highly skilled knowledge workers and professionals as they create new knowledge and try to integrate it into the firm. Group collaboration and support systems support the creation and

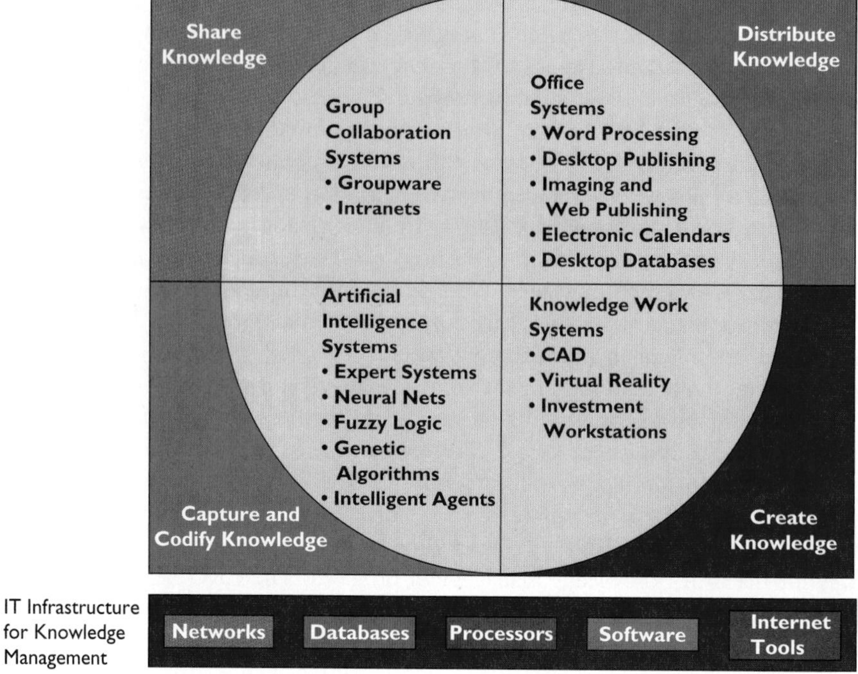


***Figure 12-1*** Knowledge management requires an information technology (IT) infrastructure that facilitates the collection and sharing of knowledge as well as software for distributing information and making it more meaningful. The information systems illustrated here give close-in support to information workers at many levels in the organization.

sharing of knowledge among people working in groups. Artificial intelligence systems capture new knowledge and provide organizations and managers with codified knowledge that can be reused by others in the organization. These systems require an IT infrastructure that makes heavy use of powerful processors, networks, databases, software, and Internet tools.

## KNOWLEDGE WORK AND PRODUCTIVITY

In information economies, organizational productivity depends on increasing the productivity of information and knowledge workers. Consequently, companies have made massive investments in technology to support information work. Information technology now accounts for more than 40 percent of total business expenditures on capital equipment in the United States. Much of that information technology investment has poured into offices and the service sector—all knowledge-intensive industries.

Although information technology has increased productivity in manufacturing, especially the manufacture of information technology products, the extent to which computers have enhanced the productivity of information workers remains under debate. Productivity is one measure of a firm's efficiency in converting inputs to outputs. It refers to the amount of capital and labor required to produce a *unit of output.* Some studies show that investment in information technology has not led to any appreciable growth in productivity among office workers. Corporate downsizings and cost-reduction measures have increased worker efficiency but have not yet led to sustained enhancements signifying genuine productivity gains (Roach, 1988, 1996, 2000). Cell phones, home fax machines, laptop computers, and information appliances allow highly paid knowledge workers to get more work done by working longer hours and bringing their work home, but they are not necessarily getting more work done in a specified unit of time.

However, measuring productivity—units of output—in information and knowledge industries is nearly impossible because of the problems of identifying suitable units of output for information work (Panko, 1991). How does one measure the output of a law office? Should one measure productivity by examining the number of forms completed per employee (a measure of physical unit productivity) or by examining the amount of revenue produced per employee (a measure of financial unit productivity) in an information- and knowledge-intense industry? The earlier studies used data that are over 10 years old, when computers were not as intensively used in organizations as they are today.

Other studies have focused on measuring the value of outputs (essentially revenues), profits, return on investment (ROI), and stock market capitalization as the ultimate measures of firm efficiency. These studies find that information technology investments started to generate a productivity payback in the 1990s. Several studies by Brynjolfsson and Hitt found that among 370 firms the return on investment in IT was about 60% whereas non-IT capital had a return on investment of only 7%. Hence investment in IT produced very large returns (Brynjolfsson and Hitt, 1999 and 1993). Banker (2001) and others (Brynjolfsson, Hitt and Yang 1999) have found that higher investment in IT produces higher stock valuations for firms and, further, that higher investment by an entire industry produces higher stock valuations for the entire industry. Moreover, several authors have argued IT-induced growth in firm efficiency is much higher in the late 1990s because of the learning required by organizations to use IT and the large amount of organizational change required to effectively unleash the potential of IT. The debate centers on whether these gains are short-term or represent fundamental changes in service-sector productivity that can be attributed to computers.

In addition to reducing costs, computers may increase the quality of products and services for consumers, or even create entirely new products and revenue streams. These intangible benefits are difficult to measure and consequently are not addressed by conventional productivity measures. Moreover, because of competition, the value created by computers may primarily flow to customers rather than to the company making the investments (Brynjolfsson, 1996). For instance, the investment in ATM machines by banks has not resulted in higher profitability for any single bank although the industry as a whole has prospered and consumers enjoy the benefits without paying higher fees. Hence, the returns to information technology investments have to be analyzed within the competitive context of the firm and industry. If IT lowers barriers to entry, and if firms cannot develop inimitable strategic advantages using IT, then the investment in IT will be imitated by all in an industry, driving down prices, and firms will not experience above-normal profits in the long run.

Introduction of information technology does not automatically guarantee productivity. Desktop computers, e-mail, and fax applications actually can generate more drafts, memos, spreadsheets, and messages—increasing bureaucratic red tape and paperwork. Firms are more likely to produce high returns on information technology investments if they rethink their procedures, processes, and business goals.

## 12.2 INFORMATION AND KNOWLEDGE WORK SYSTEMS

**Information work** is work that consists primarily of creating or processing information. It is carried out by information workers who usually are divided into two subcategories: **data workers,** who primarily process and disseminate information; and **knowledge workers,** who primarily create knowledge and information.

Examples of data workers include secretaries, sales personnel, bookkeepers, and draftspeople. Researchers, designers, architects, writers, and judges are examples of knowledge workers. Data workers usually can be distinguished from knowledge workers because knowledge workers usually have higher levels of education and memberships in professional organizations. In addition, knowledge workers exercise independent judgment as a routine aspect of their work. Data and knowledge workers have different information requirements and different systems to support them.

**information work**
Work that primarily consists of creating or processing information.

**data workers**
People, such as secretaries or bookkeepers, who process and disseminate the organization's information and paperwork.

**knowledge workers**
People, such as engineers, scientists, or architects, who design products or services or create knowledge for the organization.

### DISTRIBUTING KNOWLEDGE: OFFICE AND DOCUMENT MANAGEMENT SYSTEMS

Most data work and a great deal of knowledge work takes place in offices, including most of the work done by managers. The office plays a major role in coordinating the flow of information throughout the entire organization. The office has three basic functions (see Figure 12-2):

- Managing and coordinating the work of data and knowledge workers
- Connecting the work of the local information workers with all levels and functions of the organization
- Connecting the organization to the external world, including customers, suppliers, government regulators, and external auditors

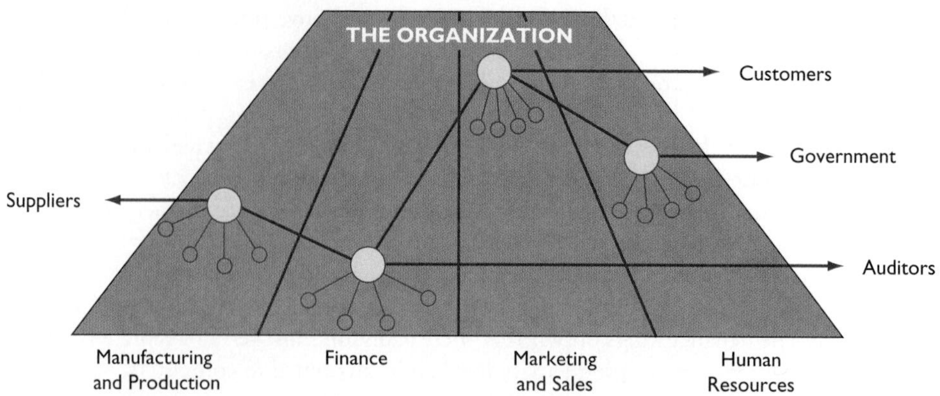


*Figure 12-2* The three major roles of offices. Offices perform three major roles. (1) They coordinate the work of local professionals and information workers. (2) They coordinate work in the organization across levels and functions. (3) They couple the organization to the external environment.

Office workers span a very broad range: professionals, managers, salespeople, and clerical workers working alone or in groups. Their major activities include the following:

- Managing documents, including document creation, storage, retrieval, and dissemination
- Scheduling for individuals and groups
- Communicating, including initiating, receiving, and managing voice, digital, and document-based communications for individuals and groups
- Managing data, such as on employees, customers, and vendors

**office systems**
Computer systems, such as word processing, voice mail, and imaging, that are designed to increase the productivity of information workers in the office.

These activities can be supported by office systems (see Table 12-1). **Office systems** are any application of information technology intended to increase productivity of information workers in the office. Fifteen years ago, office systems handled only the creation, processing, and management of documents. Today professional knowledge and information work remains highly document centered. However, digital image processing—words and documents—is also at the core of office systems, as are high-speed digital communications services. Because office work involves many people jointly engaged in projects, contemporary office systems have powerful group assistance tools like networked digital calendars. An ideal office environment would be based on a seamless network of digital machines linking professional, clerical, and managerial work groups and running a variety of types of software.

Although word processing and desktop publishing address the creation and presentation of documents, they only exacerbate the existing paper avalanche problem. Workflow problems arising from paper handling are enormous. It has been estimated that 94 percent of all business information is stored on paper (Liu and Stork, 2000). Locating and updating information in that format is a great source of organizational inefficiency.

**document imaging systems**
Systems that convert documents and images into digital form so they can be stored and accessed by the computer.

One way to reduce problems stemming from paper workflow is to employ document imaging systems. **Document imaging systems** are systems that convert documents and images into digital form so they can be stored and accessed by a computer. Such systems store, retrieve, and manipulate a digitized image of a document, allowing the document itself to be discarded. The system must contain a scanner that converts the document image into a

## TABLE 12-1 TYPICAL OFFICE SYSTEMS

| Office Activity | Technology |
|---|---|
| Managing documents | Word processing, desktop publishing, document imaging, Web publishing, workflow management |
| Scheduling | Electronic calendars, groupware, intranets |
| Communicating | E-mail, voice mail, digital answering systems, groupware, intranets |
| Managing data | Desktop databases, spreadsheets, user-friendly interfaces to mainframe databases |

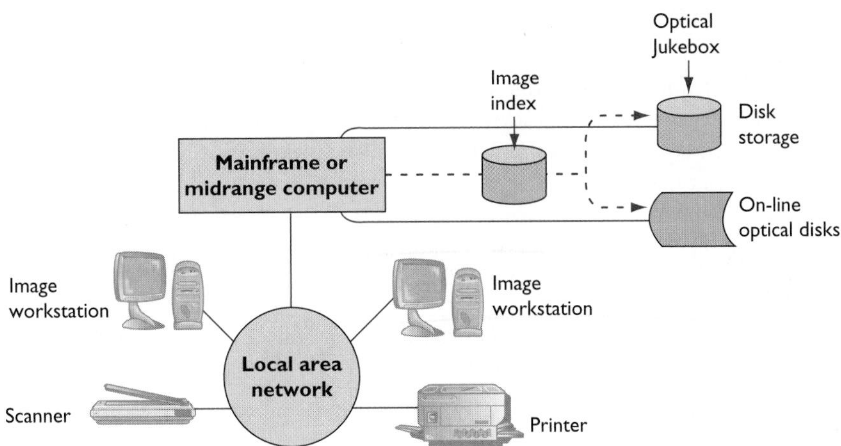


*Figure 12-3* Components of an imaging system. A typical imaging system stores and processes digitized images of documents, using scanners, an optical disk system, an image index, workstations, and printers. A midrange or small mainframe computer may be required to control the activities of a large imaging system.

bit-mapped image, storing that image as a graphic. If the document is not in active use, it usually is stored on an optical disk system. Optical disks, kept on-line in a **jukebox** (a device for storing and retrieving many optical disks), require up to a minute to retrieve the document automatically.

**jukebox**
A device for storing and retrieving many optical disks.

An imaging system also requires indexes that allow users to identify and retrieve documents when needed. Index data are entered so that a document can be retrieved in a variety of ways, depending on the application. For example, the index may contain the document scan date, the customer name and number, the document type, and some subject information. Finally, the system must include retrieval equipment, primarily workstations capable of handling graphics, although printers usually are included. Figure 12-3 illustrates the components of a typical imaging system.

Traditional document-management systems can be expensive, requiring proprietary client/server networks, special client software, and storage capabilities. Intranets provide a low-cost and universally available platform for basic document publishing, and many companies are using them for this purpose. Employees can publish information using Web-page authoring tools and post it to an intranet Web server where it can be shared and accessed throughout the company with standard Web browsers. These Weblike "documents" can be multimedia objects combining text, graphics, audio, and video along with hyperlinks. After a document has been posted to the server, it can be indexed for quicker access and linked to other documents (see Figure 12-4)

For more sophisticated document-management functions, such as controlling changes to documents, maintaining histories of activity and changes in the managed documents, and the ability to search documents on either content or index terms, commercial Web-based systems such as those from IntraNet Solutions or Open Text are available. Vendors such as FileNet and Documentum have enhanced their traditional document-management systems with Web capabilities.

To achieve the large productivity gains promised by imaging technology, organizations must redesign their workflow. In the past, the existence of only one copy of a document largely shaped workflow. Work had to be performed serially; two people could not work on the same document at the same time. Significant staff time was devoted to filing and retrieving documents. After a document has been stored electronically, workflow management can change the traditional methods of working with documents (see Chapter 10).

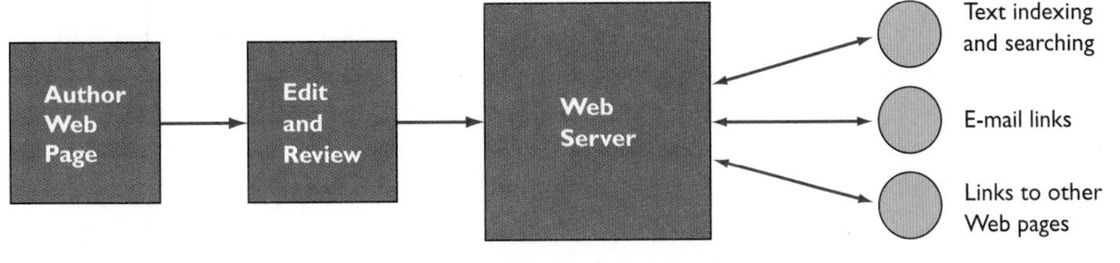


*Figure 12-4* Web publishing and document management. An author can post information on an intranet Web server, where it can be accessed through a variety of mechanisms.

## CREATING KNOWLEDGE: KNOWLEDGE WORK SYSTEMS

Knowledge work is that portion of information work that creates new knowledge and information. For example, knowledge workers create new products or find ways to improve existing ones. Knowledge work is segmented into many highly specialized fields, and each field has a different collection of **knowledge work systems (KWS)** that are specialized to support workers in that field. Knowledge workers perform three key roles that are critical to the organization and to the managers who work within the organization:

**knowledge work systems (KWS)**
Information systems that aid knowledge workers in the creation and integration of new knowledge in the organization.

- Keeping the organization up to date in knowledge as it develops in the external world—in technology, science, social thought, and the arts
- Serving as internal consultants regarding the areas of their knowledge, the changes taking place, and the opportunities
- Acting as change agents evaluating, initiating, and promoting change projects

Knowledge workers and data workers have somewhat different information systems support needs. Most knowledge workers rely on office systems such as word processors, voice mail, and calendars, but they also require more specialized knowledge work systems. Knowledge work systems are specifically designed to promote the creation of knowledge and to ensure that new knowledge and technical expertise are properly integrated into the business.

### Requirements of Knowledge Work Systems

Knowledge work systems have characteristics that reflect the special needs of knowledge workers. First, knowledge work systems must give knowledge workers the specialized tools they need, such as powerful graphics, analytical tools, and communications and document-management tools. These systems require great computing power in order to handle rapidly the sophisticated graphics or complex calculations necessary to such knowledge workers as scientific researchers, product designers, and financial analysts. Because knowledge workers are so focused on knowledge in the external world, these systems also must give the worker quick and easy access to external databases.

A user-friendly interface is very important to a knowledge worker's system. User-friendly interfaces save time by allowing the user to perform needed tasks and get to required information without having to spend a lot of time learning how to use the computer. Saving time is more important for knowledge workers than for most other employees because knowledge workers are highly paid—wasting a knowledge worker's time is simply too expensive. Figure 12-5 summarizes the requirements of knowledge work systems.

Knowledge workstations often are designed and optimized for the specific tasks to be performed, so a design engineer will require a different workstation than a lawyer. Design engineers need graphics with enough power to handle three-dimensional, computer-aided design (CAD) systems. However, financial analysts are more interested in having access to a myriad of external databases and in optical disk technology so they can access massive amounts of financial data very quickly.

### Examples of Knowledge Work Systems

Major knowledge work applications include computer-aided design (CAD) systems, virtual reality systems for simulation and modeling, and financial workstations. **Computer-aided design (CAD)** automates the creation and revision of designs, using computers and sophisticated graphics software. Using a more traditional physical design methodology, each design modification requires a mold to be made and a prototype to be physically tested. That process must be repeated many times, which is a very expensive and time-consuming process. Using a CAD workstation, the designer only needs to make a physical prototype toward the end of the design process because the design can be easily tested and changed on the computer. The ability of CAD software to provide design specifications for the tooling and the manufacturing process also saves a great deal of time and money while producing a manufacturing process with far fewer problems. For example, The Maddox Design Group of Atlanta, Georgia, uses MicroArchitect CAD software from IdeaGraphix for architectural design. Designers can quickly put the architectural background in, popping in doors and windows, and then do the engineering layout. The software can generate door and window schedules, time accounting

**computer-aided design (CAD)**
Information system that automates the creation and revision of designs using sophisticated graphics software.

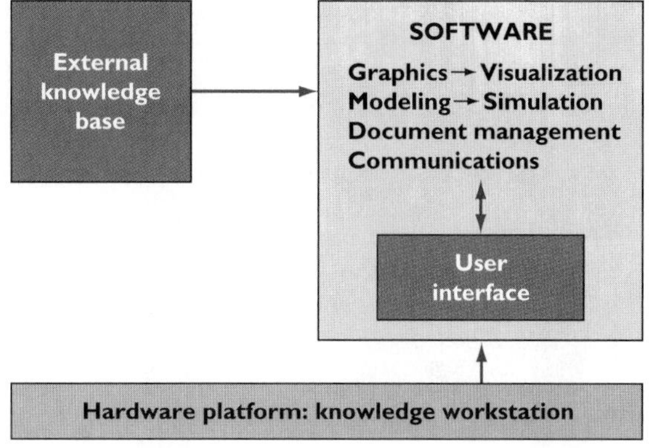


***Figure 12-5*** Requirements of knowledge work systems. Knowledge work systems require strong links to external knowledge bases in addition to specialized hardware and software.

reports, and projected costs. Additional details on CAD systems can be found in Chapter 10.

**Virtual reality systems** have visualization, rendering, and simulation capabilities that go far beyond those of conventional CAD systems. They use interactive graphics software to create computer-generated simulations that are so close to reality that users almost believe they are participating in a real-world situation. In many virtual reality systems, the user dons special clothing, headgear, and equipment, depending on the application. The clothing contains sensors that record the user's movements and immediately transmit that information back to the computer.

**virtual reality systems** Interactive graphics software and hardware, which create computer-generated simulations that provide sensations that emulate real-world activities.

Virtual reality is starting to provide benefits in educational, scientific, and business work. For example, Michael Kwartler, director of the Environmental Simulation Center in Manhattan , built a three-dimensional model of a SoHo neighborhood in lower Manhattan for a developer seeking to build a hotel in that location. Kwartler's group won community support for the project by allowing neighborhood residents to work with the model and fly around to look at things from different angles. Surgeons at Boston's Brigham and Women's Hospital are using a virtual reality system in which a three-dimensional representation of the brain using CT and MRI scans is superimposed on live video. With this version of X-ray vision, surgeons can pinpoint the location of a tumor in the brain with 0.5 millimeter accuracy.

Virtual reality applications are being developed for the Web using a standard called **Virtual Reality Modeling Language (VRML).** VRML is a set of specifications for interactive, three-dimensional modeling on the World Wide Web that can organize multiple media types, including animation, images, and audio, to put users in a simulated real-world environment. VRML is platform-independent, operates over a desktop computer, and requires little bandwidth. Users can download a three-dimensional virtual world designed using VRML from a server over the Internet using their Web browser.

**Virtual Reality Modeling Language (VRML)** A set of specifications for interactive three-dimensional modeling on the World Wide Web.

DuPont, the Wilmington, Delaware, chemical company, created a VRML application called HyperPlant, which allows users to access three-dimensional data over the Internet with Netscape Web browsers. Engineers can go through three-dimensional models as if they were physically walking through a plant, viewing objects at eye level. This level of detail reduces the number of mistakes they make during construction of oil rigs, oil plants, and other structures.

The Sharper Image's (www.sharperimage.com) 3D Enhanced Catalog for Web site visitors with high-speed Internet connections and powerful processors provides images of products in three dimensions. Visitors can rotate digitized images of many products so that they

*A group of Chrysler Corporation engineers examines a new automobile design using a computer-aided design (CAD) tool. CAD systems improve the quality and precision of product design by performing much of the design and testing work on the computer.*

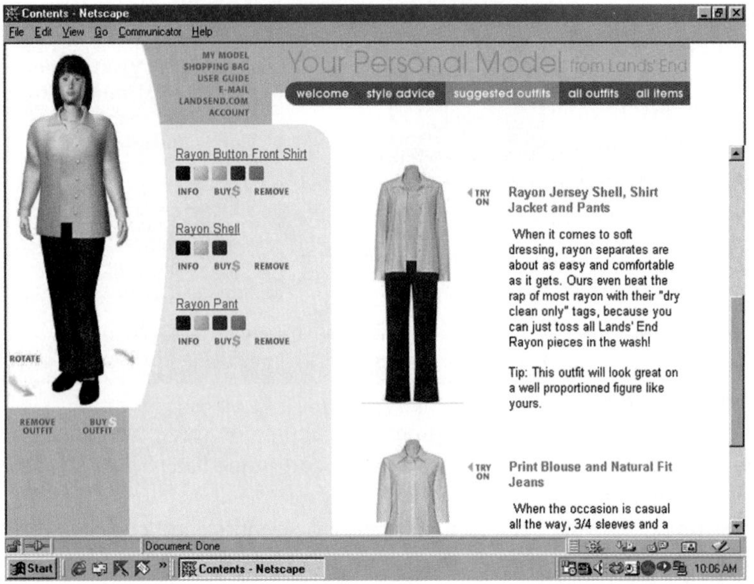


*Women can create a VRML "personal model" that approximates their physical proportions to help them visualize how they will look in clothing sold at the Lands' End Web site. The digitized image can be rotated to show how the outfits will look from all angles and users can click to change the clothes' color.*

can examine them from any angle. The user could zoom in to see specific details and manipulate the object to see how the lid opens or how it folds for storage.

**investment workstation**
Powerful desktop computer for financial specialists, which is optimized to access and manipulate massive amounts of financial data.

The financial industry is using specialized **investment workstations** to leverage the knowledge and time of its brokers, traders, and portfolio managers. Firms such as Merrill Lynch and Paine Webber have installed investment workstations that integrate a wide range of data from both internal and external sources, including contact management data, real-time and historical market data, and research reports. Previously, financial professionals had to spend considerable time accessing data from separate systems and piecing together the information they needed. By providing one-stop information faster and with fewer errors, the workstations streamline the entire investment process from stock selection to updating client records. Table 12-2 summarizes the major types of knowledge work systems.

## SHARING KNOWLEDGE: GROUP COLLABORATION SYSTEMS AND ENTERPRISE KNOWLEDGE ENVIRONMENTS

Although many knowledge and information work applications have been designed for individuals working alone, organizations have an increasing need to support people working in groups. Chapters 6, 8, and 9 introduced key technologies that can be used for group coordination and collaboration: e-mail, teleconferencing, dataconferencing, videoconferencing, groupware, and intranets. Groupware and intranets are especially valuable for this purpose.

### Groupware

Until recently, groupware (which we introduced in Chapter 6) was the primary tool for creating collaborative work environments. Groupware is built around three key principles: com-

**TABLE 12-2 EXAMPLES OF KNOWLEDGE WORK SYSTEMS**

| Knowledge Work System | Function in Organization |
|---|---|
| CAD/CAM (computer-aided design/ computer-aided manufacturing) | Provides engineers, designers, and factory managers with precise control over industrial design and manufacturing |
| Virtual reality systems | Provide drug designers, architects, engineers, retailers, and medical workers with precise, photorealistic simulations of objects |
| Investment workstations | High-end PCs used in financial sector to analyze trading situations instantaneously and facilitate portfolio management |

**TABLE 12-3** KNOWLEDGE MANAGEMENT CAPABILITIES OF GROUPWARE

| Capability | Description |
|---|---|
| Publishing | Posting documents as well as simultaneous work on the same document by multiple users along with a mechanism to track changes to these documents |
| Replication | Maintaining and updating identical data on multiple PCs and servers |
| Discussion tracking | Organizing discussions by many users on different topics |
| Document management | Storing information from various types of software in a database |
| Workflow management | Moving and tracking documents created by groups |
| Security | Preventing unauthorized access to data |
| Portability | Availability of the software for mobile use to access the corporate network from the road |
| Application development | Developing custom software applications with the software |

munication, collaboration, and coordination. It allows groups to work together on documents, schedule meetings, route electronic forms, access shared folders, develop shared databases, and send e-mail. Table 12-3 lists the capabilities of major commercial groupware products that make them such powerful platforms for capturing information and experiences, coordinating common tasks, and distributing work through time and place. Information-intensive companies such as consulting firms, law firms, and financial management companies have found groupware an especially powerful tool for leveraging their knowledge assets.

## Intranets and Enterprise Knowledge Environments

Chapters 4 and 9 described how some organizations are using intranets and Internet technologies for group collaboration, including e-mail, discussion groups, and multimedia Web documents. Some of these intranets are providing the foundation for enterprise knowledge environments in which information from a variety of sources and media, including text, sound, video, and even digital slides, can be shared, displayed, and accessed across an enterprise through a simple common interface. Examples of enterprise knowledge environments can be found in Table 12-4. These comprehensive intranets can transform decades-old processes, allowing people to disseminate information, share best practices, communicate, conduct research, and collaborate in ways that were never before possible.

Enterprise knowledge environments are so rich and vast that many organizations have built specialized corporate portals to help individuals navigate through various knowledge resources. These **enterprise information portals,** also known as *enterprise knowledge portals* direct individuals to digital knowledge objects and information system applications, helping

**enterprise information portal**
Application that enables companies to provide users with a single gateway to internal and external sources of information.

**TABLE 12-4** EXAMPLES OF ENTERPRISE KNOWLEDGE ENVIRONMENTS

| Organization | Knowledge Management Capabilities |
|---|---|
| Ford Motor Company | Intranet delivers information about news, people, processes, products, and competition to 95,000 professional employees. Employees can access on-line libraries and a Web Center of Excellence with information on best practices, standards, and recommendations. Engineers can access images on the intranet from wherever they are in the world instead of waiting for project documentation to arrive by mail. |
| Shell Oil Company | Knowledge Management System (KMS) provides a communications and collaboration environment where employees can learn about and share information about best practices. Includes information from internal sources and from external sources such as universities, consultants, other companies, and research literature. A Lotus Domino groupware application allows employees to carry on dialogues through the company intranet. The author of a best practice in the repository might use this tool to talk with colleagues about his or her experiences. |
| Booz Allen Hamilton | Knowledge Online intranet provides an on-line repository of consultants' knowledge and experience. It includes a searchable database organized around the firm's best specialties and best practices; other intellectual capital such as research reports, presentations, graphs, images, and interactive training material; and links to resumes and job histories. |

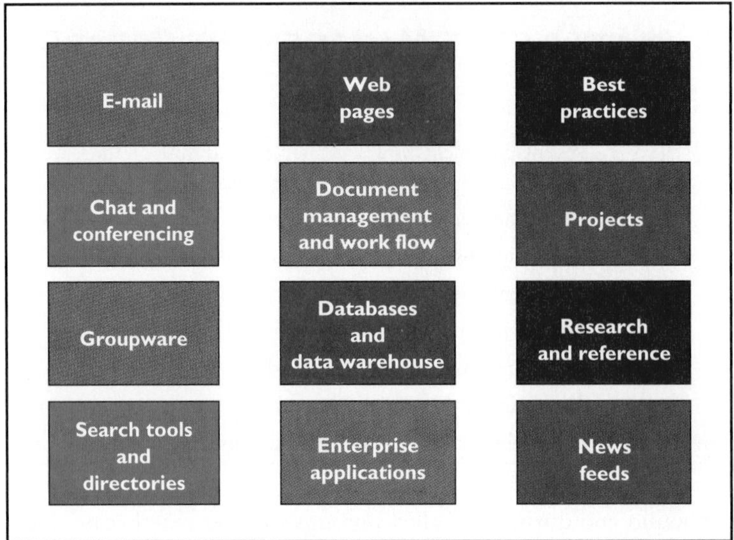


*Figure 12-6* An enterprise information portal. The portal provides a single point of access to the firm's knowledge resources and helps the firm coordinate information and people.

them make sense of the information that is available and also showing how organizational knowledge resources are interconnected. Figure 12-6 illustrates what an enterprise information portal might look like. It might include access to external sources of information, such as news feeds and research, as well as internal knowledge resources and capabilities for e-mail, chat, discussion groups, and videoconferencing. Software tools are available to build and personalize these portals. For example, Autonomy provides a tool that can analyze documents, Web pages, or e-mail to identify and rank the main ideas, categorize information by subject matter, insert hypertext links to related material, deliver information to users based on the ideas in the text they read or write, and deliver information of interest to them. Ericsson, a major manufacturer of digital phones and data communications solutions, uses Autonomy to automatically aggregate, personalize, and deliver Internet news feeds, intranet pages, internal office documents, and company e-mail to its corporate intranet portal and to users' mobile phones and handheld devices.

The collaborative and knowledge-sharing features of intranets, combined with their low cost, have made them attractive alternatives to proprietary groupware for collaborative work, especially among small and medium-size businesses. For simple tasks, such as sharing documents or document publishing, an intranet generally is less expensive to build and maintain than applications based on commercial groupware products, which require proprietary software and client/server networks.

For applications requiring extensive coordination and management, groupware software has important capabilities that intranets cannot yet provide. Groupware is more flexible when documents must be changed, updated, or edited on the fly. It can track revisions to a document as it moves through a collaborative editing process. Internal groupware-based networks are more secure than intranets. Web sites are more likely to crash or to have their servers overloaded when there are many requests for data. High-end groupware software such as Lotus Notes or OpenText Livelink is thus more appropriate for applications requiring production and publication of documents by many authors, frequent updating and document tracking, and high security and replication. Lotus Notes and other groupware products have been enhanced so they can be integrated with the Internet or private intranets.

Intranet collaboration technology works best as a central repository with a small number of authors and relatively static information that does not require frequent updating, although intranet tools for group collaboration are improving. Netscape Communications' Communicator software bundles a Web browser with messaging and collaboration tools, including e-mail, newsgroup discussions, a group scheduling and calendaring tool, and point-to-point conferencing.

**teamware**
Intranet-based software that is customized for teamwork.

Commercial software tools called teamware make intranets more useful for working in teams. **Teamware** consists of intranet-based applications for building a work team, sharing ideas and documents, brainstorming, scheduling, tracking the status of tasks and projects, and archiving decisions made or rejected by project team members for future use. Teamware

*eRoom is a secure, Web-based workplace and complete set of business collaboration tools that can be quickly tailored for specific business initiatives and easily installed. Companies can use the eRoom solution to enable distributed work teams to work closely and creatively to plan, collaborate, strategize, and make decisions across the extended enterprise.*

is similar to groupware but does not offer the powerful application development capabilities provided by sophisticated groupware products. However, it lets companies easily implement collaboration applications that can be accessed using a Web browser. eRoom Technology's eRoom, Thoroughstar's QuickTeam and Lotus Quickplace are examples of commercial teamware products. The Window on Organizations shows how companies are using collaborative development tools in the design of new products.

Group collaboration technologies alone cannot promote information sharing if team members do not believe it is in their interest to share, especially in organizations that encourage competition among employees. This technology can best enhance the work of a group if the applications are properly designed to fit the organization's needs and work practices and if management encourages a collaborative atmosphere (Alavi, 1999).

## 12.3 ARTIFICIAL INTELLIGENCE

Organizations are using artificial intelligence technology to capture individual and collective knowledge and to codify and extend their knowledge base.

### WHAT IS ARTIFICIAL INTELLIGENCE?

**Artificial intelligence (AI)** is the effort to develop computer-based systems (both hardware and software) that behave as humans. Such systems would be able to learn natural languages, accomplish coordinated physical tasks (robotics), use a perceptual apparatus that informs their physical behavior and language (visual and oral perception systems), and emulate human expertise and decision making (expert systems). Such systems also would exhibit logic, reasoning, intuition, and the just-plain-common-sense qualities that we associate with human beings. Figure 12-8 illustrates the elements of the artificial intelligence family. Another important element is intelligent machines, the physical hardware that performs these tasks.

**artificial intelligence (AI)** The effort to develop computer-based systems that can behave like humans, with the ability to learn languages, accomplish physical tasks, use a perceptual apparatus, and emulate human expertise and decision making.

Successful artificial intelligence systems are based on human expertise, knowledge, and selected reasoning patterns, but they do not exhibit the intelligence of human beings. Existing artificial intelligence systems do not come up with new and novel solutions to problems. Existing systems extend the powers of experts but in no way substitute for them or capture much of their intelligence. Briefly, existing systems lack the common sense and generality of naturally intelligent human beings.

Human intelligence is vastly complex and much broader than computer intelligence. A key factor that distinguishes human beings from other animals is their ability to develop associations and to use metaphors and analogies such as *like* and *as.* Using metaphor and analogy, humans create new rules, apply old rules to new situations, and at times act intuitively and/or instinctively without rules. Much of what we call common sense or generality in humans resides in the ability to create metaphor and analogy.

## Virtual Collaboration on the Internet

Imagine this scenario: A manufacturing manager in Chicago looks at the model of a product under development on his computer screen at the same time a supplier in Oregon is reviewing the same model on-line. Meanwhile, engineers in Europe are making changes to the model, rotating the model and changing its shape. The supplier sees gaps in the design and informs the rest of the group what changes needed to be made. All of these steps in the design process are occurring simultaneously. It sounds revolutionary but the revolution is already here. More and more companies and their business partners are engaging in collaborative product development.

Firms can use Internet technology and new design and project management tools to share design data at all phases of the product lifecycle with their design, sales, and manufacturing groups and also with their external suppliers and subcontractors. Immediate access to product data can help these groups plan resources and respond more quickly to customer expectations, saving both money and time.

Lockheed Missiles and Fire Control, a division of Lockheed Martin supplying combat and missile systems to the U.S. government, uses ipTeam from NexPrise to electronically manage bids from suppliers on-line. Lockheed can securely post complex engineering documents and bids on NexPrise servers for suppliers to review and bid on. (Some of these documents can be thousands of pages long.) Once a project is underway, Lockheed uses ipTeam to review, negotiate revisions, and track changes to designs. By replacing cumbersome manual processes and print documents with this collaboration technology, Lockheed has reduced both the labor to develop and distribute design documents and design decision cycles in half. Alliant Missile Products of Rock Center, West Virginia, was so pleased with ipTeam for making bids and managing projects with Lockheed that it brought several of its subsuppliers into the system as well.

Tight management of the product development process is essential at Seagate Technology, a leading manufacturer of data storage devices, which was acquired by Veritas Software Corporation and a group of private investors. Seagate releases 3,000 new design documents each month. The company used to maintain these documents in paper form, storing them in filing cabinets where they might be difficult to locate. If an individual in another location needed to see the document, it had to be located in the file cabinet and then faxed. According to Doug Speidel, director of Seagate's engineering information systems, when companies store their documents on microfilm or paper, "your intellectual knowledge just collects dust." Seagate now uses IQXpert's product data management software and its own collaborative Web tools to store, secure, and organize design data from around the world. These systems ensure that Seagate's product data are accurate and consistent and allow Seagate to track and control changes to these data. Employees in design, purchasing, and field service access the system an average of 10,000 times per month. Seagate has also opened the product design and change process to its largest customers, such as PC manufacturers, that use Seagate disk and tape drives inside their products. Figure 12-7 illustrates how Seagate's business processes for product development changed as a result of this system.

**To Think About:** It has been said that collaborative development is "truly an electronic revolution." Do you agree? Why or why not? How did using collaborative development technologies change the way the companies described here conducted their business?

*Sources:* Alorie Gilbert, "Online Collaboration Tools Help Simplify Product Design," *InformationWeek*, April 24, 2000; and Paul Kandarian, "All Together Now," *CIO Magazine*, September 1, 2000.

Human intelligence also includes a unique ability to impose a conceptual apparatus on the surrounding world. Metaconcepts, such as cause-and-effect and time, and concepts of a lower order such as breakfast, dinner, and lunch, are all imposed by human beings on the world around them. Thinking in terms of these concepts and acting on them are central characteristics of intelligent human behavior.

### Why Business Is Interested in Artificial Intelligence

Although artificial intelligence applications are much more limited than human intelligence, they are of great interest to business for the following reasons:

- They store information in an active form as organizational memory, creating an organizational knowledge base that many employees can examine and preserving expertise that might be lost when an acknowledged expert leaves the firm.

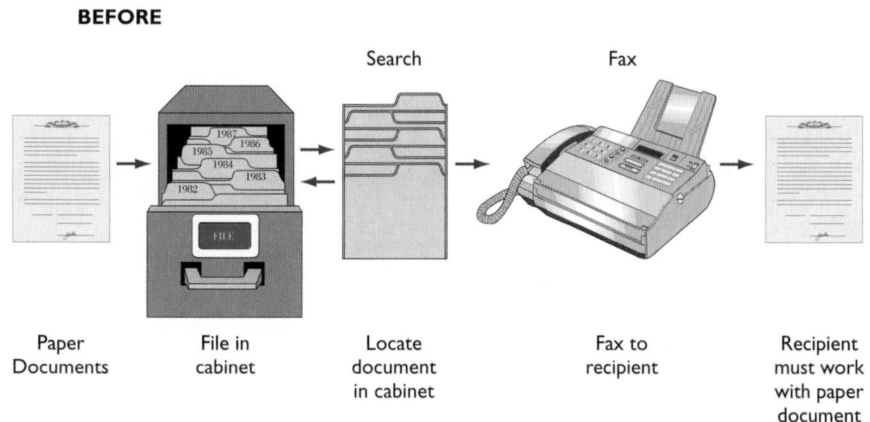


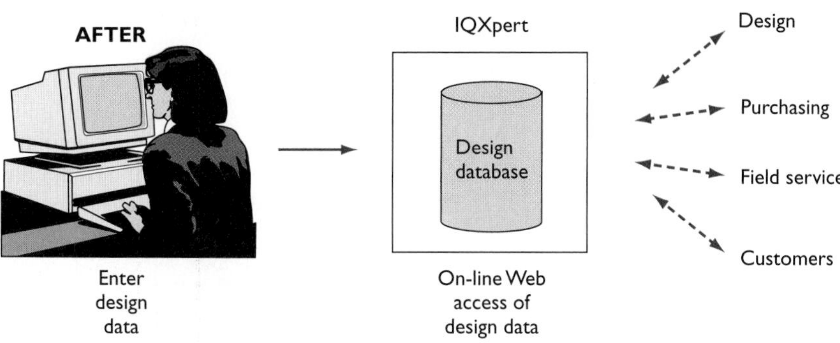


*Figure 12-7* Changes in Seagate's product development process. Seagate Technology replaced its multi-step paper-based process for product design and change with a much simpler process, using product data management software and collaborative Web tools.

- They create a mechanism that is not subject to human feelings such as fatigue and worry. This may be especially useful when jobs may be environmentally, physically, or mentally dangerous to humans. These systems also may be useful advisers in times of crisis.
- They take over routine and unsatisfying jobs held by people.
- They enhance the organization's knowledge base by suggesting solutions to specific problems that are too massive and complex to be analyzed by human beings in a short period of time.

## CAPTURING KNOWLEDGE: EXPERT SYSTEMS

In limited areas of expertise, such as diagnosing a car's ignition system or classifying biological specimens, the rules-of-thumb used by real-world experts can be understood, codified, and placed in a machine. Information systems that solve problems by capturing knowledge for a very specific and limited domain of human expertise are called **expert systems.** Expert systems capture the knowledge of skilled employees in the form of a set of rules. The set of rules in the expert system adds to the organizational memory, or stored learning, of the firm. An expert system can assist decision making by asking relevant questions and explaining the reasons for adopting certain actions.

**expert system** Knowledge-intensive computer program that captures the expertise of a human in limited domains of knowledge.

Expert systems lack the breadth of knowledge and the understanding of fundamental principles of a human expert. They are quite narrow, shallow, and brittle. They typically perform very limited tasks that can be performed by professionals in a few minutes or hours.

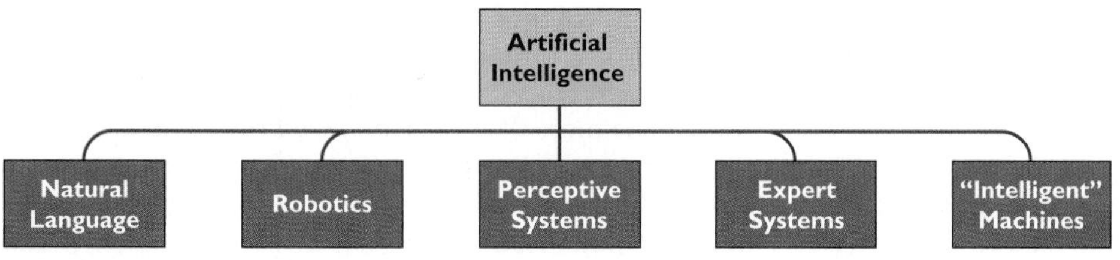


*Figure 12-8* The artificial intelligence family. The field of AI currently includes many initiatives: natural language, robotics, perceptive systems, expert systems, and intelligent machines.

## MANAGEMENT DECISION PROBLEM

### MEASURING PRODUCTIVITY FROM A KNOWLEDGE INTRANET

You head a growing electronic commerce consulting company with more than 150 employees in a fiercely competitive field. You need to recruit many junior consultants every year to replace employees who have left the firm and to fill new positions. In the past, your firm trained new employees by first sending them to a one-month training program. After completing the program, they could work full-time on projects. This process has proved very expensive and a drain on company resources. Junior consultants cannot work on any projects to generate client billings for the firm until they have finished the training program. In January 2001 your firm installed an intranet, which provides the following:

- An on-line training class in company practices and methods.
- Repository of "best practices," model proposals with search capabilities.
- Directory of employees, the projects they have worked on, and their special expertise.

You have started to compile a table showing training time and costs before and after installing the intranet. Training time goes down as the company gains experience using the intranet.

| | 2000 | 2001 | 2002 |
|---|---|---|---|
| Time to train a new consultant | 20 days | 14 days | 12 days |
| Daily training cost per consultant | $2,000 | $1,400 | $1,000 |
| Additional billings per consultant | 0 | | |

1. If your intranet trains new consultants more quickly and each trained consultant can start billing clients $1,700 per day for work on projects, how much should this new intranet increase revenue from client billings generated by newly trained consultants in 2001 and 2002? Your firm hires and trains an average of 40 new consultants each year.
2. Using only these metrics how much knowledge worker productivity has your intranet created since the intranet was installed?
3. What other capabilities would you add to the intranet to make your consultants even more productive? How could you measure productivity increases from these capabilities?

Problems that cannot be solved by human experts in the same short period of time are far too difficult for an expert system. However, by capturing human expertise in limited areas, expert systems can provide benefits, helping organizations make high-quality decisions with fewer people.

## How Expert Systems Work

**knowledge base**
Model of human knowledge that is used by expert systems.

**rule-based expert system**
An AI program that has a large number of interconnected and nested IF–THEN statements, or rules, that are the basis for the knowledge in the system.

**rule base**
The collection of knowledge in an AI system that is represented in the form of IF–THEN rules.

**knowledge frames**
A method of organizing expert system knowledge into chunks; the relationships are based on shared characteristics determined by the user.

Human knowledge must be modeled or represented in a way that a computer can process. The model of human knowledge used by expert systems is called the **knowledge base.** Two ways of representing human knowledge and expertise are rules and knowledge frames.

A standard structured programming construct (see Chapter 14) is the IF–THEN construct, in which a condition is evaluated. If the condition is true, an action is taken. For instance

IF INCOME > $45,000 (condition)
THEN PRINT NAME AND ADDRESS (action)

A series of these rules can be a knowledge base. Any reader who has written computer programs knows that virtually all traditional computer programs contain IF–THEN statements. The difference between a traditional program and a **rule-based expert system** program is one of degree and magnitude. AI programs can easily have 200 to 10,000 rules, far more than traditional programs, which may have 50 to 100 IF–THEN statements. Moreover, in an AI program the rules tend to be interconnected and nested to a far greater degree than in traditional programs, as shown in Figure 12-9. Hence the complexity of the rules in a rule-based expert system is considerable.

Could you represent the knowledge in the Encyclopedia Britannica this way? Probably not, because the **rule base** would be too large, and not all the knowledge in the encyclopedia can be represented in the form of IF–THEN rules. In general, expert systems can be efficiently used only in those situations in which the domain of knowledge is highly restricted (such as in granting credit) and involves no more than a few thousand rules.

**Knowledge frames** can be used to represent knowledge by organizing information into chunks of interrelated characteristics. The relationships are based on shared characteristics rather than a hierarchy. This approach is grounded in the belief that humans use frames, or

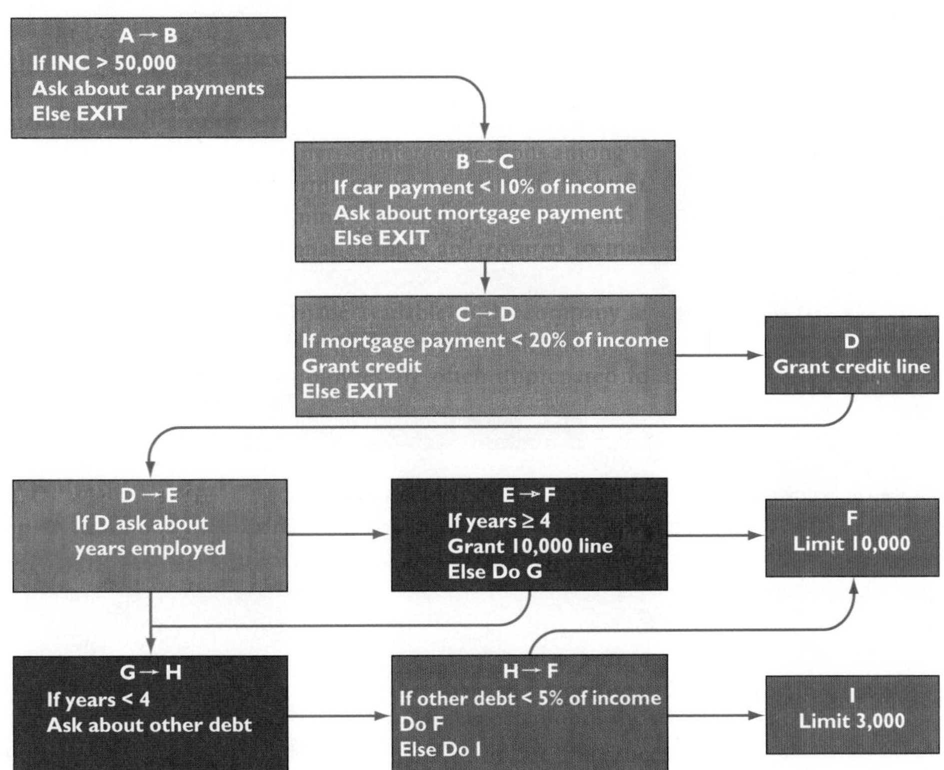


*Figure 12-9* Rules in an AI program. An expert system contains a number of rules to be followed when used. The rules themselves are interconnected; the number of outcomes is known in advance and is limited; there may be multiple paths to the same outcome; and the system can consider multiple rules at a single time. The rules illustrated are for simple credit-granting expert systems.

concepts, to make rapid sense out of perceptions. For instance, when a person is told, "Look for a tank and shoot when you see one," experts believe that humans invoke a concept, or frame, of what a tank should look like. Anything that does not fit this concept of a tank is ignored. In a similar fashion, AI researchers can organize a vast array of information into frames. The computer then is instructed to search the database of frames and list connections to other frames of interest. The user can follow the pathways pointed to by the system.

Figure 12-10 shows a part of a knowledge base organized by frames. A "CAR" is defined by characteristics or slots in a frame as a vehicle, with four wheels, a gas or diesel motor, and an action such as rolling or moving. This frame could be related to almost any other object in the database that shares any of these characteristics, such as the tank frame.

The **AI shell** is the programming environment of an expert system. In the early years of expert systems, computer scientists used specialized artificial intelligence programming languages such as LISP or Prolog that could process lists of rules efficiently. Today a growing number of expert systems use AI shells that are user-friendly development environments. AI shells can quickly generate user-interface screens, capture the knowledge base, and manage the strategies for searching the rule base.

The strategy used to search through the rule base is called the **inference engine.** Two strategies are commonly used: forward chaining and backward chaining (see Figure 12-11).

In **forward chaining** the inference engine begins with the information entered by the user and searches the rule base to arrive at a conclusion. The strategy is to fire, or carry out, the action of the rule when a condition is true. In Figure 12-11, beginning on the left, if the user enters a client with income greater than $100,000, the engine will fire all rules in sequence from left to right. If the user then enters information indicating that the same client owns real estate, another pass of the rule base will occur and more rules will fire. Processing continues until no more rules can be fired.

In **backward chaining** the strategy for searching the rule base starts with a hypothesis and proceeds by asking the user questions about selected facts until the hypothesis is either confirmed or disproved. In our example, in Figure 12-11, ask the question, "Should we add this person to the prospect database?" Begin on the right of the diagram and work toward the left. You can see that the person should be added to the database if a sales representative is sent, term insurance is granted, or a financial advisor visits the client.

**AI shell**
The programming environment of an expert system.

**inference engine**
The strategy used to search through the rule base in an expert system; can be forward or backward chaining.

**forward chaining**
A strategy for searching the rule base in an expert system that begins with the information entered by the user and searches the rule base to arrive at a conclusion.

**backward chaining**
A strategy for searching the rule base in an expert system that acts like a problem solver by beginning with a hypothesis and seeking out more information until the hypothesis is either proved or disproved.

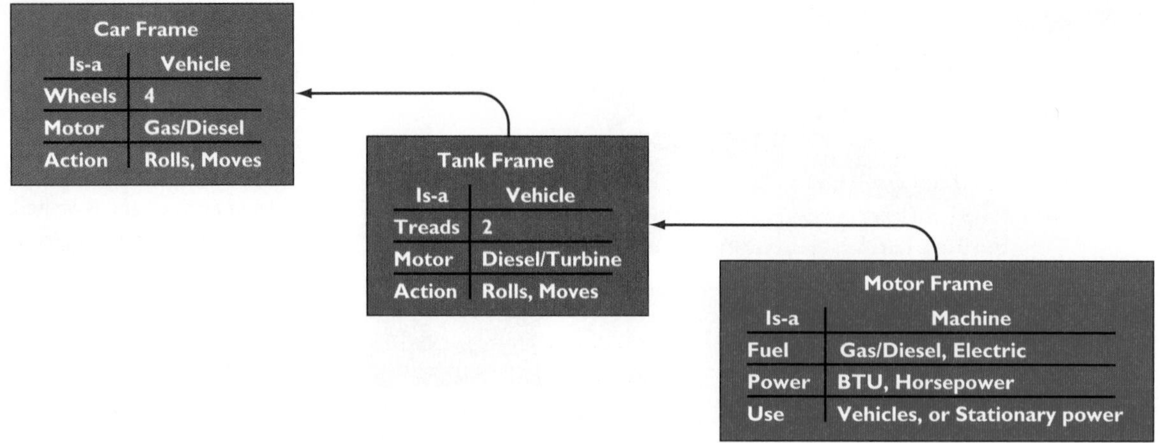


*Figure 12-10* Frames to model knowledge. Knowledge and information can be organized into frames. Frames capture the relevant characteristics of the objects of interest. This approach is based on the belief that humans use "frames" or concepts to narrow the range of possibilities when scanning incoming information to make rapid sense out of perceptions.

## Building an Expert System

Building an expert system is similar to building other information systems, although building expert systems is an iterative process with each phase possibly requiring several iterations before a full system is developed. Typically, the environment in which an expert system operates is continually changing so that the expert system must also continually change. Some expert systems, especially large ones, are so complex that in a few years the maintenance costs will equal the development costs.

An AI development team is composed of one or more experts, who have a thorough command of the knowledge base, and one or more knowledge engineers, who can translate the knowledge (as described by the expert) into a set of rules or frames. A **knowledge engineer** is similar to a traditional systems analyst but has special expertise in eliciting information and expertise from other professionals.

**knowledge engineer**
A specialist who elicits information and expertise from other professionals and translates it into a set of rules or frames for an expert system.

The team members must select a problem appropriate for an expert system. The project will balance potential savings from the proposed system against the cost. The team members will develop a prototype system to test assumptions about how to encode the knowledge of experts. Next, they will develop a full-scale system, focusing mainly on the addition of a very large number of rules. The complexity of the entire system grows with the number of rules, so the comprehensibility of the system may be threatened. Generally, the system will be pruned to achieve simplicity and power. The system is tested by a range of experts within the

*Figure 12-11* Inference engines in expert systems. An inference engine works by searching through the rules and "firing" those rules that are triggered by facts gathered and entered by the user.

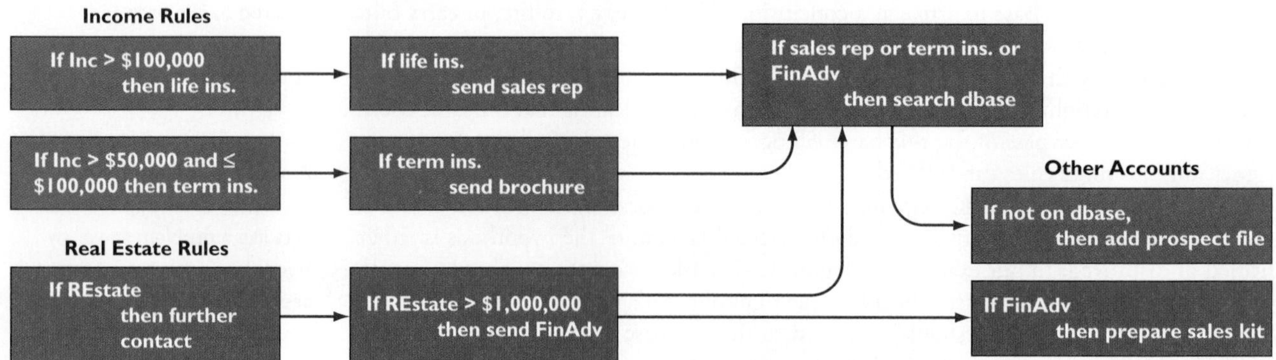

organization against the performance criteria established earlier. Once tested, the system will be integrated into the data flow and work patterns of the organization.

## Examples of Successful Expert Systems

There is no accepted definition of a successful expert system. What is successful to an academic ("It works!") may not be successful to a corporation ("It costs a million dollars!"). The following are examples of expert systems that provide organizations with an array of benefits, including reduced errors, reduced cost, reduced training time, improved decisions, and improved quality and service.

BlueCross BlueShield of North Carolina used Aion, an AI shell, to build an automated medical underwriting system (AMUS). AMUS links to an IBM IMS hierarchical database and BlueCross BlueShield's in-house system for rate quoting, policy writing, and risk management. The system determines whether to underwrite applicants for health insurance after assessing their eligibility and medical risks. Underwriters can make changes to the rules as needed. This expert system enabled BlueCross BlueShield to reduce the time required to make an underwriting decision from one week to one day. The productivity gains from the system also enabled the company to eliminate or redeploy 8 underwriters and 15 support personnel, replacing them with four underwriting processors. Since adopting AMUS, the accuracy of underwriting decisions has improved (Kay, 2000).

Countrywide Funding Corp. in Pasadena, California, is a loan-underwriting firm with about 400 underwriters in 150 offices around the country. The company developed a PC-based expert system in 1992 to make preliminary creditworthiness decisions on loan requests. The company had experienced rapid, continuing growth and wanted the system to help ensure consistent, high-quality loan decisions. CLUES (Countrywide's Loan Underwriting Expert System) has about 400 rules. Countrywide tested the system by sending every loan application handled by a human underwriter to CLUES as well. The system was refined until it agreed with the underwriters in 95 percent of the cases.

Countrywide does not rely on CLUES to reject loans, because the expert system cannot be programmed to handle exceptional situations such as those involving a self-employed person or those with complex financial schemes. An underwriter reviews all rejected loans and makes the final decision. Traditionally, an underwriter could handle six or seven applications a day. Using CLUES, the same underwriter can evaluate at least 16 per day. Countrywide now is using the rules in its expert system to answer inquiries from visitors to its Web site who want to know if they qualify for a loan.

The United Nations developed an expert system to help calculate employees' salaries, taking into account numerous and complex rules for calculating entitlements such as benefits based on location of work and an employee's contract. The knowledge base for the system

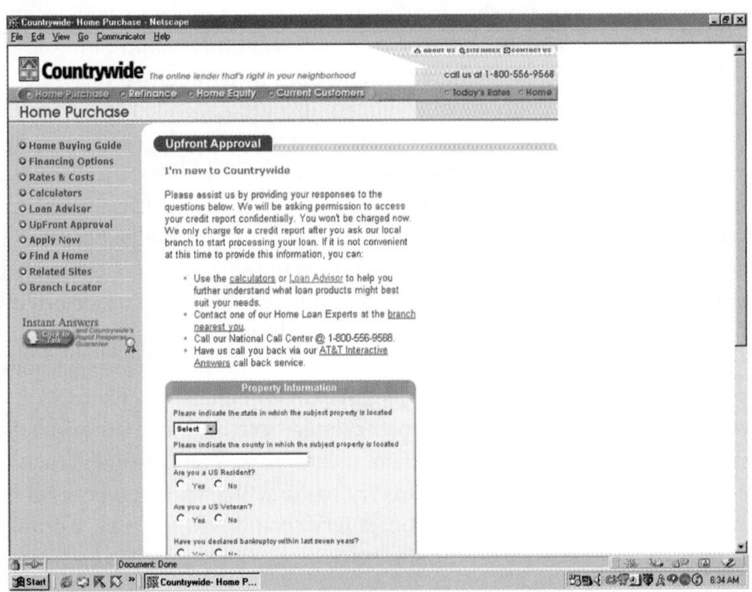


*Countrywide Funding Corporation developed an expert system called CLUES to evaluate the creditworthiness of loan applicants. Countrywide is using the rules in this system to answer inquiries from visitors to its Web site who want to know if they can qualify for a loan.*

is on-line and is capable of applying entitlements automatically in payroll calculations. The system also reassesses when a change to an employee's status is approved and generates the appropriate salary for the next payroll.

Although expert systems lack the robust and general intelligence of human beings, they can provide benefits to organizations if their limitations are well understood. Only certain classes of problems can be solved using expert systems. Virtually all successful expert systems deal with problems of classification in which there are relatively few alternative outcomes and in which these possible outcomes are all known in advance. Many expert systems require large, lengthy, and expensive development efforts. Hiring or training more experts may be less expensive than building an expert system.

The knowledge base of expert systems is fragile and brittle; they cannot learn or change over time. In fast-moving fields, such as medicine or the computer sciences, keeping the knowledge base up to date is a critical problem. For example, Digital Equipment Corporation stopped using its XCON expert system for configuring VAX computers because its product line was constantly changing and it was too difficult to keep updating the system to capture these changes. Expert systems can only represent limited forms of knowledge. IF–THEN knowledge exists primarily in textbooks. There are no adequate representations for deep causal models or temporal trends. No expert system, for instance, can write a textbook on information systems or engage in other creative activities not explicitly foreseen by system designers. Many experts cannot express their knowledge using an IF–THEN format. Expert systems cannot yet replicate knowledge that is intuitive, based on analogy and on a sense of things.

Contrary to early promises, expert systems are most effective in automating lower-level clerical functions. They can provide electronic checklists for lower-level employees in service bureaucracies such as banking, insurance, sales, and welfare agencies. The applicability of expert systems to managerial problems is very limited. Managerial problems generally involve drawing facts and interpretations from divergent sources, evaluating the facts, and comparing one interpretation of the facts with another, and are not limited to simple classification. Expert systems based on the prior knowledge of a few known alternatives are unsuitable to the problems managers face on a daily basis.

## ORGANIZATIONAL INTELLIGENCE: CASE-BASED REASONING

**case-based reasoning (CBR)** Artificial intelligence technology that represents knowledge as a database of cases and solutions.

Expert systems primarily capture the knowledge of individual experts, but organizations also have collective knowledge and expertise that they have built up over the years. This organizational knowledge can be captured and stored using case-based reasoning. In **case-based reasoning (CBR),** descriptions of past experiences of human specialists, represented as cases, are stored in a database for later retrieval when the user encounters a new case with similar parameters. The system searches for stored cases with problem characteristics similar to the new one, finds the closest fit, and applies the solutions of the old case to the new case. Successful solutions are tagged to the new case and both are stored together with the other cases in the knowledge base. Unsuccessful solutions also are appended to the case database along with explanations as to why the solutions did not work (see Figure 12-12).

Expert systems work by applying a set of IF–THEN–ELSE rules against a knowledge base, both of which are extracted from human experts. Case-based reasoning, in contrast, represents knowledge as a series of cases, and this knowledge base is continuously expanded and refined by users. For example, let us examine Compaq Computer of Houston, Texas, a company that operates in a highly competitive, customer service-oriented business environment and is daily flooded with customer phone calls crying for help. Keeping those customers satisfied requires Compaq to spend millions of dollars annually to maintain large, technically skilled, customer-support staffs. When customers call with problems, they must describe the problems to the customer service staff and then wait on hold while customer service transfers the calls to appropriate technicians. The customers then describe the problem all over again while the technicians try to come up with answers—all in all, a most frustrating experience. To improve customer service and rein in costs, Compaq began giving away expensive case-based reasoning software to customers purchasing their Pagemarq printer.

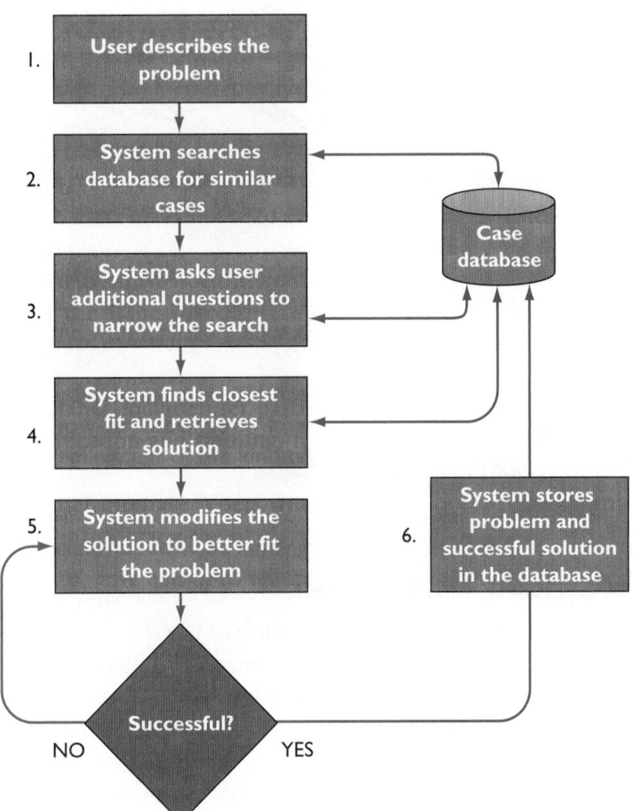


*Figure 12-12* How case-based reasoning works. Case-based reasoning represents knowledge as a database of past cases and their solutions. The system uses a six-step process to generate solutions to new problems encountered by the user.

The software knowledge base is a series of several hundred actual cases of Pagemarq printer problems—actual war stories about smudged copies, printer memory problems, jammed printers—all the typical problems people face with laser printers. Trained CBR staff entered case descriptions in textual format into the CBR system. They entered key words necessary to categorize the problem, such as smudge, smear, lines, streaks, and paper jam. They also entered a series of questions that might be needed to allow the software to further narrow the problem. Finally, solutions also were attached to each case.

With the Compaq-supplied CBR system running on their computer, owners usually do not need to call Compaq's service department. Instead they run the software and describe the problem to the software. The system swiftly searches actual cases, discarding unrelated ones, selecting related ones. If necessary to further narrow the search results, the software will ask the user for more information. In the end, one or more cases relevant to the specific problem are displayed, along with their solutions. Now, customers can solve most of their own problems quickly without a telephone call, and Compaq saves $10 million to $20 million annually in customer-support costs.

New commercial software products, such as Inference's CasePoint WebServer, allow customers to access a case database through the Web. Using case-based reasoning, the server asks customers to answer a series of questions to narrow down the problems. CasePoint then extracts solutions from the database and passes them on to customers. Audio-product manufacturer Kenwood USA used this tool to put its manuals and technical-support solutions on the Web.

## 12.4 OTHER INTELLIGENT TECHNIQUES

Organizations are using other intelligent computing techniques to extend their knowledge base by providing solutions to problems that are too massive or complex to be handled by people with limited resources. Neural networks, fuzzy logic, genetic algorithms, and intelligent agents are developing into promising business applications.

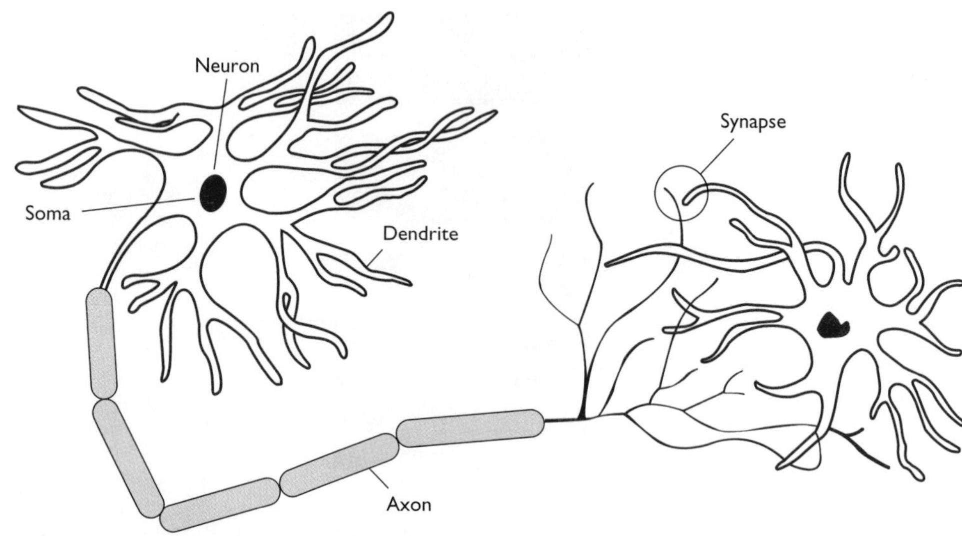


***Figure 12-13*** Biological neurons of a leech. Simple biological models, like the neurons of a leech, have influenced the development of artificial or computational neural networks in which the biological cells are replaced by transistors or entire processors. *Source:* Defense Advance Research Projects Agency (DARPA), 1988. Unclassified.

## NEURAL NETWORKS

There has been an exciting resurgence of interest in bottom-up approaches to artificial intelligence in which machines are designed to imitate the physical thought process of the biological brain. Figure 12-13 shows two neurons from a leech's brain. The soma, or nerve cell, at the center acts like a switch, stimulating other neurons and being stimulated in turn. Emanating from the neuron is an axon, which is an electrically active link to the dendrites of other neurons. Axons and dendrites are the "wires" that electrically connect neurons to one another. The junction of the two is called a synapse. This simple biological model is the metaphor for the development of neural networks. A **neural network** consists of hardware or software that attempts to emulate the processing patterns of the biological brain.

**neural network**
Hardware or software that attempts to emulate the processing patterns of the biological brain.

The human brain has about 100 billion ($10^{11}$) neurons, each having about 1,000 dendrites, which form 100,000 billion ($10^{14}$) synapses. The brain's neurons operate in parallel, and the human brain can accomplish about $10^{16}$, or ten million billion, interconnections per second. This far exceeds the capacity of any known machine or any machine planned or ever likely to be built with current technology.

However, complex networks of neurons have been simulated on computers. Figure 12-14 shows an artificial neural network with two neurons. The resistors in the circuits are variable and can be used to teach the network. When the network makes a mistake (i.e., chooses the wrong pathway through the network and arrives at a false conclusion), resistance can be raised on some circuits, forcing other neurons to fire. If this learning process continues for thousands of cycles, the machine learns the correct response. The neurons are highly interconnected and operate in parallel.

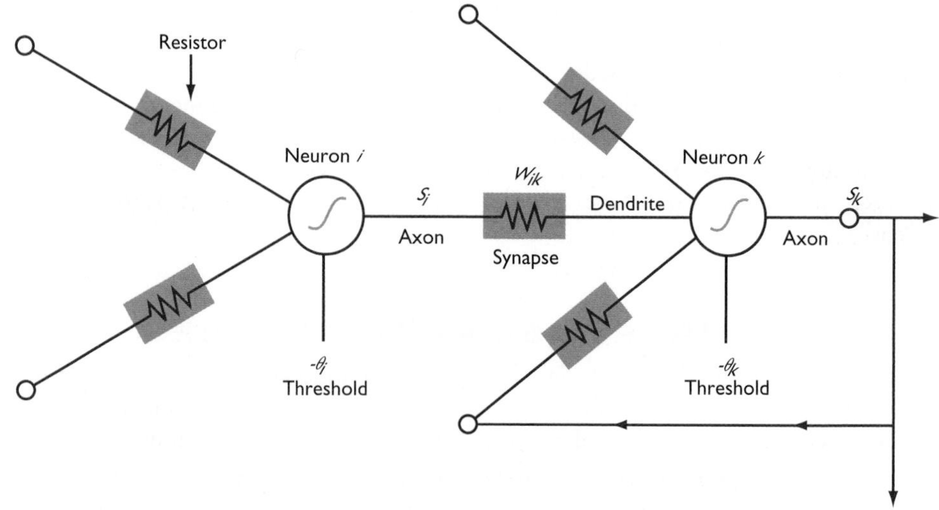


***Figure 12-14*** Artificial neural network with two neurons. In artificial neurons, the biological neurons become processing elements (switches), the axons and dendrites become wires, and the synapses become variable resistors that carry weighted inputs (currents) that represent data. *Source:* DARPA, 1988. Unclassified.

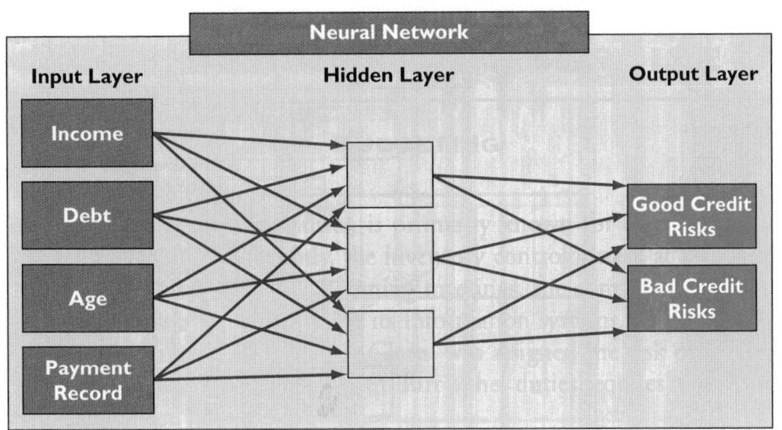


**Figure 12-15** A neural network uses rules it "learns" from patterns in data to construct a hidden layer of logic. The hidden layer processes inputs, classifying them based on the experience of the model.
*Source:* Herb Edelstein, "Technology How-To: Mining Data Warehouses," *Information Week,* January 8, 1996. Copyright © 1996 CMP Media, Inc., 600 Community Drive, Manhasset, NY 11030. Reprinted with permission.

A neural net has a large number of sensing and processing nodes that continuously interact with each other. Figure 12-15 represents a neural network comprising an input layer, an output layer, and a hidden processing layer. The network is fed a training set of data for which the inputs produce a known set of outputs or conclusions. This helps the computer learn the correct solution by example. As the computer is fed more data, each case is compared with the known outcome. If it differs, a correction is calculated and applied to the nodes in the hidden processing layer. These steps are repeated until a condition, such as corrections being less than a certain amount, is reached. The neural network in Figure 12-15 has "learned" how to identify a good credit risk.

## The Difference Between Neural Networks and Expert Systems

What is different about neural networks? Expert systems seek to emulate or model a human expert's way of solving problems, but neural network builders claim that they do not model human intelligence, do not program solutions, and do not aim to solve specific problems per se. Instead, neural network designers seek to put intelligence into the hardware in the form of a generalized capability to learn. In contrast, the expert system is highly specific to a given problem and cannot be easily retrained.

Neural network applications are emerging in medicine, science, and business to address problems in pattern classification, prediction and financial analysis, and control and optimization. Papnet is a neural net-based system that distinguishes between normal and abnormal cells when examining Pap smears for cervical cancer that has far greater accuracy than visual examinations by technicians. The computer is not able to make a final decision, so a technician will review any selected abnormal cells. Using Papnet, a technician requires one-fifth the time to review a smear while attaining perhaps ten times the accuracy of the existing manual method.

Neural networks are being used by the financial industry to discern patterns in vast pools of data that might help investment firms predict the performance of equities, corporate bond ratings, or corporate bankruptcies (Walczak, 1999). VISA International Inc. is using a neural network to help detect credit card fraud by monitoring all VISA transactions for sudden changes in the buying patterns of cardholders. The Window on Technology illustrates other neural net applications for pattern recognition.

Unlike expert systems, which typically provide explanations for their solutions, neural networks cannot always explain why they arrived at a particular solution. Moreover, they cannot always guarantee a completely certain solution, arrive at the same solution again with the same input data, or always guarantee the best solution (Trippi and Turban, 1989–1990). They are very sensitive and may not perform well if their training covers too little or too much data. In most current applications, neural networks are best used as aids to human decision makers instead of substitutes for them.

### FUZZY LOGIC

Traditional computer programs require precision: on–off, yes–no, right–wrong. However, we human beings do not experience the world this way. We might all agree that +120 degrees is

## NEURAL NETS HELP SYSTEMS MANAGEMENT AND SCOTLAND YARD

When Computer Associates (CA) first developed its neural network software, it hoped to use this technology to enhance its software for managing IT infrastructure. A neural net learns from relationships from historical data to recognize a pattern and apply the learned knowledge to detect changes and predict results. CA wanted to enlist neural network agents dubbed "neugents" to help its CA Unicenter TNG enterprise system management software administer large complex networked systems. By watching the behavior of systems, the neugent trains itself better with every event so that it can eventually predict system problems before they occur. For instance, a neugent observing an e-mail server could discern in a pattern of message queues that would soon cause the server to fail. Other neugents could detect situations such as service slowdowns, outages, or virus activity; forecast workloads; and recommend system configurations.

AGF Brasil, a subsidiary of the AGF International insurance company, works with 15,000 registered brokers and agents in Brazil. Providing brokers and agents with up-to-the-minute information on the company's insurance products is vital to its success. AGF Brazil has built an 800-node network called AGF NET consisting of IBM AIX (Unix) servers, Dell servers running Windows NT, and 50 local area networks for this purpose. The company uses CA Unicenter TNG to provide a single point of control for managing its entire IT infrastructure, including servers, desktop computers, printers, routers, and hubs. CA neugents help with performance monitoring. They have alerted system administrators to a variety of processor, network, memory, and database bottlenecks as well as the need to provide additional Web capacity. Neugents support AGF's mix of different types of servers equally well because they "learn" the machines' individual idiosyncracies. Using this neural network technology, AGF can keep important services running smoothly around the clock without high staffing levels.

Other applications can benefit from neugents as well. New Scotland Yard in London is experimenting with neugents to help with data analysis. Facing a rising crime rate and falling numbers of police officers, London's Metropolitan Police Service was looking for a way to make better use of its crime data. New Scotland Yard assigned neugents to look at data from five databases, including crime reports, forensic evidence, and mug shots, hoping the neugents would detect patterns, especially in burglaries, to help the police identify serial burglars.

Neural network technology does not require defined fields in data to detect patterns. The software can look for string searches in text such as police reports. According to Patrick Dryden, an analyst at Illuminata Group in Nashua, New Hampshire, neural networks can throw brute force at large numbers to identify interesting trends. But businesspeople still have to look at those trends and decide what is important.

**To Think About:** How useful is neural network technology for the applications described here? Would you trust the management of a large complex client/server system to a neugent? Why or why not?

*Sources:* Sami Lais, "CA Bundles Neural Net, App Development Tools," *Computerworld,* August 7, 2000; www.ca.com/products/neugents and www.security7.com/products/neugents.

hot and −40 degrees is cold; but is 75 degrees hot, warm, comfortable, or cool? The answer depends on many factors: the wind, the humidity, the individual experiencing the temperature, one's clothing, and one's expectations. Many of our activities also are inexact. Tractor-trailer drivers would find it nearly impossible to back their rig into a space precisely specified to less than an inch on all sides.

**fuzzy logic**
Rule-based AI that tolerates imprecision by using imprecisely defined terms called membership functions to solve problems.

**Fuzzy logic,** a relatively new, rule-based development in AI, tolerates imprecision and even uses it to solve problems we could not have solved before. Fuzzy logic consists of a variety of concepts and techniques for representing and inferring knowledge that is imprecise, uncertain, or unreliable. Fuzzy logic can create rules that use approximate or subjective values and incomplete or ambiguous data. By expressing logic with some carefully defined imprecision, fuzzy logic is closer to the way people actually think than traditional IF–THEN rules.

Ford Motor Co. developed a fuzzy logic application that backs a simulated tractor-trailer into a parking space. The application uses the following three rules:

IF the truck is *near* jackknifing, THEN *reduce* the steering angle.

IF the truck is *far away* from the dock, THEN steer *toward* the dock.

IF the truck is *near* the dock, THEN point the trailer *directly* at the dock.

This logic makes sense to us as human beings, for it represents how we think as we back that truck into its berth.

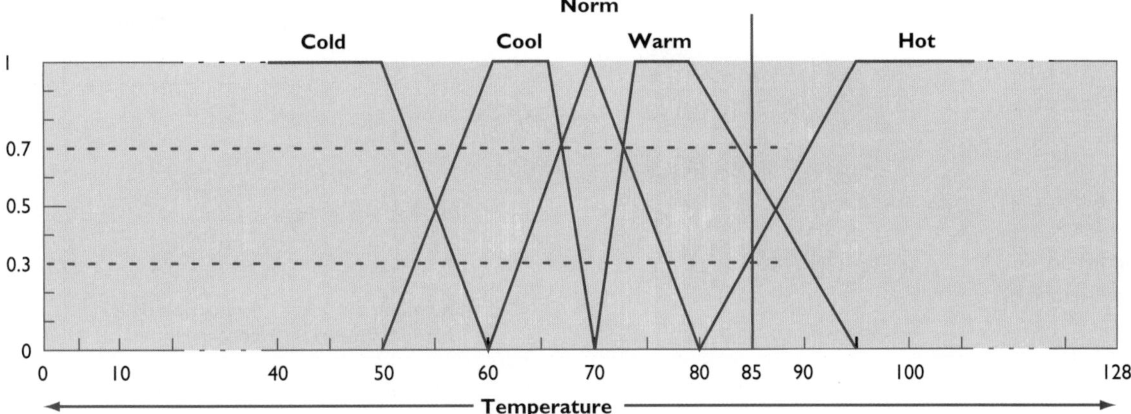


*Figure 12-16* Implementing fuzzy logic rules in hardware. The membership functions for the input called temperature are in the logic of the thermostat to control the room temperature. Membership functions help translate linguistic expressions such as "warm" into numbers that the computer can manipulate.

*Source:* James M. Sibigtroth, "Implementing Fuzzy Expert Rules in Hardware," *AI Expert,* April 1992. © 1992 Miller Freeman, Inc. Reprinted with permission.

How does the computer make sense of this programming? The answer is relatively simple. The terms (known as *membership functions*) are imprecisely defined so that, for example, in Figure 12-16, cool is between 50 degrees and 70 degrees, although the temperature is most clearly cool between about 60 degrees and 67 degrees. Note that *cool* is overlapped by *cold* or *norm.* To control the room environment using this logic, the programmer would develop similarly imprecise definitions for humidity and other factors such as outdoor wind and temperature. The rules might include one that says, *"If the temperature is cool or cold and the humidity is low while the outdoor wind is high and the outdoor temperature is low, raise the heat and humidity in the room."* The computer would combine the membership function readings in a weighted manner and, using all the rules, raise and lower the temperature and humidity.

Fuzzy logic is widely used in Japan and is gaining popularity in the United States. Its popularity has occurred partially because managers find they can use it to reduce costs and shorten development time. Fuzzy logic code requires fewer IF–THEN rules, making it simpler than traditional code. The rules required in the previous trucking example, plus its term definitions, might require hundreds of IF–THEN statements to implement in traditional logic. Compact code requires less computer capacity, allowing Sanyo Fisher USA to implement camcorder controls without adding expensive memory to their product.

Fuzzy logic also allows us to solve problems not previously solvable, thus improving product quality. In Japan, Sendai's subway system uses fuzzy logic controls to accelerate so smoothly that standing passengers need not hold on. Mitsubishi Heavy Industries in Tokyo has been able to reduce the power consumption of its air conditioners by 20 percent through implementing control programs in fuzzy logic. The autofocus device in our cameras is only possible because of fuzzy logic.

Management also has found fuzzy logic useful for decision making and organizational control. A Wall Street firm had a system developed that selects companies for potential acquisition, using the language stock traders understand. Recently, a system has been developed to detect possible fraud in medical claims submitted by healthcare providers anywhere in the United States.

## GENETIC ALGORITHMS

**genetic algorithms**
Problem-solving methods that promote the evolution of solutions to specified problems using the model of living organisms adapting to their environment.

**Genetic algorithms** (also referred to as adaptive computation) refer to a variety of problem-solving techniques that are conceptually based on the method that living organisms use to adapt to their environment—the process of evolution. They are programmed to work the way populations solve problems—by changing and reorganizing their component parts using processes such as reproduction, mutation, and natural selection. Thus, genetic algorithms promote the

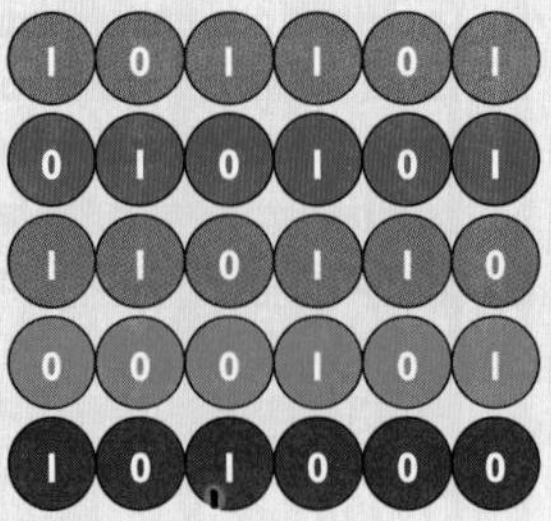

| Chromosome | | Color | Speed | Intelligence | Fitness |
|---|---|---|---|---|---|
| 1 0 1 1 0 1 | 1 | White | Medium | Dumb | 40 |
| 0 1 0 1 0 1 | 2 | Black | Slow | Dumb | 43 |
| 1 1 0 1 1 0 | 3 | White | Slow | Very Dumb | 22 |
| 0 0 0 1 0 1 | 4 | Black | Fast | Dumb | 71 |
| 1 0 1 0 0 0 | 5 | White | Medium | Very Smart | 53 |
| A population of chromosomes | | | Decoding of chromosomes | Evaluation of chromosomes | |

*Figure 12-17* The components of a genetic algorithm. This example illustrates an initial population of "chromosomes," each representing a different solution. The genetic algorithm uses an iterative process to refine the initial solutions so that the better ones, those with the higher fitness, are more likely to emerge as the best solution.

*Source:* From *Intelligent Decision Support Methods* by Vasant Dhar and Roger Stein, p. 65, © 1997. Reprinted by permission of Prentice-Hall, Upper Saddle River, NJ.

evolution of solutions to particular problems, controlling the generation, variation, adaptation, and selection of possible solutions using genetically based processes. As solutions alter and combine, the worst ones are discarded and the better ones survive to go on to produce even better solutions. Genetic algorithms breed programs that solve problems even when no person can fully understand their structure (Holland, 1992).

A genetic algorithm works by representing information as a string of 0s and 1s. A possible solution can be represented by a long string of these digits. The genetic algorithm provides methods of searching all possible combinations of digits to identify the right string representing the best possible structure for the problem.

In one method, the programmer first randomly generates a population of strings consisting of combinations of binary digits (see Figure 12-17). Each string corresponds to one of the variables in the problem. One applies a test for fitness, ranking the strings in the population according to their level of desirability as possible solutions. After the initial population is evaluated for fitness, the algorithm then produces the next generation of strings, consisting of strings that survived the fitness test plus offspring strings produced from mating pairs of strings, and tests their fitness. The process continues until a solution is reached.

Solutions to certain types of problems in areas of optimization, product design, and the monitoring of industrial systems are especially appropriate for genetic algorithms. Many business problems require optimization, because they deal with issues such as minimization of costs, maximization of profits, efficient scheduling, and use of resources. If these situations are very dynamic and complex, involving hundreds of variables or hundreds of formulas, genetic algorithms can expedite the solution, because they can evaluate many different solution alternatives quickly to find the best one. For example, General Electric engineers used genetic algorithms to help optimize the design for jet turbine aircraft engines, where each design change required changes in up to 100 variables. Coors Brewing Company and the U.S. Navy used genetic algorithms to help them with scheduling problems (Burtka, 1993).

## Hybrid AI Systems

**hybrid AI systems**
Integration of multiple AI technologies into a single application to take advantage of the best features of these technologies.

Genetic algorithms, fuzzy logic, neural networks, and expert systems can be integrated into a single application to take advantage of the best features of these technologies. Such systems are called **hybrid AI systems.** Hybrid applications in business are growing. In Japan, Hitachi, Mitsubishi, Ricoh, Sanyo, and others are starting to incorporate hybrid AI in products such as home appliances, factory machinery, and office equipment. Matsushita has developed a "neurofuzzy" washing machine that combines fuzzy logic with neural networks. Nikko Securities has been working on a neurofuzzy system to forecast convertible-bond ratings.

## Intelligent Agents

**intelligent agent**
Software program that uses a built-in or learned knowledge base to carry out specific, repetitive, and predictable tasks for an individual user, business process, or software application.

**Intelligent agents** are software programs that work in the background to carry out specific, repetitive, and predictable tasks for an individual user, business process, or software application. The agent uses a built-in or learned knowledge base to accomplish tasks or make decisions on the user's behalf. Intelligent agents can be programmed to make decisions based on the user's personal preferences—for example, to delete junk e-mail, schedule appointments, or travel over interconnected networks to find the cheapest airfare to California. The agent can be likened to a personal digital assistant collaborating with the user in the same work environment. It can help the user by performing tasks on the user's behalf, training or teaching the user, hiding the complexity of difficult tasks, helping the user collaborate with other users, or monitoring events and procedures (Maes, 1994).

There are many intelligent agent applications today in operating systems, application software, e-mail systems, mobile computing software, and network tools. For example, the Wizards found in Microsoft Office software tools have built-in capabilities to show users how to accomplish various tasks, such as formatting documents or creating graphs, and to anticipate when users need assistance. Of special interest to business are intelligent agents for cruising networks, including the Internet, in search of information. Chapter 9 described how *shopping bots* can help consumers find products they want and assist them in comparing prices and other features. Because these mobile agents are personalized, semiautonomous, and continuously running, they can help automate several of the most time-consuming stages of the buying process and thus reduce transaction costs. Increased use of XML (extensible markup language), Java, and distributed objects (see Chapter 6) will allow software agents and other automated processes to access and interact with Web-based information more easily (Glushko, Tenenbaum, and Meltzer, 1999; Wong, Paciorek, and Moore, 1999).

## APPLICATION SOFTWARE EXERCISE

### EXPERT SYSTEM SOFTWARE EXERCISE: BUILDING EXPERT SYSTEM SUPPORT FOR RETIREMENT PLANNING

Katy Roberts is a benefits specialist for Clean Air Products, a regional heating and air conditioning parts manufacturer. Many of Clean Air's employees have been with the company since the early 1960s and on retirement are given cash bonuses. These cash bonuses are based on the length of employment and the retiree's age. In order to receive a bonus, an employee must be at least 50 years of age and have worked for the company for a minimum of 5 years. The following table summarizes the criteria for determining bonuses.

| Length of Employment | Bonus |
|---|---|
| Less than 5 years | No bonus |
| 6–10 years | 20 percent of current annual salary |
| 11–15 years | 30 percent of current annual salary |
| 16–20 years | 40 percent of current annual salary |
| 20–25 years | 50 percent of current annual salary |
| 26 or more years | 100 percent of current annual salary |

Many vendors sell and make demonstration copies of their expert systems available via the Web. Use a search engine to locate and then download a demonstration copy of an expert system.

Using the information provided in the scenario, help Katy build a simple expert system for determining employee retirement bonuses. Feel free to make any assumptions that you feel are necessary; however, document your assumptions in writing. Once you have built the expert system, prepare a written report that summarizes the development process. Was the product easy to use? Why or why not? What other features should the retirement planning expert system include? Why?

## MANAGEMENT WRAP-UP

Leveraging and managing organizational knowledge have become core management responsibilities. Managers need to identify the knowledge assets of their organizations and make sure that appropriate systems and processes are in place to maximize their use.

Systems for knowledge and information work and artificial intelligence can enhance organizational processes in a number of ways. They can facilitate communication, collaboration, and coordination; bring more analytical power to bear in the development of solutions; or reduce the amount of human intervention in organizational processes.

An array of technologies is available to support knowledge management, including artificial intelligence technologies and tools for knowledge and information work and group collaboration. Managers should understand the costs, benefits, and capabilities of each technology and the knowledge management problem for which each is best suited.

*For Discussion*

1. Discuss some of the ways that knowledge management provides organizations with strategic advantage. How strategic are knowledge management systems?
2. How much can the use of artificial intelligence change the management process?

## SUMMARY

1. *Assess the importance of knowledge management in contemporary organizations.* Knowledge management is the process of systematically and actively managing and leveraging the stores of knowledge in an organization. Knowledge is a central productive and strategic asset in an information economy. Information systems can play a valuable role in knowledge management, helping the organization optimize its flow of information and capture its knowledge base. Office systems, knowledge work systems (KWS), group collaboration systems, and artificial intelligence applications are especially useful for knowledge management because they focus on supporting information and knowledge work and on defining and codifying the organization's knowledge base.
2. *Describe the applications that are most useful for distributing, creating, and sharing knowledge in the firm.* Offices coordinate information work in the organization, link the work of diverse groups in the organization, and couple the organization to its external environment. Office systems support these functions by automating document management, communications, scheduling, and data management. Word processing, desktop publishing, Web publishing, and digital imaging systems support document management activities. Electronic-mail systems and groupware support communications activities. Electronic calendar applications and groupware support scheduling activities.

   Knowledge work systems support the creation of knowledge and its integration into the organization. KWS require easy access to an external knowledge base; powerful computer hardware that can support software with intensive graphics, analysis, document management, and communications capabilities; and a friendly user interface. KWS often run on workstations that are customized for the work they must perform. Computer-aided design (CAD) systems and virtual reality systems, which create interactive simulations that behave like the real world, require graphics and powerful modeling capabilities. KWS for financial professionals provide access to external databases and the ability to analyze massive amounts of financial data very quickly.

   Groupware is special software to support information-intensive activities in which people work collaboratively in groups. Intranets can perform many group collaboration and support functions and allow organizations to use Web publishing capabilities for document management.
3. *Evaluate the role of artificial intelligence in knowledge management.* Artificial intelligence is the development of computer-based systems that behave like humans. There are five members of the artificial intelligence family tree: natural language, robotics, perceptive systems, expert systems, and intelligent machines. Artificial intelligence lacks the flexibility, breadth, and generality of human intelligence, but it can be used to capture and codify organizational knowledge.
4. *Demonstrate how organizations can use expert systems and case-based reasoning to capture knowledge.* Expert systems are knowledge-intensive computer programs that solve problems that heretofore required human expertise. The systems capture a limited domain of human knowledge using rules or frames. The strategy to search through the knowledge base, called the inference engine, can use either forward or backward chaining. Expert systems are most useful for problems of classification or diagnosis. Case-based reasoning represents

organizational knowledge as a database of cases that can be continually expanded and refined. When the user encounters a new case, the system searches for similar cases, finds the closest fit, and applies the solutions of the old case to the new case. The new case is stored with successful solutions in the case database.

5. *Explain how organizations can use neural networks and other intelligent techniques to improve their knowledge base.* Neural networks consist of hardware and software that attempt to mimic the thought processes of the human brain. Neural networks are notable for their ability to learn without programming and to recognize patterns that cannot be easily discerned by humans. They are being used in science, medicine, and business primarily to discriminate patterns in massive amounts of data.

Fuzzy logic is a software technology that expresses logic with some carefully defined imprecision so that it is closer to the way people actually think than traditional IF–THEN rules. Fuzzy logic has been used for controlling physical devices and is starting to be used for limited decision-making applications.

Genetic algorithms develop solutions to particular problems using genetically based processes such as fitness, crossover, and mutation. Genetic algorithms are beginning to be applied to problems involving optimization, product design, and monitoring industrial systems.

Intelligent agents are software programs with built-in or learned knowledge bases that carry out specific, repetitive, and predictable tasks for an individual user, business process, or software application. Intelligent agents can be programmed to search for information or conduct transactions on networks, including the Internet.

## KEY TERMS

**AI shell, 387**
**Artificial intelligence (AI), 383**
**Backward chaining, 387**
**Best practices, 373**
**Case-based reasoning (CBR), 390**
**Chief knowledge officer (CKO), 373**
**Computer-aided design (CAD), 378**
**Data workers, 375**
**Document imaging systems, 376**
**Enterprise information portal, 381**
**Expert system, 385**
**Forward chaining, 387**
**Fuzzy logic, 394**
**Genetic algorithms, 395**
**Hybrid AI systems, 396**
**Inference engine, 387**
**Information work, 375**
**Intelligent agent, 396**
**Investment workstation, 380**
**Jukebox, 377**
**Knowledge base, 386**
**Knowledge engineer, 388**
**Knowledge frames, 386**
**Knowledge management, 373**
**Knowledge workers, 375**
**Knowledge work systems (KWS), 378**
**Neural network, 392**
**Office systems, 376**
**Organizational learning, 372**
**Organizational memory, 373**
**Rule base, 386**
**Rule-based expert system, 386**
**Tacit knowledge, 373**
**Teamware, 382**
**Virtual Reality Modeling Language (VRML), 379**
**Virtual reality systems, 379**

## REVIEW QUESTIONS

1. What is knowledge management? List and briefly describe the information systems that support it and the kind of information technology (IT) infrastructure it requires.
2. How does knowledge management promote organizational learning?
3. What is the relationship between information work and productivity in contemporary organizations?
4. Describe the roles of the office in organizations. What are the major activities that take place in offices?
5. What are the principal types of information systems that support information worker activities in the office?
6. What are the generic requirements of knowledge work systems? Why?
7. Describe how the following systems support knowledge work: computer-aided design (CAD), virtual reality, investment workstations.
8. How does groupware support information work? Describe its capabilities and Internet and intranet capabilities for collaborative work.
9. What is artificial intelligence? Why is it of interest to business?
10. What is the difference between artificial intelligence and natural or human intelligence?
11. Define an expert system and describe how it can help organizations use their knowledge assets.
12. Define and describe the role of the following in expert systems: rule base, frames, inference engine.
13. What is case-based reasoning? How does it differ from an expert system?
14. Describe three problems of expert systems.
15. Describe a neural network. At what kinds of tasks would a neural network excel?
16. Define and describe fuzzy logic. For what kinds of applications is it suited?
17. What are genetic algorithms? How can they help organizations solve problems? For what kinds of problems are they suited?
18. What are intelligent agents? How can they be used to benefit businesses?

## Group Project

With a group of classmates, select two groupware products such as Lotus Notes and OpenText LiveLink and compare their features and capabilities. To prepare your analysis, use articles from computer magazines and the Web sites for the groupware vendors. If possible, use electronic presentation software to present your findings to the class.

## Tools for Interactive Learning

### Internet Connection

The Internet Connection for this chapter will take you to the National Aeronautics and Space Administration (NASA) Web site, where you can complete an exercise showing how this Web site can be used by knowledge workers. You can also use the Interactive Study Guide to test your knowledge of the topics in this chapter and get instant feedback where you need more practice.

### Electronic Commerce Project

The Electronic Commerce project for this chapter will direct you to Web sites where you can compare the capabilities of two shopping bots for the Web.

### CD-ROM

If you use the Multimedia Edition CD-ROM with this chapter, you will find two interactive exercises. The first asks you to choose the proper software tools for solving a series of knowledge management problems. The second asks you to select an appropriate AI technology to solve another series of problems. You can also find a video clip illustrating how the Papnet neural network is used for medical testing, an audio overview of the major themes of this chapter, and bullet text summarizing the key points of the chapter.

## Case Study *Hill & Knowlton Looks for a New Knowledge Management System*

What does a company have to do to increase the likelihood of success when installing a knowledge management system? Or to put it another way, why do about half the knowledge management projects fail? These are the questions that Hill & Knowlton (H&K) faced in early 1999 when it realized its current knowledge management system was not helping the company.

H&K is a global public relations firm headquartered in New York City with 1,900 employees and 68 offices in 34 countries around the world. As in so many other fields today, knowledge is central to public relations. Moreover, because public relations firms are project-centered, their employees and their clients must constantly share large amounts of information. Specifically, H&K employees need to be able to share information not only with their project mates but also with other H&K employees who have experience working with similar clients or experience working on similar products. Then they also must continually exchange information with their clients. In addition, all parties often need external information, such as market data, which they want to be able to access through the company's knowledge management system. Finally, the company needs to preserve its organizational memory, the collective, stored learning of the firm, to minimize the impact when employees leave. This memory is not only critical for H&K employees to carry out their daily work but it is also vital in training new employees quickly and effectively.

H&K had previously built an intranet to facilitate the sharing and management of its project knowledge. However, the current system was seldom used and so Ted Graham, H&K's worldwide knowledge management director, had to identify the reasons why and then either fix the old system or build a new one that employees would actually use. To examine the problem, Graham turned to H&K's worldwide advisory group. The group traditionally meets once every two years to work on long-range company issues. In this case it collected feedback from around the world and learned that H&K employees saw many problems with the existing system. Most important, however, they simply had little reason to use it. They indicated the data were out of date, inaccurate, and often irrelevant. For example, they noted that the staff biographies were quite outdated, even so far as to still contain biographies on former staff members who had left the company as much as two years earlier. Biographies are essential to H&K clients because they want to know the skills and experience of the H&K staff assigned to their accounts. H&K employees use biographies to help them identify someone with relevant experience that they can turn to for advice and help. Moreover, employees indicated they wanted a system that was easy to use where they could find one-stop shopping for all kinds of knowledge, rather than having to go to four or five different places to fulfill their needs.

The project established a new portal-type extranet, which it named hk.net. The site is password protected so that employees and clients can access only the internal data they need to see. One of the first problems the project team faced was updating and consolidating the history of all recent projects, which could be found in past e-mails that were stored without any order. The team needed to organize the e-mails and then to make them easily searchable. The project team turned to Intraspect Software of Los Altos, California, and particularly to their package called Salsa. The software enables users to store with ease e-mails and their attachments by project team and by client. Each e-mail is immediately indexed by subject and can be searched by key phrases or words. For the first time team members could find needed past information without spending a lot of search time and effort.

Easily accessible e-mail solved other problems for the company. When H&K employees or their clients' employees were assigned to a project, they were immediately told to read the archived project e-mails. In this way they were quickly and inexpensively brought up to date. "The client likes this because they're not paying for the new person to become educated," explained Graham, "and we like it because it lowers the cost of replacing employees."

The extranet captures three essential "buckets" of knowledge identified by the project team as essential to HK business processes: internal knowledge of H&K's own products and services; external knowledge, such as research, industry news, and economic forecasts; and client knowledge, such as account activity, budgets, and templates. H&K can customize the company's Web site for each of its clients using hk.net, so that when a client's staff member logs on to its hk.net channel, they are greeted with the client's company logo. All information on hk.net is accessible through on-screen folders, one each, for example, for e-mails, administrative information, and case studies, plus an H&K directory including staff biographies. These folders are arranged according to the preferences of the client.

Andrea Bartolucci, a Toronto-based H&K employee, has realized huge time savings by using hk.net. She spends half her time marketing the company to prospective clients and must assemble "credential packages" that highlight the H&K's experience in a particular industry. The package includes descriptions of past projects and biographies of H&K staff members who might be assigned to the account. Because much of this information has already been assembled by H&K in a package for another client, she can repackage it instead of starting from scratch.

Connectivity is one problem that the team could not fully solve. Because of the local infrastructures, the data are carried at different speeds in different locations. For example the Toronto and New York offices operate at high speed because both use T1 connections. The Paris office, however, has an available bandwidth of only 14.4 kilobits per second. H&K was able to use some crude workarounds to improve usage in Paris, but they were unable to fully solve the problem.

Persuading employees and clients to use the system was a big challenge. "Technology alone can't make things right," says Bartolucci. "People need to be trained to get used to it." Employees were reluctant to post information to the extranet as a matter of routine. The company offered training, but, in addition, it also offered incentives. Bonuses were given to the managers of groups that contributed the most to their project sites, and the managers were responsible for deciding how to share the funds with their team members. In addition, the company offers recognition to those whose contributions are accessed the most by others by listing the authors on a company "best-seller" list. Such a "reputational" incentive causes an individual to become recognized as an expert by co-workers. Graham also believes that those who are so recognized will "end up with better assignments, [such as flying] to South America to work on an exciting new project." H&K is also using its power by making knowledge sharing part of performance reviews.

To encourage employees to use the extranet to find out information, H&K has embedded a form of micropayment called "beenz" throughout the site. Every time an individual opens a document or contributes information, that person stands a chance of collecting beenz, which can be redeemed for books, CDs, and even vacations. H&K is also posting its internal announcements on the extranet and sending employees the links instead of e-mailing the announcements directly. Once on the extranet, employees are more likely to explore other hk.net information resources.

**Sources:** Eric Berkman, "Don't Lose Your Mind Share," *CIO Magazine,* October 1, 2000; Larry Stevens, "Incentives for Sharing," *Knowledge Management,* October 2000; and Steve Barth, "KM Horror Stories," *Knowledge Management,* October 2000.

### *CASE STUDY QUESTIONS*

1. Describe the value of a knowledge sharing system to a knowledge-based company such as Hill & Knowlton. How is knowledge management related to the firm's business strategy?
2. Explain why H&K's existing system was not fulfilling its needs.
3. What management, organization, and technical problems do you think installing the new system presented to H&K?
4. How successful is hk.net? Explain.
5. What problems do you think H&K might have faced because of their use of various incentives to increase system utilization?
6. Why do you think H&K decided to post company and industry news on hk.net? What problems might it have created for the company? How might it have helped the company?

chapter

# 13 Enhancing Management Decision Making

objectives

**After completing this chapter, you will be able to:**

1. *Differentiate a decision-support system (DSS) and a group decision-support system (GDSS).*
2. *Describe the components of decision-support systems and group decision-support systems.*
3. *Demonstrate how decision-support systems and group decision-support systems can enhance decision making.*
4. *Evaluate the capabilities of executive support systems (ESS).*
5. *Assess the benefits of executive support systems.*

## IBM Boosts Manufacturing Capacity Planning with CAPS

Manufacturing semiconductors requires hundreds of operations per product, several hundred tool groups, and weeks of manufacturing time. The lead time for purchasing a tool, which can cost up to $10 million, may be up to one year. Capacity planners base their decision of which tools to purchase on long-term demand forecasts. However, such planning is complicated by the need to consider several different tools that may be capable of each process step and the fact that the time for each process step depends on both the product and the tool.

Until recently, capacity planners dealt with a change in demand by running multiple product-mix scenarios through a spreadsheet, guessing how to change the volume or tool assignment for each product to maximize profit and minimize additional tool purchases. They could only analyze a few scenarios and had no way of knowing whether the best solution they found was actually optimal.

IBM Research worked with IBM managers to develop a Capacity Optimization Planning System (CAPS) that would identify the optimal product mix, optimally assign products to tools, and determine a minimum set of tools required to produce output to satisfy a given demand.

They built a DSS using a model with decision variables representing the production value of each product and the allocation of each product to each tool. The model considered production limits, the required process steps, and the available tool capacity. IBM refined the model to capture the preferred order in which tools are used to help identify bottlenecks. CAPS runs on a PC client that presents data to the user in a graphical interface with a convenient spreadsheet format for easy editing. IBM adopted CAPS at its largest semiconductor manufacturing plant in Burlington, Vermont.

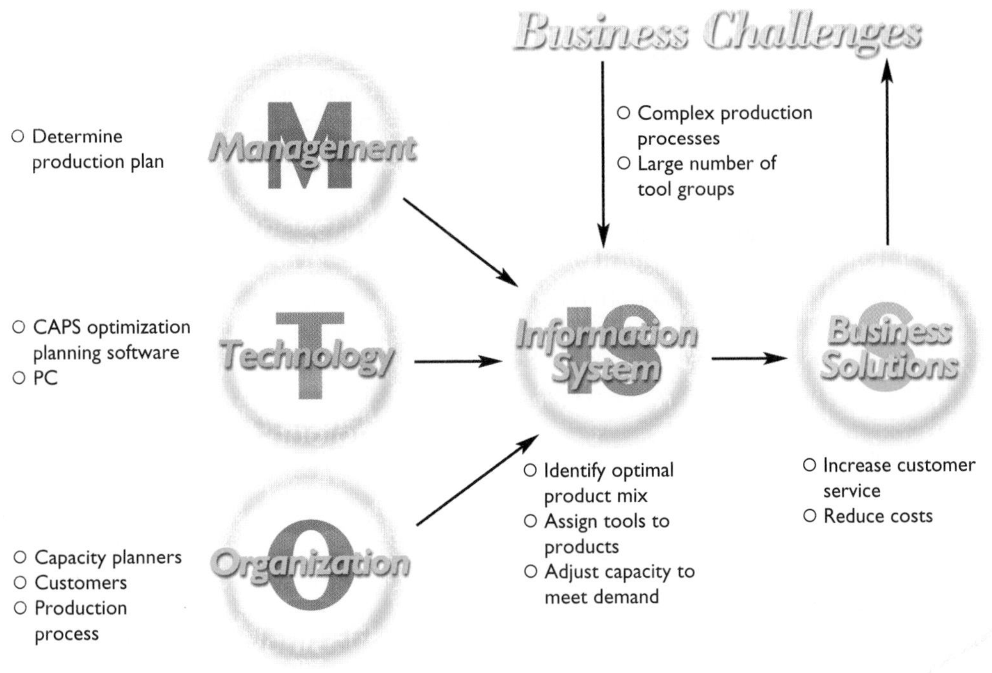


IBM planners use CAPS to adjust manufacturing capacity to meet demand forecasts. For example, when a customer asked for an increase of several hundred silicon wafers per day, planners were able to use CAPS to adjust capacity so that IBM could respond very quickly to this request. IBM planners also use CAPS to balance product portfolio offerings and to analyze the impact of cycle time commitments on fabricator output. Since its adoption in 1995, CAPS has saved IBM millions of dollars in capital expenditures.

**Sources:** Brenda Dietrich, Nick Donofrio, Grace Lin, and Jane Snowdon, "Big Benefits for Big Blue," *OR/MS Today,* June 2000; and Alexandra Barrett, "Optimize the Enterprise," *Information Week,* June 6, 2000.

## IBM Boosts Manufacturing Capacity Planning with CAPS

**MANAGEMENT CHALLENGES**

## Management Challenges

IBM's CAPS system for manufacturing capacity planning is an example of a decision-support system (DSS). Such systems have powerful analytic capabilities to support managers during the process of arriving at a decision. Other systems in this category are group decision-support systems (GDSS), which support decision making in groups, and executive support systems (ESS), which provide information for making strategic-level decisions. These systems can enhance organizational performance, but they raise the following management challenges:

1. **Building information systems that can actually fulfill executive information requirements.** Even with the use of critical success factors and other information requirements determination methods, it may still be difficult to establish information requirements for ESS and DSS serving senior management. Chapter 3 described why certain aspects of senior management decision making cannot be supported by information systems because the decisions are too unstructured and fluid. Even if a problem can be addressed by an information system, senior management may not fully understand its actual information needs. For instance, senior managers may not agree on the firm's critical success factors, or the critical success factors they describe may be inappropriate or outdated if the firm is confronting a crisis requiring a major strategic change.

2. **Creating meaningful reporting and management decision-making processes.** Enterprise systems and data warehouses have made it much easier to supply DSS and ESS with data from many different systems than in the past. The remaining challenge is changing management thinking to use the data that are available to maximum advantage, to develop better reporting categories for measuring firm performance, and to inform new types of decisions. Many managers use the new capabilities in DSS and ESS to obtain the same information as before. Major changes in management thinking will be required to get managers to ask better questions of the data.

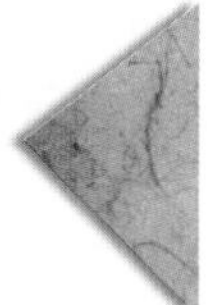

Most information systems described throughout this text help people make decisions in one way or another, but DSS, GDSS, and ESS are part of a special category of information systems that are explicitly designed to enhance managerial decision making. By taking advantage of more accurate firmwide data provided by enterprise systems and the new information technology infrastructure, these systems can support very fine-grained decisions for guiding the firm, coordinating work activities across the enterprise, and responding rapidly to changing markets and customers. Many of these managerial decision-making applications are now Web enabled. This chapter describes the characteristics of each of these types of information systems, showing how each enhances the managerial decision-making process and ultimately the performance of the organization.

DSS, GDSS, and ESS can support decision making in a number of ways. They can automate certain decision procedures (for example, determining the highest price that can be charged for a product to maintain market share or the right amount of materials to maintain in inventory to maximize efficient customer response and product profitability). They can provide information about different aspects of the decision situation and the decision process, such as what opportunities or problems triggered the decision process, what solution alternatives were generated or explored, and how the decision was reached. Finally, they can stimulate innovation in decision making by helping managers question existing decision procedures or explore different solution designs (Dutta, Wierenga, and Dalebout, 1997). The ability to explore the outcomes of alternative organizational scenarios, use precise firmwide information, and provide tools to facilitate group decision processes can help managers make decisions that help the firm achieve its strategic objectives (Forgionne and Kohli, 2000).

**decision-support system (DSS)**
Computer system at the management level of an organization that combines data, analytical tools, and models to support semistructured and unstructured decision making.

## *13.1* Decision-Support Systems (DSS)

As noted in Chapter 2, a **decision-support system (DSS)** assists management decision making by combining data, sophisticated analytical models and tools, and user-friendly software into a single powerful system that can support semistructured or unstructured decision making. A DSS provides users with a flexible set of tools and capabilities for analyzing important blocks of data.

## MIS AND DSS

Some of the earliest applications for supporting management decision making were *management information systems (MIS),* which we introduced in Chapter 2. MIS primarily provide information on the firm's performance to help managers in monitoring and controlling the business. They typically produce fixed, regularly scheduled reports based on data extracted and summarized from the organization's underlying transaction processing systems (TPS). The format from these reports is often specified in advance. A typical MIS report might show a summary of monthly sales for each of the major sales territories of a company. Sometimes MIS reports are exception reports, highlighting only exceptional conditions, such as when the sales quotas for a specific territory fall below an anticipated level or employees who have exceeded their spending limit in a dental care plan. Traditional MIS produced primarily hard copy reports. Today these reports might be available on-line through an intranet, and more MIS reports can be generated on-demand. Table 13-1 provides some examples of MIS applications.

DSS provide new sets of capabilities for nonroutine decisions and user control. An MIS provides managers with reports based on routine flows of data and assists in the general control of the organization, whereas a DSS emphasizes change, flexibility, and a rapid response. With a DSS there is less of an effort to link users to structured information flows and a correspondingly greater emphasis on models, assumptions, ad hoc queries, and display graphics.

Chapter 3 introduced the distinction between structured, semistructured, and unstructured decisions. Structured problems are repetitive and routine, for which known algorithms provide solutions. Unstructured problems are novel and nonroutine, for which there are no algorithms for solutions. One can discuss, decide, and ruminate about unstructured problems, but they are not solved in the sense that one finds an answer to an equation. Semistructured problems fall between structured and unstructured problems. Whereas MIS primarily address structured problems, DSS support semistructured and unstructured problem analysis. Chapter 3 also introduced Simon's description of decision making, which consists of four stages: intelligence, design, choice, and implementation. Decision-support systems are intended to help design and evaluate alternatives and monitor the adoption or implementation process.

## TYPES OF DECISION-SUPPORT SYSTEMS

The earliest DSS tended to draw on small subsets of corporate data and were heavily model driven. Recent advances in computer processing and database technology have expanded the definition of a DSS to include systems that can support decision making by analyzing vast quantities of data, including firmwide data from enterprise systems and transaction data from the Web.

### TABLE 13-1 EXAMPLES OF MIS APPLICATIONS

| Organization | MIS Application |
|---|---|
| California Pizza Kitchen | Inventory Express application "remembers" each restaurant's ordering patterns and compares the amount of ingredients used per menu item to predefined portion measurements established by management. The system identifies restaurants with out-of-line portions and notifies their management so that corrective action can be taken. |
| PharMark | Extranet MIS identifies patients with drug-use patterns that place them at risk for adverse outcomes. |
| Black & Veatch | Intranet MIS tracks construction costs for its various projects across the United States. |
| Taco Bell | TACO (Total Automation of Company Operations) system provides information on food cost, labor cost and period-to-date costs for each restaurant. |

**model-driven DSS**
Primarily stand-alone system that uses some type of model to perform "what-if" and other kinds of analyses.

**data-driven DSS**
A system that supports decision making by allowing users to extract and analyze useful information that was previously buried in large databases.

Today there are two basic types of decision-support systems, model driven and data driven (Dhar and Stein, 1997). **Model-driven DSS** were primarily stand-alone systems isolated from major organizational information systems that used some type of model to perform "what-if" and other kinds of analyses. Such systems were often developed by end-user divisions or groups not under central IS control. Their analysis capabilities were based on a strong theory or model combined with a good user interface that made the model easy to use. IBM's Capacity Optimization Planning System described in the chapter opening vignette and the voyage-estimating DSS described in Chapter 2 are examples of model-driven DSS.

The second type of DSS is a **data-driven DSS.** These systems analyze large pools of data found in major organizational systems. They support decision making by allowing users to extract useful information that previously was buried in large quantities of data. Often data from transaction processing systems (TPS) are collected in data warehouses for this purpose. On-line analytical processing (OLAP) and datamining can then be used to analyze the data. Companies are starting to build data-driven DSS to mine customer data gathered from their Web sites as well as data from enterprise systems.

Traditional database queries answer such questions as, "How many units of product 403 were shipped in November 2000?" OLAP, or multidimensional analysis, supports much more complex requests for information, such as, "Compare sales of product 403 relative to plan by quarter and sales region for the past two years." We described OLAP and multidimensional data analysis in Chapter 7. With OLAP and query-oriented data analysis, users need to have a good idea about the information for which they are looking.

Datamining is more discovery driven. *Datamining,* which was introduced in Chapter 7, provides insights into corporate data that cannot be obtained with OLAP by finding hidden patterns and relationships in large databases and inferring rules from them to predict future behavior. The patterns and rules then can be used to guide decision making and forecast the effect of those decisions. The types of information that can be yielded from datamining include associations, sequences, classifications, clusters, and forecasts.

*Associations* are occurrences linked to a single event. For instance, a study of supermarket purchasing patterns might reveal that when corn chips are purchased, a cola drink is purchased 65 percent of the time, but when there is a promotion, cola is purchased 85 percent of the time. With this information, managers can make better decisions because they have learned the profitability of a promotion.

In *sequences,* events are linked over time. One might find, for example, that if a house is purchased, then a new refrigerator will be purchased within two weeks 65 percent of the time, and an oven will be bought within one month of the home purchase 45 percent of the time.

*Classification* recognizes patterns that describe the group to which an item belongs by examining existing items that have been classified and by inferring a set of rules. For example, businesses such as credit card or telephone companies worry about the loss of steady customers. Classification can help discover the characteristics of customers who are likely to leave and can provide a model to help managers predict who they are so that they can devise special campaigns to retain such customers.

*Clustering* works in a manner similar to classification when no groups have yet been defined. A datamining tool will discover different groupings within data, such as finding affinity groups for bank cards or partitioning a database into groups of customers based on demographics and types of personal investments.

Although these applications involve predictions, *forecasting* uses predictions in a different way. It uses a series of existing values to forecast what other values will be. For example, forecasting might find patterns in data to help managers estimate the future value of continuous variables such as sales figures.

Datamining uses statistical analysis tools as well as neural networks, fuzzy logic, genetic algorithms, or rule-based and other intelligent techniques (described in Chapter 12).

As noted in Chapter 3, it is a mistake to think that only individuals in large organizations make decisions. In fact, most decisions are made collectively. Frequently, decisions must be coordinated with several groups before being finalized. In large organizations, decision making is inherently a group process, and a DSS can be designed to facilitate group decision making. Section 13.2 deals with this issue.

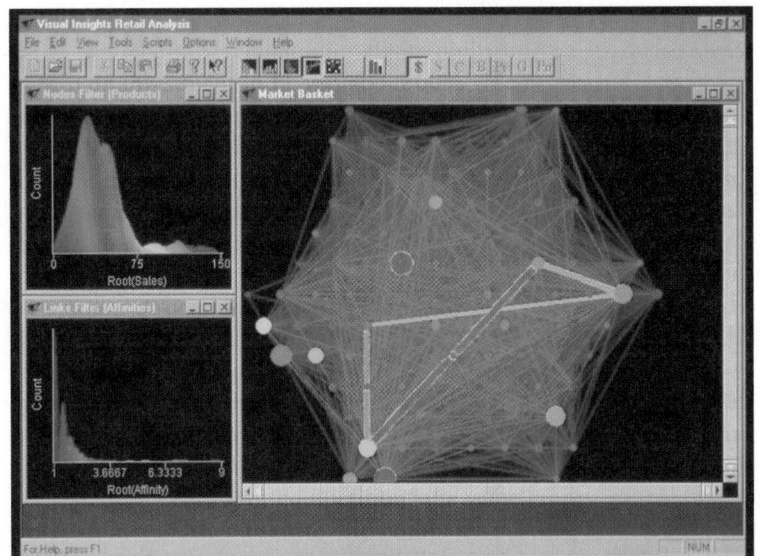


*Lucent Technologies Visual Insights software can help businesses detect patterns in their data. Each dot in this example represents items purchased at one supermarket, with lines drawn between the purchases of individual shoppers. The software shows links between different purchase items, such as cookies and milk.*

## COMPONENTS OF DSS

Figure 13-1 illustrates the components of a DSS. They include a database of data used for query and analysis, a software system with models, datamining and other analytical tools, and a user interface.

The **DSS database** is a collection of current or historical data from a number of applications or groups. It may be a small database residing on a PC that contains a subset of corporate data that has been downloaded and possibly combined with external data. Alternatively, the DSS database may be a massive data warehouse that is continuously updated by major organizational TPS (including enterprise systems and data generated by Web site transactions.) The data in DSS databases are generally extracts or copies of production databases so that using the DSS does not interfere with critical operational systems.

The **DSS software system** contains the software tools that are used for data analysis. It may contain various OLAP tools, datamining tools, or a collection of mathematical and analytical models that easily can be made accessible to the DSS user. A **model** is an abstract representation that illustrates the components or relationships of a phenomenon. A model can be a physical model (such as a model airplane), a mathematical model (such as an equation), or a verbal model (such as a description of a procedure for writing an order). Each decision-support system is built for a specific set of purposes and will make different collections of models available depending on those purposes.

**DSS database**
A collection of current or historical data from a number of applications or groups. Can be a small PC database or a massive data warehouse.

**DSS software system**
Collection of software tools that are used for data analysis, such as OLAP tools, datamining tools, or a collection of mathematical and analytical models.

**model**
An abstract representation that illustrates the components or relationships of a phenomenon.

Perhaps the most common models are libraries of statistical models. Such libraries usually contain the full range of expected statistical functions including means, medians, deviations, and scatter plots. The software has the ability to project future outcomes by analyzing a series of data. Statistical modeling software can be used to help establish relationships, such as relating product sales to differences in age, income, or other factors between communities. Optimization models, often using linear programming, determine optimal resource allocation to maximize or minimize specified variables such as cost or time. A classic use of optimization models is to determine the proper mix of products within a given market to maximize profits.

Forecasting models often are used to forecast sales. The user of this type of model might supply a range of historical data to project future conditions and the sales that might result from those conditions.

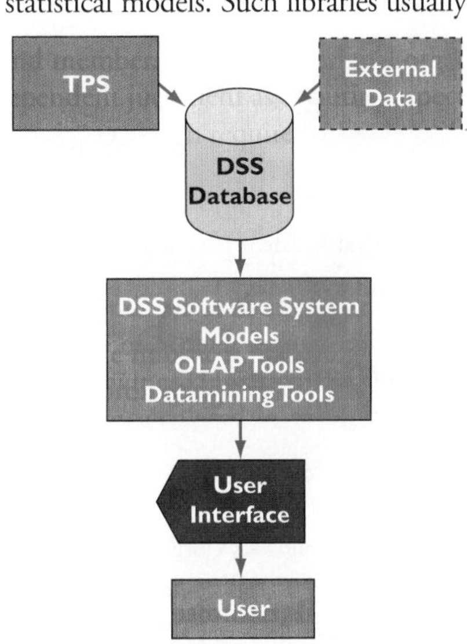


*Figure 13-1* Overview of a decision-support system (DSS). The main components of the DSS are the DSS database, the DSS software system, and the user interface. The DSS database may be a small database residing on a PC or a massive data warehouse.

| | | | | | | |
|---|---|---|---|---|---|---|
| Total fixed costs | 19000 | | | | | |
| Variable cost per unit | 3 | | | | | |
| Average sales price | 17 | | | | | |
| Contribution margin | 14 | | | | | |
| Breakeven point | 1357 | | | | | |
| | | Variable Cost per Unit | | | | |
| **Sales** | 1357 | 2 | 3 | 4 | 5 | 6 |
| **Price** | 14 | 1583 | 1727 | 1900 | 2111 | 2375 |
| | 15 | 1462 | 1583 | 1727 | 1900 | 2111 |
| | 16 | 1357 | 1462 | 1583 | 1727 | 1900 |
| | 17 | 1267 | 1357 | 1462 | 1583 | 1727 |
| | 18 | 1188 | 1267 | 1357 | 1462 | 1583 |

*Figure 13-2* Sensitivity analysis. This table displays the results of a sensitivity analysis of the effect of changing the sales price of a necktie and the cost per unit on the product's breakeven point. It answers the question "What happens to the breakeven point if the sales price and the cost to make each unit increase or decrease?"

The decision-maker could vary those future conditions (entering, for example, a rise in raw materials costs or the entry of a new, low-priced competitor in the market) to determine how these new conditions might affect sales. Companies often use this software to predict the actions of competitors. Model libraries exist for specific functions, such as financial and risk analysis models.

**sensitivity analysis**
Models that ask "what-if" questions repeatedly to determine the impact of changes in one or more factors on outcomes.

Among the most widely used models are **sensitivity analysis** models that ask "what-if" questions repeatedly to determine the impact of changes in one or more factors on outcomes. "What-if" analysis—working forward from known or assumed conditions—allows the user to vary certain values to test results in order to better predict outcomes if changes occur in those values. "What happens if" we raise the price by 5 percent or increase the advertising budget by $100,000? What happens if we keep the price and advertising budget the same? Desktop spreadsheet software, such as Microsoft Excel or Lotus 1-2-3, often is used for this purpose (see Figure 13-2). Backward sensitivity analysis software is used for goal seeking: If I want to sell one million product units next year, how much must I reduce the price of the product?

The DSS user interface permits easy interaction between users of the system and the DSS software tools. A graphic, easy-to-use, flexible user interface supports the dialogue between the user and the DSS. The DSS users can be managers or employees with no patience for learning a complex tool, so the interface must be relatively intuitive. Many DSS today are being built with Web-based interfaces to take advantage of the Web's ease of use, interactivity, and capabilities for personalization and customization. Building successful DSS requires a high level of user participation and, often, the use of prototyping to ensure these requirements are met.

## DSS Applications and the Digital Firm

There are many ways in which DSS can be used to support decision making. Table 13-2 lists examples of DSS in well-known organizations. Both data-driven and model-driven DSS have become very powerful and sophisticated, providing fine-grained information for deci-

### TABLE 13-2 Examples of Decision-Support Systems

| Organization | DSS Application |
|---|---|
| General Accident Insurance | Customer buying patterns and fraud detection |
| Bank of America | Customer profiles |
| Frito-Lay, Inc. | Price, advertising, and promotion selection |
| Burlington Coat Factory | Store location and inventory mix |
| KeyCorp | Targeting direct mail marketing customers |
| National Gypsum | Corporate planning and forecasting |
| Southern Railway | Train dispatching and routing |
| Texas Oil and Gas Corporation | Evaluation of potential drilling sites |
| United Airlines | Flight scheduling, passenger demand forecasting |
| U.S. Department of Defense | Defense contract analysis |

# MANAGEMENT DECISION PROBLEM

## MAKING A CAPITAL BUDGETING DECISION

Your firm, Wilmington Tool and Die Corporation, is considering purchasing four new CAD workstations for a total of $250,000 to improve productivity by translating designs for new dies more efficiently into finished products with fewer defects. You believe that this investment would increase the firm's after-tax income by $60,000 per year over a five-year period by reducing production costs. At the end of five years, your firm plans to sell the workstations for a total of $50,000. The amount the firm would recover when it sells the used equipment is called the salvage value of the equipment.

You would like to evaluate this expenditure to determine whether it is a good investment. To be considered worthwhile a capital expenditure must produce at least the same rate of return on the money invested as if the amount of the investment were invested somewhere else, such as at a bank, at a certain rate of interest specified by the firm.

Review the discussion of capital budgeting methods for information system investments in Chapter 11. The following spreadsheet shows the results of using the net present value method for Wilmington's investment in the new CAD equipment. The total cash flow is the sum of the additional income produced by the investment plus any salvage value of the equipment.

To arrive at the return from the investment in today's dollars, one must first calculate the present value of the total cash flow from this new equipment discounted at the prevailing interest rate for borrowing money. The initial purchase price of the equipment in today's dollars is then subtracted from the present value of the total cash flow from the investment to arrive at the net present value of the investment. If the net present value for the investment is positive, it is a worthwhile investment. If it is negative, the investment should be rejected.

The spreadsheet shows the results of your calculations assuming that interest rates are 8 percent and that the investment is producing $60,000 each year in additional income for the firm. Because investments are highly sensitive to changes in interest rates and economic conditions, you have added a sensitivity analysis to determine whether the machine tool is a good investment under a wide range of situations. The data table shows the impact on net present value if the interest rate and the annual income from using the new equipment are lower or higher than the original assumptions.

1. Should the company make this investment or should it be rejected? Explain your answer.
2. What other variables or circumstances besides interest rate and the additional income produced by the new equipment might also affect the return on investment?
3. What other actions can management take to ensure a positive return on the investment?

**Assumptions**

| | |
|---|---|
| Interest rate | 8.0% |
| Salvage value | $50,000 |
| Annual additional income | 60,000 |

**Wilmington Tool and Die Company Capital Budgeting Analysis**

| | 2001 | 2002 | 2003 | 2004 | 2005 |
|---|---|---|---|---|---|
| Annual additional income | $ 60,000 | $60,000 | $60,000 | $60,000 | $ 60,000 |
| Salvage value | | | | | 50,000 |
| Annual cash flow | $ 60,000 | $60,000 | $60,000 | $60,000 | $110,000 |
| Total cash flow | 350,000 | | | | |
| Present value | 273,592 | | | | |
| Cost of investment | 250,000 | | | | |
| Net present value | 23,592 | | | | |

| | | Interest rates | | | | |
|---|---|---|---|---|---|---|
| | $23,592 | 6.0% | 7.0% | 8.0% | 9.0% | 10.0% |
| | 40,000 | (44,143) | (50,343) | (56,262) | (61,917) | (67,322) |
| | 45,000 | (23,081) | (29,842) | (36,299) | (42,469) | (48,369) |
| **Annual additional income** | 50,000 | (2,019) | (9,341) | (16,335) | (23,021) | (29,415) |
| | 55,000 | 19,043 | 11,160 | 3,628 | (3,573) | (10,461) |
| | 60,000 | 40,105 | 31,661 | 23,592 | 15,876 | 8,493 |
| | 65,000 | 61,167 | 52,162 | 43,555 | 35,324 | 27,447 |
| | 70,000 | 82,228 | 72,663 | 63,519 | 54,772 | 46,401 |

sions that enable the firm to coordinate both internal and external business processes much more precisely. Some of these DSS are helping companies improve supply chain management or plan scenarios for changing business conditions. Some can be used to fine-tune relationships with customers. Some take advantage of the company-wide data provided by enterprise systems. DSS today can also harness the interactive capabilities of the Web to provide decision-support tools to both employees and customers.

To illustrate the range of capabilities of a DSS, we describe some successful DSS applications. San Miguel's supply chain management system, IBM's supply chain management systems described in the Window on Technology, IBM's CAPS manufacturing capacity planning system described in the chapter opening vignette, and Pioneer Natural Resources' business simulation system are examples of model-driven DSS. Royal Bank of Canada's customer segmentation system described in the Window on Organizations and Della.com's customer analysis system are examples of data-driven DSS. We also examine some applications of geographic information systems (GIS), a special category of DSS for visualizing data geographically.

## DSS for Supply Chain Management

Supply chain decisions involve determining "who, what, when, and where" from purchasing and transporting materials and parts through manufacturing products and distributing and delivering those products to customers. DSS can help managers examine this complex chain comprehensively and search among a huge number of alternatives for the combinations that are most efficient and cost effective. The prime management goal might be to reduce overall costs while increasing the speed and accuracy of filling customer orders. The Window on Technology illustrates how IBM uses DSS for supply chain management.

San Miguel Corporation uses DSS for supply chain management to help it distribute more than 300 products, such as beer, liquor, dairy products, and feedgrains to every corner of the Philippine archipelago. A Production Load Allocation system determines the quantity of products to produce for each bottling line and how production output should be assigned to warehouses. It balances ordering, carrying, and stockout costs while considering frequency of deliveries and minimum order quantities, saving the company $180,000 in inventory costs in one year. The DSS can generate optimal production allocation plans based on either minimizing cost or maximizing profit. San Miguel's system also helps it reassign deliveries and warehouse facilities to counter imbalances in capacity and demand. Managers used information from the system to move more of San Miguel's delivery business to third-party logistics providers so that its own delivery trucks could be used more efficiently. The company found that it could reduce the number of routes serving sales districts in metropolitan Manila alone by 43 percent (del Rosanò, 1999).

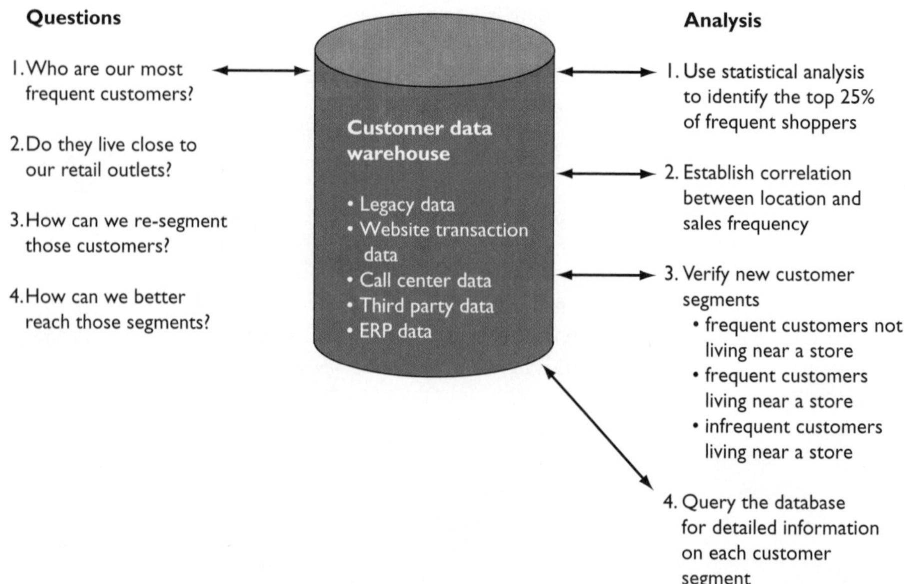


*Figure 13-3* DSS for customer analysis and segmentation. This DSS allows companies to segment their customer base with a high level of precision where it can be used to drive a marketing campaign. Based on the results of datamining, a firm can develop specific marketing campaigns for each customer segment. For example, it could target frequent customers living near a store with coupons for products of interest and with rewards for frequent shoppers.

## OPTIMIZING THE SUPPLY CHAIN AT IBM

In 1994, IBM began a global supply chain reengineering initiative to reduce inventory levels yet maintain enough inventory in the supply chain to respond quickly to customer demands. IBM Research developed an advanced supply chain optimization and simulation tool called the asset management tool (AMT) for this purpose.

AMT deals with a range of entities in the supply chain, including targets for inventory and customer service levels, product structure, channel assembly, supplier terms and conditions, and lead-time reduction. Users of AMT can evaluate supply chains in terms of financial trade-offs associated with various configurations and operational policies.

The IBM Personal Systems Group (PSG) used AMT to reduce supply chain costs to cope with the large volumes, dropping prices, and slim profit margins in the personal computer market. PSG was able to reduce overall pipeline inventory by more than 50 percent in 1997 and 1998. The system helped PSG reduce payments made to distributors and resellers to compensate for product price reductions by more than $750 million in 1998. PSG's cycle time from component procurement to product sale was reduced by four to six weeks, bringing reductions of 5 to 7 percent in overall product cost.

IBM's AS/400 midrange computer division used AMT to analyze and quantify the impact of product complexity. Information from the system helped IBM reduce the number of product features, substitute alternate parts, and delay customization. AMT also provided an analysis of the trade-off between serviceability and inventory in IBM's QuickShip Program, helping the company reduce operational costs by up to 50 percent.

According to Jean-Pierre Briant, former IBM vice president for Integrated Supply Chain, "AMT helps us understand our extended supply chain, from our suppliers' suppliers to our customers' customers." IBM has been able to use AMT to help its business partners improve management of their supply chains. For instance, supply chain analysis helped Piancor, one of IBM's major distributors, identify opportunities for optimizing the product flow between the two companies.

IBM's Microelectronics division improved its supply chain management by using a combination of software tools. This division needed to change its supply chain processes as it shifted from supplying semiconductors and packaged goods exclusively to IBM's PC and server divisions to supplying parts to outside organizations such as Advanced Micro Devices, Dell Computer, Cisco Systems, and Qualcomm. The division replaced an old homegrown system with SAP's manufacturing resource planning software to capture and store orders and track current inventory. It installed Aspen Technology's Mimi toolkit to schedule the production of products and match demand with available resources. The Microelectronics division also started transmitting purchase orders, shipping dates, logistics, and payment information to customers over the Internet.

**To Think About:** How did the systems described here help IBM promote its business strategy? How did they change the way IBM ran its business?

*Sources:* Brenda Dietrich, Nick Donofrio, Grace Lin, and Jane Snowdon, "Big Benefits for Big Blue," *OR/MS Today*, June 2000; and Judy Democker, "Businesses Seek to Cut Weak Links from Supply Chains," *Information Week*, March 6, 2000.

## DSS for Customer Relationship Management

DSS for customer relationship management use datamining to guide decisions about pricing, customer retention, market share, and new revenue streams. These systems typically consolidate customer information from a variety of systems into massive data warehouses and use various analytical tools to slice it into tiny segments for one-to-one marketing (see Figure 13-3). The Window on Organizations illustrates how the Royal Bank of Canada benefited from using a DSS for this purpose.

Some of these DSS for customer relationship management use data gathered from the Web. Chapter 9 described how each action a visitor takes when visiting a particular Web site can be captured on that Web site's log. Companies can store these data in Webhouses (see Chapter 9) and mine these data to answer questions, such as what customers are purchasing and what promotions are generating the most traffic. The results can help companies tailor marketing programs more effectively, redesign Web sites to optimize traffic, and create personalized buying experiences for Web site visitors. Upon analyzing its Website traffic data, SmarterKids.com learned that many visitors left frustrated because their searches for popular toys such as Pokemon ended with a message that "no results were found." The company then redesigned its Website to automatically list some of the products it sells.

Other DSS combine Web site transaction data with data from enterprise systems. Della.com, a gift registry and wish-list aggregator, feeds sales order data from its enterprise system and Web logs into a customer data warehouse. It uses E.piphany's marketing analysis

## Royal Bank Banks on a Data-driven DSS

"Gone are the days where we had mass buckets of customers that would receive the same treatment or same offer on a monthly basis," says Shauneen Bruder, the Royal Bank of Canada's senior vice president for North America. Instead of sending customers the same marketing information, Royal Bank has developed a DSS for customer segmentation that tailors messages to very small groups of people and offers them products, services, and prices that are likely to appeal to them. Royal Bank's customer segmentation is so effective that it can achieve a response rate as high as 30 percent to its marketing campaigns, compared to an average of 3 percent for the banking industry.

The technology behind this DSS system is based on consolidating data from various systems in the organization into a data warehouse. The Royal Bank's main customer database is its marketing information file (MIF). The database even contains customer transaction data. MIF is fed data from every document a customer fills out as well as data from checking accounts, credit cards, and the Royal Bank's enterprise and billing systems. Bank analysts have a range of tools at their fingertips as they access MIF, including SAS data analysis software.

By querying the database, analysts can identify customers based on the products they might buy and the likelihood they will leave the bank and combine these data with demographic data from external sources. Royal Bank can then identify one or a group of profitable customers who appear to be getting ready to leave the bank. To identify such customers, the bank examines the customer's bank balance (recently being kept low), credit card payments (also reduced in amount and perhaps paid later than in the past), and deposits (which have become sporadic). These signs could indicate a customer who is recently unemployed, but they could also highlight a profitable customer preparing to switch to another bank. The Royal Bank, using its vast stored data, can quickly learn that it has profited from this customer's business. They do this by examining past ongoing balances, use of the Royal Bank's line of credit, and the car loan or mortgage from the bank. They also deduce from lifestyle and family data that this customer is probably at a stage in life that will need more bank loans and other bank services.

Having identified such customer(s), the bank's marketing department might put together a tempting package of banking services at a low price, such as Internet banking, bill payment, unlimited ATM access, and a limited number of branch transactions, all for a fee of $9.95 per month. The bank knows that customers who use such service packages stay with the bank for about three years longer than do those who have no such package. If the customer is not satisfied with the specific package, marketing can even tailor a package specifically for the customer. Royal Bank is linking its customer database and legacy systems to the Web so that it can offer customers service packages instantly on-line as they access their accounts over the Internet.

**To Think About:** How did Royal Bank's customer DSS change the way it conducted its business?

*Sources:* Meridith Wilson, "Slices of Life," *CIO Magazine*, August 15, 2000; and Alan Radding, "Analyze Your Customers," *Datamation*, September 25, 2000.

software to identify customer trends, such as where customers are coming from, how long they stay on the site, and what advertising vehicles draw their most profitable customers. Della.com had started out as a wedding registry, but the system showed that its high-end customers were more seasonal than originally anticipated. Acting on this information management turned the Web site into a general gift registry (Stackpole, 2000).

## DSS for Simulating Business Scenarios

We have described the capabilities of model-driven DSS for performing "what-if" analyses of problems in specific areas of the firm. DSS with very powerful "what-if" and modeling capabilities have been developed for modeling entire business scenarios. Such DSS use information from both internal and external sources to help managers tune strategy to a constantly changing array of conditions and variables.

In the oil and gas industry, for example, there are many variables associated with running an energy company, including development and production costs and the ratio of gas and oil in a field. The number and complex relationship among these variables makes it difficult for managers to determine the cost effectiveness of their business decisions. Pioneer Natural Resources (PNR) in Las Colinas, Texas, decided to create a DSS that could provide more precise information for those decisions.

In 1995, PNR executives started identifying all of the management variables and diagrammed all of the business processes in their company to create a model that could show the impact on the business when one or more of those variables changed. The company built a prototype DSS using Powersim, a simulation development tool from Powersim Corporation in Herndon, Virginia. PNR executives first tested the prototype to simulate PNR's volatile Gulf Coast division, which had very long production time lines.

The company primarily uses Powersim to create a model for scenario planning and what-if analyses. For example, by modeling different scenarios with Powersim, PNR management can determine how much more to pay a service company to put a well into production earlier and yet still earn a profit. Powersim runs on a Windows-based PC and uses Microsoft Excel spreadsheet software and Access database software for the input and output of business variables.

The company believes that each of its five divisions could potentially raise revenues by 25 to 40 percent using Powersim to model scenarios and adjust business variables. In addition, the simulation technology provides management with more control by helping managers determine the specific actions necessary to arrive at a desired business result or model the result of each business decision under consideration (Baldwin, 1998).

## Geographic Information Systems (GIS)

**Geographic information systems (GIS)** are a special category of DSS that can analyze and display data for planning and decision making using digitized maps. The software can assemble, store, manipulate, and display geographically referenced information, tying data to points, lines, and areas on a map. GIS can thus be used to support decisions that require knowledge about the geographic distribution of people or other resources in scientific research, resource management, and development planning. For example, GIS might be used to help state and local governments calculate emergency response times to natural disasters or to help banks identify the best locations for installing new branches or ATM terminals. GIS tools have become affordable even for small businesses, and some can be used on the Web.

**geographic information system (GIS)**
System with software that can analyze and display data using digitized maps to enhance planning and decision making.

GIS have modeling capabilities, allowing managers to change data and automatically revise business scenarios to find better solutions. Johanna Dairies of Union, New Jersey, used GIS software to display its customers on a map and then design the most efficient delivery routes, saving the company $100,000 annually for each route that was eliminated. Sonny's Bar-B-Q, the Gainesville, Florida-based restaurant chain, used GIS with federal and local census data on median age, household income, total population, and population distribution to help management decide where to open new restaurants. The company's growth plan specifies that it will only expand into regions where barbecue food is very popular but where the number of barbecue restaurants is very small. Sonny's restaurants must be at least seven miles away from each other. Quaker Oats has used GIS to display and analyze sales and customer data by store locations. This information helps the company determine the best

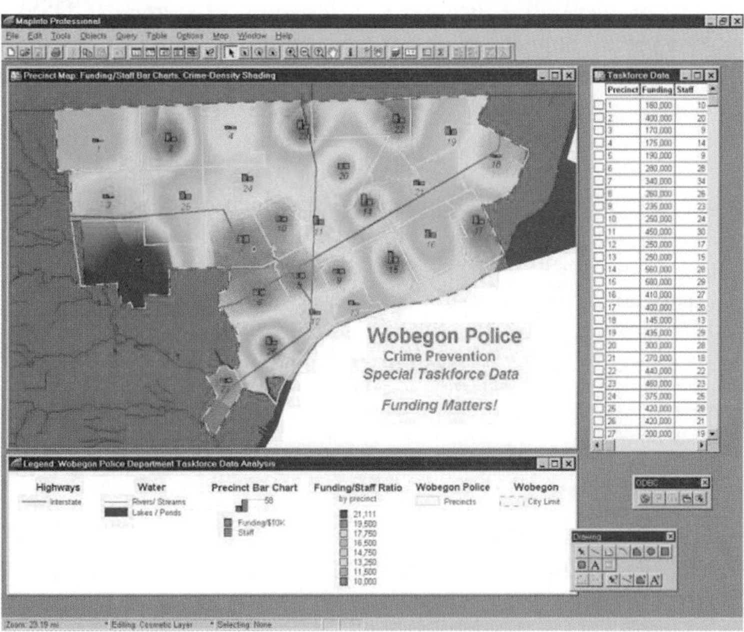


*Geographic information system (GIS) software presents and analyzes data geographically, tying data to points, lines, and areas on a map. This map can help decision makers with crime analysis by mapping each incident and relating crime hotspots to distribution of police staff.*

## TABLE 13-3 EXAMPLES OF WEB-BASED DSS

| DSS | Description |
|---|---|
| Prescription Management Solutions | HMO clients can examine and manipulate pharmaceutical purchase information over the Web to analyze prescription drug buying patterns. They can use predefined on-line reports or ad hoc information requests to identify trends, forecast pharmacy expenditures, and design benefits to control pharmacy expenses. |
| General Electric Plastics | Web site provides a searchable repository of product-specification information that can be updated weekly. Visitors can use on-line, continuous-simulation models that automatically generate graphs and diagrams in response to customer inputs. (For example, a simulation model might show how a particular plastic would behave at very high temperatures.) An e-mail capability allows visitors to forward technical questions to engineers, who then contact the customer. |
| Fidelity Investments | Web site features an on-line, interactive decision-support application to help clients make decisions about investment savings plans and investment portfolio allocations. The application allows visitors to experiment with numerous "what-if" scenarios to design investment savings plans for retirement or a child's college education. If the user enters information about his or her finances, time horizon, and tolerance for risk, the system will suggest appropriate portfolios of mutual funds. The application performs the required number-crunching and displays the changing return on investment as the user alters these assumptions. |

product mix for each retail store that carries Quaker Oats products and design advertising campaigns targeted specifically to each store's customers.

### WEB-BASED CUSTOMER DECISION-SUPPORT SYSTEMS

The growth of electronic commerce has encouraged many companies to develop DSS where customers and employees can take advantage of Internet information resources and Web capabilities for interactivity and personalization. DSS based on the Web and the Internet can support decision making by providing on-line access to various databases and information pools along with software for data analysis. Some of these DSS are targeted toward management, but many have been developed to attract customers by providing information and tools to assist their decision making as they select products and services. Companies are finding that deciding which products and services to purchase has become increasingly information intensive. People are now using more information from multiple sources to make purchasing decisions (such as purchasing a car or computer) before they interact with the product or sales staff. **Customer decision-support systems (CDSS)** support the decision-making process of an existing or potential customer.

**customer decision-support system (CDSS)**
System to support the decision-making process of an existing or potential customer.

People interested in purchasing a product or service can use Internet search engines, intelligent agents, on-line catalogs, Web directories, newsgroup discussions, e-mail, and other tools to help them locate the information they need to help with their decision. Information brokers, such as Travelocity, described in Chapter 4, are also sources of summarized, structured information for specific products or industries and may provide models for evaluating the information. Companies also have developed specific customer Web sites where all the information, models, or other analytical tools for evaluating alternatives are concentrated in one location. Web-based DSS have become especially popular in the financial services area because so many people are trying to manage their own assets and retirement savings. Table 13-3 lists some examples.

## 13.2 GROUP DECISION-SUPPORT SYSTEMS (GDSS)

Early DSS focused largely on supporting individual decision making. However, because so much work is accomplished in groups within organizations, system developers and scholars began to focus on how computers can support group and organizational decision making. A new category of systems developed known as group decision-support systems (GDSS).

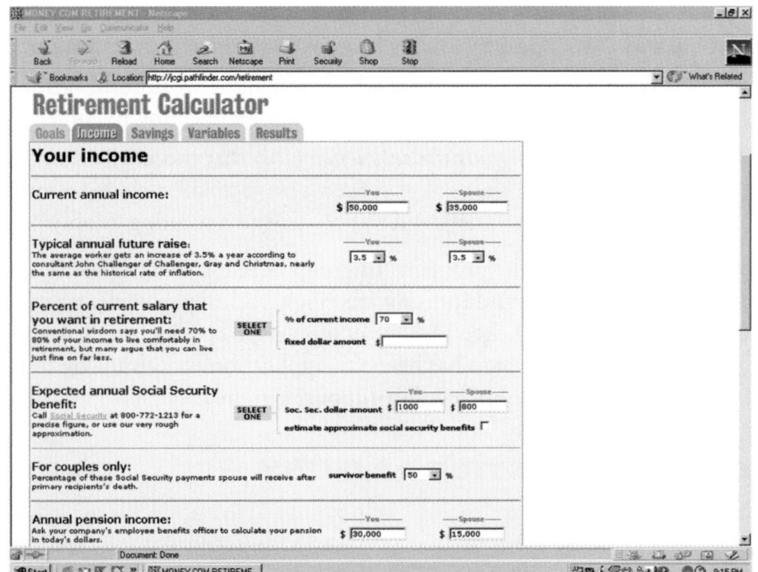


*The Money.com Web site features on-line tools to help visitors make decisions about retirement planning options. DSS based on the Web can provide information from multiple sources and analytical tools to help potential customers select products and services.*

## WHAT IS A GDSS?

A **group decision-support system (GDSS)** is an interactive computer-based system to facilitate the solution of unstructured problems by a set of decision-makers working together as a group (DeSanctis and Gallupe, 1987).

**group decision-support system (GDSS)** An interactive computer-based system to facilitate the solution to unstructured problems by a set of decision-makers working together as a group.

Groupware and Web-based tools for videoconferencing and electronic meetings described earlier in this text can support some group decision processes, but their focus is primarily on communication. This section focuses on the tools and technologies geared explicitly toward group decision making. GDSS were developed in response to a growing concern over the quality and effectiveness of meetings. The underlying problems in group decision making have been the explosion of decision-maker meetings, the growing length of those meetings, and the increased number of attendees. Estimates on the amount of a manager's time spent in meetings range from 35 to 70 percent.

Meeting facilitators, organizational development professionals, and information systems scholars have been focusing on this issue and have identified a number of discrete meeting elements that need to be addressed (Grobowski et al., 1990; Kraemer and King, 1988; Nunamaker et al., 1991). Among these elements are the following:

1. *Improved preplanning* to make meetings more effective and efficient.
2. *Increased participation,* so that all attendees will be able to contribute fully even if the number of attendees is large. Free riding (attending the meeting but not contributing) must also be addressed.
3. *Open, collaborative meeting atmosphere,* in which attendees from various organizational levels feel free to contribute. The lower-level attendees must be able to participate without fear of being judged by their management; higher-status participants must be able to participate without having their presence or ideas dominate the meeting and result in unwanted conformity.
4. *Criticism-free idea generation,* enabling attendees to contribute without undue fear of being personally criticized.
5. *Evaluation objectivity,* creating an atmosphere in which an idea will be evaluated on its merits rather than on the basis of the source of the idea.
6. *Idea organization and evaluation,* which require keeping the focus on the meeting objectives, finding efficient ways to organize the many ideas that can be generated in a brainstorming session, and evaluating those ideas not only on their merits but also within appropriate time constraints.
7. *Setting priorities and making decisions,* which require finding ways to encompass the thinking of all the attendees in making these judgments.

8. *Documentation of meetings,* so that attendees will have as complete and organized a record of the meeting as may be needed to continue the work of the project.
9. *Access to external information,* which will allow significant, factual disagreements to be settled in a timely fashion, thus enabling the meeting to continue and be productive.
10. *Preservation of "organizational memory,"* so that those who do not attend the meeting can also work on the project. Often a project will include teams at different locations who will need to understand the content of a meeting at only one of the affected sites.

One response to the problems of group decision making has been the adoption of new methods of organizing and running meetings. Techniques such as facilitated meetings, brainstorming, and criticism-free idea generation have become popular and are now accepted as standard. Another response has been the application of technology to the problems resulting in the emergence of group decision-support systems.

## CHARACTERISTICS OF GDSS

How can information technology help groups arrive at decisions? Scholars have identified at least three basic elements of a GDSS: hardware, software tools, and people. *Hardware* refers to the conference facility itself, including the room, the tables, and the chairs. Such a facility must be physically laid out in a manner that supports group collaboration. It must include some electronic hardware, such as electronic display boards, as well as audiovisual, computer, and networking equipment.

A wide range of *software tools,* including tools for organizing ideas, gathering information, ranking and setting priorities, and other aspects of collaborative work are being used to support decision-making meetings. We describe these tools in the next section. *People* refers not only to the participants but also to a trained facilitator and often to a staff that supports the hardware and software. Together these elements have led to the creation of a range of different kinds of GDSS, from simple electronic boardrooms to elaborate collaboration laboratories. In a collaboration laboratory, individuals work on their own desktop PCs or workstations. Their input is integrated on a file server and is viewable on a common screen at the front of the room; in most systems the integrated input is also viewable on the individual participant's computer screen. See Figure 13-4 for an illustration of an actual GDSS collaborative meeting room.

## GDSS SOFTWARE TOOLS

Some features of groupware tools for collaborative work described in Chapters 6 and 12 can be used to support group decision making. There also are specific GDSS software tools for supporting group meetings. These tools were originally developed for meetings in which all participants are in the same room, but they also can be used for networked meetings in which participants are in different locations. Specific GDSS software tools include the following:

***Figure 13-4*** The Gjensidige Insurance collaborative meeting room. There is one microphone for every two seats and a speaker system on the wall. This equipment is used for same-time meetings between Gjensidige's offices in Oslo and Trondheim.
*Source:* 

*Electronic questionnaires* aid the organizers in premeeting planning by identifying issues of concern and by helping to ensure that key planning information is not overlooked.

*Electronic brainstorming tools* allow individuals simultaneously and anonymously to contribute ideas on the topics of the meeting.

*Idea organizers* facilitate the organized integration and synthesis of ideas generated during brainstorming.

*Questionnaire tools* support the facilitators and group leaders as they gather information before and during the process of setting priorities.

*Tools for voting or setting priorities* make available a range of methods from simple voting, to ranking in order, to a range of weighted techniques for setting priorities or voting (see Figure 13-5).

*Stakeholder identification and analysis tools* use structured approaches to evaluate the impact of an emerging proposal on the organization and to identify stakeholders and evaluate the potential impact of those stakeholders on the proposed project.

*Policy formation tools* provide structured support for developing agreement on the wording of policy statements.

*Group dictionaries* document group agreement on definitions of words and terms central to the project.

Additional tools are available, such as group outlining and writing tools, software that stores and reads project files, and software that allows the attendees to view internal operational data stored by the organization's production computer systems.

## Overview of a GDSS Meeting

An **electronic meeting system (EMS)** is a type of collaborative GDSS that uses information technology to make group meetings more productive by facilitating communication as well as decision making. It supports any activity in which people come together, whether at the same place at the same time or in different places at different times (Dennis et al., 1988; Nunamaker et al., 1991). IBM has a number of EMSs installed at various sites. Each attendee has a workstation. The workstations are networked and are connected to the facilitator's console, which serves as both the facilitator's workstation and control panel and the meeting's file server. All data that the attendees forward from their workstations to the group are collected and saved on the file server. The facilitator is able to project computer images onto the projection screen at the front center of the room. The facilitator also has an overhead projector available. Whiteboards are visible on either side of the projection screen. Many electronic meeting rooms are arranged in a semicircle and are tiered in legislative style to accommodate a large number of attendees.

**electronic meeting system (EMS)**
A collaborative GDSS that uses information technology to make group meetings more productive by facilitating communication as well as decision making. Supports meetings at the same place and time or at different places and times.

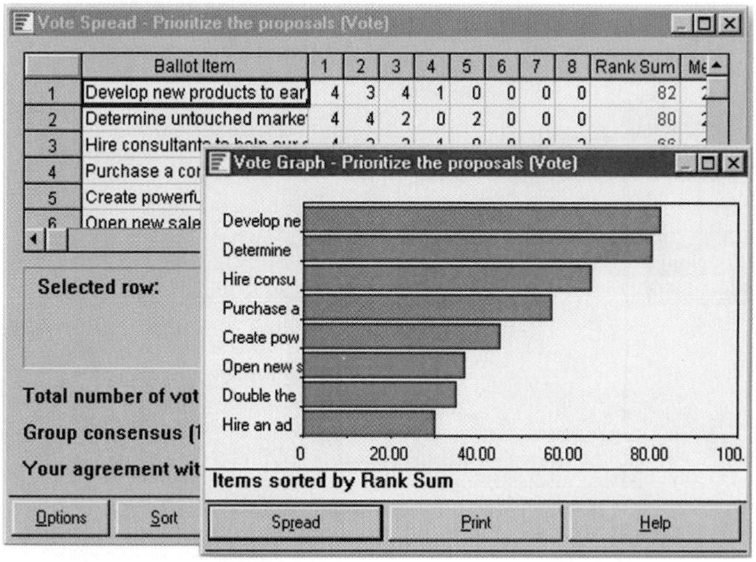

***Figure 13-5*** GDSS software tools. The Ventana Corporation's Group Systems electronic meeting software helps people create, share, record, organize, and evaluate ideas in meetings, between offices, or around the world.

The facilitator controls the use of tools during the meeting, often selecting from a large tool box that is part of the organization's GDSS. Tool selection is part of the premeeting planning process. Which tools are selected depends on the subject matter, the goals of the meeting, and the facilitation methodology the facilitator will use.

Attendees have full control over their own desktop computers. An attendee is able to view the agenda (and other planning documents), look at the integrated screen (or screens as the session progresses), use ordinary desktop PC tools (such as a word processor or a spreadsheet), tap into production data that have been made available, or work on the screen associated with the current meeting step and tool (such as a brainstorming screen). However, no one can view anyone else's screen so participants' work is confidential until it is released to the file server for integration with the work of others. All input to the file server is anonymous—at each step everyone's input to the file server (brainstorming ideas, idea evaluation and criticism, comments, voting, etc.) can be seen by all attendees on the integrated screens, but no information is available to identify the source of specific inputs. Attendees enter their data simultaneously rather than in round-robin fashion as is done in meetings that have little or no electronic systems support.

Figure 13-6 shows the sequence of activities at a typical EMS meeting. For each activity it also indicates the type of tools used and the output of those tools. During the meeting all input to the integrated screens is saved on the file server. As a result, when the meeting is completed, a full record of the meeting (both raw material and resultant output) is available to the attendees and can be made available to anyone else with a need for access.

## How GDSS Can Enhance Group Decision Making

GDSS are being used more widely, so we are able to understand some of their benefits and evaluate some of the tools. We look again at how a GDSS affects the 10 group meeting issues raised earlier.

1. *Improved preplanning.* Electronic questionnaires, supplemented by word processors, outlining software, and other desktop PC software, can structure planning, thereby improving it. The availability of the planning information at the actual meeting also can serve to enhance the quality of the meeting. Experts seem to believe that these tools add significance and emphasis to meeting preplanning.
2. *Increased participation.* Studies show that in traditional decision-making meetings without GDSS support the optimal meeting size is three to five attendees. Beyond

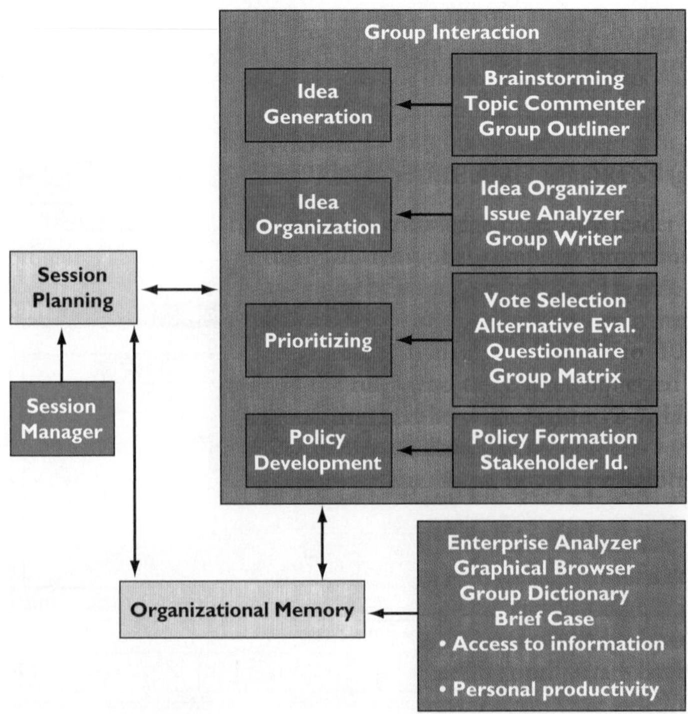


*Figure 13-6* Group system tools. The sequence of activities and collaborative support tools used in an electronic meeting system (EMS) facilitates communication among attendees and generates a full record of the meeting.
*Source:* From Nunamaker et al., "Electronic Meeting Systems to Support Group Work" in *Communications of the ACM*, July 1991. Reprinted by permission.

that size, the meeting process begins to break down. Using GDSS software, studies show the meeting size can increase while productivity also increases. One reason for this is that attendees contribute simultaneously rather than one at a time, which makes more efficient use of the meeting time. Interviews of GDSS meeting attendees indicate that the quality of participation is higher than in traditional meetings.

3. *Open, collaborative meeting atmosphere.* A GDSS contributes to a more collaborative atmosphere in several ways. First, anonymity of input is essentially guaranteed. Individuals need not be afraid of being judged by their boss for contributing a possibly offbeat idea. Second, anonymity reduces or eliminates the deadening effect that often occurs when high-status individuals contribute. And third, the numbing pressures of social cues are reduced or eliminated.
4. *Criticism-free idea generation.* Anonymity ensures that attendees can contribute without fear of personally being criticized or of having their ideas rejected because of the identity of the contributor. Several studies have shown that interactive GDSS meetings generate more ideas and more satisfaction with those ideas than verbally interactive meetings (Nunamaker et al., 1991). GDSS can help reduce unproductive interpersonal conflict (Miranda and Bostrum, 1993–1994).
5. *Evaluation objectivity.* Anonymity prevents criticism of the source of ideas, thus supporting an atmosphere in which attendees focus on evaluating the ideas themselves. The same anonymity allows participants to detach from their own ideas, so they are able to view them from a critical perspective. Evidence suggests that evaluation in an anonymous atmosphere increases the free flow of critical feedback and even stimulates the generation of new ideas during the evaluation process.
6. *Idea organization and evaluation.* GDSS software tools used for this purpose are structured and are based on methodology. They usually allow individuals to organize and then submit their results to the group (still anonymously). The group then iteratively modifies and develops the organized ideas until a document is completed. Attendees generally have viewed this approach as productive.
7. *Setting priorities and making decisions.* Anonymity helps lower-level participants have their positions taken into consideration along with the higher-level attendees.
8. *Documentation of meetings.* Evidence at IBM indicates that postmeeting use of the data is crucial. Attendees use the data to continue their dialogues after the meetings, to discuss the ideas with those who did not attend, and even to make presentations (Grobowski et al., 1990). Some tools enable the user to zoom in to more details on specific information.
9. *Access to external information.* Often a great deal of meeting time is devoted to factual disagreements. More experience with GDSS will indicate whether GDSS technology reduces this problem.
10. *Preservation of "organizational memory."* Specific tools have been developed to facilitate access to the data generated during a GDSS meeting, allowing nonattendees to locate needed information after the meeting. The documentation of a meeting by one group at one site has also successfully been used as input to another meeting on the same project at another site. GDSS could be further enhanced to integrate meeting memory with other organizational memory and supply this information to other parts of the organization (Schwabe, 1999).

Studies to date suggest that GDSS meetings can be more effective, make more efficient use of time, and produce the desired results in fewer meetings. GDSS seem most useful for tasks involving idea generation, complex problems, and large groups (Fjermestad and Hiltz, 2000–2001; 1998–1999). One problem with understanding the value of GDSS is their complexity. A GDSS can be configured in an almost infinite variety of ways. In addition, the effectiveness of the tools will partially depend the facilitator's effectiveness, the quality of the planning, the cooperation of the attendees, and the appropriateness of tools selected for different types of meetings. GDSS can enable groups to exchange more information, but can't always help participants process the information effectively or reach better decisions (Dennis, 1996).

Researchers have noted that the design of an electronic meeting system and its technology is only one of a number of contingencies that affect the outcome of group meetings. Other factors, including the nature of the group, the task, the manner in which the problem is presented to the group, and the organizational context (including the organization's culture and environment) also affect the process of group meetings and meeting outcomes (Hilmer and Dennis, 2000–2001; Dennis et al., 1999; Fjermestad, 1998; Caouette and O'Connor, 1998; Dennis et al., 1988, 1996; Nunamaker et al., 1991; Watson, Ho, and Raman, 1994). New types of group support systems with easy-to-use, Web-based interfaces and multimedia capabilities may provide additional benefits.

## 13.3 Executive Support in the Enterprise

**executive support system (ESS)**
Information system at the strategic level of an organization designed to address unstructured decision making through advanced graphics and communications.

We have described how DSS and GDSS help managers make unstructured and semistructured decisions. **Executive support systems (ESS)** also help managers with unstructured problems, focusing on the information needs of senior management. Combining data from internal and external sources, ESS create a generalized computing and communications environment that can be focused and applied to a changing array of problems. ESS help senior executives monitor organizational performance, track activities of competitors, spot problems, identify opportunities, and forecast trends.

### The Role of Executive Support Systems in the Organization

Before ESS, it was common for executives to receive numerous fixed-format reports, often hundreds of pages every month (or even every week). Today, an ESS can bring together data from all parts of the organization and allow managers to select, access, and tailor them as needed using easy-to-use desktop analytical tools and on-line data displays. Use of the systems has migrated down several organizational levels so that the executive and any subordinates are able to look at the same data in the same way.

Today's systems try to avoid the problem of data overload so common in paper reports, because the data can be filtered or viewed in graphic format (if the user so chooses). ESS systems have the ability to **drill down,** moving from a piece of summary data to lower and lower levels of detail. The ability to drill down is useful not only to senior executives but to employees at lower levels of the organization who need to analyze data. OLAP tools for analyzing large databases are one source of this capability.

**drill down**
The ability to move from summary data down to lower and lower levels of detail.

A major challenge of building executive support systems has been to integrate data from systems designed for very different purposes so that senior executives can review organizational performance from a firmwide perspective. Often data critical to the senior executive had been unavailable. For example, sales data coming from an order-entry transaction processing system might not be linked to marketing information, a linkage the executive would find useful. In the traditional firm, which typically had hundreds or even thousands of incompatible systems, pulling such information together and making sense out of it was a major task. When the information was assembled, it was likely to be out of date, incomplete, and inaccurate. Making decisions under these conditions was like a dart game with the bull's-eye swinging on a pendulum. Today, properly configured and implemented enterprise systems can provide managers with timely, comprehensive, and accurate firmwide information. Executive support systems based on such data can be considered logical extensions of enterprise system functionality.

External data, including data from the Web, now are easily available in many ESS as well. Executives need a wide range of external data from current stock market news to competitor information, industry trends, and even projected legislative action. Through their ESS, many managers have access to news services, financial market databases, economic information, and whatever other public data they may require.

Contemporary ESS include tools for modeling and analysis. With only a minimum of experience, most managers find they can use these tools to create graphic comparisons of data by time, region, product, price range, and so on. (Whereas DSS use such tools primarily for modeling and analysis in a fairly narrow range of decision situations, ESS use them primarily to provide status information about organizational performance.)

## Developing ESS

ESS are executive systems, and must be designed so that high-level managers and others can use them without much training. One area that merits special attention is the determination of executive information requirements. ESS need to have some facility for environmental scanning. A key information requirement of managers at the strategic level is the capability to detect signals of problems in the organizational environment that indicate strategic threats and opportunities (Walls et al., 1992). The ESS needs to be designed so that both external and internal sources of information can be used for environmental scanning purposes.

ESS potentially could give top executives the capability of examining other managers' work without their knowledge, so there may be some resistance to ESS at lower levels of the organization. Implementation of ESS should be carefully managed to neutralize such opposition (see Chapter 11).

Cost justification presents a different type of problem with an ESS. Because much of an executive's work is unstructured, how does one quantify benefits for a system that primarily supports such unstructured work? An ESS often is justified in advance by the intuitive feeling that it will pay for itself (Watson et al., 1991). If ESS benefits can ever be quantified, it is only after the system is operational.

# Benefits of Executive Support Systems

Much of the value of ESS is found in their flexibility. These systems put data and tools in the hands of executives without addressing specific problems or imposing solutions. Executives are free to shape the problems as necessary, using the system as an extension of their own thinking processes. These are not decision-making systems; they are tools to aid executives in making decisions.

The most visible benefit of ESS is their ability to analyze, compare, and highlight trends. The easy use of graphics allows the user to look at more data in less time with greater clarity and insight than paper-based systems can provide. In the past, executives obtained the same information by taking up days and weeks of their staffs' valuable time. By using ESS, those staffs and the executives themselves are freed up for more creative analysis and decision making in their jobs. ESS capabilities for drilling down and highlighting trends also may enhance the quality of such analysis and can speed up decision making (Leidner and Elam, 1993–1994).

Executives are using ESS to monitor performance more successfully in their own areas of responsibility. Some companies are using these systems to monitor key performance indicators for the entire firm and to measure firm performance against changes in the external environment. The timeliness and availability of the data result in needed actions being identified and taken earlier. Problems can be handled before they become too damaging; opportunities also can be identified earlier. These systems can thus help organizations move toward a "sense and respond" strategy.

A well-designed ESS could dramatically improve management performance and increase upper management's span of control. Immediate access to so much data allows executives to better monitor activities of lower units reporting to them. That very monitoring ability could allow decision making to be decentralized and to take place at lower-operating levels. Executives are often willing to push decision making further down into the organization as long as they can be assured that all is going well. Alternatively, executive support systems based on enterprise-wide data could potentially increase management centralization, enabling senior executives to monitor the performance of subordinates across the company and direct them to take appropriate action when conditions change.

# Executive Support Systems and the Digital Firm

To illustrate the ways in which an ESS can enhance management decision making, we now describe important types of ESS applications for gathering business intelligence and monitoring corporate performance, including ESS based on enterprise systems.

## ESS for Business Intelligence

Today, customer expectations, Internet technology, and new business models can alter the competitive landscape so rapidly that managers need special capabilities for competitive intelligence gathering. ESS can help managers identify changing market conditions, formulate responses, track implementation efforts, and learn from feedback.

BP Sony NV, the Netherlands branch of the multinational electronics giant, wanted more insight from the marketplace to drive its competitive strategy. Until recently, its management reports were based primarily on financial and administrative data that took at least 24 hours to generate. Management wanted to be able to make meaningful decisions based on marketing and sales data as well, so it could respond quickly to marketplace changes. Sony Netherlands constructed a data warehouse and executive information system (EIS) for this purpose.

The EIS is now available to 78 users in management, marketing, and sales. They can use the system to help them define strategies, search for opportunities, identify problems, and substantiate actions. Using a drill-down function, they can examine the underlying numbers behind the total result. For instance, whereas senior management can obtain sales results by business unit or product group, a marketing manager can use the system to look only at the group of products for which he or she is responsible. The manager can produce a report to indicate exactly which products are strong or weak performers or to rank dealers by performance. The system is flexible, easy to use, and can provide much of this information to the user on-line (Information Builders, 2000).

Cookson Electronics of Foxborough, Massachusetts, a supplier of materials used in printed circuit boards and semiconductor packaging, has 14 divisions around the world. Each is responsible for a different point in the electronics lifecycle, providing parts for computers, cell phones, and other consumer electronics. The semiconductor field has highly cyclical fluctuations in business, and Cookson divisions responsible for this part of the business can help the entire firm predict demand by anticipating industry cycles. Working with senior managers, Cookson's senior intelligence officer, Yann Morvan, developed a list of key intelligence topics (KITs) linked to strategic decisions. For example, a KIT might cover the firm's top five competitors, suppliers, customers, or technologies.

The Cookson Electronic Business Intelligence System (CEBIS), based on Lotus Notes, enables Cookson's 6,000 worldwide employees to access and contribute competitive intelligence information, such as competitor strategic alliances or geographic extensions or significant investments in research and development. Senior managers can use CEBIS to subscribe to the latest information on a specific KIT and receive news and analysis via e-mail or fax. Cookson expects the information from CEBIS to help managers counter threats and anticipate changes (Shand, 2000).

## Monitoring Corporate Performance: Balanced Scorecard Systems

Companies have traditionally measured value using financial metrics such as return on investment (ROI), which we described in Chapter 11. Many firms are now implementing a **balanced scorecard** model that supplements traditional financial measures with measurements from additional perspectives, such as customers, internal business processes, and learning and growth. Managers can use balanced scorecard systems to see how well the firm is meeting its strategic goals. The goals and measures for the balanced scorecard vary from company to company. Companies are setting up information systems to populate the scorecard for management.

**balanced scorecard**
Model for analyzing firm performance that supplements traditional financial measures with measurements from additional business perspectives, such as customers, internal business processes, and learning and growth.

Aurora Consolidated Laboratories, a division of Aurora Health Care, is Wisconsin's largest private employer, with 13 hospitals, dozens of clinics and health centers, and 3,500 physicians reporting through more than 100 cost centers. In addition to monitoring costs closely, management wanted to measure customer satisfaction, the efficiency of Aurora's lab processes, satisfaction of key partners and suppliers, and employee motivation and productivity. The company implemented a Web-based reporting and communications system based on WebFOCUS from Information Builders Inc., which uses data from more than 35 databases consolidated in a data warehouse to give managers a scorecard on how well they are progressing. The system provides up-to-date data on corporate performance, graphs and charts to spot trends and anomalies, and the capability to drill down to see detailed data behind the trends. Users can save reports from the system as HTML files for later viewing with their Web browsers. The system was initially available to 25 users, including senior managers, vice presidents, and selected supervisors but is being gradually opened to other managers (Information Builders 2000).

Amsterdam-based ING Bank, which is part of the ING Group global financial services firm, adopted a balanced scorecard approach when it reorganized. Management wanted to shift from a product to a client orientation and to develop appropriate performance indicators to measure progress in this new direction. In 1997 the bank built a Web-based balanced scorecard application using SAS tools for data warehousing and statistical analysis to measure progress with 21 indicators. Data to fill out the scorecard, from sources such as financial ledger applications and client retention and market penetration ratios, feed a central data warehouse. The data come from systems running on Lotus Notes, Microsoft Excel spreadsheets, and Oracle and DB2 databases. The data warehouse and balanced scorecard software run on IBM RS/6000 servers. ING initially made the balanced scorecard system available only to midrange executives in sales, but later expanded it to 3,000 users, including people at nearly every level of its relationship management group. (McCune, 2000)

## Enterprise-wide Reporting and Analysis

Enterprise system vendors are now providing capabilities to extend the usefulness of data captured in operational systems to give management a picture of the overall performance of the firm. Some provide reporting of metrics for balanced scorecard analysis as well as more traditional financial and operating metrics. Table 13-4 describes strategic performance management tools for each of the major enterprise system vendors.

Companies can use these new enterprise reporting capabilities to create measures of firm performance that were not previously available. The head of strategic planning at Dow Chemical led a cross-functional steering team to develop a set of measures and reports based on data from the company's SAP enterprise system. Process experts in different areas of the company defined reporting categories such as expense management, inventory management,

### TABLE 13-4 STRATEGIC PERFORMANCE MANAGEMENT TOOLS FOR ENTERPRISE SYSTEMS

| Enterprise System Vendor | Description |
|---|---|
| SAP | Web-enabled Strategic Enterprise Management module provides reports giving managers a comprehensive view of firm performance. Features corporate performance metrics, simulation, and planning tools. Managers can model and communicate key performance indicators for a balanced scorecard. Another measurement tool called the Management Cockpit can be used to structure and visualize performance indicators using ergonomic, easy-to-understand, graphical displays. |
| PeopleSoft | Enterprise Performance Management (EPM) features four modules: Enterprise Warehouse to analyze business transactions; Business Intelligence to integrate external data such as surveys; Balanced Scorecard, providing tools for measurement and communication of the scorecard; and Financial Workbench. |
| Oracle | Strategic Enterprise Management includes support for the balanced scorecard, activity-based management, and budgeting. A value-based management module under development will help companies develop and apply new accounting methods for quantifying intellectual capital. |

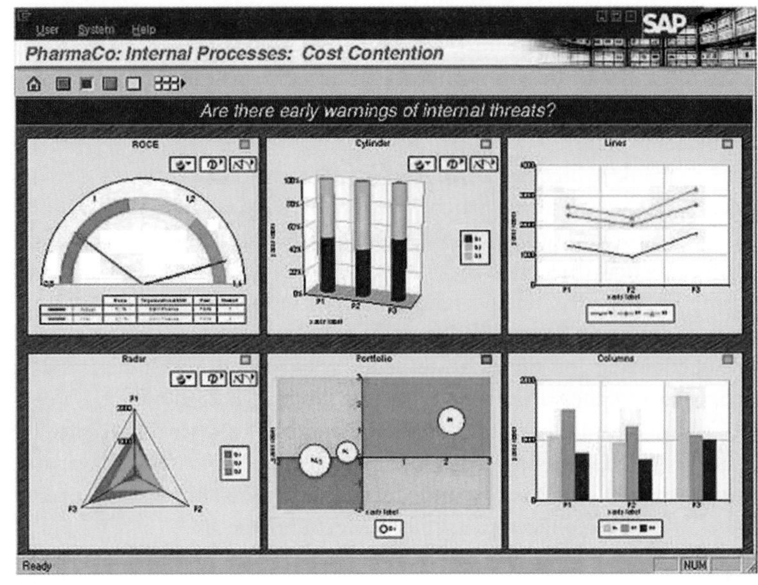


*The Management Cockpit is an ergonomic concept for structuring and visualizing firm performance indicators using easy-to-understand displays. This display is based on SAP's Strategic Enterprise Management module, which uses Web technology to provide management with a comprehensive view of firm performance.*

and sales. Dow then developed a data mart for each type of data, amounting to more than 20 data marts. The data marts are integrated so that the numbers for the "business results" mart balance with numbers in the expenses and sales marts. Dow also implemented a new set of performance measures based on shareholder value and activity-based costing. (Activity-based costing is a budgeting and analysis model that identifies all the resources, processes, and costs, including overhead and operating expenses, required to produce a specific product or service. It allows managers to ascertain which products or services are profitable, so they can determine the changes required to maximize firm profitability.) Instead of reporting in terms of product and income, the system can focus on contribution margins and customer accounts, with the ability to calculate the current and lifetime value of each account. The system is used by more than 5,000 people, ranging from Dow's CEO to plant floor workers (Davenport, 2000).

Management of Nissan Motor Company of Australia must oversee the activities of 550 people in 23 sites across the Australian continent. The company is primarily involved in Nissan's import and distribution activities for 35,000 automobiles each year. As with other automotive companies, Nissan Australia has extensive reporting requirements, including detailed controlling reports for financial accounts and monthly accounts. Managers need detailed reports down to the model level, with controlling reports for each department. When Nissan used an old legacy mainframe system, it would take up to two weeks to create and distribute reports to the company's board of directors.

In 1997, Nissan Australia installed SAP's R/3 enterprise software, serving as a pilot for the rest of the Nissan organization. The company also installed Information Builders' SNAPpack Power Reporter to create custom reports with a Web interface and powerful drill-down capabilities that did not require extensive programming to produce. These reports can be generated immediately and include profit-and-loss reports, gross margin analyses, balance sheets, and wholesale and retail vehicles. Management requests for more profit analysis reports by model, state, and other variables can be easily satisfied (Information Builders, 2000).

## APPLICATION SOFTWARE EXERCISE

### SPREADSHEET EXERCISE: BREAKEVEN ANALYSIS AT STANLEY'S COOKWARE

Stanley's Cookware produces premiere cookware products, and sells these products as sets to retailers. A typical Stanley Premiere Kitchen Set includes a Dutch oven, frying pan, stockpot, casserole, and saucepan. Each set is sold for $200 and costs the company approximately $125 to produce.

Production at the cookware company's manufacturing plant will soon reach capacity, and management must decide whether to expand the existing facility or relocate to a new plant. Existing facility expansion has associated fixed costs of $2,500,000 and a capacity of 45,000 sets. If relocation occurs, fixed costs are estimated at $4,500,000, variable costs will drop to $110, and capacity will increase to 100,000 sets.

Prepare a spreadsheet to support the decision-making needs of Stanley's Cookware's managers. The spreadsheet should summarize the fixed costs, variable costs, revenue, unit profit margin, and breakeven points for both options.

Your spreadsheet product should provide reporting and scenario analysis features. How can these features provide support for this decision problem? If an optimistic forecast suggests that 75,000 sets will be sold, which site is the better choice? If a pessimistic forecast suggests that only 30,000 sets will be sold, which site is the better choice? Company management may increase the price of a Stanley Premiere Kitchen Set to $210. What impact, if any, does this information have on your analysis? Summarize your findings in a report, and submit this report to your professor.

## MANAGEMENT WRAP-UP

Management is responsible for determining where management support systems can make their greatest contribution to organizational performance and for allocating the resources to build them. Management needs to work closely with system builders to make sure that these systems effectively capture the right set of information requirements and decision processes for guiding the firm.

Management support systems can improve organizational performance by speeding up decision making or improving the quality of management decisions themselves. However, some of these decision processes may not be clearly understood. A management support system will be most effective when system builders have a clear idea of its objectives, the nature of the decisions to be supported, and how the system will actually support decision making.

Systems to support management decision making can be developed with a range of technologies, including the use of large databases, modeling tools, graphics tools, datamining and analysis tools, and electronic meeting technology. Identifying the right technology for the decision or decision process to be supported is a key technology decision.

*For Discussion*

1. As a manager or user of information systems, what would you need to know to participate in the design and use of a DSS or an ESS? Why?
2. If businesses used DSS, GDSS, and ESS more widely, would they make better decisions? Explain.

## SUMMARY


1. *Differentiate a decision-support system (DSS) and a group decision-support system (GDSS).* A decision-support system (DSS) is an interactive system under user control that combines data, sophisticated analytical models and tools, and user-friendly software into a single powerful system that can support semistructured or unstructured decision making. There are two kinds of DSS: model-driven DSS and data-driven DSS. DSS targeted toward customers as well as managers are becoming available on the Web. A group decision-support system (GDSS) is an interactive, computer-based system to facilitate the solution of unstructured problems by a set of decision-makers working together as a group rather than individually.
2. *Describe the components of decision-support systems and group decision-support systems.* The components of a DSS are the DSS database, the DSS software system, and the user interface. The DSS database is a collection of current or historical data from a number of applications or groups that can be used for analysis. The data can come from both internal and external sources including enterprise systems and the Web. The DSS software system consists of OLAP and datamining tools or mathematical and analytical models that are used for analyzing the data in the database. The user interface allows users to interact with the DSS software tools directly.
   Group decision-support systems (GDSS) have hardware, software, and people components. Hardware components consist of the conference room facilities, including seating arrangements and computer and other electronic hardware. Software components include tools for organizing ideas, gathering information, ranking and setting priorities, and documenting meeting sessions. People components include participants, a trained facilitator, and staff to support the hardware and software.
3. *Demonstrate how decision-support systems and group decision-support systems can enhance decision making.* Both DSS and GDSS support steps in the process of arriving at decisions. A DSS provides results of model-based or data-driven analysis that help managers design and evaluate alternatives and monitor the progress of the solution that was adopted. DSS can help support decisions for supply chain management and customer relationship management as well as model alternative business scenarios. A GDSS helps decision makers meeting together to arrive at a decision efficiently and is especially useful for increasing the productivity of meetings larger than four or five people. However, the effectiveness of GDSS is contingent on the nature of the group, the task, and the context of the meeting.
4. *Evaluate the capabilities of executive support systems (ESS).* Executive support systems help managers with unstructured problems that occur at the strategic level of management. ESS provide data from both internal and external sources and provide a generalized computing and communications environment that can be focused and applied to a changing array of problems. ESS help senior executives monitor firm performance, spot problems, identify opportunities, and forecast trends. These systems can filter out extraneous details for high-level overviews, or they can drill down to provide senior managers with detailed transaction data if required. ESS are starting to take advantage of firmwide data provided by enterprise systems.
5. *Assess the benefits of executive support systems.* ESS help senior managers analyze, compare, and highlight trends so that they more easily may monitor organizational performance or identify strategic problems and opportunities. ESS can increase the span of control of senior management, allowing them to oversee more people with fewer resources.


## KEY TERMS

**Balanced scorecard, 422**
**Customer decision-support system (CDSS), 414**
**Data-driven DSS, 406**
**Decision-support system (DSS), 404**
**Drill down, 420**
**DSS database, 407**
**DSS software system, 407**
**Electronic meeting system (EMS), 417**
**Executive support system (ESS), 420**
**Geographic information system (GIS), 413**
**Group decision-support system (GDSS), 415**
**Model, 407**
**Model-driven DSS, 406**
**Sensitivity analysis, 408**

## REVIEW QUESTIONS

1. What is a decision-support system (DSS)? How does it differ from a management information system (MIS)?
2. How can a DSS support unstructured or semistructured decision making?
3. What is the difference between a data-driven DSS and a model-driven DSS? Give examples.
4. What are the three basic components of a DSS? Briefly describe each.
5. How can DSS help firms manage supply chain management and customer relationship management?
6. What is a geographic information system (GIS)? How can it support decision-making?

7. What is a customer decision-support system? How can the Internet be used for this purpose?
8. What is a group decision-support system (GDSS)? How does it differ from a DSS?
9. What are the three underlying problems in group decision making that have led to the development of GDSS?
10. Describe the three elements of a GDSS.
11. Name and describe five GDSS software tools.
12. What is an electronic meeting system (EMS)? Describe its capabilities.
13. For each of the three underlying problems in group decision making referred to in question 9, describe one or two ways GDSS can contribute to a solution.
14. Define and describe the capabilities of an executive support system (ESS).
15. How can the Internet and enterprise systems provide capabilities for executive support systems?
16. What are the benefits of ESS? How do these systems enhance managerial decision making?

## GROUP PROJECT

With three or four of your classmates, identify several groups in your university that could benefit from a GDSS. Design a GDSS for one of those groups, describing its hardware, software, and people elements. If possible, use electronic presentation software to present your findings to the class.

## TOOLS FOR INTERACTIVE LEARNING

### INTERNET CONNECTION

The Internet Connection for this chapter will take you to a series of Web sites where you can complete an exercise using Web-based DSS. You can also use the Interactive Study Guide to test your knowledge of the topics in this chapter and get instant feedback where you need more practice.

### ELECTRONIC COMMERCE PROJECT

At the Lauden Web site for Chapter 13, you will find an Electronic Commerce project that will use the interactive software at the Fidelity Investments Web site for investment portfolio analysis.

### CD-ROM

If you use the Multimedia Edition CD-ROM with this chapter, you can complete an interactive exercise asking you to design a group decision-support system (GDSS). You can also find a video clip illustrating the use of Intel videoconferencing technology, an audio overview of the major themes of this chapter, and bullet text summarizing the key points of the chapter.

## CASE STUDY *Merck-Medco Finds the Right Prescription to Combat Dot.com Fever*

The Internet has changed everything. In the new economy the small dot.com companies with the right ideas and a small amount of money can nimbly use Web sites to steal markets right out from under the noses of the giant corporations. Right? Well, don't tell that to Per Lofberg because he doesn't believe it. Lofberg, the chairman of Merck-Medco Managed Care, L.L.C., took on the drugstore start-ups such as Drugstore.com and PlanetRx, which allow customers to fill their drug prescriptions on-line.

Merck-Medco is a division of Merck & Co., the giant drug company headquartered in Whitehouse Station, New Jersey. Medco was founded as small, single, mail-service pharmacy in 1983 and was purchased by Merck in 1993. Today it is the largest pharmacy-benefit manager (PBM) in the United States. PBMs provide prescription drug services for all types of group health plans. Merck-Medco's clients include one-fourth of the Fortune 500 corporations, more than 100 local, state, and federal employee and retiree groups, many Blue Cross/Blue Shield plans, a number of unions, and other medical insurance plans. Altogether the company has 1,100 clients with more than 52 million beneficiaries (customers). In one week on average Merck-Medco fills 1.2 million prescriptions by mail while paying benefits for another 5.9 million filled weekly at local pharmacies. Altogether in 1999 the company filled or paid for about 370 million prescriptions. Merck-Medco also offers patients valuable information such as warnings on harmful drug interactions and on drug age and gender issues.

Although prescriptions-by-mail only accounted for about 10 percent of the total national prescription market (or about $12.6 billion dollars), in 1999, that market has been growing by 22 percent annually. Although the company profits from every prescription filled through its network, when customers eliminate the local drugstore by ordering directly from Merck-Medco, its profits rise while customers pay less because Merck-Medco costs are so much lower.

To fill so many prescriptions and to process and pay for millions of others, Merck-Medco had to build a giant and complex infrastructure that cannot be quickly or easily matched by the start-up dot.coms. The company not only has a large staff that includes many with expertise in pharmaceuticals, but it also includes employees who are skilled in the complexities of prescription filling, shipping, and reimbursements. In addition it has built 12 mail-service pharmacies, three calling centers, and two high-tech drug warehouses that automate the entire prescription-filling process for 75 percent of the prescriptions received. All of this has reduced turnaround time from up to two weeks after the prescription has been received to only two days or less. Lofberg and the rest of Merck-Medco's leadership team understood that creating the Web site was the easy part. Winning and servicing customers is much more difficult.

Lofberg believed that merely reimbursing customers or filling their prescriptions would not be acceptable service in the long run. Many customers were using the Internet and they knew it could mean a faster, simpler way to order a prescription refill. They also knew it could be an instant source of relevant, desired information on demand. Lofberg was convinced his company had to quickly make use of the Internet or begin to lose clients. So in 1998 he had Merck-Medco build its own Web site, merckmedco.com [http://merckmedco.com]. In the year 2000 about 20 percent of its customer transactions, including prescription refills, occurred through this Web site. That amounted to processing 80,000 prescriptions per week, a ten-fold increase from its first year. In the year 2000 the site brought in $8.5 million in revenues.

PBMs are crucial to the prescription portion of organized healthcare, yet few people have even heard of them because only a few PBMs exist, and those that do work behind the scenes. Together they fill or reimburse about 80 percent of all prescription drug sales in the United States. When they sensed a possible threat from the new Internet dot.com companies, they handled it by simply refusing to deal with them. Therefore, individuals with healthcare plans who tried to buy prescription drugs through the Net found they could not be reimbursed for their purchases. The only way the dot.com start-ups could gain a significant portion of the prescription business was to sell a major share of their ownership to a PBM or to a drug chain with large holdings in a PBM.

Merck-Medco management viewed its new Web site as a way to handle sales more efficiently, to enable the company to respond quickly and inexpensively to such customer service requests as order status information and billing inquiries, and to use it to offer health information to their customers at the customers' convenience. They also planned to promote the use of their Web-based service, thereby shifting more transactions there because Web-based transaction costs are much lower than other types of transactions. The issue became even more important when the company decided it would soon add the sale of over-the-counter products to its merckmedco.com operation.

Merck-Medco decided it should use direct-mail promotions to increase the use of its Web site. Almost all increased customer activity on the Web would be replacements for actions the same customers would have executed in another way—by mail, telephone, or fax. The dollar value to Merck-Medco of increased Web activity is actually the difference in the company's costs to complete the specific transactions using the Net versus the same transactions executed via the other alternatives. To be successful, marketing needed to understand who to target with which promotional mailings and what the content of those mailings should be. The company's Information Research (IR) group developed scoring models to help predict which of its customers would be likely to respond to a specific mailing. The models also measure the change in Web transaction volume for a brief period after a promotion. The underlying assumption is that any change in customer behavior could likely be attributed to the mailing.

To carry out its modeling and analysis, Merck-Medco needed data. PBMs need a great deal of data to operate. They usually have a service database that tracks claims placed by or for individual patients, including such information as member (and patient) identification, service date, the pharmaceutical cost, and quantity of medication dispensed expressed in terms of the number of days' supply. In a separate database they track customer service histories including member identification, service date, and reason for the service (such as order status inquiry or billing inquiry). The companies usually also track data on direct-mail promotions to its customers. The IR group brought all Merck-Medco's data together by building an e-commerce datamart.

IR employed a number of models as it studied its past and present e-commerce customers, including various classification and regression analyses. Using these statistical models to study the target populations, the analysis of its first promotional mailing showed that 2 percent of those in the study accounted for 32 percent of the increase in Web transactions. The study also showed that the 2 percent were different from most of the others because they had previously used the Web site but had not done so for 2 or more months. As the studies went on, the results led IR to develop a hierarchy of four user types, each of whom required a different business strategy and different promotion. The types are (1) current e-commerce users who should be rewarded for their ongoing patronage, (2) prior e-commerce users who needed to be reminded to execute their transaction through the Web, (3) other customer service users who used the telephone and fax and needed to be redirected to using the Web instead, and (4) noncustomer service users who used mail and needed to be recruited to the customer service approach.

Because of the scoring models IR developed, Merck-Medco is now able to achieve the same response rate with a promotional mailing one-sixth the size of the earlier mailings that were based only on local area demographics. Thus, Merck-Medco is able to increase the use of the more profitable Web site while simultaneously reducing its promotion costs. IR has since begun studying ways to further refine the scoring model by encompassing a value estimate of a given transaction. The company then will be able to target those people whose activities will bring the company the greatest profit. IR has also developed a forecasting and ad hoc reporting tool to predict future growth for its Web site that can be used for planning.

**Sources:** Edward S. Binkowski and Moshe B. Rosenwein, "Prescription for Online Pharmacy Success," *OR/MS Today,* August 2000; Gardiner Harris, "How Merck Unit Beat Dot-coms in Web Foray," *The Wall Street Journal,* April 13, 2000; and Elizabeth Corcoran, "The E Gang," *Forbes,* July 24, 2000.

### *CASE STUDY QUESTIONS*

1. Evaluate Merck-Medco using the value chain and competitive forces models. What is Merck-Medco's business strategy?

scoring models

2. What problems did Merck-Medco face that caused it to move into the Web site business? How did its Web site fit into its business strategy?
3. Why do you think Merck-Medco management chose to build its own Web site instead of purchasing one that already existed and was functioning?
4. What kind of decision support system did Merck-Medco's IR unit develop? What types of decisions does it support?
5. What management, organization, and technical issues did Merck-Medco have to address to develop and use the new system? How did the success of the system impact Merck-Medco's management, organization and technology?

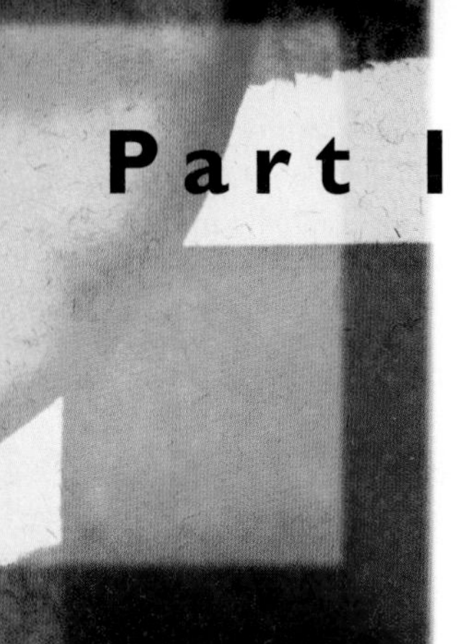

# Part IV Project

## Designing an Enterprise Information Portal

You are the CIO of a major corporation that researches, develops, manufactures, and distributes pharmaceuticals. Your company, United States Pharma Corp., is headquartered in the state of New Jersey in the United States, but it has sites in many countries around the world. Many of the research sites are in the United States, Germany, France, Great Britain, Australia, and Switzerland. Distribution sites are not only in the United States and Europe but also in a number of countries in East and South Asia, Africa, Australia, Latin America, and the Middle East.

Your company is involved with much more than research and development of new drugs. For example, it owns two companies that produce and sell generic drugs (drugs that are no longer protected by a patent and so are copied and sold under other names). It also produces many over-the-counter drugs to combat such problems as headaches, pains, athlete's foot, and allergic reactions. The company also produces and sells some drugs that help cure or improve some animal diseases such as heartworms and fleas.

The key to the ongoing profits of the company is the research and development of new pharmaceuticals. The company researches thousands of possible drugs in order to finally develop and patent only one that is successful and becomes a widely sold pharmaceutical product. Such products take 8 to 15 years to research, develop, and test, followed by clinical trials and finally approval by the U.S. Food and Drug Administration (FDA). The staff must research both diseases and their treatments, and the potential pharmaceuticals that could become innovative new drugs. Experts who are working on the cutting edge of medical, chemical, and other fields are carrying out research in order to develop possible new drugs and medical treatments.

To undertake the research and eventually test the new products and obtain FDA approval, the researchers and other scientists must test all the possible pharmaceuticals. They must also turn to many places to obtain and share information with others both inside and outside of the company. For example they will want to communicate with the World Health Organization, the FDA, and the Centers for Disease Control and Prevention. In addition they will need to connect to the pharmaceutical industry's organizations, such as the International Federation of Pharmaceutical Manufacturers Associations (IFPMA). Health education and information sites are also critical, such as the U.S. National Library of Medicine and such private organizations as the Mayo Clinic Health Oasis.

As the CIO, you have concluded that your company needs a corporate knowledge environment portal that can enable many of the corporate employees easily to access the information they need. The users of the portal would primarily be chemical, biological, and pharmaceutical researchers as well as medical personnel involved in research, tests, and eventually clinical trials.

1. Write a brief description of the company, its key functions, and systems.
2. Design the corporate portal, providing a description that can be reviewed and approved by your senior executive committee. Your design specifications should include the following:
   - Internal systems and databases that users of the portal would need to access.
   - External sources researchers would need to access to further their research.
   - Internal and external communication and collaboration facilities the researchers would need to develop their ideas, pursue their research, and share their research and ideas with others.
   - Intranet and Internet search tools to support research.
   - Sources for relevant news relating to the company and research.
   - U.S. FDA rules and regulations regarding clinical programs, clinical trials, and patent applications.
   - Connections to pharmaceutical conferences and forums as well as professional organizations and appropriate professional journals.
   - Any additional sources of information that would prove helpful to users.

   Use the Web to research these features. Your analysis should include the qualities of a good corporate portal and a description of commercially available tools for building your portal.
3. Design a home page for your portal that you can present to management.

# PART V

# MANAGING INFORMATION SYSTEMS IN THE DIGITAL FIRM

# chapter 14 Information Systems Security and Control

objectives

**After completing this chapter, you will be able to:**

1. *Demonstrate why information systems are so vulnerable to destruction, error, abuse, and system quality problems.*
2. *Compare general controls and application controls for information systems.*
3. *Evaluate the special measures required to ensure the reliability, availability, and security of electronic commerce and digital business processes.*
4. *Describe the most important software quality assurance techniques.*
5. *Demonstrate the importance of auditing information systems and safeguarding data quality.*

## Security Planning at Keystone Mercy Health Plan

The healthcare industry is not only highly competitive but also highly regulated, at least when it comes to government restrictions on the use of patient information. The U.S. Health Insurance Portability and Accountability Act of 1996 protects the security and confidentiality of electronic health information while standardizing the exchange of data for certain administrative and financial transactions.

Keystone Mercy Health Plan, a multistate managed care company headquartered in Philadelphia with 240,000 subscribers, must follow such laws to keep its information confidential. Phil Fishgold, Keystone Mercy's manager of information security, stands vigilantly over the company's network to make sure that Keystone adheres to this act and other security regulations.

Keystone already had virus detection tools in place when Fishgold arrived in 1999, but Fishgold wanted a more stringent security plan. Keystone's information technology infrastructure is based on Hewlett-Packard and Compaq servers running Unix and Windows NT. Fishgold added tools for intrusion detection that continually monitor the most vulnerable points of corporate networks to detect and deter unauthorized individuals trying to access the networks. As a low-profile, healthcare company, Keystone is an unlikely target for hacker attacks, but the company doesn't want to take any chances. Keystone also instituted a two-step, remote-access authentication system to verify the identities of software vendors that need to access Keystone's network to make upgrades and repairs.

Fishgold insisted on consistent security standards. He knows that employees will become confused if one system has a two-character password and another has a six- or eight-character password. Keystone has adopted an alpha-numeric password policy—passwords to its systems must contain both numbers and letters because they are harder to crack.

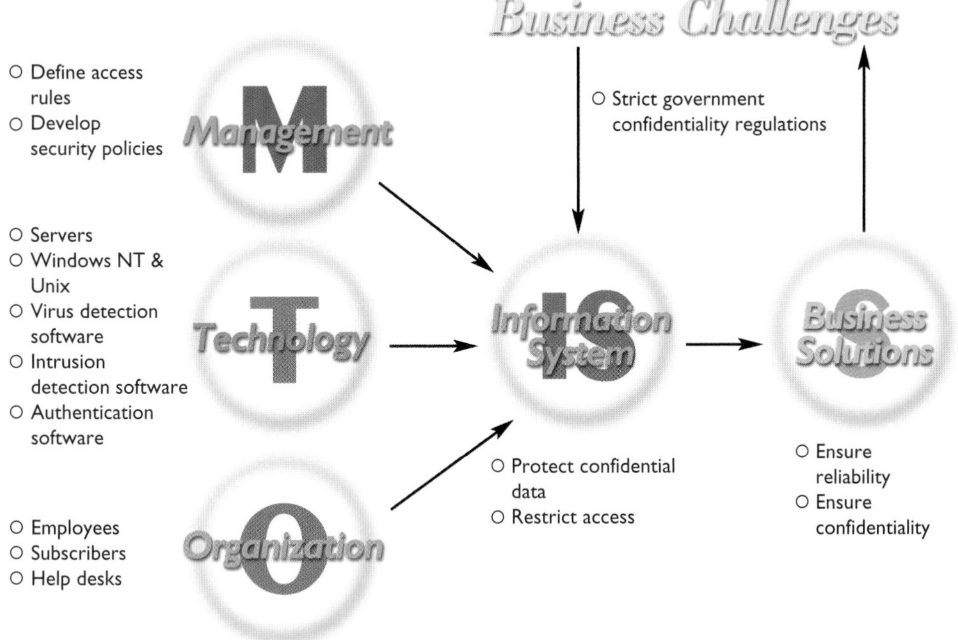


Keystone Mercy's management realizes that security is not simply a matter of selecting the right technology—employees and management must be aware of security issues and follow the right procedures when dealing with information. When all new employees undergo training, they are warned not to reveal their user identification and passwords to access the system to another person. Help desk staff are instructed not to accept calls from outsiders pretending to be employees who request access to the system. Keystone's human resources department provides the help desk staff with personal information to help verify that a caller is a legitimate employee.

According to federal and state medical confidentiality law, employees can only access confidential health-related information when it is specifically required by their job function. Fishgold works with all of Keystone's departments on developing electronic security profiles for all employees. These profiles specify what pieces of data employees may access, based on the requirements of their jobs. Management determines the access rules. Keystone senior management is committed to providing a secure business environment throughout the organization.

**Sources:** David Ward, "Keystone Mercy Strives for a Healthy Security Plan," *Information Week,* September 25, 2000; and www.keystonemercy.com.

## Security Planning at Keystone Mercy Health Plan

**MANAGEMENT CHALLENGES**

## Management Challenges

The experience of Keystone Mercy Health Plan illustrates the need for organizations to take special measures to protect their information systems. Use by unauthorized people, software failures, hardware failures, communication disruptions, natural disasters, and employee errors can prevent information systems from running properly or running at all. As you read this chapter, you should be aware of the following management challenges:

1. **Designing systems that are neither overcontrolled nor undercontrolled.** Although most security breaches and damage to information systems still come from organizational insiders, security breaches from outside the organization are increasing, because firms pursuing electronic commerce are open to outsiders through the Internet. It is difficult for organizations to determine how open or closed they should be to protect themselves. If a system requires too many passwords, authorizations, or levels of security to access information, the system will go unused. Controls that are effective but that do not prevent authorized individuals from using a system are difficult to design.

2. **Applying quality assurance standards in large systems projects.** This chapter explains why the goal of zero defects in large, complex pieces of software is impossible to achieve. If the seriousness of remaining bugs cannot be ascertained, what constitutes acceptable—if not perfect—software performance? And even if meticulous design and exhaustive testing could eliminate all defects, software projects have time and budget constraints that often prevent management from devoting as much time to thoroughly testing as it should. Under such circumstances it will be difficult for managers to define a standard for software quality and to enforce it.

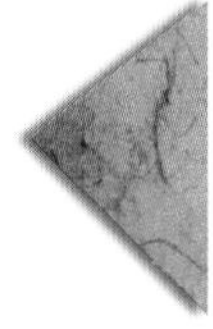

Computer systems play such a critical role in business, government, and daily life that organizations must take special steps to protect their information systems and to ensure that they are accurate and reliable. This chapter describes how information systems can be controlled and made reliable and secure so that they serve the purposes for which they are intended.

## 14.1 System Vulnerability and Abuse

Before computer automation, data about individuals or organizations were maintained and secured as paper records dispersed in separate business or organizational units. Information systems concentrate data in computer files that potentially can be accessed more easily by large numbers of people and by groups outside the organization. Consequently, automated data are more susceptible to destruction, fraud, error, and misuse.

When computer systems fail to run or work as required, firms that depend heavily on computers experience a serious loss of business function. The longer computer systems are down, the more serious the consequences for the firm. Table 14-1 describes the estimated financial losses caused by Web site outages for brokerage and auction sites. Some firms relying on computers to process their critical business transactions might experience a total loss of business function if they lose computer capability for more than a few days.

### Why Systems Are Vulnerable

When large amounts of data are stored in electronic form they are vulnerable to many more kinds of threats than when they exist in manual form. Table 14-2 lists the most common threats against computerized information systems. They can stem from technical, organizational, and environmental factors compounded by poor management decisions.

Advances in telecommunications and computer software have magnified these vulnerabilities. Through telecommunications networks, information systems in different locations can be interconnected. The potential for unauthorized access, abuse, or fraud is not limited to a single location but can occur at any access point in the network.

Additionally, more complex and diverse hardware, software, organizational, and personnel arrangements are required for telecommunications networks, creating new areas and

**TABLE 14-1** ESTIMATED FINANCIAL LOSS DUE TO A SITE OUTAGE*

| Type of Loss | Brokerage Site | Auction Site |
|---|---|---|
| Direct revenues loss | $204,000 | $341,652 |
| Compensatory loss | 0 | $943,521 |
| Inventory costs | 0 | 0 |
| Depreciation expenses | $4,110 | $6,279 |
| Lost future revenues | $4,810,320 | $1,024,955 |
| Worker downtime loss | $117,729 | $46,097 |
| Contract labor cost | $24,000 | $52,180 |
| Delay-to-market cost | $60,000 | $358,734 |
| Total financial impact | $5,220,159 | $2,773,416 |

*Based on an eight-hour brokerage site outage during the trading day and a 22-hour auction site outage.
*Source:* "Technology Spotlight: The Financial Impact of Site Outages," *The Industry Standard,* October 4, 1999. Reprinted by permission of *The Industry Standard;* www.thestandard.com.

opportunities for penetration and manipulation. Wireless networks using radio-based technology are even more vulnerable to penetration, because radio frequency bands are easy to scan. Wireless devices can form ad hoc networks that can be exploited by malicious entities to disrupt service, collect confidential information, and disseminate false information. Because wireless devices roam in and out of wireless zones, such attacks can be difficult to trace (Ghoshard Swaminathe, 2001). The Internet poses special problems, because it was explicitly designed to be accessed easily by people on different computer systems. The vulnerabilities of telecommunications networks are illustrated in Figure 14-1.

## Hackers and Computer Viruses

The explosive growth of Internet use by businesses and individuals has been accompanied by rising reports of Internet security breaches. The main concern comes from unwanted intruders, or hackers, who use the latest technology and their skills to break into supposedly secure computers or to disable them. A **hacker** is a person who gains unauthorized access to a computer network for profit, criminal mischief, or personal pleasure. There are many ways that hacker break-ins can harm businesses. Some malicious intruders have planted logic bombs, Trojan horses, and other software that can hide in a system or network until executing at a specified time. (A Trojan horse is a software program that appears legitimate but contains a second hidden function that may cause damage.) In **denial of service attacks,** hackers flood a network server or Web server with requests for information or other data in order to crash the network. The Window on Organizations describes one highly publicized denial of service attack and other problems hackers create for organizations that use the Internet.

Alarm has risen over hackers propagating **computer viruses,** rogue software programs that spread rampantly from system to system, clogging computer memory or destroying programs or data. Many thousands of viruses are known to exist, with 200 or more new viruses created each month. Table 14-3 describes the characteristics of the most common viruses.

Many viruses today are spread through the Internet from files of downloaded software or from files attached to e-mail transmissions. Viruses can also invade computerized information

**hacker**
A person who gains unauthorized access to a computer network for profit, criminal mischief, or personal pleasure.

**denial of service attack**
Overwhelming a Web server with requests for data in order to cripple the network.

**computer virus**
Rogue software programs that are difficult to detect and that spread rapidly through computer systems, destroying data or disrupting processing and memory systems.

**TABLE 14-2** THREATS TO COMPUTERIZED INFORMATION SYSTEMS

| | |
|---|---|
| Hardware failure | Fire |
| Software failure | Electrical problems |
| Personnel actions | User errors |
| Terminal access penetration | Program changes |
| Theft of data, services, or equipment | Telecommunications problems |

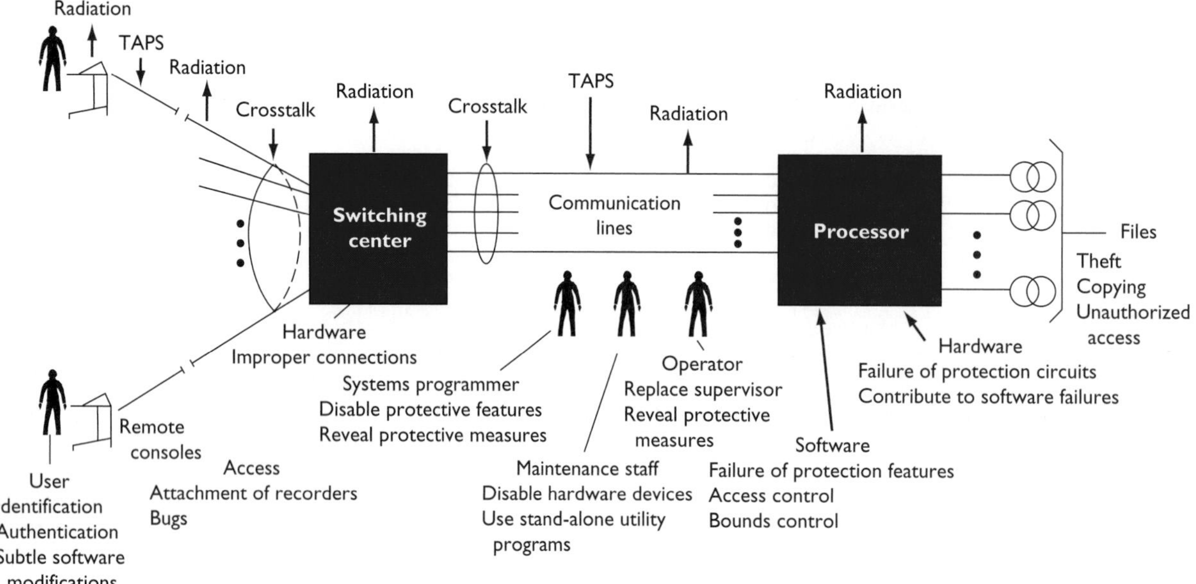


***Figure 14-1*** Telecommunications network vulnerabilities. Telecommunications networks are highly vulnerable to natural failure of hardware and software and to misuse by programmers, computer operators, maintenance staff, and end users. It is possible to tap communications lines and illegally intercept data. High-speed transmission over twisted wire communications channels causes interference called crosstalk. Radiation can disrupt a network at various points as well.

systems from other computer networks as well as from "infected" diskettes from an outside source or infected machines. The potential for massive damage and loss from future computer viruses remains. The Chernobyl, Melissa, and ILOVEYOU viruses caused extensive PC damage worldwide after spreading around the world through infected e-mail. Now viruses are spreading to wireless computing devices. Mobile device viruses could pose a serious threat to enterprise computing because so many wireless devices are now linked to corporate information systems.

**antivirus software**
Software designed to detect, and often eliminate, computer viruses from an information system.

Organizations can use antivirus software and screening procedures to reduce the chances of infection. **Antivirus software** is special software designed to check computer systems and disks for the presence of various computer viruses. Often the software can eliminate the virus from the infected area. However, most antivirus software is only effective against viruses already known when the software is written—to protect their systems, management must continually update their antivirus software.

## TABLE 14-3 EXAMPLES OF COMPUTER VIRUSES

| Virus Name | Description |
|---|---|
| Concept, Melissa | Macro viruses that exist inside executable programs called macros, which provide functions within programs such as Microsoft Word. Can be spread when Word documents are attached to e-mail. Can copy from one document to another and delete files. |
| Form | Makes a clicking sound with each keystroke but only on the eighteenth day of the month. May corrupt data on the floppy disks it infects. |
| Explore.exe | "Worm" type virus that arrives attached to e-mail. When launched tries to e-mail itself to other PCs and to destroy certain Microsoft Office and programmer files. |
| Monkey | Makes the hard disk seem as if it has failed, because Windows will not run. |
| Chernobyl | Erases a computer's hard drive and ROM BIOS (Basic Input/Output System). |
| Junkie | A "multipartite" virus that can infect files as well as the boot sector of the hard drive (the section of a PC hard drive that the PC first reads when it boots up). May cause memory conflicts. |

## Internet Hackers: Why Won't They Stop?

In early January 2000, a mysterious intruder tried to extort $100,000 from CD Universe, an Internet music retailer, claiming to have copied more than 300,000 credit card files that CD Universe had collected on its customers. The credit card numbers on these files could be used by other people to charge purchases on-line or by telephone. CD Universe refused to pay the blackmail, and the cyber-extortionist released some of the credit card files on the Internet, claiming that he had used other credit card numbers to obtain money for himself.

An e-mail trail traced the extortionist to Latvia, Bulgaria, or Russia. The extortionist had been operating a Web site called Maxus Credit Card Pipeline, where a visitor could obtain a valid credit card number, and the name and address of its owner from the site's massive database. Before the Maxus site was shut down, a traffic counter indicated that several thousand visitors had downloaded more than 25,000 credit card numbers since December 25, 1999. The extortionist claimed he had found a way to subvert ICVerify, a credit card verification program sold by Cybercash Inc. CD Universe employs ICVerify but the company was not ready to conclude that the blackmailer had obtained his credit card information by manipulating the software. The Maxus Web site extortionist claimed he hacked into a chain of shops in 1998 and obtained the ICVerify program with configuration files for transferring money.

The FBI reported in March 2001 that more than 40 businesses in 20 states have been victims of similar hacker extortion attempts and that over one million credit card numbers have been stolen. Hacker groups meeting in Russia and the Ukraine took advantage of vulnerabilities in Microsoft Corporation software. Companies that were attacked had not taken proper measures to repair these security loopholes.

During the second week of February 2000, a wave of hacker attacks temporarily disabled a series of major e-commerce sites, including Yahoo, Amazon.com, Buy.com, E*Trade, and ZDNet. These "denial of service" attacks were not designed to penetrate the Web sites but to disable them by inundating them with phony requests for data, overloading these sites' servers and preventing legitimate traffic from getting through. The Web sites were shut down for several hours, but no systems were compromised, no customer data were stolen, and financial losses from the outages were minor. After these incidents, many companies started looking for new ways to fortify their Web sites.

In early March of that year a hacker broke into the Australian government's official Web site for its new Goods and Services tax and started downloading bank account details on as many as 10,000 small businesses that had registered on-line. The hacker, known as K2 or Kelly, said on public radio that he had breached the security of the Web site by accident and wanted to publicize the risk to businesses. He started sending e-mail messages to the businesses with accounts at the Web site, detailing their bank account numbers, bank branches, tax numbers, and other private information. The Australian government immediately shut down the Web site and the Australian Federal Police launched an investigation.

All of these incidents highlight a mounting problem with Internet hackers plaguing both government and business organizations. According to ICSA, a security consulting firm, there were four times as many hacker attacks per day in North America in 2000 than there were a year earlier.

**To Think About:** How can break-ins from the Internet harm organizations? What management, organization, and technology issues should be considered when developing an Internet security plan?

*Sources:* Lee Gomes and Ted Bridis, "FBI Warns of Russian Hackers Stealing U.S. Credit-Card Data" *The Wall Street Journal,* March 9, 2001; John Markoff, "Thief Reveals Credit Card Data When Web Extortion Plot Fails," *The New York Times,* January 10, 2000; Gerard Knapp, "Hacker Strolls into Australian Tax Site," *Australia.Internet.com,* June 30, 2000; Elinor Abreu, "The Hack Attack," *The Industry Standard,* February 21, 2000; and Kelly Jackson Higgins, "Human Element Is Key to Stopping Hackers," *Information Week,* May 29, 2000.

### Concerns for System Builders and Users

The heightened vulnerability of automated data has created special concerns for the builders and users of information systems. These concerns include disaster, security, and administrative error.

#### Disaster

Computer hardware, programs, data files, and other equipment can be destroyed by fires, power failures, or other disasters. It may take many years and millions of dollars to reconstruct destroyed data files and computer programs, and some may not be replaceable. If an organization needs them to function on a day-to-day basis, it will no longer be able to operate. This is why companies such as VISA USA Inc. and National Trust employ elaborate emergency backup facilities. VISA USA Inc. has duplicate mainframes, duplicate network pathways, duplicate terminals, and duplicate power supplies. VISA even uses a duplicate data center in McLean, Virginia, to handle half of its transactions and to serve as an emergency backup to its

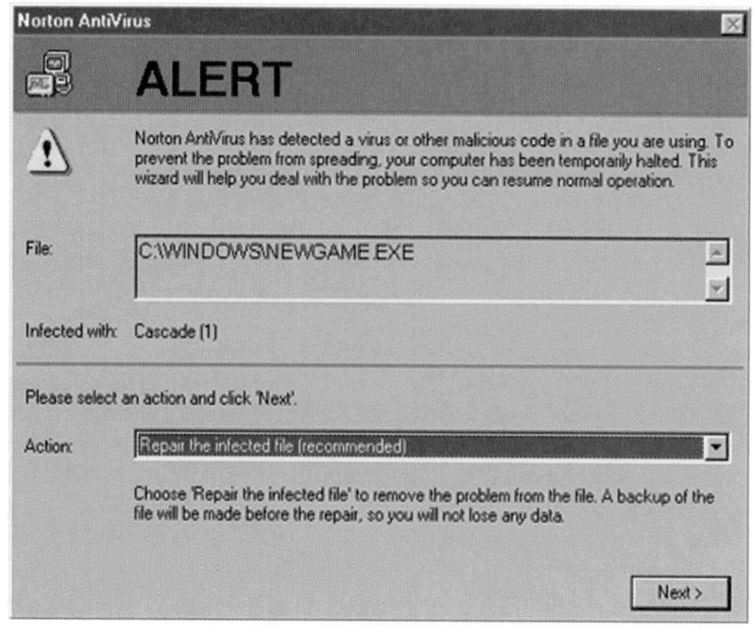


*Many organizations use antivirus software to check computer systems and disks for the presence of various computer viruses. Norton Anti Virus 2000, illustrated here, identifies viruses that have infected a system and provides tools for eradicating them.*

primary data center in San Mateo, California. National Trust, a large bank in Ontario, Canada, uses uninterruptable power supply technology provided by International Power Machines (IPM), because electrical power at its Mississauga location fluctuates frequently.

Rather than build their own backup facilities, many firms contract with disaster recovery firms, such as Comdisco Disaster Recovery Services in Rosemont, Illinois, and Sungard Recovery Services headquartered in Wayne, Pennsylvania. These disaster recovery firms provide hot sites housing spare computers at locations around the country where subscribing firms can run their critical applications in an emergency. Disaster recovery services offer backup for client/server systems as well as traditional mainframe applications. As firms become increasingly digital and depend on systems that must be constantly available, disaster recovery planning has taken on new importance. A **disaster recovery plan** includes establishing a chain of command for running the business in the event of a computer outage as well as identification of critical computer processing tasks and backup database, storage, and processing capabilities (Choy, Leong and Wong, 2000).

**disaster recovery plan**
Plan for running the business in the event of a computer outage. Includes organizational procedures as well as backup processing, storage and database capabilities.

## Security

**Security** refers to the policies, procedures, and technical measures used to prevent unauthorized access, alteration, theft, or physical damage to information systems. Security can be promoted with an array of techniques and tools to safeguard computer hardware, software, communications networks, and data. We already have discussed disaster protection measures. Other tools and techniques for promoting security are discussed in subsequent sections.

**security**
Policies, procedures, and technical measures used to prevent unauthorized access, alteration, theft, or physical damage to information systems.

## Errors

Computers also can serve as instruments of error, severely disrupting or destroying an organization's record keeping and operations. For instance, on February 25, 1991, during Operation Desert Storm, a Patriot missile defense system operating at Dharan, Saudi Arabia, failed to track and intercept an incoming Scud missile because of a software error in the system's weapons control computer. The Scud hit an army barracks, killing 28 Americans. Errors in automated systems can occur at many points in the processing cycle: through data entry, program error, computer operations, and hardware. Figure 14-2 illustrates all of the points in a typical processing cycle where errors can occur.

### SYSTEM QUALITY PROBLEMS: SOFTWARE AND DATA

In addition to disasters, viruses, and security breaches, defective software and data pose a constant threat to information systems, causing untold losses in productivity. An undiscovered error in a company's credit software or erroneous financial data can result in millions of dollars of losses. A hidden software problem in AT&T's long distance system brought down that system, bringing the New York–based financial exchanges to a halt and interfering with billions of dollars of business around the country for a number of hours. Modern passenger and commercial vehicles are increasingly dependent on computer programs for critical functions. A hidden software defect in a braking system could result in the loss of lives.

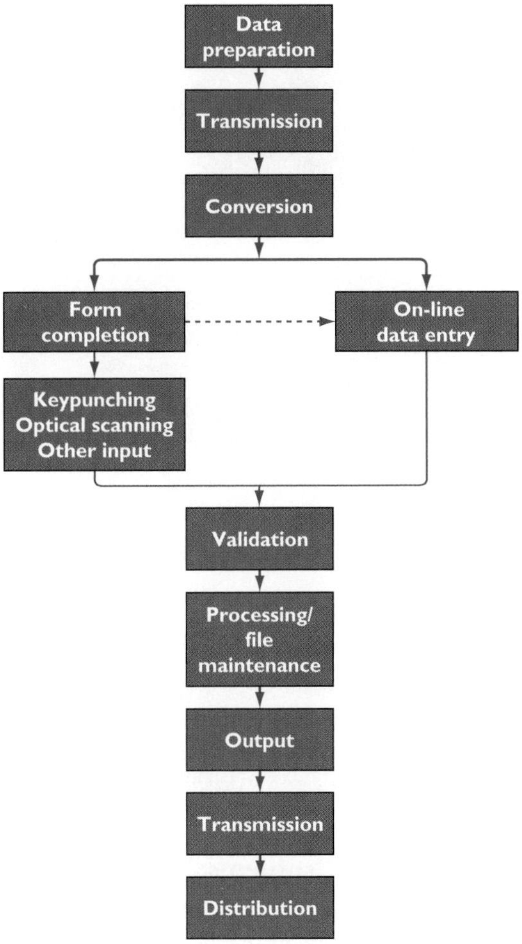

Data preparation
Transmission
Conversion
Form completion
On-line data entry
Keypunching
Optical scanning
Other input
Validation
Processing/ file maintenance
Output
Transmission
Distribution

***Figure 14-2*** Points in the processing cycle where errors can occur. Each of the points illustrated in this figure represents a control point where special automated or manual procedures should be established to reduce the risk of errors during processing.

## Bugs and Defects

A major problem with software is the presence of hidden **bugs** or program code defects. Studies have shown that it is virtually impossible to eliminate all bugs from large programs. The main source of bugs is the complexity of decision-making code. Even a relatively small program of several hundred lines will contain tens of decisions leading to hundreds or even thousands of different paths. Important programs within most corporations are usually much larger, containing tens of thousands or even millions of lines of code, each with many times the choices and paths of the smaller programs. Such complexity is difficult to document and design—designers document some reactions wrongly or fail to consider other possibilities. Studies show that about 60 percent of errors discovered during testing are a result of specifications in the design documentation that were missing, ambiguous, in error, or in conflict.

**bugs**
Program code defects or errors.

Zero defects, a goal of the total quality management movement, cannot be achieved in larger programs. Complete testing simply is not possible. Fully testing programs that contain thousands of choices and millions of paths would require thousands of years. Eliminating software bugs is an exercise in diminishing returns, because it would take proportionately longer testing to detect and eliminate obscure residual bugs (Littlewood and Strigini, 1993). Even with rigorous testing, one could not know for sure that a piece of software was dependable until the product proved itself after much operational use. The message? We cannot eliminate all bugs, and we cannot know with certainty the seriousness of the bugs that do remain.

## The Maintenance Nightmare

Another reason that systems are unreliable is that computer software traditionally has been a nightmare to maintain. Maintenance, the process of modifying a system in production use, is the most expensive phase of the systems development process. In most organizations nearly half of information systems staff time is spent in the maintenance of existing systems.

Why are maintenance costs so high? One major reason is organizational change. The firm may experience large internal changes in structure or leadership, or change may come from its surrounding environment. These organizational changes affect information requirements. Another reason appears to be software complexity, as measured by the number and size of interrelated software programs and subprograms and the complexity of the flow of program logic between them (Banker, Datar, Kemerer, and Zweig, 1993). A third common cause of long-term maintenance problems is faulty systems analysis and design, especially information requirements analysis. Some studies of large TPS systems by TRW, Inc., have found that a majority of system errors—64 percent—result from early analysis errors (Mazzucchelli, 1985).

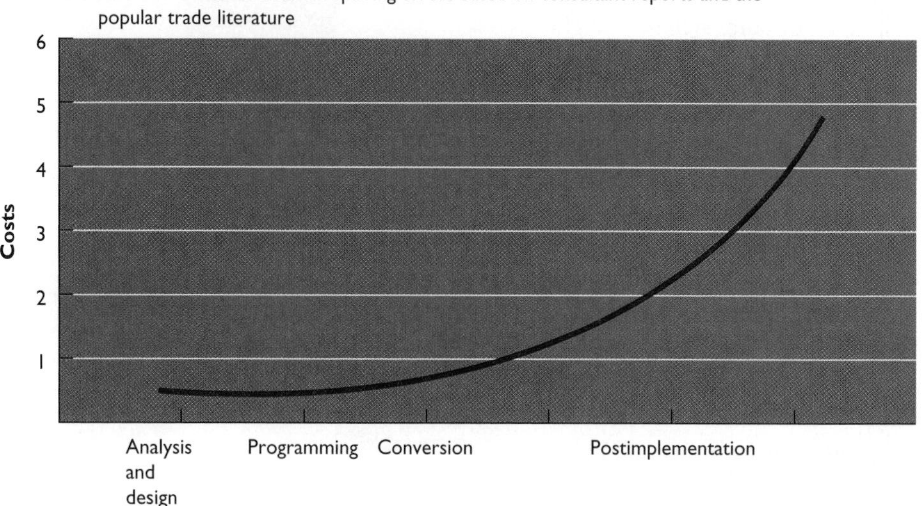


***Figure 14-3*** The cost of errors over the systems development cycle. The most common, most severe, and most expensive system errors develop in the early design stages. They involve faulty requirements analysis. Errors in program logic or syntax are much less common, less severe, and less costly to repair than design errors.
*Source:* Alberts, 1976.

Figure 14-3 illustrates the cost of correcting errors based on the experience of consultants reported in the literature. If errors are detected early, during analysis and design, the cost to the systems development effort is small. But if they are not discovered until after programming, testing, or conversion have been completed, the costs can soar astronomically. A minor logic error, for example, that could take one hour to correct during the analysis and design stage could take 10, 40, and 90 times as long to correct during programming, conversion, and postimplementation, respectively.

## Data Quality Problems

The most common source of information system failure is poor data quality. Data that are inaccurate, untimely, or inconsistent with other sources of information can create serious operational and financial problems for businesses. When bad data go unnoticed, they can lead to bad decisions, product recalls, and even financial losses (Redman, 1998). Companies cannot pursue aggressive marketing and customer relationship management strategies unless they have high-quality data about their customers. Table 14-4 describes examples of data quality problems.

Poor data quality may stem from errors during data input or faulty information system and database design (Wand and Wang, 1996; Strong, Lee, and Wang, 1997). In the following sections we examine how organizations can deal with data and software quality problems as well as other threats to information systems.

### TABLE 14-4 Examples of Data Quality Problems

| Organization | Data Quality Problem |
|---|---|
| Sears Roebuck | Could not effectively pursue cross-selling among its customers because each of its businesses, including retail, home services, credit, and Web site, had their own information systems with conflicting customer data. Sears needed to develop a massive data warehouse that consolidated and cleansed the data from all of these systems in order to create a single customer list. |
| Paint Bull | Found that nearly half the names in its purchased mailing lists of prospective customers were inaccurate or out of date. Lost $10 for every promotional package of videos and catalogs that was returned as undeliverable. |
| FBI | A study of the FBI's computerized criminal record systems found a total of 54.1 percent of the records in the National Crime Information Center System were inaccurate, ambiguous, or incomplete. The FBI has taken some steps to correct these problems, but computerized criminal history records are used to screen employees in both the public and private sectors. Inaccurate records could unjustly deny people employment. |
| Supermarkets | Several studies have established that 5 to 12 percent of bar code sales at retail supermarkets are erroneous and that the average ratio of overcharges to undercharges runs 4:1. |

## 14.2 Creating a Control Environment

To minimize errors, disaster, interruptions of service, computer crime, and breaches of security, special policies and procedures must be incorporated into the design and implementation of information systems. The combination of manual and automated measures that safeguard information systems and ensure that they perform according to management standards is termed controls. **Controls** consist of all the methods, policies, and organizational procedures that ensure the safety of the organization's assets, the accuracy and reliability of its accounting records, and operational adherence to management standards.

**controls**
All of the methods, policies, and procedures that ensure protection of the organization's assets, accuracy and reliability of its records, and operational adherence to management standards.

In the past, the control of information systems was treated as an afterthought, addressed only toward the end of implementation, just before the system was installed. Today, however, organizations are so critically dependent on information systems that vulnerabilities and control issues must be identified as early as possible. The control and security of an information system must be an integral part of its design. Users and builders of systems must pay close attention to security controls throughout the system's life span starting with requirements development (Viega, Kohno and Potter, 2001.)

### General Controls and Application Controls

Computer systems are controlled by a combination of general controls and application controls. **General controls** are those that control the design, security, and use of computer programs and the security of data files in general throughout the organization's information technology infrastructure. On the whole, general controls apply to all computerized applications and consist of a combination of hardware, software, and manual procedures that create an overall control environment.

**general controls**
Overall controls that establish a framework for controlling the design, security, and use of computer programs throughout an organization.

**Application controls** are specific controls unique to each computerized application, such as payroll, accounts receivable, and order processing. They consist of controls applied from the user functional area of a particular system and from programmed procedures.

**application controls**
Specific controls unique to each computerized application.

### General Controls

General controls are overall controls governing the organization's information technology infrastructure. They apply to all application areas. General controls include the following:

- Controls over the system implementation process
- Software controls
- Physical hardware controls
- Computer operations controls
- Data security controls
- Administrative disciplines, standards, and procedures

***Implementation Controls*** **Implementation controls** audit the systems development process at various points to ensure that the process is properly controlled and managed. The systems development audit should look for the presence of formal review points at various stages of development that enable users and management to approve or disapprove the implementation. The systems development audit also should examine the level of user involvement at each stage of implementation and check for the use of a formal cost–benefit methodology in establishing system feasibility. The audit should look for the use of controls and quality assurance techniques for program development; conversion; and testing and for complete and thorough system, user, and operations documentation.

**implementation controls**
The audit of the systems development process at various points to make sure that it is properly controlled and managed.

***Software Controls*** Controls are essential for the various categories of software used in computer systems. **Software controls** monitor the use of system software and prevent unauthorized access of software programs, system software, and computer programs. System software is an important control area, because it performs overall control functions for the programs that directly process data and data files.

**software controls**
Controls to ensure the security and reliability of software.

***Hardware Controls*** **Hardware controls** ensure that computer hardware is physically secure, and they check for equipment malfunction. Computer hardware should be physically secured so that it can be accessed only by authorized individuals. Computer equipment

**hardware controls**
Controls to ensure the physical security and correct performance of computer hardware.

should be specially protected against fires and extremes of temperature and humidity. Organizations that are critically dependent on their computers also must make provisions for backing up processing and disk storage devices or continued operation to maintain constant service. Many kinds of computer hardware contain mechanisms that check for equipment malfunction.

**computer operations controls**
Procedures to ensure that programmed procedures are consistently and correctly applied to data storage and processing.

***Computer Operations Controls*** **Computer operations controls** apply to the work of the computer department and help ensure that programmed procedures are consistently and correctly applied to the storage and processing of data. They include controls over the setup of computer processing jobs, operations software, computer operations, and backup and recovery procedures for processing that ends abnormally. Specific instructions for backup and recovery can be developed so that, in the event of a hardware or software failure, the recovery process for production programs, system software, and data files does not create erroneous changes in the system.

**data security controls**
Controls to ensure that data files on either disk or tape are not subject to unauthorized access, change, or destruction.

***Data Security Controls*** **Data security controls** ensure that valuable business data files on either disk or tape are not subject to unauthorized access, change, or destruction. Such controls are required for data files when they are in use and when they are being held for storage.

When data can be input on-line through a terminal, entry of unauthorized input must be prevented. For example, a credit note could be altered to match a sales invoice on file. In such situations, security can be developed on several levels:

- Terminals can be physically restricted so that they are available only to authorized individuals.
- System software can include the use of passwords assigned only to authorized individuals. No one can log on to the system without a valid password.
- Additional sets of passwords and security restrictions can be developed for specific systems and applications. For example, data security software can limit access to specific files, such as the files for the accounts receivable system. It can restrict the type of access so that only individuals authorized to update these specific files will have the ability to do so. All others will only be able to read the files or will be denied access altogether.
- Figure 14-4 illustrates the security allowed for two sets of users of an on-line personnel database with sensitive information such as employees' salaries, benefits, and medical histories. One set of users consists of all employees who perform clerical functions such

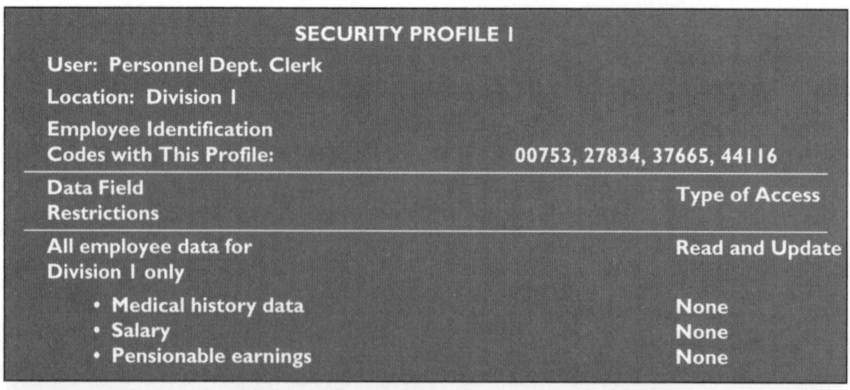

SECURITY PROFILE 1
User: Personnel Dept. Clerk
Location: Division 1
Employee Identification Codes with This Profile: 00753, 27834, 37665, 44116

| Data Field Restrictions | Type of Access |
|---|---|
| All employee data for Division 1 only | Read and Update |
| • Medical history data | None |
| • Salary | None |
| • Pensionable earnings | None |

SECURITY PROFILE 2
User: Divisional Personnel Manager
Location: Division 1
Employee Identification Codes with This Profile: 27321

| Data Field Restrictions | Type of Access |
|---|---|
| All employee data for Division 1 only | Read Only |

*Figure 14-4* Security profiles for a personnel system. These two examples represent two security profiles or data security patterns that might be found in a personnel system. Depending on the security profile, a user would have certain restrictions on access to various systems, locations, or data in an organization.

as inputting employee data into the system. All individuals with this type of profile can update the system but can neither read nor update sensitive fields such as salary, medical history, or earnings data. Another profile applies to a divisional manager, who cannot update the system but who can read all employee data fields for his or her division, including medical history and salary. These profiles would be established and maintained by a data security system. The data security system illustrated in Figure 14-5 provides very fine-grained security restrictions, such as allowing authorized personnel users to inquire about all employee information except in confidential fields such as salary or medical history. The chapter opening vignette described how Keystone Mercy Health Plan developed such data security profiles to protect confidential information.

***Administrative Controls*** **Administrative controls** are formalized standards, rules, procedures, and control disciplines to ensure that the organization's general and application controls are properly executed and enforced. The most important administrative controls are (1) segregation of functions, (2) written policies and procedures, and (3) supervision.

**administrative controls** Formalized standards, rules, procedures, and disciplines to ensure that the organization's controls are properly executed and enforced.

**Segregation of functions** means that job functions should be designed to minimize the risk of errors or fraudulent manipulation of the organization's assets. The individuals responsible for operating systems should not be the same ones who can initiate transactions that change the assets held in these systems. A typical arrangement is to have the organization's information systems department responsible for data and program files and end users responsible for initiating transactions such as payments or checks.

**segregation of functions** The principle of internal control to divide responsibilities and assign tasks among people so that job functions do not overlap, and to minimize the risk of errors and fraudulent manipulation of the organization's assets.

Written policies and procedures establish formal standards for controlling information system operations. Procedures must be formalized in writing and authorized by the appropriate level of management. Accountabilities and responsibilities must be clearly specified.

Supervision of personnel involved in control procedures ensures that the controls for an information system are performing as intended. Without adequate supervision, the best-designed set of controls may be bypassed, short circuited, or neglected.

## Application Controls

*Application controls* are specific controls within each separate computer application, such as payroll or order processing. They include automated and manual procedures that ensure that only authorized data are completely and accurately processed by that application. The controls for each application should encompass the whole sequence of processing.

Not all of the application controls discussed here are used in every information system. Some systems require more of these controls than others, depending on the importance of the data and the nature of the application. Application controls can be classified as (1) input controls, (2) processing controls, and (3) output controls.

***Input Controls*** **Input controls** check data for accuracy and completeness when they are entered into the system. There are specific input controls for input authorization, data conversion, data editing, and error handling.

**input controls** The procedures to check data for accuracy and completeness when they are entered into the system.

Input must be properly authorized, recorded, and monitored as source documents flow to the computer. For example, formal procedures can be set up to authorize only select members of the sales department to prepare sales transactions for an order entry system.

Input must be properly converted into computer transactions, with no errors as it is transcribed from one form to another. Transcription errors can be eliminated or reduced by keying input transactions directly into computer terminals or by using some form of source data automation.

**Control totals** can be established beforehand for input transactions. These totals can range from a simple document count to totals for quantity fields, such as total sales amount (for a batch of transactions). Computer programs count the totals from transactions input.

**control totals** A type of input control that requires counting transactions or quantity fields prior to processing for comparison and reconciliation after processing.

**Edit checks** include various programmed routines that can be performed to edit input data for errors before they are processed. Transactions that do not meet edit criteria are rejected. For example, data might be checked to make sure they were in the right format (e.g., nine-digit social security numbers should not contain any alphabetic characters) or that only valid codes used by the system were entered. (An employee can only have a Fair Labor Standards Act code of 1, 2, 3, 4, or 5.) The edit routines can produce lists of errors to be corrected later.

**edit checks** Routines performed to verify input data and correct errors prior to processing.

***Processing Controls*** **Processing controls** establish that data are complete and accurate during updating. The major processing controls are run control totals, computer matching, and programmed edit checks.

**processing controls** The routines for establishing that data are complete and accurate during updating.

**Run control totals** reconcile the input control totals with the totals of items that have updated the file. Updating can be controlled by generating control totals during processing. The totals, such as total transactions processed or totals for critical quantities, can be compared manually or by computer. Discrepancies are noted for investigation.

**run control totals** The procedures for controlling completeness of computer updating by generating control totals that reconcile totals before and after processing.

**Computer matching** matches the input data with information held on master or suspense files, with unmatched items noted for investigation. Most matching occurs during input, but under some circumstances it may be required to ensure completeness of updating. For example, a matching program might match employee time cards with a payroll master file and report missing or duplicate time cards.

**computer matching** The processing control that matches input data to information held on master files.

Most edit checking occurs at the time data are input. However, certain applications require some type of reasonableness or dependency check during updating. For example, consistency checks might be used by a utility company to compare a customer's electric bill with previous bills. If the bill was 500 percent higher this month compared to last month, the bill would not be processed until the meter was rechecked.

***Output Controls*** **Output controls** ensure that the results of computer processing are accurate, complete, and properly distributed. Typical output controls include the following:

**output controls** Measures that ensure that the results of computer processing are accurate, complete, and properly distributed.

- Balancing output totals with input and processing totals
- Reviews of the computer processing logs to determine that all of the correct computer jobs executed properly for processing
- Formal procedures and documentation specifying authorized recipients of output reports, checks, or other critical documents

## PROTECTING THE DIGITAL FIRM

As companies increasingly rely on digital networks for their revenue and operations, they need to take additional steps to ensure that their systems and applications are always available to support their digital business processes.

### High-Availability Computing

In a digital firm environment, information technology infrastructures must provide a continuous level of service availability across distributed computing platforms. Many factors can disrupt the performance of a Web site, including network failure, heavy Internet traffic, and exhausted server resources. Computer failures, interruptions, and downtime can translate into disgruntled customers, millions of dollars in lost sales, and the inability to perform critical internal transactions. Firms such as those in the airline and financial service industries with critical applications requiring on-line transaction processing have traditionally used fault-tolerant computer systems for many years to ensure 100 percent availability. In **on-line transaction processing,** transactions entered on-line are immediately processed by the computer. Multitudinous changes to databases, reporting, or requests for information occur each instant. **Fault-tolerant computer systems** contain redundant hardware, software, and power supply components that can back up the system and keep it running to prevent system failure. Fault-tolerant computers contain extra memory chips, processors, and disk storage devices. They use special software routines or self-checking logic built into their circuitry to detect hardware failures and automatically switch to a backup device. Parts from these computers can be removed and repaired without disruption to the computer system. E-Smart Direct Services, Inc. of Etobicoke, Ontario, in Canada, a provider of electronic payment processing and authorization services for retailers and financial institutions, needs a technology platform with 100 percent 24-hour system availability. The company uses fault-tolerant systems from Stratus for this purpose.

**on-line transaction processing** Transaction processing mode in which transactions entered on-line are immediately processed by the computer.

**fault-tolerant computer systems** Systems that contain extra hardware, software, and power supply components that can back up a system and keep it running continuously to prevent system failure.

Fault tolerance should be distinguished from **high-availability computing.** Both fault tolerance and high-availability computing are designed to maximize application and system availability. Both use backup hardware resources. However, high-availability computing helps firms recover quickly from a crash, whereas fault tolerance promises continuous availability and the elimination of recovery time altogether. High-availability computing environ-

**high-availability computing** Tools and technologies, including backup hardware resources, to enable a system to recover quickly from a crash.

ments are a minimum requirement for firms with heavy electronic commerce processing or for those that depend on digital networks for their internal operations. High-availability computing requires an assortment of tools and technologies to ensure maximum performance of computer systems and networks, including redundant servers, mirroring, load balancing, clustering, storage area networks (see Chapter 5), and a good disaster recovery plan. The firm's computing platform must be extremely robust with scalable processing power, storage, and bandwidth.

**Load balancing** distributes large numbers of access requests across multiple servers. The requests are directed to the most available server so that no single device is overwhelmed. If one server starts to get swamped, requests are forwarded to another server with more capacity. **Mirroring** uses a backup server that duplicates all the processes and transactions of the primary server. If the primary server fails, the backup server can immediately take its place without any interruption in service. However, server mirroring is very expensive, because each server must be mirrored by an identical server whose only purpose is to be available in the event of a failure. Clustering is a less expensive technique for ensuring continued availability. High-availability **clustering** links two computers together so that the second computer can act as a backup to the primary computer. If the primary computer fails, the second computer picks up its processing without any pause in the system. (Computers can also be clustered together as a single computing resource to speed up processing.) High-availability computing also requires a security infrastructure that can support electronic commerce and electronic business, as described in the following section.

**load balancing**
Distribution of large numbers of requests for access among multiple servers so that no single device is overwhelmed.

**mirroring**
Duplicating all the processes and transactions of a server on a backup server to prevent any interruption in service if the primary server fails.

**clustering**
Linking two computers together so that the second computer can act as a backup to the primary computer or speed up processing.

## Internet Security Challenges

Linking to the Internet or transmitting information via intranets and extranets requires special security measures. Large public networks, including the Internet, are vulnerable, because they are virtually open to anyone and because they are so huge that, when abuses do occur, they can have an enormously widespread impact. When the Internet becomes part of the corporate network, the organization's information systems become vulnerable to actions from outsiders. The architecture of a Web-based application typically includes a Web client, a server, and corporate information systems linked to databases (review Figure 7-21 in Chapter 7 and Figure 9-3 in Chapter 9). Each of these components presents security challenges and vulnerabilities (Joshi, Aref, Ghafoor, and Spafford, 2001.)

Computers that are constantly connected to the Internet via cable modem or DSL line are more open to penetration by outsiders, because they use a fixed Internet address where they can be more easily identified. (With dial-up service, a temporary Internet address is assigned for each session.) A fixed Internet address creates a fixed target for hackers.

Both electronic commerce and electronic business require companies to be both more open and more closed at the same time. To benefit from electronic commerce, supply chain management, and other digital business processes, companies need to be open to outsiders such as customers, suppliers, and trading partners. Corporate systems must also be extended outside the organization so that they can be accessed by employees working with wireless and other mobile computing devices. Yet these systems also must be closed to hackers and other intruders. The new information technology infrastructure requires a new security culture and infrastructure that allows businesses to straddle this fine line.

Chapter 9 described the use of *firewalls* to prevent unauthorized users from accessing private networks. As growing numbers of businesses expose their networks to Internet traffic, firewalls are becoming a necessity.

A firewall is generally placed between internal LANs and WANs and external networks such as the Internet. The firewall controls access to the organization's internal networks by acting like a gatekeeper that examines each user's credentials before allowing access to the network. The firewall identifies names, Internet Protocol (IP) addresses, applications, and other characteristics of incoming traffic. It checks this information against the access rules that have been programmed into the system by the network administrator. The firewall prevents unauthorized communication into and out of the network, allowing the organization to enforce a security policy on traffic flowing between its network and the Internet.

There are essentially two major types of firewall technologies: proxies and stateful inspection. *Proxies* stop data originating outside the organization at the firewall, inspect them, and pass a proxy to the other side of the firewall. If a user outside the company wants to communicate with a user inside the organization, the outside user first "talks" to the proxy application and the proxy application communicates with the firm's internal computer. Likewise a computer user inside the organization goes through the proxy to "talk" to computers on the outside. Because the actual message doesn't pass through the firewall, proxies are considered more secure than stateful inspection. However, they have to do a lot of work and can consume system resources, degrading network performance. The Raptor Firewall product is primarily a proxy-based firewall.

In *stateful inspection,* the firewall scans each packet of incoming data, checking its source, destination addresses, or services. It sets up state tables to track information over multiple packets. User-defined access rules must identify every type of packet that the organization does not want to admit. Although stateful inspection consumes fewer network resources than proxies, it is theoretically not as secure, because some data pass through the firewall. Cisco Systems' firewall product is an example of a stateful inspection firewall. Hybrid firewall products are being developed. For instance, Check Point is primarily a stateful inspection product, but it has incorporated some proxy capabilities for communication.

To create a good firewall, someone must write and maintain the internal rules identifying the people, applications, or addresses that are allowed or rejected in very fine detail. Firewalls can deter, but not completely prevent, network penetration from outsiders and should be viewed as one element in an overall security plan. In order to deal effectively with Internet security, broader corporate policies and procedures, user responsibilities, and security awareness training may be required (Segev, Porra, and Roldan, 1998).

**intrusion detection system**
Tools to monitor the most vulnerable points in a network to detect and deter unauthorized intruders.

In addition to firewalls, commercial security vendors now provide intrusion detection tools and services to protect against suspicious network traffic. **Intrusion detection systems** feature full-time monitoring tools placed at the most vulnerable points or "hot spots" of corporate networks to continually detect and deter intruders. Scanning software looks for known problems such as bad passwords, checks to see if important files have been removed or modified, and sends warnings of vandalism or system administration errors. Monitoring software examines events as they are happening to look for security attacks in progress. The intrusion detection tool can also be customized to shut down a particularly sensitive part of a network if it receives unauthorized traffic.

## Security and Electronic Commerce

Security of electronic communications is a major control issue for companies engaged in electronic commerce. It is essential that commerce-related data of buyers and sellers be kept private when they are transmitted electronically. The data being transmitted also must be protected against being purposefully altered by someone other than the sender, so that, for

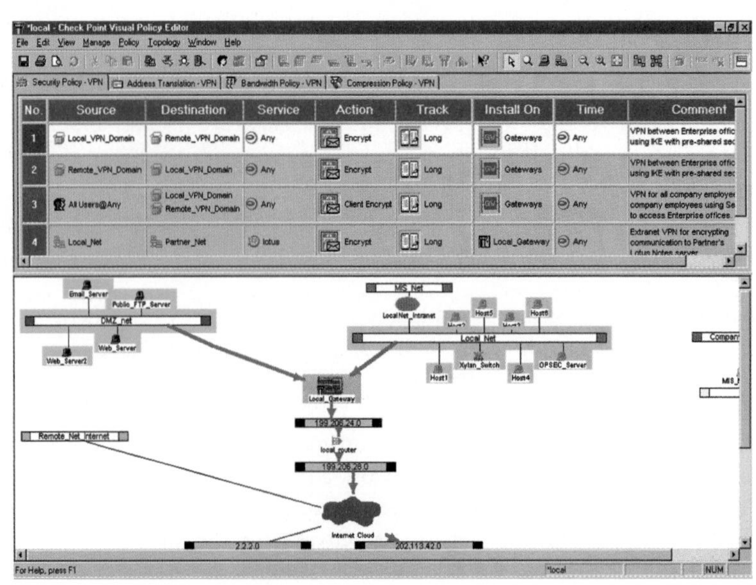


*Check Point's Firewall-1 software provides a user-friendly graphical interface for defining security rules. Firewall-1 includes tools to monitor and control what goes into and out of an organization's network.*

example, stock market execution orders or product orders accurately represent the wishes of the buyer and seller.

Much on-line commerce continues to be handled through private EDI networks usually run over VANs (value-added networks). VANs are relatively secure and reliable. However, because they have to be privately maintained and run on high-speed private lines, VANs are expensive, easily costing a company $100,000 per month. They also are inflexible, being connected only to a limited number of sites and companies. As a result, the Internet is emerging as the network technology of choice for e-commerce. EDI transactions on the Internet run from one-half to one-tenth the cost of VAN-based transactions.

Many organizations rely on encryption to protect sensitive information transmitted over the Internet and other networks. **Encryption** is the coding and scrambling of messages to prevent unauthorized access to or understanding of the data being transmitted. A message can be encrypted by applying a secret numerical code, called an encryption key, so that it is transmitted as a scrambled set of characters. (The key consists of a large group of letters, numbers, and symbols.) In order to be read, the message must be decrypted (unscrambled) with a matching key. A number of encryption standards exist. SSL (secure sockets layer) and S-HTTP (secure hypertext transport protocol) are protocols for secure information transfer over the Internet. They allow client and server computers to manage encryption and decryption activities as they communicate with each other during a secure Web session.

**encryption**
The coding and scrambling of messages to prevent their being read or accessed without authorization.

There are several alternative methods of encryption, but "public key" encryption is becoming popular. Public key encryption, illustrated in Figure 14-5, uses two different keys, one private and one public. The keys are mathematically related so that data encrypted with one key only can be decrypted using the other key. To send and receive messages, communicators first create separate pairs of private and public keys. The public key is kept in a directory and the private key must be kept secret. The sender encrypts a message with the recipient's public key. On receiving the message, the recipient uses his or her private key to decrypt it. No one else knows the private key except the recipient, ensuring that the message was kept private during transmission.

**authentication**
The ability of each party in a transaction to ascertain the identity of the other party.

**message integrity**
The ability to ascertain that a transmitted message has not been copied or altered.

Encryption helps protect transmission of payment data, such as credit card information, and addresses problems of authentication and message integrity. **Authentication** refers to the ability of each party in a transaction to know that the other parties are who they claim to be. In the nonelectronic world, we use our signatures. **Message integrity** is the ability to be certain that the message that is sent arrives without being copied or changed.

**digital signature**
A digital code that can be attached to an electronically transmitted message to uniquely identify its contents and the sender.

The Electronic Signatures in Global and National Commerce Act has given digital signatures the same legal status as those written with ink on paper. A **digital signature** uses public-key encryption to attach a digital code to an encrypted electronically transmitted message to verify the origins and contents of the message. It provides a way to associate a message with the sender, performing a function similar to a written signature.

**digital certificate**
An attachment to an electronic message to verify the identity of the sender and to provide the receiver with the means to encode a reply.

Digital certificates play a valuable role in authentication. **Digital certificates** are data files used to establish the identity of people and electronic assets for protection of on-line transactions (see Figure 14-6). A digital certificate system uses a trusted third party known as a certificate authority (CA) to validate a user's identity. The CA system can be run as a function inside an organization or by an outside company such as VeriSign Inc. in Mountain

*Figure 14-5* Public key encryption. A public key encryption system can be viewed as a series of public and private keys that lock data when they are transmitted and unlock the data when they are received. The sender locates the recipient's public key in a directory and uses it to encrypt a message. The message is sent in encrypted form over the Internet or a private network. When the encrypted message arrives, the recipient uses his or her private key to decrypt the data and read the message.

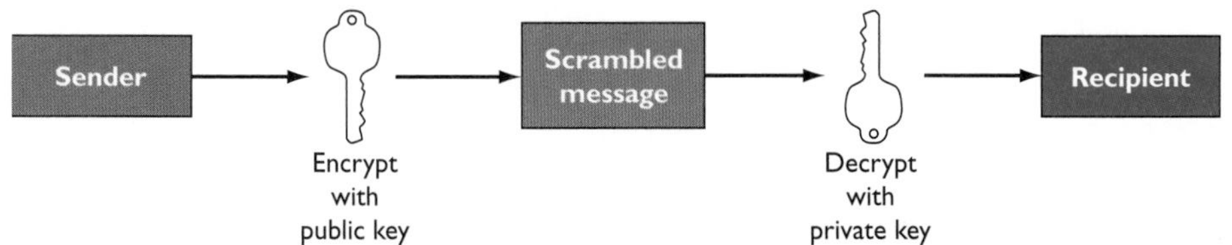

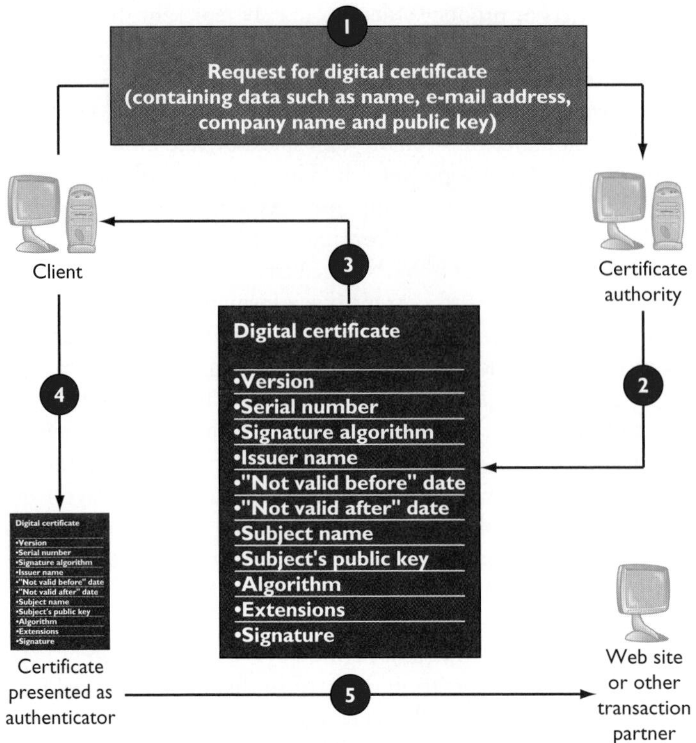


*Figure 14-6* Digital certificates. Digital certificates can be used to establish the identity of people or electronic assets. They protect on-line transactions by providing secure, encrypted on-line communication.

View, California. The CA verifies a digital certificate user's identity off-line by telephone, postal mail, or in person. This information is put into a CA server, which generates an encrypted digital certificate containing owner identification information and a copy of the owner's public key. The certificate authenticates that the public key belongs to the designated owner. The CA makes its own public key available publicly either in print or, perhaps, on the Internet. The recipient of an encrypted message uses the CA's public key to decode the digital certificate attached to the message, verifies it was issued by the CA, and then obtains the sender's public key and identification information contained in the certificate. Using this information, the recipient can send an encrypted reply. The digital certificate system would enable, for example, a credit card user and merchant to validate that their digital certificates were issued by an authorized and trusted third party before they exchange data.

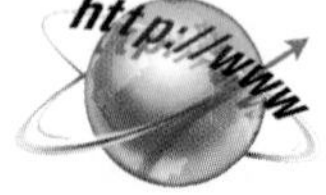


**secure electronic transaction (SET)**
A standard for securing credit card transactions over the Internet and other networks.

Many credit card payment systems use the secure sockets layer (SSL) protocol for encrypting the credit card payment data. However, SSL does not verify that the purchaser is the owner of the card being used for payment. VISA International, MasterCard International, American Express, and other major credit card companies and banks have adopted a more secure protocol, called the **secure electronic transaction (SET)** protocol, for encrypting credit card payment data over the Internet and other open networks. Figure 14-7 illustrates how SET works. A user acquires a digital certificate and SET-enabled digital wallet. The wallet and certificate specify the identity of the user and the credit card being used. When the user shops at a Web site that uses the SET payment method, the merchant's servers send a signal over the Internet that invokes the user's SET wallet. The digital wallet encrypts the payment information and sends it to the merchant. The merchant then encrypts this information and passes it on to its bank. The merchant's bank sends this encrypted information to the customer's issuing bank, which approves or denies the transaction based on credit standing. If the payment is authorized, the merchant's bank arranges for the fund transfer from user to merchant and the user's credit card account is charged for the transaction amount. The merchant then ships the merchandise to the purchaser.

## DEVELOPING A CONTROL STRUCTURE: COSTS AND BENEFITS

Information systems can make exhaustive use of all the control mechanisms previously discussed. But they may be so expensive to build and so complicated to use that the system is

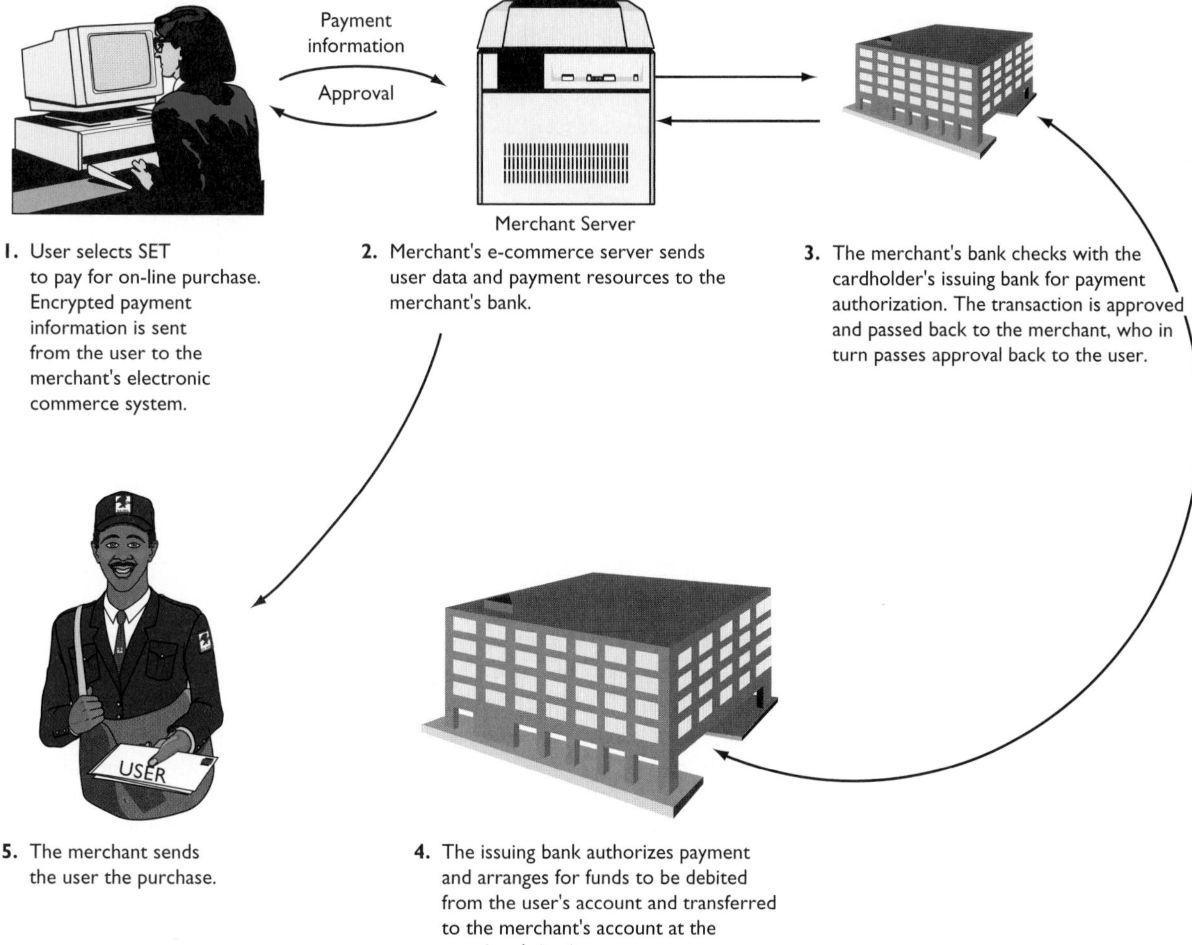

Payment information
Approval
Merchant Server
1. User selects SET to pay for on-line purchase. Encrypted payment information is sent from the user to the merchant's electronic commerce system.
2. Merchant's e-commerce server sends user data and payment resources to the merchant's bank.
3. The merchant's bank checks with the cardholder's issuing bank for payment authorization. The transaction is approved and passed back to the merchant, who in turn passes approval back to the user.
USER
5. The merchant sends the user the purchase.
4. The issuing bank authorizes payment and arranges for funds to be debited from the user's account and transferred to the merchant's account at the merchant's bank.


***Figure 14-7*** How SET (secure electronic transaction protocol) works. The SET standard for secure credit card transactions supports both sellers and buyers.

economically or operationally unfeasible. Some cost–benefit analysis must be performed to determine which control mechanisms provide the most effective safeguards without sacrificing operational efficiency or cost.

One of the criteria that determines how much control is built into a system is the importance of its data. Major financial and accounting systems, such as a payroll system or one that tracks purchases and sales on the stock exchange, must have higher standards of control than a tickler system to track dental patients and remind them that their six-month checkup is due. For instance, SwissAir invested in additional hardware and software to increase its network reliability because it was running critical reservation and ticketing applications.

The cost effectiveness of controls also will be influenced by the efficiency, complexity, and expense of each control technique. For example, complete one-for-one checking may be time consuming and operationally impossible for a system that processes hundreds of thousands of utilities payments daily. But it might be possible to use this technique to verify only critical data such as dollar amounts and account numbers, while ignoring names and addresses.

A third consideration is the level of risk if a specific activity or process is not properly controlled. System builders can undertake a **risk assessment,** determining the likely frequency of a problem and the potential damage if it were to occur. For example, if an event is likely to occur no more than once a year, with a maximum of $1,000 loss to the organization, it would not be feasible to spend $20,000 on the design and maintenance of a control to protect against that event. However, if that same event could occur at least once a day, with a potential loss of more than $300,000 a year, $100,000 spent on a control might be entirely appropriate.

**risk assessment**
Determining the potential frequency of the occurrence of a problem and the potential damage if the problem were to occur. Used to determine the cost–benefit of a control.

### TABLE 14-5 ON-LINE ORDER PROCESSING RISK ASSESSMENT

| Exposure | Probability of Occurrence (%) | Loss Range/ Average | Expected Annual Loss |
|---|---|---|---|
| Power failure | 30% | $5,000–$200,000 ($102,500) | $30,750 |
| Embezzlement | 5 | $1,000–$50,000 ($25,500) | $1,275 |
| User error | 98 | $200–$40,000 ($20,100) | $19,698 |

This chart shows the results of a risk assessment of three selected areas of an on-line order processing system. The likelihood of each exposure occurring over a one-year period is expressed as a percentage. The second column shows the highest and lowest possible loss that could be expected each time the exposure occurred and an average loss calculated by adding the highest and lowest figures together and dividing by 2. The expected annual loss of each exposure can be determined by multiplying the average loss by its probability of occurrence.

Table 14-5 illustrates sample results of a risk assessment for an on-line order processing system that processes 30,000 orders per day. The probability of a power failure occurring in a one-year period is 30 percent. Loss of order transactions while power is down could range from $5,000 to $200,000 for each occurrence, depending on how long processing is halted. The probability of embezzlement occurring over a yearly period is about 5 percent, with potential losses ranging from $1,000 to $50,000 for each occurrence. User errors have a 98 percent chance of occurring over a yearly period, with losses ranging from $200 to $40,000 for each occurrence. The average loss for each event can be weighted by multiplying it by the probability of its occurrence annually to determine the expected annual loss. Once the risks have been assessed, system builders can concentrate on the control points with the greatest vulnerability and potential loss. In this case, controls should focus on ways to minimize the risk of power failures and user errors. Increasing management awareness of the full range of actions they can take to reduce risks can substantially reduce system losses (Straub and Welke, 1998).

In some situations, organizations may not know the precise probability of threats occurring to their information systems, and they may not be able to quantify the impact of such events. In these instances, management may choose to describe risks and their likely impact in a qualitative manner (Rainer, Snyder, and Carr, 1991).

To decide which controls to use, information system builders must examine various control techniques in relation to each other and to their relative cost effectiveness. A control weakness at one point may be offset by a strong control at another. It may not be cost effective to build tight controls at every point in the processing cycle if the areas of greatest risk are secure or if compensating controls exist elsewhere. The combination of all of the controls developed for a particular application will determine its overall control structure.

## THE ROLE OF AUDITING IN THE CONTROL PROCESS

**MIS audit**
Identifies all the controls that govern individual information systems and assesses their effectiveness.

How does management know that information system controls are effective? To answer this question, organizations must conduct comprehensive and systematic audits. An **MIS audit** identifies all of the controls that govern individual information systems and assesses their effectiveness. To accomplish this, the auditor must acquire a thorough understanding of operations, physical facilities, telecommunications, control systems, data security objectives, organizational structure, personnel, manual procedures, and individual applications.

The auditor usually interviews key individuals who use and operate a specific information system concerning their activities and procedures. Application controls, overall integrity controls, and control disciplines are examined. The auditor should trace the flow of sample transactions through the system and perform tests, using, if appropriate, automated audit software.

## MANAGEMENT DECISION PROBLEM

### ANALYZING SECURITY VULNERABILITIES

A survey of your firm's information technology infrastructure has produced the following security analysis statistics:

High-risk vulnerabilities include nonauthorized users accessing applications, guessable passwords, user name matching the password, active user accounts with missing passwords, and the existence of unauthorized programs in application systems.

Medium-risk vulnerabilities include the ability of users to shut down the system without being logged on, passwords and screen saver settings that were not established for PCs, and outdated versions of software still being stored on hard drives.

Low-risk vulnerabilities include the inability of users to change their passwords, user passwords that have not been changed periodically, and passwords that were smaller than the minimum size specified by the company.

1. Calculate the total number of vulnerabilities for each platform. What is the potential impact of the security problems for each computing platform on the organization?
2. If you only have one information systems specialist in charge of security, which platforms should you address first in trying to eliminate these vulnerabilities? Second? Third? Last? Why?
3. Identify the types of control problems illustrated by these vulnerabilities and explain the measures that should be taken to solve them.
4. What does your firm risk by ignoring the security vulnerabilities identified?

**Security Vulnerabilities by Type of Computing Platform**

| Platform | Number of Computers | High Risk | Medium Risk | Low Risk | Total Vulnerabilities |
|---|---|---|---|---|---|
| Windows 2000 Server (corporate applications) | 1 | 11 | 37 | 19 | |
| Windows 2000 Workstation (high-level administrators) | 3 | 56 | 242 | 87 | |
| Linux (e-mail and printing services) | 1 | 3 | 154 | 98 | |
| Sun Solaris (Unix,) e-commerce and Web servers | 2 | 12 | 299 | 78 | |
| Windows 98 (user desktops and laptops with office productivity tools that can also be linked to the corporate network running corporate applications and the intranet) | 195 | 14 | 16 | 1,237 | |

The audit lists and ranks all control weaknesses and estimates the probability of their occurrence. It then assesses the financial and organizational impact of each threat. Figure 14-8 is a sample auditor's listing of control weaknesses for a loan system. It includes a section for notifying management of such weaknesses and for management's response. Management is expected to devise a plan for countering significant weaknesses in controls.

## *14.3* ENSURING SYSTEM QUALITY

Organizations can improve system quality by using software quality assurance techniques and by improving the quality of their data.

### SOFTWARE QUALITY ASSURANCE METHODOLOGIES AND TOOLS

Solutions to software quality problems include using an appropriate systems development methodology, proper resource allocation during systems development, the use of metrics, and attention to testing.

#### Structured Methodologies

Various tools and development methodologies have been employed to help system builders document, analyze, design, and implement information systems. A **development methodology** is a collection of methods, one or more, for every activity within every phase of a systems development project. The primary function of a development methodology is to provide discipline to the entire development process. A good development methodology establishes organization-wide standards for requirements gathering, design, programming, and testing. To produce quality software, organizations must select an appropriate methodology and then enforce its use. Specifications also must include agreed on measures of system quality so that the system can be evaluated objectively while it is being developed and once it is completed.

**development methodology** A collection of methods, one or more for every activity within every phase of a development project.

Development methodologies reflect different philosophies of systems development. Chapter 10 described object-oriented software development. The traditional structured methodologies

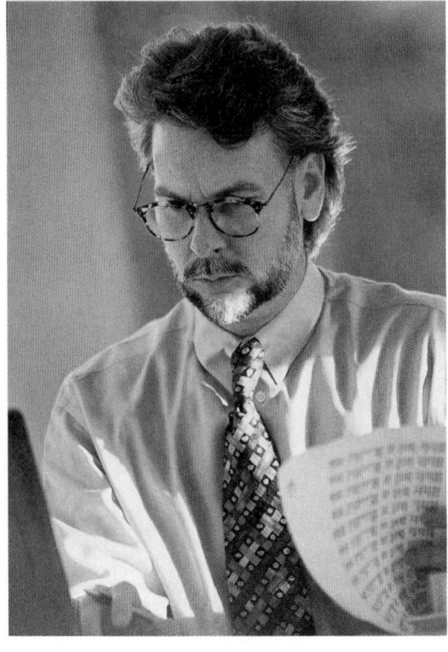

*An auditor interviews key individuals who use and operate a specific information system concerning their activities and procedures. The auditor often traces the flow of sample transactions through the system and performs tests using automated audit software.*

**structured**
Refers to the fact that techniques are carefully drawn up, step by step, with each step building on a previous one.

and computer-aided software engineering (CASE) are other important methodologies and tools for producing quality software. Structured methodologies have been used to document, analyze, and design information systems since the 1970s. **Structured** refers to the fact that the techniques are step by step, with each step building on the previous one. Structured methodologies are top-down, progressing from the highest, most abstract level to the lowest level of detail—from the general to the specific. For example, the highest level of a top-down description of a human resources system would show the main human resources functions: personnel, benefits, compensation, and Equal Employment Opportunity (EEO). Each of these would be broken down into the next layer. Benefits, for instance, might include pension, employee savings, healthcare, and insurance. Each of these layers in turn would be broken down until the lowest level of detail could be depicted.

The traditional structured methodologies are process oriented rather than data oriented. Although data descriptions are part of the methods, the methodologies focus on how the data are transformed rather than on the data themselves. These methodologies are largely linear; each phase must be completed before the next one can begin. Structured methodologies include structured analysis, structured design, structured programming and the use of flowcharts.

**structured analysis**
A method for defining system inputs, processes, and outputs and for partitioning systems into subsystems or modules that show a logical graphic model of information flow.

## Structured Analysis

**Structured analysis** is widely used to define system inputs, processes, and outputs. It offers a logical graphic model of information flow, partitioning a system into modules that show manageable levels of detail. It rigorously specifies the processes or transformations that occur within each module and the interfaces that exist between them. Its primary tool is the **data**

***Figure 14-8*** Sample auditor's list of control weaknesses. This chart is a sample page from a list of control weaknesses that an auditor might find in a loan system in a local commercial bank. This form helps auditors record and evaluate control weaknesses and shows the results of discussing those weaknesses with management, as well as any corrective actions taken by management.

Function: Personal Loans
Location: Peoria, Ill.
Prepared by: J. Ericson
Preparation date: June 16, 2001
Received by: T. Barrow
Review date: June 28, 2001

| Nature of Weakness and Impact | Chance for Substantial Error | | Effect on Audit Procedures | Notification to Management | |
|---|---|---|---|---|---|
| | Yes/ No | Justification | Required Amendment | Date of Report | Management Response |
| Loan repayment records are not reconciled to borrower's records during processing. | Yes | Without a detection control, errors in individual client balances may remain undetected. | Confirm a sample of loans. | 5/10/01 | Interest Rate Compare Report provides this control. |
| There are no regular audits of computer-generated data (interest charges). | Yes | Without a regular audit or reasonableness check, widespread miscalculations could result before errors are detected. | | 5/10/01 | Periodic audits of loans will be instituted. |
| Programs can be put into production libraries to meet target deadlines without final approval from the Standards and Controls group. | No | All programs require management authorization. The Standards and Controls group controls access to all production systems, and assigns such cases to a temporary production status. | | | |

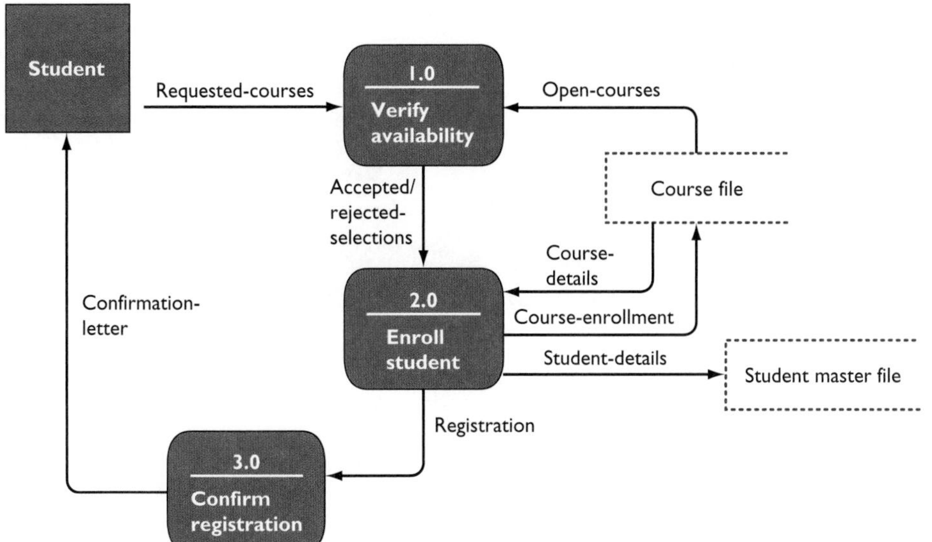


*Figure 14-9* Data flow diagram for mail-in university registration system. The system has three processes: Verify availability (1.0), Enroll student (2.0), and Confirm registration (3.0). The name and content of each of the data flows appear adjacent to each arrow. There is one external entity in this system: the student. There are two data stores: the student master file and the course file.

**flow diagram (DFD),** a graphic representation of a system's component processes and the interfaces (flow of data) between them.

**data flow diagram (DFD)** Primary tool for structured analysis that graphically illustrates a system's component processes and the flow of data between them.

Figure 14-9 shows a simple data flow diagram for a mail-in university course registration system. The rounded boxes represent processes, which portray the transformation of data. The square box represents an external entity, which is an originator or receiver of information located outside the boundaries of the system being modeled. The open rectangles represent data stores, which are either manual or automated inventories of data. The arrows represent data flows, which show the movement between processes, external entities, and data stores. They always contain packets of data with the name or content of each data flow listed beside the arrow.

This data flow diagram shows that students submit registration forms with their name, identification number, and the numbers of the courses they wish to take. In process 1.0 the system verifies that each course selected is still open by referencing the university's course file. The file distinguishes courses that are open from those that have been canceled or filled. Process 1.0 then determines which of the student's selections can be accepted or rejected. Process 2.0 enrolls the student in the courses for which he or she has been accepted. It updates the university's course file with the student's name and identification number and recalculates the class size. If maximum enrollment has been reached, the course number is flagged as closed. Process 2.0 also updates the university's student master file with information about new students or changes in address. Process 3.0 then sends each student applicant a confirmation-of-registration letter listing the courses for which he or she is registered and noting the course selections that could not be fulfilled.

The diagrams can be used to depict higher-level processes as well as lower-level details. Through leveled data flow diagrams, a complex process can be broken down into successive levels of detail. An entire system can be divided into subsystems with a high-level data flow diagram. Each subsystem, in turn, can be divided into additional subsystems with second-level data flow diagrams, and the lower-level subsystems can be broken down again until the lowest level of detail has been reached.

Another tool for structured analysis is a data dictionary, which contains information about individual pieces of data and data groupings within a system (see Chapter 7). The data dictionary defines the contents of data flows and data stores so that system builders understand exactly what pieces of data they contain. **Process specifications** describe the transformation occurring within the lowest levels of the data flow diagrams. They express the logic for each process.

**process specifications** Describe the logic of the processes occurring within the lowest levels of a data flow diagram.

## Structured Design

**Structured design** encompasses a set of design rules and techniques that promotes program clarity and simplicity, thereby reducing the time and effort required for coding, debugging,

**structured design** Software design discipline encompassing a set of design rules and techniques for designing systems from the top down in a hierarchical fashion.

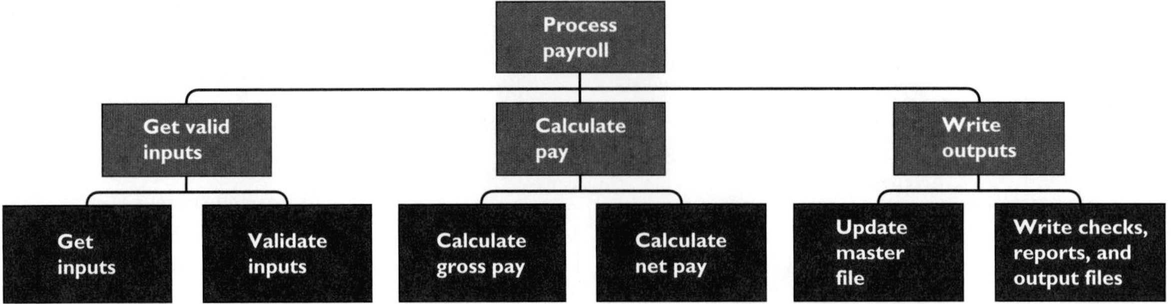


*Figure 14-10* High-level structure chart for a payroll system. This structure chart shows the highest or most abstract level of design for a payroll system, providing an overview of the entire system.

and maintenance. The main principle of structured design is that a system should be designed from the top down in hierarchical fashion and refined to greater levels of detail. The design should first consider the main function of a program or system, then break this function into subfunctions and decompose each subfunction until the lowest level of detail has been reached. The lowest level modules describe the actual processing that will occur. In this manner all high-level logic and the design model are developed before detailed program code is written. If structured analysis has been performed, the structured specification document can serve as input to the design process. Our earlier human resources top-down description provides a good overview example of structured design.

As the design is formulated, it is documented in a structure chart. The **structure chart** is a top-down chart, showing each level of design, its relationship to other levels, and its place in the overall design structure. Figure 14-10 shows a high-level structure chart for a payroll system. If a design has too many levels to fit onto one structure chart, it can be broken down further on more detailed structure charts. A structure chart may document one program, one system (a set of programs), or part of one program.

**structure chart**
System documentation showing each level of design, the relationship among the levels, and the overall place in the design structure; can document one program, one system, or part of one program.

**structured programming**
A discipline for organizing and coding programs that simplifies the control paths so that the programs can be easily understood and modified; uses the basic control structures and modules that have only one entry point and one exit point.

**module**
A logical unit of a program that performs one or several functions.

**sequence construct**
The sequential single steps or actions in the logic of a program that do not depend on the existence of any condition.

**selection construct**
The logic pattern in programming where a stated condition determines which of two alternative actions can be taken.

**iteration construct**
The logic pattern in programming where certain actions are repeated while a specified conditions occurs or until a certain condition is met.

## Structured Programming

**Structured programming** extends the principles governing structured design to the writing of programs to make software programs easier to understand and modify. It is based on the principle of modularization, which follows from top-down analysis and design. Each of the boxes in the structure chart represents a component **module** that is usually directly related to a bottom-level design module. It constitutes a logical unit that performs one or several functions. Ideally, modules should be independent of each other and should have only one entry and exit point. They should share data with as few other modules as possible. Each module should be kept to a manageable size. An individual should be able to read and understand the program code for the module and easily keep track of its functions.

Proponents of structured programming have shown that any program can be written using three basic control constructs, or instruction patterns: (1) simple sequence, (2) selection, and (3) iteration. These control constructs are illustrated in Figure 14-11.

The **sequence construct** executes statements in the order in which they appear, with control passing unconditionally from one statement to the next. The program will execute statement A and then statement B.

The **selection construct** tests a condition and executes one of two alternative instructions based on the results of the test. Condition R is tested. If R is true, statement C is executed. If R is false, statement D is executed. Control then passes to the next statement.

The **iteration construct** repeats a segment of code as long as a conditional test remains true. Condition S is tested. If S is true, statement E is executed and control returns to the test of S. If S is false, E is skipped and control passes to the next statement.

## Flowcharts

Flowcharting is an old design tool that is still in use. **System flowcharts** detail the flow of data throughout an entire information system and may be used to document physical design specifications. They can show all inputs, major files, processing, and outputs for a system, and they can document manual procedures.

Using specialized symbols and flow lines, the system flowchart traces the flow of information and work in a system, the sequence of processing steps, and the physical media on which data are input, output, and stored. Figure 14-12 shows some of the basic symbols for system flowcharting used in a high-level system flowchart for a payroll system. The plain rectangle is a general symbol for a process. Flow lines show the sequence of steps and the direction of information flow. Arrows are used to show direction if it is not apparent in the diagram.

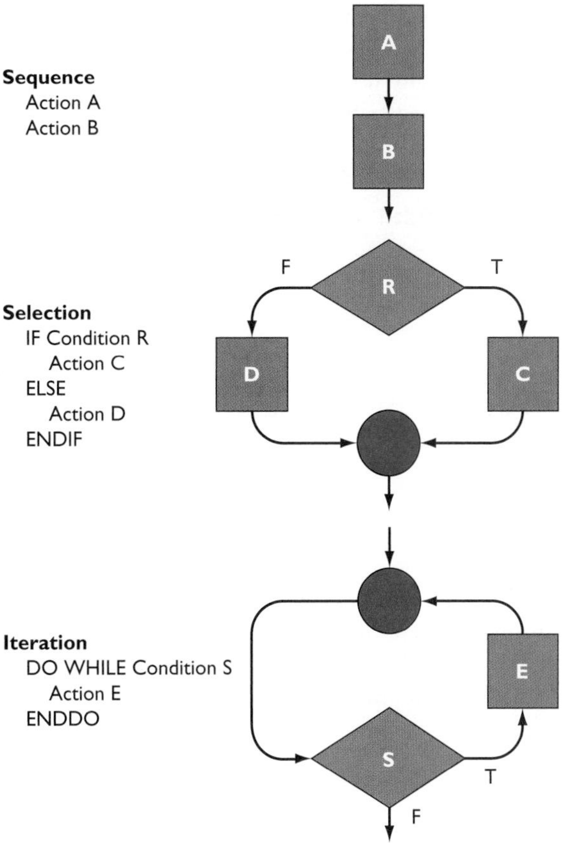

**Sequence**
Action A
Action B

**Selection**
IF Condition R
Action C
ELSE
Action D
ENDIF

**Iteration**
DO WHILE Condition S
Action E
ENDDO

A B F R T D C E S T F

***Figure 14-11*** Basic program control constructs. The three basic control constructs used in structured programming are sequence, selection, and iteration.

## Limitations of Traditional Methods

Although traditional methods are valuable, they can be inflexible and time consuming. Completion of structured analysis is required before design can begin, and programming must await the completed deliverables from design. A change in specifications requires that first the analysis documents and then the design documents must be modified before the programs can be changed to reflect the new requirement.

**system flowchart**
A graphic design tool that depicts the physical media and sequence of processing steps used in an entire information system.

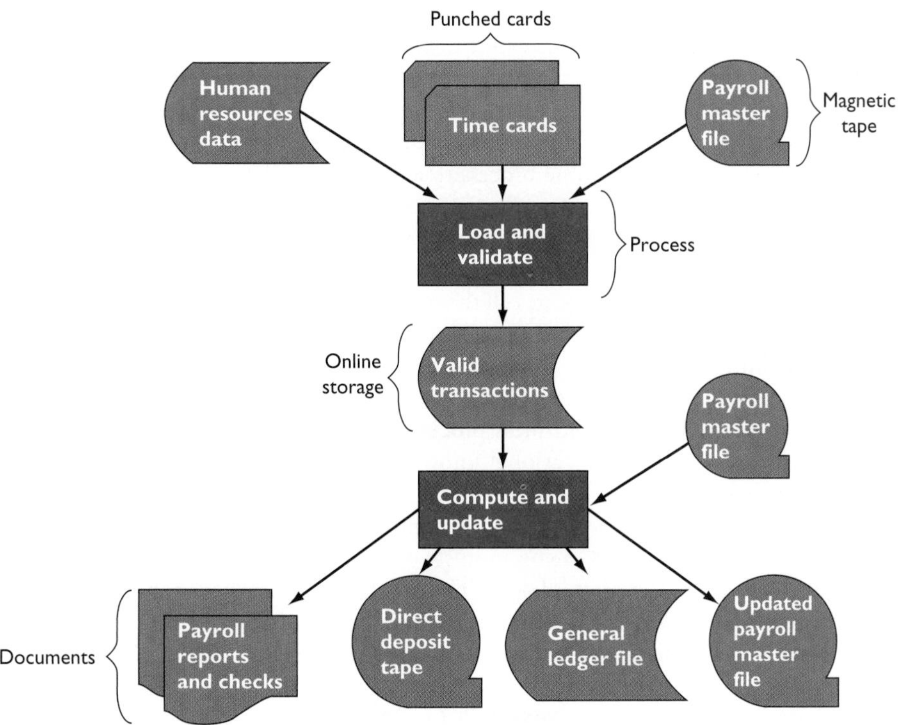


***Figure 14-12*** System flowchart for a payroll system. This is a high-level system flowchart for a batch payroll system. Only the most important processes and files are illustrated. Data are input from two sources: time cards and payroll-related data (such as salary increases) passed from the human resources system. The data are first edited and validated against the existing payroll master file before the payroll master is updated. The update process produces an updated payroll master file, various payroll reports (such as the payroll register and hours register), checks, a direct deposit tape, and a file of payment data that must be passed to the organization's general ledger system. The direct deposit tape is sent to the automated clearinghouse that serves the banks offering direct deposit services to employees.

Structured methodologies are function oriented, focusing on the processes that transform the data. Chapter 10 describes how object-oriented development addresses this problem. System builders can also use computer-aided software engineering (CASE) tools to make structured methods more flexible.

## Computer-aided Software Engineering (CASE)

**computer-aided software engineering (CASE).** The automation of step-by-step methodologies for software and systems development to reduce the amount of repetitive work the developer needs to do.

**Computer-aided software engineering (CASE)**—sometimes called *computer-aided systems engineering*—is the automation of step-by-step methodologies for software and systems development to reduce the amount of repetitive work the developer needs to do. Its adoption can free the developer for more creative problem-solving tasks. CASE tools also facilitate the creation of clear documentation and the coordination of team development efforts. Team members can share their work easily by accessing each other's files to review or modify what has been done. Some studies have found that systems developed with CASE and the newer methodologies are more reliable, and they require repairs less often (Dekleva, 1992). Modest productivity benefits can also be achieved if the tools are used properly. Many CASE tools are PC-based, with powerful graphical capabilities.

CASE tools provide automated graphics facilities for producing charts and diagrams, screen and report generators, data dictionaries, extensive reporting facilities, analysis and checking tools, code generators, and documentation generators. Most CASE tools are based on one or more of the popular structured methodologies. Some are starting to support object-oriented development. In general, CASE tools try to increase productivity and quality by doing the following:

- Enforce a standard development methodology and design discipline
- Improve communication between users and technical specialists
- Organize and correlate design components and provide rapid access to them via a design repository
- Automate tedious and error-prone portions of analysis and design
- Automate code generation, testing, and control rollout

Many CASE tools have been classified in terms of whether they support activities at the front end or the back end of the systems development process. Front-end CASE tools focus on capturing analysis and design information in the early stages of systems development, whereas back-end CASE tools address coding, testing, and maintenance activities. Back-end tools help convert specifications automatically into program code.

CASE tools automatically tie data elements to the processes where they are used. If a data flow diagram is changed from one process to another, the elements in the data dictionary would be altered automatically to reflect the change in the diagram. CASE tools also contain features for validating design diagrams and specifications. CASE tools thus support iterative design by automating revisions and changes and providing prototyping facilities.

A CASE information repository stores all the information defined by the analysts during the project. The repository includes data flow diagrams, structure charts, entity-relationship diagrams, data definitions, process specifications, screen and report formats, notes and comments, and test results. CASE tools now have features to support client/server applications, object-oriented programming, and business process redesign. Methodologies and tool sets are being created to leverage organizational knowledge of business process reengineering (Nissen, 1998).

To be used effectively, CASE tools require organizational discipline. Every member of a development project must adhere to a common set of naming conventions and standards as well as a common development methodology. The best CASE tools enforce common methods and standards, which may frustrate designer creativity and discourage their use in situations where organizational discipline is lacking, (Scott, Horvath, and Day, 2000).

**resource allocation** The determination of how costs, time, and personnel are assigned to different phases of a systems development project.

## Resource Allocation During Systems Development

Views on **resource allocation** during systems development have changed significantly over the years. Resource allocation determines the way the costs, time, and personnel are assigned

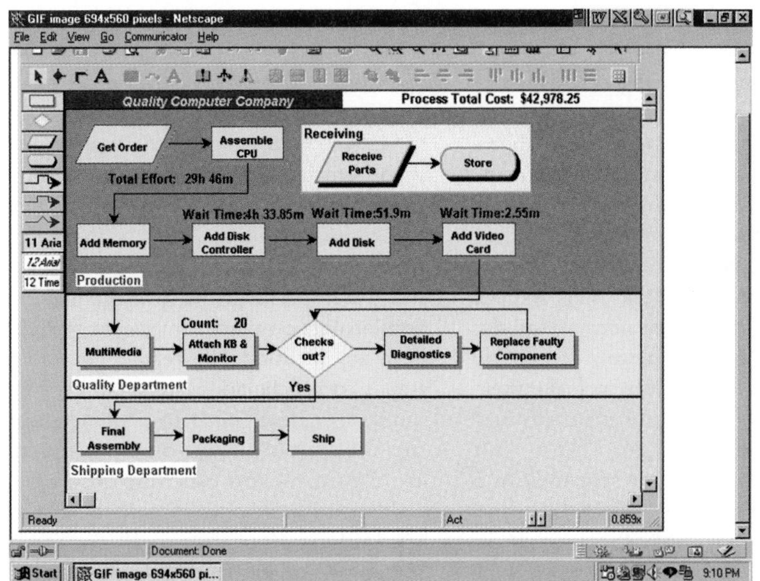


*Scitor Process provides tools to map out business processes and to simulate the processes in real-time. CASE tools facilitate the creation of clear documentation and the coordination of team development efforts.*

to different phases of the project. In earlier times, developers focused on programming, with only about 1 percent of the time and costs of a project being devoted to systems analysis (determining specifications). More time should be spent in specifications and systems analysis, decreasing the proportion of programming time and reducing the need for so much maintenance time. Documenting requirements so that they can be understood from their origin through development, specification, and continuing use can also reduce errors as well as time and costs (Domges and Pohl, 1998). Current literature suggests that about one-quarter of a project's time and cost should be expended in specifications and analysis, with perhaps 50 percent of its resources allocated to design and programming. Installation and postimplementation ideally should require only one-quarter of the project's resources. Investments in software quality initiatives early in a project are likely to provide the greatest payback (Slaughter, Harter, and Krishnan, 1998).

## Software Metrics

Software metrics can play a vital role in increasing system quality. **Software metrics** are objective assessments of the system in the form of quantified measurements. Ongoing use of metrics allows the IS department and the user jointly to measure the performance of the system and identify problems as they occur. Examples of software metrics include the number of transactions that can be processed in a specified unit of time, on-line response time, the number of payroll checks printed per hour, and the number of known bugs per hundred lines of code.

**software metrics**
The objective assessments of the software used in a system in the form of quantified measurements.

For metrics to be successful, they must be carefully designed, formal, and objective. They must measure significant aspects of the system. In addition, metrics are of no value unless they are used consistently and users agree to the measurements in advance.

## Testing

Chapter 10 described the stages of testing required to put an information system in operation—program testing, system testing, and acceptance testing. Early, regular, and thorough testing will contribute significantly to system quality. In general, software testing is often misunderstood. Many view testing as a way to prove the correctness of work they have done. In fact, we know that all sizable software is riddled with errors, and we must test to uncover these errors.

**walkthrough**
A review of a specification or design document by a small group of people carefully selected based on the skills needed for the particular objectives being tested.

Testing begins at the design phase. Because no coding yet exists, the test normally used is a **walkthrough**—a review of a specification or design document by a small group of people carefully selected based on the skills needed for the particular objectives being tested. Once coding begins, coding walkthroughs also can be used to review program code. However, code must be tested by computer runs. When errors are discovered, the source is found and eliminated through a process called **debugging.**

**debugging**
The process of discovering and eliminating the errors and defects—bugs—in program code.

## STRESS TESTING WEB SITES

Performance failures often accompany a Web site's success. Many Web site outages have been caused by large surges in the number of legitimate visitors as well as by hackers overwhelming the sites with requests for services. Serious e-commerce sites can expect spikes in traffic that run four to ten times their normal load. If a Web site can't respond quickly and accurately to visitor requests, customers are quick to go elsewhere to make their purchases. The benefits of testing Web sites for scalability and rigor are obvious.

Some companies think that gathering five or six people in a room to click on a Web site is a suitable test of scalability and performance. But to test a Web site realistically, companies need to find a way to subject the Web site to the same number of concurrent users as would actually be visiting the site at one time and to devise test plans that reflect what these people would actually be doing. For example, a retail e-commerce site should create a test scenario where there are many visitors simply browsing and a few making purchases. Developers should test for users with different types of client computers and the effect of slow telecommunication transmission speeds.

A realistic scalability test will reflect the driving factors behind each business, such as historic traffic numbers, profiles of typical Web site visitors, and metrics that are of most importance to the organization, such as page load time or number of transactions per second.

Managing spikes in Web site traffic requires a knowledge of Web site content, users, their interactions, and everything in between that can affect Web site performance. According to Jayaram Bhat, vice president of marketing for Mercury Interactive, "almost no one has a clue about their site's real performance level before testing."

Mercury Interactive is a Web site performance management service that offers real-time monitoring of virtually all Web operations. It designs test scripts to replicate what a normal Web site visitor would do—browse, shop, check orders—and to test the Web site with the desired number of user transactions from any location. These test scenarios are run before the Web site goes live with heavy loads to pinpoint any bottlenecks in hardware or design. After the Web site actually goes live, the service can monitor it to test its ongoing performance. Mercury and other performance management services can produce detailed data on every component of the Web site, any time, and from any location. The resulting data can be used to create graphs to benchmark average performance from each location and to spot slow points. By creating a test population that mirrors the actual Web site visitor population, Web site owners can find out exactly how well their site works.

Mercury Interactive often finds that a site can initially only handle about 10 percent of the designer's projected user load. Sometimes performance can be boosted by simply tuning the Web site, but there are cases where the performance problems are deeply rooted and the Web site must undergo major design changes.

Testing wireless applications poses additional challenges. The millions of new wireless users are placing a massive new burden on the Internet infrastructure for wireless service providers and for organizations with wireless Web applications. Many wireless and conventional Web applications are linked to the same back-end systems so the total load on those systems will increase dramatically as wireless users are added. Automated load testing tools that simulate thousands of simultaneous wireless Web and conventional Web browser sessions can help companies measure the impact on system performance.

**To Think About:** What management, organization, and technology issues should be addressed by Web site testing?

*Sources:* Phil Hollows, "Build High-quality E-business Applications," *e-Business Advisor,* November 2000; and James Karney, "For Good Measure," *Internet World,* July 1, 2000.

Electronic commerce and electronic business applications introduce new levels of complexity for testing to ensure high-quality performance and functionality. Behind each large Web site such as Amazon.com, eBay, or E*Trade are hundreds of servers, thousands of miles of network cable, and hundreds of software programs, creating numerous points of vulnerability. These Web sites must be built and tested to make sure that they can withstand expected—and unexpected—spikes and peaks in their load. Both Web site traffic and technical components, such as hardware, software, and networks, must be taken into consideration during application development and during testing. The Window on Technology explores this issue.

Many companies delay testing until the end of the application development phase, when design decisions have been finalized and most of the software program code has been written. Leaving Web site performance and scalability tests until the end of the application development cycle is extremely risky, because such problems often stem from the fundamental workings of the system. To minimize the chance of discovering major structural problems late in the systems development process, companies should perform this testing well before the system is complete. This makes it possible to address performance bottlenecks and other issues in each application level or system component before everything is integrated.

## DATA QUALITY AUDITS AND DATA CLEANSING

Information system quality also can be improved by identifying and correcting faulty data, making error detection a more explicit organizational goal (Klein, Goodhue, and Davis, 1997). The analysis of data quality often begins with a **data quality audit,** which is a structured survey of the accuracy and level of completeness of the data in an information system. Data quality audits are accomplished using the following methods:

**data quality audit**
A survey of files and samples of files for accuracy and completeness of data in an information system.

- Surveying end users for their perceptions of data quality
- Surveying entire data files
- Surveying samples from data files

Unless regular data quality audits are undertaken, organizations have no way of knowing to what extent their information systems contain inaccurate, incomplete, or ambiguous information.

Until recently, many organizations were not giving data quality the priority it deserved (Tayi and Ballou, 1998). Now electronic commerce and electronic business are forcing more companies to pay attention to data quality, because a digitally enabled firm cannot run efficiently without accurate data about customers and business partners. **Data cleansing** has become a core requirement for data warehousing, customer relationship management, and Web-based commerce. Companies implementing data warehousing often find inconsistencies in customer or employee information as they try to integrate information from different business units. Companies are also finding mistakes in the data provided by customers or business partners through a Web site. On-line exchanges (see Chapter 4) are especially problematic, because they use catalog data from dozens to thousands of suppliers and these data are often in different formats, with different classification schemes for product numbers, product descriptions, and other attributes. Data cleansing tools can be used to correct errors in these data and to integrate these data in a consistent company-wide format. Ameritech was able to cut the volume of its mail by 4 percent and save $250,000 per year by cleansing millions of customer names and addresses (Faden, 2000).

**data cleansing**
Correcting errors and inconsistencies in data to increase accuracy so that they can be used in a standard company-wide format.

# APPLICATION SOFTWARE EXERCISE

### SPREADSHEET EXERCISE: PERFORMING A SECURITY RISK ASSESSMENT

Mercer Paints is a paint manufacturing company located in Alabama. Although Mercer Paints is a small paint manufacturing company, the quality of its products is widely recognized. The company has a network in place, linking many of its business operations.

Although the company believes that its security is adequate, the recent addition of a Web site provided an open invitation to hackers. Just last week, someone hacked into the computer system and defaced the company's Web site. Because of this recent event, company management requested a risk assessment. The risk assessment identified several potential exposures; these exposures, associated probabilities, and average losses are summarized in the table provided on the Laudon Web site for Chapter 14. In addition to the potential exposures listed, you should identify at least three other potential threats to Mercer Paints, assign probabilities, and estimate a loss range.

Using a spreadsheet product and the risk assessment data provided on the Laudon Web site, calculate the expected annual loss for each exposure. Which control points have the greatest vulnerability? What recommendations would you make to Mercer Paints? Prepare a written report that summarizes your findings and recommendations.

## MANAGEMENT WRAP-UP

Management is responsible for developing the control structure and quality standards for the organization. Key management decisions include establishing standards for systems accuracy and reliability, determining an appropriate level of control for organizational functions, and establishing a disaster recovery plan.

The characteristics of the organization play a large role in determining its approach to quality assurance and control issues. Some organizations are more quality and control conscious than others. Their cultures and business processes support high standards of quality and performance. Creating high levels of security and quality in information systems can be a process of lengthy organizational change.

A number of technologies and methodologies are available for promoting system quality and security. Technologies such as antivirus and data security software, firewalls, fault-tolerant and high-availability computing technology, and programmed procedures, can be used to create a control environment, whereas software metrics, systems development methodologies, and automated tools for systems development can be used to improve software quality. Organizational discipline is required to use these technologies effectively.

*For Discussion*

1. It has been said that controls and security should be one of the first areas to be addressed in the design of an information system. Do you agree? Why or why not?
2. How much software testing is "enough"? What management, organization, and technology issues should you consider in answering this question?

## SUMMARY

1. *Demonstrate why information systems are so vulnerable to destruction, error, abuse, and system quality problems.* With data concentrated into electronic form and many procedures invisible through automation, computerized information systems are vulnerable to destruction, misuse, error, fraud, and hardware or software failures. On-line systems and those using the Internet are especially vulnerable, because data and files can be immediately and directly accessed through computer terminals or at many points in the network. Computer viruses can spread rampantly from system to system, clogging computer memory or destroying programs and data. Software presents problems because of the high costs of correcting errors and because software bugs may be impossible to eliminate. Data quality can also severely impact system quality and performance.
2. *Compare general controls and application controls for information systems.* Controls consist of all the methods, policies, and organizational procedures that ensure the safety of the organization's assets, the accuracy and reliability of its accounting records, and adherence to management standards. There are two main categories of controls: general controls and application controls.

   General controls handle the overall design, security, and use of computers, programs, and files for the organization's information technology infrastructure. They include physical hardware controls, software controls, data file security controls, computer operations controls, controls over the system implementation process, and administrative disciplines.

   Application controls are those unique to specific computerized applications. They focus on the completeness and accuracy of input, updating and maintenance, and the validity of the information in the system. Application controls consist of (1) input controls, (2) processing controls, and (3) output controls.

   To determine which controls are required, designers and users of systems must identify all of the control points and control weaknesses and perform risk assessment. They must also perform a cost–benefit analysis of controls and design controls that can effectively safeguard systems without making them unusable.
3. *Evaluate the special measures required to ensure the reliability, availability, and security of electronic commerce and digital business processes.* Companies require special measures to support electronic commerce and digital business processes.

They can use fault-tolerant computer systems or create high-availability computing environments to make sure that their information systems are always available and performing without interruptions. Firewalls and intrusion detection systems help safeguard private networks from unauthorized access when organizations use intranets or link to the Internet. Encryption is a widely used technology for securing electronic transmissions over the Internet. Digital certificates provide further protection of electronic transactions by authenticating a user's identity.

4. *Describe the most important software quality assurance techniques.* The quality and reliability of software can be improved by using a standard development methodology, software metrics, thorough testing procedures, and by reallocating resources to put more emphasis on the analysis and design stages of systems development.

   Structured methodologies have been used to increase software quality since the 1970s. Structured analysis highlights the flow of data and the processes through which data are transformed. Its principal tool is the data flow diagram. Structured design and programming are software design disciplines that produce reliable, well-documented software with a simple, clear structure that is easy for others to understand and maintain. System flowcharts are useful for documenting the physical aspects of system design.

   Computer-aided software engineering (CASE) automates methodologies for systems development. It promotes standards and improves coordination and consistency during systems development. CASE tools help system builders build a better model of a system and facilitate revision of design specifications to correct errors.

5. *Demonstrate the importance of auditing information systems and safeguarding data quality.* Comprehensive and systematic MIS auditing can help organizations to determine the effectiveness of the controls in their information systems. Regular data quality audits should be conducted to help organizations ensure a high level of completeness and accuracy of the data stored in their systems. Data cleansing should also be performed to create consistent and accurate data for company-wide use in electronic commerce and electronic business.

## KEY TERMS

**Administrative controls, 443**
**Antivirus software, 436**
**Application controls, 441**
**Authentication, 447**
**Bugs, 439**
**Clustering, 445**
**Computer-aided software engineering (CASE), 456**
**Computer matching, 444**
**Computer operations controls, 442**
**Computer virus, 435**
**Control totals, 443**
**Controls, 441**
**Data cleansing, 459**
**Data flow diagram (DFD), 453**
**Data quality audit, 459**
**Data security controls, 442**
**Debugging, 457**
**Denial of service attack, 435**
**Development methodology, 451**
**Digital certificate, 447**
**Digital signature, 447**
**Disaster recovery plan, 438**
**Edit checks, 443**
**Encryption, 447**
**Fault-tolerant computer systems, 444**
**General controls, 441**
**Hacker, 435**
**Hardware controls, 441**
**High-availability computing, 444**
**Implementation controls, 441**
**Input controls, 443**
**Intrusion detection system, 446**
**Iteration construct, 454**
**Load balancing, 445**
**Message integrity, 447**
**Mirroring, 445**
**Module, 454**
**MIS audit, 450**
**On-line transaction processing, 444**
**Output controls, 444**
**Process specifications, 453**
**Processing controls, 444**
**Resource allocation, 456**
**Risk assessment, 449**
**Run control totals, 444**
**Secure electronic transaction (SET), 448**
**Security, 438**
**Segregation of functions, 443**
**Selection construct, 454**
**Sequence construct, 454**
**Software controls, 441**
**Software metrics, 457**
**Structure chart, 454**
**Structured, 452**
**Structured analysis, 452**
**Structured design, 453**
**Structured programming, 454**
**System flowchart, 455**
**Walkthrough, 457**

## REVIEW QUESTIONS

1. Why are computer systems more vulnerable than manual systems to destruction, fraud, error, and misuse? Name some of the key areas where systems are most vulnerable.
2. Name some features of on-line information systems that make them difficult to control.
3. How can bad software and data quality affect system performance and reliability? Describe two software quality problems.
4. What are controls? Distinguish between general controls and application controls.

5. Name and describe the principal general controls for computerized systems.
6. List and describe the principal application controls.
7. What is security? List and describe controls that promote security for computer hardware, computer networks, computer software, and computerized data.
8. What special security measures must be taken by organizations linking to the Internet?
9. Distinguish between fault tolerant and high-availability computing.
10. Describe the role of firewalls, intrusion detection systems, and encryption systems in promoting security.
11. Why are digital signatures and digital certificates important for electronic commerce?
12. What is the function of risk assessment?
13. How does MIS auditing enhance the control process?
14. Name and describe four software quality assurance techniques.
15. What is structured analysis? What is the role of the data flow diagram in structured analysis?
16. How is structured design related to structured programming? How can both promote software quality?
17. Why are data quality audits and data cleansing essential?

## GROUP PROJECT

Form a group with two or three other students. Select a system described in one of the chapter ending cases. Write a description of the system, its functions, and its value to the organization. Then write a description of both the general and application controls that should be used to protect the organization. If possible, use electronic presentation software to present your findings to the class.

## TOOLS FOR INTERACTIVE LEARNING

### INTERNET CONNECTION

The Internet Connection for this chapter will take you to a series of Web sites where you can complete an exercise to evaluate various secure electronic payment systems for the Internet. You can also use the Interactive Study Guide to test your knowledge of the topics in this chapter and get instant feedback where you need more practice.

### ELECTRONIC COMMERCE PROJECT

At the Laudon Web site for Chapter 14, you will find an Electronic Commerce project that uses the interactive software at the Holistix Web site to remotely test an e-commerce Web site's transactions, response time, and availability.

### CD-ROM

If you use the Multimedia Edition CD-ROM with this chapter, you can complete an interactive exercise asking you to identify the security and control problems faced by a company and select appropriate solutions. You can also find a video clip illustrating the Comdisco disaster recovery service, an audio overview of the major themes of this chapter, and bullet text summarizing the key points of the chapter.

## CASE STUDY *Did the FAA Fly Off Course?*

The Federal Aviation Administration (FAA), through its air traffic controllers, controls all commercial planes in the air in the United States. With many thousands of flights daily, the airspace of the United States is very crowded. The controllers give permission for landings and takeoffs, they approve flight paths, and they monitor all airplanes in flight.

The FAA has more than 250 separate computer systems to manage. Before a flight, pilots file their flight plans, which are then entered into a computer. Once in the air, each plane continually transmits data to computers, including its flight number, location, and altitude. The computers also continually receive data from radar stations around the country and data from weather computers. The system keeps track of all planes in U.S. airspace, displaying their locations on a screen. These systems also have specialty functions, such as issuing warnings when two planes are coming too close together or are flying too low. In today's world, controllers could not manage airplane traffic without these computers.

Controller applications are divided into two major types of systems. The airport control systems at all commercial airports control all aircraft when they are within 20 to 30 miles of the airport. The others, the Air Route Traffic Control (en-route) systems, operate at 20 centers around the country and control the high-altitude planes that are flying between their points-of-origin and their destinations.

Many FAA computers were very old, particularly those used at the Air Route Traffic Control centers. Some even dated back to the 1950s and were still using vacuum tubes. Until very recently, of the 20 en-route control sites, only New York, Chicago, Washington D.C., Fort Worth, and Cleveland had modern ES/9121 mainframes. All the other 15 sites had IBM 3083 large computers that were at least 15 years old and had not even been produced or sold by IBM for 10 years.

These old computers have presented many problems. Despite their huge size, the old mainframes have less power than today's desktops. Spare parts were hard to obtain. Fewer and fewer technicians were available to keep these computers running. Being so old, these computers suffered many breakdowns. For example, from September 1994 to September 1995, 11 major breakdowns occurred. To make matters worse, the FAA employs 5,000 fewer computer technicians today than it did seven or eight years ago, despite the growing number of failures as the equipment ages. In addition to the age of the hardware, much of the software is 30 years old. Outdated software often cannot be updated because of the computers' age. Newer, more sophisticated software could make air travel much safer.

The FAA had backup systems, but they did not have many of the more sophisticated functions, such as the warnings when airplanes are too close or too low. Many were just as old as the front-line systems. In addition, the controllers' training in these systems is very limited. When the backups also fail, the controllers must switch to working with pilots, using slips of paper to keep track of each flight, an impossible task given the number of flights. At those times, many flights are not allowed to take off at the affected airports, and flights due into those airports must be put into a holding pattern or diverted to other airports. Besides increasing the risk of accidents, this situation has cost airlines hundreds of millions of dollars yearly, and it cost passengers major delays and inconveniences.

Air traffic controllers suffer major stress under the best of circumstances. Many feel that the workload on controllers has been too heavy, partially because of all the manual processing the old systems require. Peter Neumann, a specialist in computer reliability and safety, said, "Controllers are under enormous pressure, and anything that goes slightly wrong makes their job inordinately harder."

The FAA, recognizing it had potential problems, began planning for upgrading in 1983. The project, labeled AAS (Advanced Automation System), called for a complete overhaul of its computers, software, radar units, and communications network. Its original goals were to lower operating costs, to improve systems reliability and efficiency, and to make flying safer. In 1988 the AAS contract was awarded to IBM. The projected was budgeted at $4.8 billion, and completion was targeted for 1994.

The project did not go well. In December 1990, IBM announced that the project was 19 months behind schedule. By late 1992, IBM announced that the project was 33 months late, and it estimated that the cost had risen to $5.1 billion. The project was scaled back. In December 1993, the estimated cost of the now-smaller project rose to $5.9 billion. In April 1994, an independent study commissioned by the FAA concluded that the project design has "a high risk of failure."

In June 1994, the FAA announced further major changes. The contract was shifted from IBM to Lockheed Martin Corp. In addition major parts of the project were dropped, including one project to combine the two major controller systems and another to replace the hardware and software that controls aircraft near the airports. The plan to replace control tower equipment at the 150 largest airports was downsized to include only the 70 largest airports. The estimated cost of the slimmed-down project was $6 billion and the planned completion date was postponed to the year 2000.

Meanwhile, signs of system aging were multiplying. For example, in June 1995, a computer outage at Washington Air Route Traffic Control Center lasted 41 hours, and one in Chicago a year later lasted 122 hours. In August 1998, the Nashua, New Hampshire, center, which is responsible for all of New England and part of New York, went down for 37 minutes. Even before this outage, there were many complaints of frozen radar screens and minor outages.

In September 1996, a new project, the Standard Terminal Automation Replacement System (STARS), was announced. This announcement marked the end of AAS. Estimates of the cost of AAS range from $7.6 billion to $23 billion, and yet it failed to improve much of the FAA's IT infrastructure. STARS is planned to bring together flight-plan data, air-traffic automation systems, terminal-control facilities, and radar systems around the United States. The prime contractor this time is Raytheon Co., of Lexington, Massachusetts.

STARS is targeted to replace the 20-year-old systems used by air traffic controllers to control flights near the airports. Its goals are to improve safety and reduce flight delays. It was to be installed at 317 airports and military bases, with installation beginning at Boston's Logan Airport in 1998. The project, scheduled to be completed in 2007, is estimated to cost about $11 billion through 2003. The new system will have four computers at each site: one primary, one backup, and a second pair that mirrors the first (redundancy).

The FAA has been able to replace its old mainframe computers with newer ones and install color radar display screens. The system crashes, which used to force controllers to track planes on slips of paper, are now rare. But serious problems remain. The FAA could not purchase the newest IBM computers because they would not run Jovial, a programming language from the 1960s used in the FAA's software. The FAA plans to switch to a more modern programming language, but the conversion of its old software is very complex and will take some years to complete.

At present, the FAA is in the process of rolling out a series of systems that will improve the efficiency of takeoffs and landings at busy airports and allow some airplanes to fly more direct routes. However, these improvements cannot address all of the air traffic control problems facing the FAA as air traffic continues to grow.

Why did the FAA have so many problems upgrading its computers? One specific issue is the lack of an FAA systems architecture. The FAA did develop a logical architecture, called the National Airspace System (NAS). This architecture document describes the FAA's services and functions, and outlines the systems needed for both air traffic management and navigation systems. It even includes a systems plan through the year 2015. Thus, it gives a high-level overview of the business functions and the systems needed to serve them, including the interconnection between the various systems. However, the FAA did not then go on to translate this plan into the required physical or technical architecture. The FAA's air traffic control development work is assigned to one of ten teams, and the lack of a technical architecture has left all ten teams to determine their own specific standards for developing the software, hardware, communications, data management, security, and performance characteristics.

Let's look at the results of the lack of standards. Of the ten development teams, seven have no technical architecture at all. The other three developed their own architectures, and they are not the same. One result is the systems that feed the main computers use several different communications protocols and data formats. Of the three teams with standards, one architecture specifies Ethernet for networking, whereas another specifies Fiber Distributed Data Interface (the two are incompatible). Two of the architectures specify writing programs in C and C++, whereas the third one specifies Ada. Altogether the ten teams developed 54 air traffic control system applications using 53 different languages. Incompatibility is one result. Staffs are forced to spend time (and money) creating complex interfaces, which also must be supported. These translation programs also increase the possibility of data errors. Moreover, the use of multiple standards greatly increases staff training costs. A February 1998 GAO report said that the result of the lack of an FAA uniform architecture is that "the FAA permits and perpetuates" inconsistency and incompatibilities. It stresses that any organization must implement a technical architecture before it replaces an old computer system.

Congressional observers have severely criticized the culture of the FAA, characterizing its employees as being unwilling to face up to its problems. Rona B. Stillman, the GAO's chief scientist for computers, stated that the "FAA has a culture . . . that is averse to change and has entrenched autonomous organizations that tend not to respond to change."

One issue appears to be the organization of the information systems function within the agency. As described, with 10 independent development organizations, the FAA lacks needed central control. Regionalized management appears not to work well. The 1998 GAO report concluded, "No FAA organizational entity is responsible for developing and maintaining the technical Air Traffic Control architecture." In its opinion, this leaves the agency "at risk of making ill-informed decisions on critical multimillion-dollar, even billion-dollar, air-traffic-control systems." The same report, in referring to the failure of the AAS project, determined that the "FAA did not recognize the technical complexity of the effort, realistically estimate the resources required, adequately oversee its contractors' activities, or effectively control system requirements."

The IT Management Reform Act of 1996, known also as the Clinger-Cohen Act, mandates major information technology (IT) reforms in government agencies, including a requirement that federal agencies have CIOs. The reason that the FAA has no such centralized management is that the agency successfully lobbied to have itself exempted from the act.

One other problem, cited by several labor representatives from the controllers' union, is the communication gap between FAA management and the users of the traffic control systems. Management claims positive results on the STARS project, whereas the controllers apparently disagree. Controllers have often spoken out in meetings, saying that STARS is cumbersome, that the controls are complex, and the terminal displays are unclear.

*Sources:* Laurence Zuckerman and Matthew L. Wald, "Crisis for Air Traffic System: More Passengers, More Delays," *The New York Times,* September 5, 2000; Bob Brewin and Michael Meehan, "FAA Looks Abroad for Air-Traffic Control Systems," *Computerworld,* July 17, 2000; Scott McCartney, "Efforts to Ease Delays in Summer Air Travel also Produce Snarls," *The Wall Street Journal,* September 14, 2000; Patrick Thibodeau, "IBM Says FAA Air Traffic Computers Should Be Retired," *Computerworld,* January 15, 1999, and "Air Traffic Controllers Say Old Computers Hobble FAA," *Computerworld,* June 22, 1998; Matthew L. Wald, "Warning Issued on Air Traffic Computers," *The New York Times,* January 12, 1999; Thomas Hoffman, "On a Wing and a Prayer. . . ," *Computerworld,* February 2, 1999, and "Feds Slam FAA for Millennium Mess," *Computerworld,* February 9, 1998; Matt Hamblen, "IBM, Others Question FAA's 2000 Progress," *Computerworld,* July 24, 1998, "FAA: Systems Are a Go for 2000," *Computerworld,* July 24, 1998, and "FAA's IT Management Slammed," *Computerworld,* February 10, 1997; Jeff Cole, "FAA, Air Groups Agree on Traffic Plan," *The Wall Street Journal,* April 23, 1998; Mary Mosquera, "FAA Faces Year 2000 Emergency, Report Says," *TechWeb News,* February 4, 1998; Jeff Sweat, "FAA: We're Y2K OK," *Information Week,* October 5, 1998; Bruce D. Nordwall, "FAA Structural Problems Impede ATC Upgrades," *Aviation Week and Space Technology,* February 10, 1997; Gary Anthes, "Ancient Systems Put Scare in Air," and "Revamp Flies Off Course," *Computerworld,* August 5, 1996; "$1B Award to Fix Air Traffic System," *Computerworld,* September 23, 1996; and George Leopold, "FAA Sets Massive Systems Overhaul, But Will It Fly?" *TechWeb News,* October 28, 1996.

### *CASE STUDY QUESTIONS*

1. List and explain the control weaknesses in the FAA and its air traffic control systems.
2. What management, organization, and technology factors were responsible for the FAA's control weaknesses?
3. How effectively did the FAA deal with its control weaknesses? Evaluate the importance of the AAS and STARS projects for the FAA, for the air traffic controllers, and for the flying public.
4. Design a complete set of controls for the FAA to deal effectively with its control problems and the management of the FAA's information systems projects.

chapter

# 15 Ethical and Social Impact of Information Systems

objectives

**After completing this chapter, you will be able to:**

1. *Analyze the relationship among ethical, social, and political issues raised by information systems.*
2. *Identify the main moral dimensions of an information society and apply them to specific situations.*
3. *Apply an ethical analysis to difficult situations.*
4. *Examine specific ethical principles for conduct.*
5. *Design corporate policies for ethical conduct.*

## M-commerce: A New Threat to Privacy?

As the Web goes wireless, the old real estate adage "location, location, location" is taking on new importance. Location can matter in electronic commerce as people tap into the Internet while they are on the go. Web-enabled cell phones, PDA devices, or automobiles with location-tracking systems have the potential to figure out exactly where people are and put that information to use. For example, one could use location information to find the nearest restaurant or hotel, with the answer delivered on a tiny Web screen. Users could obtain this information on request or even have the information automatically delivered to them when they were in the vicinity of hotels and restaurants. Wingate Inns International is hoping to offer such personalized services as directions and last-minute reservations once location-tracking systems are more widely used. Location-based services promise to be one of the hottest areas of m-commerce.

How can a cell phone or PDA figure out your location? Users could tap in ZIP codes or nearby addresses. But there are better ways. The Federal Communications Commission has called for enhanced 911 systems that can automatically route emergency teams to a caller's location. Cell phones might be equipped with tiny Global Positioning System (GPS) devices that triangulate positions by reading signals from U.S. military satellites sending timing and location information. Automakers are starting to equip vehicles with GPS systems linked to wireless voice communications, Internet access, and onboard computers. Location-tracking technology is improving rapidly.

Businesses might even use these systems to send electronic coupons directly to a consumer's cell phone or car as the person nears a particular store or restaurant. Consumers might agree to such services in exchange for reduced equipment or service charges. But privacy groups have raised concerns about the potential threat to

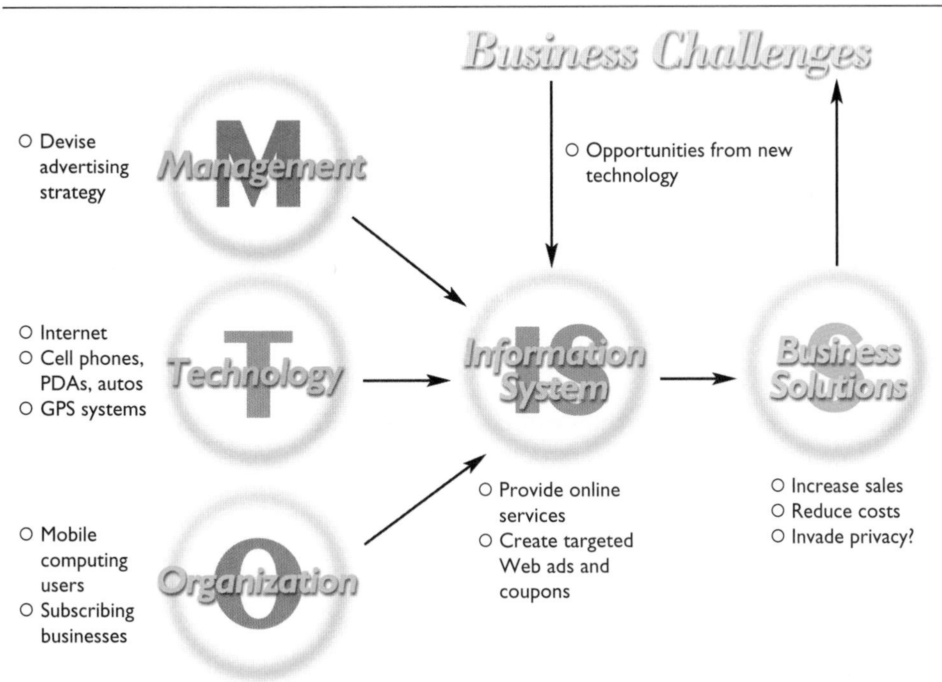


individual privacy posed by location-tracking technology. Many people may not like having their physical movements tracked so closely. Location information might help direct a tow truck to your broken-down car, but it could also be used to find out where you went on your lunch hour. According to David Sobel, general counsel at the Electronic Privacy Information Center (EPIC) in Washington, much depends on "who is going to have control over whether location information is transmitted." Worries about privacy would diminish if there were mechanisms for users to determine exactly when and how their location information could be used.

**Sources:** Thomas E. Weber, "With Wireless Gadgets, Web Companies Plan to Map Your Moves," *The Wall Street Journal,* May 8, 2000; and Patrick Thibodeau, "Satellites Will Change E-commerce Landscape," *Computerworld,* February 21, 2000.

**M-commerce: A New Threat to Privacy?**

**MANAGEMENT CHALLENGES**

Technology can be a double-edged sword. It can be the source of many benefits. One great achievement of contemporary computer systems is the ease with which digital information can be analyzed, transmitted, and shared among many people. But at the same time, this powerful capability creates new opportunities for breaking the law or taking benefits away from others. Balancing the convenience and privacy implications of creating electronic dossiers on consumers is one of the compelling ethical issues raised by contemporary information systems. As you read this chapter, you should be aware of the following management challenges:

## Management Challenges

1. **Understanding the moral risks of new technology.** Rapid technological change means that the choices facing individuals also rapidly change, and the balance of risk and reward and the probabilities of apprehension for wrongful acts change as well. Protecting individual privacy has become a serious ethical issue precisely for this reason, in addition to other issues described in this chapter. In this environment it will be important for management to conduct an ethical and social impact analysis of new technologies. One might take each of the moral dimensions described in this chapter and briefly speculate on how a new technology will impact each dimension. There may not always be right answers for how to behave, but there should be management awareness of the moral risks of new technology.
2. **Establishing corporate ethics policies that include information systems issues.** As managers you will be responsible for developing, enforcing, and explaining corporate ethics policies. Historically, corporate management has paid much more attention to financial integrity and personnel policies than to information systems. But from what you will know after reading this chapter, it is clear your corporation should have an ethics policy in the information systems area covering such issues as privacy, property, accountability, system quality, and quality of life. The challenge will be in educating non-IS managers to the need for these policies, as well as educating your workforce.

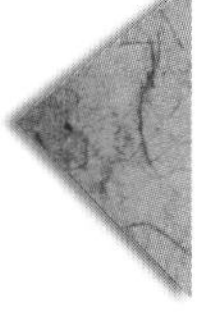

Protecting personal privacy on the Internet and establishing information rights represent one of the new ethical issues raised by the widespread use of information systems. Others include protecting intellectual property rights; establishing accountability for the consequences of information systems; setting standards to safeguard system quality that protect the safety of the individual and society; and preserving values and institutions considered essential to the quality of life in an information society. This chapter describes these issues and suggests guidelines for dealing with these questions.

## 15.1 Understanding Ethical and Social Issues Related to Systems

**ethics**
Principles of right and wrong that can be used by individuals acting as free moral agents to make choices to guide their behavior.

**Ethics** refers to the principles of right and wrong that individuals, acting as free moral agents, can use to make choices to guide their behavior. Information technology and information systems raise new ethical questions for both individuals and societies because they create opportunities for intense social change, and thus threaten existing distributions of power, money, rights, and obligations. Like other technologies, such as steam engines, electricity, telephone, and radio, information technology can be used to achieve social progress, but it can also be used to commit crimes and threaten cherished social values. The development of information technology will produce benefits for many and costs for others. When using information systems, it is essential to ask, what is the ethically and socially responsible course of action?

### A Model for Thinking About Ethical, Social, and Political Issues

Ethical, social, and political issues are closely linked. The ethical dilemma you may face as a manager of information systems typically is reflected in social and political debate. One way

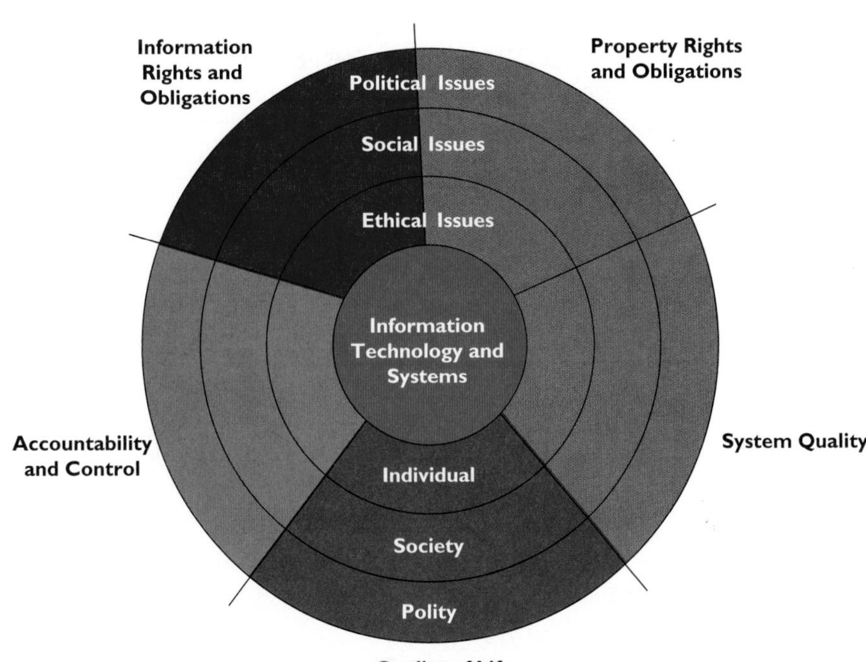


*Figure 15-1* The relationship between ethical, social, and political issues in an information society. The introduction of new information technology has a ripple effect, raising new ethical, social, and political issues that must be dealt with on the individual, social, and political levels. These issues have five moral dimensions: information rights and obligations, property rights and obligations, system quality, quality of life, and accountability and control.

to think about these relationships is given in Figure 15-1. Imagine society as a more or less calm pond on a summer day, a delicate ecosystem in partial equilibrium with individuals and with social and political institutions. Individuals know how to act in this pond because social institutions (family, education, organizations) have developed well-honed rules of behavior, and these are backed by laws developed in the political sector that prescribe behavior and promise sanctions for violations. Now toss a rock into the center of the pond. But imagine instead of a rock that the disturbing force is a powerful shock of new information technology and systems hitting a society more or less at rest. What happens? Ripples, of course.

Suddenly individual actors are confronted with new situations often not covered by the old rules. Social institutions cannot respond overnight to these ripples—it may take years to develop etiquette, expectations, social responsibility, "politically correct" attitudes, or approved rules. Political institutions also require time before developing new laws and often require the demonstration of real harm before they act. In the meantime, you may have to act. You may be forced to act in a legal "gray area."

We can use this model to illustrate the dynamics that connect ethical, social, and political issues. This model is also useful for identifying the main moral dimensions of the "information society," which cut across various levels of action—individual, social, and political.

## Five Moral Dimensions of the Information Age

A review of the literature on ethical, social, and political issues surrounding systems identifies five moral dimensions of the information age that we introduce here and explore in greater detail in Section 15.3. The five moral dimensions are as follows:

- Information rights and obligations: What **information rights** do individuals and organizations possess with respect to information about themselves? What can they protect? What obligations do individuals and organizations have concerning this information?
- Property rights and obligations: How will traditional intellectual property rights be protected in a digital society in which tracing and accounting for ownership is difficult, and ignoring such property rights is so easy?
- Accountability and control: Who can and will be held accountable and liable for the harm done to individual and collective information and property rights?
- System quality: What standards of data and system quality should we demand to protect individual rights and the safety of society?

**information rights** The rights that individuals and organizations have with respect to information that pertains to themselves.

## TABLE 15-1 TECHNOLOGY TRENDS THAT RAISE ETHICAL ISSUES

| Trend | Impact |
|---|---|
| Computing power doubles every 18 months | More organizations depend on computer systems for critical operations |
| Rapidly declining data storage costs | Organizations can easily maintain detailed databases on individuals |
| Datamining advances | Companies can analyze vast quantities of data gathered on individuals to develop detailed profiles of individual behavior |
| Networking advances and the Internet | Copying data from one location to another and accessing personal data from remote locations are much easier |

- Quality of life: What values should be preserved in an information- and knowledge-based society? What institutions should we protect from violation? What cultural values and practices are supported by the new information technology?

Before we analyze these dimensions let us briefly review the major technology and system trends that have heightened concern about these issues.

### KEY TECHNOLOGY TRENDS THAT RAISE ETHICAL ISSUES

Ethical issues long preceded information technology—they are the abiding concerns of free societies everywhere. Nevertheless, information technology has heightened ethical concerns, put stress on existing social arrangements, and made existing laws obsolete or severely crippled. There are four key technological trends responsible for these ethical stresses and they are summarized in Table 15-1.

The doubling of computing power every 18 months has made it possible for most organizations to use information systems for their core production processes. As a result, our dependence on systems and our vulnerability to system errors and poor data quality have increased. Social rules and laws have not yet adjusted to this dependence. Standards for ensuring the accuracy and reliability of information systems (see Chapter 14) are not universally accepted or enforced.

Advances in data storage techniques and rapidly declining storage costs have been responsible for the multiplying databases on individuals—employees, customers, and potential customers—maintained by private and public organizations. These advances in data storage have made the routine violation of individual privacy both cheap and effective. Already massive data storage systems are cheap enough for regional and even local retailing firms to use in identifying customers. For Example, Amazon.com built a massive data warehouse with over 3 terabytes of customer sales data and Web visitor data that could grow 1000-fold in the next few years (Whiting, 2000).

Advances in datamining techniques for large databases are a third technological trend that heightens ethical concerns, because they enable companies to find out much detailed personal information about individuals. With contemporary information systems technology, companies can assemble and combine the myriad pieces of information stored on you by computers much more easily than in the past. Think of all the ways you generate computer information about yourself—credit card purchases, telephone calls, magazine subscriptions, video rentals, mail-order purchases, banking records, and local, state, and federal government records (including court and police records). Put together and mined properly, this information could reveal not only your credit information but also your driving habits, your tastes, your associations, and your political interests.

**profiling**
The use of computers to combine data from multiple sources and create electronic dossiers of detailed information on individuals.

Companies with products to sell purchase relevant information from these sources to help them more finely target their marketing campaigns. Chapter 7 described how companies can use datamining on very large pools of data from multiple sources to rapidly identify buying patterns of customers and suggest individual responses. The use of computers to combine data from multiple sources and create electronic dossiers of detailed information on individuals is called **profiling.** For example, hundreds of Web sites allow DoubleClick

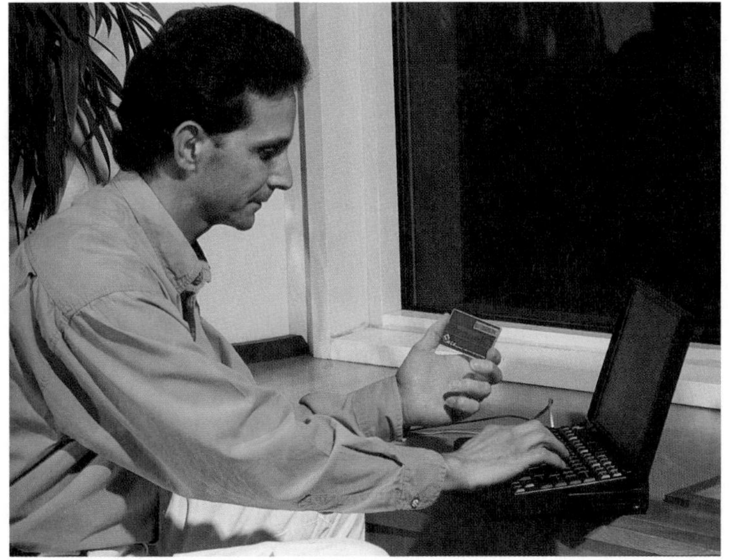

*Credit car purchases can make personal information available to market researchers, telephone marketers, and direct mail companies. Advances in information technology facilitate the invasion of privacy.*

(www.doubleclick.net), an Internet advertising broker, to track the activities of their visitors in exchange for revenue from advertisements based on visitor information DoubleClick gathers. DoubleClick uses this information to create a profile of each on-line visitor, adding more detail to the profile as the visitor visits an associated DoubleClick site. Over time DoubleClick can create a detailed dossier of a person's spending and computing habits on the Web that can be sold to companies to help them target their Web ads more precisely.

Last, advances in networking, including the Internet, promise to reduce greatly the costs of moving and accessing large quantities of data, and open the possibility of mining large pools of data remotely using small desktop machines, permitting an invasion of privacy on a scale and precision heretofore unimaginable.

The development of global digital-superhighway communication networks widely available to individuals and businesses poses many ethical and social concerns. Who will account for the flow of information over these networks? Will you be able to trace information collected about you? What will these networks do to the traditional relationships between family, work, and leisure? How will traditional job designs be altered when millions of "employees" become subcontractors using mobile offices for which they themselves must pay?

In the next section we consider some ethical principles and analytical techniques for dealing with these kinds of ethical and social concerns.

## 15.2 Ethics in an Information Society

Ethics is a concern of humans who have freedom of choice. Ethics is about individual choice: When faced with alternative courses of action, what is the correct moral choice? What are the main features of "ethical choice"?

### Basic Concepts: Responsibility, Accountability, and Liability

Ethical choices are decisions made by individuals who are responsible for the consequences of their actions. **Responsibility** is a key element of ethical action. Responsibility means that you accept the potential costs, duties, and obligations for the decisions you make. **Accountability** is a feature of systems and social institutions: It means that mechanisms are in place to determine who took responsible action, who is responsible. Systems and institutions in which it is impossible to find out who took what action are inherently incapable of ethical analysis or ethical action. Liability extends the concept of responsibility further to the area of laws. **Liability** is a feature of political systems in which a body of law is in place that permits individuals to recover the damages done to them by other actors, systems, or organizations. **Due process** is a related feature of law-governed societies and is a process in which

**responsibility**
Accepting the potential costs, duties, and obligations for the decisions one makes.

**accountability**
The mechanisms for assessing responsibility for decisions made and actions taken.

**liability**
The existence of laws that permit individuals to recover the damages done to them by other actors, systems, or organizations.

**due process**
A process in which laws are well-known and understood and there is an ability to appeal to higher authorities to ensure that laws are applied correctly.

laws are known and understood and there is an ability to appeal to higher authorities to ensure that the laws were applied correctly.

These basic concepts form the underpinning of an ethical analysis of information systems and those who manage them. First, as discussed in Chapter 3, information technologies are filtered through social institutions, organizations, and individuals. Systems do not have "impacts" by themselves. Whatever information system impacts exist are products of institutional, organizational, and individual actions and behaviors. Second, responsibility for the consequences of technology falls clearly on the institutions, organizations, and individual managers who choose to use the technology. Using information technology in a "socially responsible" manner means that you can and will be held accountable for the consequences of your actions. Third, in an ethical political society, individuals and others can recover damages done to them through a set of laws characterized by due process.

## ETHICAL ANALYSIS

When confronted with a situation that seems to present ethical issues, how should you analyze and reason about the situation? Following is a five-step process that should help:

- **Identify and describe clearly the facts.** Find out who did what to whom, and where, when, and how. In many instances, you will be surprised at the errors in the initially reported facts, and often you will find that simply getting the facts straight helps define the solution. It also helps to get the opposing parties involved in an ethical dilemma to agree on the facts.
- **Define the conflict or dilemma and identify the higher-order values involved.** Ethical, social, and political issues always reference higher values. The parties to a dispute all claim to be pursuing higher values (e.g., freedom, privacy, protection of property, and the free enterprise system). Typically, an ethical issue involves a dilemma: two diametrically opposed courses of action that support worthwhile values. For example, the chapter opening vignette and ending case study illustrate two competing values: the need for companies to use marketing to become more efficient and the need to protect individual privacy.
- **Identify the stakeholders.** Every ethical, social, and political issue has stakeholders: players in the game who have an interest in the outcome, who have invested in the situation, and who usually have vocal opinions. Find out the identity of these individuals and groups and what they want. This will be useful later when designing a solution.
- **Identify the options that you can reasonably take.** You may find that none of the options satisfy all the interests involved, but that some options do a better job than others. Sometimes arriving at a "good" or ethical solution may not always be a "balancing" of consequences to stakeholders.
- **Identify the potential consequences of your options.** Some options may be ethically correct but disastrous from other points of view. Other options may work in this one instance but not in other similar instances. Always ask yourself, "What if I choose this option consistently over time?"

Once your analysis is complete, what ethical principles or rules should you use to make a decision? What higher-order values should inform your judgment?

## CANDIDATE ETHICAL PRINCIPLES

Although you are the only one who can decide which among many ethical principles you will follow, and how you will prioritize them, it is helpful to consider some ethical principles with deep roots in many cultures that have survived throughout recorded history.

1. Do unto others as you would have them do unto you (the Golden Rule). Putting yourself into the place of others, and thinking of yourself as the object of the decision, can help you think about "fairness" in decision making.
2. If an action is not right for everyone to take, then it is not right for anyone (**Immanuel Kant's Categorical Imperative**). Ask yourself, "If everyone did this, could the organization, or society, survive?"

**Immanuel Kant's Categorical Imperative**
A principle that states that if an action is not right for everyone to take it is not right for anyone.

3. If an action cannot be taken repeatedly, then it is not right to take at all (**Descartes' rule of change**). This is the slippery-slope rule: An action may bring about a small change now that is acceptable, but if repeated it would bring unacceptable changes in the long run. In the vernacular, it might be stated as "once started down a slippery path you may not be able to stop."
4. Take the action that achieves the higher or greater value (**Utilitarian Principle**). This rule assumes you can prioritize values in a rank order and understand the consequences of various courses of action.
5. Take the action that produces the least harm or the least potential cost (**Risk Aversion Principle**). Some actions have extremely high failure costs of very low probability (e.g., building a nuclear generating facility in an urban area) or extremely high failure costs of moderate probability (speeding and automobile accidents). Avoid these high failure cost actions, paying greater attention obviously to high failure cost potential of moderate to high probability.
6. Assume that virtually all tangible and intangible objects are owned by someone else unless there is a specific declaration otherwise. (This is the **ethical "no free lunch" rule.**) If something someone else has created is useful to you, it has value and you should assume the creator wants compensation for this work.

**Descartes' rule of change**
A principle that states that if an action cannot be taken repeatedly, then it is not right to be taken at any time.

**Utilitarian Principle**
Principle that assumes one can put values in rank order and understand the consequences of various courses of action.

**Risk Aversion Principle**
Principle that one should take the action that produces the least harm or incurs the least cost.

**ethical "no free lunch" rule**
Assumption that all tangible and intangible objects are owned by someone else unless there is a specific declaration otherwise and that the creator wants compensation for this work.

Although these ethical rules cannot be absolute guides to action, actions that do not easily pass these rules deserve some very close attention and a great deal of caution. The appearance of unethical behavior may do as much harm to you and your company as actual unethical behavior.

## PROFESSIONAL CODES OF CONDUCT

When groups of people claim to be professionals, they take on special rights and obligations because of their special claims to knowledge, wisdom, and respect. Professional codes of conduct are promulgated by associations of professionals such as the American Medical Association (AMA), the American Bar Association (ABA), the Association of Information Technology Professionals (AITP), and the Association of Computing Machinery (ACM). These professional groups take responsibility for the partial regulation of their professions by determining entrance qualifications and competence. Codes of ethics are promises by professions to regulate themselves in the general interest of society. For example, avoiding harm to others, honoring property rights (including intellectual property), and respecting privacy are among the General Moral Imperatives of the ACM's Code of Ethics and Professional Conduct (ACM, 1993).

## SOME REAL-WORLD ETHICAL DILEMMAS

The recent ethical problems described in this section illustrate a wide range of issues. Some of these issues are obvious ethical dilemmas, in which one set of interests is pitted against another. Others represent some type of breach of ethics. In either instance, there are rarely any easy solutions.

***Downsizing with Technology at the Telephone Company*** Many of the large telephone companies in the United States are using information technology to reduce the sizes of their workforces. For example, AT&T is using voice recognition software to reduce the need for human operators by allowing computers to recognize a customer's responses to a series of computerized questions. AT&T planned for the new technology to eliminate 3,000 to 6,000 operator jobs nationwide, 200 to 400 management positions, and 31 offices in 21 states.

***Electronic Profiling at the Airport*** The Federal Aviation Administration instituted an electronic profiling system to identify potential terrorists. The system collects data about people from multiple sources and uses datamining and artificial intelligence to create a profile on all purchasers of airline tickets that identifies the risks each might present. The American Civil Liberties Union (ACLU) believes this type of profiling is discriminatory because it singles out people of Middle Eastern descent (Nash, 1998).

***Employee Monitoring on the Internet*** Xerox Corporation fired 40 workers in 1999 for spending too much of their work time surfing the Web. That company and many others monitor their employees' activities on the Internet to prevent them from wasting company resources on nonbusiness activities (San Jose Mercury, 2000). Many firms also claim the right to monitor the electronic mail of their employees because they own the facilities, intend their use to be for business purposes only, and create the facility for a business purpose (see the Chapter 8 case study).

In each instance, you can find competing values at work, with groups lined on either side of a debate. A company may argue, for example, that it has a right to use information systems to increase productivity and reduce the size of its workforce to lower costs and stay in business. Employees displaced by information systems may argue that employers have some responsibility for their welfare. A close analysis of the facts can sometimes produce compromised solutions that give each side "half a loaf." Try to apply some of the described principles of ethical analysis to each of these cases. What is the right thing to do?

## 15.3 THE MORAL DIMENSIONS OF INFORMATION SYSTEMS

In this section, we take a closer look at the five moral dimensions of information systems first described in Figure 15-1. In each dimension we identify the ethical, social, and political levels of analysis and use real-world examples to illustrate the values involved, the stakeholders, and the options chosen.

**privacy**
The claim of individuals to be left alone, free from surveillance or interference from other individuals, organizations, or the state.

### INFORMATION RIGHTS: PRIVACY AND FREEDOM IN AN INFORMATION SOCIETY

**Privacy** is the claim of individuals to be left alone, free from surveillance or interference from other individuals or organizations including the state. Claims to privacy are also involved at the workplace: Millions of employees are subject to electronic and other forms of high-tech

## MANAGEMENT DECISION PROBLEM

### WHAT TO DO ABOUT EMPLOYEE WEB USAGE

As the head of a small insurance company with six employees, you are concerned about how effectively your company is using its networking and human resources. Budgets are tight, and you are struggling to meet payrolls because employees are reporting many overtime hours. You do not believe that the employees have a sufficiently heavy work load to warrant working longer hours and are looking into the amount of time they spend on the Internet. Each employee uses a computer with Internet access on the job. You requested the following weekly report of employee Web usage from your company Web server.

**Web Usage Report for the Week Ending January 12, 2001**

| User Name | Minutes On-line | URL Visited |
|---|---|---|
| Kelleher, Claire | 45 | www.doubleclick.net |
| Kelleher, Claire | 57 | www.yahoo.com |
| Kelleher, Claire | 96 | www.insuremarket.com |
| McMahon, Patricia | 83 | www.e-music.com |
| Milligan, Robert | 112 | www.shopping.com |
| Milligan, Robert | 43 | www.travelocity.com |
| Olivera, Ernesto | 40 | www.internetnews.com |
| Talbot, Helen | 125 | www.etrade.com |
| Talbot, Helen | 27 | www.wine.com |
| Talbot, Helen | 35 | www.yahoo.com |
| Talbot, Helen | 73 | www.ebay.com |
| Wright, Steven | 23 | www.geocities.com |
| Wright, Steven | 15 | www.autobytel.com |

1. Calculate the total amount of time each employee spent on the Web for the week and the total amount of time that company computers were used for this purpose. Rank the employees in the order of the amount of time each spent on-line.
2. Do your findings and the contents of the report indicate any ethical problems employees are creating? Explain. Is the company creating an ethical problem by monitoring its employees' use of the Internet?
3. Use the guidelines for ethical analysis presented in this chapter to develop a solution to the problems you have identified.

surveillance. Information technology and systems threaten individual claims to privacy by making the invasion of privacy cheap, profitable, and effective.

The claim to privacy is protected in the U.S., Canadian, and German constitutions in a variety of different ways and in other countries through various statutes. In the United States, the claim to privacy is protected primarily by the First Amendment guarantees of freedom of speech and association; the Fourth Amendment protections against unreasonable search and seizure of one's personal documents or home; and the guarantee of due process.

Due process has become a key concept in defining privacy. Due process requires that a set of rules or laws exist that clearly define how information about individuals will be treated and what appeal mechanisms are available. Perhaps the best statement of due process in record keeping is given by the Fair Information Practices Doctrine developed in the early 1970s.

Most American and European privacy law is based on a regime called Fair Information Practices (FIP) first set forth in a report written in 1973 by a federal government advisory committee (U.S. Department of Health, Education, and Welfare, 1973). **Fair Information Practices (FIP)** is a set of principles governing the collection and use of information about individuals. The five Fair Information Practices principles are shown in Table 15-2.

**Fair Information Practices (FIP)**
A set of principles originally set forth in 1973 that governs the collection and use of information about individuals and forms the basis of most U.S. and European privacy laws.

FIP principles are based on the notion of a "mutuality of interest" among the record holder and the individual. The individual has an interest in engaging in a transaction, and the record keeper—usually a business or government agency—requires information about the individual to support the transaction. Once gathered, the individual maintains an interest in the record, and the record may not be used to support other activities without the individual's consent.

Fair Information Practices form the basis of the federal statutes listed in Table 15-3 that set forth the conditions for handling information about individuals in such areas as credit reporting, education, financial records, newspaper records, cable communications, electronic communications, and even video rentals. The Privacy Act of 1974 is the most important of these laws, regulating the federal government's collection, use, and disclosure of information. Most federal privacy laws apply only to the United States federal government. Only credit, banking, cable, and video rental industries have been regulated by federal privacy law.

In the United States, privacy law is enforced by individuals who must sue agencies or companies in court to recover damages. European countries and Canada define privacy in a similar manner to that in the United States, but they have chosen to enforce their privacy laws by creating privacy commissions or data protection agencies to pursue complaints brought by citizens.

## The European Directive on Data Protection

In Europe, privacy protection is much more stringent than in the United States. On October 25, 1998, the European Directive on Data Protection came into effect, broadening privacy protection in the European Union (EU) nations. The Directive requires companies to inform people when they collect information about them and disclose how it will be stored and used. Customers must provide their informed consent before any company can legally use data about them, and they have the right to access that information, correct it, and request that no further data be collected. EU member nations must translate these principles into their own laws and cannot transfer personal data to countries such as the United States that don't have similar privacy protection regulations (see Chapter 16).

### TABLE 15-2 FAIR INFORMATION PRACTICES PRINCIPLES

1. There should be no personal record systems whose existence is secret.
2. Individuals have rights of access, inspection, review, and amendment to systems that contain information about them.
3. There must be no use of personal information for purposes other than those for which it was gathered without prior consent.
4. Managers of systems are responsible and can be held accountable and liable for the damage done by systems.
5. Governments have the right to intervene in the information relationships among private parties.

**TABLE 15-3 FEDERAL PRIVACY LAWS IN THE UNITED STATES**

| |
|---|
| **1. General Federal Privacy Laws** |
| Freedom of Information Act, 1968 as Amended (5 USC 552) |
| Privacy Act of 1974 as Amended (5 USC 552a) |
| Federal Managers Financial Integrity Act of 1982 |
| Electronic Communications Privacy Act of 1986 |
| Computer Security Act of 1987 |
| Computer Matching and Privacy Protection Act of 1988 |
| **2. Privacy Laws Affecting Private Institutions** |
| Fair Credit Reporting Act of 1970 |
| Family Educational Rights and Privacy Act of 1978 |
| Right to Financial Privacy Act of 1978 |
| Privacy Protection Act of 1980 |
| Cable Communications Policy Act of 1984 |
| Electronic Communications Privacy Act of 1986 |
| Video Privacy Protection Act of 1988 |
| Communications Privacy and Consumer Empowerment Act of 1997 |
| Data Privacy Act of 1997 |
| Consumer Internet Privacy Protection Act of 1999 |

## Internet Challenges to Privacy

The Internet introduces technology that poses new challenges to the protection of individual privacy that existing Fair Information Practices principles are inadequate to address. Information sent over this vast network of networks may pass through many different computer systems before it reaches its final destination. Each of these systems is capable of monitoring, capturing, and storing communications that pass through it.

It is possible to record many on-line activities, including which on-line newsgroups or files a person has accessed, which Web sites he or she has visited, and what items that person has inspected or purchased over the Web. This information can be collected by both a subscriber's own Internet service provider and the system operators of remote Web sites that a subscriber visits. Tools to monitor visits to the World Wide Web have become popular because they help organizations determine who is visiting their Web sites and how to better target their offerings. (Some firms also monitor the Internet usage of their employees to see how they are using company network resources.) Web retailers now have access to software that lets them watch the on-line shopping behavior of individuals and groups while they are visiting a Web site and making purchases. The commercial demand for this personal information is virtually insatiable.

**cookie**
Tiny file deposited on a computer hard drive when an individual visits certain Web sites. Used to identify the visitor and track visits to the Web site.

Web sites can learn the identity of their visitors if the visitors voluntarily register at the site to purchase a product or service or to obtain a free service, such as information. Web sites can also capture information about visitors without their knowledge using "cookie" technology. **Cookies** are tiny files deposited on a computer hard drive when a user visits certain Web sites. Cookies identify the visitor's Web browser software and track visits to the Web site. When the visitor returns to a site that has stored a cookie, the Web site software will search the visitor's computer, find the cookie, and "know" what that person has done in the past. It may also update the cookie, depending on the activity during the visit. In this way, the site can customize its contents for each visitor's interests. For example, if you purchase a book on the Amazon.com Web site and return later using the same browser, the site will welcome you by name and recommend other books of interest based on your past purchases. DoubleClick, introduced earlier in this chapter, uses cookies to build its dossiers with details of on-line purchases and behavior of Web site visitors. Figure 15-2 illustrates how cookies work.

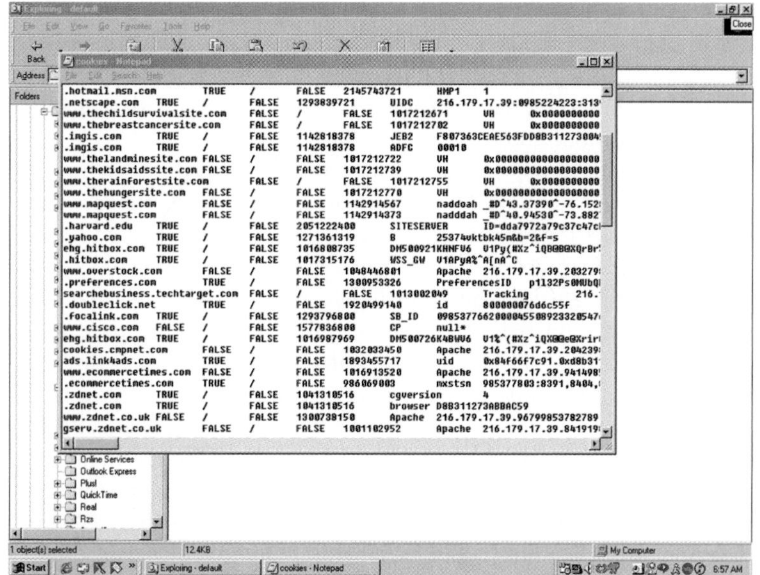

*"Cookies" are tiny files deposited on a computer hard drive when users visit certain Web sites. Although cookies can provide valuable marketing information, the practice of collecting Web-site visitor data raises worries about protecting individual privacy.*

If you are a regular Web user, search your hard drive for files named "cookie.txt" and you are likely to find some. The site may use the data collected from its cookies for itself or it may sell that data to other companies. Web sites using cookie technology cannot directly obtain visitors' names and addresses. However, if a person has registered at any other site, some of that information will be stored in a cookie. Examine the cookies on your own computer and you will see how much personal data is there. Often, scattered within the cookies, you will find your real name, your user name, your bank, and perhaps your account numbers. These cookies are not secured in any way, and Web site owners can surreptitiously search them for personal data. Thus, if one site stores your name, another will find it. The result is that many sites know a great deal more about you than you might suspect or desire.

Organizations can collect e-mail addresses to send out thousands and even hundreds of thousands of unsolicited e-mail and electronic messages. This practice is called **spamming,** and it is growing, because it only costs a few cents to send thousands of messages advertising

**spamming**
The practice of sending unsolicited e-mail and other electronic communication.

***Figure 15-2*** How cookies identify Web visitors. Cookies are written by a Web site on a visitor's hard drive. When the visitor returns to that Web site, the Web server requests the ID number from the cookie and uses it to access the data stored by that server on that visitor. The Web site can then use these data to display personalized information.
*Source:* "Personalization Explained" by Alan Zeichick, from *Red Herring,* September 1999, p. 130. Reprinted by permission.

**Don't I Know You?**

How Web servers identify their visitors.

1. The server reads the PC's browser to determine the user's operating system, browser name and version number, IP address, and other information, sometimes including the user's e-mail address.
2. The server uses the browser information to transmit tiny bits of personalized data called cookies, which the user's browser receives and stores on the PC's hard drive.
3. When the user revisits the Web site, the server requests the contents of any cookie previously provided by that site.
4. The Web server reads the cookie, identifies the user, then calls up its data on the visitor.

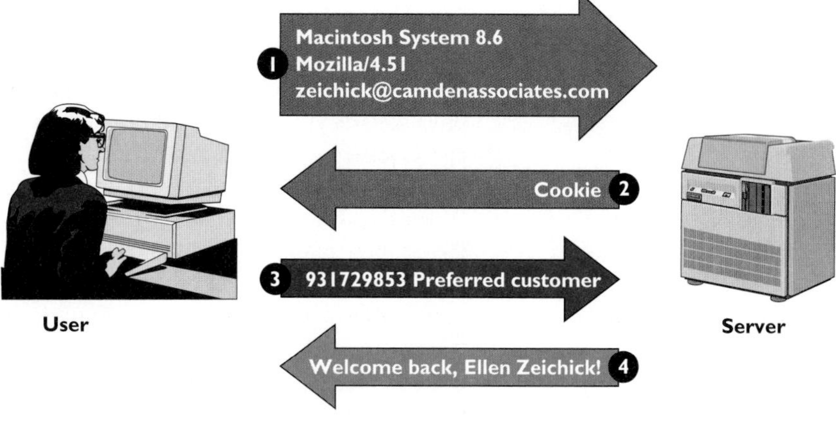

one's wares to Internet users. Marketing companies can use new technology for monitoring e-mail users to keep tabs on who opens their e-mail solicitations and at what time of the day in order to develop more personalized promotions. They can link this information to data collected through cookies to create even more detailed databases of individuals'activities on the Web (Harmon, 2000).

At present, Web site visitors can't easily find out how the information collected about them from their visits to Web sites is being used. Some free-of-charge software downloads have capabilities for leaving audit trails of users' Internet activities without their knowledge and do not alert users of these features at the time of download (Martin, Smith, Brittain, Fetch, and Wu, 2001). Only a small percentage of Web sites openly post their privacy policies or offer consumers a choice about how their personal data are to be used (Rosen and Bacheldor, 2000). To encourage self-regulation in the Internet industry, the U.S. Department of Commerce has issued guidelines for Fair Information Practices in on-line business. Industry groups such as the Online Privacy Alliance (OPA), consisting of more than 100 global corporations and associations, have also issued guidelines for self-regulation. Privacy-enhancing technologies for protecting user privacy during interactions with Web sites are being developed (Vijayan, 2000; Reiter and Rubin, 1999; Goldschlag, Reed, and Syverson, 1999; Gabber, Gibbons, Kristol, Matias, and Mayer, 1999). Additional legislation and government oversight may be required to make sure that privacy in the Internet age is properly safeguarded. The chapter ending case study explores the issue of Web site privacy in greater detail.

## Ethical Issues

The ethical privacy issue in this information age is as follows: Under what conditions should I (you) invade the privacy of others? What legitimates intruding into others' lives through unobtrusive surveillance, through market research, or by any other means? Do we have to inform people that we are eavesdropping? Do we have to inform people that we are using credit history information for employment screening purposes?

## Social Issues

The social issue of privacy concerns the development of "expectations of privacy," or privacy norms, as well as public attitudes. In what areas of life should we, as a society, encourage people to think they are in "private territory" as opposed to public view? For instance, should we, as a society, encourage people to develop expectations of privacy when using electronic mail, cellular telephones, bulletin boards, the postal system, the workplace, the street? Should expectations of privacy be extended to criminal conspirators?

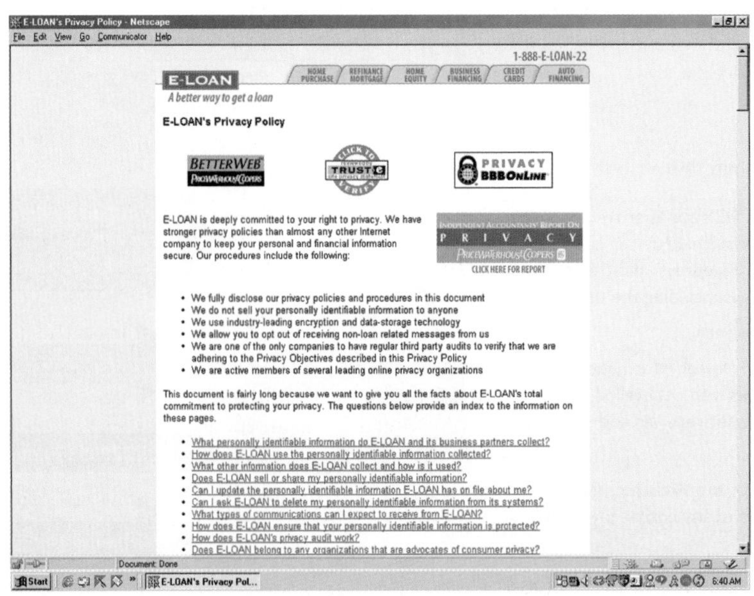


*Web sites are starting to post their privacy policies for visitors to review. The TRUSTe seal designates Web sites that have agreed to adhere to TRUSTe's established privacy principles of disclosure, choice, access, and security.*

### Political Issues

The political issue of privacy concerns the development of statutes that govern the relations between record keepers and individuals. Should we permit the FBI to prevent the commercial development of encrypted telephone transmissions so it can eavesdrop at will (Denning et al., 1993)? Should a law be passed to require direct-marketing firms to obtain the consent of individuals before using their names in mass marketing? Should e-mail privacy—regardless of who owns the equipment—be protected by law? In general, large organizations of all kinds—public and private—are reluctant to remit the advantages that come from the unfettered flow of information on individuals. Civil libertarians and other private groups have been the strongest voices supporting restraints on large organizations' information-gathering activities.

## PROPERTY RIGHTS: INTELLECTUAL PROPERTY

Contemporary information systems have severely challenged existing law and social practices that protect private intellectual property. **Intellectual property** is considered to be intangible property created by individuals or corporations. Information technology has made it difficult to protect intellectual property, because computerized information can be so easily copied or distributed on networks. Intellectual property is subject to a variety of protections under three different legal traditions: trade secret, copyright, and patent law (Graham, 1984).

**intellectual property**
Intangible property created by individuals or corporations that is subject to protections under trade secret, copyright, and patent law.

### Trade Secrets

Any intellectual work product—a formula, device, pattern, or compilation of data—used for a business purpose can be classified as a **trade secret,** provided it is not based on information in the public domain. Protections for trade secrets vary from state to state. In general, trade secret laws grant a monopoly on the ideas behind a work product, but it can be a very tenuous monopoly.

**trade secret**
Any intellectual work or product used for a business purpose that can be classified as belonging to that business, provided it is not based on information in the public domain.

Software that contains novel or unique elements, procedures, or compilations can be included as a trade secret. Trade secret law protects the actual ideas in a work product, not only their manifestation. To make this claim, the creator or owner must take care to bind employees and customers with nondisclosure agreements and to prevent the secret from falling into the public domain.

The limitation of trade secret protection is that, although virtually all software programs of any complexity contain unique elements of some sort, it is difficult to prevent the ideas in the work from falling into the public domain when the software is widely distributed.

### Copyright

**Copyright** is a statutory grant that protects creators of intellectual property from having their work copied by others for any purpose for a period of 28 years. Since the first Federal Copyright Act of 1790 and the creation of the Copyright Office to register copyrights and enforce copyright law, Congress has extended copyright protection to books, periodicals, lectures, dramas, musical compositions, maps, drawings, artwork of any kind, and motion pictures. The congressional intent behind copyright laws has been to encourage creativity and authorship by ensuring that creative people receive the financial and other benefits of their work. Most industrial nations have their own copyright laws, and there are several international conventions and bilateral agreements through which nations coordinate and enforce their laws.

**copyright**
A statutory grant that protects creators of intellectual property against copying by others for any purpose for a period of 28 years.

In the mid-1960s the Copyright Office began registering software programs, and in 1980 Congress passed the Computer Software Copyright Act, which clearly provides protection for source and object code and for copies of the original sold in commerce, and sets forth the rights of the purchaser to use the software while the creator retains legal title.

Copyright protection is clear-cut: It protects against copying of entire programs or their parts. Damages and relief are readily obtained for infringement. The drawback to copyright protection is that the underlying ideas behind a work are not protected, only their manifestation in a work. A competitor can use your software, understand how it works, and build new software that follows the same concepts without infringing on a copyright.

"Look and feel" copyright infringement lawsuits are precisely about the distinction between an idea and its expression. For instance, in the early 1990s Apple Computer sued Microsoft Corporation and Hewlett-Packard Inc. for infringement of the expression of Apple's Macintosh interface. Among other claims, Apple claimed that the defendants copied the expression of overlapping windows. The defendants counterclaimed that the idea of overlapping windows can only be expressed in a single way and, therefore, was not protectable under the "merger" doctrine of copyright law. When ideas and their expression merge, the expression cannot be copyrighted. In general, courts appear to be following the reasoning of a 1989 case—*Brown Bag Software* vs. *Symantec Corp.*—in which the court dissected the elements of software alleged to be infringing. The court found that neither similar concept, function, general functional features (e.g., drop-down menus), nor colors are protectable by copyright law (*Brown Bag* vs. *Symantec Corp.,* 1992).

## Patents

**patent**
A legal document that grants the owner an exclusive monopoly on the ideas behind an invention for 17 years; designed to ensure that inventors of new machines or methods are rewarded for their labor while making widespread use of their inventions.

A **patent** grants the owner an exclusive monopoly on the ideas behind an invention for 17 years. The congressional intent behind patent law was to ensure that inventors of new machines, devices, or methods receive the full financial and other rewards of their labor and yet still make widespread use of the invention possible by providing detailed diagrams for those wishing to use the idea under license from the patent's owner. The granting of a patent is determined by the Patent Office and relies on court rulings.

The key concepts in patent law are originality, novelty, and invention. The Patent Office did not accept applications for software patents routinely until a 1981 Supreme Court decision that held that computer programs could be a part of a patentable process. Since that time hundreds of patents have been granted and thousands await consideration.

The strength of patent protection is that it grants a monopoly on the underlying concepts and ideas of software. The difficulty is passing stringent criteria of nonobviousness (e.g., the work must reflect some special understanding and contribution), originality, and novelty, as well as years of waiting to receive protection.

## Challenges to Intellectual Property Rights

Contemporary information technologies, especially software, pose a severe challenge to existing intellectual property regimes and, therefore, create significant ethical, social, and political issues. Digital media differ from books, periodicals, and other media in terms of ease of replication; ease of transmission; ease of alteration; difficulty classifying a software work as a program, book, or even music; compactness—making theft easy; and difficulties in establishing uniqueness. Computer software has features which do not fit easily into traditional legal categories for patent and copyright protection (Burk, 2001).

The proliferation of electronic networks, including the Internet, has made it even more difficult to protect intellectual property. Before widespread use of networks, copies of software, books, magazine articles, or films had to be stored on physical media, such as paper, computer disks, or videotape, creating some hurdles to distribution. Using networks and the Web, digital, information can be more widely reproduced and distributed with technology that is available to ordinary households (Davis, 2001). Software piracy rates in some countries exceed 90%. Many countries tolerate software piracy to allow their citizens to obtain the latest software products from abroad at low prices and to keep abreast of the latest technology (Gopal and Sanders, 2000).

With the World Wide Web in particular, one can easily copy and distribute virtually anything to thousands and even millions of people around the world, even if they are using different types of computer systems. Information can be illicitly copied from one place and distributed through other systems and networks even though these parties do not willingly participate in the infringement. For example, the music industry is worried because individuals can illegally copy MP3 music files to Web sites where they can be downloaded by others who do not know that the MP3 files are not licensed for copying or distribution (see the Window on Technology). The Internet was designed to transmit information freely around the world, including copyrighted information. Intellectual property that can be easily copied is likely to be copied (Carazos, 1996; Chabrow, 1996).

## Napster and Gnutella Rock the Entertainment Industry

Would you pay $15.99 for a CD of your favorite recording artist when you could get it for free on the Web? That's what the music industry has been worrying about since the advent of Napster. Napster is a Web site that provides software and services that enable users to find and share MP3 music files. To use the company's service, users must download client software that allows them to search the hard drives of other Napster subscribers for MP3 files. The MP3 files can then be downloaded directly from the user's computer.

Napster servers do not store any files. They act as matchmakers. After you type in the name of the song you want, Napster shows all the users who are connected and who have that song on their computer available for downloading. Napster software then sets up a connection between your computer and the computer with the MP3 file, so the download can proceed. The song can then be played through computer speakers, transferred to an audio CD with a CD-R drive, or left in the shared music folder on your hard drive so other Napster users can copy it from you. Napster attracted about 38 million users in its first 18 months of existence.

Napster software can be used in a perfectly legal fashion to trade uncopyrighted music files, but many Napster users had been sharing digital MP3 music files that have been copied from commercial audio CDs. In December 1999 the Recording Industry of America representing the five major music recording companies sued Napster for violating copyright laws. This suit is one of a series of legal actions the recording industry has taken against online music companies that are violating copyrights. In February 2001, a Federal appeals court upheld an earlier lower-court ruling ordering Napster to stop allowing users to share and download copyrighted music files. On October 31, 2000, Napster announced it would join Bertelsman, one of the world's five major music companies to create a fee-based Internet music service. MP3.com also has arranged to pay the recording companies for use of their songs through its site.

But reforming Napster won't solve the problem. Other software and Web sites allow people to do the same thing. Gnutella, for example allows individuals to send and receive all kinds of files without going through a central computer. In addition to MP3 music files, digital files of any type, size, or origin, including files of films, books, TV shows, or software—anything that can be digitized—can be shared with other computers without going through a central server. Each Gnutella.net client can share files, search for files, and download files from any other user. Gnutella users have been actively trading movies as well as CDs over the Internet.

Gnutella was developed by Nullsoft, the maker of the Winamp MP3 player. Nullsoft's owner, America Online, shut down the Gnutella site immediately after it became active, but the Gnutella source code was openly distributed to developers outside the company and versions are available on the Internet. It is nearly impossible for ISPs, governments, or other groups to disable the network. According to Thomas Hale, CEO of Wired Planet, "The only way to stop [Gnutella] is to turn off the Internet."

Viewed in a positive light, Gnutella provides technology that can help break through censorship in other countries. Viewed more negatively, the same technology can be used to systematically violate copyright laws. The publishing and computer software industries are especially worried about potential losses from Gnutella and other similar programs, such as Hotline, JungleMonkey, and Freenet, because there is no central server, as in the case of Napster, that can be shut down to stop the flow of files.

**To Think About:** Should you use programs like Gnutella to obtain software, movies, or other digital files? Explain your answer.

*Sources:* Dan Goodis, "Napster Blocks over 115,000 Songs," *The Industry Standard*, March 12, 2001 and "Can Napster Change Its Tune?" *The Industry Standard*, February 18, 2001; Amy Harmon, "Napster Users Mourn End of Free Music," *The New York Times*, November 1, 2000; Amy Harmon with John Sullivan, "Music Industry Wins Ruling in U.S. Court," *The New York Times*, April 29, 2000; Hane C. Lee and Michael Laermonth, "Spawn of Napster," *The Industry Standard*, May 8, 2000; Peter H. Lewis, "Napster Rocks the Web," *The New York Times*, June 2000; Lee Gomes, "Software 'Free Spirits' Release Version of Program Mimicking Napster Product," *The Wall Street Journal*, March 15, 2000; and Don Clark and Martin Peers, "Can the Record Industry Beat Free Web Music?" *The Wall Street Journal*, June 20, 2000.

The manner in which information is obtained and presented on the Web further challenges intellectual property protections (Okerson, 1996). Web pages can be constructed from bits of text, graphics, sound, or video that may come from many different sources. Each item may belong to a different entity, creating complicated issues of ownership and compensation (see Figure 15-3). Web sites can also use a capability called "framing" to let one site construct an on-screen border around content obtained by linking to another Web site. The first site's border and logo stay on the screen, making the content of the new Web site appear to be "offered" by the previous Web site.

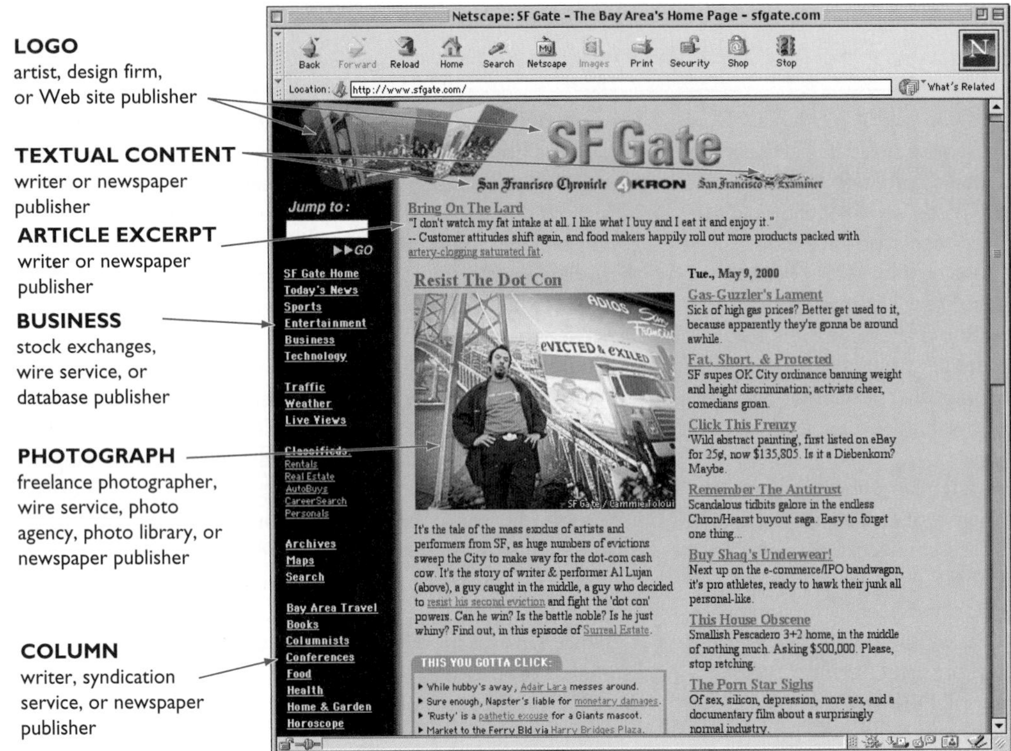


*Figure 15-3* Who owns the pieces? Anatomy of a Web page. Web pages are often constructed with elements from many different sources, clouding issues of ownership and intellectual property protection.

Mechanisms are being developed to sell and distribute books, articles, and other intellectual property on the Internet, but publishers continue to look for copyright violations because intellectual property can now be copied so easily.

## Ethical Issues

The central ethical issue posed to individuals concerns copying software: Should I (you) copy for my own use a piece of software protected by trade secret, copyright, or patent law? In the information age, it is so easy to obtain perfect, functional copies of software, that the software companies themselves have abandoned software protection schemes to increase market penetration, and enforcement of the law is rare. However, if everyone copied software, very little new software would be produced because creators could not benefit from the results of their work.

## Social Issues

There are several property-related social issues raised by new information technology. Most experts agree that the current intellectual property laws are breaking down in the information age. The vast majority of Americans report in surveys that they routinely violate some minor laws—everything from speeding to taking paper clips from work to copying software. The ease with which software can be copied contributes to making us a society of lawbreakers. These routine thefts threaten significantly to reduce the speed with which new information technologies can and will be introduced and, thereby, threaten further advances in productivity and social well-being.

## Political Issues

The main property-related political issue concerns the creation of new property protection measures to protect investments made by creators of new software. Microsoft and 1,400 other software and information content firms are represented by the Software and Information Industry Association (SIIA), which lobbies for new laws and enforcement of existing laws to protect intellectual property around the world. (SIIA was formed on January 1, 1999, from the merger of the Software Publishers Association [SPA] and the Information Industry Association [IIA].) The SIIA runs an antipiracy hotline for individuals to report piracy activities and educational programs to help organizations combat software piracy. The SIIA has developed model Employee Usage Guidelines for software, described in Table 15-4.

Allied against SIIA are a host of groups and millions of individuals who believe that antipiracy laws cannot be enforced in the digital age and that software should be free or be paid for on a voluntary basis (shareware software). According to these groups, the greater social benefit results from the free distribution of software.

## ACCOUNTABILITY, LIABILITY, AND CONTROL

Along with privacy and property laws, new information technologies are challenging existing liability law and social practices for holding individuals and institutions accountable. If a

### TABLE 15-4 EMPLOYEE USAGE GUIDELINES FOR [ORGANIZATION]

**Purpose**

Software will be used only in accordance with its license agreement. Unless otherwise provided in the license, any duplication of copyrighted software, except for backup and archival purposes by software manager or designated department, is a violation of copyright law. In addition to violating copyright law, unauthorized duplication of software is contrary to [organization's] standards of conduct. The following points are to be followed to comply with software license agreements:

1. All users must use all software in accordance with its license agreements and the [organization's] software policy. All users acknowledge that they do not own this software or its related documentation, and unless expressly authorized by software publisher, may not make additional copies except for archival purposes.
2. [Organization] will not tolerate the use of any unauthorized copies of software or fonts in our organization. Any person illegally reproducing software can be subject to civil and criminal penalties including fines and imprisonment. All users must not condone illegal copying of software under any circumstances and anyone who makes, uses, or otherwise acquires unauthorized software will be appropriately disciplined.
3. No user will give software or fonts to any outsiders including clients, customers, and others. Under no circumstances will software be used within [organization] that has been brought in from any unauthorized location under [organization's] policy, including, but not limited to, the Internet, the home, friends, and colleagues.
4. Any user who determines that there may be a misuse of software within the organization will notify the Certified Software Manager, department manager, or legal counsel.
5. All software used by the organization-owned computers will be purchased through appropriate procedures.

I have read [organization's] software code of ethics. I am fully aware of our software compliance policies and agree to abide by them. I understand that violation of any above policies may result in my termination.

________________________________________

Employee Signature

________________________________________

Date

Published by the SPA Anti-Piracy. You are given permission to duplicate and modify this policy statement so long as attribution to the original document comes from SPA Anti-Piracy.

person is injured by a machine controlled, in part, by software, who should be held accountable and, therefore, held liable? Should a public bulletin board or an electronic service such as Prodigy or America Online permit the transmission of pornographic or offensive material (as broadcasters), or should they be held harmless against any liability for what users transmit (as is true of common carriers such as the telephone system)? What about the Internet? If you outsource your information processing, can you hold the external vendor liable for injuries done to your customers? Some real-world examples may shed light on these questions.

## Some Computer Liability Problems

On March 13, 1993, a blizzard hit the East Coast of the United States, knocking out an Electronic Data Systems Inc. (EDS) computer center in Clifton, New Jersey. The center operated 5,200 ATM machines in 12 different networks across the country involving more than one million card holders. In the two weeks required to recover operations, EDS suggested its customers use alternative ATM networks operated by other banks or computer centers and offered to cover more than $50 million in cash withdrawals. Because the alternative networks did not have access to the actual customer account balances, EDS was at substantial risk of fraud. Cash withdrawals were limited to $100 per day per customer to reduce the exposure. Most service was restored by March 26. Although EDS had a disaster-recovery plan, it did not have a dedicated backup facility. Who is liable for any economic harm caused to individuals or businesses who could not access their full account balances during this period (Joes, 1993)?

In April 1990, a computer system at Shell Pipeline Corporation failed to detect a human operator error. As a result, 93,000 barrels of crude oil were shipped to the wrong trader. The error cost $2 million because the trader sold oil that should not have been delivered to him. A court ruled later that Shell Pipeline was liable for the loss of the oil because the error was caused by a human operator who entered erroneous information into the system. Shell was held liable for not developing a system that would prevent the possibility of misdeliveries (King, 1992). Whom would you have held liable—Shell Pipeline? The trader for not being more careful about deliveries? The human operator who made the error?

These cases point out the difficulties faced by information systems executives who ultimately are responsible for the harm done by systems developed by their staffs. In general, insofar as computer software is part of a machine, and the machine injures someone physically or economically, the producer of the software and the operator can be held liable for damages. Insofar as the software acts more like a book, storing and displaying information, courts have been reluctant to hold authors, publishers, and booksellers liable for contents (the exception being instances of fraud or defamation), and hence courts have been wary of holding software authors liable for "booklike" software.

In general, it is very difficult (if not impossible) to hold software producers liable for their software products when those products are considered as books, regardless of the physical or economic harm that results. Historically, print publishers, books, and periodicals have not been held liable because of fears that liability claims would interfere with First Amendment rights guaranteeing freedom of expression.

What about "software as service?" ATMs provide a service to bank customers. Should this service fail, customers will be inconvenienced and perhaps harmed economically if they cannot access their funds in a timely manner. Should liability protections be extended to software publishers and operators of defective financial, accounting, simulation, or marketing systems?

Software is very different from books. Software users may develop expectations of infallibility about software; software is less easily inspected than a book and more difficult to compare with other software products for quality; software claims actually to perform a task rather than describe a task like a book; and people come to depend on services essentially based on software. Given the centrality of software to everyday life, the chances are excellent that liability law will extend its reach to include software even when it merely provides an information service.

Telephone systems have not been held liable for the messages transmitted because they are regulated "common carriers." In return for their right to provide telephone service, they must provide access to all, at reasonable rates, and achieve acceptable reliability. But broadcasters and cable television systems are subject to a wide variety of federal and local constraints on content and facilities. Organizations can be held liable for offensive content on their Web sites; and on-line services, such as Prodigy or America Online, might be held liable for postings by their users.

### Ethical Issues

The central liability-related ethical issue raised by new information technologies is whether individuals and organizations who create, produce, and sell systems (both hardware and software) are morally responsible for the consequences of their use (see Johnson and Mulvey, 1995). If so, under what conditions? What liabilities (and responsibilities) should the user assume, and what should the provider assume?

### Social Issues

The central liability-related social issue concerns the expectations that society should allow to develop around service-providing information systems. Should individuals (and organizations) be encouraged to develop their own backup devices to cover likely or easily anticipated system failures, or should organizations be held strictly liable for system services they provide? If organizations are held strictly liable, what impact will this have on the development of new system services? Can society permit networks and bulletin boards to post libelous, inaccurate, and misleading information that will harm many persons? Or should information service companies become self-regulating, self-censoring?

### Political Issues

The leading liability-related political issue is the debate between information providers of all kinds (from software developers to network service providers), who want to be relieved of liability as much as possible (thereby maximizing their profits), and service users (individuals, organizations, communities), who want organizations to be held responsible for providing high-quality system services (thereby maximizing the quality of service). Service providers argue they will withdraw from the marketplace if they are held liable, whereas service users argue that only by holding providers liable can we guarantee a high level of service and compensate injured parties. Should legislation impose liability or restrict liability on service providers? This fundamental cleavage is at the heart of numerous political and judicial conflicts.

## System Quality: Data Quality and System Errors

The debate over liability and accountability for unintentional consequences of system use raises a related but independent moral dimension: What is an acceptable, technologically feasible level of system quality (see Chapter 14)? At what point should system managers say, "Stop testing, we've done all we can to perfect this software. Ship it!" Individuals and organizations may be held responsible for avoidable and foreseeable consequences, which they have a duty to perceive and correct. And the gray area is that some system errors are foreseeable and correctable only at very great expense, an expense so great that pursuing this level of perfection is not feasible economically—no one could afford the product. For example, although software companies try to debug their products before releasing them to the marketplace, they knowingly ship buggy products because the time and cost of fixing all minor errors would prevent these products from ever being released (Rigdon, 1995). What if the product was not offered on the marketplace? Would social welfare as a whole not advance and perhaps even decline? Carrying this further, just what is the responsibility of a producer of computer services—should they withdraw the product that can never be perfect, warn the user, or forget about the risk (let the buyer beware)?

Three principal sources of poor system performance are software bugs and errors, hardware or facility failures because of natural or other causes, and poor input data quality. Chapter 14 considers why zero defects in software code of any complexity cannot be achieved and the seriousness of remaining bugs cannot be estimated. Hence, there is a technological barrier to perfect software, and users must be aware of the potential for catastrophic failure. The software industry has not yet arrived at testing standards for producing software of acceptable, but not perfect, performance (Collins et al., 1994).

Although software bugs and facility catastrophe are likely to be widely reported in the press, by far the most common source of business system failure is data quality. Few companies routinely measure the quality of their data, but studies of individual organizations report data error rates ranging from 0.5 to 30 percent (Redman, 1998).

### Ethical Issues

The central quality-related ethical issue information systems raise is at what point should I (or you) release software or services for consumption by others? At what point can you conclude that your software or service achieves an economically and technologically adequate level of quality? What are you obliged to know about the quality of your software, its procedures for testing, and its operational characteristics?

### Social Issues

The leading quality-related social issue once again deals with expectations: As a society, do we want to encourage people to believe that systems are infallible, that data errors are impossible? Do we instead want a society where people are openly skeptical and questioning of the output of machines, where people are at least informed of the risk? By heightening awareness of system failure, do we inhibit the development of all systems, which in the end contribute to social well-being?

### Political Issues

The leading quality-related political issue concerns the laws of responsibility and accountability. Should Congress establish or direct the National Institute of Science and Technology (NIST) to develop quality standards (software, hardware, data quality) and impose those standards on industry? Or should industry associations be encouraged to develop industry-wide standards of quality? Or should Congress wait for the marketplace to punish poor system quality, recognizing that in some instances this will not work (e.g., if all retail grocers maintain poor quality systems, then customers have no alternatives)?

## QUALITY OF LIFE: EQUITY, ACCESS, BOUNDARIES

The negative social costs of introducing information technologies and systems are beginning to mount along with the power of the technology. Many of these negative social consequences are neither violations of individual rights nor property crimes. Nevertheless, these negative consequences can be extremely harmful to individuals, societies, and political institutions. Computers and information technologies potentially can destroy valuable elements of our culture and society even while they bring us benefits. If there is a balance of good and bad consequences of using information systems, whom do we hold responsible for the bad consequences? Next, we briefly examine some of the negative social consequences of systems, considering individual, social, and political responses.

### Balancing Power Center Versus Periphery

An early fear of the computer age was that huge, centralized mainframe computers would centralize power at corporate headquarters and in the nation's capital, resulting in a Big Brother society, as suggested in George Orwell's novel, *1984*. The shift toward highly decentralized computing, coupled with an ideology of "empowerment" of thousands of workers, and the decentralization of decision making to lower organizational levels, have reduced fears of power centralization in institutions. Yet much of the "empowerment" described in popular business magazines is trivial. Lower-level employees may be empowered to make minor decisions, but the key policy decisions may be as centralized as in the past.

### Rapidity of Change: Reduced Response Time to Competition

Information systems have helped to create much more efficient national and international markets. The now-more-efficient global marketplace has reduced the normal social buffers

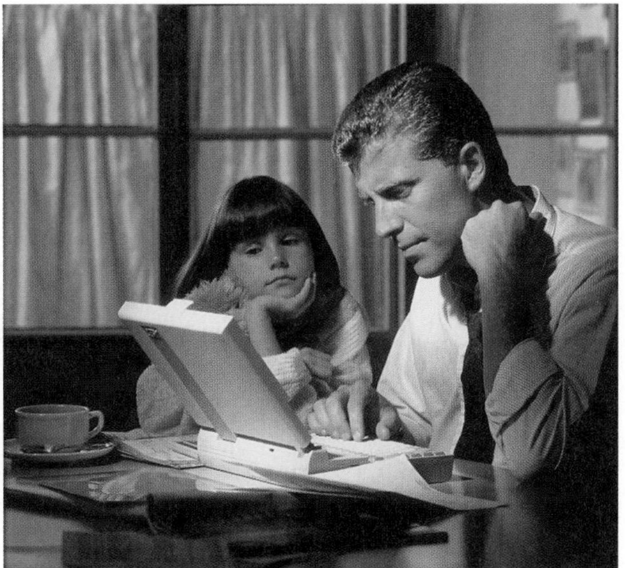

*Although some people may enjoy the convenience of working at home, the "do anything anywhere" computing environment can blur the traditional boundaries between work and family time.*

that permitted businesses many years to adjust to competition. "Time-based competition" has an ugly side: The business you work for may not have enough time to respond to global competitors and may be wiped out in a year, along with your job. We stand the risk of developing a "just-in-time society" with "just-in-time jobs" and "just-in-time" workplaces, families, and vacations.

## Maintaining Boundaries: Family, Work, Leisure

Parts of this book were produced on trains and planes, as well as on family "vacations" and what otherwise might have been "family" time. The danger of ubiquitous computing, telecommuting, nomad computing, and the "do anything anywhere" computing environment, is that it might actually come true. If so, the traditional boundaries that separate work from family and leisure will be weakened. Although authors have traditionally worked just about anywhere (typewriters have been portable for nearly a century), the advent of information systems, coupled with the growth of knowledge-work occupations, means that more and more people will be working when traditionally they would have been playing or communicating with family and friends. The "work umbrella" now extends far beyond the eight-hour day.

Weakening these institutions poses clear-cut risks. Family and friends historically have provided powerful support mechanisms for individuals, and they act as balance points in a society by preserving "private life," providing a place for one to collect one's thoughts, think in ways contrary to one's employer, and dream.

## Dependence and Vulnerability

Today, our businesses, governments, schools, and private associations such as churches are incredibly dependent on information systems and are, therefore, highly vulnerable if these systems should fail. With systems now as ubiquitous as the telephone system, it is startling to remember that there are no regulatory or standard-setting forces in place similar to telephone, electrical, radio, television, or other public-utility technologies. The absence of standards and the criticality of some system applications will probably call forth demands for national standards and perhaps regulatory oversight.

## Computer Crime and Abuse

Many new technologies in the industrial era have created new opportunities for committing crime. Technologies, including computers, create new valuable items to steal, new ways to steal them, and new ways to harm others. **Computer crime** is the commission of illegal acts through the use of a computer or against a computer system. Computers or computer systems can be the object of the crime (destroying a company's computer center or a company's computer files) as well as the instrument of a crime (stealing computer lists by illegally

**computer crime**
The commission of illegal acts through the use of a computer or against a computer system.

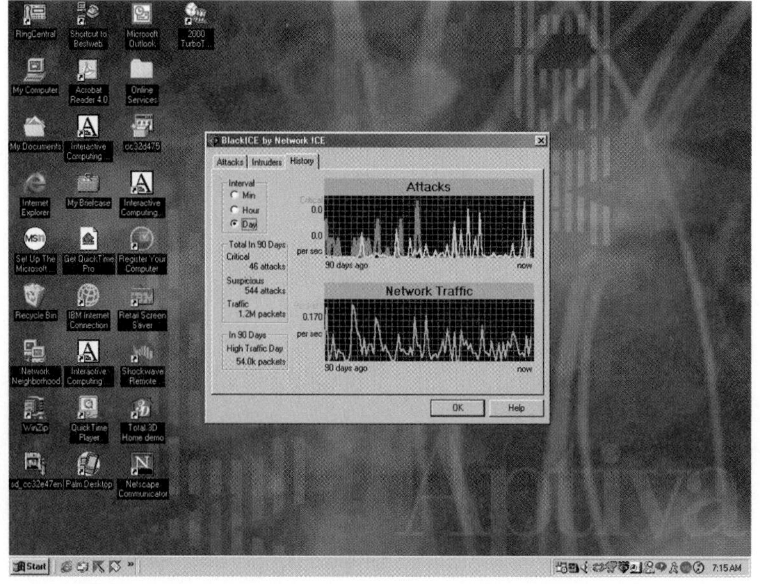


*The Black ICE Defender Firewall protects home and small office systems from hacker attacks and provides reports documenting attempted attacks. Hackers illegally accessing systems can cause widespread disruption and harm.*

gaining access to a computer system using a home computer). Simply accessing a computer system without authorization, or intent to do harm, even by accident, is now a federal crime. **Computer abuse** is the commission of acts involving a computer that may not be illegal but are considered unethical.

**computer abuse**
The commission of acts involving a computer that may not be illegal but are considered unethical.

No one knows the magnitude of the computer crime problem—how many systems are invaded, how many people engage in the practice, or what the total economic damage is, but it is estimated to cost more than $1 billion in the United States alone. Many companies are reluctant to report computer crimes, because they may involve employees. The most economically damaging kinds of computer crime are introducing viruses, theft of services, and disruption of computer systems. "Hackers" is the pejorative term for persons who use computers in illegal ways. Hacker attacks are on the rise, posing new threats to organizations linked to the Internet (see Chapter 14).

Computer viruses have grown exponentially during the past decade. More than 20,000 viruses have been documented, many causing huge losses because of lost data or crippled computers. Although many firms now use antivirus software, the proliferation of computer networks will increase the probability of infections. Following are some illustrative computer crimes:

- An 11-member group of hackers dubbed "The Phonemasters" by the FBI gained access to telephone networks of companies including British Telecommunications, AT&T Corporation, MCI, Southwestern Bell, and Sprint. They were able to access credit-reporting databases belonging to Equifax and TRW Inc., as well as databases owned by Nexis/Lexis and Dunn & Bradstreet information services. Members of the ring sold credit reports, criminal records, and other data they pilfered from the databases, causing $1.85 million in losses. The FBI apprehended group members Calvin Cantrell, Corey Lindsley, and John Bosanac, and they were sentenced to jail terms of two to four years in federal prison. Other members remain at large (Simons, 1999).
- Santo Polanco, an 18-year-old student at the New York Institute of Technology and 26-year-old Eric Bilejhy were charged with a scheme to defraud in First District Court in New York. Both men allegedly raised at least $16,000 through fraudulent sales at eBay, Yahoo, and other Web sites, offering computers for auction that were never delivered after purchasers paid them thousands of dollars (Angwin, 2000).
- Timothy Lloyd, a former chief computer network administrator at Omega Engineering Inc. in Bridgeport, New Jersey, was charged with planting a "logic bomb" that deleted all of the firm's software programs on July 30, 1996. A "logic bomb" is a malicious program that is set to trigger at a specified time. The company suffered $10 million in damages. Lloyd had been recently dismissed from his job. Federal prosecutors also charged Lloyd

TABLE 15-5 INTERNET CRIME AND ABUSE

| Problem | Description |
|---|---|
| Hacking | Hackers exploit weaknesses in Web site security to obtain access to proprietary data such as customer information and passwords. They may use "Trojan horses" posing as legitimate software to obtain information from the host computer. |
| Jamming | Jammers use software routines to tie up the computer hosting a Web site so that legitimate visitors can't access the site. |
| Malicious software | Cyber vandals use data flowing through the Internet to transmit computer viruses, which can disable computers that they "infect"(see Chapter 14). |
| Sniffing | Sniffing, a form of electronic eavesdropping, involves placing a piece of software to intercept information passing from a user to the computer hosting a Web site. This information can include credit card numbers and other confidential data. |
| Spoofing | Spoofers fraudulently misrepresent themselves as other organizations, setting up false Web sites where they can collect confidential information from unsuspecting visitors to the site. |

with stealing about $50,000 of computer equipment, which included a backup tape that could have allowed Omega to recover its lost files (Chen, 1998).

In general, it is employees—insiders—who have inflicted the most injurious computer crimes because they have the knowledge, access, and frequently a job-related motive to commit such crimes.

Congress responded to the threat of computer crime in 1986 with the Computer Fraud and Abuse Act. This act makes it illegal to access a computer system without authorization. Most states have similar laws, and nations in Europe have similar legislation. Other existing legislation covering wiretapping, fraud, and conspiracy by any means, regardless of technology employed, is adequate to cover computer crimes committed thus far.

The Internet's ease of use and accessibility have created new opportunities for computer crime and abuse. Table 15-5 describes some of the most common areas where the Internet has been used for illegal or malicious purposes.

## Employment: Trickle-down Technology and Reengineering Job Loss

Reengineering work (see Chapter 10) is typically hailed in the information systems community as a major benefit of new information technology. It is much less frequently noted that redesigning business processes could potentially cause millions of middle-level managers and clerical workers to lose their jobs. One economist has raised the possibility that we will create a society run by a small "high tech elite of corporate professionals . . . in a nation of the permanently unemployed" (Rifkin, 1993).

Other economists are much more sanguine about the potential job losses. They believe relieving bright, educated workers from reengineered jobs will result in these workers moving to better jobs in fast-growth industries. Left out of this equation are blue-collar workers, and older, less well educated middle managers. It is not clear that these groups can be retrained easily for high-quality (high-paying) jobs. Careful planning and sensitivity to employee needs can help companies redesign work to minimize job losses.

## Equity and Access: Increasing Racial and Social Class Cleavages

Does everyone have an equal opportunity to participate in the digital age? Will the social, economic, and cultural gaps that exist in America and other societies be reduced by information systems technology? Or will the cleavages be increased, permitting the "better off" to become even better off relative to others?

These questions have not yet been fully answered because the impact of systems technology on various groups in society is not well studied. What is known is that information, knowledge, computers, and access to these resources through educational institutions and public libraries, are inequitably distributed along racial and social class lines, as are many

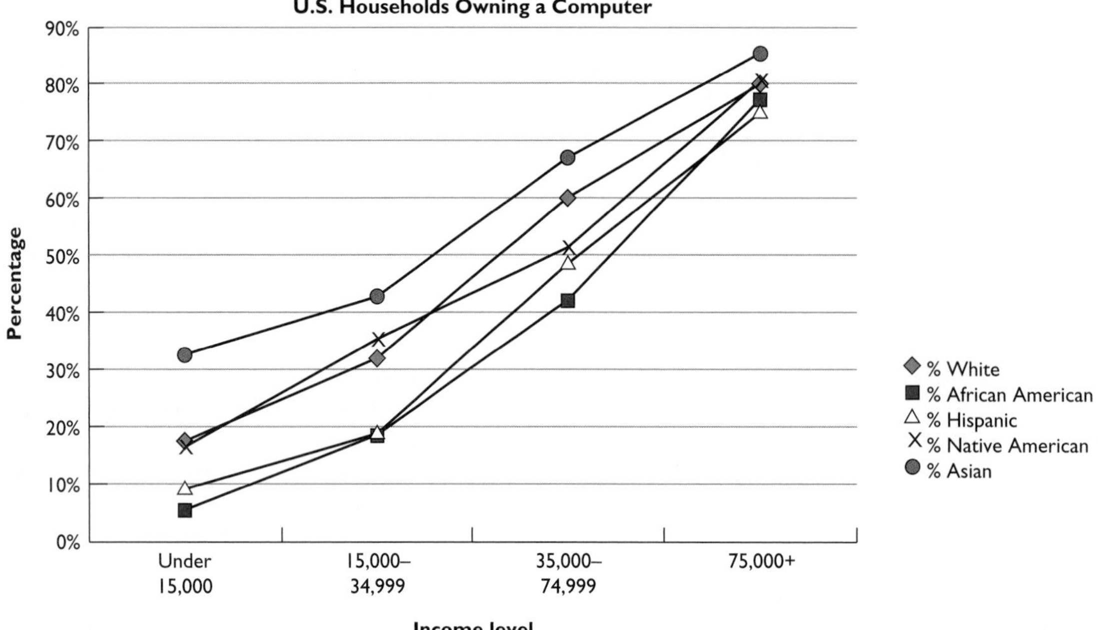


*Figure 15-4* The widening digital divide. Households at the lowest income levels are up to nine times less likely to have a computer at home than those with incomes of $75,000 or higher. Home computer ownership among African American and Hispanic households is also lower than among other ethnic groups.

*Source:* U.S. Department of Commerce, National Telecommunications and Information Association, "Falling Through the Net: Defining the Digital Divide," July 8, 1999.

other information resources. Figure 15-4 illustrates the differences in Internet use based on income and ethnicity. Left uncorrected, we could end up creating a society of information haves, computer literate and skilled, versus a large group of information have-nots, computer illiterate and unskilled.

Public interest groups want to narrow this "digital divide" by making digital information services—including the Internet—available to "virtually everyone" just as basic telephone service is now. An amendment to the Telecommunications Act of 1996, which widened telecommunications deregulation, stipulates subsidies for schools and libraries so that people of all backgrounds have access to the tools of information technology. This is only a partial solution to the problem.

## Health Risks: RSI, CVS, and Technostress

**repetitive stress injury (RSI)** Occupational disease that occurs when muscle groups are forced through repetitive actions with high-impact loads or thousands of repetitions with low-impact loads.

**carpal tunnel syndrome (CTS)** Type of RSI in which pressure on the median nerve through the wrist's bony carpal tunnel structure produces pain.

The most important occupational disease today is **repetitive stress injury (RSI).** RSI occurs when muscle groups are forced through repetitive actions often with high-impact loads (such as tennis) or tens of thousands of repetitions under low-impact loads (such as working at a computer keyboard).

The single largest source of RSI is computer keyboards. About 50 million Americans use computers at work. The most common kind of computer-related RSI is **carpal tunnel syndrome (CTS),** in which pressure on the median nerve through the wrist's bony structure, called a "carpal tunnel," produces pain. The pressure is caused by constant repetition of keystrokes: In a single shift, a word processor may perform 23,000 keystrokes. Symptoms of carpal tunnel syndrome include numbness, shooting pain, inability to grasp objects, and tingling. Millions of workers have been diagnosed with carpal tunnel syndrome.

RSI is avoidable. Designing workstations for a neutral wrist position (using a wrist rest to support the wrist), proper monitor stands, and footrests all contribute to proper posture and reduced RSI. New, ergonomically correct keyboards are also an option, although their effectiveness has yet to be clearly established. These measures should be backed by frequent rest breaks, rotation of employees to different jobs, and moving toward voice or scanner data entry. RSI presents a serious challenge to management, as the Window on Management illustrates.

## MANAGING RSI

Ergonomic injuries, including repetitive stress injury (RSI) from computer use are attracting more attention now than ever. Such injuries have become more numerous, and their costs—in lost productivity, high medical bills, and workers' compensation claims—are rising. Workers for Web sites and Web site graphics and development firms are even more at risk than those doing general office and computing tasks, because they spend protracted hours at their terminals.

In November 2000, the U.S. Occupational Safety and Health Administration issued rules requiring that every company that has more than one repetitive stress injury develop an ergonomic program to analyze job hazards and risks, provide training, and institute injury management procedures. Industry groups have opposed the regulations, claiming they would cost $18 billion to $120 billion a year to implement and would create hardships for small and midsize businesses.

Others claim such preventive measures are relatively inexpensive compared with the bills for lost workdays, medical treatments, and increased insurance premiums. The Office of Ergonomics Research Committee, a business-sponsored group counting Delta Air Lines, IBM, Compaq, and Aetna among its members, has been examining carpal tunnel syndrome and the effect of ergonomic intervention and stress management on workers. Bob Bettendorf, an ergonomic consultant who heads the Committee, says that many ergonomic solutions aren't costly and don't necessarily require special equipment. Rather, they require employees to change the way they work. For example, one Committee study found that users strike computer keys with four to seven times the necessary force, contributing to hand and finger injuries.

SAS Institute Inc. established an ergonomic lab in 1996 to house ergonomic office equipment such as keyboards, computer mice, footrests, and adjustable chairs. The ergonomic lab conducted more than 545 employee ergonomic assessments in 1999. To help Jude Redman, an employee at SAS's Cary, North Carolina, headquarters, ease discomfort and pain from a musculoskeletal disorder, the office recommended refitting Redman's workplace with ergonomic equipment that she could test herself in the lab. She switched to a split keyboard to ease her hand pain and found that adjusting the height of her computer monitor and incorporating wrist-support devices lessened her shoulder ache. To prevent future injuries, the ergonomic lab taught Redman how to sit correctly at her desk. SAS ergonomic coordinator Kathleen Kitts believes the ergonomic program can be justified from a cost–benefit standpoint. She estimates that one carpal tunnel injury costs the company at least $20,000 in medical bills and lost productivity, whereas helping an employee facing ergonomic injuries costs $1,500 at most.

Botwater, which owns and operates eight pulp and paper mills in the United States, Canada, and Korea, instituted an ergonomic plan about five years ago when its customer service personnel expressed concerns about increased worker injuries from their growing use of PCs. Worker-safety teams at the mills and headquarters attend a 40-hour training course at an ergonomics educational facility. So far no employees have reported an ergonomic injury.

**To Think About:** If you were a corporate vice president with responsibility for corporate safety, what policies would you recommend regarding RSI? Explain your recommendations.

*Sources:* Steven Greenhouse, "Ergonomics Report Cites Job Injuries," *The New York Times*, January 18, 2001; Judith N. Mottl, "Computer-related Injuries: IT Helps Ease the Pain," *Information Week*, June 19, 2000, and Steven Greenhouse, "Battle Lines Drawn over Ergonomic Rules," *The New York Times*, November 18, 2000.

RSI is not the only occupational illness computers cause. Back and neck pain, leg stress, and foot pain also result from poor ergonomic designs of workstations.

**Computer vision syndrome (CVS)** refers to any eye strain condition related to computer display screen use. Its symptoms, usually temporary, include headaches, blurred vision, and dry and irritated eyes.

**computer vision syndrome (CVS)**
Eye strain condition related to computer display screen use, with symptoms including headaches, blurred vision, and dry, irritated eyes.

The newest computer-related malady is **technostress,** which is stress induced by computer use. Its symptoms include aggravation, hostility toward humans, impatience, and fatigue. The problem, according to experts, is that humans working continuously with computers come to expect other humans and human institutions to behave like computers, providing instant response, attentiveness, and with an absence of emotion. Computer-intense workers are aggravated when put on hold during a phone call and become incensed or alarmed when their PCs take a few seconds longer to perform a task. Technostress is thought to be related to high levels of job turnover in the computer industry, high levels of early retirement from computer-intense occupations, and elevated levels of drug and alcohol abuse.

**technostress**
Stress induced by computer use, with symptoms including aggravation, hostility toward humans, impatience, and enervation.

The incidence of technostress is not known but is thought to be in the millions in the United States and growing rapidly. Computer-related jobs now top the list of stressful occupations based on health statistics in several industrialized countries.

*Repetitive stress injury (RSI) is the leading occupational disease today. The single largest cause of RSI is computer keyboard work.*

To date the role of radiation from computer display screens in occupational disease has not been proved. Video display terminals (VDTs) emit nonionizing electric and magnetic fields at low frequencies. These rays enter the body and have unknown effects on enzymes, molecules, chromosomes, and cell membranes. Long-term studies are investigating low-level electromagnetic fields and birth defects, stress, low birth weight, and other diseases. All manufacturers have reduced display screen emissions since the early 1980s, and European countries such as Sweden have adopted stiff radiation emission standards.

The computer has become a part of our lives—personally as well as socially, culturally, and politically. It is unlikely the issues and our choices will become easier as information technology continues to transform our world. The growth of the Internet and the information economy suggests that all the ethical and social issues we have described will be heightened further as we move into the first digital century.

## Management Actions: A Corporate Code of Ethics

Some corporations have developed far-reaching corporate IS codes of ethics. Federal Express, IBM, American Express, and Merck and Co. are just a few. Most firms, however, have not developed these codes of ethics, leaving their employees in the dark about expected correct behavior. There is some dispute concerning a general code of ethics versus a specific information systems code of ethics. As managers, you should strive to develop an IS-specific set of ethical standards for each of the five moral dimensions:

- Information rights and obligations: A code should cover topics such as employee e-mail privacy, workplace monitoring, treatment of corporate information, and policies on customer information.
- Property rights and obligations: A code should cover topics such as software licenses, ownership of firm data and facilities, ownership of software created by employees on company hardware, and software copyrights. Specific guidelines for contractual relationships with third parties should be covered as well.

- Accountability and control: The code should specify a single individual responsible for all information systems, and underneath this individual others who are responsible for individual rights, the protection of property rights, system quality, and quality of life (e.g., job design, ergonomics, employee satisfaction). Responsibilities for control of systems, audits, and management should be clearly defined. The potential liabilities of systems officers and the corporation should be detailed in a separate document.
- System quality: The code should describe the general levels of data quality and system error that can be tolerated with detailed specifications left to specific projects. The code should require that all systems attempt to estimate data quality and system error probabilities.
- Quality of life: The code should state that the purpose of systems is to improve the quality of life for customers and for employees by achieving high levels of product quality, customer service, and employee satisfaction and human dignity through proper ergonomics, job and work flow design, and human resource development.

## APPLICATION SOFTWARE EXERCISE

### CASE TOOL EXERCISE: DIAGRAMMING PROCESSING ACTIVITIES AT MICKEY'S BURGER HOUSE

Mickey's Burger House is a local fast-food restaurant operating in the Houston, Texas, area. Since the restaurant first opened in the 1970s, Mickey's has gained a reputation for providing quality, low-priced meals to the public. Mickey's Burger House is renowned for its 32-ounce chocolate milk shakes, foot-long hot dogs with a special sauce, and hickory-smoked, Texas-size burgers. Although Mickey's food quality has remained superior, its internal operations have grown antiquated. Customers have complained about long wait times; suppliers are not always paid on time, thus causing late fees to be assessed, and inventory items are not always replenished in a timely fashion. Michelle, Mickey's granddaughter, has decided it is now time to reengineer the restaurant's internal operations. Because you are an MIS major, she asks you to help her with this systems development project.

At your first meeting with Michelle, the two of you discuss Mickey's major processing activities: Michelle identifies the following activities. A customer walks up to the counter and places an order. A waitress manually records the order on an order ticket, rings up the sale on an old cash register, makes change, and gives the customer a sales receipt and order number. The order ticket is given to the cook who prepares the order. Once the order is prepared, the order ticket and order are placed on the delivery countertop; a waitress then calls the order number and hands the order to the waiting customer. Each night Michelle reconciles the cash on hand with the order tickets, performs a visual check of inventory, and makes a list of items that are low in stock. The next morning, Michelle places orders for all items that are low in stock, receives orders from suppliers, updates inventory counts, and makes deposits at a local bank.

What problems do you recognize with Mickey's processes? How would you approach this problem? What solutions are available?

You would like to document the activities described in this problem using a CASE tool. Locate several CASE tool vendors, and download demonstration copies of their CASE tools from their Web sites. What features does each CASE tool provide? Select one of the CASE tools and prepare a data flow diagram to represent the activities at Mickey's Burger House. Prepare a written analysis of your findings. Be sure to include a copy of your data flow diagram with your written analysis. Next, use presentation software to prepare a formal presentation of your findings and present your findings to the class.

## MANAGEMENT WRAP-UP

Managers are ethical rule makers for their organizations (Green, 1994). They are charged with creating the policies and procedures to establish ethical conduct, including the ethical use of information systems. Managers are also responsible for identifying, analyzing, and resolving the ethical dilemmas that invariably crop up as they balance conflicting needs and interests.

Rapid changes fueled by information technology are creating new situations where existing laws or rules of conduct may not be relevant. New "gray areas" are emerging in which ethical standards have not yet been codified into law. A new system of ethics for the information age is required to guide individual and organizational choices and actions.

Information technology is introducing changes that create new ethical issues for societies to debate and resolve. Increasing computing power, storage, and networking capabilities—including the Internet—can expand the reach of individual and organizational actions and magnify their impact. The ease and anonymity with which information can be communicated, copied, and manipulated in on-line environments are challenging traditional rules of right and wrong behavior.

*For Discussion*

1. Should producers of software-based services such as ATMs be held liable for economic injuries suffered when their systems fail?
2. Should companies be responsible for unemployment caused by their information systems? Why or why not?

## SUMMARY

1. *Analyze the relationship among ethical, social, and political issues raised by information systems.* Ethical, social, and political issues are closely related in an information society. Ethical issues confront individuals who must choose a course of action, often in a situation in which two or more ethical principles are in conflict (a dilemma). Social issues spring from ethical issues. Societies must develop expectations in individuals about the correct course of action, and social issues then become debates about the kinds of situations and expectations that societies should develop so that individuals behave correctly. Political issues spring from social conflict and have to do largely with laws that prescribe behavior and seek to create situations in which individuals behave correctly.
2. *Identify the main moral dimensions of an information society and apply them to specific situations.* There are five main moral dimensions that tie together ethical, social, and political issues in an information society. These moral dimensions are information rights and obligations, property rights and obligations, accountability and control, system quality, and quality of life.
3. *Apply an ethical analysis to difficult situations.* An ethical analysis is a five-step methodology for analyzing a situation. The method involves identifying the facts, values, stakeholders, options, and consequences of actions. Once completed, you can begin to consider what ethical principle you should apply to a situation to arrive at a judgment.
4. *Examine specific ethical principles for conduct.* Six ethical principles are available to judge your own conduct (and that of others). These principles are derived independently from several cultural, religious, and intellectual traditions. They are not hard-and-fast rules and may not apply in all situations. The principles are the Golden Rule, Immanuel Kant's Categorical Imperative, Descartes' rule of change, the Utilitarian Principle, the Risk Aversion Principle, and the ethical "no free lunch" rule.
5. *Design corporate policies for ethical conduct.* For each of the five moral dimensions, corporations should develop an ethics policy statement to assist individuals and to encourage the correct decisions. The policy areas are as follows. Individual information rights: Spell out corporate privacy and due process policies. Property rights: Clarify how the corporation will treat property rights of software owners. Accountability and control: Clarify who is responsible and accountable for information. System quality: Identify methodologies and quality standards to be achieved. Quality of life: Identify corporate policies on family, computer crime, decision making, vulnerability, job loss, and health risks.

## KEY TERMS

**Accountability, 471**
**Carpal tunnel syndrome (CTS), 490**
**Computer abuse, 488**
**Computer crime, 487**
**Computer vision syndrome (CVS), 491**
**Cookie, 476**
**Copyright, 479**
**Descartes' rule of change, 473**
**Due process, 471**
**Ethical "no free lunch" rule, 473**
**Ethics, 468**
**Fair Information Practices (FIP), 475**
**Immanuel Kant's Categorical Imperative, 472**
**Information rights, 469**
**Intellectual property, 479**
**Liability, 471**
**Patent, 480**
**Privacy, 474**
**Profiling, 470**
**Repetitive stress injury (RSI), 490**
**Responsibility, 471**
**Risk Aversion Principle, 473**
**Spamming, 477**
**Technostress, 491**
**Trade secret, 479**
**Utilitarian Principle, 473**

## REVIEW QUESTIONS

1. In what ways are ethical, social, and political issues connected? Give some examples.
2. What are the key technological trends that heighten ethical concerns?
3. What are the differences between responsibility, accountability, and liability?
4. What are the five steps in an ethical analysis?
5. Identify and describe six ethical principles.
6. What is a professional code of conduct?
7. What are meant by "privacy" and "fair information practices"?
8. How is the Internet challenging the protection of individual privacy?
9. What are the three different regimes that protect intellectual property rights? What challenges to intellectual property rights are posed by the Internet?
10. Why is it so difficult to hold software services liable for failure or injury?
11. What is the most common cause of system quality problems?
12. Name and describe four "quality of life" impacts of computers and information systems.
13. What is technostress, and how would you identify it?
14. Name three management actions that could reduce RSIs.

## GROUP PROJECT

With three or four of your classmates, develop a corporate ethics code on privacy that addresses both employee privacy and the privacy of customers and users of the corporate Web site. Be sure to consider e-mail privacy and employer monitoring of worksites, as well as corporate use of information about employees concerning their off-job behavior (e.g., lifestyle, marital arrangements, and so forth). If possible, use electronic presentation software to present your ethics code to the class.

## TOOLS FOR INTERACTIVE LEARNING

### INTERNET CONNECTION

The Internet Connection for this chapter will direct you to a series of Web sites where you can learn more about the privacy issues raised by the use of the Internet and the Web. You can complete an exercise to analyze the privacy implications of existing technologies for tracking Web site visitors. You can also use the Interactive Study Guide to test your knowledge of the topics in this chapter, and get instant feedback where you need more practice.

### ELECTRONIC COMMERCE PROJECT

At the Laudon Web site for Chapter 15, you will find an Electronic Commerce project that uses the interactive software at the Deja.com Web site to explore the use of Internet discussion groups for targeted marketing.

### CD-ROM

If you use the Multimedia Edition CD-ROM with this chapter, you can complete an interactive exercise asking you to perform an ethical analysis of problems encountered by a business. You can also find a video clip on software piracy, an audio overview of the major themes of this chapter, and bullet text summarizing the key points of the chapter.

## CASE STUDY *Web Site Privacy: How Much Should We Worry?*

The Internet has quickly become one of the most important sources of personal data. Obviously, we openly volunteer personal information such as our names, addresses, and e-mail addresses when we register to gain access to a Web site, or when we subscribe to an on-line newsletter. If you bank through the Net or invest through an on-line brokerage firm, you must give out a great deal more personal data. Although you give this information freely, you rarely have any control over what the site will do with it. Additionally many sites are gathering much more personal information without our even being aware of it using "cookies" and other tools for gathering personal data from Web visitors.

Once these data are collected they are often merged with other personal data about the individual to develop detailed profiles of customer behavior for marketing campaigns. Many companies sell personal data in order to obtain income. Acxiom Corp. has collected data on 176 million individuals, data that is for sale. "They follow you more closely than the U.S. government," says Anthony Picardi, a software analyst at International Data Corp.

Public institutions, such as hospitals, schools, and the police, also collect massive amounts of data on their clients (patients, students, and citizens). Medical data in particular are becoming more and more centralized into huge databases. Many medical institutions are private and, without government regulation, are free to sell their data. Moreover, organizations are occasionally privatized, merged, or closed, and so their data could end up in the hands of someone who would sell them. For example, the Federal Trade Commission (FTC) filed suit in July 2000 against Toysmart.com, the failed on-line retailer of children's toys, to block the company from selling its customer data as part of its assets. Toysmart.com's databases included information such as children's names, birth dates, and toy wish lists, and the firm's privacy policy promised that personal information voluntarily submitted by Web site visitors would never be shared with a third party. The case was settled when the FTC said Toysmart.com could sell the information provided the buyer purchase the entire company and adhere to Toysmart's privacy policy. Two other expiring Internet companies, Boo.com and CraftShop.com, were also discovered trying to sell private customer information, such as home addresses, telephone and credit card numbers, and data on shopping habits.

Why does this lucrative trade in personal data exist? Obviously, one reason is to increase sales. Many businesses use the information to locate good sales prospects or to target repeat customers with new offers of items to purchase. Web sites even use their own data to direct visitors to other sites in exchange for a fee. Insurance companies, lawyers, bail bondspersons, manufacturers of home security equipment, and even funeral parlors want personal data on recent crime victims in the hope of finding new clients.

Increasing sales is not the only reason for interest in these data, however. Organizations can use data on your Web travels to draw implications about you, implications that can be wrong and harmful. Job applicants may find that trouble they had in elementary school has followed them the rest of their lives. Or the employer may find that an applicant has visited a number of sites relating to AIDS. The candidate may then be denied employment based on the conclusion that the candidate has AIDS even though the person may have visited them for many reasons, such as curiosity, research (for work, school), or to help a friend. Compounding this problem, data errors are likely to abound. Data can be inaccurate, false, and out of date and still be sold repeatedly or used in ways that harms the individual.

Because personal data can help as well as harm, its collection presents many people with a dilemma. "There's no question that this technology could be hugely invasive," explains Christine Varney, who was the Internet expert for the Federal Trade Commission (FTC) until August 1997 and now heads the Online Privacy Alliance. "But," she continues, "it could also be enormously empowering by allowing individuals to make their own choices and by saving us all time and money." Studies do show that most users want some protection from indiscriminate use of their personal data, but they will supply it as long as they benefit from the proffered information and are fully informed as to how the data will be used.

Many individuals and organizations are addressing the Internet privacy issue. Self-regulation (that is, regulation by the industry rather than by the government) is a major approach involving some of the leading Internet companies. Online Privacy Alliance is a trade association of about 100 companies including America Online Inc., Yahoo, Microsoft, Hewlett-Packard, IBM, and the Direct Marketing Association. The alliance recommends four guidelines that it urges all companies on the Internet to adopt:

- Notify visitors of data collection practices:
- Give visitors the choice of opting out of the site collecting personal data:
- Give visitors access to their own personal data;
- Assure visitors that their personal data are secure.

A major goal of the alliance is to persuade the government and U.S. citizens that little government Internet privacy regulation is needed, because the industry can adequately regulate itself.

TRUSTe is also an industry organization promoting self-regulation. It issues a seal of approval that qualifying Web sites can display. To obtain permission to display its seal of approval, a Web site must agree to comply with TRUSTe's consumer privacy guidelines. If a Web site uses the personal information it has gathered in ways that the customer was not explicitly informed about, a violation would occur. Hundreds of companies now display the TRUSTe seal of approval. However, many question its value. When the Microsoft collection of private data on users who had registered for Windows 98 was disclosed, TRUSTe refused to revoke its seal of approval. Each Windows 98 user's unique serial number could be used to identify owners of documents transmitted over the Internet. TRUSTe claimed that the storing of the serial number was unrelated to Microsoft's Web site.

Some companies take Web site privacy very seriously. Some companies, including Disney, IBM, and Microsoft, have announced they will not work with advertisers who don't have a baseline privacy policy for their Web sites. E-loan, a Web site company based in Dublin, California, decided to establish ongoing quarterly privacy audits despite the expense. Chris Larsen, E-loan's CEO, has concerns about state and federal financial regulatory agencies and a desire to give its customers the confidence that their loan data will not be shared with other organizations. Some companies are taking action because they fear being sued and conclude that a good privacy policy will cost less than successful lawsuits. IBM and other companies have established a position for a chief privacy officer who would oversee the firm's privacy policies, practices, and initiatives to strengthen consumer privacy protection.

The main reasons companies don't establish or enforce privacy policies are cost and revenue loss. It can be expensive to hire auditors or experts who can help the company establish and enforce a privacy policy. In addition, enforcing such policies often requires a whole redesign of the Web site and of its databases. The other side of the coin is that companies can sell private information and thereby generate a good income.

Privacy advocates have developed a Web browsers' bill of rights that can be used to measure the success of existing efforts to protect Web privacy. The bill of rights is based on two principles: Visitors' must control their own data, and sites must disclose their privacy policies. The bill of rights states that site browsers must have the right to prevent uses of the information beyond the clear purposes of the site unless the visitor is explicitly notified and is given the opportunity to prohibit such expanded uses. Visitors must have the right to prevent the Web site from distributing the information on the visitor outside the Web site's own organization unless the visitor has explicitly given permission. In addition, visitors must also have the right to correct existing errors in their personal data, including the right to modify outdated information.

A survey released in April 2000 by Eponymous.com, a San Diego provider of privacy-related products and services, showed that 77 percent of the busiest Web sites still don't have a stated privacy policy. Of those that do, many don't offer policies providing much protection.

Addressing these concerns in November 1999, a group of leading Internet advertising and data-profiling companies, including DoubleClick and CMGI, agreed to develop voluntary privacy-protection guidelines that would notify consumers about their data collection practices and allow them to "opt out" of the profiling technology. These data-profiling companies are also encouraging other Web sites that work with them to clearly state they are using their services.

Marc Rotenberg, the executive director of the Electronic Privacy Information Center, a Washington D.C. civil liberties advocacy group, believes that posted privacy policies actually protect the site operators rather than the visitors because the site operators are then free to do as they wish. "It becomes a privacy policy as a disclaimer," says Rotenberg. His organization is supporting technical changes to the Internet that would allow individuals to surf the Net anonymously.

The FTC already has rules that require companies to enforce any privacy policies that they publicly post. Critics claim that the problem with this FTC requirement is that the FTC does not enforce its own rules. The commission has several times warned companies that have sold or exchanged data after public promises not to do so, and it has even worked with them to stop the practice. However, as of this writing it has never fined or otherwise punished any company.

In the spring of 2000 the FTC started expanding its activities for monitoring Internet commerce. It proposed rules for financial institutions to safeguard customer information and called on Congress for more rigorous protection of the privacy of online consumers. Members of Congress are sponsoring numerous bills for tougher privacy protection laws, and a number of states are pushing for even stricter privacy laws.

Commercial vendors are also developing privacy tools that help users gain more control over their personal information. These tools include software to enable people to surf the Web using fictitious identities and to send and receive e-mail that can never be traced back to them. Other tools block the use of cookies, scramble Internet Protocol(IP) addresses to prevent others from learning one's fixed Internet address, and help users determine the kind of personal data that can be extracted by Web sites. Microsoft Corporation incorporated privacy-protection features into the latest version of its Internet Explorer Web browser. Users of the browser will be able to set their own levels of privacy protection for sharing of cookies and other interactions with business Web sites.

**Sources:** L. Scott Tillett, "Microsoft Unveils Browser Privacy Functions," *Internet Week,* March 21, 2001; Glen R. Simpson, "As Congress Makes New Web-Privacy Laws, Microsoft Pushes System Tied to Its Browser," *The Wall Street Journal,* March 21, 2001; Linda Rosencrance, "IBM Follows Chief Privacy Officer Trend," *Computerworld,* December 4, 2000; Cheryl Rosen and Beth Bacheldor, "The Politics of Privacy Protection," *Information Week,* July 17, 2000; DeWayne Lehman, "Privacy Policies Missing on 77% of Web Sites," *Computerworld,* April 17, 2000; Jaikumar Vijayan, "Caught in the Middle," *Computerworld,* July 24, 2000; Keith Perine, "The Privacy Police," *The Industry Standard,* February 21, 2000; Michelle V. Rafter, "Trust or Bust?" *The Industry Standard,* March 13, 2000; Steve Lohr, "Internet Companies Set Policies to Help Protect Consumer Privacy," *The New York Times,* November 5, 1999; "Seizing the Initiative on Privacy" *The New York Times,* October 11, 1999; Jon G. Auerbach, "To Get IBM Ad, Sites Must Post Privacy Policies," *The Wall Street Journal,* April 30, 1999; Edward C. Baig, Marcia Stepanek, and Neil Gross, "Privacy," *Business Week,* April 5, 1999; and Alex Lash, "Privacy, Practically Speaking," *The Industry Standard,* August 2–9, 1999.

### *CASE STUDY QUESTIONS*

1. Is Web site privacy a serious problem? Why or why not?
2. What are the gains for the Web-based businesses if they collect, use, sell, and otherwise disseminate information on their visitors or use it in ways not explicitly approved by the visitor? The losses (costs)?
3. Apply an ethical analysis to the issue of Web site visitors' privacy rights.
4. Should Web sites be allowed to collect information on their visitors that is not voluntarily provided?
5. How should Web site privacy be promoted? What role should the government play? What role should private business play? What role should technology play?

chapter

# 16 Managing International Information Systems

objectives

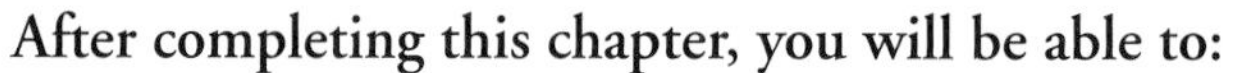

**After completing this chapter, you will be able to:**

1. *Identify the major factors behind the growing internationalization of business.*
2. *Compare global strategies for developing business.*
3. *Demonstrate how information systems support different global strategies.*
4. *Plan the development of international information systems.*
5. *Evaluate the main technical alternatives in developing global systems.*

## Nestlé Turns to Enterprise Systems for Global Coordination

Nestlé SA, headquartered in Vevey, Switzerland, is a giant food and pharmaceuticals company that operates virtually all over the world, with more than 230,000 employees at 500 facilities in 80 countries. Although it is best known for its chocolate, coffee, and milk products, Nestlé sells thousands of other items, which are adapted to fit local markets and culture.

The firm had been allowing each factory to conduct business as it saw fit, taking into account different local conditions and business cultures. With 80 different information technology units, Nestlé's information technology infrastructure has been described as a veritable Tower of Babel. Its operations around the world run on nearly 900 IBM AS/400 midrange computers, 15 mainframes, and 200 Unix systems. There was no corporate computer center.

Nestlé's management found that allowing these local differences created inefficiencies and extra costs that could prevent the company from competing effectively in electronic commerce. The lack of standard business processes prevented Nestlé from, for example, leveraging its worldwide buying power to obtain lower prices for its raw materials. Even though each factory uses the same global suppliers, it negotiated its own deals and prices.

Several years ago, Nestlé embarked on a program to standardize and coordinate its information systems and business processes. The company initially installed SAP's R/3 enterprise resource planning (ERP) software to integrate material, distribution, and accounting applications in the United States, Europe, and Canada. Now it is extending its enterprise systems to all of its 500 facilities to make them act as a single-minded e-business.

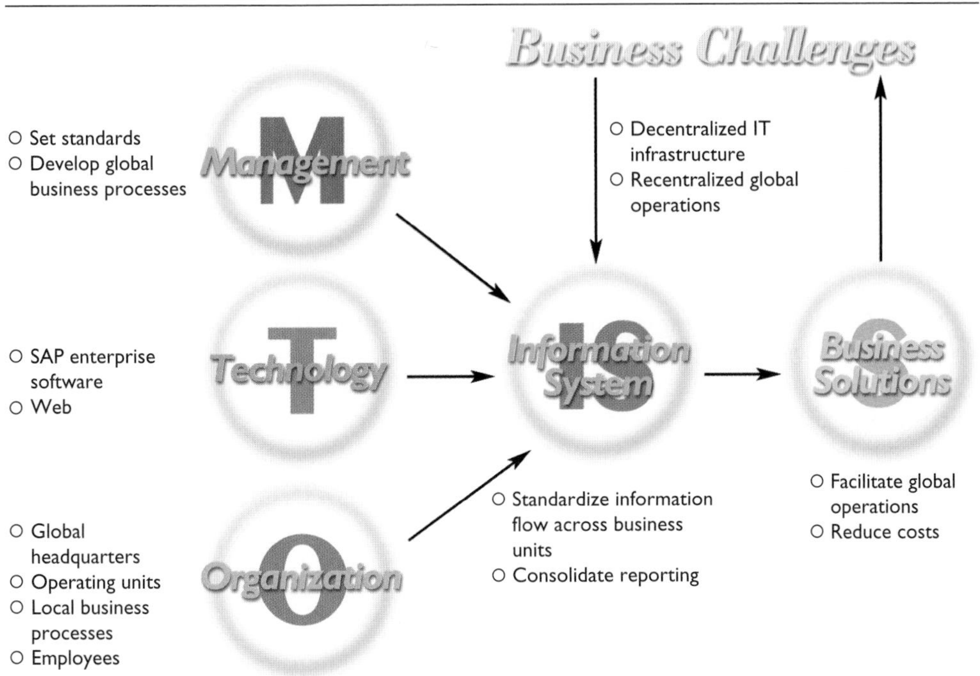


In June 2000 Nestlé contracted with SAP to deploy mySAP.com, which extends SAP's enterprise software to the Web. The new system allows each Nestlé employee to start work from a personalized Web page linked to his or her job function. The employee's job is structured to conform to the "best practices" defined by SAP for each of 300 work roles. These roles mandate precise steps for executing a business process that must be followed in a prescribed sequence. For instance, an invoice for an order can't be referred to accounts payable until the system shows that the order was received. According to Jean Claud Dispaux, senior Nestlé vice president for group information systems, "it's an exceptionally simple way to make sure that everyone does the same job the same way."

Nestlé is also creating up to five computer centers around the world to run mySAP.com enterprise financial, accounts payable, accounts receivable, planning, production management, supply chain management, and business intelligence software. Once this project is completed Nestlé will be able to use sales information from retailers on a global basis to measure the effectiveness of its promotional activities and reduce overstocking and spoilage caused by having products sit around too long on grocery shelves.

Implementing the enterprise software throughout the company will take about three years and cost nearly $300 million. Many employees will have to change the way they work in order to conform to the roles defined by the new system. Nestlé is providing individualized training to help employees make the transition. "It won't be a nice project," Dispaux says, "but it's necessary."

**Source:** Steve Konicki, "Nestlé Taps SAP for E-business," *Information Week*, June 26, 2000 and Marc L. Songini "Exxon Mobil Adopts my SAP as Its Primary Backbone," *Computerworld*, October 23, 2000.

**Nestlé Turns to Enterprise Systems for Global Coordination**

## Management Challenges

Nestlé is one of many business firms moving toward global forms of organization that transcend national boundaries. Nestlé could not make this move unless it reorganized its information systems and standardized some of its business processes so that the same information could be used by disparate business units in different countries. The opening vignette shows that such changes are not always easy to make, and they raise the following management challenges:

1. **Lines of business and global strategy.** Firms must decide whether some or all of their lines of business should be managed on a global basis. There are some lines of business in which local variations are slight, and the possibility exists to reap large rewards by organizing globally. PCs and power tools may fit this pattern, as well as industrial raw materials. Other consumer goods may be quite different by country or region. It is likely that firms with many lines of business will have to maintain a mixed organizational structure.
2. **The difficulties of managing change in a multicultural firm.** Although engineering change in a single corporation in a single nation can be difficult, costly, and long term, bringing about significant change in very large-scale global corporations can be daunting. Both the agreement on "core business processes" in a transnational context and the decision to use common systems require extraordinary insight, a lengthy process of consensus building, or the exercise of sheer power.

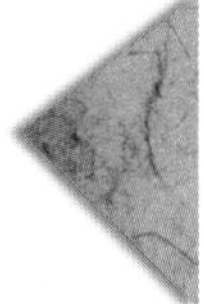

The changes Nestlé seeks reflect some of the changes in international information systems architecture—the basic systems needed to coordinate worldwide trade and other activities—that organizations need to consider if they want to operate across the globe. This chapter explores how to organize, manage, and control the development of international information systems.

## *16.1* The Growth of International Information Systems

We already have described two powerful worldwide changes driven by advances in information technology that have transformed the business environment and posed new challenges for management. One is the transformation of industrial economies and societies into knowledge- and information-based economies. The other is the emergence of a global economy and global world order.

The new world order will sweep away many national corporations, national industries, and national economies controlled by domestic politicians. Many firms will be replaced by fast-moving, networked corporations that transcend national boundaries. The growth of international trade has radically altered domestic economies around the globe. About $1 trillion worth of goods, services, and financial instruments—one-fifth of the annual U.S. gross national product—changes hands each day in global trade.

Consider a laptop computer as an example: The CPU is likely to have been designed and built in the United States; the DRAM (or dynamic random access memory, which makes up the majority of primary storage in a computer) was designed in the United States but built in Malaysia; the screen was designed and assembled in Japan using American patents; the keyboard is from Taiwan; and it was all assembled in Japan, where the case also was made. Management of the project, located in Silicon Valley, California, along with marketing, sales, and finance, coordinated all the activities from financing and production to shipping and sales efforts. None of this would be possible without powerful international information and telecommunication systems.

To be effective, managers need a global perspective on business and an understanding of the support systems needed to conduct business on an international scale.

## Developing the International Information Systems Architecture

This chapter describes how to go about building an international information systems architecture suitable for your international strategy. An **international information systems architecture** consists of the basic information systems required by organizations to coordinate worldwide trade and other activities. Figure 16-1 illustrates the reasoning we follow throughout the chapter and depicts the major dimensions of an international information systems architecture.

**international information systems architecture**
The basic information systems required by organizations to coordinate worldwide trade and other activities.

The basic strategy to follow when building an international system is to understand the global environment in which your firm is operating. This means understanding the overall market forces, or business drivers, that are pushing your industry toward global competition. A **business driver** is a force in the environment to which businesses must respond and that influences the direction of the business. Likewise, examine carefully the inhibitors or negative factors that create *management challenges*—factors that could scuttle the development of a global business. Once you have examined the global environment, you will need to consider a corporate strategy for competing in that environment. How will your firm respond? You could ignore the global market and focus on domestic competition only, sell to the globe from a domestic base, or organize production and distribution around the globe. There are many in-between choices.

**business driver**
A force in the environment to which businesses must respond and that influences the direction of business.

After you have developed a strategy, consider how to structure your organization so it can pursue the strategy. How will you accomplish a division of labor across a global environment? Where will production, administration, accounting, marketing, and human resource functions be located? Who will handle the systems function?

Next, consider the management issues in implementing your strategy and making the organization design come alive. Key here will be the design of business processes. How can you discover and manage user requirements? How can you induce change in local units to conform to international requirements? How can you reengineer on a global scale, and how can you coordinate systems development?

The last issue to consider is the technology platform. Although changing technology is a key driving factor leading toward global markets, you need to have a corporate strategy and structure before you can rationally choose the right technology.

After you have completed this process of reasoning, you will be well on your way toward an appropriate international information systems architecture capable of achieving your corporate goals. Let us begin by looking at the overall global environment.

## The Global Environment: Business Drivers and Challenges

Table 16-1 illustrates the business drivers in the global environment that are leading all industries toward global markets and competition.

The global business drivers can be divided into two groups: general cultural factors and specific business factors. There are easily recognized general cultural factors driving internationalization since World War II. Information, communication, and transportation technologies have created a *global village* in which communication (by telephone, television, radio, or computer network) around the globe is no more difficult and not much more expensive than communication down the block. Moving goods and services to and from geographically dispersed locations has declined dramatically in cost.

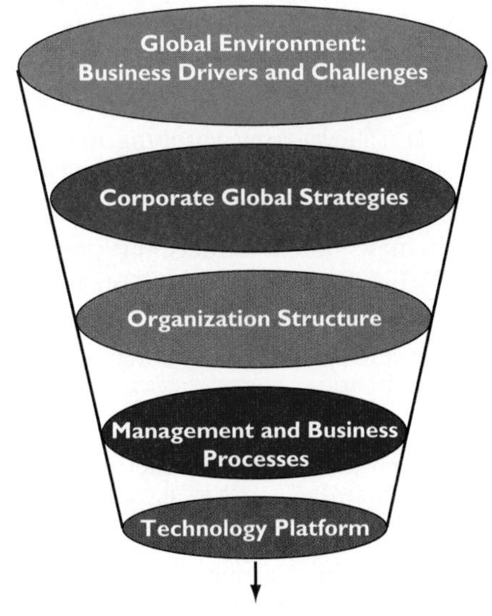


*Figure 16-1* International information systems architecture. The major dimensions for developing an international information systems architecture are the global environment, the corporate global strategies, the structure of the organization, the management and business processes, and the technology platform.

**TABLE 16-1 THE GLOBAL BUSINESS DRIVERS**

| **General Cultural Factors** |
|---|
| Global communication and transportation technologies |
| Global culture |
| Global social norms |
| Political stability |
| Global knowledge base |
| **Specific Business Factors** |
| Global markets |
| Global production and operations |
| Global coordination |
| Global workforce |
| Global economies of scale |

**global culture**
The development of common expectations, shared artifacts, and social norms among different cultures and peoples.

The development of global communications has created a global village in a second sense: There is now a **global culture** created by television and other globally shared media, such as movies, that permits different cultures and peoples to develop common expectations about right and wrong, desirable and undesirable, heroic and cowardly. The collapse of the Eastern bloc has speeded up the growth of a world culture enormously, increased support for capitalism and business, and reduced the level of cultural conflict considerably.

A last factor to consider is the growth of a global knowledge base. At the end of World War II, knowledge, education, science, and industrial skills were highly concentrated in North America, Europe, and Japan, with the rest of the world euphemistically called the *Third World.* This is no longer true. Latin America, China, Southern Asia, and Eastern Europe have developed powerful educational, industrial, and scientific centers, resulting in a much more democratically and widely dispersed knowledge base.

These general cultural factors leading toward internationalization result in specific business globalization factors that affect most industries. The growth of powerful communications technologies and the emergence of world cultures create the condition for *global markets*—global consumers interested in consuming similar products that are culturally approved. Coca-Cola, American sneakers (made in Korea but designed in Los Angeles), and CNN News (a television show) can now be sold in Latin America, Africa, and Asia.

Responding to this demand, global production and operations have emerged with precise on-line coordination between far-flung production facilities and central headquarters thousands of miles away. At Sealand Transportation, a major global shipping company based in Newark, New Jersey, shipping managers in Newark can watch the loading of ships in Rotterdam on-line, check trim and ballast, and trace packages to specific ship locations as the activity proceeds. This is all possible through an international satellite link.

The new global markets and pressure toward global production and operation have called forth whole new information system capabilities for global coordination of all factors of production. Not only production but also accounting, marketing and sales, human resources, and systems development (all the major business functions) can be coordinated on a global scale. Frito Lay, for instance, can develop a marketing sales force automation system in the United States and, once provided, may try the same techniques and technologies in Spain. Micromarketing—marketing to very small geographic and social units—no longer means marketing to neighborhoods in the United States, but to neighborhoods throughout the world! These new levels of global coordination permit for the first time in history the location of business activity according to comparative advantage. Design should be located where it is best accomplished, as should marketing, production, and finance.

Finally, global markets, production, and administration create the conditions for powerful, sustained global economies of scale. Production driven by worldwide global demand can be concentrated where it can be best accomplished, fixed resources can be allocated over larger production runs, and production runs in larger plants can be scheduled more efficiently and precisely estimated. Lower-cost factors of production can be exploited wherever they emerge. The result is a powerful strategic advantage to firms that can organize globally. These general and specific business drivers have greatly enlarged world trade and commerce.

*Businesses need an international information systems architecture to coordinate the activities of their sales, manufacturing, and warehouse units worldwide.*

Not all industries are similarly affected by these trends. Clearly, manufacturing has been much more affected than services, which still tend to be domestic and highly inefficient. However, the localism of services is breaking down in telecommunications, entertainment, transportation, financial services, and general business services including law. Clearly those firms within an industry that can understand the internationalization of the industry and respond appropriately will reap enormous gains in productivity and stability.

## Business Challenges

Although the possibilities of globalization for business success are significant, fundamental forces are operating to inhibit a global economy and to disrupt international business. Table 16-2 lists the most common and powerful challenges to the development of global systems.

At a cultural level, **particularism,** making judgments and taking action on the basis of narrow or personal characteristics, in all its forms (religious, nationalistic, ethnic, regionalism, geopolitical position) rejects the very concept of a shared global culture and rejects the penetration of domestic markets by foreign goods and services. Differences among cultures produce differences in social expectations, politics, and ultimately legal rules. In certain countries, such as the United States, consumers expect domestic name-brand products to be built domestically and are disappointed to learn that much of what they thought of as domestically produced is in fact foreign made.

**particularism**
Making judgments and taking actions on the basis of narrow or personal characteristics.

Different cultures produce different political regimes. Among the many countries of the world there are different laws governing the movement of information, information privacy of citizens, origins of software and hardware in systems, and radio and satellite telecommunications. Even the hours of business and the terms of business trade vary greatly across political cultures. These different legal regimes complicate global business and must be considered when building global systems.

### TABLE 16-2 CHALLENGES AND OBSTACLES TO GLOBAL BUSINESS SYSTEMS

**General**

Cultural particularism: regionalism, nationalism, language differences

Social expectations: brand name expectations; work hours

Political laws: transborder data and privacy laws, commercial regulations

**Specific**

Standards: different EDI, e-mail, telecommunications standards

Reliability: phone networks not uniformly reliable

Speed: different data transfer speeds, many slower than in the United States

Personnel: shortages of skilled consultants

**transsborder data flow**
The movement of information across international boundaries in any form.

For instance, European countries have very strict laws concerning transborder data flow and privacy. **Transborder data flow** is defined as the movement of information across international boundaries in any form. Some European countries prohibit the processing of financial information outside their boundaries or the movement of personal information to foreign countries. The European Union Data Protection Directive, which went into effect in October 1998, restricts the flow of any personal information to countries (such as the United States) that do not meet strict European laws on personal information. (A "safe harbor" agreement approved two years later allows U.S. and other companies willing to accept European privacy protection standards to collect personal data originating in Europe.) In response, most multinational firms develop information systems within each European country to avoid the cost and uncertainty of moving information across national boundaries.

Cultural and political differences profoundly affect organizations' standard operating procedures. A host of specific barriers arise from the general cultural differences, everything from different reliability of phone networks to the shortage of skilled consultants (see Steinbart and Nath, 1992).

National laws and traditions have created disparate accounting practices in various countries, which impact the ways profits and losses are analyzed. German companies generally do not recognize the profit from a venture until the project is completely finished and they have been paid. Conversely, British firms begin posting profits before a project is completed, when they are reasonably certain they will get the money.

These accounting practices are tightly intertwined with each country's legal system, business philosophy, and tax code. British, U.S., and Dutch firms share a predominantly Anglo-Saxon outlook that separates tax calculations from reports to shareholders to focus on showing shareholders how fast profits are growing. Continental European accounting practices are less oriented toward impressing investors, focusing rather on demonstrating compliance with strict rules and minimizing tax liabilities. These diverging accounting practices make it difficult for large international companies with units in different countries to evaluate their performance. Cultural differences can also affect the way organizations use information technology. For example, Japanese firms fax extensively but have been hesitant to take full advantage of the capabilities of e-mail.

Language remains a significant barrier. Although English has become a kind of standard business language, this is truer at higher levels of companies and not throughout the middle and lower ranks. Software may have to be built with local language interfaces before a new information system can be successfully implemented.

Currency fluctuations can wreak havoc with planning models and projections. A product that appears profitable in Mexico or Japan may actually produce a loss because of changes in foreign exchange rates. Some of these problems will diminish as the euro becomes more widely used.

These inhibiting factors must be taken into account when you are designing and building international systems for your business. For example, companies trying to implement "lean production" systems spanning national boundaries typically underestimate the time, expense, and logistical difficulties of making goods and information flow freely across different countries (Levy, 1997).

## STATE OF THE ART

One might think, given the opportunities for achieving competitive advantages as outlined previously and the interest in future applications, that most international companies have rationally developed marvelous international systems architectures. Nothing could be further from the truth. Most companies have inherited patchwork international systems from the distant past, often based on concepts of information processing developed in the 1960s—batch-oriented reporting from independent foreign divisions to corporate headquarters, with little on-line control and communication. Corporations in this situation increasingly will face powerful competitive challenges in the marketplace from firms that have rationally designed truly international systems. Still other companies have recently built technology platforms for an international information systems architecture but have nowhere to go because they lack global strategy.

As it turns out, there are significant difficulties in building appropriate international systems architectures. The difficulties involve planning a system appropriate to the firm's global strategy, structuring the organization of systems and business units, solving implementation issues, and choosing the right technical platform. Let us examine these problems in greater detail.

## 16.2 ORGANIZING INTERNATIONAL INFORMATION SYSTEMS

There are three organizational issues facing corporations seeking a global position: choosing a strategy, organizing the business, and organizing the systems management area. The first two are closely connected, so we discuss them together.

### GLOBAL STRATEGIES AND BUSINESS ORGANIZATION

Four main global strategies form the basis for global firms' organizational structure. These are domestic exporter, multinational, franchiser, and transnational. Each of these strategies is pursued with a specific business organizational structure (see Table 16-3). For simplicity's sake, we describe three kinds of organizational structure or governance: centralized (in the home country), decentralized (to local foreign units), and coordinated (all units participate as equals).

The **domestic exporter** strategy is characterized by heavy centralization of corporate activities in the home country of origin. Nearly all international companies begin this way, and some move on to other forms. Production, finance/accounting, sales/marketing, human resources, and strategic management are set up to optimize resources in the home country. International sales are sometimes dispersed using agency agreements or subsidiaries, but even here foreign marketing is totally reliant on the domestic home base for marketing themes and strategies. Caterpillar Corporation and other heavy capital-equipment manufacturers fall into this category of firm.

**domestic exporter**
A strategy characterized by heavy centralization of corporate activities in the home country of origin.

The **multinational** strategy concentrates financial management and control out of a central home base while decentralizing production, sales, and marketing operations to units in other countries. The products and services on sale in different countries are adapted to suit local market conditions. The organization becomes a far-flung confederation of production and marketing facilities in different countries. Many financial service firms, along with a host of manufacturers, such as General Motors, Chrysler, and Intel, fit this pattern.

**multinational**
A global strategy that concentrates financial management and control out of a central home base while decentralizing production, sales, and marketing operations to units in other countries.

**Franchisers** are an interesting mix of old and new. On the one hand, the product is created, designed, financed, and initially produced in the home country, but for product-specific reasons the firm must rely heavily on foreign personnel for further production, marketing, and human resources. Food franchisers such as McDonald's, Mrs. Fields Cookies, and Kentucky Fried Chicken fit this pattern. McDonald's created a new form of fast-food chain in the United States and continues to rely largely on the United States for inspiration of new products, strategic management, and financing. On the other hand, because the product must be produced locally—it is perishable—extensive coordination and dispersal of production, local marketing, and local recruitment of personnel are required. Generally, foreign franchisees are clones of the mother country units, but fully coordinated worldwide production that could optimize factors of production is not possible. For instance, potatoes and beef can generally not be bought where they are cheapest on world markets but must be produced reasonably close to the area of consumption.

**franchiser**
A firm in which a product is created, designed, financed, and initially produced in the home country, but for product-specific reasons the firm must rely heavily on foreign personnel for further production, marketing, and human resources.

**TABLE 16-3** GLOBAL BUSINESS STRATEGY AND STRUCTURE

| | | STRATEGY | | |
|---|---|---|---|---|
| **Business Function** | **Domestic Exporter** | **Multinational** | **Franchiser** | **Transnational** |
| Production | Centralized | Dispersed | Coordinated | Coordinated |
| Finance/accounting | Centralized | Centralized | Centralized | Coordinated |
| Sales/marketing | Mixed | Dispersed | Coordinated | Coordinated |
| Human resources | Centralized | Centralized | Coordinated | Coordinated |
| Strategic management | Centralized | Centralized | Centralized | Coordinated |

Transnational firms are the stateless, truly globally managed firms that may represent a larger part of international business in the future. Transnational firms have no single national headquarters but instead have many regional headquarters and perhaps a world headquarters. In a **transnational** strategy, nearly all the value-adding activities are managed from a global perspective without reference to national borders, optimizing sources of supply and demand wherever they appear, and taking advantage of any local competitive advantages. Transnational firms take the globe, not the home country, as their management frame of reference. The governance of these firms has been likened to a federal structure in which there is a strong central management core of decision making, but considerable dispersal of power and financial muscle throughout the global divisions. Few companies have actually attained transnational status, but Citigroup, Sony, Ford, and others are attempting this transition.

**transnational**
Truly globally managed firms that have no national headquarters; value-added activities are managed from a global perspective without reference to national borders, optimizing sources of supply and demand and taking advantage of any local competitive advantage.

## Global Systems to Fit the Strategy

Information technology and improvements in global telecommunications are giving international firms more flexibility to shape their global strategies. The configuration, management, and development of systems tend to follow the global strategy chosen (Roche, 1992; Ives and Jarvenpaa, 1991). Figure 16-2 depicts the typical arrangements. By *systems* we mean the full range of activities involved in building information systems: conception and alignment with the strategic business plan, systems development, and ongoing operation. For the sake of simplicity, we consider four types of systems configuration. *Centralized systems* are those in which systems development and operation occur totally at the domestic home base. *Duplicated systems* are those in which development occurs at the home base but operations are handed over to autonomous units in foreign locations. *Decentralized systems* are those in which each foreign unit designs its own unique solutions and systems. *Networked systems* are those in which systems development and operations occur in an integrated and coordinated fashion across all units.

As can be seen in Figure 16-2, domestic exporters tend to have highly centralized systems in which a single domestic systems development staff develops worldwide applications. Multinationals offer a direct and striking contrast: Here foreign units devise their own systems solutions based on local needs with few if any applications in common with headquarters (the exceptions being financial reporting and some telecommunications applications). Franchisers have the simplest systems structure: Like the products they sell, franchisers develop a single system usually at the home base and then replicate it around the world. Each unit, no matter where it is located, has identical applications. Last, the most ambitious form of systems development is found in the transnational: Networked systems are those in which there is a solid, singular global environment for developing and operating systems. This usually presupposes a powerful telecommunications backbone, a culture of shared applications development, and a shared management culture that crosses national barriers. The networked systems structure is the most visible in financial services where the homogeneity of the product—money and money instruments—seems to overcome cultural barriers.

## Reorganizing the Business

How should a firm organize itself for doing business on an international scale? To develop a global company and an information systems support structure, a firm needs to follow these principles:

*Figure 16-2* Global strategy and systems configurations. The large Xs show the dominant patterns, and the small Xs show the emerging patterns. For instance, domestic exporters rely predominantly on centralized systems, but there is continual pressure and some development of decentralized systems in local marketing regions.

| SYSTEM CONFIGURATION | STRATEGY | | | |
|---|---|---|---|---|
| | Domestic Exporter | Multinational | Franchiser | Transnational |
| Centralized | X | | | |
| Duplicated | | | X | |
| Decentralized | x | X | x | |
| Networked | | x | | X |

1. Organize value-adding activities along lines of comparative advantage. For instance, marketing/sales functions should be located where they can best be performed, for least cost and maximum impact; likewise with production, finance, human resources, and information systems.
2. Develop and operate systems units at each level of corporate activity—regional, national, and international. To serve local needs, there should be *host country systems units* of some magnitude. *Regional systems units* should handle telecommunications and systems development across national boundaries that take place within major geographic regions (European, Asian, American). *Transnational systems units* should be established to create the linkages across major regional areas and coordinate the development and operation of international telecommunications and systems development (Roche, 1992).
3. Establish at world headquarters a single office responsible for development of international systems, a global chief information officer (CIO) position.

Many successful companies have devised organizational systems structures along these principles. The success of these companies relies not only on the proper organization of activities, but also on a key ingredient—a management team that understands the risks and benefits of international systems and that can devise strategies for overcoming the risks. We turn to these management topics next.

## 16.3 Managing Global Systems

Table 16-4 lists the principal management problems posed by developing international systems. It is interesting to note that most of these problems are the chief difficulties managers experience in developing ordinary domestic systems as well! But these are enormously complicated in the international environment

### A Typical Scenario: Disorganization on a Global Scale

Let us look at a common scenario. A traditional multinational consumer-goods company based in the United States and operating in Europe would like to expand into Asian markets and knows that it must develop a transnational strategy and a supportive information systems structure. Like most multinationals it has dispersed production and marketing to regional and national centers while maintaining a world headquarters and strategic management in the United States. Historically, it has allowed each of the subsidiary foreign divisions to develop its own systems. The only centrally coordinated system is financial controls and reporting. The central systems group in the United States focuses only on domestic functions and production. The result is a hodgepodge of hardware, software, and telecommunications. The e-mail systems between Europe and the United States are incompatible. Each production facility uses a different manufacturing resources planning system (or a different version with local variations) and different marketing, sales, and human resource systems. The technology platforms are widely different: Europe is using mostly Unix-based file servers and IBM PC clones on desktops. Communications between different sites are poor, given the high cost and low quality of European intercountry communications. The U.S. group is moving from an IBM mainframe environment centralized at headquarters to a highly

**TABLE 16-4** Management Challenges in Developing Global Systems

| |
|---|
| Agreeing on common user requirements |
| Introducing changes in business processes |
| Coordinating applications development |
| Coordinating software releases |
| Encouraging local users to support global systems |

distributed network architecture based on a national value-added network, with local sites developing their own local area networks. The central systems group at headquarters recently was decimated and dispersed to the U.S. local sites in the hope of serving local needs better and reducing costs.

What do you recommend to the senior management leaders of this company, who now want to pursue a transnational strategy and develop an information systems infrastructure to support a highly coordinated global systems environment? Consider the problems you face by reexamining Table 16–4. The foreign divisions will resist efforts to agree on common user requirements; they have never thought about much other than their own units' needs. The systems groups in American local sites, which have been enlarged recently and told to focus on local needs, will not easily accept guidance from anyone recommending a transnational strategy. It will be difficult to convince local managers anywhere in the world that they should change their business procedures to align with other units in the world, especially if this might interfere with their local performance. After all, local managers are rewarded in this company for meeting local objectives of their division or plant. Finally, it will be difficult to coordinate development of projects around the world in the absence of a powerful telecommunications network and, therefore, difficult to encourage local users to take on ownership in the systems developed.

## STRATEGY: DIVIDE, CONQUER, APPEASE

**core systems**
Systems that support functions that are absolutely critical to the organization.

Figure 16-3 lays out the main dimensions of a solution. First, consider that not all systems should be coordinated on a transnational basis; only some core systems are truly worth sharing from a cost and feasibility point of view. **Core systems** are systems that support functions that are absolutely critical to the organization. Other systems should be partially coordinated because they share key elements, but they do not have to be totally common across national boundaries. For such systems, a good deal of local variation is possible and desirable. A final group of systems are peripheral, truly provincial, and are needed to suit local requirements only.

### Define the Core Business Processes

How do you identify *core systems?* The first step is to define a short list of critical core business processes. Business processes were defined in Chapters 1 and 2, which you should review. Briefly, business processes are sets of logically related tasks, such as shipping out correct orders to customers or delivering innovative products to the market. Each business process typically involves many functional areas communicating and coordinating work, information, and knowledge.

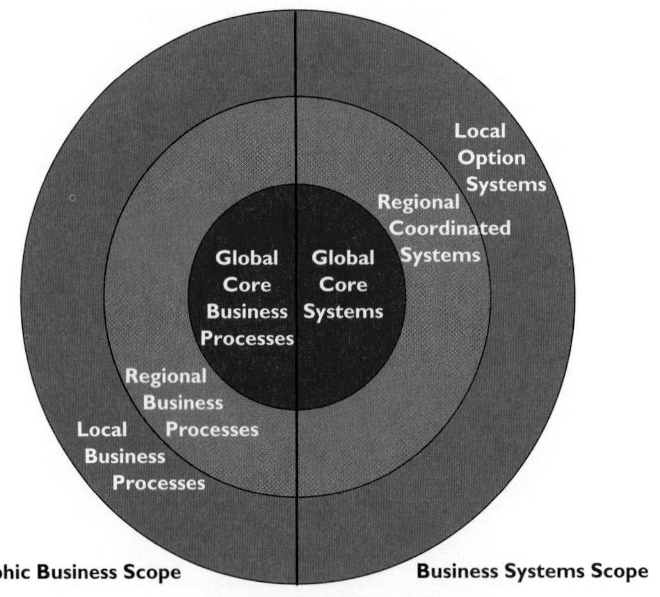


***Figure 16-3*** Agency and other coordination costs increase as the firm moves from local option systems toward regional and global systems. However, transaction costs of participating in global markets probably decrease as firms develop global systems. A sensible strategy is to reduce agency costs by developing only a few core global systems that are vital for global operations, leaving other systems in the hands of regional and local units.
*Source:* From *Managing Information Technology in Multinational Corporations* by Edward M. Roche, © 1993. Adapted by permission of Prentice-Hall, Inc., Upper Saddle River, NJ.

The way to identify these core business processes is to conduct a workflow analysis. How are customer orders taken, what happens to them once they are taken, who fills the orders, how are they shipped to the customers? What about suppliers? Do they have access to manufacturing resource planning systems so that supply is automatic? You should be able to identify and set priorities in a short list of 10 business processes that are absolutely critical for the firm.

Next, can you identify centers of excellence for these processes? Is the customer order fulfillment superior in the United States, manufacturing process control superior in Germany, and human resources superior in Asia? You should be able to identify some areas of the company, for some lines of business, where a division or unit stands out in the performance of one or several business functions.

When you understand the business processes of a firm, you can rank-order them. You then can decide which processes should be core applications, centrally coordinated, designed, and implemented around the globe, and which should be regional and local. At the same time, by identifying the critical business processes, the really important ones, you have gone a long way to defining a vision of the future that you should be working toward.

## Identify the Core Systems to Coordinate Centrally

By identifying the critical core business processes, you begin to see opportunities for transnational systems. The second strategic step is to conquer the core systems and define these systems as truly transnational. The financial and political costs of defining and implementing transnational systems are extremely high. Therefore, keep the list to an absolute minimum, letting experience be the guide and erring on the side of minimalism. By dividing off a small group of systems as absolutely critical, you divide opposition to a transnational strategy. At the same time, you can appease those who oppose the central worldwide coordination implied by transnational systems by permitting peripheral systems development to progress unabated, with the exception of some technical platform requirements.

## Choose an Approach: Incremental, Grand Design, Evolutionary

A third step is to choose an approach. Avoid piecemeal approaches. These surely will fail for lack of visibility, opposition from all who stand to lose from transnational development, and lack of power to convince senior management that the transnational systems are worth it. Likewise, avoid grand design approaches that try to do everything at once. These also tend to fail, because of an inability to focus resources. Nothing gets done properly, and opposition to organizational change is needlessly strengthened because the effort requires huge resources. An alternative approach is to evolve transnational applications from existing applications with a precise and clear vision of the transnational capabilities the organization should have in five years.

## Make the Benefits Clear

What is in it for the company? One of the worst situations to avoid is to build global systems for the sake of building global systems. From the beginning, it is crucial that senior management at headquarters and foreign division managers clearly understand the benefits that will come to the company as well as to individual units. Although each system offers unique benefits to a particular budget, the overall contribution of global systems lies in four areas.

Global systems—truly integrated, distributed, and transnational systems—contribute to superior management and coordination. A simple price tag cannot be put on the value of this contribution, and the benefit will not show up in any capital budgeting model. This is the ability to switch suppliers on a moment's notice from one region to another in a crisis, the ability to move production in response to natural disasters, and the ability to use excess capacity in one region to meet raging demand in another.

A second major contribution is vast improvement in production, operation, and supply and distribution. Imagine a global value chain, with global suppliers and a global distribution network. For the first time, senior managers can locate value-adding activities in regions where they are most economically performed.

Third, global systems mean global customers and global marketing. Fixed costs around the world can be amortized over a much larger customer base. This will unleash new economies of scale at production facilities.

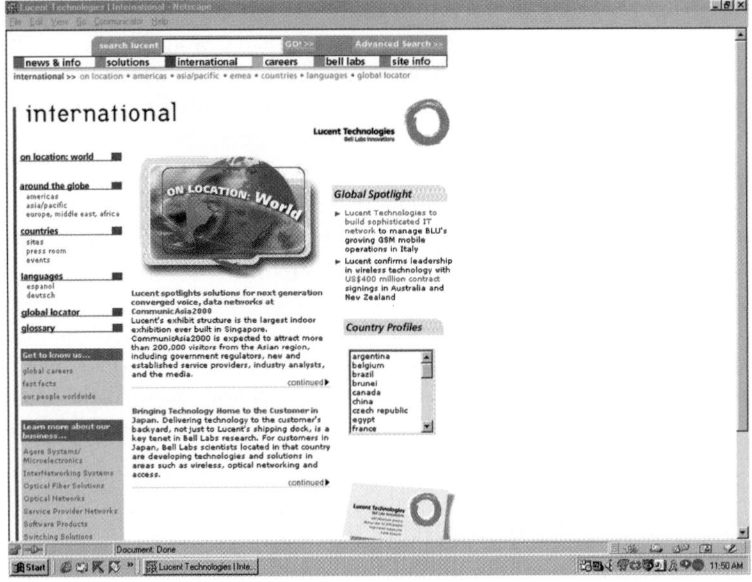


*Lucent Technologies installed an enterprise system to coordinate materials, processes, schedules, logistics, and accounting information among its production facilities in different countries. The new system gives Lucent a global view of its supply chain.*

Last, global systems mean the ability to optimize the use of corporate funds over a much larger capital base. This means, for instance, that capital in a surplus region can be moved efficiently to expand production of capital-starved regions; that cash can be managed more effectively within the company and put to use more effectively.

These strategies will not by themselves create global systems. You will have to implement what you strategize and this is a whole new challenge.

## Implementation Tactics: Cooptation

**cooptation**
Bringing the opposition into the process of designing and implementing the solution without giving up control of the direction and nature of the change.

The overall tactic for dealing with resistant local units in a transnational company is cooptation. **Cooptation** is defined as bringing the opposition into the process of designing and implementing the solution without giving up control of the direction and nature of the change. As much as possible, raw power should be avoided. Minimally, however, local units must agree on a short list of transnational systems, and raw power may be required to solidify the idea that transnational systems of some sort are truly required.

How should cooptation proceed? Several alternatives are possible. One alternative is to permit each country unit the opportunity to develop one transnational application first in its home territory, and then throughout the world. In this manner, each major country systems group is given a piece of the action in developing a transnational system, and local units have a sense of ownership in the transnational effort. On the downside, this assumes the ability to develop high-quality systems is widely distributed, and that, say, the German team can successfully implement systems in France and Italy. This will not always be the case. Also, the transnational effort will have low visibility.

A second tactic is to develop new transnational centers of excellence, or a single center of excellence. There may be several centers around the globe that focus on specific business processes. These centers draw heavily from local national units, are based on multinational teams, and must report to worldwide management—their first line of responsibility is to the core applications. Centers of excellence perform the initial identification and specification of the business process, define the information requirements, perform the business and systems analysis, and accomplish all design and testing. Implementation, however, and pilot testing occur in world pilot regions where new applications are installed and tested first. Later, they are rolled out to other parts of the globe. This phased rollout strategy is precisely how national applications are successfully developed.

## The Management Solution

We now can reconsider how to handle the most vexing problems facing managers developing global systems that were described in Table 16-4.

- *Agreeing on common user requirements:* Establishing a short list of the core business processes and core support systems will begin a process of rational comparison across the many divisions of the company, develop a common language for discussing the business, and naturally lead to an understanding of common elements (as well as the unique qualities that must remain local).
- *Introducing changes in business processes:* Your success as a change agent will depend on your legitimacy, your actual raw power, and your ability to involve users in the change design process. **Legitimacy** is defined as the extent to which your authority is accepted on grounds of competence, vision, or other qualities. The selection of a viable change strategy, which we have defined as evolutionary but with a vision, should assist you in convincing others that change is feasible and desirable. Involving people in change, assuring them that change is in the best interests of the company and their local units, is a key tactic.

**legitimacy**
The extent to which one's authority is accepted on grounds of competence, vision, or other qualities.

- *Coordinating applications development:* Choice of change strategy is critical for this problem. At the global level there is far too much complexity to attempt a grand design strategy of change. It is far easier to coordinate change by making small incremental steps toward a larger vision. Imagine a five-year plan of action rather than a two-year plan of action, and reduce the set of transnational systems to a bare minimum to reduce coordination costs.
- *Coordinating software releases:* Firms can institute procedures to ensure that all operating units convert to new software updates at the same time so that everyone's software is compatible.
- *Encouraging local users to support global systems:* The key to this problem is to involve users in the creation of the design without giving up control over the development of the project to parochial interests. Recruiting a wide range of local individuals to transnational centers of excellence helps send the message that all significant groups are involved in the design and will have an influence.

Even with the proper organizational structure and appropriate management choices, it is still possible to stumble over technological issues. Choices of technology, platforms, networks, hardware, and software are the final elements in building global systems.

## 16.4 TECHNOLOGY ISSUES AND OPPORTUNITIES FOR GLOBAL VALUE CHAINS

Information technology is itself a powerful business driver for encouraging the development of global systems and global value chains, where firms can coordinate commercial transactions and production with other firms across many different locations throughout the world. Companies pursuing electronic commerce and electronic business on a global scale and digital integration with their customers and value partners face many challenges (Farhoomand, Tuunainen, and Yee, 2000).

### MAIN TECHNICAL ISSUES

Hardware, software, and telecommunications pose special technical challenges in an international setting. The major hardware challenge is finding some way to standardize the firm's computer hardware platform when there is so much variation from operating unit to operating unit and from country to country. Managers need to think carefully about where to locate the firm's computer centers and how to select hardware suppliers. The major global software challenge is finding applications that are user friendly and that truly enhance the productivity of international work teams. The major telecommunications challenge is making data flow seamlessly across networks shaped by disparate national standards. Overcoming these challenges requires systems integration and connectivity on a global basis.

#### Hardware and Systems Integration

The development of global systems based on the concept of core systems raises questions about how the new core systems will fit in with the existing suite of applications developed around the globe by different divisions, different people, and for different kinds of computing hardware. The goal is to develop global, distributed, and integrated systems. Briefly, these are the same problems faced by any large domestic systems development effort. However, the problems are more complex because of the international environment. For instance, in the United States, IBM operating systems have played the predominant role in building core systems for large organizations, whereas in Europe, Unix was much more commonly used for large systems. How can the two be integrated in a common transnational system?

The correct solution often will depend on the history of the company's systems and the extent of commitment to proprietary systems. For instance, finance and insurance firms typically have relied almost exclusively on IBM proprietary equipment and architectures, and it would be extremely difficult and cost ineffective to abandon that equipment and software. Newer firms and manufacturing firms generally find it much easier to adopt open Unix systems for international systems.

After a hardware platform is chosen, the question of standards must be addressed. Just because all sites use the same hardware does not guarantee common, integrated systems. Some central authority in the firm must establish data, as well as other technical standards, with which sites are to comply. For instance, technical accounting terms, such as the beginning and end of the fiscal year, must be standardized (review our earlier discussion of the cultural challenges to building global businesses), as well as the acceptable interfaces between systems, communication speeds and architectures, and network software.

## Connectivity

The heart of the international systems problem is telecommunications—linking together the systems and people of a global firm into a single integrated network just like the phone system but capable of voice, data, and image transmissions. However, integrated global networks are extremely difficult to create (see Table 16-5). For example, many countries cannot fulfill basic business telecommunications needs such as obtaining reliable circuits, coordinating among different carriers and the regional telecommunications authority, obtaining bills in a common currency standard, and obtaining standard agreements for the level of telecommunications service provided.

Despite moves toward economic unity, Europe remains a hodgepodge of disparate national technical standards and service levels. The problem is especially critical for banks or airlines that must move massive volumes of data around the world. Although most circuits leased by multinational corporations are fault free more than 99.8 percent of the time, line quality and service vary widely from the north to the south of Europe. Network service is much more unreliable in southern Europe.

Existing European standards for networking and EDI (electronic data interchange) are very industry specific and country specific. Most European banks use the SWIFT (Society for Worldwide Interbank Financial Telecommunications) protocol for international funds transfer, whereas automobile companies and food producers often use industry-specific or country-specific versions of standard protocols for EDI. Complicating matters further, the United States standard for EDI is ANSI (American National Standards Institute) X.12. The

**TABLE 16-5 PROBLEMS OF INTERNATIONAL NETWORKS**

Costs and tariffs
Network management
Installation delays
Poor quality of international service
Regulatory constraints
Changing user requirements
Disparate standards
Network capacity

Open Systems Interconnect (OSI) reference model for linking networks is more popular in Europe than it is in the United States. Various industry groups have standardized on other networking architectures, such as Transmission Control Protocol/Internet Protocol (TCP/IP) or IBM's proprietary Systems Network Architecture (SNA). Even standards such as ISDN (integrated services digital network) vary from country to country.

Firms have several options for providing international connectivity: build their own international private network, rely on a network service based on the public switched networks throughout the world, or use the Internet and intranets.

One possibility is for the firm to put together its own private network based on leased lines from each country's PTT (post, telegraph, and telephone authorities). Each country, however, has different restrictions on data exchange, technical standards, and acceptable vendors of equipment. These problems magnify in certain parts of the world. Despite such limitations, in Europe and the United States, reliance on PTTs still makes sense while these public networks expand services to compete with private providers.

The second major alternative to building one's own network is to use one of several expanding network services. With deregulation of telecommunications around the globe, private providers have sprung up to service business customers' data needs, along with some voice and image communication.

Already common in the United States, IVANs (international value-added network services) are expanding in Europe and Asia. These private firms offer value-added telecommunications capacity, usually rented from local PTTs or international satellite authorities, and then resell it to corporate users. IVANs add value by providing protocol conversion, operating mailboxes and mail systems, and offering integrated billing that permits a firm to track its data communications costs. Currently, these systems are limited to data transmissions, but in the future they will expand to voice and image.

The third alternative, which is becoming increasingly attractive, is to create global intranets and extranets to use the Internet for international communication. However, the Internet is not yet a worldwide tool, because many countries lack the communications infrastructure for extensive Internet use. Countries face high costs, government control, or government monitoring. Many countries also do not have the speedy and reliable postal and package delivery services that are essential for electronic commerce (DePalma, 2000).

Western Europe faces both high-transmission costs and lack of common technology, because it is not politically unified and because European telecommunications systems are still in the process of shedding their government monopolies. The lack of an infrastructure and the high costs of installing one is even more widespread in the rest of the world. The International Telecommunications Union estimates that only 500 million of the world's 1.5 billion households have basic telephone services (Wysocki, 2000). Low penetration of PCs and widespread illiteracy limit demand for Internet service in India (Burkhardt, Goodman, Mehta, and Press, 1999). Where an infrastructure exists in less-developed countries, it is often outdated, lacks digital circuits, and has very noisy lines. Figure 16-4 illustrates some of these global disparities in the pricing and cost of Internet service. The purchasing power of most people in developing counties makes access to Internet services very expensive (Petrazzini and Kibati, 1999).

Many countries monitor transmissions. The governments in China and Singapore monitor Internet traffic and block access to Web sites considered morally or politically offensive (Smith, 2000; Blanning, 1999). Corporations may be discouraged from using this medium. Companies planning international operations through the Internet still will have many hurdles. The Window on Organizations explores Internet availability and other issues for companies attempting to develop an international Web strategy.

## Software

Compatible hardware and communications provide a platform but not the total solution. Also critical to global core infrastructure is software. The development of core systems poses unique challenges for software: How will the old systems interface with the new? Entirely new interfaces must be built and tested if old systems are kept in local areas (which is common). These interfaces can be costly and messy to build. If new software must be created,

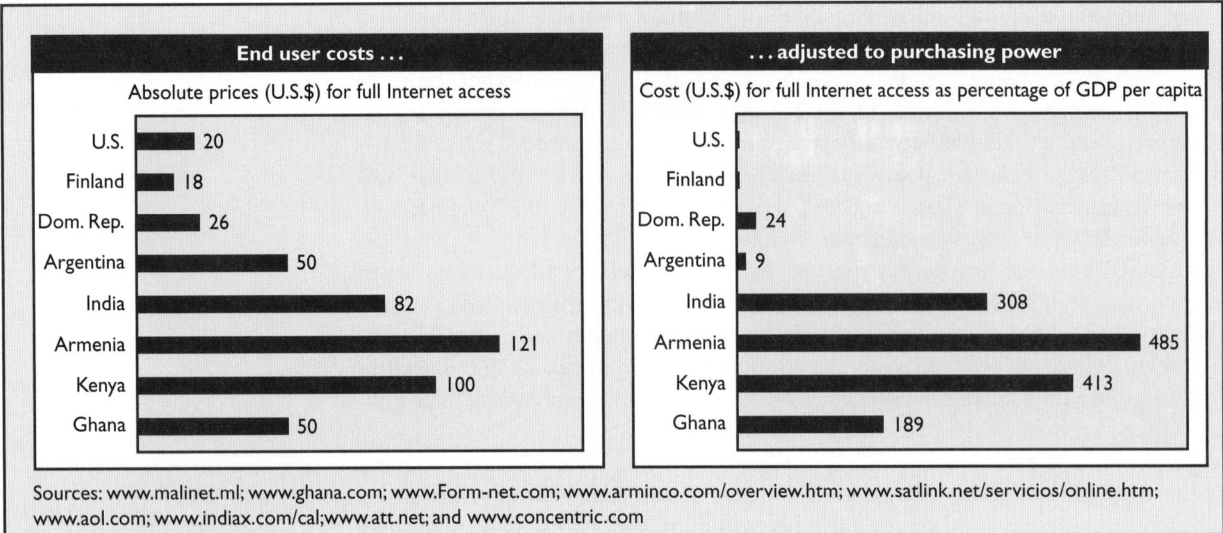


***Figure 16-4*** End-user costs for full Internet access. The cost of accessing the Internet is much higher in developing countries than in the United States and Western Europe. These disparities are even greater when users' purchasing power is taken into account.
*Source:* From "The Internet in Developing Countries," by Ben Petrazzini and Mugo Kibati in *Communications of the ACM* 42, no. 6, June 1999. Reprinted by permission.

another challenge is to build software that can be realistically used by multiple business units from different countries because these business units are accustomed to their own unique business processes and definitions of data.

Aside from integrating the new with the old systems, there are problems of human interface design and functionality of systems. For instance, to be truly useful for enhancing productivity of a global workforce, software interfaces must be easily understood and able to be mastered quickly. Graphical user interfaces are ideal for this but presuppose a common language—often English. When international systems involve knowledge workers only, English may be the assumed international standard. But as international systems penetrate deeper into management and clerical groups, a common language may not be assumed and human interfaces must be built to accommodate different languages and even conventions.

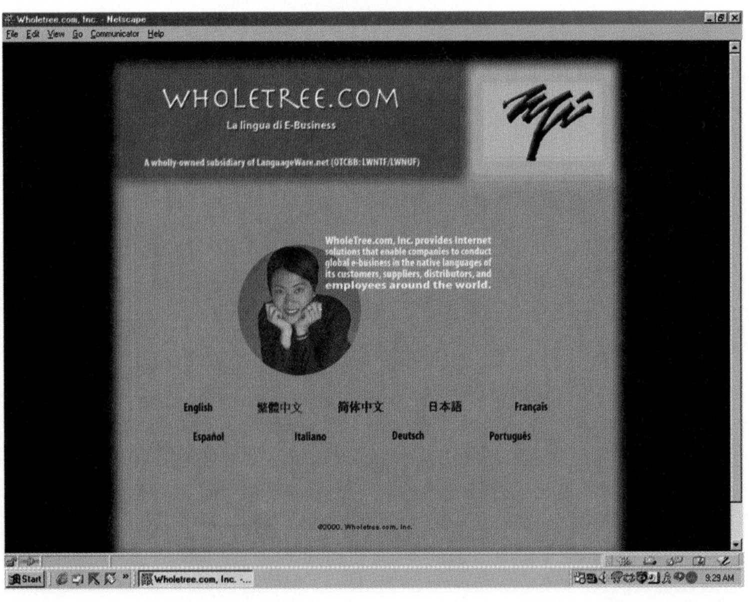


*WholeTree.com provides technology and services for developing multilingual Web sites. Web sites and software interfaces for global systems may have to be translated to accommodate users in other parts of the world.*

## E-GLOBALIZATION PITFALLS

All Internet sites are accessible to anyone in the world unless the site owners establish security restrictions. However, doing business in distant lands has many pitfalls. Even the smallest organization attempting to conduct business abroad must deal with many differences, from technology, law, and custom to foreign languages or differences in terminology. Let us look at some of the hazards.

Technology and the quality of that technology differ all over the world. For example although the United States, Finland, and Sweden have developed adequate bandwidth for high-speed connections, the telecommunications infrastructures in Greece and Turkey are not so well developed, and in some countries such an infrastructure barely exists. One effect of a less developed infrastructure is that visitors from those countries will access the site at a very slow speed and will even slow down visitors from other countries. Therefore, Web site owners may want to establish multiple regional sites to better serve those who are used to rapid responses on the Web.

Law can present important obstacles as organizations attempt to expand. "We [Americans] take it for granted that when we log on a site, it recognizes us and displays preferences," says Victoria Bracewell-Short, a global e-commerce consultant with iXL Enterprises Inc. in Atlanta, Georgia. However, she points out, other countries, such as Germany, have privacy laws that prevent the gathering of the kind of data necessary to be able to tailor the screen to the specific user. Just asking for such personal data as the visitor's name, mailing address, or e-mail address can be either illegal or outside the accepted customs and mores of the specific country. Sites must be developed to accommodate different laws in different countries.

Many question the use of language translation software created for foreign language sites, because they can produce clumsy language or even culturally unacceptable terms (see Chase Manhattan's position on this issue in this chapter's case study). However, screens developed in one country can even present translation problems in foreign countries that speak the same language. Let us look at Manheim Auctions Inc. as an example.

Manheim is an Atlanta, Georgia-based company that is the world's largest reseller of used cars. As the director of on-line operations for Manheim, Donald Foy ran into many unexpected problems when Manheim decided to go international. The company first targeted Australia and Great Britain, which seemed logical because they both speak English. However, a number of problems immediately emerged. For example, the company's logo displayed a globe showing North and South America. Australians were not willing to be so ignored, and the logo had to be redesigned. Foy explained that his group had missed that issue altogether, and he added, "We have to be sensitive to their business and culture." To operate in both countries the database had to be expanded to encompass national differences in terminology. For example, what the people in the United States call a car's hood the British refer to as the bonnet. The database must also incorporate differences in measurements, because the United States uses miles, whereas the British and Australians use kilometers.

**To Think About:** What management, organization, and technology issues should be addressed when developing a global Web strategy?

*Sources:* Donald DePalma, "Which Markets First?", *E-Business* Advisor, January 2001; Dawne Shand, "All Information Is Local," *Computerworld,* April 10, 2000; and Dermot McGrath, "Going Native," *Tornado-Insider.com,* May 2000.

What are the most important software applications? Many international systems focus on basic transaction and MIS systems. Increasingly, firms such as Lucent Technologies, described in the Window on Technology, are turning to enterprise systems to standardize their business processes on a global basis and to create coordinated global supply chains. However, enterprise systems are not always compatible with differences in languages and business practices (Soh, Kien, and Tay-Yap, 2000). Company units in countries that are not technically sophisticated may also encounter problems trying to manage the technical complexities of enterprise software.

EDI—electronic data interchange—is a common global transaction processing application used by manufacturing and distribution firms to connect units of the same company, as well as customers and suppliers on a global basis. Groupware systems, electronic mail, and videoconferencing are especially important worldwide collaboration tools for knowledge- and data-based firms, such as advertising firms, research-based firms in medicine and engineering, and graphics and publishing firms. The Internet will be increasingly used for such purposes.

## Lucent's Enterprise System Speeds Its Global Supply Chain

Competition in the manufacture and sales of cellular phones is so fierce that a new phone model can retain its original value for only two to three months. After that, newer models from competitors with newer functions and capabilities make existing models somewhat obsolete. To compete successfully in such a market, speed is critical. Cellular phone manufacturers must be able to improve their products every several months and to shift to the manufacture of their new products within days or hours. This market presented a huge problem for the Lucent Microelectronics Group, which produces the chips that are the heart of many cellular phones. Lucent Microelectronics is a part of Lucent Technologies, the giant Murray Hill, New Jersey, telecommunications technology company and offspring of AT&T.

Lucent silicon wafers are produced in plants in Pennsylvania, Florida, and Spain. They are then assembled into integrated circuits in other plants in Pennsylvania, Thailand, and Singapore, where they are also tested. From there they are shipped to customers such as L. M. Ericsson, a telecommunications equipment maker in Stockholm, Sweden. Prior to 1999 Lucent factories were run by legacy systems that often did not communicate with each other. Each factory had its own supply chain, production schedule, and manufacturing systems. "Gathering data across the enterprise was difficult, if not impossible," according to Lucent CIO William Stuckey.

The solution involved putting all Lucent factories on the same set of information systems and installing an Oracle enterprise system in June 1999 to help the company coordinate materials, processes, schedules, logistics, and accounting information. The new system gives Lucent a global view of its supply chain within three minutes of any transaction. For example, once a purchase order from Ericsson for chips has been entered into the system, the system verifies customer data and checks whether the product is available. If it is, the system instructs the Lucent integrated circuit assembly plants to pick and pack the chips and hand then over to DHL for delivery. At the same time, the system sends Ericsson an EDI confirmation. DHL can deliver the order to an Ericsson plant in Sweden about 56 hours after it has been received.

The ERP system has reduced processes that used to take 10 to 15 days to less than eight hours. Lucent is able to manage all of its global factories as if they were a single factory. If, for instance, a natural catastrophe hits a plant, Lucent can shift any critical production to another plant within eight hours. Customers can even use the Web to track the status of their own orders at any time.

Although DHL's rapid delivery service is more expensive than the slower previous companies Lucent had relied on, it is actually saving Lucent money. Previously, logistics costs, including personnel, warehousing, stocking, and transportation, ran about 1.5 percent of revenue, whereas today they have dropped to less than 1 percent. This is so because Lucent has lowered warehousing and inventory expenses by substituting "information for inventory."

**To Think About:** What competitive forces drove Lucent to a new ERP system and to installing the same systems around the world? How did this technology help solve Lucent's supply chain problems?

*Sources:* David Baum, "The Future Is Calling," *Profit,* August 2000; Eric Chabrow, "Supply Chains Go Global," *Information Week,* April 3, 2000; and "Tighter Supply Chain Helps Lucent Speed Deliveries," *Information Week,* April 3, 2000.

## New Technical Opportunities and the Internet

Technical advances described in Chapter 8 such as wireless and digital subscriber line (DSL) services, should continue to fall in price and gain in power, facilitating the creation and operation of global networks. Networks that *communicate and compute any time, anywhere,* based on satellite systems, digital cellular phones, and personal communications services, will make it even easier to coordinate work and information in many parts of the globe that cannot be reached by existing ground-based systems. Thus, a salesperson in China could send an order-confirmation request to the home office in London effortlessly and expect an instant reply.

Companies are using Internet technology to construct virtual private networks (VPNs) to reduce wide area network (WAN) costs and staffing requirements. Instead of using private, leased telephone lines or frame-relay connections, companies outsource the VPN to an Internet service provider. The VPN comprises WAN links, security products, and routers, providing a secure and encrypted connection between two points across the Internet to transmit corporate data. These VPNs from Internet service providers can provide many features of a private network to firms operating internationally.

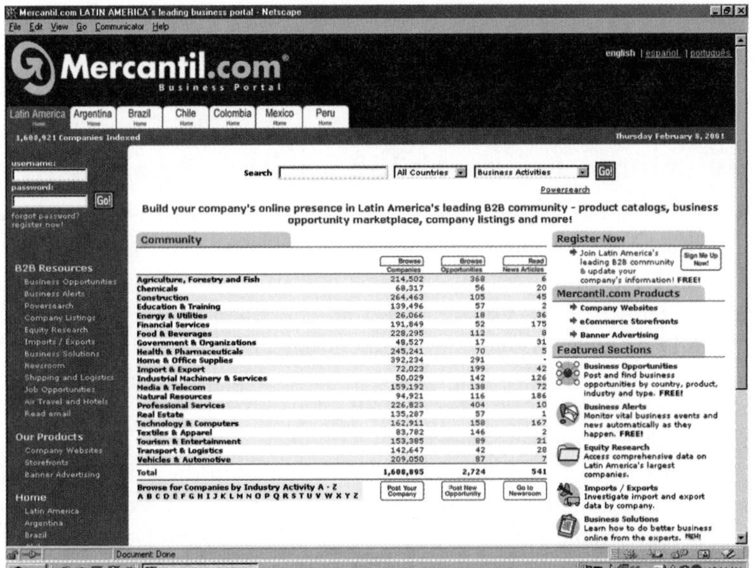


*Mercantil.com is a portal for promoting business in Latin America. It includes descriptions of business opportunities, a directory of businesses, and search capabilities for locating businesses and products of interest to visitors.*

However, VPNs may not provide the same level of quick and predictable response as private networks, especially during times of the day when Internet traffic is very congested. VPNs may not be able to support large numbers of remote users.

Throughout this text we have shown how the Internet facilitates global coordination, communication, and electronic business. As Internet technology becomes more widespread outside the United States, it will expand opportunities for electronic commerce and international trade. The global connectivity and low cost of Internet technology will further remove obstacles of geography and time zones for companies seeking to expand operations and sell their wares abroad. Companies in Asia, Latin America, or Africa that do not have the financial or technical resources to handle EDI transactions can use Internet technology to exchange information rapidly with business partners in their supply chains. Small companies may especially benefit from using the Internet to speed delivery of products and manage their supply chains (Chabrow, 2000; Quelch and Klein, 1996).

## MANAGEMENT DECISION PROBLEM

### PLANNING A GLOBAL WEB SITE

Your company manufactures and sells tennis rackets and would like to start selling its products to countries outside the United States. You are in charge of developing a global Web strategy. Based on the statistics in the following table, what countries would you target first? (Gross domestic product [GDP] per capita is a measure of relative purchasing power.)

| Country | Total Population (in millions) | Percentage On-line | Total On-line Population (in millions) | GDP per Capita |
|---|---|---|---|---|
| Brazil | 172 | 4.0% | | $ 6,100 |
| China | 1,247 | .05 | | 3,600 |
| Germany | 82 | 15.0 | | 22,100 |
| Italy | 57 | 8.4 | | 20,800 |
| Japan | 126 | 14.4 | | 23,100 |
| Sweden | 9 | 43.3 | | 19,700 |

1. Calculate the total number of people in each country who have Internet access.
2. Based on these statistics alone, what countries would you target first for selling your products? Why?
3. Using what you have learned in this chapter, what other considerations should you address in your Web strategy? What additional information would be helpful to make sure your Web sales effort is successful?
4. What features would you put on your Web site to attract buyers from the countries you target?

# APPLICATION SOFTWARE EXERCISE

## DATABASE AND WEB-PAGE DEVELOPMENT TOOL EXERCISE: BUILDING A JOB DATABASE AND WEB PAGE AT KTP CONSULTING

KTP Consulting operates in various locations around the world. KTP specializes in designing, developing, and implementing enterprise systems for medium- to large-size companies. KTP offers its employees opportunities to travel, live, and work in various locations throughout the United States, Europe, and Asia.

KTP's human resources department has a simple database that enables its staff to track job vacancies. When an employee is interested in relocating, she or he contacts the human resources department for a list of KTP job vacancies. KTP also posts its employment opportunities on the company Web site.

What type of data do you think is included in the KTP job vacancies database? What information should not be included in this database? Based on your answers to these questions, build a replica of how you think the KTP job vacancies database should look. Populate the database with at least 20 records. You should also build a simple Web page that incorporates job vacancy data from your newly created database. Submit a disk containing a copy of the KTP database and Web page to your professor.

# MANAGEMENT WRAP-UP

Managers are responsible for devising an appropriate organizational and technological framework for international business. Choosing a global business strategy, identifying core business processes, organizing the firm to conduct business on an international scale, and selecting an international information systems architecture are key management decisions.

Cultural, political, and language diversity magnifies differences in organizational culture and standard operating procedures when companies operate internationally. These differences create barriers to the development of global information systems that transcend national boundaries.

The main technology decision in building international systems is finding a set of workable standards in hardware, software, and networking for the firm's international information systems infrastructure and architecture. The Internet and intranets are increasingly used to provide global connectivity and to serve as a foundation for global systems, but many companies still need proprietary systems for certain functions, and, therefore, international standards.

*For Discussion*

1. If you were a manager in a company that operates in many countries, what criteria would you use to determine whether an application should be developed as a global application or as a local application?
2. Describe ways the Internet can be used in international information systems.

# SUMMARY

1. *Identify the major factors behind the growing internationalization of business.* There are general cultural factors and specific business factors to consider. The growth of cheap international communication and transportation has created a world culture with stable expectations or norms. Political stability and a growing global knowledge base that is widely shared contribute also to the world culture. These general factors create the conditions for global markets, global production, coordination, distribution, and global economies of scale.

2. *Compare global strategies for developing business.* There are four basic international strategies: domestic exporter, multinational, franchiser, and transnational. In a transnational strategy, all factors of production are coordinated on a global scale. However, the choice of strategy is a function of the type of business and product.
3. *Demonstrate how information systems support different global strategies.* There is a connection between firm strategy and information systems design. Transnational firms must develop networked system configurations and permit considerable decentralization of development and operations. Franchisers almost always duplicate systems across many countries and use centralized financial controls. Multinationals typically rely on decentralized independence among foreign units with some movement toward development of networks. Domestic exporters typically are centralized in domestic headquarters with some decentralized operations permitted.
4. *Plan the development of international information systems.* Implementing a global system requires an implementation strategy. Typically, global systems have evolved without a conscious plan. The remedy is to define a small subset of core business processes and focus on building systems that could support these processes. Tactically, you will have to coopt widely dispersed foreign units to participate in the development and operation of these systems, being careful to maintain overall control.
5. *Evaluate the main technical alternatives in developing global systems.* The main hardware and telecommunications issues are systems integration and connectivity. The choices for integration are to go either with a proprietary architecture or with an open systems technology such as Unix. Global networks are extremely difficult to build and operate. Some measure of connectivity may be achieved by relying on local PTT authorities to provide connections, building a system oneself, relying on private providers to supply communications capacity, or using the Internet and intranets. Companies can use Internet services to create virtual private networks (VPNs) as low-cost alternatives to global private networks. The main software issue concerns building interfaces to existing systems and providing much needed group support software.

## KEY TERMS

**Business driver, 501**
**Cooptation, 510**
**Core systems, 508**
**Domestic exporter, 505**
**Franchiser, 505**
**Global culture, 502**
**International information systems architecture, 501**
**Legitimacy, 511**
**Multinational, 505**
**Particularism, 503**
**Transborder data flow, 504**
**Transnational, 506**

## REVIEW QUESTIONS

1. What are the five major factors to consider when building an international information systems architecture?
2. Describe the five general cultural factors leading toward growth in global business and the four specific business factors. Describe the interconnection among these factors.
3. What is meant by a *global culture?*
4. What are the major challenges to the development of global systems?
5. Why have firms not planned for the development of international systems?
6. Describe the four main strategies for global business and organizational structure.
7. Describe the four different system configurations that can be used to support different global strategies.
8. What are the major management issues in developing international systems?
9. What are three principles to follow when organizing a firm for global business?
10. What are three steps of a management strategy for developing and implementing global systems?
11. What is meant by *cooptation,* and how can it be used in building global systems?
12. Describe the main technical issues facing global systems.
13. Describe three new technologies that can help firms develop global systems.

## GROUP PROJECT

With a group of students, identify an area of information technology and explore how this technology might be useful for supporting global business strategies. For instance, you might choose an area such as digital telecommunications (e.g., electronic mail, wireless communications, value-added networks), enterprise systems, collaborative work group software, or the Internet. It will be necessary to choose a business scenario to discuss the technology. You might choose, for instance, an automobile parts franchise or a clothing franchise such as the Limited Express as example businesses. What applications would you make global, what core business processes would you choose, and how would the technology be helpful? If possible, use presentation software to present your findings to the class.

# TOOLS FOR INTERACTIVE LEARNING

## INTERNET CONNECTION

The Internet Connection for this chapter will take you to a series of Web sites where you can complete an exercise to evaluate the capabilities of various global package tracking and delivery services. You can also use the Interactive Study Guide to test your knowledge of the topics in this chapter and get instant feedback where you need more practice.

## ELECTRONIC COMMERCE PROJECT

At the Laudon Web site for Chapter 16, you will find an Electronic Commerce project for international marketing and pricing.

## CD-ROM

If you use the Multimedia Edition CD-ROM with this chapter, you can complete an interactive exercise asking you to design a global network for a multinational corporation. You can also find a video clip illustrating the United Parcel Service International Shipping and Processing System (ISPS), an audio overview of the major themes of this chapter, and bullet text summarizing the key points of the chapter.

# CASE STUDY *Chase.com's Quest for a Global Web Presence*

On July 24, 2000, Chase.com, a subsidiary of the Chase Manhattan Corp. (the parent of the Chase Manhattan Bank) issued a request-for-proposal (RFP) to application service providers (ASPs). The purpose of the RFP was to find a partner to aid Chase.com in establishing "international Web sites in all of its major international locations by spring 2001." After reading this case study, your major task will be to propose a system solution for Chase.com.

The modern Chase Manhattan Bank was created in 1955 from the merger of the Bank of the Manhattan Company and The Chase National Bank. The new bank was basically a domestic bank that also had a few offices abroad. However, by 1960, under the leadership of David Rockefeller, the bank had become an international bank (as well as a domestic bank), with 40 offices in 17 countries in Europe, Asia, the Middle East, and South America.

In the late 1980s the bank decided that information technology was critical to its future, and it began to spend $500 million a year to modernize its technology. Its goals were to give Chase a competitive edge in both wholesale and retail banking while simultaneously cutting costs. The bank also began thinking even more internationally by focusing on helping its corporate customers manage their global risks. In March 1996 Chase merged with the Chemical Banking Corporation of New York, creating the largest bank holding company in the United States. In September 2000, Chase acquired the prestigious investment bank J.P. Morgan. This new merger creates a powerhouse in commercial banking that would further strengthen Chase's presence overseas. Chase is also focusing on selling more consumer banking services such as credit cards, mortgages, and mutual funds.

By the late 1990s the general business environment had undergone two fundamental changes that were to profoundly affect Chase. First, globalization was fast becoming a reality, and this meant that Chase's domestic customers now were competing with rivals all over the world. Chase, in turn, had to be able to offer these customers top-quality service wherever they were carrying out their business. Second, continuing advances in telecommunications, including the growth of the Internet, forced Chase (and all major banks) to use telecommunications to compete globally.

After Bill Harrison was appointed Chase Manhattan's CEO in early 1999, he created Chase.com, with the goal of making Chase's older businesses Internet-enabled. Its mission was to invest in promising Web-related businesses and to establish and nurture new wired ventures. These investments were to be in ventures that would enhance Chase's already-advanced technological position and help it better use and benefit from the technology.

Management described Chase.com as "a massive opportunity to change the way business is done." Chase.com was purposely kept small, with only 120 employees. In the year 2000 it invested about $400 million in Web-based enterprises, and with diversification as a guiding principal, by mid-2000 the new venture had already become involved in dozens of projects.

Let us briefly examine several examples of the types of projects Chase.com was already engaged in when it issued its RFP. It joined with consulting firm Deloitte & Touche to offer an Internet procurement service in late 2000. The software comes from Intelisys Electronic Commerce, a majority of which is owned by Chase. This service offers thousands of Chase's small-business clients a payment infrastructure and trading network, and Deloitte & Touche offers its breadth of expertise. This project not only serves Chase's existing customer base, but also helps Chase gain new business, because it handles the electronic payments for all transactions.

Chase became involved with Spectrum EBP L.L.C. for very different reasons. Chase originally joined with two other banks, First Union and Wells Fargo, to create a network that would enable businesses to bill customers through the Web and receive payments the same way. Very quickly 18 other banks joined the venture. With this project the company is battling for customer loyalty and retention. The problem for all these banks is that another such network, CheckFree Holdings Corp., already exists. This giant already had signed up three million consumers, 1,000 business, and 350 financial institutional customers when Spectrum was established. Chase fears not getting a piece of that payment business. If that were to happen, Chase's management fears, Chase would not be able to compete, and their clients' ties to the bank will be weakened.

In more than one venture Chase has even gone into competition with itself—in order to capture or maintain business that is migrating to the Internet. For example, although Chase has its own on-line mortgage site, Chase Manhattan Mortgage, it has partnered with Microsoft to create HomeAdvisor on-line.

Chase.com's July 2000 RFP, which was directed at ASPs, said, "Chase.com's objective is to have international Web sites in place in all of its major international locations by spring 2001." They want a few regional sites, at least in Brazil, Hong Kong, Japan, and the United Kingdom, all connected to Chase.com's headquarters in New York City (Chase already has its own sites in Brazil and Hong Kong, but they only offer basic information about services available in regional offices). Ultimately, Chase's goal is to offer to international business customers the same on-line facilities they offer businesses within the United States, such as access to corporate account information. An investment bank portal, on-line portfolio management, funds-transfer service, and international currency exchange capabilities would also be desirable. Chase's international customers are almost exclusively business and private institutional clients. (Chase is not chartered to offer consumer banking services outside the United States.)

The international Web sites are to be in the local, native languages, and their content is to be synchronized with Chase's domestic business sites. Chase will not accept auto-translation, because the translations can be very awkward. Local Web site administrators in international locations will be notified automatically when any content changes are made on the Chase.com U.S. Web site. Once notified, the administrators can decide whether to update the content immediately or schedule the update for a later time. As of this writing Chase can be found operating in 180 countries on all six inhabited continents.

Chase management has made clear that it wants to avoid the possible future loss of even one international business or institutional customer because such a loss might negatively impact revenue growth. Chase's Global Services currently moves trillions of dollars in securities and cash across international borders every day. Competitors such as Citibank and Hong Kong's Shanghai Banking Corporation already offer on-line services for their international institutional clients. To nurture its good and trusted banking name, Chase has made its number one project priority the maintenance of both security and professionalism. Thus the RFP specifies that the "principal requirement . . . is drum-tight security." It further stipulates that "The hosted systems will serve as a pass-through for banking information, which means that the systems won't house any customer data." The data will be maintained on Chase's own computers where the ASP cannot access them. Strong operational and change control procedures are essential.

The Chase.com Web sites will have to supply interfaces to Chase.com's back-end systems. These back-end systems, which process and maintain client transactions, run on IBM mainframes, AS/400 midrange computers, and Tandem and Windows NT clusters. Data are stored on Oracle databases. Chase.com's U.S. Web servers run on hardware that uses either the Windows NT or Unix operating system. Chase.com uses search engine technology from Verity Inc. and content management software from Open Market Inc.

Given the importance of security, why is Chase turning to outsourcing? Management claims that when banking customers use self-service software, there's a heavy need for back-end support that requires additional staff. However, Chase.com has stressed its need to keep its own staff limited. Its operations model is to outsource noncore services like Web servers, search engines, domain name system servers, and MIS capabilities. Chase's job is to design, develop, implement, and optimize the business applications that need to be linked to these noncore services. Chase thinks an ASP will be better able to hire top-notch technical personnel. Interestingly, Chase.com made clear in the RFP that the size and culture of the partner is also important. "Chase.com is looking to partner with a large-scale, established ASP, but one not too bureaucratic."

**Sources:** Riva D. Atlas, "Ambitious Plans at Chase Manhattan," *The New York Times,* February 8, 2001; Steven Lipin, Jathan Sapsford, Paul Beckett, and Charles Gasparino, "Chase Agrees to Buy J.P. Morgan & Co. In a Historic Linkup," *The Wall Street Journal,* September 13, 2000; Claudia Graziano, "Chase.com Goes Global," *Information Week,* July 24, 2000; Alorie Gilbert, "Chase.com's Agenda," *Information Week,* May 15, 2000; Chase Manhattan Corp., "Chase.com's RFP Specifics," *Information Week,* July 24, 2000; and "History of the Chase Manhattan Corporation," http://www.chase.com.

### *CASE STUDY QUESTIONS*

1. Evaluate Chase using the competitive forces and value chain models.
2. What were the problems and issues faced by Chase Manhattan that caused the bank to establish Chase.com? Do you think it was the necessary or correct response to establish a semi-independent subsidiary? Explain your answer.
3. What do you think were the reasons that Chase.com decided to turn to an ASP to help it establish itself as a global force in on-line business banking? Was it a correct decision to turn to an outsourcing organization, or would it have been better to develop and run the systems in-house? Explain your response.
4. Acting as the CIO of an ASP, propose a specific system solution for Chase.com. Your analysis should describe the objectives of the solution; the requirements to be met by the new system (or series of systems); and the technical, operational, and economic feasibility of your proposal. Include an overview of the systems you would recommend and explain how those systems would address the problems listed in your analysis. Your analysis should consider organizational and management issues to be addressed by the solution as well as technology issues.
5. If you were the ASP's systems analyst for this project, list five questions you would ask Chase Manhattan and Chase.com users during interviews to elicit the information you need for your systems study report.

# Part V Project

# Assessing the Total Cost of Ownership (TCO) of a Web Site

Your advertising company has about 65 employees and you would like to set up a Web site originally devoted to attracting new clients by advertising and showcasing your work. Most of your work consists of printed magazine advertisements and television commercials. You have not yet established a presence on the Web. You have been asked to prepare an estimate of how much it would cost to establish and operate your own Web site for two years.

At first your company will not be selling anything. Instead, it will be displaying about 400 Web pages showing samples of your ads, with photographs, line art, text, and short video clips. It will also include links to customer Web sites (for those customers who agree to be linked). The site should have the capability of accepting on-line requests for additional information from visitors and should display information about how to contact the company by telephone, e-mail, or conventional mail. You anticipate your Web site will require two gigabytes of storage to start. You also anticipate a maximum of 50 concurrent visitors at first.

You have been instructed that your company will almost certainly want to expand usage of the site in the future, perhaps actually selling ads through the Net, or perhaps using the site for working together with existing clients. You have been asked to provide a solution that can handle other possible future uses as well.

To carry out this task, use the Web to find the information you need to complete your assignment. Use several search engines to locate a quality overview describing the process of building a Web site. You will need information on the most fundamental item, the Web server. After selecting and pricing Web server software, you will need to price the cost of hardware, personnel, and other software required to run your Web site. Your employees are already equipped with desktop computers running Windows 2000, which they use for their work. Your Web site will need its own dedicated server along with appropriate software, networking, and human resources, and you would like to use hardware and software that works with your existing computing environment. Your management does not want to install content management or personalization tools at this time.

To calculate the Total Cost of Ownership (TCO) of creating and operating your Web site, you should consider the following cost components (and any others you determine will be necessary):

- Web server software.
- Computer hardware to house your Web site.
- Operating system software.
- Web site development software for creating your Web site.
- Software to analyze the performance of your Web site, including analysis of Web site traffic and analysis of links between Web pages.
- Firewall and antivirus software.
- Web site design and creation costs, including the following:
  a. Cost to design and set up the original Web site. (A Web site development firm has agreed to do this work for $15,000.)
  b. Initial Web page layouts, including custom graphics, photographs, line art, audio, and video elements. Your firm can use its own staff to create these pages at a cost of $200 per page.
  c. Domain name registration fee.
  d. Development of search engine keywords to direct visitors to your site and to register with search engines.
- Ongoing maintenance costs. Costs to update the Web site, change existing pages, and create new pages. Your company estimates making changes to eight pages per month. Your company does not anticipate additional hardware or software upgrades for the next two years.
- Additional personnel costs:
  a. A marketing specialist in charge of Web site content.
  b. An information systems specialist to maintain the Web site.
  c. Training of current and new staff, estimated at 15 people requiring 10 hours each annually.
- Additional monthly telephone expenses for the cost of a leased T1 line.

To research this topic, again use Web search engines. You may also find some of these sites helpful:

**Web Servers**

Picking the Right Web Server (http://www.microtimes.com/183/webserver.html)

Planning for Your Web Server (http://www.ucfv.bc.ca/cis/merzv/COMP355/Class%20Notes/Comp_355_Lesson2_Planning_web_server.htm)

The Best Bets for Web Development (http://www.nwc.com/1020/1020f1.html)

Netcraft Web Site Finder (http://www.netcraft.com/)

Serving Up Web Server Basics (http://webcompare.internet.com/webbasics/index.html)

Web Server Compare: The Definitive Guide to Web Server and HTTP Specs (http://webcompare.internet.com/)

Apache Project (http://www.apache.org/httpd.html)

Microsoft Internet Information Services Features (http://www.microsoft.com/windows2000/guide/server/features/web.asp)

Netscape Enterprise Server (http://home.netscape.com/enterprise/v3.6/)

**Operating System Software**

Microsoft (www.microsoft.com)

Sun (www.sun.com)

Linux (www.linux.org)

**Hardware**

IBM (www.ibm.com)

Dell (www.dell.com)

Sun (www.sun.com)

Compaq (www.compaq.com)

**Web Site Development Software**

Microsoft FrontPage (www.microsoft.com)

Dreamweaver (www.macromedia.com)

Cold Fusion (www.allaire.com)

PageMill (www.adobe.com)

Netscape Composer (www.netscape.com)

**Web Site Analysis Software**

Webtrends (www.webtrends.com)

Summary.net (www.summary.net)

Web Site Tools (www.web-site-tools.com)

**Firewall Software**

Check Point Software Technologies (www.checkpoint.com)

Cyberguard (www.cyberguard.com)

Symantec (www.symantec.com)

BorderWare Firewall Server (www.borderware.de)

**Antivirus Software**

Symantec (www.symantec.com)

IBM (www.ibm.com)

McAfee (www.mcafee.com)

**Personnel Costs**

CareerMosaic.com

Monster.com

Headhunter.net

# INTERNATIONAL CASE STUDY

## CASE STUDY 1: GINORMOUS LIFE INSURANCE COMPANY

*Len Fertuck, University of Toronto (Canada)*

Ginormous Life is an insurance company with a long tradition. The company has four divisions that each operate their own computers. The IS group provides analysis, design, and programming services to all of the divisions. The divisions are actuarial, marketing, operations, and investment. All divisions are located at the corporate headquarters building. Marketing also has field offices in 20 cities across the country.

- **The Actuarial Division** is responsible for the design and pricing of new kinds of policies. They use purchased industry data and weekly summaries of data obtained from the Operations Division. They have their own DEC VAX minicomputer, running the Unix operating system, to store data files. They do most of their analysis on PCs and Sun workstations, either on spreadsheets or with a specialized interactive language called APL.
- **The Marketing Division** is responsible for selling policies to new customers and for follow-up of existing customers in case they need changes to their current insurance. All sales orders are sent to the Operations Division for data entry and billing. They use purchased external data for market research and weekly copies of data from operations for follow-ups. They have their own IBM AS/400 minicomputer with dumb terminals for clerks to enter sales data. There are also many PCs used to analyze market data using statistical packages like SAS.
- **The Operations Division** is responsible for processing all mission-critical financial transactions including payroll. They record all new policies, send regular bills to customers, evaluate and pay all claims, and cancel lapsed policies. They have all their data and programs on two IBM ES/9000 mainframes running under the OS/390 operating system. The programs are often large and complex because they must service not only the 15 products currently being sold but also the 75 old kinds of policies that are no longer being sold but still have existing policy holders. Clerks use dumb terminals to enter and update data. Applications written in the last five years have used an SQL relational database to store data, but most programs are still written in COBOL. The average age of the transaction processing programs is about 10 years.
- **The Investment Division** is responsible for investing premiums until they are needed to pay claims. Their data consist primarily of internal portfolio data and research data obtained by direct links to data services. They have a DEC minicomputer to store their data. The internal data are received by a weekly download of cash flows from the Operations Division. External data are obtained as needed. They use PCs to analyze data obtained either from the mini or from commercial data services.

A controlling interest in Ginormous Life has recently been purchased by Financial Behemoth Corp. The management of Financial Behemoth has decided that the firm's efficiency and profitability must be improved. Their first move has been to put Dan D. Mann, a hotshot information systems specialist from Financial Behemoth, in charge of the Information Systems Division. He has been given the objective of modernizing and streamlining the computer facilities without any increase in budget.

In the first week on the job, Dan discovered that only seven junior members of the staff of 200 information systems specialists know anything about CASE tools, End-User Computing, or LANs. They have no experience in implementing PC systems. There is no evidence of any formal decision-support systems or executive information systems in the organization. New applications in the last five years have been implemented in COBOL on DB2, a relational database product purchased from IBM. Over two-thirds of applications are still based on COBOL flat files. One of the benefits of using DB2 is that it is now possible to deliver reports quickly based on ad hoc queries. This is creating a snowballing demand for conversion of more systems to a relational database so that other managers can get similar service.

There have been some problems with the older systems. Maintenance is difficult and costly because almost every change to the data structure of applications in operations requires corresponding changes to applications in the other divisions. There has been a growing demand in other divisions for faster access to operations data. For instance the Investment Division claims that they could make more profitable investments if they had continuous access to the cash position in operations. Marketing complains that they get calls from clients about claims and cannot answer them because they do not have current access to the status of the claim. Management wants current access to a wide variety of data in summary form so they can get a better understanding of the business. The IS group says that it would be difficult to provide access to data in operations because of security considerations. It is difficult to ensure that users do not make unauthorized changes to the COBOL files.

The IS group complains that they cannot deliver all the applications that users want because they are short-staffed. They spend 90 percent of their time maintaining the existing systems. The programmers are mostly old and experienced and employee turnover is unusually low, so there is not likely to be much room for improvement by further training in programming. Employees often remark that the company is a very pleasant and benevolent place to work. At least they did until rumors of deregulation and foreign competition started to sweep the industry.

Dan foresees that there will be an increasing need for computer capacity as more and more applications are converted to on-line transaction processing and more users begin to make ad hoc queries. Dan is also wondering if intranets or the Internet should become part of any new software.

Dan began to look for ways to solve the many problems of the Information Systems Division. He solicited proposals from various vendors and consultants in the computer industry. After a preliminary review of the proposals, Dan was left with three broad options suggested by IBM, Oracle Corp., and Datamotion, a local consulting firm. The proposals are briefly described below.

**IBM proposes an integrated solution** using IBM hardware and software. The main elements of the proposal are

- **Data and applications will remain on a mainframe.** The IBM ES/9000 series of hardware running their OS/390 operating system will provide mainframe services. Mainframe hardware capacity will have to be approximately doubled by adding two more ES/9000 series machines. The four machines will run under OS/390 with Parallel Sysplex clustering technology that allows for future growth. The Parallel Sysplex system can be scaled by connecting up to 32 servers to work in parallel and be treated as a single system for scheduling and system management. The OS/390 operating system can also run Unix applications.
- **AS/400 minicomputers running under the OS/400 operating system** will replace DEC minicomputers.
- **RS/6000 workstations running AIX**—a flavor of the Unix operating system—can be used for actuarial computations. All hardware will be interconnected with IBM's proprietary SNA network architecture. PCs will run under the OS/2 operating system and the IBM LAN Server to support both Microsoft Windows applications and locally designed applications that communicate with mainframe databases.
- **A DB2 relational database will store all data on-line.** Users will be able to access any data they need through their terminals or through PCs that communicate with the mainframe.
- **Legacy systems will be converted using reengineering tools,** like Design Recovery and Maintenance Workbench from Intersolv, Inc. These will have the advantage that they will continue to use the COBOL code that the existing programmers are familiar with. New work will be done using CASE tools with code generators that produce COBOL code.
- **Proven technology.** The IBM systems are widely used by many customers and vendors. Many mission-critical application programs are available on the market that address a wide variety of business needs.

**Oracle Corp. proposed that all systems be converted to use their Oracle database** product and its associated screen and report generators. They said that such a conversion would have the following advantages:

- **Over 90 hardware platforms are supported.** This means that the company is no longer bound to stay with a single hardware vendor. Oracle databases and application programs can be easily moved from one manufacturer's machine to another manufacturer's machine by a relatively simple export and import operation as long as applications are created with Oracle tools. Thus the most economical hardware platform can be used for the application. Oracle will also access data stored in an IBM DB2 database.
- **Integrated CASE tools and application generators.** Oracle has its own design and development tools called Designer/2000 and Developer/2000. Applications designed with Designer/2000 can be automatically created for a wide variety of terminals or for the World Wide Web. The same design can be implemented in Windows, on a Macintosh, or on X-Windows in Unix. Applications are created using graphic tools that eliminate the need for a language like COBOL. The designer works entirely with visual prototyping specifications.
- **Vertically integrated applications.** Oracle sells a number of common applications, like accounting programs, that can be used as building blocks in developing a complete system. These applications could eliminate the need to redevelop some applications.
- **Distributed network support.** A wide variety of common network protocols like SNA, DecNet, Novell, and TCP/IP are supported. Different parts of the database can be distributed to different machines on the network and accessed or updated by any application. All data are stored on-line for instant access. The data can be stored on one machine and the applications can be run on a different machine, including a PC or workstation, to provide a client/server environment. The ability to distribute a database allows a large database on an expensive mainframe to be distributed to a number of cheaper minicomputers.

**Datamotion proposed a data warehouse approach** using software tools from Information Builders Inc. Existing applications would be linked using EDA, a middleware data warehouse server that acts as a bridge between the existing data files and the users performing enquiries. New applications would be developed using an application tool called Cactus. The advantages of this approach are:

- **Data Location Transparency.** EDA Hub Server provides a single connection point from which applications can access multiple data sources anywhere in the enterprise. In addition, users can join data between any supported EDA database—locally, cross-server, or cross-platform. Users can easily access remote data sources for enhanced decision-making capabilities.
- **The EDA server can reach most nonrelational databases** and file systems through its SQL translation engine. EDA also supports 3GL, 4GL, static SQL, CICS, IMS/TM, and proprietary database stored procedure processing.
- **Extensive network and operating system support.** EDA supports 14 major network protocols and provides protocol translation between dissimilar networks. EDA also runs on 35 different processing platforms. EDA servers support optimized SQL against any RDBMS. And the EDA server can automatically generate the dialect of SQL optimal for the targeted data source. It is available on Windows 3.x, Windows 95/98, Windows NT, OS/2, MVS, Unix, CICS, VM, OpenVMS, Tandem, and AS/400.

- **Comprehensive Internet Support.** With EDA's Internet services, users can issue requests from a standard Web browser to any EDA-supported data source and receive answer sets formatted as HTML pages.
- **Cactus promotes modern development methods.** Cactus allows the developer to partition an application, keeping presentation logic, business logic, and data access logic separate. This partitioning of functionality can occur across a large number of enterprise platforms to allow greater flexibility in achieving scalability, performance, and maintenance. Cactus provides all the tools needed to deal with every aspect of developing, testing, packaging, and deploying client/server traditional applications or Web-based applications.

Dan is not sure which approach to take for the future of Ginormous Life. Whichever route he follows, the technology will have an enormous impact on the kinds of applications his staff will be able to produce in the future and the way in which they will produce them. While industry trends toward downsizing and distribution of systems may eventually prove to be more efficient, Dan's staff does not have much experience with the new technologies that would be required. He is uncertain about whether there will be a sufficient payoff to justify the organizational turmoil that will result from a major change in direction. Ideally he would like to move quickly to a modern client/server system with minimal disturbance to existing staff and development methods, but he fears that both of these are not simultaneously possible.

**Source:** Reprinted by permission of Len Fertuck, University of Toronto, Canada.

### *CASE STUDY QUESTIONS*

Dan must prepare a strategy for the renewal of the Information Systems Division over the next three years. As his assistant, prepare an outline, in point form, containing the following items:

1. A list of factors or issues that must be considered in selecting a technology platform for the firm.
2. Weights for each factor obtained by dividing up 100 points among the factors in proportion to their importance.
3. A score from 0 to 10 of how each of the three proposals performs on each factor.
4. A grand score for each proposal obtained by summing the product of the proposal score times the factor weight for each proposal.
5. The technology that you would recommend that Dan adopt and the reason for choosing the particular technology that you recommend.
6. The order in which each component of the technology should be introduced and the reason for selecting the order.

# INTERNATIONAL CASE STUDY

## CASE STUDY 2: FROM ANALYSIS TO EVALUATION—THE EXAMPLE OF CUPARLA

*Gerhard Schwabe, University of Koblenz—Landau (Germany)*

### *Analysis and Design*

Just like in other towns, members of the Stuttgart City Council have a large workload: In addition to their primary profession (e.g., as an engineer at Daimler Benz) they devote more than 40 hours a week to local politics. This extra work has to be done under fairly unfavorable conditions. Only council sessions and party meetings take place in the city hall; the deputies of the local council do not have an office in the city hall to prepare or coordinate their work. This means, for example, that they have to read and file all official documents at home. In a city with more than 500,000 inhabitants they receive a very large number of documents. Furthermore, council members feel that they could be better informed by the administration and better use could be made of their time. Therefore Hohenheim University and partners* launched the Cuparla project to improve the information access and collaboration of council members.

A detailed analysis of their work revealed the following characteristics of council work:

- Since council members are very mobile, support has to be available to them any time and in any place.
- Council members collaborate and behave differently in different contexts: While they act informally and rather open in the context of their own party, they behave more controlled and formal in official council sessions.
- A closer investigation of council work reveals a low degree of process structure. Every council member has the right of initiative and can inform and involve other members and members of the administration in any order.
- Council members rarely are power computer users. Computer support for them has to be very straightforward and intuitive to use.

When designing computer support we initially had to decide on the basic orientation of our software. We soon abandoned a workflow model as there are merely a few steps and there is little order in the collaboration of local politicians. Imposing a new structure into this situation would have been too restrictive for the council members. We then turned to pure document-orientation, imposing no structure at all on the council members' work. We created a single large database with all the documents any member of the city council ever needs. However, working with this database turned out to be too complex for the council members. In addition, they need to control the access to certain documents at all stages of the decision-making process. For example, a party may not want to reveal a proposal to other parties before it has officially been brought up in the city council. Controlling access to each document individually and changing the access control list was not feasible.

Therefore, the working context was chosen as a basis of our design. Each working context of a council member can be symbolized by a "room." A private office corresponds to the council member working at home; there is a party room, where he collaborates with his party colleagues, and a committee room symbolises the place for committee meetings. In addition, there is a room for working groups, a private post office, and a library for filed information. All rooms hence have an electronic equivalent in the Cuparla software. When a council member opens the Cuparla software, he sees all the rooms from the entrance hall (Figure 1).

The council member creates a document in one room (e.g., his private office) and then shares it with other council members in other rooms. If he moves a document into the room of his party, he shares it with his party colleagues; if he hands it on to the administration, he shares it with the mayors, administration officials, and all council members.

The interface of the electronic rooms resembles the setup of the original rooms. Figure 2 shows the example of the room for a parliamentary party. On the left hand side of the screen there are document locations, whereas, on the right hand side, the documents of the selected location are presented. Documents that are currently being worked on are displayed on the "desk." These documents have the connotation that they need to be worked on without an additional outside trigger. If a document is in the files, it belongs to a topic that is still on the political agenda. However, a trigger is necessary to move it off of the shelf. If a topic is not on the political agenda any more, all documents belonging to it are moved to the archive.

The other locations support the collaboration within the party. The conference desk contains all documents for the next (weekly) party meeting. Any council member of the party can put documents there. When a council member prepares for the meeting, he or she merely has to check the conference desk for relevant information. The mailbox for the chairman contains all documents that the chairman needs to decide on. In contrast to his e-mail account all members have access to the mailbox. Double work is avoided as every council member is aware of the chairman's agenda. The mailbox of the assistant contains tasks for the party assistants; the mailbox for the secretary, assignments for the secretary (e.g., a draft for a letter). The inbox contains documents that have been moved from other rooms into this room.

**Figure 1** Entrance hall

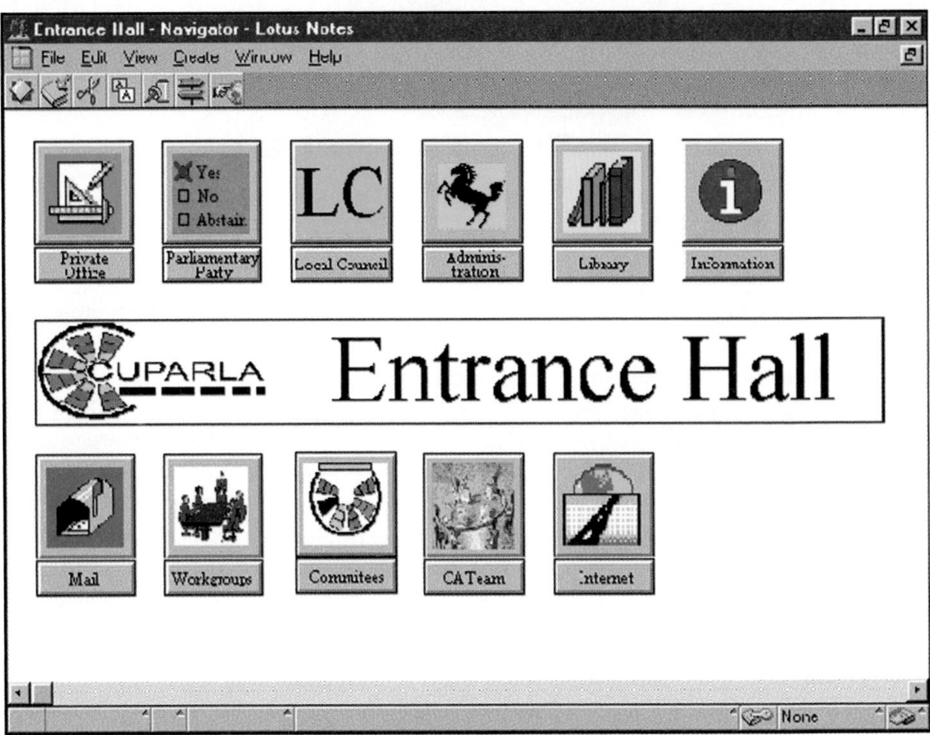


Thus, in the electronic room all locations correspond to the current manual situation. Council members do not have to relearn their work. Instead, they collaborate in the shared environment they are accustomed to with shared expectations about the other peoples' behaviour. Feedback from the pilot users indicates that this approach is appropriate.

Some specific design features make the software easy to use. The software on purpose does not have a fancy three-dimensional interface that has the same look as a real room. Buttons (in the entrance hall) and lists (in the rooms) are much easier to use and do not distract the user from the essential parts. Each location (e.g., the desk) has a little arrow. If a user clicks on this arrow, a document is moved to the location. This operation is much easier for a beginner than proceeding by "drag and drop."

Furthermore, software design is not restricted to building an electronic equivalent of a manual situation. If one wants to truly

**Figure 2** Parliamentary party room

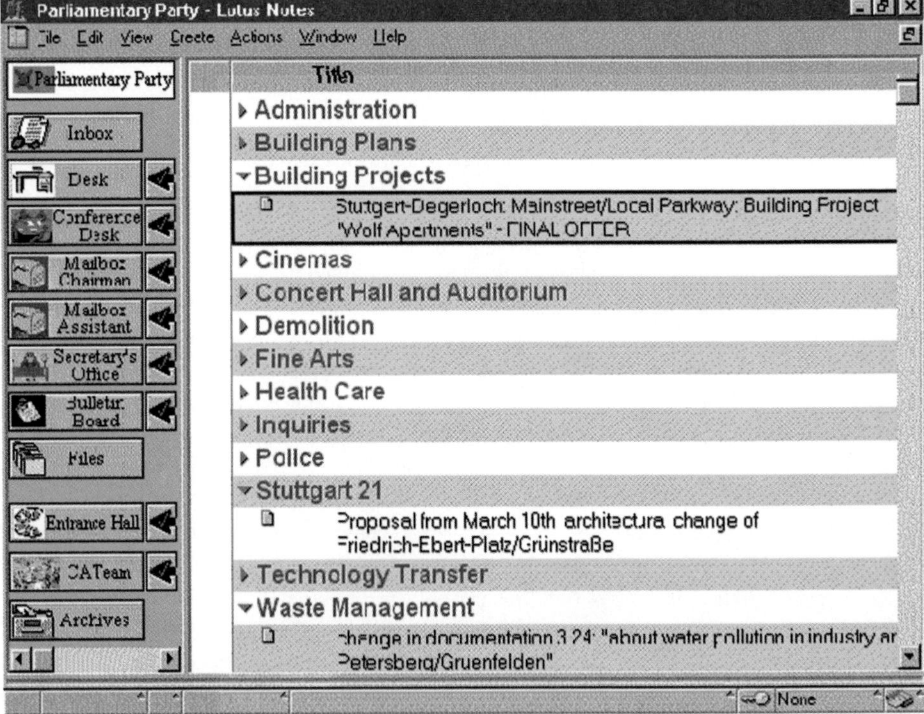

benefit from the opportunities of electronic collaboration support systems, one has to include new tools that are not possible in the manual setting. For example, additional cross-location and room search features are needed to make it easy for the council member to retrieve information. The challenge of interface design is to give the user a starting point that is close to the situation he is used to. A next step is to provide the user with options to improve and adjust his working behavior to the opportunities offered by the use of a computer.

## *Organizational Implementation*

Building the appropriate software is only one success factor for a groupware project. Organizational implementation typically is at least as difficult. Groupware often has a free rider problem: All want to gain the benefit and nobody wants to do the work. Furthermore, many features are only beneficial if all participate actively. For example, if a significant part of a council faction insists on using paper documents for their work, providing and sharing electronic documents actually means additional work for the others. This can easily lead to the situation that groupware usage never really gets started. To "bootstrap" usage we started with the (socially) simple activities and ended with the (socially) complex activities (Figure 3).

In the first step we provided the basic council information in digital form. The city council has the power to demand this initial organizational learning process from the administration. Once there is sufficient information the individual council member can already benefit from the system without relying on the usage of his fellow councillors. The usage conventions are therefore socially simple. As better information is a competitive advantage for a council member, there was an incentive for the individual effort required to learn the system. Communication support (e-mail, fax) is a more complex process, because its success depends on reliable usage patterns by all communication partners. The usage patterns are straightforward and easy to learn. We therefore implemented them in a second phase. Coordination activities (sharing to-do lists, sharing calendars) and cooperation activities (sharing documents and room locations, electronic meetings) depend on the observance of socially complex usage conventions by all group members. For example, the council member had to learn that her activities had effects on the documents and containers of all others and that "surprises" typically resulted from ill-coordinated activities of several group members. The council has to go through an intensive organizational learning process to benefit from the features. For example, the party's business processes had to be reorganized.

We offered collaboration and coordination support in the same phase to the council members. Their appropriation depended on the party's culture: A hierarchically organized party preferred to use the coordination features and requested to turn off many collaborative features. In another party most councillors had equal rights. This party preferred the collaborative features.

***Figure 3*** Steps of groupware implementation

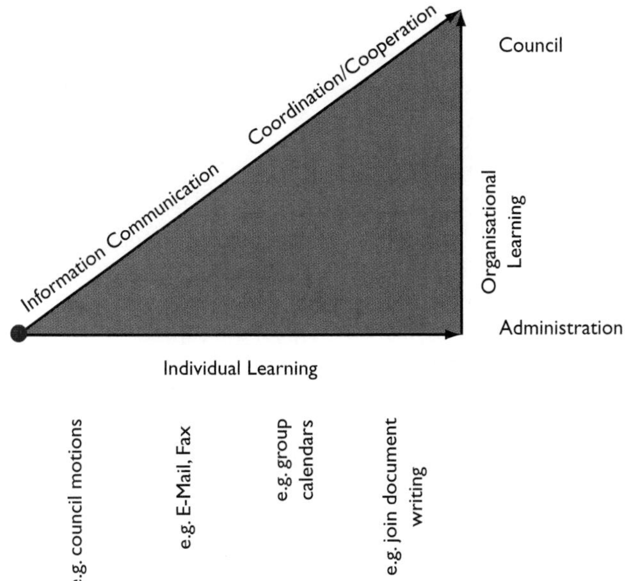


## *Economic Benefits*

The ultimate success of any IS project is not only determined by the quality of the developed technology but also by its economic benefits. Thus, the economic benefit of Cuparla was evaluated in the first quarter of 1998 after about four months of use by the whole city council (pilot users had been using the system for more than a year). Evaluating the economic benefits of innovative software is notoriously difficult. Reasons for that include

1. It is difficult to attribute costs to a single project. For example, the city of Stuttgart had to wire part of their city hall for Cuparla—is this a cost of the project? And how about the servers bought for Cuparla and co-used for other purposes? And the cost for the information that was collected for the city council and is now being used in the administration's intranet?
2. Many benefits cannot be quantified in monetary terms. For instance, how much is it worth if the council members make better informed decisions? Or, how much is it worth if council membership becomes more attractive?
3. What is the appropriate level of aggregation for economic benefits? Should it be the cost and benefit for the individual council member? Or the parties? Or the whole city council? Or even the whole city of Stuttgart? Or should the improved processes be measured?

The evaluation of Cuparla was therefore not based on purely monetary terms; rather evaluation results were aggregated on five sets of criteria (cost, time, quality, flexibility, and human situation) and four levels of aggregation (individual, group, process, organization) resulting in a 4 × 5 matrix (Figure 4).

The trick is to attribute the effects only to the lowest possible level, e.g., if one can attribute the cost of an individual PC to an individual council member, it counts only there and not on the group level. On the other hand, a server probably can only be attributed to the group of all council members and so on. We will now briefly go through the major effects:

**Costs:** Both on the individual and the group level costs have gone up significantly (notebooks, ISDN, printer, server,

*Figure 4* Aggregated evaluation of Cuparla (March 1998)

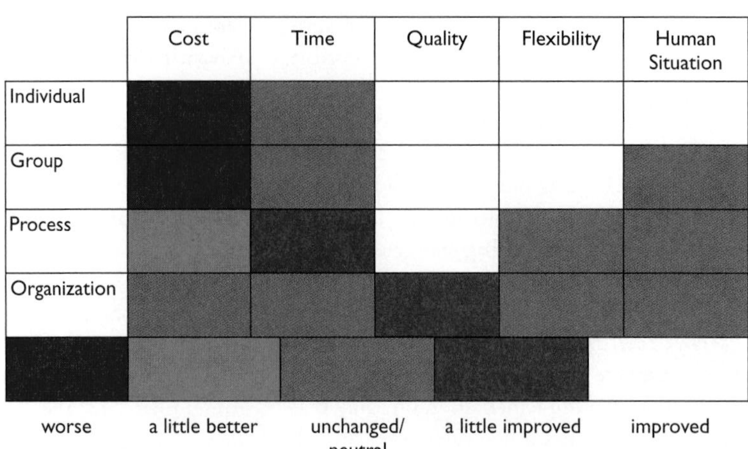


etc.). There is a potential for cost savings if the council members forgo the delivery of paper copies of the documents. There have been some additional costs on the process level, but not as much as on the two levels below. There may have been direct cost savings by the provision of electronic documents in the council-related business processes, but we were not able to identify them. As the administration was reluctant to really reorganize its internal business processes, many potential cost savings could not be realized. As all costs could be attributed to the levels business process, group or individual, we noted a cost neutrality for the level "organization" (the costs for provisionally wiring the city hall were negligible).

**Time:** During the pilot phase, the system did not save time for the councillors; to the contrary, the individual councillors had to work longer in order to learn how to use the Cuparla system. However, the councillors also indicated that they used their time more productively, i.e., the overtime was well invested. Thus, we decided to summarize the effects on the individual level as "neutral." Cuparla had also not yet led to faster or more efficient decisions in the council or its subgroups. Therefore the effects are graded "unchanged." The council members see potential here, but the speed of decisions is not only a matter of work efficiency but also has a political dimension and politics does not change that fast. Some business processes were rated as being faster, particularly the processes at the interface between council and administration (e.g., the process of writing the meeting minutes). There was no effect on the organization as a whole; i.e., the city of Stuttgart was not faster at reacting to external challenges and opportunities.

**Quality:** The council members reported a remarkable improvement of quality of their work. The council members feel that the quality of their decisions has been improved by the much better access to information. The work of the parties has benefited from the e-mail and the collaboration features of Cuparla as well as the computer support of strategic party meetings. As the interface between different subprocesses of council work has fewer media changes and the (partially erroneous) duplication of information has been reduced, the council members and members of the administration also reported an improved quality of their business processes. The creation of an organization-wide database of council-related information even contributed to a somewhat better work in the whole administration.

**Flexibility:** Improved individual flexibility was the most important benefit of Cuparla. This holds true for spatial, temporal, and interpersonal flexibility. People can work and access other people any place and any time they want. On the group level Cuparla has enhanced the flexibility within parties as it has become easier to coordinate the actions of the council members. There have not been any significant changes to the flexibility on the process or organizational levels.

**Human situation:** Cuparla has made council membership more attractive because it has become easier to reconcile one's primary job, council work, and private life. Furthermore Cuparla is regarded as an opportunity for the council member's individual development. There were no significant changes to the human situation on the group, process, or organizational levels.

As mentioned above, these effects were measured after a relatively short period of usage. By the time of writing this case study, (January 2000), Cuparla had become an indispensable part of council work. When the system was down for a week in the beginning of 2000 because of router problems, the council members were so annoyed that the local newspaper reported their unanimous complaint in a committee meeting.

## Additional English Literature

**Schwabe, G., and Krcmar, H.** "Digital Material in a Political Work Context—The Case of Cuparla." Appears in the *Proceedings of the European Conference on Information Systems,* ECIS 2000 in Vienna.

**Schwabe, G., and Krcmar, H.** "Piloting a Sociotechnical Innovation." Appears in the *Proceedings of the European Conference on Information Systems,* ECIS 2000 in Vienna.

**Schwabe, G.** "Understanding and Supporting Knowledge Management and Organizational Memory in a City Council." In Hawaii International Conference on System Sciences 1999 (HICSS99), CD-ROM, 12 pages.

**Schwabe, G., and Krcmar, H.** "Electronic Meeting Support for Councils." Appears in *Journal of AI and Society,* 1999.

## *CASE STUDY QUESTIONS*

1. Analyze the management, organization, and technology issues that had to be addressed by the Cuparla project.
2. Analyze the interface and design of the Cuparla system. What problems does it solve? What organizational processes does it support? How effective is it?
3. How successful was the Cuparla project? Describe the implementation issues, costs, and benefits.

**Source:** From "Analysis to Interface Design—The Example of Cuparla," by Gerhard Schwabe, Stephen Wilczek, and Helmut Krcmar. Reprinted by permission.

*The project partners were Hohenheim University (Coordinator), Datenzentrale Baden-Württemberg and GroupVision Softwaresysteme GmbH. The project was funded as part of its R&D program by DeTeBerkom GmbH, a 100% subsidiary of German Telekom.

# INTERNATIONAL CASE STUDY

## CASE STUDY 3: CITIBANK ASIA PACIFIC: MANAGING INFORMATION TECHNOLOGY CONSOLIDATION, CHANGE, AND NEW CHALLENGES

*Christina Soh and Neo Boon Siong, Information Management Research Center (IMARC), Nanyang Business School, Nanyang Technological University (Singapore)*

### *I. Citicorp*

> Citicorp in 1991 recorded a net loss of $457 million,[1] suspended the dividend on its common stock, and saw the price of that stock fall to a long-time low before rebounding after year end. Nevertheless, and despite the magnitude of our problems, 1991 for Citicorp was in key respects a transitional, turnaround year.

John Reed, Citicorp's chairman, acknowledged Citicorp's problems in his letter to stockholders in the 1991 annual report. The bank had been struggling with a large Third World loan portfolio, as well as significant problems with its commercial property loans, and with its financing of highly leveraged transactions in the U.S. The bank needed more equity but Third World debt costs prevented Citicorp from increasing its equity through retention of earnings.

The severe storms that Citicorp had been subjected to prompted significant changes. To combat the slowdown in revenue growth, and the rise in consumer and credit write-offs, Citicorp aggressively reduced expenses in order to improve the operating margin, issued stock to improve their capital ratio, and made structural changes at the senior executive level which were aimed at providing more focused direction to the business. John Reed articulated three requirements for being a "great bank in the 1990s"—meeting customer needs, having financial strength, and "marshalling human and **technological** resources . . . **more imaginative and cost-effectively** than one's competitors" (emphasis added).

In the midst of this organizational turbulence, one of Citicorp's undisputed strengths was its global presence. It is unrivalled in its network of banks in more than 90 countries. Its overseas consumer banking operations in particular, were showing healthy growth. Global consumer banking includes mortgage and insurance business and non-U.S. credit card business. Citicorp only entered the field of consumer banking in the mid-70s. John Reed's vision was to pursue growth in the consumer banking area, and to pursue it through global expansion and leveraging information technology.

The primary vision in consumer banking is "Citibanking"—combining relationship banking with technology that enables Citibank to serve its customers anywhere anytime with the high standard of service that they receive in their home countries. In the early 1990s, this involved technology-enabled innovations such as having a one-stop account opening with paperless relationship opening, instant card and check issuance, and instant account availability; having a customer relationship database that supports cross-product relationships; creation of hybrid and customized products; and relationship pricing that more closely matches the value to the customer. The Citicard is the "key" to Citibanking services such as checking, money market, and bankcard accounts. Consumer banking products are distributed through bank branches, Citicard centres, and Citiphone banking, which gives 24-hour, 7-day-a-week service. The global services available to customers were augmented in 1991 when Citibank joined the CIRRUS ATM network, allowing Citicard holders access to cash around the world.

Today, the Internet provides another channel for delivery of Citibank services and products, and the Citibanking strategy now includes ensuring that the bank is "one mile, one phone call, or one click" away from anyone on earth.[2] The multiple delivery channels has also led Citibank to emphasize consistency of experience for all customers by establishing design standards to ensure that every Citibank access point is instantly recognizable.[3] The Citibanking concept has also evolved to include building lifelong relationships by providing product sets to match customers' needs at each stage of their financial lives[4]—"offering all the banking products needed as young people complete their education, enter the workforce, establish a household, rear a family, and eventually retire. . . ."[5]

The results of operating and structural changes made in the early 1990s, as well as the impact of the growing Asian consumer market, contributed to the turnaround at Citicorp, where the 1992 net earning was $772 million. This earned it an A minus credit rating from Standard and Poor, which also upgraded the bank's outlook from negative to stable. Citicorp share price also moved up to $36.88 during 1993, from a low of $23 in 1990. In early 1994, the bank was also given permission by the U.S. regulatory agency to resume issuing dividends. By the end of 1997, the share price had risen to $126, and net income in 1998 was $5.8b.[6]

In 1998, Citicorp merged with Travelers to form Citigroup. Each brings to Citigroup complementary products and services—Citicorp's strengths are in consumer and corporate banking, and Traveler's strengths are in insurance, securities, and investment banking. Their combined customer list is 100m and the "stretch target" is 1 billion customers by 2010.[7] In 1999, Citigroup had almost $10b in net incomes worldwide, and its stock has risen 63%.[8]

## *II. Citibank in Asia Pacific*

Citicorp has been in Asia since 1902 when it set up finance houses in a number of Asian ports, such as Shanghai and Singapore. It has built up an understanding of the local markets in which it operates. Citicorp's major competitors in terms of established presence throughout Asia are Hong Kong and Shanghai Bank, and Standard Chartered Bank, but neither has the global reach that Citicorp offers.

Citibank began pursuing consumer banking in earnest in 1986, and since then Asian accounts have increased from 1 million to 6 million in 1997. Asian consumer deposits grew sixfold to $13.6 billion between 1983 and 1992, while loans grew seventeenfold to $10.8 billion over the same period.[9] This growth is a reflection of the region's high gross savings rate (about 35%), and high GNP growth. Critics had suggested that Citicorp may run into credit problems because Asians had little experience with personal debt. Although revenue decreased between 1996 and 1997 due to the Asian financial crisis, there has been strong growth in the customer deposits and accounts.[10] In 1998, accounts increased 19%, and customer deposits 18%.[11] Since then accounts and customer deposits have grown by more than 20% across the Asia Pacific region,[12] continuing to fuel the growth in consumer banking in Citibank.

Citibank made significant innovations in packaging financial services for the relatively rich customer, and has managed to cream the Asian market. They pioneered the concept of consumer credit in Asia, with then innovative offerings such as round-the-clock phone banking and automated teller cards. Interestingly, some innovations such as phone-banking, were motivated by local regulations that severely restricted the number of branches that it may operate. More recent innovations include International Personal Banking, which offers a broad and flexible range of investment opportunities, time deposits, overdraft facilities, and the ability to trade and deposit in any of 18 international currencies. This is to tap the fast-growing offshore banking component of Asian consumer banking.[13]

## *III. Previous Technology Infrastructure*

In the early 1990s, each of Citibank's Asia Pacific countries belonged to one of three automation platforms—MVS, AS/400, or Unix—and had one of two consumer banking applications—COSMOS or CORE. COSMOS was the earlier set of applications, and was fairly typical of most U.S. banks' offshore banking applications. It was written in COBOL in order to provide flexibility in complying with varying regulatory reporting formats, and it provided backroom support for standard areas such as current accounts, general ledger, and some loans processing. Subsequently, Citibank began to replace COSMOS with CORE, which was to provide an all encompassing system to run on IBM's minicomputers, the AS/400s. CORE was used in a number of countries with smaller operations, like Indonesia. It was not suitable for countries, such as India, where IBM did not have a presence, and in countries with high volumes, like Hong Kong. Both COSMOS and CORE were subject to many country-specific modifications over time, as the local banks responded to varying regulatory and business requirements. The wholesale banking division also used COSMOS, and it ran on large IBM mainframes. Over time, the wholesale banking version of COSMOS has also proliferated. The result is significant differences in each country's basic banking software.

The underlying philosophy of customizing to meet local customer needs resulted in each country having its own IT infrastructure and unique applications. While it worked adequately in the past, the local-markets approach did not allow Citibank to integrate its products, services, and information to serve its highly sophisticated, mobile and increasingly demanding global customers. Further, there are substantial economies of scale that may be gained from standardizing and consolidating bank products and processing across the diverse countries of the Asia Pacific region. The key to achieving these goals lay in re-architecting the technology infrastructure that enables the consumer banking business.

## *IV. Regional Card Centre as Prototype of the New Strategy*

A significant piece of Citibank's Asian Pacific IT infrastructure that provided the prototype for subsequent consolidation in consumer banking is the Regional Card Centre. The RCC was set up in Singapore in 1989 to support start-up credit card businesses in South East Asia. Country managers whose credit card data processing was to be centralized demanded exacting performance standards from the centre because of its direct impact on their operating performance. Ajit Kanagasundram, who used to run the data centre for Citibank Singapore, was given the mandate to set up and run the centre. He explained the rationale for the centre:

> The purpose of the RCC was to jump-start the credit card businesses in Citibank countries in South East Asia. Setting up the processing infrastructure before offering credit card services in each country would take too long and be too costly for start-up businesses. The time constraint to make the RCC operational also dictated our approach, which was to get the operational software requirements from a couple of lead businesses, in this case, Citibank Hong Kong and Singapore. Trying to get requirements from all countries would be too time consuming and result in missed market opportunities. Further, 80% of credit card operational requirements are stipulated by the card associations and were common across countries. We recruited a few staff experienced in credit card operations, used our own production experience, plus on-site consultants to modify the package software, CARDPAC, and got the RCC operational in eight months.
>
> By 1990, we had reduced the processing cost per credit card by 45% and we were given the mandate to extend our operations to cover the Middle East and North Asia, excluding Hong Kong. By 1994, in the midst of heightened cost consciousness because of corporate financial troubles, our cost per card was down to 32% of the 1989 cost. None of the country managers asked for decentralization of the credit card operations—who wants cost per card to triple overnight?

In 1993, Citibank beat out other regional rivals to become the issuer of affinity Visa and Mastercard for Passages, a joint frequent-flyer program of 15 Asian airlines. Citibank credits its ability to launch and support the cards regionally, enabled by the RCC, as being a key factor for being selected. By 1999, the RCC was processing credit cards for 27 countries—12 countries in Asia, 7 in Central Europe and the Middle East, and 8 in Latin America. The cost economies offered by the RCC made it obvious for countries to join it rather than go on their own. Average costs in 1999 were 40% less than they were 3 years earlier, and it is projected that the marginal cost of adding 5 million cards will be a third of the current average costs. The creation of "starter kits" also means that new countries can be added with relative ease and at far less expense. The decreasing costs of telecommunications and the cost savings from standardizing hardware, software, and procedures enable RCC to reap ever increasing economies of scale as each new country joins its fold, and as businesses of member countries grow.

The RCC concept combines both centralization and decentralization ideas to meet specific local business needs and low costs of processing at the same time. The business strategy, marketing, credit evaluation, and customer service for credit cards continue to be decentralized in each country to cater to local market conditions and needs. The front-end data capture and printing of customer statements are also decentralized to each country. What is centralized is the back-end transaction processing and data repository. The control and active management of credit card businesses continue to be with country managers and the business gains are reflected in the financial performance of each country. The RCC provides the technology infrastructure for lowering operational costs, diffusing best practices, and attracting the needed technical talent.

The RCC experience provided the experiential base for subsequent re-architecting of the technology of the consumer bank. The experience and expertise that RCC had built up would be repositioned to serve the processing requirements of the Asia-Pacific Consumer Bank.

## *V. Re-Architecting the IT Infrastructure*

The appointment of George DiNardo as the new Chief Technology Officer signalled the bank's strategic intent to develop a new technology infrastructure for capitalizing the opportunities from rapid economic growth in Asian countries which is expected to continue well into the twenty-first century. Recipient of **Information Week's** CIO of the Year Award for 1988, DiNardo had been with Mellon Bank in Pittsburgh from 1969 to 1991 and was its executive vice president of their information systems function from 1985 to 1991. Prior to joining Citicorp, he was a consulting partner for Coopers and Lybrand, and professor of information systems at a leading university. He crisply summed up his job portfolio at Citicorp:

> My job is to introduce the most advanced technology possible in Asia and I spent 35 years doing that for other banks, Bankers Trust and Mellon Bank. I am truly a bank businessman and a technologist . . . I have also been given the responsibility for all reengineering efforts in Citibank Asia.

According to George DiNardo, the Citibanking vision requires that

> a customer going anywhere in the world is able to transact the same way wherever he goes. It is moving to (the concept of) Citibank recognizes you, and relationship manages you. If you have $100,000 with Citibank, you have certain services free, and it will be the same wherever you go. It's the ability to use the ATM wherever you are.

Moving toward this level of global banking requires that a Citibank branch anywhere in the world have access to the customer's addresses, customary services, and relationships anywhere else in the world. It would have been costly to achieve this with the current decentralized computing structure, where each country in the Asia Pacific has its own host computer and where each country has a different technology platform. It would also be difficult to ensure simultaneous roll-out across countries of new products. Hence, the foundational changes to computing at Citibank Asia Pacific begin with the centralization of processing, and having a uniform backroom platform. The bank standardized on an IBM MVS platform. DiNardo explained the logic of centralization for Citibank Asia:

> The old days of having the computer centre next to you are gone. Where should your computer centre be—remote! Now, with fibre, put your console, command centre in your main office, and your big box is remote. Our command centre is here in Singapore. . . . The telecommunications are improving enough that we can centralize. The economies of large IBMs are important to banking. I have promised that if we regionalize on a new single system, we will get a saving. It will cost $50m to do this, but we will break even in year two, and we should have a $50m running rate cost reduction at the end of year four. We will put the largest IBM box we can get in a centre in Singapore. I have promised a 10–20% computing reduction every year. How am I going to do that? You buy the biggest building, so you can pull any computer in anytime, backup for 100% uptime, 99.9% on-time completion of batch jobs. Therefore you don't need backup all over Asia. You put in all the other countries account processing, and transmit all the rest.

Initially, the major saving will come from avoiding the building of another computer centre in Hong Kong. Savings arise also from having all processing in one site, with only one other hot backup site, as compared to having processing distributed in 14 countries, with each country having its own backup. Citibank will be leveraging off the networks that are already in place as a result of the regional card centre. Another significant source of savings comes from the centralization of software development.

Citibank is aiming for uniformity in its backroom processing software. Citibank replaced individual country systems that have evolved over time with a $20 million integrated back-office banking applications package from Systematics. The strength of the Systematics package is that it has evolved significantly through its sale to more than 400 banks, and therefore offers many functions and features. It uses a traditional design based on the MVS/CICS/COBOL platform, and has been proven to support high volumes. According to DiNardo, the idea is to not reinvent the wheel by writing yet another in-house back-office processing system, but to take this package and "turn the 2000 Citibank systems professionals loose on innovation . . . its delivery and panache that counts . . . to create reusable modules to be called in through Systematics user exits. Systematics has promised to keep the exits constant through time." The plan also calls for eventual conversion of all other programs to the Systematics format, for example, using the same approach to data modelling, COBOL programming, and naming conventions.

A new Asia-Pacific data center running an IBM ES/9000 model 821 mainframe was set up in Singapore's Science Park on the western part of the island in October 1994. The hot-site backup running an IBM ES/9000 model 500 was located in Singapore's Chai Chee Industrial Park on the eastern part of the island.

The conversion of the Asia Pacific countries to Systematics was completed by the end of 1997. Work then began on Y2k certification. Citibank has one of the more stringent Y2k certification processes in the world, and is estimated to have spent $600m globally over three years on Y2k certification.[14] However, a senior executive noted that Y2k certification was easier and probably less costly in Citibank Asia Pacific because the backend systems had been centralized and standardized prior to the certification process.

## *VI. Building Common Front-End Systems*

Running in parallel with the IT infrastructure changes was a reengineering effort. Peter Mills, then director of business improvement, noted that the goal was to

> create common business processes that may result in common front-end systems that are compatible with our back-end platforms. As part of the re-architecting of Citibank's technology infrastructure, we initiated several process reengineering projects to develop new process templates for Asia-Pacific. For example, we will use the redesigned Australian mortgage process and the new Taiwan auto business process as templates for other countries.

A common thread that emerged from both the reengineering and infrastructural change efforts is the idea of incorporating best practice. In the area of software development, the emphasis on adopting best practice among the Citibank countries is a guard against the common trap of settling for the lowest common denominator in the process of standardization. The commitment to develop a reengineering template incorporating the best redesigned processes from each country, for use in developing common systems is another embodiment of this idea. DiNardo explained what is being practised in Citibank Asia Pacific:

> The purchase of the Systematics package provides the bank with increased functionality and standardized processing without significant systems development effort. In-house development effort will be focused on strategic products such as those for currency trading, Citiplus, and the SABRE front-end teller and platform systems. The approach to future systems development will no longer be one of letting "a hundred flowers bloom." There will no longer be systems development or enhancement only for individual countries. Any country requiring any change needs to convince at least two other countries to support it. Any changes made would then be made for all Citibank countries in Asia. Several countries have now been identified as likely centers of excellence for front-end software development: Taiwan for auto loans processing, Australia for mortgage products, Hong Kong for personal finance products; India, Philippines, and Singapore will become centers for application software development, design, and the generation of high quality code at competitive cost.

The reengineering of business processes in Singapore provides a glimpse of how Citibank intends to introduce best practices in banking products and service delivery, which would be built into common front-end systems. Citibank has been in Singapore for more than 90 years. It started out as a wholesale bank. The consumer bank business was started later in the 1960s. Being a foreign bank, it is allowed to set up only three branches in Singapore. Nonetheless, Citibank has done very well in Singapore. Customer accounts have more than tripled since 1989, largely due to the successful introduction of Citibank's Visa card business. There has been an accompanying tenfold increase in profit in the same period.

The increase in account volume however, has been accomplished without any major increase in staff or changes in processes. Staff, processes, and infrastructure that were originally designed to support about 50,000 accounts are strained when they have to support an account volume of about 250,000. This has contributed to a drop in customers' perception of service levels. Annual surveys conducted indicated that customer satisfaction has dropped from a high of 90% in 1987 to a low of 65% in 1993. Some departments are experiencing high overtime and employee turnover. A cultural assessment study conducted by consultants confirmed that some employees did not feel valued and trusted. Frontline operations were also paper intensive and perceived to have significant opportunities for improvements. In addition, there was the need to achieve the vision of Citibanking, which required cross-product integration as a basis for relationship banking.

The project was carried out in three phases: (1) building the case for action, (2) design, and (3) implementation. In the first two phases, the consultants worked closely with four Citibankers who were assigned full time to the reengineering project. After six months, the team had completed phase two and had come up with a list of 28 recommended process changes. Three core processes were identified for change—delivery of services to the customer, marketing, and transaction processing. The delivery process included account opening and servicing, credit, and customer problem resolution. The team found that it was encumbered with many hand-offs, a "maker-checker" mindset where transactions had to be checked by someone other than the originating employee, and unclear accountability for problem resolution. The transaction processing process was basically the back-end processing for the transactions originating in the branches. The major observation here was that the processing was fragmented by product or system. The marketing processes were currently also product focused, and there was limited understanding of customer segments and individual customers.

The vision that the team presented included a streamlined front-end delivery process with clear accountability and quick turnaround on customer problem resolution, a unified approach to transaction processing, and segment-focused, cross-product marketing. They felt that the most radical change required would be that of the organizational culture. One aspect of culture manifested in the many "maker-checker" was a legacy of the days when the bank was a wholesale bank, and each transaction value was very high while volume was relatively low. In the retail bank business, the high volume and low individual value of transactions required a different mindset. Other aspects of Citibank culture that would need to change included the emphasis and the incentive system that rewarded product innovation and individuality. The process changes required a culture that focused more on relationships with customers and on team efforts.

The team also set detailed targets for each of the core processes. Among the many set for the delivery processes, examples are a rise in the percentage of customers who were highly satisfied from 64% to 80%, an increase in the percentage of customers served within 5 minutes from 71% to 80%, and improved transaction processing accuracy from 2 errors per 5,000 transactions to 1 error per 5,000 transactions. Detailed targets for productivity and cost improvements were also set. These targets were in effect also a list of measures that would be used to evaluate each process on a recurring basis.

In phase three, three implementation teams—service delivery, operations, and product development and marketing—involving many more employees were formed. Each team was headed by the vice president in charge of the function. The role of the consultants in phase three was scaled back. Some resistance was encountered to the recommended changes. George DiNardo and Peter Mills addressed the problem of resistance by having discussions with key stakeholders of the processes to be reengineered, and by focusing on a number of projects. Before the end of the first year, the consultants had been phased out. The Citibank implementation teams were driving their own implementation.

A major part of implementation was to develop and implement the information systems needed to support the reengineered processes. One resulting new system is SABRE (Strategic Asia Pacific Branch Retail Environment). SABRE consists of two complementary subsystems: SABRE I is at the teller level and provides automated support for signature verification, paperless teller transactions, and Citicard transactions. SABRE II includes the phone banking systems, together with facilities for telemarketing and cross-product marketing at the branches. The bank developed the SABRE system in-house, because it considers this to be a strategic product. SABRE I has been a great success and is considered to be best of breed. Today, the SABRE platform itself is of strategic importance as a vehicle to deliver Citibanking to customers, and to enable cross-selling of multiple products to customers.

## *VII. Managing Change*

The changes to the IT architecture and business processes are not trivial. George DiNardo, as chief technology officer, was a catalyst for change, and his ability to communicate convincingly with senior officers of the bank in corporate headquarters and in Asia was an important asset. He brought a different perspective to technology management, starting from the premise that the IT infrastructure had to be standardized to obtain the maximum benefit for the bank. Countries wanting to be different will have to justify it, quite a change from the days when country managers decided the types of technology they wanted for each country.

The RCC experience provides a useful model for the current consumer bank consolidation. The in-depth technical expertise gained from running a regional data centre would be directly relevant to the new infrastructure that Citibank is putting in place for Consumer Banking. Not surprisingly, Ajit was asked to set up and run the data centre for the new Asian Pacific Consumer Banking technology infrastructure. However, the new infrastructure is more than just scaling up to process more transactions. The business of Citibanking in Global Consumer Banking is more diverse and complex than cards and requires the internalization of many business parameters in developing software to support back-end banking operations. Correspondingly, the business impact is also far greater. Citibank, as an American bank operating in Asia, is subjected to restrictions on the number of branches allowed in each country. The reliance on an electronic interface with customers and for an electronic channel for delivery of banking services is significantly higher than many local banks. Citibank sees the new technological infrastructure as a key enabler for flexibility in its product and service offerings throughout Asia at a competitive cost.

The conversion to a new technology infrastructure at Citibank Asia Pacific meant some loss of control over computing for the Citibank country managers. DiNardo felt that there had not been serious opposition to the changes, although country managers were understandably "nervous" about the sweeping changes. He stated

> It's an idea whose time has come. The Asia Pacific high profit margin must be maintained! They all know this. They know the value of what we're doing. Computer costs will be down for them, it will affect their bottom line. There is no longer any desire for the sophisticated manager to have his/her own mainframe computer. They know that I have done it 700 times already. No one objects to the logic of the idea. We will insist on a postimplementation audit. The country managers in Asia did see that to survive the next 10 years something like this is necessary. It's all about customer service.

However, it is the level of service and support from the center that country managers are concerned about. The standardization and centralization strategy obviously restricted flexibility in country operations. It was adopted consciously and the gain in integrated customer service and economies of scale is substantial. Nonetheless, the issue of responsiveness to local needs is unlikely to go away, and there are concerns about how priorities for enhancements will be handled if there are not enough resources and capacity to meet requests in a timely manner. In 1999, George DiNardo retired from Citibank. Without his forceful personality to enforce standardization, countries' requests for customization will be more difficult to resist.

## *VIII. New Challenges: Merger and the Internet*

By 1998, when Citicorp merged with Travelers, Citibank Asia Pacific had largely completed its centralization of back-end processing for consumer banking. The other regions began a little later but had also been centralizing their IT infrastructure for several years. At the time of the merger, Citicorp was three-quarters of the way through a huge back-office restructuring effort, under Mary Taylor, head of Citibank's operations and technology division. She took restructuring one step further, pulling together the operations and technology for the corporate and consumer sides of the bank. Today, Citibank's data centers have gone from 66 to 12 worldwide. Ms. Taylor notes that

> The consumer bank handles huge volumes of transactions that are of much smaller value. The corporate bank handles fewer transactions but with large dollar value. There are real synergies you can take advantage of because you can add more transactions without really impacting capacity.[15]

Outside of the United States, the main data centers are now in Dublin, London, Singapore, Hong Kong, and Sydney, and together serve over 100 countries.

The merger with the Travelers Group posed another set of challenges to the bank's infrastructure. The merger offered the opportunity of providing a financial services supermarket to customers. However, to do so requires integration of information systems, customer databases, product lines, and multiple transaction types.[16] The integration options that are open to Citigroup are broadly "total integration of platforms, servers, risk management and front- and back-office operations—or instead establish a data warehouse for customer information, accessed by object-oriented middleware."[17] The latter option is more expedient and avoids the need for risky reengineering of business processes. However, total system integration offers more effective cross-selling of products and risk management. The decisions made are likely to have implications for the IT infrastructure in the Asia Pacific given the bank's desire for increasing standardization globally.

The other global trend that affects Citibank Asia Pacific is the rise of Internet banking. E-banking offers some unique opportunities and threats to established banks. For example, Internet transactions cost about one-tenth of traditional bank counter transactions, according to William Lo, chief executive of Citibank Hong Kong's consumer banking operations.[18] Citibank, with its long tradition of technology-enabled banking initiatives appears well placed to take advantage of the Internet. However, it has not been smooth sailing.

Citigroup has spent about $400m on e-banking, more than other large banks.[19] In 1999, Citigroup recorded a $172m net loss in e-banking.[20] Citigroup's biggest consumer banking initiatives are either in test phase, or have only been soft-launched. Citi f/i, (f/i stands for financial interactive) rolled out quietly in mid-1999, and will not be widely marketed yet.[21] There are those who believe that Internet banking will take off when the most common devices for connecting to the Web are mobile phones. This may be particularly true in Asia where mobile phone ownership is much higher than PC ownership. In 1999, a trial service began in Singapore with carrier Mobile One to let users perform retail banking functions using cell phones. The long-term goal is to allow customers to switch easily among banking, credit card, insurance and brokerage services using the cell phone.[22]

In contrast to retail e-banking initiatives, Citibank's corporate e-banking initiatives appear to be more well received. In 1999, Citibank launched a well-regarded small-business site—Bizzed.com, which is expected to make a profit in two years.[23] In May 1999, Citibank also launched a B-to-B e-commerce system—Citibank Commerce—that lets customers order products, monitor order status, complete settlement and reconciliation processes. Interestingly, it was first made available in the Asia Pacific region.[24] It targets 8,000 Citibank corporate customers in the Asia Pacific region and will be introduced to the United States, Europe, and Latin America later in 2000.[25] The service has its competitors even in the region. For example, the Singapore government and Visa International recently launched an on-line business-to-business trading network for companies and financial institutions in Singapore, called the Commerce Exchange.

The rise of Internet banking also has strong implications for the bank's IT infrastructure. Citicorp is converting its technology platforms to make them more Web compatible. For example, its internal data networks are being converted worldwide to TCP/1P, with the help of AT&T. E-Citi, Citigroup's Internet banking innovation group, is developing middleware that links the mainframe environment to the Web architecture.[26] At present, most of the core products will remain on mainframes, but they will increasingly be linked to Web-based front-ends. Internet-based direct banking initiatives are already using different core banking systems. Sanchez, a client/server based core banking system, is being used to support Citi f/i. Citibank is also considering Sanchez as "part of an ongoing effort to standardize operations and processes across the bank's various consumer businesses."[27] To that end, all four of Citibank's regional consumer banking operations have the option to independently acquire Sanchez for their core retail banking system. Sanchez's potential advantages compared to mainframe core retail banking systems, such as Systematics, are responsiveness to time-to-market demands, and channel integration requirements. Questions about scalability of client/server systems to meet traditional retail banking volumes however remain.

While Citibank Asia Pacific has managed the transition to centralized back-end processing, it continues to face new challenges from global trends in bank mergers and Internet banking. Virtual banks without brick and mortar compete with established banks and have the advantage of lower overheads, greater agility and speed of response to the market. Nonbank companies like AOL and Microsoft are also offering financial services and compete on the pervasiveness of their customer reach, as well as the large set of potentially complementary products and services. Sunil Sreenivasan, chief executive of Citibank Singapore, clearly recognizes the implications for Citibank:

> In the future, the list of competitors in financial services will include unfamiliar names such as telcos, power companies, and dot-com companies. What is frightening to us traditionalists is that we will have to cannibalize our own products in order to avoid others cannibalizing those very same products. Or put more extremely, we may in certain respects need to commit suicide in order to survive.[28]

Clearly, the competitive environment will be very different in the future. Will the economics of large-scale, centralized computing hold sway? To what extent will the major infrastructural changes made in the 1990s be a help or a hindrance to the next wave of changes brought on by the changing business environment?

### *CASE STUDY QUESTIONS*

1. What business strategy has Citicorp been pursuing in Asia?
2. Evaluate Citibank's Asia Pacific information technology (IT) infrastructure and systems in light of this strategy. How well do they support it?
3. How well do Citibank's infrastructural changes made in the 1990s support the merger with Travelers Group and Citigroup's efforts to deal with the impact of the Internet on the banking and financial services industries? What management, organization, and technology issues will Citibank need to address?

**Source:** From Boon Siong Neo and Christina Soh, Information Management Research Center (IMARC), Nanyang Business School, Nanyang Technological University, Singapore. Reprinted by permission.

[1]All financial figures are in US$ unless otherwise stated.
[2]"Legacy Systems Under Strain," *US Banker,* May 1998, pp. 103–107.
[3]Brand, A., Weill, P., Soh, C., and Periasamy, "Citibank—Asia Pacific: Positioning IT as a Strategic Resource," Melbourne Business School Case Study, 1999.
[4]Ibid.
[5]Citigroup Annual Report 1998, p. 9.
[6]Ibid.
[7]Clark, D., "Megadeal Challenges Citicorp to Meld Systems Successfully," American Banker Online, April 9, 1998. http://www.americanbanker.
[8]Flanigan, J., "Citigroup as Barometer and Business Model," *LA Times,* January 23, 2000, http://www.latimes.com:80/.
[9]"Thinking Globally, Acting Locally," The China Business Review, May–June, 1993, pp. 23–25.
[10]Brand, A., Weill, P., Soh, C., and Periasamy, "Citibank—Asia Pacific: Positioning IT as a Strategic Resource," Melbourne Business School Case Study, 1999.
[11]Citicorp Annual Report 1998, p. 13.
[12]Citigroup press release, April 19, 1999. http://www.citi.com/citigroup/pr/news/pr95.htm.
[13]TimesNet Asia, http://web3.asia1.com.sg/timesnet/data/ab/docs/ab1406.html.
[14]Clark, D., "Megadeal Challenges Citicorp to Meld Systems Successfully," American Banker Online, April 9, 1998. http://www.americanbanker.
[15]Power, C., "Citibank Exec Finishing a Systems Harnessing," American Banker Online, October 27, 1998. http://www.americanbanker.
[16]Schmerken, I., "The Big Gamble: Mergers and Technology," WST Online Magazine, July 1998. http://www.wstonline.com/mfwt.
[17]Helland, E., "Can Citigroup Reign in Citicorp's Decentralized IT Strategy?" WST Online Magazine, July 1998. http://www.wstonline.com/mfwt.
[18]Bickers, C., "Net Returns," Far Eastern Economic Review Interactive Edition, May 6, 1999.
[19]Beckett, P. "Citigroup Struggles to Gain Momentum in New Business," *Wall Street Journal,* January 21, 2000.
[20]Flanigan, J., "Citigroup as Barometer and Business Model," *LA Times,* January 23, 2000, http://www.latimes.com:80/.
[21]"E-Citi's Soft Launch Raises Eyebrows," Future Banker, November 1999, http://www.thebankingchannel.com/fb/fbnov99-5.
[22]Violino, B., "Banking on E-Business" Information Week Online, May 3 1999. http://www.informationweek.com/.
[23]Beckett, P. "Citigroup Struggles to Gain Momentum in New Business," *Wall Street Journal,* January 21, 2000.
[24]Violino, B., "Banking on E-Business" Information Week Online, May 3 1999. http://www.informationweek.com/.
[25]"Cyberspace Race," CitiComerce.com: In the News, http://www.citibank.com/singapore.
[26]Violino, B., "Banking on E-Business," Information Week Online, May 3 1999. http://www.informationweek.com/.
[27]Costanzo, C., "Software Deal May Signal End of Citi's Mainframes," American Banker Online, July 16, 1999. http://www.americanbanker.
[28]Sunil Sreenivasan, "Banking in a Brave New World," *The Business Times,* February 2, 2000.

# INTERNATIONAL CASE STUDY

## CASE STUDY 4: ENERLINE RESTORATIONS INC.: STAY WITH AN ASP?

*Jane Movold and Scott Schneberger, University of Western Ontario*

On April 1, 2000, Ron Hozjan, chief financial officer (CFO) of Enerline Restorations Inc. (Enerline) in Calgary, Alberta, Canada, had a decision to make. Enerline had more than doubled in size since Hozjan signed the initial contract with the company's application service provider (ASP), FutureLink, in February 1999, and the existing arrangement was no longer adequate. Hozjan needed to determine if the ASP model was still appropriate for Enerline, given the continued rapid growth and change the company was experiencing, or whether it was time to invest in building an internal information technology infrastructure.

### *Enerline Restorations Inc. Background*

Enerline was Canada's leader in both pipeline liner systems for corrosion, and production tubing liner systems for progressive cavity pumping, rod pumping, injection, and disposal well applications. Enerline opened for business in May 1996, with a staff of three employees. By the year 2000, the company's technologies were field-proven with several hundred pipeline liner systems in service, as well as over 1,000 lined tubing strings in producing oil wells. Enerline was a 100 percent Canadian, privately owned business that had grown to 30 employees. The company had more than doubled its annual revenues to approximately $3.5 million, with projected revenues of $7.4 million for the year 2000.

The original division within the organization was the Ener-Liner division which offered pipeline liner systems. The subsequently formed Ener-Core Tubing Liner division offered the pumping and disposal well applications and was still considered to be in its infancy in 1999. The head office in Calgary was the base for a small manufacturing shop and for the liner crews. The construction of a larger manufacturing plant in Stettler, Alberta, for the growing Ener-Core product line had been completed by January 2000 and was operating at full production capacity by June of that year. Additional locations were likely to be acquired or constructed in the near future, as this rate of rapid growth due to increasing product demand was expected to continue. However, as Hozjan explains,

> Capital was definitely tight during this time due to plant construction combined with the development of a new product line. Therefore, this constrained economic environment weighed heavily in my decision-making process for acquiring all new operational items, including a much-needed information system.

Ener-Core was the company's product solution designed to increase runtime to their customers' producing, injection, and disposal wells. Ener-Core was a high-density, polyethylene-lined production tubing that guaranteed reduced friction and rod torques, elimination of tubing wear, power savings, and corrosion protection, while it also resolved wax and paraffin problems. The Ener-Core tubing liner was used in heavy oil producing areas in Alberta and Saskatchewan, and Enerline was rapidly expanding to other areas of Canada and the United States.

C.E. Franklin was the company's distributor for the Ener-Core product, with 40 locations in western Canada. Said Edwin Quinn, Enerline's sales manager,

> We formed a strong relationship with C.E. Franklin early before commencing production at our Stettler facility. C.E. Franklin is convinced that our liner system will greatly impact the way producers operate wells in the future. Even when oil prices dipped below $11 a barrel, C.E. Franklin was still willing to commit a generous amount of new tubing to be lined with Ener-Core liner.

The increased demand for this product was evidence of the ongoing cost savings realized by its customers.

### *Ron Hozjan, CFO*

Ron Hozjan joined Enerline as chief financial officer in June 1998. In this position, he was responsible for the overall management and control of the operations and financial areas of the business. All Enerline employees reported to Hozjan; Hozjan reported directly to the president, Graham Illingworth, and also had a dotted-line reporting relationship to the five-member board of directors. The Enerline organizational chart appears in Appendix B. Hozjan would periodically meet with the board of directors to keep them informed of his decisions and actions toward improvement within the organization. The board of directors empowered him to make decisions and implement the solutions for improvement within the organization.

This responsibility for the overall operations within the organization included the area of computerization and information systems. Hozjan was well aware that much effort would be required in this area to transform Enerline's operations into an efficient and competitive business environment. He also knew that he would need to make some key decisions regarding the company's systems and operations in a timely manner to be successful. At this time, Enerline had only one stand-alone personal computer which was running Simply Accounting, on-line banking, and Microsoft Office. Hozjan explained that, "Enerline was operating at least 10 years behind the times when I joined the company, and it was obvious that its operations and information systems infrastructure needed to be upgraded if the company was going to succeed." Over the ensuing five months, Hozjan familiarized himself with the Enerline business and the potential ramifications of the projected areas of business growth. Hozjan had previous experience within a similar industry; therefore, he had already gained a solid understanding of the general operational requirements for conducting business successfully within this marketplace.

## *Search for a Financial Information System Solution*

In November 1998, Hozjan launched an organized and focused search for a complete information system solution to meet Enerline's needs. Several alternative solutions were evaluated in detail. Hozjan decided that the selected solution would be one that was either at one end of the spectrum, where absolutely every part of the system was hosted at a provider's site, or would be a solution that was entirely resident in-house. He had ultimately determined that building a partial information system infrastructure within the organization would not be a valid option, based on his evaluation of existing hybrid solutions. He reached this decision because he realized that a hybrid solution would require him to allocate internal resources or hire information systems staff to maintain this partial infrastructure, while also allocating monetary resources to the external solution provider.

Hozjan's evaluation of the aspects involved in this all-or-nothing scenario (such as in-house staffing, training, his management time, and constrained monetary issues) clearly led him to the criteria by which he would select the optimum solution. He was searching for an on-line ASP that would meet every one of his information system and infrastructure needs. Ideally, he wanted an ASP that would supply his hardware, software, communications, consulting, ongoing maintenance, support and system backup functions. As Hozjan explained, "One-stop shopping that resulted in a reliable solution was exactly what I was looking for." He was well aware that Internet connectivity between Enerline and the ASP in this one-stop-shopping scenario would be a key element of the overall solution, as well as the ASP's ability to host the financial software of his choice.

If Hozjan found such an organization, he planned to compare the financial and operational aspects of the ASP model to the conventional in-house information system infrastructure setup to which he was accustomed. In a conventional IS shop, hired in-house specialists, trained and experienced in information technology, would design, develop, test, implement, and maintain information system components. The decision to move forward with the on-line ASP model and enter a business relationship with FutureLink was made prior to the selection of the specific financial software to be used. Hozjan felt confident at this point that the financial software package selected could be hosted in this flexible ASP environment. Hozjan's 1998 comparison of the ASP model versus the in-house setup appears in Appendix A. It was this comparison that led him to establish the business relationship between Enerline and FutureLink.

## *FutureLink ASP*

The on-line ASP industry was still in its infancy in 1998 when Hozjan launched his search for the ideal provider. In fact, Hozjan explained that FutureLink was really the only ASP based in Canada at the time, and there were no more than five ASPs in North America. FutureLink was the Canadian pioneer in this industry at that time, with 50 to 60 employees offering a variety of IS services. The ASP model was so new at this point that there were not even any FutureLink pricing models in existence when Enerline joined FutureLink as its first customer in February 1999.

Hozjan was introduced to FutureLink via a former employee of Sysgold, a company that had successfully set up an internal network of approximately 10 personal computers and an Internet solution for him at a previous place of employment. He had developed a positive business relationship with Sysgold as their work had been reliable and the network they implemented was easily maintained.

Hozjan interacted primarily with FutureLink's founder and president at the time, Cameron Shell, to establish the initial contract and parameters for their ongoing business relationship. Throughout the negotiations, Hozjan found FutureLink a flexible organization and claimed that they were open to hosting any software application if they were given approximately four weeks to successfully test the new software in their environment. This ongoing flexibility and openness to explore new solutions was critical in the positive development of the business relationship between the two organizations. Hozjan reported that,

> I do not feel bound or constrained to consider only specific information systems solutions, as my ASP has not established a rigid scope of applications which they are prepared to host. This freedom of choice is very important to me as I am responsible for the operations of a rapidly growing organization with changing and expanding needs.

## *Alternative Financial Software Solutions Evaluated*

Several specific financial software solutions were considered to determine which was best suited for the Enerline operations.

The Great Plains accounting software solution was evaluated. This solution would cost Enerline approximately US$30,000 to US$40,000 to purchase and implement for a five-user license, plus additional maintenance fees—a sizable sum for Enerline at the time. Great Plains was located in Seattle, and the fact that Great Plains did not have a local Canadian presence or close relationship with other local IS-related vendors that Enerline dealt with was a disadvantage. Software customizations would also be required with this solution.

The PeachTree software solution was evaluated and was a much less costly solution for Enerline—Cdn$1,500 to purchase and implement for a five-user license. This software package was more prevalent in the local community and was already hosted by FutureLink for other customers. However, Hozjan determined that this software package was not sufficiently sophisticated to meet Enerline's financial reporting requirements.

QByte was an industry-specific financial software package that included general ledger, accounts payable, and accounts receivable modules, as well as some reporting functionality. It was developed by the PriceWaterhouseCoopers accounting firm with input from various oil and gas producers and was already offered on a time-share basis for smaller organizations. The monthly access cost of the QByte software was $900 plus $145 per month for dedicated connectivity. Hozjan was intimately familiar with QByte's application offerings as he had implemented this software for a previous employer and was quite satisfied, from a functionality perspective, with its capabilities. Microsoft Access and Excel were already utilized for generating Enerline internal financial statements by using exported data from the existing Simply Accounting system; this existing financial reporting process was intended to be continued. This same process of utilizing the importing and exporting functionality within the QByte software for ease of financial data manipulation was also previously utilized successfully by Hozjan. This was a solution he was certain would meet Enerline's existing information requirements. Many large corporations in the industry, such as Canadian Natural Resource, used the QByte software, as well as many smaller companies similar in size to Enerline. This software was offered on a time-share basis; therefore, any ASP could connect to the QByte host and, in turn, could provide the link to their customers if they so desired.

Ultimately, Hozjan chose the QByte software solution for Enerline.

## *The Enerline—FutureLink Existing Business Arrangement*

The three-year contract between Enerline and FutureLink was signed in February 1999. Hozjan decided to enter the three-year contract with FutureLink at $1,800 per month, rather than a one-year commitment at $3,000 per month to reduce the company's overall cash outflow.

The contract included five thin client workstations (monitor, keyboard, box to run the Citrix software), five dedicated connections to the FutureLink ServerFarm, five licences to run MS Office Pro suite, QByte software implementation and system access for two users, a laser printer, firewall security, Internet access, consulting, maintenance, and system backup activities and 24-hour support. All of the hardware and software was owned by FutureLink.

The FutureLink contract stipulated that their organization guaranteed 99.9 percent uptime for their customers during normal business hours of operation between 8 A.M. and 5 P.M. If this quality of service was not delivered, the customer was allowed to exit the contract agreement with no penalty fee, or to receive one month of FutureLink services free of charge. The penalty for exiting the contract without cause was equal to six months of service fees (6 × $1,800 = $10,800).

FutureLink established a help-desk department with four priorities of service calls. Hozjan indicated that he had used the help-desk services several times, even on the weekends, and they were successful in meeting their service objectives. Hozjan explained, "The help-desk can even 'shadow' your screen and take control of your system to further assist in resolving the problem in a timely manner. It's great!" Hozjan also added, "I am working with my third monitor and second keyboard. However, the parts were replaced at no charge, on the same or next day, by FutureLink, depending upon the urgency of the situation, which resulted in little interruption of service."

By mid-March 1999, FutureLink had the hardware and communications setup completed, and the five users from Enerline were connected to FutureLink for their work in Outlook e-mail and MS Office Pro. All Enerline company files were stored at the FutureLink location.

In late-March 1999, it was actually the FutureLink ASP organization that assisted Hozjan in evaluating financial packages. Hozjan communicated the particular Enerline business information requirements to FutureLink, and FutureLink responded with their evaluation, based on his criteria, for him to review. Ultimately, Hozjan decided on the recommended QByte solution, and FutureLink successfully implemented this solution for Enerline's two key users within the next 60 days. Although QByte remained the host for this application, FutureLink established a dedicated line between their own server and the QByte location. Therefore, Enerline received easy access to the QByte software because of their existing connection to FutureLink. This stable, direct communications connection was key to Enerline users as they were constantly importing or exporting data between MS Excel or Access, which was hosted on the FutureLink ServerFarm and the QByte software.

Enerline also had remote users who relied on their information systems to conduct business, and these sales personnel regularly dialed up to FutureLink through the Internet. Two members of Enerline's sales staff were on the road 60 percent to 70 percent of the time.

The Enerline Stettler production facility relied heavily on a Microsoft Access-based system, developed by FutureLink programmers, which was the driving force for their daily production activity. The Stettler production site had a dedicated Telus Planet phone line to the FutureLink server farm site where the Access database resided.

## *Challenges Introduced*

In September 1999, Hozjan was informed by FutureLink's founder and president, Cameron Shell, that FutureLink was experiencing serious financial difficulty. This information was a complete and unpleasant surprise to Hozjan. There had been no previous mention of FutureLink's financial difficulties when Hozjan signed the business contract, or subsequently. Now, seven months into a three-year contract, Hozjan discovered that the ASP hosting all of his applications was in financial trouble. Although receiving this information was unsettling and did not contribute toward further development of a strong business relationship, Hozjan reported that Enerline had not experienced any evident degradation of service due to FutureLink's financial difficulties.

In November 1999, FutureLink merged with a California-based organization. The head office for FutureLink was subsequently moved to California, and significant turnover within all levels of the existing FutureLink organization began to occur. Hozjan commented,

> It was very difficult as everyone I had dealt with at FutureLink left the organization. There was significant turnover from the top on down, including FutureLink's founder and president, Cameron Shell. Even all of the original technical staff had left since November of last year. The California-based management team had taken over.

Hozjan added that, "Although things were different and 1999 was a bad year for FutureLink, Enerline was still receiving reliable service, and the new management was still agreeable to changes that were requested in their business agreement."

In November 1999, when the merger took place, the stock price of the new FutureLink Corporation skyrocketed from $10 per share to between $30 and $40 per share for almost a five-month period. However, by late March 2000, and early April, the stock price had plummeted back to below $10 per share. Certainly, from the perspective of a growing customer base, the development of key industry partnerships, and tremendous growth in annual revenues due to acquisitions, prospects appeared to be very bright for the new FutureLink Corporation. However, their overall financial picture was not a bright one, and large losses were growing. The new California-based FutureLink organization reported that their higher losses reflected the expansion of the ASP business. By this time, the ASP marketplace was an environment with increased competition.

## *Changes in the Information System Industry*

During the previous two years, there had been several major changes in the information system industry that directly affected the ASP marketplace. A critical element of the ASP model was the communications infrastructure between the customer and the provider. The ongoing communications cost and the cost of initial setup for communications within the previous two years had decreased significantly as technology improved and competition increased. Also, this decrease in communications cost was combined with further advances in technology that allowed improvements in the standard communication speeds offered to customers. This evolution in the communications area ultimately resulted in speedier access for users at less cost, and also played a major role in making the ASP model much more attractive and competitive, especially when compared to in-house or hybrid solutions.

Another change within the information systems industry revolved around the Internet. A dramatically increasing number of popular enterprise resource planning (ERP) packages and other software applications had been redesigned and developed for Internet-based deployment. This Internet-based phenomenon made the hosting of popular applications much easier and less costly for ASPs. Therefore, the cost-savings in providing these services could be passed on to customers, which further assisted in making the ASP model more competitive.

E-business and e-commerce business models were major evolutions within the information systems industry over the past two years. Implementing these business models combined well with an ASP solution for many customers launching into this new arena.

## *Going Forward*

As the available options were analyzed and system implementation decisions were being made, Enerline was rapidly growing. Hozjan said,

> It was like trying to hit a moving target! The business needs were growing as we were trying to make the appropriate decisions. The key to making appropriate decisions is to allow for growth. But when your organization doubles in size and expects the same rate of growth for the near future, this decision-making process is a difficult task.

Hozjan indicated,

> Since I joined the company in 1998, it was in a serious growth period where we were building a new large production plant, and new product lines were being developed. The economic environment within the organization was a key factor in selecting the ASP model to meet our immediate information needs. I knew roughly what the equipment and infrastructure would cost the company to purchase and set up, so the monthly cost of the ASP fees was merely that lump-sum amount distributed over a three-year period. It was a no-lose situation from an economic perspective, as most of the equipment has a three-year life span at most anyway. The only real concern at the time was whether the ASP would be reliable enough to provide ongoing, stable service to Enerline for a sustained period of time. I had faith in the people and in the technology, so with the economic analysis making sense due to the monthly cash outlay—I said "Let's do it!" Internal staff and capital resources were scarce, so it was basically a "no-brainer" at the time.

Two years later, Enerline had grown substantially and had developed a solid market presence with the continued success of their established product lines. The world of information systems had also changed during that two-year period. Enerline needed additional communications infrastructure, as their business operations in new locations were actually being driven by production-oriented applications that were hosted at the FutureLink location. Enerline was also purchasing companies in the United States that had to be brought on-line with their systems. Enerline was becoming increasingly dependent on their information systems for actual daily production activity and business transactions, making the nature of their information systems much more mission-critical. Hozjan needed to determine whether renegotiations to upgrade the information system services with FutureLink would be of benefit to Enerline, or whether it was time, based on the considerable growth and expected rapid pace of change, for Enerline to provide for themselves from an information systems perspective. Given FutureLink's financial problems, should he seek a different ASP to replace FutureLink? And while an ASP had seemed perfect for Enerline's needs two years earlier, would it meet the company's current needs, or its needs two years in the future?

### *CASE STUDY QUESTIONS*

1. Why did Enerline initially decide to use an ASP? Was this a good decision? Why or why not? Identify the issues that were involved in this decision.
2. Should Enerline continue using an ASP? What management, organization, and technology issues should be addressed by this decision?
3. If Enerline decides to continue with an ASP, what criteria should it use to evaluate alternative ASPs?

**Source:** Jane Movold prepared this case under the supervision of Professor Scott Schneberger solely to provide material for class discussion.

# Appendix A

## 1998 Internal Infrastructure Setup Versus ASP Model Comparison

1. Internal Infrastructure Setup — $80,000 in year 1
(Then increasing due to further staff resources and training required in this area as Enerline grows and the IS infrastructure demands full-time management.)

- Microsoft NT server and software
- Five personal computers
- Five MS Office Pro licenses
- Five QByte licenses
- Internet access
- Firewall router and security software
- Backup software and tape drive equipment
- Staff training and resource allocation to this area
- Consulting, implementation, and setup fees
- Support
- Communications

2. ASP Model — $1,800 per month for year 1 of the contract = $21,600 of sunk cost.
$1,600 per month was renegotiated for the remaining 2 years of the contract = $38,400.

Includes all of the above.

*Note:* The $1,800 per month fee in year 1 included a five-user setup. The $1,600 per month fee for years 2 and 3 was negotiated for a seven-user setup.

# APPENDIX B

## ORGANIZATIONAL CHART (AS OF APRIL 1, 2000)

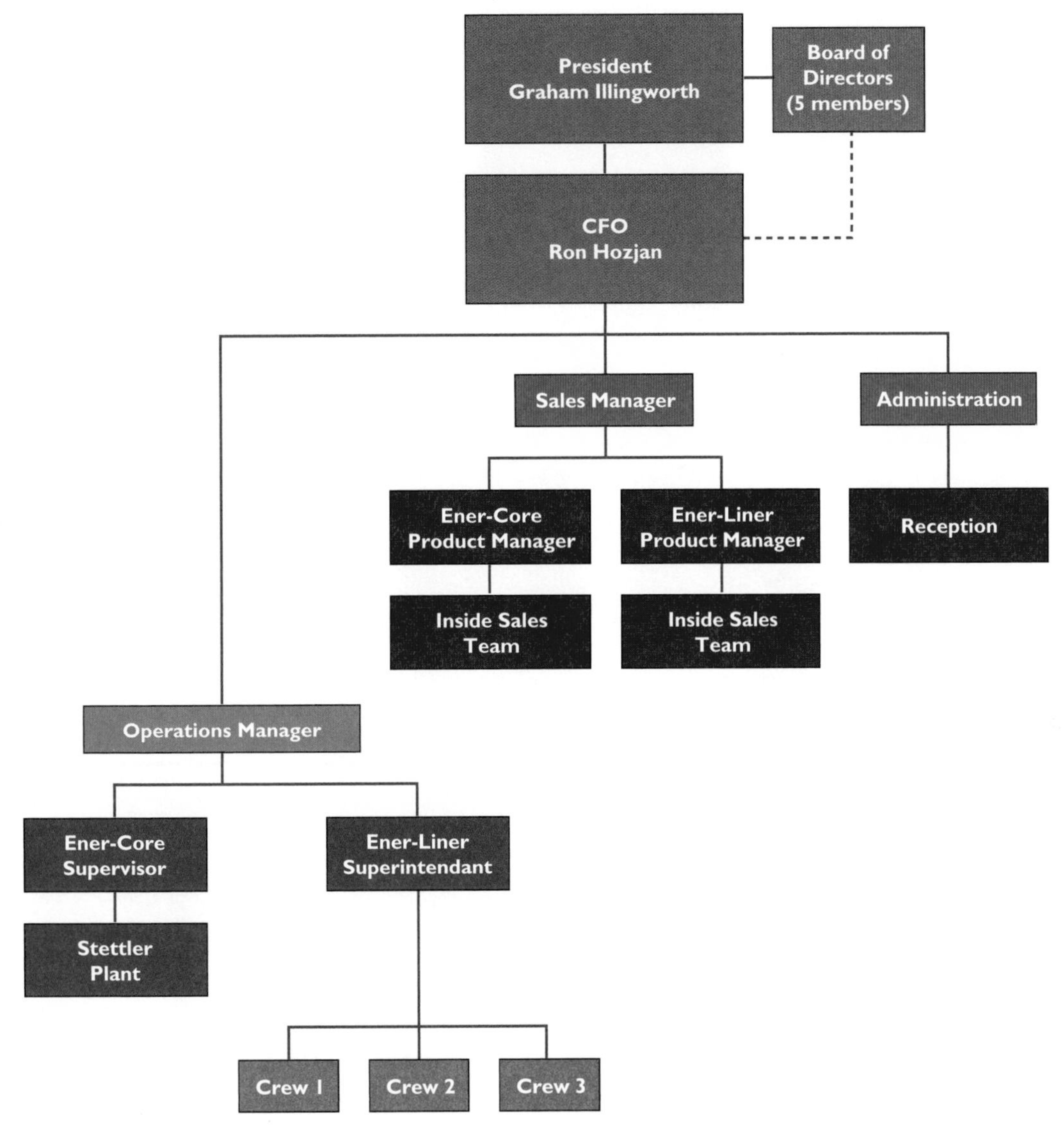

# REFERENCES


CHAPTER 1

**Ackoff, R. L.** "Management Misinformation System." *Management Science* 14, no. 4 (December 1967), B140–B116.

**Allen, Brandt R.,** and **Andrew C. Boynton.** "Information Architecture: In Search of Efficient Flexibility." *MIS Quarterly* 15, no. 4 (December 1991).

**Applegate, Lynda,** and **Janice Gogan.** "Electronic Commerce: Trends and Opportunities." Harvard Business School, 9-196-006 (October 6, 1995).

**Applegate, Lynda M., Clyde W. Holsapple, Ravi Kalakota, Franz J. Radermacher,** and **Andrew B. Whinston.** "Electronic Commerce: Building Blocks of New Business Opportunity." *Journal of Organizational Computing and Electronic Commerce* 6, no. 1 (1996).

**Bakos, J. Yannis.** "The Emerging Role of Electronic Marketplaces on the Internet." *Communications of the ACM* 41, no. 8 (August 1998).

**Barrett, Stephanie S.** "Strategic Alternatives and Interorganizational System Implementations: An Overview." *Journal of Management Information Systems* (Winter 1986–1987).

**Benjamin, Robert,** and **Rolf Wigand.** "Electronic Markets and Virtual Value Chains on the Information Superhighway." *Sloan Management Review* (Winter 1995).

**Brynjolfsson, E. T., T. W. Malone, V. Gurbaxani,** and **A. Kambil.** "Does Information Technology Lead to Smaller Firms?" *Management Science* 40, no. 12 (1994).

**Davis, Gordon B.,** and **Margrethe H. Olson.** *Management Information Systems: Conceptual Foundations, Structure, and Development,* 2nd ed. New York: McGraw-Hill (1985).

**Deans, Candace P.,** and **Michael J. Kane.** *International Dimensions of Information Systems and Technology.* Boston, MA: PWS-Kent (1992).

**"Eastman is Keen on E-Commerce."** *Information Week* (August 2, 2000).

**Engler, Natalie.** "Small but Nimble." *Information Week* (January 18, 1999).

**Fedorowicz, Jane,** and **Benn Konsynski.** "Organization Support Systems: Bridging Business and Decision Processes." *Journal of Management Information Systems* 8, no. 4 (Spring 1992).

**Feeny, David E.,** and **Leslie P. Willcocks.** "Core IS Capabilities for Exploiting Information Technology." *Sloan Management Review* 39, no. 3 (Spring 1998).

**Gallupe, R. Brent.** "Images of Information Systems in the Early 21st Century." *Communications of the Association for Information Systems* 3, no. 3 (February 2000).

**Gilmore, James H.,** and **B. Joseph Pine, II.** "The Four Faces of Mass Customization." *Harvard Business Review* (January–February 1997).

**Gorry, G. A.,** and **M. S. Scott Morton.** "A Framework for Management Information Systems." *Sloan Management Review* 13, no. 1 (1971).

**Johnston, Russell,** and **Michael J. Vitale.** "Creating Competitive Advantage with Interorganizational Information Systems." *MIS Quarterly* 12, no. 2 (June 1988).

**Joy, Bill.** "Design for the Digital Revolution." *Fortune* (March 6, 2000).

**Keen, Peter G. W.** *Shaping the Future: Business Design Through Information Technology.* Cambridge, MA: Harvard Business School Press (1991).

**King, John.** "Centralized vs. Decentralized Computing: Organizational Considerations and Management Options." *Computing Surveys* (October 1984).

**Kling, Rob,** and **William H. Dutton.** "The Computer Package: Dynamic Complexity." In *Computers and Politics,* edited by James Danziger, William H. Dutton, Rob Kling, and Kenneth Kraemer. New York: Columbia University Press (1982).

**Laudon, Kenneth C.** "A General Model for Understanding the Relationship Between Information Technology and Organizations." Working paper, Center for Research on Information Systems, New York University (1989).

**Leonard-Barton, Dorothy.** *Wellsprings of Knowledge.* Boston, MA: Harvard Business School Press (1995).

**Liker, Jeffrey K., David B. Roitman,** and **Ethel Roskies.** "Changing Everything All at Once: Work Life and Technological Change." *Sloan Management Review* (Summer 1987).

**Malone, T. W.,** and **J. F. Rockart.** "Computers, Networks and the Corporation." *Scientific American* 265, no. 3 (September 1991).

**Malone, Thomas W., JoAnne Yates,** and **Robert I. Benjamin.** "Electronic Markets and Electronic Hierarchies." *Communications of the ACM* (June 1987).

———. "The Logic of Electronic Markets." *Harvard Business Review* (May–June 1989).

**McFarlan, F. Warren, James L. McKenney,** and **Philip Pyburn.** "The Information Archipelago—Plotting a Course." *Harvard Business Review* (January–February 1983).

———. "Governing the New World." *Harvard Business Review* (July–August 1983).

**McKenney, James L.,** and **F. Warren McFarlan.** "The Information Archipelago—Maps and Bridges." *Harvard Business Review* (September–October 1982).

**Orlikowski, Wanda J.,** and **Jack J. Baroudi.** "Studying Information Technology in Organizations: Research Approaches and Assumptions." *Information Systems Research* 2, no. 1 (March 1991).

**Quinn, James Brian.** "Strategic Outsourcing: Leveraging Knowledge Capabilities." *Sloan Management Review* 40, no. 4 (Summer 1999).

**Roche, Edward M.** "Planning for Competitive Use of Information Technology in Multinational Corporations." AIB UK Region, Brighton Polytechnic, Brighton, UK, Conference Paper (March 1992). Edward M. Roche, W. Paul Stillman School of Business, Seton Hall University.

**Rockart, John F.**, and **James E. Short.** "IT in the 1990s: Managing Organizational Interdependence." *Sloan Management Review* 30, no. 2 (Winter 1989).

**Sambamurthy, V.** and **Robert W. Zmud.** "Research Commentary: The Organizing Logic for an Enterprise's IT Activities in the Digital Era-A Prognosis of Practice and a Call to Research." *Information Systems Research* 11, No. 2 (June 2000).

**Scott Morton, Michael, ed.** *The Corporation in the 1990s.* New York: Oxford University Press (1991).

**Slywotzky, Adrian J.** and **David J. Morrison.** *How Digital Is Your Business?* New York: Crown Business (2001).

**Tornatsky, Louis G., J. D. Eveland, Myles G. Boylan, W. A. Hertzner, E. C. Johnson, D. Roitman,** and **J. Schneider.** "The Process of Technological Innovation: Reviewing the Literature." Washington, DC: National Science Foundation (1983).

**Tuomi, Ilkka.** "Data Is More Than Knowledge." *Journal of Management Information Systems* 16, no. 3 (Winter 1999-2000).

**Weill, Peter,** and **Marianne Broadbent.** *Leveraging the New Infrastructure.* Cambridge, MA: Harvard Business School Press (1998).

———. "Management by Maxim: How Business and IT Managers Can Create IT Infrastructures," *Sloan Management Review* (Spring 1997).

### CHAPTER 2

**Anthony, R. N.** *Planning and Control Systems: A Framework for Analysis.* Cambridge, MA: Harvard University Press (1965).

**Bensaou, M.** "Portfolios of Buyer-Supplier Relationships," *Sloan Management Review* 40, no. 4 (Summer 1999).

**Berry, Leonard L.,** and **A. Parasuraman.** "Listening to the Customer—the Concept of a Service-Quality Information System." *Sloan Management Review* (Spring 1997).

**Concours Group.** "ESII: Capitalizing on Enterprise Systems and Infrastructure." (1999).

**Culnan, Mary J.** "Transaction Processing Applications as Organizational Message Systems: Implications for the Intelligent Organization." Working paper no. 88-10, Twenty-second Hawaii International Conference on Systems Sciences (January 1989).

**Davenport, Tom.** *Mission Critical: Realizing the Promise of Enterprise Systems.* Boston, MA: Harvard Business School Press (2000).

———. "Putting the Enterprise into Enterprise Systems." *Harvard Business Review* (July–August 1998).

**Fisher, Marshall L.** "What Is the Right Supply Chain for Your Product?" *Harvard Business Review* (March–April 1997).

**Houdeshel, George,** and **Hugh J. Watson.** "The Management Information and Decision Support (MIDS) System at Lockheed Georgia." *MIS Quarterly* 11, no. 1 (March 1987).

**Huber, George P.** "Organizational Information Systems: Determinants of Their Performance and Behavior." *Management Science* 28, no. 2 (1984).

**Kalakota, Ravi,** and **Marcia Robinson.** *e-Business2.0: Roadmap for Success.* Reading, MA: Addison-Wesley (2001).

**Keen, Peter G. W.,** and **M. S. Morton.** *Decision Support Systems: An Organizational Perspective.* Reading, MA: Addison-Wesley (1978).

**King, John.** "Centralized vs. Decentralized Computing: Organizational Considerations and Management Options." *Computing Surveys* (October 1984).

**Lee, Hau, L., V. Padmanabhan,** and **Seugin Whang.** "The Bullwhip Effect in Supply Chains." *Sloan Management Review* (Spring 1997).

**Levy, David.** "Lean Production in an International Supply Chain." *Sloan Management Review* (Winter 1997).

**Malone, Thomas M., Kevin Crowston, Jintae Lee,** and **Brian Pentland.** "Tools for Inventing Organizations: Toward a Handbook of Organizational Processes." *Management Science* 45, no. 3 (March 1999).

**Palaniswamy, Rajagopal,** and **Tyler Frank.** "Enhancing Manufacturing Performance with ERP Systems." *Information Systems Management* (Summer 2000).

**Patton, Susannah.** "The Truth About CRM." *CIO Magazine* (May 1, 2001).

**Rockart, John F.,** and **Michael E. Treacy.** "The CEO Goes On-line." *Harvard Business Review* (January–February 1982).

**Seybold, Patricia B.** "Get Inside the Lives of Your Customers." *Harvard Business Review* (May 2001).

**Sprague, Ralph H., Jr.,** and **Eric D. Carlson.** *Building Effective Decision Support Systems.* Englewood Cliffs, NJ: Prentice Hall (1982).

### CHAPTER 3

**Allison, Graham T.** *Essence of Decision-Explaining the Cuban Missile Crisis.* Boston: Little Brown (1971).

**Alter, Steven,** and **Michael Ginzberg.** "Managing Uncertainty in MIS Implementation." *Sloan Management Review* 20, no. 1 (Fall 1978).

**Anthony, R. N.** *Planning and Control Systems: A Framework for Analysis.* Cambridge, MA: Harvard University Press (1965).

**Argyris, Chris.** *Interpersonal Competence and Organizational Effectiveness.* Homewood, IL: Dorsey Press (1962).

**Attewell, Paul,** and **James Rule.** "Computing and Organizations: What We Know and What We Don't Know." *Communications of the ACM* 27, no. 12 (December 1984).

**Bakos, J. Yannis,** and **Michael E. Treacy.** "Information Technology and Corporate Strategy: A Research Perspective." *MIS Quarterly* (June 1986).

**Beer, Michael, Russell A. Eisenstat,** and **Bert Spector.** "Why Change Programs Don't Produce Change." *Harvard Business Review* (November–December 1990).

**Bikson, T. K.,** and **J. D. Eveland.** "Integrating New Tools into Information Work." The Rand Corporation (1992). RAND/RP-106.

**Blau, Peter,** and **W. Richard Scott.** *Formal Organizations.* San Francisco: Chandler Press (1962).

**Brancheau, James C., Brian D. Janz,** and **James C. Wetherbe.** "Key Issues in Information Systems Management: 1994–1995 SIM Delphi Results." *MIS Quarterly* 20, no. 2 (June 1996).

**Caldwell, Bruce.** "A Cure for Hospital Woes." *Information Week* (September 9, 1991).

**Cash, J. I.,** and **Benn R. Konsynski.** "IS Redraws Competitive Boundaries." *Harvard Business Review* (March–April 1985).

**Chan, Yolande E., Sid L. Huff, Donald W. Barclay,** and **Duncan G. Copeland.** "Business Strategic Orientation, Information Systems Strategic Orientation, and Strategic Alignment." *Information Systems Research* 8, no. 2 (June 1997).

**Christensen, Clayton.** "The Past and Future of Competitive Advantage." **Sloan Management Review** 42, no. 2 (Winter 2001).

**Clemons, Eric K.** "Evaluation of Strategic Investments in Information Technology." *Communications of the ACM* (January 1991).

**Clemons, Eric K.,** and **Bruce W. Weber.** "Segmentation, Differentiation, and Flexible Pricing: Experience with

Information Technology and Segment-Tailored Strategies." *Journal of Management Information Systems* 11, no. 2 (Fall 1994).

**Clemons, Eric K.,** and **Michael Row.** "McKesson Drug Co.: Case Study of a Strategic Information System." *Journal of Management Information Systems* (Summer 1988).

———. "Sustaining IT Advantage: The Role of Structural Differences." *MIS Quarterly* 15, no. 3 (September 1991).

———. "Limits to Interfirm Coordination through IT." *Journal of Management Information Systems* 10, no. 1 (Summer 1993).

———, and **Il-Horn Hann.** "Rosenbluth International: Strategic Transformation." *Journal of Management Information Systems* 16, no. 2 (Fall 1999).

**Coase, Ronald H.** "The Nature of the Firm."(1937) in Putterman, Louis and Randall Kroszner. *The Economic Nature of the Firm: A Reader.* Cambridge University Press, 1995.

**Cohen, Michael, James March,** and **Johan Olsen.** "A Garbage Can Model of Organizational Choice." *Administrative Science Quarterly* 17 (1972).

**Copeland, Duncan G.,** and **James L. McKenney.** "Airline Reservations Systems: Lessons from History." *MIS Quarterly* 12, no. 3 (September 1988).

**Davenport, Thomas H.,** and **Keri Pearlson.** "Two Cheers for the Virtual Office." *Sloan Management Review* 39, no. 4 (Summer 1998).

———, **Jeanne G. Harris,** and **Ajay K. Kohli.** "How Do They Know Their Customers So Well?" *Sloan Management Review* 42, no. 2 (Winter 2001).

**Drucker, Peter.** "The Coming of the New Organization." *Harvard Business Review* (January–February 1988).

**Eardley, Alan, David Avison,** and **Philip Powell.** "Developing Information Systems to Support Flexible Strategy." *Journal of Organizational Computing and Electronic Commerce* 7, no. 1 (1997).

**Earl, Michael J.,** and **Jeffrey L. Sampler.** "Market Management to Transform the IT Organization." *Sloan Management Review* 39, no. 4 (Summer 1998).

**El Sawy, Omar A.** "Implementation by Cultural Infusion: An Approach for Managing the Introduction of Information Technologies." *MIS Quarterly* (June 1985).

**Etzioni, Amitai.** *A Comparative Analysis of Complex Organizations.* New York: Free Press (1975).

**Fayol, Henri.** *Administration industrielle et generale.* Paris: Dunods (1950, first published in 1916).

**Feeny, David.** "Making Business Sense of the E-Opportunity." *Sloan Management Review* 42, no. 2 (Winter 2001).

**Feeny, David E.,** and **Blake Ives.** "In Search of Sustainability: Reaping Long-Term Advantage from Investments in Information Technology." *Journal of Management Information Systems* (Summer 1990).

**Fisher, Marshall L., Ananth Raman,** and **Anne Sheen McClelland.** "Rocket Science Retailing Is Almost Here: Are You Ready?" *Harvard Business Review* (July–August 2000).

**Freeman, John, Glenn R. Carroll,** and **Michael T. Hannan.** "The Liability of Newness: Age Dependence in Organizational Death Rates." *American Sociological Review* 48 (1983).

**Fritz, Mary Beth Watson, Sridhar Narasimhan,** and **Hyeun-Suk Rhee.** "Communication and Coordination in the Virtual Office." *Journal of Management Information Systems* 14, no. 4 (Spring 1998).

**Fulk, Janet,** and **Geraldine DeSanctis.** "Electronic Communication and Changing Organizational Forms." *Organization Science* 6, no. 4 (July–August 1995).

**Garvin, David A.** "The Processes of Organization and Management." *Sloan Management Review* 39, no. 4 (Summer 1998).

**Glazer, Rashi.** "Winning in Smart Markets." *Sloan Management Review* 40, no. 4 (Summer 1999).

**Henderson, John C.,** and **John J. Sifonis.** "The Value of Strategic IS Planning: Understanding Consistency, Validity, and IS Markets." *MIS Quarterly* 12, no. 2 (June 1988).

**Hopper, Max.** "Rattling SABRE-New Ways to Compete on Information." *Harvard Business Review* (May–June 1990).

**Gorry, G. Anthony,** and **Michael S. Scott Morton.** "A Framework for Management Information Systems." *Sloan Management Review* 13, no. 1 (Fall 1971).

**Gurbaxani, V.,** and **S. Whang,** "The Impact of Information Systems on Organizations and Markets." *Communications of the ACM* 34, no. 1 (Jan. 1991).

**Hinds, Pamela,** and **Sara Kiesler.** "Communication across Boundaries: Work, Structure, and Use of Communication Technologies in a Large Organization." *Organization Science* 6, no. 4 (July–August 1995).

**Hitt, Lorin M.** "Information Technology and Firm Boundaries: Evidence from Panel Data." *Information Systems Research* 10, no. 2 (June 1999).

**Hitt, Lorin M.,** and **Erik Brynjolfsson.** "Information Technology and Internal Firm Organization: An Exploratory Analysis." *Journal of Management Information Systems* 14, no. 2 (Fall 1997).

**Huber, George.** "Organizational Learning: The Contributing Processes and Literature." *Organization Science,* 2 (1991), pp. 88–115.

———. "The Nature and Design of Post-Industrial Organizations." *Management Science* 30, no. 8 (August 1984).

**Huber, George P.** "Cognitive Style as a Basis for MIS and DSS Designs: Much Ado About Nothing?" *Management Science* 29 (May 1983).

**Isenberg, Daniel J.** "How Senior Managers Think." *Harvard Business Review* (November–December 1984).

**Jensen, M.,** and **W. Meckling.** "Theory of the Firm: Managerial Behavior, Agency Costs, and Ownership Structure." *Journal of Financial Economics* 3 (1976).

**Jensen, M. C.,** and **W. H. Meckling.** "Specific and General Knowledge and Organizational Science." In *Contract Economics,* edited by L. Wetin and J. Wijkander. Oxford: Basil Blackwell (1992).

**Johnston, David Cay.** "A Kinder, Smarter Tax System for Kansas." *The New York Times* (June 22, 1998).

**Johnston, Russell,** and **Michael R. Vitale.** "Creating Competitive Advantage with Interorganizational Information Systems." *MIS Quarterly* 12, no. 2 (June 1988).

**Kambil, Ajit,** and **James E. Short.** "Electronic Integration and Business Network Redesign: A Roles-Linkage Perspective." *Journal of Management Information Systems* 10, no. 4 (Spring 1994).

**Kanter, Rosabeth Moss.** "The New Managerial Work." *Harvard Business Review* (November–December 1989).

**Keen, Peter G. W.** *Competing in Time: Using Telecommunications for Competitive Advantage.* Cambridge, MA: Ballinger Publishing Company (1986).

———. *Shaping the Future: Business Design Through Information Technology.* Cambridge, MA: Harvard Business School Press (1991).

———. "Information Systems and Organizational Change." *Communications of the ACM* 24, no. 1 (January 1981).

———. *The Process Edge.* Boston, MA: Harvard Business School Press (1997).

**Kettinger, William J., Varun Grover, Subashish Guhan,** and **Albert H. Segors.** "Strategic Information Systems Revisited: A Study in Sustainability and Performance." *MIS Quarterly* 18, no. 1 (March 1994).

**King, J. L., V. Gurbaxani, K. L. Kraemer, F. W. McFarlan, K. S. Raman,** and **C. S. Yap.** "Institutional Factors in Information Technology Innovation." *Information Systems Research* 5, no. 2 (June 1994).

**King, W. R.** "Creating a Strategic Capabilities Architecture." *Information Systems Management* 12, no. 1 (Winter 1995).

**Kling, Rob.** "Social Analyses of Computing: Theoretical Perspectives in Recent Empirical Research." *Computing Survey* 12, no. 1 (March 1980).

**Kling, Rob,** and **William H. Dutton.** "The Computer Package: Dynamic Complexity." In *Computers and Politics,* edited by James Danziger, William Dutton, Rob Kling, and Kenneth Kraemer. New York: Columbia University Press (1982).

**Kolb, D. A.,** and **A. L. Frohman.** "An Organization Development Approach to Consulting." *Sloan Management Review* 12, no. 1 (Fall 1970).

**Konsynski, Benn R.,** and **F. Warren McFarlan.** "Information Partnerships—Shared Data, Shared Scale." *Harvard Business Review* (September–October 1990).

**Kotter, John T.** "What Effective General Managers Really Do." *Harvard Business Review* (November–December 1982).

**Kraemer, Kenneth, John King, Debora Dunkle,** and **Joe Lane.** *Managing Information Systems.* Los Angeles: Jossey-Bass (1989).

**Kraut, Robert, Charles Steinfield, Alice P Chan, Brian Butler,** and **Anne Hoag.** "Coordination and Virtualization: The Role of Electronic Networks and Personal Relationships. *Organization Science* 10, no. 6 (November–December 1999).

**Kumar, Kuldeep,** and **Jos Van Hillegersberg.** "ERP Experiences and Revolution." *Communications of the ACM* 43, no. 4 (April 2000).

**Laudon, Kenneth C.** *Computers and Bureaucratic Reform.* New York: Wiley (1974).

———. *Dossier Society: Value Choices in the Design of National Information Systems.* New York: Columbia University Press (1986).

———. "Environmental and Institutional Models of Systems Development." *Communications of the ACM* 28, no. 7 (July 1985).

———. "A General Model of the Relationship Between Information Technology and Organizations." Center for Research on Information Systems, New York University. Working paper, National Science Foundation (1989).

———. "The Promise and Potential of Enterprise Systems and Industrial Networks." Working paper, The Concours Group. Copyright Kenneth C. Laudon (1999).

**Lawrence, Paul,** and **Jay Lorsch.** *Organization and Environment.* Cambridge, MA: Harvard University Press (1969).

**Leavitt, Harold J.** "Applying Organizational Change in Industry: Structural, Technological, and Humanistic Approaches." In *Handbook of Organizations,* edited by James G. March. Chicago: Rand McNally (1965).

**Leavitt, Harold J.,** and **Thomas L. Whisler.** "Management in the 1980s." *Harvard Business Review* (November–December 1958).

**Lee, Ho-Geun.** "Do Electronic Marketplaces Lower the Price of Goods?" *Communications of the ACM* 41, no. 1 (January 1998).

**Lindblom, C. E.** "The Science of Muddling Through." *Public Administration Review* 19 (1959).

**Machlup, Fritz.** *The Production and Distribution of Knowledge in the United States.* Princeton, NJ: Princeton University Press (1962).

**Maier, Jerry L., R. Kelly Rainer, Jr.,** and **Charles A. Snyder.** "Environmental Scanning for Information Technology: An Empirical Investigation." *Journal of Management Information Systems* 14, no. 2 (Fall 1997).

**Main, Thomas J.,** and **James E. Short.** "Managing the Merger: Building Partnership Through IT Planning at the New Baxter." *MIS Quarterly* 13, no. 4 (December 1989).

**Malcolm, Andrew H.** "How the Oil Spilled and Spread: Delay and Confusion Off Alaska." *The New York Times* (April 16, 1989).

**Malone, Thomas W.** "Is Empowerment Just a Fad? Control, Decision-Making, and IT." *Sloan Management Review* (Winter 1997).

**March, James G.,** and **Herbert A. Simon.** *Organizations.* New York: Wiley (1958).

**March, James G.,** and **G. Sevon.** "Gossip, Information, and Decision Making." In *Advances in Information Processing in Organizations,* edited by Lee S. Sproull and J. P. Crecine. vol. 1. Hillsdale, NJ: Erlbaum (1984).

**Markus, M. L.** "Power, Politics, and MIS Implementation." *Communications of the ACM* 26, no. 6 (June 1983).

**Mata, Franciso J., William L. Fuerst,** and **Jay B. Barney.** "Information Technology and Sustained Competitive Advantage: A Resource-Based Analysis." *MIS Quarterly* 19, no. 4 (December 1995).

**McFarlan, F. Warren.** "Information Technology Changes the Way You Compete." *Harvard Business Review* (May–June 1984).

**McKenney, James L.,** and **Peter G. W. Keen.** "How Managers' Minds Work." *Harvard Business Review* (May–June 1974).

**Mendelson, Haim,** and **Ravindra R. Pillai.** "Clock Speed and Informational Response: Evidence from the Information Technology Industry." *Information Systems Research* 9, no. 4 (December 1998).

**Mintzberg, Henry.** "Managerial Work: Analysis from Observation." *Management Science* 18 (October 1971).

———. *The Structuring of Organizations.* Englewood Cliffs, NJ: Prentice Hall (1979).

———. *The Nature of Managerial Work.* New York: Harper & Row (1973).

**Orlikowski, Wanda J.,** and **Daniel Robey.** "Information Technology and the Structuring of Organizations." *Information Systems Research* 2, no. 2 (June 1991).

**Pindyck, Robert S.,** and **Daniel L. Rubinfeld.** *Microeconomics, Fifth Ed.* Upper Saddle River, NJ: Prentice Hall (2001).

**Porter, Michael.** *Competitive Strategy.* New York: Free Press (1980).

———. *Competitive Advantage.* New York: Free Press (1985).

———. "How Information Can Help You Compete." *Harvard Business Review* (August–September 1985a).

———. "Strategy and the Internet." *Harvard Business Review* (March 2001).

**Rangan, V. Kasturi,** and **Marie Bell.** "Dell Online." Harvard Business School Case 9-598-116 (1998).

**Rebello, Joseph.** "State Street Boston's Allure for Investors Starts to Fade." *The Wall Street Journal* (January 4, 1995).

**Reich, Blaize Horner,** and **Izak Benbasat.** "Factors that Influence the Social Dimension of Alignment between Business and Information Technology Objectives." *MIS Quarterly 24,* no. 1 (March 2000).

**Robey, Daniel,** and **Marie-Claude Boudreau.** "Accounting for the Contradictory Organizational Consequences of Information Technology: Theoretical Directions and Methodological Implications." *Information Systems Research* 10, no. 42 (June 1999).

**Robey, Daniel,** and **Sundeep Sahay.** "Transforming Work through Information Technology: A Comparative Case Study of Geographic Information Systems in County Government." *Information Systems Research* 7, no. 1 (March 1996).

**Sauter, Vicki L.** "Intuitive Decision-Making." *Communications of the ACM* 42, no 6 (June 1999).

**Schein, Edgar H.** *Organizational Culture and Leadership.* San Francisco: Jossey-Bass (1985).

**Schwenk, C. R.** "Cognitive Simplification Processes in Strategic Decision Making." *Strategic Management Journal,* 5 (1984).

**Shapiro, Carl,** and **Hal R. Varian.** *Information Rules.* Boston, MA: Harvard Business School Press (1999).

**Shore, Edwin B.** "Reshaping the IS Organization." *MIS Quarterly* (December 1983).

**Short, James E.,** and **N. Venkatraman.** "Beyond Business Process Redesign: Redefining Baxter's Business Network." *Sloan Management Review* (Fall 1992).

**Simon, H. A.** *The New Science of Management Decision.* New York: Harper & Row (1960).

**Simon, Herbert A.** "Applying Information Technology to Organization Design." *Public Administration Review* (May–June 1973).

**Staples, D. Sandy, John S. Hulland,** and **Christopher A. Higgins.** "A Self-Efficacy Theory Explanation for the Management of Remote Workers in Virtual Organizations." *Organization Science* 10, no. 6 (November–December 1999).

**Starbuck, William H.** "Organizations as Action Generators." *American Sociological Review* 48 (1983).

**Starbuck, William H.,** and **Frances J. Milliken.** "Executives' Perceptual Filters: What They Notice and How They Make Sense." In *The Executive Effect: Concepts and Methods for Studying Top Managers,* edited by D. C. Hambrick. Greenwich, CT: JAI Press (1988).

**Straub, Detmar,** and **James C. Wetherbe.** "Information Technologies for the 1990s: An Organizational Impact Perspective." *Communications of the ACM* 32, no. 11 (November 1989).

**Turner, Jon A.** "Computer Mediated Work: The Interplay Between Technology and Structured Jobs." *Communications of the ACM* 27, no. 12 (December 1984).

**Turner, Jon A.,** and **Robert A. Karasek, Jr.** "Software Ergonomics: Effects of Computer Application Design Parameters on Operator Task Performance and Health." *Ergonomics* 27, no. 6 (1984).

**Tushman, Michael L.,** and **Philip Anderson.** "Technological Discontinuities and Organizational Environments." *Administrative Science Quarterly* 31 (September 1986).

**Tversky, A.,** and **D. Kahneman.** "The Framing of Decisions and the Psychology of Choice." *Science* 211 (January 1981).

**Uslaner, Eric M.** "Social Capital and the Net." *Communications of the ACM* 43, no. 12 (December 2000).

**Weber, Max.** *The Theory of Social and Economic Organization.* Translated by Talcott Parsons. New York: Free Press (1947).

**Williamson, Oliver E.** *The Economic Institutions of Capitalism.* New York: Free Press, (1985).

**Wiseman, Charles.** *Strategic Information Systems.* Homewood, IL: Richard D. Irwin (1988).

**Wrapp, H. Edward.** "Good Managers Don't Make Policy Decisions." *Harvard Business Review* (July–August 1984).

## Chapter 4

**Andrew, James P., Andy Blackburn,** and **Harold L. Sirkin.** "The Business-to-Business Opportunity." Boston Consulting Group (October 2000).

**Armstrong, Arthur,** and **John Hagel, III.** "The Real Value of On-line Communities." *Harvard Business Review* (May–June 1996).

**Bakos, Yannis.** "The Emerging Role of Electronic Marketplaces and the Internet." *Communications of the ACM* 41, no. 8 (August 1998).

**Bannan, Karen J.** "Chatting Up a Sale." *The Wall Street Journal* (October 23, 2000).

**Baron, John P., Michael J. Shaw,** and **Andrew D. Bailey, Jr.** "Web-based E-catalog Systems in B2B Procurement." *Communications of the ACM* 43, no.5 (May 2000).

**Barua, Anitesh, Sury Ravindran,** and **Andrew B. Whinston.** "Efficient Selection of Suppliers over the Internet." *Journal of Management Information Systems* 13, no. 4 (Spring 1997).

**Baum, David.** "E-xchange This." *Profit Magazine* (August 2000).

**Chaudhury, Abhijit, Debasish Mallick,** and **H. Raghav Rao.** "Web Channels in E-Commerce." *Communications of the ACM* 44, No. 1 (January 2001).

**Choi, Soon-Yong, Dale O. Stahl,** and **Andrew B. Whinston.** *The Economics of Electronic Commerce.* Indianapolis, IN: Macmillan Technical Publishing (1997).

**"Compaq Intranet Case Study."** *Intranet Design Magazine* (January 17, 2001).

**Corcoran, Cate T.** "The Auction Economy." *Red Herring* (August 1999).

**Crede, Andreas.** "Electronic Commerce and the Banking Industry: The Requirement and Opportunities for New Payment Systems Using the Internet." *JCMC* 1, no. 3 (December 1995).

**Cronin, Mary.** *The Internet Strategy Handbook.* Boston, MA: Harvard Business School Press (1996).

**Dalton, Gregory.** "Going, Going, Gone!" *Information Week* (October 4, 1999).

**Downes, Larry,** and **Chunka Mui.** *Unleashing the Killer App: Digital Strategies for Market Dominance.* Boston, MA: Harvard Business School Press (1998).

**El Sawy, Omar A., Arvind Malhotra, Sanjay Gosain,** and **Kerry M. Young,** "IT-Intensive Value Innovation in the Electronic Economy: Insights from Marshall Industries, " *MIS Quarterly* 23, no. 3, (September 1999).

**Elofson, Greg,** and **William N. Robinson.** "Creating a Custom Mass Production Channel on the Internet." *Communications of the ACM* 41, no. 3 (March 1998).

**Enos, Lori.** "Report: B2B Still Driving E-Commerce." *E-Commerce Times* (December 11, 2000).

**Evans, Philip,** and **Thomas S. Wurster.** *Blown to Bits: How the New Economics of Information Transforms Strategy.* Boston, MA: Harvard Business School Press (2000).

**Evans, Philip,** and **Thomas S. Wurster.** "Getting Real about Virtual Commerce." *Harvard Business Review* (November–December 1999).

———. "Strategy and the New Economics of Information." *Harvard Business Review* (September–October 1997).

**Ghosh, Shikhar.** "Making Business Sense of the Internet." *Harvard Business Review* (March–April 1998).

**Grover, Varun,** and **Pradipkumar Ramanlal.** "Six Myths of Information and Markets: Information Technology Networks, Electronic Commerce, and the Battle for Consumer Surplus." *MIS Quarterly* 23, no. 4 (December 1999).

———, and **James T. C. Teng.** "E-Commerce and the Information Market." *Communications of the ACM* 44, no. 4 (April 2001).

**Gulati, Ranjay,** and **Jason Garino.** "Get the Right Mix of Bricks and Clicks." *Harvard Business Review* (May–June 2000).

**Hagel, John III,** and **Marc Singer.** *Net Worth.* Boston, MA: Harvard Business School Press (1999).

———. "Unbundling the Corporation." *Harvard Business Review* (March–April 1999).

**Hoffman, Donna L., William D. Kalsbeek,** and **Thomas P. Novak.** "Internet and Web Use in the U.S." *Communications of the ACM* 39, no. 12 (December 1996).

**Hogan, Kevin,** and **Matt Beer.** "The New Economy: Five Who Get It and Five Who Don't." *Business 2.0* (June 2000).

**Jahnke, Art.** "It Takes a Village." *CIO WebBusiness* (February 1, 1998).

**Jones, Sara, Marc Wilikens, Philip Morris,** and **Marcelo Masera.** "Trust Requirements in E-Business." *Communications of the ACM* 43, no. 12 (December 2000).

**Kalakota, Ravi,** and **Andrew B. Whinston.** *Electronic Commerce: A Manager's Guide.* Reading MA: Addison-Wesley (1997).

**Kanan, P. K., Ai-Mei Chang,** and **Andrew B. Whinston.** "Marketing Information on the I-Way." *Communications of the ACM* 41, no. 3 (March 1998).

**Kaplan, Steven,** and **Mohanbir Sawhney.** "E-Hubs: the New B2B Marketplaces." *Harvard Business Review* (May–June 2000).

**Kenny, David,** and **John F. Marshall.** "Contextual Marketing." *Harvard Business Review* (November–December 2000).

**Lee, Ho Geun.** "Do Electronic Marketplaces Lower the Price of Goods?" *Communications of the ACM* 41, no. 1 (January 1998).

**Lee, Ho Geun,** and **Theodore H. Clark.** "Market Process Reengineering through Electronic Market Systems: Opportunities and Challenges." *Journal of Management Information Systems* 13, no. 3 (Winter 1997).

**McWilliam, Gil.** "Building Stronger Brands through Online Communities." *Sloan Management Review* 41, no. 3 (Spring 2000).

**Mougayar, Walid.** *Opening Digital Markets,* 2nd ed. New York: McGraw-Hill (1998).

**Mullich, Joe.** "Reinvent Your Intranet." *Datamation* (June 1999).

**O'Leary, Daniel E., Daniel Koukka,** and **Robert Plant.** "Artificial Intelligence and Virtual Organizations." *Communications of the ACM* 40, no. 1 (January 1997).

**Palmer, Jonathan W.,** and **David A. Griffith.** "An Emerging Model of Web Site Design for Marketing." *Communications of the ACM* 41, no. 3 (March 1998).

**Prahalad, C. K.,** and **Venkatram Ramaswamy.** "Coopting Consumer Competence." *Harvard Business Review* (January–February 2000).

**Quelch, John A.,** and **Lisa R. Klein.** "The Internet and International Marketing." *Sloan Management Review* (Spring 1996).

**Rafter, Michelle V.** "Can We Talk?" *The Industry Standard* (February 15, 1999).

**Rayport, J. F.,** and **J. J. Sviokla.** "Managing in the Marketspace." *Harvard Business Review* (November–December 1994).

**Redburn, Tom.** "How Much Am I Bid for this Imperfect Marketplace?" *The New York Times E-Commerce Section* (December 13, 2000).

**Reichheld, Frederick E.,** and **Phil Schefter.** "E-Loyalty: Your Secret Weapon on the Web." *Harvard Business Review* (July–August 2000).

**Sarkar, Mitra Barun, Brian Butler,** and **Charles Steinfield.** "Intermediaries and Cybermediaries: A Continuing Role for Mediating Players in the Electronic Marketplace." *JCMC* 1, no. 3 (December 1995).

**Schoder, Detlef,** and **Pai-ling Yin.** "Building Firm Trust Online." *Communications of the ACM* 43, no. 12 (December 2000).

**Singh, Surendra N.,** and **Nikunj P. Dalal.** "Web Home Pages as Advertisements." *Communications of the ACM* 42, no. 8 (August 1999).

**Smith, Michael D., Joseph Bailey,** and **Erik Brynjolfsson.** "Understanding Digital Markets: Review and Assessment" in Erik Brynjolfsson and Brian Kahin, ed. *Understanding the Digital Economy.* Cambridge, MA: MIT Press (1999).

**Steinfield, Charles.** "The Impact of Electronic Commerce on Buyer-Seller Relationships." *JCMC* 1, no. 3 (December 1995).

**Sterne, Jim.** "Customer Interface." *CIO WebBusiness* (February 1, 1998).

**Venkatraman, N.** "Five Steps to a Dot-Com Strategy: How to Find Your Footing on the Web." *Sloan Management Review* 41, no. 3 (Spring 2000).

**Werbach, Kevin.** "Syndication: The Emerging Model for Business in the Internet Era." *Harvard Business Review* (May–June 2000).

**Wigand, Rolf T.,** and **Robert Benjamin.** "Electronic Commerce: Effects on Electronic Markets." *JCMC* 1, no. 3 (December 1995).

**Wise, Richard,** and **David Morrison.** "Beyond the Exchange: The Future of B2B." *Harvard Business Review* (November–December 2000).

**Young, Eric.** "B2B's Broken Models." *The Industry Standard* (November 6, 2000).

## CHAPTER 5

**Alison, Diana.** "IT Takes on Handheld Management." *Information Week* (May 29, 2000).

**Anthes, Gary H.** "Supercomputers Make a Comeback." *Computerworld* (July 3, 2000).

**Brannigan, Mary.** "Bill Payments Over the Internet Get a Big Boost." *The Wall Street Journal* (January 28, 1999).

**Fitzmaurice, George W., Rvain Balakrishnan,** and **Gordon Kurtenbach.** "Sampling, Synthesis, and Input Devices." *Communications of the ACM* 42, no. 8 (August 1999).

**Fulton, Susan M.** "Speak Softly, Carry a Big Chip," *The New York Times Circuits* (March 30, 2000).

**Garber, Angela R.** "Ready, Set, Grow." *Small Business Computing* (September 2000).

**Gibson, Garth A.,** and **Rodney Van Meter.** "Network Attached Storage Architecture." *Communications of the ACM* 43, no. 11 (November 2000).

**Hardaway, Don,** and **Richard P. Will.** "Digital Multimedia Offers Key to Educational Reform." *Communications of the ACM* 40, no. 4 (April 1997).

**Jacobs, April.** "The Network Computer: Where It's Going." *Computerworld* (December 23, 1997/January 2, 1998).

**Lohr, Steve.** "The Network Computer as the PC's Evil Twin," *The New York Times* (November 4, 1996).

**Markoff, John.** "Computer Scientists are Poised for Revolution on a Tiny Scale." *The New York Times* (November 1, 1999).

———. "Tiniest Circuits Hold Prospect of Explosive Computer Speeds," *The New York Times* (July 16, 1999).

**Messina, Paul, David Culler, Wayne Pfeiffer, William Martin, J. Tinsley Oden,** and **Gary Smith.** "Architecture." *Communications of the ACM* 41, no. 11 (November 1998).

**Paul, Lauren Gibbons.** "What Price Ownership?" *Datamation* (December/January 1998).

**Peleg, Alex, Sam Wilkie,** and **Uri Weiser.** "Intel MMX for Multimedia PCs." *Communications of the ACM* 40, no. 1 (January 1997).

**Post, Gerald V.** "How Often Should a Firm Buy New PCs?" *Communications of the ACM* 42, no. 5 (May 1999).

**Robinson, Teri.** "NASDAQ Is Bullish on Technology." *Information Week* (May 22, w2000).

**Selker, Ted.** "New Paradigms for Using Computers." *Communications of the ACM* 39, no. 8 (August 1996).

**Tennenhouse, David.** "Proactive Computing." *Communications of the ACM* 43, no. 5 (May 2000).

**Weiser, Mark.** "Some Computer Science Issues in Ubiquitous Computing." *Communications of the ACM* 36, no. 7 (July 1993).

## CHAPTER 6

**Barrett, Jim, Kevin Knight, Inderject Man,** and **Elaine Rich.** "Knowledge and Natural Language Processing." *Communications of the ACM* 33, no. 8 (August 1990).

**Bosak, Jon,** and **Tim Bray.** "XML and the Second-Generation Web." *Scientific American* (May 1999).

**Clark, Don.** "Sun Microsystems Still Has a Legion of Believers." *The Wall Street Journal* (March 23, 1998).

———. "The End of Software." *The Wall Street Journal Technology Report* (November 15, 1999).

**Fayad, Mohamed,** and **Marshall P. Cline.** "Aspects of Software Adaptability." *Communications of the ACM* 39, no. 10 (October 1996).

**Flynn, Jim,** and **Bill Clarke.** "How Java Makes Network-Centric Computing Real." *Datamation* (March 1, 1996).

**Gomes, Lee.** "Somebody Else's Problem." *The Wall Street Journal Technology Report* (November 15, 1999).

**Gowan, J. Arthur, Chris Jesse,** and **Richard G. Mathieu.** "Y2K Compliance and the Distributed Enterprise." *Communications of the ACM* 42, no. 2 (February 1999).

**Haavind, Robert.** "Software's New Object Lesson," *Technology Review* (February–March 1992).

**Johnson, Ralph E.** "Frameworks 5 (Components 1 Patterns)." *Communications of the ACM* 40, no. 10 (October 1997).

**Kappelman, Leon A., Darla Fent, Kellie B. Keeling,** and **Victor Prybutok.** "Calculating the Cost of Year 2000 Compliance." *Communications of the ACM* 41, no. 2 (February 1998).

**Kim, Yongbeom,** and **Edward A. Stohr.** "Software Reuse." *Journal of Management Information Systems* 14, no. 4 (Spring 1998).

**Korson, Tim,** and **John D. McGregor.** "Understanding Object-Oriented: A Unifying Paradigm." *Communications of the ACM* 33, no. 9 (September 1990).

**Linthicum, David S.** "EAI Application Integration Exposed." *Software Magazine* (February/March 2000).

**Mandelkern, David.** "Graphical User Interfaces: The Next Generation." *Communications of the ACM* 36, no. 4 (April 1993).

**Meyer, Marc H.,** and **Robert Seliger,** "Product Platforms in Software Development." *Sloan Management Review* 40, no. 1 (Fall 1998).

**Morse, Alan,** and **George Reynolds.** "Overcoming Current Growth Limits in UI Development." *Communications of the ACM* 36, no. 4 (April 1993).

**Nilsen, Kelvin.** "Adding Real-Time Capabilities to Java." *Communications of the ACM* 41, no. 6 (June 1998).

**Noffsinger, W. B., Robert Niedbalski, Michael Blanks,** and **Niall Emmart.** "Legacy Object Modeling Speeds Software Integration." *Communications of the ACM* 41, no. 12 (December 1998).

**Poulin, Jeffrey S.** "Reuse: Been There, Done That." *Communications of the ACM* 42, no. 5 (May 1999).

**Prahalad, C. K.,** and **M.S. Krishnan.** "The New Meaning of Quality in the Information Age." *Harvard Business Review* (September–October 1999).

**Purao, Sandeep, Hemant Jain,** and **Derek Nazareth.** "Effective Distribution of Object-Oriented Applications." *Communications of the ACM* 41, no. 8 (August 1998).

**Satzinger, John W.,** and **Lorne Olfman.** "User Interface Consistency Across Applications." *Journal of Management Infomation Systems* 14, no. 4 (Spring 1998).

**Sheetz, Steven D., Gretchen Irwin, David P. Tegarden, H. James Nelson,** and **David E. Monarchi.** "Exploring the Difficulties of Learning Object-Oriented Techniques." *Journal of Management Information Systems* 14, no. 2 (Fall 1997).

**Tyma, Paul.** "Why Are We Using Java Again?" *Communications of the ACM* 41, no. 6 (June 1998).

**Vassiliou, Yannis.** "On the Interactive Use of Databases: Query Languages." *Journal of Management Information Systems* 1 (Winter 1984–1985).

**Wilkes, Maurice V.** "The Long-Term Future of Operating Systems." *Communications of the ACM* 35, no. 11 (November 1992).

## CHAPTER 7

**Belkin, Nicholas J.,** and **W. Bruce Croft.** "Information Filtering and Information Retrieval: Two Sides of the Same Coin?" *Communications of the ACM* 35, no. 12 (November 1992).

**Chang, Shih-Fu, John R. Amith, Mandis Beigi,** and **Ana Benitez.** "Visual Information Retrieval from Large Distributed On-line Repositories." *Communications of the ACM* 40, no. 12 (December 1997).

**Clifford, James, Albert Croker,** and **Alex Tuzhilin.** "On Data Representation and Use in a Temporal Relational DBMS." *Information Systems Research* 7, no. 3 (September 1996).

**Cooper, Brian L., Hugh J. Watson, Barbara H. Wixom,** and **Dale L. Goodhue.** "Data Warehousing Supports Corporate Strategy at First American Corporation." *MIS Quarterly* (December 2000).

**Fiori, Rich.** "The Information Warehouse." *Relational Database Journal* (January–February 1995).

**Gardner, Stephen R.** "Building the Data Warehouse." *Communications of the ACM* 41, no. 9 (September 1998).

**Goldstein, R. C.,** and **J. B. McCririck.** "What Do Data Administrators Really Do?" *Datamation* 26 (August 1980).

**Goodhue, Dale L., Judith A. Quillard,** and **John F. Rockart.** "Managing the Data Resource: A Contingency Perspective." *MIS Quarterly* (September 1988).

**Goodhue, Dale L., Laurie J. Kirsch, Judith A. Quillard,** and **Michael D. Wybo.** "Strategic Data Planning: Lessons from the Field." *MIS Quarterly* 16, no. 1 (March 1992).

**Goodhue, Dale L., Michael D. Wybo,** and **Laurie J. Kirsch.** "The Impact of Data Integration on the Costs and Benefits of Information Systems." *MIS Quarterly* 16, no. 3 (September 1992).

**Greengard, Samuel.** "Assembling a Hybrid Data Warehouse." *Beyond Computing* (March 1999).

**Grosky, William I.** "Managing Multimedia Information in Database Systems." *Communications of the ACM* 40, no. 12 (December 1997).

**Grover, Varun,** and **James Teng.** "How Effective Is Data Resource Management?" *Journal of Information Systems Management* (Summer 1991).

**Gupta, Amarnath,** and **Ranesh Jain.** "Visual Information Retrieval." *Communications of the ACM* 40, no. 5 (May 1997).

**Inman, W. H.** "The Data Warehouse and Data Mining." *Communications of the ACM* 39, no. 11 (November 1996).

**Kahn, Beverly K.** "Some Realities of Data Administration." *Communications of the ACM* 26 (October 1983).

**King, John L.,** and **Kenneth Kraemer.** "Information Resource Management Cannot Work." *Information and Management* (1988).

**Kroenke, David.** *Database Processing: Fundamentals, Design, and Implementation,* 7th ed. Upper Saddle River, NJ: Prentice Hall (2000).

**Lange, Danny B.** "An Object-Oriented Design Approach for Developing Hypermedia Information Systems." *Journal of Organizational Computing and Electronic Commerce* 6, no. 2 (1996).

**March, Salvatore T.**, and **Young-Gul Kim.** "Information Resource Management: A Metadata Perspective." *Journal of Management Information Systems* 5, no. 3 (Winter 1988–1989).

**McCarthy, John.** "Phenomenal Data Mining." *Communications of the ACM* 43, no. 8 (August 2000).

**McFadden, Fred R., Jeffrey A. Hoffer,** and **Mary B. Prescott.** *Modern Database Management,* Fifth Edition. Upper Saddle River, NJ: Prentice-Hall (1999).

**Rundensteiner, Elke A, Andreas Koeller,** and **Xin Zhang.** "Maintaining Data Warehouses over Changing Information Sources." *Communications of the ACM* 43, no. 6 (June 2000).

**Silberschatz, Avi, Michael Stonebraker,** and **Jeff Ullman,** eds. "Database Systems: Achievements and Opportunities." *Communications of the ACM* 34, no. 10 (October 1991).

**Smith, John B.,** and **Stephen F. Weiss.** "Hypertext." *Communications of the ACM* 31, no. 7 (July 1988).

**Truman, Gregory E.** "Integration in Electronic Exchange Environments." *Journal of Management Information Systems* 17, no. 1 (Summer 2000).

**Watson, Hugh J.,** and **Barbara J. Haley.** "Managerial Considerations." *Communications of the ACM* 41, no. 9 (September 1998).

**Woods, Tony,** and **Kate O'Rourke.** "Keeping Track of Customers." *E-Doc* (May/June 2000).

## CHAPTER 8

**Boston Consulting Group.** "Mobile Commerce: Winning the On-Air Consumer" (November 2000).

**Chatfield, Akemi Takeoka,** and **Philip Yetton.** "Strategic Payoff from EDI as a Function of EDI Embeddedness." *Journal of Management Information Systems* 16, no. 4 (Spring 2000).

**Chatterjee, Samir.** "Requirements for Success in Gigabit Networking." *Communications of the ACM* 40, no. 7 (July 1997).

**Chatterjee, Samir,** and **Suzanne Pawlowski.** "All-Optical Networks." *Communications of the ACM* 42, no. 6 (June 1999).

**Concours Group.** "Managing and Exploiting Corporate Intranets" (1999).

**Duchessi, Peter,** and **InduShobha Chengalur-Smith.** "Client/Server Benefits, Problems, Best Practices." *Communications of the ACM* 41, no. 5 (May 1998).

**Gefen, David,** and **Detmar W. Straub.** "Gender Differences in the Perception and Use of E-Mail: An Extension to the Technology Acceptance Model." *MIS Quarterly* 21, no. 4 (December 1997).

**Grover, Varun,** and **Martin D. Goslar.** "Initiation, Adoption, and Implementation of Telecommunications Technologies in U.S. Organizations." *Journal of Management Information Systems* 10, no. 1 (Summer 1993).

**Hansen, James V.,** and **Ned C. Hill.** "Control and Audit of Electronic Data Interchange." *MIS Quarterly* 13, no. 4 (December 1989).

**Hart, Paul J.,** and **Carol Stoak Saunders.** "Emerging Electronic Partnerships: Antecedents and Dimensions of EDI Use from the Supplier's Perspective." *Journal of Management Information Systems* 14, no. 4 (Spring 1998).

**Heywood, Peter.** "Charge of the Light Brigade." *Red Herring* (February 2000).

**Hill, G. Christian.** "First Voice, Now Data." *The Wall Street Journal* (September 20, 1999).

**Imielinski, Tomasz,** and **B. R. Badrinath.** "Mobile Wireless Computing: Challenges in Data Management." *Communications of the ACM* 37, no. 10 (October 1994).

**Karahanna, Elena,** and **Moez Limayem.** "E-Mail and V-Mail Usage: Generalizing Across Technologies." *Journal of Organizational Computing and Electronic Commerce* 10, no. 1 (2000).

**Keen, Peter G. W.** *Competing in Time.* Cambridge, MA: Ballinger Publishing Company (1986).

**Kim, B. G.,** and **P. Wang.** "ATM Network: Goals and Challenges." *Communications of the ACM* 38, no. 2 (February 1995).

**Lee, Ho Geun, Theodore Clark,** and **Kar Yan Tam.** "Research Report: Can EDI Benefit Adopters?" *Information Systems Research* 10, no. 2 (June 1999).

**Massetti, Brenda,** and **Robert W. Zmud.** "Measuring the Extent of EDI Usage in Complex Organizations. Strategies and Illustrative Examples." *MIS Quarterly* 20, no. 3 (September 1996).

**Mears, Rena,** and **Jason Salzetti.** "The New Wireless Enterprise." *Information Week* (September 18, 2000).

**Meister, Frank, Jeetu Patel,** and **Joe Fenner.** "E-Commerce Platforms Mature." *Information Week* (October 23, 2000).

**Mueller, Milton.** "Universal Service and the Telecommunications Act: Myth Made Law." *Communications of the ACM* 40, no. 3 (March 1997).

**Nakamura, Kiyoh, Toshihiro Ide,** and **Yukio Kiyokane.** "Roles of Multimedia Technology in Telework." *Journal of Organizational Computing and Electronic Commerce* 6, no. 4 (1996).

**Ngwenyama, Ojelanki,** and **Allen S. Lee.** "Communication Richness in Electronic Mail: Critical Social Theory and the Contextuality of Meaning." *MIS Quarterly* 21, no. 2 (June 1997).

**Passmore, David.** "Scaling Large E-Commerce Infrastructures." *Packet Magazine* (Third Quarter 1999).

**"Plans and Policies for Client/Server Technology."** *I/S Analyzer* 30, no. 4 (April 1992).

**Pottie, G.J.,** and **W.J Kaiser.** "Wireless Integrated Network Sensors." *Communications of the ACM* 43, no. 5 (May 2000).

**Premkumar, G., K. Ramamurthy,** and **Sree Nilakanta.** "Implementation of Electronic Data Interchange: An Innovation Diffusion Perspective." *Journal of Management Information Systems* 11, no. 2 (Fall 1994).

**Raymond, Louis,** and **Francois Bergeron.** "EDI Success in Small- and Medium-sized Enterprises: A Field Study." *Journal of Organizational Computing and Electronic Commerce* 6, no. 2 (1996).

**Roche, Edward M.** *Telecommunications and Business Strategy.* Chicago: The Dryden Press (1991).

**Sharda, Nalin.** "Multimedia Networks: Fundamentals and Future Directions." *Communications of the Association for Information Systems* (February 1999).

**Sinha, Alok.** "Client-Server Computing." *Communications of the ACM* 35, no. 7 (July 1992).

**Teo, Hock-Hai, Bernard C. Y. Tan,** and **Kwok-Kee Wei.** "Organizational Transformation Using Electronic Data Interchange: The Case of TradeNet in Singapore." *Journal of Management Information Systems* 13, no. 4 (Spring 1997).

**Thompson, Marjorie Sarbough,** and **Martha S. Feldman.** "Electronic Mail and Organizational Communication." *Organization Science* 9, no. 6 (November–December 1998).

**Torkzadeh, Gholamreza,** and **Weidong Xia.** "Managing Telecommunications Strategy by Steering Committee." *MIS Quarterly* 16, no. 2 (June 1992).

**Varshney, Upkar.** "Networking Support for Mobile Computing." *Communications of the Association for Information Systems* 1 (January 1999).

———, and **Ron Vetter.** "Emerging Mobile and Wireless Networks. *Communications of the ACM* 42, no. 6 (June 2000).

**Vetter, Ronald J.** "ATM Concepts, Architectures, and Protocols." *Communications of the ACM* 38, no. 2 (February 1995).

**Waldo, Jim.** "The Jini Architecture for Network-centric Computing." *Communications of the ACM 42,* no. 7 (July 1999).

**Whitman, Michael E., Anthony M. Townsend,** and **Robert J. Aalberts.** "Considerations for Effective Telecommunications-Use Policy." *Communications of the ACM* 42, no. 6 (June 1999).

## Chapter 9

**Amor, Daniel.** *The E-Business Revolution.* Upper Saddle River, NJ: Prentice-Hall (2000).

**Applegate, Lynda,** and **Janice Gogan.** "Paving the Information Superhighway: Introduction to the Internet," *Harvard Business School* 9-195-202 (August 1995).

**Berners-Lee, Tim, Robert Cailliau, Ari Luotonen, Henrik Frystyk Nielsen,** and **Arthur Secret.** "The World-Wide Web." *Communications of the ACM* 37, no. 8 (August 1994).

**Bikson, Tora K., Cathleen Stasz,** and **Donald A. Monkin.** "Computer-Mediated Work: Individual and Organizational Impact on One Corporate Headquarters." Rand Corporation (1985).

**Borriello, Gaetano,** and **Roy Want.** "Embedded Computation Meets the World Wide Web." *Communications of the ACM* 43, no. 5 (May 2000).

**Byrd, Terry Anthony.** "Measuring the Flexibility of Information Technology Infrastructure: Exploratory Analysis of a Construct." *Journal of Management Information Systems* 17, no. 1 (Summer 2000).

**Cheyne, Tanya L.,** and **Frank E. Ritter.** "Targeting Audiences on the Internet." *Communications of the ACM* 44, no. 4 (April 2001).

**Garner, Rochelle.** "Internet2. . . and Counting." *CIO Magazine* (September 1, 1999).

**Goodman, S. E., L. I. Press, S. R. Ruth,** and **A. M. Rutkowski.** "The Global Diffusion of the Internet: Patterns and Problems." *Communications of the ACM* 37, no. 8 (August 1994).

**Greengard, Samuel.** "All for One." *Internet World* (March 1, 2001).

**Hardman, Vicky, Martina Angela Sasse,** and **Isidor Kouvelas.** "Successful Multiparty Audio Communication over the Internet." *Communications of the ACM* 41, no. 5 (May 1998).

**Huff, Sid, Malcolm C. Munro,** and **Barbara H. Martin.** "Growth Stages of End User Computing." *Communications of the ACM* (May 1988).

**Isakowitz, Tomas, Michael Bieber,** and **Fabio Vitali.** "Web Information Systems." *Communications of the ACM* 41, no. 7 (July 1998).

**Kanter, Rosabeth Moss.** "The Ten Deadly Mistakes of Wanna-Dots." *Harvard Business Review* (January 2001).

**Kautz, Henry, Bart Selman,** and **Mehul Shah.** "ReferralWeb: Combining Social Networks and Collaborative Filtering." *Communications of the ACM* 40, no. 3 (March 1997).

**Keen, Peter.** "Ready for the 'New' B2B?" *Computerworld* (September 11, 2000).

**Kendall, Kenneth E.,** and **Julie E. Kendall.** "Information Delivery Systems: An Exploration of Web Push and Pull Technologies." *Communications of the Association for Information Systems* 1 (April 1999).

**Kuo, Geng-Sheng,** and **Jing-Pei Lin.** "New Design Concepts for an Intelligent Internet." *Communications of the ACM* 41, no. 11 (November 1998).

**Laudon, Kenneth C.** "From PCs to Managerial Workstations." In Matthias Jarke, *Managers, Micros, and Mainframes.* New York: John Wiley (1986).

**Lewis, Nicole.** "Internet Telephony: The Business Connection." *Beyond Computing* (July/August 1999).

**Lohse, Gerald L.,** and **Peter Spiller.** "Electronic Shopping." *Communications of the ACM* 41, no. 7 (July 1998).

**Mike P. Papazoglou.** "Agent-Oriented Technology in Support of E-Business." *Communications of the ACM* 44, no. 4 (April 2001).

**Sweeney, Terry.** "Voice Over IP Builds Momentum." *Information Week* (November 20, 2000).

**Valera, Francisco, Jorge E. López de Vergara, José I. Moreno, Víctor A. Villagrá,** and **Julio Berrocal.** "Communication Management Experiences in E-commerce." *Communications of the ACM* 44, no. 4 (April 2001).

**Vetter, Ron.** "The Wireless Web." *Communications of the ACM* 44, no. 3 (March 2001).

**Westin, Alan F., Heather A. Schweder, Michael A. Baker,** and **Sheila Lehman.** *The Changing Workplace.* New York: Knowledge Industries (1995).

## Chapter 10

**Agarwal, Ritu, Jayesh Prasad, Mohan Tanniru,** and **John Lynch.** "Risks of Rapid Application Development." *Communications of the ACM* 43, no. 11es (November 2000).

**Agarwal, Ritu, Prabudda De, Atish P. Sinha,** and **Mohan Tanniru.** "On the Usability of OO Representations." *Communications of the ACM* 43, no. 10 (October 2000).

**Ahituv, Niv,** and **Seev Neumann.** "A Flexible Approach to Information System Development." *MIS Quarterly* (June 1984).

**Aiken, Peter, Alice Muntz,** and **Russ Richards.** "DOD Legacy Systems: Reverse Engineering Data Requirements." *Communications of the ACM* 37, no. 5 (May 1994).

**Alavi, Maryam.** "An Assessment of the Prototyping Approach to Information System Development." *Communications of the ACM* 27 (June 1984).

**Alavi, Maryam, R. Ryan Nelson,** and **Ira R. Weiss.** "Strategies for End-User Computing: An Integrative Framework." *Journal of Management Information Systems* 4, no. 3 (Winter 1987–1988).

**Anderson, Evan A.** "Choice Models for the Evaluation and Selection of Software Packages." *Journal of Management Information Systems* 6, no. 4 (Spring 1990).

**Barua, Anitesh, Sophie C. H. Lee,** and **Andrew B. Whinston.** "The Calculus of Reengineering." *Information Systems Research* 7, no. 4 (December 1996).

**Baskerville, Richard L.,** and **Jan Stage.** "Controlling Prototype Development through Risk Analysis." *MIS Quarterly* 20, no. 4 (December 1996).

**Brier, Tom, Jerry Luftman,** and **Raymond Papp.** " Enablers and Inhibitors of Business—IT Alignment." *Communications of the Association for Information Systems* 1 (March 1999).

**Broadbent, Marianne, Peter Weill,** and **Don St. Clair.** "The Implications of Information Technology Infrastructure for Business Process Redesign." *MIS Quarterly* 23, no. 2 (June 1999).

**Bullen, Christine,** and **John F. Rockart.** "A Primer on Critical Success Factors." Cambridge, MA: Center for Information Systems Research, Sloan School of Management (1981).

**Cline, Marshall,** and **Mike Girou.** "Enduring Business Themes." *Communications of the ACM* 43, no. 5 (May 2000).

**Davenport, Thomas H.,** and **James E. Short.** "The New Industrial Engineering: Information Technology and Business Process Redesign." *Sloan Management Review* 31, no. 4 (Summer 1990).

**Davidson, W. H.** "Beyond Engineering: The Three Phases of Business Transformation." *IBM Systems Journal* 32, no. 1 (1993).

**Davis, Gordon B.** "Determining Management Information Needs: A Comparison of Methods." *MIS Quarterly* 1 (June 1977).

———. "Information Analysis for Information System Development." In *Systems Analysis and Design: A Foundation for the 1980's,* edited by W. W. Cotterman. J. D. Cougar, N. L. Enger, and F. Harold. New York: Wiley (1981).

———. "Strategies for Information Requirements Determination." *IBM Systems Journal* 1 (1982).

**Ein Dor Philip,** and **Eli Segev.** "Strategic Planning for Management Information Systems." *Management Science* 24, no. 15 (1978).

**Fingar, Peter.** "Component-Based Frameworks for E-Commerce." *Communications of the ACM* 43, no. 10 (October 2000).

**Hammer, Michael.** "Reengineering Work: Don't Automate, Obliterate." *Harvard Business Review* (July–August 1990).

**Hammer, Michael,** and **James Champy.** *Reengineering the Corporation.* New York: HarperCollins Publishers (1993).

**Hammer, Michael,** and **Steven A. Stanton.** *The Reengineering Revolution.* New York: HarperCollins (1995).

**Hirscheim, Rudy,** and **Mary Lacity.** "The Myths and Realities of Information Technology Insourcing." *Communications of the ACM* 43, no. 2 (February 2000).

**Hopkins, Jon.** "Component Primer." *Communications of the ACM* 43, no. 10 (October 2000).

**Huizing, Ard, Esther Koster,** and **Wim Bouman.** "Balance in Business Process Reengineering: An Empirical Study of Fit and Performance." *Journal of Management Information Systems* 14, no. 1 (Summer 1997).

**Ivari, Juhani, Rudy Hirscheim,** and **Heinz K. Klein.** "A Dynamic Framework for Classifying Information Systems Development Methodologies and Approaches." *Journal of Management Information Systems* 17, no. 3 (Winter 2000-2001).

**Jesser, Ryan, Rodney Smith, Mark Stupeck,** and **William F. Wright.** "Information Technology Process Reengineering and Performance Measurement." *Communications of the Association for Information Systems* 1 (February 1999).

**Johnson, Richard A.** "The Ups and Downs of Object-Oriented Systems Development." *Communications of the ACM* 43, no.10 (October 2000).

**Kendall, Kenneth E.,** and **Julie E. Kendall.** *Systems Analysis and Design,* 4th ed. Upper Saddle River, NJ: Prentice Hall (1999).

**Lee, Jae Nam,** and **Young-Gul Kim.** "Effect of Partnership Quality on IS Outsourcing Success." *Journal of Management Information Systems* 15, no. 4 (Spring 1999).

**Martin, J.,** and **C. McClure.** "Buying Software Off the Rack." *Harvard Business Review* (November–December 1983).

**Martin, James.** *Application Development without Programmers.* Englewood Cliffs, NJ: Prentice Hall (1982).

**Mason, R. E. A.,** and **T. T. Carey.** "Prototyping Interactive Information Systems." *Communications of the ACM* 26 (May 1983).

**Matos, Victor M.,** and **Paul J. Jalics.** "An Experimental Analysis of the Performance of Fourth-Generation Tools on PCs." *Communications of the ACM* 32, no. 11 (November 1989).

**McIntyre, Scott C.,** and **Lexis F. Higgins.** "Object-Oriented Analysis and Design: Methodology and Application." *Journal of Management Information Systems* 5, no. 1 (Summer 1988).

**Nerson, Jean-Marc.** "Applying Object-Oriented Analysis and Design." *Communications of the ACM* 35, no. 9 (September 1992).

**Nissen, Mark E.** "Redesigning Reengineering through Measurement-Driven Inference," *MIS Quarterly* 22, no. 4 (December 1998).

**Pancake, Cherri M.** "The Promise and the Cost of Object Technology: A Five-Year Forecast." *Communications of the ACM* 38, no. 10 (October 1995).

**Parker, M. M.** "Enterprise Information Analysis: Cost-Benefit Analysis and the Data-Managed System." *IBM Systems Journal* 21 (1982).

**Rivard, Suzanne,** and **Sid L. Huff.** "Factors of Success for End-User Computing." *Communications of the ACM* 31, no. 5 (May 1988).

**Rockart, John F.** "Chief Executives Define Their Own Data Needs." *Harvard Business Review* (March–April 1979).

**Rockart, John F.,** and **Lauren S. Flannery.** "The Management of End-User Computing." *Communications of the ACM* 26, no. 10 (October 1983).

**Rockart, John F.,** and **Michael E. Treacy.** "The CEO Goes On-Line." *Harvard Business Review* (January–February 1982).

**Sabherwahl, Rajiv.** "The Role of Trust in IS Outsourcing Development Projects." *Communications of the ACM* 42, no. 2 (February 1999).

**Schmidt, Douglas C.,** and **Mohamed E. Fayad.** "Lessons Learned Building Reusable OO Frameworks for Distributed Software." *Communications of the ACM* 40, no. 10 (October 1997).

**Segars, Albert H.,** and **Varun Grover.** "Profiles of Strategic Information Systems Planning." *Information Systems Research* 10, no. 3 (September 1999).

**Shank, Michael E., Andrew C. Boynton,** and **Robert W. Zmud.** "Critical Success Factor Analysis as a Methodology for MIS Planning." *MIS Quarterly* (June 1985).

**Sprott, David.** "Componentizing the Enterprise Application Packages." *Communications of the ACM* 43, no. 3 (April 2000).

**Swanson, E. Burton** and **Enrique Dans.** "System Life Expectancy and the Maintenance Effort: Exploring their Equilibration." *MIS Quarterly* 24, no. 2 (June 2000).

**Thong, James Y.L., Chee-Sing Yap** and **Kin-Lee Seah.** "Business Process Reengineering in the Public Sector: The Case of the Housing Development Board in Singapore." *Journal of Management Information Systems* 17, no. 1 (Summer 2000).

**Venkatraman, N.** "Beyond Outsourcing: Managing IT Resources as a Value Center." *Sloan Management Review* (Spring 1997).

**Vessey, Iris,** and **Sue A. Conger.** "Requirements Specification: Learning Object, Process, and Data Methodologies." *Communications of the ACM* 37, no. 5 (May 1994).

**Vessey, Iris,** and **Sue Conger.** "Learning to Specify Information Requirements: The Relationship between Application and Methodology." *Journal of Management Information Systems* 10, no. 2 (Fall 1993).

**Vitalari, Nicholas P.** "Knowledge as a Basis for Expertise in Systems Analysis: Empirical Study." *MIS Quarterly* (September 1985).

**Watad, Mahmoud M.,** and **Frank J. DiSanzo.** "Case Study: The Synergism of Telecommuting and Office Automation." *Sloan Management Review* 41, no. 2 (Winter 2000).

**Willis, T. Hillman,** and **Debbie B. Tesch.** "An Assessment of Systems Development Methodologies." *Journal of Information Technology Management* 2, no. 2 (1991).

**Zachman, J. A.** "Business Systems Planning and Business Information Control Study: A Comparison." *IBM Systems Journal* 21 (1982).

## Chapter 11


**Alter, Steven,** and **Michael Ginzberg.** "Managing Uncertainty in MIS Implementation." *Sloan Management Review* 20 (Fall 1978).

**Armstrong, Curtis P.,** and **V. Sambamurthy.** "Information Technology Assimilation in Firms: The Influence of Senior Leadership and IT Infrastructures." *Information Systems Research* 10, no. 4 (December 1999).

**Attewell, Paul.** "Technology Diffusion and Organizational Learning: The Case of Business Computing." *Organization Science,* no. 3 (1992).

**Beath, Cynthia Mathis,** and **Wanda J. Orlikowski.** "The Contradictory Structure of Systems Development Methodologies: Deconstructing the IS-User Relationship in Information Engineering." *Information Systems Research* 5, no. 4 (December 1994).

**Benaroch, Michel,** and **Robert J. Kauffman.** "Justifying Electronic Banking Network Expansion Using Real Options Analysis." *MIS Quarterly* 24, no. 2 (June 2000).

**Bharadwaj, Anandhi.** "A Resource-Based Perspective on Information Technology Capability and Firm Performance." *MIS Quarterly* 24, no. 1 (March 2000).

**Bhattacharjee, Sudip,** and **R. Ramesh.** "Enterprise Computing Environments and Cost Assessment." *Communications of the ACM* 43, no. 10 (October 2000).

**Bostrom, R. P.,** and **J. S. Heinen.** "MIS Problems and Failures: A Socio-Technical Perspective. Part I: The Causes." *MIS Quarterly* 1 (September 1977); "Part II: The Application of Socio-Technical Theory." *MIS Quarterly* 1 (December 1977).

**Brooks, Frederick P.** "The Mythical Man-Month." *Datamation* (December 1974).

**Buss, Martin D. J.** "How to Rank Computer Projects." *Harvard Business Review* (January 1983).

**Clement, Andrew,** and **Peter Van den Besselaar.** "A Retrospective Look at PD Projects." *Communications of the ACM* 36, no. 4 (June 1993).

**Concours Group.** "Delivering Large-Scale System Projects." (2000).

**Cooper, Randolph B.** "Information Technology Development Creativity: A Case Study of Attempted Radical Change." *MIS Quarterly* 24, no. 2 (June 2000).

**Davenport, Thomas H.** *Mission Critical: Realizing the Promise of Enterprise Systems.* Boston, MA: Harvard Business School Press, (2000).

**Davern, Michael J.,** and **Robert J. Kauffman.** "Discovering Potential and Realizing Value from Information Technology Investments. " *Journal of Management Information Systems* 16, no. 4 (Spring 2000).

**Davis, Fred R.** "Perceived Usefulness, Ease of Use, and User Acceptance of Information Technology." *MIS Quarterly* 13, no. 3 (September 1989).

**Desmarais, Michel C., Richard Leclair, Jean-Yves Fiset,** and **Hichem Talbi.** "Cost-Justifying Electronic Performance Support Systems." *Communications of the ACM* 40, no. 7 (July 1997).

**Doll, William J.** "Avenues for Top Management Involvement in Successful MIS Development." *MIS Quarterly* (March 1985).

**Dos Santos, Brian.** "Justifying Investments in New Information Technologies." *Journal of Management Information Systems* 7, no. 4 (Spring 1991).

**Ein-Dor, Philip,** and **Eli Segev.** "Organizational Context and the Success of Management Information Systems." *Management Science* 24 (June 1978).

**El Sawy, Omar,** and **Burt Nanus.** "Toward the Design of Robust Information Systems." *Journal of Management Information Systems* 5, no. 4 (Spring 1989).

**Emery, James C.** "Cost/Benefit Analysis of Information Systems." Chicago: Society for Management Information Systems Workshop Report No. 1 (1971).

**Fichman, Robert G.,** and **Scott A. Moses.** "An Incremental Process for Software Implementation." *Sloan Management Review* 40, no. 2 (Winter 1999).

**Franz, Charles,** and **Daniel Robey.** "An Investigation of User-Led System Design: Rational and Political Perspectives." *Communications of the ACM* 27 (December 1984).

**Gardner, Julia.** "Strengthening the Focus on Users' Working Practices." *Communications of the ACM* 42, no. 5 (May 1999)

**Giaglis, George.** "Focus Issue on Legacy Information Systems and Business Process Change: On the Integrated Design and Evaluation of Business Processes and Information Systems." *Communications of the AIS* 2, (July 1999).

**Ginzberg, Michael J.** "Early Diagnosis of MIS Implementation Failure: Promising Results and Unanswered Questions." *Management Science* 27 (April 1981).

**Gogan, Janis L., Jane Fedorowicz,** and **Ashok Rao.** "Assessing Risks in Two Projects: A Strategic Opportunity and a Necessary Evil." *Communications of the Association for Information Systems* 1 (May 1999).

**Grover, Varun.** "IS Investment Priorities in Contemporary Organizations." *Communications of the ACM* 41, no. 2 (February 1998).

**Helms, Glenn L.,** and **Ira R. Weiss.** "The Cost of Internally Developed Applications: Analysis of Problems and Cost Control Methods." *Journal of Management Information Systems* (Fall 1986).

**Hunton, James E.,** and **Beeler, Jesse D.,** "Effects of User Participation in Systems Development: A Longitudinal Field Study." *MIS Quarterly* 21, no. 4 (December 1997).

**Irani, Zahir,** and **Peter E.D. Love.** "The Propagation of Technology Management Taxonomies for Evaluating Investments in Information Systems." *Journal of Management Information Systems* 17, no.3 (Winter 2000–2001).

**Joshi, Kailash.** "A Model of Users' Perspective on Change: The Case of Information Systems Technology Implementation." *MIS Quarterly* 15, no. 2 (June 1991).

**Karat, John.** "Evolving the Scope of User-Centered Design." *Communications of the ACM* 40, no. 7 (July 1997).

**Keen, Peter W.** "Information Systems and Organizational Change." *Communications of the ACM* 24 (January 1981).

**Keil, Mark, Bernard C.Y. Tan, Kwok-Kee Wei, Timo Saarinen, Virpi Tuunainen,** and **Arjen Waassenaar.** "A Cross-Cultural Study on Escalation of Commitment Behavior in Software Projects." *MIS Quarterly* 24, no. 2 (June 2000).

**Keil, Mark,** and **Daniel Robey.** "Blowing the Whistle on Troubled Software Projects." *Communications of the ACM* 44, no. 4 (April 2001).

**Keil, Mark, Joan Mann,** and **Arun Rai.** "Why Software Projects Escalate: An Empirical Analysis and Test of Four Theoretical Models." *MIS Quarterly* 24, no. 4 (December 2000).

**Keil, Mark, Paul E. Cule, Kalle Lyytinen,** and **Roy C. Schmidt.** "A Framework for Identifying Software Project Risks." *Communications of the ACM* 41, 11 (November 1998).

**Keil, Mark,** and **Ramiro Montealegre.** "Cutting Your Losses: Extricating Your Organization When a Big Project Goes Awry." *Sloan Management Review* 41, no. 3 (Spring 2000).

**Keil, Mark, Richard Mixon, Timo Saarinen,** and **Virpi Tuunairen.** "Understanding Runaway IT Projects." *Journal of Management Information Systems* 11, no. 3 (Winter 1994–95).

**Kelly, Sue, Nicola Gibson, Christopher P. Holland,** and **Ben Light.** "Focus Issue on Legacy Information Systems and Business Process Change: A Business Perspective of Legacy Information Systems." *Communications of the AIS* 2 (July 1999).

**King, Julia.** "Reengineering Slammed." *Computerworld* (June 13, 1994).

**Kolb, D. A.,** and **A. L. Frohman.** "An Organization Development Approach to Consulting." *Sloan Management Review* 12 (Fall 1970).

**Lassila, Kathy S.,** and **James C. Brancheau.** "Adoption and Utilization of Commercial Software Packages: Exploring Utilization Equilibria, Transitions, Triggers, and Tracks." *Journal of Management Information Systems* 16, no. 2 (Fall 1999).

**Laudon, Kenneth C.** "CIOs Beware: Very Large Scale Systems." Center for Research on Information Systems, New York University Stern School of Business, working paper (1989).

**Lederer, Albert,** and **Jayesh Prasad.** "Nine Management Guidelines for Better Cost Estimating." *Communications of the ACM* 35, no. 2 (February 1992).

**Lientz, Bennett P.,** and **E. Burton Swanson.** *Software Maintenance Management.* Reading, MA: Addison-Wesley (1980).

**Lipin, Steven,** and **Nikhil Deogun.** "Big Mergers of 90s Prove Disappointing to Shareholders." *The Wall Street Journal* (October 30, 2000).

**Lohse, Gerald L.,** and **Peter Spiller.** "Internet Retail Store Design: How the User Interface Influences Traffic and Sales." *Journal of Computer-Mediated Communication* 5, no. 2 (December 1999).

**Lucas, Henry C., Jr.** *Implementation: The Key to Successful Information Systems.* New York: Columbia University Press (1981).

**Markus, M. Lynne, Conelis Tanis,** and **Paul C. van Fenema.** "Multisite ERP Implementations." *Communications of the ACM* 43, no. 3 (April 2000).

**Markus, M. Lynne,** and **Mark Keil.** "If We Build It, They Will Come: Designing Information Systems That People Want to Use." *Sloan Management Review* (Summer 1994).

**Markus, M. Lynne,** and **Robert I. Benjamin.** "Change Agentry—The Next IS Frontier." *MIS Quarterly* 20, no. 4 (December 1996).

**Markus, M. Lynne,** and **Robert I. Benjamin.** "The Magic Bullet Theory of IT-Enabled Transformation." *Sloan Management Review* (Winter 1997).

**Matlin, Gerald.** "What Is the Value of Investment in Information Systems?" *MIS Quarterly* 13, no. 3 (September 1989).

**McCormack, Alan.** "Product-Development Practices that Work: How Internet Companies Build Software." *Sloan Management Review* 42, no. 2 (Winter 2001).

**McFarlan, F. Warren.** "Portfolio Approach to Information Systems." *Harvard Business Review* (September–October 1981).

**McKeen, James D.,** and **Tor Guimaraes.** "Successful Strategies for User Participation in Systems Development." *Journal of Management Information Systems* 14, no. 2 (Fall 1997).

**Mumford, Enid,** and **Mary Weir.** *Computer Systems in Work Design: The ETHICS Method.* New York: John Wiley (1979).

**Nambisan, Satish,** and **Yu-Ming Wang.** "Web Technology Adoption and Knowledge Barriers." *Journal of Organizational Computing and Electronic Commerce* 10, no. 2 (2000).

**Orlikowski, Wanda J.,** and **J. Debra Hofman.** "An Improvisational Change Model for Change Management: The Case of Groupware Technologies." *Sloan Management Review* (Winter 1997).

**Rai, Arun, Ravi Patnayakuni,** and **Nainika Patnayakuni.** "Technology Investment and Business Performance." *Communications of the ACM* 40, no. 7 (July 1997).

**Randall, Dave, John Hughes, Jon O'Brien, Tom Rodden, Mark Rouncefield, Ian Sommerville,** and **Peter Tolmie.** "Focus Issue on Legacy Information Systems and Business Process Change: Banking on the Old Technology: Understanding the Organisational Context of 'Legacy' Issues." *Communications of the AIS* 2 (July 1999).

**Robey, Daniel,** and **M. Lynne Markus.** "Rituals in Information System Design." *MIS Quarterly* (March 1984).

**Ryan, Sherry D.,** and **David A. Harrison.** "Considering Social Subsystem Costs and Benefits in Information Technology Investment Decisions: A View from the Field on Anticipated Payoffs." *Journal of Management Information Systems* 16, no. 4 (Spring 2000).

**Scheer, August-Wilhelm,** and **Frank Habermann.** "Making ERP a Success." *Communications of the ACM* 43, no. 3 (April 2000).

**Schneiderman, Ben.** "Universal Usability." *Communications of the ACM* 43, no. 5 (May 2000).

**Sia, Siew Kien,** and **Boon Siong Neo.** "Reengineering Effectiveness and the Redesign of Organizational Control: A Case Study of the Inland Revenue Authority in Singapore." *Journal of Management Information Systems* 14, no. 1 (Summer 1997).

**Swanson, E. Burton.** *Information System Implementation.* Homewood, IL: Richard D. Irwin (1988).

**Tallon, Paul P, Kenneth L. Kraemer,** and **Vijay Gurbaxani.** "Executives' Perceptions of the Business Value of Information Technology: A Process-Oriented Approach." *Journal of Management Information Systems* 16, no. 4 (Spring 2000).

**Taudes, Alfred, Markus Feurstein,** and **Andreas Mild.** "Options Analysis of Software Platform Decisions: A Case Study." *MIS Quarterly* 24, no. 2 (June 2000).

**Teng, James T. C., Seung Ryul Jeong,** and **Varun Grover.** "Profiling Successful Reengineering Projects." *Communications of the ACM* 41, no. 6 (June 1998).

**Tornatsky, Louis G., J. D. Eveland, M. G. Boylan, W. A. Hetzner, E. C. Johnson, D. Roitman,** and **J. Schneider.** *The Process of Technological Innovation: Reviewing the Literature.* Washington, DC: National Science Foundation (1983).

**Truex, Duane P., Richard Baskerville,** and **Heinz Klein.** "Growing Systems in Emergent Organizations." *Communications of the ACM* 42, no. 8 (August 1999).

**Turner, Jon A.** "Computer Mediated Work: The Interplay Between Technology and Structured Jobs." *Communications of the ACM* 27 (December 1984).

**Wastell, David G.** "Learning Dysfunctions in Information Systems Development: Overcoming the Social Defenses with Transitional Objects." *MIS Quarterly* 23, no. 1 (December 1999).

**Yin, Robert K.** "Life Histories of Innovations: How New Practices Become Routinized." *Public Administration Review* (January–February 1981).

## CHAPTER 12

**Ackerman, Mark S.,** and **Christine A. Halverson.** "Reexamining Organizational Memory." *Communications of the ACM* 43, no. 1 (January 2000).

**Alavi, Maryam,** and **Dorothy Leidner.** "Knowledge Management Systems: Issues, Challenges, and Benefits." *Communications of the Association for Information Systems* 1 (February 1999).

**Allen, Bradley P.** "CASE-Based Reasoning: Business Applications." *Communications of the ACM* 37, no. 3 (March 1994).

**Asakawa, Kazuo,** and **Hideyuki Takagi.** "Neural Networks in Japan." *Communications of the ACM* 37, no. 3 (March 1994).

**Badler, Norman I., Martha S. Palmer,** and **Rama Bindiganavale.** "Animation Control for Real-time Virtual Humans." *Communications of the ACM* 42, no. 8 (August 1999).

**Balasubramanian, V.,** and **Alf Bashian.** "Document Management and Web Technologies: Alice Marries the Mad Hatter." *Communications of the ACM* 41, no. 7 (July 1998).

**Banker, Rajiv.** "Value Implications of Relative Investments in Information Technology." Department of Information Systems and Center for Digital Economy Research, University of Texas at Dallas, January 23, 2001.

**Barker, Virginia E.,** and **Dennis E. O'Connor.** "Expert Systems for Configuration at Digital: XCON and Beyond." *Communications of the ACM* (March 1989).

**Beer, Randall D., Roger D. Quinn, Hillel J. Chiel,** and **Roy E. Ritzman.** "Biologically Inspired Approaches to Robots." *Communications of the ACM* 40, no. 3 (March 1997).

**Blanning, Robert W., David R. King, James R. Marsden,** and **Ann C. Seror.** "Intelligent Models of Human Organizations: The State of the Art." *Journal of Organizational Computing* 2, no. 2 (1992).

**Brutzman, Don.** "The Virtual Reality Modeling Language and Java." *Communications of the ACM* 41, no. 6 (June 1998).

**Brynjolfsson, Erik.** "The Contribution of Information Technology to Consumer Welfare." *Information Systems Research* 7, no. 3 (September 1996).

———. "The Productivity Paradox of Information Technology." *Communications of the ACM* 36, no. 12 (December 1993).

**Brynjolfsson, Erik,** and **Lorin M. Hitt.** "Information Technology and Organizational Design: Evidence from Micro Data." (January 1998).

**Brynjolfsson, Erik,** and **Lorin M. Hitt.** "Beyond the Productivity Paradox." *Communications of the ACM* 41, no. 8 (August 1998).

———. "New Evidence on the Returns to Information Systems." MIT Sloan School of Management (October 1993).

**Brynjolfsson, Erik,** and **S. Yang.** "Intangible Assets: How the Interaction of Computers and Organizational Structure Affects Stock Markets." MIT Sloan School of Management (2000).

**Burtka, Michael.** "Generic Algorithms." *The Stern Information Systems Review* 1, no. 1 (Spring 1993).

**Busch, Elizabeth, Matti Hamalainen, Clyde W. Holsapple, Yongmoo Suh,** and **Andrew B. Whinston.** "Issues and Obstacles in the Development of Team Support Systems." *Journal of Organizational Computing* 1, no. 2 (April–June 1991).

**Cho, Sungzoon, Chigeun Han, Dae Hee Han,** and **Hyung-Il Kim.** "Web-Based Keystroke Dynamics Identity Verification Using Neural Network." *Journal of Organizational Computing and Electronic Commerce* 10, no. 4 (2000).

**Churchland, Paul M.,** and **Patricia Smith Churchland.** "Could a Machine Think?" *Scientific American* (January 1990).

**Cole, Kevin, Olivier Fischer,** and **Phyllis Saltzman.** "Just-in-Time Knowledge Delivery." *Communications of the ACM* 40, no. 7 (July 1997).

**Cole-Gomolski, Barbara.** "Customer Service with a :-)" *Computerworld* (March 30, 1998).

**Cross, Rob,** and **Lloyd Baird.** "Technology is Not Enough: Improving Performance by Building Organizational Memory." *Sloan Management Review* 41, no. 3 (Spring 2000).

**Davenport, Thomas H., David W. DeLong,** and **Michael C. Beers.** "Successful Knowledge Management Projects." *Sloan Management Review* 39, no. 2 (Winter 1998).

**Davenport, Thomas H.,** and **Lawrence Prusak.** *Working Knowledge: How Organizations Manage What They Know.* Boston, MA: Harvard Business School Press (1997).

**Dhar, Vasant.** "Plausibility and Scope of Expert Systems in Management." *Journal of Management Information Systems* (Summer 1987).

**Dhar, Vasant,** and **Roger Stein.** *Intelligent Decision Support Methods: The Science of Knowledge Work.* Upper Saddle River, NJ: Prentice Hall (1997).

**Earl, Michael J.,** and **Ian A. Scott.** "What Is a Chief Knowledge Officer?" *Sloan Management Review* 40, no. 2 (Winter 1999).

**El Najdawi, M. K.,** and **Anthony C. Stylianou.** "Expert Support Systems: Integrating AI Technologies." *Communications of the ACM* 36, no. 12 (December 1993).

**Favela, Jesus.** "Capture and Dissemination of Specialized Knowledge in Network Organizations." *Journal of Organizational Computing and Electronic Commerce* 7, nos. 2 and 3 (1997).

**Feigenbaum, Edward A.** "The Art of Artificial Intelligence: Themes and Case Studies in Knowledge Engineering." *Proceedings of the IJCAI* (1977).

**Gelernter, David.** "The Metamorphosis of Information Management." *Scientific American* (August 1989).

**Giuliao, Vincent E.** "The Mechanization of Office Work." *Scientific American* (September 1982).

**Glushko, Robert J., Jay M. Tenenbaum,** and **Bart Meltzer.** "An XML Framework for Agent-Based E-Commerce." *Communications of the ACM* 42, no. 3 (March 1999).

**Goldberg, David E.** "Genetic and Evolutionary Algorithms Come of Age." *Communications of the ACM* 37, no. 3 (March 1994).

**Grant, Robert M.** "Prospering in Dynamically-Competitive Environments: Organizational Capability as Knowledge Integration." *Organization Science* 7, no. 4 (July–August 1996).

**Gregor, Shirley,** and **Izak Benbasat.** "Explanations from Intelligent Systems: Theoretical Foundations and Implications for Practice." *MIS Quarterly* 23, no. 4 (December 1999).

**Hansen, Morton,** and **Bolko von Oetinger.** "Introducing T-Shaped Managers: Knowledge Management's Next Generation." *Harvard Business Review* (March 2001).

**Hansen, Morton T., Nitin Nohria,** and **Thomas Tierney.** "What's Your Strategy for Knowledge Management?" *Harvard Business Review* (March–April 1999).

**Hayes-Roth, Frederick.** "Knowledge-Based Expert Systems." *Spectrum IEEE* (October 1987).

**Hayes-Roth, Frederick,** and **Neil Jacobstein.** "The State of Knowledge-Based Systems." *Communications of the ACM* 37, no. 3 (March 1994).

**Hinton, Gregory.** "How Neural Networks Learn from Experience." *Scientific American* (September 1992).

**Holland, John H.** "Genetic Algorithms." *Scientific American* (July 1992).

**Johansen, Robert.** "Groupware: Future Directions and Wild Cards." *Journal of Organizational Computing* 1, no. 2 (April–June 1991).

**Kanade, Takeo, Michael L. Reed,** and **Lee E. Weiss.** "New Technologies and Applications in Robotics." *Communications of the ACM* 37, no. 3 (March 1994).

**Kock, Ned,** and **Robert J. McQueen.** "An Action Research Study of Effects of Asynchronous Groupware Support on Productivity and Outcome Quality in Process Redesign Groups." *Journal of Organizational Computing and Electronic Commerce* 8, no. 2 (1998).

**Lee, Soonchul.** "The Impact of Office Information Systems on Power and Influence." *Journal of Management Information Systems* 8, no. 2 (Fall 1991).

**Leonard-Barton, Dorothy,** and **John J. Sviokla.** "Putting Expert Systems to Work." *Harvard Business Review* (March–April 1988).

**Liu, Ziming,** and **David G. Stork.** "Is Paperless Really More?" *Communications of the ACM* 43, no. 11 (November 2000).

**Lou, Hao,** and **Richard W. Scannell.** "Acceptance of Groupware: The Relationships Among Use, Satisfaction, and Outcomes." *Journal of Organizational Computing and Electronic Commerce* 6, no. 2 (1996).

**Maes, Patti.** "Agents that Reduce Work and Information Overload." *Communications of the ACM* 38, no. 7 (July 1994).

**Maes, Patti, Robert H. Guttman,** and **Alexandros G. Moukas.** "Agents that Buy and Sell." *Communications of the ACM* 42, no. 3 (March 1999).

**Malhotra, Yogesh.** "Toward a Knowledge Ecology for Organizational White-Waters." Keynote Presentations for the Knowledge Ecology Fair '98 (1998).

**McCarthy, John.** "Generality in Artificial Intelligence." *Communications of the ACM* (December 1987).

**Munakata, Toshinori,** and **Yashvant Jani.** "Fuzzy Systems: An Overview." *Communications of the ACM* 37, no. 3 (March 1994).

**Nash, Jim.** "State of the Market, Art, Union, and Technology." *AI Expert* (January 1993).

**O'Leary, Daniel, Daniel Kuokka,** and **Robert Plant.** "Artificial Intelligence and Virtual Organizations." *Communications of the ACM* 40, no. 1 (January 1997).

**O'Leary, Daniel,** and **Peter Selfridge.** "Knowledge Management for Best Practices." *Communications of the ACM* 43, no. 11es (November 2000).

**Orlikowski, Wanda J.** "Learning from Notes: Organizational Issues in Groupware Implementation." Sloan Working Paper, no. 3428. Cambridge, MA: Sloan School of Management, Massachusetts Institute of Technology.

**Panko, Raymond R.** "Is Office Productivity Stagnant?" *MIS Quarterly* 15, no. 2 (June 1991).

**Porat, Marc.** "The Information Economy: Definition and Measurement." Washington, DC: U.S. Department of Commerce, Office of Telecommunications (May 1977).

**Press, Lawrence.** "Lotus Notes (Groupware) in Context." *Journal of Organizational Computing* 2, nos. 3 and 4 (1992b).

**Roach, Stephen S.** "Industrialization of the Information Economy." New York: Morgan Stanley and Co. (1984).

———. "Making Technology Work." New York: Morgan Stanley and Co. (1993).

———. "Services Under Siege—The Restructuring Imperative." *Harvard Business Review* (September–October 1991).

———. "Technology and the Service Sector." *Technological Forecasting and Social Change* 34, no. 4 (December 1988).

———. "The Hollow Ring of the Productivity Revival." *Harvard Business Review* (November–December 1996).

**Ruhleder, Karen,** and **John Leslie King.** "Computer Support for Work Across Space, Time, and Social Worlds." *Journal of Organizational Computing* 1, no. 4 (1991).

**Rumelhart, David E., Bernard Widrow,** and **Michael A. Lehr.** "The Basic Ideas in Neural Networks." *Communications of the ACM* 37, no. 3 (March 1994).

**Salisbury, J. Kenneth, Jr.** "Making Graphics Physically Tangible." *Communications of the ACM* 42, no. 8 (August 1999).

**Schultze, Ulrike,** and **Betty Vandenbosch.** "Information Overload in a Groupware Environment: Now You See It, Now You Don't." *Journal of Organizational Computing and Electronic Commerce* 8, no. 2 (1998).

**Selker, Ted.** "Coach: A Teaching Agent that Learns." *Communications of the ACM* 37, no. 7 (July 1994).

**Sibigtroth, James M.** "Implementing Fuzzy Expert Rules in Hardware." *AI Expert* (April 1992).

**Sircar, Sumit, Joe L. Turnbow,** and **Bijoy Bordoloi.** "A Framework for Assessing the Relationship between Information Technology Investments and Firm Performance." *Journal of Management Information Systems* 16, no. 4 (Spring 2000).

**Slatalla, Michelle.** "Shopper's Virtual Home Tour Satisfies that Peeping Urge." *The New York Times Circuits* (August 31, 2000).

**Sproull, Lee,** and **Sara Kiesler.** *Connections: New Ways of Working in the Networked Organization.* Cambridge, MA: MIT Press (1992).

**Starbuck, William H.** "Learning by Knowledge-Intensive Firms." *Journal of Management Studies* 29, no. 6 (November 1992).

**Stirland, Sarah.** "Armed with Insight." *Wall Street and Technology* 16, no. 8 (August 1998).

**Storey, Veda C.,** and **Robert C. Goldstein.** "Knowledge-Based Approaches to Database Design," *MIS Quarterly* 17, no. 1 (March 1993).

**Stylianou, Anthony C., Gregory R. Madey,** and **Robert D. Smith.** "Selection Criteria for Expert System Shells: A Socio-Technical Framework." *Communications of the ACM* 35, no. 10 (October 1992).

**Sukhatme, Gaurav S.,** and **Maja J. Mataric.** "Embedding Robots into the Internet." *Communications of the ACM* 43, no. 5 (May 2000).

**Sviokla, John J.** "An Examination of the Impact of Expert Systems on the Firm: The Case of XCON." *MIS Quarterly* 14, no. 5 (June 1990).

———. "Expert Systems and Their Impact on the Firm: The Effects of PlanPower Use on the Information Processing Capacity of the Financial Collaborative." *Journal of Management Information Systems* 6, no. 3 (Winter 1989–1990).

**Trippi, Robert,** and **Efraim Turban.** "The Impact of Parallel and Neural Computing on Managerial Decision Making." *Journal of Management Information Systems* 6, no. 3 (Winter 1989–1990).

**Turban, Efraim,** and **Paul R. Watkins.** "Integrating Expert Systems and Decision Support Systems." *MIS Quarterly* (June 1986).

**Vandenbosch, Betty,** and **Michael J. Ginzberg.** "Lotus Notes and Collaboration: Plus ca change . . ." *Journal of Management Information Systems* 13, no. 3 (Winter 1997).

**Walczak, Steven.** "Gaining Competitive Advantage for Trading in Emerging Capital Markets with Neural Networks." *Journal of Management Information Systems* 16, no. 2 (Fall 1999).

**Weitzel, John R.,** and **Larry Kerschberg.** "Developing Knowledge Based Systems: Reorganizing the System Development Life Cycle." *Communications of the ACM* (April 1989).

**Widrow, Bernard, David E. Rumelhart,** and **Michael A. Lehr.** "Neural Networks: Applications in Industry, Business, and Science." *Communications of the ACM* 37, no. 3 (March 1994).

**Wijnhoven, Fons.** "Designing Organizational Memories: Concept and Method." *Journal of Organizational Computing and Electronic Commerce* 8, no. 1 (1998).

**Wong, David, Noemi Paciorek,** and **Dana Moore.** "Java-Based Mobile Agents." *Communications of the ACM* 42, no. 3 (March 1999).

**Zadeh, Lotfi A.** "The Calculus of Fuzzy If/Then Rules." *AI Expert* (March 1992).

**Zadeh, Lotfi A.** "Fuzzy Logic, Neural Networks, and Soft Computing." *Communications of the ACM* 37, no. 3 (March 1994).

**Zhao, J. Leon, Akhil Kumar,** and **Edward W. Stohr.** "Workflow-Centric Information Distribution through E-Mail." *Journal of Management Information Systems* 17, no. 3 (Winter 2000–2001).

**CHAPTER 13**

**Alavi, Maryam**, and **Erich A. Joachimsthaler.** "Revisiting DSS Implementation Research: A Meta-Analysis of the Literature and Suggestions for Researchers." *MIS Quarterly* 16, no. 1 (March 1992).

**Anthes, Gary H.** "Notes System Sends Federal Property Data Nationwide." *Computerworld* (August 8, 1994).

**Brachman, Ronald J., Tom Khabaza, Willi Kloesgen, Gregory Piatetsky-Shapiro,** and **Evangelos Simoudis.** "Mining Business Databases." *Communications of the ACM* 39, no. 11 (November 1996).

**Caouette, Margarette J.**, and **Bridget N. O'Connor.** "The Impact of Group Support Systems on Corporate Teams' Stages of Development." *Journal of Organizational Computing and Electronic Commerce* 8, no. 1 (1998).

**Chidambaram, Laku.** "Relational Development in Computer-Supported Groups." *MIS Quarterly* 20, no. 2 (June 1996).

**Dennis, Alan R.** "Information Exchange and Use in Group Decision Making: You Can Lead a Group to Information, but You Can't Make It Think." *MIS Quarterly* 20, no. 4 (December 1996).

**Dennis, Alan R., Craig K. Tyran, Douglas R. Vogel,** and **Jay Nunamaker, Jr.** "Group Support Systems for Strategic Planning." *Journal of Management Information Systems* 14, no. 1 (Summer 1997).

**Dennis, Alan R., Jay E. Aronson, William G. Henriger,** and **Edward D. Walker III.** "Structuring Time and Task in Electronic Brainstorming." *MIS Quarterly* 23, no. 1 (March 1999).

**Dennis, Alan R., Jay F. Nunamaker, Jr.,** and **Douglas R. Vogel.** "A Comparison of Laboratory and Field Research in the Study of Electronic Meeting Systems." *Journal of Management Information Systems* 7, no. 3 (Winter 1990–1991).

**Dennis, Alan R., Joey F. George, Len M. Jessup, Jay F. Nunamaker,** and **Douglas R. Vogel.** "Information Technology to Support Electronic Meetings." *MIS Quarterly* 12, no. 4 (December 1988).

**Dennis, Alan R., Sridar K. Pootheri,** and **Vijaya L. Natarajan.** "Lessons from Early Adopters of Web Groupware." *Journal of Management Information Systems* 14, no. 4 (Spring 1998).

**DeSanctis, Geraldine,** and **R. Brent Gallupe.** "A Foundation for the Study of Group Decision Support Systems." *Management Science* 33, no. 5 (May 1987).

**Dutta, Soumitra, Berend Wierenga,** and **Arco Dalebout.** "Designing Management Support Systems Using an Integrative Perspective." *Communications of the ACM* 40, no. 6 (June 1997).

**Edelstein, Herb.** "Technology How To: Mining Data Warehouses." *Information Week* (January 8, 1996).

**El Sawy, Omar.** "Personal Information Systems for Strategic Scanning in Turbulent Environments." *MIS Quarterly* 9, no. 1 (March 1985).

**El Sherif, Hisham,** and **Omar A. El Sawy.** "Issue-Based Decision Support Systems for the Egyptian Cabinet." *MIS Quarterly* 12, no. 4 (December 1988).

**Etzioni, Oren.** "The World-Wide Web: Quagmire or Gold Mine?" *Communications of the ACM* 39, no. 11 (November 1996).

**Fjermestad, Jerry.** "An Integrated Framework for Group Support Systems." *Journal of Organizational Computing and Electronic Commerce* 8, no. 2 (1998).

**Fjermestad, Jerry,** and **Starr Roxanne Hiltz.** "An Assessment of Group Support Systems Experimental Research: Methodology, and Results." *Journal of Management Information Systems* 15, no. 3 (Winter, 1998–1999).

———. "Group Support Systems: A Descriptive Evaluation of Case and Field Studies." *Journal of Management Information Systems* 17, no. 3 (Winter 2000–2001).

**Forgionne, Guiseppe.** "Management Support System Effectiveness: Further Empirical Evidence." *Journal of the Association for Information Systems* 1 (May 2000).

**Gallupe, R. Brent, Geraldine DeSanctis,** and **Gary W. Dickson.** "Computer-Based Support for Group Problem-Finding: An Experimental Investigation." *MIS Quarterly* 12, no. 2 (June 1988).

**George, Joey.** "Organizational Decision Support Systems." *Journal of Management Information Systems* 8, no. 3 (Winter 1991–1992).

**Ginzberg, Michael J., W. R. Reitman,** and **E. A. Stohr,** eds. *Decision Support Systems.* New York: North Holland Publishing Co. (1982).

**Grobowski, Ron, Chris McGoff, Doug Vogel, Ben Martz,** and **Jay Nunamaker.** "Implementing Electronic Meeting Systems at IBM: Lessons Learned and Success Factors." *MIS Quarterly* 14, no. 4 (December 1990).

**Henderson, John C.,** and **David A. Schilling.** "Design and Implementation of Decision Support Systems in the Public Sector." *MIS Quarterly* (June 1985).

**Hilmer, Kelly M.,** and **Alan R. Dennis.** "Stimulating Thinking: Cultivating Better Decisions with Groupware through Categorization." *Journal of Management Information Systems* 17, no. 3 (Winter 2000–2001).

**Ho, T. H.,** and **K. S. Raman.** "The Effect of GDSS on Small Group Meetings." *Journal of Management Information Systems* 8, no. 2 (Fall 1991).

**Hogue, Jack T.** "Decision Support Systems and the Traditional Computer Information System Function: An Examination of Relationships During DSS Application Development." *Journal of Management Information Systems* (Summer 1985).

**Hogue, Jack T.** "A Framework for the Examination of Management Involvement in Decision Support Systems." *Journal of Management Information Systems* 4, no. 1 (Summer 1987).

**Houdeshel, George,** and **Hugh J. Watson.** "The Management Information and Decision Support (MIDS) System at Lockheed, Georgia." *MIS Quarterly* 11, no. 2 (March 1987).

**Jessup, Leonard M., Terry Connolly,** and **Jolene Galegher.** "The Effects of Anonymity on GDSS Group Process with an Idea-Generating Task." *MIS Quarterly* 14, no. 3 (September 1990).

**Jones, Jack William, Carol Saunders,** and **Raymond McLeod, Jr.,** "Media Usage and Velocity in Executive Information Acquisition: An Exploratory Study." *European Journal of Information Systems* 2 (1993).

**Kalakota, Ravi, Jan Stallaert,** and **Andrew B. Whinston.** "Worldwide Real-Time Decision Support Systems for Electronic Commerce Applications." *Journal of Organizational Computing and Electronic Commerce* 6, no. 1 (1996).

**Keen, Peter G. W.,** and **M. S. Scott Morton.** *Decision Support Systems: An Organizational Perspective.* Reading, MA: Addison-Wesley (1982).

**King, John.** "Successful Implementation of Large Scale Decision Support Systems: Computerized Models in U.S. Economic Policy Making." *Systems Objectives Solutions* (November 1983).

**Kraemer, Kenneth L.,** and **John Leslie King.** "Computer-Based Systems for Cooperative Work and Group Decision Making." *ACM Computing Surveys* 20, no. 2 (June 1988).

**Laudon, Kenneth C.** *Communications Technology and Democratic Participation.* New York: Praeger (1977).

**Leidner, Dorothy E.,** and **Joyce Elam.** "Executive Information Systems: Their Impact on Executive Decision Making." *Journal of Management Information Systems* (Winter 1993–1994).

**Leidner, Dorothy E.,** and **Joyce Elam.** "The Impact of Executive Information Systems on Organizational Design, Intelligence, and Decision Making." *Organization Science* 6, no. 6 (November–December 1995).

**Lewe, Henrik,** and **Helmut Krcmar.** "A Computer-Supported Cooperative Work Research Laboratory." *Journal of Management Information Systems* 8, no. 3 (Winter 1991–1992).

**McCune, Jenny C.** "Measuring Value." *Beyond Computing* (July/August 2000).

**Miranda, Shaila M.,** and **Robert P. Bostrum.** "The Impact of Group Support Systems on Group Conflict and Conflict Management." *Journal of Management Information Systems* 10, no. 3 (Winter 1993–1994).

———. "Meeting Facilitation: Process versus Content Interventions." *Journal of Management Information Systems* 15, no. 4 (Spring 1999).

**Nidumolu, Sarma R., Seymour E. Goodman, Douglas R. Vogel,** and **Ann K. Danowitz.** "Information Technology for Local Administration Support: The Governorates Project in Egypt." *MIS Quarterly* 20, no. 2 (June 1996).

**Niederman, Fred, Catherine M. Beise,** and **Peggy M. Beranek.** "Issues and Concerns about Computer-Supported Meetings: The Facilitator's Perspective." *MIS Quarterly* 20, no. 1 (March 1996).

**Nunamaker, J. F., Alan R. Dennis, Joseph S. Valacich, Douglas R. Vogel,** and **Joey F. George.** "Electronic Meeting Systems to Support Group Work." *Communications of the ACM* 34, no. 7 (July 1991).

**Nunamaker, Jay, Robert O. Briggs, Daniel D. Mittleman, Douglas R. Vogel,** and **Pierre A. Balthazard.** "Lessons from a Dozen Years of Group Support Systems Research: A Discussion of Lab and Field Findings." *Journal of Management Information Systems* 13, no. 3 (Winter 1997).

**O'Keefe, Robert M.,** and **Tim McEachern.** "Web-based Customer Decision Support Systems." *Communications of the ACM* 41, no. 3 (March 1998).

**Pinsonneault, Alain, Henri Barki, R. Brent Gallupe,** and **Norberto Hoppen.** "Electronic Brainstorming: The Illusion of Productivity." *Information Systems Research* 10, no. 2 (July 1999).

**Rockart, John F.,** and **David W. DeLong.** *Executive Support Systems: The Emergence of Top Management Computer Use.* Homewood, IL: Dow-Jones Irwin (1988).

**Schwabe, Gerhard.** "Providing for Organizational Memory in Computer-Supported Meetings." *Journal of Organizational Computing and Electronic Commerce* 9, no. 2 and 3 (1999).

**Shand, Dawne.** "Making It Up as You Go." *Knowledge Management* (April 2000).

**Sharda, Ramesh,** and **David M. Steiger.** "Inductive Model Analysis Systems: Enhancing Model Analysis in Decision Support Systems." *Information Systems Research* 7, no. 3 (September 1996).

**Silver, Mark S.** "Decision Support Systems: Directed and Nondirected Change." *Information Systems Research* 1, no. 1 (March 1990).

**Sprague, R. H.,** and **E. D. Carlson.** *Building Effective Decision Support Systems.* Englewood Cliffs, NJ: Prentice Hall (1982).

**Stackpole, Beth.** "Targeting One Buyer-Or a Million." *Datamation* (March 2000).

**Todd, Peter,** and **Izak Benbasat.** "Evaluating the Impact of DSS, Cognitive Effort, and Incentives on Strategy Selection. *Information Systems Research* 10, no. 4 (December 1999).

**"The New Role for 'Executive Information Systems.' "** *I/S Analyzer* (January 1992).

**Turban, Efraim,** and **Jay E. Aronson.** *Decision Support Systems and Intelligent Systems: Management Support Systems,* 5th ed. Upper Saddle River, NJ: Prentice Hall (1998).

**Tyran, Craig K., Alan R. Dennis, Douglas R. Vogel,** and **J. F. Nunamaker, Jr.** "The Application of Electronic Meeting Technology to Support Senior Management." *MIS Quarterly* 16, no. 3 (September 1992).

**Van der Zee, J. T. M.** and **Berend de Jong.** "Alignment Is Not Enough: Integrating Business and Information Technology Management." *Journal of Management Information Systems* 16, no. 2 (Fall 1999).

**Vedder, Richard G., Michael T. Vanacek, C. Stephen Guynes,** and **James J. Cappel.** "CEO and CIO Perspectives on Competitive Intelligence." *Communications of the ACM 42,* no. 8 (August 1999).

**Vogel, Douglas R., Jay F. Nunamaker, William Benjamin Martz, Jr., Ronald Grobowski,** and **Christopher McGoff.** "Electronic Meeting System Experience at IBM." *Journal of Management Information Systems* 6, no. 3 (Winter 1989–1990).

**Volonino, Linda,** and **Hugh J. Watson.** "The Strategic Business Objectives Method for EIS Development." *Journal of Management Information Systems* 7, no. 3 (Winter 1990–1991).

**Walls, Joseph G., George R. Widmeyer,** and **Omar A. El Sawy.** "Building an Information System Design Theory for Vigilant EIS." *Information Systems Research* 3, no. 1 (March 1992).

**Watson, Hugh J., Astrid Lipp, Pamela Z. Jackson, Abdelhafid Dahmani,** and **William B. Fredenberger.** "Organizational Support for Decision Support Systems." *Journal of Management Information Systems* 5, no. 4 (Spring 1989).

**Watson, Hugh J., R. Kelly Rainer, Jr.,** and **Chang E. Koh.** "Executive Information Systems: A Framework for Development and a Survey of Current Practices." *MIS Quarterly* 15, no. 1 (March 1991).

**Watson, Richard T., Geraldine DeSanctis,** and **Marshall Scott Poole.** "Using a GDSS to Facilitate Group Consensus: Some Intended and Unintended Consequences." *MIS Quarterly* 12, no. 3 (September 1988).

**Watson, Richard T., Teck-Hua Ho,** and **K. S. Raman.** "Culture: A Fourth Dimension of Group Support Systems." *Communications of the ACM* 37, no. 10 (October 1994).

**Wilder, Clinton.** "Tapping the Pipeline." *Information Week* (March 15, 1999).

**Wreden, Nick.** "Business Intelligence: Turning on Success," *Beyond Computing* (September 1997).

## CHAPTER 14

**Abdel-Hamid, Tarek K. Kishore Sengupta,** and **Clint Swett.** "The Impact of Goals on Software Project Management: An Experimental Investigation." *MIS Quarterly* 23, no. 4 (December 1999).

**Alberts, David S.** "The Economics of Software Quality Assurance." Washington, DC: National Computer Conference, 1976 Proceedings.

**Banker, Rajiv D.,** and **Chris F. Kemerer.** "Performance Evaluation Metrics in Information Systems Development: A Principal-Agent Model." *Information Systems Research* 3, no. 4 (December 1992).

**Banker, Rajiv D., Robert J. Kaufmann,** and **Rachna Kumar.** "An Empirical Test of Object-Based Output Measurement Metrics in a Computer-Aided Software Engineering (CASE) Environment."

*Journal of Management Information Systems* 8, no. 3 (Winter 1991–1992).

**Banker, Rajiv D., Srikant M. Datar, Chris F. Kemerer,** and **Dani Zweig.** "Software Complexity and Maintenance Costs." *Communications of the ACM* 36, no. 11 (November 1993).

**Bertino, Elisa, Elena Pagani, Gian Paolo Rossi,** and **Pierangela Samarati.** "Protecting Information on the Web." *Communications of the ACM* 43, no.11 (Novemer 2000).

**Blackburn, Joseph, Gary Scudder,** and **Luk N. Van Wassenhove.** "Concurrent Software Development." *Communications of the ACM* 43, no. 11es (November 2000).

**Boehm, Barry W.** "Understanding and Controlling Software Costs." *IEEE Transactions on Software Engineering* 14, no. 10 (October 1988).

**Chin, Shu-Kai.** "High-Confidence Design for Security." *Communications of the ACM* 42, no. 7 (July 1999).

**Choy, Manhoi, Hong Va Leong,** and **Man Hon Wong.** "Disaster Recovery Techniques for Database Systems." *Communications of the ACM* 43, no. 11 (November 2000).

**Corbato, Fernando J.** "On Building Systems that Will Fail." *Communications of the ACM* 34, no. 9 (September 1991).

**Dekleva, Sasa M.** "The Influence of Information Systems Development Approach on Maintenance." *MIS Quarterly* 16, no. 3 (September 1992).

**DeMarco, Tom.** *Structured Analysis and System Specification.* New York: Yourdon Press (1978).

**Dijkstra, E.** "Structured Programming." In *Classics in Software Engineering,* edited by Edward Nash Yourdon. New York: Yourdon Press (1979).

**Domges, Rolf,** and **Klaus Pohl.** "Adapting Traceability Environments to Project-Specific Needs." *Communications of the ACM* 41, no. 12 (December 1998).

**Durst, Robert, Terrence Champion, Brian Witten, Eric Miller,** and **Luigi Spagnuolo.** "Testing and Evaluating Computer Intrusion Detection Systems." *Communications of the ACM 42,* no. 7 (July 1999).

**Dutta, Soumitra, Luk N. Van Wassenhove,** and **Selvan Kulandaiswamy.** "Benchmarking European Software Management Practices." *Communications of the ACM* 41, no. 6 (June 1998).

**Forrest, Stephanie, Steven A. Hofmeyr,** and **Anil Somayaji.** "Computer Immunology." *Communications of the ACM* 40, no. 10 (October 1997).

**Fraser, Martin D.,** and **Vijay K. Vaishnavi.** "A Formal Specifications Maturity Model." *Communications of the ACM* 40, no. 12 (December 1997).

**Gane, Chris,** and **Trish Sarson.** *Structured Systems Analysis: Tools and Techniques.* Englewood Cliffs, NJ: Prentice Hall (1979).

**Ghosh, Anup K.,** and **Jeffrey M. Voas.** "Inoculating Software for Survivability." *Communications of the ACM* 42, no. 7 (July 1999).

**Ghosh, Anup K.,** and **Tara M. Swaminatha.** "Software Security and Privacy Risks in Mobile E-Commerce." *Communications of the ACM* 44, no. 2 (February 2001).

**Goan, Terrance.** "A Cop on the Beat: Collecting and Appraising Intrusion Evidence." *Communications of the ACM* 42, no. 7 (July 1999).

**Goslar, Martin.** "The New E-Security Frontier." *Information Week* (July 10, 2000).

**Jajoda, Sushil, Catherine D. McCollum,** and **Paul Ammann.** "Trusted Recovery." *Communications of the ACM* 42, no. 7 (July 1999).

**Jarzabek, Stan,** and **Riri Huang.** "The Case for User-Centered CASE Tools." *Communications of the ACM* 41, no. 8 (August 1998).

**Johnson, Philip M.** "Reengineering Inspection." *Communications of the ACM* 41, no. 2 (February 1998).

**Joshi, James B. D., Walid G. Aref, Arif Ghafoor,** and **Eugene H. Spafford.** "Security Models for Web-Based Applications." *Communications of the ACM* 44, no. 2 (February 2001).

**Kaplan, David, Ramayya Krishnan, Rema Padman,** and **James Peters.** "Assessing Data Quality in Accounting Information Systems." *Communications of the ACM* 41, no. 2 (February 1998).

**Kemerer, Chris F.** "Progress, Obstacles, and Opportunities in Software Engineering Economics." *Communications of the ACM* 41, no. 8 (August 1998).

**Klein, Barbara D., Dale L. Goodhue,** and **Gordon B. Davis.** "Can Humans Detect Errors in Data?" *MIS Quarterly* 21, no. 2 (June 1997).

**Knowles, Ann.** "EDI Experiments with the Net." *Software Magazine* (January 1997).

**Laudon, Kenneth C.** "Data Quality and Due Process in Large Interorganizational Record Systems." *Communications of the ACM* 29 (January 1986a).

———. *Dossier Society: Value Choices in the Design of National Information Systems.* New York: Columbia University Press (1986b).

**Lientz, Bennett P.,** and **E. Burton Swanson.** *Software Maintenance Management.* Reading, MA: Addison-Wesley (1980).

**Littlewood, Bev,** and **Lorenzo Strigini.** "The Risks of Software." *Scientific American* 267, no. 5 (November 1992).

———. "Validation of Ultra-high Dependability for Software-based Systems." *Communications of the ACM* 36, no. 11 (November 1993).

**Loch, Karen D., Houston H. Carr,** and **Merrill E. Warkentin.** "Threats to Information Systems: Today's Reality, Yesterday's Understanding." *MIS Quarterly* 16, no. 2 (June 1992).

**Martin, James,** and **Carma McClure.** *Structured Techniques: The Basis of CASE.* Englewood Cliffs, NJ: Prentice Hall (1988).

**Mazzucchelli, Louis.** "Structured Analysis Can Streamline Software Design." *Computerworld* (December 9, 1985).

**Needham, Roger M.** "Denial of Service: An Example." *Communications of the ACM* 37, no. 11 (November 1994).

**Nerson, Jean-Marc.** "Applying Object-Oriented Analysis and Design." *Communications of the ACM* 35, no. 9 (September 1992).

**Neumann, Peter G.** "Risks Considered Global(ly)." *Communications of the ACM* 35, no. 1 (January 1993).

**Oppliger, Rolf.** "Internet Security, Firewalls, and Beyond." *Communications of the ACM* 40, no.7 (May 1997).

**Orr, Kenneth.** "Data Quality and Systems Theory." *Communications of the ACM* 41, no. 2 (February 1998).

**Parsons, Jeffrey,** and **Yair Wand.** "Using Objects for Systems Analysis." *Communications of the ACM* 40, no. 12 (December 1997).

**Rainer, Rex Kelley, Jr., Charles A. Snyder,** and **Houston H. Carr.** "Risk Analysis for Information Technology." *Journal of Management Information Systems* 8, no. 1 (Summer 1991).

**Ravichandran, T.,** and **Arun Rai.** "Total Quality Management in Information Systems Development." *Journal of Management Information Systems* 16, no. 3 (Winter 1999–2000).

**Redman, Thomas.** "The Impact of Poor Data Quality on the Typical Enterprise." *Communications of the ACM* 41, no. 2 (February 1998).

**Scott, Louise, Levente Horvath,** and **Donald Day.** "Characterizing CASE Constraints." *Communications of the ACM* 43, no. 11 (November 2000).

**Segev, Arie, Janna Porra,** and **Malu Roldan.** "Internet Security and the Case of Bank of America." *Communications of the ACM* 41, no. 10 (October 1998).

**Sharma, Srinarayan,** and **Arun Rai.** "CASE Deployment in IS Organizations." *Communications of the ACM* 43, no. 1 (January 2000).

**Slaughter, Sandra A., Donald E. Harter,** and **Mayuram S. Krishnan.** "Evaluating the Cost of Software Quality." *Communications of the ACM* 41, no. 8 (August 1998).

**Stillerman, Matthew, Carla Marceau,** and **Maureen Stillman.** "Intrusion Detection for Distributed Applications." *Communications of the ACM* 42, no. 7 (July 1999).

**Straub, Detmar W.,** and **Richard J. Welke.** "Coping with Systems Risk: Security Planning Models for Management Decision Making." *MIS Quarterly* 22, no. 4 (December 1998).

**Strong, Diane M., Yang W. Lee,** and **Richard Y. Wang.** "Data Quality in Context." *Communications of the ACM* 40, no. 5 (May 1997).

**Swanson, Kent, Dave McComb, Jill Smith,** and **Don McCubbrey.** "The Application Software Factory: Applying Total Quality Techniques to Systems Development." *MIS Quarterly* 15, no. 4 (December 1991).

**Tayi, Giri Kumar,** and **Donald P. Ballou.** "Examining Data Quality." *Communications of the ACM* 41, no. 2 (February 1998).

**United States General Accounting Office.** "Patriot Missile Defense: Software Problem Led to System Failure at Dharan, Saudi Arabia." GAO/IMTEC-92-26 (February 1992).

**Viega, John, Tadayoshi Koho,** and **Bruce Potter.** "Trust (and Mistrust) in Secure Applications." *Communications of the ACM* 44, no. 2 (February 2001).

**Wand, Yair,** and **Richard Y. Wang.** "Anchoring Data Quality Dimensions in Ontological Foundations." *Communications of the ACM* 39, no. 11 (November 1996).

**Wang, Richard.** "A Product Perspective on Total Data Quality Management." *Communications of the ACM* 41, no. 2 (February 1998).

**Wang, Richard Y., Yang W. Lee, Leo L. Pipino,** and **Diane M. Strong.** "Manage Your Information as a Product." *Sloan Management Review* 39, no. 4 (Summer 1998).

**Weber, Ron.** *EDP Auditing: Conceptual Foundations and Practice,* 2nd ed. New York: McGraw-Hill (1988).

**Yourdon, Edward,** and **L. L. Constantine.** *Structured Design.* New York: Yourdon Press (1978).

### CHAPTER 15

**Angwin, Julia.** "How an E-Posse Led to Arrests in Online Fraud." *The Wall Street Journal* (May 4, 2000).

**Association of Computing Machinery.** "ACM's Code of Ethics and Professional Conduct." *Communications of the ACM* 36, no. 12 (December 1993).

**Baig, Edward C., Marcia Stepanek,** and **Neill Gross.** "Privacy." *Business Week* (April 5, 1999).

**Bellman, Steven, Eric J. Johnson,** and **Gerald L. Lohse.** "To Opt-in or Opt-out? It Depends on the Question." *Communications of the ACM* 44, no. 2 (February 2001).

**Berdichevsky, Daniel,** and **Erik Neunschwander.** "Toward an Ethics of Persuasive Technology." *Communications of the ACM* 42, no. 5 (May 1999).

**Bjerklie, David.** "Does E-Mail Mean Everyone's Mail?" *Information Week* (January 3, 1994).

**Bowen, Jonathan.** "The Ethics of Safety-Critical Systems." *Communications of the ACM* 43, no. 3 (April 2000).

**Brod, Craig.** *Techno Stress—The Human Cost of the Computer Revolution.* Reading MA: Addison-Wesley (1982).

***Brown Bag Software vs. Symantec Corp.*** 960 F2D 1465 (Ninth Circuit, 1992).

**Burk, Dan L.** "Copyrightable Functions and Patentable Speech." *Communications of the ACM* 44, no. 2 (February 2001).

**Cavazos, Edward A.** "The Legal Risks of Setting up Shop in Cyberspace." *Journal of Organizational Computing* 6, no. 1 (1996).

**Chabrow, Eric R.** "The Internet: Copyrights." *Information Week* (March 25, 1996).

**Chen, David W.** "Man Charged with Sabotage of Computers." *The New York Times* (February 18, 1998).

**Cheng, Hsing K., Ronald R. Sims,** and **Hildy Teegen.** "To Purchase or to Pirate Software: An Empirical Study." *Journal of Management Information Systems* 13, no. 4 (Spring 1997).

**Clarke, Roger.** "Internet Privacy Concerns Confirm the Case for Intervention." *Communications of the ACM* 42, no. 2 (February 1999).

**Collins, W. Robert, Keith W. Miller, Bethany J. Spielman,** and **Phillip Wherry.** "How Good Is Good Enough? An Ethical Analysis of Software Construction and Use." *Communications of the ACM* 37, no. 1 (January 1994).

**Computer Systems Policy Project.** "Perspectives on the National Information Infrastructure." (January 12, 1993).

**Couger, J. Daniel.** "Preparing IS Students to Deal with Ethical Issues." *MIS Quarterly* 13, no. 2 (June 1989).

**Cranor, Lorrie Faith,** and **Brian A. LaMacchia.** "Spam!" *Communications of the ACM* 41, no. 8 (August 1998).

**Dalton, Gregory.** "Online Data's Fine Line." *Information Week* (March 29, 1999).

**Davis, Randall.** "The Digital Dilemma." *Communications of the ACM* 44, no. 2 (February 2001).

**Dejoie, Roy, George Fowler,** and **David Paradice,** eds. *Ethical Issues in Information Systems.* Boston: Boyd & Fraser (1991).

**Denning, Dorothy E.,** et al., "To Tap or Not to Tap." *Communications of the ACM* 36, no. 3 ( March 1993).

**Diamond, Edwin,** and **Stephen Bates.** "Law and Order Comes to Cyberspace." *Technology Review* (October 1995).

**Friedman, Batya, Peter H. Kahn, Jr.,** and **Daniel C. Howek.** "Trust Online." *Communications of the ACM* 43, no. 12 (December 2000).

**Froomkin, A. Michael.** "The Collision of Trademarks, Domain Names, and Due Process in Cyberspace." *Communications of the ACM* 44, no. 2 (February 2001).

**Gattiker, Urs E.,** and **Helen Kelley.** "Morality and Computers: Attitudes and Differences in Judgments." *Information Systems Research* 10, no. 3 (September 1999).

**Gopal, Ram D.,** and **G. Lawrence Sanders.** "Preventive and Deterrent Controls for Software Piracy." *Journal of Management Information Systems* 13, no. 4 (Spring 1997).

———. "Global Software Piracy: You Can't Get Blood Out of a Turnip." *Communications of the ACM* 43, no. 9 (September 2000).

**Graham, Robert L.** "The Legal Protection of Computer Software." *Communications of the ACM* (May 1984).

**Green, R. H.** *The Ethical Manager.* New York: Macmillan (1994).

**Hafner, Katie.** " For the Well Connected, All the World's an Office," *The New York Times Circuits* (March 30, 2000).

**Harmon, Amy.** "Software that Tracks E-Mail is Raising Privacy Concerns." *The New York Times* (November 22, 2000).

**Harrington, Susan J.** "The Effect of Codes of Ethics and Personal Denial of Responsibility on Computer Abuse Judgments and Intentions." *MIS Quarterly* 20, no. 2 (September 1996).

**Huff, Chuck,** and **C. Dianne Martin.** "Computing Consequences: A Framework for Teaching Ethical Computing." *Communications of the ACM* 38, no. 12 (December 1995).

**Joes, Kathryn.** "EDS Set to Restore Cash-Machine Network." *The New York Times* (March 26, 1993).

**Johnson, Deborah G.** "Ethics Online." *Communications of the ACM* 40, no. 1 (January 1997).

**Johnson, Deborah G.,** and **John M. Mulvey.** "Accountability and Computer Decision Systems." *Communications of the ACM* 38, no. 12 (December 1995).

**King, Julia.** "It's CYA Time." *Computerworld* (March 30, 1992).

**Kling, Rob.** "When Organizations Are Perpetrators: The Conditions of Computer Abuse and Computer Crime." In *Computerization & Controversy: Value Conflicts & Social Choices,* edited by Charles Dunlop and Rob Kling. New York: Academic Press (1991).

**Kreie, Jennifer,** and **Timothy Paul Cronan.** "Making Ethical Decisions." *Communications of the ACM* 43, no. 12 (December 2000).

**Laudon, Kenneth C.** "Ethical Concepts and Information Technology." *Communications of the ACM* 38, no. 12 (December 1995).

**Lohr, Steve.** "A Nation Ponders Its Growing Digital Divide." *The New York Times* (October 21, 1996).

**Markoff, John.** "Growing Compatibility Issue: Computers and User Privacy." *The New York Times* (March 3, 1999).

**Martin, Jr. David M., Richard M. Smith, Michael Brittain, Ivan Fetch,** and **Hailin Wu.** "The Privacy Practices of Web Browser Extensions." *Communications of the ACM* 44, no. 2 (February 2001).

**Mason, Richard O.** "Applying Ethics to Information Technology Issues." *Communications of the ACM* 38, no. 12 (December 1995).

**Mason, Richard O.** "Four Ethical Issues in the Information Age." *MIS Quarterly* 10, no. 1 (March 1986).

**Memon, Nasir,** and **Ping Wah Wong.** "Protecting Digital Media Content." *Communications of the ACM* 41, no. 7 (July 1998).

**Milberg, Sandra J., Sandra J. Burke, H. Jeff Smith,** and **Ernest A. Kallman.** "Values, Personal Information Privacy, and Regulatory Approaches." *Communications of the ACM* 38, no. 12 (December 1995).

**Moores, Trevor,** and **Gurpreet Dhillon.** "Software Piracy: A View from Hong Kong." *Communications of the ACM* 43, no. 12, (December 2000).

**Mykytyn, Kathleen, Peter P. Mykytyn, Jr.,** and **Craig W. Slinkman.** "Expert Systems: A Question of Liability." *MIS Quarterly* 14, no. 1 (March 1990).

**National Telecommunications & Information Administration,** U.S. Department of Commerce. "Falling Through the Net: Defining the Digital Divide." July 8, 1999

**Neumann, Peter G.** "Inside RISKS: Computers, Ethics and Values." *Communications of the ACM* 34, no. 7 (July 1991).

———. "Inside RISKS: Fraud by Computer." *Communications of the ACM* 35, no. 8 (August 1992).

**Nissenbaum, Helen.** "Computing and Accountability." *Communications of the ACM* 37, no. 1 (January 1994).

**Okerson, Ann.** "Who Owns Digital Works?" *Scientific American* (July 1996).

**O'Rourke, Maureen A.** "Is Virtual Trespass an Apt Analogy?" *Communications of the ACM* 44, no. 2 (February 2001).

**Oz, Effy.** "Ethical Standards for Information Systems Professionals," *MIS Quarterly* 16, no. 4 (December 1992).

———. *Ethics for the Information Age.* Dubuque, Iowa: W. C. Brown (1994).

**Reagle, Joseph,** and **Lorrie Faith Cranor.** "The Platform for Privacy Preferences." *Communications of the ACM* 42, no. 2 (February 1999).

**Redman, Thomas C.** "The Impact of Poor Data Quality on the Typical Enterprise." *Communications of the ACM* 41, no. 2 (February 1998).

**Rifkin, Jeremy.** "Watch Out for Trickle-Down Technology." *The New York Times* (March 16, 1993).

**Rigdon, Joan E.** "Frequent Glitches in New Software Bug Users." *The Wall Street Journal* (January 18, 1995).

**Rotenberg, Marc.** "Communications Privacy: Implications for Network Design." *Communications of the ACM* 36, no. 8 (August 1993).

———. "Inside RISKS: Protecting Privacy." *Communications of the ACM* 35, no. 4 (April 1992).

**Samuelson, Pamela.** "Computer Programs and Copyright's Fair Use Doctrine." *Communications of the ACM* 36, no. 9 (September 1993).

———. "Copyright's Fair Use Doctrine and Digital Data." *Communications of the ACM* 37, no. 1 (January 1994).

———. "Liability for Defective Electronic Information." *Communications of the ACM* 36, no. 1 (January 1993).

———. "Self Plagiarism or Fair Use?" *Communications of the ACM* 37, no. 8 (August 1994).

———. "The Ups and Downs of Look and Feel." *Communications of the ACM* 36, no. 4 (April 1993).

**San Jose Mercury News.** "Dow Chemical Fires 50 workers after E-Mail Investigation." (July 27, 2000).

**Sipior, Janice C.,** and **Burke T. Ward.** "The Dark Side of Employee Email." *Communications of the ACM* 42, no. 7 (July 1999).

———. "The Ethical and Legal Quandary of E-mail Privacy." *Communications of the ACM* 38, no. 12 (December 1995).

**Smith, H. Jeff.** "Privacy Policies and Practices: Inside the Organizational Maze." *Communications of the ACM* 36, no. 12, (December 1993).

**Smith, H. Jeff,** and **John Hasnas.** "Ethics and Information Systems: The Corporate Domain." *MIS Quarterly* 23, no. 1 (March 1999).

**Smith, H. Jeff, Sandra J. Milberg,** and **Sandra J. Burke.** "Information Privacy: Measuring Individuals' Concerns about Organizational Practices." *MIS Quarterly* 20, no. 2 (June 1996).

**Straub, Detmar W., Jr.,** and **Rosann Webb Collins.** "Key Information Liability Issues Facing Managers: Software Piracy, Proprietary Databases, and Individual Rights to Privacy." *MIS Quarterly* 14, no. 2 (June 1990).

**Straub, Detmar W., Jr.,** and **William D. Nance.** "Discovering and Disciplining Computer Abuse in Organizations: A Field Study." *MIS Quarterly* 14, no. 1 (March 1990).

**The Telecommunications Policy Roundtable.** "Renewing the Commitment to a Public Interest Telecommunications Policy." *Communications of the ACM* 37, no. 1 (January 1994).

**Thong, James Y. L.,** and **Chee-Sing Yap.** "Testing an Ethical Decision-Making Theory." *Journal of Management Information Systems* 15, no. 1 (Summer 1998).

**Tuttle, Brad, Adrian Harrell,** and **Paul Harrison.** "Moral Hazard, Ethical Considerations, and the Decision to Implement an Information System." *Journal of Management Information Systems* 13, no. 4 (Spring 1997).

**United States Department of Health, Education, and Welfare.** *Records, Computers, and the Rights of Citizens.* Cambridge: MIT Press (1973).

**Vijayan, Jaikumar.** "Caught in the Middle." *Computerworld* (July 24, 2000).

**Volokh, Eugene.** "Personalization and Privacy." *Communications of the ACM* 43, no. 8 (August 2000).

**Wang, Huaiqing, Matthew K. O. Lee,** and **Chen Wang.** "Consumer Privacy Concerns about Internet Marketing." *Communications of the ACM* 41, no. 3 (March 1998).

**Whiting, Rich.** "Mind Your Business." *Information Week* (March 6, 2000).

**Wilder, Clinton.** "Feds Allege Internet Scam." *Information Week* (June 10, 1996).

**Zviran, Moshe,** and **William J. Haga.** "Password Security: An Empirical Study." *Journal of Management Information Systems* 15, no. 4 (Spring 1999).

## CHAPTER 16

**Agarwal, P.K.** "Building India's National Internet Backbone." *Communications of the ACM* 42, no. 6 (June 1999).

**Blanning, Robert W.** "Establishing a Corporate Presence on the Internet in Singapore." *Journal of Organizational Computing and Electronic Commerce* 9, no. 1 (1999).

**Burkhardt, Grey E., Seymour E. Goodman, Arun Mehta,** and **Larry Press.** "The Internet in India: Better Times Ahead?" *Communications of the ACM* 41, no. 11 (November 1998).

**Chabrow, Eric.** "Supply Chains Go Global." *Information Week* (April 3, 2000).

**Chismar, William G.,** and **Laku Chidambaram.** "Telecommunications and the Structuring of U.S. Multinational Corporations." *International Information Systems* 1, no. 4 (October 1992).

**Cox, Butler.** *Globalization: The IT Challenge.* Sunnyvale, CA: Amdahl Executive Institute (1991).

**Deans, Candace P., Kirk R. Karwan, Martin D. Goslar, David A. Ricks,** and **Brian Toyne.** "Key International Issues in U.S.-Based Multinational Corporations." *Journal of Management Information Systems* 7, no. 4 (Spring 1991).

**Deans, Candace P.,** and **Michael J. Kane.** *International Dimensions of Information Systems and Technology.* Boston, MA: PWS-Kent (1992).

**DePalma, Anthony.** "Getting There is Challenge for Latin American E-tailing." *The New York Times (*August 17, 2000).

**Dutta, Amitava.** "Telecommunications Infrastructure in Developing Nations." *International Information Systems* 1, no. 3 (July 1992).

**Ein-Dor, Philip, Seymour E. Goodman,** and **Peter Wolcott.** "From Via Maris to Electronic Highway: The Internet in Canaan." *Communications of the ACM* 43, no. 7 (July 2000).

**Farhoomand, Ali, Virpi Kristiina Tuunainen,** and **Lester W. Yee.** "Barrier to Global Electronic Commerce: A Cross-Country Study of Hong Kong and Finland." *Journal of Organizational Computing and Electronic Commerce* 10, no. 1 (2000).

**Holland, Christopher, Geoff Lockett,** and **Ian Blackman.** "Electronic Data Interchange Implementation: A Comparison of U.S. and European Cases." *International Information Systems* 1, no. 4 (October 1992).

**Ives, Blake,** and **Sirkka Jarvenpaa.** "Applications of Global Information Technology: Key Issues for Management." *MIS Quarterly* 15, no. 1 (March 1991).

———. "Global Business Drivers: Aligning Information Technology to Global Business Strategy". *IBM Systems Journal* 32, no. 1 (1993).

———. "Global Information Technology: Some Lessons from Practice." *International Information Systems* 1, no. 3 (July 1992).

**Jarvenpaa, Sirkka L., Kathleen Knoll,** and **Dorothy Leidner.** "Is Anybody Out There? Antecedents of Trust in Global Virtual Teams." *Journal of Management Information Systems* 14, no. 4 (Spring 1998).

**Karin, Jahangir,** and **Benn R. Konsynski.** "Globalization and Information Management Strategies." *Journal of Management Information Systems* 7 (Spring 1991).

**Keen, Peter.** *Shaping the Future.* Cambridge, MA: Harvard Business School Press (1991).

**Kibati, Mugo,** and **Donyaprueth Krairit.** "Building India's National Internet Backbone." *Communications of the ACM* 42, no. 6 (June 1999).

**King, William R.,** and **Vikram Sethi.** "An Empirical Analysis of the Organization of Transnational Information Systems." *Journal of Management Information Systems* 15, no. 4 (Spring 1999).

**Levy, David.** "Lean Production in an International Supply Chain." *Sloan Management Review* (Winter 1997).

**Mannheim, Marvin L.** "Global Information Technology: Issues and Strategic Opportunities." *International Information Systems* 1, no. 1 (January 1992).

**Neumann, Seev.** "Issues and Opportunities in International Information Systems." *International Information Systems* 1, no. 4 (October 1992).

**Palvia, Shailendra, Prashant Palvia,** and **Ronald Zigli,** eds. *The Global Issues of Information Technology Management.* Harrisburg, PA: Idea Group Publishing (1992).

**Petrazzini, Ben,** and **Mugo Kibati.** "The Internet in Developing Countries." *Communications of the ACM* 42, no. 6 (June 1999).

**Quelch, John A.,** and **Lisa R. Klein.** "The Internet and International Marketing." *Sloan Management Review* (Spring 1996).

**Roche, Edward M.** *Managing Information Technology in Multinational Corporations.* New York: Macmillan (1992).

**Smith, Craig S.** "Ambivalence in China on Expanding Net Access." *The New York Times* (August 11, 2000).

**Soh, Christina, Sia Siew Kien,** and **Joanne Tay-Yap.** "Cultural Fits and Misfits: Is ERP a Universal Solution?" *Communications of the ACM* 43, no. 3 (April 2000).

**Steinbart, Paul John,** and **Ravinder Nath.** "Problems and Issues in the Management of International Data Networks." *MIS Quarterly* 16, no. 1 (March 1992).

**Straub, Detmar W.** "The Effect of Culture on IT Diffusion: E-Mail and FAX in Japan and the U.S." *Information Systems Research* 5, no. 1 (March 1994).

**Taggart, Stewart.** "The Other Side of the Divide." *The Industry Standard* (September 11, 2000).

**Tan, Zixiang (Alex), Milton Mueller,** and **Will Foster.** "China's New Internet Regulations: Two Steps Forward, One Step Backward." *Communications of the ACM* 40, no. 12 (December 1997).

**Tan, Zixiang, William Foster,** and **Seymour Goodman.** "China's State-Coordinated Internet Infrastructure." *Communications of the ACM* 42, no. 6 (June 1999).

**Tractinsky, Noam,** and **Sirkka L. Jarvenpaa.** "Information Systems Design Decisions in a Global Versus Domestic Context." *MIS Quarterly* 19, no. 4 (December 1995).

**Walsham, Geoffrey,** and **Sundeys Sahay.** "GIS and District Level Administration in India: Problems and Opportunities." *MIS Quarterly* 23, no. 1 (March 1999).

**Watson, Richard T., Gigi G. Kelly, Robert D. Galliers,** and **James C. Brancheau.** "Key Issues in Information Systems Management: An International Perspective." *Journal of Management Information Systems* 13, no. 4 (Spring 1997).

**Wong, Poh-Kam.** "Leveraging the Global Information Revolution for Economic Development: Singapore's Evolving Information Industry Strategy." *Information Systems Research* 9, no. 4 (December 1998).

**Wysocki, Bernard.** "The Big Bang." *The Wall Street Journal* (January 1, 2000).

# INDEXES

## NAME INDEX

## ORGANIZATIONS INDEX

## International Organizations Index



## Subject Index

# Photo and Screen Shot Credits

| Page | Photographer/Source |
|---|---|

## Preface

| | |
|---|---|
| xxiv | Courtesy of United Parcel Service |

## Chapter 1

| | |
|---|---|
| 8 | Cisco Systems |
| 11 | "UPS and UPS shield design are registered trademarks of United Parcel Service of America, Inc. Used with permission." |
| 17 | Courtesy of Lucent Technologies |
| 18 | Midnight Sun Products |
| 25 | Drugstore. com |

## Chapter 2

| | |
|---|---|
| 43 | Michael Newman, Photo Edit |
| 48 | Robert Essel, The Stock Market |
| 52 | Chris Gardner, AP Wide World Photos |
| 55 | Charles Grupton, The Stock Market |

## Chapter 3

| | |
|---|---|
| 78 | Courtesy of International Business Machines Corporation. Unauthorized use not permitted. |
| 80 | Jose Luis Palaez, The Stock Market |
| 90 | Dell Computer Corporation |
| 91 | Bonnie Kamin, Photo Edit |

## Chapter 4

| | |
|---|---|
| 107 | Datek Online Brokerage Service |
| 109 | © 2001 FortuneCity. Com, Inc. |
| 113 | © 2000 Vanguard Group, Inc. Reprinted with permission of The Vanguard Group. All rights reserved. Vanguard Marketing Corporation, Distributor |
| 117 | Free Markets, Inc. |
| 120 | The Gator Company |
| 125 | Enwisen, Inc. (www. enwisen. com) |
| 128 | LogNet, Inc. |

## Chapter 5

| | |
|---|---|
| 147 | Photo Courtesy of Intel Corp. |
| 150 | (right) Bonnie Kamin, Photo Edit |
| 150 | (left) Tom Prettyman, Photo Edit |
| 153 | Novastock, Photo Edit |
| 155 | (top) Charles Grupton, The Stock Market |
| 155 | (bottom) Reprinted by permission of CNN |
| 159 | (top) Courtesy of International Business Machines Corporation. Unauthorized use not permitted. |
| 159 | (bottom) SETI@home |

## Chapter 6

| | |
|---|---|
| 178 | Screen shot reprinted by permission of Microsoft Corporation. |
| 184 | Screen shot reprinted by permission of Microsoft Corporation. |
| 185 | Screen shot reprinted by permission of Microsoft Corporation. |
| 186 | Screen shot reprinted by permission of Microsoft Corporation. |
| 187 | Livelink Guided Tour® Copyright © 1995, 2001 Open Text Inc. All rights reserved. |
| 190 | Courtesy of International Business Machines Corporation. Unauthorized use not permitted. |
| 196 | Salesforce.com |

## Chapter 7

| | |
|---|---|
| 222 | SAS |
| 225 | National Oceanic Atmospheric Administration |
| 226 | The Enviromental Protection Agency |

## Chapter 8

| | |
|---|---|
| 240 | Lucido Studio, Inc., The Stock Market |
| 242 | (left) Copyright © 2000 Acme, Inc. |
| 242 | (center) Nokia |
| 242 | (right) Research in Motion |
| 252 | "Netscape Communicator browser window © 1999 Netscape Communications Corporation. Netscape Commnications has not authorized, sponsored, endorsed, or approved this publication and is not responsible for its content. Used with permission." |
| 253 | Courtesy of International Business Machines Corporation. Unauthorized use not permitted. |
| 254 | "AOL.com website © 2001 America Online, Inc. Screenshot used with permission." |
| 255 | Blackboard |

## Chapter 9

| | |
|---|---|
| 271 | Lands' End |
| 274 | Alta Vista Company |
| 275 | mySimon |
| 276 | Desktop News |
| 278 | Tellme Networks, Inc. |
| 279 | Nokia |
| 288 | © 2001 WebTrends Corporation |

## Chapter 10

311 Cemex
318 Courtesy of International Business Machines Corporation. Unauthorized use is not permitted.
326 Portions © 2001 NetObjects, Inc. All rights reserved.
329 Gatsby Software

## Chapter 11

341 Elke Hesser, The Stock Market
349 CarsDirect
356 Roger Ball, The Stock Market
357 Courtesy of International Business Machines Corporation. Unauthorized use is not permitted.

## Chapter 12

379 Alan Levinson, Stone
380 Lands' End
383 eRoom Technology, Inc.
389 Countrywide Home Loans

## Chapter 13

407 Stephen G. Elck: Visual Insights/Lucent Technologies
413 Courtesy of MapInfo Corporation (www.mapinfo.com)
415 Money Magazine
416 Ventana Corporation
417 Group Systems® Courtesy of Ventana Corporation
424 "SAP" any my SAP.com are trademarks of SAPAktiengesellschaft, Systems, Applications and Products in Data processing, Neurottstrasse 16, 69190 Waldorf, Germany. The publisher gratefully acknowledges SAP's kind permission to use its trademark in this publication. SAP AG is not the publisher of this book and is not responsible under any aspect of press law.

## Chapter 14

438 Symantec Corporation
446 Check Point Software Technologies
452 Steven Peters, Stone
457 Scitor Corporation

## Chapter 15

471 Courtesy of International Business Machines Corporation. Unauthorized use is not permitted.
478 E-Loan, Inc.
482 © The San Francisco Chronicle
487 Frank Herholdt, Stone
488 Black ICE Defender. Screen shot courtesy of Network Ice Corp.
492 Stephen Ferry, Liaison Agency, Inc.

## Chapter 16

503 Charles Thatcher, Stone
510 Lucent Technologies
514 Wholetree.com
517 Mercantile.com

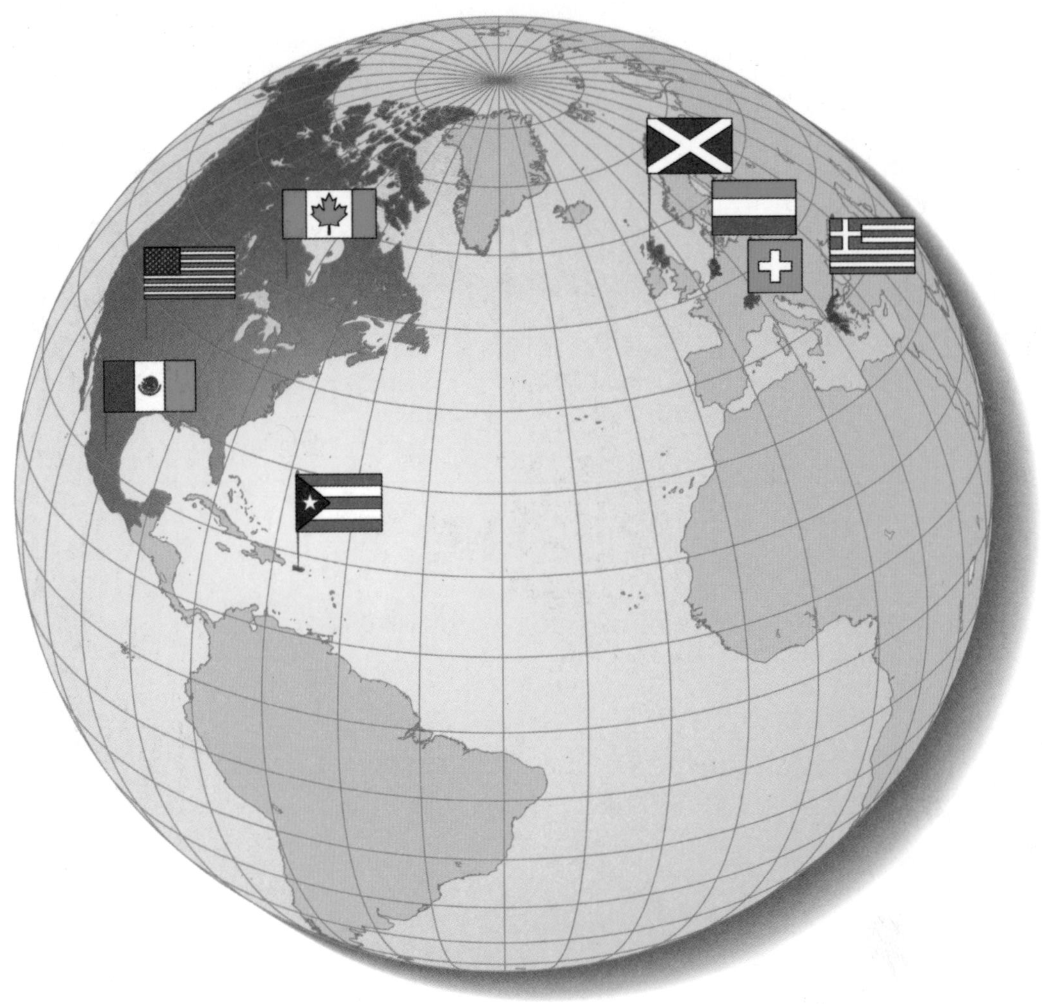

**Contributors**

CANADA

**Len Fertuck**, University of Toronto
**Jane Movold**, University of Western Ontario
**Scott Schneberger**, University of Western Ontario

GERMANY

**Helmut Krcmar**, University of Hohenheim
**Gerhard Schwabe**, University of Hohenheim
**Stephen Wilczek**, University of Hohenheim

SINGAPORE

**Boon Siong Neo**, Nanyang Technological University
**Christina Soh**, Nanyang Technological University

**Consultants**

AUSTRALIA

**Robert MacGregor**, University of Wollongong
**Alan Underwood**, Queensland University of Technology
**Peter Weill**, University of Melbourne

CANADA

**Wynne W. Chin**, University of Calgary
**Len Fertuck**, University of Toronto
**Robert C. Goldstein**, University of British Columbia
**Rebecca Grant**, University of Victoria
**Kevin Leonard**, Wilfrid Laurier University
**Anne B. Pidduck**, University of Waterloo

GREECE

**Anastasios V. Katos**, University of Macedonia

HONG KONG

**Enoch Tse**, Hong Kong Baptist University

INDIA

**Sanjiv D. Vaidya**, Indian Institute of Management, Calcutta

ISRAEL

**Phillip Ein-Dor**, Tel-Aviv University
**Peretz Shoval**, Ben Gurion University

MEXICO

**Noe Urzua Bustamante**, Universidad Tecnológica de México

NETHERLANDS

**E.O. de Brock**, University of Groningen
**Theo Thiadens**, University of Twente
**Charles Van Der Mast**, Delft University of Technology

PUERTO RICO, **Commonwealth of the United States**

**Brunilda Marrero**, University of Puerto Rico

SWEDEN

**Mats Daniels**, Uppsala University

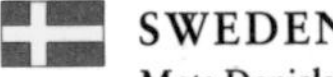

SWITZERLAND

**Andrew C. Boynton**, International Institute for Management Development

UNITED KINGDOM

ENGLAND

**G.R. Hidderley**, University of Central England, Birmingham
**Christopher Kimble**, University of York
**Jonathan Liebenau**, London School of Economics and Political Science
**Kecheng Liu**, Staffordshire University

SCOTLAND

**William N. Dyer**, Falkirk College of Technology